CSE 148 Business Computing

Miami University custom edition

CENGAGE
Learning

Australia • Brazil • Japan • Korea • Mexico • Singapore • Spain • United Kingdom • United States

CENGAGE Learning

CSE 148 Business Computing
Miami University custom edition

Senior Manager, Student Engagement:
Linda deStefano

Manager, Student Engagement:
Julie Dierig

Manager, Student Engagement:
Janey Moeller

Senior Marketing Manager:
Heather Kramer

Manager, Production Editorial:
Kim Fry

Manager, Intellectual Property Project Manager:
Brian Methe

Senior Manager, Production and Manufacturing:
Donna M. Brown

Manager, Production:
Terri Daley

Compositor:
GEX Publishing Services

Printed in the United States of America

New Perspectives on Microsoft Excel 2013, Comprehensive
June Jamrich Parsons | Dan Oja | Roy Ageloff | Patrick Carey | Carol A. DesJardins

© 2014 Cengage Learning. All rights reserved.

Some of the product names and company names used in this book have been used for identification purposes only and may be trademarks or registered trademarks of their respective manufacturers and sellers.

Microsoft and the Office logo are either registered trademarks or trademarks of Microsoft Corporation in the United States and/or other countries. Course Technology, Cengage Learning is an independent entity from the Microsoft Corporation, and not affiliated with Microsoft in any manner.

Disclaimer: Any fictional data related to persons or companies or URLS used throughout this book is intended for instructional purposes only. At the time this book was printed, any such data was fictional and not belonging to any real persons or companies.

Library of Congress Control Number: 2013950930

ALL RIGHTS RESERVED. No part of this work covered by the copyright herein may be reproduced, transmitted, stored or used in any form or by any means graphic, electronic, or mechanical, including but not limited to photocopying, recording, scanning, digitizing, taping, Web distribution, information networks, or information storage and retrieval systems, except as permitted under Section 107 or 108 of the 1976 United States Copyright Act, without the prior written permission of the publisher.

> For product information and technology assistance, contact us at
> **Cengage Learning Customer & Sales Support, 1-800-354-9706**
> For permission to use material from this text or product,
> submit all requests online at **cengage.com/permissions**
> Further permissions questions can be emailed to
> **permissionrequest@cengage.com**

This book contains select works from existing Cengage Learning resources and was produced by Cengage Learning Custom Solutions for collegiate use. As such, those adopting and/or contributing to this work are responsible for editorial content accuracy, continuity and completeness.

Compilation © 2014 Cengage Learning
ISBN-13: 978-1-305-00638-6

ISBN-10: 1-305-00638-0

WCN: 01-100-101
Cengage Learning
5191 Natorp Boulevard
Mason, Ohio 45040
USA
Cengage Learning is a leading provider of customized learning solutions with office locations around the globe, including Singapore, the United Kingdom, Australia, Mexico, Brazil, and Japan. Locate your local office at:
international.cengage.com/region.

Cengage Learning products are represented in Canada by Nelson Education, Ltd.
For your lifelong learning solutions, visit **www.cengage.com/custom.**
Visit our corporate website at **www.cengage.com.**

Preface

The New Perspectives Series' critical-thinking, problem-solving approach is the ideal way to prepare students to transcend point-and-click skills and take advantage of all that Microsoft Office 2013 has to offer.

In developing the New Perspectives Series, our goal was to create books that give students the software concepts and practical skills they need to succeed beyond the classroom. We've updated our proven case-based pedagogy with more practical content to make learning skills more meaningful to students.

With the New Perspectives Series, students understand *why* they are learning *what* they are learning, and are fully prepared to apply their skills to real-life situations.

About This Book

"This text presents students with scenarios that reflect real-world Excel problems they must analyze and solve. I recommend my students keep this text to use as a reference when they attempt to solve similar problems in the future."
— Peggy Foreman
Texas State University

This book provides complete coverage of Microsoft Excel 2013, and includes the following:
- Detailed, hands-on instruction of Microsoft Excel 2013, including creating and formatting a workbook; working with formulas and functions; creating charts, tables, and PivotTables; managing multiple workbooks; developing an Excel application; consolidating data from various sources; and collaborating on a shared workbook
- Coverage of important spreadsheet concepts, including order of precedence in formulas, function syntax, absolute and relative cell references, what-if analysis, and data validation
- Exploration of features new to Excel 2013, including Flash Fill, the Quick Analysis tool, and the recommended charts tool

New for this edition!
- Each tutorial has been updated with new case scenarios throughout, which provide a rich and realistic context for students to apply the concepts and skills presented.
- A new Troubleshoot type of Case Problem, in which certain steps of the exercise require students to identify and correct errors—which are intentionally placed in the files students work with—promotes problem solving and critical thinking.
- The content has been developed so that students and instructors can work seamlessly on either the Windows 7 or Windows 8 operating system.

System Requirements

This book assumes a typical installation of Microsoft Excel 2013 and Microsoft Windows 8 Professional. (You can also complete the material in this text using another version of Windows 8 or using Windows 7. You may see only minor differences in how some windows look.) The browser used for any steps that require a browser is Internet Explorer 10.

www.cengage.com/series/newperspectives

"The clear step-by-step instructions, real-world data files, and helpful figures make New Perspectives texts excellent for courses taught in the classroom, the hybrid/blended format, or entirely online."
—Sylvia Amito'elau
Coastline Community College

The New Perspectives Approach

Context
Each tutorial begins with a problem presented in a "real-world" case that is meaningful to students. The case sets the scene to help students understand what they will do in the tutorial.

Hands-on Approach
Each tutorial is divided into manageable sessions that combine reading and hands-on, step-by-step work. Colorful screenshots help guide students through the steps. **Trouble?** tips anticipate common mistakes or problems to help students stay on track and continue with the tutorial.

VISUAL OVERVIEW
Visual Overviews
Each session begins with a Visual Overview, a two-page spread that includes colorful, enlarged screenshots with numerous callouts and key term definitions, giving students a comprehensive preview of the topics covered in the session, as well as a handy study guide.

PROSKILLS
ProSkills Boxes and Exercises
ProSkills boxes provide guidance for how to use the software in real-world, professional situations, and related ProSkills exercises integrate the technology skills students learn with one or more of the following soft skills: decision making, problem solving, teamwork, verbal communication, and written communication.

KEY STEP
Key Steps
Important steps are highlighted in yellow with attached margin notes to help students pay close attention to completing the steps correctly and avoid time-consuming rework.

INSIGHT
InSight Boxes
InSight boxes offer expert advice and best practices to help students achieve a deeper understanding of the concepts behind the software features and skills.

TIP
Margin Tips
Margin Tips provide helpful hints and shortcuts for more efficient use of the software. The Tips appear in the margin at key points throughout each tutorial, giving students extra information when and where they need it.

REVIEW
APPLY
Assessment
Retention is a key component to learning. At the end of each session, a series of Quick Check questions helps students test their understanding of the material before moving on. Engaging end-of-tutorial Review Assignments and Case Problems have always been a hallmark feature of the New Perspectives Series. Colorful bars and headings identify the type of exercise, making it easy to understand both the goal and level of challenge a particular assignment holds.

REFERENCE
TASK REFERENCE
GLOSSARY/INDEX
Reference
Within each tutorial, Reference boxes appear before a set of steps to provide a succinct summary and preview of how to perform a task. In addition, a complete Task Reference at the back of the book provides quick access to information on how to carry out common tasks. Finally, each book includes a combination Glossary/Index to promote easy reference of material.

www.cengage.com/series/newperspectives

Our Complete System of Instruction

Coverage To Meet Your Needs
Whether you're looking for just a small amount of coverage or enough to fill a semester-long class, we can provide you with a textbook that meets your needs.
- Brief books typically cover the essential skills in just 2 to 4 tutorials.
- Introductory books build and expand on those skills and contain an average of 5 to 8 tutorials.
- Comprehensive books are great for a full-semester class, and contain 9 to 12+ tutorials.

So if the book you're holding does not provide the right amount of coverage for you, there's probably another offering available. Go to our Web site or contact your Cengage Learning sales representative to find out what else we offer.

CourseCasts – Learning on the Go. Always available...always relevant.
Want to keep up with the latest technology trends relevant to you? Visit http://coursecasts.course.com to find a library of weekly updated podcasts, CourseCasts, and download them to your mp3 player.

Ken Baldauf, host of CourseCasts, is a faculty member of the Florida State University Computer Science Department where he is responsible for teaching technology classes to thousands of FSU students each year. Ken is an expert in the latest technology trends; he gathers and sorts through the most pertinent news and information for CourseCasts so your students can spend their time enjoying technology, rather than trying to figure it out. Open or close your lecture with a discussion based on the latest CourseCast.

Visit us at http://coursecasts.course.com to learn on the go!

Instructor Resources
We offer more than just a book. We have all the tools you need to enhance your lectures, check students' work, and generate exams in a new, easier-to-use and completely revised package. This book's Instructor's Manual, ExamView testbank, PowerPoint presentations, data files, solution files, figure files, and a sample syllabus are all available on a single CD-ROM or for downloading at http://www.cengage.com.

SAM: Skills Assessment Manager
Get your students workplace-ready with SAM, the premier proficiency-based assessment and training solution for Microsoft Office! SAM's active, hands-on environment helps students master computer skills and concepts that are essential to academic and career success.

Skill-based assessments, interactive trainings, business-centric projects, and comprehensive remediation engage students in mastering the latest Microsoft Office programs on their own, allowing instructors to spend class time teaching. SAM's efficient course setup and robust grading features provide faculty with consistency across sections. Fully interactive MindTap Readers integrate market-leading Cengage Learning content with SAM, creating a comprehensive online student learning environment.

www.cengage.com/series/newperspectives

Certification Prep Tool

This textbook was developed to instruct on the Microsoft® Office® 2013 certification objectives. Microsoft Corporation has developed a set of standardized, performance-based examinations that you can take to demonstrate your overall expertise with Microsoft Office 2013 programs. Microsoft Office 2013 certification provides a number of benefits for you:

- Differentiate yourself in the employment marketplace from those who are not Microsoft Office Specialist or Expert certified.
- Prove skills and expertise when using Microsoft Office 2013.
- Perform at a higher skill level in your job.
- Work at a higher professional level than those who are not certified.
- Broaden your employment opportunities and advance your career more rapidly.

For more information about Microsoft Office 2013 certification, including a complete list of certification objectives, visit the Microsoft web site, http://www.microsoft.com/learning. To see which Microsoft Office 2013 certification objectives are addressed by the contents of this text and where each is included in the text, visit the Certification resource on the Student Companion Site located on www.cengagebrain.com. For detailed instructions about accessing available resources, visit www.cengage.com/ct/student download or contact your instructor for information about accessing the required files.

Acknowledgments

We would like to thank the many people whose invaluable contributions made this book possible. First, sincere thanks go to our reviewers: Will Demeré, Michigan State University; Peggy Foreman, Texas State University; Martha Huggins, Pitt Community College; Steve Luzier, Fortis Institute; and Paul Smith, Brown Mackie College. At Cengage Learning we would like to thank Donna Gridley, Executive Editor for the New Perspectives Series; Leigh Hefferon, Product Development Manager; Amanda Lyons, Associate Acquisitions Editor; Julia Leroux-Lindsey, Product Manager; Melissa Stehler, Editorial Assistant; Jennifer Goguen McGrail, Senior Content Project Manager; Chris Scriver, Manuscript Quality Assurance (MQA) Project Leader; and John Freitas, Serge Palladino, Susan Pedicini, Danielle Shaw, Ashlee Welz Smith, and Susan Whalen, MQA Testers. Special thanks to Robin Romer, Developmental Editor, for her exceptional efforts in improving this text; and to Kathy Finnegan, Senior Product Manager, for keeping us on task and focused.

– June Jamrich Parsons
– Dan Oja
– Roy Ageloff
– Patrick Carey
– Carol A. DesJardins

www.cengage.com/series/newperspectives

BRIEF CONTENTS

FILE MANAGEMENT

Managing Your Files .... FM 1
Organizing Files and Folders with Windows 8

EXCEL

Tutorial 1 Getting Started with Excel .... EX 1
Creating a Customer Order Report

Tutorial 2 Formatting Workbook Text and Data .... EX 67
Designing a Sales Report

Tutorial 3 Calculating Data with Formulas and Functions .... EX 131
Creating a Fitness Tracker

Tutorial 4 Analyzing and Charting Financial Data .... EX 189
Presenting Data for a Business Plan

Tutorial 5 Working with Excel Tables, PivotTables, and PivotCharts ... EX 257
Tracking Cash Receipts

Tutorial 6 Managing Multiple Worksheets and Workbooks .... EX 327
Summarizing Recycling Data

Tutorial 7 Developing an Excel Application .... EX 389
Creating a Receipt

Tutorial 8 Working with Advanced Functions .... EX 463
Calculating Employee Compensation and Benefits

Tutorial 9 Exploring Financial Tools and Functions .... EX 529
Analyzing a Business Plan

Tutorial 10 Performing What-If Analyses .... EX 595
Analyzing Financial Data to Maximize Profits

Tutorial 11 Connecting to External Data .... EX 657
Building a Financial Report from Several Data Sources

Tutorial 12 Collaborating on a Shared Workbook .... EX 725
Working with Others to Create a Stockholder's Report

Additional Cases .... EX ADD 1

Appendix A Working with Text Functions and Creating Custom Formats .. EX A1
Cleaning Data in a Spreadsheet

Appendix B Advanced Filters, Database Functions, and Summary IFS Functions .... EX B1
Filtering and Summarizing Database Information

Appendix C Enhancing Excel with Visual Basic for Applications .... EX C1
Designing a Stock Report Application

Appendix D Working with Enhanced Formatting Tools .... EX D1
Formatting a Chemistry Report

Glossary/Index   REF 1

Task Reference   REF 15

New Perspectives Series

TABLE OF CONTENTS

Preface iii

Managing Your Files
Organizing Files and Folders with Windows 8 ...... **FM 1**

Visual Overview: Comparing Windows 7 & Windows 8 .... FM 2
Exploring the Differences Between Windows 7 and Windows 8 .... FM 4
Organizing Files and Folders .... FM 5
   Understanding How to Organize Files and Folders .... FM 6
Exploring Files and Folders .... FM 8
   Navigating to Your Data Files .... FM 10
   Changing the View .... FM 12
Managing Files and Folders .... FM 14
   Opening a File .... FM 15
   Saving a File .... FM 16
   Creating Folders .... FM 19
   Moving and Copying Files and Folders .... FM 20
   Deleting Files and Folders .... FM 25
   Renaming Files .... FM 26
Working with Compressed Files .... FM 26
Quick Check .... FM 29
Review Assignments .... FM 30
Case Problems .... FM 31

Tutorial 1 Getting Started with Excel
Creating a Customer Order Report .... **EX 1**

Session 1.1 Visual Overview: The Excel Window ... EX 2
Introducing Excel and Spreadsheets .... EX 4
   Opening an Existing Workbook .... EX 4
   Using Keyboard Shortcuts to Work Faster ...... EX 6
   Getting Help .... EX 6
   Using Excel 2013 in Touch Mode .... EX 6
Exploring a Workbook .... EX 7
   Changing the Active Sheet .... EX 8
   Navigating Within a Worksheet .... EX 9
   Selecting a Cell Range .... EX 11
Closing a Workbook .... EX 13

Planning a Workbook .... EX 13
Creating a New Workbook .... EX 15
   Renaming and Inserting Worksheets .... EX 16
   Moving Worksheets .... EX 16
   Deleting Worksheets .... EX 17
   Saving a Workbook .... EX 17
Entering Text, Dates, and Numbers .... EX 17
   Entering Text .... EX 18
   Undoing and Redoing an Action .... EX 19
   Editing Cell Content .... EX 19
   Understanding AutoComplete .... EX 20
   Displaying Numbers as Text .... EX 21
   Entering Dates .... EX 22
   Entering Numbers .... EX 24
Resizing Columns and Rows .... EX 25
   Changing Column Widths .... EX 25
   Wrapping Text Within a Cell .... EX 28
   Changing Row Heights .... EX 29
Session 1.1 Quick Check .... EX 29
Session 1.2 Visual Overview: Formulas and Functions .... EX 30
Adding Formulas to a Worksheet .... EX 32
   Entering a Formula .... EX 32
   Copying and Pasting Formulas .... EX 35
Simplifying Formulas with Functions .... EX 36
   Introducing Function Syntax .... EX 36
   Entering Functions with AutoSum .... EX 36
Modifying a Worksheet .... EX 40
   Moving and Copying a Cell or Range .... EX 40
   Using the COUNT Function .... EX 42
   Inserting a Column or Row .... EX 43
   Deleting a Row or Column .... EX 45
   Inserting and Deleting a Range .... EX 46
Using Flash Fill .... EX 48
Formatting a Worksheet .... EX 49
   Adding Cell Borders .... EX 50
   Changing the Font Size .... EX 51

Microsoft Excel 2013, Comprehensive ix

Printing a Workbook	EX 51
Changing Worksheet Views	EX 51
Changing the Page Orientation	EX 53
Setting the Scaling Options	EX 54
Setting the Print Options	EX 55
Viewing Worksheet Formulas	EX 56
Saving a Workbook with a New Filename	EX 57
Session 1.2 Quick Check	EX 58
Review Assignments	EX 59
Case Problems	EX 61

Tutorial 2 Formatting Workbook Text and Data
Designing a Sales Report . . . . **EX 67**

Session 2.1 Visual Overview: Worksheet with Formatting	EX 68
Formatting Cell Text	EX 70
Applying Fonts and Font Styles	EX 71
Applying a Font Color	EX 73
Formatting Text Selections	EX 75
Working with Fill Colors and Backgrounds	EX 76
Changing a Fill Color	EX 76
Adding a Background Image	EX 77
Using Functions and Formulas to Calculate Sales Data	EX 78
Formatting Numbers	EX 82
Applying Number Formats	EX 82
Formatting Dates and Times	EX 86
Formatting Worksheet Cells	EX 87
Aligning Cell Content	EX 87
Indenting Cell Content	EX 88
Adding Cell Borders	EX 88
Merging Cells	EX 90
Rotating Cell Contents	EX 91
Exploring the Format Cells Dialog Box	EX 92
Session 2.1 Quick Check	EX 95
Session 2.2 Visual Overview: Worksheet Formatted for Printing	EX 96
Using the Average Function	EX 98
Applying Cell Styles	EX 99

Copying and Pasting Formats	EX 101
Copying Formats with the Format Painter	EX 101
Copying Formats with the Paste Options Button	EX 103
Copying Formats with Paste Special	EX 104
Finding and Replacing Text and Formats	EX 104
Working with Themes	EX 106
Highlighting Cells with Conditional Formats	EX 108
Highlighting Cells Based on Their Values	EX 109
Highlighting Cells with a Top/Bottom Rule	EX 110
Clearing a Conditional Format	EX 112
Creating a Conditional Formatting Legend	EX 112
Formatting a Worksheet for Printing	EX 114
Using Page Break Preview	EX 114
Defining the Print Area	EX 115
Inserting Page Breaks	EX 116
Adding Print Titles	EX 117
Creating Headers and Footers	EX 119
Setting the Page Margins	EX 121
Session 2.2 Quick Check	EX 122
Review Assignments	EX 123
Case Problems	EX 125

Tutorial 3 Calculating Data with Formulas and Functions
Creating a Fitness Tracker . . . . **EX 131**

Session 3.1 Visual Overview: Functions and Cell References	EX 132
Making Workbooks User-Friendly	EX 134
Documenting Formulas	EX 135
Using Constants in Formulas	EX 135
Identifying Notes, Input Values, and Calculated Values	EX 138
Using Excel Functions	EX 140
Exploring Function Syntax	EX 141
Entering Functions with the Quick Analysis Tool	EX 142
Entering Functions with the Insert Function Dialog Box	EX 145

Referencing Function Results in a Formula	EX 149	Creating a Chart	EX 197
Interpreting Error Values	EX 150	Selecting a Chart's Data Source	EX 198
Exploring Cell References	EX 152	Exploring Chart Types and Subtypes	EX 199
Understanding Relative References	EX 152	Inserting a Pie Chart with the Quick Analysis Tool	EX 200
Understanding Absolute References	EX 154	Moving and Resizing a Chart	EX 202
Understanding Mixed References	EX 154	Working with Chart Elements	EX 203
Changing Cell References in a Formula	EX 156	Choosing a Chart Style	EX 204
Planning Which Cell Reference to Use in a Formula	EX 157	Formatting the Pie Chart Legend	EX 205
Session 3.1 Quick Check	EX 159	Formatting Pie Chart Data Labels	EX 207
Session 3.2 Visual Overview: Logical and Lookup Functions	EX 160	Setting the Pie Slice Colors	EX 208
AutoFilling Formulas and Data	EX 162	Formatting the Chart Area	EX 209
Using the Fill Handle	EX 162	Performing What-If Analyses with Charts	EX 210
Using the Auto Fill Options Button	EX 163	Creating a Column Chart	EX 211
Filling a Series	EX 164	Comparing Column Chart Subtypes	EX 212
Working with Date Functions	EX 166	Creating a Clustered Column Chart	EX 212
Displaying the Current Date with the TODAY function	EX 167	Moving a Chart to a Different Worksheet	EX 214
Finding the Next Weekday with the WORKDAY function	EX 168	Changing and Formatting a Chart Title	EX 214
Counting Cells	EX 170	Creating a Stacked Column Chart	EX 215
Working with Logical Functions	EX 172	Session 4.1 Quick Check	EX 217
Using the IF Function	EX 172	Session 4.2 Visual Overview: Charts, Sparklines, and Data Bars	EX 218
Using a Lookup Function	EX 176	Creating a Line Chart	EX 220
Finding an Exact Match with the VLOOKUP Function	EX 177	Working with Axes and Gridlines	EX 222
Performing What-If Analysis	EX 179	Editing the Scale of the Vertical Axis	EX 222
Using Trial and Error	EX 179	Adding Gridlines	EX 223
Using Goal Seek	EX 180	Working with Column Widths	EX 224
Session 3.2 Quick Check	EX 182	Formatting Data Markers	EX 225
Review Assignments	EX 183	Formatting the Plot Area	EX 227
Case Problems	EX 184	Creating a Combination Chart	EX 230
		Working with Primary and Secondary Axes	EX 232
Tutorial 4 Analyzing and Charting Financial Data		Editing a Chart Data Source	EX 234
Presenting Data for a Business Plan	**EX 189**	Creating Sparklines	EX 238
Session 4.1 Visual Overview: Chart Elements	EX 190	Formatting the Sparkline Axis	EX 240
Introduction to Financial Functions	EX 192	Working with Sparkline Groups	EX 240
Using the PMT Function	EX 193	Creating Data Bars	EX 242
		Modifying a Data Bar Rule	EX 243
		Inserting a Watermark	EX 245

Microsoft Excel 2013, Comprehensive   xi

Session 4.2 Quick Check	EX 247
Review Assignments	EX 248
Case Problems	EX 249
ProSkills Exercise: Decision Making	EX 254

Tutorial 5 Working with Excel Tables, PivotTables, and PivotCharts
Tracking Cash Receipts .... **EX 257**

Session 5.1 Visual Overview: Elements of an Excel Table	EX 258
Planning a Structured Range of Data	EX 260
Freezing Rows and Columns	EX 262
Creating an Excel Table	EX 264
Renaming an Excel Table	EX 266
Modifying an Excel Table	EX 266
Maintaining Data in an Excel Table	EX 267
Adding Records	EX 268
Finding and Editing Records	EX 269
Deleting a Record	EX 270
Sorting Data	EX 271
Sorting One Column Using the Sort Buttons	EX 271
Sorting Multiple Columns Using the Sort Dialog Box	EX 272
Sorting Using a Custom List	EX 274
Session 5.1 Quick Check	EX 275
Session 5.2 Visual Overview: Filtering Table Data	EX 276
Filtering Data	EX 278
Filtering Using One Column	EX 278
Filtering Using Multiple Columns	EX 280
Clearing Filters	EX 281
Selecting Multiple Filter Items	EX 281
Creating Criteria Filters to Specify More Complex Criteria	EX 282
Creating a Slicer to Filter Data in an Excel Table	EX 285
Using the Total Row to Calculate Summary Statistics	EX 287
Splitting the Worksheet Window into Panes	EX 290

Inserting Subtotals	EX 292
Using the Subtotal Outline View	EX 295
Session 5.2 Quick Check	EX 297
Session 5.3 Visual Overview: PivotTable and PivotChart	EX 298
Analyzing Data with PivotTables	EX 300
Creating a PivotTable	EX 300
Adding Fields to a PivotTable	EX 303
Changing the Layout of a PivotTable	EX 305
Formatting a PivotTable	EX 306
Filtering a PivotTable	EX 308
Adding a Field to the FILTERS Area	EX 308
Filtering PivotTable Fields	EX 309
Creating a Slicer to Filter a PivotTable	EX 310
Refreshing a PivotTable	EX 312
Creating a Recommended PivotTable	EX 314
Creating a PivotChart	EX 316
Session 5.3 Quick Check	EX 318
Review Assignments	EX 319
Case Problems	EX 320

Tutorial 6 Managing Multiple Worksheets and Workbooks
Summarizing Recycling Data .... **EX 327**

Session 6.1 Visual Overview: Worksheet Groups and 3-D References	EX 328
Grouping Worksheets	EX 330
Entering Headings and Formulas in a Worksheet Group	EX 332
Formatting a Worksheet Group	EX 334
Ungrouping Worksheets	EX 335
Working with Multiple Worksheets	EX 336
Copying Worksheets	EX 336
Referencing Cells and Ranges in Other Worksheets	EX 339
Using 3-D References to Add Values Across Worksheets	EX 342
Printing a Worksheet Group	EX 347
Session 6.1 Quick Check	EX 349

Session 6.2 Visual Overview: Links and External References . . . . EX 350
Linking Workbooks . . . . EX 352
    Navigating Multiple Workbooks . . . . EX 353
    Arranging Multiple Workbooks . . . . EX 354
    Creating Formulas with External References . . EX 355
Updating Linked Workbooks . . . . EX 361
    Updating a Destination Workbook with Source Workbooks Open . . . . EX 361
    Updating a Destination Workbook with Source Workbooks Closed . . . . EX 363
    Managing Links . . . . EX 365
Session 6.2 Quick Check . . . . EX 367
Session 6.3 Visual Overview: Templates and Hyperlinks . . . . EX 368
Creating a Hyperlink . . . . EX 370
    Inserting a Hyperlink . . . . EX 370
    Editing a Hyperlink . . . . EX 372
Using Templates . . . . EX 372
    Creating a Workbook Based on an Existing Template . . . . EX 373
    Creating a Custom Workbook Template . . . . . EX 376
    Creating a New Workbook from a Template . . EX 380
Session 6.3 Quick Check . . . . EX 382
Review Assignments . . . . EX 383
Case Problems . . . . EX 384

Tutorial 7 Developing an Excel Application
Creating a Receipt . . . . **EX 389**

Session 7.1 Visual Overview: Excel Application and Defined Names . . . . EX 390
Planning an Excel Application . . . . EX 392
Naming Cells and Ranges . . . . EX 394
    Using the Name Box to Create Defined Names . . . . EX 395
    Selecting Cells and Ranges by Their Defined Names . . . . EX 396
    Creating Defined Names by Selection . . . . EX 397
    Editing and Deleting Defined Names . . . . EX 398
    Using the Paste Names Command . . . . EX 399

Using Defined Names in Formulas . . . . EX 400
    Using Defined Names in Formulas . . . . EX 401
    Adding Defined Names to Existing Formulas . . EX 405
Session 7.1 Quick Check . . . . EX 407
Session 7.2 Visual Overview: Data Validation and Protection . . . . EX 408
Validating Data Entry . . . . EX 410
    Specifying Validation Criteria . . . . EX 410
    Creating an Error Alert Style and Message . . . EX 412
    Creating an Input Message . . . . EX 413
    Creating a List Validation Rule . . . . EX 414
    Testing Data Validation Rules . . . . EX 418
Protecting a Worksheet and a Workbook . . . . . . EX 420
    Locking and Unlocking Cells . . . . EX 420
    Protecting a Worksheet . . . . EX 421
    Protecting a Workbook . . . . EX 423
    Unprotecting a Worksheet and a Workbook . . EX 424
Inserting Comments . . . . EX 425
Session 7.2 Quick Check . . . . EX 427
Session 7.3 Visual Overview: Working with Macros . . . . EX 428
Automating Tasks with Macros . . . . EX 430
Protecting Against Macro Viruses . . . . EX 431
    Macro Security Settings . . . . EX 431
Recording a Macro . . . . EX 433
Running a Macro . . . . EX 437
Creating the TransferData Macro . . . . EX 439
    Fixing Macro Errors . . . . EX 441
Working with the Visual Basic Editor . . . . EX 441
    Understanding the Structure of Macros . . . . . EX 443
    Editing a Macro Using the Visual Basic Editor . . EX 443
Creating Macro Buttons . . . . EX 444
Saving a Workbook with Macros . . . . EX 450
Opening a Workbook with Macros . . . . EX 451
Removing a Tab from the Ribbon . . . . EX 452
Session 7.3 Quick Check . . . . EX 452
Review Assignments . . . . EX 453
Case Problems . . . . EX 455

Tutorial 8 Working with Advanced Functions
Calculating Employee Compensation and Benefits .... **EX 463**

Session 8.1 Visual Overview: Logical Functions .. EX 464
Working with Logical Functions .... EX 466
   Inserting Calculated Columns in an Excel Table .... EX 467
   Using the IF Function .... EX 467
   Using the AND Function .... EX 470
   Using the OR Function .... EX 475
Using Structured References to Create Formulas in Excel Tables .... EX 477
Session 8.1 Quick Check .... EX 481
Session 8.2 Visual Overview: Nested IFs and Lookup Tables .... EX 482
Creating Nested IFs .... EX 484
Using LOOKUP Functions .... EX 489
   Using the VLOOKUP Function to Find an Exact Match .... EX 491
   Using the VLOOKUP Function to Find an Approximate Match .... EX 493
   Using the HLOOKUP Function to Find an Exact Match .... EX 497
Using the IFERROR Function .... EX 500
Session 8.2 Quick Check .... EX 503
Session 8.3 Visual Overview: Conditional Formatting and Functions .... EX 504
Applying Conditional Formatting .... EX 506
   Highlighting Duplicate Values .... EX 506
   Using the Conditional Formatting Rules Manager .... EX 508
Using Functions to Summarize Data Conditionally .... EX 511
   Using the COUNTIF Function .... EX 512
   Using the SUMIF Function .... EX 514
   Using the AVERAGEIF Function .... EX 515
Session 8.3 Quick Check .... EX 519
Review Assignments .... EX 520
Case Problems .... EX 521
ProSkills Exercise: Problem Solving .... EX 526

Tutorial 9 Exploring Financial Tools and Functions
Analyzing a Business Plan .... **EX 529**

Session 9.1 Loan and Investment Functions ..... EX 530
Calculating Borrowing Costs .... EX 532
   Calculating a Payment with the PMT Function EX 532
   Calculating a Future Value with the FV Function .... EX 534
   Calculating the Payment Period with the NPER Function .... EX 536
   Calculating the Present Value with the PV Function .... EX 537
Creating an Amortization Schedule .... EX 540
   Calculating Interest and Principal Payments .. EX 541
   Calculating Cumulative Interest and Principal Payments .... EX 543
Session 9.1 Quick Check .... EX 547
Session 9.2 Visual Overview: Income Statement and Depreciation .... EX 548
Projecting Future Income and Expenses .... EX 550
   Exploring Linear and Growth Trends .... EX 550
   Interpolating from a Starting Value to an Ending Value .... EX 551
   Calculating the Cost of Sales .... EX 553
   Extrapolating from a Series of Values .... EX 555
Calculating Depreciation of Assets .... EX 557
   Straight-Line Depreciation .... EX 558
   Declining Balance Depreciation .... EX 558
   Adding Depreciation to an Income Statement EX 563
Adding Taxes and Interest Expenses to an Income Statement .... EX 563
Session 9.2 Quick Check .... EX 565
Session 9.3 Visual Overview: NPV and IRR Functions and Auditing .... EX 566
Calculating Interest Rates with the RATE function .. EX 568
Viewing the Payback Period of an Investment ... EX 569
Calculating Net Present Value .... EX 571
   The Time Value of Money .... EX 571
   Using the NPV Function .... EX 571
   Choosing a Rate of Return .... EX 572

Calculating the Internal Rate of Return......... EX 574
    Using the IRR Function................... EX 575
    Exploring the XNPV and XIRR Functions..... EX 577
Auditing a Workbook...................... EX 580
    Tracing an Error......................... EX 581
    Evaluating a Formula.................... EX 583
    Using the Watch Window.................. EX 585
Session 9.3 Quick Check.................... EX 587
Review Assignments........................ EX 588
Case Problems............................ EX 590

Tutorial 10 Performing What-If Analyses
Analyzing Financial Data to Maximize Profits..... **EX 595**

Session 10.1 Visual Overview: Data Tables and
What-If Analysis........................... EX 596
Understanding Cost-Volume Relationships..... EX 598
    Comparing Expenses and Revenue......... EX 598
    Exploring the Break-Even Point........... EX 600
    Finding the Break-Even Point with What-If
    Analysis................................ EX 601
Working with Data Tables................... EX 603
    Creating a One-Variable Data Table........ EX 603
    Charting a One-Variable Data Table........ EX 607
    Modifying a Data Table.................. EX 607
    Creating a Two-Variable Data Table......... EX 609
    Formatting the Result Cell................ EX 610
    Charting a Two-Variable Data Table......... EX 612
Session 10.1 Quick Check................... EX 615
Session 10.2 Visual Overview: What-If Scenarios. EX 616
Developing Financial Scenarios with the
Scenario Manager.......................... EX 618
    Defining a Scenario..................... EX 619
    Viewing Scenarios....................... EX 622
    Editing a Scenario...................... EX 624
Creating Scenario Summary Reports.......... EX 625
Session 10.2 Quick Check................... EX 629
Session 10.3 Visual Overview: Optimal Solutions
with Solver............................... EX 630
Introducing Product Mix.................... EX 632

Finding an Optimal Solution Using Solver...... EX 633
    Activating Solver........................ EX 634
    Setting the Objective Cell and Variable Cells. EX 635
    Adding Constraints to Solver............... EX 637
Creating a Solver Answer Report............. EX 642
Saving and Loading Solver Models............ EX 645
Session 10.3 Quick Check................... EX 649
Review Assignments....................... EX 650
Case Problems............................ EX 651

Tutorial 11 Connecting to External Data
*Building a Financial Report from Several
Data Sources................................* **EX 657**

Session 11.1 Visual Overview: Retrieving
Text Data................................. EX 658
Exploring External Data Sources............. EX 660
Importing Data from Text Files............... EX 661
    Understanding Text File Formats........... EX 662
    Starting the Text Import Wizard........... EX 663
    Specifying the Starting Row............... EX 664
    Editing Column Breaks................... EX 664
    Formatting and Trimming Incoming Data.... EX 665
Exploring External Data Ranges and Data
Connections.............................. EX 668
    Viewing a Data Connection............... EX 669
    Modifying Data Connection Properties...... EX 670
Defining a Trusted Location.................. EX 673
Session 11.1 Quick Check................... EX 675
Session 11.2 Visual Overview: Excel Databases
and Queries............................... EX 676
An Introduction to Databases................ EX 678
Retrieving Data with Microsoft Query......... EX 680
    Connecting to a Data Source.............. EX 681
    Choosing Tables and Fields............... EX 681
    Filtering and Sorting Data................ EX 683
    Editing a Query........................ EX 686
Importing Data from Multiple Tables
into a PivotTable.......................... EX 689
Exploring the Data Model and PowerPivot..... EX 692

Installing the PowerPivot Add-In	EX 693
Adding a Table to the Data Model	EX 693
Viewing the Data Model	EX 694
Managing Relationships in the Data Model	EX 695
Session 11.2 Quick Check	EX 699
Session 11.3 Visual Overview: Web and XML Connections	EX 700
Creating a Web Query	EX 702
Formatting a Web Query	EX 705
Saving a Web Query	EX 706
Retrieving Data Using Office Apps	EX 707
Inserting an Office App	EX 707
Retrieving Stock Market Data	EX 708
Importing Data from XML	EX 711
Editing an XML File	EX 713
Loading an XML Data Map	EX 713
Binding XML Elements to a Worksheet	EX 714
Importing XML Data	EX 715
Using Real-Time Data Acquisition	EX 717
Session 11.3 Quick Check	EX 718
Review Assignments	EX 719
Case Problems	EX 720

Tutorial 12 Collaborating on a Shared Workbook
Working with Others to Create a Stockholder's Report .... **EX 725**

Session 12.1 Visual Overview: Collaborating on a Workbook	EX 726
Sharing a Workbook Among Multiple Users	EX 728
Setting Privacy Options	EX 728
Enable Workbook Sharing	EX 729
Tracking Changes in a Workbook	EX 730
Reviewing Comments in a Shared Workbook	EX 731
Reviewing Changes Using the Tracking Log	EX 733
Accepting and Rejecting Edits	EX 735
Merge and Compare Workbooks	EX 737
Collaborating on the Web	EX 740
Saving a Workbook to a File Hosting Service	EX 740
Editing a Shared Workbook	EX 741
Sharing Workbooks on the Cloud	EX 741
Session 12.1 Quick Check	EX 743

Session 12.2 Visual Overview: Finalizing a Workbook	EX 745
Preparing the Final Workbook Version	EX 746
Setting Document Properties	EX 746
Inspecting a Workbook	EX 748
Protecting a Workbook	EX 752
Marking a Workbook as Final	EX 753
Signing Off on a Workbook	EX 754
Integrating Excel with Other Office Applications	EX 756
Copying and Pasting Data	EX 756
Object Linking and Embedding	EX 757
Customizing Excel for Your Working Preferences	EX 764
Developing a Workbook for International Clients	EX 768
Saving a Worksheet as a PDF File	EX 772
Session 12.2 Quick Check	EX 774
Review Assignments	EX 775
Case Problems	EX 776
ProSkills Exercise: Teamwork	EX 781

Additional Case 1 Creating a Grading Workbook .... **ADD 1**

Additional Case 2 Finding an Optimal Product Mix .... **ADD 3**

Additional Case 3 Creating an Interactive Order Form .... **ADD 4**

Additional Case 4 Analyzing a Sales Database .... **ADD 9**

Appendix A Working with Text Functions and Creating Custom Formats
Cleaning Data in a Spreadsheet .... **EX A1**

Opening and Saving Workbooks Created in Earlier Versions of Excel	EX A2
Using Text Functions	EX A3
Using the LEN and LEFT Functions	EX A4
Using the Paste Values Command	EX A6
Using the PROPER Function and the CONCATENATE Function	EX A7

Applying the Text to Columns Command	EX A8
Using the UPPER Function to Convert Case	EX A10
Using the SUBSTITUTE Function	EX A11
Using Special Formats	EX A13
Creating Custom Formats	EX A14
Creating a Custom Number Format	EX A14
Creating a Custom Date Format	EX A16
Using the Compatibility Checker	EX A17
Review Assignments	EX A19
Case Problems	EX A19

Appendix B Advanced Filters, Database Functions, and Summary IFS Functions
Filtering and Summarizing Database Information .... **EX B1**

Using Advanced Filters	EX B2
Understanding the Criteria Range	EX B3
Creating a Criteria Range	EX B5
Using Database Functions to Summarize Data	EX B9
Summarizing Data Using the COUNTIFS, SUMIFS, and AVERAGEIFS Functions	EX B13
Review Assignments	EX B19
Case Problems	EX B19

Appendix C Enhancing Excel with Visual Basic for Applications
Designing a Stock Report Application .... **EX C1**

Developing an Excel Application	EX C2
Working with the Visual Basic Editor	EX C3
Examining Project Explorer	EX C4
Modifying a Project's Properties	EX C5
Working with Sub Procedures	EX C6
Copying and Pasting a Sub Procedure	EX C7
Running a Sub Procedure	EX C9
Assigning a Sub Procedure to a Macro Button	EX C11
An Introduction to Visual Basic for Applications	EX C12
Modifying Properties	EX C13
Applying Methods	EX C15
Writing a Visual Basic Sub Procedure	EX C16
Working with Variables and Values	EX C19
Declaring a Variable	EX C20
Assigning a Value to a Variable	EX C20
Referencing a Variable	EX C22
Exploring Conditional Statements	EX C25
Using the If Statement	EX C25
Testing for Multiple Conditions	EX C25
Using Comparison and Logical Operators	EX C26
An Introduction to Custom Functions	EX C27
Review Assignments	EX C29
Case Problems	EX C30

Appendix D Working with Enhanced Formatting Tools
Formatting a Chemistry Report .... **EX D1**

Creating a Custom Cell Style	EX D2
Creating a Custom Table Style	EX D4
Working with Conditional Formats	EX D7
Highlighting Cells	EX D7
Modifying a Conditional Formatting Rule	EX D9
Working with Color Scales	EX D10
Working with Icon Sets	EX D13
Using Formulas to Apply Conditional Formatting	EX D15
Working with Pictures and SmartArt Graphics	EX D16
Adding Text Labels to SmartArt Graphics	EX D18
Applying SmartArt Styles	EX D19
Inserting and Editing a Picture	EX D19
Positioning a SmartArt Graphic	EX D23
Working with Themes	EX D24
Modifying a Theme's Fonts and Colors	EX D25
Saving a Custom Theme	EX D27
Review Assignments	EX D29
Case Problems	EX D30
GLOSSARY/INDEX	**REF 1**
TASK REFERENCE	**REF 15**

Managing Your Files

Organizing Files and Folders with Windows 8

OBJECTIVES

- Explore the differences between Windows 7 and Windows 8
- Plan the organization of files and folders
- Use File Explorer to view and manage libraries, folders, and files
- Open and save files
- Create folders
- Copy and move files and folders
- Compress and extract files

Case | Savvy Traveler

After spending a summer traveling in Italy, Matt Marino started Savvy Traveler, a travel company that organizes small tours in Europe. To market his company, Matt created flyers, brochures, webpages, and other materials that describe the tours he offers. Matt uses the Savvy Traveler office computer to locate and store photos, illustrations, and text documents he can include in his marketing materials. He recently hired you to help manage the office. To keep Matt connected to the office while traveling, he just purchased a new laptop computer running Windows 8. He is familiar with Windows 7, so he needs an overview explaining how Windows 8 is different. Matt asks you to train him on using Windows 8 to organize his files and folders. Although he has only a few files, he knows it's a good idea to set up a logical organization now so he can find his work later as he stores more files and folders on the computer.

In this tutorial, you'll explore the differences between Windows 7 and Windows 8, especially those related to file management tools. You'll also work with Matt to devise a plan for managing his files. You'll learn how Windows 8 organizes files and folders, and then create files and folders yourself and organize them on Matt's computer. You'll also use techniques to display the information you need in folder windows, and explore options for working with compressed files.

STARTING DATA FILES

FM

Tutorial
Artists.rtf
Chianti.jpg
Florence.jpg
List.rtf
Logo.png
Market.jpg
Marketing.txt
Tour Rates.rtf
Tuscany.rtf

Review
Banner.png
Colosseum.jpg
Lectures.xlsx
Rome.jpg
Rome.rtf
Schedule.rtf
Tours.rtf

Case1
Fall Classes.rtf
Instructors.txt
Kings Canyon.jpg
Mojave.jpg
Redwoods.jpg
Spring Classes.rtf
Summer Classes.rtf
Winter Classes.rtf
Workshops.rtf
Yosemite.jpg

Case2
Budget1.xlsx
Budget2.xlsx
Report1.xlsx
Report2.xlsx
Report3.xlsx
Report4.xlsx
Tips1.rtf
Tips1 – Copy.rtf
Tips2.rtf
Tips2 – Copy.rtf

Microsoft product screenshots used with permission from Microsoft Corporation.

FM 2 Windows 8 | Managing Your Files

Visual Overview:

In Windows 7, you use **Windows Explorer** to navigate the contents of your computer.

Use the arrow buttons in the Address bar to navigate to other locations on your computer.

The **file path** is a notation that indicates a file's location on your computer.

You use the Change your view button to change the size of the icons in the window.

Use the Search box to search for files in the current folder.

The Windows Explorer **toolbar** provides buttons for completing tasks.

Windows Explorer includes a **navigation pane**, which displays icons and links to resources and locations on your computer.

By default, Windows Explorer includes the **Details pane** at the bottom of the window, which displays the properties of the selected object.

Windows provides **libraries** so you can organize files by category—documents, music, pictures, and video.

A thumbnail image previews the file contents for certain types of files.

The zipped folder icon indicates a **compressed folder**, which stores files so they take up less disk space.

Windows 7

Photos courtesy of Lisa Ruffolo

Managing Your Files | Windows 8 FM 3

Comparing Windows 7 & Windows 8

The **View tab** on the ribbon contains options for specifying how the information displays in File Explorer.

Windows provides **libraries** so you can organize files by category—documents, music, pictures, and videos.

The **Quick Access toolbar** contains buttons for viewing properties and creating a folder.

Use the arrow buttons in the Address bar to navigate to other locations on your computer.

The **file path** in the Address bar shows a file's location on your computer.

In Windows 8, you use **File Explorer** to navigate the contents of your computer.

File Explorer includes a ribbon with tools organized on tabs for working with files and folders.

A thumbnail image previews the file contents for certain types of files.

A **filename** is the name you give to a file when you save it to identify the file's contents.

A **file icon** indicates the file type.

Clicking the Computer icon in the navigation pane shows the drives on your computer.

You can use the Large icons view button on the status bar or in the Layout group on the View tab to switch to Large icons view.

Data Files for this tutorial are stored on a removable disk on this computer.

File Explorer includes a **navigation pane**, which displays icons and links to resources and locations on your computer.

Windows 8

Exploring the Differences Between Windows 7 and Windows 8

Windows 8, the most recent version of the Microsoft operating system, is significantly different from Windows 7, the previous version. The major difference is that Windows 8 is designed for touchscreen computers such as tablets and laptops with touch-activated displays, though it runs on computers with more traditional pointing devices such as a mouse or a trackpad. This design change affects many of the fundamental Windows features you use to work on a computer. Figure 1 compares how to perform typical tasks in Windows 7 and Windows 8.

Figure 1 — Comparing Windows 7 and Windows 8

Task	Windows 7 Method	Windows 8 Method
Start applications (sometimes called apps)	**Start menu** Open the Start menu by clicking the Start button.	**Start screen** The Start screen appears when you start Windows.
Access applications, documents, settings, and other resources	**Start menu** Use the Start menu, All Programs list, and Search box.	**Charms bar** The Charms bar appears when you point to the upper-right or lower-right corner of the screen, and displays buttons, called charms, for interacting with Windows 8 and accessing applications.
Select objects and commands	**Icons** Icons are small and detailed, designed for interaction with mechanical pointing devices.	**Icons and tiles** Icons and tiles are large and simplified, designed for interaction with your fingertips.
Open and work in applications	**Desktop** Applications all use a single desktop interface featuring windows and dialog boxes.	**Windows 8 and desktop** Applications use one of two interfaces: the Windows 8 interface (featuring tiles and a full-screen layout) or the desktop.
Display content out of view	**Vertical scrolling** Applications allow more vertical scrolling than horizontal scrolling.	**Horizontal scrolling** The Start screen and applications allow more horizontal scrolling than vertical scrolling to take advantage of wide-screen monitors.
Store files	**Physical storage devices** Windows primarily provides access to disks physically connected to the computer.	**Cloud storage locations** A Microsoft user account provides access to information stored online.
Enter text	**Physical keyboard** Type on the keyboard attached to the computer.	**On-screen keyboard** If your computer does not have a physical keyboard, type using the on-screen keyboard.

© 2014 Cengage Learning

Although Windows 7 introduced a few gestures for touchscreen users, Windows 8 expands the use of gestures and interactions. In Windows 8, you can use touch gestures to do nearly everything you can do with a pointing device. Figure 2 lists common Windows 8 interactions and their touch and mouse equivalents.

Figure 2 — Windows 8 touch and mouse interactions

Interaction	Touch Gesture	Mouse Action
Display a ScreenTip, text that identifies the name or purpose of the button	Touch and hold (or press) an object such as a button.	Point to an object such as a button.
Display an Apps bar, which displays options related to the current task and access to the Apps screen	Swipe from the top or bottom of the screen toward the center.	Right-click the bottom edge of the screen.
Display the Charms bar	Swipe from the right edge of the screen toward the center.	Point to the upper-right or lower-right corner of the screen.
Display thumbnails of open apps (the Switch List)	Swipe from the left edge of the screen toward the center.	Point to the upper-left corner of the screen, and then drag the pointer down.
Drag an object	Press and then drag.	Click, hold, and then drag.
Scroll the Start screen	Swipe from the right edge of the screen to the left.	Click the scroll arrows, or drag the scroll bar.
Select an object or perform an action such as starting an app	Tap the object.	Click the object.
Zoom	Pinch two fingers to zoom out or move the fingers apart to zoom in.	Click the Zoom button.

© 2014 Cengage Learning

Despite the substantial differences between how you interact with Windows 7 and Windows 8, the steps you follow to perform work in either operating system are the same. In a typical computer session, you start an application and open a **file**, often referred to as a document, which is a collection of data that has a name and is stored on a computer. You view, add, or change the file contents, and then save and close the file. You can complete all of these steps using Windows 7 or Windows 8. Because most of your work involves files, you need to understand how to save and organize files so you can easily find and open them when necessary.

Organizing Files and Folders

Knowing how to save, locate, and organize computer files makes you more productive when you are working with a computer. After you create a file, you can open it, edit its contents, print the file, and save it again—usually using the same application you used to create the file. You organize files by storing them in folders. A **folder** is a container for files. You need to organize files and folders so that you can find them easily and work efficiently.

A file cabinet is a common metaphor for computer file organization. As shown in Figure 3, a computer is like a file cabinet that has two or more drawers—each drawer is a storage device, or **disk**. Each disk contains folders that hold files. To make it easy to retrieve files, you arrange them logically into folders. For example, one folder might contain financial data, another might contain your creative work, and another could contain information you're gathering for an upcoming vacation.

Figure 3   Computer as a file cabinet

disks contain folders

folders contain files

each drawer is a storage device, or disk

© 2014 Cengage Learning

    A computer can store folders and files on different types of disks, ranging from removable media—such as **USB drives** (also called USB flash drives) and digital video discs (DVDs)—to **hard disks**, or fixed disks, which are permanently housed in a computer. Hard disks are the most popular type of computer storage because they provide an economical way to store many gigabytes of data. (A **gigabyte**, or **GB**, is about 1 billion bytes, with each byte roughly equivalent to a character of data.)

    To have your computer access a removable disk, you must insert the disk into a **drive**, which is a device that can retrieve and sometimes record data on a disk. A computer's hard disk is already contained in a drive inside the computer, so you don't need to insert it each time you use the computer.

    A computer distinguishes one drive from another by assigning each a drive letter. The hard disk is assigned to drive C. The remaining drives can have any other letters, but are usually assigned in the order that the drives were installed on the computer—so your USB drive might be drive D or drive F.

Understanding How to Organize Files and Folders

Windows stores thousands of files in many folders on the hard disk of your computer. These are system files that Windows needs to display the Start screen and desktop, use drives, and perform other operating system tasks. To keep the system stable and to find files quickly, Windows organizes the folders and files in a hierarchy, or **file system**. At the top of the hierarchy, Windows stores folders and important files that it needs when you turn on the computer. This location is called the **root directory** and is usually drive C (the hard disk). As Figure 4 shows, the root directory contains all the other folders and files on the computer. The figure also shows that folders can contain other folders. An effectively organized computer contains a few folders in the root directory, and those folders contain other folders, also called **subfolders**.

Figure 4 — Organizing folders and files on a hard disk

- Top level of file system: Hard disk (C:), Removable disk (F:)
- Level 2: Windows, Applications, User
- Level 3: My Documents
- Level 4 (folders created for each course): Basic Accounting, Computer Concepts, Management Skills, Professional Writing
- Level 5 (files for the Professional Writing course): Memo, Procedure, Proposal, Report

© 2014 Cengage Learning

The root directory is the top level of the hard disk and is for system files and folders only. You should not store your own work in the root directory because your files could interfere with Windows or an application. (If you are working in a computer lab, you might not be allowed to access the root directory.)

Do not delete or move any files or folders from the root directory of the hard disk; doing so could disrupt the system so that you can't start or run the computer. In fact, you should not reorganize or change any folder that contains installed software because Windows 8 expects to find the files for specific applications within certain folders. In Figure 4, folders containing software are stored at Level 2 of the file system. If you reorganize or change these folders, Windows 8 can't locate and start the applications stored in those folders. Likewise, you should not make changes to the folder (usually named Windows) that contains the Windows 8 operating system.

Level 2 of the file system also includes a folder for your user account, such as the User folder. This folder contains all of your system settings, preferences, and other user account information. It also contains subfolders, such as the My Documents folder, for your personal files. The folders in Level 3 of the file system are designed to contain subfolders for your personal files. You can create as many subfolders at Level 4 of the file system as you need to store other folders and files and keep them organized.

Figure 4 shows how you could organize your files on a hard disk if you were taking a full semester of business classes. To duplicate this organization, you would open the main folder for your documents, such as My Documents, create four folders—one each for the Basic Accounting, Computer Concepts, Management Skills, and Professional Writing courses—and then store the writing assignments you complete in the Professional Writing folder.

If you store your files on removable media, such as a USB drive, you can use a simpler organization because you do not have to account for system files. In general, the larger the storage medium, the more levels of folders you should use because large media can store more files and, therefore, need better organization. For example, if you were organizing your files on a 12 GB USB drive, you could create folders in the top level of the USB drive for each general category of documents you store—one each for Courses, Creative, Financials, and Vacation. The Courses folder could then include one folder for each course (Basic Accounting, Computer Concepts, Management Skills, and Professional Writing), and each of those folders could contain the appropriate files.

PROSKILLS

Decision Making: Determining Where to Store Files

When you create and save files on your computer's hard disk, you should store them in subfolders. The top level of the hard disk is off-limits for your files because they could interfere with system files. If you are working on your own computer, store your files within the My Documents folder in the Documents library, which is where many applications save your files by default. When you use a computer on the job, your employer might assign a main folder to you for storing your work. In either case, if you simply store all your files in one folder, you will soon have trouble finding the files you want. Instead, you should create subfolders within a main folder to separate files in a way that makes sense for you.

Even if you store most of your files on removable media, such as USB drives, you still need to organize those files into folders and subfolders. Before you start creating folders, whether on a hard disk or removable disk, you need to plan the organization you will use. Following your plan increases your efficiency because you don't have to pause and decide which folder to use when you save your files. A file organization plan also makes you more productive in your computer work—the next time you need a particular file, you'll know where to find it.

Exploring Files and Folders

As shown in the Visual Overview, you use File Explorer in Windows 8 to explore the files and folders on your computer. File Explorer displays the contents of your computer by using icons to represent drives, folders, and files. When you open File Explorer, it shows the contents of the Windows built-in libraries by default. Windows provides these libraries so you can organize files by category—documents, music, pictures, and video. A library can display these categories of files together, no matter where the files are actually stored. For example, you might keep some music files in a folder named Albums on your hard disk. You might also keep music files in a Songs folder on a USB drive. Although the Albums and Songs folders are physically stored in different locations, you can set up the Music library to display both folders in the same File Explorer window. You can then search and arrange the files as a single collection to quickly find the music you want to open and play. In this way, you use libraries to organize your files into categories so you can easily locate and work with files.

The File Explorer window is divided into two sections, called panes. The left pane is the navigation pane, which contains icons and links to locations on your computer. The right pane displays the contents of the location selected in the navigation pane. If the navigation pane showed all the contents on your computer at once, it could be a very long list. Instead, you open drives and folders only when you want to see what they contain. For example, to display the hierarchy of the folders and other locations on your computer, you select the Computer icon in the navigation pane, and then select the icon for a drive, such as Local Disk (C:) or Removable Disk (F:). You can then open and explore folders on that drive.

If a folder contains undisplayed subfolders, an expand icon appears to the left of the folder icon. (The same is true for drives.) To view the folders contained in an object, you click the expand icon. A collapse icon then appears next to the folder icon; click the collapse icon to hide the folder's subfolders. To view the files contained in a folder, you click the folder icon, and the files appear in the right pane. See Figure 5.

Figure 5 — Viewing files in File Explorer

Using the navigation pane helps you explore your computer and orients you to your current location. As you move, copy, delete, and perform other tasks with the files and folders in the right pane of File Explorer, you can refer to the navigation pane to see how your changes affect the overall organization of the selected location.

In addition to using the navigation pane, you can explore your computer in File Explorer using the following navigation techniques:

- Opening drives and folders in the right pane—To view the contents of a drive or folder, double-click the drive or folder icon in the right pane of File Explorer.
- Using the Address bar—You can use the Address bar to navigate to a different folder. The Address bar displays the file path for your current folder. (Recall that a file path shows the location of a folder or file.) Click a folder name such as My Documents in the Address bar to navigate to that folder, or click an arrow button to navigate to a different location in the folder's hierarchy.
- Clicking the Back, Forward, Recent locations, and Up to buttons—Use the Back, Forward, and Recent locations buttons to navigate to other folders you have already opened. Use the Up to button to navigate up to the folder containing the current folder.
- Using the Search box—To find a file or folder stored in the current folder or its subfolders, type a word or phrase in the Search box. The search begins as soon as you

start typing. Windows finds files based on text in the filename, text within the file, and other properties of the file.

You'll practice using some of these navigation techniques later in the tutorial. Right now, you'll show Matt how to open File Explorer. Your computer should be turned on and displaying the Start screen.

To open File Explorer:

1. On the Start screen, click the **Desktop** tile to display the desktop.
2. On the taskbar, click the **File Explorer** button. The File Explorer window opens, displaying the contents of the default libraries.
3. In the Libraries section of the navigation pane, click the **expand** icon next to the Documents icon. The folders in the Documents library appear in the navigation pane; see Figure 6. The contents of your computer will differ.

Figure 6 — Viewing the contents of the Documents library

- four tabs on the File Explorer ribbon
- Documents library is expanded to display its folders
- My Documents and Public Documents folders are included in the Documents library by default
- four default libraries provided with Windows 8

Trouble? If your window displays icons in a size or arrangement different from the one shown in the figure, you can still explore files and folders. The same is true for all the figures in this tutorial.

TIP
When you are working in the navigation pane, you only need to click a folder to open it; you do not need to double-click it.

4. In the navigation pane, click the **My Documents** folder to display its contents in the right pane.

As Figure 6 shows, the File Explorer window includes a ribbon, which is collapsed by default so it displays only tab names, such as File, Home, Share, and View. The Visual Overview shows the expanded ribbon, which displays the options for the selected tab. You'll work with the ribbon and learn how to expand it later in the tutorial.

Navigating to Your Data Files

To navigate to the files you want, it helps to know the file path because the file path tells you exactly where the file is stored in the hierarchy of drives and folders on your computer. For example, Matt has a file named "Logo," which contains an image of the company's logo. If Matt stored the Logo file in a folder named "Marketing" and saved that folder in a folder named "Savvy Traveler" on drive F (a USB drive) on his computer, the Address bar would show the following file path for the Logo file:

Managing Your Files | Windows 8   FM 11

Computer ▸ Removable Disk (F:) ▸ Savvy Traveler ▸ Marketing ▸ Logo.png

This path has five parts, with each part separated by an arrow button:

- Computer—The main container for the file, such as "Computer" or "Network"
- Removable Disk (F:)—The drive name, including the drive letter followed by a colon, which indicates a drive rather than a folder
- Savvy Traveler—The top-level folder on drive F
- Marketing—A subfolder in the Savvy Traveler folder
- Logo.png—The name of the file

Although File Explorer uses arrow buttons to separate locations in a file path, printed documents use backslashes (\ ). For example, if you read an instruction to open the Logo file in the Savvy Traveler\Marketing folder on your USB drive, you know you must navigate to the USB drive attached to your computer, open the Savvy Traveler folder, and then open the Marketing folder to find the Logo file.

File Explorer displays the file path in the Address bar so you can keep track of your current location as you navigate between drives and folders. You can use File Explorer to navigate to the Data Files you need for this tutorial. Before you perform the following steps, you should know where you stored your Data Files, such as on a USB drive. The following steps assume that drive is Removable Disk (F:), a USB drive. If necessary, substitute the appropriate drive on your system when you perform the steps.

To navigate to your Data Files:

1. Make sure your computer can access your Data Files for this tutorial. For example, if you are using a USB drive, insert the drive into the USB port.

   Trouble? If you don't have the starting Data Files, you need to get them before you can proceed. Your instructor will either give you the Data Files or ask you to obtain them from a specified location (such as a network drive). If you have any questions about the Data Files, see your instructor or technical support person for assistance.

2. In the navigation pane of File Explorer, click the **expand** icon ▷ next to the Computer icon to display the drives on your computer, if necessary.

3. Click the **expand** icon ▷ next to the drive containing your Data Files, such as Removable Disk (F:). A list of the folders on that drive appears below the drive name.

4. If the list of folders does not include the FM folder, continue clicking the **expand** icon ▷ to navigate to the folder that contains the FM folder.

5. Click the **expand** icon ▷ next to the FM folder to expand the folder, and then click the **FM** folder so that its contents appear in the navigation pane and in the right pane of the folder window. The FM folder contains the Case1, Case2, Review, and Tutorial folders, as shown in Figure 7. The other folders on your computer might vary.

Figure 7 — Navigating to the FM folder

- file path displayed in the Address bar
- the name of the selected folder appears in the File Explorer title bar
- contents of the FM folder; your Date modified information might differ
- your Data Files might be stored on a different drive
- selected FM folder is expanded in the navigation pane
- Tutorial folder

6. In the navigation pane, click the **Tutorial** folder. The files it contains appear in the right pane.

You can change the appearance of the File Explorer window to suit your preferences. You'll do so next so you can see more details about folders and files.

Changing the View

TIP

The default view for any folder in the Pictures library is Large icons view, which provides a thumbnail image of the file contents.

File Explorer provides eight ways to view the contents of a folder: Extra large icons, Large icons, Medium icons, Small icons, List, Details, Tiles, and Content. For example, the files in the Tutorial folder are currently displayed in Details view, which is the default view for all folders except those stored in the Pictures library. Details view displays a small icon to identify each file's type and lists file details in columns, such as the date the file was last modified, the file type, and the size of the file. Although only Details view lists the file details, you can see these details in any other view by pointing to a file to display a ScreenTip.

To change the view of File Explorer to any of the eight views, you use the View tab on the ribbon. To switch to Details view or Large icons view, you can use the view buttons on the status bar.

REFERENCE

Changing the View in File Explorer

- Click a view button on the status bar.

or

- Click the View tab on the ribbon.
- In the Layout group, click the view option; or click the More button, if necessary, and then click a view option.

You'll show Matt how to change the view of the Tutorial folder in the File Explorer window.

Managing Your Files | Windows 8   FM 13

To change the view of the Tutorial folder in File Explorer:

1. On the ribbon, click the **View** tab.
2. In the Layout group, click **Medium icons**. The files appear in Medium icons view in File Explorer. See Figure 8.

Figure 8   Files in the Tutorial folder in Medium icons view

- View tab on the ribbon
- Expand the Ribbon button
- icons are displayed in Medium icons view
- thumbnail image previews the file contents for certain file types
- file icon identifies the file type; your icons might be different
- Tutorial folder is selected in the navigation pane
- Details view button

Photos courtesy of Lisa Ruffolo

Because the icons used to identify types of files depend on the applications installed on your computer, the file icons that appear in your window might be different.

TIP
When you change the view, it only changes the view for the currently selected folder.

3. On the status bar, click the **Large icons view** button. The window shows the files with large icons and no file details.

When you clicked the View tab in the previous steps, the ribbon expanded so you could select an option and then collapsed after you clicked the Medium icons option. You can keep the ribbon expanded in the File Explorer window so you can easily access all of its options. You'll show Matt how to expand the ribbon and then use the View tab to switch to Details view.

To expand the ribbon in File Explorer:

1. Click the **Expand the Ribbon** button to expand the ribbon. The Expand the Ribbon button changes to the Minimize the Ribbon button, which you could click if you wanted to collapse the ribbon.
2. On the View tab, in the Layout group, click **Details**. The window shows the files with small icons and lists the file details.

No matter which view you use, you can sort the file list by the name of the files or another detail, such as size, type, or date. When you **sort** files, you list them in ascending order (A to Z, 0 to 9, or earliest to latest date) or descending order (Z to A, 9 to 0, or latest to earliest date) by a file detail. If you're viewing music files, you can sort by details such as contributing artists or album title; and if you're viewing picture files, you can sort by details such as date taken or size. Sorting can help you find a particular file in a long file listing. For example, suppose you want to work on a document that you know you edited on June 4, 2016, but you can't remember the name of the file. You can sort the file list by date modified to find the file you want.

When you are working in Details view in File Explorer, you sort by clicking a column heading that appears at the top of the file list. In other views, you use the View tab on the ribbon to sort. In the Current view group, click the Sort by button, and then click a file detail.

> **TIP**
> To sort by a file detail that does not appear as a column heading, right-click any column heading and then select a file detail.

To sort the file list by date modified:

1. At the top of the file list, click the **Date modified** column heading button. The down arrow that appears above the label of the Date modified button indicates that the files are sorted in descending (newest to oldest) order by the date the file was modified. At the top of the list is the List file, which was modified on June 18, 2016.

   Trouble? If your folder window does not contain a Date modified column, right-click any column heading, click Date modified on the shortcut menu, and then repeat Step 1.

2. Click the **Date modified** column heading button again. The up arrow on the Date modified button indicates that the sort order is reversed, with the files listed in ascending (oldest to newest) order.

3. Click the **Name** column heading button to sort the files in alphabetical order by name. The Artists file is now listed first.

Now that Matt is comfortable working in File Explorer, you're ready to show him how to manage his files and folders.

Managing Files and Folders

As discussed earlier, you manage your personal files and folders by storing them according to a logical organization so that they are easy to find later. You can organize files as you create, edit, and save them, or you can do so later by creating folders, if necessary, and then moving and copying files into the folders.

To create a file-organization plan for Matt's files, you can review Figure 8 and look for files that logically belong together. In the Tutorial folder, Chianti, Florence, Logo, and Market are all graphics files that Matt uses for marketing and sales. He created the Artists and Tuscany files to describe Italian tours. The Marketing and Tour Rates files relate to business finances. Matt thinks the List file contains a task list for completing a project, but he isn't sure of its contents. He does recall creating the file using WordPad.

If the List file does contain a project task list, you can organize the files by creating four folders—one for graphics, one for tours, another for the financial files, and a fourth folder for projects. When you create a folder, you give it a name, preferably one that describes its contents. A folder name can have up to 255 characters, and any character is allowed, except / \ : * ? " < > and |. Considering these conventions, you could create four folders to contain Matt's files, as follows:

- Marketing Graphics folder—Chianti, Florence, Logo, and Market files
- Tours folder—Artists and Tuscany files
- Financial folder—Marketing and Tour Rates files
- Projects folder—List file

Before you start creating folders according to this plan, you need to verify the contents of the List file. You can do so by opening the file.

Opening a File

You can open a file from a running application or from File Explorer. To open a file in a running application, you select the application's Open command to access the Open dialog box, which you use to navigate to the file you want, select the file, and then open it. In the Open dialog box, you use the same tools that are available in File Explorer to navigate to the file you want to open. If the application you want to use is not running, you can open a file by double-clicking it in the right pane of File Explorer. The file usually opens in the application that you used to create or edit it.

Occasionally, File Explorer will open the file in an application other than the one you want to use to work with the file. For example, double-clicking a digital picture file usually opens the picture in a picture viewer application. If you want to edit the picture, you must open the file in a graphics editing application. When you need to specify an application to open a file, you can right-click the file, point to Open with on the shortcut menu, and then click the name of the application that you want to use.

Matt says that he might want to edit the List file to add another task. You'll show him how to use File Explorer to open the file in WordPad, which he used to create the file, and then edit it.

> **TIP**
>
> To select the default application for opening a file, right-click the file in File Explorer, point to Open with, and then click Choose default application. Click an application in the list that opens, and then click OK.

To open and edit the List file:

1. In the right pane of File Explorer, right-click the **List** file, and then point to **Open with** on the shortcut menu to display a list of applications that can open the file. See Figure 9.

   Trouble? If a list does not appear when you point to Open with on the shortcut menu, click Open with to display a window asking how you want to open this file.

Figure 9 — Shortcut menu for opening a file

List is the selected file

Open with command

applications on this computer that can open the List file

TIP

In File Explorer, you can also double-click a file to open it in the default application for that file type.

2. Click **WordPad** to open the List file in WordPad. The file contains a task list for the marketing project, which includes three items.

   Trouble? If you had to click Open with instead of pointing to it, in the window that asks how you want to open this file, click Keep using WordPad.

3. Press the **Ctrl+End** keys to move the insertion point to the end of the document, press the **Enter** key if necessary to start a new line, and then type **4. Review the Tours in Italy webpage.**

Now that you've added text to the List file, you need to save it to preserve the changes you made.

Saving a File

As you are creating or editing a file, you should save it frequently so you don't lose your work. When you save a file, you need to decide what name to use for the file and where to store it. Most applications provide a default location for saving a file, which makes it easy to find the file again later. However, you can select a different location depending on where you want to store the file.

Besides a storage location, every file must have a filename, which provides important information about the file, including its contents and purpose. A filename such as Italian Tours.docx has the following three parts:

- Main part of the filename—When you save a file, you need to provide only the main part of the filename, such as "Italian Tours."
- Dot—The dot (.) separates the main part of the filename from the extension.
- Extension—The **extension** includes the three or four characters that follow the dot in the filename and identify the file's type.

Similar to folder names, the main part of a filename can have up to 255 characters. This gives you plenty of room to name your file accurately enough so that you'll recognize the contents of the file just by looking at the filename. You can use spaces and certain punctuation symbols in your filenames. However, filenames cannot contain the symbols / \ : * ? " < > or | because these characters have special meanings in Windows 8.

Windows and other software add the dot and the extension to a filename, though File Explorer does not display them by default. Instead, File Explorer shows the file icon associated with the extension or a thumbnail for some types of files, such as graphics. For example, in a file named Italian Tours.docx, the docx extension identifies the file as one created in Microsoft Word, a word-processing application. File Explorer displays this file using a Microsoft Word icon and the main part of its filename. For a file named Italian Tours.png, the png extension identifies the file as one created in a graphics application such as Paint. In Details view or List view, File Explorer displays this file using a Paint icon and the main part of its filename. In other views, File Explorer does not use an icon, but displays the file contents in a thumbnail. File Explorer treats the Italian Tours.docx and Italian Tours.png files differently because their extensions distinguish them as different types of files, even though the main parts of their filenames are identical.

When you save a new file, you use the Save As dialog box to provide a filename and select a location for the file. You can create a folder for the new file at the same time you save the file. When you edit a file you saved previously, you can use the application's Save command to save your changes to the file, keeping the same name and location. If you want to save the edited file with a different name or in a different location, however, you need to use the Save As dialog box to specify the new name or location.

As with the Open dialog box, you specify the file location in the Save As dialog box using the same navigation techniques and tools that are available in File Explorer. You might need to click the Browse Folders button to expand the Save As dialog box so it displays these tools. In addition, the Save As dialog box always includes a File name box where you specify a filename.

> ### INSIGHT
>
> ### Saving Files on SkyDrive
>
> Some Windows 8 applications, such as Microsoft Office, include SkyDrive as a location for saving and opening files. **SkyDrive** is a Microsoft service that provides up to 7 GB of online storage space for your files at no charge. You can purchase additional space if you need it. For example, if you create a document in Microsoft Word, your SkyDrive appears as a location for saving the document. (Your SkyDrive appears with your username, such as Matt's SkyDrive.) If you have a Microsoft account, you can select a folder on your SkyDrive to save the document online. (If you don't have a Microsoft account, you can sign up for one by visiting the SkyDrive website.) Because the file is stored online, it takes up no storage space on your computer and is available from any computer with an Internet connection. You access the document by opening it in Word or by visiting the SkyDrive website, and then signing in to your Microsoft account. To share the document with other people, you can send them a link to the document via email. They can use the link to access the document even if they do not have a Microsoft account.

One reason that Matt had trouble remembering the contents of the List file is that "List" is not a descriptive name. A better name for this file is Task List. You will save this document in the Tutorial subfolder of the FM folder provided with your Data Files. You will also use the Save As dialog box to specify a new name for the file as you save it.

Windows 8 | Managing Your Files

To save the List file with a new name:

1. On the ribbon in the WordPad window, click the **File** tab to display commands for working with files.

2. Click **Save as** to open the Save As dialog box, as shown in Figure 10. The Tutorial folder is selected as the storage location for this file because you opened the file from this folder.

Figure 10	Saving a file using the Save As dialog box

use the navigation pane or the Address bar to navigate to a different location for saving the file

type the name for the file in the File name box

clicking the Hide Folders button collapses the dialog box

toolbar

the Save As dialog box displays the original location of the file as the default storage location

Save as type box

Trouble? If the navigation pane does not appear in the Save As dialog box, click the Browse Folders button. The Browse Folders button toggles to become the Hide Folders button.

3. With the current filename selected in the File name box, type **Task List**. The Save as type box shows that WordPad will save this file as a Rich Text Format (RTF) file, which is the default file type for WordPad files.

   Trouble? If the current filename is not selected in the File name box, drag to select the text in the File name box and then type Task List.

4. Click the **Save** button. The Save As dialog box closes, WordPad saves the Task List file in the Tutorial folder, and the new filename appears in the WordPad title bar.

5. On the title bar, click the **Close** button ✕ to close WordPad.

TIP
To change the file type, click the Save as type box, and then click a file type such as Text Document.

Now you're ready to start creating the folders you need to organize Matt's files.

Managing Your Files | Windows 8   FM 19

Creating Folders

You originally proposed creating four new folders for Matt's files: Marketing Graphics, Tours, Financial, and Projects. Matt asks you to create these folders now. After that, you'll move his files to the appropriate folders. You create folders in File Explorer using one of three methods: using the New folder button in the New group on the Home tab; using the New folder button on the Quick Access Toolbar; or right-clicking to display a shortcut menu that includes the New command.

> **INSIGHT**
>
> ### Guidelines for Creating Folders
>
> Consider the following guidelines as you create folders:
> - Keep folder names short yet descriptive of the folder's contents. Long folder names can be more difficult to display in their entirety in folder windows, so use names that are short but clear. Choose names that will be meaningful later, such as project names or course numbers.
> - Create subfolders to organize files. If a file list in File Explorer is so long that you must scroll the window, you should probably organize those files into subfolders.
> - Develop standards for naming folders. Use a consistent naming scheme that is clear to you, such as one that uses a project name as the name of the main folder, and includes step numbers in each subfolder name (for example, 1-Outline, 2-First Draft, 3-Final Draft, and so on).

In the following steps, you will create the four folders for Matt in your Tutorial folder. Because it is easier to work with files using large file icons, you'll switch to Large icons view first.

To create the folders:

1. On the status bar in the File Explorer window, click the **Large icons view** button to switch to Large icons view.
2. Click the **Home** tab to display the Home tab on the ribbon.
3. In the New group, click the **New folder** button. A folder icon with the label "New folder" appears in the right pane of the File Explorer window. See Figure 11.

Windows 8 | Managing Your Files

Figure 11 — Creating a new folder in the Tutorial folder

Quick Access Toolbar

new folder; its location on your screen might differ

type to replace the selected text with a different folder name

Photos courtesy of Lisa Ruffolo

Trouble? If the "New folder" name is not selected, right-click the new folder, click Rename on the shortcut menu, and then continue with Step 4.

Windows uses "New folder" as a placeholder, and selects the text so that you can replace it immediately by typing a new name. You do not need to press the Backspace or Delete key to delete the text.

▶ 4. Type **Marketing Graphics** as the folder name, and then press the **Enter** key. The new folder is named Marketing Graphics and is the selected item in the right pane. To create a second folder, you can use a shortcut menu.

▶ 5. In the right pane, right-click a blank area, point to **New** on the shortcut menu, and then click **Folder**. A folder icon appears in the right pane with the "New folder" text selected.

▶ 6. Type **Tours** as the name of the new folder, and then press the **Enter** key. To create the third folder, you can use the Quick Access Toolbar.

▶ 7. On the Quick Access Toolbar, click the **New folder** button, type **Financial**, and then press the **Enter** key to create and name the folder.

▶ 8. Create a new folder in the Tutorial folder named **Projects**.

After creating four folders, you're ready to organize Matt's files by moving them into the appropriate folders.

Moving and Copying Files and Folders

You can either move or copy a file from its current location to a new location. **Moving** a file removes it from its current location and places it in a new location that you specify. **Copying** a file places a duplicate version of the file in a new location that you specify, while leaving the original file intact in its current location. You can also move and copy folders. When you do, you move or copy all the files contained in the folder. (You'll practice copying folders in a Case Problem at the end of this tutorial.)

Managing Your Files | Windows 8 FM 21

In File Explorer, you can move and copy files by using the Move to or Copy to buttons in the Organize group on the Home tab; using the Copy and Cut commands on a file's shortcut menu; or using keyboard shortcuts. When you copy or move files using these methods, you are using the **Clipboard**, a temporary storage area for files and information that you copy or move from one location to place in another.

You can also move files by dragging the files in the File Explorer window. You will now organize Matt's files by moving them to the appropriate folders you have created. You'll start by moving the Marketing file to the Financial folder by dragging the file.

To move the Marketing file by dragging it:

1. In File Explorer, point to the **Marketing** file in the right pane, and then press and hold the mouse button.

2. While still pressing the mouse button, drag the **Marketing** file to the **Financial** folder. See Figure 12.

| Figure 12 | Dragging a file to move it to a folder |

Marketing file is selected

Financial folder

Move to Financial ScreenTip

TIP

If you drag a file or folder to a location on a different drive, the file is copied, not moved, to preserve the file in its original location.

3. When the Move to Financial ScreenTip appears, release the mouse button. The Marketing file is removed from the main Tutorial folder and stored in the Financial subfolder.

Trouble? If you released the mouse button before the Move to Financial ScreenTip appeared, press the Ctrl+Z keys to undo the move, and then repeat Steps 1–3.

Trouble? If you moved the Market file instead of the Marketing file, press the Ctrl+Z keys to undo the move, and then repeat Steps 1–3.

4. In the right pane, double-click the **Financial** folder to verify that it contains the Marketing file.

Trouble? If the Marketing file does not appear in the Financial folder, you probably moved it to a different folder. Press the Ctrl+Z keys to undo the move, and then repeat Steps 1–3.

5. Click the **Back** button on the Address bar to return to the Tutorial folder.

You'll move the remaining files into the folders using the Clipboard.

To move files using the Clipboard:

1. Right-click the **Artists** file, and then click **Cut** on the shortcut menu. Although the file icon still appears selected in the right pane of File Explorer, Windows removes the Artists file from the Tutorial folder and stores it on the Clipboard.

2. In the right pane, right-click the **Tours** folder, and then click **Paste** on the shortcut menu. Windows pastes the Artists file from the Clipboard to the Tours folder. The Artists file icon no longer appears in the File Explorer window, which is currently displaying the contents of the Tutorial folder.

3. In the navigation pane, click the **expand** icon next to the Tutorial folder, if necessary, to display its contents, and then click the **Tours** folder to view its contents in the right pane. The Tours folder now contains the Artists file. See Figure 13.

Figure 13 — Artists file in its new location

Artists file is now stored in the Tours folder

selected folder

Next, you'll use the Clipboard again to move the Tuscany file from the Tutorial folder to the Tours folder. But this time, you'll access the Clipboard using the ribbon.

Managing Your Files | Windows 8 FM 23

> 4. On the Address bar, point to the **Up to** button to display its ScreenTip (Up to "Tutorial"), click the **Up to** button to return to the Tutorial folder, and then click the **Tuscany** file to select it.

> 5. On the Home tab, in the Clipboard group, click the **Cut** button to remove the Tuscany file from the Tutorial folder and temporarily store it on the Clipboard.

> 6. In the Address bar, click the **arrow** button to the right of "Tutorial" to display a list of subfolders in the Tutorial folder, and then click **Tours** to display the contents of the Tours folder in File Explorer.

> 7. In the Clipboard group, click the **Paste** button to paste the Tuscany file in the Tours folder. The Tours folder now contains the Artists and Tuscany files.

Finally, you'll move the Task List file from the Tutorial folder to the Projects folder using the Move to button in the Organize group on the Home tab. This button and the Copy to button are ideal when you want to move or copy files without leaving the current folder. When you select a file and then click the Move to or Copy to button, a list of locations appears, including all of the Windows libraries and one or more folders you open frequently. You can click a location in the list to move the selected file to that library or folder. You can also select the Choose location option to open the Move Items or Copy Items dialog box, and then select a location for the file, which you'll do in the following steps.

To move the Task List file using the Move to button:

> 1. In the Address bar, click **Tutorial** to return to the Tutorial folder, and then click the **Task List** file to select it.

> 2. On the Home tab, in the Organize group, click the **Move to** button to display a list of locations to which you can move the selected file. The Projects folder is not included on this list because you haven't opened it yet.

> 3. Click **Choose location** to open the Move Items dialog box. See Figure 14.

Figure 14   **Move Items dialog box**

[locations on your computer; yours might differ]

Move Items
Select the place where you want to move 'Task List', then click the Move button.
- Desktop
  - Libraries
  - Homegroup
  - User
  - Computer
    - Local Disk (C:)
    - DVD RW Drive (D:)

Folder: User

Make New Folder   Move   Cancel

> 4. If necessary, scroll the list of locations, and then click the **expand** icon next to the drive containing your Data Files, such as Removable Disk (F:).

5. Navigate to the FM ▶ Tutorial folder, and then click the **Projects** folder to select it.

6. Click the **Move** button to close the dialog box and move the Task List file to the Projects folder.

7. Open the Projects folder to confirm that it contains the Task List file.

One way to save steps when moving or copying multiple files or folders is to select all the files and folders you want to move or copy, and then work with them as a group. You can use several techniques to select multiple files or folders at the same time, which are described in Figure 15.

Figure 15 | **Selecting multiple files or folders**

Items to Select in the Right Pane of File Explorer	Method
Files or folders listed together	Click the first item, press and hold the Shift key, click the last item, and then release the Shift key.
	or
	Drag the pointer to create a selection box around all the items you want to include.
Files or folders not listed together	Press and hold the Ctrl key, click each item you want to select, and then release the Ctrl key.
All files and folders	On the Home tab, in the Select group, click the Select all button.

Items to Deselect in the Right Pane of File Explorer	Method
Single file or folder in a selected group	Press and hold the Ctrl key, click each item you want to remove from the selection, and then release the Ctrl key.
All selected files and folders	Click a blank area of the File Explorer window.

© 2014 Cengage Learning

Next, you'll copy the four graphics files from the Tutorial folder to the Marketing Graphics folder using the Clipboard. To do this efficiently, you will select multiple files at once.

To copy multiple files at once using the Clipboard:

1. Display the contents of the Tutorial folder in File Explorer.

2. Click the **Chianti** file, press and hold the **Shift** key, click the **Market** file, and then release the **Shift** key.

3. Press and hold the **Ctrl** key, click the **List** file to deselect it, and then release the **Ctrl** key. Four files—Chianti, Florence, Logo, and Market—are selected in the Tutorial folder window.

4. Right-click a selected file, and then click **Copy** on the shortcut menu. Windows copies the selected files to the Clipboard.

5. Right-click the **Marketing Graphics** folder, and then click **Paste** on the shortcut menu.

6. Open the **Marketing Graphics** folder to verify it contains the four files you copied, and then return to the Tutorial folder.

7. Right-click the **Tour Rates** file, and then click **Copy** on the shortcut menu.
8. In the right pane, double-click the **Financial** folder to open it, right-click a blank area of the right pane, and then click **Paste** on the shortcut menu.

> **INSIGHT**
>
> ### Duplicating Your Folder Organization
>
> If you work on two computers, such as one computer at an office or school and another computer at home, you can duplicate the folders you use on both computers to simplify the process of transferring files from one computer to another. For example, if you have four folders in your My Documents folder on your work computer, create these same four folders on a USB drive and in the My Documents folder of your home computer. If you change a file on the hard disk of your home computer, you can copy the most recent version of the file to the corresponding folder on your USB drive so the file is available when you are at work. You also then have a **backup**, or duplicate copy, of important files. Having a backup of your files is invaluable if your computer has a fatal error.

All the files that originally appeared in the Tutorial folder are now stored in appropriate subfolders. You can streamline the organization of the Tutorial folder by deleting the duplicate files you no longer need.

Deleting Files and Folders

TIP
In most cases, a file deleted from a USB drive does not go into the Recycle Bin. Instead, it is deleted when Windows 8 removes its icon, and the file cannot be recovered.

You should periodically delete files and folders you no longer need so that your main folders and disks don't get cluttered. In File Explorer, you delete a file or folder by deleting its icon. When you delete a file from a hard disk, Windows 8 removes the file from the folder but stores the file contents in the Recycle Bin. The Recycle Bin is an area on your hard disk that holds deleted files until you remove them permanently. When you delete a folder from the hard disk, the folder and all of its files are stored in the Recycle Bin. If you change your mind and want to retrieve a deleted file or folder, you can double-click the Recycle Bin on the desktop, right-click the file or folder you want to retrieve, and then click Restore. However, after you empty the Recycle Bin, you can no longer recover the files it contained.

Because you copied the Chianti, Florence, Logo, Market, and Tour Rates files to the subfolders in the Tutorial folder, you can safely delete the original files. You can also delete the List file because you no longer need it. You can delete a file or folder using various methods, including using a shortcut menu or selecting one or more files and then pressing the Delete key.

To delete files in the Tutorial folder:

1. Display the Tutorial folder in the File Explorer window.
2. In the right pane, click **Chianti**, press and hold the **Shift** key, click **Tour Rates**, and then release the **Shift** key. All files in the Tutorial folder are now selected. None of the subfolders should be selected.

Make sure you have copied the selected files to the Marketing Graphics and Financial folders before completing this step.

3. Right-click the selected files, and then click **Delete** on the shortcut menu. A message box appears, asking if you're sure you want to permanently delete these files.
4. Click the **Yes** button to confirm that you want to delete the files.

Renaming Files

After creating and naming a file or folder, you might realize that a different name would be more meaningful or descriptive. You can easily rename a file or folder by using the Rename command on the file's shortcut menu.

Now that you've organized Matt's files into folders, he reviews your work and notes that the Artists file was originally created to store text specifically about Florentine painters and sculptors. You can rename that file to give it a more descriptive filename.

> **TIP**
> To rename a file, you can also click the file, pause, click it again to select the filename, and then type to enter a new filename.

To rename the Artists file:

1. In the right pane of the File Explorer window, double-click the **Tours** folder to display its contents.
2. Right-click the **Artists** file, and then click **Rename** on the shortcut menu. The filename is highlighted and a box appears around it.
3. Type **Florentine Artists**, and then press the **Enter** key. The file now appears with the new name.

   Trouble? If you make a mistake while typing and you haven't pressed the Enter key yet, press the Backspace key until you delete the mistake and then complete Step 3. If you've already pressed the Enter key, repeat Steps 2 and 3 to rename the file again.

   Trouble? If your computer is set to display filename extensions, a message might appear asking if you are sure you want to change the filename extension. Click the No button, and then repeat Steps 2 and 3.

Working with Compressed Files

You compress a file or a folder of files so it occupies less space on the disk. It can be useful to compress files before transferring them from one location to another, such as from your hard disk to a removable disk or vice versa, or from one computer to another via email. You can then transfer the files more quickly. Also, if you or your email contacts can send and receive files only up to a certain size, compressing large files might make them small enough to send and receive. Compare two folders—a folder named Photos that contains files totaling about 8.6 MB, and a compressed folder containing the same files but requiring only 6.5 MB of disk space. In this case, the compressed files use about 25 percent less disk space than the uncompressed files.

You can compress one or more files in File Explorer using the Zip button, which is located in the Send group on the Share tab of the ribbon. Windows stores the compressed files in a special type of folder called an **archive**, or a compressed folder. File Explorer uses an icon of a folder with a zipper to represent a compressed folder. To compress additional files or folders, you drag them into the compressed folder. You can open a file directly from a compressed folder, although you cannot modify the file. To edit and save a compressed file, you must **extract** it first. When you extract a file, you create an uncompressed copy of the file in a folder you specify. The original file remains in the compressed folder.

Matt suggests that you compress the files and folders in the Tutorial folder so that you can more quickly transfer them to another location.

Managing Your Files | Windows 8 FM 27

To compress the folders and files in the Tutorial folder:

TIP
Another way to compress files is to select the files, right-click the selection, point to Send to on the shortcut menu, and then click Compressed (zipped) folder.

1. In File Explorer, navigate to the Tutorial folder, and then select all the folders in the Tutorial folder.
2. Click the **Share** tab on the ribbon.
3. In the Send group, click the **Zip** button. After a few moments, a new compressed folder appears in the Tutorial window with the filename selected. By default, File Explorer uses the name of the first selected item as the name of the compressed folder. You'll replace the name with a more descriptive one.
4. Type **Savvy Traveler**, and then press the **Enter** key to rename the compressed folder. See Figure 16.

Figure 16 — Compressing files and folders

[Screenshot of File Explorer showing the Tutorial folder with Financial, Marketing Graphics, Projects, Tours folders and the Savvy Traveler zipped folder. Callout: "zipped folder contains all the files and folders in the Tutorial folder"]

5. Double-click the **Savvy Traveler** compressed folder to open it, open the **Tours** folder, and then note the size of the compressed Tuscany file, which is 1,815 KB.
6. Navigate back to the Tutorial folder.

You can move and copy the files and folders from an opened compressed folder to other locations, although you cannot rename the files. More often, you extract all of the files from the compressed folder to a new location that you specify, preserving the files in their original folders as appropriate.

To extract the compressed files:

1. Click the **Savvy Traveler** compressed folder to select it, and then click the **Compressed Folder Tools Extract** tab on the ribbon.
2. In the Extract all group, click the **Extract all** button. The Extract Compressed (Zipped) Folders Wizard starts and opens the Select a Destination and Extract Files dialog box.
3. Press the **End** key to deselect the path in the box and move the insertion point to the end of the path, press the **Backspace** key as many times as necessary to delete the Savvy Traveler text, and then type **Backups**. The final three parts of the path in the box should be \FM\Tutorial\Backups. See Figure 17.

Figure 17   **Extracting files from a compressed folder**

your path might differ, but should end with FM\Tutorial\Backups

check box should be selected

4. Make sure the Show extracted files when complete check box is checked, and then click the **Extract** button. Windows extracts the files and then opens the Backups folder, showing the Financial, Marketing Graphics, Projects, and Tours folders.

5. Open each folder to make sure it contains the files you worked with in this tutorial. When you open the Tours folder, note the uncompressed size of the Tuscany file, which is about four times as large as its compressed version.

6. Close all open windows.

In this tutorial, you examined the purpose of organizing files and folders, and you planned and created an organization for a set of related files and folders. You also explored your computer using File Explorer and learned how to navigate to your Data Files using the navigation pane. You used File Explorer to manage files and folders by opening and saving files; creating folders; and selecting, moving, and copying files. You also renamed and deleted files according to your organization plan. Finally, you compressed and extracted files.

REVIEW

Quick Check

1. You organize files by storing them in _____.
2. What is the purpose of the Address bar in File Explorer?
3. A filename _____ identifies the file's type and indicates the application that created the file.
4. Explain how to use File Explorer to navigate to a file in the following location: E: ▸ Courses ▸ Computer Basics ▸ Operating Systems.txt.
5. One way to move files and folders is to use the _____, a temporary storage area for files and information that you copied or moved from one place and plan to use somewhere else.
6. What happens if you click the first file in a folder window, press the Shift key, click the last file, and then release the Shift key?
7. When you delete a file from a hard disk, Windows removes the file from the folder but stores the file contents in the _____.
8. Describe how to compress a file or folder.
9. What are the benefits of compressing files and folders?

Review Assignments

Data Files needed for the Review Assignments: Banner.png, Colosseum.jpg, Lectures.xlsx, Rome.jpg, Rome.rtf, Schedule.rtf, Tours.rtf

Matt has saved a few files from his old computer to a removable disk. He gives you these files in a single, unorganized folder, and asks you to organize them logically into subfolders. To do this, you will need to devise a plan for managing the files, and then create the subfolders you need. Next, you will rename, copy, move, and delete files, and then perform other management tasks to make it easy for Matt to work with these files and folders. Complete the following steps:

1. Use File Explorer to navigate to and open the FM ▶ Review folder provided with your Data Files. Examine the seven files in this folder and consider the best way to organize the files.
2. Open the **Rome** text file in WordPad, and then add the following tip to the end of the document: **Dine on the Italian schedule, with the main meal in the middle of the day.**
3. Save the document as **Rome Dining Tips** in the Review folder. Close the WordPad window.
4. In the Review folder, create three folders: **Business**, **Destinations**, and **Supplements**.
5. To organize the files into the correct folders, complete the following steps:
   - Move the Banner and Schedule files from the Review folder to the Business folder.
   - Move the Colosseum and Rome JPEG image files and the Rome Dining Tips and Tours text files to the Destinations folder.
   - Copy the Lectures file to the Supplements folder.
6. Copy the Tours file in the Destinations folder to the Business folder.
7. Rename the Schedule file in the Business folder as **2016 Schedule**. Rename the Lectures file in the Supplements folder as **On-site Lectures**.
8. Delete the Lectures file and the Rome text file from the Review folder.
9. Create a compressed (zipped) folder in the Review folder named **Rome** that contains all the files and folders in the Review folder.
10. Extract the contents of the Rome compressed folder to a new folder named **Rome Backups** in the Review folder. (*Hint:* The file path will end with \FM\Review\Rome Backups.)
11. Close the File Explorer window.

Case Problem 1

See the Starting Data Files section at the beginning of this tutorial for the list of Data Files needed for this Case Problem.

Bay Shore Arts Center   Casey Sullivan started the Bay Shore Arts Center in Monterey, California, to provide workshops and courses on art and photography. Attracting students from the San Francisco and San José areas, Casey's business has grown and she now holds classes five days a week. She recently started a course on fine art landscape photography, which has quickly become her most popular offering. Casey hired you to help her design new classes and manage other parts of her growing business, including maintaining electronic business files and communications. Your first task is to organize the files on her new Windows 8 computer. Complete the following steps:

1. Open File Explorer. In the FM ▶ Case1 folder provided with your Data Files, create three folders: **Classes**, **Landscapes**, and **Management**.
2. Move the Fall Classes, Spring Classes, Summer Classes, and Winter Classes files from the Case1 folder to the Classes folder.
3. Rename the four files in the Classes folder by deleting the word "Classes" from each filename.
4. Move the four JPEG image files from the Case1 folder to the Landscapes folder.
5. Copy the remaining two files to the Management folder.
6. Copy the Workshops file to the Classes folder.
7. Delete the Instructors and Workshops files from the Case1 folder.
8. Make a copy of the Landscapes folder in the Case1 folder. The name of the duplicate folder appears as Landscapes – Copy. Rename the Landscapes – Copy folder as **California Photos**.
9. Copy the Workshops file from the Classes folder to the California Photos folder. Rename this file **California Workshops**.
10. Compress the graphics files in the California Photos folder in a new compressed folder named **Photos**.
11. Move the compressed Photos folder to the Case1 folder.
12. Close File Explorer.

Case Problem 2

See the Starting Data Files section at the beginning of this tutorial for the list of Data Files needed for this Case Problem.

Charlotte Area Business Incubator Antoine Jackson is the director of the Charlotte Area Business Incubator, a service run by the University of North Carolina in Charlotte to consult with new and struggling small businesses. You work as an intern at the business incubator and spend part of your time organizing client files. Since Antoine started using Windows 8, he has been having trouble finding files on his computer. He sometimes creates duplicates of files and then doesn't know which copy is the most current. Complete the following steps:

1. Navigate to the FM ▶ Case2 folder provided with your Data Files, and then examine the files in this folder. Based on the filenames and file types, begin to create an organization plan for the files.
2. **Troubleshoot** Open the Tips1 and the Tips1 – Copy files and consider the problem these files could cause. Close the files and then fix the problem, renaming one or more files as necessary to reflect the contents.
3. **Troubleshoot** Open the Tips2 and the Tips2 – Copy files and compare their contents. Change the filenames to clarify the purpose and contents of the files.
4. Complete the organization plan for Antoine's files. In the FM ▶ Case2 folder, create the subfolders you need according to your plan.
5. Move the files in the Case2 folder to the subfolders you created. When you finish, the Case2 folder should contain at least two subfolders containing files.
6. Rename the spreadsheet files in each subfolder according to the following descriptions.
   - Budget1: **Website budget**
   - Budget2: **Marketing budget**
   - Report1: **Travel expense report**
   - Report2: **Project expense report**
   - Report3: **Balance sheet**
   - Report4: **Event budget**
7. **Troubleshoot** Make sure all files have descriptive names that accurately reflect their contents.
8. **Troubleshoot** Based on the work you did in Steps 6 and 7, move files as necessary to improve the file organization.
9. Close File Explorer.

TUTORIAL 1

Getting Started with Excel

Creating a Customer Order Report

OBJECTIVES

Session 1.1
- Open and close a workbook
- Navigate through a workbook and worksheet
- Select cells and ranges
- Plan and create a workbook
- Insert, rename, and move worksheets
- Enter text, dates, and numbers
- Undo and redo actions
- Resize columns and rows

Session 1.2
- Enter formulas and the SUM and COUNT functions
- Copy and paste formulas
- Move or copy cells and ranges
- Insert and delete rows, columns, and ranges
- Create patterned text with Flash Fill
- Add cell borders and change font size
- Change worksheet views
- Prepare a workbook for printing
- Save a workbook with a new filename

Case | *Sparrow & Pond*

Sally Hughes is part owner of Sparrow & Pond, a small bookstore in Hudson, New Hampshire. Among her many tasks is to purchase new books from publishers. She also purchases rare and first edition books from online auctions as well as local library, estate, and garage sales.

Sally needs to quickly track sales data, compile customer profiles, and generate financial reports. She can perform all of these tasks with **Microsoft Excel 2013** (or **Excel**), an application used to enter, analyze, and present quantitative data. Sally asks you to use Excel to record a recent book order from a regular Sparrow & Pond customer.

STARTING DATA FILES

- Excel1 → Tutorial — SP Finances.xlsx
- Review — (none)
- Case1 — Pacific.xlsx
- Case2 — Tropical.xlsx
- Case3 — Physics.xlsx
- Case4 — Turf.xlsx

Microsoft product screenshots used with permission from Microsoft Corporation.

EX 2   Excel | Tutorial 1 Getting Started with Excel

Session 1.1 Visual Overview:

The **ribbon** contains buttons that you click to execute commands to work with Excel. You can pin the ribbon to leave it fully displayed, as shown here.

The ribbon is organized into tabs. Each **tab** has commands related to particular activities or tasks.

The **formula bar** displays the value or formula entered in the active cell.

Excel stores spreadsheets in files called **workbooks**. The name of the current workbook appears in the title bar.

SP Finances - Ex

FILE | HOME | INSERT | PAGE LAYOUT | FORMULAS | DATA | REVIEW | VIE

B10   Cost of Goods

The **Name box** displays the cell reference of the active cell. In this case, the active cell is cell B104.

	A	B	C	D
1		Sparrow & Pond		
2		Income Statement		
3		January 1, 2015 to December 31, 2015		
4				
5		Income		
6		Gross Sales	$ 258,500	
7		Less returns and allowances	24,500	
8		Net Sales	234,000	
9				
10		Cost of Goods		
11		Inventory, January 1	121,000	
12		Purchases	72,000	
13		Delivery Charges	12,000	
14		Total Merchandise Handled	205,000	
15				
16		mber 31	133,500	
17				
18		Cost of Goods Sold	71,500	

A group of cells in a rectangular block is called a **cell range** (or **range**). If the blocks are not connected, as shown here, it is a **nonadjacent range**.

The currently selected cell is the **active cell**.

The **row headings** are numbers along the left side of the workbook window that identify the different rows of the worksheet.

A workbook is made up of **sheets**. Each sheet is identified by a sheet name, which appears in a **sheet tab**.

Documentation | Income Statement | Expenses | Balance Sheet

READY   AVERAGE: 132428.5

The **status bar** provides information about the workbook.

Inactive sheets are not visible in the workbook window. Their sheet tabs are not underlined and the sheet name is black.

The sheet currently displayed in the workbook window is the **active sheet**. Its sheet tab is underlined and the sheet name is green and bold.

Tutorial 1 Getting Started with Excel | Excel   EX 3

The Excel Window

The **Ribbon Display Options** button is used to display all, part, or none of the ribbon.

The **Restore Down button** returns a window to its previous size. If the **Maximize button** appears, it expands the window to fill the screen.

The **Minimize button** hides a window so that only its program button is visible on the taskbar.

Buttons for related commands are organized on a tab in **groups**.

The **column headings** are letters along the top of the workbook window that identify the different columns in the worksheet.

Each intersection of a row and a column is a **cell**. Each cell contains a separate value.

The contents of a **worksheet** are laid out in a grid of rows and columns in the **workbook window**.

The **Zoom controls** increase or decrease the magnification of the worksheet content. These tutorials show worksheets zoomed to 120%.

Introducing Excel and Spreadsheets

A **spreadsheet** is a grouping of text and numbers in a rectangular grid or table. Spreadsheets are often used in business for budgeting, inventory management, and financial reporting because they unite text, numbers, and charts within one document. They can also be employed for personal use for planning a personal budget, tracking expenses, or creating a list of personal items. The advantage of an electronic spreadsheet is that the content can be easily edited and updated to reflect changing financial conditions.

To start Excel:

1. Display the Windows Start screen, if necessary.

   Using Windows 7? To complete Step 1, click the Start button on the taskbar.

2. Click the **Excel 2013** tile. Excel starts and displays the Recent screen in Backstage view. **Backstage view** provides access to various screens with commands that allow you to manage files and Excel options. On the left is a list of recently opened workbooks. On the right are options for creating new workbooks. See Figure 1-1.

Figure 1-1   Recent screen in Backstage view

- you might see a list of recently opened workbooks here
- link to the Open screen
- opens a blank workbook
- preview of a template

Trouble? If you don't see the Excel 2013 tile on your Start screen, type Excel to display the Apps screen with the Excel 2013 tile highlighted, and then click the tile.

Using Windows 7? To complete Step 2, point to All Programs on the Start menu, click Microsoft Office 2013, and then click Excel 2013.

Opening an Existing Workbook

Excel documents are called workbooks. From the Recent screen in Backstage view, you can open a blank workbook, open an existing workbook, or create a new workbook based on a template. A **template** is a preformatted workbook with many design features and some content already filled in. Templates can speed up the process of creating a workbook because much of the work in designing the appearance of the workbook and entering its data and formulas is already done for you.

Sally created an Excel workbook that contains several worksheets describing the current financial status of Sparrow & Pond. You will open that workbook now.

To open Sally's workbook:

1. In the navigation bar on the Recent screen, click the **Open Other Workbooks** link. The Open screen is displayed and provides access to different locations where you might store files. The Recent Workbooks list shows the workbooks that were most recently opened on your computer.

2. Click **Computer**. The list of recently opened workbooks is replaced with a list of recently accessed folders on your computer and a Browse button.

   Trouble? If you are storing your files on your SkyDrive, click SkyDrive, and then log in if necessary.

3. Click the **Browse** button. The Open dialog box appears.

4. Navigate to the **Excel1 ▶ Tutorial** folder included with your Data Files.

   Trouble? If you don't have the starting Data Files, you need to get them before you can proceed. Your instructor will either give you the Data Files or ask you to obtain them from a specified location (such as a network drive). If you have any questions about the Data Files, see your instructor or technical support person for assistance.

5. Click **SP Finances** in the file list to select it.

6. Click the **Open** button. The SP Finances workbook opens in Excel.

   Trouble? If you don't see the full ribbon as shown in the Session 1.1 Visual Overview, the ribbon may be partially or fully hidden. To pin the ribbon so that the tabs and groups are fully displayed and remain visible, click the Ribbon Display Options button, and then click Show Tabs and Commands.

7. If the Excel window doesn't fill the screen, click the **Maximize** button in the upper-right corner of the title bar. See Figure 1-2.

Figure 1-2   SP Finances workbook

Using Keyboard Shortcuts to Work Faster

Keyboard shortcuts can help you work faster and more efficiently because you can keep your hands on the keyboard. A **keyboard shortcut** is a key or combination of keys that you press to access a feature or perform a command. Excel provides keyboard shortcuts for many commonly used commands. For example, Ctrl+S is the keyboard shortcut for the Save command, which means you hold down the Ctrl key while you press the S key to save the workbook. (Note that the plus sign is not pressed; it is used to indicate that an additional key is pressed.) When available, a keyboard shortcut is listed next to the command's name in a ScreenTip. A **ScreenTip** is a box with descriptive text about a command that appears when you point to a button on the ribbon. Figure 1-3 lists some of the keyboard shortcuts commonly used in Excel. The tutorials in this text show the corresponding keyboard shortcuts for accomplishing an action when available.

Figure 1-3 Excel keyboard shortcuts

Press	To	Press	To
Alt	Display the Key Tips for the commands and tools on the ribbon	Ctrl+V	Paste content that was cut or copied
Ctrl+A	Select all objects in a range	Ctrl+W	Close the current workbook
Ctrl+C	Copy the selected object(s)	Ctrl+X	Cut the selected object(s)
Ctrl+G	Go to a location in the workbook	Ctrl+Y	Repeat the last command
Ctrl+N	Open a new blank workbook	Ctrl+Z	Undo the last command
Ctrl+O	Open a saved workbook file	F1	Display the Excel Help window
Ctrl+P	Print the current workbook	F5	Go to a location in the workbook
Ctrl+S	Save the current workbook	F12	Save the current workbook with a new name or to a new location

© 2014 Cengage Learning

You can also use the keyboard to quickly select commands on the ribbon. First, you press the Alt key to display the **Key Tips**, which are labels that appear over each tab and command on the ribbon. Then, you press the key or keys indicated to access the corresponding tab, command, or button while your hands remain on the keyboard.

Getting Help

If you are unsure about the function of an Excel command or you want information about how to accomplish a particular task, you can use the Help system. To access Excel Help, you either press the F1 key or click the Microsoft Excel Help button in the title bar of the Excel window or dialog boxes. From the Excel Help window, you can search for a specific topic or click a topic in a category.

Using Excel 2013 in Touch Mode

In Office 2013, you can work with a mouse or, if you have a touchscreen, you can work in Touch Mode. In **Touch Mode**, the ribbon increases in height, the buttons are bigger, and more space appears around each button so you can more easily use your finger or a stylus to tap the button you need. As you work with Excel on a touchscreen, you tap objects instead of clicking them. Note that the figures in these tutorials show the screen with Mouse Mode on, but it's helpful to learn how to switch back and forth between Touch Mode and Mouse Mode. You'll switch to Touch Mode and then back to Mouse Mode now.

Note: The following steps assume that you are using a mouse. If you are instead using a touch device, please read these steps but don't complete them, so that you remain working in Touch Mode.

To switch between Touch Mode and Mouse Mode:

▶ 1. On the Quick Access Toolbar, click the **Customize Quick Access Toolbar** button. A menu opens listing buttons you can add to the Quick Access Toolbar as well as other options for customizing the toolbar.

   Trouble? If the Touch/Mouse Mode command on the menu has a checkmark next to it, press the Esc key to close the menu, and then skip Step 2.

▶ 2. Click **Touch/Mouse Mode**. The Quick Access Toolbar now contains the Touch/Mouse Mode button, which you can use to switch between Mouse Mode, the default display, and Touch Mode.

▶ 3. On the Quick Access Toolbar, click the **Touch/Mouse Mode** button. A menu opens listing Mouse and Touch, and the icon next to Mouse is shaded to indicate it is selected.

   Trouble? If the icon next to Touch is shaded, press the Esc key to close the menu and skip Step 4.

▶ 4. Click **Touch**. The display switches to Touch Mode with more space between the commands and buttons on the ribbon. See Figure 1-4.

Figure 1-4   Ribbon displayed in Touch Mode

- Touch/Mouse Mode button
- buttons are larger with more space around them

Now you'll return to Mouse Mode.

   Trouble? If you are working with a touchscreen and want to use Touch Mode, skip Steps 5 and 6.

▶ 5. On the Quick Access Toolbar, click the **Touch/Mouse Mode** button, and then click **Mouse**. The ribbon returns to the Mouse Mode display shown in Figure 1-2.

▶ 6. On the Quick Access Toolbar, click the **Customize Quick Access Toolbar** button, and then click **Touch/Mouse Mode** to deselect it. The Touch/Mouse Mode button is removed from the Quick Access Toolbar.

Exploring a Workbook

Workbooks are organized into separate pages called sheets. Excel supports two types of sheets: worksheets and chart sheets. A worksheet contains a grid of rows and columns into which you can enter text, numbers, dates, and formulas, and display charts. A **chart sheet** contains a chart that provides a visual representation of worksheet data. The contents of a workbook are shown in the workbook window.

EX 8　Excel | Tutorial 1 Getting Started with Excel

Changing the Active Sheet

The sheets in a workbook are identified in the sheet tabs at the bottom of the workbook window. The SP Finances workbook includes five sheets labeled Documentation, Income Statement, Expenses, Balance Sheet, and Cash Flow. The sheet currently displayed in the workbook window is the active sheet, which in this case is the Documentation sheet. To make a different sheet active and visible, you click its sheet tab. You can tell which sheet is active because its name appears in bold green.

If a workbook includes so many sheets that not all of the sheet tabs can be displayed at the same time in the workbook window, you can use the sheet tab scrolling buttons to scroll through the list of tabs. Scrolling the sheet tabs does not change the active sheet; it only changes which sheet tabs are visible.

You will view the different sheets in the SP Finances workbook.

To change the active sheet:

1. Click the **Income Statement** sheet tab. The Income Statement worksheet becomes the active sheet, and its name is in bold green type. See Figure 1-5.

Figure 1-5　Income Statement worksheet

- Name box
- sheet tab for the active worksheet
- sheet tab scrolling buttons

2. Click the **Expenses** sheet tab to make it the active sheet. The Expenses sheet is an example of a chart sheet containing only an Excel chart. See Figure 1-6.

Figure 1-6　Expenses chart sheet

- chart sheet contains a chart but no grid of text and data
- sheet tab for the active worksheet

> **TIP**
> You can move to the previous or next sheet in the workbook by pressing the Ctrl+PgUp or Ctrl+PgDn keys.

> 3. Click the **Balance Sheet** sheet tab to make it the active sheet. Note that this sheet contains a chart embedded into the grid of data values. A worksheet can contain data values, charts, pictures, and other design elements.
>
> 4. Click the **Cash Flow** sheet tab. The worksheet with information about the company's cash flow is now active.
>
> 5. Click the **Income Statement** sheet tab to make the Income Statement worksheet the active sheet.

Navigating Within a Worksheet

The worksheet is organized into individual cells. Each cell is identified by a **cell reference**, which is based on the cell's column and row location. For example, in Figure 1-5, the company name, Sparrow & Pond, is in cell B1, which is the intersection of column B and row 1. The column letter always appears before the row number in any cell reference. The cell that is currently selected in the worksheet is referred to as the active cell. The active cell is highlighted with a thick green border, its cell reference appears in the Name box, and the corresponding column and row headings are highlighted. The active cell in Figure 1-5 is cell A1.

Row numbers range from 1 to 1,048,576, and column labels are letters in alphabetical order. The first 26 column headings range from A to Z. After Z, the next column headings are labeled AA, AB, AC, and so forth. Excel allows a maximum of 16,384 columns in a worksheet (the last column has the heading XFD). This means that you can create large worksheets whose content extends well beyond what is visible in the workbook window.

To move different parts of the worksheet into view, you can use the horizontal and vertical scroll bars located at the bottom and right edges of the workbook window, respectively. A scroll bar has arrow buttons that you can click to shift the worksheet one column or row in the specified direction, and a scroll box that you can drag to shift the worksheet in the direction you drag.

You will scroll the active worksheet so you can review the rest of the Sparrow & Pond income statement.

> **To scroll through the Income Statement worksheet:**
>
> 1. On the vertical scroll bar, click the down arrow button to scroll down the Income Statement worksheet until you see cell C36, which displays the company's net income value of $4,600.
>
> 2. On the horizontal scroll bar, click the right arrow button three times. The worksheet scrolls three columns to the right, moving columns A through C out of view.
>
> 3. On the horizontal scroll bar, drag the scroll box to the left until you see column A.
>
> 4. On the vertical scroll bar, drag the scroll box up until you see the top of the worksheet and cell A1.

Scrolling the worksheet does not change the location of the active cell. Although the active cell might shift out of view, you can always see the location of the active cell in the Name box. To make a different cell active, you can either click a new cell or use the keyboard to move between cells, as described in Figure 1-7.

Figure 1-7 Excel navigation keys

Press	To move the active cell
↑ ↓ ← →	Up, down, left, or right one cell
Home	To column A of the current row
Ctrl+Home	To cell A1
Ctrl+End	To the last cell in the worksheet that contains data
Enter	Down one row or to the start of the next row of data
Shift+Enter	Up one row
Tab	One column to the right
Shift+Tab	One column to the left
PgUp, PgDn	Up or down one screen
Ctrl+PgUp, Ctrl+PgDn	To the previous or next sheet in the workbook

© 2014 Cengage Learning

You will use both your mouse and your keyboard to change the location of the active cell in the Income Statement worksheet.

To change the active cell:

1. Move your pointer over cell **B5**, and then click the mouse button. The active cell moves from cell A1 to cell B5. A green border appears around cell B5, the column heading for column B and the row heading for row 5 are both highlighted, and the cell reference in the Name box changes from A1 to B5.

2. Press the → key. The active cell moves one cell to the right to cell C5.

3. Press the **PgDn** key. The active cell moves down one full screen.

4. Press the **PgUp** key. The active cell moves up one full screen, returning to cell C5.

5. Press the **Ctrl+Home** keys. The active cell returns to the first cell in the worksheet, cell A1.

The mouse and keyboard provide quick ways to navigate the active worksheet. For larger worksheets that span several screens, you can move directly to a specific cell using the Go To command or by typing a cell reference in the Name box. You will try both of these methods.

To use the Go To dialog box and the Name box:

1. On the HOME tab, in the Editing group, click the **Find & Select** button, and then click **Go To** on the menu that opens (or press the **F5** key). The Go To dialog box opens.

2. Type **C36** in the Reference box. See Figure 1-8.

Tutorial 1 Getting Started with Excel | Excel EX 11

Figure 1-8   Go To dialog box

cell reference of the cell you want to make active → Reference: C36

3. Click the **OK** button. Cell C36 becomes the active cell, displaying $4,600, which is Sparrow & Pond's net income for the year. Because cell C36 is the active cell, its cell reference appears in the Name box.

4. Click in the Name box, type **A1**, and then press the **Enter** key. Cell A1 is again the active cell.

Selecting a Cell Range

Many tasks in Excel require you to work with a group of cells. You can use your mouse or keyboard to select those cells. A group of cells in a rectangular block is called a cell range (or simply a range). Each range is identified with a **range reference** that includes the cell reference of the upper-left cell of the rectangular block and the cell reference of the lower-right cell separated by a colon. For example, the range reference A1:G5 refers to all of the cells in the rectangular block from cell A1 through cell G5.

As with individual cells, you can select cell ranges using your mouse, the keyboard, or commands. You will select a range in the Income Statement worksheet.

To select a cell range:

1. Click cell **B5** to select it, and without releasing the mouse button, drag down to cell **C8**.

2. Release the mouse button. The range B5:C8 is selected. See Figure 1-9. The selected cells are highlighted and surrounded by a green border. The first cell you selected in the range, cell B5, is the active cell in the worksheet. The active cell in a selected range is white. The Quick Analysis button appears, providing options for working with the range; you will use this button in another tutorial.

TIP

You can also select a range by clicking the upper-left cell of the range, holding down the Shift key as you click the lower-right cell in the range, and then releasing the Shift key.

EX 12 Excel | Tutorial 1 Getting Started with Excel

Figure 1-9   **Range B5:C8 selected**

[Screenshot of Excel worksheet showing Sparrow & Pond Income Statement with range B5:C8 selected, with callouts labeling "active cell in the selected range" and "Quick Analysis button"]

3. Click cell **A1** to deselect the range.

A nonadjacent range is a collection of separate ranges. The range reference for a nonadjacent range includes the range reference to each range separated by a semicolon. For example, the range reference A1:G5;A10:G15 includes two ranges—the first range is the rectangular block of cells from cell A1 to cell G5, and the second range is the rectangular block of cells from cell A10 to cell G15.

You will select a nonadjacent range in the Income Statement worksheet.

To select a nonadjacent range in the Income Statement worksheet:

1. Click cell **B5**, hold down the **Shift** key as you click cell **C8**, and then release the **Shift** key to select the range B5:C8.

2. Hold down the **Ctrl** key as you select the range **B10:C14**, and then release the **Ctrl** key. The two separate blocks of cells in the nonadjacent range B5:C8;B10:C14 are selected. See Figure 1-10.

Figure 1-10 Nonadjacent range B5:C8;B10:C14 selected

	A	B	C	D
1		Sparrow & Pond		
2		Income Statement		
3		January 1, 2015 to December 31, 2015		
4				
5		**Income**		
6		Gross Sales	$ 258,500	
7		Less returns and allowances	24,500	
8		Net Sales	234,000	
9				
10		Cost of Goods		
11		Inventory, January 1	121,000	
12		Purchases	72,000	
13		Delivery Charges	12,000	
14		Total Merchandise Handled	205,000	
15				
16		Less Inventory, December 31	133,500	
17				
18		Cost of Goods Sold	71,500	

- active cell in the selected range
- selected range B5:C8
- selected range B10:C14

▶ **3.** Click cell **A1** to deselect the range.

Closing a Workbook

When you close a workbook, a dialog box might open, asking whether you want to save the workbook. If you have made changes that you want to keep, you should save the workbook. You have finished reviewing the SP Finances workbook, so you will close it. You will not save the workbook because you want the original version to remain unchanged.

To close the SP Finances workbook:

▶ **1.** On the ribbon, click the **FILE** tab to display Backstage view, and then click **Close** in the navigation bar (or press the **Ctrl+W** keys).

▶ **2.** If a dialog box opens asking whether you want to save your changes to the workbook, click the **Don't Save** button. The workbook closes without saving any changes. Excel remains opens, ready for you to create or open another workbook.

Planning a Workbook

Before you begin creating a new workbook, you should develop a plan. You can do this by using a **planning analysis sheet**, which includes the following questions that help you think about the workbook's purpose and how to achieve your desired results:

  1. **What problems do I want to solve?** The answer identifies the goal or purpose of the workbook. For example, Sally needs an easy way to record customer orders and analyze details from these orders.

2. **What data do I need?** The answer identifies the type of data that you need to collect and enter into the workbook. For example, Sally needs customer contact information, an order ID number, the date the order shipped, the shipping method, a list of books ordered, the quantity of each book ordered, and the price of each book.
3. **What calculations do I need to enter?** The answer identifies the formulas you need to apply to the data you have collected and entered. For example, Sally needs to calculate the charge for each book ordered, the number of books ordered, the shipping cost, the sales tax, and the total cost of the order.
4. **What form should my solution take?** The answer describes the appearance of the workbook content and how it should be presented to others. For example, Sally wants the information stored in a single worksheet that is easy to read and prints clearly.

Based on Sally's plan, you will create a workbook containing the details of a recent customer order. Sally will use this workbook as a model for future workbooks detailing other customer orders.

PROSKILLS

Written Communication: Creating Effective Workbooks

Workbooks convey information in written form. As with any type of writing, the final product creates an impression and provides an indicator of your interest, knowledge, and attention to detail. To create the best impression, all workbooks—especially those you intend to share with others such as coworkers and clients—should be well planned, well organized, and well written.

A well-designed workbook should clearly identify its overall goal and present information in an organized format. The data it includes—both the entered values and the calculated values—should be accurate. The process of developing an effective workbook includes the following steps:

- Determine the workbook's purpose, content, and organization before you start.
- Create a list of the sheets used in the workbook, noting each sheet's purpose.
- Insert a documentation sheet that describes the workbook's purpose and organization. Include the name of the workbook author, the date the workbook was created, and any additional information that will help others to track the workbook to its source.
- Enter all of the data in the workbook. Add labels to indicate what the values represent and, if possible, where they originated so others can view the source of your data.
- Enter formulas for calculated items rather than entering the calculated values into the workbook. For more complicated calculations, provide documentation explaining them.
- Test the workbook with a variety of values; edit the data and formulas to correct errors.
- Save the workbook and create a backup copy when the project is completed. Print the workbook's contents if you need to provide a hard-copy version to others or for your files.
- Maintain a history of your workbook as it goes through different versions, so that you and others can quickly see how the workbook has changed during revisions.

By including clearly written documentation, explanatory text, a logical organization, and accurate data and formulas, you will create effective workbooks that others can use easily.

Tutorial 1 Getting Started with Excel | Excel   EX 15

Creating a New Workbook

You create new workbooks from the New screen in Backstage view. Similar to the Recent screen that opened when you started Excel, the New screen include templates for a variety of workbook types. You can see a preview of what the different workbooks will look like. You will create a new workbook from the Blank workbook template, in which you can add all of the content and design Sally wants for the Sparrow & Pond customer order worksheet.

To start a new, blank workbook:

TIP
You can also create a new, blank workbook by pressing the Ctrl+N keys.

1. On the ribbon, click the **FILE** tab to display Backstage view.
2. Click **New** in the navigation bar to display the New screen, which includes access to templates for a variety of workbooks.
3. Click the **Blank workbook** tile. A blank workbook opens. See Figure 1-11.

Figure 1-11   Blank workbook

- Save button on the Quick Access Toolbar
- workbook is named Book1 until you save it with a new name
- Restore Down button appears when the window is maximized
- active sheet is named Sheet1
- inserts a new sheet
- zoom controls

In these tutorials, the workbook window is zoomed to 120% for better readability. If you want to zoom your workbook window to match the figures, complete Step 4. If you prefer to work in the default zoom of 100% or at another zoom level, read but do not complete Step 4; you might see more or less of the worksheet on your screen, but this will not affect your work in the tutorials.

4. If you want your workbook window zoomed to 120% to match the figures, click the **Zoom In** button ➕ on the status bar twice to increase the zoom level to 120%. The 120% magnification increases the size of each cell, but reduces the number of worksheet cells visible in the workbook window.

The name of the active workbook, Book1, appears in the title bar. If you open multiple blank workbooks, they are named Book1, Book2, Book3, and so forth until you save them with a more descriptive name.

Renaming and Inserting Worksheets

Blank workbooks open with a single blank sheet named Sheet1. You can give sheets more descriptive and meaningful names. This is a good practice so that you and others can easily tell what a sheet contains. Sheet names cannot exceed 31 characters, but they can contain blank spaces and include upper- and lowercase letters.

Because Sheet1 is not a very descriptive name, Sally wants you to rename the worksheet as Customer Order.

To rename the Sheet1 worksheet:

1. Double-click the **Sheet1** tab. The Sheet1 label in the tab is selected.
2. Type **Customer Order** as the new name, and then press the **Enter** key. The width of the sheet tab expands to fit the longer sheet name.

Many workbooks include multiple sheets so that data can be organized in logical groups. A common business practice is to include a worksheet named Documentation that contains a description of the workbook, the name of the person who prepared the workbook, and the date it was created.

You will create two new worksheets. You will rename one worksheet as Documentation and you will rename the other worksheet as Customer Contact to record the customer's contact information.

To insert and name the Documentation and Customer Contact worksheets:

1. To the right of the Customer Order sheet tab, click the **New sheet** button ⊕. A new sheet named Sheet2 is inserted to the right of the Customer Order sheet.
2. Double-click the **Sheet2** sheet tab, type **Documentation** as the new name, and then press the **Enter** key. The second worksheet is renamed.
3. To the right of the Documentation sheet, click the **New sheet** button ⊕, and then rename the inserted worksheet as **Customer Contact**.

Moving Worksheets

A good practice is to place the most important sheets at the beginning of the workbook (the leftmost sheet tabs) and less important sheets at the end (the rightmost sheet tabs). To change the placement of sheets in a workbook, you drag them by their sheet tabs to the new location.

Sally wants you to move the Documentation worksheet to the front of the workbook, so that it appears before the Customer Order sheet.

To move the Documentation worksheet:

1. Point to the **Documentation** sheet tab.
2. Press and hold the mouse button. The pointer changes to ▯, and a small arrow appears in the upper-left corner of the tab.
3. Drag to the left until the small arrow appears in the upper-left corner of the Customer Order sheet tab, and then release the mouse button. The Documentation worksheet is now the first sheet in the workbook.

TIP
To copy a sheet, hold down the Ctrl key as you drag and drop its sheet tab.

Deleting Worksheets

In some workbooks, you will want to delete an existing sheet. The easiest way to delete a sheet is by using a **shortcut menu**, which is a list of commands related to a selection that opens when you click the right mouse button. Sally asks you to include the customer's contact information on the Customer Order worksheet so all of the information is on one sheet.

To delete the Customer Contact worksheet from the workbook:

1. Right-click the **Customer Contact** sheet tab. A shortcut menu opens.
2. Click **Delete**. The Customer Contact worksheet is removed from the workbook.

Saving a Workbook

As you modify a workbook, you should save it regularly—every 10 minutes or so is a good practice. The first time you save a workbook, the Save As dialog box opens so you can name the file and choose where to save it. You can save the workbook on your computer or network, or to your account on SkyDrive.

To save your workbook for the first time:

1. On the Quick Access Toolbar, click the **Save** button 🖫 (or press the **Ctrl+S** keys). The Save As screen in Backstage view opens.
2. Click **Computer** in the Places list, and then click the **Browse** button. The Save As dialog box opens.

   Trouble? If your instructor wants you to save your files to your SkyDrive account, click SkyDrive, and then log in to your account, if necessary.

3. Navigate to the location specified by your instructor.
4. In the File name box, select **Book1** (the suggested name) if it is not already selected, and then type **SP Customer Order**.
5. Verify that **Excel Workbook** appears in the Save as type box.
6. Click the **Save** button. The workbook is saved, the dialog box closes, and the workbook window reappears with the new filename in the title bar.

As you modify the workbook, you will need to resave the file. Because you already saved the workbook with a filename, the next time you save, the Save command saves the changes you made to the workbook without opening the Save As dialog box.

Entering Text, Dates, and Numbers

Workbook content is entered into worksheet cells. Those cells can contain text, numbers, or dates and times. **Text data** is any combination of letters, numbers, and symbols. Text data is often referred to as a **text string** because it contains a series, or string, of text characters. **Numeric data** is any number that can be used in a mathematical calculation. **Date** and **time data** are commonly recognized formats for date and time values. For example, Excel interprets the cell entry April 15, 2016 as a date and not as text. New data is placed into the active cell of the current worksheet. As you enter data, the entry appears in both the active cell and the formula bar. By default, text is left-aligned in cells, and numbers, dates, and times are right-aligned.

Entering Text

Text is often used in worksheets to label other data and to identify areas of a sheet. Sally wants you to enter some of the information from the planning analysis sheet into the Documentation sheet.

To enter the text for the Documentation sheet:

1. Press the **Ctrl+Home** keys to make sure cell A1 is the active cell on the Documentation sheet.

2. Type **Sparrow and Pond** in cell A1. As you type, the text appears in cell A1 and in the formula bar.

3. Press the **Enter** key twice. The text is entered into cell A1 and the active cell moves down two rows to cell A3.

4. Type **Author** in cell A3, and then press the **Tab** key. The text is entered and the active cell moves one column to the right to cell B3.

5. Type your name in cell B3, and then press the **Enter** key. The text is entered and the active cell moves one cell down and to the left to cell A4.

6. Type **Date** in cell A4, and then press the **Tab** key. The text is entered and the active cell moves one column to the right to cell B4, where you would enter the date you created the worksheet. For now, you will leave the cell for the date blank.

7. Click cell **A5** to make it the active cell, type **Purpose** in the cell, and then press the **Tab** key. The active cell moves one column to the right to cell B5.

8. Type **To record customer book orders.** in cell B5, and then press the **Enter** key. Figure 1-12 shows the text entered in the Documentation sheet.

Figure 1-12 — Documentation sheet

text overflows into the empty cell to the right

	A	B
1	Sparrow and Pond	
2		
3	Author	Sally Hughes
4	Date	
5	Purpose	To record customer book orders
6		

your name appears here

The text you entered in cell A1 is so long that it appears to overflow into cell B1. The same is true for the text you entered in cells B3 and B5. Any text you enter in a cell that doesn't fit within that cell will cover the adjacent cells to the right as long as they are empty. If the adjacent cells contain data, only the text that fits into the cell is displayed. The rest of the text entry is hidden from view. The text itself is not affected. The complete text is still entered in the cell; it is just not displayed. (You will learn how to display all text in a cell in the next session.)

Undoing and Redoing an Action

As you enter data in a workbook, you might need to undo a previous action. Excel maintains a list of the actions you performed in the workbook during the current session, so you can undo most of your actions. You can use the Undo button on the Quick Access Toolbar or press the Ctrl+Z keys to reverse your most recent actions one at a time. If you want to undo more than one action, you can click the Undo button arrow and then select the earliest action you want to undo—all of the actions after the earliest action you selected are also undone.

You will undo the most recent change you made to the Documentation sheet—the text you entered into cell B5. Then you will enter more descriptive and accurate description of the worksheet's purpose.

To undo the text entry in cell B5:

1. On the Quick Access Toolbar, click the **Undo** button (or press the **Ctrl+Z** keys). The last action is reversed, removing the text you entered in cell B5.

2. In cell B5, type **To record book orders from a Sparrow & Pond customer.** and then press the **Enter** key.

If you want to restore actions you have undone, you can redo them. To redo one action at a time, you can click the Redo button on the Quick Access Toolbar or press the Ctrl+Y keys. To redo multiple actions at once, you can click the Redo button arrow and then click the earliest action you want to redo. After you undo or redo an action, Excel continues the action list starting from any new changes you make to the workbook.

Editing Cell Content

As you work, you might find mistakes you need to correct or entries that you want to change. If you want to replace all of the content in a cell, you simply select the cell and then type the new entry to overwrite the previous entry. However, if you need to replace only part of a cell's content, you can work in **Edit mode**. To switch to Edit mode, you double-click the cell. A blinking insertion point indicates where the new content you type will be inserted. In the cell or formula bar, the pointer changes to an I-beam, which you can use to select text in the cell. Anything you type replaces the selected content.

You need to edit the text in cell A1 to Sparrow & Pond. You will switch to Edit mode to correct the text.

To edit the text in cell A1:

1. Double-click cell **A1** to select the cell and switch to Edit mode. A blinking insertion point appears within the text of cell A1. The status bar displays EDIT instead of READY to indicate that the cell is in Edit mode.

2. Press the arrow keys to move the insertion point directly to the right of the word "and" in the company name.

3. Press the **Backspace** key three times to delete the word "and."

4. Type **&** to enter the new text, and then press the **Enter** key. The cell text changes to Sparrow & Pond. See Figure 1-13.

Figure 1-13 | Revised Documentation sheet

- Undo button
- Redo button
- cell A1 in Edit mode
- Sparrow & Pond
- company name changed to Sparrow & Pond

5. Press the **Enter** key to exit the cell and return to Ready mode.

Understanding AutoComplete

As you type text in the active cell, Excel tries to anticipate the remaining characters by displaying text that begins with the same letters as a previous entry in the same column. This feature, known as **AutoComplete**, helps make entering repetitive text easier. To accept the suggested text, press the Tab or Enter key. To override the suggested text, continue to type the text you want to enter in the cell. AutoComplete does not work with dates or numbers, or when a blank cell is between the previous entry and the text you are typing.

Next, you will enter the contact information for Tobias Gregson, a customer who recently placed an order with Sparrow & Pond. You will enter the contact information on the Customer Order worksheet.

To enter Tobias Gregson's contact information:

1. Click the **Customer Order** sheet tab to make it the active sheet.
2. In cell A1, type **Customer Order** as the worksheet title, and then press the **Enter** key twice. The worksheet title is entered in cell A1, and the active cell is cell A3.
3. Type **Ship To** in cell A3, and then press the **Enter** key. The label is entered in the cell, and the active cell is now cell A4.
4. In the range A4:A10, enter the following labels, pressing the **Enter** key after each entry and ignoring any AutoComplete suggestions: **First Name**, **Last Name**, **Address**, **City**, **State**, **Postal Code**, and **Phone**.
5. Click cell **B4** to make that cell the active cell.

Tutorial 1 Getting Started with Excel | Excel   EX 21

▶ **6.** In the range B4:B10, enter the following contact information, pressing the **Enter** key after each entry and ignoring any AutoComplete suggestions: **Tobias**, **Gregson**, **412 Apple Grove St.**, **Nashua**, **NH**, **03061**, and **(603) 555-4128**. See Figure 1-14.

Figure 1-14 Text entered in the Customer Order worksheet

text in cells A4, A5, and A9 is partially hidden

postal code is missing its leading zero

	A	B
1	Customer Order	
2		
3	Ship To	
4	First Name	Tobias
5	Last Name	Gregson
6	Address	412 Apple Grove St.
7	City	Nashua
8	State	NH
9	Postal Code	3061
10	Phone	(603) 555-4128

Displaying Numbers as Text

When you type numbers in the active cell, Excel treats the entry as a number and ignores any leading zero. For example, in cell B9, the first digit of the postal code 03061 is missing; Excel displays 3061 because the numbers 3061 and 03061 have the same value. To specify that a number entry should be considered text and all digits should be displayed, you include an apostrophe (') before the numbers.

You will make this change in cell B9 so that Excel treats the postal code as text and displays all of the digits you type.

To enter the postal code as text:

▶ **1.** Click cell **B9** to select it. Notice that the postal code is right-aligned in the cell, unlike the other text entries, which are left-aligned—another indication that the entry is being treated as a number.

▶ **2.** Type **'03061** in cell B9, and then press the **Enter** key. The text 03061 appears in cell B9 and is left-aligned in the cell, matching all of the other text entries. See Figure 1-15.

Figure 1-15   Number displayed as text

(Screenshot of Excel worksheet showing the SP Customer Order workbook. Cell B10 is selected with value (603) 555-4128. The worksheet contains:)

	A	B
1	Customer Order	
2		
3	Ship To	
4	First Name	Tobias
5	Last Name	Gregson
6	Address	412 Apple Grove St.
7	City	Nashua
8	State	NH
9	Postal Code	03061
10	Phone	(603) 555-4128

Callouts:
- green triangle warns about a potential error (pointing to B9)
- postal code is left-aligned in the cell (pointing to B9)

TIP
To remove a green triangle, click the cell, click the yellow caution icon that appears to the left of the cell, and then click Ignore Error.

Notice that a green triangle appears in the upper-left corner of cell B9. Excel uses green triangles to flag potential errors in cells. In this case, it is simply a warning that you entered a number as a text string. Because this is intentional, you do not have to edit the cell to fix the "error." Green triangles appear only in the workbook window and not in any printouts of the worksheet.

Entering Dates

You can enter dates in any of the standard date formats. For example, all of the following entries are recognized by Excel as the same date:

- 4/6/2016
- 4/6/16
- 4-6-2016
- April 6, 2016
- 6-Apr-16

Even though you enter a date as text, Excel stores the date as a number equal to the number of days between the specified date and January 0, 1900. Times are also entered as text and stored as fractions of a 24-hour day. For example, the date and time April 4, 2016 @ 6:00 PM is stored by Excel as 42,464.75. Dates and times are stored as numbers so that Excel can easily perform date and time calculations, such as determining the elapsed time between one date and another.

Based on the default date format your computer uses, Excel might alter the format of a date after you type it. For example, if you enter the date 4/6/16 into the active cell, Excel might display the date with the four-digit year value, 4/6/2016; if you enter the text April 6, 2016, Excel might convert the date format to 6-Apr-16. Changing the date or time format does not affect the underlying date or time value.

INSIGHT

International Date Formats

As business transactions become more international in scope, you may need to adopt international standards for expressing dates, times, and currency values in your workbooks. For example, a worksheet cell might contain 06/05/16. This format could represent any of the following dates: the 5th of June, 2016; the 6th of May, 2016; and the 16th of May, 2006.

The date depends on which country the workbook has been designed for. You can avoid this problem by entering the full date, as in June 5, 2016. However, this might not work with documents written in foreign languages, such as Japanese, that use different character symbols.

To solve this problem, many international businesses adopt ISO (International Organization for Standardization) dates in the format *yyyy-mm-dd*, where *yyyy* is the four-digit year value, *mm* is the two-digit month value, and *dd* is the two-digit day value. So, a date such as June 5, 2016 is entered as 2016/06/05. If you choose to use this international date format, make sure that people using your workbook understand this format so they do not misinterpret the dates. You can include information about the date format in the Documentation sheet.

For the SP Customer Order workbook, you will enter dates in the format *mm/dd/yyyy*, where *mm* is the 2-digit month number, *dd* is the 2-digit day number, and *yyyy* is the 4-digit year number.

To enter the current date into the Documentation sheet:

1. Click the **Documentation** sheet tab to make the Documentation sheet the active worksheet.

2. Click cell **B4** to make it active, type the current date in the *mm/dd/yyyy* format, and then press the **Enter** key. The date is entered in the cell.

    Trouble? Depending on your system configuration, Excel might change the date to the date format *dd-mmm-yy*. This difference will not affect your work.

3. Make the **Customer Order** worksheet the active sheet.

The next part of the Customer Order worksheet will list the books the customer purchased from Sparrow & Pond. As shown in Figure 1-16, the list includes identifying information about each book, its price, and the quantity ordered.

Figure 1-16   **Book order from Tobias Gregson**

ISBN	CATEGORY	BINDING	TITLE	AUTHOR(S)	PRICE	QTY
0-374-25385-4	Used	Hardcover	Samurai William: The Englishman Who Opened Japan	Milton, Giles	$5.95	2
4-889-96213-1	New	Softcover	Floral Origami Globes	Fuse, Tomoko	$24.95	3
0-500-27062-7	New	Hardcover	Tao Magic: The Secret Language of Diagrams and Calligraphy	Legeza, Laszlo	$8.95	1
0-785-82169-4	Used	Hardcover	The Holy Grail	Morgan, Giles	$3.75	1
0-854-56516-7	New	Softcover	Murder on the Links	Christie, Agatha	$7.50	2

© 2014 Cengage Learning

You will enter the first five columns of the book order into the worksheet.

To enter the first part of the book order:

1. In the Customer Order worksheet, click cell **A12** to make it the active cell, type **ISBN** as the column label, and then press the **Tab** key to move to cell B12.

2. In the range B12:E12, type the following labels, pressing the **Tab** key to move to the next cell: **CATEGORY**, **BINDING**, **TITLE**, and **AUTHOR(S)**.

3. Press the **Enter** key to go to the next row of the worksheet, making cell A13 the active cell.

4. In the range A13:E17, enter the ISBN, category, binding, title, and author text for the five books listed in Figure 1-16, pressing the **Tab** key to move from one cell to the next, and pressing the **Enter** key to move to a new row. See Figure 1-17. The text in some cells will be partially hidden; you will fix that problem shortly.

Figure 1-17   Tobias Gregson's partial book order

	A	B	C	D	E
11					
12	ISBN	CATEGORY	BINDING	TITLE	AUTHOR(S)
13	0-374-253	Used	Hardcover	Samurai W	Milton, Giles
14	4-889-962	New	Softcover	Floral Orig	Fuse, Tomoko
15	0-500-270	New	Hardcover	Tao Magic	Legeza, Laszlo
16	0-785-821	Used	Hardcover	The Holy (	Morgan, Giles
17	0-854-565	New	Softcover	Murder or	Christie, Agatha
18					
19					

- text is left-aligned
- text overlaps the next column
- text is partially hidden

Documentation | **Customer Order**
READY

Entering Numbers

TIP
If a number exceeds its cell size, you see ###### instead of the number. You can display the entire number by increasing the column width.

In Excel, numbers can be integers such as 378, decimals such as 1.95, or negatives such as −5.2. In the case of currency and percentages, you can include the currency symbol and percent sign when you enter the value. Excel treats a currency value such as $87.25 as the number 87.25, and a percentage such as 95% as the decimal 0.95. Much like dates, currency and percentages are formatted in a convenient way for you to read, but only the number is stored within the cell. This makes it easier to perform calculations with currency and percentage values.

You will complete the information for Tobias Gregson's order by entering the price for each title and the quantity of each title he ordered.

To enter the price and quantity of books ordered:

1. In the range F12:G12, enter **PRICE** and **QTY** as the labels.

2. In cell F13, enter **$5.95** as the price of the first book. The book price is stored as a number but displayed with the $ symbol.

3. In cell G13, enter **2** as the quantity of books ordered.

4. In the range F14:G17, enter the remaining prices and quantities shown in Figure 1-16. See Figure 1-18.

Figure 1-18 Price and quantity data

	A	B	C	D	E	F	G
11							
12	ISBN	CATEGORY	BINDING	TITLE	AUTHOR(S)	PRICE	QTY
13	0-374-253	Used	Hardcover	Samurai W	Milton, Gil	$5.95	2
14	4-889-962	New	Softcover	Floral Orig	Fuse, Tom	$24.95	3
15	0-500-270	New	Hardcover	Tao Magic	Legeza, La	$8.95	1
16	0-785-821	Used	Hardcover	The Holy (	Morgan, G	$3.75	1
17	0-854-565	New	Softcover	Murder or	Christie, A	$7.50	2

numbers are right-aligned

price stored as a number formatted as currency

5. On the Quick Access Toolbar, click the **Save** button (or press the **Ctrl+S** keys) to save the workbook.

Resizing Columns and Rows

Much of the information in the Customer Order worksheet is difficult to read because of the hidden text. You can make the cell content easier to read by changing the size of the columns and rows in the worksheet.

Changing Column Widths

Column widths are expressed as the number of characters the column can contain. The default column width is 8.43 standard-sized characters. In general, this means that you can type eight characters in a cell; any additional text is hidden or overlaps the adjacent cell. Column widths are also expressed in terms of pixels. A **pixel** is a single point on a computer monitor or printout. A column width of 8.43 characters is equivalent to 64 pixels.

> **INSIGHT**
>
> ### Setting Column Widths
>
> On a computer monitor, pixel size is based on screen resolution. As a result, cell contents that look fine on one screen might appear very different when viewed on a screen with a different resolution. If you work on multiple computers or share your workbooks with others, you should set column widths based on the maximum number of characters you want displayed in the cells rather than pixel size. This ensures that everyone sees the cell contents the way you intended.

You will increase the width of column A so that the contact information labels in cells A4 and A5 and the ISBN numbers in the range A13:A17 are completely displayed.

To increase the width of column A:

1. Move the pointer over the right border of the column A heading until the pointer changes to ↔.

2. Click and drag to the right until the width of the column heading reaches **15** characters, but do not release the mouse button. The ScreenTip that appears as you resize the column shows the new column width in characters and in pixels.

3. Release the mouse button. The width of column A expands to 15 characters, and all of the text within that column is visible within the cells. See Figure 1-19.

Figure 1-19   **Width of column A increased**

ScreenTip shows the column width in characters and pixels

pointer for resizing the column

text in column A fits within the cells

You will increase the widths of columns B and C to 18 characters so that their complete entries are visible. Rather than resizing each column separately, you can select both columns and adjust their widths at the same time.

To increase the widths of columns B and C:

1. Click the **column B** heading. The entire column is selected.

2. Hold down the **Ctrl** key, click the **column C** heading, and then release the **Ctrl** key. Both columns B and C are selected.

3. Move the pointer to the right border of the column C heading until the pointer changes to ✥.

4. Drag to the right until the column width changes to **18** characters, and then release the mouse button. Both column widths increase to 18 characters and display all of the entered text.

TIP

To select multiple columns, you can also click and drag the pointer over multiple column headings.

The book titles in column D are partially hidden. You will increase the width of this column to 30 characters. Rather than using your mouse, you can set the column width using the Format command on the HOME tab. The Format command gives you precise control over setting column widths and row heights.

To set the width of column D with the Format command:

1. Click the **column D** heading. The entire column is selected.
2. On the HOME tab, in the Cells group, click the **Format** button, and then click **Column Width**. The Column Width dialog box opens.
3. Type **30** in the Column width box to specify the new column width.
4. Click the **OK** button. The width of column D changes to 30 characters.
5. Change the width of column E to **15** characters.
6. Click cell **A1**. The revised column widths are shown in Figure 1-20.

Figure 1-20   **Resized columns**

[Screenshot of Excel worksheet showing resized columns with callouts: "18 characters in each column" pointing to columns B and C, "30 characters" pointing to column D, "15 characters" pointing to column E, and "15 characters" pointing to column A. The worksheet contains a Customer Order with Ship To info (Tobias Gregson, 412 Apple Grove St., Nashua, NH, 03061, (603) 555-4128) and a book order list with ISBN, CATEGORY, BINDING, TITLE, AUTHOR(S), PRICE, QTY columns.]

	A	B	C	D	E	F	G
1	Customer Order						
2							
3	Ship To						
4	First Name	Tobias					
5	Last Name	Gregson					
6	Address	412 Apple Grove St.					
7	City	Nashua					
8	State	NH					
9	Postal Code	03061					
10	Phone	(603) 555-4128					
11							
12	ISBN	CATEGORY	BINDING	TITLE	AUTHOR(S)	PRICE	QTY
13	0-374-25385-4	Used	Hardcover	Samurai William: The Englishman W	Milton, Giles	$5.95	2
14	4-889-96213-1	New	Softcover	Floral Origami Globes	Fuse, Tomoko	$24.95	3
15	0-500-27062-7	New	Hardcover	Tao Magic: The Secret Language of	Legeza, Laszlo	$8.95	1
16	0-785-82169-4	Used	Hardcover	The Holy Grail	Morgan, Giles	$3.75	1
17	0-854-56516-7	New	Softcover	Murder on the Links	Christie, Agatha	$7.50	2

> **TIP**
> If the row or column is blank, autofitting restores its default height or width.

Even with the width of column D increased, some of the book titles still don't fit within the allotted space. Instead of manually changing the column width to display all of the text, you can autofit the column. **AutoFit** changes the column width or row height to display the longest or tallest entry within the column or row. You autofit a column or a row by double-clicking the right border of the column heading or the bottom border of the row heading.

To autofit the contents of column D:

1. Move the pointer over the right border of column D until the pointer changes to ↔.
2. Double-click the right border of the column D heading. The width of column D increases to about 54 characters so that the longest book title is completely visible.

Wrapping Text Within a Cell

Sometimes, resizing a column width to display all of the text entered in the cells makes the worksheet more difficult to read. This is the case with column D in the Customer Order worksheet. Another way to display long text entries is to wrap text to a new line when it extends beyond the column width. When text wraps within a cell, the row height increases so that all of the text within the cell is displayed.

You will resize column D, and then wrap the text entries in the column.

To wrap text in column D:

1. Resize the width of column D to **30** characters.
2. Select the range **D13:D17**. These cells include the titles that extend beyond the new cell width.
3. On the HOME tab, in the Alignment group, click the **Wrap Text** button. The Wrap Text button is toggled on, and text in the selected cells that exceeds the column width wraps to a new line.
4. Click cell **A12** to make it the active cell. See Figure 1-21.

Figure 1-21   **Text wrapped within cells**

5	Last Name	Gregson				
6	Address	412 Apple Grove St.				
7	City	Nashua				
8	State	NH				
9	Postal Code	03061				
10	Phone	(603) 555-4128				
11						
12	ISBN	CATEGORY	BINDING	TITLE	AUTHOR(S)	PRICE	QTY
13	0-374-25385-4	Used	Hardcover	Samurai William: The Englishman Who Opened Japan	Milton, Giles	$5.95	
14	4-889-96213-1	New	Softcover	Floral Origami Globes	Fuse, Tomoko	$24.95	
15	0-500-27062-7	New	Hardcover	Tao Magic: The Secret Language of Diagrams and Calligraphy	Legeza, Laszlo	$8.95	
16	0-785-82169-4	Used	Hardcover	The Holy Grail	Morgan, Giles	$3.75	
17	0-854-56516-7	New	Softcover	Murder on the Links	Christie, Agatha	$7.50	

- column width set to 30 characters
- titles wrapped within the cells
- row heights increased to accommodate the wrapped text

If you want to create a new line within a cell, press the Alt+Enter keys to move the insertion point to the next line within the cell. Whatever you type next will appear on the new line in the cell.

Changing Row Heights

The height of a row is measured in points or pixels. A **point** is approximately 1/72 of an inch. The default row height is 15 points or 20 pixels. Row heights are set in the same way as column widths. You can drag the bottom border of the row heading to a new row height, specify a row height using the Format command, or autofit the row's height to match its content.

Sanjit wants you add more space above the labels in the book list by resizing row 12.

To increase the height of row 12:

1. Move the pointer over the bottom border of the row 12 heading until the pointer changes to ✥.

2. Drag the bottom border down until the height of the row is equal to **30** points (or **40** pixels), and then release the mouse button. The height of row 12 is set to 30 points.

3. Press the **Ctrl+S** keys to save the workbook.

TIP
You can also set the row height by clicking the Format button in the Cells group on the HOME tab and then using the Row Height command.

You have entered most of the data for Tobias Gregson's order at Sparrow & Pond. In the next session, you will calculate the total charge for the order and print the worksheet.

Session 1.1 Quick Check

1. What are the two types of sheets used in a workbook?
2. What is the cell reference for the cell located in the fourth column and third row of a worksheet?
3. What is the range reference for the block of cells B10 through C15?
4. What is the reference for the nonadjacent block of cells B10 through C15 and cells B20 through D25?
5. What keyboard shortcut changes the active cell to cell A1?
6. What is text data?
7. Cell A4 contains *May 3, 2016*; why doesn't Excel consider this entry a text string?
8. How do you resize a column or row?

EX 30   Excel | Tutorial 1 Getting Started with Excel

Session 1.2 Visual Overview:

The font size refers to how big the text is.

You use the PAGE LAYOUT tab to change how the worksheet will appear on the printed page.

In Excel, every formula begins with an equal sign (=).

When the active cell contains a formula, the formula appears in the formula bar but the result of the formula appears in the cell.

The gridlines that surround cells appear on the worksheet as a guide; they do not print.

A **border** is a line you can add along an edge of a cell. Borders are used to improve the readability of data.

SP Customer Order

FILE | HOME | INSERT | PAGE LAYOUT | FORMULAS | DATA | REVIEW | VIE

Calibri 11 Currency

Clipboard | Font | Alignment | Number

I23   =G23*H23

	A	B	C	D
9	Ship To			
10	First Name	Tobias		
11	Last Name	Gregson		
12	Address	412 Apple Grove St.		
13	City	Nashua		
14	State	NH		
15	Postal Code	03061		
16	Phone	(603) 555-4128		
17				
18	BOOK ID	ISBN	CATEGORY	BINDING	TITLE
19	25385-Used	0-374-25385-4	Used	Hardcover	Samurai William: Who Opened Ja
20	96213-New	4-889-96213-1	New	Softcover	Floral Origami G
21	01089-Used	0-151-01089-7	Used	Hardcover	Pops: A Life of Lo
22	27062-New	0-500-27062-7	New	Hardcover	Tao Magic: The S Diagrams and Ca
23	56516-New	0-854-56516-7	New	Softcover	Murder on the Li
24				
25				
26				
27				
28				

Documentation | **Customer Order**

READY

© 2014 Cengage Learning

Formulas and Functions

AutoSum quickly inserts functions to sum, average, or count values in a range, or find the minimum or maximum value in a range.

A **function** is a named operation that replaces the action of an arithmetic expression.

=G19*H19
=G20*H20
=G21*H21

A **formula** is an expression that calculates a value. These formulas multiply values in different cells.

The **SUM** function adds the values in the specified range.

	AUTHOR(S)	PRICE	QTY	CHARGE
			Sales Tax	5%
ai William: The Englishman				
pened Japan	Milton, Giles	$5.95	2	$11.90
Origami Globes	Fuse, Tomoko	$24.95	3	$74.85
A Life of Louis Armstrong	Teachout, Terry	$11.95	2	$23.90
gic: The Secret Language of				
ms and Calligraphy	Legeza, Laszlo	$8.95	1	$8.95
r on the Links	ie, Agatha	$7.50	2	$15.00
			Subtotal	$134.60
			Tax	$6.73
			Handling	$15.30
			TOTAL	$156.63

=SUM(I19:I23)
=I17*I25
15.3
=SUM(I25:I27)

Page Break Preview shows the location of page breaks in the printed sheet.

Normal view shows the contents of the active sheet in the workbook window.

Page Layout view shows how the sheet will appear when printed.

Tutorial 1 Getting Started with Excel | Excel   EX 31

Adding Formulas to a Worksheet

So far you have entered text, numbers, and dates in the worksheet. However, the main reason for using Excel is to display values calculated from data. For example, Sally wants the workbook to calculate the number of books the customer ordered and how much revenue the order will generate. Such calculations are added to a worksheet using formulas and functions.

Entering a Formula

A formula is an expression that returns a value. In most cases, this is a number—though it could also be text or a date. In Excel, every formula begins with an equal sign (=) followed by an expression describing the operation that returns the value. If you don't begin the formula with the equal sign, Excel assumes that you are entering text and will not treat the cell contents as a formula.

A formula is written using **operators** that combine different values, resulting in a single value that is then displayed in the cell. The most common operators are **arithmetic operators** that perform addition, subtraction, multiplication, division, and exponentiation. For example, the following formula adds 5 and 7, returning a value of 12:

=5+7

Most Excel formulas contain references to cells rather than specific values. This allows you to change the values used in the calculation without having to modify the formula itself. For example, the following formula returns the result of adding the values stored in cells A1 and B2:

=A1+B2

If the value 5 is stored in cell A1 and the value 7 is stored in cell B2, this formula would also return a value of 12. If you later changed the value in cell A1 to 10, the formula would return a value of 17. Figure 1-22 describes the different arithmetic operators and provides examples of formulas.

Figure 1-22   Arithmetic operators

Operation	Arithmetic Operator	Example	Description
Addition	+	=B1+B2+B3	Adds the values in cells B1, B2, and B3
Subtraction	–	=C9–B2	Subtracts the value in cell B2 from the value in cell C9
Multiplication	*	=C9*B9	Multiplies the values in cells C9 and B9
Division	/	=C9/B9	Divides the value in cell C9 by the value in cell B9
Exponentiation	^	=B5^3	Raises the value of cell B5 to the third power

© 2014 Cengage Learning

If a formula contains more than one arithmetic operator, Excel performs the calculation using the same order of operations you might have already seen in math classes. The **order of operations** is a set of predefined rules used to determine the sequence in which operators are applied in a calculation. Excel first calculates the value of any operation within parentheses, then it applies exponentiation (^), multiplication (*), and division (/), and finally it performs addition (+) and subtraction (–). For example, the following formula returns the value 23 because multiplying 4 by 5 takes precedence over adding 3:

=3+4*5

If a formula contains two or more operators with the same level of priority, the operators are applied in order from left to right. In the following formula, Excel first multiplies 4 by 10 and then divides that result by 8 to return the value 5:

=4*10/8

When parentheses are used, the value inside them is calculated first. In the following formula, Excel calculates (3+4) first, and then multiplies that result by 5 to return the value 35:

=(3+4)*5

Figure 1-23 shows how slight changes in a formula affect the order of operations and the result of the formula.

Figure 1-23   **Order of operations applied to Excel formulas**

Formula	Application of the Order of Operations	Result
=50+10*5	10*5 calculated first and then 50 is added	100
=(50+10)*5	(50+10) calculated first and then 60 is multiplied by 5	300
=50/10–5	50/10 calculated first and then 5 is subtracted	0
=50/(10–5)	(10–5) calculated first and then 50 is divided by that value	10
=50/10*5	Two operators at same precedence level, so the calculation is done left to right in the expression	25
=50/(10*5)	(10*5) is calculated first and then 50 is divided by that value	1

© 2014 Cengage Learning

Sally wants the Customer Order worksheet to include the total amount charged for each book. The charge is equal to the number of books ordered multiplied by the book's price. You already entered this information in columns F and G. Now you will enter a formula to calculate the charge for books ordered in column H.

To enter the formula to calculate the charge for the first book order:

1. Make cell **H12** the active cell, type **CHARGE** as the column label, and then press the **Enter** key. The label text is entered in cell H12, and cell H13 is now the active cell.

2. Type **=F13*G13** (the price of the book multiplied by the quantity of books ordered). As you type the formula, a list of Excel function names appears in a ScreenTip, which provides a quick method for entering functions. The list will close when you complete the formula. You will learn more about Excel functions shortly. Also, as you type each cell reference, Excel color codes the cell reference with the cell. See Figure 1-24.

Figure 1-24 Formula being entered in a cell

- formula displayed in the formula bar
- formula in cell H13 multiplies the values in cells F13 and G13
- cell references are color coded

> 3. Press the **Enter** key. The formula is entered in cell H13, which displays the value $11.90. The result is displayed as currency because cell F13, which is referenced in the formula, contains a currency value.
>
> 4. Click cell **H13** to make it the active cell. The cell displays the result of the formula, and the formula bar displays the formula you entered.

For the first book, you entered the formula by typing each cell reference in the expression. You can also insert a cell reference by clicking the cell as you type the formula. This technique reduces the possibility of error caused by typing an incorrect cell reference. You will use this method to enter the formula to calculate the charge for the second book.

To enter the cell references in the formula using the mouse:

> 1. Click cell **H14** to make it the active cell.
>
> 2. Type **=**. The equal sign indicates that you are entering a formula. Any cell you click from now on inserts the cell reference of the selected cell into the formula until you complete the formula by pressing the Enter or Tab key.
>
> 3. Click cell **F14**. The cell reference is inserted into the formula in the formula bar. At this point, any cell you click changes the cell reference used in the formula. The cell reference isn't locked until you type an operator.
>
> 4. Type ***** to enter the multiplication operator. The cell reference for cell F14 is locked in the formula, and the next cell you click will be inserted after the operator.
>
> 5. Click cell **G14** to enter its cell reference in the formula. The formula is complete.
>
> 6. Press the **Enter** key. Cell H14 displays the value $74.85, which is the total charge for the second book.

Be sure to type = as the first part of the entry; otherwise, Excel will not interpret the entry as a formula.

Tutorial 1 Getting Started with Excel | Excel   EX 35

Copying and Pasting Formulas

Sometimes you will need to repeat the same formula throughout a worksheet. Rather than retyping the formula, you can copy a formula from one cell and paste it into another cell. When you copy a formula, Excel places the formula into the **Clipboard**, which is a temporary storage location for text and graphics. When you paste, Excel takes the formula from the Clipboard and inserts it into the selected cell or range. Excel adjusts the cell references in the formula to reflect the formula's new location in the worksheet. This occurs because you usually want to copy the actions of a formula rather than the specific value the formula generates. In this case, the formula's action is to multiply the price of the book by the quantity. By copying and pasting the formula, you can quickly repeat that action for every book listed in the worksheet.

You will copy the formula you entered in cell H14 to the range H15:H17 to calculate the charges on the remaining three books in Tobias Gregson's order. By copying and pasting the formula, you will save time and avoid potential mistakes from retyping the formula.

To copy and paste the formula:

1. Click cell **H14** to select the cell that contains the formula you want to copy.
2. On the HOME tab, in the Clipboard group, click the **Copy** button (or press the **Ctrl+C** keys). Excel copies the formula to the Clipboard.
3. Select the range **H15:H17**. You want to paste the formula into these cells.
4. In the Clipboard group, click the **Paste** button (or press the **Ctrl+V** keys). Excel pastes the formula into the selected cells, adjusting each formula so that the total charges calculated for the books are based on the corresponding values within each row. A button appears below the selected range, providing options for pasting formulas and values. See Figure 1-25.

Figure 1-25   Copied and pasted formula

> **5.** Click cell **H15** and verify that the formula =F15*G15 appears in the formula bar. The formula was updated to reflect the cell references in the corresponding row.
>
> **6.** Click the other cells in column H and verify that the corresponding formulas are entered in those cells.

Simplifying Formulas with Functions

In addition to cell references and operators, formulas can also contain functions. A function is a named operation that replaces the arithmetic expression in a formula. Functions are used to simplify long or complex formulas. For example, to add the values from cells A1 through A10, you could enter the following long formula:

=A1+A2+A3+A4+A5+A6+A7+A8+A9+A10

Or, you could use the SUM function to calculate the sum of those cell values by entering the following formula:

=SUM(A1:A10)

In both instances, Excel adds the values in cells A1 through A10, but the SUM function is faster and simpler to enter and less prone to a typing error. You should always use a function, if one is available, in place of a long, complex formula. Excel supports more than 300 different functions from the fields of finance, business, science, and engineering. Excel provides functions that work with numbers, text, and dates.

Introducing Function Syntax

Every function follows a set of rules, or **syntax**, which specifies how the function should be written. The general syntax of all Excel functions is

`FUNCTION (argument1, argument2, ...)`

where `FUNCTION` is the function name, and `argument1`, `argument2`, and so forth are values used by that function. For example, the SUM function shown above uses a single argument, A1:A10, which is the range reference of the cells whose values will be added. Some functions do not require any arguments and are entered as `FUNCTION()`. Functions without arguments still require the opening and closing parentheses, but do not include a value within the parentheses.

Entering Functions with AutoSum

A fast and convenient way to enter commonly used functions is with AutoSum. The AutoSum button includes options to insert the SUM, AVERAGE, COUNT, MIN, and MAX functions to generate the following:

- Sum of the values in the specified range
- Average value in the specified range
- Total count of numeric values in the specified range
- Minimum value in the specified range
- Maximum value in the specified range

After you select one of the AutoSum options, Excel determines the most appropriate range from the available data and enters it as the function's argument. You should always verify that the range included in the AutoSum function matches the range that you want to use.

Tutorial 1 Getting Started with Excel | Excel   EX 37

You will use AutoSum to enter the SUM function to add the total charges for Tobias Gregson's order.

To use AutoSum to enter the SUM function:

1. Click cell **G18** to make it the active cell, type **Subtotal** as the label, and then press the **Tab** key to make cell H18 the active cell.

2. On the HOME tab, in the Editing group, click the **AutoSum button arrow**. The button's menu opens and displays five common summary functions: Sum, Average, Count Numbers, Max (for maximum), and Min (for minimum).

TIP
You can quickly insert the SUM function by pressing the Alt+= keys.

3. Click **Sum** to enter the SUM function. The formula =SUM(H13:H17) is entered in cell H18. The cells involved in calculating the sum are selected and highlighted on the worksheet so you can quickly confirm that Excel selected the most appropriate range from the available data. A ScreenTip appears below the formula describing the function's syntax. See Figure 1-26.

Figure 1-26   SUM function being entered with the AutoSum button

4. Press the **Enter** key to accept the formula. The subtotal of the book charges returned by the SUM function is $114.45.

AutoSum makes entering a commonly used formula such as the SUM function fast and easy. However, AutoSum can determine the appropriate range reference to include only when the function is adjacent to the cells containing the values you want to summarize. If you need to use a function elsewhere in the worksheet, you will have to select the range reference to include or type the function yourself.

Each sale made by Sparrow & Pond is subject to a 5 percent sales tax and a $15.30 handling fee. You will add these to the Customer Order worksheet so you can calculate the total charge for the order.

To add the sales tax and handling fee to the worksheet:

1. Click cell **G11**, type **Sales Tax** as the label, and then press the **Tab** key to make cell H11 the active cell.

2. In cell H11, type **5%** as the sales tax rate, and then press the **Enter** key. The sales tax rate is entered in the cell, and can be used in other calculations. The value is displayed with the % symbol, but is stored as the equivalent decimal value 0.05.

3. Click cell **G19** to make it the active cell, type **Tax** as the label, and then press the **Tab** key to make cell H19 the active cell.

4. Type **=H11*H18** as the formula to calculate the sales tax on the book order, and then press the **Enter** key. The formula multiples the sales tax value in cell H11 by the order subtotal value in cell H18. The value $5.72 is displayed in cell H19, which is 5 percent of the book order subtotal of $114.45.

5. In cell G20, type **Handling** as the label, and then press the **Tab** key to make cell H20 the active cell. You will enter the handling fee in this cell.

6. Type **$15.30** as the handling fee, and then press the **Enter** key.

The last part of the customer order is to calculate the total cost by adding the subtotal, the tax, and the handling fee. Rather than using AutoSum, you will type the SUM function so you can enter the correct range reference for the function. You can type the range reference or select the range in the worksheet. Remember, that you must type parentheses around the range reference.

To calculate the total order cost:

1. In cell G21, type **TOTAL** as the label, and then press the **Tab** key.

2. Type **=SUM(** in cell H21 to enter the function name and the opening parenthesis. As you begin to type the function, a ScreenTip lists the names of all functions that start with S.

3. Type **H18:H20** to specify the range reference of the cells you want to add. The cells referenced in the function are selected and highlighted on the worksheet so you can quickly confirm that you entered the correct range reference.

> Make sure the cell reference in the function matches the range you want to calculate.

4. Type **)** to complete the function, and then press the **Enter** key. The value of the SUM function appears in cell H21, indicating that the total charge for the order is $135.47. See Figure 1-27.

Figure 1-27   **Total charge for the customer order**

5% sales tax stored as 0.05

*tax is 5% of the subtotal, calculated as =H11*H18*

handling fee is $15.30

total charge is the sum of the range H18:H20, calculated as =SUM(H18:H20)

The SUM function makes it simple to quickly add the values in a group of cells.

Problem Solving: Writing Effective Formulas

You can use formulas to quickly perform calculations and solve problems. First, identify the problem you need to solve. Then, gather the data needed to solve the problem. Finally, create accurate and effective formulas that use the data to answer or resolve the problem. Follow these guidelines:

- **Keep formulas simple.** Use functions in place of long, complex formulas whenever possible. For example, use the SUM function instead of entering a formula that adds individual cells, which makes it easier to confirm that the formula is making an accurate calculation as it provides answers needed to evaluate the problem.
- **Do not hide data values within formulas.** The worksheet displays formula results, not the actual formula. For example, to calculate a 5 percent interest rate on a currency value in cell A5, you could enter the formula =0.05*A5. However, this doesn't show how the value is calculated. A better approach places the value 0.05 in a cell accompanied by a descriptive label and uses the cell reference in the formula. If you place 0.05 in cell A6, the formula =A6*A5 would calculate the interest value. Other people can then easily see the interest rate as well as the resulting interest, ensuring that the formula is solving the right problem.
- **Break up formulas to show intermediate results.** When a worksheet contains complex computations, other people can more easily comprehend how the formula results are calculated when different parts of the formula are distinguished. For example, the formula =SUM(A1:A10)/SUM(B1:B10) calculates the ratio of two sums, but hides the two sum values. Instead, enter each SUM function in a separate cell, such as cells A11 and B11, and use the formula =A11/B11 to calculate the ratio. Other people can see both sums and the value of their ratio in the worksheet and better understand the final result, which makes it more likely that the best problem resolution will be selected.
- **Test formulas with simple values.** Use values you can calculate in your head to confirm that your formula works as intended. For example, using 1s or 10s as the input values lets you easily figure out the answer and verify the formula.

Finding a solution to a problem requires accurate data and analysis. With workbooks, this means using formulas that are easy to understand, clearly show the data being used in the calculations, and demonstrate how the results are calculated. Only then can you be confident that you are choosing the best problem resolution.

Modifying a Worksheet

As you develop a worksheet, you might need to modify its content and structure to create a more logical organization. Some ways you can modify a worksheet include moving cells and ranges, inserting rows and columns, deleting rows and columns, and inserting and deleting cells.

Moving and Copying a Cell or Range

One way to move a cell or range is to select it, position the pointer over the bottom border of the selection, drag the selection to a new location, and then release the mouse button. This technique is called **drag and drop** because you are dragging the range and dropping it in a new location. If the drop location is not visible, drag the selection to the edge of the workbook window to scroll the worksheet, and then drop the selection.

You can also use the drag-and-drop technique to copy cells by pressing the Ctrl key as you drag the selected range to its new location. A copy of the original range is placed in the new location without removing the original range from the worksheet.

Tutorial 1 Getting Started with Excel | Excel   EX 41

REFERENCE

Moving or Copying a Cell or Range

- Select the cell or range you want to move or copy.
- Move the pointer over the border of the selection until the pointer changes shape.
- To move the range, click the border and drag the selection to a new location (or to copy the range, hold down the Ctrl key and drag the selection to a new location).

or

- Select the cell or range you want to move or copy.
- On the HOME tab, in the Clipboard group, click the Cut or Copy button (or right-click the selection, and then click Cut or Copy on the shortcut menu, or press the Ctrl+X or Ctrl+C keys).
- Select the cell or the upper-left cell of the range where you want to paste the content.
- In the Clipboard group, click the Paste button (or right-click the selection and then click Paste on the shortcut menu, or press the Ctrl+V keys).

Sally wants the subtotal, tax, handling, and total values in the range G18:H21 moved down one row to the range G19:H22 to provide more space from the book orders. You will use the drag-and-drop method to move the range.

To drag and drop the range G18:H21:

1. Select the range **G18:H21**. These are the cells you want to move.

2. Move the pointer over the bottom border of the selected range so that the pointer changes to ⊹.

3. Press and hold the mouse button to change the pointer to ▷, and then drag the selection down one row. Do not release the mouse button. A ScreenTip appears, indicating that the new range of the selected cells will be G19:H22. A darker border also appears around the new range. See Figure 1-28.

Figure 1-28 Range G18:H21 being moved to range G19:H22

| 16 | 0-785-82169-4 | Used | Hardcover | The Holy Grail | Morgan, Giles | $3.75 | 1 | $3.75 |
| 17 | 0-854-56516-7 | New | Softcover | Murder on the Links | Christie, Agatha | $7.50 | 2 | $15.00 |

Subtotal $114.45
Tax $5.72
Handling $15.30
TOTAL $135.47

darker border outlines the new range

G19:H22

ScreenTip indicates the new range reference of the cells being moved

4. Make sure the ScreenTip displays the range **G19:H22**, and then release the mouse button. The selected cells move to their new location.

Some people find dragging and dropping a difficult and awkward way to move a selection, particularly if the selected range is large or needs to move a long distance in the worksheet. In those situations, it is often more efficient to cut or copy and paste the cell contents. Cutting moves the selected content, whereas copying duplicates the selected content. Pasting places the selected content in the new location.

Sally wants the worksheet to include a summary of the customer order starting in row 3. You will cut the customer contact information and the book listing from range A3:A22 and paste it into range A9:H23, freeing up space for the order information.

To cut and paste the customer contact information and book listing:

1. Click cell **A3** to select it.

2. Press the **Ctrl+Shift+End** keys to extend the selection to the last cell in the lower-right corner of the worksheet (cell H22).

3. On the HOME tab, in the Clipboard group, click the **Cut** button (or press the **Ctrl+X** keys). The range is surrounded by a moving border, indicating that it has been cut.

4. Click cell **A9** to select it. This is the upper-left corner of the range where you want to paste the range that you cut.

5. In the Clipboard group, click the **Paste** button (or press the **Ctrl+V** keys). The range A3:H22 is pasted into the range A9:H28. All of the formulas in the moved range were automatically updated to reflect their new locations.

Using the COUNT Function

Sometimes you will want to know how many unique items are included in a range, such as the number of different books in the customer order. To calculate that value, you use the COUNT function, which has the syntax

=COUNT(*range*)

where *range* is the range of cells containing numeric values to be counted. Note that any cell in the range containing a non-numeric value is not counted in the final tally.

You will include the count of the number of different books for the order in the summary information. The summary will also display the order ID (a unique number assigned by Sparrow & Pond to the order), the shipping date, and the type of delivery (overnight, two-day, or standard) in the freed-up space at the top of the worksheet. In addition, Sally wants the total charge for the order to be displayed with the order summary so she does not have to scroll to the bottom of the worksheet to find that value.

To add the order summary:

1. Click cell **A3**, type **Order ID** as the label, press the **Tab** key, type **14123** in cell B3, and then press the **Enter** key. The order ID is entered, and cell A4 is the active cell.

2. Type **Shipping Date** as the label in cell A4, press the **Tab** key, type **4/3/2016** in cell B4, and then press the **Enter** key. The shipping date is entered, and cell A5 is the active cell.

3. Type **Delivery** as the label in cell A5, press the **Tab** key, type **Overnight** in cell B5, and then press the **Enter** key. The delivery type is entered, and cell A6 is the active cell.

4. Type **Items Ordered** as the label in cell A6, and then press the **Tab** key. Cell B6 is the active cell. You will enter the COUNT function to determine the number of different books ordered.

5. In cell B6, type **=COUNT(** to begin the function.

Tutorial 1 Getting Started with Excel | Excel EX 43

6. With the insertion point still blinking in cell B6, select the range **G19:G23**. The range reference is entered as the argument for the COUNT function.

7. Type **)** to complete the function, and then press the **Enter** key. Cell B6 displays the value 5, indicating that five items were ordered by Tobias Gregson. Cell A7 is the active cell.

8. Type **Total Charge** as the label in cell A7, and then press the **Tab** key to make cell B7 the active cell.

9. Type **=** to start the formula, and then click cell **H28** to enter its cell reference in the formula in cell B7. The formula =H28 tells Excel to display the contents of cell H28 in the current cell.

10. Press the **Enter** key to complete the formula. See Figure 1-29.

Figure 1-29 Customer order summary

[Screenshot of Excel worksheet showing:]

	A	B
1	Customer Order	
2		
3	Order ID	14123
4	Shipping Date	4/3/2016
5	Delivery	Overnight
6	Items Ordered	5
7	Total Charge	$135.47
8		
9	Ship To	
10	First Name	Tobias
11	Last Name	Gregson
12	Address	412 Apple Grove St.
13	City	Nashua
14	State	NH
15	Postal Code	03061
16	Phone	(603) 555-4128
17		
18	ISBN	CATEGORY

Callouts: order summary; total book items in the order calculated using the formula =COUNT(G19:G23); total charge references the value in cell H28 using the formula =H28

Inserting a Column or Row

You can insert a new column or row anywhere within a worksheet. When you insert a new column, the existing columns are shifted to the right and the new column has the same width as the column directly to its left. When you insert a new row, the existing rows are shifted down and the new row has the same height as the row above it. Because inserting a new row or column moves the location of the other cells in the worksheet, any cell references in a formula or function are updated to reflect the new layout.

> **REFERENCE**
>
> ### Inserting or Deleting a Column or Row
>
> **To insert a column or row:**
> - Select the column(s) or row(s) where you want to insert the new column(s) or row(s). Excel will insert the same number of columns or rows as you select to the *left* of the selected columns or *above* the selected rows.
> - On the HOME tab, in the Cells group, click the Insert button (or right-click a column or row heading or selected column and row headings, and then click Insert on the shortcut menu; or press the Ctrl+Shift+= keys).
>
> **To delete a column or row:**
> - Select the column(s) or row(s) you want to delete.
> - On the HOME tab, in the Cells group, click the Delete button (or right-click a column or row heading or selected column and row headings, and then click Delete on the shortcut menu; or press the Ctrl+− keys).

Tobias Gregson's order is missing an item. You need to insert a row directly below *Floral Origami Globes* in which to enter the additional book.

To insert a new row for the missing book order:

1. Click the **row 21** heading to select the entire row.

2. On the HOME tab, in the Cells group, click the **Insert** button (or press the **Ctrl+Shift+=** keys). A new row is inserted below row 20 and becomes the new row 21.

3. Enter **0-151-01089-7** in cell A21, enter **Used** in cell B21, enter **Hardcover** in cell C21, enter **Pops: A Life of Louis Armstrong** in cell D21, enter **Teachout, Terry** in cell E21, enter **$11.95** in cell F21, and then enter **2** in cell G21.

4. Click cell **H20** to select the cell with the formula for calculating the book charge, and then press the **Ctrl+C** keys to copy the formula in that cell.

5. Click cell **H21** to select the cell where you want to insert the formula, and then press the **Ctrl+V** keys to paste the formula into the cell.

6. Click cell **H26**. The formula in this cell is now =SUM(H19:H24); the range reference was updated to reflect the inserted row. Also, the tax amount increased to $6.92 based on the new subtotal value of $138.35, and the total charge increased to $160.57 because of the added book order. See Figure 1-30. Also, the result of the COUNT function in cell B6 increased to 6 to reflect the item added to the book order.

> **TIP**
>
> You can insert multiple columns or rows by selecting that number of column or row headings, and then clicking the Insert button or pressing the Ctrl+Shift+= keys.

Figure 1-30 New row inserted

	A	B	C	D	E	F	G	H
16	Phone	(603) 555-4128						
17							Sales Tax	5%
18	ISBN	CATEGORY	BINDING	TITLE	AUTHOR(S)	PRICE	QTY	CHARGE
19	0-374-25385-4	Used	Hardcover	Samurai William: The Englishman Who Opened Japan	Milton, Giles	$5.95	2	$11.90
20	4-889-96213-1	New	Softcover	Floral Origami Globes	Fuse, Tomoko	$24.95	3	$74.85
21	0-151-01089-7	Used	Hardcover	Pops: A Life of Louis Armstrong	Teachout, Terry	$11.95	2	$23.90
22	0-500-27062-7	New	Hardcover	Tao Magic: The Secret Language of Diagrams and Calligraphy	Legeza, Laszlo	$8.95	1	$8.95
23	0-785-82169-4	Used	Hardcover	The Holy Grail	Morgan, Giles	$3.75	1	$3.75
24	0-854-56516-7	New	Softcover	Murder on the Links	Christie, Agatha	$7.50	2	$15.00
25								
26							Subtotal	$138.35
27							Tax	$6.92
28							Handling	$15.30
29							TOTAL	$160.57

Cell H26 formula: =SUM(H19:H24)

- cell references adjusted to match the new layout
- new row inserted in the worksheet
- rows below shifted down
- subtotal, sales tax, and total charge automatically updated to include the new item

Deleting a Row or Column

You can delete rows or columns from a worksheet. **Deleting** removes the data from the row or column as well as the row or column itself. The rows below the deleted row shift up to fill the vacated space. Likewise, the columns to the right of the deleted column shift left to fill the vacated space. Also, all cell references in the worksheet are adjusted to reflect the change. You click the Delete button in the Cells group on the HOME tab to delete selected rows or columns.

Deleting a column or row is not the same as clearing a column or row. **Clearing** removes the data from the selected row or column but leaves the blank row or column in the worksheet. You press the Delete key to clear the contents of the selected row or column, which leaves the worksheet structure unchanged.

Tobias Gregson did not order *The Holy Grail* by Giles Morgan, so that book needs to be removed from the order. You will delete the row containing that book.

To delete the *The Holy Grail* row from the book order:

1. Click the **row 23** heading to select the entire row.
2. On the HOME tab, in the Cells group, click the **Delete** button (or press the **Ctrl+–** keys). Row 23 is deleted, and the rows below it shift up to fill the space.

All of the cell references in the worksheet are again updated automatically to reflect the impact of deleting row 23. The subtotal value in cell H25 now returns a value of $134.60 based on the sum of the cells in the range H19:H23. The sales tax amount in cell H26 decreases to $6.73. The total cost of the order decreases to $156.63. Also, the result of the COUNT function in cell B6 decreases to 5 to reflect the item deleted from the book order. As you can see, one of the great advantages of using Excel is that it modifies the formulas to reflect the additions and deletions you make to the worksheet.

Inserting and Deleting a Range

You can also insert or delete ranges within a worksheet. When you use the Insert button to insert a range of cells, the existing cells shift down when the selected range is wider than it is long, and they shift right when the selected range is longer than it is wide, as shown in Figure 1-31. When you use the Insert Cells command, you specify whether the existing cells shift right or down, or whether to insert an entire row or column into the new range.

Figure 1-31 Cells being inserted in a worksheet

© 2014 Cengage Learning

The process works in reverse when you delete a range. As with deleting a row or column, the cells adjacent to the deleted range either move up or left to fill in the space vacated by the deleted cells. The Delete Cells command lets you specify whether you want to shift the adjacent cells left or up, or whether you want to delete the entire column or row.

When you insert or delete a range, cells that shift to a new location adopt the width of the columns they move into. As a result, you might need to resize columns and rows in the worksheet.

REFERENCE

Inserting or Deleting a Range

- Select a range that matches the range you want to insert or delete.
- On the HOME tab, in the Cells group, click the Insert button or the Delete button.

or

- Select the range that matches the range you want to insert or delete.
- On the HOME tab, in the Cells group, click the Insert button arrow and then click Insert Cells, or click the Delete button arrow and then click Delete Cells (or right-click the selected range, and then click Insert or Delete on the shortcut menu).
- Click the option button for the direction to shift the cells, columns, or rows.
- Click the OK button.

Sally wants you to insert cells in the book list that will contain the Sparrow & Pond book ID for each book. You will insert these new cells into the range A17:A28, shifting the adjacent cells to the right.

Tutorial 1 Getting Started with Excel | Excel **EX 47**

To insert a range in the book list:

1. Select the range **A17:A28**. You want to insert cells in this range.
2. On the HOME tab, in the Cells group, click the **Insert button arrow**. A menu of insert options appears.
3. Click **Insert Cells**. The Insert dialog box opens.
4. Verify that the **Shift cells right** option button is selected.
5. Click the **OK** button. New cells are inserted into the selected range, and the adjacent cells move to the right. The cell contents do not fit well in the columns and rows they shifted into, so you will resize the columns and rows.
6. Resize columns C and D to **12** characters, resize column E to **30** characters, and then resize column F to **15** characters. The text is easier to read in the resized columns.
7. Select the row **19** through row **23** headings.
8. In the Cells group, click the **Format** button, and then click **AutoFit Row Height**. The selected rows autofit to their contents.
9. Click cell **A18**, type **BOOK ID** as the label, and then press the **Enter** key. See Figure 1-32.

> **TIP**
> You can also autofit by double-clicking the bottom border of row 23.

Figure 1-32 Range added to the worksheet

[Screenshot of Excel worksheet showing:
- Callout "inserted range" pointing to column A
- Callout "adjacent cells shifted to the right" pointing to columns B onward
- Callout "columns and rows resized to better display the data" pointing to columns C-F
- Row 16: Phone (603) 555-4128
- Row 17: Sales Tax 5%
- Row 18: BOOK ID | ISBN | CATEGORY | BINDING | TITLE | AUTHOR(S) | PRICE | QTY | CHARGE
- Row 19: 0-374-25385-4 | Used | Hardcover | Samurai William: The Englishman Who Opened Japan | Milton, Giles | $5.95 | 2 | $11.90
- Row 20: 4-889-96213-1 | New | Softcover | Floral Origami Globes | Fuse, Tomoko | $24.95 | 3 | $74.85
- Row 21: 0-151-01089-7 | Used | Hardcover | Pops: A Life of Louis Armstrong | Teachout, Terry | $11.95 | 2 | $23.90
- Row 22: 0-500-27062-7 | New | Hardcover | Tao Magic: The Secret Language of Diagrams and Calligraphy | Legeza, Laszlo | $8.95 | 1 | $8.95
- Row 23: 0-854-56516-7 | New | Softcover | Murder on the Links | Christie, Agatha | $7.50 | 2 | $15.00
- Row 25: Subtotal $134.60
- Row 26: Tax $6.73
- Row 27: Handling $15.30
- Row 28: TOTAL $156.63]

Why did you insert cells in the range A17:A28 even though the book ID values will be entered only in the range A18:A23? You did this to retain the layout of the page design. Selecting the additional rows ensures that the sales tax and summary values still line up with the QTY and CHARGE columns. Whenever you insert a new range, be sure to consider its impact on the layout of the entire worksheet.

INSIGHT

Hiding and Unhiding Rows, Columns, and Worksheets

Workbooks can become long and complicated, filled with formulas and data that are important for performing calculations but are of little interest to readers. In those situations, you can simplify these workbooks for readers by **hiding** rows, columns, and even worksheets. Although the contents of hidden cells cannot be seen, the data in those cells is still available for use in formulas and functions throughout the workbook.

Hiding a row or column essentially decreases that row height or column width to 0 pixels. To a hide a row or column, select the row or column heading, click the Format button in the Cells group on the HOME tab, point to Hide & Unhide on the menu that appears, and then click Hide Rows or Hide Columns. The border of the row or column heading is doubled to mark the location of hidden rows or columns.

A worksheet often is hidden when the entire worksheet contains data that is not of interest to the reader and is better summarized elsewhere in the document. To hide a worksheet, make that worksheet active, click the Format button in the Cells group on the HOME tab, point to Hide & Unhide, and then click Hide Sheet.

Unhiding redisplays the hidden content in the workbook. To unhide a row or column, click in a cell below the hidden row or to the right of the hidden column, click the Format button, point to Hide & Unhide, and then click Unhide Rows or Unhide Columns. To unhide a worksheet, click the Format button, point to Hide & Unhide, and then click Unhide Sheet. The Unhide dialog box opens. Click the sheet you want to unhide, and then click the OK button. The hidden content is redisplayed in the workbook.

Although hiding data can make a worksheet and workbook easier to read, be sure never to hide information that is important to the reader.

Sally wants you to add one more piece of data to the worksheet—a book ID that is used by Sparrow & Pond to identify each book in stock. You will use Flash Fill to create the book IDs.

Using Flash Fill

Flash Fill enters text based on patterns it finds in the data. As shown in Figure 1-33, Flash Fill generates customer names from the first and last names stored in the adjacent columns in the worksheet. To enter the rest of the names, you press the Enter key; to continue typing the names yourself, you press the Esc key.

Figure 1-33   **Entering text with Flash Fill**

	A	B	C	D	E
1	First	M.I.	Last	Full Name	
2	Tobias	A.	Gregson	Tobias Gregson	you enter the full name twice to begin the pattern
3	Maria	R.	Sanchez	Maria Sanchez	
4	Andrew	T.	Lewis	Andrew Lewis	
5	Brett	K.	Carls	Brett Carls	Flash Fill generates the remaining full names based on the pattern in the first two cells
6	Carmen	A.	Hzu	Carmen Hzu	
7	Karen	M.	Schultz	Karen Schultz	
8	Howard	P.	Gary	Howard Gary	
9	Natalia	N.	Shapiro	Natalia Shapiro	
10	Paul	O.	Douglas	Paul Douglas	
11					

Flash Fill works best when the pattern is clearly recognized from the values in the data. Be sure to enter the data pattern in the column or row right next to the related data. The data used to generate the pattern must be in a rectangular grid and cannot have blank columns or rows. Also, Flash Fill enters text, not formulas. If you edit or replace an entry originally used by Flash Fill, the content generated by Flash Fill will not be updated.

The Sparrow & Pond book ID combines five digits of the book's ISBN and its category (used or new). For example, *Floral Origami Globes* has the ISBN 4-889-96213-1 and is new, so its book ID is 96213-New. The book IDs follow a consistent and logical pattern. Rather than typing every book ID, you will use Flash Fill to enter the book IDs into the worksheet.

To enter the book IDs using Flash Fill:

1. Make sure that cell **A19** is the active cell.

2. Type **25385-Used** as the ID for the first book in the list, and then press the **Enter** key.

3. Type **9** in cell A20. As soon as you start typing, Flash Fill generates the remaining entries in the column based on the pattern you entered. See Figure 1-34.

Figure 1-34   **Book IDs generated by Flash Fill**

[Screenshot showing Excel worksheet with book ID column being filled by Flash Fill. Callouts indicate "book ID is based on the ISBN and Category values" and "book ID values suggested by Flash Fill". Cell A20 contains 96213-New, with additional suggested entries 01089-Used, 27062-New, and 56516-New below it.]

4. Press the **Enter** key to accept the suggested entries.

Formatting a Worksheet

Formatting changes a workbook's appearance to make the content of a worksheet easier to read. Two common formatting changes are adding borders to cells and changing the font size of text.

Adding Cell Borders

Sometimes you want to include lines along the edges of cells to enhance the readability of rows and columns of data. You can do this by adding borders to the left, top, right, or bottom edge of a cell or range. You can also specify the thickness of and the number of lines in the border. This is especially helpful when a worksheet is printed because the gridlines that surround the cells are not printed by default; they appear on the worksheet only as a guide.

Sally wants add borders around the cells that contain content in the Customer Order worksheet to make the content easier to read.

To add borders around the worksheet cells:

1. Select the range **A3:B7**. You will add borders around all of the cells in the selected range.

2. On the HOME tab, in the Font group, click the **Borders button arrow**, and then click **All Borders**. Borders are added around each cell in the range. The Borders button changes to reflect the last selected border option, which in this case is All Borders. The name of the selected border option appears in the button's ScreenTip.

3. Select the nonadjacent range **A9:B16;H17:I17**. You will add borders around each cell in the selected range.

4. In the Font group, click the **All Borders** button to add borders to all of the cells in the selected range.

5. Click cell **A17** to deselect the cells. See Figure 1-35.

Figure 1-35   **Borders added to selected cells**

6. Select the nonadjacent range **A18:I23;H25:I28**, and then click the **All Borders** button to add borders to all of the cells in the selected range.

Tutorial 1 Getting Started with Excel | Excel   EX 51

Changing the Font Size

Changing the size of text in a sheet provides a way to identify different parts of a worksheet, such as distinguishing a title or section heading from data. The size of the text is referred to as the font size and is measured in points. The default font size for worksheets is 11 points, but it can be made larger or smaller as needed. You can resize text in selected cells using the Font Size button in the Font group on the HOME tab. You can also use the Increase Font Size and Decrease Font Size buttons to resize cell content to the next higher or lower standard font size.

Sally wants you to increase the size of the worksheet title to 26 points to make it stand out more.

To change the font size of the worksheet title:

1. Click cell **A1** to select it. The worksheet title is in this cell.
2. On the HOME tab, in the Font group, click the **Font Size button arrow** to display a list of font sizes, and then click **28**. The worksheet title changes to 28 points. See Figure 1-36.

Figure 1-36   Font size of cell content increased

- Font Size button arrow
- title is now 28 points

3. Press the **Ctrl+S** keys to save the workbook.

Printing a Workbook

Now that you have finished the workbook, Sally wants you to print a copy of the book order. Before you print a workbook, you should preview it to ensure that it will print correctly.

Changing Worksheet Views

You can view a worksheet in three ways. Normal view, which you have been using throughout this tutorial, shows the contents of the worksheet. Page Layout view shows how the worksheet will appear when printed. Page Break Preview displays the location of the different page breaks within the worksheet. This is useful when a worksheet will span several printed pages and you need to control what content appears on each page.

Sally wants you to see how the Customer Order worksheet will appear on printed pages. You will do this by switching between views.

To switch the Customer Order worksheet to different views:

1. Click the **Page Layout** button on the status bar. The page layout of the worksheet appears in the workbook window.

2. Drag the **Zoom slider** to reduce the zoom level to 50%. The reduced magnification makes it clear that the worksheet will spread over two pages when printed. See Figure 1-37.

Figure 1-37   **Worksheet in Page Layout view**

worksheet will span two printed pages

TIP

You can relocate a page break by dragging the dotted blue border in the Page Break Preview window.

3. Click the **Page Break Preview** button on the status bar. The view switches to Page Break Preview, which shows only those parts of the current worksheet that will print. A dotted blue border separates one page from another.

4. Zoom the worksheet to **70%** so that you can more easily read the contents of the worksheet. See Figure 1-38.

Tutorial 1 Getting Started with Excel | Excel   EX 53

Figure 1-38   **Worksheet in Page Break Preview**

[Screenshot of Excel worksheet in Page Break Preview showing the Customer Order worksheet split across page 1 (columns A–D) and page 2 (columns E–I), with callouts labeling "page 1 of the printout" and "page 2 of the printout."]

> 5. Click the **Normal** button on the status bar. The worksheet returns to Normal view. A dotted black line indicates where the page break will occur.

Changing the Page Orientation

Page orientation specifies in which direction content is printed on the page. In **portrait orientation**, the page is taller than it is wide. In **landscape orientation**, the page is wider than it is tall. By default, Excel displays pages in portrait orientation. Changing the page orientation affects only the active sheet.

As you saw in Page Layout view and Page Break Preview, the Customer Order worksheet will print on two pages—columns A through D will print on the first page, and columns E through I will print on the second page, although the columns that print on each page may differ slightly depending on the printer. Sally wants the entire worksheet to print on a single page, so you'll change the page orientation from portrait to landscape.

> **To change the page orientation of the Customer Order worksheet:**
>
> 1. On the ribbon, click the **PAGE LAYOUT** tab. The tab includes options for changing how the worksheet is arranged.
>
> 2. In the Page Setup group, click the **Orientation** button, and then click **Landscape**. The worksheet switches to landscape orientation.
>
> 3. Click the **Page Layout** button on the status bar to switch to Page Layout view. The worksheet will still print on two pages.

Setting the Scaling Options

You change the size of the worksheet on the printed page by **scaling** it. You can scale the width or the height of the printout so that all of the columns or all of the rows fit on a single page. You can also scale the printout to fit the entire worksheet (both columns and rows) on a single page. If the worksheet is too large to fit on one page, you can scale the print to fit on the number of pages you select. You can also scale the worksheet to a percentage of its size. For example, scaling a worksheet to 50% reduces the size of the sheet by half when it is sent to the printer. When scaling a printout, make sure that the worksheet is still readable after shrinking. Scaling affects only the active worksheet, so you can scale each worksheet to best fit its contents.

Sally asks you to scale the printout so that all of the Customer Order worksheet fits on one page in landscape orientation.

To scale the printout of the Customer Order worksheet:

1. On the PAGE LAYOUT tab, in the Scale to Fit group, click the **Width arrow**, and then click **1 page** on the menu that appears. All of the columns in the worksheet now fit on one page.

2. In the Scale to Fit group, click the **Height arrow**, and then click **1 page**. All of the rows in the worksheet now fit on one page. See Figure 1-39.

Figure 1-39 Printout scaled to fit on one page

printout scaled to fit all of the rows and columns on one page

Tutorial 1 Getting Started with Excel | Excel **EX 55**

Setting the Print Options

TIP

To print the gridlines or the column and row headings, click the corresponding Print check box in the Sheet Options group on the PAGE LAYOUT tab.

You can print the contents of a workbook by using the Print screen in Backstage view. The Print screen provides options for choosing where to print, what to print, and how to print. For example, you can specify the number of copies to print, which printer to use, and what to print. You can choose to print only the selected cells, only the active sheets, or all of the worksheets in the workbook that contain data. The printout will include only the data in the worksheet. The other elements in the worksheet, such as the row and column headings and the gridlines around the worksheet cells, will not print by default. The preview shows you exactly how the printed pages will look with the current settings. You should always preview before printing to ensure that the printout looks exactly as you intended and avoid unnecessary reprinting.

Sally asks you to preview and print the Sparrow & Pond workbook now.

Note: Check with your instructor first to make sure you should complete the steps for printing the workbook.

To preview and print the workbook:

1. On the ribbon, click the **FILE** tab to display Backstage view.

2. Click **Print** in the navigation bar. The Print screen appears with the print options and a preview of the Customer Order worksheet printout. See Figure 1-40.

Figure 1-40   **Print screen in Backstage view**

- Back button closes Backstage view
- selected printer
- part of the workbook selected to print
- printer options
- preview of the printout
- buttons to scroll through the print preview

3. Click the **Printer** button, and then click the printer to which you want to print, if it is not already selected. By default, Excel will print only the active sheet.

4. In the Settings options, click the top button, and then click **Print Entire Workbook** to print all of the sheets in the workbook—in this case, both the Documentation and the Customer Order worksheets. The preview shows the first sheet in the workbook—the Documentation worksheet. Note that this sheet is still in the default portrait orientation.

5. Below the preview, click the **Next Page** button ▶ to view the Customer Order worksheet. As you can see, the Customer Order worksheet will print on a single page in landscape orientation.

6. If you are instructed to print, click the **Print** button to send the contents of the workbook to the specified printer. If you are not instructed to print, click the **Back** button in the navigation bar to exit Backstage view.

Viewing Worksheet Formulas

Most of the time, you will be interested in only the final results of a worksheet, not the formulas used to calculate those results. However, in some cases, you might want to view the formulas used to develop the workbook. This is particularly useful when you encounter unexpected results and you want to examine the underlying formulas, or you want to discuss your formulas with a colleague. You can display the formulas instead of the resulting values in cells.

If you print the worksheet while the formulas are displayed, the printout shows the formulas instead of the values. To make the printout easier to read, you should print the worksheet gridlines as well as the row and column headings so that cell references in the formulas are easy to find in the printed version of the worksheet.

You will look at the Customer Order worksheet with the formulas displayed.

To display the formulas in cells in the Customer Order worksheet:

1. Make sure the Customer Order worksheet is in Page Layout view.

2. Press the **Ctrl+`** keys (the grave accent symbol ` is usually located above the Tab key). The worksheet changes to display all of the formulas instead of the resulting values. Notice that the columns widen to display all of the formula text in the cells.

3. Look at the entry in cell B4. The underlying numeric value of the shipping date (42463) is displayed instead of the formatted date value (4/3/2016). See Figure 1-41.

TIP

You can also display formulas in a worksheet by clicking the Show Formulas button in the Formula Auditing group on the FORMULAS tab.

Tutorial 1 Getting Started with Excel | Excel   EX 57

Figure 1-41   Worksheet with formulas displayed

(Screenshot of Excel worksheet showing the Page Layout tab with formulas displayed instead of results. Callouts indicate:)
- option to print the gridlines
- option to print the row and column headings
- date displayed as a number
- formulas displayed instead of results
- text and numbers displayed as usual

It's good practice to hide the formulas when you are done reviewing them.

▸ **4.** Press the **Ctrl+`** keys to hide the formulas and display the resulting values.

▸ **5.** Click the **Normal** button on the status bar to return the workbook to Normal view.

Saving a Workbook with a New Filename

Whenever you click the Save button on the Quick Access Toolbar or press the Ctrl+S keys, the workbook file is updated to reflect the latest content. If you want to save a copy of the workbook with a new filename or to a different location, you need to use the Save As command. When you save a workbook with a new filename or to a different location, the previous version of the workbook remains stored as well.

You have completed the SP Customer Order workbook. Sally wants to use the workbook as a model for other customer order reports. You will save the workbook with a new filename to avoid overwriting the Tobias Gregson book order. Then you'll clear the information related to Tobias Gregson, leaving the formulas intact. This new, revised workbook will then be ready for a new customer order.

To save the workbook with a new filename:

1. Press the **Ctrl+S** keys to save the workbook. This ensures that the final copy of the SP Customer Order workbook contains the latest content.

2. On the ribbon, click the **FILE** tab to display Backstage view, and then click **Save As** on the navigation bar. The Save As screen is displayed.

3. Click **Computer**, and then click the **Browse** button. The Save As dialog box opens so you can save the workbook with a new filename or to a new location.

4. Navigate to the location specified by your instructor.

5. In the File name box, type **SP Customer Order Form** as the new filename.

6. Click the **Save** button. The workbook is saved with the new filename and is open in Excel.

7. Select the range **B3:B5**, right-click the selected range to open the shortcut menu, and then click **Clear Contents** to clear the contents of the order ID, shipping date, and delivery type cells.

8. Select the nonadjacent range **B10:B16;A19:H23**, and then press the **Delete** key to clear the contact information for Tobias Gregson and the list of books he ordered from those cells.

9. Select cell **I27**, and then clear the handling fee.

10. Click cell **A3** to make that cell the active cell. The next time someone opens this workbook, cell A3 will still be the active cell.

11. Press the **Ctrl+S** keys to save the workbook.

12. Click the **Close** button ☒ on the title bar (or press the **Ctrl+W** keys). The workbook closes, and the Excel program closes.

> **TIP**
> Save the workbook with the new name *before* making your changes to avoid inadvertently saving your edits to the wrong file.

Sally is pleased with the workbook you created. With the calculations already in place in the new workbook, she will be able to quickly enter new customer orders and see the calculated book charges without having to recreate the worksheet.

Session 1.2 Quick Check

1. What formula would you enter to add the values in cells B4, B5, and B6? What function would you enter to achieve the same result?
2. What formula would you enter to count the number of numeric values in the range B2:B100?
3. What formula would you enter to find the maximum value of the cells in the range B2:B100?
4. If you insert cells into the range C1:D10 shifting the cells to the right, what is the new location of the data that was previously in cell E5?
5. Cell E11 contains the formula =SUM(E1:E10). How does this formula change if a new row is inserted above row 5?
6. Describe four ways of viewing the content of a workbook in Excel.
7. How are page breaks indicated in Page Break Preview?
8. How do you display the formulas used in a worksheet instead of the formula results?

Tutorial 1 Getting Started with Excel | Excel EX 59

SAM Projects

Put your skills into practice with SAM Projects! SAM Projects for this tutorial can be found online. If you have a SAM account, go to www.cengage.com/sam2013 to download the most recent Project Instructions and Start Files.

Review Assignments

There are no Data Files needed for the Review Assignments.

Sally wants you to create a workbook to record the recent book purchases made by Sparrow & Pond. The workbook should list the recent acquisitions from private sellers, libraries, and other vendors; include a description of each book; and calculate the total number of books acquired and the total amount spent by Sparrow & Pond. Complete the following:

1. Create a new, blank workbook, and then save the workbook as **Book List** in the location specified by your instructor.
2. Rename the Sheet1 worksheet as **Documentation**, and then enter the data shown in Figure 1-42 in the specified cells.

Figure 1-42   Documentation sheet data

Cell	Data
A1	Sparrow & Pond
A3	Author
A4	Date
A5	Purpose
B3	your name
B4	current date
B5	To record book acquisitions by Sparrow & Pond

© 2014 Cengage Learning

3. Set the font size of the title text in cell A1 to 26 points.
4. Add a new worksheet after the Documentation sheet, and then rename the sheet as **Books**.
5. In cell A1, enter the text **Book Acquisitions**. Set the font size of this text to 26 points.
6. In cell A2, enter the text **DATE** as the label. In cell B2, enter the date **4/3/2016**.
7. In the range A4:G9, enter the data shown in Figure 1-43.

Figure 1-43   Book list

ISBN	STATUS	BINDING	TITLE	AUTHOR	CONDITION	PRICE
0-670-02103-2	New	Softcover	Rocket Men: The Epic Story of the First Men on the Moon	Nelson, Craig	Excellent	$12.95
0-195-09076-4	Used	Hardcover	Buildings of Colorado	Noel, Thomas J.	Good	$22.50
0-375-70365-9	New	Softcover	American Visions: The Epic History of Art in America	Hughes, Robert	Excellent	$22.50
1-564-77848-7	New	Softcover	Simple Comforts: 12 Cozy Lap Quilts	Diehl, Kim	Very Good	$9.25
1-851-70006-4	Used	Hardcover	Beautiful Stories About Children	Dickens, Charles	Good	$33.50

© 2014 Cengage Learning

8. Insert cells into the range A4:A9, shifting the other cells to the right.
9. Enter the label **BOOK ID** in cell A4, type **02103-New** in cell A5, and then type **09076-Used** in cell A6.
10. Use Flash Fill to fill in the remaining book IDs.
11. Set the width of columns A through D to 15 characters each. Set the width of column E to 30 characters. Set the width of column F to 20 characters. Set the width of column G to 15 characters.
12. Set the book titles in the range E4:E9 to wrap to a new line.
13. Autofit the heights of rows 4 through 9.
14. Move the book list in the range A4:H9 to the range A8:H13.
15. In cell G15, enter the text **TOTAL**. In cell H15, enter a function to add the prices in the range H9:H13.
16. In cell A4, enter the text **TOTAL BOOKS**. In cell B4, enter a function to count the number of numeric values in the range H9:H13.
17. In cell A5, enter the text **TOTAL PRICE**. In cell B5, display the value from cell H15.
18. In cell A6, enter the text **AVERAGE PRICE**. In cell B6, enter a formula to calculate the total price paid for the books (listed in cell B5) divided by the number of books purchased (listed in cell B4).
19. Add borders around each cell in the nonadjacent range A4:B6;A8:H13;G15:H15.
20. For the Books worksheet, change the page orientation to landscape and scale the worksheet to print on a single page for both the width and the height. If you are instructed to print, print the entire workbook.
21. Display the formulas in the Books worksheet, and set the gridlines and row/column headings to print. If you are instructed to print, print the entire worksheet.
22. Save and close the workbook.

Case Problem 1

Data File needed for this Case Problem: Pacific.xlsx

American Wheel Tours Kevin Bennett is a tours manager at American Wheel Tours, a bicycle touring company located in Philadelphia, Pennsylvania, that specializes in one- and two-week supported tours in destinations across the United States. Kevin wants you to create a workbook that details the itinerary of the company's Pacific Coast tour. The workbook will list the tour itinerary shown in Figure 1-44 and calculate the total number of riding days, total mileage, and average mileage per ride.

Figure 1-44   Pacific Tour itinerary

DATE	START	FINISH	CAMPSITE	MILES	DESCRIPTION
10-Oct-16	Eugene	Eugene	Richardson Park		Orientation day. Meet at Richardson Park, located at the Fern Ridge Reservoir.
11-Oct-16	Eugene	Florence	Honeyman State Park	66	Cycle over Low Pass to Honeyman State Park.
12-Oct-16	Florence	Charleston	Sunset Bay State Park	56	Cycle through Oregon Dunes National Recreation Area to Sunset Bay State Park.
13-Oct-16	Charleston	Port Orford	Humbug Mountain State Park	60	Cycle around Bullards Beach State Park and camp at Humbug Mountain State Park.
14-Oct-16	Port Orford	Brookings	Harris Beach State Park	52	Cycle past the mouth of the Rogue River to Harris Beach State Park.
15-Oct-16	Brookings	Crescent City	Jedediah State Park	48	Pass into California and camp at Jedediah State Park.
16-Oct-16	Crescent City	Eureka	Eureka Fairgrounds	72	A long day through Del Norte Coast Redwoods State Park to Eureka.

© 2014 Cengage Learning

Complete the following:

1. Open the **Pacific** workbook located in the Excel1 ▸ Case1 folder included with your Data Files, and then save the workbook as **Pacific Coast** in the location specified by your instructor.
2. In the Documentation worksheet, enter your name in cell B3 and the date in cell B4.
3. Add a new sheet to the end of the workbook and rename it as **Itinerary**.
4. In cell A1, enter the text **Pacific Coast Tour** and set the font size to 28 points.
5. In the range A3:A8, enter the following labels: **Start Date**, **End Date**, **Total Days**, **Riding Days**, **Total Miles**, and **Miles per Day**.
6. Enter the date **October 10, 2016** in cell B3, and then enter the date **October 16, 2016** in cell B4.
7. In the range D3:D8, enter the labels **Type**, **Surface**, **Difficulty**, **Tour Leader**, **Cost**, and **Deposit**.
8. In the range E3:E8, enter **Van Supported**, **Paved**, **Intermediate**, **Kevin Bennett**, **$1,250**, and **$350**.
9. In the range A11:F18, enter the data shown in Figure 1-44, including the column labels. Leave the mileage value for October 10th blank.
10. In cell B5, enter a formula to calculate the total number of days in the tour by subtracting the starting date (cell B3) from the ending date (cell B4) and adding 1.

11. In cell B6, enter a function to count the total number of riding days based on the numbers in the range E12:E18.
12. In cell B7, enter a function to add the total number of miles in the range E12:E18.
13. In cell B8, enter a formula to calculate the average miles per day by dividing the total miles by the number of riding days.
14. Insert cells in the range A11:A18, shifting the cells to the right. In cell A11, enter **DAY**. In the range A12:A18, enter the numbers 1 through 7 to number each day of the tour.
15. Set the column widths so that column A is 12 characters, columns B through E are 14 characters each, column F is 6 characters, and column G is 50 characters.
16. Wrap text in the range A11:G18 as needed so that any hidden entries are displayed on multiple lines within the cell.
17. Autofit the height of rows 11 through 18.
18. Add borders around the ranges A3:B8, D3:E8, and A11:G18.
19. Format the Itinerary worksheet so that it prints on a single page in landscape orientation. If you are instructed to print, print the entire workbook.
20. Display the formulas in the Itinerary worksheet, and set the gridlines and column/row headings to print. If you are instructed to print, print the worksheet.
21. Return the Itinerary worksheet to Normal view, hide the formulas, set the gridlines and column/row headings so that they won't print, and then save the workbook.
22. Save the workbook as **Pacific Coast Revised** in the location specified by your instructor.
23. Determine what the total mileage and average mileage per day of the tour would be if Kevin adds a 10-mile warm-up ride on October 10th but decreases the length of the October 15th ride to 41 miles. Save the workbook.

Case Problem 2

APPLY

Data File needed for this Case Problem: Tropical.xlsx

Tropical Foods Tropical Foods is a health food grocery store located in Keizer, Oregon. Monica Li is working on the store's annual financial report. One part of the financial report will be the company's balance sheet for the previous two years. Monica already entered the labels for the balance sheet. You will enter the numeric data and formulas to perform the financial calculations. Complete the following:

1. Open the **Tropical** workbook located in the Excel1 ▶ Case2 folder included with your Data Files, and then save the workbook as **Tropical Foods Balance Sheet** in the location specified by your instructor.
2. In cells B3 and B4 of the Documentation sheet, enter your name and the date. In cell A1, increase the font size of the title to 28 points.
3. Go to the Balance Sheet worksheet. Increase the font size of the title in cell A1 to 28 points, and then increase the font size of the subtitle in cell A2 to 20 points.
4. In the corresponding cells of columns C and D, enter the numbers shown in Figure 1-45 for the company's assets and liabilities.

Figure 1-45 — Tropical Foods assets and liabilities

		2015	2014
Assets	Cash	$645,785	$627,858
	Accounts Receivable	431,982	405,811
	Inventories	417,615	395,648
	Prepaid Expenses	2,152	4,151
	Other Assets	31,252	26,298
	Fixed Assets @ Cost	1,800,000	1,750,000
	Accumulated Depreciation	82,164	$77,939
Liabilities	Accounts Payable	$241,191	$193,644
	Accrued Expenses	31,115	32,151
	Current Portion of Debt	120,000	100,000
	Income Taxes Payable	144,135	126,524
	Long-Term Debt	815,000	850,000
	Capital Stock	1,560,000	1,525,000
	Retain Earnings	335,181	304,508

© 2014 Cengage Learning

5. Set the width of column A to 12 characters, column B to 28 characters, columns C and D to 14 characters each, column E to 2 characters, and column F to 10 characters.
6. In cells C8 and D8, enter formulas to calculate the current assets value for 2014 and 2015, which is equal to the sum of the cash, accounts receivable, inventories, and prepaid expenses values.
7. In cells C14 and D14, enter formulas to calculate the net fixed assets value for 2014 and 2015, which is equal to the difference between the fixed assets value and the accumulated depreciation value.
8. In cells C16 and D16, enter formulas to calculate the total assets value for 2014 and 2015, which is equal to the sum of the current assets, other assets, and net fixed assets value.
9. In cells C23 and D23, enter formulas to calculate the sum of the accounts payable, accrued expenses, current portion of debt, and income taxes payable values for 2014 and 2015.
10. In cells C29 and D29, enter formulas to calculate the shareholders' equity value for 2014 and 2015, which is equal to the sum of the capital stock and retained earnings.
11. In cells C31 and D31, enter formulas to calculate the total liabilities & equity value for 2014 and 2015, which is equal to the sum of the current liabilities, long-term debt, and shareholders' equity.
12. In a balance sheet, the total assets should equal the total liabilities & equity. Compare the values in cells C16 and C31, and then compare the values in cells D16 and D31 to confirm that this is the case for the Tropical Foods balance sheet in 2014 and 2015. If the account doesn't balance, check your worksheet for errors in either values or formulas.
13. In cell F4, enter a formula to calculate the percentage change in cash from 2014 to 2015, which is equal to (C4–D4)/D4.

14. Copy the formula in cell F4 and paste it in the nonadjacent range F5:F8;F10;F12:F14;F16; F19:F23;F25;F27:F29;F31 to show the percentage change in all values of the balance sheet.
15. Add borders around the cells in columns B, C, D, and F of the balance sheet, excluding the cells in rows 9, 11, 15, 17, 18, 24, 26, and 30.
16. Set the page layout of the Balance Sheet worksheet to portrait orientation and scaled to print on a single page. If you are instructed to print, print the entire workbook.
17. Display the formulas in the Balance Sheet worksheet, and then set the gridlines and row/column headings to print. If you are instructed to print, print the worksheet.
18. Display the Balance Sheet worksheet in Normal view, hide the formulas, set the gridlines and column/row headings so that they won't print, and then save the workbook.

Case Problem 3

Data File needed for this Case Problem: Physics.xlsx

Gladstone Country Day School Beatrix Melendez teaches Introduction to Physics at Gladstone Country Day School in Gladstone, Missouri. She wants to record students' quiz scores, and then calculate each student's total and average scores. She also wants to calculate the class average, high score, and low score for each quiz in her records. Beatrix has entered scores from 10 quizzes for 20 students in a worksheet. You will summarize these grades by student and by quiz using the functions listed in Figure 1-46.

Figure 1-46 Excel summary functions

Function	Description
=AVERAGE (range)	Calculates the average of the values from the specified range
=MEDIAN (range)	Calculates the median or midpoint of the values from the specified range
=MIN (range)	Calculates the minimum of the values from the specified range
=MAX (range)	Calculates the maximum of the values from the specified range

© 2014 Cengage Learning

Complete the following:
1. Open the **Physics** workbook located in the Excel1 ▸ Case3 folder included with your Data Files, and then save the workbook as **Physics Grading Sheet** in the location specified by your instructor.
2. In the Documentation sheet, enter your name in cell B3 and the date in cell B4. Increase the font size of the title in cell A1 to 28 points.
3. Go to the Grades worksheet. Increase the font size of cell A1 to 28 points, and then increase the font size of cell A2 to 22 points.
4. **Explore** In cell M5, enter a formula to calculate the median or midpoint of the quiz scores for Debra Alt. In cell N5, enter a formula to calculate the average of Debra Alt's quiz scores.
5. Copy the formulas in the range M5:N5 to the range M6:N24 to summarize the scores for the remaining students.
6. **Explore** In cell B26, enter a formula to calculate the minimum class score from the first quiz. In cell B27, enter a formula to calculate the median class score.
7. **Explore** In cell B28, use the MAX function to calculate the high score from the first quiz.
8. In cell B30, enter a formula to calculate the average score from the first quiz.
9. Copy the formulas in the range B26:B30 to the range C26:K30 to calculate the summary statistics for the rest of the quizzes.

10. Insert 10 new rows above row 4, shifting the student grade table and summary from the range A4:N30 to the range A14:N40. You will enter a summary of all of the students from all of the quizzes at the top of the worksheet.
11. In cell A4, enter the text **Class Size**. In cell B4, enter a formula to calculate the count of scores from the range N15:N34.
12. In the range A6:A9, enter the labels **Overall Scores**, **Lowest Average**, **Median Average**, and **Highest Average**. In cell A11, enter **Class Average**.
13. Using the average scores in the range N15:N34, enter formulas to calculate the overall lowest average score in cell B7, the median of the class averages in cell B8, the overall highest average in cell B9, and the average overall class score in cell B11.
14. Add cell borders around the ranges A4:B4, A7:B9, A11:B11, A14:K34, M14:N34, A36:K38, and A40:K40.
15. Set the page layout of the Grades worksheet to landscape orientation and scaled to print on a single page. If you are instructed to print, print the entire workbook.
16. Display the formulas in the Grades worksheet. Set the gridlines and the row/column headings to print. If you are instructed to print, print the worksheet.
17. Display the Grades worksheet in Normal view, hide the formulas, set the gridlines and column/row headings so that they won't print, and then save the workbook.
18. Determine the effect of raising each student's score on the first quiz by 10 points to curve the results. Report what impact this has on the overall class average from all 10 quizzes.
19. Save the workbook as **Physics Grading Sheet Revised**. If you are instructed to print, print the Grades worksheet.

Case Problem 4

Data File needed for this Case Problem: Turf.xlsx

Turf Toughs Tim Gables is the owner and operator of Turf Toughs, a lawn and tree removal service located in Chicopee, Massachusetts. He created a workbook to record and analyze the service calls made by his company. So far, the workbook calculates the cost of each service call, the total charges for all of the calls, and the total number of billable hours. Unfortunately, the workbook contains several errors. You will fix these errors and then complete the workbook. Complete the following:

1. Open the **Turf** workbook located in the Excel1 ▸ Case4 folder included with your Data Files, and then save the workbook as **Turf Toughs Service Calls** in the location specified by your instructor.
2. In the Documentation sheet, enter your name in cell B3 and the date in cell B4.
3. Go to the Service Log worksheet. The log lists the contact information and the service calls for each customer.

   Tim wants you to insert a column of IDs for each customer. The customer ID is in the form *last-phone*, where *last* is the customer's last name and *phone* is the last four digits of the customer's phone number.
4. Insert cells in the range A4:A34, shifting the other cells to the right. Type **Cust ID** in cell A4, and then enter **Morris-4380** as the customer ID for Michael Morris. Use Flash Fill to fill in the remaining customer IDs in the column.
5. Add borders around the cells in the range A4:A32.
6. **Troubleshoot** There is a problem with the all of the customer zip codes. Each zip code should begin with zero. Make the necessary changes to fix this problem.
7. Resize the columns of the worksheet so that all of the column labels in the service calls list are displayed entirely.
8. **Troubleshoot** The formula in cell L5 is not correctly calculating the number of hours for each service call. Fix the formula so that it multiplies the difference between the starting and ending time by 24.

9. Copy the formula you created for cell L5 to the range L6:L32, replacing the previous calculated values.
10. Calculate the service charge for each service call so that it equals the base fee added to the hourly rate times the number of hours worked.

Troubleshoot 11. Cell N34 contains a formula to calculate the total service charges for all customer visits. Is it calculating the value correctly? If not, edit the formula to fix any errors you find.

12. Above row 4, insert six new rows, shifting the range A4:N34 down to the range A10:N40.
13. In the range A4:A8, enter the labels **From**, **To**, **Total Service Calls**, **Billable Hours**, and **Total Charges**.
14. In cell B4, calculate the starting date of the service calls by entering a formula that finds the minimum value of the dates in the Date column.
15. In cell B5, calculate the ending date of the service calls by entering a formula that finds the maximum value of the dates in the Date column.
16. In cell B6, enter a formula that counts the total number of service calls using the values in the Date column.
17. In cell B7, enter a formula that calculates the sum of hours from the Hours column.
18. In cell B8, enter a formula that references the value of cell N40.
19. Add borders around each cell in the range A4:B8.
20. Set the page layout of the Service Log worksheet so that it prints on a single page in landscape orientation. If you are instructed to print, print the entire workbook.
21. Display the formulas in the Service Log worksheet, scale the worksheet to fit on a single page, and then set the gridlines and row/column headings to print. If you are instructed to print, print the Service Log worksheet.
22. Return the Service Log worksheet to Normal view, hide the formulas, set the gridlines and column/row headings so that they won't print, and then save the workbook.

TUTORIAL 2

Formatting Workbook Text and Data

Designing a Sales Report

OBJECTIVES

Session 2.1
- Change fonts, font style, and font color
- Add fill colors and a background image
- Create formulas to calculate sales data
- Apply Currency and Accounting formats and the Percent style
- Format dates and times
- Align, indent, and rotate cell contents
- Merge a group of cells

Session 2.2
- Use the AVERAGE function
- Apply cell styles
- Copy and paste formats with the Format Painter
- Find and replace text and formatting
- Change workbook themes
- Highlight cells with conditional formats
- Format a worksheet for printing
- Set the print area, insert page breaks, add print titles, create headers and footers, and set margins

Case | Big Red Wraps

Sanjit Chandra is a sales manager for Big Red Wraps, a growing restaurant chain that specializes in preparing made-to-order sandwich wraps, seasonal soups, and fresh salads. The first Big Red Wraps opened in Madison, Wisconsin, and has since expanded to 20 restaurants across six states. Four of these restaurants were opened this year. Each spring, the company has a sales conference where the restaurant managers meet to discuss sales concerns and review marketing plans for the upcoming year. Sanjit created a workbook that summarizes the sales data for the previous year and is part of a sales report that will be given to all conference attendees. He wants you to calculate some summary statistics and format the workbook.

STARTING DATA FILES

Excel2 →

Tutorial
Background.jpg
Sales.xlsx

Review
Background2.png
Menu.xlsx

Case1
Salon.xlsx

Case2
Waist.xlsx

Access3 →
Wind.xlsx

Case4
Office.xlsx

Microsoft product screenshots used with permission from Microsoft Corporation.

EX 68   Excel | Tutorial 2 Formatting Workbook Text and Data

Session 2.1 Visual Overview:

You use the Font button to change the font of selected text or numbers.

Every font can be formatted with a font style, such as bold, *italic*, or underline.

You can format a text string within a cell in Edit mode.

A font is a set of characters that employ the same typeface, such as Arial, Times New Roman, and Courier.

You can merge, or combine, several cells into one cell. This content is merged and centered across the range A17:A20.

You can rotate content in a cell.

The Alignment group has buttons for setting the horizontal and vertical alignment, the orientation, indents, and text wrapping of text in a cell, as well as merging cells.

Big Flavor, Small Price

Sales Statistics

Category	2015	2014	Net Change	% Change
Gross Sales	$ 7,000,000	$ 8,424,000	$ (1,424,000)	-16.90%
Cost of Sales	3,374,000	2,784,000	590,000	21.19%
Operating Expenses	5,032,000	4,376,000	656,000	14.99%
Net Profit/Loss	$ (1,406,000)	$ 1,264,000	$ (2,670,000)	-211.23%

2015 Monthly Gross Sales

State	Jan	Feb	Mar	Apr	May
Iowa	26,000	24,000	27,000	28,000	29,000
				51,000	53,000
				47,000	47,000
				27,000	28,000
Kansas	44,000	43,000	48,000	50,000	51,000
	29,000	26,000	30,000	31,000	35,000
	20,000	21,000	24,000	25,000	28,000
	46,000	43,000	52,000	51,000	54,000
Colorado	38,000	35,000	43,000	42,000	44,000
Nebr					
	27,000	28,000			
	38,000	39,000	45,000	47,000	46,000

The Accounting format lines up numbers within a column by their currency symbol and decimal point; negative numbers are enclosed in parentheses.

The Percent style formats numbers as percentages with the % symbol after the number and no decimal places. You can change the number of decimal places that are displayed, as shown here.

Documentation | **Sales Report**

READY

Tutorial 2 Formatting Workbook Text and Data | Excel EX 69

Worksheet with Formatting

The Number group has buttons for formatting numbers in the Accounting format, Percent style, and Comma style, as well as changing the number of decimal places displayed.

A fill color is a background color that can be added to cells to help differentiate parts of a worksheet or highlight data.

You can increase or decrease the number of decimal places that are displayed in a value. These values show no decimal places.

The Comma style adds a thousands separator to numbers, adds two decimal places, and lines up values within a column by their decimal points. You can change the number of decimal places that are displayed, as shown here.

Jun	Jul	Aug	Sep	Oct	Nov
32,000	33,000	34,000	30,000	32,000	30,000
54,000	54,000	58,000	54,000	55,000	51,000
51,000	52,000	54,000	50,000	49,000	46,000
29,000	32,000	30,000	30,000	28,000	27,000
54,000	54,000	55,000	54,000	52,000	51,000
34,000	37,000	37,000	34,000	34,000	34,000
27,000	27,000	29,000	24,000	26,000	24,000
54,000	58,000	58,000	55,000	54,000	50,000
44,000	47,000	48,000	47,000	48,000	44,000
37,000	37,000	38,000	35,000	33,000	35,000
49,000	51,000	49,000	47,000	49,000	47,000

Formatting Cell Text

You can add formatting to a workbook by choosing its fonts, styles, colors, and decorative features. Formatting changes only the appearance of data—it does not affect the data itself. In Excel, formatting options are organized into themes. A **theme** is a collection of formatting for text, colors, and graphical effects that are applied throughout a workbook to create a specific look and feel. Each theme has a name. Although the Office theme is the default theme, you can apply other themes or create your own. You can also add formatting to a workbook using fonts and colors that are not part of the current theme.

As you format a workbook, galleries and Live Preview show how a workbook would be affected by a formatting selection. A **gallery** is a menu or grid that shows a visual representation of the options available for the selected button. As you point to options in a gallery, **Live Preview** shows the results of clicking each option. By pointing to different options, you can quickly see different results before selecting the format you want.

PROSKILLS

Written Communication: Formatting Workbooks for Readability and Appeal

Designing a workbook requires the same care as designing any written document or report. A well-formatted workbook is easy to read and establishes a sense of professionalism with readers. Do the following to improve the appearance of your workbooks:

- **Clearly identify each worksheet's purpose.** Include column or row titles and a descriptive sheet name.
- **Include only one or two topics on each worksheet.** Don't crowd individual worksheets with too much information. Place extra topics on separate sheets. Readers should be able to interpret each worksheet with a minimal amount of horizontal and vertical scrolling.
- **Place worksheets with the most important information first in the workbook.** Position worksheets summarizing your findings near the front of the workbook. Position worksheets with detailed and involved analysis near the end as an appendix.
- **Use consistent formatting throughout the workbook.** If negative values appear in red on one worksheet, format them in the same way on all sheets. Also, be consistent in the use of thousands separators, decimal places, and percentages.
- **Pay attention to the format of the printed workbook.** Make sure your printouts are legible with informative headers and footers. Check that the content of the printout is scaled correctly to the page size, and that page breaks divide the information into logical sections.

Excel provides many formatting tools. However, too much formatting can be intrusive, overwhelm data, and make the document difficult to read. Remember that the goal of formatting is not simply to make a "pretty workbook," but also to accentuate important trends and relationships in the data. A well-formatted workbook should seamlessly convey your data to the reader. If the reader is thinking about how your workbook looks, it means he or she is not thinking about your data.

Sanjit has already entered the data and some formulas in a workbook, which is only a rough draft of what he wants to submit to the company. The Documentation sheet describes the workbook's purpose and content. The Sales Report sheet displays a summary of the previous year's sales including a table of monthly gross sales broken down by the 20 franchise stores. In its current form, the data is difficult to read and interpret. Sanjit wants you to format the contents of the workbook to improve its readability and visual appeal.

Tutorial 2 Formatting Workbook Text and Data | Excel   EX 71

To open the workbook:

1. Open the **Sales** workbook located in the Excel2 ▸ Tutorial folder included with your Data Files, and then save the workbook as **Sales Report** in the location specified by your instructor.

2. In the Documentation sheet, enter your name in cell B4 and the date in cell B5.

Applying Fonts and Font Styles

Excel organizes fonts into theme and non-theme fonts. A **theme font** is associated with a particular theme and used for headings and body text in the workbook. These fonts change automatically when you change the theme applied to the workbook. Text formatted with a **non-theme font** retains its appearance no matter what theme is used with the workbook.

Fonts appear in different character styles. **Serif fonts**, such as Times New Roman, have extra strokes at the end of each character that aid in reading passages of text. **Sans serif fonts**, such as Arial, do not include these extra strokes. Other fonts are purely decorative, such as a font used for specialized logos. Every font can be further formatted with a font style such as *italic*, **bold**, or ***bold italic***; with underline; and with special effects such as ~~strikethrough~~ and color. You can also increase or decrease the font size.

REFERENCE

Formatting Cell Content

- To change the font, select the cell or range. On the HOME tab, in the Font group, click the Font arrow, and then click a font.
- To change the font size, select the cell or range. On the HOME tab, in the Font group, click the Font Size arrow, and then click a font size.
- To change a font style, select the cell or range. On the HOME tab, in the Font group, click the Bold, Italic, or Underline button.
- To change a font color, select the cell or range. On the HOME tab, in the Font group, click the Font Color button arrow, and then click a color.
- To format a text selection, double-click the cell to enter Edit mode, and then select the text to format. Change the font, size, style, or color, and then press the Enter key.

Sanjit wants the company name at the top of each worksheet to appear in large, bold letters using the default heading font from the Office theme. He wants the slogan "Big Flavor, Small Price" displayed below the company name to appear in the heading font, but in smaller, italicized letters.

To format the company name and slogan in the Documentation sheet:

1. In the Documentation sheet, select cell **A1** to make it the active cell. The cell with the company name is selected.

2. On the HOME tab, in the Font group, click the **Font button arrow** to display a gallery of fonts available on your computer. Each name is displayed in its corresponding font. When you point to a font in the gallery, Live Preview shows how the text in the selected cell will look with that font. The first two fonts are the theme fonts for headings and body text—Calibri Light and Calibri.

EX 72 Excel | Tutorial 2 Formatting Workbook Text and Data

3. Point to **Algerian** (or another font) in the All Fonts list. Live Preview shows the effect of the Algerian font on the text in cell A1. See Figure 2-1.

Figure 2-1 Font gallery

fonts in the Office theme
Live Preview of the Algerian font
all available fonts
pointer on the Algerian font

4. Point to three other fonts in the Font gallery to see the Live Preview showing how cell A1 could look with those fonts.

5. Click **Calibri Light** in the Theme Fonts list. The company name in cell A1 changes to the Calibri Light font, the default headings font in the current theme.

6. In the Font group, click the **Font Size button arrow** to display a list of font sizes, and then click **26**. The company name changes to 26 points.

7. In the Font group, click the **Bold** button B (or press the **Ctrl+B** keys). The company name is set in bold.

8. Select cell **A2** to make it active. The cell with the slogan text is selected.

9. In the Font group, click the **Font Size button arrow**, and then click **10**. The slogan text changes to 10 points.

10. In the Font group, click the **Italic** button I (or press the **Ctrl+I** keys). The slogan in cell A2 is italicized.

11. Select the range **A4:A6**, and then press the **Ctrl+B** keys to change the font to bold.

12. Select cell **A7** to deselect the range. The column labels are set in bold. See Figure 2-2.

Figure 2-2   **Formatted cell text**

- Bold button
- Italic button
- company name in 26-point bold Calibri Light font → **Big Red Wraps**
- slogan in 10-point italic Calibri font → *Big Flavor, Small Price*
- headings in bold → Author, Date, Purpose
  - Author: Sanjit Chandra
  - Date: 3/1/2016
  - Purpose: To display sales information for the upcoming Big Red Wraps sales conference

Applying a Font Color

Color can transform a plain workbook filled with numbers and text into a powerful presentation that captures the user's attention and adds visual emphasis to the points you want to make. By default, Excel displays text in a black font color.

Like fonts, colors are organized into theme and non-theme colors. **Theme colors** are the 12 colors that belong to the workbook's theme. Four colors are designated for text and backgrounds, six colors are used for accents and highlights, and two colors are used for hyperlinks (followed and not followed links). These 12 colors are designed to work well together and to remain readable in all combinations. Each theme color has five variations, or accents, in which a different tint or shading is applied to the theme color.

Ten **standard colors**—dark red, red, orange, yellow, light green, green, light blue, blue, dark blue, and purple—are always available regardless of the workbook's theme. You can open an extended palette of 134 standard colors. You can also create a custom color by specifying a mixture of red, blue, and green color values, making available 16.7 million custom colors—more colors than the human eye can distinguish. Some dialog boxes have an automatic color option that uses your Windows default text and background colors, usually black text on a white background.

EX 74 Excel | Tutorial 2 Formatting Workbook Text and Data

INSIGHT

Creating Custom Colors

Custom colors let you add subtle and striking colors to a formatted workbook. To create custom colors, you use the **RGB Color model** in which each color is expressed with varying intensities of red, green, and blue. RGB color values are often represented as a set of numbers in the format

(`red`, `green`, `blue`)

where `red` is an intensity value assigned to red light, `green` is an intensity value assigned to green light, and `blue` is an intensity value assigned to blue light. The intensities are measured on a scale of 0 to 255—0 indicates no intensity (or the absence of the color) and 255 indicates the highest intensity. So, the RGB color value (255, 255, 0) represents a mixture of high-intensity red (255) and high-intensity green (255) with the absence of blue (0), which creates the color yellow.

To create colors in Excel using the RGB model, click the More Colors option located in a color menu or dialog box to open the Colors dialog box. In the Colors dialog box, click the Custom tab, and then enter the red, green, and blue intensity values. A preview box shows the resulting RGB color.

Sanjit wants the labels in the Documentation sheet to stand out, so you will change the Big Red Wraps company name and slogan to red.

To change the company name and slogan font color:

1. Select the range **A1:A2**. The company name and slogan are selected.

2. On the HOME tab, in the Font group, click the **Font Color button arrow** to display the gallery of theme and standard colors. (The two colors for hyperlinked text are not shown.)

3. Point to the **Red** color (the second color) in the Standard Colors section. The color name appears in a ScreenTip and you see a Live Preview of the text with the red font color. See Figure 2-3.

Figure 2-3   Font color gallery

- Live Preview of the Red font color
- 10 theme colors (each with five variations)
- standard colors available in all themes
- pointer on the Red font color

4. Click the **Red** color. The company name and slogan change to red.

Tutorial 2 Formatting Workbook Text and Data | Excel   EX 75

Formatting Text Selections

TIP

The **Mini toolbar** contains buttons for common formatting options used for the selection. These same buttons appear on the ribbon.

In Edit mode, you can select and format selections of text within a cell. When the Big Red Wraps slogan is used in marketing materials, "Big Flavor" is set slightly larger than "Small Price." Sanjit wants you to recreate this effect in the workbook by increasing the font size of "Big Flavor" while leaving the rest of the text unchanged. You will use Edit mode to apply a different format to part of the cell text.

To format part of the company slogan:

1. Double-click cell **A2** to select the cell and enter Edit mode (or click cell **A2** and press the **F2** key). The status bar shows EDIT to indicate that you are working with the cell in Edit mode. The pointer changes to the I-beam pointer.

2. Drag the pointer over the phrase **Big Flavor** to select it. The Mini toolbar appears above the selected text with buttons to change the font, size, style, and color of the selected text in the cell. See Figure 2-4.

Figure 2-4   Mini toolbar in Edit mode

Mini toolbar includes common formatting options

3. On the Mini toolbar, click the **Font Size button arrow**, and then click **14**. The font size of the selected text increases to 14 points.

4. Select cell **A7** to deselect cell A2. See Figure 2-5.

Figure 2-5   Formatted text selection

font size increased to 14 points

Working with Fill Colors and Backgrounds

Another way to distinguish sections of a worksheet is by formatting the cell background. You can fill the cell background with color or an image. Sanjit wants you to add fill colors and background images to the Documentation worksheet.

> **INSIGHT**
>
> ### Using Color to Enhance a Workbook
>
> When used wisely, color can enhance any workbook. However, when used improperly, color can distract the user, making the workbook more difficult to read. As you format a workbook, keep in mind the following tips:
>
> - Use colors from the same theme to maintain a consistent look and feel across the worksheets. If the built-in themes do not fit your needs, you can create a custom theme.
> - Use colors to differentiate types of cell content and to direct users where to enter data. For example, format a worksheet so that formula results appear in cells without a fill color and users enter data in cells with a light gray fill color.
> - Avoid color combinations that are difficult to read.
> - Print the workbook on both color and black-and-white printers to ensure that the printed copy is readable in both versions.
> - Understand your printer's limitations and features. Colors that look good on your monitor might not look as good when printed.
> - Be sensitive to your audience. About 8 percent of all men and 0.5 percent of all women have some type of color blindness and might not be able to see the text when certain color combinations are used. Red-green color blindness is the most common, so avoid using red text on a green background or green text on a red background.

Changing a Fill Color

> **TIP**
>
> You can also change a sheet tab's color. Right-click a sheet tab, point to Tab Color on the shortcut menu, and then click a color.

By default, worksheet cells do not include any background color. But background colors, also known as fill colors, can be helpful for distinguishing different parts of a worksheet or adding visual interest. You add fill colors to selected cells in the worksheet from the Fill Color gallery, which has the same options as the Font Color gallery.

Sanjit wants the labels and text in the Documentation sheet to stand out. You will format the labels in a white font on a red background, and then you'll format the author's name, current date, and purpose of the worksheet in a red font on a white background.

To change the fill and font colors in the Documentation worksheet:

1. Select the range **A4:A6**.

2. On the HOME tab, in the Font group, click the **Fill Color button arrow**, and then click the **Red** color (the second color) in the Standard Colors section.

3. In the Font group, click the **Font Color button arrow**, and then click the **White, Background 1** color in the Theme Colors section. The labels are formatted in white text on a red background.

4. Select the range **B4:B6**, and then format the cells with a red font and a white background.

5. Increase the width of column B to **30** characters, and then wrap the text in the selected range.

Tutorial 2 Formatting Workbook Text and Data | Excel   EX 77

▸ 6. Select the range **A4:B6**, and then add all borders around each of the selected cells.

▸ 7. Click cell **A7** to deselect the range. See Figure 2-6.

| Figure 2-6 | Font and fill colors in the Documentation sheet |

[Screenshot of Excel Documentation sheet showing "Big Red Wraps" title in orange, "Big Flavor, Small Price" subtitle, and a table with Author: Sanjit Chandra, Date: 3/1/2016, Purpose: To display sales information for the upcoming Big Red Wraps sales conference]

Callouts:
- width of column B is 30 characters
- labels are white text on a red background
- red text on a white background
- text wrapped in the cell

Adding a Background Image

A background image can provide a textured appearance, like that of granite, wood, or fibered paper, to a worksheet. The image is repeated until it fills the entire sheet. The background image does not affect any cell's format or content. Fill colors added to cells appear on top of the image, covering that portion of the image. Background images are visible only on the screen; they do not print.

Sanjit has provided an image that he wants you to use as the background of the Documentation sheet.

To add a background image to the Documentation sheet:

▸ 1. On the ribbon, click the **PAGE LAYOUT** tab to display the page layout options.

▸ 2. In the Page Setup group, click the **Background** button. The Insert Pictures dialog box opens with options to select a picture from a file, select Office.com Clip Art, or perform a Bing Image Search.

▸ 3. Click the **Browse** button next to the From a file label. The Sheet Background dialog box opens.

▸ 4. Navigate to the **Excel2 ▸ Tutorial** folder included with your Data Files, click the **Background** JPEG image file, and then click the **Insert** button. The image is added to the background of the Documentation sheet, and the Background button changes to the Delete Background button, which you can use to remove the background image. See Figure 2-7.

Figure 2-7 Background image in the Documentation sheet

background image appears behind text

button to remove the background image

fill color appears on top of the background image

Background image courtesy of Patrick Carey

Using Functions and Formulas to Calculate Sales Data

In the Sales Report worksheet, you will format the gross sales from each of the store's 20 restaurants and the summary statistics for those stores. The Sales Report worksheet is divided into two areas. The table at the bottom of the worksheet displays gross sales for the past year for each month by restaurant. The section at the top of the worksheet summarizes the sales data for the past two years. Sanjit collected the following sales data:

- **Gross Sales**—the total amount of sales at all of the restaurants
- **Cost of Sales**—the cost of producing the store's menu items
- **Operating Expenses**—the cost of running the stores including the employment and insurance costs
- **Net Profit/Loss**—the difference between the income from the gross sales and the total cost of sales and operating expenses
- **Units Sold**—the total number of menu items sold by the company during the year
- **Customers Served**—the total number of customers served by the company during the year

Sanjit wants you to calculate these sales statistics for the entire company and per store so he can track how well the stores are performing. First, you will calculate the total gross sales for Big Red Wraps and the company's overall net profit and loss.

To calculate the company's sales and profit/loss:

1. Click the **Sales Report** sheet tab to make the Sales Report worksheet active.

> 2. Click cell **C6**, type the formula **=SUM(C27:N46)** to calculate the total gross sales from all stores in the previous year, and then press the **Enter** key. Cell C6 displays 9514000, which means that Big Red Wraps' total gross sales for the previous year were more than $9.5 million.
>
> 3. In cell **C9**, enter the formula **=C6−(C7+C8)** to calculate the current year's net profit/loss, which is equal to the difference between the gross sales and the sum of the cost of sales and operating expenses. Cell C9 displays 1108000, which means that the company's net profit for 2015 was more than $1.1 million.
>
> 4. Copy the formula in cell **C9**, and then paste it into cell **D9** to calculate the net profit/loss for 2014. Cell D9 displays 1264000, which means that the company's net profit for that year was more than $1.26 million.

TIP
To enter content in a cell, you select the cell, type the specified content, and then press the Enter key.

Next, Sanjit asks you to summarize the sales statistics for each store. Sanjit wants the same per-store statistics calculated for the 2015 and 2014 sales data. Per-store sales statistics are calculated by dividing the overall statistics by the number of stores. In this case, you will divide the overall statistics by the value in cell C23, which contains the total number of stores in the Big Red Wraps chain. After you enter the 2015 formulas, you can copy and paste them to calculate the 2014 results.

To calculate the per-store statistics:

> 1. In cell **C16**, enter the formula **=C6/C23** to calculate the gross sales per store in 2015. The formula returns 475700, which means that the annual gross sales amount for a Big Red Wraps store in 2015 was more than $475,000.
>
> 2. In cell **C17**, enter the formula **=C7/C23** to calculate the cost of sales per store in 2015. The formula returns the value 168700, which means that the cost of sales for a Big Red Wraps store in 2015 was typically $168,700.
>
> 3. In cell **C18**, enter the formula **=C8/C23** to calculate the operating expenses per store in 2015. The formula returns the value 251600, which means that operating expenses of a typical store in 2015 were $251,600.
>
> 4. In cell **C19**, enter the formula **=C9/C23** to calculate the net profit/loss per store in 2015. The formula returns the value 55400, indicating that the net profit/loss of a typical store in 2015 was $55,400.
>
> 5. In cell **C21**, enter the formula **=C11/C23** to calculate the units sold per store in 2015. The formula returns the value 67200, indicating that a typical store sold 67,200 units during 2015.
>
> 6. In cell **C22**, enter the formula **=C12/C23** to calculate the customers served per store in 2015. The formula returns the value 7770, indicating that a typical store served 7,770 customers during that year.
>
> 7. Copy the formulas in the range **C16:C22** and paste them into the range **D16:D22**. The cell references in the formulas change to calculate the sales data for the year 2014.
>
> 8. Select cell **B24** to deselect the range. See Figure 2-8.

Figure 2-8 — Sales statistics for the entire company and per store

	A	B	C	D	E	F
5		Category	2015	2014	Net Change	% Change
6		Gross Sales	9514000	8424000		
7		Cost of Sales	3374000	2784000		
8		Operating Expenses	5032000	4376000		
9		Net Profit/Loss	1108000	1264000		
10						
11		Units Sold	1344000	1104000		
12		Customers Served	155400	129600		
13						
14		Sales Statistics per Store				
15		Category	2015	2014	Net Change	% Change
16		Gross Sales	475700	526500		
17		Cost of Sales	168700	174000		
18		Operating Expenses	251600	273500		
19		Net Profit/Loss	55400	79000		
20						
21		Units Sold	67200	69000		
22		Customers Served	7770	8100		
23		Stores	20	16		

- overall store sales statistics
- per-store sales statistics are calculated by dividing the overall statistics by the number of stores
- number of stores in 2014 and 2015

Sanjit also wants to explore how the company's sales and expenses have changed from 2014 to 2015. To do this, you will calculate the net change in sales from 2014 to 2015 as well as the percent change. The percent change is calculated using the following formula:

$$\text{percent change} = \frac{2015\ value - 2014\ value}{2014\ value}$$

You will calculate the net and percent changes for all of the sales statistics.

To calculate the net and percent changes for 2015 and 2014:

1. In cell **E6**, enter the formula **=C6–D6** to calculate the difference between the 2015 and 2014 gross sales. The formula returns 1090000, indicating that gross sales increased by $1.09 million between 2014 and 2015.

2. In cell **F6**, enter the formula **=(C6–D6)/D6** to calculate the percent change in gross sales from 2014 to 2015. The formula returns 0.129392213, indicating a nearly 13% increase in gross sales from 2014 to 2015.

   Be sure to include the parentheses as shown to calculate the percent change correctly.

   Next, you'll copy and paste the formulas in cells E6 and F6 to the rest of the sales data to calculate the net change and percent change from 2014 to 2015.

3. Select the range **E6:F6**, and then copy the selected range. The two formulas are copied to the Clipboard.

4. Select the nonadjacent range **E7:F9;E11:F12;E16:F19;E21:F23**, and then paste the formulas from the Clipboard into the selected range. The net and percent changes are calculated for the remaining sales data.

5. Click cell **B24** to deselect the range, and then scroll the worksheet up to display row 5. See Figure 2-9.

Tutorial 2 Formatting Workbook Text and Data | Excel   EX 81

Figure 2-9 — Net and percent changes calculated

column E displays the change in sales values from 2014 to 2015

column F displays the percent change in sales values from 2014 to 2015

percentages are displayed as decimals

	A	B	C	D	E	F	G	H	I	J	K
5		Category	2015	2014	Net Change	% Change					
6		Gross Sales	9514000	8424000	1090000	0.129392213					
7		Cost of Sales	3374000	2784000	590000	0.211925287					
8		Operating Expenses	5032000	4376000	656000	0.149908592					
9		Net Profit/Loss	1108000	1264000	-156000	-0.12341772					
10											
11		Units Sold	1344000	1104000	240000	0.217391304					
12		Customers Served	155400	129600	25800	0.199074074					
13											
14		Sales Statistics per Store									
15		Category	2015	2014	Net Change	% Change					
16		Gross Sales	475700	526500	-50800	-0.09648623					
17		Cost of Sales	168700	174000	-5300	-0.03045977					
18		Operating Expenses	251600	273500	-21900	-0.08007313					
19		Net Profit/Loss	55400	79000	-23600	-0.29873418					
20											
21		Units Sold	67200	69000	-1800	-0.02608696					
22		Customers Served	7770	8100	-330	-0.04074074					
23		Stores	20	16	4	0.25					

The bottom part of the worksheet contains the sales for each restaurant from 2015. You will use the SUM function to calculate the total gross sales for each restaurant during the entire year, the total monthly sales of all 20 restaurants, and the total gross sales of all restaurants and months.

To calculate different subtotals of the gross sales:

1. Select cell **O26**, type **TOTAL** as the label, and then press the **Enter** key. Cell O27 is now the active cell.

2. On the HOME tab, in the Editing group, click the **AutoSum** button, and then press the **Enter** key to accept the suggested range reference and enter the formula =SUM(C27:N27) in cell O27. The cell displays 355000, indicating gross sales in 2015 for the 411 Elm Drive restaurant were $355,000.

3. Copy the formula in cell **O27**, and then paste that formula into the range **O28:O46** to calculate the total sales for each of the remaining 19 restaurants in the Big Red Wraps chain.

4. Select cell **B47**, type **TOTAL** as the label, and then press the **Tab** key. Cell C47 is now the active cell.

5. Select the range **C47:O47** so that you can calculate the total monthly sales for all of the stores.

6. On the HOME tab, in the Editing group, click the **AutoSum** button, and then press the **Enter** key to calculate the total sales for each month as well as the total sales for all months. For example, cell C47 displays 680000, indicating that monthly sales for January 2015 for all stores were $680,000.

7. Select cell **O48** to deselect the range. See Figure 2-10.

Figure 2-10   Gross sales summarized by store and month

row 47 displays the total gross sales for each month for all 20 stores

column O displays the gross sales for each store for all months

	E	F	G	H	I	J	K	L	M	N	O
42	31000	33000	32000	37000	37000	38000	35000	33000	35000	33000	399000
43	45000	47000	46000	49000	51000	49000	47000	49000	47000	48000	555000
44	49000	53000	55000	56000	56000	59000	54000	55000	51000	53000	632000
45	34000	36000	37000	38000	37000	38000	36000	36000	35000	38000	427000
46	53000	53000	56000	55000	59000	58000	56000	58000	53000	57000	650000
47	757000	779000	815000	830000	861000	876000	819000	828000	783000	827000	9514000

cell O47 displays the total gross sales for all stores and months

Formatting Numbers

The goal in formatting any workbook is to make the content easier to interpret. For numbers, this can mean adding a comma to separate thousands, setting the number of decimal places, and using percentage and currency symbols to make numbers easier to read and understand. Sanjit asks you to format the numbers in the Sales Report worksheet to improve their readability.

Applying Number Formats

You can use a number format to display values in a way that makes them easier to read and understand. Changing the number format of the displayed value does not affect the stored value. Numbers are originally formatted in the **General format**, which, for the most part, displays numbers exactly as they are typed. If the number is calculated from a formula or function, the cell displays as many digits after the decimal point as will fit in the cell with the last digit rounded. Calculated values too large to fit into the cell are displayed in scientific notation.

The General format is fine for small numbers, but some values require additional formatting to make the numbers easier to interpret. For example, you might want to:

- Change the number of digits displayed to the right of the decimal point
- Add commas to separate thousands in large numbers
- Apply currency symbols to numbers to identify the monetary unit being used
- Display percentages using the % symbol

TIP
To apply the Currency format, click the Number Format button arrow and click Currency, or press the Ctrl+Shift+$ keys.

Excel supports two monetary formats: currency and accounting. Both formats add a thousands separator to the currency values and display two digits to the right of the decimal point. However, the **Currency format** places a currency symbol directly to the left of the first digit of the currency value and displays negative numbers with a negative sign. The **Accounting format** fixes a currency symbol at the left edge of the column, and displays negative numbers within parentheses and zero values with a dash. It also slightly indents the values from the right edge of the cell to allow room for parentheses around negative values. Figure 2-11 compares the two formats.

Figure 2-11   **Currency and Accounting number formats**

Currency Format	Accounting Format
$95,000.00	$ 95,000.00
-$3,300.00	$ (3,300.00)
$0.00	$ -
$1,108.00	$ 1,108.00

- negative values displayed with a negative sign
- $ symbols placed to the left of the leading digit
- negative values displayed in parentheses
- zeros displayed with a dash
- $ symbols fixed on the left edge of the cell
- values slightly indented from the right cell edge

PROSKILLS

Written Communication: Formatting Monetary Values

Spreadsheets commonly include monetary values. To make these values simpler to read and comprehend, keep in mind the following guidelines when formatting the currency data in a worksheet:

- **Format for your audience.** For general financial reports, round values to the nearest hundred, thousand, or million. Investors are generally more interested in the big picture than in exact values. However, for accounting reports, accuracy is important and often legally required. So, for those reports, be sure to display the exact monetary value.
- **Use thousands separators.** Large strings of numbers can be challenging to read. For monetary values, use a thousands separator to make the amounts easier to comprehend.
- **Apply the Accounting format to columns of monetary values.** The Accounting format makes columns of numbers easier to read than the Currency format. Use the Currency format for individual cells that are not part of long columns of numbers.
- **Use only two currency symbols in a column of monetary values.** Standard accounting format displays one currency symbol with the first monetary value in the column, and optionally displays a second currency symbol with the last value in that column. Use the Accounting format to fix the currency symbols, lining them up within the column.

Following these standard accounting principles will make your financial data easier to read both on the screen and in printouts.

Sanjit wants you to format the gross sales amounts in the Accounting format so that they are easier to read.

TIP

To select other currency symbols, click the Accounting Number Format button arrow, and then click a currency symbol.

To format the gross sales in the Accounting format:

1. Select the range **C6:E6** with the gross sales.

2. On the HOME tab, in the Number group, click the **Accounting Number Format** button $. The numbers are formatted in the Accounting format. You cannot see the format because the cells display ##########.

The cells display ########## because the formatted number doesn't fit into the column. One reason for this is that monetary values, by default, show both dollars and cents in the cell. However, you can increase or decrease the number of decimal places displayed in a cell. The displayed value might then be rounded. For example, the stored value 11.7 will appear in the cell as 12 if no decimal places are displayed to the right of the decimal point. Changing the number of decimal places displayed in a cell does not change the value stored in the cell.

Because Sanjit and the other conference attendees are interested only in whole dollar amounts, he wants you to hide the cents values of the gross sales by decreasing the number of decimal places to zero.

To decrease the number of decimal places displayed in the gross sales:

1. Make sure the range **C6:E6** is selected.

2. On the HOME tab, in the Number group, click the **Decrease Decimal** button twice. The cents are hidden for gross sales.

3. Select cell **C4** to deselect the range. See Figure 2-12.

Figure 2-12   Formatted gross sales values

	A	B	C	D	E
1	Big Red Wraps				
2	Big Flavor, Small Price				
3					
4		Sales Statistics			
5		Category	2015	2014	Net Change	% Change
6		Gross Sales	$ 9,514,000	$ 8,424,000	$ 1,090,000	0.129392213

Accounting Format button

gross sales values displayed in the Accounting format with no decimal places

Increase Decimal button

Decrease Decimal button

The Comma style is identical to the Accounting format except that it does not fix a currency symbol to the left of the number. The advantage of using the Comma style and the Accounting format together is that the numbers will be aligned in the column.

Sanjit asks you to apply the Comma style to the remaining sales statistics.

Tutorial 2 Formatting Workbook Text and Data | Excel EX 85

To apply the Comma style to the sales statistics:

1. Select the nonadjacent range **C7:E9;C11:E12** containing the sales figures for all stores in 2014 and 2015.

2. On the HOME tab, in the Number group, click the **Comma Style** button. In some instances, the number is now too large to be displayed in the cell.

3. In the Number group, click the **Decrease Decimal** button twice to remove two decimal places. Digits to the right of the decimal point are hidden for all of the selected cells.

4. Select cell **C13** to deselect the range. See Figure 2-13.

Figure 2-13 Formatted sales values

		2015	2014	Net Change	% Change
4	Sales Statistics				
5	Category	2015	2014	Net Change	% Change
6	Gross Sales	$ 9,514,000	$ 8,424,000	$ 1,090,000	0.129392213
7	Cost of Sales	3,374,000	2,784,000	590,000	0.211925287
8	Operating Expenses	5,032,000	4,376,000	656,000	0.149908592
9	Net Profit/Loss	1,108,000	1,264,000	(156,000)	-0.12341772
10					
11	Units Sold	1,344,000	1,104,000	240,000	0.217391304
12	Customers Served	155,400	129,600	25,800	0.199074074
13					
14	Sales Statistics per Store				
15	Category	2015	2014	Net Change	% Change
16	Gross Sales	475700	526500	-50800	-0.09648623
17	Cost of Sales	168700	174000	-5300	-0.03045977
18	Operating Expenses	251600	273500	-21900	-0.08007313
19	Net Profit/Loss	55400	79000	-23600	-0.29873418

numbers with the Accounting format and no decimal places

numbers with the Comma style and no decimal places

numbers aligned within each column

The Percent style formats numbers as percentages. When you format values as percentages, the % symbol appears after the number and no digits appear to the right of the decimal point. You can always change how many decimal places are displayed in the cell if that is important to show with your data.

Sanjit wants you to format the percent change from the 2014 to 2015 sales statistics with a percent symbol to make the percent values easier to read.

To format percentages:

1. Select the nonadjacent range **F6:F9;F11:F12** containing the percent change values.

2. On the HOME tab, in the Number group, click the **Percent Style** button (or press the **Ctrl+Shift+%** keys). The values are displayed as percentages.

3. In the Number group, click the **Increase Decimal** button twice. The displayed number includes two decimal places.

4. Select cell **F13** to deselect the range. See Figure 2-14.

EX 86 Excel | Tutorial 2 Formatting Workbook Text and Data

Figure 2-14 Formatted percent changes

Percent Style button — points to the % button in the Number group on the HOME tab.

percentages displayed to two decimal places — points to column F values.

	A	B	C	D	E	F
1	Big Red Wraps					
2	Big Flavor, Small Price					
3						
4		Sales Statistics				
5		Category	2015	2014	Net Change	% Change
6		Gross Sales	$ 9,514,000	$ 8,424,000	$ 1,090,000	12.94%
7		Cost of Sales	3,374,000	2,784,000	590,000	21.19%
8		Operating Expenses	5,032,000	4,376,000	656,000	14.99%
9		Net Profit/Loss	1,108,000	1,264,000	(156,000)	-12.34%
10						
11		Units Sold	1,344,000	1,104,000	240,000	21.74%
12		Customers Served	155,400	129,600	25,800	19.91%
13						

With the data reformatted, the worksheet clearly shows that Big Red Wraps' gross sales increased from 2014 to 2015 by almost 13 percent. However, both the cost of sales and the operating expenses increased by about 21.2 percent and 15 percent, respectively, probably due to the cost of building four new stores. As a result, the company's net profit decreased by $156,000 or about 12.3 percent.

Formatting Dates and Times

TIP

To view the underlying date and time value, apply the General format to the cell or display the formulas instead of the formula results.

Because Excel stores dates and times as numbers and not as text, you can apply different formats without affecting the date and time value. The abbreviated format, *mm/dd/yyyy*, entered in the Documentation sheet is referred to as the **Short Date format**. You can also apply a **Long Date format** that displays the day of the week and the full month name in addition to the day of the month and the year. Other built-in formats include formats for displaying time values in 12- or 24-hour time format.

You will change the date in the Documentation sheet to the Long Date format.

To format the date in the Long Date format:

1. Go to the **Documentation** sheet, and then select cell **B5**.

2. On the ribbon, make sure the HOME tab is displayed.

3. In the Number group, click the **Number Format button arrow** to display a list of number formats, and then click **Long Date**. The date is displayed with the weekday name, month name, day, and year. Notice that the date in the formula bar did not change because you changed only the display format, not the date value.

Tutorial 2 Formatting Workbook Text and Data | Excel   EX 87

Formatting Worksheet Cells

You can format the appearance of individual cells by modifying the alignment of text within the cell, indenting cell text, or adding borders of different styles and colors.

Aligning Cell Content

By default, text is aligned with the left and bottom borders of a cell, and numbers are aligned with the right and bottom borders. You might want to change the alignment to make the text and numbers more readable or visually appealing. In general, you should center column titles, left-align other text, and right-align numbers to keep their decimal places lined up within a column. Figure 2-15 describes the buttons you use to set these alignment options, which are located in the Alignment group on the HOME tab.

Figure 2-15   **Alignment buttons**

Button	Name	Description
	Top Align	Aligns the cell content with the cell's top edge
	Middle Align	Vertically centers the cell content within the cell
	Bottom Align	Aligns the cell content with the cell's bottom edge
	Align Left	Aligns the cell content with the cell's left edge
	Center	Horizontally centers the cell content within the cell
	Align Right	Aligns the cell content with the cell's right edge
	Decrease Indent	Decreases the size of the indentation used in the cell
	Increase Indent	Increases the size of the indentation used in the cell
	Orientation	Rotates the cell content to any angle within the cell
	Wrap Text	Forces the cell text to wrap within the cell borders
	Merge & Center	Merges the selected cells into a single cell

© 2014 Cengage Learning

The date in the Documentation sheet is right-aligned in the cell because Excel treats dates and times as numbers. Sanjit wants you to left-align the date and center the column titles in the Sales Report worksheet.

To left-align the date and center the column titles:

1. In the Documentation sheet, make sure cell **B5** is still selected.
2. On the HOME tab, in the Alignment group, click the **Align Left** button. The date shifts to the left edge of the cell.
3. Make the **Sales Report** worksheet the active worksheet.
4. Select the range **C5:F5**. The column titles are selected.
5. In the Alignment group, click the **Center** button. The column titles are centered in the cells.

Indenting Cell Content

Sometimes you want a cell's content moved a few spaces from the cell's left edge. This is particularly useful to create subsections in a worksheet or to set off some entries from others. You can increase the indent to shift the contents of a cell away from the left edge of the cell, or you can decrease the indent to shift a cell's contents closer to the left edge of the cell.

Sanjit wants the Cost of Sales and Operating Expenses labels in the sales statistics table offset from the other labels because they represent expenses to the company. You will increase the indent for the expense categories.

To indent the expense categories:

1. Select the range **B7:B8** containing the expense categories.
2. On the HOME tab, in the Alignment group, click the **Increase Indent** button twice to indent each label two spaces in its cell.

Adding Cell Borders

Common accounting practices provide guidelines on when to add borders to cells. In general, a single black border appears above a subtotal, a single bottom border is added below a calculated number, and a double black bottom border appears below the total.

Sanjit wants you to follow these common accounting practices in the Sales Report worksheet. You will add borders below the column titles and below the gross sales values. You will add a top border to the net profit/loss values. Finally, you will add a top and bottom border to the Units Sold and Customers Served rows.

To add borders to the sales statistics data:

1. Select the range **B5:F5** containing the table headings.
2. On the HOME tab, in the Font group, click the **All Borders button arrow**, and then click **Bottom Border**. A border is added below the column titles.
3. Select the range **B6:F6** containing the gross sales amounts.
4. In the Font group, click the **Bottom Border** button to add a border below the selected gross sales amounts.
5. Select the range **B9:F9**, click the **Bottom Border button arrow**, and then click **Top Border** to add a border above the net profit/loss amounts.

   The Units Sold and Customers Served rows do not contain monetary values as the other rows do. You will distinguish these rows by adding a top and bottom border.

6. Select the range **B11:F12**, click the **Top Border button arrow**, and then click **Top and Bottom** to add a border above the number of units sold and below the number of customers served.
7. Select cell **B3** to deselect the range. See Figure 2-16.

Tutorial 2 Formatting Workbook Text and Data | Excel   EX 89

Figure 2-16   Worksheet with formatted cells

(Screenshot of an Excel worksheet showing the Home tab ribbon with Clipboard, Font, Alignment, and Number groups. Callouts point to: "alignment buttons" (Alignment group in ribbon), "centered text" (column headers 2015, 2014, Net Change, % Change), "indented text" (Cost of Sales, Operating Expenses rows), and "borders added above and below cell content" (Units Sold, Customers Served rows).)

	A	B	C	D	E	F
1	Big Red Wraps					
2	Big Flavor, Small Price					
3						
4		Sales Statistics				
5		Category	2015	2014	Net Change	% Change
6		Gross Sales	$ 9,514,000	$ 8,424,000	$ 1,090,000	12.94%
7		Cost of Sales	3,374,000	2,784,000	590,000	21.19%
8		Operating Expenses	5,032,000	4,376,000	656,000	14.99%
9		Net Profit/Loss	1,108,000	1,264,000	(156,000)	-12.34%
10						
11		Units Sold	1,344,000	1,104,000	240,000	21.74%
12		Customers Served	155,400	129,600	25,800	19.91%
13						

You can apply multiple formats to the same cell to create the look that best fits the data. For example, one cell might be formatted with a number format, alignments, borders, indents, fonts, font sizes, and so on. The monthly sales data needs to be formatted with number styles, alignment, indents, and borders. You'll add these formats now.

To format the monthly sales table:

1. Click the **Name** box to select the cell reference, type **C27:O47**, and then press the **Enter** key to quickly select the range C27:O47 containing the monthly gross sales for each restaurant.

2. On the HOME tab, in the Number group, click the **Comma Style** button to add a thousands separator to the values.

3. In the Number group, click the **Decrease Decimal** button twice to hide the cents from the sales results.

4. In the Alignment group, click the **Top Align** button to align the sales numbers with the top of each cell.

5. Select the range **C26:O26** containing the labels for the month abbreviations and the TOTAL column.

6. In the Alignment group, click the **Center** button to center the column labels.

7. Select the range **B27:B46** containing the store addresses.

8. Reduce the font size of the store addresses to **9** points.

9. In the Alignment group, click the **Increase Indent** button to indent the store addresses.

10. In the Alignment group, click the **Top Align** button to align the addresses at the top of each cell.

11. Select the range **B47:O47** containing the monthly totals.

EX 90 Excel | Tutorial 2 Formatting Workbook Text and Data

▸ 12. In the Font group, click the **Top and Bottom Borders button arrow**, and then click **All Borders** to add borders around each monthly totals cell.

▸ 13. Select the range **O26:O46**, which contains the annual totals for each restaurant, and then click the **All Borders** button to add borders around each restaurant total.

▸ 14. Select cell **A24** to deselect the range. See Figure 2-17.

Figure 2-17   **Formatted monthly gross sales figures**

gross sales values aligned with the top of the cell

month abbreviations are centered

	A	B	...	E	F	G	...	K	...
24									
25	2015 Monthly Gross Sales								
26	State	Store		Jan	Feb	Mar	Apr	May	Jun	Jul	Aug	Sep
27	Wisconsin	411 Elm Dr. Madison, WI 53713 (608) 555 - 3005		26,000	24,000	27,000	28,000	29,000	32,000	33,000	34,000	30,000
28		54 North St. Madison, WI 53704 (608) 555 - 6313		45,000	45,000	52,000	51,000	54,000	56,000	56,000	59,000	54,000
29		3 Ashford Ln. Monroe, WI 53566 (779) 555 - 2401		19,000	21,000	23,000	25,000	26,000	26,000	28,000	26,000	25,000
30		100 East Troy Ave. Platteville, WI 53818 (608) 555 - 4555		26,000	27,000	30,000	29,000	34,000	31,000	34,000	36,000	31,000
31		902 South Dr. Janesville, WI 53545 (608) 555 - 8174		45,000	41,000	49,000	51,000	53,000	54,000	54,000	58,000	54,000
32		15 Watts Rd. Dodgeville, WI 53533 (608) 555 - 4904		41,000	39,000	46,000	47,000	47,000	51,000	52,000	54,000	50,000
		791 East River Dr. La Crosse, WI 54601		24,000	22,000	25,000	27,000	28,000	29,000	32,000	30,000	30,000

address text is 9 points

thousands separators displayed

Merging Cells

You can merge, or combine, several cells into one cell. A merged cell contains two or more cells with a single cell reference. When you merge cells, only the content from the upper-left cell in the range is retained. The cell reference for the merged cell is the upper-left cell reference. So, if you merge cells A1 and A2, the merged cell reference is cell A1. After you merge cells, you can align the content within the merged cell. The Merge & Center button in the Alignment group on the HOME tab includes the following options:

- **Merge & Center**—merges the range into one cell and horizontally centers the content
- **Merge Across**—merges each row in the selected range across the columns in the range
- **Merge Cells**—merges the range into a single cell, but does not horizontally center the cell content
- **Unmerge Cells**—reverses a merge, returning the merged cell to a range of individual cells

The first column of the monthly sales data lists the states in which Big Red Wraps has stores. You will merge the cells for each state name.

To merge the state name cells:

▸ 1. Select the range **A27:A33** containing the cells for the Wisconsin stores. You will merge these seven cells into a single cell.

2. On the HOME tab, in the Alignment group, click the **Merge & Center** button. The range A27:A33 merges into one cell with the cell reference A27, and the text is centered and bottom-aligned within the cell.

3. Select the range **A34:A36**, and then click the **Merge & Center** button in the Alignment group to merge and center the Minnesota cells.

4. Select the range **A37:A40**, and then click the **Merge & Center** button to merge and center the Iowa cells.

5. Select cell **A41**, and then center it horizontally to align the Colorado text with the text in the other state cells.

6. Merge and center the range **A42:A43** containing the Nebraska cells.

7. Merge and center the range **A44:A46** containing the Kansas cells. See Figure 2-18. The merged cells make it easier to distinguish restaurants in each state.

Figure 2-18 Merged cells

	A	B	C	D	E	F	G
40	Iowa	414 Main St. Des Moines, IA 50311 (515) 555 - 3134	46,000	43,000	52,000	51,000	54
41	Colorado	112 Reservoir Ln. Greeley, CO 80631 (970) 555 - 2138	38,000	35,000	43,000	42,000	44
42		5155 Pocane Dr. Grand Island, NE 68801 (402) 555 - 7734	27,000	28,000	31,000	33,000	32
43	Nebraska	42 East River Rd. Omaha, NE 68111 (402) 555 - 9148	38,000	39,000	45,000	47,000	46
44		975 Business Dr. Manhattan, KS 66502 (785) 555 - 0444	46,000	45,000	49,000	53,000	55
45		47 Valley View Ln. Topeka, KS 66604 (785) 555 - 6106	31,000	31,000	34,000	36,000	37
46	Kansas	87210 Causeway Dr. Salina, KS 67401 (785) 555 - 8103	47,000	45,000	53,000	53,000	56
47		TOTAL	680,000	659,000	757,000	779,000	815
48							

merged cell A42 contains the range A42:A43

merged cell A44 contains the range A44:A46

Rotating Cell Contents

Text and numbers are displayed horizontally within cells. However, you can rotate cell text to any angle to save space or to provide visual interest to a worksheet. The state names at the bottom of the merged cells would look better and take up less room if they were rotated vertically within their cells. Sanjit asks you to rotate the state names.

To rotate the state names:

1. Select the merged cell **A27**.

2. On the HOME tab, in the Alignment group, click the **Orientation** button to display a list of rotation options, and then click **Rotate Text Up**. The state name rotates 90 degrees counterclockwise.

3. In the Alignment group, click the **Middle Align** button to vertically center the rotated text in the merged cell.

4. Select the merged cell range **A34:A44**, and then repeat Steps 2 and 3 to rotate and vertically center the rest of the state names in their cells.

5. Select cell **A41** to deselect the range, and then increase the height of row 41 (the Colorado row) to **75** points (**100** pixels) so that the entire state name appears in the cell.

6. Reduce the width of column A to **7** characters because the rotated state names take up less space.

7. Select cell **A47**. See Figure 2-19.

Figure 2-19   Rotated cell content

Exploring the Format Cells Dialog Box

The buttons on the HOME tab provide quick access to the most commonly used formatting choices. For more options, you can use the Format Cells dialog box. You can apply the formats in this dialog box to the selected worksheet cells. The Format Cells dialog box has six tabs, each focusing on a different set of formatting options, as described below:

- **Number**—provides options for formatting the appearance of numbers, including dates and numbers treated as text such as telephone or Social Security numbers
- **Alignment**—provides options for how data is aligned within a cell
- **Font**—provides options for selecting font types, sizes, styles, and other formatting attributes such as underlining and font colors

Tutorial 2 Formatting Workbook Text and Data | Excel   EX 93

- **Border**—provides options for adding and removing cell borders as well as selecting a line style and color
- **Fill**—provides options for creating and applying background colors and patterns to cells
- **Protection**—provides options for locking or hiding cells to prevent other users from modifying their contents

Although you have applied many of these formats from the HOME tab, the Format Cells dialog box presents them in a different way and provides more choices. You will use the Font and Fill tabs to format the column titles with a white font on a red background.

To use the Format Cells dialog box to format the column labels:

1. Select the range **A26:O26** containing the column labels for the table.

2. On the HOME tab, in the Number group, click the **Dialog Box Launcher** located to the right of the group name (refer to Figure 2-19). The Format Cells dialog box opens with the Number tab displayed.

3. Click the **Font** tab to display the font formatting options.

4. Click the **Color** box to display the color palette, and then click the **White, Background 1** theme color. The font is set to white. See Figure 2-20.

TIP

You can also open the Format Cells dialog box by right-clicking the selected range, and then clicking Format Cells on the shortcut menu.

Figure 2-20   Font tab in the Format Cells dialog box

5. Click the **Fill** tab to display background options.

6. In the Background Color palette, click the **red** standard color (the second color in the last row). The background is set to red, as you can see in the Sample box.

7. Click the **OK** button. The dialog box closes, and the font and fill options you selected are applied to the column titles.

You will also use the Format Cells dialog box to change the appearance of the row titles. You'll format them to be displayed in a larger white font on a gray background.

To format the row labels:

1. Select the range **A27:A46** containing the rotated state names.
2. Right-click the selected range, and then click **Format Cells** on the shortcut menu. The Format Cells dialog box opens with the last tab used displayed—in this case, the Fill tab.
3. In the Background Color palette, click the **gray** theme color (the first color in the seventh column). Its preview is shown in the Sample box.
4. Click the **Font** tab to display the font formatting options.
5. Click the **Color** box, and then click the **White, Background 1** theme color to set the font color to white.
6. Scroll down the **Size** box, and then click **16** to set the font size to 16 points.
7. Click the **OK** button. The dialog box closes, and the font and fill formats are applied to the state names.

The Border tab in the Format Cells dialog box provides options for changing the border style and color as well as placing the border anywhere around a cell or cells in a selected range. Sanjit wants you to format the borders in the monthly sales data so that the sales result from each state is surrounded by a double border.

To add a double border to the state results:

1. Select the range **A27:O33** containing the monthly sales totals for the Wisconsin restaurants.
2. Open the Format Cells dialog box, and then click the **Border** tab to display the border options.
3. In the Style box, click the **double line** in the lower-right corner of the box.
4. In the Presets section, click the **Outline** option. The double border appears around the outside of the selected cells in the Border preview. See Figure 2-21.

Figure 2-21   Border tab in the Format Cells dialog box

Tutorial 2 Formatting Workbook Text and Data | Excel   EX 95

> 5. Click the **OK** button. The selected border is applied to the Wisconsin monthly sales.
> 6. Repeat Steps 2 through 5 to apply double borders to the ranges **A34:O36**, **A37:O40**, **A41:O41**, **A42:O43**, and **A44:O46**.
> 7. Select cell **A48** to deselect the range. See Figure 2-22.

Figure 2-22   Worksheet with font, fill, and border formatting

state names in a 16-point white font on a gray background

double borders around state sales rows

	A	B	C	D	E	F	G
41	Colorado	112 Reservoir Ln. Greeley, CO 80631 (970) 555 - 2138	38,000	35,000	43,000	42,000	44,000
42	Nebraska	5155 Pocane Dr. Grand Island, NE 68801 (402) 555 - 7734	27,000	28,000	31,000	33,000	32,000
43		42 East River Rd. Omaha, NE 68111 (402) 555 - 9148	38,000	39,000	45,000	47,000	46,000
44	Kansas	975 Business Dr. Manhattan, KS 66502 (785) 555 - 0444	46,000	45,000	49,000	53,000	55,000
45		47 Valley View Ln. Topeka, KS 66604 (785) 555 - 6106	31,000	31,000	34,000	36,000	37,000
46		87210 Causeway Dr. Salina, KS 67401 (785) 555 - 8103	47,000	45,000	53,000	53,000	56,000
47		TOTAL	680,000	659,000	757,000	779,000	815,000
48							

Documentation | Sales Report

READY

> 8. Save the Sales Report worksheet.

You have completed much of the formatting that Sanjit wants in the Sales Report worksheet for the Big Red Wraps sales conference. In the next session, you will explore other formatting options.

Session 2.1 Quick Check

REVIEW

1. What is the difference between a serif font and a sans serif font?
2. What is the difference between a theme color and a standard color?
3. A cell containing a number displays #######. Why does this occur and what can you do to fix it?
4. What is the General format?
5. Describe the differences between Currency format and Accounting format.
6. The range A1:C5 is merged into a single cell. What is its cell reference?
7. How do you format text so that it is set vertically within the cell?
8. Where can you access all the formatting options for worksheet cells?

EX 96   Excel | Tutorial 2 Formatting Workbook Text and Data

Session 2.2 Visual Overview:

The PAGE LAYOUT tab has options for setting how the worksheet will print.

The **Format Painter** copies and pastes formatting from one cell or range to another without duplicating any data.

Print titles are rows and columns that are included on every page of the printout. In this case, the text in rows 1 and 2 will print on every page.

A **manual page break** is one you set to indicate where a new page of the printout should start and is identified by a solid blue line.

Tutorial 2 Formatting Workbook Text and Data | Excel   EX 97

Worksheet Formatted for Printing

The Find and Replace commands, which are available from the Find & Select button, are used to quickly make content and format changes throughout a workbook.

The **print area** is a range or ranges in a worksheet that you specify to be printed. In Page Break Preview, the print area is not grayed out.

Cell styles contain predefined formatting options that can be applied to cells in the workbook.

Cell highlighting is a conditional format that changes a cell's font color or fill color based on the cell's value.

An **automatic page break** is set by Excel when the page of the printout is full and is identified by a dotted blue line.

Page Break Preview shows the location of the print area and all page breaks.

Jul	Aug	Sep	Oct	Nov	Dec	TOTAL	AVERAGE
33,000	34,000	30,000	32,000	30,000	30,000	355,000	29,583
56,000	59,000	54,000	55,000	51,000	56,000	634,000	52,833
28,000	26,000	25,000	26,000	25,000	25,000	295,000	24,583
34,000	36,000	31,000	31,000	31,000	35,000	375,000	31,250
54,000	58,000	54,000	55,000	51,000	52,000	617,000	51,417
52,000	54,000	50,000	49,000	46,000	50,000	572,000	47,667
32,000	30,000	30,000	28,000	27,000	30,000	332,000	27,667
43,000	44,000	42,000	43,000	40,000	43,000	484,000	40,333
36,000	38,000	35,000	38,000	32,000	37,000	414,000	34,500
30,000	28,000	26,000	26,000	26,000	26,000	312,000	26,000
54,000	55,000	54,000	52,000	51,000	54,000	610,000	50,833

Using the Average Function

The **AVERAGE function** calculates the average value from a collection of numbers. The syntax of the Average function is

```
AVERAGE (number1, number2, number3, ...)
```

where *number1*, *number2*, *number3*, and so forth are either numbers or cell references to the cells or a range where the numbers are stored. For example, the following formula uses the AVERAGE function to calculate the average of 1, 2, 5, and 8, returning the value 4:

```
=AVERAGE(1, 2, 5, 8)
```

However, functions usually reference values entered in a worksheet. So, if the range A1:A4 contains the values 1, 2, 5, and 8, the following formula also returns the value 4:

```
=AVERAGE(A1:A4)
```

The advantage of using cell references is that the values used in the function are visible and can be easily edited.

Sanjit wants to show the average monthly sales for each of the 20 Big Red Wraps stores in addition to the total sales for each store. You will use the AVERAGE function to calculate these values.

To calculate the average monthly sales for each store:

1. If you took a break after the previous session, make sure the Sales Report workbook is open and the Sales Report worksheet is active.

2. In cell **P26**, enter the text **AVERAGE** as the label.

3. Select cell **P27**. You will enter the AVERAGE function in this cell to calculate the average monthly sales for the store on 411 Elm Drive in Madison, Wisconsin.

4. On the HOME tab, in the Editing group, click the **AutoSum button arrow**, and then click **AVERAGE**. The formula =AVERAGE(C27:O27) appears in the cell. The range reference that was included in the function is incorrect. It includes cell O27, which contains the total gross sales for all months. You need to correct the range reference.

5. Select **O27** in the function's argument, and then click cell **N27** to replace the cell reference. The range reference now correctly includes only the gross sales for each month.

6. Press the **Enter** key to complete the formula. The formula results show 29,583, which is the monthly gross sales from the store on 411 Elm Drive in Madison, Wisconsin.

7. Select cell **P27**, and then change the alignment to **Top Align** so that the calculated value is aligned with the top of the cell.

8. Copy the formula in cell **P27**, and then paste the copied formula into the range **P28:P47**.

9. Select cell **P48** to deselect the range. As shown in Figure 2-23, the average monthly sales from all of the stores are $792,833. Individual stores have average monthly gross sales ranging from about $25,000 up to almost $55,000.

Figure 2-23   **AVERAGE function results**

average gross sales for each store per month

	F	G	H	I	J	K	L	M	N	O	P	Q	R
	42,000	44,000	44,000	47,000	48,000	47,000	48,000	44,000	46,000	526,000	43,833		
41													
42	33,000	32,000	37,000	37,000	38,000	35,000	33,000	35,000	33,000	399,000	33,250		
43	47,000	46,000	49,000	51,000	49,000	47,000	49,000	47,000	48,000	555,000	46,250		
44	53,000	55,000	56,000	56,000	59,000	54,000	55,000	51,000	53,000	632,000	52,667		
45	36,000	37,000	38,000	37,000	38,000	36,000	36,000	35,000	38,000	427,000	35,583		
46	53,000	56,000	55,000	59,000	58,000	56,000	58,000	53,000	57,000	650,000	54,167		
47	779,000	815,000	830,000	861,000	876,000	819,000	828,000	783,000	827,000	9,514,000	792,833		
48													

average gross sales for all stores per month

With the last formulas added to the worksheet, Sanjit wants you to continue formatting the workbook.

Applying Cell Styles

A workbook often contains several cells that store the same type of data. For example, each worksheet might have a cell displaying the sheet title, or a range of financial data might have several cells containing totals and averages. It is good design practice to apply the same format to worksheet cells that contain the same type of data.

One way to ensure that similar data is displayed consistently is with styles. A **style** is a collection of formatting options that include a specified font, font size, font styles, font color, fill color, and borders. The Cell Styles gallery includes a variety of built-in styles that you can use to format titles and headings, different types of data such as totals or calculations, and cells that you want to emphasize. For example, you can use the Heading 1 style to display sheet titles in a bold, blue-gray, 15-point Calibri font with no fill color and a blue bottom border. You can then apply the Heading 1 style to all titles in the workbook. If you later revise the style, the appearance of any cell formatted with that style is updated automatically. This saves you the time and effort of reformatting each cell individually.

You already used built-in styles when you formatted data in the Sales Report worksheet with the Accounting, Comma, and Percent styles. You can also create your own cell styles by clicking New Cell Style at the bottom of the Cell Styles gallery.

REFERENCE

Applying a Cell Style

- Select the cell or range to which you want to apply a style.
- On the HOME tab, in the Styles group, click the Cell Styles button.
- Point to each style in the Cell Styles gallery to see a Live Preview of that style on the selected cell or range.
- Click the style you want to apply to the selected cell or range.

Sanjit wants you to add more color and visual interest to the Sales Report worksheet. You'll use some of the styles in the Cell Styles gallery to do this.

To apply cell styles to the Sales Report worksheet:

1. Select cell **B4** containing the text "Sales Statistics."

2. On the HOME tab, in the Styles group, click the **Cell Styles** button. The Cell Styles gallery opens.

3. Point to the **Heading 1** style in the Titles and Headings section. Live Preview shows cell B4 in a 15-point, bold font with a solid blue bottom border. See Figure 2-24.

Figure 2-24   **Cell Styles gallery**

4. Move the pointer over different styles in the Cell Styles gallery to see cell B4 with a Live Preview of each style.

5. Click the **Title** style. The Title style is applied to cell B4.

6. Select the range **B5:F5** containing the column labels for the Sales Statistics data.

7. In the Styles group, click the **Cell Styles** button, and then click the **Accent3** style in the Themed Cell Styles section of the Cell Styles gallery.

8. Select cell **A25** containing the text "2015 Monthly Gross Sales," and then apply the **Title** cell style to the cell.

9. Select cell **A3**. See Figure 2-25.

Figure 2-25 Cell styles applied to the worksheet

Accent3 style applied to the range B5:F5

Title style applied to cell B4

Copying and Pasting Formats

Large workbooks often use the same formatting on similar data throughout the workbook, sometimes in widely scattered cells. Rather than repeating the same steps to format these cells, you can copy the format of one cell or range and paste it to another.

Copying Formats with the Format Painter

The Format Painter provides a fast and efficient way of copying and pasting formats, ensuring that a workbook has a consistent look and feel. The Format Painter does not copy formatting applied to selected text within a cell, and it does not copy data.

Sanjit wants the Sales Report worksheet to use the same formats you applied to the Big Red Wraps company name and slogan in the Documentation sheet. You will use the Format Painter to copy and paste the formats.

To use the Format Painter to copy and paste a format:

1. Go to the **Documentation** worksheet, and then select the range **A1:A2**.

2. On the HOME tab, in the Clipboard group, click the **Format Painter** button. The formats from the selected cells are copied to the Clipboard, and a flashing border appears around the selected range and the pointer changes to ✥🖌.

3. Return to the **Sales Report** worksheet, and then click cell **A1**. The formatting from the Documentation worksheet is removed from the Clipboard and applied to the range A1:A2. Notice that the larger font size you applied to the text "Big Flavor" was not included in the pasted formats.

4. Double-click cell **A2** to enter Edit mode, select **Big Flavor**, and then increase the font size to **14** points. The format for the slogan now matches the slogan on the Documentation sheet.

5. Select cell **A3** to exit Edit mode. See Figure 2-26.

TIP

To paste the same format multiple times, double-click the Format Painter button to leave the Format Painter on until you click the button again or press the Esc key.

Figure 2-26 Formats pasted in the Sales Report worksheet

- Format Painter button
- format copied from Documentation sheet

You can use the Format Painter to copy all of the formats within a selected range and then apply those formats to another range that has the same size and shape by clicking the upper-left cell of the range. Sanjit wants you to copy all of the formats you applied to the Sales Statistics data to the sales statistics per store.

TIP

If the range in which you paste the formats is bigger than the range you copied, Format Painter will repeat the copied formats to fill the pasted range.

To copy and paste multiple formats:

1. Select the range **B4:F12** in the Sales Report worksheet.
2. On the HOME tab, in the Clipboard group, click the **Format Painter** button.
3. Click cell **B14**. All of the number formats, cell borders, fonts, and fill colors are pasted into the range B14:F22.
4. Select the range **C23:E23**.
5. On the HOME tab, in the Number group, click the **Comma Style** button, and then click the **Decrease Decimal** button twice to remove the decimal places to the right of the decimal point. The numbers are vertically aligned in their columns.
6. Select cell **F23**.
7. In the Number group, click the **Percent Style** button to change the number to a percentage, and then click the **Increase Decimal** button twice to display two decimal places in the percentage.
8. Click cell **B24**. See Figure 2-27.

Tutorial 2 Formatting Workbook Text and Data | Excel   EX 103

Figure 2-27 Formats pasted from a range

	A	B	C	D	E	F	G	H
6		Gross Sales	$ 9,514,000	$ 8,424,000	$ 1,090,000	12.94%		
7		Cost of Sales	3,374,000	2,784,000	590,000	21.19%		
8		Operating Expenses	5,032,000	4,376,000	656,000	14.99%		
9		Net Profit/Loss	1,108,000	1,264,000	(156,000)	-12.34%		
10								
11		Units Sold	1,344,000	1,104,000	240,000	21.74%		
12		Customers Served	155,400	129,600	25,800	19.91%		
13								
14		Sales Statistics per Store						
15		Category	2015	2014	Net Change	% Change		
16		Gross Sales	$ 475,700	$ 526,500	$ (50,800)	-9.65%		
17		Cost of Sales	168,700	174,000	(5,300)	-3.05%		
18		Operating Expenses	251,600	273,500	(21,900)	-8.01%		
19		Net Profit/Loss	55,400	79,000	(23,600)	-29.87%		
20								
21		Units Sold	67,200	69,000	(1,800)	-2.61%		
22		Customers Served	7,770	8,100	(330)	-4.07%		
23		Stores	20	16	4	25.00%		
24								

- copied formats
- pasted formats

Copying Formats with the Paste Options Button

Another way to copy and paste formats is with the Paste Options button [icon] (Ctrl)▼, which provides options for pasting only values, only formats, or some combination of values and formats. Each time you paste, the Paste Options button appears in the lower-right corner of the pasted cell or range. You click the Paste Options button to open a list of pasting options, shown in Figure 2-28, such as pasting only the values or only the formatting. You can also click the Transpose button to paste the column data into a row, or to paste the row data into a column.

Figure 2-28 Paste Options button

- options to paste formulas and borders with or without formatting
- Transpose button
- options to paste values with or without formatting
- options to paste hypertext links, pictures, and formats only
- button appears in the lower-left corner of the pasted range

Copying Formats with Paste Special

The Paste Special command provides another way to control what you paste from the Clipboard. To use Paste Special, select and copy a range, select the range where you want to paste the Clipboard contents, click the Paste button arrow in the Clipboard group on the HOME tab, and then click Paste Special to open the dialog box shown in Figure 2-29.

Figure 2-29   **Paste Special dialog box**

specifies what to paste

applies the specified arithmetic operation to the copied value

avoids pasting into empty cells

pastes column data into a row or row data into a column

From the Paste Special dialog box, you can control exactly how to paste the copied range.

Finding and Replacing Text and Formats

The Find and Replace commands let you make content and design changes to a worksheet or the entire workbook quickly. The Find command searches through the current worksheet or workbook for the content or formatting you want to locate, and the Replace command then substitutes it with the new content or formatting you specify.

Sanjit wants you to replace all the street title abbreviations (such as Ave.) in the Sales Report with their full names (such as Avenue). You will use Find and Replace to make these changes.

To find and replace the street title abbreviations:

1. On the HOME tab, in the Editing group, click the **Find & Select** button, and then click **Replace** (or press the **Ctrl+H** keys). The Find and Replace dialog box opens.

2. Type **Ave.** in the Find what box.

3. Press the **Tab** key to move the insertion point to the Replace with box, and then type **Avenue**. See Figure 2-30.

Tutorial 2 Formatting Workbook Text and Data | Excel   EX 105

Figure 2-30 **Find and Replace dialog box**

[Figure 2-30: Find and Replace dialog box with callouts — search text (Find what: Ave.), replacement text (Replace with: Avenue), highlights all occurrences, locates the next occurrence, replaces every occurrence (Replace All), replaces the current occurrence (Replace)]

You can choose to find each occurrence of the search text one at a time and decide whether to replace it. You can choose to highlight all occurrences of the search text in the worksheet. Or, you can choose to replace all occurrences at once without reviewing them. In this case, you want to replace every occurrence of the search text with the replacement text.

▶ 4. Click the **Replace All** button to replace all occurrences of the search text without reviewing them. A dialog box opens, reporting that three replacements were made in the worksheet.

▶ 5. Click the **OK** button to return to the Find and Replace dialog box.

Next, you will replace the other street title abbreviations.

▶ 6. Repeat Steps 2 through 5 to replace all occurrences of each of the following: **St.** with **Street**, **Ln.** with **Lane**, **Dr.** with **Drive**, and **Rd.** with **Road**.

▶ 7. Click the **Close** button to close the Find and Replace dialog box.

▶ 8. Scroll through the Sales Report worksheet to verify that all street title abbreviations were replaced with their full names.

The Find and Replace dialog box can also be used to replace one format with another or to replace both text and a format simultaneously. Sanjit wants you to replace all occurrences of the white text in the Sales Report worksheet with light yellow text. You'll use the Find and Replace dialog box to make this formatting change.

To replace white text with yellow text:

▶ 1. On the HOME tab, in the Editing group, click the **Find & Select** button, and then click **Replace** (or press the **Ctrl+H** keys). The Find and Replace dialog box opens.

▶ 2. Click the **Options** button to expand the dialog box.

▶ 3. Click the **Format** button in the Find what row to open the Find Format dialog box, which is similar to the Format Cells dialog box you used earlier to format a range.

▶ 4. Click the **Font** tab to make it active, click the **Color** box, and then click the **White, Background 1** theme color.

▶ 5. Click the **OK** button to close the dialog box and return to the Find and Replace dialog box.

▶ 6. Click the **Format** button in the Replace with row to open the Replace Format dialog box.

7. Click the **Color** box, and then click the **Yellow** standard color.
8. Click the **OK** button to close the dialog box and return to the Find and Replace dialog box. See Figure 2-31.

Figure 2-31   Expanded Find and Replace dialog box

limits the search to the current worksheet
search format
replacement format
shows or hides the additional options

9. Verify that the Within box lists **Sheet** to limit the search to the current worksheet.
10. Click the **Replace All** button to replace all occurrences of white text in the Sales Report worksheet with yellow text. A dialog box appears, reporting that 32 replacements were made.
11. Click the **OK** button to return to the Find and Replace dialog box.

    It is a good idea to clear the find and replace formats after you are done so that they won't affect any future searches and replacements. You'll remove the formats from the Find and Replace dialog box.

12. Click the **Format button arrow** in the Find what row, and then click **Clear Find Format**. The search format is removed.
13. Click the **Format button arrow** in the Replace with row, and then click **Clear Replace Format**. The replacement format is removed.
14. Click the **Close** button to return to the worksheet. Notice that every cell in the worksheet that had white text now has yellow text.

Working with Themes

Recall that a theme is a coordinated selection of fonts, colors, and graphical effects that are applied throughout a workbook to create a specific look and feel. When you switch to a different theme, the theme-related fonts, colors, and effects change throughout the workbook to reflect the new theme. The appearance of non-theme fonts, colors, and effects remains unchanged no matter which theme is applied to the workbook.

Most of the formatting you have applied to the Sales Report workbook is based on the Office theme. Sanjit wants you to change the theme to see how it affects the workbook's appearance.

Tutorial 2 Formatting Workbook Text and Data | Excel   EX 107

To change the workbook's theme:

1. Click the **PAGE LAYOUT** tab on the ribbon.
2. In the Themes group, click the **Themes** button. The Themes gallery opens. Office—the current theme—is the default.
3. Point to the **Organic** theme in the Themes gallery. Live Preview shows how the appearance of the Sales Report worksheet will change if you select the Organic theme. See Figure 2-32.

Figure 2-32 Live Preview of the Organic theme

4. Point to several other themes in the Themes gallery to see how the worksheet appearance would change.
5. Click the **Wisp** theme to apply that theme to the workbook.

Changing the theme made a significant difference in the worksheet's appearance. The most obvious changes to the worksheet are the fill colors and the fonts. Only formatting options directly tied to a theme change when you select a different theme. Any formatting options you selected that were not theme-based remain unaffected by the change. For example, the yellow standard color you just applied to the different column labels is still yellow, even with the Wisp theme applied, because yellow is not a theme color. For the same reason, the red fill color used in the column labels of the monthly sales table remains unchanged under the new theme.

Sanjit informs you that Big Red Wraps requires all documents to be formatted with the Office theme. You will reapply the Office theme to the workbook.

To reapply the Office theme to the workbook:

▶ 1. On the PAGE LAYOUT tab, in the Themes group, click the **Themes** button, and then click the **Office** theme from the gallery of themes.

The workbook now complies with the company's standard formatting.

INSIGHT

Sharing Styles and Themes

Using a consistent look and feel for all the files you create in Microsoft Office is a simple way to project a professional image. This consistency is especially important when a team is collaborating on a set of documents. When all team members work from a common set of style and design themes, readers will not be distracted by inconsistent or clashing formatting.

To quickly copy the styles from one workbook to another, open the workbook with the styles you want to copy, and then open the workbook in which you want to copy those styles. On the HOME tab, in the Styles group, click the Cell Styles button, and then click Merge Styles. The Merge Styles dialog box opens, listing the currently open workbooks. Select the workbook with the styles you want to copy, and then click the OK button to copy those styles into the current workbook. If you modify any styles, you must copy the styles to the other workbook; Excel does not update styles between workbooks.

Because other Office files, including those created with Word or PowerPoint, use the same file format for themes, you can create one theme to use with all of your Office files. To save a theme, click the Themes button in the Themes group on the PAGE LAYOUT tab, and then click Save Current Theme. The Save Current Theme dialog box opens. Select a save location (in a default Theme folder on your computer or another folder), type a descriptive name in the File name box, and then click the Save button. If you saved the theme file in a default Theme folder, the theme appears in the Themes gallery, and any changes made to the theme are reflected in any Office file that uses that theme.

Highlighting Cells with Conditional Formats

Conditional formats are often used to help analyze data. A **conditional format** applies formatting to a cell when its value meets a specified condition. For example, a conditional format can be used to format negative numbers in red and positive numbers in black. Conditional formats are dynamic, which means that the formatting can change when the cell's value changes. Each conditional format has a set of rules that define how the formatting should be applied and under what conditions the format will be changed.

REFERENCE

Highlighting Cells with a Conditional Format

- Select the range in which you want to highlight cells.
- On the HOME tab, in the Styles group, click the Conditional Formatting button, point to Highlight Cells Rules or Top/Bottom Rules, and then click the appropriate rule.
- Select the appropriate options in the dialog box.
- Click the OK button.

Excel has four conditional formats—data bars, highlighting, color scales, and icon sets. In this tutorial, you will apply cell highlighting, which changes the cell's font color or fill color based on the cell's value, as described in Figure 2-33. You can enter a value or a cell reference if you want to compare other cells with the value in a certain cell.

Figure 2-33 | **Highlight Cells rules**

Rule	Highlights Cell Values
Greater Than	Greater than a specified number
Less Than	Less than a specified number
Between	Between two specified numbers
Equal To	Equal to a specified number
Text that Contains	That contain specified text
A Date Occurring	That contain a specified date
Duplicate Values	That contain duplicate or unique values

© 2014 Cengage Learning

Highlighting Cells Based on Their Values

Sanjit wants to highlight important trends and sales values in the Sales Report worksheet. He wants you to use a conditional format to display sales statistics that showed a negative net or percent change in a red font so that they stand out. You will do this by creating a rule to format the cells in ranges E6:F12 and E16:F22 with numbers that are less than 0.

To highlight negative numbers in red:

1. Select the nonadjacent range **E6:F12;E16:F22** in the Sales Report worksheet.
2. On the ribbon, click the **HOME** tab.
3. In the Styles group, click the **Conditional Formatting** button, and then point to **Highlight Cells Rules** to display a menu of the available rules.
4. Click **Less Than**. The Less Than dialog box opens so you can select the value and formatting to highlight negative values.
5. Type **0** (a zero) in the Format cells that are LESS THAN box, click the **with** arrow, and then click **Red Text**. Live Preview shows that the rule formats any cells in the selected range that have a negative value in a red font. See Figure 2-34.

Figure 2-34   Live Preview of the Less Than conditional format

6. Click the **OK** button to apply the highlighting rule. You will verify that this format is conditional.

7. In cell D8, enter **4,576,000** to change the Operating Expenses value. The now positive values in cells E9 and F9 are formatted in a black font.

8. Press the **Ctrl+Z** keys to return the value in cell D8 to 4,376,000. The values in cells E9 and F9 are again negative and in a red font.

The highlighted values show at a glance that Big Red Wraps' gross sales, units sold, and customers served increased from 2014 to 2015, while the company's net profit declined during the same period. The average gross sales per store also declined in 2015. Big Red Wraps opened four new stores in 2015, and Sanjit will argue that the cost of this expansion and low sales from the new stores caused this apparent decline.

Highlighting Cells with a Top/Bottom Rule

Another way of applying conditional formats is with the Quick Analysis tool. The **Quick Analysis tool**, which appears whenever you select a range of cells, provides access to the most common tools for data analysis and formatting. The FORMATTING category includes buttons for the Greater Than and Top 10% conditional formatting rules. You can highlight cells based on their values in comparison to other cells. For example, you can highlight cells with the 10 highest or lowest values in a selected range, or you can highlight the cells with above-average values in a range.

Tutorial 2 Formatting Workbook Text and Data | Excel   EX 111

Sanjit wants you to highlight the five stores in the Big Red Wraps chain that had the highest gross sales in the last fiscal year. You will use a Top/Bottom rule to do this.

To use a Top/Bottom Rule to highlight the stores with the highest gross sales:

1. Select the range **P27:P46** containing the average monthly gross sales for each of the 20 Big Red Wraps stores. The Quick Analysis button appears in the lower-right corner of the selected range.

2. Click the **Quick Analysis** button, and then point to **Top 10%**. Live Preview colors the cells in the top 10 percent with red font and a red fill. See Figure 2-35.

Figure 2-35   Quick Analysis tool

Sanjit wants to see the top five items rather than the cells with values in the top 10 percent, so you won't apply this conditional formatting.

3. Press the **Esc** key to close the Quick Analysis tool. The range P27:P46 remains selected.

4. On the HOME tab, in the Styles group, click the **Conditional Formatting** button, and then point to **Top/Bottom Rules** to display a menu of available rules.

5. Click **Top 10 Items** to open the Top 10 Items dialog box.

6. Click the down arrow on the spin box five times to change the value from 10 to 5. This specifies that the top five values in the selected range will be formatted.

7. Click the **with** arrow, and then click **Green Fill with Dark Green Text** to specify the formatting to apply to the five cells with the top values. Live Preview highlights the top five stores in terms of gross sales. See Figure 2-36.

Figure 2-36 Live Preview of the top five selling stores

	F	G	H	I	J	K	L	M	N	O	P	Q
42	33,000	32,000	37,000	37,000	38,000	35,000	33,000	35,000	33,000	399,000	33,250	
43	47,000	46,000	49,000				49,000	47,000	48,000	555,000	46,250	
44			56,000				55,000	51,000	53,000	632,000	52,667	
45	36,000	37,000	38,000				36,000	35,000	38,000	427,000	35,583	
46	53,000	56,000	55,000	59,000	58,000	56,000	58,000	53,000	57,000	650,000	54,167	
47	779,000	815,000	830,000	861,000	876,000	819,000	828,000	783,000	827,000	9,514,000	792,833	

- displays the five largest values
- Top 10 Items dialog: Format cells that rank in the TOP: 5 with Green Fill with Dark Green Text
- formats cells that meet the criteria in a dark green font on a light green background
- two of the five top sellers at Big Red Wraps

▸ 8. Click the **OK** button to accept the conditional formatting.

The Top/Bottom rule highlights the average monthly gross sales for the five top-selling stores: the North Street store in Madison, Wisconsin; the South Drive store in Janesville, Wisconsin; the Main Street store in Des Moines, Iowa; the Business Drive store in Manhattan, Kansas; and the Causeway Drive store in Salina, Kansas.

Clearing a Conditional Format

You can remove a conditional format at any time without affecting the underlying data by selecting the range containing the conditional format, clicking the Conditional Formatting button, and then clicking the Clear Rules button. A menu opens, providing options to clear the conditional formatting rules from the selected cells or the entire worksheet. You can also click the Quick Analysis button that appears in the lower-right corner of the selected range, and then click the Clear Format button in the FORMATTING category.

Creating a Conditional Formatting Legend

When you use conditional formatting to highlight cells in a worksheet, the purpose of the formatting is not always immediately apparent. To ensure that everyone knows why certain cells are highlighted, you should include a **legend**, which is a key that identifies each color and its meaning.

You will add a legend to the Sales Report worksheet to document the Top 5 highlighting rule you just created.

To create a conditional formatting legend:

▸ 1. Select cell **P49**, type **light green**, and then press the **Enter** key. You will use a highlight rule to fill this cell with a dark green font on a light green fill.

▸ 2. Select cell **P49** to make it the active cell.

▸ 3. On the HOME tab, in the Styles group, click the **Conditional Formatting** button, point to **Highlight Cells Rules**, and then click **Text that Contains**. The Text That Contains dialog box opens.

Tutorial 2 Formatting Workbook Text and Data | Excel   EX 113

▶ 4. Verify that **light green** appears in the Format cells that contain the text box. The box shows the text entered in the selected cell.

▶ 5. Click the **with** arrow, and then click **Green Fill with Dark Green Text** to format cell P49 with the same format used for the top five gross sales.

▶ 6. Click the **OK** button. Cell P49 remains selected.

▶ 7. In the Alignment group, click the **Center** button to center the text in the cell.

▶ 8. In cell O49, enter **Top 5 Stores** to identify the format's purpose, and then select cell **O49**.

▶ 9. In the Styles group, click the **Cell Styles** button, and then click the **Explanatory Text** style (the third style in the first row of the Data and Model section). The cell style is applied to the selected cell.

▶ 10. Click cell **O51**. The legend is complete, as shown in Figure 2-37.

Figure 2-37   **Conditional formatting legend**

45											
46	53,000	56,000	55,000	59,000	58,000	56,000	58,000	53,000	57,000	650,000	54,167
47	779,000	815,000	830,000	861,000	876,000	819,000	828,000	783,000	827,000	9,514,000	792,833
48											
49										Top 5 Stores	light green
50											
51											
52				legend explains the							
53				purpose of the formatting							

The conditional formatting makes the top-selling stores stand out.

Written Communication: Using Conditional Formatting Effectively

Conditional formatting is an excellent way to highlight important trends and data values to clients and colleagues. However, be sure to use it judiciously. Overusing conditional formatting might obscure the very data you want to emphasize. Keep in mind the following tips as you make decisions about what to highlight and how it should be highlighted:

- **Document the conditional formats you use.** If a bold, green font means that a sales number is in the top 10 percent of all sales, include that information in a legend in the worksheet.
- **Don't clutter data with too much highlighting.** Limit highlighting rules to one or two per data set. Highlights are designed to draw attention to points of interest. If you use too many, you will end up highlighting everything—and, therefore, nothing.
- **Use color sparingly in worksheets with highlights.** It is difficult to tell a highlight color from a regular fill color, especially when fill colors are used in every cell.
- **Consider alternatives to conditional formats.** If you want to highlight the top 10 sales regions, it might be more effective to simply sort the data with the best-selling regions at the top of the list.

Remember that the goal of highlighting is to provide a strong visual clue to important data or results. Careful use of conditional formatting helps readers to focus on the important points you want to make rather than distracting them with secondary issues and facts.

Formatting a Worksheet for Printing

You should format any worksheets you plan to print so that they are easy to read and understand. You can do this using the print settings, which enable you to set the page orientation, the print area, page breaks, print titles, and headers and footers. Print settings can be applied to an entire workbook or to individual sheets. Because other people will likely see your printed worksheets, you should format the printed output as carefully as you format the electronic version. Sanjit wants you to format the Sales Report worksheet so he can distribute the printed version at the upcoming sales conference.

Using Page Break Preview

Page Break Preview shows only those parts of the active sheet that will print and how the content will be split across pages. A dotted blue border indicates a page break, which separates one page from another. As you format the worksheet for printing, you can use this view to control what content appears on each page.

Sanjit wants to know how the Sales Report worksheet would print in portrait orientation and how many pages would be required. You will look at the worksheet in Page Break Preview to find these answers.

To view the Sales Report worksheet in Page Break Preview:

1. Click the **Page Break Preview** button on the status bar. The worksheet switches to Page Break Preview.

2. Change the zoom level of the worksheet to **30%** so you can view the entire contents of this large worksheet. See Figure 2-38.

Figure 2-38   **Sales Report worksheet in Page Break Preview**

> **Trouble?** If you see a different page layout or the worksheet is split onto a different number of pages, don't worry. Each printer is different, so the layout and pages might differ from what is shown in Figure 2-38.

Page Break Preview shows that a printout of the Sales Report worksheet requires six pages in portrait orientation, and that pages 3 and 5 would be mostly blank. Note that each printer is different, so your Page Break Preview might show a different number of pages. With this layout, each page would be difficult to interpret because the data is separated from the descriptive labels. Sanjit wants you to fix the layout so that the contents are easier to read and understand.

Defining the Print Area

By default, all cells in a worksheet containing text, formulas, or values are printed. If you want to print only part of a worksheet, you can set a print area, which is the region of the worksheet that is sent to the printer. Each worksheet has its own print area. Although you can set the print area in any view, Page Break Preview shades the areas of the worksheet that are not included in the print area, making it simple to confirm what will print.

Sanjit doesn't want the empty cells in the range G1:O24 to print, so you will set the print area to eliminate those cells.

To set the print area of the Sales Report worksheet:

1. Change the zoom level of the worksheet to **80%** to make it easier to select cells and ranges.

2. Select the nonadjacent range **A1:F24;A25:P49** containing the cells with content.

3. On the ribbon, click the **PAGE LAYOUT** tab.

4. In the Page Setup group, click the **Print Area** button, and then click **Set Print Area**. The print area changes to cover only the nonadjacent range A1:F24;A25:P49. The rest of the worksheet content is shaded to indicate that it will not be part of the printout.

5. Select cell **A1** to deselect the range.

6. Change the zoom level to **50%** so you can view more of the worksheet. See Figure 2-39.

Figure 2-39   Print area set for the Sales Report worksheet

- range A1:F24 prints on its own page
- print area covers the nonadjacent range A1:F24;A25:P49
- solid line indicates a manual page break
- dotted lines indicate automatic page breaks

Inserting Page Breaks

Often, the contents of a worksheet will not fit onto a single printed page. When this happens, Excel prints as much of the content that fits on a single page without resizing, and then inserts automatic page breaks to continue printing the remaining worksheet content on successive pages. The resulting printouts might split worksheet content in awkward places, such as within a table of data.

To split the printout into logical segments, you can insert manual page breaks. Page Break Preview identifies manual page breaks with a solid blue line and automatic page breaks with a dotted blue line. When you specify a print area for a nonadjacent range, as you did for the Sales Report worksheet, you also insert manual page breaks around the adjacent ranges. So a manual page break already appears in the print area you defined (see Figure 2-39). You can remove a page break in Page Break Preview by dragging it out of the print area.

TIP

When you remove a page break, Excel will automatically rescale the printout to fit into the allotted pages.

REFERENCE

Inserting and Removing Page Breaks

To insert a page break:
- Click the first cell below the row where you want to insert a page break, click a column heading, or click a row heading.
- On the PAGE LAYOUT tab, in the Page Setup group, click the Breaks button, and then click Insert Page Break.

To remove a page break:
- Select any cell below or to the right of the page break you want to remove.
- On the PAGE LAYOUT tab, in the Page Setup group, click the Breaks button, and then click Remove Page Break.

or

- In Page Break Preview, drag the page break line out of the print area.

Tutorial 2 Formatting Workbook Text and Data | Excel EX 117

The Sales Report worksheet has automatic page breaks along columns F and L. You will remove these automatic page breaks from the Sales Report worksheet.

To remove the automatic page breaks and insert manual page breaks:

1. Point to the dotted blue page break directly to the right of column L until the pointer changes to ↔.

2. Drag the page break to the right and out of the print area. The page break is removed from the worksheet.

3. Point to the page break located in cell F31 until the pointer changes to ↔, and then drag the page break to the right and out of the print area.

   On the PAGE LAYOUT tab, in the Scale to Fit section, notice that the Scale box shows 43%. After removing the two page breaks from the Sales Report printout, Excel scaled the printout from 100% of its actual size to 43% to fit the printout onto two pages.

4. Click the **column I** heading to select the entire column. You will add a manual page break between columns H and I to split the monthly gross sales data onto two pages so the printout will be larger and easier to read.

5. On the PAGE LAYOUT tab, in the Page Setup group, click the **Breaks** button, and then click **Insert Page Break**. A manual page break is added between columns H and I, forcing the monthly gross sales onto a new page after the June data.

6. Select cell **A1** to deselect the column. The printout of the Sales Report worksheet is now limited to three pages. However, the gross sales data in the range A25:O49 is split across pages. See Figure 2-40.

Figure 2-40 Manual page break added to the print area

manual page break splits the data onto two pages

Adding Print Titles

It is a good practice to include descriptive information such as the company name, logo, and worksheet title on each page of a printout in case a page becomes separated from the other pages. You can repeat information, such as the company name, by specifying which rows or columns in the worksheet act as print titles. If a worksheet contains a large table, you can print the table's column headings and row headings on every page of the printout by designating those columns and rows as print titles.

In the Sales Report worksheet, the company name and slogan currently appear on the first page of the printout, but do not appear on subsequent pages. Also, the descriptive row labels for the monthly sales table in column A do not appear on the third page of the printout. You will add print titles to fix these issues.

To set the print titles:

1. On the PAGE LAYOUT tab, in the Page Setup group, click the **Print Titles** button. The Page Setup dialog box opens with the Sheet tab displayed.

2. In the Print titles section, click the **Rows to repeat at top** box, move the pointer over the worksheet, and then select the range **A1:A2**. A flashing border appears around the first two rows of the worksheet to indicate that the contents of the first two rows will be repeated on each page of the printout. The row reference $1:$2 appears in the Rows to repeat at top box.

3. Click the **Columns to repeat at left** box, and then select columns A and B from the worksheet. The column reference $A:$B appears in the Columns to repeat at left box. See Figure 2-41.

> **TIP**
> You can also open the Page Setup dialog box by clicking the Dialog Box Launcher in the Page Setup group on the PAGE LAYOUT tab.

Figure 2-41 Sheet tab in the Page Setup dialog box

4. Click the **Page** tab in the Page Setup dialog box. You will rescale the worksheet so that it doesn't appear too small in the printout.

5. In the Scaling section, change the Adjust to amount to **65%** of normal size.

6. Click the **Print Preview** button to preview the three pages of printed material on the Print screen in Backstage view.

7. Verify that each of the three pages has the Big Red Wraps title and slogan at the top of the page, and that the state and store names appear in the leftmost columns of pages 2 and 3. See Figure 2-42.

Figure 2-42 Print titles on page 3 of the Sales Report worksheet

- first two rows repeat on every page
- link opens the Page Setup dialog box
- first two columns repeat on every page

Trouble? If your printout doesn't fit on three pages, reduce the scaling factor from 65% to a slightly lower percentage until it does fit on three pages.

Creating Headers and Footers

You can also use headers and footers to repeat information on each printed page. A **header** appears at the top of each printed page; a **footer** appears at the bottom of each printed page. Headers and footers contain helpful and descriptive text that is usually not found within the worksheet, such as the workbook's author, the current date, or the workbook's filename. If the printout spans multiple pages, you can display the page number and the total number of pages in the printout to help ensure you and others have all the pages.

Each header and footer has three sections—a left section, a center section, and a right section. Within each section, you type the text you want to appear, or you insert elements such as the worksheet name or the current date and time. These header and footer elements are dynamic; if you rename the worksheet, for example, the name is automatically updated in the header or footer. Also, you can create one set of headers and footers for even and odd pages, and you can create another set for the first page in the printout.

Sanjit wants the printout to display the workbook's filename in the header's left section, and the current date in the header's right section. He wants the center footer to display the page number and the total number of pages in the printout, and the right footer to display your name as the workbook's author.

To create the header and footer:

1. Click the **Page Setup** link near the bottom of the Print screen to open the Page Setup dialog box.

2. Click the **Header/Footer** tab to display the header and footer options.

3. Click the **Different first page** check box to select it. This lets you create one set of headers and footers for the first page, and one set for the rest of the pages. See Figure 2-43.

Figure 2-43   Header/Footer tab in the Page Setup dialog box

when selected, displays a different header and footer for even- and odd-numbered pages

displays a different header or footer for the first page

4. Click the **Custom Header** button to open the Header dialog box. The dialog box contains two tabs—Header and First Page Header—because you selected the Different first page option.

5. On the Header tab, type **Filename:** in the Left section box, press the **spacebar**, and then click the **Insert File Name** button. The code &[File], which displays the filename of the current workbook, is added to the left section of the header.

TIP

You can create or edit headers and footers in Page Layout view by clicking in the header/footer section and using the tools on the DESIGN tab.

6. Press the **Tab** key twice to move to the right section of the header, and then click the **Insert Current Date** button. The code &[Date] is added to the right section of the header. See Figure 2-44.

Figure 2-44   Header dialog box

inserts the current date

inserts the workbook's filename

code to print the workbook's filename

code to print the current date

7. Click the **OK** button to return to the Header/Footer tab in the Page Setup dialog box. You did not define a header for the first page of the printout, so no header information will be added to that page.

Tutorial 2 Formatting Workbook Text and Data | Excel   EX 121

Now you will format the page footer for all pages of the printout.

8. Click the **Custom Footer** button to open the Footer dialog box, which is similar to the Header dialog box.

9. Click the **Center section** box, type **Page**, press the **spacebar**, and then click the **Insert Page Number** button. The code &[Page], which inserts the current page number, appears after the label "Page."

10. Press the **spacebar**, type **of**, press the **spacebar**, and then click the **Insert Number of Pages** button. The code &[Pages], which inserts the total number of pages in the printout, is added to the Center section box. See Figure 2-45.

Figure 2-45 Footer dialog box

click to set footer options for the first page

inserts the total number of pages

inserts the page number

prints the current page number out of the total page count

Center section: Page &[Page] of &[Pages]

11. Click the **First Page Footer** tab so you can create the footer for the first page of the printout.

12. Click the **Right section** box, type **Prepared by:**, press the **spacebar**, and then type your name.

13. Click the **OK** button to return to the Page Setup dialog box.

Setting the Page Margins

A **margin** is the space between the page content and the edges of the page. By default, Excel sets the page margins to 0.7 inch on the left and right sides, and 0.75 inch on the top and bottom; and it allows for 0.3-inch margins around the header and footer. You can reduce or increase these margins as needed by selecting predefined margin sizes or setting your own.

Sanjit's reports need a wider margin along the left side of the page to accommodate the binding. He asks you to increase the left margin for the printout from 0.7 inch to 1 inch.

To set the left margin:

1. Click the **Margins** tab in the Page Setup dialog box to display options for changing the page margins.

2. Double-click the **Left** box to select the setting, and then type **1** to increase the size of the left margin. See Figure 2-46.

> **TIP**
> To select preset margins, click the Margins button in the Page Setup group on the PAGE LAYOUT tab.

EX 122   Excel | Tutorial 2 Formatting Workbook Text and Data

Figure 2-46   **Margins tab in the Page Setup dialog box**

sets the size of individual page margins

centers the workbook contents horizontally or vertically on the printout

3. Click the **OK** button to close the dialog box and return to the worksheet.

Sanjit is happy with the appearance of the worksheet and the layout of the printout. You'll save the workbook, and then print the Documentation and Sales Report sheets.

To save and print the workbook:

1. Return the Sales Report worksheet to **Normal** view, and then save the workbook.
2. Display the Print screen in Backstage view, and then change the first Settings box to **Print Entire Workbook**. Both the Sales Report worksheet and the Documentation sheet appear in the preview. As you can see, the printout will include a header with the filename and date on every page except the first page, and a footer with your name on the first page and the page number along with the total number of pages on subsequent pages.
3. If you are instructed to print, print the entire workbook, and then close it.

Session 2.2 Quick Check

REVIEW

1. Describe two methods of applying the same format to different ranges.
2. Red is a standard color. What happens to red text when you change the workbook's theme?
3. What is a conditional format?
4. How would you highlight the top five values in the range A1:C20?
5. How do you insert a manual page break in a worksheet?
6. What is a print area?
7. What are print titles?
8. Describe how to add the workbook filename to the center section of the footer on every page of the printout.

SAM Projects

Put your skills into practice with SAM Projects! SAM Projects for this tutorial can be found online. If you have a SAM account, go to www.cengage.com/sam2013 to download the most recent Project Instructions and Start Files.

Review Assignments

Data Files needed for the Review Assignments: Menu.xlsx, Background2.png

Sanjit has a worksheet that details the sales of individual items from the Big Red Wraps menu. He asks you to format the sales figures and design a layout for the printed sheet as you did for the Sales Report workbook. Complete the following:

1. Open the **Menu** workbook located in the Excel2 ▸ Review folder included with your Data Files, and then save the workbook as **Menu Sales** in the location specified by your instructor.
2. In the Documentation sheet, enter your name in cell B4 and the date in cell B5.
3. Make the following formatting changes to the Documentation sheet:
    a. Set the background image to the **Background2.png** file located in the Excel2 ▸ Review folder.
    b. Format the text in cell A1 in red 26-point bold Calibri Light.
    c. Format the text in cell A2 to red 10-point italic Calibri Light. Change the text string "Big Flavor" to 14 points.
    d. Apply the Accent2 cell style to the range A4:A6.
    e. Change the font color of range B4:B6 to red and change its fill color to white.
    f. Format the date in the Long Date format and left-align the cell contents.
4. Use the Format Painter to copy the formatting in the range A1:A2 in the Documentation sheet and paste it to the same range in the Menu Sales worksheet. (*Hint*: You must increase the size of the text "Big Flavor" manually.)
5. Apply the Title cell style to the titles in cells B4, B12, and A20.
6. Make the following changes to the Units Sold table in the range B5:F10:
    a. In cell C6, calculate the total number of wraps sold by the company (found in the range C22:N31). In cell C7, calculate the total number of soups. In cell C8, calculate the total number of sides. In cell C9, calculate the total number of salads.
    b. In cell C10, calculate the sum of the range C6:C9. Copy the formula to cell D10.
    c. In the range E6:E10, calculate the difference between the 2015 and 2014 values. In the range F6:F10, calculate the percent change from 2014 to 2015.
    d. Apply the Accent2 cell style to the headings in the range B5:F5. Center the headings in the range C5:F5.
    e. Apply the Comma style to the values in the range C6:E10. Do not display any numbers to the right of the decimal point.
    f. Apply the Percent style to the values in the range F6:F10 and show two decimal places.
    g. Add a top border to the values in the range B10:F10.
7. Make the following changes to the range B13:F18:
    a. In cells C18 and D18, calculate the totals of the 2014 and 2015 sales. In the range E14:F18, calculate the change in sales and the percent change.
    b. Copy the format from the range B5:F10 and paste it into the range B13:F18.
    c. Change the format for the values in the ranges C14:E14 and C18:E18 to Accounting format with no decimal places.

8. Make the following changes to the Units Sold per Month table in the range A21:O46:
   a. In the range O22:O45, calculate the total units sold for each menu item. In the range C46:O46, calculate the total items sold per month and overall.
   b. Format the headings in the range A21:O21 with the Accent2 cell style. Center the headings in the range C21:O21.
   c. Format the units sold values in the range C22:O46 with the Comma style and no decimal places.
   d. Change the fill color of the subtotals in the range O22:O45 and C46:N46 to White, Background 1, Darker 15% (the first color in the third row of the theme colors).
   e. Merge each of the menu categories in the range A22:A45 into single cells. Rotate the text of the cells up. Increase the font size to 18 points and middle-align the cell contents.
   f. Format cell A22 with the "Wraps" label in a white font on a Gray-25%, Background 2, Darker 50% fill. Format cell A32 with the "Soups" label in a white font on Blue, Accent 1, Darker 25% fill. Format of cell A37 with the "Sides" label in a white font on a Gold, Accent 4, Darker 25% fill. Format cell A42 with the "Salads" label in a white font on a Green, Accent 6, Darker 25% fill.
   g. Add a thick box border around each category of menu item in the ranges A22:O31, A32:O36, A37:O41, and A42:O45.
9. Create a conditional format for the subtotals in the range O22:O45 highlighting the top five selling items with a yellow fill and dark yellow text.
10. Create a legend for the conditional format. Enter the text **Top 5 Sellers** in cell O48. Add a thick box border around the cell, and then use a conditional format that displays this text in dark yellow text on a yellow fill.
11. Set the following print formats for the Menu Sales worksheet:
    a. Set the print area to the nonadjacent range A1:F19;A20:O48.
    b. Remove any automatic page breaks in the large Units Sold table. Insert a manual page break to separate the June and July sales figures. The printout of the Menu Sales worksheet should fit on three pages.
    c. Scale the printout to 70 percent of normal size.
    d. Define the print titles to repeat the first three rows at the top of the sheet, and the first two columns at the left of the sheet.
    e. Increase the left margin of the printout from 0.7 inch to 1 inch.
    f. Create headers and footers for the printout with a different header for the first page.
    g. For the first page header, print **Prepared by** *your name* in the right section. For every other page, print **Filename:** *file* in the left section and *date* in the right section, where *file* is the name of the workbook file and *date* is the current date. (*Hint*: Use the buttons in the Header dialog box to insert the filename and date.)
    h. For every footer, print **Page** *page* **of** *pages* in the center section, where *page* is the page number and *pages* is the total number of pages in the printout.
12. If you are instructed to print, print the entire workbook in portrait orientation. Verify that the company name and slogan appear on every page of the Menu Sales worksheet printout, and that the menu category and menu item name appear on both pages with the Units Sold table.
13. Save and close the workbook.

Case Problem 1

Data File needed for this Case Problem: Salon.xlsx

Special Highlights Hair Salon Sarah Jones is developing a business plan for a new hair salon, Special Highlights Hair Salon, located in Hatton, North Dakota. As part of the business plan, she needs a projected income statement for the company. You will help her develop and format the income statement. Complete the following:

1. Open the **Salon** workbook located in the Excel2 ▸ Case1 folder included with your Data Files, and then save the workbook as **Salon Income Statement** in the location specified by your instructor.
2. In the Documentation sheet, enter your name in cell B3 and the date in cell B4.
3. Apply the following formatting to the Documentation sheet:
    a. Format cell A1 using the Title cell style.
    b. Format the range A3:A5 using the Accent6 cell style.
    c. In cell B4, format the date value using the long date format, and left-align the cell contents.
    d. In cell B5, format the text string "Special Highlights Hair Salon" in italic.
4. In the Income Statement worksheet, format cell A1 using the Title cell style.
5. Calculate the following items in the Income Statement worksheet:
    a. In cell C7, calculate the Gross Profit, which is equal to the Gross Sales minus the Cost of Sales.
    b. In cell C21, calculate the Total Operating Expenses, which is equal to the sum of the operating expenses.
    c. In cell C22, calculate the Total Operating Profit/Loss, which is equal to the Gross Profit minus the Total Operating Expenses.
    d. In cell C23, calculate the projected Income Taxes, which is equal to 35 percent of the Total Operating Profit/Loss.
    e. In cell C24, calculate the Net Profit/Loss, which is equal to the Total Operating Profit/Loss minus the projected Income Taxes.
6. Set the following formats to the Income Statement worksheet:
    a. Format cells A3 and A26 using the Heading 2 cell style.
    b. Format cells A4 and A9 and the range A27:A38 in bold.
    c. Format cells B5, C7, B10, C21, and C24 using the Accounting format with no decimal places.
    d. Format cells B6, B11:B19, C22, and C23 using the Comma style with no decimal places.
    e. Indent the text in the ranges A5:A6 and A10:A19 two spaces. Indent the text in cell A7 and the range A21:A24 four spaces.
    f. Add a bottom border to cells B6, C7, C21, C22, and C23. Add a double bottom border to cell C24.
7. Merge cells A26:E26 and then left-align the merged cell's contents.
8. Merge the contents of the range B27:E27. Left-align the merged cell's contents and wrap the text within the cell. Increase the height of row 27 to display the entire contents of the cell.
9. Top-align and left-align the range A27:B38.
10. Copy the format from the range A27:B27 to the range A28:B38. Merge columns B through E in each row, left-align the text, and resize the row heights to display the complete contents of the cells.
11. Italicize the text string "National Salon News" in cells B27 and B28.

12. Set the following printing formats to the Income Statement worksheet:
    a. Insert a manual page break directly above row 26 so that the Income Statement prints on two pages.
    b. Set rows 1 and 2 as a print title to print on both pages.
    c. Change the page margins to 1 inch on every side.
    d. On the first page of the printout, print **Prepared by** *your name* in the left section of the header, where *your name* is your name. Print the **current date** in the right section of the header. Do not display header text on any other page.
    e. For every page, add a footer that prints the workbook *filename* in the left section, **Page** *page* in the center section, and the *worksheet name* in the right section.
13. If you are instructed to print, print the entire contents of the workbook in portrait orientation.
14. Save and close the workbook.

Case Problem 2

Data File needed for this Case Problem: Waist.xlsx

Waist Trainers Alexandra Roulez is a dietician at Waist Trainers, a company in Fort Smith, Arkansas, that specializes in personal improvement, particularly in areas of health and fitness. Alexandra wants to create a meal-planning workbook for her clients who want to lose weight and improve their health. One goal of meal planning is to decrease the percentage of fat in the diet. Alexandra thinks it would be helpful to highlight foods that have a high percentage of fat as well as list their total fat calories. She already created a workbook that contains a few sample food items and lists the number of calories and grams of fat in each item. She wants you to format this workbook. Complete the following:

1. Open the **Waist** workbook located in the Excel2 ▸ Case2 folder included with your Data Files, and then save the workbook as **Waist Trainers Nutrition Table** in the location specified by your instructor.
2. In the Documentation sheet, enter your name in cell B3 and the date in cell B4.
3. Set the following formatting to the Documentation sheet:
    a. In cell A1, apply the Title cell style, increase the font size to 24 points, and then change the font color to a medium orange.
    b. Apply the Accent2 cell style to the range A3:A5.
    c. Wrap the text within the range B3:B5, and then left- and top-align the text in the cells.
    d. Change the format of the date in cell B4 to the long date format.
    e. Add borders around all of the cells in the range A3:B5.
4. Copy the cell format for cell A1 in the Documentation sheet to cell A1 in the Meal Planner worksheet.
5. In cell F4, enter the text **Calories from Fat**. In cell G4, enter the text **Fat Percentage**.
6. In the range F5:F54, calculate the calories from fat for each food item, which is equal to the Grams of Fat multiplied by 9. In the range G5:G54, calculate the fat percentage of each food item, which is equal to the Calories from Fat divided by the Calories.
7. Format cell A3 using the Heading 4 cell style.
8. Format the range A4:G4 using the Accent2 cell style.
9. Format the range D5:F54 with the Comma style and display one decimal place.
10. Format the range G5:G54 with the Percent style and display two decimal places.
11. Merge the cells in the range A5:A8, rotate the text up, and then center-align the cell content both horizontally and vertically. Change the fill color to medium gold, increase the font size to 14 points, and then change the font color to white.

12. Place a thick box border around the beef food items in the range A5:G8.
13. Repeat Steps 11 and 12 for the other six food categories.
14. For good health, the FDA recommends that the fat percentage in a person's diet should not exceed 30 percent of the total calories per day. Create a Conditional Formatting rule for the fat percentages to highlight those food items that exceed the FDA recommendation in dark red text on a light red fill.
15. In cell G2, enter the text **High Fat Food**. Center the text in the cell. Change the format of the cell to dark red text on a light red fill. Add a thick black border around the cell.
16. Set the following print formats for the Meal Planner worksheet:
    a. Change the page orientation to landscape.
    b. Scale the printout so that the width of the worksheet fits on a single page.
    c. If necessary, create manual page breaks directly above row 25 and above row 44. The worksheet should print on three separate pages.
    d. Repeat the first four rows of the worksheet on every printed page.
    e. For every page, add a footer that prints **Prepared by** *your name* in the left section, **Page** *page* in the center section, and the *worksheet name* in the right section.
17. If you are instructed to print, print the entire contents of the workbook.
18. Save and close the workbook.

Case Problem 3

Data File needed for this Case Problem: Wind.xlsx

Winds of Change Odette Ferris is a researcher at Winds of Change, a privately run wind farm providing supplemental power for communities near Topeka, Kansas. One of Odette's jobs is to record wind speeds from different sectors of the wind farm. She has entered the wind speed data into a workbook as a table with wind speed measures laid out in a grid. Because the numbers are difficult to read and interpret, she wants you to color code the wind speed values using conditional formatting. Complete the following:

1. Open the **Wind** workbook located in the Excel2 ▶ Case3 folder included with your Data Files, and then save the workbook as **Wind Speed Grid** in the location specified by your instructor.
2. In the Documentation sheet, enter your name in cell B3 and the date in cell B4.
3. In the Wind Speed Grid worksheet, merge the range A1:V1, and then apply the Heading 1 cell style to the merged cell and set the font size to 20 points.
4. Format the range B3:V3 as white text on a black background. Copy this formatting to the grid coordinates in the range A4:A64.
5. **Explore** Create a conditional format that highlights cells in the range B4:V64 whose value equals 18 with fill color equal to (99, 37, 35). (*Hint*: In the Equal To dialog box, select Custom Format in the with box to open the Format Cells dialog box. On the Fill tab, in the Background Color section, click the More Colors button, and then click the Custom tab to enter the RGB color value.)
6. **Explore** Repeat Step 5 to continue creating conditional formats that set highlight colors for the wind speed values in the range B4:V64 using the wind speeds and color values shown in Figure 2-47.

Figure 2-47   Wind speed color values

Wind Speed	RGB Color Value
16 m/s	(150, 54, 52)
14 m/s	(218, 150, 148)
12 m/s	(230, 184, 183)
10 m/s	(242, 220, 219)
8 m/s	(242, 242, 242)
6 m/s	(255, 255, 255)
4 m/s	(197, 217, 241)
2 m/s	(141, 180, 226)
0 m/s	(83, 141, 213)

© 2014 Cengage Learning

7. Reduce the font size of the values in the range B4:V64 to 1 point.

Explore 8. Enclose each cell in the range B4:V64 in a light gray border. (*Hint*: Use the Border tab in the Format Cells dialog box.)

9. Use the Format Painter to copy the formats from the range B4:V64 and apply them to the range X3:X12. Increase the font size of the cells in that range to 11 points.

10. Merge the range Y3:Y12, center the contents of the merged cell horizontally and vertically, and then rotate the text down. Format the text in a bold 18-point font.

11. Set the following print formats to the Wind Speed Grid worksheet:
    a. Change the page orientation to landscape.
    b. Set the print area to the range A1:Y64.
    c. Scale the worksheet so that the width and the height of the sheet fit on a single page.
    d. Add a header to the printed page with your name in the left section of the header and the worksheet name in the right section of the header.

12. Save and close the workbook.

Case Problem 4

Data File needed for this Case Problem: Office.xlsx

Office Cart   Robert Trenton is a shipping manager at Office Cart, an online office supply store located in Muncie, Indiana. He wants to use an Excel workbook to track shipping orders. Robert asks you to create and format a worksheet that he can use to enter information for packing slips. Complete the following:

1. Open the **Office** workbook located in the Excel2 ▸ Case4 folder included with your Data Files, and then save the workbook as **Office Cart Packing Slip** in the location specified by your instructor.

2. In the Documentation sheet, enter your name in cell B3 and the date in cell B4.

3. Set the following formats in the Documentation sheet:
    a. Merge cells A1 and B1, and then left-align the contents of the merged cell. Change the font to 28-point white Calibri Light on a dark green background.
    b. Change the font of the range A3:A5 to 14-point white Calibri Light on a dark green background.
    c. Change the format of the date value in cell B4 to the Long Date style, and then left-align the date in the cell.
    d. Italicize the text "Office Cart" in cell B5.
    e. Add a border around each cell in the range A3:B5.

4. Insert a new worksheet at the end of the workbook and name it **Packing Slip**.
5. In the Packing Slip worksheet, select all of the cells in the worksheet. (*Hint*: Click the Select All button at the intersection of the row and column headings, or press the Ctrl+A keys.) Change the font to 10-point dark green Calibri.
6. Add a thick box border around the range A1:D40.
7. For the range A1:D3, change the format to a white Calibri Light font on a dark green background.
8. Set the width of column A to 15 characters. Set the width of column B to 20 characters. Set the width of column C to 30 characters. Set the width of column D to 20 characters.
9. Merge the range A1:B3. Merge the range C1:D3, and then right- and top-align the merged cell. Set the row height of row 1 to 36 points and the heights of rows 2 and 3 to 15 points.
10. In cell A1, enter the following three lines of text, pressing the Alt+Enter keys to start a new line within the cell:
    Office Cart
    14 Trenke Lane
    Muncie, IN 47303
    Format the first line in a 26-point bold font.
11. In cell C1, enter **Packing Slip**, and then format the text in a 26-point bold font using the Headings font of the current theme.
12. In the range A5:A7, enter the following three lines of text in a bold font, and then right-align the text and indent the text one character:
    Order Date
    Order Number
    Purchase Order
13. Format cell B5 in the Long Date format and left-align the cell contents. Insert border lines around each of the cells in the range B5:B7.
14. In the range C5:C7, enter the following three lines of text, and then use the Format Painter to copy the formats from the range A5:B7 to the range C5:D7:
    Date
    Sales Rep
    Account Num
15. In cell B9, enter **Ship To**. In cell D9, enter **Bill To**. Format the text in both cells in bold.
16. In cell A10, enter **Address**, format the text in bold, right-align the text, and then indent it one character.
17. Merge the cells in the range B10:B15, left- and top-align the cell contents, insert a border around the merged cell, and then wrap the text within this cell.
18. In cell C10, enter **Address**. Copy the format from the range A10:B15 to the range C10:D15.
19. Enter the following data in the indicated cells in the worksheet:
    cell A17: **Item**
    cell B17: **Product No.**
    cell C17: **Description**
    cell D17: **Order Quantity**
20. Format the range A17:D17 in bold white Calibri on a dark green background.
21. Format the range A18:D18 with a bottom border and a light green background. Format the range A19:D19 with a bottom border and a white background. Copy the format in the range A18:D19 to the range A20:D27.
22. Apply a Top and Double Bottom Border to the range A28:D28. Merge the contents of the range A28:C28. Enter **Total** in cell A28, bold the text, and right-align the cell contents.
23. In cell D28, enter a formula to calculate the sum of the values in the range D18:D27. Bold the text.
24. In cell A30, enter **Comments** and then bold the text.
25. Merge the range A31:D39, left- and top-align the cell contents, and then add a thick box border around the merged cell.

26. In cell D40, enter **Thank you for your business!** in italic 16-point Calibri, and then right-align the cell contents.
27. Make sure the worksheet is set to portrait orientation, and then add a footer that displays your name in the left section, the filename in the center section, and the current date in the right section. Scale the printout so that it fits onto a single page.
28. Enter the packing slip data shown in Figure 2-48. Save and close the workbook.

Figure 2-48   Office Cart packing slip form

Office Cart

14 Trenke Lane
Muncie, IN 47303

Packing Slip

Order Date	Thursday, June 09, 2016	Date	Thursday, June 09, 2016
Order Number	OC414-0608	Sales Rep	Helen Richards
Purchase Order	OC912-1418-3	Account Num	97

Ship To

Address: c/o Kevin Davidson
Unger and Associates
550 Commerce Drive
Jefferson City, MO 65101

Bill To

Address: Unger and Associates
550 Commerce Drive
Jefferson City, MO

Item	Product No.	Description	Order Quantity
1	MC10R	Multiuse Copy Paper 10 ream	5
2	SGP10	Select Gel Pens	15
3	QCLPT4C	QS Laser Print Toner Kit	2
4	OCBE200	OC Business Envelopes (200 ct)	3
5	OCSL200	OC Shipping Labels (200 ct)	5
6			
7			
8			
9			
10			
		Total	30

Comments

Please contact shipping manager Robert Trenton (ext. 311) regarding discount shipping rates.

Thank you for your business!

TUTORIAL 3

Calculating Data with Formulas and Functions

Creating a Fitness Tracker

OBJECTIVES

Session 3.1
- Make a workbook user-friendly
- Translate an equation into an Excel formula
- Understand function syntax
- Enter formulas and functions with the Quick Analysis tool
- Enter functions with the Insert Function dialog box
- Interpret error values
- Change cell references between relative and absolute

Session 3.2
- Use the AutoFill tool to enter formulas and data and complete a series
- Display the current date with the TODAY function
- Find the next weekday with the WORKDAY function
- Use the COUNT and COUNTA functions to tally cells
- Use an IF function to return a value based on a condition
- Perform an exact match lookup with the VLOOKUP function
- Perform what-if analysis using trial and error and Goal Seek

Case | Fit Fathers Inc.

Ken Dorsett is a certified fitness professional and founder of Fit Fathers Inc., which is a fitness program he developed to help fathers stay fit and active. From its beginnings in Blue Springs, Missouri, where Ken led daily workouts with three other dads, his program has grown to an enrollment of 318 fathers in five different cities in the northwest corner of the state.

Ken wants to help his members evaluate their fitness goals and track their workouts. He has been working on an Excel workbook that can assess each participant's fitness level and track his workout progress. Ken has developed the basic structure of the workbook, but still needs to enter the formulas to calculate the different statistics and data that are important for his clients. He asks you to enter the appropriate formulas to complete the workbook. To do this, you will use a variety of formulas and functions.

STARTING DATA FILES

Excel3

- Tutorial — Fitness.xlsx
- Review — Mothers.xlsx
- Case1 — Hernandez.xlsx
- Case2 — Econ.xlsx
- Case3 — Homes.xlsx
- Case4 — Quality.xlsx

Microsoft product screenshots used with permission from Microsoft Corporation.

Session 3.1 Visual Overview:

Functions are organized by category in the Function Library group. Select a function to open the Function Arguments dialog box.

The Insert Function button opens the Insert Function dialog box from which you can select a function.

The SUM function adds the values in the range.

The AVERAGE function calculates the average value of the range.

The MEDIAN function determines the middle value in the range.

The MAX function displays the maximum value in the range.

The MIN function displays the minimum value in the range.

	Exercise Statistics	Jogging	Calisthenics	Strength
14				
15	SUM	278	245	347
16	AVERAGE	16.4	14.4	20.4
17	MEDIAN	15.0	15.0	20.0
18	MAX	22	20	30
19	MIN	10	8	12

Cell J17: =MEDIAN(K23:K45)

Jogging (min.)
=SUM(I23:I45)
=AVERAGE(I23:I45)
=MEDIAN(I23:I45)
=MAX(I23:I45)
=MIN(I23:I45)

Documentation | Fitness Report | Explanation of Formulas

READY

© 2014 Cengage Learning

Tutorial 3 Calculating Data with Formulas and Functions | Excel   EX 133

Functions and Cell References

The Function Arguments dialog box displays the arguments used by each function. **Arguments** are the numbers, text, or cell references used by the function to return a value.

Required arguments are needed for the function to return a value. These are displayed in bold.

Optional arguments are not required for the function to return a value.

A **relative reference** is a cell reference that is interpreted in relation to the location of the cell containing the formula. For example, M23 is a relative reference to cell M23.

An **absolute reference** is a cell reference that remains fixed when the cell formula is copied to a new location. It includes a $ in front of the column letter and row number. For example, $M$23 is the absolute reference to cell M23.

Making Workbooks User-Friendly

Every workbook should be accessible to its intended users. When a workbook is user-friendly, anyone who needs to enter data in the workbook or interpret its results can understand the workbook's contents, including any jargon or unusual terms, what is being calculated, and how the equations make those calculations.

Many of the fitness calculations needed for Ken's workbook involve terms and equations that are unfamiliar to people not in the fitness industry. Because both trainers and clients will access this workbook, these terms and equations need to be explained. Ken has already included information about the fitness equations in the workbook. You will open the workbook, and examine its layout and structure.

To open and review the Fitness workbook:

1. Open the **Fitness** workbook located in the Excel3 ▸ Tutorial folder included with your Data Files, and then save the workbook as **Fitness Tracker** in the location specified by your instructor.

2. In the Documentation sheet, enter your name in cell B3 and the date in cell B4.

3. Go to the **Fitness Report** worksheet. See Figure 3-1.

Figure 3-1   Fitness Tracker workbook

The Fitness Report worksheet is divided into three sections. The Fitness Evaluation in columns B through D will store the client's personal data and calculate his fitness status. The Workout Report in columns F through M will contain monthly reports on the client's workout routine and calculate the results from his workouts. The Fitness Tables in columns O through P contain different fitness values that will be used in the calculations.

The Fitness Evaluation contains a section for personal information on a Fit Fathers client. Ken wants you to enter the personal data for Daniel Pridham, a Fit Fathers client, to help you test the calculations you enter in the workbook.

To enter Daniel's personal data:

1. In cell **C8**, enter **Daniel Pridham** as the client's name.
2. In cell **C9**, enter **Sedentary** to describe Daniel's activity level.
3. In the range **C10:C14**, enter **45** for his age, **193** for his weight in pounds, **70** for his height in inches, **37** for his waist size in inches, and **15.5** for his neck size in inches.

Documenting Formulas

Documenting the contents of a workbook helps to avoid errors and confusion. This type of information can make a workbook easier for other people to understand. For workbooks that include many calculations, as the Fitness Tracker workbook does, it is helpful to explain the formulas and terms used in the calculations. Such documentation also can serve as a check that the equations are accurate. Another way to document formulas and terms is to include notes of explanation within the worksheet where the equations are used.

Ken has included explanations of different fitness terms and equations in the Explanation of Formulas worksheet, and explanatory notes in cells B26 and F46 of the Fitness Report worksheet. Before proceeding, he wants you to review the documentation in these worksheets.

To review the documentation in the Fitness Tracker workbook:

1. Click the **Explanation of Formulas** sheet tab to make it the active sheet.
2. Read the sheet contents, reviewing the descriptions of common fitness terms and formulas. As you continue developing the Fitness Tracker workbook, you'll learn about these terms and formulas in more detail.
3. Click the **Fitness Report** sheet tab to return to the Fitness Report worksheet.
4. Read the explanatory notes in cells B26 and F46.

Using Constants in Formulas

The first fitness equation Ken wants you to enter is BMI, or body mass index, which estimates the amount of human body fat. The BMI equation is based on the individual's body weight divided by the square of his or her height. The specific formula is

$$BMI = \frac{703w}{h^2}$$

where w is the body weight in pounds and h is the height in inches. BMI values from 18.5 to 24.9 are considered normal; anything higher is considered overweight.

One common skill you need when creating a workbook is to translate an equation like the BMI equation into an Excel formula. Some equations use constants. A **constant** is a value in a formula that doesn't change. In the BMI equation, 703 is a constant because that value never changes when calculating the body mass index.

> **INSIGHT**
>
> ### Deciding Where to Place a Constant
>
> Should a constant be entered directly into the formula or placed in a separate worksheet cell and referenced in the formula? The answer depends on the constant being used, the purpose of the workbook, and the intended audience. Placing constants in separate cells that you reference in the formulas can help users better understand the worksheet because no values are hidden within the formulas. Also, when a constant is entered in a cell, you can add explanatory text next to each constant to document how it is being used in the formula. On the other hand, you don't want a user to inadvertently change the value of a constant and throw off all the formula results. You will need to evaluate how important it is for other people to immediately see the constant, and whether the constant requires any explanation for other people to understand the formula. For example, Ken wants you to include the 703 constant in the BMI formula rather than in a separate cell because he doesn't feel that clients need to see this constant to understand BMI.

To convert the BMI equation into a formula, you need to replace *w* and *h* in the equation with Daniel's actual weight and height. Because Daniel's weight is stored in cell C11 and his height is stored in cell C12, you replace the *w* in the formula with the C11 cell reference, and replace the *h* in the formula with the C12 cell reference. The resulting Excel formula is:

```
=703*C11/C12^2
```

Note that the exponent operator ^ is used to square the height value in the denominator of the fraction. Recall that exponentiation raises a value to a power; in this case, the value in cell C12 is raised to the second power, or squared. Following the order of operations, Excel will first square the height value, then multiply the weight value by 703, and finally divide that product by the squared height. You will enter the BMI formula in the Fitness Report worksheet now.

To enter the BMI formula in the Fitness Report worksheet:

1. In cell **C19**, enter the formula **=703*C11/C12^2**. The formula multiplies the weight in cell C11 by the constant 703, and then divides the resulting value by the square of the height in cell C12. The calculated BMI value that is displayed in cell C19 is 27.68959184.

   Trouble? If your BMI formula results differ from 27.68959184, you probably entered the formula incorrectly. Edit your formula as needed so that the numbers and cell references match those shown in the formula in Step 1.

2. Select cell **C19**, and then reduce the number of displayed decimals to one. Cell C19 displays 27.7 as the formula results.

The next fitness equation, which calculates the individual's resting basal metabolic rate (BMR), includes four constants. The resting BMR estimates the number of calories a person expends daily (not counting any actual activity). For men, the BMR is calculated with the equation

$BMR = 6.23w + 12.7h - 6.76a + 66$

where *w* is the weight in pounds, *h* is the height in inches, and *a* is the age in years. BMR is calculated by multiplying the weight, height, and age by different constants, and then adding the results to another constant. Heavier and taller people require more daily calories to sustain them. As people age, their metabolism slows, resulting in a lower BMR. Daniel's weight, height, and age are stored in cells C11, C12, and C10, respectively, so the BMR equation translates to the following Excel formula:

```
=6.23*C11+12.7*C12-6.76*C10+66
```

You will enter this formula in the Fitness Report worksheet to calculate Daniel's BMR.

To enter the BMR formula in the Fitness Report worksheet:

▶ **1.** In cell **C21**, enter the formula **=6.23*C11+12.7*C12−6.76*C10+66**. Cell C21 displays 1853.19, indicating that Daniel burns about 1853 calories per day before performing any activity.

   Trouble? If your BMR formula results differ from 1853.19, you might have entered the formula incorrectly. Edit the formula as needed so that the numbers and cell references match those shown in the formula in Step 1.

▶ **2.** Select cell **C21**, and then reduce the number of decimals displayed in the cell to zero. The number of calories per day displayed in cell C21 is 1853.

The 1853 calories per day amount assumes no physical activity. However, even the most sedentary person moves a little bit during the day, which increases the BMR value. The table in the range O7:P12 in the Fitness Report worksheet lists the constant multipliers for different activity levels. For example, the BMR of a sedentary man like Daniel is multiplied by 1.2 (shown in cell P8) to account for daily movements. If Daniel were to increase his activities to a moderate level, the multiplier would increase to 1.55 (as shown in cell P10).

You will enter the formula to calculate Daniel's active BMR based on his sedentary lifestyle. Ken wants you to use the constant value stored in the table rather entering it into the formula because he anticipates that Daniel will increase his activity level under the direction of Fit Fathers, and it is easier to update the amount in a cell rather than editing a formula.

To calculate Daniel's active BMR:

▶ **1.** In cell **C22**, enter the formula **=C21*P8** to multiply Daniel's resting BMR by the sedentary activity level. Based on this calculation, Daniel's active BMR is 2223.828 calories per day.

▶ **2.** Select cell **C22**, and then decrease the number of decimal places displayed in the cell to zero. The displayed value changes to 2224. See Figure 3-2.

Figure 3-2 BMI and BMR calculated values

client's personal data → (points to B8:C14 personal data area)

estimate of daily metabolism while at rest and active → (points to C21:C22)

estimate of body mass index → (points to C19)

The active BMR shows that Daniel needs about 2224 calories per day to maintain his current weight.

Identifying Notes, Input Values, and Calculated Values

When worksheets involve notes and many calculations, it is useful to distinguish input values that are used in formulas from calculated values that are returned by formulas. Formatting that clearly differentiates input values from calculated values helps others more easily understand the worksheet. Such formatting also helps prevent anyone from entering a value in a cell that contains a formula.

You can use cell styles to identify cells as containing explanatory text, input values, and calculated values. When you use cell styles or other formatting to identify a cell's purpose, you should include a legend in the worksheet describing the purpose of the formatting.

Ken wants to be sure that whenever he and his staff members update a client's workbook, they can easily see where to enter numbers. You will apply cell styles to distinguish between notes, input cells, and formula cells.

To apply cell styles to differentiate cells with notes, input values, and calculated values:

1. Select the merged cell **B26**.
2. On the HOME tab, in the Styles group, click the **Cell Styles** button to open the Cell Styles gallery.
3. Click the **Explanatory Text** cell style located in the Data and Model group. Cell B26 is formatted with the Explanatory Text cell style.
4. Format cell **F46** with the **Explanatory Text** cell style.

Tutorial 3 Calculating Data with Formulas and Functions | Excel EX 139

5. Format the range **C8:C14** with the **Input** cell style. These cells contain the personal information about Daniel that you entered earlier.

6. Format the nonadjacent range **C19;C21:C22** containing the calculated BMI and BMR values with the **Calculation** cell style.

7. Format the range **G22:J44** with the **Input** cell style. These cells store information about Daniel's workout routine, which Ken enters after each workout.

   Next, you'll create a legend to identify which cells are input cells and which cells are calculated cells.

8. In cell **C2**, enter **Input Values** as the label, format the cell with the **Explanatory Text** cell style, and then right-align the text in the cell.

9. In cell **C4**, enter **Calculated Values** as the label, and then use the Format Painter to copy the formatting in cell C2 and paste it to cell C4.

10. Format cell **D2** with the **Input** cell style, and then format cell **D4** with the **Calculation** cell style.

11. Select cell **C19**. See Figure 3-3.

Figure 3-3 | Input and calculated values formatted with cell styles

- BMI formula → C19 =703*C11/C12^2
- legend explains formatting → Input Values / Calculated Values (row 2 and row 4)
- input values → Personal Data: Name Daniel Pridham; Activity Level Sedentary; Age (years) 45; Weight (lb.) 193; Height (in.) 70; Waist (in.) 37; Neck (in.) 15.5
- calculated value → BMI 27.7

Workout Report: Current Date; Workout Summary: Start Date, End Date, Workouts Scheduled, Workouts Attended, Workouts Missed; Exercise Statistics: Jogging (min.), Calisthenics — SUM, AVERAGE, MEDIAN, MINIMUM, MAXIMUM

Fitness Assessment

Documentation | Fitness Report | Explanation of Formulas

READY

The built-in cell styles are a quick way of marking different types of values in your worksheet. If the formats do not match what you want for your workbook, you can create your own cell styles. However you design your worksheet, your purpose is to make the values easy to interpret.

PROSKILLS

Written Communication: Displaying Significant Digits

Excel stores numbers with up to 15 digits and displays as many digits as will fit into the cell. So even the result of a simple formula such as =10/3 will display 3.33333333333333 if the cell is wide enough.

A number with 15 digits is difficult to read, and calculations rarely need that level of accuracy. Many scientific disciplines, such as chemistry or physics, have rules for specifying exactly how many digits should be displayed with any calculation. These digits are called **significant digits** because they indicate the accuracy of the measured and calculated values. For example, an input value of 19.32 has four significant digits.

The rules are based on several factors and vary from one discipline to another. Generally, a calculated value should display no more digits than are found in any of the input values. For example, because the input value 19.32 has four significant digits, any calculated value based on that input should have no more than four significant digits. Showing more digits would be misleading because it implies a level of accuracy beyond that which was actually measured.

Because Excel displays calculated values with as many digits as can fit into a cell, you need to know the standards for your profession and change the display of your calculated values accordingly.

Using Excel Functions

Functions provide a quick way to calculate summary data such as the total, average, and median values in a collection of values. Ken recorded the amount of time Daniel spent at each workout doing brisk jogging, calisthenics, and strength exercise. Ken wants you to analyze the results from Daniel's workout routine. You will use Excel functions to summarize these results.

Excel supports an extensive library of functions, organized into the 12 categories shown in Figure 3-4. You can use Excel functions to perform statistical analysis, work with financial data, retrieve information from databases, and generate text strings, among many other tasks.

Figure 3-4   Excel function categories

Category	Description
Cube	Retrieve data from multidimensional databases involving online analytical processing (OLAP)
Database	Retrieve and analyze data stored in databases
Date & Time	Analyze or create date and time values and time intervals
Engineering	Analyze engineering problems
Financial	Analyze information for business and finance
Information	Return information about the format, location, or contents of worksheet cells
Logical	Return logical (true-false) values
Lookup & Reference	Look up and return data matching a set of specified conditions from a range
Math & Trig	Perform math and trigonometry calculations
Statistical	Provide statistical analyses of data sets
Text	Return text values or evaluate text
Web	Provide information on web-based connections

© 2014 Cengage Learning

The Excel Help system provides information on all of the Excel functions.

Exploring Function Syntax

Before you use functions, you should understand the function syntax. Recall that the syntax of an Excel function follows the general pattern

```
FUNCTION(argument1,argument2,...)
```

where `FUNCTION` is the name of the function, and `argument1`, `argument2`, and so forth are arguments used by the function. An argument can be any type of value including text, numbers, cell references, or even other formulas or functions. Not all functions require arguments.

Some arguments are optional. You can include an optional argument in the function or omit it from the function. Some optional arguments have default values associated with them, so that if you omit the optional argument, Excel will use the default value. These tutorials show optional arguments within square brackets along with the argument's default value (if any), as

```
FUNCTION(argument1[, argument2=value2,...])
```

where `argument1` is a required argument, `argument2` is optional, and `value2` is the default value for `argument2`. As you work with specific functions, you will learn which arguments are required and which are optional as well as any default values associated with optional arguments.

Figure 3-5 describes some of the more common Math, Trig, and Statistical functions and provides the syntax of those functions.

TIP
Optional arguments are always placed last in the argument list.

Figure 3-5   **Common Math, Trig, and Statistical functions**

Function	Category	Description
`AVERAGE(number1[, number2, number3, ...])`	Statistical	Calculates the average of a collection of numbers, where `number1`, `number2`, and so forth are numbers or cell references; only `number1` is required
`COUNT(value1[, value2, value3, ...])`	Statistical	Counts how many cells in a range contain numbers, where `value1`, `value2`, and so forth are text, numbers, or cell references; only `value1` is required
`COUNTA(value1[, value2, value3, ...])`	Statistical	Counts how many cells are not empty in ranges `value1`, `value2`, and so forth, or how many numbers are listed within `value1`, `value2`, etc.
`INT(number)`	Math & Trig	Displays the integer portion of `number`
`MAX(number1[, number2, number3, ...])`	Statistical	Calculates the maximum value of a collection of numbers, where `number1`, `number2`, and so forth are either numbers or cell references
`MEDIAN(number1[, number2, number3, ...])`	Statistical	Calculates the median, or middle, value of a collection of numbers, where `number1`, `number2`, and so forth are either numbers or cell references
`MIN(number1[, number2, number3, ...])`	Statistical	Calculates the minimum value of a collection of numbers, where `number1`, `number2`, and so forth are either numbers or cell references
`RAND()`	Math & Trig	Returns a random number between 0 and 1
`ROUND(number, num_digits)`	Math & Trig	Rounds `number` to the number of digits specified by `num_digits`
`SUM(number1[, number2, number3, ...])`	Math & Trig	Adds a collection of numbers, where `number1`, `number2`, and so forth are either numbers or cell references

© 2014 Cengage Learning

For example, the ROUND function rounds a number to a specified number of decimal places and has the syntax

`ROUND(number, num_digits)`

where `number` is the number to be rounded and `num_digits` is the number of decimal places to which you want to round the `number` argument. The following function rounds 2.718282 to two decimal places, resulting in 2.72:

`ROUND(2.718282, 2)`

However, you usually reference data values stored in worksheet cells rather than entering the numbers directly in the function. For example, the following function rounds the number in cell A10 to three decimal places:

`ROUND(A10, 3)`

Both arguments in the ROUND function are required. An example of a function that uses optional arguments is the AVERAGE function, which can calculate averages from several ranges or entered values. For example, the function

`AVERAGE(A1:A10)`

averages the values in the range A1:A10, while the function

`AVERAGE(A1:A10, C5:C10, E10)`

includes two optional arguments and averages the values from the cells in range A1:A10, range C5:C10, and cell E10.

Functions can be included as part of larger formulas. The following formula calculates the average of the values in the range A1:A100, and then squares that result using the ^ operator:

`=AVERAGE(A1:A100)^2`

Functions can also be placed inside another function, or **nested**. If a formula contains several functions, Excel starts with the innermost function and then moves outward. For example, the following formula first calculates the average of the values in the range A1:A100 using the AVERAGE function, and then rounds that value to two decimal places:

`=ROUND(AVERAGE(A1:A100),2)`

One challenge of nesting functions is to make sure that you include all of the parentheses. You can check this by counting the number of opening parentheses and making sure that number matches the number of closing parentheses. Excel also displays each level of nested parentheses in different colors to make it easier for you to match the opening and closing parentheses in the formula. If the number of parentheses doesn't match, Excel will not accept the formula and will provide a suggestion for how to rewrite the formula so the number of opening and closing parentheses does match.

There are several ways to enter a function. You have already entered a function by typing directly in a cell and using the AutoSum button. Another way to enter a function is with the Quick Analysis tool.

Entering Functions with the Quick Analysis Tool

The Quick Analysis tool, which you have already used to apply conditional formats that highlight specific data values, can also be used to generate columns and rows of summary statistics that can be used for analyzing data.

Tutorial 3 Calculating Data with Formulas and Functions | Excel   EX 143

Columns F through M in the Fitness Report worksheet will contain the workout report. The range H22:J44 records the number of minutes Daniel spent at each workout jogging, doing calisthenics, and doing strength training. Ken needs to know the total minutes Daniel spent at each exercise to evaluate Daniel's workout effort during the past month. The most efficient way to calculate these totals is with the SUM function. You will use the Quick Analysis tool to enter the SUM function to calculate the total minutes spent at each exercise.

To calculate the total minutes spent on each exercise:

1. Select the range **H22:J44** containing the minutes spent on each exercise during each workout. The Quick Analysis button appears in the lower-right corner of the selected range.

2. Click the **Quick Analysis** button (or press the **Ctrl+Q** keys) to display the Quick Analysis tool.

3. Click the **TOTALS** category to display Quick Analysis tools for calculating totals.

4. Point to the **Sum** button. Live Preview shows the results of Sum. See Figure 3-6.

Figure 3-6   Quick Analysis tool to calculate totals

5. Click **Sum** to enter the SUM function for each cell in the selected range. The results show that Daniel spent 278 minutes jogging, 245 minutes doing calisthenics, and 347 minutes doing strength exercises during the previous month's workouts.

    The Quick Analysis tool automatically inserts the formulas containing the SUM function at the bottom of the table. Ken wants you to move this information near the top of the worksheet where it can be viewed first.

6. Select the range **H45:J45**, and then cut the selected range.

7. Select cell **G14**, and then paste the formulas with the SUM functions. The totals now appear in the range G14:I14.

The Quick Analysis tool can also be used to quickly calculate averages. An average provides an estimate of the most typical value from a data sample. Ken wants to know the average number of minutes that Daniel spent on each exercise during his sessions.

To calculate the average minutes spent per exercise:

1. Select the range **H22:J44**, and then click the **Quick Analysis** button that appears in the lower-right corner of the selected range (or press the **Ctrl+Q** keys).

2. Click the **TOTALS** category, and then click **Average** to enter the AVERAGE function in the range H45:J45 and calculate the average minutes per exercise type.

3. Cut the formulas from the range **H45:J45**, and then paste them into the range **G15:I15**.

   Excel displays the averages to eight decimal places, which implies a far greater accuracy in measuring the exercise time than could be recorded.

4. In the range **G15:I15**, decrease the number of decimal places displayed to one. On average, Daniel spent about 16.4 minutes per session jogging, 14.4 minutes on calisthenics, and 20.4 minutes on strength exercises. See Figure 3-7.

Figure 3-7   **Sums and averages of exercise times**

The Quick Analysis tool can be used to summarize values across rows as well as down columns. Ken wants to calculate how long Daniel worked out each day. You will use the Quick Analysis tool to calculate the total exercise minutes per workout.

To calculate the total workout times per session:

1. In cell **K21**, enter **Total Minutes** as the heading.

2. Select the range **H22:J44**, and then open the Quick Analysis tool.

3. Click the **TOTALS** category, and then click the right scroll button to scroll to the right through the list of calculations.

4. Click the **Sum** button for the column of summary statistics. SUM functions are entered in the range K22:K44, calculating the sum of the workout minutes per session.

   The Quick Analysis tool applies its own style to the formulas it generates. Instead of the bold text, you want the formulas to be formatted with the Calculation style.

5. Format the range **K22:K44** with the **Calculation** cell style.

Tutorial 3 Calculating Data with Formulas and Functions | Excel   EX 145

▶ 6. In cell **J13**, enter **Total Minutes** as the heading.

▶ 7. Copy the formulas in the range **I14:I15**, and then paste them into the range **J14:J15** to calculate the sum and average of the total exercise minutes from all of the workouts. As shown in Figure 3-8, Daniel worked out for 870 minutes during the month with an average of 37.8 minutes per workout.

Figure 3-8 Total exercise time per workout

Entering Functions with the Insert Function Dialog Box

Functions are organized in the Function Library group on the FORMULAS tab. In the Function Library, you can select a function from a function category. You can also open the Insert Function dialog box to search for a particular function based on a description you enter. When you select a function, the Function Arguments dialog box opens, listing all of the arguments associated with that function. Required arguments are in bold type; optional arguments are in normal type.

Ken wants his report to include the median exercise times for the three exercise categories. The **median** provides the middle value from a data sample. You can use the MEDIAN function to determine the middle value in a range of numbers. The Quick Analysis tool doesn't include median, so you will use the Insert Function and Function Arguments dialog boxes to help you correctly insert the MEDIAN function.

To calculate the median exercise time:

▶ 1. Select cell **G16**. This is the cell in which you will enter the MEDIAN function.

▶ 2. Click the **Insert Function** button *fx* to the left of the formula bar to open the Insert Function dialog box. From the Insert Function dialog box, you can describe the function you want to search for.

▶ 3. In the Search for a function box, type **middle value**, and then click the **Go** button. Functions for finding a middle value appear in the Select a function box. The second entry in the list, MEDIAN, is the one you want to use. See Figure 3-9.

Excel | Tutorial 3 Calculating Data with Formulas and Functions

Figure 3-9 Insert Function dialog box

- description of the function you want to find
- functions that match your search description
- description of the selected function

4. In the Select a function box, click **MEDIAN** to select it, and then click the **OK** button. The Function Arguments dialog box opens with the arguments for the MEDIAN function.

5. With the insertion point in the Number1 box, click the **Collapse Dialog Box** button to shrink the dialog box so you can see more of the worksheet.

6. In the worksheet, select the range **H22:H44**. These cells contain the times Daniel spent jogging.

7. In the Function Arguments dialog box, click the **Expand Dialog Box** button to redisplay the entire dialog box. The dialog box now shows a preview of the MEDIAN function and the value it will return to the formula. See Figure 3-10.

Figure 3-10 Function Arguments dialog box

- numbers contained in the range reference
- range reference for the first argument
- required arguments appear in bold
- optional arguments are not set in bold
- preview of the function value
- description of the MEDIAN function
- preview of the formula result
- click to view help about the function
- description of the selected argument

▶ 8. Click the **OK** button. The formula =MEDIAN(H22:H44) is entered in cell G16, which displays 15 (the median exercise time for jogging).

▶ 9. Copy cell **G16**, and then paste the copied formula into the range **H16:J16** to calculate the median exercise times for calisthenics, strength training, and all exercises. See Figure 3-11.

Figure 3-11   **Median exercise times**

	Exercise Statistics	Jogging (min.)	Calisthenics (min.)	Strength (min.)	Total Minutes
13					
14	SUM	278	245	347	870
15	AVERAGE	16.4	14.4	20.4	37.8
16	MEDIAN	15	15	20	50
17	MINIMUM				
18	MAXIMUM				

Insert Function button

MEDIAN function formula calculates the middle exercise times

median minutes for each exercise

Daniel spent a median time of 15 minutes on calisthenics and 20 minutes on strength training. The median total exercise time was 50 minutes, which is quite a bit higher than the average total exercise time of 37.8 minutes. Why this difference? One reason is that averages are greatly influenced by extremely low or high values. Because Daniel missed several workouts, his exercise time for those days was 0, bringing down the overall average. A median, or middle value, is not as affected by these extreme values, which is why some statisticians advocate medians over averages for analyzing data with widely spaced values.

Ken also wants to know the minimum and maximum minutes Daniel spent exercising during the month. You can access functions by scrolling through the Function Library. You will use this method to enter the functions to calculate the minimum and maximum exercise times.

To calculate the minimum and maximum minutes of exercise:

▶ 1. Select cell **G17**, which is where you will calculate the minimum exercise time.

▶ 2. On the ribbon, click the **FORMULAS** tab to display the function categories in the Function Library.

▶ 3. Click the **More Functions** button to display the rest of the function categories. Calculations involving maximums and minimums are included with the Statistical functions.

▶ 4. Click **Statistical** to display the statistical functions, and then scroll down and point to **MIN**. A ScreenTip appears, displaying the MIN function syntax and a description of the function. See Figure 3-12.

Figure 3-12   MIN function in the Function Library

functions organized into categories

syntax of the selected function

list of statistical functions

> 5. Click **MIN** to open the Function Arguments dialog box.
>
> 6. With the insertion point in the Number1 box, select the range **H22:H44** in the worksheet. These cells store the amount of time Daniel spent jogging.
>
> 7. Click the **OK** button. The dialog box closes, and the formula =MIN(H22:H44) is entered in cell G17, which displays 10, the minimum minutes that Daniel spent jogging during the month.
>
> 8. Select cell **G18**, click the **More Functions** button in the Function Library group, click **Statistical**, and then scroll down and click **MAX**. The Function Arguments dialog box opens.
>
> 9. With the insertion point in the Number1 box, select the range **H22:H44** in the worksheet, and then click the **OK** button. The formula =MAX(H22:H44) is entered in cell G18, which displays 22, the maximum minutes that Daniel spent jogging.
>
> 10. Copy the range **G17:G18**, and then paste the formulas in the range **H17:J18** to calculate the minimum and maximum times for the other exercises and overall.
>
> 11. Format the range **G14:J18** with the **Calculation** cell style, and then select cell **F19**. See Figure 3-13.

Figure 3-13 Summary statistics of the exercise times

sum, average, median, minimum, and maximum values of each exercise time

Exercise Statistics	Jogging (min.)	Calisthenics (min.)	Strength (min.)	Total Minutes
SUM	278	245	347	870
AVERAGE	16.4	14.4	20.4	37.8
MEDIAN	15	15	20	50
MINIMUM	10	8	12	0
MAXIMUM	22	20	30	60

Referencing Function Results in a Formula

The amount of calories burned during exercise is a function of intensity and time. The more intense the exercise or the longer it lasts, the more calories burned. Ken uses the fitness equation

$$\text{Calories} = \frac{\text{METS} \times w \times t}{125.7143}$$

to calculate how many calories will be used during exercise, where *METS* is a metabolic factor that measures the intensity of the exercise, *w* is the individual's weight in pounds, *t* is the exercise time in minutes, and 125.7143 is a constant that converts the quantity into calories. Ken listed the METS values for the different workout routines he created in the range O15:P25 of the Fitness Report worksheet. For example, the METS for Workout Routine 5 is 7.0 and the METS for Workout Routine 10 is 16.0. Using the METS information and the weight and exercise times, you can calculate the total calories burned during each workout.

The fitness equation that calculates calories burned during the first workout translates into the formula

```
=P20*C11*K22/125.7143
```

where `P20` references the cell with the METS for Workout Routine 5, `C11` references the cell that stores Daniel's weight, and `K22` references the cell that calculates the total exercise time of the first workout.

You will enter this formula in cell L22, and then copy it to the remaining cells in the column to calculate the calories burned during each workout.

To calculate the calories burned during Daniel's first workout:

1. In cell **L21**, enter **Calories Burned** as the label.
2. In cell **L22**, enter the formula **=P20*C11*K22/125.7143** to calculate the calories Daniel burned at his first workout. Cell P20 stores the METS value, cell C11 contains Daniel's weight, and cell K22 is the total exercise time for Workout Routine 5 on the first day of the month. Cell L22 displays 376.1306391, which is the number of calories burned at the first workout.

Trouble? If your value differs from 376.1306391, edit your formula as needed so it exactly matches the formula shown in Step 2.

3. Select cell **L22**, and then decrease the number of decimal places shown to one. The displayed value is 376.1.

4. Copy the formula in cell **L22**, and then paste the formula to the range **L23:L44** to calculate the calories burned for the rest of the workouts. See Figure 3-14.

Figure 3-14 Formulas incorrectly calculating the calories burned per workout

The first few values seem somewhat reasonable, but then several workouts show no calories burned. These are followed by cells displaying #VALUE! rather than a number. Obviously something went wrong when you copied and pasted the formula.

Interpreting Error Values

The #VALUE! that appears in some of the cells in the Fitness Report worksheet is an error value. An **error value** indicates that some part of a formula is preventing Excel from returning a calculated value. An error value begins with a pound sign (#) followed by an error name that indicates the type of error. Figure 3-15 describes common error values that you might see instead of the results from formulas and functions. For example, the error value #VALUE! indicates that the wrong type of value is used in a function or formula. You will need to examine the formulas in the cells with error values to determine exactly what went wrong.

Figure 3-15   Excel error values

Error Value	Description
#DIV/0!	The formula or function contains a number divided by 0.
#NAME?	Excel doesn't recognize text in the formula or function, such as when the function name is misspelled.
#N/A	A value is not available to a function or formula, which can occur when a workbook is initially set up prior to entering actual data values.
#NULL!	A formula or function requires two cell ranges to intersect, but they don't.
#NUM!	Invalid numbers are used in a formula or function, such as text entered in a function that requires a number.
#REF!	A cell reference used in a formula or function is no longer valid, which can occur when the cell used by the function was deleted from the worksheet.
#VALUE!	The wrong type of argument is used in a function or formula. This can occur when you reference a text value for an argument that should be strictly numeric.

© 2014 Cengage Learning

The error value messages are not particularly descriptive or helpful. To help you locate the error, an error indicator appears in the upper-left corner of the cell with the error value. When you point to the error indicator, a ScreenTip appears with more information about the source of the error.

INSIGHT

Deciding When to Correct an Error Value

An error value does not mean that you must correct the cell's formula or function. Some error values appear simply because you have not yet entered any data into the workbook. For example, if you use the AVERAGE function to find the average value of an empty column, the #DIV/0! error value appears because the formula cannot calculate the average of a collection of empty cells. However, as soon as you begin entering data, the #DIV/0! message will disappear.

Ken wants you to figure out why the #VALUE error value appears in some of the cells where you copied the calories burned formula. To figure this out, you will examine the formula in cell L31, which is the first cell that displays the error value instead of the expected number results.

To view the formula in cell L31 that results in an error value:

1. Double-click cell **L31**, which displays the #VALUE! error value. In Edit mode, the cell references used in the formula are color coded to match the corresponding cells, making it easier to see which cells are used in the formula.

2. Observe that cell L31 contains the formula =P29*C20*K31/125.7143.

> 3. Look at the first cell reference in the formula. The first cell reference is to cell P29 containing the text "Fitness Level" instead of cell P20 containing the METS value for Workout Routine 5. The formula is attempting to multiply the text in cell P29, but multiplication can be done only with numbers. This is the problem causing the #VALUE! error value.
> 4. Look at the second cell reference in the formula. The second cell reference is to cell C20, an empty cell, rather than to cell C11 containing Daniel's weight.
> 5. Look at the third cell reference in the formula. The third cell reference is to cell K31, which contains the total exercise times for the tenth workout—the correct cell reference.

Exploring Cell References

Most workbooks include data entered in cells that are then referenced in formulas to perform calculations on that data. The formulas can be simple, such as the formulas you entered to add the total minutes of each workout, or they can be more complex, such as the formulas you entered to calculate the calories burned during each workout. Each of these formulas includes one or more cell references.

Understanding Relative References

When a formula includes a cell reference, Excel interprets that cell reference as being located relative to the position of the current cell. For example, Excel interprets the following formula entered in cell A1 to mean "add the value of the cell one column to the right of this cell to the value of the cell one column to the right and one row below this cell":

`=B1+B2`

This relative interpretation is retained when the formula is copied to a new location. So, if the formula in cell A1 is copied to cell A3 (two rows down in the worksheet), the relative references in the formula also shift two rows down, resulting in the following formula:

`=B3+B4`

Figure 3-16 shows another example of how relative references change when a formula is copied to new cell locations. In this figure, the formula =A4 entered in cell D7 displays 10, which is the number entered in cell A4. When pasted to a new location, each of the pasted formulas contains a reference to a cell that is three rows up and three rows to the left of the current cell's location.

Figure 3-16   Formulas using relative references

formula references a cell three rows up and three columns to the left of the active cell

when copied to new cells, each formula still references a cell three rows up and three columns to the left

values returned by each formula

© 2014 Cengage Learning

This explains what happened with the relative references you used to calculate calories burned for each workout. When you entered the following formula in cell L22, cell C11 correctly references the client's weight and the other cells correctly reference the METS for Workout Routine 5 and the total exercise time:

```
=P20*C11*K22/125.7143
```

When you copied the formula down to cell L31, all of the cell references contained in that formula also shifted down nine rows, resulting in the following formula, which accurately references the total exercise time for the corresponding workout but no longer references Daniel's weight or the METS for Workout Routine 5—both of which are necessary for the calculation:

```
=P29*C20*K31/125.7143
```

What you need is a cell reference that remains fixed when the formula is copied to a new location.

Understanding Absolute References

A fixed reference—one that always references the same cell no matter where it is moved—is called an absolute reference. In Excel, absolute references include a $ (dollar sign) before each column and row designation. For example, B8 is a relative reference to cell B8, and $B$8 is an absolute reference to that cell. When you copy a formula that contains an absolute reference to a new location, that cell reference does not change.

Figure 3-17 shows an example of how copying a formula with an absolute reference results in the same cell reference being pasted in different cells regardless of their position compared to the location of the original copied cell. In this example, the formula =$A$4 will always reference cell A4 no matter where the formula is copied to, because the cell is referenced with the absolute reference $A$4.

Figure 3-17   Formulas using absolute references

© 2014 Cengage Learning

Understanding Mixed References

A formula can also include cell references that are mixed. A **mixed reference** contains both relative and absolute references. For example, a mixed reference for cell A2 can be either $A2 or A$2. In the mixed reference $A2, the reference to column A is absolute and the reference to row 2 is relative. In the mixed reference A$2, the column reference is relative and the row reference is absolute. A mixed reference "locks" one part of the cell reference while the other part can change. When you copy and paste a cell with a mixed reference to a new location, the absolute portion of the cell reference remains fixed and the relative portion shifts along with the new location of the pasted cell.

Figure 3-18 shows an example of using mixed references to complete a multiplication table. The first cell in the table, cell B3, contains the formula =$A3*B$2, which multiplies the first column entry (A3) by the first row entry (B2), returning 1. When this formula is copied to another cell, the absolute portions of the cell references remain unchanged and the relative portions of the references change. For example, if the formula is copied to cell E6, the first mixed cell reference changes to $A6 because the column reference is absolute and the row reference is relative, and the second cell reference changes to E$2 because the row reference is absolute and the column reference is relative. The result is that cell E6 contains the formula =$A6*E$2 and returns 16. Other cells in the multiplication table are similarly modified so that each entry returns the multiplication of the intersection of the row and column headings.

Figure 3-18 Formulas using mixed references

mixed cell reference that fixes the column reference for the first term and the row reference for the second term

	A	B	C	D	E	F	G
1			Multiplication Table				
2		1	2	3	4	5	
3	1	=$A3*B$2					
4	2						
5	3						
6	4						
7	5						
8							

when copied to the B3:B7 range, the fixed references remain unchanged and the relative references are shifted

	A	B	C	D	E	F	G
1			Multiplication Table				
2		1	2	3	4	5	
3	1	=$A3*B$2	=$A3*C$2	=$A3*D$2	=$A3*E$2	=$A3*F$2	
4	2	=$A4*B$2	=$A4*C$2	=$A4*D$2	=$A4*E$2	=$A4*F$2	
5	3	=$A5*B$2	=$A5*C$2	=$A5*D$2	=$A5*E$2	=$A5*F$2	
6	4	=$A6*B$2	=$A6*C$2	=$A6*D$2	=$A6*E$2	=$A6*F$2	
7	5	=$A7*B$2	=$A7*C$2	=$A7*D$2	=$A7*E$2	=$A7*F$2	
8							

values returned by each formula

	A	B	C	D	E	F	G
1			Multiplication Table				
2		1	2	3	4	5	
3	1	1	2	3	4	5	
4	2	2	4	6	8	10	
5	3	3	6	9	12	15	
6	4	4	8	12	16	20	
7	5	5	10	15	20	25	
8							

Changing Cell References in a Formula

You can quickly switch a cell reference from relative to absolute or mixed. Rather than retyping the formula, you can select the cell reference in Edit mode and then press the F4 key. As you press the F4 key, Excel cycles through the different reference types—starting with the relative reference, followed by the absolute reference, then to a mixed reference with the row absolute, and finally to a mixed reference with the column absolute.

Ken wants you to fix the problem with the cell references in the calories burned formulas. You need to revise the formula to use absolute references to Daniel's weight and the METS value that will not change when the formula is copied to new locations. You will leave the relative reference to the total exercise time so that the copied formulas will retrieve the exercise times from the corresponding workouts. The revised formula in cell L22 uses an absolute reference to the METS values in $P$20 and an absolute reference to Daniel's weight in $C$11, as follows:

```
=$P$20*$C$11*K22/125.7143
```

You will edit the calories burned formula in cell L22, and then paste it to the rest of the workouts.

To revise the calories burned formulas to use absolute references:

1. Double-click cell **L22** to select it and enter Edit mode.

2. Click immediately to the left of cell reference **P20** in the formula to move the insertion point before the letter P, type **$** to change the column reference to absolute, press the → key to move the insertion point between the letter P and 20, and then type **$** to change the row reference to absolute. The complete absolute reference is now $P$20.

3. Double-click the cell reference **C11** in the formula to select it, and then press the **F4** key to change it to the absolute reference $C$11. The formula is now =$P$20*$C$11*K22/125.7143.

4. Press the **Enter** key to complete the edit. The 376.1 calories burned displayed in the cell is unchanged because the relative references were accurate in this first formula.

5. Copy cell **L22** and paste it into the range **L23:L44**. The worksheet shows 322.4 calories burned for the second workout and 483.6 calories burned for the third workout. The next row in the list shows 0 calories burned because Daniel did not work out that day. As you can see, the remaining formulas now correctly calculate the calories burned at each workout.

6. Format the range **L22:L44** with the **Calculation** cell style. See Figure 3-19.

> Select only the cell reference you want to change before you press the F4 key.

Figure 3-19 Formulas with absolute and relative references

Planning Which Cell Reference to Use in a Formula

You can include the correct type of cell reference in a formula as you create the formula. This requires a little more thought up front, as you consider how each cell in a formula needs to be referenced before you create the formula. Ken wants you to create a running total of the calories burned during each workout. You can use the SUM function with a combination of absolute and relative cell references to add the values in a range. The formula to calculate the total in the first cell is:

=SUM($L$22:L22)

In this formula, the starting cell of the range is fixed at cell L22, but the ending cell of the range is relative. When you copy this formula down the column, the starting cell remains absolutely referenced to cell L22, but the ending cell changes to include the current row. For example, when the formula is pasted three rows down, the formula changes to add the numbers in cells L22, L23, L24, and L25, as follows:

=SUM($L$22:L25)

Continuing in this way, the last cell will contain the sum of all of the calories burned totals using the following formula:

=SUM($L$22:L44)

Instead of entering the formulas yourself, you can use the Quick Analysis tool to calculate the total calories burned up through the end of each workout session.

To calculate the running total of calories burned:

1. In cell **M21**, enter **Calories Subtotal** as the label.
2. Select the range **L22:L44** containing the calories burned during each workout, and then click the **Quick Analysis** button (or press the **Ctrl+Q** keys).
3. Click the **TOTALS** category, and then scroll right to the end of the TOTALS tools.

4. Click **Running Total** (the last entry in the list, which is the Running Total of a column). The range M22:M44 displays the total calories burned up through the end of each workout session.

5. Format the range **M22:M44** with the **Calculation** cell style. See Figure 3-20.

Figure 3-20 Formulas calculating the running total of calories burned

[Screenshot showing Excel spreadsheet with:]
- formula contains absolute and relative references (pointing to =SUM($L$22:L22))
- running totals of the calories burned through the end of each workout (pointing to column M values: 5642.0, 6233.0, 6233.0, 6877.8, 6877.8, 6877.8, 7468.9, 8113.7, 8758.5, 9349.5)

Daniel burned 698.5 calories during the first two workouts and more than 1180 calories after the first three workouts. The formula used to calculate the running totals for the column includes both absolute and relative references. You will review the formulas in column M to see the formulas calculating the running totals.

To view the formulas for the running totals:

1. Select cell **M22**, and then review the formula, which is =SUM($L$22:L22). Notice the absolute and relative references to cell L22.

2. Select cell **M23**, and then review the formula, which is =SUM($L$22:L23). Notice that the absolute reference to cell L22 remains unchanged, but the relative reference is now cell L23, expanding the range being added with the SUM function.

3. Select each cell in column M and review its formula, noticing that the absolute reference $L$22 always appears as the top cell of the range but the relative reference for the last cell of the range changes.

4. Save the workbook.

You can see that the running total is calculated with the SUM function using a combination of absolute and relative cell references. The top of the range used in the SUM function is locked at cell L22, but the bottom of the range is relative, expanding in size as the formula was copied down column M. Entered this way, with absolute and relative cell references, the SUM function calculates partial sums, providing the total calories burned up through the end of each workout session.

INSIGHT

Understanding When to Use Relative, Absolute, and Mixed References

Part of effective workbook design is knowing when to use relative, absolute, and mixed references. Use relative references when you want to apply the same formula with input cells that share a common layout or pattern. Relative references are commonly used when copying a formula that calculates summary statistics across columns or rows of data values. Use absolute references when you want your copied formulas to always refer to the same cell. This usually occurs when a cell contains a constant value, such as a tax rate, that will be referenced in formulas throughout the worksheet. Mixed references are seldom used other than when creating tables of calculated values such as a multiplication table in which the values of the formula or function can be found at the intersection of the rows and columns of the table.

So far, you have entered the fitness formulas and summary statistics in the Fitness Tracker workbook. In the next session, you will explore date and time functions, and then look up values to use in formulas and functions.

REVIEW

Session 3.1 Quick Check

1. What is an optional argument? What does Excel do if you do not include an optional argument?
2. Write the function to return the middle value from the values in the range X1:X10.
3. Write the function to round the value in cell A5 to the fourth decimal place.
4. The range of a set of values is defined as the maximum value minus the minimum value. Write the formula to calculate the range of values in the range Y1:Y10.
5. If cell A11 contains the formula =SUME(A1:A10), what error value will appear in the cell?
6. You need to reference cell Q57 in a formula. What is its relative reference? What is its absolute reference? What are the two mixed references?
7. If cell R10 contains the formula =R1+R2, which is then copied to cell S20, what formula is entered in cell S20?
8. If cell V10 contains the formula = AVERAGE($U1:$U5), which is then copied to cell W20, what formula is entered in cell W20?

EX 160 Excel | Tutorial 3 Calculating Data with Formulas and Functions

Session 3.2 Visual Overview:

A lookup table stores the data you want to retrieve in categories. This is a vertical lookup table that organizes the categories in the first column of the table.

Compare values are the categories located in the first column of the lookup table and are used for matching to a lookup value specified by the user.

Return values are the data values you want to retrieve from the lookup table and are located in the second and subsequent columns.

A lookup value is the category you want to find in a lookup table.

The VLOOKUP function returns values from a vertical lookup table by specifying the lookup value to match to a compare value, the location of the lookup table, and the column in the table that contains the return values.

Basal Metabolic Rate Activity Factors

Activity Level	BMR Factor
Sedentary	1.200
Light	1.375
Moderate	1.550
High	1.725
Extreme	1.900

Personal Data

Name	Daniel Pridham
Activity Level	Light
Age (years)	45
Weight (lb.)	173
Height (in.)	70
Waist (in.)	37
Neck (in.)	15.5

Fitness Assessment

BMI	24.8
Resting BMR (cal./day)	1729
Active BMR (cal./d...)	2377

Notes

=6.23*C11+12.7*C12-6.76*C10+...
=VLOOKUP(C9,O8:P12,2,FALSE)

Workout Summary

Start Date	8/1/201...
Ending Date	8/31/201...
Workouts Scheduled	
Workouts Attended	
Workouts Missed	

Exercise Statistics — Jogging (min.)

SUM	27...
AVERAGE	16...
MEDIAN	15...
MAXIMUM	22...
MINIMUM	10...

Workout Routine 5

Day	Attended (x)
8/1/2016	x
8/2/2016	x
8/3/2016	x
8/4/2016	
8/5/2016	x
8/8/2016	x
8/9/2016	
8/10/2016	x
8/11/2016	x
8/12/2016	x

© 2014 Cengage Learning

Logical and Lookup Functions

Tutorial 3 Calculating Data with Formulas and Functions | Excel EX 161

The COUNT function tallies how many cells in the specified range contain numbers or dates.

=F44
=COUNT(F22:F44)
=COUNTA(G22:G44)
=G9-G10

The COUNTA function tallies how many cells in the specified range are not blank (contain numbers, dates, or text).

Total Minutes
=IF(G22="x",SUM(H22:J22),"")
=IF(G23="x",SUM(H23:J23),"")
=IF(G24="x",SUM(H24:J24),"")
=IF(G25="x",SUM(H25:J25),"")
=IF(G26="x",SUM(H26:J26),"")

A **logical function** is a function that works with statements that are either true or false. This logical function tests whether the value of cell G22 equals x.

The IF function is a logical function that tests a condition and then returns one value if the condition is true and another value if the condition is false.

=G7
=WORKDAY(F22,1)
=WORKDAY(F23,1)
=WORKDAY(F24,1)
=WORKDAY(F25,1)

The WORKDAY function displays the date of a weekday that is a specified number of weekdays past a starting date.

AutoFilling Formulas and Data

AutoFill provides a quick way to enter content and formatting in cells based on existing entries in adjacent cells. Ken wants you to include summary statistics for calories burned across all of the scheduled workouts. To add these statistics, you'll use the AutoFill tool.

REFERENCE

Copying Formulas and Formats with AutoFill
- Select the cell or range that contains the formula or formulas you want to copy.
- Drag the fill handle in the direction you want to copy the formula(s), and then release the mouse button.
- To copy only the formats or only the formulas, click the Auto Fill Options button and select the appropriate option.

or
- Select the cell or range that contains the formula or formulas you want to copy.
- On the HOME tab, in the Editing group, click the Fill button.
- Select a fill direction and fill type.

or
- On the HOME tab, in the Editing group, click Series.
- Enter the desired fill series options, and then click the OK button.

Using the Fill Handle

After you select a range, a **fill handle** appears in the lower-right corner of the selection. When you drag the fill handle over an adjacent cell or range, AutoFill copies the content and formats from the original cell or range into the adjacent cell or range. This process is often more efficient than the two-step process of copying and pasting.

Ken wants you to calculate the same summary statistics for the calories burned during the workouts as you did for the total minutes of each workout. Because the total minutes formulas use relative references, you can use the fill handle to copy these for the calories burned statistics.

To copy the calories burned summary statistics and formatting with the fill handle:

1. In cell **K13**, enter **Calories Burned** as the label.
2. Select the range **J14:J18**, which contains the cells with formulas for calculating the sum, average, median, minimum, and maximum total minutes. A fill handle appears in the lower-right corner of the selected range, directly above and to the left of the Quick Analysis button.
3. Point to the **fill handle**. The pointer changes to ✚.
4. Click and drag the fill handle over the range **K14:K18**. A solid outline appears around the selected range as you move the pointer.
5. Release the mouse button. The selected range is filled in with the formulas and formatting from the range J14:J18, and the Auto Fill Options button appears in the lower-right corner of the selected cells. See Figure 3-21.

> **TIP**
> You can also fill a series to the right by selecting both the cells to copy and the cells to be filled in, and then pressing the Ctrl+R keys.

Tutorial 3 Calculating Data with Formulas and Functions | Excel **EX 163**

Figure 3-21 Formulas and formatting copied with AutoFill

	E	F	G	H	I	J	K
13		Exercise Statistics	Jogging (min.)	Calisthenics (min.)	Strength (min.)	Total Minutes	Calories Burned
14		SUM	278	245	347	870	9349.533028
15		AVERAGE	16.4	14.4	20.4	37.8	406.5
16		MEDIAN	15	15	20	50	537.3294844
17		MINIMUM	10	8	12	0	0
18		MAXIMUM	22	20	30	60	644.7953813

Annotations: formulas and formatting filled into the K14:K18 range; Auto Fill Options button; fill handle.

> 6. Format the range **K14:K18** to display one decimal place.

Based on the summary statistics, Ken can see that Daniel burned 9349.5 calories during the month, burned an average of 406.5 calories per session, burned a median of 537.3 calories per session, and burned a minimum of 0.0 calories and a maximum of 644.8 calories per session during the month.

Using the Auto Fill Options Button

By default, AutoFill copies both the content and the formatting of the original range to the selected range. However, sometimes you might want to copy only the content or only the formatting. The Auto Fill Options button that appears after you release the mouse button lets you specify what is copied. As shown in Figure 3-22, clicking this button provides a menu of AutoFill options. The Copy Cells option, which is the default, copies both the content and the formatting. The Fill Formatting Only option copies the formatting into the selected cells but not any content. The Fill Without Formatting option copies the content but not the formatting.

Figure 3-22 Auto Fill Options button

- Copy Cells — copies the formatting and the formulas
- Fill Formatting Only — copies only the formatting but not the formulas
- Fill Without Formatting — copies only the formulas but not the formatting

Because you want to copy the content and the formatting of the summary statistics, you don't need to use the Auto Fill Options button.

Filling a Series

AutoFill can also be used to create a series of numbers, dates, or text based on a pattern. To create a series of numbers, you enter the initial values in the series in a selected range and then use AutoFill to complete the series.

> **REFERENCE**
>
> **Creating a Series with AutoFill**
>
> - Enter the first few values of the series into a range.
> - Select the range, and then drag the fill handle of the selected range over the cells you want to fill.
>
> or
>
> - Enter the first few values of the series into a range.
> - Select the entire range into which you want to extend the series.
> - On the HOME tab, in the Editing group, click the Fill button, and then click Down, Right, Up, Left, Series, or Justify to set the direction in which you want to extend the series.

Figure 3-23 shows how AutoFill can be used to insert the numbers from 1 to 10 in a selected range. You enter the first few numbers in the range A2:A4 to establish the pattern you want AutoFill to use—consecutive positive numbers in this example. Then, you select the range and drag its fill handle over the cells where you want the pattern continued—in this case, the range A5:A11—and Excel fills in the rest of the series.

Figure 3-23   AutoFill extends a numeric sequence

© 2014 Cengage Learning

AutoFill can extend a wide variety of series, including dates and times and patterned text. Figure 3-24 shows some examples of series that AutoFill can generate. In each case, you must provide enough information for AutoFill to identify the pattern. AutoFill can recognize some patterns from only a single entry—such as Jan or January, to create a series of month abbreviations or names, or Mon or Monday, to create a series of the days of the week. A text pattern that includes text and a number such as Region 1, Region 2, and so on can also be automatically extended using AutoFill. You can start the series at any point, such as Weds, June, or Region 10, and AutoFill will complete the next days, months, or text.

Tutorial 3 Calculating Data with Formulas and Functions | Excel   EX 165

Figure 3-24   AutoFill extends numbers, dates and times, and patterned text

Type	Initial Pattern	Extended Series
Numbers	1, 2, 3	4, 5, 6, ..
	2, 4, 6	8, 10, 12, …
Dates and Times	Jan	Feb, Mar, Apr, …
	January	February, March, April, …
	15-Jan, 15-Feb	15-Mar, 15-Apr, 15-May, …
	12/30/2016	12/31/2016, 1/1/2017, 1/2/2017, …
	12/31/2016, 1/31/2017	2/29/2017, 3/31/2017, 4/30/2017, …
	Mon	Tue, Wed, Thu, …
	Monday	Tuesday, Wednesday, Thursday, …
	11:00AM	12:00PM, 1:00PM, 2:00PM, …
Patterned Text	1st period	2nd period, 3rd period, 4th period, …
	Region 1	Region 2, Region 3, Region 4, …
	Quarter 3	Quarter 4, Quarter 1, Quarter 2, …
	Qtr3	Qtr4, Qtr1, Qtr2, …

© 2014 Cengage Learning

Ken wants you to fill in the dates of the workouts, replacing the numbers in the range F22:F44. You will use AutoFill to insert the calendar dates starting with 8/1/2016.

To use AutoFill to enter the calendar dates:

1. In cell **F22**, enter **8/1/2016**. This is the first date you want to use for the series.
2. Select cell **F22** to select the cell with the first date in the series.
3. Drag the fill handle over the range **F23:F44**.
4. Release the mouse button. AutoFill enters the calendar dates ending with 8/23/2016 in cell F44.

TIP

You can also fill a series down by selecting both the cells to copy and the cells to be filled in, and then pressing the Ctrl+D keys.

For more complex AutoFill patterns, you can use the Series dialog box to specify a linear or growth series for numbers; a date series for dates that increase by day, weekday, month, or year; or an AutoFill series for patterned text. With numbers, you can also specify the step value (how much each number increases over the previous entry) and a stop value (the endpoint for the entire series).

Ken notices that the workout dates are wrong in the Fitness Report worksheet. Fit Fathers meets only Monday through Friday. He asks you to change the fill pattern to include only weekdays. You will use the Series dialog box to set the fill pattern for the rest of the weekdays in the month.

To fill the dates of weekdays in August:

1. Make sure the range **F22:F44** is selected. Cell F22 contains the first value for the series that will be entered in the range F23:F44.
2. On the HOME tab, in the Editing group, click the **Fill** button, and then click **Series**. The Series dialog box opens.
3. In the Type section, make sure that the **Date** option button is selected.

4. In the Date unit section, click the **Weekday** option button so that the series includes only dates for Mondays through Fridays. See Figure 3-25.

Figure 3-25 **Series dialog box**

- fills the series columns
- specifies date as the type of series
- specifies weekdays as the date unit

5. Click the **OK** button. The dates of weekdays in August are filled into the selected range ending with 8/31/2016. See Figure 3-26.

Figure 3-26 **Weekday values filled in**

only weekdays are entered in the selected range

	E	F	G	H	I	J
20		Workout Routine 5				
21		Day	Attended (x)	Jogging (min.)	Calisthenics (min.)	Strength (min.)	Tota
22		8/1/2016	x	10	10	15	
23		8/2/2016	x	10	8	12	
24		8/3/2016	x	12	18	15	
25		8/4/2016					
26		8/5/2016	x	12	15	18	
27		8/8/2016	x	15	10	15	
28		8/9/2016					
29		8/10/2016	x	15	15	20	
30		8/11/2016	x	15	13	22	
31		8/12/2016	x	20	15	25	
32		8/15/2016	x	20	15	20	
33		8/16/2016	x	22	8	30	
34		8/17/2016					
35		8/18/2016	x	12	18	25	
36		8/19/2016	x	15	20	20	
37		8/22/2016					
38		8/23/2016	x	20	17	23	

Working with Date Functions

Excel has several functions that work with dates and times. **Date functions** insert or calculate dates and times. They are particularly useful in business workbooks that involve production schedules and calendar applications. Figure 3-27 describes some of the commonly used Date functions.

Figure 3-27 Date functions

Function	Description
DATE(year, month, day)	Creates a date value for the date represented by the year, month, and day arguments
DAY(date)	Extracts the day of the month from date
MONTH(date)	Extracts the month number from date where 1=January, 2=February, and so forth
YEAR(date)	Extracts the year number from date
NETWORKDAYS(start, end[, holidays])	Calculates the number of whole working days between start and end; to exclude holidays, add the optional holidays argument containing a list of holiday dates to skip
WEEKDAY(date[, return_type])	Calculates the weekday from date, where 1=Sunday, 2=Monday, and so forth; to choose a different numbering scheme, set return_type to 1 (1=Sunday, 2=Monday, ...), 2 (1=Monday, 2=Tuesday, ...), or 3 (0=Monday, 1=Tuesday, ...)
WORKDAY(start, days[, holidays])	Returns the workday after days workdays have passed since the start date; to exclude holidays, add the optional holidays argument containing a list of holiday dates to skip
NOW( )	Returns the current date and time
TODAY( )	Returns the current date

© 2014 Cengage Learning

Displaying the Current Date with the TODAY function

Many workbooks include the current date. You can use the **TODAY function** to display the current date in a worksheet. The TODAY function has the following syntax:

=TODAY()

TIP

To display the current date and time, which is updated each time the workbook is reopened, use the NOW function.

Note that although the TODAY function doesn't have any arguments, you still must include the parentheses for the function to work. The date displayed by the TODAY function is updated automatically whenever you reopen the workbook or enter a new calculation.

Ken wants the Fitness Report worksheet to show the current date each time it is used or printed. You will use the TODAY function to display the current date in cell G2.

To display the current date with the TODAY function:

▶ 1. Select cell **G2**.
▶ 2. On the FORMULAS tab, in the Function Library group, click the **Date & Time** button to display the date and time functions.
▶ 3. Click **TODAY**. The Function Arguments dialog box opens and indicates that the TODAY function requires no arguments.
▶ 4. Click the **OK** button. The formula =TODAY() is entered in cell G2.
▶ 5. Verify that the current date is displayed in the cell.
▶ 6. Format the cell using the **Calculation** style.

Finding the Next Weekday with the WORKDAY function

Instead of using AutoFill to enter a series of dates in a range, you can use the WORKDAY function to fill in the remaining weekdays based on the start date you specify. The WORKDAY function displays the date of the weekday a specific number of weekdays past a starting date. The syntax of the WORKDAY function is

TIP

You can enter the dates to skip into worksheet cells, and then reference that range in the *holiday* argument of the WORKDAY function.

```
=WORKDAY(start, days[, holiday])
```

where *start* is a start date, *days* is the number of weekdays after *start*, and *holiday* is an optional list of dates to skip. If you do not include anything for the optional *holiday* argument, the WORKDAY function does not skip any days. For example, if cell A1 contains the date 11/4/2016, a Friday, the following formula displays the date 11/9/2016, a Wednesday that is three working days after 11/4/2016:

```
=WORKDAY(A1, 3)
```

Ken wants to automate the process of inserting the exercise dates. You will use the WORKDAY function to do this.

To insert the exercise dates using the WORKDAY function:

1. In cell **G7**, enter **8/1/2016** to specify the date the workouts will begin, and then format the cell using the **Input** cell style.

2. In cell **G8**, enter the formula **=F44** to display the date of the last scheduled workout, which is 8/31/2016 in this instance, and then format the cell using the **Calculation** cell style.

3. In cell **F22**, enter the formula **=G7** to replace the date with a reference to the start date you specified in cell G7. The cell still displays 8/1/2016.

4. Select cell **F23**, if necessary, and then click the **Insert Function** button next to the formula bar. The Insert Function dialog box opens.

5. Type **working days** in the Search for a function box, and then click the **Go** button to find all of the functions related to working days.

6. In the Select a function box, click **WORKDAY** to select the function, and then click the **OK** button. The WORKDAY Function Arguments dialog box opens.

7. In the Start_date box, type the cell reference **F22** to specify that cell F22 contains the start date you want to use.

8. In the Days box, type **1** to specify the number of workdays after the date in cell F22 that you want the formula results to show. See Figure 3-28.

Figure 3-28 Function Arguments dialog box for the WORKDAY function

cell reference for the cell with the start date

number of workdays after the start date

preview of the formula result

TIP

To select a working day prior to the start date, enter a negative number rather than a positive number.

9. Click the **OK** button. Cell F23 contains the formula =WORKDAY(F22, 1) and displays the date 8/2/2016, which is the next workday after 8/1/2016.

   You want to use the same formula to calculate the rest of the workout dates. You can use AutoFill to quickly repeat the formula.

10. Select cell **F23**, and then drag the fill handle down over the range **F23:F44** to copy the formula and enter the rest of the workdays in the month.

    Because the copied formulas use relative references, each cell displays a date that is one workday after the date in the previous cell. The dates should not be different from the dates you entered previously using AutoFill.

11. Format the range **F22:F44** with the **Calculation** cell style to show that these dates are calculated by a formula rather than entered manually.

    You will test that the formulas in the range F22:F44 are working correctly by entering a different start date.

12. In cell **G7**, enter **9/1/2016** as the new start date.

13. Review the dates in the range F22:F44, verifying that the workout dates start with 9/2/2016 in cell F23, continue with 9/5/2016 in cell F24, and end with 10/3/2016 in cell F44.

    Trouble? If the workout dates do not end with 10/3/2016, compare the formula in cell F23 to the formula shown in Step 9, make any edits needed, and then repeat Step 10.

14. In cell **G7**, enter **8/1/2016** to return to the original start date.

INSIGHT

Selecting the Days in the Work Week

Different countries, regions, and even businesses might have different rules for what constitutes a workday. If you need to create a schedule that doesn't follow the standard U.S. business days (Monday through Friday), you can use the WORKDAY.INTL function to specify the days to use as the work week. The syntax of the WORKDAY.INTL function is:

```
=WORKDAY.INTL(start, days[, weekend=1, holidays])
```

The only difference between the syntax of the WORKDAY.INTL function and the syntax of the WORKDAY function is the optional *weekend* argument, which specifies the days of the week considered to be weekend or nonworking days. If you omit the *weekend* argument, weekends are considered to occur only on Saturday and Sunday. If you include the *weekend* argument, you enter one of the following numbers to specify the two days or the one day to consider as the weekend:

Weekend	Two-Day Weekend	Weekend	One-Day Weekend
1	Saturday, Sunday	11	Sunday
2	Sunday, Monday	12	Monday
3	Monday, Tuesday	13	Tuesday
...		...	
7	Friday, Saturday	17	Saturday

For example, a business that is open every day except Sunday would use a *weekend* value of 11 to indicate that only Sunday is considered a nonworking day, and a business that is closed on Monday and Tuesday would use a *weekend* value of 3 to specify a work week of Wednesday through Sunday. For other working week schedules, you can enter text to specify which days are workdays. See Excel Help for more information.

Counting Cells

Excel has two functions for counting cells—the COUNT function and the COUNTA function. The COUNT function tallies how many cells in a range contain numbers or dates (because they are stored as numeric values). The COUNT function does not count blank cells or cells that contain text. Its syntax is

```
COUNT(value1[, value2, value3, ...])
```

where *value1* is the first item or cell reference containing the numbers you want to count. The remaining *value* arguments are used primarily when you want to count numbers and dates in nonadjacent ranges. For example, the following function counts how many cells in the range A1:A10, the range C1:C5, and cell E5 contain numbers or dates:

```
COUNT(A1:A10, C1:C5, E5)
```

If you want to know how many cells contain entries—whether those entries are numbers, dates, or text—you use the COUNTA function, which tallies the nonblank cells in a range. The following is the syntax of the COUNTA function, which has the same arguments as the COUNT function:

```
COUNTA(value1[, value2, value3, ...])
```

Ken wants the Workout Summary to show the total number of scheduled workouts for the month, the number of attended workouts, and the number of missed workouts. You will use the COUNT function to count the total number of workout dates in the Workout Routine 5 table. Then, you will use the COUNTA function to count the number of workouts actually attended. Each attended workout is marked by an "x" in column G of the Workout Routine 5 table; missing workouts are left blank. Finally, you will enter a formula to calculate the missed workouts.

To count the scheduled, attended, and missed workouts:

1. In cell **G9**, enter the formula **=COUNT(F22:F44)**. Cell G9 displays 23, indicating that Ken scheduled 23 workouts for the month.

2. In cell **G10**, enter the formula **=COUNTA(G22:G44)**. Cell G10 displays 17, indicating that Daniel attended 17 of the 23 scheduled workouts.

3. In cell **G11**, enter the formula **=G9–G10** to calculate the difference between the number of scheduled workouts and the number of attended workouts. Cell G11 displays 6, which is the number of missed workouts.

4. Format the range **G9:G11** with the **Calculation** cell style.

5. Select cell **G10**. See Figure 3-29.

Figure 3-29 | Completed Workout Summary

COUNTA function counts the number of nonblank cells in the specified range

Cell G10: `=COUNTA(G22:G44)`

	E	F	G
6		Workout Summary	
7		Start Date	8/1/2016
8		End Date	8/31/2016
9		Workouts Scheduled	23
10		Workouts Attended	17
11		Workouts Missed	6
13		Exercise Statistics	Jogging (min.) Calisthenics (min.) Strength (min.) Total Minutes Calor

number of scheduled workouts

workouts marked with an "x" in the Attended column

difference between the scheduled and attended workouts

It is important to understand the difference between the COUNT and COUNTA functions. For example, if you had used the COUNT function in cell G10 to tally the number of attended workouts, the result would have been 0 because the range G22:G44 contains no entries with numbers.

Like the COUNT function, many of Excel's statistical functions ignore cells that are blank or contain text. This can create unexpected results with calculated values if you are not careful. Figure 3-30 shows how some of the common summary statistics change when blank cells are used in place of zeroes.

Figure 3-30 | Calculations involving blank cells and zeroes

	A	B	C	D
1		Zero Values	Blank Cells	
2		7	7	
3		0		
4		8	8	
5		5	5	
6		6	6	
7		0		
8		4	4	
9	Sum	30	30	
10	Count	7	5	
11	Average	4.29	6	
12	Median	5	6	
13	Minimum	0	4	
14	Maximum	8	8	

cells with zeroes

cells left blank

Excel returns a different value depending on whether zeroes or blank cells are used

Some of the fitness statistics for total exercise minutes and calories burned include the six workouts that Daniel missed. For example, the minimum exercise minutes and calories burned are both listed as 0 because the calculated values show up as 0 in the worksheet when the workout session was missed. Ken wants the summary statistics based on only the workouts actually attended. One way to exclude missed workouts is to delete the zeroes, leaving blank cells. However, Ken wants the worksheet to be user-friendly and not require anyone to double-check and edit entries for missed workouts. Instead of editing the worksheet, you can use a logical function to automatically replace zeroes with blanks for missed workouts.

Working with Logical Functions

A logical function returns a different value depending on whether the given condition is true or false, such as whether or not a scheduled workout was attended. In Excel, the condition is expressed as a formula. Consider a condition that includes the expression A5=3. If cell A5 is equal to 3, this expression and condition are true; if cell A5 is not equal to 3, this expression and condition are false. The IF function is one of the many logical functions you can use in Excel.

Using the IF Function

The IF function is a logical function that returns one value if a condition is true, and returns a different value if that condition is false. The syntax of the IF function is

```
IF(logical_test, value_if_true, value_if_false)
```

where `logical_test` is a condition that is either true or false, `value_if_true` is the value returned by the function if the condition is true, and `value_if_false` is the value returned if the condition is false. The value can be a number, text, a date, or a cell reference. For example, the following formula tests whether the value in cell A1 is equal to the value in cell B1:

```
=IF(A1=B1, 100, 50)
```

If the value in cell A1 equals the value in cell B1, the formula result is 100; otherwise, the formula result is 50.

In many cases, however, you will not use values directly in the IF function. The following formula uses cell references, returning the value of cell C1 if A1 equals B1; otherwise, it returns the value of cell C2:

```
=IF(A1=B1, C1, C2)
```

The = symbol in these formulas is a comparison operator. A **comparison operator** is a symbol that indicates the relationship between two values. Figure 3-31 describes the comparison operators that can be used within a logical function.

Figure 3-31   Comparison operators

Operator	Expression	Description
=	A1 = B1	Tests whether the value in cell A1 is equal to the value in cell B1
>	A1 > B1	Tests whether the value in cell A1 is greater than the value in cell B1
<	A1 < B1	Tests whether the value in cell A1 is less than the value in cell B1
>=	A1 >= B1	Tests whether the value in cell A1 is greater than or equal to the value in cell B1
<=	A1 <= B1	Tests whether the value in cell A1 is less than or equal to the value in cell B1
<>	A1 <> B1	Tests whether the value in cell A1 is not equal to the value in cell B1

© 2014 Cengage Learning

The IF function also works with text. For example, the following formula tests whether the value of cell A1 is equal to "yes":

```
=IF(A1="yes", "done", "restart")
```

If true (the value of cell A1 is equal to "yes"), the formula returns the text "done"; otherwise, it returns the text "restart". Notice that the text in the function is enclosed in quotation marks.

In addition, you can nest other functions inside an IF statement. The following formula first tests whether cell A5 is equal to the maximum of values within the range A1:A100:

```
=IF(A5=MAX(A1:A100), "Maximum", "")
```

TIP

For the formula result to show no text, include opening and closing quotation marks with nothing between them.

If it is, the formula returns the text "Maximum"; otherwise, it returns no text.

In the Fitness Report worksheet, you need to rewrite the formulas that calculate the total minutes and total calories from each workout as IF functions that test whether Daniel actually attended the workout. Because every attended workout is marked with an "x" in column G, you can test whether the cell entry in column G is an "x". For example, the following formula in cell K22 is currently being used to calculate the total minutes from the first workout:

```
=SUM(H22:J22)
```

This formula can be revised to the following IF function, which first determines if cell G22 contains an "x" (indicating that the workout was attended), and then uses the SUM function to calculate the total minutes if there is an "x":

```
=IF(G22="x", SUM(H22:J22), "")
```

Otherwise, the formula displays nothing, leaving the cell blank.

You will use relative references in the revised formula so that you can copy it for the other workouts and total columns. You will create the formula with the IF function for the total minutes column now.

To use an IF function to calculate total minutes for attended workouts:

1. Select cell **K22**, and then press the **Delete** key to clear the original formula from the cell.

2. Click the **Insert Function** button f_x next to the formula bar to open the Insert Function dialog box.

3. Type **if function** in the Search for a function box, and then press the **Enter** key. Functions that match your description appear in the Select a function box.

4. Click **IF** in the Select a function box, and then click the **OK** button to open the Function Arguments dialog box.

5. In the Logical_test box, type **G22="x"** as the expression that tests whether cell G22 is equal to x.

6. Press the **Tab** key to move the insertion point to the Value_if_true box, and then type **SUM(H22:J22)**. If cell G22 does contain an x (the logical test is true), the sum of the values in the range H22:J22 will be displayed in cell K22.

7. Press the **Tab** key to move the insertion point to the Value_if_false box, and then type **""** (opening and closing quotation marks). If cell G22 does not contain an x (the logical test is false), the cell will be left blank. See Figure 3-32.

EX 174 Excel | Tutorial 3 Calculating Data with Formulas and Functions

Figure 3-32   **Function Arguments dialog box for the IF function**

- statement to evaluate as true or false
- Logical_test: G22="x" = TRUE
- Value_if_true: SUM(H22:J22) = 35
- Value_if_false: "" = ""
- calculates the sum if the statement is true
- displays nothing if the statement is false
- preview of the formula result: Formula result = 35

Checks whether a condition is met, and returns one value if TRUE, and another value if FALSE.

Value_if_false is the value that is returned if Logical_test is FALSE. If omitted, FALSE is returned.

▶ 8. Click the **OK** button. The formula =IF(G22="x", SUM(H22:J22), "") is entered into cell K22. The cell displays 35, which is the number of minutes Daniel spent exercising at that workout session.

You will copy the formula with the IF function to calculate the total minutes for the rest of the workouts.

▶ 9. Select cell **K22**, and then drag the fill handle down over the range **K22:K44** to copy the IF formula to the remaining cells in the column. The total number of minutes for each workout is recalculated so that the missed workouts in cells K25, K28, K34, K37, K39, and K40 are now left blank.

▶ 10. Select cell **K22**. The #VALUE! error value appears in columns L and M for each of the missed workouts because the current formulas cannot calculate calories burned when no total minutes are provided. See Figure 3-33.

Figure 3-33   **IF function excludes the total minutes for missed workouts**

- IF function tests whether the workout was attended (marked with an "x") before calculating the total minutes of exercise
- Total Minutes summary statistics no longer include missed workouts
- error values appear because formulas need a total minutes value to calculate
- attended workouts marked with an "x"
- missed workouts displayed as blank cells

K22 =IF(G22="x",SUM(H22:J22),"")

	E	F	G	H	I	J	K
13	Exercise Statistics		Jogging (min.)	Calisthenics (min.)	Strength (min.)	Total Minutes	Calories Burned
14	SUM		278	245	347	870	#VALUE!
15	AVERAGE		16.4	14.4	20.4	51.2	#VALUE!
16	MEDIAN		15	15	20	55	#VALUE!
17	MINIMUM		10	8	12	30	#VALUE!
18	MAXIMUM		22	20	30	60	#VALUE!
20	Workout Routine 5						
21	Day	Attended (x)	Jogging (min.)	Calisthenics (min.)	Strength (min.)	Total Minutes	Calories Burned
22	8/1/2016	x	10	10	15	35	376.1
23	8/2/2016	x	10	8	12	30	322.4
24	8/3/2016	x	12	18	15	45	483.6
25	016						#VALUE!
26	016	x			18	45	483.6
27	016	x			15	40	429.9
28	016						#VALUE!
29	016	x	15	15	20	50	537.3
30	8/11/2016	x	15	13	22	50	537.3
31	8/12/2016	x	20	15	25	60	644.8

Tutorial 3 Calculating Data with Formulas and Functions | Excel **EX 175**

Next, you will update the calories burned formulas so that they don't display the #VALUE! error value when a workout is missed. This requires another IF statement similar to the one you used to calculate total minutes. As with the total minutes calculation, any missed workout will display a blank cell for the calories burned in place of a 0. Rather than reentering the complete formula for calories burned, you can edit the existing formula, inserting the IF function.

To change the calories burned formulas to IF functions:

1. Double-click cell **L22** to enter Edit mode.

2. Press the **Home** key to move the insertion point to the beginning of the formula, and then press the → key to move the insertion point one space to the right, directly after = (the equal sign). You will begin the IF function after the equal sign.

3. Type **IF(G22="x",** to insert the function name and the expression for the logical test.

4. Press the **Ctrl+End** keys to move the insertion point to the end of the formula.

5. Type **, "")** to enter the value if false and complete the IF function. The complete formula is now =IF(G22="x", $P$20*$C$11*K22/125.7143, "").

    Make sure your formula matches the one shown here.

6. Press the **Enter** key to exit Edit mode and make cell L23 active. Cell L22 still displays 376.1 because Ken did not miss the first workout.

    You will use AutoFill to copy the IF function to the rest of the cells in the Calories Burned column.

7. Select cell **L22**, and then drag the fill handle down over the range **L22:L44**. As shown in Figure 3-34, the missed workouts now display blank cells instead of zeroes, and the attended workouts show the same calculated values as earlier.

Figure 3-34   IF function excludes the calories burned for missed workouts

By excluding the missed workouts, Daniel's average exercise time increased from 37.8 minutes to 51.2 minutes, and the average calories burned increased to 550 calories. These averages more closely match the median values because zeroes were removed from the calculations. The minimum values for Total Minutes and Calories Burned now also reflect only attended workouts, changing from 0 (when they were based on a missed workout) to 30 minutes and 322.4 calories, respectively. These measures reflect the true results of the workouts Daniel attended.

Using a Lookup Function

Lookup functions find values in tables of data and insert them in another location in the worksheet such as cells or in formulas. For example, consider the active BMR calculated in cell C22, which adjusts the calculation of Daniel's metabolic rate to account for his activity level. The more active Daniel is, the more calories he can consume without gaining weight. The multiplying factors for each activity level (Sedentary, Light, Moderate, High, or Extreme) are stored in a table in the range O8:P12; you used the value in cell P8 to adjust Daniel's BMR value for his sedentary lifestyle. Instead of including a direct reference to one of the multiplying factors in the table, you can use a function to have Excel choose the multiplying factor that corresponds to the specified activity level.

The table that stores the data you want to retrieve is called a lookup table. A lookup table organizes numbers or text into categories. This particular lookup table organizes the BMR factors by activity levels, as shown in Figure 3-35. Every activity level category in the first column of the lookup table has a corresponding BMR factor in the second column of the table. This table is a vertical lookup table because the categories are arranged vertically. The entries in the first column of a vertical lookup table are referred to as the compare values because they are compared to the category you want to find (called the lookup value). When a match is found, the corresponding value in one of the subsequent columns is returned. For example, to find the return value for the Moderate lookup value, you look down the first column of the lookup table until you find the Moderate entry. Then, you move to the second column to locate the corresponding return value, which is 1.550, in this case.

Figure 3-35 Finding an exact match from a vertical lookup table

Lookup Value = "Moderate"

go down the first column until the lookup value exactly matches the compare value

Basal Metabolic Rate Activity Factors

Activity Level	BMR Factor
Sedentary	1.200
Light	1.375
Moderate	1.550
High	1.725
Extreme	1.900

return the corresponding value from the second column of the table

Return Value = 1.550

© 2014 Cengage Learning

Lookup tables can be constructed for exact match or approximate match lookups. An **exact match lookup** is when the lookup value must match one of the compare values in the first column of the lookup table. The table in Figure 3-35 is an exact match lookup because the activity level must match one of the compare values in the table or a value is not returned. An **approximate match lookup** occurs when the lookup value falls within a range of numbers in the first column of the lookup table. You will work with exact match lookups in this tutorial.

Finding an Exact Match with the VLOOKUP Function

To retrieve the return value from a vertical lookup table, you use the VLOOKUP function. The syntax of the VLOOKUP function is

```
VLOOKUP(lookup_value, table_array, col_index_num[, range_lookup=TRUE])
```

where `lookup_value` is the compare value to find in the first column of the lookup table, `table_array` is the range reference to the lookup table, and `col_index_num` is the number of the column in the lookup table that contains the return value. Keep in mind that `col_index_num` refers to the number of the column within the lookup table, not the worksheet column. For example, `col_index_num` 2 refers to the second column of the table, `col_index_num` 3 refers to the third column of the table, and so forth. Finally, `range_lookup` is an optional argument that specifies whether the compare values are an exact match or a range of values (for an approximate match). For an exact match, you set the `range_lookup` value to FALSE. For approximate match lookups, you set the `range_lookup` value to TRUE or you can omit it because its default value is TRUE.

For example, the following formula performs an exact match lookup to find the BMR factor for an Extreme activity level based on the values from the lookup table in the range O8:P12 (shown earlier in Figure 3-35):

```
=VLOOKUP("Extreme", O8:P12, 2, FALSE)
```

> **TIP**
>
> If the VLOOKUP function cannot find the lookup value, the #N/A error value is displayed in the cell.

The `col_index_num` is 2 because the BMR factors are in the second column of the table. The `range_lookup` is FALSE because this is an exact match. The function looks through the compare values in the first column of the table to locate the "Extreme" entry. When the exact entry is found, the function returns the corresponding value in the second column of the table, which in this case is 1.900.

Daniel's activity level in cell C9 is entered as Sedentary, which has a BMR factor of 1.2. The following active BMR formula you entered earlier calculated that Daniel can consume about 2224 calories per day and maintain his current weight:

```
=P8*C21
```

In this formula, `P8` references the Sedentary BMR value in cell P8 and `C21` references Daniel's base or resting metabolic rate. To have Excel look up the BMR value, you need to replace the P8 cell reference with a VLOOKUP function, as follows:

```
=VLOOKUP(C9, O8:P12, 2, FALSE)*C21
```

In this formula, `C9` contains Daniel's activity level (Sedentary), `O8:P12` references the lookup table, 2 specifies the table column to find the BMR factors, and `FALSE` indicates that this is an exact match lookup. You will enter this formula into the worksheet now.

To use the VLOOKUP function to calculate Daniel's active BMR:

1. Select cell **C22**, and then press the **Delete** key to clear the formula currently in the cell.

2. On the ribbon, click the **FORMULAS** tab. Because VLOOKUP has several arguments to manage, you will enter the function using the Function Arguments dialog box.

3. In the Function Library group, click **Lookup & Reference** to display a list of functions, and then click **VLOOKUP**. The Function Arguments dialog box opens.

4. With the insertion point in the Lookup_value box, click cell **C9** in the worksheet to enter that cell reference as the location containing the value to look up in the first column of the lookup table.

5. Press the **Tab** key to move the insertion point into the Table_array box, and then select the range **O8:P12**, which contains the vertical lookup table in the worksheet.

6. Press the **Tab** key to move the insertion point to the Col_index_num box, and then type **2** to return a value from the second column of the lookup table.

7. Press the **Tab** key to move the insertion point to the Range_lookup box, and then type **FALSE** to specify an exact match lookup. The dialog box shows the resulting value of the function with these arguments, which in this case is 1.2. See Figure 3-36.

Figure 3-36   Function Arguments dialog box for the VLOOKUP function

- cell with the value to look up in the first column of the table
- range with the lookup table
- return value is in the second column of the lookup table
- returns a value only if an exact match is found
- value returned from the lookup table

8. Click the **OK** button to close the dialog box.

9. Double-click cell **C22** to enter Edit mode, press the **Ctrl+End** keys to move the insertion point to the end of the formula, type ***C21** to complete the formula, and then press the **Enter** key. The completed formula in cell C22 is =VLOOKUP(C9,O8:P12,2,FALSE)*C21, resulting in an active BMR of 2224 calories per day for a Sedentary activity level.

You will change the activity level to ensure that the formula works correctly.

10. In cell **C9**, enter **Moderate** to change the activity level from Sedentary. The active BMR value changes to 2872 because the VLOOKUP function returns a 1.55 BMR factor from the lookup table.

Ken decides that Light is a more accurate description of Daniel's activity level.

11. In cell **C9**, enter **Light** as the activity level. At that activity level, the active BMR changes to 2548. With a Light activity level, Daniel can consume about 2548 calories per day and maintain his current weight.

12. Select cell **C22** to view the formula. See Figure 3-37.

TIP

Exact matches are not case sensitive, so the lookup values Light, light, and LIGHT are considered to be the same.

Figure 3-37 VLOOKUP function calculates the active BMR

- VLOOKUP function looks up the BMR factor from the table in the range O8:P12
- updated activity level
- formula results show the daily calories for light activity

Performing What-If Analysis

A **what-if analysis** lets you explore the impact that changing input values has on the calculated values in the workbook. For example, Ken could perform a what-if analysis to determine how many pounds Daniel needs to lose to reach a more healthy weight. Current fitness standards suggest that a body mass index between 18.5 and 24.9 is considered to be within the "normal" classification. Daniel's body mass index is 27.7, which is rated as overweight. So Ken wants to know how many pounds Daniel needs to lose to reduce his body mass index to 24.9.

Using Trial and Error

One way to perform a what-if analysis is by changing one or more of the input values to see how they affect the calculated results. This **trial-and-error method** requires some guesswork as you estimate which values to change and by how much. In this case, Ken wants you to find out the weight at which Daniel would reach a BMI of 24.9. You'll start by checking the resulting body mass index if Daniel were to lose 10 pounds, reducing his weight to 183 pounds.

To perform a what-if analysis by trial and error:

1. In cell **C11**, change the weight from 193 pounds to **183** pounds. Daniel's body mass index decreases from 27.7 to 26.3, as shown in cell C19. At this weight, he is still considered overweight.

2. In cell **C11**, enter **163** pounds. At this weight, Daniel's BMI shown in cell C19 is 23.4. So losing 30 pounds is more than enough to classify Daniel's body weight as normal.

    Ken wants to know if Daniel can lose fewer than 30 pounds to reach that classification.

3. In cell **C11**, enter **168** pounds. At this weight, Daniel's BMI value is 24.1, which is still within the normal classification, but not exactly equal to 24.9.

If you want to find the exact weight that will result in a body mass index of 24.9, you would have to continue trying different weight values as you close in on the correct weight. This is why the method is called "trial and error." For some calculations, trial and error can be a very time-consuming way to locate the exact input value. A more direct approach to this problem is to use Goal Seek.

Using Goal Seek

TIP

Goal Seek can only be used with calculated numbers, not text or a value from a lookup table.

Goal Seek automates the trial-and-error process by allowing you to specify a value for a calculated item, which Excel uses to determine the input value needed to reach that goal. In this case, because Ken wants to know how Daniel can reach a body mass index of exactly 24.9 (the upper level of the normal classification), the question that Goal Seek answers is: "What weight value is required to reach that goal?" Goal Seek starts by setting the calculated value and works backward to determine the correct input value.

REFERENCE

Performing What-If Analysis and Goal Seek

To perform a what-if analysis by trial and error:
- Change the value of a worksheet cell (the input cell).
- Observe its impact on one or more calculated cells (the result cells).
- Repeat until the desired results are achieved.

To perform a what-if analysis using Goal Seek:
- On the DATA tab, in the Data Tools group, click the What-If Analysis button, and then click Goal Seek.
- Select the result cell in the Set cell box, and then specify its value (goal) in the To value box.
- In the By changing cell box, specify the input cell.
- Click the OK button. The value of the input cell changes to set the value of the result cell.

You will use Goal Seek to find the weight that will result in Daniel's BMI reaching exactly 24.9.

To use Goal Seek to find a weight resulting in a 24.9 BMI:

1. On the ribbon, click the **DATA** tab.

2. In the Data Tools group, click the **What-If Analysis** button, and then click **Goal Seek**. The Goal Seek dialog box opens.

3. Make sure the value in the Set cell box is selected, and then click cell **C19** in the Fitness Report worksheet. The absolute cell reference $C$19 appears in the Set cell box. The set cell is the calculated value you want Goal Seek to change to meet your goal.

Tutorial 3 Calculating Data with Formulas and Functions | Excel   EX 181

▸ 4. Press the **Tab** key to move the insertion point to the To value box, and then type **24.9**. This indicates that you want Goal Seek to set this value to 24.9 (the highest body mass index in the normal classification).

▸ 5. Press the **Tab** key to move the insertion point to the By changing cell box. There are often various input values you can change to meet a goal. In this case, you want to change the weight value in cell C11.

▸ 6. Click cell **C11**. The absolute reference $C$11 appears in the By changing cell box. See Figure 3-38.

Figure 3-38 Goal Seek dialog box

Goal Seek dialog box:
- Set cell: $C$19 — cell whose value should be set
- To value: 24.9 — value to set cell to
- By changing cell: $C$11 — input cell whose value should be changed to meet the set goal

▸ 7. Click the **OK** button. The Goal Seek dialog box closes, and the Goal Seek Status dialog box opens, indicating that Goal Seek found a solution.

▸ 8. Click the **OK** button. A weight value of about 173 pounds is displayed in cell C11. Daniel would need to lose roughly 20 pounds, reducing his weight to 173 pounds to reach a weight within the normal classification for BMI. See Figure 3-39.

Figure 3-39 Target weight determined by Goal Seek

	A	B	C	D	E	F	G	H
6		Personal Data				Workout Summary		
7						Start Date	8/1/2016	
8		Name	Daniel Pridham			End Date	8/31/2016	
9		Activity Level	Light			Workouts Scheduled	23	
10		Age (years)	45			Workouts Attended	17	
11		Weight (lb.)	173.5561878			Workouts Missed	6	
12		Height (in.)	70					
13		Waist (in.)	37			Exercise Statistics	Jogging (min.)	Calistheni
14		Neck (in.)	15.5			SUM	278	
15						AVERAGE	16.4	
16						MEDIAN	15	
17		Fitness Assessment				MINIMUM	10	
18						MAXIMUM	22	
19		BMI	24.9					
20						Workout Routine 5		
21		Resting BMR (cal./day)	1732			Day	Attended (x)	Jogging
22		Active BMR (cal./day)	2382			8/1/2016	x	
23						8/2/2016	x	
24						8/3/2016	x	

- solution weight (C11: 173.5561878)
- desired BMI (C19: 24.9)

Sheet tabs: Documentation | Fitness Report | Explanation of Formulas

READY

▸ 9. Save and close the workbook.

Ken appreciates all of the work you have done in developing the Fitness Tracker workbook. He will use this workbook as a model for all of his other clients at Fit Fathers.

REVIEW

Session 3.2 Quick Check

1. The first three values in a selected series are 3, 6, and 9. What are the next three values that will be inserted by AutoFill?
2. Write a formula to display the current date.
3. Write a formula to find the date four workdays after the date value stored in cell B10. There are no holidays.
4. Explain the difference between the COUNT function and the COUNTA function.
5. If cell Q3 is greater than cell Q4, you want to display the text "OK"; otherwise, display the text "RETRY". Write the formula that accomplishes this.
6. Jan is entering hundreds of temperature values into an Excel worksheet for a climate research project, and she wants to save time on data entry by leaving freezing point values as blanks rather than typing zeroes. Will this cause complications if she later tries to calculate an average temperature from her data values? Explain why or why not.
7. Provide the formula to perform an exact match lookup with the lookup value from cell G5 using a lookup table located in the range A1:F50. Return the value from the third column of the table.
8. What is the difference between a what-if analysis by trial and error and by Goal Seek?

Tutorial 3 Calculating Data with Formulas and Functions | Excel

SAM Projects

Put your skills into practice with SAM Projects! SAM Projects for this tutorial can be found online. If you have a SAM account, go to www.cengage.com/sam2013 to download the most recent Project Instructions and Start Files.

Review Assignments

Data File needed for the Review Assignments: Mothers.xlsx

Ken and his wife, Sally, are expanding the business, changing its name to Fit Fathers and Mothers Inc., and adding fitness classes for mothers with a special emphasis on pregnant women. The fitness equations for women are different from those for men. Ken and Sally want you to create a workbook similar to the one you created for fathers, but focused on the fitness needs of women. Sally also wants you to calculate the total fat burned in the course of completing the workout schedule. She has already designed much of the workbook's contents, but she needs you to add the formulas and functions. Complete the following:

1. Open the **Mothers** workbook located in the Excel3 ▸ Review folder included with your Data Files, and then save the workbook as **Mothers Fitness** in the location specified by your instructor.
2. In the Documentation sheet, enter your name and the date.
3. Go to the Fitness Analysis worksheet. In the range C8:C15, enter the personal data for **Dorothy Young**. Her activity level is **Moderate**, she is **38** years old, **152** pounds, **64** inches tall, with a **33**-inch waist, **35**-inch hips, and a **14**-inch neck.
4. In cell C20, enter a formula to calculate Dorothy's body mass index based on the equation
   $$BMI = 703w/h^2$$
   where w is the weight in pounds and h is the height in inches. Display the formula results with one decimal place.
5. In cell C22, enter a formula to calculate the resting metabolism rate for women based on the equation
   $$BMR = 4.338w + 4.698h - 4.68a + 655$$
   where w is the weight in pounds, h is the height in inches, and a is the age in years. Display the formula results with no decimal places.
6. In cell C23, enter a formula using the VLOOKUP function to calculate the active BMR based on the equation
   $$Active\ BMR = Activity\ Factor \times BMR$$
   where *Activity Factor* is an exact match lookup for the value in the range O8:Q12 that corresponds to the activity level entered in cell C9, and *BMR* is the value in cell C22. Display the formula results with no decimal places.
7. In cell K22, enter a formula using an IF function to calculate the total minutes for the first workout that displays a blank cell if Dorothy did not attend a workout that day.
8. Use AuotFill to copy the formula you entered in cell K22 to the range K23:K44 to calculate the total minutes for each workout.
9. In cell L22, enter a formula to calculate the calories burned at the first workout based on the equation
   $$Calories = \frac{METS \times w \times t}{125.7143}$$
   where *METS* is the metabolic factor for the exercise, w is the client's weight, and t is the exercise time. Use the METS value located in cell P19, the weight value located in cell C11, and the time value located in the corresponding cell in column K. Be sure to use an absolute reference for both weight and METS.

10. Edit the formula you entered in cell L22 to be included as part of an IF function that returns a blank cell if Dorothy did not attend the workout that day. Display the formula results with one decimal place.
11. Use AutoFill to copy the formula you entered in cell L22 to the range L23:L44 to calculate the calories burned at each workout.
12. In the range M22:M44, use the Quick Analysis tool to calculate a column running total of the calories burned in the range L22:L44. Display the formula results with two decimal places.
13. Complete the exercise statistics in the range G14:K18 by entering formulas calculating the sum, average, median, maximum, and minimum values of the exercise times, and calories burned values from the workout log. Display the averages and the calories burned statistics with one decimal place.
14. In cell G2, use a function to display the current date whenever the workbook is opened.
15. In cell F22, enter a formula to reference the start date entered in cell G7.
16. In the range F23:F44, use a function to increase the value of the date in the previous row by 1 workday. Format the formula results with the Short Date format.
17. In cell G8, enter a formula to display the ending date entered in cell F44.
18. In cell G9, enter a formula to count the number of days included in the range F22:F44.
19. In cell G10, enter a formula to count the number of attended workouts as indicated in the range G22:G44.
20. In cell G11, enter a formula to calculate the difference between the number of scheduled workouts and the number of attended workouts. Save the workbook.
21. Use Goal Seek to determine the weight Dorothy must attain to reach a body mass index of 22.
22. Save the revised workbook as **Mothers Fitness Goal**, and then close the workbook.

Case Problem 1

APPLY

Data File needed for this Case Problem: Hernandez.xlsx

Hernandez Family Juan and Olivia Hernandez are a recently married couple in Fort Wayne, Indiana. Juan is currently in graduate school and Olivia is the manager at a local bakery. They want to use Excel to help manage their family budget, but they need help setting up the formulas and functions to project their monthly expenses and help them meet their financial goals. Complete the following:

1. Open the **Hernandez** workbook located in the Excel3 ► Case1 folder included with your Data Files, and then save the workbook as **Hernandez Budget** in the location specified by your instructor.
2. In the Documentation sheet, enter your name and the date.
3. Go to the Budget worksheet. In cell B7, calculate the couple's total monthly income.
4. In row 23, use AutoFill to replace the numbers 1 through 12 with the month abbreviations **Jan** through **Dec**.
5. In rows 24 and 25, enter the couple's monthly income by referencing the monthly income estimates in cells B5 and B6. Use an absolute cell reference.
6. In row 26, calculate the couple's monthly income.
7. In row 37, enter formulas to calculate the total estimated expenses for each month.
8. In row 38, calculate each month's net cash flow, which is equal to the total income minus the total expenses.
9. In row 39, calculate the running total of the net cash flow so that Olivia and Juan can see how their net cash flow changes as the year progresses.
10. In the range B10:B19, calculate the average monthly expenses by category based on the values previously entered in rows 27 through 36.
11. In cell B20, calculate the total average monthly expenses.

12. The couple currently has $7,350 in their savings account. Each month the couple will either take money out of their savings account or deposit money. In row 41, calculate the end-of-month balance in their savings account by adding the value in cell E5 to the running total values of the net cash flow in row 39. Use an absolute cell reference for cell E5.
13. In cell E6, enter a formula to display the value of the savings balance at the end of December.
14. Juan and Olivia would like to have $15,000 in their savings account by the end of the year. Olivia is planning to ask for a raise at her job. Use Goal Seek to determine the value of cell B6 that will achieve a final savings balance of $15,000.
15. Save and close the workbook.

Case Problem 2

Data File needed for this Case Problem: Econ.xlsx

Introduction to Economics 102   Alice Keyes teaches Introduction to Economics 102 at Mountain View Business School in Huntington, West Virginia. She wants to use Excel to track the grades from her class. Alice has already entered the homework, quiz, and final exam scores for all of her students in a workbook, and she has asked you to set up the formulas and functions for her.

You will calculate each student's final average based on his or her homework score, quiz scores, and final exam. Homework counts for 20 percent of the student's final grade. The first two quizzes count for 10 percent each. The second two quizzes count for 15 percent each. The final exam counts for 30 percent of the final grade.

You will also calculate each student's rank in the class. The rank will display which student placed first in terms of his or her overall score, which student placed second, and so forth. Ranks are calculated using the function

```
RANK(number, ref, [order=0])
```

where *number* is the value to be ranked, *ref* is a reference to the cell range containing the values against which the ranking is done, and *order* is an optional argument that specifies whether to rank in descending order or ascending order. The default *order* value is 0 to rank the values in descending order.

Finally, you will create formulas that will look up information on a particular student based on that student's ID so Alice doesn't have to scroll through the complete class roster to find a particular student. Complete the following:

1. Open the **Econ** workbook located in the Excel3 ▸ Case2 folder included with your Data Files, and then save the workbook as **Econ Grades** in the location specified by your instructor.
2. In the Documentation sheet, enter your name and the date.
3. Go to the Grade Book worksheet. In cell B5, count the number of student IDs in the range A22:A57.
4. **Explore** Cells C15 through H15 contain the weights assigned to each assignment, quiz, or exam. In cell J22, calculate the weighted average of the first student's scores by entering a formula that multiplies each score by its corresponding weight and adds the resulting products.
5. Edit the formula in cell J22, changing the references to the weights in cells C15 through H15 from relative references to absolute references.
6. Use AutoFill to copy the formula from cell J22 into the range J23:J57.
7. **Explore** In cell K22, use the RANK function to calculate how the first student compares to the other students in the class. Use the weighted average from cell J22 for the *number* argument and the range of weighted averages in the cell range $J$22:$J$57 for the *ref* argument. You do not need to specify a value for the *order* argument.
8. Use AutoFill to copy the formula you entered in cell K22 into the range K23:K57.
9. In the range C16:H18, calculate the class average, minimum, and maximum for each of the six grading components (homework, quizzes, and final exam).
10. In cell B8, enter the student ID **14858**.

Explore 11. Using the VLOOKUP function with an exact match and the student data table in the range A22:K57, retrieve the first name, last name, weighted average, and class rank for student 14858 in the range B9:B12. Use an absolute reference to the lookup table. Note that the first name is found in the third column of the student data table, the last name is found in the second column, the weighted average is found in the tenth column, and the class rank is found in the eleventh column.

12. Brenda Dunford missed the final exam and will be taking a make-up exam. She wants to know what score she would need on the final exam to achieve an overall weighted average of 90. Use Goal Seek to calculate what final exam score Brenda needs to result in a weighted average of 90.

13. Save and close the workbook.

Case Problem 3

Data File needed for this Case Problem: Homes.xlsx

Homes of Dreams Larry Helt is a carpenter and a woodcrafter in Coventry, Rhode Island, who loves to design and build custom dollhouses. He started his business, Homes of Dreams, a few years ago and it has expanded into a very profitable sideline to his ongoing carpentry work. Larry wants to create a shipping form that will calculate the cost for the purchased items, including taxes, shipping, and handling. Larry already designed the worksheet, which includes a table of shipping rates, shipping surcharges, and items sold by Homes of Dreams. He asks you to complete the worksheet. Complete the following:

1. Open the **Homes** workbook located in the Excel3 ▸ Case3 folder included with your Data Files, and then save the workbook as **Homes of Dreams** in the location specified by your instructor.
2. In the Documentation sheet, enter your name and the date.
3. Go to the Order Form worksheet.
4. In cell B21, enter the Item ID **DH007**.
5. In cell C21, enter the VLOOKUP function with an exact match to return the name of the item referenced in cell B21. Reference the lookup table in the range M4:O50 using an absolute cell reference. Return the value from the second column of the table.
6. In cell E21, enter the VLOOKUP function with an exact match to return the price of the item referenced in cell B21. Use an absolute reference to the lookup table in the range M4:O50. Return the value from the third column of the table.
7. In cell F21, enter **1** as the quantity of the item ordered.
8. In cell G21, calculate the price of the item multiplied by the quantity ordered.
9. **Explore** Revise your formulas in cells C21, E21, and G21, nesting them within an IF formula. For each cell, test whether the value of cell B21 is not equal to "" (a blank). If it is not, return the value of the VLOOKUP function in cells C21 and E21 and the calculated value in cell G21. Otherwise, those cells should return a blank ("") value.
10. Use AutoFill to copy the formulas in cells C21, E21, and G21 through row 30 in the order items table.
11. In row 22, enter **BD002** as the Item ID and **3** as the quantity of items ordered. Verify that the formulas you created automatically enter the name, price, and charge for the item.
12. In rows 23 through 25, enter **1** order for item **BH003**, **1** order for item **DR002**, and **1** order for item **KR009**.
13. In cell G32, calculate the sum of the item charges from all possible orders.
14. In cell G33, calculate the sales tax on the order, which is equal to the subtotal multiplied by the tax rate (entered in cell J9).
15. In cell C15, enter a function to insert the current date whenever the workbook is opened.
16. In cell C16, enter **3 Day** as the type of delivery for this order.

17. In cell C17, calculate the number of working days it will take to ship the order by inserting a VLOOKUP function using an exact match lookup. Use the delivery type in cell C16 as the lookup value, and use the shipping data in the range I4:K7 as the lookup table. Return the value from the third column of the table.

Explore 18. In cell C18, estimate the date of delivery. Use cell C15 as the start date and cell C17 as the number of working days after the start date.

Explore 19. The shipping and handling fee is based on the delivery method (Standard, 3 Day, 2 Day, or Overnight). In cell G34, calculate the shipping and handling fee for the order using an exact match lookup with the data in the range I4:J7. Use the delivery method specified in cell C16 to find the corresponding shipping and handling fee in the Delivery table.

20. In cell G36, calculate the sum of the merchandise subtotal, sales tax, and shipping and handling fee.
21. Save the workbook, and then delete the item IDs and quantities from the order table.
22. Save the workbook as **Homes of Dreams 2**, calculate the cost of ordering 1 of item BD001 using overnight delivery, and then save the workbook.
23. Save the workbook as **Homes of Dreams 3**, and then delete the item IDs and quantities from the order table. Calculate the cost of ordering 1 of item KR001, 2 of item BH004, and 1 of item DR001 using standard delivery. Save and close the workbook.

Case Problem 4

TROUBLESHOOT

Data File needed for this Case Problem: Quality.xlsx

Karleton Manufacturing Carmen Garza is a quality control manager at Karleton Manufacturing, a manufacturing plant located in Trotwood, Ohio. One project that Carmen oversees is the manufacture of tin cans for a major food company. The can widths must be consistent. To compensate for the fact that metal working tools tend to wear down during the day, the pressure behind the tools is increased as the blades become worn. Quality control technicians monitor the process to check that it remains "in control" creating cans whose widths are neither too narrow nor too wide. Carmen has recorded the widths of four cans from 39 batches in an Excel workbook that she wants to use to determine whether the process is "in control." One standard for determining whether a process is "in control" is whether the average value from a process batch falls within the lower and upper control limits. The workbook itself is in need of quality control as some of the formulas are not calculating correctly. You will fix these and then enter the remainder of the formulas needed in the worksheet. Complete the following:

1. Open the **Quality** workbook located in the Excel3 ▸ Case4 folder included with your Data Files, and then save the workbook as **Quality Control Analysis** in the location specified by your instructor.
2. In the Documentation sheet, enter your name and the date.
3. In the Quality Control worksheet, use AutoFill with the value in cell A7 and fill the series of batch numbers from B-1 to B-39 into the range A7:A45.

Troubleshoot 4. In the Quality Control worksheet, cells M3 and M4 display the #NAME? error value instead of the averages. Make the necessary changes to correct the formulas.

Troubleshoot 5. The formulas in the range H7:H45 are supposed to calculate the range of values (maximum minus minimum) within each batch. However, the formula results display 6.2 for every batch. Make the necessary changes in the formulas to fix the problem.

Troubleshoot 6. The formulas in the range I7:I45 are supposed to calculate the average width of the four cans tested in each batch. Unfortunately, the formulas' results don't equal the average widths. Make the necessary changes in the formulas to fix the problem.

7. In cell J7, calculate the lower control limit for the first batch based on the equation

    $LCL = XBAR - A2 \times RBAR$

    where LCL is the lower and upper control limits, $XBAR$ is the average value from all batches, $RBAR$ is the average range from all batches, and $A2$ is a correction factor that depends on the sample size of the batch. In this case, use the $XBAR$ value from cell M3 and the $RBAR$ value from cell M4. Determine the $A2$ value using an exact match lookup with the sample size in cell G7 as the reference value, and the second column from the table in the range O7:P30 as the return value.

8. AutoFill the lower control limit formula from cell J7 into the rest of the LCL column in the Control Limits table. Check to make sure your formulas were properly copied and that they still reference the correct cells.

9. In cell K7, calculate the upper control limit for the first batch based on the equation

    $UCL = XBAR + A2 \times RBAR$

    where UCL is the upper control limit. Copy your formula into the rest of the UCL column in the Control Limits table.

10. In cell L7, indicate whether the B-1 batch process is "in control low" by testing whether the batch's average is less than its LCL value. If it is, display "NO"; otherwise, display a blank cell.

11. In cell M7, indicate whether the B-1 batch process is "in control high" by testing whether the batch's average is greater than its UCL value. If it is, display "NO"; otherwise, display a blank cell.

12. Fill the in control low and in control high formulas for the rest of the batches.

13. Add conditional formatting to the range L7:M45 so that cells displaying "NO" are formatted in dark red text on a light red background.

Troubleshoot 14. The computer program that recorded the width values entered a missing width value as a 0 instead of leaving the cells blank. This affects the calculations about sample size and which batches are in control. Fix this in the data set and any formulas so that the worksheet accurately indicates which batches are not in control on the low side or not in control on the high side.

15. Save and close the workbook.

TUTORIAL 4

Analyzing and Charting Financial Data

Presenting Data for a Business Plan

OBJECTIVES

Session 4.1
- Use the PMT function to calculate a loan payment
- Create an embedded pie chart
- Apply styles to a chart
- Add data labels to a pie chart
- Format a chart legend
- Create a clustered column chart
- Create a stacked column chart

Session 4.2
- Create a line chart
- Create a combination chart
- Format chart elements
- Modify the chart's data source
- Add sparklines to a worksheet
- Format cells with data bars
- Insert a watermark

Case | Levitt Winery

Bob and Carol Levitt want to establish a new winery in Northern Michigan near the town of Traverse City. After many years of working as a winemaker for other wineries, Bob is eager to strike out on his own. Carol will handle the business and finances side of the business, building on her experience managing other companies.

To establish Levitt Winery, Bob and Carol need to borrow money to supplement their personal funds. Bob and Carol are in the process of applying for a business loan. They plan to use this money to help cover the startup costs for their winery. As part of the business loan application, Bob and Carol need to develop a 10-year business plan. They have analyzed the market and made reasonable projections for future production, expenses, and revenue. This information is compiled in an Excel workbook.

Because they are providing a lot of detailed information, Bob and Carol want to include charts in their Excel workbook to make this information easy to read and interpret. Before you create the financial charts that Bob and Carol need for their workbook, you will complete the contents of this worksheet by calculating the cost of the business loan they will need to get started.

STARTING DATA FILES

Excel4 → Tutorial
Draft.png
Levitt.xlsx

Review
Market.xlsx
Watermark.png

Case1
Bertrand.xlsx

Case2
PetroChart.xlsx

Case3
Confidential.png
Frame.xlsx

Case4
Mortgage.xlsx

Microsoft product screenshots used with permission from Microsoft Corporation.

EX 189

EX 190   Excel | Tutorial 4 Analyzing and Charting Financial Data

Session 4.1 Visual Overview:

A **chart**, or **graph**, is a visual representation of a set of data values. Charts show trends or relationships that may not be readily apparent from numbers alone.

An **embedded chart** is an object in a worksheet.

The **chart area** contains the chart and all of the other chart elements.

A **data label** is text associated with an individual data marker, such as the percentage value next to a pie slice.

Each chart has a **data source**, which is the range that contains the data displayed in the chart. The data source for the pie chart is the range B29:C34.

The **category values** are the groups or categories that the data series values belong to. These category values show the different wines produced.

A **data series** contains the actual values that are plotted or displayed on the chart. This data series shows the total cases that will be produced for each wine.

The **vertical axis**, or **value axis**, displays the values from the data series.

Tutorial 4 Analyzing and Charting Financial Data | Excel

Chart Elements

Chart elements are individual parts of the chart, such as the title or the legend.

The CHART TOOLS contextual tabs appear on the ribbon when a chart is selected.

The **Format pane** provides a collection of commands to format chart elements. The options change based on the selected chart element.

The **chart title** is a descriptive label or name for the chart.

A **data marker** displays an individual value from a data series. These data markers are columns.

A **legend** identifies which data markers are associated with each data series.

The **horizontal axis**, or **category axis**, displays the category values from each data series.

Introduction to Financial Functions

Excel provides a wide range of financial functions related to loans and investments. One of these is the **PMT function**, which can be used to calculate the payment schedule required to completely repay a mortgage or other type of loan. Figure 4-1 describes the PMT function and some of the other financial functions often used to develop budgets and financial projections.

Figure 4-1   Financial functions for loans and investments

Function	Description
`FV(rate, nper, pmt [,pv=0] [,type=0])`	Calculates the future value of an investment, where *rate* is the interest rate per period, *nper* is the total number of periods, *pmt* is the payment in each period, *pv* is the present value of the investment, and *type* indicates whether payments should be made at the end of the period (0) or the beginning of the period (1)
`PMT(rate, nper, pv [,fv=0] [,type=0])`	Calculates the payments required each period on a loan or an investment, where *fv* is the future value of the investment
`IPMT(rate, per, nper, pv [,fv=0] [,type=0])`	Calculates the amount of a loan payment devoted to paying the loan interest, where *per* is the number of the payment period
`PPMT(rate, per, nper, pv [,fv=0] [,type=0])`	Calculates the amount of a loan payment devoted to paying off the principal of a loan
`PV(rate, nper, pmt [,fv=0] [,type=0])`	Calculates the present value of a loan or an investment based on periodic, constant payments
`NPER(rate, pmt, pv [,fv=0] [,type=0])`	Calculates the number of periods required to pay off a loan or an investment
`RATE(nper, pmt, pv [,fv=0] [,type=0])`	Calculates the interest rate of a loan or an investment based on periodic, constant payments

© 2014 Cengage Learning

    Before you can use the PMT function, you need to understand some of the concepts and definitions associated with loans. The cost of a loan to the borrower is largely based on three factors—the principal, the interest, and the time required to repay the loan. **Principal** is the amount of money being loaned. **Interest** is the amount added to the principal by the lender. You can think of interest as a kind of "user fee" because the borrower is paying for the right to use the lender's money for an interval of time. Generally, interest is expressed at an annual percentage rate, or APR. For example, an 8 percent APR means that the annual interest rate on the loan is 8 percent of the amount owed to the lender.

    An annual interest rate is divided by the number of payments per year (often monthly or quarterly). So, if the 8 percent annual interest rate is paid monthly, the resulting monthly interest rate is 1/12 of 8 percent, which is about 0.67 percent per month. If payments are made quarterly, then the interest rate per quarter would be 1/4 of 8 percent, which is 2 percent per quarter.

    The third factor in calculating the cost of a loan is the time required to repay the loan, which is specified as the number of payment periods. The number of payment periods is based on the length of the loan multiplied by the number of payments per year. For example, a 10-year loan that is paid monthly has 120 payment periods (that is, 10 years × 12 months per year). If that same 10-year loan is paid quarterly, it has 40 payment periods (that is, 10 years × 4 quarters per year).

Using the PMT Function

To calculate the costs associated with a loan, such as the one that Bob and Carol need to start their winery, you must have the following information:

- The annual interest rate
- The number of payment periods per year
- The length of the loan in terms of the total number of payment periods
- The amount being borrowed
- When loan payments are due

The PMT function uses this information to calculate the payment required in each period to pay back the loan. The syntax of the PMT function is

```
PMT(rate, nper, pv [, fv=0] [, type=0])
```

where *rate* is the interest rate for each payment period, *nper* is the total number of payment periods required to repay the loan, and *pv* is the present value of the loan or the amount that needs to be borrowed. The PMT function has two optional arguments—*fv* and *type*. The *fv* argument is the future value of the loan. Because the intent with most loans is to repay them completely, the future value is equal to 0 by default. The *type* argument specifies when the interest is charged on the loan, either at the end of the payment period (*type*=0), which is the default, or at the beginning of the payment period (*type*=1).

For example, you can use the PMT function to calculate the monthly payments required to repay a car loan of $10,000 over a 5-year period at an annual interest rate of 9 percent. The *rate* or interest rate per period argument is equal to 9 percent divided by 12 monthly payments, which is 0.75 percent per month. The *nper* or total number of payments argument is equal to 12 × 5 (12 monthly payments over 5 years), which is 60. The *pv* or present value of the loan is 10,000. In this case, because the loan will be repaid completely and payments will be made at the end of the month, you can accept the default values for the *fv* and *type* arguments. The resulting PMT function

```
PMT(0.09/12, 5*12, 10000)
```

returns the value −207.58, or a monthly loan payment of $207.58. The PMT function results in a negative value because that value represents an expense to the borrower. Essentially, the loan is money you subtract from your funds to repay the loan.

Rather than entering the argument values directly in the PMT function, you should include the loan terms in worksheet cells that are referenced in the function. This makes it clear what values are being used in the loan calculation. It also makes it easier to perform a what-if analysis exploring other loan options.

Bob and Carol want to borrow $310,000 for their winery at an 8 percent annual interest rate. They plan to repay the loan in 10 years with monthly payments. You will enter these loan terms in the Overview worksheet.

To enter the loan information in the Overview worksheet:

1. Open the **Levitt** workbook located in the Excel4 ▸ Tutorial folder included with your Data Files, and then save the workbook as **Levitt Winery**.

2. In the Documentation sheet, enter your name in cell B4 and the date in cell B5.

3. Go to the **Overview** worksheet. The Overview worksheet provides a summary of Bob and Carol's business plan, including their loan request and business forecasts.

4. In cell **C5**, enter **310,000** as the loan amount.

5. In cell **C6**, enter **8%** as the annual interest rate.

6. In cell **C7**, enter **12** as the number of payments per year. Twelve payments indicate monthly payments.

7. In cell **C8**, enter the formula **=C6/C7** to calculate the interest rate per period. In this case, the 8 percent interest rate is divided by 12 payments per year, calculating the monthly interest rate of 0.67 percent.

8. In cell **C9**, enter **10** as the number of years in the loan.

9. In cell **C10**, enter **=C7*C9** to multiply the number of payments per year by the number of years in the loan, calculating the total number of payments on the loan, which is 120.

The Overview worksheet includes all the data you need to calculate the monthly payment required to repay the $310,000 loan in 10 years at an 8 percent annual interest rate paid monthly. Next, you will use the PMT function to calculate the monthly payment needed to repay the loan.

To use the PMT function to calculate Bob and Carol's monthly payment:

1. Select cell **C12** to make it the active cell. You will enter the PMT function in this cell.

2. On the ribbon, click the **FORMULAS** tab to display the function library.

3. In the Function Library group, click the **Financial** button, and then scroll down and click **PMT** in the list of financial functions. The Function Arguments dialog box opens.

4. With the insertion point in the Rate box, click cell **C8** in the worksheet to enter the reference to the cell with the interest rate per month.

5. Click in the **Nper** box, and then click cell **C10** in the worksheet to enter the reference to the cell with the total number of monthly payments required to repay the loan.

6. Click in the **Pv** box, and then click cell **C5** in the worksheet to enter the reference to the cell with the present value of the loan. See Figure 4-2.

TIP
Be sure to enter the interest rate per month (not per year) for the Rate argument for any loan or investment that has monthly payments.

Figure 4-2 Function Arguments dialog box for the PMT function

▶ 7. Click the **OK** button. The monthly payment amount ($3,761.16) appears in cell C12. The number is displayed in parentheses to indicate a negative amount, specifying the amount to be paid.

▶ 8. In cell **C13**, enter the formula **=C7*C12** to multiply the number of payments per year by the monthly payment amount, calculating the total payments for the entire year. The annual payments would be ($45,133.87), shown as a negative number to indicate money being paid out.

▶ 9. Select cell **C12**. See Figure 4-3.

Figure 4-3 Monthly and annual costs of the business loan

	B	C	D
		=PMT(C8,C10,C5) — PMT function calculates the loan payment	
1	Levitt Winery		
2	Business Plan Overview		
4	Business Loan Request		
5	Loan Amount (PV)	$ 310,000	
6	Annual Interest Rate	8.00%	
7	Payments per Year	12	monthly payment is negative to indicate an expense
8	Interest Rate per Period (RATE)	0.67%	
9	Number of Years	10	
10	Total Payments (NPER)	120	
12	Monthly Payment	($3,761.16)	
13	Annual Total	($45,133.87)	annual payment
15	Estimated Production		

Carol wants to see the financial impact of taking out a smaller loan.

▶ 10. In cell **C5**, change the loan amount to **250,000**. With a loan of that size, the monthly payment drops to $3,033 and the annual total decreases to $36,398.

Although the lower loan amount will save money, Bob feels that the winery cannot get off the ground with less than a $310,000 loan.

▶ 11. In cell **C5**, return the loan amount to **310,000**.

Based on your analysis, the Levitts would spend about $45,000 a year repaying the $310,000 business loan. Carol and Bob want this information included in the Projected Cash Flow worksheet, which estimates Levitt Winery's annual revenue, expenses, and cash flow for the first 10 years. You will enter that amount as an expense for each year, completing the projected cash flow calculations.

To enter the loan repayment amount in the Projected Cash Flow worksheet:

1. Go to the **Projected Cash Flow** worksheet and review the estimated annual revenue, expenses, and cash flow for the next decade.

2. In cell **C17**, enter **45,000** as the projected yearly amount of the loan repayment. Because the projected cash flow is a rough estimate of the projected income and expenses, it is not necessary to include the exact dollar-and-cents cost of the loan.

3. Copy the annual loan payment in cell **C17** into the range **D17:L17** to enter the projected annual loan payment in each year of the cash flow projections. See Figure 4-4.

Figure 4-4   Completed Projected Cash Flow worksheet

	A	B	C	D	E	F	G	H	I	J	K	L
12		Expenses										
13		Grapes	$ 35,000	$ 70,000	$ 100,000	$ 150,000	$ 175,000	$ 175,000	$ 200,000	$ 250,000	$ 275,000	$ 325,000
14		Labor	100,000	120,000	140,000	170,000	240,000	250,000	275,000	275,000	300,000	350,000
15		Maintenance	20,000	35,000	50,000	50,000	50,000	50,000	60,000	70,000	80,000	90,000
16		Miscellaneous	50,000	35,000	25,000	25,000	35,000	50,000	50,000	50,000	75,000	75,000
17		Loan Repayment	45,000	45,000	45,000	45,000	45,000	45,000	45,000	45,000	45,000	45,000
18		Total Expenses	$ 250,000	$ 305,000	$ 360,000	$ 440,000	$ 545,000	$ 570,000	$ 630,000	$ 690,000	$ 775,000	$ 885,000
19												
20		Gross Income	$ (250,000)	$ (245,000)	$ (240,000)	$ (175,000)	$ (170,000)	$ 20,000	$ 200,000	$ 360,000	$ 600,000	$ 865,000
21		Loss Carry Forward	(250,000)	(495,000)	(735,000)	(910,000)	(1,080,000)				-	-
22		Income Tax @35%	-	-	-	-	-	-	-	-	(210,000)	(302,750)
23		Net Income	$ (250,000)	$ (245,000)	$ (240,000)	$ (175,000)	$ (170,000)	$ 20,000	$ 200,000	$ 360,000	$ 390,000	$ 562,250
24												
25		Capital Purchases	$ (310,000)	$ (50,000)	$ (50,000)	$ (50,000)	$ (50,000)	$ (50,000)		$ (75,000)	$ (85,000)
26		Depreciation	30,000	75,000	72,000	70,000	65,000		30,000	25,000	25,000
27		Cash Flow	$ (530,000)	$ (220,000)	$ (218,000)	$ (155,000)	$ (155,000)	$ 35,000	$ 210,000	$ 340,000	$ 340,000	$ 502,250

- yearly loan payments
- total expenses projected over the next 10 years
- net income projected over the next 10 years
- end-of-the-year cash receipts projected over the next 10 years

After including the projected annual loan payments, the Projected Cash Flow worksheet shows that the winery's projected net income at the end of the tenth year would be about $560,000, assuming all of the other projections are accurate. Based on these figures, the winery should have about $500,000 in cash at that time as well.

INSIGHT

Using Functions to Manage Personal Finances

Excel has many financial functions to manage personal finances. The following list can help you determine which function to use for the most common personal finance calculations:

- To determine how much an investment will be worth after a series of monthly payments at some future time, use the FV (future value) function.
- To determine how much you have to spend each month to repay a loan or mortgage within a set period of time, use the PMT (payment) function.
- To determine how much of your monthly loan payment is used to pay the interest, use the IPMT (interest payment) function.
- To determine how much of your monthly loan payment is used for repaying the principal, use the PPMT (principal payment) function.
- To determine the largest loan or mortgage you can afford given a set monthly payment, use the PV (present value) function.
- To determine how long it will take to pay off a loan with constant monthly payments, use the NPER (number of periods) function.

For most loan and investment calculations, you need to enter the annual interest rate divided by the number of times the interest is compounded during the year. If interest is compounded monthly, divide the annual interest rate by 12; if interest is compounded quarterly, divide the annual rate by 4. You must also convert the length of the loan or investment to the number of payments per year. If you will make payments monthly, multiply the number of years of the loan or investment by 12.

Now that you have completed the cash flow projections for the winery, you can begin displaying this information in charts.

Creating a Chart

Charts show trends or relationships in data that are easier to see than by looking at the actual numbers. Creating a chart is a several-step process that involves selecting the data to display in the chart, choosing the chart type, moving the chart to a specific location in the workbook, sizing the chart so that it matches the layout of the worksheet, and formatting the chart's appearance. When creating a chart, remember that your goal is to convey important information that would be more difficult to interpret from columns of data in a worksheet.

REFERENCE

Creating a Chart

- Select the range containing the data you want to chart.
- On the INSERT tab, in the Charts group, click the Recommended Chart button or a chart type button, and then click the chart you want to create (or click the Quick Analysis button, click the CHARTS category, and then click the chart you want to create).
- On the CHART TOOLS DESIGN tab, in the Location group, click the Move Chart button, select whether to embed the chart in a worksheet or place it in a chart sheet, and then click the OK button.

Selecting a Chart's Data Source

The data displayed in a chart comes from the chart's data source. A data source includes one or more data series and a series of category values. A data series contains the actual values that are plotted on the chart, whereas the category values provide descriptive labels for each data series or data value. Category values are usually located in the first column or first row of the data source. The data series are usually placed in subsequent columns or rows. However, you can select category and data values from anywhere within a workbook.

Bob and Carol want a chart to display information about the winery's estimated production in 10 years. The data source for this chart is located in the range B28:C34 of the Overview worksheet. You will select this range now as the data source for the chart.

To select the data source for a chart showing the projected production:

1. Go to the **Overview** worksheet. The production projections are included in this worksheet.

2. Select the range **B28:C34** containing the production estimates as the data source for the chart. See Figure 4-5.

Figure 4-5   Selected chart data source

	A	B	C	D	E	F	G
27							
28		Wine	Production Goal (Cases)	10-Year Production			
29		Chardonnay	3,500				
30		Riesling	2,000				
31		Pinot Grigio	1,500				
32		Pinot Noir	1,250				
33		Cabernet Franc	1,875				
34		Ruby Cabernet	1,000				
35							
36		Proposed Bottle Price (Retail)					
37		Wine	First Label	Second Label			
38		Chardonnay		$16			
39		Riesling		$11			
40		Pinot Grigio	$18	$12			
41		Pinot Noir	$27	$21			
42		Cabernet Franc	$22	$17			
43		Ruby Cabernet	$15	$13			

(data source: B28:C34; category values in column B; data series values in column C)

This data source includes two columns. The category values are located in the first column, and the one and only data series is located in the second column. When the selected range is taller than it is wide, Excel assumes that the category values and data series are laid out in columns. Conversely, a data source that is wider than it is tall is assumed to have the category values and data series laid out in rows. Note that the first row in this selected data source contains labels that identify the category values (Wine) and the data series (Production Goal).

Now that you've selected the data source for the chart, you want to consider the type of chart to create.

Exploring Chart Types and Subtypes

Excel provides 53 types of charts organized into the 10 categories described in Figure 4-6. Each category includes variations of the same chart type, which are called **chart subtypes**. You can also design your own custom chart types to meet the specific needs of your reports and projects.

Figure 4-6 Excel chart types

Chart Type	Description
Column	Compares values from different categories. Values are indicated by the height of the columns.
Line	Compares values from different categories. Values are indicated by the height of the lines. Often used to show trends and changes over time.
Pie	Compares relative values of different categories to the whole. Values are indicated by the areas of the pie slices.
Bar	Compares values from different categories. Values are indicated by the length of the bars.
Area	Compares values from different categories. Similar to the line chart except that areas under the lines contain a fill color.
X Y (Scatter)	Shows the patterns or relationship between two or more sets of values. Often used in scientific studies and statistical analyses.
Stock	Displays stock market data, including the high, low, opening, and closing prices of a stock.
Surface	Compares three sets of values in a three-dimensional chart.
Radar	Compares a collection of values from several different data sets.
Combo	Combines two or more chart types to make the data easy to visualize, especially when the data is widely varied.

© 2014 Cengage Learning

For example, Figure 4-7 presents the same labor cost data displayed as a line chart, a bar chart, and column charts. The column charts are shown with both a 2-D subtype that has two-dimensional or flat columns and a 3-D subtype that gives the illusion of three-dimensional columns. The various charts and chart subtypes are better suited for different data. You should choose the one that makes the data easiest to interpret.

Figure 4-7 Chart types and subtypes

Line chart

Bar chart

2-D Column chart

3-D Column chart

The first chart you will create is a pie chart. A **pie chart** is a chart in the shape of a circle divided into slices like a pie. Each slice represents a single value from a data series. Larger data values are represented with bigger pie slices. The relative sizes of the slices let you visually compare the data values and see how much each contributes to the whole. Pie charts are most effective with six or fewer slices, and when each slice is large enough to view easily.

TIP
Most charts should include only the category labels and data values and not row or column totals because Excel will treat those totals as another category to be graphed.

Inserting a Pie Chart with the Quick Analysis Tool

After you select an adjacent range to use as a chart's data source, the Quick Analysis tool appears. It includes a category for creating charts. The CHART category lists recommended chart types, which are the charts that are most appropriate for the data source you selected.

For the wine production data, a pie chart provides the best way to compare the production levels for the six wines Levitt Winery plans to produce. You will use the Quick Analysis tool to create a pie chart of the projected wine production data that you selected.

To create a pie chart with the Quick Analysis tool:

1. Make sure the range **B28:C34** is selected.
2. Click the **Quick Analysis** button in the lower-right corner of the selected range (or press the **Ctrl+Q** keys) to open the Quick Analysis tool.
3. Click the **CHARTS** category. The chart types you will most likely want to use with the selected data source are listed. See Figure 4-8.

TIP
You can also insert a chart by selecting a chart type in the Charts group on the INSERT tab.

Tutorial 4 Analyzing and Charting Financial Data | Excel EX 201

Figure 4-8 — CHARTS category of the Quick Analysis tool

chart types recommended based on the selected data source

displays other chart types that can be used with the data

4. Click **Pie**. A pie chart appears in the Overview worksheet. Each slice is a different size based on its value in the data series. The biggest slice represents the 3500 cases of Chardonnay that the Levitts estimate they will produce. The smallest slice of the pie represents 1000 cases of Ruby Cabernet. See Figure 4-9.

Figure 4-9 — Pie chart in the Overview worksheet

CHART TOOLS contextual tabs appear when a chart is selected

Chart Elements button

Chart Styles button

Chart Filters button

embedded pie chart

When you create or select a chart, two CHART TOOLS contextual tabs appear on the ribbon. The DESIGN tab provides commands to specify the chart's overall design. The FORMAT tab supplies the tools needed to format the graphic shapes found in the chart, such as the chart's border or the slices from a pie chart. When you select a worksheet cell or another object that is not a chart, the CHART TOOLS contextual tabs disappear until you reselect the chart.

Three buttons appear to the right of the selected chart. The Chart Elements button ➕ is used for adding, removing, or changing elements displayed in the chart. The Chart Styles button 🖌 sets the style and color scheme of the chart. The Chart Filters button 🔻 enables you to edit the data points and names displayed on the chart.

Moving and Resizing a Chart

Excel charts are either placed in their own chart sheets or embedded in a worksheet. When you create a chart, it is embedded in the worksheet that contains the data source. For example, the chart shown in Figure 4-9 is embedded in the Overview worksheet. The advantage of an embedded chart is that you can display the chart alongside its data source and any text that describes the chart's meaning and purpose. Because an embedded chart covers worksheet cells, you might have to move or resize the chart so that important information is not hidden.

Before you can move or resize a chart, it must be selected. When a chart is selected, a **selection box** appears around the selected chart that is used to move or resize the chart. **Sizing handles** appear along the edges of the selection box and are used to change the chart's width and height.

Bob and Carol want the wine production chart to appear above its data source in the Overview worksheet. You will move and resize the chart to fit this location.

> **TIP**
> You can print an embedded chart with the rest of the worksheet, or you can select the embedded chart and print only the chart without the rest of the worksheet.

> Be sure to drag the chart from an empty part of the chart area so the entire chart moves, not just chart elements within the chart.

To move and resize the wine production pie chart:

1. Move the pointer over an empty area of the selected chart until the pointer changes to ✥ and "Chart Area" appears in a ScreenTip.

2. Hold down the **Alt** key, drag the chart up and to the left until its upper-left corner snaps to the upper-left corner of cell B16, and then release the mouse button and the **Alt** key. The upper-left corner of the chart is aligned with the upper-left corner of cell B16.

   Trouble? If the pie chart resizes or does not move to the new location, you probably didn't drag the chart from an empty part of the chart area. Press the Ctrl+Z keys to undo your last action, and then repeat Steps 1 and 2, being sure to drag the pie chart from the chart area.

   The chart moves to a new location, but it still covers some data and needs to be resized.

3. Move the pointer over the sizing handle in the lower-right corner of the selection box until the pointer changes to ⤡.

4. Hold down the **Alt** key, drag the sizing handle up to the lower-right corner of cell D27, and then release the mouse button and the **Alt** key. The chart resizes to cover the range B16:D27 and remains selected. See Figure 4-10.

Tutorial 4 Analyzing and Charting Financial Data | Excel EX 203

Figure 4-10 Moved and resized chart

- chart covers the range B16:D27
- selection box
- chart title (linked with cell C28)
- lower-right corner sizing handle
- chart legend (linked with the category values in the range B29:B34)

Working with Chart Elements

Every chart contains elements that can be formatted, added to the chart, or removed from the chart. For example, a pie chart has three elements—the chart title, the chart legend identifying each pie slice, and data labels that can be displayed next to each slice providing the data value or percentage associated with that slice. The Chart Elements button that appears next to a selected chart lists the elements associated with that chart. You can use this button to add, remove, and format individual elements. When you add or remove a chart element, the other elements resize to fit in the space. Live Preview shows how changing an element will affect the chart's appearance.

Carol doesn't want the pie chart to include a title because the text in cell B15 and the data in the range B28:D34 sufficiently explain the chart's purpose. However, she does want to display the data values next to the pie slices. You will remove the chart title element and add the data labels element.

To remove the pie chart title and add data labels to the slices:

1. Click the **pie chart** to select it. The selection box appears around the chart.

2. To the right of the selected chart, click the **Chart Elements** button ⊕. A menu of chart elements that are available for the pie chart opens. As the checkmarks indicate, only the chart title and the chart legend are displayed in the pie chart.

3. Click the **Chart Title** check box to deselect it. The chart title is removed from the pie chart and the chart elements resize to fill the space.

4. Point to the **Data Labels** check box. Live Preview shows how the chart will look when the data labels showing the production goal for each wine are added to the pie slices.

5. Click the **Data Labels** check box to select it. The data labels are added to the chart. See Figure 4-11.

TIP

To add and remove chart elements, you can also use the Add Chart Element button in the Chart Layouts group on the CHART TOOLS DESIGN tab.

Figure 4-11 Chart elements

data labels show the values from the range C29:C34

chart legend

Chart Elements button

checked elements are displayed in the chart

Choosing a Chart Style

When you create a chart, the chart is formatted with a style. Recall that a style is a collection of formats that are saved with a name and can then be applied at one time. In the pie chart you just created, the format of the chart title, the location of the legend, and the colors of the pie slices are all part of the default pie chart style. You can quickly change the appearance of a chart by selecting a different style from the Chart Styles gallery. Live Preview shows how a chart style will affect the chart.

Carol wants the pie slices to have a raised, three-dimensional look. You will explore different chart styles to find a style that best fulfills her request.

To choose a different chart style for the wine production pie chart:

1. Click the **Chart Styles** button next to the selected pie chart. The Chart Styles gallery opens.

2. Point to different styles in the gallery. Live Preview shows the impact of each chart style on the pie chart's appearance.

3. Scroll to the bottom of the gallery, and then click the **Style 12** chart style. The chart style is applied to the pie chart. See Figure 4-12.

TIP

You can also select a chart style from the Chart Styles gallery in the Chart Styles group on the CHART TOOLS DESIGN tab.

Tutorial 4 Analyzing and Charting Financial Data | Excel   EX 205

Figure 4-12   **Chart Styles gallery**

pie chart formatted with the Style 12 chart style

gallery of pie chart styles

Chart Styles button

Style 12 chart style

Formatting the Pie Chart Legend

You can fine-tune a chart style by formatting individual chart elements. From the Chart Elements button, you can open a submenu for each element that includes formatting options, such as the element's location within the chart. You can also open a Format pane, which has more options for formatting the selected chart element.

The default location for the pie chart legend is alongside the chart's bottom edge. Carol thinks the chart would look better if the legend were aligned with the right edge of the chart.

To reposition the pie chart legend:

1. Click the **Chart Elements** button ➕ next to the selected pie chart.

2. Point to **Legend** in the CHART ELEMENTS menu to display a right arrow icon, and then click the **right arrow** icon ▶. A submenu opens with formatting options available for the selected chart element. For a chart legend, the submenu offers placement options.

3. Point to **Left** to see a Live Preview of that formatting. The legend is aligned along the left side of the chart area, and the pie moves to the right to occupy the remaining space.

4. Click **Right** to place the legend along the right side of the chart area. The pie shifts to the left to make room for the legend.

The Chart Elements button also provides access to the Format pane, which has more design options. Carol wants you to add a drop shadow to the legend similar to the pie chart's drop shadow, change the fill color to a light gold, and add a light gray border. You'll use the Format pane to make these changes.

TIP

You can also open the Format pane by double-clicking any chart element.

To format the chart legend:

1. On the CHART ELEMENTS menu, click the **right arrow** icon next to the Legend entry to display a submenu, and then click **More Options**. The Format pane opens on the right side of the workbook window. The pane's title, "Format Legend," indicates that the options relate to formatting the chart legend.

2. Click the **Fill & Line** button near the top of the Format pane to display options for setting the fill color and border style of the legend.

3. Click **FILL** to display fill options, and then click the **Solid fill** option button to apply a solid fill color to the legend. Color and Transparency options appear below the fill color options.

4. Click the **Fill Color** button, and then click the **Gold, Accent 4, Lighter 60%** theme color located in the third row and eighth column of the color palette to add a light gold fill color to the legend.

5. Click **BORDER** to display the border options, and then click the **Solid line** option button. Additional border options appear below the border options.

6. Click the **Outline color** button, and then click the **Gray - 50%, Accent 3, Lighter 80%** theme color located in the second row and seventh column of the color palette to add a light gray border around the legend.

7. At the top of the Format Legend pane, click the **Effects** button to display options for special visual effects.

8. Click **Shadow** to display the shadow options, and then next to the Presets label, click the **Shadow** button to display a gallery of shadow effects.

9. Click the **Offset Diagonal Button Right** button in the first row and first column to apply the drop shadow effect to the legend. See Figure 4-13.

Figure 4-13   Formatted chart legend

Formatting Pie Chart Data Labels

You can modify the content and appearance of data labels, selecting what the labels contain as well as where the labels are positioned. By default, data labels are placed where they will keep the chart nicely proportioned, but you can specify a different location. For pie chart labels, you can move the labels to the center of the pie slices or place them outside of the slices. Another option is to set the labels as data callouts, with each label placed within a text bubble and connected to the slice with a callout line. Likewise, you can change the text and number styles used in the data labels as well. These options are all available in the Format pane. You can also drag and drop individual data labels, placing them anywhere within the chart. When a data label is placed far from its pie slice, a **leader line** is added to connect the data label to its pie slice.

The pie chart data labels display the production goal values for the different wines, but this information also appears on the worksheet directly below the chart. The Levitts want to include data labels that add new information to the chart—in this case, the percentage that each wine varietal adds to the whole. You will make this change.

To display percentages in the wine production pie chart:

> **TIP**
> You can also format chart elements using the formatting buttons on the HOME tab or on the CHART TOOLS FORMAT tab.

1. At the top of the Format pane, click the **Legend Options** arrow to display a menu of chart elements, and then click **Series "Production Goal (Cases)" Data Labels** to display the formatting options for data labels. The title of the Format pane changes to "Format Data Labels" and includes formatting options for data labels. Selection boxes appear around every data label in the pie chart.

2. Click the **Label Options** button near the top of the pane to display the options for the label contents and position. Data labels can contain series names, category names, values, and percentages.

3. Click the **Percentage** check box to display the percentage associated with each data label in the pie chart next to its value.

4. Click the **Value** check box to deselect it, removing the data series values from the data labels. The pie chart shows that Chardonnay accounts for 31.5 percent of the estimated wine production.

5. Click the **Outside End** option button to move the labels outside of the pie slices. The labels are easier to read in this location.

   The percentages are displayed with no decimal places, but Carol wants them to show one decimal place to provide a bit more accuracy in the chart.

6. Scroll down the Format pane, and then click **NUMBER** to show the formatting options for numbers.

7. Scroll down the Format pane, click the **Category** box to display the number formats, and then click **Percentage**. The percentages in the data labels include two decimal places.

8. In the Decimal places box, replace the value 2 with **1**, and then press the **Enter** key. The percentages display one decimal place. See Figure 4-14.

Figure 4-14 Formatted data labels

- data labels display the percentages associated with each slice
- no leader lines appear because the data labels are close to their pie slices
- arrow to select a different chart element to format
- labels contain checked items
- Label Options button
- selection box and sizing handles appear around each data label
- labels are placed at the outside end of each slice
- Percentage format applied to the data label values

Setting the Pie Slice Colors

A pie slice is an example of a data marker that represents a single data value from a data series. You can format the appearance of individual data markers to make them stand out from the others. Pie slice colors should be as distinct as possible to avoid confusion. Depending on the printer quality or the monitor resolution, it might be difficult to distinguish between similarly colored slices. If data labels are displayed within the slice, you also need enough contrast between the slice color and the data label color to make the text readable.

The Levitts are concerned that the blue color of the Cabernet Franc slice will appear too dark when printed, and they want you to change it to a light shade of green.

To change the color of the Cabernet Franc pie slice:

1. Click any pie slice to select all of the slices in the pie chart.

2. Click the **Cabernet Franc** slice, which is the darker blue slice that represents 16.9 percent of the pie. Only that slice is selected, as you can see from the handles that appear at each corner of the slice.

3. Click the **HOME** tab, click the **Fill Color button arrow** in the Font group, and then click the **Green, Accent 6, Lighter 40%** theme color in the fourth row and last column of the gallery. The Cabernet Franc pie slice changes to a light green and the chart legend automatically updates to reflect that change.

You can also change the colors of all the pie slices by clicking the Chart Styles button next to the selected chart, clicking the COLOR heading, and then selecting a color scheme.

INSIGHT

Exploding a Pie Chart

Pie slices do not need to be fixed within the pie. An **exploded pie chart** moves one slice away from the others as if someone were taking the piece away from the pie. Exploded pie charts are useful for emphasizing one category above all of the others. For example, to emphasize the fact that Levitt Winery will be producing more Chardonnay than any other wine, you could explode that single slice, moving it away from the other slices.

To explode a pie slice, first click the pie to select all of the slices, and then click the single slide you want to move. Make sure that a selection box appears around only that slice. Drag the slice away from the pie to offset it from the others. You can explode multiple slices by selecting each slice in turn and dragging them away. To explode all of the slices, select the entire pie and drag the pointer away from the pie's center. Each slice will be exploded and separated from the others. Although you can explode more than one slice, the resulting pie chart is rarely effective as a visual aid to the reader.

Formatting the Chart Area

The chart's background, which is called the chart area, can also be formatted using fill colors, border styles, and special effects such as drop shadows and blurred edges. The chart area fill color used in the pie chart is white, which blends in with the worksheet background. Carol wants you to change the fill color to a light gold to match the worksheet's color scheme, and to make the chart stand out better.

To change the chart area of the pie chart to light gold:

> **TIP**
> You can select any chart element using the Chart Elements box in the Current Selection group on the CHART TOOLS FORMAT tab.

1. Click a blank area within the chart, not containing either a pie slice or the chart legend. The chart area is selected, which you can verify because the Format pane title changes to "Format Chart Area."

2. On the HOME tab, in the Font group, click the **Fill Color button arrow**, and then click the **Gold, Accent 4, Lighter 80%** theme color in the second row and eighth column. The chart area fill color is now light gold. See Figure 4-15.

Figure 4-15   Chart area fill color

> You are done formatting the pie chart, so you will close the Format pane to keep the window uncluttered.
>
> 3. Click the **Close** button ❌ on the title bar of the Format pane. The pane closes, leaving more space for viewing the worksheet contents.

Performing What-If Analyses with Charts

A chart is linked to its data source. For the wine production pie chart, the chart title is linked to the text of cell C28, the size of the pie slices is based on the production goals in the range C29:C34, and the category names are linked to the category values in the range B29:B34. Any changes to these cells affect the chart's content and appearance. This makes charts a powerful tool for data exploration and what-if analysis. Excel uses **chart animation** to slow down the effect of changing data source values, making it easier to see how changing one value affects the chart.

Bob and Carol want to see how the pie chart would change if they were to alter some of their production goals. You will edit the data source to see how the changes affect the chart.

> **To apply a what-if analysis to the pie chart:**
>
> 1. In cell **C29**, enter **5500** to increase the production goal for Chardonnay by 2000 cases. The pie slice associated with Chardonnay becomes larger, slowly changing from 31.5 percent to 41.9 percent because of the chart animation. The size of the remaining slices and their percentages are reduced to compensate.
>
> 2. In cell **C29**, restore the value to **3,500**. The pie slices return to their initial sizes and the percentages return to their initial values.
>
> 3. In cell **C30**, change the production goal for Riesling from 2,000 to **4,000**. The orange slice representing Riesling is now the largest slice in the pie, comprising 30.5 percent of the projected production.
>
> 4. In cell **C30**, restore the value to **2,000**.
>
>   Bob points out that the legend entry "Riesling" should be changed to "White Riesling" to distinguish it from other Riesling varietals.
>
> 5. In cells **B30** and **B39**, change the text to **White Riesling**. The chart legend automatically updates to show the revised wine name.

Another type of what-if analysis is to limit the data to a subset of the original values in a process called **filtering**. For example, the pie chart shows the estimated production for all six varietals of wine that Levitt Winery will produce. Sometimes, however, Carol and Bob might want to see information on only the red wines or only the white wines. Rather than creating a new chart that includes only those wines, you can filter an existing chart.

Levitt Winery plans to produce three white wines—Chardonnay, White Riesling, and Pinot Grigio. Carol and Bob want to see the different percentages of white wine. You will use the Chart Filters button to limit the pie chart to those three wines.

Tutorial 4 Analyzing and Charting Financial Data | Excel   EX 211

To filter the pie chart to show only white wines:

1. Click the pie chart to select it.
2. Click the **Chart Filters** button next to the chart to open a menu listing the categories in the chart. In this case, the categories are the different types of wines.
3. Click the **Pinot Noir**, **Cabernet Franc**, and **Ruby Cabernet** check boxes to deselect them, leaving only the Chardonnay, White Riesling, and Pinot Grigio check boxes selected.
4. At the bottom of the Chart Filters menu, click the **Apply** button. Excel filters the chart, showing only the white wines. After filtering the data, the chart shows that 50 percent of the white wines produced will be Chardonnay. See Figure 4-16.

Figure 4-16   **Filtered pie chart**

pie chart shows only the white wines

Chart Filters button

only values for selected categories appear in the chart

5. In the CATEGORIES section of the Chart Filters menu, double-click the **Select All** check box to reselect all six wines.
6. Click the **Apply** button to update the chart's appearance.
7. Press the **Esc** key to close the menu, leaving the chart selected.

The pie chart that displays the winery's projected level of production for different wines is complete. Next, you'll use column charts to examine the winery's financial projections for the next 10 years.

Creating a Column Chart

A **column chart** displays data values as columns with the height of each column based on the data value. A column chart turned on its side is called a **bar chart**, with the length of the bar determined by the data value. It is better to use column and bar charts than pie charts when the number of categories is large or the data values are close in value. For example, Figure 4-17 displays the same data as a pie chart and a column chart. As you can see, it's difficult to determine which pie slice is biggest and by how much. It is much simpler to see the differences in a column or bar chart.

Figure 4-17 Data displayed as a pie chart and a column chart

Comparing Column Chart Subtypes

Unlike pie charts, which can show only one data series, column and bar charts can display multiple data series. For example, you can plot three data series (such as the wine production of Chardonnay, White Riesling, and Cabernet Franc) against one category (such as Years). Figure 4-18 shows the same data charted on the three column chart subtypes available to display data from multiple series.

Figure 4-18 Column chart subtypes

Clustered Column   Stacked Column   100% Stacked Column

The **clustered column chart** displays the data series in separate columns side-by-side so that you can compare the relative heights of the columns in the three series. The clustered column chart in Figure 4-18 compares the number of cases of each wine produced in Year 1 through Year 5. Note that the winery produces mostly Chardonnay with the other varietals increasing in volume in the later years.

The **stacked column chart** places the data series values within combined columns showing how much is contributed by each series. The stacked column chart in Figure 4-18 gives information on the total number of wine cases produced each year, and how each year's production is split among the three wine varietals.

Finally, the **100% stacked column chart** makes the same comparison as the stacked column chart except that the stacked sections are expressed as percentages. As you can see from the 100% stacked column chart in Figure 4-18, Chardonnay accounts for about 75 percent of the wine produced in Year 1, and that percentage steadily declines to about 50 percent in Year 5 as more cases of White Riesling and Cabernet Franc are produced.

The chart subtype you use depends on what you want to highlight with your data.

Creating a Clustered Column Chart

The process for creating a column chart is the same as for creating a pie chart. First, you select the data source. Then, you select the type of chart you want to create. After the chart is embedded in the worksheet, you can move and resize the chart as well as change the chart's design, layout, and format.

Tutorial 4 Analyzing and Charting Financial Data | Excel   EX 213

Bob and Carol want to show the projected revenue and expenses for each of the next 10 years. Because this requires comparing the data series values, you will create a clustered column chart.

To create a column chart for the revenue and expenses data:

1. Go to the **Projected Cash Flow** worksheet.

2. Select the nonadjacent range **B4:L4;B10:L10;B18:L18** containing the Year categories in row 4, the Total Revenue data series in row 10, and the Total Expenses data series in row 18. Because you selected a nonadjacent range, the Quick Analysis tool is not available.

TIP
You can also open the Insert Chart dialog box to see the chart types recommended for the selected data source.

3. On the ribbon, click the **INSERT** tab. The Charts group contains buttons for inserting different types of charts.

4. In the Charts group, click the **Recommended Charts** button. The Insert Chart dialog box opens with the Recommended Charts tab displayed. The charts show how the selected data would appear in that chart type. See Figure 4-19.

Figure 4-19 Clustered column chart being created

5. Make sure the **Clustered Column** chart is selected, and then click the **OK** button. The clustered column chart is embedded in the Projected Cash Flow worksheet.

6. Click the **Chart Styles** button next to the selected column chart.

7. In the STYLE gallery, scroll down and click the **Style 14** chart style to format the columns with drop shadows.

8. Click the **Chart Styles** button to close the STYLE gallery.

INSIGHT

Changing a Chart Type

After creating a chart, you can easily switch the chart to a different chart type without having to recreate the chart from scratch. For example, if the data in a column chart would be more effective presented as a line chart, you can change its chart type rather than creating a new chart. Clicking the Change Chart Type button in the Type group on the CHART TOOLS DESIGN tab opens a dialog box similar to the Insert Chart dialog box, from which you can select a new chart type.

Moving a Chart to a Different Worksheet

You can move a chart from one worksheet to another, or you can place the chart in its own chart sheet. In a chart sheet, the chart is enlarged to fill the entire workspace. The Move Chart dialog box provides options for moving charts between worksheets and chart sheets. You can also cut and paste a chart between workbooks.

Bob and Carol want all of the charts to be displayed in the Overview worksheet. You will move the clustered column chart to the Overview worksheet, and then resize it.

To move the clustered column chart to the Overview worksheet:

1. Make sure the clustered column chart is selected.
2. On the CHART TOOLS DESIGN tab, in the Location group, click the **Move Chart** button. The Move Chart dialog box opens.
3. Click the **Object in** arrow to display a list of the worksheets in the active workbook, and then click **Overview**.
4. Click the **OK** button. The embedded chart moves from the Projected Cash Flow worksheet to the Overview worksheet, and remains selected.
5. Hold down the **Alt** key as you drag the chart so that its upper-left corner is aligned with the upper-left corner of cell F16, and then release the mouse button and the **Alt** key to snap the upper-left corner of the chart to the worksheet.
6. Hold down the **Alt** key as you drag the lower-right sizing handle of the clustered column chart to the lower-right corner of cell **M29**, and then release the mouse button and the **Alt** key. The chart now covers the range F16:M29.

TIP

To set an exact chart size, enter the height and width values in the Size group on the CHART TOOLS FORMAT tab.

The revenue and expenses chart shows that the winery will produce little revenue during its first few years as it establishes itself and its customer base. It is only during Year 6 that the revenue will outpace the expenses. After that, Bob and Carol hope that the winery's revenue will increase rapidly while expenses grow at a more moderate pace.

Changing and Formatting a Chart Title

When a chart has a single data series, the name of the data series is used for the chart title. When a chart has more than one data series, the "Chart Title" placeholder appears as the temporary title of the chart. You can then replace the placeholder text with a more descriptive title.

The clustered column chart includes the Chart Title placeholder. Bob and Carol want you to replace this with a more descriptive title.

Tutorial 4 Analyzing and Charting Financial Data | Excel   EX 215

To change the title of the column chart:

1. At the top of the column chart, click **Chart Title** to select the placeholder text.

2. Type **Projected Revenue and Expenses** as the new title, and then press the **Enter** key. The new title is entered into the chart, and the chart title element remains selected.

3. Click the **HOME** tab, and then use the buttons in the Font group to remove the bold from the chart title, change the font to **Calibri Light**, and change the font color to the **Blue, Accent 1** theme color. See Figure 4-20.

Figure 4-20 Column chart

Creating a Stacked Column Chart

The next chart that the Levitts want added to the Overview worksheet is a chart that projects the expenses incurred by the winery over the next 10 years broken down by category. Because this chart looks at how different parts of the whole vary across time, it would be better to display that information in a stacked column chart. You will create this chart based on the data located in the Projected Cash Flow worksheet.

To create a stacked column chart:

1. Go to the **Projected Cash Flow** worksheet, and then select the nonadjacent range **B4:L4;B13:L17** containing the year categories and five data series for different types of expenses.

2. Click the **INSERT** tab, and then click the **Insert Column Chart** button in the Charts group. A list of column chart subtypes appears.

3. Click the **Stacked Column** icon (the second icon in the 2-D Column section). The stacked column chart is embedded in the Projected Cash Flow worksheet.

4. With the chart still selected, click the **Chart Styles** button, and then apply the **Style 11** chart style located at the bottom of the style gallery.

You'll place this stacked column chart on the Overview worksheet.

5. On the CHART TOOLS DESIGN tab, in the Location group, click the **Move Chart** button to open the Move Chart dialog box.

6. Click the **Object in** arrow, and then click the **Overview** worksheet.

7. Click the **OK** button. The stacked column chart is moved to the Overview worksheet.

As with the clustered column chart, you'll move and resize the stacked column chart and add a descriptive chart title.

TIP

To retain the chart's proportions as you resize it, hold down the Shift key as you drag the sizing handle.

To edit the stacked column chart:

1. Move and resize the stacked column chart so that it covers the range **F31:M43** in the Overview worksheet. Use the Alt key to help you align the chart's location and size with the underlying worksheet grid.

2. Select the chart title, type **Breakdown of Business Expenses** as the new title, and then press the **Enter** key.

3. With the chart title still selected, change the font style to **non-bold**; **Blue, Accent 1**; **Calibri Light** font to match the clustered column chart. See Figure 4-21.

Figure 4-21   Stacked column chart

- revised chart title
- stacked column chart covers the range F31:M43
- grapes and labor are the source of most of the expenses
- expenses are projected to increase for the winery over the next 10 years

4. Save the workbook.

The chart clearly shows that the winery's main expenses over the next 10 years will come from the purchase of grapes and labor costs. General maintenance, miscellaneous, and the business loan repayment constitute a smaller portion of the company's projected expenses. The overall yearly expense of running the winery is expected to increase from about $250,000 in Year 1 to almost $900,000 by Year 10.

PROSKILLS

Written Communication: Communicating Effectively with Charts

Studies show that people more easily interpret information when it is presented as a graphic rather than in a table. As a result, charts can help communicate the real story underlying the facts and figures you present to colleagues and clients. A well-designed chart can illuminate the bigger picture that might be hidden by viewing only the numbers. However, poorly designed charts can mislead readers and make it more difficult to interpret data.

To create effective and useful charts, keep in mind the following tips as you design charts:

- **Keep it simple.** Do not clutter a chart with too many graphical elements. Focus attention on the data rather than on decorative elements that do not inform.
- **Focus on the message.** Design the chart to highlight the points you want to convey to readers.
- **Limit the number of data series.** Most charts should display no more than four or five data series. Pie charts should have no more than six slices.
- **Choose colors carefully.** Display different data series in contrasting colors to make it easier to distinguish one series from another. Modify the default colors as needed to make them distinct on the screen and in the printed copy.
- **Limit your chart to a few text styles.** Use a maximum of two or three different text styles in the same chart. Having too many text styles in one chart can distract attention from the data.

The goal of written communication is always to inform the reader in the simplest, most accurate, and most direct way possible. When creating worksheets and charts, everything in the workbook should be directed toward that end.

So far, you have determined monthly payments by using the PMT function, and created and formatted a pie chart and two column charts. In the next session, you'll continue your work on the winery's business plan by creating line charts, combination charts, sparklines, and data bars.

REVIEW

Session 4.1 Quick Check

1. You want to take out a loan for $130,000. The annual interest on the loan is 5 percent with payments due monthly. You plan to repay the loan in 15 years. Write the formula to calculate the monthly payment required to completely repay the loan under those conditions.
2. What function do you use to determine how many payment periods are required to repay a loan?
3. What three chart elements are included in a pie chart?
4. A data series contains values grouped into 10 categories. Would this data be better displayed as a pie chart or a column chart? Explain why.
5. A research firm wants to create a chart that displays the total population growth of a county over a 10-year period broken down by five ethnicities. Which chart type best displays this information? Explain why.
6. If the research firm wants to display the changing ethnic profile of the county over time as a percentage of the county population, which chart type should it use? Explain why.
7. If the research firm is interested in comparing the numeric sizes of different ethnic groups over time, which chart should it use? Explain why.
8. If the research firm wants to display the ethnic profile of the county only for the current year, which chart should it use? Explain why.
9. How does chart animation help you perform a what-if analysis?

Excel | Tutorial 4 Analyzing and Charting Financial Data

Session 4.2 Visual Overview:

The SPARKLINE TOOLS DESIGN contextual tab provides commands to format sparklines.

A sparkline is a chart that is displayed within a cell. You can create line, column, and win/loss sparklines.

Line sparklines can contain data markers to identify the high and low points, negative points, first and last points, and all points.

These column sparklines have been ungrouped and formatted individually.

A data bar is a conditional format that adds a horizontal bar to the background of a cell proportional in length to the cell's value.

Wine	Production Goal (Cases)	10-Year Production
Chardonnay	3,500	
White Riesling	2,000	
Pinot Grigio	1,500	
Pinot Noir	1,250	
Cabernet Franc	1,875	
Ruby Cabernet	1,000	

Wine	First Label	Second Label
Chardonnay	$20	$16
White Riesling	$16	$11
Pinot Grigio	$18	$12
Pinot Noir	$27	$21
Cabernet Franc	$22	$17
Ruby Cabernet	$15	$13

Tutorial 4 Analyzing and Charting Financial Data | Excel   EX 219

Charts, Sparklines, and Data Bars

Sparklines can be grouped or ungrouped. **Grouped sparklines** share a common format. **Ungrouped sparklines** can be formatted individually.

The **plot area** is the part of the chart that contains the graphical representation of the data series.

A **combination chart** combines two or more Excel chart types into a single graph. This chart combines a column chart and a line chart.

An **axis title** is descriptive text that appears next to an axis.

Data callouts are data labels that appear as callout bubbles pointing to data markers.

A **line chart** displays data values using a connected line rather than columns or bars.

Gridlines extend the values of the major or minor tick marks across the plot area.

Creating a Line Chart

Line charts are typically used when the data consists of values drawn from categories that follow a sequential order at evenly spaced intervals, such as historical data that is recorded monthly, quarterly, or yearly. Like column charts, a line chart can be used with one or more data series. When multiple data series are included, the data values are plotted on different lines with varying line colors.

Bob and Carol want to use a line chart to show the winery's potential cash flow over the next decade. Cash flow measures the amount of cash flowing into and out of a business annually; it is one measure of a business's financial health and ability to make its payments. Because the cash flow values are the only data series, only one line will appear on the chart. You will create the line chart now.

To create the projected cash flow line chart:

1. If you took a break at the end of the previous session, make sure the Levitt Winery workbook is open.

2. Go to the **Projected Cash Flow** worksheet, and then select the nonadjacent range **B4:L4;B27:L27** containing the Year categories from row 4 and the Cash Flow data series from row 27.

3. Click the **INSERT** tab, and then click the **Recommended Charts** button in the Charts group. The Insert Chart dialog box opens, showing different ways to chart the selected data.

4. Click the second chart listed (the Line chart), and then click the **OK** button. The line chart of the year-end cash flow values is embedded in the Projected Cash Flow worksheet.

5. Format the line chart with the **Style 15** chart style to give the line a raised 3-D appearance.

6. Move the chart to the **Overview** worksheet.

7. Move and resize the line chart in the Overview worksheet so that it covers the range **B45:D58**.

8. Format the chart title with the same **non-bold**; **Blue, Accent 1**; **Calibri Light** font you applied to the two column charts. See Figure 4-22.

> When charting table values, do not include the summary totals because they will be treated as another category.

Tutorial 4 Analyzing and Charting Financial Data | Excel EX 221

Figure 4-22 Line chart of the projected cash flow

- chart title formatted to match other chart titles
- chart moved and resized
- chart line has a 3-D appearance
- positive cash flow values
- initial cash flow values are negative

The line chart shows that Levitt Winery will have a negative cash flow in its early years and that the annual cash flow will increase throughout the decade, showing a positive cash flow starting in its sixth year.

INSIGHT

Line Charts and Scatter Charts

Line charts can sometimes be confused with XY (Scatter) charts; but they are very different chart types. A line chart is more like a column chart that uses lines instead of columns. In a line chart, the data series are plotted against category values. These categories are assumed to have some sequential order. If the categories represent dates or times, they must be evenly spaced in time. For example, the Cash Flow line chart plotted the cash flow values against categories that ranged sequentially from Year 1 to Year 10.

A scatter chart has no category values. Instead, one series of data values is plotted against another. For example, if you were analyzing the relationship between height and weight among high school students, you would use a scatter chart because both weight and height are data values. On the other hand, if you charted height measures against weight categories (Underweight, Normal, Overweight), a line chart would be more appropriate.

Scatter charts are more often used in statistical analysis and scientific studies in which the researcher is attempting to find a relationship between one variable and another. For that purpose, Excel includes several statistical tools to augment scatter charts, such as trendlines that provide the best fitting line or curve to the data. You can add a trendline by right-clicking the data series in the chart, and then clicking Add Trendline on the shortcut menu. From the Format Trendline pane that opens you can select different types of trendlines, including exponential and logarithmic lines as well as linear (straight) lines.

You have created three charts that provide a visual picture of the Levitt Winery business plan. Bob and Carol anticipate lean years as the winery becomes established; but they expect that by the end of 10 years, the winery will be profitable and stable. Next, you'll look at other tools to fine-tune the formatting of these charts. You'll start by looking at the scale applied to the chart values.

Working with Axes and Gridlines

A chart's vertical and horizontal axes are based on the values in the data series and the category values. In many cases, the axes display the data in the most visually effective and informative way. Sometimes, however, you will want to modify the axes' scale, add gridlines, and make other changes to better highlight the chart data.

Editing the Scale of the Vertical Axis

The range of values, or **scale**, of an axis is based on the values in the data source. The default scale usually ranges from 0 (if the data source has no negative values) to the maximum value. If the scale includes negative values, it ranges from the minimum value to the maximum value. The vertical, or value, axis shows the range of values in the data series; the horizontal, or category, axis shows the category values.

Excel divides the scale into regular intervals, which are marked on the axis with **tick marks** and labels. For example, the scale of the vertical axis for the Projected Revenue and Expenses chart ranges from $0 up to $2,000,000 in increments of $200,000. Having more tick marks at smaller intervals could make the chart difficult to read because the tick mark labels might start to overlap. Likewise, having fewer tick marks at larger intervals could make the chart less informative. **Major tick marks** identify the main units on the chart axis while **minor tick marks** identify the smaller intervals between the major tick marks.

Some charts involve multiple data series that have vastly different values. In those instances, you can create dual axis charts. You can plot one data series against a **primary axis**, which usually appears along the left side of the chart, and the other against a **secondary axis**, which is usually placed on the right side of the chart. The two axes can be based on entirely different scales.

By default, no titles appear next to the value and category axes. This is fine when the axis labels are self-explanatory. Otherwise, you can add descriptive axis titles. In general, you should avoid cluttering a chart with extra elements such as axis titles when that information is easily understood from other parts of the chart.

The Levitts think that the value axis scale for the Projected Revenue and Expenses chart is too crowded, and they want tick marks placed at intervals of $250,000 ranging from $0 to $1,750,000. You will modify the scale of the value axis.

To change the scale of the vertical axis:

1. Double-click the vertical axis of the Projected Revenue and Expenses chart to open the Format pane.

   The Format Axis pane has options to modify the value axis. The Bounds section provides the minimum and maximum boundaries of the axis, which in this case are set from 0.0 to 2.0E6 (which stands for 2,000,000). Note that minimum and maximum values are set to Auto, which means that Excel automatically set these boundaries based on the data values.

2. In the Bounds section of the AXIS OPTIONS, click in the **Maximum** box, delete the current value, type **1750000** as the new value, and then press the **Enter** key. Excel changes the maximum value of the vertical axis to $1,750,000.

TIP

To return a scale value to Auto, click the Reset button next to the value in the Format pane.

Tutorial 4 Analyzing and Charting Financial Data | Excel   EX 223

The Units section provides the intervals between the major tick marks and between minor tick marks. These intervals are also set automatically by Excel.

3. In the Units section, click in the **Major** box, delete the current value, type **250000** as the new interval between major tick marks, and then press the **Enter** key. The scale of the value axis has been changed. See Figure 4-23.

Figure 4-23   **Formatted value axis**

The revised axis scale makes the values easier to read and interpret.

INSIGHT

Displaying Unit Labels

When a chart involves large numbers, the axis labels can take up a lot of the available chart area and be difficult to read. You can simplify the chart's appearance by displaying units of measure more appropriate to the data values. For example, you can display the value 20 to represent 20,000 or 20,000,000. This is particularly useful when space is at a premium, such as in an embedded chart confined to a small area of the worksheet.

To display a units label, you double-click the axis to open the Format pane displaying options to format the axis. Select the units type from the Display units box. You can choose unit labels to represent values measured in the hundreds up to the trillions. Excel will modify the numbers on the selected axis and add a label so that readers will know what the axis values represent.

Adding Gridlines

Gridlines are horizontal and vertical lines that help you compare data and category values. Depending on the chart style, gridlines may or may not appear in a chart, though you can add or remove them separately. Gridlines are placed at the major tick marks on the axes, or you can set them to appear at the minor tick marks.

The chart style used for the two column charts and the line chart includes horizontal gridlines. Carol and Bob want you to add vertical gridlines to help further separate one set of year values from another. You'll add major vertical gridlines to the Projected Revenue and Expenses chart.

To add vertical gridlines to the Projected Revenue and Expenses chart:

1. With the Projected Revenue and Expenses chart still selected, click the **Chart Elements** button ➕ next to the selected column chart. The menu of chart elements appears.

2. Point to **Gridlines**, and then click the **right arrow** that appears to open a submenu of gridline options.

3. Click the **Primary Major Vertical** check box to add vertical gridlines at the major tick marks on the chart. See Figure 4-24.

Figure 4-24 Vertical gridlines added to the column chart

4. Press the **Esc** key to close the Chart Elements menu.

Working with Column Widths

Category values do not have the scale options used with data values. However, you can set the spacing between one column and another in your column charts. You can also define the width of the columns. As with the vertical axis, the default spacing and width are set automatically by Excel. A column chart with several categories will naturally make those columns thinner and more tightly packed.

The Levitts think that the columns in the Projected Revenue and Expenses chart are spaced too closely, making it difficult to distinguish one year's values from another. They want you to increase the gap between the columns.

To format the chart columns:

1. Make sure the Projected Revenue and Expenses chart is still selected and the Format pane is still open.

2. In the Format pane, click the **AXIS OPTIONS arrow**, and then click **Series "Total Revenue"** from the list of chart elements. The Format pane title changes to "Format Data Series" and all of the columns that show total revenue values are selected.

Tutorial 4 Analyzing and Charting Financial Data | Excel   EX 225

TIP

You can use the up and down spin arrows in the Gap Width box to fine-tune the gap width in 1 percent increments.

3. In the Format pane, click **SERIES OPTIONS** to display the list of options, if necessary. Series Overlap sets the amount of overlap between columns of different data series. Gap Width sets the amount of space between one group of columns and the next.

4. Drag the **Gap Width** slider until **150%** appears in the Gap Width box. The gap between groups of columns increases and the individual column widths decrease to make room for the larger gap. See Figure 4-25.

Figure 4-25   Gap width between columns

Formatting Data Markers

Each value from a data series is represented by a data marker. In pie charts, the data markers are the individual pie slices. In column charts, the columns are the data markers. In a line chart, the data markers are the points connected by the line. Depending on the line chart style, these data marker points can be displayed or hidden.

In the Cash Flow line chart, the data marker points are hidden and only the line connecting them is visible. Carol wants you to display these data markers and change their fill color to white so that they stand out, making the chart easier to understand.

To display and format the line chart data markers:

1. Scroll down the worksheet to display the Cash Flow line chart, and then double-click the line to change the Format pane to the Format Data Series pane.

2. Click the **Fill & Line** button. You can choose to display the format options for lines or data markers.

3. Click **MARKER**, if necessary, and then click **MARKER OPTIONS** to display a list of options for the line chart data markers. Currently, the None option button is selected to hide the data markers.

4. Click the **Automatic** option button to automatically display the markers. The data markers are now visible in the line chart, but they have a blue fill color. You will change this fill color to white.

- 5. Click **FILL**, if necessary, to expand the fill options.
- 6. Click the **Solid fill** option button, click the **Fill Color** button, and then click the **White, Background 1** theme color. The fill color for the data markers in the line chart changes to white.
- 7. Press the **Esc** key to deselect the data markers in the line chart.

In many charts, you will want to highlight an important data point. Data labels provide a way to identify the different values in a chart. Whether you include data labels depends on the chart, the complexity of the data and presentation, and the chart's purpose. You can include data labels for every data marker, or you can include data labels for individual data points.

Carol and Bob want to highlight that at the end of the tenth year, the winery should have an annual cash flow that exceeds $500,000. They want you to add a data label that displays the value of the last data marker in the chart at that data point.

To add a data label to the last data marker in the line chart:

- 1. Click the line in the line chart to select the entire data series, including all of the data markers.
- 2. Click the last data marker to select it. Selection handles appear around this data marker, but not any of the others.
- 3. Click the **Chart Elements** button [+] next to the line chart, and then click the **Data Labels** check box to insert a checkmark. The data label appears above only the selected data marker.
- 4. Click the **Data Labels arrow** to display a menu of data label positions and options, and then click **Data Callout**. The data label is changed to a data callout box that includes both the category value and the data value, displaying "Year 10, $502,250." You will modify this callout to display only the data value.
- 5. Double-click the data callout to select it. The Format pane is titled "Format Data Labels."
- 6. Click the **Label Options** button, and then click **LABEL OPTIONS**, if necessary, to display those options.
- 7. Click the **Category Name** check box to deselect it.
- 8. Press the **Esc** key to deselect the data label. The data callout now displays only $502,250. See Figure 4-26.

Tutorial 4 Analyzing and Charting Financial Data | Excel **EX 227**

| Figure 4-26 | Formatted data markers and data label |

[Screenshot showing a Cash Flow line chart with annotations: "data label displayed as a data callout" pointing to $502,250, and "data markers with a white fill" pointing to the line chart markers. The CHART ELEMENTS pane is visible on the right with Axes, Chart Title, Data Labels, and Gridlines checked.]

Formatting the Plot Area

The chart area covers the entire background of the chart, whereas the plot area includes only that portion of the chart in which the data markers, such as the columns in a column chart, have been placed or plotted. You can format the plot area by changing its fill and borders, and by adding visual effects. Changes to the plot area are often made in conjunction with the chart area.

Carol and Bob want you to format the chart area and plot area of the Projected Revenue and Expenses chart. You'll set the chart area fill color to a light gold to match the pie chart, and the plot area fill color to white.

To change the fill colors of the chart and plot areas:

1. Scroll the worksheet up and select the Projected Revenue and Expenses chart.

2. On the ribbon, click the **CHART TOOLS FORMAT** tab.

3. In the Current Selection group, click the **Chart Elements** arrow to display a list of chart elements in the current chart, and then click **Chart Area**. The chart area is selected in the chart.

4. In the Shape Styles group, click the **Shape Fill** button, and then click the **Gold, Accent 4, Lighter 80%** theme color in the second row and eighth column. The entire background of the chart changes to light gold.

5. In the Current Selection group, click the **Chart Elements** arrow, and then click **Plot Area** to select that chart element.

6. Change the fill color of the plot area to **white**. See Figure 4-27.

EX 228 Excel | Tutorial 4 Analyzing and Charting Financial Data

Figure 4-27 **Final Projected Revenue and Expenses chart**

- selection box for selecting chart elements
- Shape Fill button for setting the fill color of the selected shape
- chart area is light gold
- plot area is white

Bob and Carol like the appearance of the Projected Revenue and Expenses chart, and they want the same general design applied to the Breakdown of Business Expenses column chart and the Cash Flow line chart. You will add vertical gridlines to each chart, and then change the chart area fill color to light gold and the plot area fill color to white.

To format the Breakdown of Business Expenses column chart and the Cash Flow line chart:

1. Select the **Breakdown of Business Expenses** column chart.

2. Select the **chart area**, and then set the fill color of the chart area to the **Gold, Accent 4, Lighter 80%** theme color.

3. Select the **plot area**, and then change the fill color to **white**.

   Next, you'll add vertical gridlines to the chart. You can also use the CHART TOOLS DESIGN tab to add chart elements such as gridlines.

4. On the ribbon, click the **CHART TOOLS DESIGN** tab.

5. In the Chart Layouts group, click the **Add Chart Element** button, scroll down the chart elements, point to **Gridlines**, and then click **Primary Major Vertical** on the submenu. Vertical gridlines are added to the chart. See Figure 4-28.

Figure 4-28   Final Breakdown of Business Expenses chart

6. Scroll down the worksheet, select the **Cash Flow** line chart, and then repeat Steps 2 through 5 to set the chart area fill color to light gold, set the plot area fill color to white, and add major gridlines to the chart's primary axis.

The Breakdown of Business Expenses column chart and the Cash Flow line chart are now formatted with the same design.

INSIGHT

Overlaying Chart Elements

An embedded chart takes up less space than a chart sheet. However, it can be challenging to fit all of the chart elements into that smaller space. One solution is to overlay one element on top of another. The most commonly overlaid elements are the chart title and the chart legend. To overlay the chart title, click the Chart Title arrow from the list of Chart Elements and select Centered Overlay from the list of position options. Excel will place the chart title on top of the plot area, freeing up more space for other chart elements. Chart legends can also be overlaid by opening the Format pane for the legend and deselecting the Show the legend without overlapping the chart check box in the LEGEND OPTIONS section. Other chart elements can be overlaid by dragging them to new locations in the chart area and then resizing the plot area to recover the empty space.

Don't overuse the technique of overlaying chart elements. Too much overlaying of chart elements can make your chart difficult to read.

Creating a Combination Chart

A combination chart combines two chart types, such as a column chart and a line chart, within a single chart. Combination charts enable you to show two sets of data using the chart type that is best for each data set. Combination charts can have data series with vastly different values. In those instances, you can create dual axis charts, using primary and secondary axes.

Bob and Carol want to include a chart that projects the net income and cases sold by Levitt Winery over the next 10 years. Because these two data series are measuring different things (dollars and wine cases), the chart might be better understood if the Net Income data series was displayed as a column chart and the Cases Produced and Sold data series was displayed as a line chart.

To create a combination chart that shows net income and sales data:

1. Go to the **Projected Cash Flow** worksheet, and then select the nonadjacent range **B4:L5;B23:L23** containing the Year category values, the data series for Cases Produced and Sold, and the data series for Net Income.

2. On the ribbon, click the **INSERT** tab.

3. In the Charts group, click the **Recommended Charts** button. The Insert Chart dialog box opens.

4. Click the **All Charts** tab to view a list of all chart types and subtypes.

5. Click **Combo** in the list of chart types, and then click the **Custom Combination** icon (the fourth subtype). At the bottom of the dialog box, you choose the chart type for each data series and whether that data series is plotted on the primary or secondary axis.

6. For the Cases Produced and Sold data series, click the **Chart Type** arrow, and then click **Line**.

7. Click the **Secondary Axis** check box to display the values for that series on a secondary axis.

8. For the Net Income data series, click the **Chart Type** arrow, and then click **Clustered Column**. See Figure 4-29.

Tutorial 4 Analyzing and Charting Financial Data | Excel   EX 231

Figure 4-29   **Combo chart type**

Combo chart type → Combo

data displayed as a line chart on the secondary axis → Cases Produced and Sold / Line / Secondary Axis checked

Custom Combination subtype

data displayed as a column chart on the primary axis → Net Income / Clustered Column

▶ 9. Click the **OK** button. The combination chart is embedded in the Projected Cash Flow worksheet.

▶ 10. Format the combination chart with the **Style 8** chart style to give both the line and the columns a raised 3-D effect.

Bob and Carol want the combination chart to appear in the Overview worksheet and be formatted to resemble the other charts. You will make those changes now.

To move and format the combination chart:

▶ 1. Move the combination chart to the **Overview** worksheet.

▶ 2. Position and resize the combination chart so that it covers the range **F45:M58**.

▶ 3. Change the title of the combination chart to **Sales Projections**, and then format the title in the same **non-bold**; **Blue**, **Accent 1**; **Calibri Light** font you used with the other chart titles.

▶ 4. Remove the **Legend** chart element from the combination chart.

▶ 5. Add **Primary Major Vertical** gridlines to the combination chart.

▶ 6. Change the fill color of the plot area to **white**, and then change the fill color of the chart area to the same light gold (**Gold, Accent 4, Lighter 80%**) as the other charts. See Figure 4-30.

Figure 4-30 — Initial Sales Projections combination chart

- primary axis
- secondary axis
- wine cases produced and sold shown as a line chart
- yearly net income shown as a column chart

The primary axis scale for the net income values is shown on the left side of the chart; the secondary axis scale for the number of cases produced and sold appears on the right side. The chart clearly shows that the winery will have a negative income for the first five years, while the number of cases produced and sold will start at 0 and increase steadily to more than 9,000 cases by Year 10.

Working with Primary and Secondary Axes

When a chart has primary and secondary vertical axes, it is helpful to identify exactly what each axis is measuring. You can do this by adding an axis title to the chart. An axis title is descriptive text that appears next to the axis. As with other chart elements, you can add, remove, and format axis titles.

Bob and Carol want the Sales Projections chart to include labels describing what is being measured by the primary and secondary axes. You will add descriptive axis titles to the primary and secondary vertical axes.

To add axis titles to the primary and secondary vertical axes:

1. Click the **Chart Elements** button ➕ next to the combination chart, and then click the **Axis Title** check box to select it. Titles with the placeholders "Axis Title" are added to the primary and secondary axes.

2. Click the left axis title to select it, type **Net Income** as the descriptive title, and then press the **Enter** key.

3. With the left axis title selected, change the font color to the **Orange, Accent 2, Darker 25%** theme color to match the color of the columns in the chart.

4. Select the numbers on the left axis scale, and then change the font color to the **Orange, Accent 2, Darker 25%** theme color. The left axis title and scale are now the same color as the columns that reference that axis.

5. Select the right axis title, type **Cases Sold** as the descriptive title, and then press the **Enter** key.

Tutorial 4 Analyzing and Charting Financial Data | Excel   EX 233

6. With the right axis title still selected, change the font color to the **Blue, Accent 1, Darker 25%** theme color to match the color of the line in the chart.

7. Change the orientation of the right axis title to **Rotate Text Down**. The text is easier to read in this orientation.

8. Select the numbers on the right axis scale, and then change the font color to the **Blue, Accent 1, Darker 25%** theme color. The right axis title and scale are now the same color as the line that references that axis.

   Excel added the "Axis Title" placeholder to the horizontal category values axis. You can remove this title, freeing up more space for other chart elements.

9. Click the horizontal axis title to select it, and then press the **Delete** key to remove it from the chart. See Figure 4-31.

Figure 4-31   Combination chart with axis titles

The Levitts are concerned that the line chart portion of the graph makes it look as if the number of cases produced and sold was negative for the first five years. This is because the secondary axis scale, which is automatically generated by Excel, goes from a minimum of 0 to a maximum of 10,000. You will change the scale so that the 0 tick mark for Cases Sold better aligns with the $0 for Net Income.

To modify the secondary axis scale:

1. Double-click the secondary axis scale to select it and open the Format pane.

2. Verify that the **AXIS OPTIONS** list of commands is displayed.

3. Click the **Minimum** box, change the value from 0.0 to **–4000**, and then press the **Enter** key. The secondary axis scale is modified. The Cases Sold scale is now better aligned with the Net Income scale, providing a more realistic picture of the data.

4. Close the Format pane, and then press the **Esc** key to deselect the secondary axis. See Figure 4-32.

Figure 4-32   **Final combination chart**

[Screenshot of Excel showing two charts: a "Cash Flow" line chart with values ranging from $(600,000) to $600,000 across Year 1 to Year 10, with a final value of $502,250; and a "Sales Projections" combination chart showing Net Income bars and Cases Sold line across Year 1 to Year 10, with a secondary axis ranging from (4,000) to 10,000. An annotation points to the secondary axis labeled "secondary axis rescaled".]

You have completed the charts portion of the Overview worksheet. These charts provide a good overview of the financial picture of the winery that Bob and Carol plan to open.

> ### INSIGHT
> #### Copying and Pasting a Chart Format
>
> You will often want to use the same design over and over again for the charts in your worksheet. Rather than repeating the same commands, you can copy the formatting from one chart to another. To copy a chart format, first select the chart with the existing design that you want to replicate, and then click the Copy button in the Clipboard group on the HOME tab (or press the Ctrl+C keys). Next, select the chart that you want to format, click the Paste button arrow in the Clipboard group, and then click Paste Special to open the Paste Special dialog box. In the Paste Special dialog box, select the Formats option button, and then click the OK button. All of the copied formats from the original chart—including fill colors, font styles, axis scales, and chart types—are then pasted into the new chart. Be aware that the pasted formats will overwrite any formats previously used in the new chart.

Editing a Chart Data Source

Excel automates most of the process of creating and formatting a chart. However, sometimes the rendered chart does not appear the way you expected. One situation where this happens is when the selected cells contain numbers you want to treat as categories, but Excel treats them as a data series. When this happens, you can modify the data source to specify exactly which ranges should be treated as category values and which ranges should be treated as data values.

Tutorial 4 Analyzing and Charting Financial Data | Excel   **EX 235**

> **REFERENCE**
>
> **Modifying a Chart's Data Source**
> - Click the chart to select it.
> - On the CHART TOOLS DESIGN tab, in the Data group, click the Select Data button.
> - In the Legend Entries (Series) section of the Select Data Source dialog box, click the Add button to add another data series to the chart, or click the Remove button to remove a data series from the chart.
> - Click the Edit button in the Horizontal (Category) Axis Labels section to select the category values for the chart.

The Yearly Gross Income worksheet contains a table that projects the winery's gross income for 2015 through 2024. Carol wants to see a simple line chart of this data.

To create the line chart:

1. Go to the **Yearly Gross Income** worksheet, and then select the range **B4:C14**.
2. On the ribbon, click the **INSERT** tab.
3. In the Charts group, click the **Insert Line Chart** button.
4. In the 2-D Line charts section, click the **Line with Markers** subtype (the first subtype in the second row). The 2-D line chart is created. See Figure 4-33.

Figure 4-33   **Line chart with Year treated as a data series**

	A	B	C
1		Levitt Winery	
2		Yearly Gross Income	
4		Year	Gross Income
5		2015	$ (250,000)
6		2016	(245,000)
7		2017	(240,000)
8		2018	(175,000)
9		2019	(170,000)
10		2020	20,000
11		2021	200,000
12		2022	360,000
13		2023	600,000
14		2024	865,000

Year values should be treated as categories

Year appears in the chart legend as a data series

The line chart is incorrect because the Year values from the range B5:B14 are treated as another data series rather than category values. The line chart actually doesn't even have category values; the values are charted sequentially from the first value to the tenth. You can correct this problem from the Select Data dialog box by identifying the data series and category values to use in the chart.

To edit the chart's data source:

1. On the CHART TOOLS DESIGN tab, in the Data group, click the **Select Data** button. The Select Data Source dialog box opens. Note that Year is selected as a legend entry and the category values are simply the numbers 1 through 10. See Figure 4-34.

Figure 4-34	Select Data Source dialog box

range of the data source
edits the category values used in the chart
edits the highlighted data series
adds a new data series to the chart
data series used in the chart
deletes the highlighted data series
category values displayed in the chart

TIP

You can organize your data series in rows rather than columns by clicking the Switch Row/Column button in the Select Data Source dialog box.

2. With Year selected (highlighted in gray) in the list of legend entries, click the **Remove** button. Year is removed from the line chart.

3. Click the **Edit** button for the Horizontal (Category) Axis Labels. You'll specify that Year should be used as the category values.

4. Select the range **B5:B14** containing the Year values, and then click the **OK** button. The values 2015 through 2024 now appear in the list of category values.

5. Click the **OK** button to close the Select Data Source dialog box. The line chart now displays Year as the category values and Gross Income as the only data series. See Figure 4-35.

Tutorial 4 Analyzing and Charting Financial Data | Excel **EX 237**

| Figure 4-35 | **Revised Gross Income line chart** |

[Screenshot of Excel worksheet showing Levitt Winery Yearly Gross Income data and line chart]

Year	Gross Income
2015	$ (250,000)
2016	(245,000)
2017	(240,000)
2018	(175,000)
2019	(170,000)
2020	20,000
2021	200,000
2022	360,000
2023	600,000
2024	865,000

years displayed on the category axis

The Select Data Source dialog box is also useful when you want to add more data series to a chart. For example, if Bob and Carol wanted to include other financial estimates in an existing chart, they could add the data series to the existing chart rather than creating a new chart. To add a data series to a chart, select the chart, click the Select Data button in the Data group on the CHART TOOLS DESIGN tab to open the Select Data Source dialog box, click the Add button, and then select the range for the data series.

PROSKILLS

Decision Making: Choosing the Right Chart

Excel supports a wide variety of charts and chart styles. To decide which type of chart to use, you must evaluate your data and determine the ultimate purpose or goal of the chart. Consider how your data will appear in each type of chart before making a final decision.

- In general, pie charts should be used only when the number of categories is small and the relative sizes of the different slices can be easily distinguished. If you have several categories, use a column or bar chart.
- Line charts are best for categories that follow a sequential order. Be aware, however, that the time intervals must be a constant length if used in a line chart. Line charts will distort data that occurs at irregular time intervals, making it appear that the data values occurred at regular intervals when they did not.
- Pie, column, bar, and line charts assume that numbers are plotted against categories. In science and engineering applications, you will often want to plot two numeric values against one another. For that data, use **XY scatter charts**, which show the patterns or relationship between two or more sets of values. XY scatter charts are also useful for data recorded at irregular time intervals.
- If you still can't find the right chart to meet your needs, you can create a custom chart based on the built-in chart types. Third-party vendors also sell software to allow Excel to create chart types that are not built into the software.

Choosing the right chart and chart style can make your presentation more effective and informative.

Creating Sparklines

A sparkline is a chart that is displayed entirely within a worksheet cell. Because sparklines are compact in size, they don't include chart elements such as legends, titles, or gridlines. The goal of a sparkline is to convey the maximum amount of information within a very small space. As a result, sparklines are useful when you don't want charts to overwhelm the rest of your worksheet or take up valuable page space.

You can create the following three types of sparklines:

- A line sparkline for highlighting trends
- A column sparkline for column charts
- A win/loss sparkline for highlighting positive and negative values

Figure 4-36 shows examples of each sparkline type. The line sparklines show the sales history from each department and across all four departments of a computer manufacturer. The sparklines provide enough information for you to examine the sales trend within and across departments. Notice that although total sales rose steadily during the year, some departments, such as Printers, showed a sales decline midway through the year.

Figure 4-36 Types of sparklines

Tutorial 4 Analyzing and Charting Financial Data | Excel   EX 239

The column sparklines present a record of monthly temperature averages for four cities. Temperatures above 0 degrees Celsius are presented in blue columns; temperatures below 0 degrees Celsius are presented in red columns that extend downward. The height of each column is related to the magnitude of the value it represents.

Finally, the win/loss sparklines reveal a snapshot of the season results for four sports teams. Wins are displayed in blue; losses are in red. From the sparklines, you can quickly see that the Cutler Tigers finished their 10–2 season with six straight wins and the Liddleton Lions finished their 3–9 season with four straight losses.

To create a set of sparklines, you first select the data you want to graph, and then select the location range where you want the sparklines to appear. Note that the cells in which you insert the sparklines do not need to be blank. Sparklines are added as part of the cell background and do not replace any cell content.

REFERENCE

Creating and Editing Sparklines

- On the INSERT tab, in the Sparklines group, click the Line, Column, or Win/Loss button.
- In the Data Range box, enter the range for the data source of the sparkline.
- In the Location Range box, enter the range into which to place the sparkline.
- Click the OK button.
- To edit a sparkline's appearance, click the SPARKLINE TOOLS DESIGN tab.
- In the Show group, click the appropriate check boxes to specify which markers to display on the sparkline.
- In the Group group, click the Axis button, and then click Show Axis to add an axis to the sparkline.

The Levitts' business plan involves rolling out the different wine types gradually, starting with Chardonnay and Cabernet Franc and then adding more varietals over the first five years. They won't start producing all six wines until Year 6. They want you to add a column sparkline to the Overview worksheet that displays this 10-year production plan.

To insert column sparklines showing the 10-year production plan in the Overview worksheet:

1. Go to the **Overview** worksheet, and then select the range **D29:D34**. This is the location range into which you will insert the sparklines.

2. On the INSERT tab, in the Sparklines group, click the **Column** button. The Create Sparklines dialog box opens. The location range is already entered because you selected it before opening the dialog box.

3. With the insertion point in the Data Range box, click the **Estimated Production** sheet tab, and then select the data in the range **C6:L11**. This is the range that contains the data you want to chart in the sparklines.

4. Click the **OK** button. The Create Sparklines dialog box closes and the column sparklines are added to the location range in the Overview worksheet. See Figure 4-37.

Figure 4-37 Column sparklines of annual wine production

sparklines are added to the background of the location range

	Wine	Production Goal (Cases)	10-Year Production
29	Chardonnay	3,500	
30	White Riesling	2,000	
31	Pinot Grigio	1,500	
32	Pinot Noir	1,250	
33	Cabernet Franc	1,875	
34	Ruby Cabernet	1,000	

The column sparklines make it clear how the wines are placed into production at different times—Chardonnay and Cabernet Franc first, and Pinot Grigio in Year 6. Each wine, once it is introduced, is steadily produced in greater quantities as the decade progresses.

Formatting the Sparkline Axis

Because of their compact size, you have few formatting options with sparklines. One thing you can change is the scale of the vertical axis. The vertical axis will range from the minimum value to the maximum value. By default, this range is defined differently for each cell to maximize the available space. But this can be misleading. For example, the column sparklines in Figure 4-37 seem to show that Levitt Winery will be producing the same amount of each wine by the end of Year 10 because the heights of the last columns are all the same. You can change the vertical axis scale to be the same for the related sparklines.

Carol and Bob want to use the same vertical axis range for each sparkline showing the 10-year production. You will set the scale of the vertical axis to range from 0 cases to 3500 cases.

To set the scale of the vertical axis of the column sparklines:

1. If necessary, select the range **D29:D34**. Because you have selected the sparklines, the SPARKLINE TOOLS DESIGN tab appears on the ribbon.

2. On the SPARKLINE TOOLS DESIGN tab, in the Group group, click the **Axis** button, and then click **Custom Value** in the Vertical Axis Maximum Value Options section. The Sparkline Vertical Axis Setting dialog box opens.

3. Replace the value in the box with **3500**, and then click the **OK** button. You do not have to set the vertical axis minimum value because Excel assumes this to be 0 for all of the column sparklines. The column sparklines are now based on the same vertical scale, and the height of each column is based on the number of cases produced per year.

Working with Sparkline Groups

The sparklines in the location range are part of a single group. Clicking any cell in the location range selects all of the sparklines in the group. Any formatting you apply to one sparkline affects all of the sparklines in the group, as you saw when you set the range of the vertical axis. This ensures that the sparklines for related data are formatted consistently. To format each sparkline differently, you must first ungroup them.

Tutorial 4 Analyzing and Charting Financial Data | Excel   EX 241

Carol and Bob think that the column sparklines would look better if they used the same colors as the pie chart for the different wines. You will first ungroup the sparklines so you can format them separately, and then you will apply a different fill color to each sparkline.

To ungroup and format the column sparklines:

1. Make sure the range **D29:D34** is still selected.
2. On the DESIGN tab, in the Group group, click the **Ungroup** button. The sparklines are ungrouped, and selecting any one of the sparklines will no longer select the entire group.
3. Click cell **D30** to select it and its sparkline.
4. On the DESIGN tab, in the Style group, click the **Sparkline Color** button, and then click the **Orange, Accent 2, Darker 25%** theme color in the sixth row and fifth column. The fill color of the column sparkline changes to a medium orange.
5. Click cell **D31**, click the **Sparkline Color** button, and then click the **Gray-50%, Accent 3** theme color.
6. Set the color of the sparkline in cell **D32** to **Gold, Accent 4**, set the color of the sparkline in cell **D33** to **Green, Accent 6, Lighter 60%**, and then set the color of the sparkline in cell D34 to **Green, Accent 6**.
7. Select cell **B35** to deselect the sparklines. See Figure 4-38.

Figure 4-38   **Formatted sparklines**

To regroup sparklines, you select all of the cells in the location range containing the sparklines, and then click the Group button in the Group group on the SPARKLINE TOOLS DESIGN tab. Be aware that regrouping sparklines causes them to share a common format, so you will lose any formatting applied to individual sparklines.

The Sparkline Color button applied a single color to the entire sparkline. You can also apply colors to individual markers within a sparkline by clicking the Marker Color button. Using this button, you can set a distinct color for negative values, maximum values, minimum values, first values, and last values. This is useful with line sparklines that track data across a time range in which you might want to identify the maximum value within that range or the minimum value.

Creating Data Bars

A data bar is a conditional format that adds a horizontal bar to the background of a cell containing a number. When applied to a range of cells, the data bars have the same appearance as a bar chart, with each cell containing one bar. The lengths of data bars are based on the value of each cell in the selected range. Cells with larger values have longer bars; cells with smaller values have shorter bars. Data bars are dynamic, which means that if one cell's value changes, the lengths of the data bars in the selected range are automatically updated.

Data bars differ from sparklines in that the bars are always placed in the cells containing the value they represent, and each cell represents only a single bar from the bar chart. By contrast, a column sparkline can be inserted anywhere within the workbook and can represent data from several rows or columns. However, like sparklines, data bars can be used to create compact graphs that can be easily integrated alongside the text and values stored in worksheet cells.

REFERENCE

Creating Data Bars

- Select the range containing the data you want to chart.
- On the HOME tab, in the Styles group, click the Conditional Formatting button, point to Data Bars, and then click the data bar style you want to use.
- To modify the data bar rules, click the Conditional Formatting button, and then click Manage Rules.

As part of their business plan, Bob and Carol have added a table with the proposed bottle prices for their six wines under the designation First Label (highest quality) and Second Label (average quality). They want these bottle prices to be displayed graphically. You will do this using data bars.

To add data bars to the proposed bottle prices:

1. In the Overview worksheet, select the range **C38:D43**.
2. On the HOME tab, in the Styles group, click the **Conditional Formatting** button, and then click **Data Bars**. A gallery of data bar styles opens.
3. Click the **Blue Data Bar** style in the Gradient Fill section. Blue data bars are added to each of the bottle price cells.
4. Select cell **B44** to deselect the range. See Figure 4-39.

Tutorial 4 Analyzing and Charting Financial Data | Excel   EX 243

Figure 4-39   Data bars added to the Overview worksheet

[Screenshot of Excel worksheet showing Proposed Bottle Price (Retail) table with data bars in columns C and D. Callouts indicate "largest cell value in the range has the longest bar, filling the width of the cell" and "data bars".]

Wine	First Label	Second Label
Chardonnay	$20	$16
White Riesling	$16	$11
Pinot Grigio	$18	$12
Pinot Noir	$27	$21
Cabernet Franc	$22	$17
Ruby Cabernet	$15	$13

The data bars make it easy to visually compare the proposed prices of the different wines. Pinot Noir will be the most expensive wine sold by the Levitts; White Riesling and Ruby Cabernet will be the least expensive.

Modifying a Data Bar Rule

The lengths of the data bars are determined based on the values in the selected range. The cell with the largest value contains a data bar that extends across the entire width of the cell, and the lengths of the other bars in the selected range are determined relative to that bar. In some cases, this will result in the longest data bar overlapping its cell's data value, making it difficult to read. You can modify the length of the data bars by altering the rules of the conditional format.

The first label price for Pinot Noir in cell C41 contains the largest value ($27) in the range C38:D43 and has the longest data bar. The data bar for the second label price for Ruby Cabernet ($13) fills only half the cell width by comparison. The Levitts don't want data bars to overlap the cell values. You will change the data bar rule that sets the maximum length of the data bars to 35 so that the longest bar no longer fills the entire cell.

TIP

When data bars are used with negative values, the data bars originate from the center of the cell—negative bars extend to the left, and positive bars extend to the right.

To modify the data bar rule:

1. Select the range **C38:D43** containing the data bars.

2. On the HOME tab, in the Styles group, click the **Conditional Formatting** button, and then click **Manage Rules**. The Conditional Formatting Rules Manager dialog box opens, displaying all the rules applied to any conditional format in the workbook.

3. Make sure **Current Selection** appears in the Show formatting rules for box. You'll edit the rule applied to the current selection—the data bars in the Sectors worksheet.

4. Click the **Edit Rule** button. The Edit Formatting Rule dialog box opens. You want to modify this rule so that the maximum value for the data bar is set to 35. All data bar lengths will then be defined relative to this value.

5. In the Type row, click the **Maximum** arrow, and then click **Number**.

EX 244   Excel | Tutorial 4 Analyzing and Charting Financial Data

▶ 6. Press the **Tab** key to move the insertion point to the Maximum box in the Value row, and then type **35**. See Figure 4-40.

Figure 4-40   **Edit Formatting Rule dialog box**

- hides the cell value
- value used for the shortest data bar
- value used for the longest data bar
- sets the fill and border colors of the data bars
- defines how negative values will be presented

▶ 7. Click the **OK** button in each dialog box, and then select cell **B44**. The lengths of the data bars are reduced so that the longest bar covers about three-fourths of the cell width. See Figure 4-41.

Figure 4-41   **Revised data bars**

- longest data bar leaves the data value uncovered
- data bar lengths are expressed relative to a maximum value of 35

	B	C	D
36	Proposed Bottle Price (Retail)		
37	Wine	First Label	Second Label
38	Chardonnay	$20	$16
39	White Riesling	$16	$11
40	Pinot Grigio	$18	$12
41	Pinot Noir	$27	$21
42	Cabernet Franc	$22	$17
43	Ruby Cabernet	$15	$13
44			

The data bars provide a good visual of the wine prices.

Tutorial 4 Analyzing and Charting Financial Data | Excel   EX 245

INSIGHT

Edward Tufte and Chart Design Theory

Any serious study of charts will include the works of Edward Tufte, who pioneered the field of information design. One of Tufte's most important works is *The Visual Display of Quantitative Information*, in which he laid out several principles for the design of charts and graphics.

Tufte was concerned with what he termed as "chart junk," in which a proliferation of chart elements—chosen because they look "nice"—confuse and distract the reader. One measure of chart junk is Tufte's data-ink ratio, which is the amount of "ink" used to display quantitative information compared to the total ink required by the chart. Tufte advocated limiting the use of non-data ink. Non-data ink is any part of the chart that does not convey information about the data. One way of measuring the data-ink ratio is to determine how much of the chart you can erase without affecting the user's ability to interpret the chart. Tufte would argue for high data-ink ratios with a minimum of extraneous elements and graphics.

To this end, Tufte helped develop sparklines, which convey information with a high data-ink ratio within a compact space. Tufte believed that charts that can be viewed and comprehended at a glance have a greater impact on the reader than large and cluttered graphs, no matter how attractive they might be.

Inserting a Watermark

TIP

Fill colors hide a watermark. So if a sheet has a watermark, don't use a fill color for the worksheet background.

Many businesses distinguish works in progress from final versions by including the word "Draft" as a watermark on each page. A **watermark** is text or an image that appears in the background behind other content. You insert a watermark into the header or footer of a worksheet. Even though the watermark is inserted into the header or footer, a large watermark will overflow those sections and appear on the entire sheet. Generally, watermarks are given a "washed-out" appearance and are placed behind text or charts on the sheet so that they don't obscure any of the other content on the sheet. Because the watermark is included in the header/footer section, it is visible in Page Layout view and Page Break Preview but not in Normal view.

Because the current business plan for Levitt Winery will change as Bob and Carol continue to explore their financial options and the status of the wine market, they want to include a watermark with the word "Draft" on the Overview worksheet.

To insert a watermark into the worksheet:

1. On the ribbon, click the **PAGE LAYOUT** tab.

2. In the Page Setup group, click the **Dialog Box Launcher** to open the Page Setup dialog box.

3. Click the **Header/Footer** tab to display options for the header or footer of the current worksheet.

4. Click the **Custom Header** button to open the Header dialog box.

5. Click the **Center section** box. You want to insert the watermark in the center section of the header.

6. Click the **Insert Picture** button to open the Insert Pictures dialog box.

7. Click the **From a file**, navigate to the **Excel4 ▸ Tutorial** folder included with your Data Files, click the **Draft.png** file, and then click the **Insert** button. Code for the inserted picture is added to the center section of the header. See Figure 4-42.

Figure 4-42   Inserting a watermark graphic image

[Header dialog box screenshot with callouts: "Insert Picture button", "Format Picture button", and "&[Picture] indicates that a picture will be inserted" pointing to the Center section containing &[Picture]; Right section contains &[Date]]

Generally, watermarks are lighter or washed out so that they don't obscure or distract from the sheet content. You can format the appearance of the watermark from the Header dialog box.

To format the appearance of the watermark:

1. In the Header dialog box, click the **Format Picture** button to open the Format Picture dialog box.

2. Click the **Picture** tab, click the **Color** box, and then click **Washout** from the color options.

3. Click the **OK** button in each dialog box to return to the Page Setup dialog box.

4. Click the **Print Preview** button to preview the printed worksheet in Backstage view. As shown in Figure 4-43, the Draft graphic image appears in the background, faded out so as to not obscure the sheet contents.

Tutorial 4 Analyzing and Charting Financial Data | Excel   EX 247

| Figure 4-43 | Print preview of the worksheet with the watermark |

Watermark courtesy of Patrick Carey

5. Click the **Back** button ⬅ to return to the workbook.
6. Save and close the workbook.

The Levitts are pleased with the charts and graphics you have created. They provide useful visuals for anyone who is studying the Levitts' proposal.

Session 4.2 Quick Check

1. What is the difference between a line chart and a scatter chart?
2. A researcher wants to plot weight versus blood pressure. Should the researcher use a line chart or a scatter chart? Explain why.
3. What are major tick marks, minor tick marks, and gridlines?
4. How do you change the scale of a chart axis?
5. What is the difference between the chart area and the plot area?
6. What are sparklines? Describe the three types of sparklines.
7. What are data bars? How do data bars differ from sparklines?
8. What is a watermark?

SAM Projects

Put your skills into practice with SAM Projects! SAM Projects for this tutorial can be found online. If you have a SAM account, go to www.cengage.com/sam2013 to download the most recent Project Instructions and Start Files.

Review Assignments

Data Files needed for the Review Assignments: Market.xlsx, Watermark.png

Another part of Carol and Bob Levitt's business plan for the new Levitt Winery is to analyze current market conditions. The Levitts have created a workbook that explores customer preferences and sales of wine in the United States. The workbook also explores the current wineries in Michigan against which the Levitt Winery will be competing. Bob and Carol asked you to complete their workbook by presenting this data in graphic form using Excel charts. Complete the following:

1. Open the **Market** workbook located in the Excel4 ▸ Review folder included with your Data Files, and then save the workbook as **Market Analysis** in the location specified by your instructor.
2. In the Documentation sheet, enter your name in cell B3 and the date in cell B4.
3. In the Loan Analysis sheet, enter the data values and formulas required to calculate the monthly payment on a business loan of **$225,000** at **8.2** percent annual interest to be repaid in **15** years.
4. In the Market Summary worksheet, use the data in the range E21:F27 showing the types of grapes cultivated by Michigan wineries to create a pie chart comparing production rates. Embed the pie chart in the Market Summary worksheet covering the range B5:G18.
5. Format the pie chart by removing the chart title, applying the Style 11 chart style, and aligning the legend with the right edge of the chart area.
6. In the Michigan Wineries worksheet, create a line chart based on the data in the nonadjacent range B4:B16;F4:F16 showing the increase in the number of wineries in Michigan over the past 12 years. Embed the line chart in the Market Summary worksheet covering the range I5:O16.
7. Format the line chart by making the following changes:
    a. Format the chart with the Style 14 chart style.
    b. Change the chart title to **Michigan Wineries**.
    c. Change the fill color of the chart area to light blue and the plot area to white.
    d. Add primary major vertical gridlines to the plot area.
    e. Change the scale of the primary axis to range from **50** to **140** in steps of **10** units.
8. In the Michigan Wineries worksheet, create a clustered column chart using the data in the range B4:E16 showing the growth of Michigan wineries by region. Embed the chart in the Market Summary worksheet over the range I18:O28.
9. Format the column chart by making the following changes:
    a. Format the chart with the Style 13 chart style.
    b. Change the chart title to **Michigan Wineries** and reduce its font size to 14 points.
    c. Set the fill color of the chart area to light blue and the plot area to white.
    d. Add primary major vertical gridlines to the plot area.
10. In the U.S. Wine Sales worksheet, create a stacked column chart using the data in the range B3:E15 showing the breakout of the wine market into table wines, dessert wines, and sparkling wines or champagne. Embed the stacked column chart in the range B30:G43 of the Market Summary worksheet.

11. Format the stacked column chart by making the following changes:
    a. Format the chart with the Style 6 chart style.
    b. Change the chart title to **U.S. Wine Sales** and set its font size to 14 points.
    c. Add a primary vertical axis title with the text **Millions of Cases** and remove the primary horizontal axis title.
    d. Add primary major vertical gridlines.
    e. Set the fill color of the chart area to light blue and the plot area to white.
12. In the U.S. Wine Consumption worksheet, create a combination chart based on the data in the range B3:D15 showing how much wine Americans consume annually. Display the Gallons (millions) data series as a clustered column chart on the primary axis, and then display the Gallons (per Capita) data series as a line chart on the secondary axis.
13. Move the combination chart to the Market Summary worksheet; embed it over the range I30:O43.
14. Format the combination chart by making the following changes:
    a. Format the chart with the Style 4 chart style.
    b. Change the chart title to **U.S. Wine Consumption** and set its font size to 14 points.
    c. Add the primary axis title **Gallons (millions)** and the secondary axis title **Gallons (per Capita)**. Change the font color of the axis titles and scales to match the column and line markers.
    d. Remove the horizontal axis title and chart legend.
    e. Change the rotation of the secondary axis title to Rotate Text Down.
    f. Change the primary axis scale to range from **650** to **950** in intervals of **50**. Change the scale of the secondary axis to range from **2.2** to **3.0** in steps of **0.1** units.
    g. Change the fill color of the chart area to light blue and the plot area to white.
    h. Add primary major vertical gridlines to the chart.
15. Insert column sparklines in the range G21:G27 of the Market Summary worksheet based on the data in the range C5:N11 of the Michigan Grapes worksheet to show whether the number of wineries growing their own grapes has increased over the past 12 years.
16. Set the axis of the sparklines so that the column heights range from **0** to a maximum of **26** for each sparkline. Ungroup the sparklines and set the color of each to match the color of the corresponding grape in the pie chart.
17. Because the Levitts plan to grow their own grapes rather than purchasing them from out-of-state vendors, they are interested in knowing how many wineries in Michigan also grow their own grapes. The results of their survey are shown in the range B20:C22 in the Market Summary worksheet. Add data bars to the values in the range C20:C22 using the blue gradient fill. Define a rule that sets the maximum length of the data bars in those cells to a value of **100**.
18. Insert the **Watermark.png** graphic file located in the Excel4 ▶ Review folder as a washed-out watermark in the center section of the header of the Market Summary worksheet.
19. Save the workbook, and then close it.

Case Problem 1

Data File needed for this Case Problem: Bertrand.xlsx

Bertrand Family Budget Andrew and Maria Bertrand of Santa Fe, New Mexico, are hoping to purchase their first home and they are using Excel to help manage their family budget. The couple needs to estimate the monthly payments required for a $275,000 mortgage. They want to track their income and expenses using tables, charts, data bars, and sparklines. You will help them do all of these tasks. Complete the following:

1. Open the **Bertrand** workbook located in the Excel4 ▶ Case1 folder included with your Data Files, and then save the workbook as **Bertrand Budget** in the location specified by your instructor.
2. In the Documentation sheet, enter your name in cell B3 and the date in cell B4.

3. In the Budget worksheet, in the range O4:O6, enter the parameters of a **$275,000** loan that is repaid at an annual interest rate of **4.35** percent over **30** years.
4. In the range O8:O9, calculate the total number of months to repay the loan and the interest rate per month.
5. In cell O11, use the PMT function to calculate the monthly payment. Multiply the PMT function by –1 so that the result appears as a positive currency value rather than a negative value.
6. In the range D25:O25, enter the value of the monthly mortgage payment by creating an absolute reference to the value in cell O11.
7. In the range D18:O18, calculate the total income per month. In the range D27:O27, calculate the total expenses incurred each month. In the range D28:O28, calculate the couple's net income (total income minus total expenses) each month.
8. In the range C4:C11, calculate the average monthly value of each expense category.
9. Add green gradient data bars to the values in the range C4:C11. Set the maximum length of the data bars to a value of **2500**.
10. **Explore** Insert line sparklines in the range D4:D11 using the expense values in the range D19:O26. On the SPARKLINE TOOLS DESIGN tab, in the Show group, click the High Point check box to mark the high point of each sparkline.
11. Create a clustered column chart of the income, expenses, and net income for each month of the year based on the data in the nonadjacent range D15:O15;D18:O18;D27:O28. Place the chart within the range E2:K13.
12. Format the clustered column chart by making the following changes:
    a. Format the chart with the Style 8 chart style.
    b. Change the chart title to **Income and Expenses** and format it in a Calibri, non-bold 12-point font.
    c. Change the vertical scale of the chart to range from **–1000** to **6500** in steps of **1000**.
    d. Change the series overlap of the columns to **0%** and the gap width to **200%**.
13. Save the workbook.
14. Perform a what-if analysis by changing the length of the loan from 30 years to **15** years. Determine the monthly payments under this new mortgage plan, and then analyze its impact on the couple's projected income and expenses.
15. Save the workbook as **Bertrand Budget 2**, and then close it.

Case Problem 2

APPLY

Data File needed for this Case Problem: PetroChart.xlsx

PetroChart Reports William Rawlings runs a blog called *PetroChart Reports* that deals with the energy market with special emphasis on crude oil production and consumption. William likes to augment his writing with informative charts and graphics. He has an Excel workbook with some historic data on the crude oil market. He has asked you to create charts from that data that he can use in an article that reviews the history of oil production and consumption, and their impact on the size of the proven world oil reserves. Complete the following:

1. Open the **PetroChart** workbook located in the Excel4 ▶ Case2 folder included with your Data Files, and then save the workbook as **PetroChart Reports**.
2. In the Documentation sheet, enter your name in cell B3 and the date in cell B4.
3. In the World Oil Production worksheet, create a line chart of world oil production from 1980 to 2010 using the data from the range A6:G37. Move the chart to the Summary worksheet covering the range B4:H19.
4. Format the chart with the Style 9 chart style, and then change the chart title to **Oil Production Historic Trends**.
5. Change the line color for the North America data series to white, which is easier to read against the black backdrop.

Explore 6. Revise the vertical axis scale so that the display unit is expressed in terms of thousands (most oil production reports are quoted in terms of thousands of barrels per day). Change the text of the display unit from Thousands to **Thousands of Barrels per Day**.

7. In the World Oil Production worksheet, create a pie chart that displays the relative size of the oil production values for different regions in 2010 based on the data in the nonadjacent range B6:G6;B37:G37. Move the pie chart to the Summary worksheet covering the range J4:P19.

8. Make the following changes to the pie chart:
   a. Format the chart with the Style 7 chart style.
   b. Change the chart title to **2010 Oil Production** and reduce its font size to 14 points.
   c. Move the chart legend to the left edge of the chart area.
   d. Add data labels outside of the pie slices showing the percentage associated with each region.
   e. Change the color of the pie slice for the North America region to white.

9. In the World Oil Consumption worksheet, create a line chart that shows how oil consumption changed from 1980 to 2010 based on the data in the range A6:G37. Move the chart to the Summary worksheet covering the range B21:H36.

10. Change the chart title to **Oil Consumption Historic Trends**.

Explore 11. Copy the Oil Production Historic Trends line chart. Use Paste Special to paste the format of that chart into the Oil Consumption Historic Trends line chart.

12. In the World Oil Consumption worksheet, create a pie chart showing the 2010 regional breakdown of oil consumption based on the data in the range B6:G6;B37:G37. Move the chart to the Summary worksheet covering the range J21:P36.

Explore 13. Change the chart title to **2010 Oil Consumption**. Use Paste Special to copy the 2010 Oil Production pie chart and paste its format into the 2010 Oil Consumption pie chart.

14. There was a fear that with increased oil production and consumption from 1980 to 2010, there would be decreasing amounts of proven reserves. Was this the case? In the Proven Reserves worksheet, create a combination chart based on the data in the range A5:D36. Display the Oil Production and Oil Consumption data series as line charts on the primary axis. Display the Proven Reserves data series as an area chart on the secondary axis. Move the chart to the Summary worksheet covering the range E38:M53.

15. Make the following changes to the combination chart:
   a. Format the chart with the Style 6 chart style.
   b. Change the chart title to **Historic Trends in Proven Oil Reserves**; reduce the font size to 12 points.
   c. Change the primary axis scale to range from **50,000** to **90,000** in steps of **5,000**.
   d. Change the line color of the Oil Production data series to white.

16. Save the workbook, and then close it.

Case Problem 3

CHALLENGE

Data Files needed for this Case Problem: Frame.xlsx, Confidential.png

Frame Financial Jeri Carbone is the owner of Frame Financial, a small financial consulting firm in Marion, Iowa. Among her many tasks is to maintain Excel workbooks with information on companies and their stock market activity. One of her workbooks contains information on Harriman Scientific, a company traded on the stock exchange. She wants you to complete the workbook by adding charts that describe the company's financial status and stock charts to display recent values of the company's stock. The stock chart should display the stock's daily opening, high, low, and closing values, and the number of shares traded for each day of the past few weeks. The volume of shares traded should be expressed in terms of millions of shares. Complete the following:

1. Open the **Frame** workbook located in the Excel4 ▸ Case3 folder included with your Data Files, and then save the workbook as **Frame Financial** in the location specified by your instructor.

2. In the Documentation sheet, enter your name in cell B3 and the date in cell B4.

3. Insert the **Confidential.png** graphics file located in the Excel4 ▸ Case3 folder as a washed-out watermark in the center section of the header of the Documentation worksheet.
4. In the Overview worksheet, create a 3-D pie chart describing the company's shareholders based on the data source values in the range K4:L6.
5. Remove the chart title and chart legend, and then resize the chart so that it is contained within the range M3:O7.
6. Change the fill colors of the ranges K4:L4, K5:L5, and K6:L6 to match their corresponding pie slice colors. Change the font color in those ranges to white.
7. Add pink gradient-colored data bars to the values in the range L10:O14. Edit the data bar rules so that the maximum data bar length corresponds to a value of **15,000**, and the bar direction goes from right to left.
8. In the Income Statement worksheet, create a 3-D clustered column chart of the company's net revenue and operating expenses using the data values in the nonadjacent range B4:F4;B6:F6;B12:F12. Move the chart to the Overview worksheet.
 Explore 9. On the CHART TOOLS FORMAT tab, use the Size group to set the height of the chart to 2.44" and the width to 3.51". Move the chart so that its upper-left corner is aligned with the upper-left corner of cell B17.
10. Format the chart with the Style 11 chart style, change the chart title to **Revenue and Expenses**, and then reduce the font size of the chart title to 11 points.
11. In the Balance Sheet worksheet, create a 3-D clustered column chart of the company's assets and liabilities using the data in the range B4:F4;B18:F18;B26:F26. Move the chart to the Overview worksheet. Set its size to 2.44" high by 3.51" wide and place the chart so that it is directly to the right of the Revenue and Expenses chart.
 Explore 12. Change the chart title to **Assets and Liabilities**. Copy and paste the format used with the Revenue and Expenses chart into this chart.
13. In the Cash Flow Statement worksheet, create a 2-D line chart of the data in the range C4:F4;C28:F28. Move the chart to the Overview worksheet. Resize the chart to 2.44" high by 3.51" wide and place the chart directly to the right of the Assets and Liabilities chart.
14. In the line chart, apply the Style 15 chart style, change the chart title to **Net Cash Flow**, and then reduce the font size of the chart title to 11 points.
15. In the Income Statement, Balance Sheet, and Cash Flow Statement worksheets, add line sparklines in the Trend column based on the financial values for 2012 through 2015.
 Explore 16. In the Stock Values worksheet, select the range A4:F34, and then insert a Volume-Open-High-Low-Close stock chart.
 Explore 17. Move the chart to a new chart sheet named **Stock History**.
18. Make the following changes to the stock chart:
    a. Change the chart title to **Recent Stock History** and increase the font size to 24 points.
    b. Set the font size of the horizontal and vertical axes to 12 points.
    c. Add Axis titles to the chart. Set the primary vertical axis title to **Volume of Shares Traded**, the secondary vertical axis title to **Stock Value**, and the horizontal axis title to **Date**.
    d. Set the font size of the axis titles to 16 points and rotate the text of the secondary axis title down.
    e. Remove the chart legend.
    f. Change the scale of the primary vertical axis to range from **200,000** to **2,000,000**, and then change the display unit of the primary vertical axis to Thousands.
    g. Change the scale of the secondary vertical axis to range from **10** to **35**.
    h. Add primary major horizontal and vertical gridlines, and remove any secondary gridlines.
    i. Set the gap width of the columns in the stock chart to **20%**.
19. Save the workbook, and then close it.

Case Problem 4

Data File needed for this Case Problem: Mortgage.xlsx

The Mortgage White Paper Kyle Lewis of Rockford, Illinois, runs a newsletter and blog called *The Mortgage White Paper* containing valuable financial information for investors, entrepreneurs, and homeowners. Kyle's emphasis is on tracking the world of home mortgages and home equity loans. Kyle's assistant has been creating an Excel workbook with an updated listing of the 15-year and 30-year interest rates on home loans. Now, his assistant reports that the formulas and charts in the workbook aren't working correctly. Kyle has asked you to fix the problems and finish the workbook. Complete the following:

1. Open the **Mortgage** workbook located in the Excel4 ▸ Case4 folder included with your Data Files, and then save the workbook as **Mortgage Report**.
2. In the Documentation sheet, enter your name in cell B3 and the date in cell B4.
3. In the Mortgage Calculator worksheet, calculate the monthly payments required to repay loans of different amounts, which are listed in the range A9:A24. The annual interest rate and length of the loan in years are provided in the range B5:C6 for 15-year and 30-year fixed loans.
4. **Troubleshoot** The formulas used to calculate the monthly payments are displaying error values. Kyle is sure that the value in cell B9 is correct, but something happened when the formula was copied to the range B9:C24. Make the necessary changes so that the formula results are shown instead of the error values.
5. **Troubleshoot** The line chart that displays the monthly payments for the 15-year and 30-year fixed rate loans is showing the loan amounts plotted as a third data series rather than as category values. Find the problem and fix it.
6. Format the line chart with the chart style and design you think is most appropriate for the data. Make sure the finished chart is easy to read and interpret.
7. **Troubleshoot** In the Mortgage Trends worksheet, the data bars that were added to the Mortgage Application Index values in the range D7:D56 all have the same length. Fix the data bars so that reasonable bar lengths are displayed in the cells.
8. Create a combination chart that displays the 15-year and 30-year fixed rates in a line chart on the primary axis, and the Mortgage Application Index in an area chart on the secondary axis. Move and resize the chart to cover the range F6:M22.
9. Make the following changes to the chart:
   a. Format the chart with the Style 1 chart style.
   b. Change the chart title to **Interest Rates vs. Mortgage Applications** and reduce the font size of the title text to 14 points.
   c. Move the legend to the bottom of the chart area.
   d. Add the axis title **Interest Rate** to the primary vertical axis, and then add the axis title **Application Index** to the secondary vertical axis.
   e. Rotate the text of the secondary vertical axis title down.
   f. Change the scale of the primary vertical axis to range from 2 percent to 4.5 percent in increments of 0.5 percent, and then change the scale of the secondary vertical axis to range from 500 to 1000 in increments of 50.
   g. Add primary major vertical gridlines to the plot area.
   h. Set the fill color of the plot area to white and the fill color of the chart area to Brown, Accent 3, Lighter 80%.
10. Save the workbook.
11. Return to the Mortgage Calculator worksheet. One of Kyle's clients wants to take out a $200,000 mortgage but can afford only an $850 monthly payment. Use Goal Seek to determine how low the 30-year fixed rate needs to be to meet that goal.
12. Save the workbook as **Mortgage Report 2**, and then close it.

Decision Making

Creating a Budget Worksheet to Make Financial Decisions

Decision making is the process of choosing between alternative courses of action, usually in response to a problem that needs to be solved. Having an understanding of decision-making processes will lead to better decisions and greater confidence in carrying out those decisions. This is especially important when making financial decisions.

Gather Relevant Information

Begin by collecting data and information related to the decision you need to make. This information can include data expressed as currency or numbers, as well as data that cannot be measured numerically. For example, when creating a budget, numerical data includes your income and expenses, current savings, future savings and purchases, and so on. Other data might include the amount of savings you need in order to feel comfortable before making a large purchase, such as buying a car or paying tuition.

Evaluate the Gathered Information and Develop Alternatives

Evaluate the data you collected and determine possible alternatives. Excel workbooks are well suited to evaluating numerical data. You can also use workbooks to evaluate potential outcomes based on other data by assigning numerical weights to them. For example, you can enter your monthly income and fixed expenses into a worksheet along with variable expenses to determine your cash flow. You can then consider this information along with your current savings to determine how much money to contribute to savings or earmark for a purchase. Based on these results, you can develop alternatives for how to distribute your available money among variable expenses (such as entertainment), savings, and a large purchase.

Select the Best Alternative

Carefully evaluate the alternatives you developed based on your analysis. Before making a decision, be sure to take into account all factors. Consider such questions as:

- Does this alternative make sense for the long term? For example, does this budget allow you to achieve all your financial goals?
- Can you realistically carry out this alternative? For example, does this budget provide enough for necessities such as food and housing as well as for luxuries such as entertainment?
- Will this alternative be acceptable even if its outcome is not perfect or some unconsidered factors emerge? For example, will this budget cover unforeseen expenses such as car repairs or an unexpected trip?
- How comfortable are you with this decision? For example, does this budget relieve or add stress about managing your finances?

After analyzing all the factors, one alternative should begin to emerge as the best alternative. If it doesn't, you might need to develop additional alternatives.

Prepare an Action Plan

After making a decision, you need to plan how to implement that decision. Consider what steps you need to take to achieve the final outcome. For example, do you need to open a bank account or change services to reduce expenses (such as switching to a less expensive cell phone plan)? Determine a reasonable time table. When do you want to start? How long will each task take? What tasks must be completed before others start? Can tasks be performed at the same time? Develop milestones to track the success of your plan. For example, one milestone might be to increase your savings by 10 percent in three months. Finally, identify what resources you need to be successful. For example, do you need to talk to a financial advisor at your bank?

Take Action and Monitor the Results

After you develop the action plan, the actual plan begins. For example, you can open bank accounts, change telephone services, and so forth as outlined in your action plan. Be sure to check off completed tasks and assess how well those actions produce the desired outcome. For example, is the budget achieving the financial goals you set? If so, then continue to follow the established plan. If not, you may need to modify the action plan or reevaluate your decision.

Develop a Budget Worksheet

Excel is valuable to a wide audience of users: from accountants of Fortune 500 companies to homeowners managing their budgets. An Excel workbook can be a complex document, recording data from thousands of financial transactions, or it can track a few monthly household expenses. Anyone who has to balance a budget, track expenses, or project future income can use the financial tools in Excel to help them make good financial decisions about their financing and future expenditures.

In this exercise, you will use Excel to create a sample budget workbook that will contain information of your choice, using the Excel skills and features presented in Tutorials 1 through 4. Use the following steps as a guide to completing your workbook.

Note: Please be sure *not* to include any personal information of a sensitive nature in any workbooks you create to be submitted to your instructor for this exercise. Later, you can update the workbooks with such information for your personal use.

1. Gather the data related to your monthly cash inflows and outflows. For example, how much do you take home in your paychecks each month? What other sources of income do you have? What expenses do you have—rent, utilities, gas, insurance, groceries, entertainment, car payments, and so on?

2. Create a new workbook for the sample financial data. Use the first worksheet as a documentation sheet that includes your name, the date on which you start creating the workbook, and a brief description of the workbook's purpose.

3. Plan the structure of the second worksheet, which will contain the budget. Include a section to enter values that remain consistent from month to month, such as monthly income and expenses. As you develop the budget worksheet, reference these cells in formulas that require those values. Later, you can update any of these values and see the changes immediately reflected throughout the budget.

4. In the budget worksheet, enter realistic monthly earnings for each month of the year. Use formulas to calculate the total earnings each month, the average monthly earnings, and the total earnings for the entire year.

5. In the budget worksheet, enter realistic personal expenses for each month. Divide the expenses into at least three categories, providing subtotals for each category and a grand total of all the monthly expenses. Calculate the average monthly expenses and total expenses for the year.

6. Calculate the monthly net cash flow (the value of total income minus total expenses).

7. Use the cash flow values to track the savings throughout the year. Use a realistic amount for savings at the beginning of the year. Use the monthly net cash flow values to add or subtract from this value. Project the end-of-year balance in the savings account under your proposed budget.
8. Format the worksheet's contents using appropriate text and number formats. Add colors and borders to make the content easier to read and interpret. Use cell styles and themes to provide your worksheet with a uniform appearance.
9. Use conditional formatting to automatically highlight negative net cash flow months.
10. Insert a pie chart that compares the monthly expenses for the categories.
11. Insert a column chart that charts all of the monthly expenses regardless of the category.
12. Insert a line chart or sparkline that shows the change in the savings balance throughout the 12 months of the year.
13. Insert new rows at the top of the worksheet and enter titles that describe the worksheet's contents.
14. Examine your assumptions. How likely are certain events to occur? Perform several what-if analyses on your budget, providing the impact of (a) reducing income with expenses remaining constant; (b) increasing expenses with income remaining constant; (c) reducing income and expenses; and (d) increasing income and expenses. Discuss the different scenarios you explored. How much cushion does your projected income give you if expenses increase? What are some things you can do in your budget to accommodate this scenario?
15. Think of a major purchase you might want to make—for example, a car or a house. Determine the amount of the purchase and the current annual interest rate charged by your local bank. Provide a reasonable length of time to repay the loan, such as five years for a car loan or 20 to 30 years for a home loan. Use the PMT function to determine how much you would have to spend each month on the payments for your purchase. You can do these calculations in a separate worksheet.
16. Add the loan information to your monthly budget and evaluate the purchase of this item on your budget. Is it affordable? Examine other possible loans you might pursue and evaluate their impact on your budget. Come up with the most realistic way of paying off the loan while still maintaining a reasonable monthly cash flow and a cushion against unexpected expenses. If the payment exceeds your budget, reduce the estimated price of the item you're thinking of purchasing until you determine the monthly payment you can afford under the conditions of the loan.
17. After settling on a budget and the terms of a loan that you can afford, develop an action plan for putting your budget into place. What are some potential pitfalls that will prohibit you from following through on your proposed budget? How can you increase the likelihood that you will follow the budget? Be specific, and write down a list of goals and benchmarks that you'll use to monitor your progress in following your financial plan.
18. With the worksheet set up and your budget in place, you can take action and monitor your results. You will want to update your worksheet each month as income or expense items change to be sure you remain on track to meet your goals. You will also want to confirm that you made a good decision. If not, evaluate your budget and determine what new action you need to take to get yourself back on track.
19. Format the worksheets for your printer. Include headers and footers that display the workbook filename, the workbook's author, and the date on which the report is printed. If the report extends across several pages, repeat appropriate print titles on all of the pages, and include page numbers and the total number of pages on every printed page.
20. Save and close the workbook.

TUTORIAL 5

Working with Excel Tables, PivotTables, and PivotCharts

Tracking Cash Receipts

OBJECTIVES

Session 5.1
- Explore a structured range of data
- Freeze rows and columns
- Plan and create an Excel table
- Rename and format an Excel table
- Add, edit, and delete records in an Excel table
- Sort data

Session 5.2
- Filter data using filter buttons
- Filter an Excel table with a slicer
- Insert a Total row to summarize an Excel table
- Split a worksheet into two panes
- Insert subtotals into a range of data
- Use the Outline buttons to show or hide details

Session 5.3
- Create and modify a PivotTable
- Apply PivotTable styles and formatting
- Filter a PivotTable
- Insert a slicer to filter a PivotTable
- Insert a recommended PivotTable
- Create a PivotChart

Case | Laurie's Coffeehouse

Laurie Kye's dream of opening Laurie's Coffeehouse became a reality three months ago. Laurie's Coffeehouse serves coffee blends and specialty drinks, along with breakfast and lunch items. To keep the shop interesting, Laurie sells unique handcrafted gifts at the counter. The coffeehouse is located in Cave Creek, Arizona, which is a popular tourist attraction and close to a community college campus, so it attracts heavy foot traffic. Recently, the coffeehouse has become a weekend meeting place for many motorcyclists and bikers.

Now that Laurie's Coffeehouse has settled into a smooth routine, Laurie wants to analyze her business operations more carefully. She wants to determine what is working best, and what is selling most each day. In addition, Laurie wants information to help her make ordering and staffing decisions. She has entered the January cash receipts data into an Excel workbook, and has asked you to help her analyze the data. You'll work with the data as an Excel table so you can easily edit, sort, and filter the data. You'll also summarize the data using the Subtotals command, a PivotTable, and a PivotChart.

STARTING DATA FILES

Excel5 → Tutorial
January.xlsx

Review
February.xlsx

Case1
Student.xlsx

Case2
Players.xlsx

Case3
Cooking.xlsx

Case4
Benjis.xlsx

Excel | Tutorial 5 Working with Excel Tables, PivotTables, and PivotCharts

Session 5.1 Visual Overview:

Every Excel table has a table name, which you can change to a descriptive name.

The filter button changes to a sort icon as a reminder that the data is sorted by that field.

The first row of the range contains field names and is called the **header row**. Although the header row often is row 1, it can begin in any row.

Each row represents a **record**, which is a group of related fields.

You can rearrange, or **sort**, the records in a table or a range based on one or more fields. This table is sorted by the Trn Date field, which is the **sort field**.

You can use a predefined list to sort data in chronological rather than alphabetical order, such as by day of the week.

Cash Receipts January - Excel

FILE | HOME | INSERT | PAGE LAYOUT | FORMULAS | DATA | REVIEW | VIEW

Table Name: JanuaryData
Resize Table
Summarize with PivotTable
Remove Duplicates
Convert to Range
Insert Slicer
Export
Refresh
Header Row
Total Row
Banded Rows

Properties | Tools | External Table Data

D13 — Spec Drink

	A	B	C	D
1	Trn Date	Day	Week #	Segment
2	1/1/2016	Friday	1	Coffee
3	1/1/2016	Friday	1	Food
4	1/1/2016	Friday	1	Gifts
5	1/1/2016	Friday	1	Spec Drink
6	1/2/2016	Saturday	1	Coffee
7	1/2/2016	Saturday	1	Food
8	1/2/2016	Saturday	1	Gifts
9	1/2/2016	Saturday	1	Spec Drink
10	1/3/2016	Sunday	2	Coffee
11	1/3/2016	Sunday	2	Food
12	1/3/2016	Sunday	2	Gifts
13	1/3/2016	Sunday	2	Spec Drink
14	1/4/2016	Monday	2	Coffee
15	1/4/2016	Monday	2	Food
16	1/4/2016	Monday	2	Gifts
17	1/4/2016	Monday	2	Spec Drink
18	1/5/2016	Tuesday	2	Coffee
19	1/5/2016	Tuesday	2	Food
20	1/5/2016	Tuesday	2	Gifts

Documentation | Cash Receipts

READY

Tutorial 5 Working with Excel Tables, PivotTables, and PivotCharts | Excel   EX 259

Elements of an Excel Table

Table styles provide a way to quickly format an entire table using a preset style definition.

A **field name**, or **column header**, is a unique label that describes the contents of the data in a column.

You can click a filter button to sort the table by data in that column.

An **Excel table** is a range of related data that is managed independently from other data in the worksheet.

Amount
$ 152.15
$ 221.26
$ 57.17
$ 380.64
$ 92.37
$ 206.32
$ 183.59
$ 126.09
$ 175.62
$ 116.43
$ 117.67
$ 437.50
$ 209.25
$ 409.66
$ 136.91
$ 140.79
$ 221.29
$ 252.61
$ 147.89

Each column represents a **field**, which is a single piece of data. A field describes a characteristic of a person, place, or thing, such as a last name, a city, or a product.

Planning a Structured Range of Data

A worksheet is often used to manage related data, such as lists of clients, products, or transactions. For example, the January cash receipts for Laurie's Coffeehouse that Laurie entered in the Cash Receipts worksheet, which is shown in Figure 5-1, are a collection of related data. Related data that is organized in columns and rows, such as the January cash receipts, is sometimes referred to as a structured range of data. Each column represents a field, which is a single piece of data. Each row represents a record, which is a group of related fields. In the Cash Receipts worksheet, the columns labeled Trn Date, Day, Week #, Segment, and Amount are fields that store different pieces of data. Each row in the worksheet is a record that stores one day's cash receipts for a specific segment that includes the Trn Date, Day, Week #, Segment, and Amount fields. All of the cash receipts records make up the structured range of data. A structured range of data is commonly referred to as a list or table.

TIP

In Excel, a range of data is any block of cells, whereas a structured range of data has related records and fields organized in rows and columns.

Figure 5-1 January cash receipts data

each column is a field

	A	B	C	D	E
1	Trn Date	Day	Week #	Segment	Amount
2	1/1/2016	Friday	1	Spec Drink	380.64
3	1/1/2016	Friday	1	Food	221.26
4	1/1/2016	Friday	1	Coffee	152.15
5	1/1/2016	Friday	1	Gifts	57.17
6	1/2/2016	Saturday	1	Food	206.32
7	1/2/2016	Saturday	1	Gifts	183.59
8	1/2/2016	Saturday	1	Spec Drink	126.09
9	1/2/2016	Saturday	1	Coffee	92.37
10	1/3/2016	Sunday	2	Spec Drink	437.50
11	1/3/2016	Sunday	2	Coffee	175.62
12	1/3/2016	Sunday	2	Gifts	117.67
13	1/3/2016	Sunday	2	Food	116.43
14	1/4/2016	Monday	2	Food	309.66
15	1/4/2016	Monday	2	Coffee	209.25
16	1/4/2016	Monday	2	Spec Drink	140.79
17	1/4/2016	Monday	2	Gifts	136.91
18	1/5/2016	Tuesday	2	Spec Drink	262.04
19	1/5/2016	Tuesday	2	Food	252.61
20	1/5/2016	Tuesday	2	Coffee	221.29

each row is a record

You can easily add and delete data, edit data, sort data, find subsets of data, summarize data, and create reports about related data.

PROSKILLS

Decision Making: The Importance of Planning

Before you create a structured range of data, you should create a plan. Planning involves gathering relevant information about the data and deciding your goals. The end results you want to achieve will help you determine the kind of data to include in each record and how to divide that data into fields. Specifically, you should do the following to create an effective plan:

- Spend time thinking about how you will use the data.
- Consider what reports you want to create for different audiences (supervisors, customers, directors, and so forth) and the fields needed to produce those reports.
- Think about the various questions, or *queries*, you want answered and the fields needed to create those results.

This information is often documented in a **data definition table**, which lists the fields to be maintained for each record, a description of the information each field will include, and the type of data (such as numbers, text, or dates) stored in each field. Careful and thorough planning will help you avoid having to redesign a structured range of data later.

Before creating the list of cash receipts, Laurie carefully considered what information she needs and how she wants to use it. Laurie plans to use the data to track daily cash receipts for each segment of business activity, which she has identified as coffee, specialty drinks, food, and gifts. She wants to be able to create reports that show specific lists of cash receipts, such as all the cash receipts for a specific date, day of the week, or week of the year. Based on this information, Laurie developed the data definition table shown in Figure 5-2.

Figure 5-2 Data definition table for the cash receipts

Data Definition Table			
Field	Description	Data Type	Notes
Trn Date	Date of the cash receipts	Date	Transaction Date (abbreviated to Trn Date) Use the *mm/dd/yyyy* format
Day	Day of the week	Text	Sunday, Monday, Tuesday, …
Week #	Week of the year	Number	1–52
Segment	Business category for the cash receipts	Text	Coffee, Spec Drink, Food, Gifts
Amount	Cash receipts total for a specific transaction date and segment	Number	Use the Accounting format and show two decimal places

After you determine the fields and records you need, you can enter the data in a worksheet. You can then work with the data in many ways, including the following common operations:

- Add, edit, and delete data in the range.
- Sort the data range.
- Filter to display only rows that meet specified criteria.
- Insert formulas to calculate subtotals.
- Create summary tables based on the data in the range (usually with PivotTables).

You'll perform many of these operations on the cash receipts data.

INSIGHT

Creating an Effective Structured Range of Data

For a range of data to be used effectively, it must have the same structure throughout. Keep in mind the following guidelines:

- **Enter field names in the top row of the range.** This clearly identifies each field.
- **Use short, descriptive field names.** Shorter field names are easier to remember and enable more fields to appear in the workbook window at once.
- **Format field names.** Use formatting to distinguish the header row from the data. For example, apply bold, color, and a different font size.
- **Enter the same kind of data in a field.** Each field should store the smallest bit of information and be consistent from record to record. For example, enter Los Angeles, Tucson, or Chicago in a City field, but do not include states, such as CA, AZ, or IL, in the same column of data.
- **Separate the data from the rest of the worksheet.** The data, which includes the header row, should be separated from other information in the worksheet by *at least* one blank row and one blank column. The blank row and column enable Excel to accurately determine the range of the data.

Laurie created a workbook and entered the cash receipts data for January based on the plan outlined in the data definition table. You'll open this workbook and review its structure.

To open and review Laurie's workbook:

1. Open the **January** workbook located in the Excel5 ▸ Tutorial folder included with your Data Files, and then save the workbook as **Cash Receipts January** in the location specified by your instructor.

2. In the Documentation sheet, enter your name in cell B3 and the date in cell B4.

3. In the range A7:D13, review the data definition table. This table, which was shown in Figure 5-2, describes the different fields that are used in the Cash Receipts worksheet.

4. Go to the **Cash Receipts** worksheet. This worksheet, which was shown in Figure 5-1, contains data about the coffeehouse's cash receipts. Currently, the worksheet includes 121 cash receipts. Each cash receipt record is a separate row (rows 2 through 122) and contains five fields (columns A through E). Row 1, the header row, contains labels that describe the data in each column.

5. Scroll the worksheet to row **122**, which is the last record. The column headers in row 1 are no longer visible. Without seeing the column headers, it is difficult to know what the data entered in each column represents.

Freezing Rows and Columns

You can select rows and columns to remain visible in the workbook window as you scroll the worksheet. **Freezing** a row or column lets you keep the headers visible as you work with the data in a large worksheet. You can freeze the top row, freeze the first column, or freeze the rows and columns above and to the left of the selected cell. If you freeze the top row, row 1 remains on the screen as you scroll, leaving column headers visible and making it easier to identify the data in each record.

Tutorial 5 Working with Excel Tables, PivotTables, and PivotCharts | Excel   EX 263

Laurie wants to see the column headers as she scrolls the cash receipts data. You'll freeze row 1, which contains the column headers.

To freeze row 1 of the worksheet:

1. Press the **Ctrl+Home** keys to return to cell A1. You want to freeze row 1.
2. On the ribbon, click the **VIEW** tab.
3. In the Window group, click the **Freeze Panes** button, and then click **Freeze Top Row**. A horizontal line appears below the column labels to indicate which row is frozen.
4. Scroll the worksheet to row **122**. This time, the column headers remain visible as you scroll. See Figure 5-3.

TIP

To freeze the columns and rows above and to the right of the selected cell, click the Freeze Panes button, and then click Freeze Panes.

Figure 5-3   Top row of the worksheet is frozen

	A	B	C	D	E
1	Trn Date	Day	Week #	Segment	Amount
115	1/29/2016	Friday	5	Spec Drink	276.44
116	1/29/2016	Friday	5	Food	275.18
117	1/29/2016	Friday	5	Gifts	124.40
118	1/29/2016	Friday	5	Coffee	117.89
119	1/30/2016	Saturday	5	Spec Drink	425.50
120	1/30/2016	Saturday	5	Food	348.08
121	1/30/2016	Saturday	5	Coffee	323.35
122	1/30/2016	Saturday	5	Gifts	169.29

header row remains visible as you scroll the worksheet

Freeze Panes button

rows above the line are frozen

5. Press the **Ctrl+Home** keys. Cell A2, the cell directly below the frozen row, becomes the active cell.

After you freeze panes, the first option on the Freeze Panes button menu changes to Unfreeze Panes. This option releases the frozen panes so that all the columns and rows in the worksheet shift when you scroll. Laurie wants you to use a different method to keep the column headers visible, so you will unfreeze the top row of the worksheet.

To unfreeze the top row of the worksheet:

1. On the VIEW tab, in the Window group, click the **Freeze Panes** button. The first Freeze Panes option is now Unfreeze Panes.
2. Click **Unfreeze Panes**. The headers are no longer frozen, and the dark, horizontal line below the column headers is removed. You can now scroll all the rows and columns in the worksheet.

Creating an Excel Table

You can convert a structured range of data, such as the cash receipts data in the range A1:E122, to an Excel table. An Excel table makes it easier to identify, manage, and analyze the groups of related data. When a structured range of data is converted into an Excel table, you see the following:

- A filter button in each cell of the header row
- The range formatted with a table style
- A sizing handle (a small triangle) in the lower-right corner of the last cell of the table
- The TABLE TOOLS DESIGN tab on the ribbon

You can create more than one Excel table in a worksheet. Although you can leave the cash receipts data as a structured range of data and still perform all of the tasks in this section, creating an Excel table helps you to be more efficient and accurate.

INSIGHT

Saving Time with Excel Tables

Although you can perform the same operations for both a structured range of data and an Excel table, using Excel tables provides many advantages to help you be more productive and reduce the chance of error, such as the following:

- Format the Excel table quickly using a table style.
- Add new rows and columns to the Excel table that automatically expand the range.
- Add a Total row to calculate the summary function you select, such as SUM, AVERAGE, COUNT, MIN, and MAX.
- Enter a formula in one table cell that is automatically copied to all other cells in that table column.
- Create formulas that reference cells in a table by using table and column names instead of cell addresses.

These Excel table features let you focus on analyzing and understanding the data, leaving the more time-consuming tasks for the program to perform.

Laurie wants you to create an Excel table from the cash receipts data in the Cash Receipts worksheet. You'll be able to work with the Excel tables to analyze Laurie's data effectively.

To create an Excel table from the cash receipts data:

1. If necessary, select any cell in the range of cash receipts data to make it the active cell.
2. On the ribbon, click the **INSERT** tab.
3. In the Tables group, click the **Table** button. The Create Table dialog box opens. The range of data you want to use for the table is selected in the worksheet, and a formula with its range reference, =$A$1:$E$122, is entered in the dialog box.
4. Verify that the **My table has headers** check box is selected. The headers are the field names entered in row 1. If the first row did not contain field names, the My table has headers check box would be unchecked and Excel would insert a row of headers with the names Column1, Column2, and so on.

Tutorial 5 Working with Excel Tables, PivotTables, and PivotCharts | Excel   EX 265

5. Click the **OK** button. The dialog box closes, and the range of data is converted to an Excel table, which is selected. Filter buttons appear in the header row, the sizing handle appears in the lower-right corner of the last cell of the table, the table is formatted with a predefined table style, and the TABLE TOOLS DESIGN tab appears on the ribbon. See Figure 5-4.

Figure 5-4   **Excel table with the cash receipts data**

contextual tab appears on the ribbon

filter buttons appear in the header row

table style applied

6. Select any cell in the table, and then scroll down the table. The field names in the header row replace the standard lettered column headers (A, B, C, and so on) as you scroll, so you don't need to freeze panes to keep the header row visible. See Figure 5-5.

Figure 5-5   **Cash receipts table scrolled**

header row replaces the column headings

7. Press the **Ctrl+Home** keys to make cell A1 the active cell. The column headers return to the standard display, and the Excel table header row scrolls back into view as row 1.

Renaming an Excel Table

Each Excel table in a workbook must have a unique name. Excel assigns the name Table1 to the first Excel table created in a workbook. Any additional Excel tables you create in the workbook are named consecutively as Table2, Table3, and so forth. You can assign a more descriptive name to a table, making it easier to identify a particular table by its content. Descriptive names are especially useful when you create more than one Excel table in the same workbook because they make it easier to reference the different Excel tables. Table names must start with a letter or an underscore but can use any combination of letters, numbers, and underscores for the rest of the name. Table names cannot include spaces, but you can use an underscore or uppercase letters instead of spaces to separate words in a table name, such as January_Data or JanuaryData.

Laurie wants you to rename the Excel table you just created from the January cash receipts data.

TIP

If you copy a worksheet that contains a table, Excel adds the next consecutive number at the end of the table name to create a unique table name.

To rename the Table1 table:

▸ 1. On the TABLE TOOLS DESIGN tab, in the Properties group, select **Table1** in the Table Name box. See Figure 5-6.

Figure 5-6 Table Name box

enter a descriptive table name

▸ 2. Type **JanuaryData** as the descriptive name, and then press the **Enter** key. The Excel table is renamed as "JanuaryData."

Modifying an Excel Table

You can modify an Excel table by adding or removing table elements or by changing the table's formatting. For every Excel table, you can display or hide the following elements:

- **Header row**—The first row of the table that includes the field names
- **Total row**—A row at the bottom of the table that applies a function to the column values
- **First column**—Formatting added to the leftmost column of the table
- **Last column**—Formatting added to the rightmost column of the table
- **Banded rows**—Formatting added to alternating rows so that even and odd rows are different colors, making it simpler to distinguish records
- **Banded columns**—Formatting added to alternating columns so they are different colors, making it simpler to distinguish fields
- **Filter buttons**—Buttons that appear in each column of the header row and open a menu with options for sorting and filtering the table data

Tutorial 5 Working with Excel Tables, PivotTables, and PivotCharts | Excel   EX 267

You can also modify a table by applying a table style. As with other styles, a table style formats all of the selected table elements with a consistent, unified design. You can change the font, fill, alignment, number formats, column widths and row heights, and other formatting of selected cells in the table the same way you would for other cells in the worksheet.

Laurie wants the JanuaryData table to have a format that makes the table easier to read. You will apply a table style and make other formatting changes to the table.

To format the JanuaryData table:

1. On the TABLE TOOLS DESIGN tab, in the Table Styles group, click the **More** button. A gallery of table styles opens.

2. In the Table Styles gallery, in the Medium section, click **Table Style Medium 3**. The table now has an orange style.

3. In the Table Style Options group, click the **Banded Rows** check box. The alternating row colors disappear. The table is more challenging to read this way, so you will reapply the banded rows formatting.

4. In the Table Style Options group, click the **Banded Rows** check box to select it. The alternating row colors reappear.

5. Change the width of columns A through E to **12** characters. The entire column headers and all values will now be visible.

6. Select the **Amount** column, and then change the values to the **Accounting** format. See Figure 5-7.

> **TIP**
> To display or hide alternating column colors, click the Banded Columns check box in the Table Style Options group.

Figure 5-7   Modified JanuaryData table

[Screenshot of Excel spreadsheet showing the modified JanuaryData table with callouts: "columns A through E widened to 12 characters", "table formatted with Table Style Medium 3", and "Amount column formatted with the Accounting format". Table shows Trn Date, Day, Week #, Segment, Amount columns with rows: 1/1/2016 Friday 1 Spec Drink $380.64; 1/1/2016 Friday 1 Food $221.26; 1/1/2016 Friday 1 Coffee $152.15; 1/1/2016 Friday 1 Gifts $57.17; 1/2/2016 Saturday 1 Food $206.32; 1/2/2016 Saturday 1 Gifts $183.59; 1/2/2016 Saturday 1 Spec Drink $126.09]

7. Select cell **A1** to make it the active cell.

Maintaining Data in an Excel Table

As you develop a worksheet with an Excel table, you may need to add new records to the table, find and edit existing records in the table, and delete records from the table. Laurie wants you to make several changes to the data in the JanuaryData table.

Adding Records

As you maintain data in an Excel table, you often need to add new records. You add a record to an Excel table in a blank row. The simplest and most convenient way to add a record to an Excel table is to enter the data in the first blank row below the last record. You can then sort the data to arrange the table in the order you want. If you want the record in a specific location, you can also insert a row within the table for the new record.

The cash receipts records for January 31 are missing from the JanuaryData table. Laurie asks you to add to the table four new records that contain the missing data.

To add four records to the JanuaryData table:

1. Press the **End** key, and then press the ↓ key to make cell A122 the active cell. This cell is in the last row of the table.

2. Press the ↓ key to move the active cell to cell A123, which is in the first blank row below the table.

3. In cell A123, type **1/31/2016**, and then press the **Tab** key. Cell B123 in the Day column becomes the active cell. The table expands to include a new row with the same formatting as the rest of the table. The AutoCorrect Options button appears so you can undo the table formatting if you hadn't intended the new data to be part of the existing table. The sizing handle moves to the lower-right corner of cell E123, which is now the cell in the lower-right corner of the table. See Figure 5-8.

TIP
You can drag the sizing handle to add columns or rows to the Excel table or delete them from it.

Figure 5-8   New row added to the JanuaryData table

120	1/30/2016	Saturday	5	Food	$	348.08
121	1/30/2016	Saturday	5	Coffee	$	323.35
122	1/30/2016	Saturday	5	Gifts	$	169.29
123	1/31/2016					

AutoCorrect Options button
sizing handle

Trouble? If cell A124 is the active cell, you probably pressed the Enter key instead of the Tab key. Click cell B123 and then continue entering the data in Step 4.

4. In the range **B123:E123**, enter **Sunday** as the Day, **6** as the Week #, **Food** as the Segment, and **164.50** as the Amount, pressing the **Tab** key after each entry. Cell A124 becomes the active cell and the table expands to include row 124.

5. In the range **A124:E126**, enter the following cash receipts:

1/31/2016	Sunday	6	Coffee	278.98
1/31/2016	Sunday	6	Gifts	178.17
1/31/2016	Sunday	6	Spec Drink	345.88

6. Press the **Enter** key. The records are added to the table. See Figure 5-9.

Figure 5-9   **Records added to the JanuaryData table**

121	1/30/2016	Saturday	5	Coffee	$	323.35
122	1/30/2016	Saturday	5	Gifts	$	169.29
123	1/31/2016	Sunday	6	Food	$	164.50
124	1/31/2016	Sunday	6	Coffee	$	278.98
125	1/31/2016	Sunday	6	Gifts	$	178.17
126	1/31/2016	Sunday	6	Spec Drink	$	345.88
127						

four new records → (rows 123–126)

Documentation | **Cash Receipts**

READY

Trouble? If a new row is added to the table, you probably pressed the Tab key instead of the Enter key after the last entry in the record. On the Quick Access Toolbar, click the Undo button ↶ to remove the extra row.

Finding and Editing Records

Although you can manually scroll through the table to find a specific record, often a quicker way to locate a record is to use the Find command. When using the Find or Replace command, it is best to start at the top of a worksheet to ensure that all cells in the table are searched. You edit the data in a table the same way as you edit data in a worksheet cell.

Laurie wants you to update the January 20 cash receipts for the Gifts segment. You'll use the Find command to locate the record, which is currently blank. Then, you'll edit the record in the table to change the amount to $154.25.

To find and edit the record for Gifts on 1/20/2016:

1. Press the **Ctrl+Home** keys to make cell A1 the active cell so that all cells in the table will be searched.

2. On the HOME tab, in the Editing group, click the **Find & Select** button, and then click **Find** (or press the **Ctrl+F** keys). The Find and Replace dialog box opens.

3. In the Find what box, type **1/20/2016**, and then click the **Find Next** button. Cell A79, which contains the Coffee segment, is selected. This is not the record you want.

4. Click the **Find Next** button three times to display the record for Gifts on 1/20/2016.

5. Click the **Close** button. The Find and Replace dialog box closes.

6. Press the **Tab** key four times to move the active cell to the Amount column, type **154.25**, and then press the **Enter** key. The record is updated.

7. Press the **Ctrl+Home** keys to make cell A1 the active cell.

Deleting a Record

As you work with the data in an Excel table, you might find records that are outdated or duplicated. In these instances, you can delete the records. To delete records that are incorrect, out of date, or no longer needed, select a cell in each record you want to delete, click the Delete button arrow in the Cells group on the HOME tab, and then click Delete Table Rows. You can also delete a field by selecting a cell in the field you want to delete, clicking the Delete button arrow, and then clicking Delete Table Columns. In addition, you can use the Remove Duplicates dialog box to locate and remove records that have the same data in selected columns. The Remove Duplicates dialog box lists all columns in the table. Usually, all columns in a table are selected to identify duplicate records.

Laurie thinks that one of the cash receipts was entered twice. You'll use the Remove Duplicates dialog box to locate and delete the duplicate record from the table.

To find and delete the duplicate record from the JanuaryData table:

1. Scroll to row **64**, and observe that the entries in row 64 and row 65 are exactly the same. One of these records needs to be deleted.

2. On the ribbon, click the **TABLE TOOLS DESIGN** tab.

3. In the Tools group, click the **Remove Duplicates** button. The Remove Duplicates dialog box opens, and all of the columns in the table are selected. Excel looks for repeated data in the selected columns to determine whether any duplicate records exist. If duplicates are found, all but one of the records are deleted. See Figure 5-10.

Figure 5-10   Remove Duplicates dialog box

values in all of the selected columns must be equal for the row to be considered a duplicate

You want to search all columns in the table for duplicated data so that you don't inadvertently delete a record that has duplicate values in all of the selected fields but a unique value in the deselected field.

4. Click the **OK** button. A dialog box opens, reporting "1 duplicate values found and removed; 124 unique values remain."

5. Click the **OK** button.

Trouble? If you deleted records you did not intend to delete, you can reverse the action. On the Quick Access Toolbar, click the Undo button, and then repeat Steps 3 through 5.

6. Press the **Ctrl+Home** keys to make cell A1 the active cell.

Tutorial 5 Working with Excel Tables, PivotTables, and PivotCharts | Excel **EX 271**

Sorting Data

The records in an Excel table initially appear in the order they were entered. As you work, however, you may want to view the same records in a different order. For example, Laurie might want to view the cash receipts by segment or day of the week. You can sort data in ascending or descending order. **Ascending order** arranges text alphabetically from A to Z, numbers from smallest to largest, and dates from oldest to newest. **Descending order** arranges text in reverse alphabetical order from Z to A, numbers from largest to smallest, and dates from newest to oldest. In both ascending and descending order, blank cells are placed at the end of the table.

Sorting One Column Using the Sort Buttons

You can quickly sort data with one sort field using the Sort A to Z button or the Sort Z to A button. Laurie wants you to sort the cash receipts in ascending order by the Segment column. This will rearrange the table data so that the records appear in alphabetical order by Segment.

To sort the JanuaryData table in ascending order by the Segment column:

1. Select any cell in the Segment column. You do not need to select the entire JanuaryData table, which consists of the range A1:E125. Excel determines the table's range when you click any cell in the table.

2. On the ribbon, click the **DATA** tab.

3. In the Sort & Filter group, click the **Sort A to Z** button. The data is sorted in ascending order by Segment. The Segment filter button changes to show that the data is sorted by that column. See Figure 5-11.

TIP
You can also use the Sort & Filter button in the Editing group on the HOME tab.

Figure 5-11 JanuaryData table sorted by the Segment field

- Sort buttons
- sort icon appears in the filter button
- cash receipts appear in alphabetical order by Segment

	A	B	C	D	E
1	Trn Date	Day	Week #	Segment	Amount
2	1/1/2016	Friday	1	Coffee	$ 152.15
3	1/2/2016	Saturday	1	Coffee	$ 92.37
4	1/3/2016	Sunday	2	Coffee	$ 175.62
5	1/4/2016	Monday	2	Coffee	$ 209.25
6	1/5/2016	Tuesday	2	Coffee	$ 221.29
7	1/6/2016	Wednesday	2	Coffee	$ 231.03
8	1/7/2016	Thursday	2	Coffee	$ 127.68
9	1/8/2016	Friday	2	Coffee	$ 163.20
10	1/9/2016	Saturday	2	Coffee	$ 155.84
11	1/10/2016	Sunday	3	Coffee	$ 138.90
12	1/11/2016	Monday	3	Coffee	$ 88.55
13	1/12/2016	Tuesday	3	Coffee	$ 148.00

Trouble? If the data is sorted in the wrong order, you might have clicked in a different column than the Segment column. Repeat Steps 1 through 3.

Sorting Multiple Columns Using the Sort Dialog Box

Sometimes one sort field is not adequate for your needs. For example, Laurie wants to arrange the JanuaryData table so that the cash receipts are ordered first by Day (Sunday, Monday, and so forth), then by Segment for each day of the week, and then by Amount (highest to lowest). You must sort by more than one column to accomplish this. The first sort field is called the **primary sort field**, the second sort field is called the **secondary sort field**, and so forth. Although you can include up to 64 sort fields in a single sort, you typically will use one to three sort fields. In this case, the Day field is the primary sort field, the Segment field is the secondary sort field, and the Amount field is the tertiary sort field. When you have more than one sort field, you should use the Sort dialog box to specify the sort criteria.

REFERENCE

Sorting Data Using Multiple Sort Fields

- Select any cell in a table or range.
- On the DATA tab, in the Sort & Filter group, click the Sort button.
- If necessary, click the Add Level button to insert the Sort by row.
- Click the Sort by arrow, select the column heading for the primary sort field, click the Sort On arrow to select the type of data, and then click the Order arrow to select the sort order.
- For each additional column to sort, click the Add Level button, click the Then by arrow, select the column heading for the secondary sort field, click the Sort On arrow to select the type of data, and then click the Order arrow to select the sort order.
- Click the OK button.

Laurie wants to see the cash receipts sorted by day, and then within day by segment, and then within segment by amount, with the highest amounts appearing before the smaller ones for each segment. This will make it easier for Laurie to evaluate business on specific days of the week in each segment.

To sort the JanuaryData table by three sort fields:

1. Select cell **A1** in the JanuaryData table. Cell A1 is the active cell—although you can select any cell in the table to sort the table data.

2. On the DATA tab, in the Sort & Filter group, click the **Sort** button. The Sort dialog box opens. Any sort specifications (sort field, type of data sorted on, and sort order) from the last sort appear in the dialog box.

3. Click the **Sort by** arrow to display the list of the column headers in the JanuaryData table, and then click **Day**. The primary sort field is set to the Day field.

4. If necessary, click the **Sort On** arrow to display the type of sort, and then click **Values**. Typically, you want to sort by the numbers, text, or dates stored in the cells, which are all values. You can also sort by formats such as cell color, font color, and cell icon (a graphic that appears in a cell due to a conditional format).

5. If necessary, click the **Order** arrow to display sort order options, and then click **A to Z**. The sort order is set to ascending.

6. Click the **Add Level** button. A Then by row is added below the primary sort field.

7. Click the **Then by** arrow and click **Segment**, and then verify that **Values** appears in the Sort On box and **A to Z** appears in the Order box.

Tutorial 5 Working with Excel Tables, PivotTables, and PivotCharts | Excel **EX 273**

▸ 8. Click the **Add Level** button to add a second Then by row.
▸ 9. Click the second **Then by** arrow, click **Amount**, verify that **Values** appears in the Sort On box, click the **Order** arrow, and then click **Largest to smallest** to specify a descending sort order for the Amount values. See Figure 5-12.

Figure 5-12 | Sort dialog box with three sort fields

- adds a sort field
- deletes the selected sort field
- moves the selected sort field up or down in the sort order
- order is based on the column's value
- arranges the data in the specified order

Sort dialog:
Column	Sort On	Order
Sort by: Day	Values	A to Z
Then by: Segment	Values	A to Z
Then by: Amount	Values	Largest to Smallest

▸ 10. Click the **OK** button. Excel sorts the table records first in ascending order by the Day field, then within each Day in ascending order by the Segment field, and then within each Segment in descending order by the Amount field. For example, the first 20 records are Friday cash receipts. Of these records, the first five are Coffee, the next five are Food, and so on. Finally, the Friday Coffee receipts are arranged from highest to lowest in the Amount column. See Figure 5-13.

Figure 5-13 | Cash receipts sorted by Day, then by Segment, and then by Amount

- secondary sort field
- primary sort field
- tertiary sort field
- up arrow indicates an ascending sort order
- down arrow indicates a descending sort order

	A	B	C	D	E
1	Trn Date	Day	Week #	Segment	Amount
2	1/22/2016	Friday	4	Coffee	$ 171.53
3	1/8/2016	Friday	2	Coffee	$ 163.20
4	1/1/2016	Friday	1	Coffee	$ 152.15
5	1/29/2016	Friday	5	Coffee	$ 117.89
6	1/15/2016	Friday	3	Coffee	$ 106.95
7	1/29/2016	Friday	5	Food	$ 275.18
8	1/15/2016	Friday	3	Food	$ 267.87
9	1/1/2016	Friday	1	Food	$ 221.26
10	1/22/2016	Friday	4	Food	$ 180.91
11	1/8/2016	Friday	2	Food	$ 179.17
12	1/22/2016	Friday	4	Gifts	$ 169.62
13	1/8/2016	Friday	2	Gifts	$ 126.44
14	1/29/2016	Friday	5	Gifts	$ 124.40

▸ 11. Scroll the table to view the sorted table data.

The table data is sorted in alphabetical order by the day of the week: Friday, Monday, Saturday, and so forth. This default sort order for fields with text values is not appropriate for days of the week. Instead, Laurie wants you to base the sort on chronological rather than alphabetical order. You'll use a custom sort list to set up the sort order Laurie wants.

Sorting Using a Custom List

Text is sorted in ascending or descending alphabetical order unless you specify a different order using a custom list. A **custom list** indicates the sequence in which you want data ordered. Excel has two predefined custom lists—day-of-the-week (Sun, Mon, Tues, … and Sunday, Monday, Tuesday, …) and month-of-the-year (Jan, Feb, Mar, Apr, … and January, February, March, April, …). If a column consists of day or month labels, you can sort them in their correct chronological order using one of these predefined custom lists.

You can also create custom lists to sort records in a sequence you define. For example, you can create a custom list to logically order high-school or college students based on their admittance date (freshman, sophomore, junior, and senior) rather than alphabetical order (freshman, junior, senior, and sophomore).

REFERENCE

Sorting Using a Custom List

- On the DATA tab, in the Sort & Filter group, click the Sort button.
- Click the Order arrow, and then click Custom List.
- If necessary, in the List entries box, type each entry for the custom list (in the desired order) and press the Enter key, and then click the Add button.
- In the Custom lists box, select the predefined custom list.
- Click the OK button.

You'll use a predefined custom list to sort the records by the Day column in chronological order rather than alphabetical order.

To use a predefined custom list to sort the Day column:

1. Make sure the active cell is in the JanuaryData table.

2. On the DATA tab, in the Sort & Filter group, click the **Sort** button. The Sort dialog box opens, showing the sort specifications from the previous sort.

3. In the Sort by Day row, click the **Order** arrow to display the sort order options, and then click **Custom List**. The Custom Lists dialog box opens.

4. In the Custom lists box, click **Sunday, Monday, Tuesday, …** to place the days in the List entries box. See Figure 5-14.

Tutorial 5 Working with Excel Tables, PivotTables, and PivotCharts | Excel EX 275

Figure 5-14   **Custom Lists dialog box**

- adds new custom list entries to the Custom lists box
- predefined list selected
- permanently removes a selected user-created custom list
- sort order for days of the week

> 5. Click the **OK** button to return to the Sort dialog box. The custom sort list—Sunday, Monday, Tuesday, …—appears in the Order box.
>
> 7. Click the **OK** button. The table is sorted based on the predefined custom list.
>
> 8. Scroll the sorted table to verify that the cash receipts are sorted by their chronological day order—Sunday, Monday, Tuesday, Wednesday, Thursday, Friday, Saturday.

So far, you created an Excel table for the cash receipts, and then named and formatted the table. You updated the table by adding, editing, and deleting records. You also sorted the records and used a predefined custom list to sort the Day field by its chronological order. In the next session, you will continue to work with the JanuaryData table.

Session 5.1 Quick Check

REVIEW

1. In Excel, what is the difference between a range of data and a structured range of data?
2. Explain the difference between a field and a record.
3. What is the purpose of the Freeze Panes button in the Window group on the VIEW tab? Why is this feature helpful?
4. What three elements indicate that a range of data is an Excel table?
5. How can you quickly find and delete duplicate records from an Excel table?
6. If you sort table data from the most recent purchase date to the oldest purchase date, in what order have you sorted the data?
7. An Excel table of college students tracks each student's first name, last name, major, and year of graduation. How can you order the table so that students graduating in the same year appear together in alphabetical order by the student's last name?
8. An Excel table of sales data includes the Month field with the values Jan, Feb, Mar, … Dec. How can you sort the data so the sales data is sorted by Month in chronological order (Jan, Feb, Mar, … Dec)?

EX 276　Excel | Tutorial 5 Working with Excel Tables, PivotTables, and PivotCharts

Session 5.2 Visual Overview:

Filtering is the process of displaying a subset of rows in an Excel table or a structured range of data that meets the criteria you specify. In this case, the table is filtered to show the cash receipts for Week 2.

If you want to change an Excel table back to a structured range of data, you click the Convert to Range button.

The filter button opens the Filter menu, which includes options to sort and filter the table based on the data in that column.

As a reminder that the records are filtered, only the row numbers of the records that match the filter appear (leaving gaps in the consecutive numbering) and are blue. Rows of records that don't match the filter are hidden.

The selection list displays the unique items in the selected column. You can select one item or multiple items from the list to filter the table by.

The **Total row** is used to calculate summary statistics (including sum, average, count, maximum, and minimum) for any column in an Excel table.

The status bar indicates that the table is filtered.

Tutorial 5 Working with Excel Tables, PivotTables, and PivotCharts | Excel   EX 277

Filtering Table Data

A **slicer** is an object used to filter data in an Excel table. It includes a button for each unique value in the field—in this case, each Week #.

Selected buttons that match the color of the slicer style are included in the filter. Gray buttons are not selected.

To view different areas of a large worksheet, you can split the window into two or four resizable areas. Each area is called a **pane**.

The **split bar** indicates the division between the panes. You can drag the split bar to resize the panes.

Each pane has its own set of scroll bars for shifting different parts of the worksheet into view in that pane.

Amount
$ 175.62
$ 116.43
$ 117.67
$ 437.50
$ 209.25
$ 409.66
$ 136.91
$ 140.79
$ 221.29
$ 252.61
$ 147.89
$ 262.04
$ 231.03
$ 285.49
$ 144.04
$ 165.83
$ 127.68
$ 5,818.25

Week #: 1, 2, 3, 4, 5, 6

Filtering Data

Laurie needs to determine if she should increase food orders on Saturdays, her busiest day. She wants to see a list of all Food receipts on Saturdays. Although you could sort the receipts by Segment and Day to group the records of interest to Laurie, the entire table would still be visible. A better solution is to display only the specific records you want. Filtering temporarily hides any records that do not meet the specified criteria. After data is filtered, you can sort, copy, format, chart, and print it.

Filtering Using One Column

When you create an Excel table, a filter button appears in each column header. You click a filter button to open the Filter menu for that field. You can use options on the Filter menu to create three types of filters. You can filter a column of data by its cell colors or font colors. You can filter a column of data by a specific text, number, or date filter, although the choices depend on the type of data in the column. Or, you can filter a column of data by selecting the exact values by which you want to filter in the column. After you filter a column, the Clear Filter command becomes available so you can remove the filter and redisplay all the records.

Laurie wants to see the cash receipts for only Food orders. You'll filter the JanuaryData table to show only those records with the value Food in the Segment column.

> **TIP**
>
> To show or hide filter buttons for an Excel table or a structured range of data, click the Filter button in the Sort & Filter group on the DATA tab.

To filter the JanuaryData table to show only the Food segment:

1. If you took a break after the previous session, make sure the Cash Receipts January workbook is open, the Cash Receipts worksheet is the active sheet, and the JanuaryData table is active.

2. Click the **Segment** filter button. The Filter menu opens, as shown in Figure 5-15, listing the unique entries in the Segment field—Coffee, Food, Gifts, and Spec Drink. All of the items are selected, but you can set which items to use to filter the data. In this case, you want to select Food.

Figure 5-15   Filter menu for the Segment column

use the Search box with large data sets to find the entered text

items in the Segment column

Tutorial 5 Working with Excel Tables, PivotTables, and PivotCharts | Excel   EX 279

> 3. Click the **(Select All)** check box to remove the checkmarks from all of the Segment items.

> 4. Click the **Food** check box to insert a checkmark. The filter will show only records that match the checked item, and will hide records that contain the unchecked items.

> 5. Click the **OK** button. The filter is applied. The status bar lists the number of Food rows found in the entire table—in this case, 31 of the 124 records in the table are displayed. See Figure 5-16.

Figure 5-16   JanuaryData table filtered to show only Food

icon indicates that this column is being used to filter the table

row numbers of the filtered records are blue

only records with the segment value Food are displayed

status bar indicates the number of records displayed

	A	B	C	D	E
1	Trn Date	Day	Week #	Segment	Amount
7	1/31/2016	Sunday	6	Food	$ 164.50
8	1/24/2016	Sunday	5	Food	$ 151.27
9	1/17/2016	Sunday	4	Food	$ 140.25
10	1/10/2016	Sunday	3	Food	$ 122.50
11	1/3/2016	Sunday	2	Food	$ 116.43
26	1/4/2016	Monday	2	Food	$ 309.66
27	1/25/2016	Monday	5	Food	$ 241.35
28	1/11/2016	Monday	3	Food	$ 211.26
29	1/18/2016	Monday	4	Food	$ 117.49
42	1/5/2016	Tuesday	2	Food	$ 252.61
43	1/12/2016	Tuesday	3	Food	$ 242.03
44	1/26/2016	Tuesday	5	Food	$ 206.59
45	1/19/2016	Tuesday	4	Food	$ 148.23
58	1/6/2016	Wednesday	2	Food	$ 285.49
59	1/20/2016	Wednesday	4	Food	$ 262.27
60	1/27/2016	Wednesday	5	Food	$ 217.94
61	1/13/2016	Wednesday	3	Food	$ 101.81
74	1/21/2016	Thursday	4	Food	$ 330.02
75	1/14/2016	Thursday	3	Food	$ 272.49

READY   31 OF 124 RECORDS FOUND

> 6. Review the records to verify that only records with Food in the Segment column are visible. All other records in this column are hidden, leaving gaps in the row numbers.

> 7. Point to the **Segment** filter button. A ScreenTip—Segment: Equals "Food"—describes the filter applied to the column.

    The Filter menu includes options to Sort by Color and Filter by Color. These options enable you to filter and sort data using color, one of many cell attributes. Laurie could use specific cell background colors for certain receipts in the JanuaryData table. For example, she might want to highlight the dates when the coffeehouse could have used an additional employee. So cells in the Trn Date column for busy days would be formatted with yellow as a reminder. You could click the Sort by Color option to display a list of available colors by which to sort, and then click the specific color so that all the records for the days when she needed more help in the store (formatted with yellow) would appear together. Similarly, you could click the Filter by Color option to display a submenu with the available colors by which to filter, and then click a color.

INSIGHT

Exploring Text Filters

You can use different text filters to display the records you want. If you know only part of a text value or if you want to match a certain pattern, you can use the Begins With, Ends With, and Contains operators to filter a text field to match the pattern you specify. The following examples are based on a student directory table that includes First Name, Last Name, Address, City, State, and Zip fields:

- To find a student named Smith, Smithe, or Smythe, create a text filter using the Begins With operator. In this example, use "Begins With Sm" to display all records that have "Sm" at the beginning of the text value.
- To Find anyone whose Last Name ends in "son" (such as Robertson, Anderson, Dawson, or Gibson), create a text filter using the Ends With operator. In this example, use "Ends With son" to display all records that have "son" as the last characters in the text value.
- To find anyone whose street address includes "Central" (such as 101 Central Ave., 1024 Central Road, or 457 Avenue De Central), create a text filter using the Contains operator. In this example, use "Contains Central" to display all records that have "Central" anywhere in the text value.

When you create a text filter, determine what results you want. Then, consider what text filter you can use to best achieve those results.

Filtering Using Multiple Columns

If you need to further restrict the records that appear in a filtered table, you can filter by one or more of the other columns. Each additional filter is applied to the currently filtered data and further reduces the number of records that are displayed.

Laurie wants to see only Saturday Food receipts, rather than all of the Food receipts in the JanuaryData table. To do this, you need to filter the Food records to display only those with the value Saturday in the Day column. You'll use the filter button in the Day column to add this second filter criterion to the filtered data.

To filter the Food records to show only Saturday:

1. Click the **Day** filter button. The Filter menu opens.
2. Click the **(Select All)** check box to remove the checkmarks from all of the Day check boxes.
3. Click the **Saturday** check box.
4. Click the **OK** button. The JanuaryData table is further filtered and shows the five rows of Saturday Food receipts in January. See Figure 5-17.

Tutorial 5 Working with Excel Tables, PivotTables, and PivotCharts | Excel   EX 281

Figure 5-17 JanuaryData table filtered to show Food on Saturday

icons indicate that these columns are being used to filter the table

five records include the Food segment on Saturday

	A	B	C	D	E
1	Trn Date	Day	Week #	Segment	Amount
111	1/30/2016	Saturday	5	Food	$ 348.08
112	1/23/2016	Saturday	4	Food	$ 337.82
113	1/16/2016	Saturday	3	Food	$ 326.01
114	1/9/2016	Saturday	2	Food	$ 248.15
115	1/2/2016	Saturday	1	Food	$ 206.32

Clearing Filters

When you want to redisplay all of the data in a filtered table, you need to **clear** (or remove) the filters. When you clear a filter from a column, any other filters are still applied. For example, in the JanuaryData table, you would see all the food receipts in the table if you cleared the filter from the Day field. Similarly, you would see all the cash receipts on Saturday if you cleared the filter from the Segment field. To redisplay all the cash receipts in the table, you need to clear both the Day filter and the Segment filter. You will do this now to redisplay the entire table of cash receipts.

To clear the filters to show all the records in the JanuaryData table:

1. Click the **Day** filter button, and then click **Clear Filter From "Day"**. The Day filter is removed from the table. The table shows only Food receipts because the Segment filter is still in effect.

2. Click the **Segment** filter button, and then click **Clear Filter From "Segment"**. The Segment filter is removed, and all the records in the JanuaryData table are now displayed.

Selecting Multiple Filter Items

You can often find the information you need by selecting a single filter item from a list of filter items. Sometimes, however, you need to specify a more complex set of criteria to find the records you want. Earlier, you selected one filter item for the Segment column and one filter item for the Day column to display the records whose Segment field value equals Food *and* whose Day field value equals Saturday. A record had to contain both values to be displayed. Now you want the Segment column to display records whose Segment field value equals Coffee *or* Spec Drink. The records must have one of these values to be displayed. You do this by selecting two filter items from the list of filter items. For example, checking the Coffee and Spec Drink check boxes in the Segment filter items creates the filter "Segment equals Coffee" *or* "Segment equals Spec Drink."

Laurie wants a list of all Coffee and Spec Drink items on days when cash receipts in a segment are greater than $300. You'll create a filter with multiple items selected to find this information.

> **To select multiple filter items:**
>
> 1. Click the **Segment** filter button, and then click the **Gifts** and **Food** check boxes to remove the checkmarks.
> 2. Verify that the **Coffee** and **Spec Drink** check boxes remain checked. Selecting more than one item creates a multiselect filter.
> 3. Click the **OK** button. The JanuaryData table is filtered, and the status bar indicates that 62 of 124 records are either coffee or a specialty drink.

Creating Criteria Filters to Specify More Complex Criteria

Filter items enable you to filter a range of data or an Excel table based on exact values in a column. However, many times you need broader criteria. With **criteria filters**, you can specify various conditions in addition to those that are based on an equals criterion. For example, you might want to find all cash receipts that are greater than $500 or that occurred after 1/15/2016. You use criteria filters to create these conditions.

The types of criteria filters available change depending on whether the data in a column contains text, numbers, or dates. Figure 5-18 shows some of the options for text, number, and date criteria filters.

Figure 5-18 | Options for text, number, and date criteria filters

Filter	Criteria	Records Displayed
Text	Equals	Exactly match the specified text
	Does Not Equal	Do not exactly match the specified text
	Begins With	Begin with the specified text
	Ends With	End with the specified text
	Contains	Have the specified text anywhere
	Does Not Contain	Do not have the specified text anywhere
Number	Equals	Exactly match the specified number
	Greater Than or Equal to	Are greater than or equal to the specified number
	Less Than	Are less than the specified number
	Between	Are greater than or equal to *and* less than or equal to the specified numbers
	Top 10	Are the top or bottom 10 (or the specified number)
	Above Average	Are greater than the average
Date	Today	Have the current date
	Last Week	Are in the prior week
	Next Month	Are in the month following the current month
	Last Quarter	Are in the previous quarter of the year (quarters defined as Jan, Feb, Mar; Apr, May, June; and so on)
	Year to Date	Are since January 1 of the current year to the current date
	Last Year	Are in the previous year (based on the current date)

© 2014 Cengage Learning

PROSKILLS

Problem Solving: Using Filters to Find Appropriate Data

Problem solving often requires finding information from a set of data to answer specific questions. When you're working with a range of data or an Excel table that contains hundreds or thousands of records, filters help you find that information without having to review each record in the table. For example, a human resources manager can use a filter to narrow the search for a specific employee out of the 2500 working at the company knowing only that the employee's first name is Elliot.

Filtering limits the data to display only the specific records that meet the criteria you set, enabling you to more effectively analyze the data. The following examples further illustrate how filtering can help people to quickly locate the data they need to answer a particular question:

- A customer service representative can use a filter to search a list of 10,000 products to find all products priced between $500 and $1000.
- A donations coordinator can use a filter to prepare a report that shows the donations received during the first quarter of the current year.
- An academic dean can use a filter to retrieve the names of all students with GPAs below 2.0 (probation) or above 3.5 (high honors).
- A professor who has 300 students in a psychology class can use a filter to develop a list of potential student assistants for next semester from the names the professor has highlighted in blue because their work was impressive. Filtering by the blue color generates a list of students to interview.
- The author of a guide to celebrity autographs can use a filter to determine whether an entry for a specific celebrity already exists in an Excel table and, if it does, determine whether the entry needs to be updated. If the entry does not exist, the author will know to add the autograph data to the table.

As these examples show, filtering is a useful tool for locating the answers to a wide variety of questions. You then can use this information to help you resolve problems.

Laurie wants you to display the records for coffee or specialty drinks that were greater than $300. You'll modify the filtered JanuaryData table to add a criteria filter that includes cash receipts with values greater than $300.

To create a number filter that shows cash receipts greater than $300:

1. Click the **Amount** filter button, and then point to **Number Filters**. A menu opens, displaying the comparison operators available for columns of numbers.

2. Click **Greater Than**. The Custom AutoFilter dialog box opens. The upper-left box displays *is greater than*, which is the comparison operator you want to use to filter the Amount column. You enter the value you want to use for the filter criteria in the upper-right box, which, in this case, is $300.

3. Type **300** in the upper-right box. See Figure 5-19. You use the lower set of boxes if you want the filter to meet a second condition. You click the And option button to display rows that meet both criteria. You click the Or option button to display rows that meet either of the two criteria. You only want to set one criterion for this filter, so you'll leave the lower boxes empty.

Figure 5-19   **Custom AutoFilter dialog box**

- column being filtered
- logical operators used when there are two conditions
- operator for the first condition
- criterion for the first condition
- boxes to specify a second condition for the list

▸ 4. Click the **OK** button. The status bar indicates that 17 of 124 records were found. The 17 records that appear in the JanuaryData table are either Coffee or Spec Drink, and have an Amount greater than $300.

Next, you'll sort the filtered data to show the largest Amount first. Although you can sort the data using Sort buttons, as you did earlier, these sort options are also available on the Filter menu. If you want to perform a more complex sort, you still need to use the Sort dialog box.

To sort the filtered table data:

▸ 1. Click the **Amount** filter button. The Filter menu opens. The sort options are at the top of the menu.

▸ 2. Click **Sort Largest to Smallest**. The filtered table now displays Coffee and Spec Drink categories with daily receipts greater than $300 sorted in descending order. See Figure 5-20.

Figure 5-20   **Filtered and sorted JanuaryData table**

- icon shows that this column is filtered
- Spec Drink or Coffee with daily amount greater than $300 sorted in descending order by Amount
- icon shows that this column is filtered and sorted

	A	B	C	D	E
1	Trn Date	Day	Week #	Segment	Amount
17	1/23/2016	Saturday	4	Spec Drink	$ 454.14
18	1/3/2016	Sunday	2	Spec Drink	$ 437.50
19	1/30/2016	Saturday	5	Spec Drink	$ 425.50
20	1/1/2016	Friday	1	Spec Drink	$ 380.64
34	1/9/2016	Saturday	2	Spec Drink	$ 374.25
50	1/13/2016	Wednesday	3	Spec Drink	$ 360.50
66	1/22/2016	Friday	4	Spec Drink	$ 353.50
82	1/31/2016	Sunday	6	Spec Drink	$ 345.88
101	1/8/2016	Friday	2	Spec Drink	$ 344.79
102	1/18/2016	Monday	4	Spec Drink	$ 330.99
103	1/24/2016	Sunday	5	Spec Drink	$ 327.89
106	1/30/2016	Saturday	5	Coffee	$ 323.35
107	1/19/2016	Tuesday	4	Spec Drink	$ 322.65
121	1/17/2016	Sunday	4	Spec Drink	$ 316.39
122	1/16/2016	Saturday	3	Spec Drink	$ 314.66
123	1/23/2016	Saturday	4	Coffee	$ 308.43
124	1/28/2016	Thursday	5	Spec Drink	$ 305.42

Documentation   **Cash Receipts**

READY   17 OF 124 RECORDS FOUND

Tutorial 5 Working with Excel Tables, PivotTables, and PivotCharts | Excel **EX 285**

Laurie will use this data to help her decide on which days she may hire additional workers. You need to restore the entire table of cash receipts, which you can do by clearing all the filters at one time.

To clear all the filters from the JanuaryData table:

▶ 1. On the ribbon, click the **DATA** tab, if necessary.

▶ 2. In the Sort & Filter group, click the **Clear** button. All of the records are redisplayed in the table.

Creating a Slicer to Filter Data in an Excel Table

Another way to filter an Excel table is with slicers. You can create a slicer for any field in the Excel table. You also can create more than one slicer for a table. Every slicer consists of an object that contains a button for each unique value in that field. For example, a slicer created for the Day field would include seven buttons—one for each day of the week. One advantage of a slicer is that it clearly shows what filters are currently applied—the buttons for selected values are a different color. However, a slicer can take up a lot of space or hide data if there isn't a big enough blank area near the table. You can format the slicer and its buttons, changing its style, height, and width.

Laurie wants to be able to quickly filter the table to show cash receipts for a specific week. You will add a slicer for the Week # field so she can do this.

To add the Week # slicer to the JanuaryData table:

▶ 1. On the ribbon, click the **TABLE TOOLS DESIGN** tab.

▶ 2. In the Tools group, click the **Insert Slicer** button. The Insert Slicers dialog box opens, listing every available field in all tables in the workbook. You can select any or all of the fields.

▶ 3. Click the **Week #** check box to insert a checkmark, and then click the **OK** button. The Week # slicer appears on the worksheet. All of the slicer buttons are selected, indicating that every Week # is included in the table.

▶ 4. Drag the **Week #** slicer to the right of the JanuaryData table, placing its upper-left corner in cell G1.

▶ 5. If necessary, click the **Week #** slicer to select it. The SLICER TOOLS OPTIONS tab appears on the ribbon and is selected.

▶ 6. In the Size group, enter **2.2"** in the Height box and **1"** in the Width box. The slicer is resized, eliminating the extra space below the buttons and to the right of the labels.

▶ 7. In the Slicer Styles group, click the **More** button, and then click **Slicer Style Dark 2**. The slicer colors now match the formatting of the Excel table. See Figure 5-21.

Figure 5-21 JanuaryData table with the Week # slicer

[Screenshot of Excel showing the JanuaryData table with a Week # slicer. Annotations point to: "button height and width", "slicer height and width", "slicer for the Week # field", and "button for each unique value in the Week # column".]

Table data:

	A	B	C	D	E
1	Trn Date	Day	Week #	Segment	Amount
2	1/31/2016	Sunday	6	Coffee	$ 278.98
3	1/3/2016	Sunday	2	Coffee	$ 175.62
4	1/17/2016	Sunday	4	Coffee	$ 140.83
5	1/10/2016	Sunday	3	Coffee	$ 138.90
6	1/24/2016	Sunday	5	Coffee	$ 98.41
7	1/31/2016	Sunday	6	Food	$ 164.50
8	1/24/2016	Sunday	5	Food	$ 151.27
9	1/17/2016	Sunday	4	Food	$ 140.25
10	1/10/2016	Sunday	3	Food	$ 122.50
11	1/3/2016	Sunday	2	Food	$ 116.43
12	1/31/2016	Sunday	6	Gifts	$ 178.17

You can use the slicer to quickly filter records in an Excel table. Just click the slicer button corresponding to the data you want to display in the table. If you want to show more than one week, hold down the Ctrl key as you click the buttons that correspond to the additional data you want to show.

Laurie wants you to filter the JanuaryData table to display cash receipts for Week 1 and Week 5. You will use the Week # slicer to do this.

To filter the JanuaryData table using the Week # slicer:

1. On the Week # slicer, click the **1** button. Only Week 1 data appears in the JanuaryData table. All of the other buttons are gray, indicating that these weeks are not included in the filtered data.

2. Press and hold the **Ctrl** key, click the **5** button, and then release the **Ctrl** key. Cash receipts for Week 5 are now added to the JanuaryData filtered table. See Figure 5-22.

Tutorial 5 Working with Excel Tables, PivotTables, and PivotCharts | Excel   EX 287

Figure 5-22 JanuaryData table filtered to show Weeks 1 and 5

icon shows that this column is filtered

button to clear the current filter

	A	B	C	D	E		G
1	Trn Date	Day	Week #	Segment	Amount		Week #
6	1/24/2016	Sunday	5	Coffee	$ 98.41		1
8	1/24/2016	Sunday	5	Food	$ 151.27		2
16	1/24/2016	Sunday	5	Gifts	$ 35.29		3
19	1/30/2016	Saturday	5	Spec Drink	$ 425.50		4
20	1/1/2016	Friday	1	Spec Drink	$ 380.64		5
24	1/25/2016	Monday	5	Coffee	$ 164.73		6
27	1/25/2016	Monday	5	Food	$ 241.35		
33	1/25/2016	Monday	5	Gifts	$ 120.30		
36	1/25/2016	Monday	5	Spec Drink	$ 178.86		
40	1/26/2016	Tuesday	5	Coffee	$ 162.09		
44	1/26/2016	Tuesday	5	Food	$ 206.59		
48	1/26/2016	Tuesday	5	Gifts	$ 146.12		
51	1/26/2016	Tuesday	5	Spec Drink	$ 296.22		
55	1/27/2016	Wednesday	5	Coffee	$ 165.97		
60	1/27/2016	Wednesday	5	Food	$ 217.94		
64	1/27/2016	Wednesday	5	Gifts	$ 108.29		
68	1/27/2016	Wednesday	5	Spec Drink	$ 168.71		
72	1/28/2016	Thursday	5	Coffee	$ 144.60		
76	1/28/2016	Thursday	5	Food	$ 228.12		

filtered table shows only Weeks 1 and 5

orange button values are included in the filter

gray buttons are not included in the filter

READY 36 OF 124 RECORDS FOUND

Laurie no longer needs to see the JanuaryData table filtered, so you can clear the filter.

TIP
To remove a slicer from the worksheet, select it and then press the Delete key.

3. On the Week # slicer, click the **Clear Filter** button (or press the **Alt+C** keys). All filters from the Week # slicer are cleared from the JanuaryData table. All of the cash receipts for January are now displayed.

Using the Total Row to Calculate Summary Statistics

The Total row is used to calculate summary statistics (including sum, average, count, maximum, and minimum) for any column in an Excel table. The Total row is inserted immediately after the last row of data in the table. A double-line border is inserted to indicate that the following row contains totals, and the label Total is added to the leftmost cell of the row. By default, the Total row adds the numbers in the last column of the Excel table or counts the number of records if the data in the last column contains text. When you click in each cell of the Total row, an arrow appears that you can click to open a list of the most commonly used functions. You can also select other functions by opening the Insert Functions dialog box.

Laurie wants to see the total amount of cash receipts in January and the total number of records being displayed. You will add a Total row to the JanuaryData table, and then use the SUM and COUNT functions to calculate these statistics for Laurie.

To add a Total row to sum the Amount column and count the Day column:

1. Select any cell in the JanuaryData table to display the TABLE TOOLS contextual tab.

2. On the ribbon, click the **TABLE TOOLS DESIGN** tab.

3. In the Table Style Options group, click the **Total Row** check box to insert a checkmark. The worksheet scrolls to the end of the table. The Total row is now the last row in the table, the label Total appears in the leftmost cell of the row, and $24,612.67 appears in the rightmost cell of the row (at the bottom of the Amount column). See Figure 5-23.

Figure 5-23   Total row added to the JanuaryData table

when checked, the Total row appears at the bottom of the table

Total label

sum of the values in the Amount column

	Trn Date	Day	Week #	Segment	Amount		
116	1/2/2016	Saturday	1	Gifts	$ 183.59		
117	1/23/2016	Saturday	4	Gifts	$ 182.00		
118	1/30/2016	Saturday	5	Gifts	$ 169.29		
119	1/9/2016	Saturday	2	Gifts	$ 147.11		
120	1/16/2016	Saturday	3	Gifts	$ 142.02		
121	1/17/2016	Sunday	4	Spec Drink	$ 316.39		
122	1/16/2016	Saturday	3	Spec Drink	$ 314.66		
123	1/23/2016	Saturday	4	Coffee	$ 308.43		
124	1/28/2016	Thursday	5	Spec Drink	$ 305.42		
125	1/2/2016	Saturday	1	Spec Drink	$ 126.09		
126	Total				$ 24,612.67		
127							

Next, you will use the COUNT function to add the number of records displayed.

4. Click cell **B126** (the Day cell in the Total row), and then click the **arrow** button to display a list of functions. None is the default function in all columns except the last column. See Figure 5-24.

Tutorial 5 Working with Excel Tables, PivotTables, and PivotCharts | Excel   EX 289

Figure 5-24   Total row functions

	Trn Date	Day	Week #	Segment	Amount	F	G
116	1/2/2016	Saturday	1	Gifts	$ 183.59		
117	1/23/2016	Saturday	4	Gifts	$ 182.00		
118	1/30/2016	Saturday	5	Gifts	$ 169.29		
119	1/9/2016	Saturday	2	Gifts	$ 147.11		
120	1/16/2016	Saturday	3	Gifts	$ 142.02		
121	1/17/2016	Sunday	4	Spec Drink	$ 316.39		
122	1/16/2016	Saturday	3	Spec Drink	$ 314.66		
123	1/23/2016	Saturday	4	Coffee	$ 308.43		
124	1/28/2016	Thursday	5	Spec Drink	$ 305.42		
125	1/2/2016	Saturday	1	Spec Drink	$ 126.09		
126	Total				$ 24,612.67		

functions available in the Total row → None, Average, Count, Count Numbers, Max, Min, Sum, StdDev, Var, More Functions...

arrow button appears in the active cell of the Total row

opens the Insert Function dialog box

TIP

When you select Sum, Count, or Average, Excel uses the SUBTOTAL function to calculate the summary statistic in the Total row.

5. Click **Count**. The number 124, which is the number of records in the JanuaryData table, appears in the cell.

As you add, edit, or delete data in the table, the Total row values change. This also happens if you filter the table to show only some of the table data. Laurie wants the total cash receipts to include only weeks in January with seven days. You will filter the table to exclude Weeks 1 and 6, displaying the total Amount for Weeks 2 through 5 only. The COUNT function will also change to show only the number of transactions for the filtered data.

To filter cash receipts by excluding receipts from Week 1 and Week 6:

1. Press the **Ctrl+Home** keys to make cell A1 the active cell.

2. On the Week # slicer, click the **2** slicer button, press and hold the **Ctrl** key as you click the **3**, **4**, and **5** slicer buttons, and then release the **Ctrl** key. The JanuaryData table is filtered to display cash receipts for the four full weeks in January.

3. Scroll to the end of the table. The Total row shows that the 112 records contain total cash receipts of $22,225.55. See Figure 5-25.

Figure 5-25   Summary statistics in the filtered table

	Trn Date	Day	Week #	Segment	Amount
114	1/9/2016	Saturday	2	Food	$ 248.15
117	1/23/2016	Saturday	4	Gifts	$ 182.00
118	1/30/2016	Saturday	5	Gifts	$ 169.29
119	1/9/2016	Saturday	2	Gifts	$ 147.11
120	1/16/2016	Saturday	3	Gifts	$ 142.02
121	1/17/2016	Sunday	4	Spec Drink	$ 316.39
122	1/16/2016	Saturday	3	Spec Drink	$ 314.66
123	1/23/2016	Saturday	4	Coffee	$ 308.43
124	1/28/2016	Thursday	5	Spec Drink	$ 305.42
126	**Total**		112		$ 22,225.55

- number of records displayed
- Amount total for the displayed records

Splitting the Worksheet Window into Panes

You can split the worksheet window into two or four separate panes. This allows you to easily view data from several areas of the worksheet at the same time. Each pane has its own scroll bars so you can navigate easily within one pane or display different parts of the worksheet. You can move between panes using the mouse. To create two panes, select a cell in row 1 to split the worksheet vertically, or select a cell in column A to split the worksheet horizontally; to create four panes, select any other cell in the worksheet.

Laurie wants to view the JanuaryData summary totals at the same time she views the data on individual cash receipts. You will divide the worksheet into two horizontal panes to view the cash receipt records in the top pane and the totals in the bottom pane.

To split the Cash Receipts worksheet window into panes:

1. Press the **Ctrl+Home** keys to make cell A1 at the top of the table the active cell.

2. Select the cell in column A that is two rows above the last row visible on your screen.

3. On the ribbon, click the **VIEW** tab.

4. In the Window group, click the **Split** button. The worksheet window splits into two panes. Each pane has its own set of scroll bars. The active cell is in the bottom pane below the split bar. See Figure 5-26.

Tutorial 5 Working with Excel Tables, PivotTables, and PivotCharts | Excel **EX 291**

Figure 5-26   Worksheet split into two panes

[Screenshot of Excel worksheet with annotations: "splits the window into panes" pointing to the Split button; "top horizontal pane" and "bottom horizontal pane" labels; "each pane has separate scroll bars"; "split bar divides the two panes".]

Trouble? If the window splits into four panes rather than two, click the Split button to remove all panes, and then repeat Step 1 through 4.

5. Using the lower scroll bar, scroll down until the Total row appears immediately below the split bar. See Figure 5-27.

Figure 5-27   Total row displayed in the bottom pane

14	1/17/2016	Sunday	4	Gifts	$ 116.75
15	1/10/2016	Sunday	3	Gifts	$ 88.63
16	1/24/2016	Sunday	5	Gifts	$ 35.29
17	1/23/2016	Saturday	4	Spec Drink	$ 454.14
18	1/3/2016	Sunday	2	Spec Drink	$ 437.50
19	1/30/2016	Saturday	5	Spec Drink	$ 425.50
21	1/10/2016	Sunday	3	Spec Drink	$ 199.61
22	1/4/2016	Monday	2	Coffee	$ 209.25
126	**Total**		112		$ 22,225.55
127					

Annotation: "Total row appears immediately below the split bar"

Laurie discovered a data entry error in the receipts amount for Coffee on 1/28/2016. It was entered as 144.60; the correct amount is 244.60. You will change the amount.

To update the amount of the Coffee receipts on 1/28/2016:

1. Select any cell in the top pane.
2. Use the Find command to locate the 1/28/2016 receipts for Coffee. The amount is 144.60.
3. In the Amount column, enter **244.60**. The total receipts amount in the bottom pane changes from $22,225.55 to $22,325.55.

When you want to see a worksheet in a single pane, you remove the split panes from the worksheet window. You will do this now.

To remove the split panes from the Cash Receipts worksheet window:

1. On the ribbon, click the **VIEW** tab, if necessary.
2. In the Window group, click the **Split** button. The split bar is removed, and the worksheet is again a single window.

TIP
You can also double-click the split bar to remove the panes.

Now, you will hide the Total row and clear the filter. If you later redisplay the Total row, the functions you last used will appear even after you save, close, and then reopen the workbook.

To hide the Total row and clear the filter from the JanuaryData table:

1. On the ribbon, click the **TABLE TOOLS DESIGN** tab.
2. In the Table Style Options group, click the **Total Row** check box to remove the checkmark. The Total row is no longer visible.
3. Press the **Ctrl+Home** keys to make cell A1 the active cell.
4. On the Week # slicer, click the **Clear Filter** button to remove the filters from the JanuaryData table. All of the cash receipts for January are displayed.

Inserting Subtotals

You can summarize data in a range by inserting subtotals. The Subtotal command offers many kinds of summary information, including counts, sums, averages, minimums, and maximums. The Subtotal command inserts a subtotal row into the range for each group of data and adds a grand total row below the last row of data. Because Excel inserts subtotals whenever the value in a specified field changes, you need to sort the data so that records with the same value in a specified field are grouped together *before* you use the Subtotal command. The Subtotal command cannot be used in an Excel table, so you must first convert the Excel table to a normal range.

Tutorial 5 Working with Excel Tables, PivotTables, and PivotCharts | Excel **EX 293**

REFERENCE

Calculating Subtotals for a Range of Data

- Sort the data by the column for which you want a subtotal.
- If the data is in an Excel table, on the TABLE TOOLS DESIGN tab, in the Tools group, click the Convert to Range button, and then click the Yes button to convert the Excel table to a range.
- On the DATA tab, in the Outline group, click the Subtotal button.
- Click the At each change in arrow, and then click the column that contains the group you want to subtotal.
- Click the Use function arrow, and then click the function you want to use to summarize the data.
- In the Add subtotal to box, click the check box for each column that contains the values you want to summarize.
- To calculate another category of subtotals, click the Replace current subtotals check box to remove the checkmark, and then repeat the previous three steps.
- Click the OK button.

Laurie wants to create a report that shows all the coffeehouse's cash receipts sorted by Trn Date with the total amount of the cash receipts for each date. She also wants to see the total amount for each receipt date after the last item of that date. The Subtotal command is a simple way to provide the information Laurie needs. First, you will sort the cash receipts by Trn Date, then you will convert the Excel table to a normal range, and finally you will calculate subtotals in the Amount column for each Trn Date grouping to produce the results Laurie needs.

To sort the cash receipts and convert the table to a range:

> Be sure to sort the table and then convert the table to a range before calculating subtotals.

1. Click the **Trn Date** filter button, and then click **Sort Oldest to Newest** on the Filter menu. The JanuaryData table is sorted in ascending order by the Trn Date field. This ensures one subtotal is created for each date.

2. On the TABLE TOOLS DESIGN tab, in the Tools group, click the **Convert to Range** button. A dialog box opens, asking if you want to convert the table to a normal range.

3. Click the **Yes** button. The Excel table is converted to a range, and the HOME tab is selected on the ribbon. You can tell the table data is now a normal range because the filter buttons, the TABLE TOOLS DESIGN tab, and the slicer disappear.

Next, you'll calculate the subtotals.

To calculate the cash receipts amount subtotals for each date:

1. On the ribbon, click the **DATA** tab.

2. In the Outline group, click the **Subtotal** button. The Subtotal dialog box opens. See Figure 5-28.

Figure 5-28   Subtotal dialog box

records must be sorted by Trn Date

function to use for the subtotals

field to be subtotaled

removes subtotals from the data

column in which to insert the subtotals

	A	B	C	D	E
1	Trn Date	Day	Week #	Segment	Amount
2	1/1/2016	Friday	1	Spec Drink	$ 380.64
3	1/1/2016	Friday	1	Coffee	$ 152.15
4	1/1/2016	Friday	1	Food	$ 221.26
5	1/1/2016	Friday	1	Gifts	$ 57.17
6	1/2/2016	Saturday	1	Coffee	$ 92.37
7	1/2/2016	Saturday	1	Food	$ 206.32
8	1/2/2016	Saturday	1	Gifts	$ 183.59
9	1/2/2016	Saturday	1	Spec Drink	$ 126.09
10	1/3/2016	Sunday	2	Coffee	$ 175.62
11	1/3/2016	Sunday	2	Food	$ 116.43
12	1/3/2016	Sunday	2	Gifts	$ 117.67
13	1/3/2016	Sunday	2	Spec Drink	$ 437.50
14	1/4/2016	Monday	2	Coffee	$ 209.25
15	1/4/2016	Monday	2	Food	$ 309.66
16	1/4/2016	Monday	2	Gifts	$ 136.91
17	1/4/2016	Monday	2	Spec Drink	$ 140.79
18	1/5/2016	Tuesday	2	Coffee	$ 221.29
19	1/5/2016	Tuesday	2	Food	$ 252.61
20	1/5/2016	Tuesday	2	Gifts	

3. If necessary, click the **At each change in** arrow, and then click **Trn Date**. This is the column you want Excel to use to determine where to insert the subtotals; it is the column you sorted. A subtotal will be calculated at every change in the Trn Date value.

4. If necessary, click the **Use function** arrow, and then click **Sum**. The Use function list provides several options for subtotaling data, including counts, averages, minimums, maximums, and products.

5. In the Add subtotal to box, make sure only the **Amount** check box is checked. This specifies the Amount field as the field to be subtotaled.

   If the data already included subtotals, you would check the Replace current subtotals check box to replace the existing subtotals, or uncheck the option to display the new subtotals on separate rows above the existing subtotals. Because the data has no subtotals, it makes no difference whether you select this option.

6. Make sure the **Summary below data** check box is checked. This option places the subtotals below each group of data instead of above the first entry in each group, and places the grand total at the end of the data instead of at the top of the column just below the row of column headings.

7. Click the **OK** button. Excel inserts rows below each Trn Date group and displays the subtotals for the Amount of each Trn Date in the Amount column. A series of Outline buttons appears to the left of the worksheet so you can display or hide the detail rows within each subtotal.

   Trouble? If each item has a subtotal following it, or repeating subtotals appear for the same item, you probably forgot to sort the data by Trn Date. Click the Undo button on the Quick Access Toolbar, sort the data by Trn Date, and then repeat Steps 1 through 7.

8. Scroll through the data to see the subtotals below each category and the grand total at the end of the data. See Figure 5-29.

Tutorial 5 Working with Excel Tables, PivotTables, and PivotCharts | Excel   EX 295

Figure 5-29   Subtotals and grand total added to the cash receipts data

Outline buttons

	A	B	C	D	E
138	1/28/2016	Thursday	5	Food	$ 228.12
139	1/28/2016	Thursday	5	Gifts	$ 41.05
140	1/28/2016	Thursday	5	Spec Drink	$ 305.42
141	1/28/2016 Total				$ 819.19
142	1/29/2016	Friday	5	Coffee	$ 117.89
143	1/29/2016	Friday	5	Food	$ 275.18
144	1/29/2016	Friday	5	Gifts	$ 124.40
145	1/29/2016	Friday	5	Spec Drink	$ 276.44
146	1/29/2016 Total				$ 793.91
147	1/30/2016	Saturday	5	Spec Drink	$ 425.50
148	1/30/2016	Saturday	5	Coffee	$ 323.35
149	1/30/2016	Saturday	5	Food	$ 348.08
150	1/30/2016	Saturday	5	Gifts	$ 169.29
151	1/30/2016 Total				$ 1,266.22
152	1/31/2016	Sunday	6	Coffee	$ 278.98
153	1/31/2016	Sunday	6	Food	$ 164.50
154	1/31/2016	Sunday	6	Gifts	$ 178.17
155	1/31/2016	Sunday	6	Spec Drink	$ 345.88
156	1/31/2016 Total				$ 967.53
157	Grand Total				$ 24,712.67

new rows with the subtotal added below each Trn Date

new row with the grand total added at the end of the table

Using the Subtotal Outline View

The Subtotal feature "outlines" the worksheet so you can control the level of detail that is displayed. The three Outline buttons at the top of the outline area, shown in Figure 5-29, allow you to show or hide different levels of detail in the worksheet. By default, the highest level is active; in this case, Level 3. Level 3 displays the most detail—the individual cash receipt records, the subtotals, and the grand total. Level 2 displays the subtotals and the grand total, but not the individual records. Level 1 displays only the grand total.

Laurie wants you to isolate the different subtotal sections so that she can focus on them individually. You will use the Outline buttons to prepare a report for Laurie that includes only subtotals and the grand total.

To use the Outline buttons to hide records:

1. Click the **Level 2 Outline** button 2, and then scroll to view the daily subtotals and grand total. The individual cash receipt records are hidden; only the subtotals for each Trn Date and the grand total are displayed. See Figure 5-30.

Figure 5-30 — Level 2 outline

	A	B	C	D	E	F
71	1/14/2016 Total				$ 669.17	
76	1/15/2016 Total				$ 638.34	
81	1/16/2016 Total				$ 1,065.74	
86	1/17/2016 Total				$ 714.22	
91	1/18/2016 Total				$ 750.72	
96	1/19/2016 Total				$ 732.97	
101	1/20/2016 Total				$ 738.27	
106	1/21/2016 Total				$ 818.60	
111	1/22/2016 Total				$ 875.56	
116	1/23/2016 Total				$ 1,282.39	
121	1/24/2016 Total				$ 612.86	
126	1/25/2016 Total				$ 705.24	
131	1/26/2016 Total				$ 811.02	
136	1/27/2016 Total				$ 660.91	
141	1/28/2016 Total				$ 819.19	
146	1/29/2016 Total				$ 793.91	
151	1/30/2016 Total				$ 1,266.22	
156	1/31/2016 Total				$ 967.53	
157	**Grand Total**				$ 24,712.67	
158						

Callouts: Outline buttons; Show Detail button; Hide Detail button; subtotals and grand total displayed.

TIP
To collapse the outline and hide the rows with details, click the Hide Detail button.

2. Click the **Show Detail** button ⊞ to the left of 1/31/2016 to expand the outline and show the details of daily receipts by unhiding rows for this date. Cash receipts for each segment on 1/31/2016 are now displayed.

3. Click the **Level 1 Outline** button ①. The individual cash receipt records and the subtotals for each Trn Date are hidden. Only the grand total remains visible.

4. Click the **Level 3 Outline** button ③, and then scroll up. All the records along with the subtotals and the grand total are visible.

Laurie has completed her review of the daily cash receipts report for January. She asks you to remove the subtotals from the data.

To remove the subtotals from the cash receipts data:

1. On the DATA tab, in the Outline group, click the **Subtotal** button. The Subtotal dialog box opens.

2. Click the **Remove All** button. The subtotals are removed from the data, and only the records appear in the worksheet.

   You'll reset the cash receipts data as an Excel table.

3. Make sure the active cell is a cell within the normal range of data.

4. On the ribbon, click the **INSERT** tab.

5. In the Tables group, click the **Table** button. The Create Table dialog box opens.

Tutorial 5 Working with Excel Tables, PivotTables, and PivotCharts | Excel   EX 297

> 6. Click the **OK** button to create the Excel table, and then click any cell in the table. The table structure is active.
>
> 7. On the TABLE TOOLS DESIGN tab, in the Properties group, type **JanuaryData** in the Table Name box, and then press the **Enter** key. The Excel table is again named JanuaryData.

In this session, you filtered the table data, inserted a Total row, and determined totals and subtotals for the data. In the next session, you will work with PivotTables and PivotCharts to gather the information to help Laurie with staffing and ordering decisions.

Session 5.2 Quick Check

1. Explain filtering.
2. What is a slicer and how does it work?
3. How can you display a list of Economics majors with a GPA less than 2.5 from an Excel table with records for 1000 students?
4. An Excel table includes records for 500 employees. What can you use to calculate the average salary of employees in the finance department?
5. If you have a list of employees that includes fields for gender and salary, among others, how can you determine the average salary for females using the Total row feature?
6. Explain the relationship between the Sort and Subtotal commands.
7. After you display subtotals, how can you use the Outline buttons?

EX 298 Excel | Tutorial 5 Working with Excel Tables, PivotTables, and PivotCharts

Session 5.3 Visual Overview:

This PivotTable uses the data from the Segment field as column labels.

A PivotTable is an interactive table used to group and summarize either a range of data or an Excel table into a concise, tabular format for reporting and analysis.

This PivotTable uses the data from the Day field as row labels.

Values fields are the fields that contain summary data in a PivotTable. This PivotTable uses the total of Cash Receipts as the values field.

A PivotChart is a graphical representation of the data in a PivotTable.

Cash Receipts January - Excel

A8 — Thursday

Sum of Amount	Column Labels			
Row Labels	Coffee	Food	Spec Drink	Grand Total
Monday	$643.01	$979.76	$893.26	$2,516.03
Tuesday	$719.25	$849.46	$1,147.56	$2,716.27
Wednesday	$661.89	$867.51	$871.82	$2,401.22
Thursday	$733.37	$949.32	$986.47	$2,669.16
Friday	$711.72	$1,124.39	$1,585.96	$3,422.07
Grand Total	$3,469.24	$4,770.44	$5,485.07	$13,724.75

Sum of Amount

Cash Recepts By Day

Day | Trn Date

Documentation | WeeklySummaryPivotTable | **DailyReceiptsPivotTable**

READY

Tutorial 5 Working with Excel Tables, PivotTables, and PivotCharts | Excel   EX 299

PivotTable and PivotChart

You create a PivotTable using the PivotTable Fields pane. The upper section displays names of each field in the Excel table, and the lower section displays four areas in which you place fields to define the PivotTable.

You can add a slicer to a PivotTable or PivotChart to filter data. You click one or more slicer buttons to filter the PivotTable or PivotChart.

Fields in the FILTERS area create a filtered view of the PivotTable, showing summarized data in the report.

Category fields are the fields that group the values in a PivotTable. Category fields appear in PivotTables as row labels, column labels, and report filters.

Fields in the ROWS area are displayed as rows in the PivotTable.

Fields in the COLUMNS area are displayed as columns at the top of the PivotTable.

Fields in the VALUES area are summarized in the PivotTable.

Analyzing Data with PivotTables

An Excel table can contain a wealth of information. However, when the table contains large amounts of detailed data, it often becomes more difficult to obtain a clear, overall view of that information. You can use a PivotTable to help organize the data into a meaningful summary. A PivotTable groups data into categories and then uses functions such as COUNT, SUM, AVERAGE, MAX, and MIN to summarize that data. For example, Laurie wants to see the daily cash receipts for each segment (Coffee, Spec Drink, Food, Gifts) grouped by week. Although there are several ways to generate the information Laurie needs, you can use a PivotTable like the one shown in the Session 5.3 Visual Overview to generate this information quickly and present it concisely.

You can easily rearrange, hide, and display different category columns in the PivotTable to provide alternative views of the data. This ability to "pivot" the table—for example, change row headings to column positions and vice versa—gives the PivotTable its name and makes it a powerful analytical tool.

Written Communication: Summarizing Data with a PivotTable

PivotTables are a great way to summarize data from selected fields of an Excel table or range. The PivotTable omits all the detailed data, enabling readers to focus on the bigger picture. This makes it easier for readers to understand the results and gain insights about the topic. It can also help you back up or support specific points in written documents.

You can show summaries in written documents based on function results in PivotTables. The SUM function is probably the most frequently used function. For example, you might show the total sales for a region. However, you can use many other functions to summarize the data, including COUNT, AVERAGE, MIN, MAX, PRODUCT, COUNT NUMBERS, STDDEV, STDDEVP, VAR, and VARP. Using the functions, you might show the average sales for a region, the minimum price of a product, or a count of the number of students by major.

When you write a report, you want supporting data to be presented in the way that best communicates your points. With PivotTables, you display the values in different views. For example, to compare one item to another item in the PivotTable, you can show the values as a percentage of a total. You can display the data in each row as a percentage of the total for the row. You can also display the data in each column as a percentage of the total for the column, or display the data as a percentage of the grand total of all the data in the PivotTable. Viewing data as a percentage of the total is useful for analyses such as comparing product sales with total sales within a region, or comparing expense categories to total expenses for the year.

As you can see, PivotTables provide great flexibility in how you analyze and display data. This makes it easier to present data in a way that highlights and supports the points you are communicating, making your written documents much more effective.

Creating a PivotTable

A useful first step in creating a PivotTable is to plan its layout. Figure 5-31 shows the PivotTable that Laurie wants you to create. As you can see in the figure, the PivotTable will show the total Amount of the cash receipts organized by Week #, Trn Date, and Segment.

Tutorial 5 Working with Excel Tables, PivotTables, and PivotCharts | Excel   EX 301

Figure 5-31   PivotTable plan

Week #	xxxx				
Total Cash Receipts					
Trn Date		Coffee	Food	Gifts	Spec Drink	Total
Total						

© 2014 Cengage Learning

You are ready to create the PivotTable summarizing the total cash receipts for Laurie.

REFERENCE

Creating a PivotTable

- Click in the Excel table or select the range of data for the PivotTable.
- On the INSERT tab, in the Tables group, click the PivotTable button.
- Click the Select a table or range option button, and then verify the reference in the Table/Range box.
- Click the New Worksheet option button, or click the Existing Worksheet option button and specify a cell.
- Click the OK button.
- Click the check boxes for the fields you want to add to the PivotTable (or drag fields to the appropriate box in the layout section).
- If needed, drag fields to different boxes in the layout section.

When you create a PivotTable, you need to specify where to find the data for the PivotTable. The data can be in an Excel table or range in the current workbook, or an external data source such as an Access database file. You also must specify whether to place the PivotTable in a new or an existing worksheet. If you place the PivotTable in an existing worksheet, you must also specify the cell in which you want the upper-left corner of the PivotTable to appear.

To create the PivotTable that will provide the information Laurie needs, you will use the JanuaryData table and place the PivotTable in a new worksheet.

To create a PivotTable using the JanuaryData table:

1. If you took a break after the previous session, make sure the Cash Receipts January workbook is open, the Cash Receipts worksheet is the active sheet, and the JanuaryData table is active.

2. On the ribbon, click the **INSERT** tab.

3. In the Tables group, click the **PivotTable** button. The Create PivotTable dialog box opens. See Figure 5-32.

TIP
You can also click the Summarize with PivotTable button in the Tools group on the TABLE TOOLS DESIGN tab.

EX 302 Excel | Tutorial 5 Working with Excel Tables, PivotTables, and PivotCharts

Figure 5-32   Create PivotTable dialog box

data source for the PivotTable

location for the PivotTable

4. Make sure the **Select a table or range** option button is selected and **JanuaryData** appears in the Table/Range box.

5. Click the **New Worksheet** option button, if necessary. This sets the PivotTable report to be placed in a new worksheet.

6. Click the **OK** button. A new worksheet, Sheet1, is inserted to the left of the Cash Receipts worksheet. On the left is the empty PivotTable report area, where the finished PivotTable will be placed. On the right is the PivotTable Fields pane, which you use to build the PivotTable. The PIVOTTABLE TOOLS tabs appear on the ribbon. See Figure 5-33.

Figure 5-33   Empty PivotTable report

you can enter a name for the PivotTable

PivotTable Fields pane

fields (columns) in the JanuaryData table

PivotTable report area

four areas that represent the PivotTable layout

Trouble? If the PivotTable Fields pane is not displayed, you need to display it. On the PIVOTTABLE TOOLS ANALYZE tab, in the Show group, click the Field List button.

Tutorial 5 Working with Excel Tables, PivotTables, and PivotCharts | Excel   EX 303

Adding Fields to a PivotTable

In order to display data in a PivotTable, you add fields to the PivotTable. In PivotTable terminology, fields that contain summary data are Values fields, and fields that group the values in the PivotTable are Category fields. Category fields appear in PivotTables as row labels, column labels, and filters. You add fields to a PivotTable from the PivotTable Fields pane, which is divided into two sections. The upper section, often referred to as the Fields section, lists the names of each field in the data source, which is the JanuaryData table, in this case. You select a field check box or drag the field into the lower section to add that field to the FILTERS, ROWS, COLUMNS, or VALUES area (described in Figure 5-34). The placement of fields in the area boxes determines the layout of the PivotTable.

Figure 5-34   **Layout areas for a PivotTable**

Area	Description
ROWS	Fields placed in this area appear as Row Labels on the left side of the PivotTable. Each unique item in this field is displayed in a separate row. Row fields can be nested.
COLUMNS	Fields placed in this area appear as Column Labels at the top of the PivotTable. Each unique item in a field is displayed in a separate column. Column fields can be nested.
FILTERS	Fields placed in this area appear as top-level filters above the PivotTable. These fields are used to select one or more items to display in the PivotTable.
VALUES	Fields placed in this area are the numbers that are summarized in the PivotTable.

© 2014 Cengage Learning

Typically, fields with text or nonnumeric data are placed in the ROWS area. Fields with numeric data are most often placed in the VALUES area and by default are summarized with the SUM function. If you want to use a different function, click the field button in the VALUES area, click Value Field Settings to open the Value Field Settings dialog box, select a different function such as AVERAGE, COUNT, MIN, MAX, etc., and then click the OK button. You can move fields between the areas at any time to change how data is displayed in the PivotTable. You can also add the same field to the VALUES area more than once so you can calculate its sum, average, and count in one PivotTable.

TIP
By default, Excel uses the COUNT function for nonnumeric fields placed in the VALUES area.

Laurie wants to see the total value of cash receipts first by Week #. Within each Week #, she wants to see total cash receipts for each Day. Finally, she wants each Day further divided to display cash receipts for each Segment. You'll add fields to the PivotTable so that the Week #, Trn Date, and Segment fields are row labels, and the Amount field is the data to be summarized as the Values field.

To add fields to the PivotTable:

1. In the PivotTable Fields pane, drag **Week #** from the upper section to the ROWS area in the lower section. The Week # field appears in the ROWS area, and the unique values in the Week # field—1, 2, 3, 4, 5, and 6—appear in the PivotTable report area. See Figure 5-35.

Figure 5-35   PivotTable with the Week # field values as row labels

[Screenshot of PivotTable with Row Labels column containing values 1 through 6 and Grand Total; callouts indicate "Week # field values entered as the row labels," "Week # check box is selected," and "Week # field in the ROWS area."]

Trouble? If the Week # field appears in the VALUES area, you probably checked the Week # field, which places fields with numeric values in the VALUES area. Drag the Week # field from the VALUES area to the ROWS area.

2. In the PivotTable Fields pane, click the **Amount** check box. The Sum of Amount button is placed in the VALUES box because the field contains numeric values. The PivotTable groups the items from the JanuaryData table by Week # and calculates the total Amount for each week. The grand total appears at the bottom of the PivotTable. See Figure 5-36.

Figure 5-36   PivotTable shows the sum of the Amounts field for each Week #

[Screenshot of PivotTable with the following data:]

Row Labels	Sum of Amount
1	1419.59
2	5718.25
3	5025.22
4	5912.73
5	5669.35
6	967.53
Grand Total	24712.67

[Callouts: "total cash receipts for each week," "Grand Total of the January cash receipts," "Week #," "Amount field in the VALUES area."]

Next, you'll add the Trn Date and Segment fields to the PivotTable.

3. In the PivotTable Fields pane, click the **Trn Date** check box. The Trn Date field appears in the ROWS area box below the Week # field, and the unique items in the Trn Date field are indented below each Week # field item in the PivotTable report.

Tutorial 5 Working with Excel Tables, PivotTables, and PivotCharts | Excel   EX 305

Trouble? If the PivotTable Fields pane is not visible, the active cell is probably not in the PivotTable. Click any cell within the PivotTable to redisplay the PivotTable Fields pane. If the PivotTable Fields pane is still not visible, click the PIVOTTABLE TOOLS ANALYZE tab, and then click the Field List button in the Show group.

4. In the PivotTable Fields pane, click the **Segment** check box. The Segment field appears in the ROWS area below the Trn Date field, and its unique items are indented below the Week # and Trn Date fields already in the PivotTable. See Figure 5-37.

Figure 5-37   PivotTable with Week #, Trn Date, and Segment field items as row labels

Row Labels	Sum of Amount
⊟ 1	1419.59
⊟ 1/1/2016	811.22
Coffee	152.15
Food	221.26
Gifts	57.17
Spec Drink	380.64
⊟ 1/2/2016	608.37
Coffee	92.37
Food	206.32
Gifts	183.59
Spec Drink	126.09
⊟ 2	5718.25
⊟ 1/3/2016	847.22
Coffee	175.62
Food	116.43
Gifts	117.67
Spec Drink	437.5

- items first arranged by Week #
- then items arranged by Trn Date within each Week #
- then items arranged by Segment within each Trn Date
- drag the dotted line to view more field buttons
- field order in the ROWS area determines the PivotTable's organization

PivotTable Fields — Choose fields to add to report:
- ☑ Trn Date
- ☐ Day
- ☑ Week #
- ☑ Segment
- ☑ Amount

MORE TABLES...

Drag fields between areas below:

FILTERS | COLUMNS

ROWS: Week #, Trn Date, Segment
Σ VALUES: Sum of Amou...

☐ Defer Layout Update   UPDATE

Trouble? If the Segment field button is not visible in the ROWS area, drag the dotted line above the "Drag fields between areas below" label up until the Segment field button is visible.

If a PivotTable becomes too detailed or confusing, you can always remove one of its fields. In the PivotTable Fields pane, click the check box of the field you want to remove. The field is then deleted from the PivotTable and the area box.

Changing the Layout of a PivotTable

You can add, remove, and rearrange fields to change the PivotTable's layout. Recall that the benefit of a PivotTable is that it summarizes large amounts of data into a readable format. After you create a PivotTable, you can view the same data in different ways. Each time you make a change in the areas section of the PivotTable Fields pane, the PivotTable layout is rearranged. This ability to "pivot" the table—for example, change row headings to column positions and vice versa—makes the PivotTable a powerful analytical tool.

Based on Laurie's PivotTable plan that was shown in Figure 5-31, the Segment field items should be positioned as columns instead of rows in the PivotTable. You'll move the Segment field now to produce the layout Laurie wants.

To move the Segment field to the COLUMNS area:

1. In the PivotTable Fields pane, locate the **Segment** field button in the ROWS area.

2. Drag the **Segment** field button from the ROWS area to the COLUMNS area. The PivotTable is rearranged so that the Segment field is a column label instead of a row label. See Figure 5-38.

Figure 5-38   PivotTable rearranged with Segment as a column label

	B	C	D	E	F
2					
3	Sum of Amount	Column Labels			
4	Row Labels	Coffee	Food	Gifts	Spec Drink	Grand Total
5	⊟1	244.52	427.58	240.76	506.73	1419.59
6	1/1/2016	152.15	221.26	57.17	380.64	811.22
7	1/2/2016	92.37	206.32	183.59	126.09	608.37
8	⊟2	1283.91	1510.2	938.81	1985.33	5718.25
9	1/3/2016	175.62	116.43	117.67	437.5	847.22
10	1/4/2016	209.25	309.66	136.91	140.79	796.61
11	1/5/2016	221.29	252.61	147.89	262.04	883.83
12	1/6/2016	231.03	285.49	144.04	165.83	826.39
13	1/7/2016	127.68	118.69	118.75	260.13	625.25
14	1/8/2016	163.2	179.17	126.44	344.79	813.6
15	1/9/2016	155.84	248.15	147.11	374.25	925.35
16	⊟3	1091.71	1543.97	632.89	1756.65	5025.22
17	1/10/2016	138.9	122.5	88.63	199.61	549.64
18	1/11/2016	88.55	211.26	146.01	242.62	688.44
19	1/12/2016	148	242.03	146.38	266.65	803.06
20	1/13/2016	119.92	101.81	28.6	360.5	610.83

field headers

Segment items appear in the PivotTable as column labels

field moved from the ROWS area into the COLUMNS area

PivotTable Fields

Choose fields to add to report:
- ☑ Trn Date
- ☐ Day
- ☑ Week #
- ☑ Segment
- ☑ Amount

MORE TABLES...

Drag fields between areas below:

▼ FILTERS   ▥ COLUMNS
                  Segment ▼

▤ ROWS   Σ VALUES
Week # ▼   Sum of Amou... ▼
Trn Date ▼

☐ Defer Layout Update   UPDATE

The PivotTable now has the layout that Laurie wants.

INSIGHT

Choosing a Report Layout

There are three different report layouts available for PivotTables. The report layout shown in Figure 5-38, which is referred to as the Compact Form, is the default layout. It places all fields from the ROWS area in a single column, and indents the items from each field below the outer fields. In the Outline Form layout, each field in the ROWS area takes a column in the PivotTable. The subtotal for each group appears above every group. The Tabular Form layout displays one column for each field and leaves space for column headers. A total for each group appears below each group. To select a different report layout, click the Report Layout button in the Layout group on the PIVOTTABLE TOOLS DESIGN tab.

Formatting a PivotTable

Like worksheet cells and Excel tables, you can quickly format a PivotTable report using one of the built-in styles available in the PivotTable Styles gallery. As with cell and table styles, you can point to any style in the gallery to see a Live Preview of the PivotTable with that style. You also can modify the appearance of PivotTables by adding or removing banded rows, banded columns, row headers, and column headers.

Tutorial 5 Working with Excel Tables, PivotTables, and PivotCharts | Excel   EX 307

Laurie wants you to apply the Pivot Style Medium 10 style, which makes each group in the PivotTable stand out and makes subtotals in the report easier to find.

To apply the Pivot Style Medium 10 style to the PivotTable:

1. Make sure the active cell is in the PivotTable.
2. On the ribbon, click the **PIVOTTABLE TOOLS DESIGN** tab.
3. In the PivotTable Styles group, click the **More** button to open the PivotTable Styles gallery.
4. Move the pointer over each style to see the Live Preview of the PivotTable report with that style.
5. Click the **Pivot Style Medium 10** style (the third style in the second row of the Medium section). The style is applied to the PivotTable.

You can format cells in a PivotTable the same way that you format cells in a worksheet. This enables you to further customize the look of the PivotTable by changing the font, color, alignment, and number formats of specific cells in the PivotTable. Laurie wants the numbers in the PivotTable to be quickly recognized as dollars. You'll change the total Amount values in the PivotTable to the Currency style.

To format the Amount field in the PivotTable as currency:

1. In the VALUES area of the PivotTable Fields pane, click the **Sum of Amount** button. A shortcut menu opens with options related to that field.
2. Click the **Value Field Settings** button on the shortcut menu. The Value Field Settings dialog box opens. See Figure 5-39.

Figure 5-39   Value Field Settings dialog box

3. In the Custom Name box, type **Total Cash Receipts** as the label for the field. You will leave Sum as the summary function for the field; however, you could select a different function.
4. Click the **Number Format** button. The Format Cells dialog box opens. This is the same dialog box you have used before to format numbers in worksheet cells.

TIP

You can also right-click in the PivotTable data area and click Number Format or Format Cells to quickly format the PivotTable.

5. In the Category box, click **Currency**. You will use the default number of decimal places, currency symbol, and negative number format.

6. Click the **OK** button. The numbers in the PivotTable will be formatted as currency with two decimal places.

7. Click the **OK** button. The Value Field Settings dialog box closes. The PivotTable changes to reflect the label you entered, and the number format for the field changes to currency.

Filtering a PivotTable

As you analyze the data in a PivotTable, you might want to show only a portion of the total data. You can do this by filtering the PivotTable. Filtering a field lets you focus on a subset of items in that field.

Adding a Field to the FILTERS Area

You can drag one or more fields to the FILTERS area of the PivotTable Fields pane to change what values are displayed in the PivotTable. A field placed in the FILTERS area provides a way to filter the PivotTable so that it displays summarized data for one or more items or all items in that field. For example, placing the Week # field in the FILTERS area allows you to view or print the total cash receipts for all weeks, a specific week such as Week 1, or multiple weeks such as Weeks 2 through 5.

Laurie wants you to move the Week # field from the ROWS area to the FILTERS area so that she can focus on specific subsets of the cash receipts.

To add the Week # field to the FILTERS area:

1. In the PivotTable Fields pane, drag the **Week #** button from the ROWS area to the FILTERS area. By default, the Filter field item shows "(All)" to indicate that the PivotTable displays all the summarized data associated with the Week # field. See Figure 5-40.

Figure 5-40   PivotTable with the Week # filter

Next, you'll filter the summarized report to show only cash receipts for Week 2.

2. In cell B1, click the **filter** button. The Filter menu opens, showing the field items displayed.

3. In the Filter menu, click **2**, and then click the **OK** button. The PivotTable displays the total Amount of cash receipts for the dates in Week 2. The filter button changes to indicate the PivotTable is currently filtered. See Figure 5-41.

Figure 5-41 — Week # filter set to show cash receipts in Week 2

PivotTable is filtered to show only Week 2 data

Row Labels	Coffee	Food	Gifts	Spec Drink	Grand Total
1/3/2016	$175.62	$116.43	$117.67	$437.50	$847.22
1/4/2016	$209.25	$309.66	$136.91	$140.79	$796.61
1/5/2016	$221.29	$252.61	$147.89	$262.04	$883.83
1/6/2016	$231.03	$285.49	$144.04	$165.83	$826.39
1/7/2016	$127.68	$118.69	$118.75	$260.13	$625.25
1/8/2016	$163.20	$179.17	$126.44	$344.79	$813.60
1/9/2016	$155.84	$248.15	$147.11	$374.25	$925.35
Grand Total	$1,283.91	$1,510.20	$938.81	$1,985.33	$5,718.25

Week # : 2
Total Cash Receipts Column Labels

Filtering PivotTable Fields

Another way that you can filter field items in the PivotTable is by using the Filter menu, which you open by clicking the Row Labels filter button or the Column Labels filter button. You then check or uncheck items to show or hide them, respectively, in the PivotTable.

Laurie wants to exclude Gifts from her analysis. She asks you to remove the cash receipts for Gifts from the PivotTable.

To filter Gifts from the Segment column labels:

1. In the PivotTable, click the **Column Labels** filter button. The Filter menu opens, listing the items in the Segment field.

2. Click the **Gifts** check box to remove the checkmark. The Select All check box is filled with black indicating that all items are not selected.

3. Click the **OK** button. The Gifts column is removed from the PivotTable. The PivotTable includes only cash receipts from Coffee, Food, and Spec Drink (specialty drinks). See Figure 5-42. You can show the hidden objects by clicking the Column Labels filter button and checking the Gifts check box.

Figure 5-42 **PivotTable report filtered by Segment**

[Screenshot of Excel PivotTable showing Cash Receipts January filtered to Week # 2, with columns for Coffee, Food, Spec Drink, and Grand Total across dates 1/3/2016 through 1/9/2016. Callout: "filtered PivotTable hides cash receipts for Gifts"]

Row Labels	Coffee	Food	Spec Drink	Grand Total
1/3/2016	$175.62	$116.43	$437.50	$729.55
1/4/2016	$209.25	$309.66	$140.79	$659.70
1/5/2016	$221.29	$252.61	$262.04	$735.94
1/6/2016	$231.03	$285.49	$165.83	$682.35
1/7/2016	$127.68	$118.69	$260.13	$506.50
1/8/2016	$163.20	$179.17	$344.79	$687.16
1/9/2016	$155.84	$248.15	$374.25	$778.24
Grand Total	$1,283.91	$1,510.20	$1,985.33	$4,779.44

Creating a Slicer to Filter a PivotTable

Another way to filter a PivotTable is with a slicer just like the slicer you created to filter an Excel table. You can create a slicer for any field in the PivotTable Fields pane. The slicer contains a button for each unique value in that field. You can format the slicer and its buttons, changing its style, height, and width. You also can create more than one slicer at a time. For example, you can have a slicer for Week # that has a button for each unique Week # value, and a second slicer for Segment. This allows you to filter a PivotTable report so that it displays the cash receipts for Week 2 sales of coffee, food, and specialty drinks by clicking the corresponding slicer buttons.

Laurie wants flexibility in how she views the data in the PivotTable, so she asks you to add a slicer for the Week # field to the current PivotTable.

To add the Week # slicer to the PivotTable:

1. On the ribbon, click the **PIVOTTABLE TOOLS ANALYZE** tab.

2. In the Filter group, click the **Insert Slicer** button. The Insert Slicers dialog box opens, displaying a list of available PivotTable Fields. You can select any or all of the fields.

3. Click the **Week #** check box to insert a checkmark, and then click the **OK** button. The Week # slicer appears on the worksheet. Because the PivotTable is already filtered to display only the results for Week # 2, the 2 button is selected. The other slicer buttons are white because those weeks have been filtered and are not part of the PivotTable.

4. If necessary, click the **Week #** slicer to select it. The SLICER TOOLS OPTIONS tab appears on the ribbon.

5. On the SLICER TOOLS OPTIONS tab, in the Size group, change the height to **2.2"** and change the width to **1"**. The slicer object is resized, eliminating the extra space below the buttons and to the right of the labels.

Tutorial 5 Working with Excel Tables, PivotTables, and PivotCharts | Excel   EX 311

▶ 6. In the Slicer Styles group, click the **More** button, and then click **Slicer Style Dark 2**. The slicer colors now match the PivotTable.

▶ 7. Drag the **Week #** slicer to the right of the PivotTable, placing its upper-left corner in cell G3. See Figure 5-43.

Figure 5-43   Week # slicer

Laurie wants you to display the results of the PivotTable for all the full weeks in January—Weeks 2, 3, 4, and 5. You can do this quickly using the Week # slicer.

To filter the PivotTable using the Week # slicer:

▶ 1. Press and hold the **Ctrl** key, click the **3** button, and then release the **Ctrl** key. Week 3 data also appears in the PivotTable.

▶ 2. Press and hold the **Ctrl** key, click the **4** button, click the **5** button, and then release the **Ctrl** key. Data for Weeks 4 and 5 is added to the PivotTable.

▶ 3. Click the **Week # 2** slicer button. Only the cash receipts for Week 2 are displayed in the PivotTable.

TIP

To remove all filters from the PivotTable, click the Clear Filter button in the upper-right corner of the slicer.

After you have finished creating a PivotTable, you can hide the PivotTable Fields pane so that it won't appear when a cell is selected in the PivotTable. You can also assign more descriptive names to the PivotTable as well as the worksheet that contains the PivotTable.

To hide the PivotTable Fields pane and rename the PivotTable and worksheet:

▶ 1. Click in the PivotTable to display the PIVOTTABLE TOOLS contextual tabs on the ribbon.

▶ 2. Click the **PIVOTTABLE TOOLS ANALYZE** tab.

▶ 3. In the Show group, click the **Field List** button. The PivotTable Fields pane is hidden and won't reappear when a cell in the PivotTable is selected.

4. In the PivotTable group, select the default name in the PivotTable Name box, type **WeeklySummary** as the descriptive PivotTable name, and then press the **Enter** key.

5. Rename the worksheet as **Weekly Summary PivotTable**.

Refreshing a PivotTable

You cannot change data directly in a PivotTable. Instead, you must edit the data source on which the PivotTable is created. However, PivotTables are not updated automatically when the source data for the PivotTable is updated. After you edit the underlying data, you must **refresh**, or update, the PivotTable report to reflect the revised calculations.

> **INSIGHT**
>
> ### Displaying the Data Source for a PivotTable Cell
>
> As you have seen, PivotTables are a great way to summarize the results of an Excel table. However, at some point, you may question the accuracy of a specific calculation in your PivotTable. In these cases, you can "drill down" to view the source data for a summary cell in a PivotTable. You simply double-click a summary cell, and the corresponding source data of the records for the PivotTable cell is displayed in a new worksheet.

The cash receipts entry for Food on 1/4/2016 should have been $409.66 (not $309.66 as currently listed). You'll edit the record in the JanuaryData table, which is the underlying data source for the PivotTable. This one change will affect the PivotTable in several locations—the Grand Total value of receipts in Week 2 is $1,510.20 for the Food, $659.70 for 1/4/2016, and $4,779.44 overall.

To update the JanuaryData table and refresh the PivotTable:

1. Go to the **Cash Receipts** worksheet, and then find the Food cash receipts for 1/4/2016. The amount is $309.66.

2. Click the record's **Amount** cell, and then enter **409.66**. The receipt's Amount is updated in the table. You'll return to the PivotTable report to see the effect of this change.

3. Go to the **Weekly Summary PivotTable** worksheet. The Amount for Food on 1/4/2016 is still $309.66, the Grand Total for Food is still $1,510.20, the Grand Total for 1/4/2016 is still $659.70, and the overall Grand Total is still $4,779.44. The PivotTable was not automatically updated when the data in its source table changed, so you need to refresh the PivotTable.

4. Click any cell in the PivotTable.

5. On the ribbon, click the **PIVOTTABLE TOOLS ANALYZE** tab.

6. In the Data group, click the **Refresh** button. The PivotTable report is updated. The totals are now $409.66, $1,610.20, $759.70, and $4,879.44. See Figure 5-44.

Figure 5-44 | **Refreshed PivotTable**

(screenshot of Excel PivotTable showing Refresh button on Analyze tab and updated cash receipts values)

Row Labels	Coffee	Food	Spec Drink	Grand Total
1/3/2016	$175.62	$116.43	$437.50	$729.55
1/4/2016	$209.25	$409.66	$140.79	$759.70
1/5/2016	$221.29	$252.61	$262.04	$735.94
1/6/2016	$231.03	$285.49	$165.83	$682.35
1/7/2016	$127.68	$118.69	$260.13	$506.50
1/8/2016	$163.20	$179.17	$344.79	$687.16
1/9/2016	$155.84	$248.15	$374.25	$778.24
Grand Total	**$1,283.91**	**$1,610.20**	**$1,985.33**	**$4,879.44**

Week # = 2

> ### INSIGHT
>
> ### Creating Different Types of PivotTables
>
> This tutorial only scratched the surface of the variety of PivotTables you can create. Here are a few more examples:
>
> - Most PivotTable summaries are based on numeric data; Excel uses SUM as the default calculation. If your analysis requires a different calculation, you can select any of the 11 built-in summary calculations. For example, you could build a report that displays the minimum, maximum, and average receipts for each week in January.
> - You can use PivotTables to combine row label and column label items into groups. If items are numbers or dates, they can be grouped automatically using the Grouping dialog box, or they can be grouped manually using the Ctrl key to select items in a group and then clicking Group Selection from the shortcut menu. For example, you can manually combine Saturday and Sunday receipts into a Weekend group, and combine Monday through Friday receipts into a Weekday group, and then display total receipts by these groups within the PivotTable. Over time, you will also be able to group the Trn Date field to summarize daily cash receipts by month, quarter, and year.
> - You can develop PivotTables that use the percent of row, percent of column, or percent of total calculation to view each item in the PivotTable as a percent of the total in the current row, current column, or grand total. For example, you can display the total weekly receipts as a percent of the total monthly receipts.
> - You can develop PivotTables that display how the current month/quarter/year compares to the previous month/quarter/year. For example, you can compare this month's receipts for each category to the corresponding receipts for the previous month to display the difference between the two months.
>
> Being able to enhance PivotTables by changing summary calculations, consolidating data into larger groups, and creating custom calculations based on other data in the VALUES area gives you flexibility in your analysis.

Creating a Recommended PivotTable

The Recommended PivotTables dialog box shows previews of PivotTables based on the source data. This lets you see different options for how to create the PivotTable, and you can choose the one that best meets your needs.

Laurie wants to summarize sales by days-of-the-week so she can gain insights into staffing and ordering for each day. You will see if a recommended PivotTable meets Laurie's request.

To create a recommended PivotTable:

1. Go to the **Cash Receipts** worksheet, and then select any cell in the Excel table.
2. On the ribbon, click the **INSERT** tab.
3. In the Tables group, click the **Recommended PivotTables** button. The Recommended PivotTables dialog box opens. You can select from several PivotTables. See Figure 5-45.

Figure 5-45   Recommended PivotTable dialog box

recommended PivotTables based on your data

preview of the selected PivotTable

The Sum of Amount by Day PivotTable meets Laurie's request.

4. Click **Sum of Amount by Day** (the fourth PivotTable in the left pane). An enlarged version of the selected PivotTable is displayed in the right pane of the dialog box.
5. Click the **OK** button. A PivotTable of the cash receipts by day appears in a new worksheet. See Figure 5-46.

Tutorial 5 Working with Excel Tables, PivotTables, and PivotCharts | Excel   EX 315

Figure 5-46   PivotTable of cash receipts by day

Row Labels	Sum of Amount
⊞ Sunday	3691.47
⊞ Monday	3041.01
⊞ Tuesday	3230.88
⊞ Wednesday	2836.4
⊞ Thursday	2932.21
⊞ Friday	3932.63
⊞ Saturday	5148.07
Grand Total	24812.67

▶ 6. In the PivotTable Fields pane, in the VALUES area, click the **Sum of Amount** button, and then click **Value Field Settings** on the shortcut menu. The Value Field Settings dialog box opens.

▶ 7. Click the **Number Format** button. The Format Cells dialog box opens.

▶ 8. In the Category box, click **Currency**, and then click the **OK** button.

▶ 9. Click the **OK** button. The numbers in the PivotTable are formatted as currency with two decimal places.

▶ 10. On the ribbon, click the **PIVOTTABLE TOOLS DESIGN** tab.

▶ 11. In the PivotTable Styles group, click the **More** button to open the PivotTable Styles gallery, and then click the **Pivot Style Medium 10** style. The style is applied to the PivotTable.

▶ 12. Rename the worksheet as **Daily Receipts PivotTable**.

Laurie will use the summary of sales by days-of-the-week in the Daily Receipts PivotTable worksheet to evaluate staffing and ordering for each day.

INSIGHT

Adding a Calculated Field to a PivotTable Report

Occasionally, you might need to display more information than a PivotTable is designed to show, but it doesn't make sense to alter your data source to include this additional information. For example, you might want to include a field that shows an 8 percent sales tax on each value in an Amount field. In these instances, you can add a calculated field to the PivotTable. A **calculated field** is a formula you define to generate PivotTable values that otherwise would not appear in the PivotTable. The calculated field formula looks like a regular worksheet formula.

To add a calculated field to a PivotTable, complete the following steps:

1. Select any cell in the PivotTable report.
2. On the ANALYZE tab, in the Calculations group, click Fields, Items & Sets, and then click Calculated Field.
3. In the Name box, type a name for the field, such as Sales Tax.
4. In the Formula box, enter the formula for the field. To use data from another field, click the field in the Fields box, and then click Insert Field. For example, to calculate an 8 percent sales tax on each value in the Amount field, enter =Amount*8%.
5. Click the Add button.
6. Click the OK button. The calculated field is added PivotTable's data area and to the PivotTable Field List

As you can see, you can use calculated fields to include additional information in a PivotTable.

Creating a PivotChart

A PivotChart is a graphical representation of the data in a PivotTable. You can create a PivotChart from a PivotTable. A PivotChart allows you to interactively add, remove, filter, and refresh data fields in the PivotChart similar to working with a PivotTable. PivotCharts can have all the same formatting as other charts, including layouts and styles. You can move and resize chart elements, or change formatting of individual data points.

Laurie wants you to add a PivotChart next to the Sum of Amount by Day PivotTable. You will prepare a clustered column chart next to the PivotTable.

TIP

You can also create a PivotChart based directly on an Excel table, which creates both a PivotTable and a PivotChart.

To create and format the PivotChart:

1. Select any cell in the PivotTable.
2. On the ribbon, click the **PIVOTTABLE TOOLS ANALYZE** tab.
3. In the Tools group, click the **PivotChart** button. The Insert Chart dialog box opens.
4. If necessary, click the **Clustered Column** chart (the first chart in the Column charts section), and then click the **OK** button. A PivotChart appears next to the PivotTable along with the PivotChart Fields pane.

   Trouble? If you selected the wrong PivotChart, delete the PivotChart you just created, and then repeat Steps 1 through 4.

5. On the ribbon, click the **PIVOTCHART TOOLS DESIGN** tab.
6. In the Chart Layouts group, click the **Add Chart Element** button, point to **Legend**, and then click **None**. The legend is removed from the PivotChart. You do not need a legend because the PivotChart has only one data series.

Tutorial 5 Working with Excel Tables, PivotTables, and PivotCharts | Excel   EX 317

7. In the PivotChart, right-click the chart title, and then click **Edit Text** on the shortcut menu. The insertion point appears in the title so you can edit it.

8. Select the title, type **Cash Receipts by Day** as the new title, and then click the chart area to deselect the title.

9. Right-click any column to select the series, and then use the **Fill** button on the Mini toolbar above the shortcut menu to change its fill color to the **Orange, Accent 2** theme color.

10. Drag the PivotChart so its upper-left corner is in cell **D3**. The PivotChart is aligned with the PivotTable. See Figure 5-47.

Figure 5-47   PivotChart added to the PivotTable report

	A	B
3	Row Labels	Sum of Amount
4	Sunday	$3,691.47
5	Monday	$3,041.01
6	Tuesday	$3,230.88
7	Wednesday	$2,836.40
8	Thursday	$2,932.21
9	Friday	$3,932.63
10	Saturday	$5,148.07
11	Grand Total	$24,812.67

PivotChart based on the PivotTable data

chart filter buttons

The PIVOTCHART TOOLS contextual tabs enable you to work with and format the selected PivotChart the same way as an ordinary chart. A PivotChart and its associated PivotTable are linked. When you modify one, the other also changes. You can quickly display different views of the PivotChart by using the chart filter buttons on the PivotChart to filter the data.

Laurie wants you to display cash receipts for only Monday through Friday. You will filter the PivotChart to display only those items.

To filter the PivotChart to display cash receipts for Monday through Friday:

1. Make sure the PivotChart is selected, and then click the **Day** axis field button in the PivotChart. The Filter menu opens.

2. Click the **Sunday** and **Saturday** check boxes to remove their checkmarks.

3. Click the **OK** button. The PivotChart displays only cash receipts for the weekdays. The PivotTable is automatically filtered to display the same results.

4. Select cell **A1**. See Figure 5-48.

Figure 5-48   **Filtered PivotChart**

Day axis field button shows that the items are filtered in the PivotChart

5. Save the workbook, and then close it.

Laurie is pleased with the PivotTable and PivotChart. Both show the cash receipts arranged by day of the week, which will help her make ordering and staffing decisions.

Session 5.3 Quick Check

REVIEW

1. What is a PivotTable?
2. How do you add fields to a PivotTable?
3. How are fields such as region, state, and country most likely to appear in a PivotTable?
4. How are fields such as revenue, costs, and profits most likely to appear in a PivotTable?
5. A list of college students includes a code to indicate the student's gender (male or female) and a field to identify the student's major. Would you use a filter or a PivotTable to (a) create a list of all females majoring in history, and (b) count the number of males and females in each major?
6. An Excel table of professional baseball player data consists of team name, player name, position, and salary. What area of a PivotTable report would be used for the Team name field if you wanted to display the average salaries by position for all teams or an individual team?
7. After you update data in an Excel table, what must you do to a PivotTable based on that Excel table?
8. What is a PivotChart?

Review Assignments

Data File needed for the Review Assignments: February.xlsx

Laurie wants to analyze the cash receipts data for February. She entered this data into a new workbook and wants you to sort and filter the data, as well as create summary reports using the Subtotal command, PivotTables, and PivotCharts. Complete the following:

1. Open the **February** workbook located in the Excel5 ▸ Review folder included with your Data Files, and then save the workbook as **Cash Receipts February**.
2. In the Documentation worksheet, enter your name and the date.
3. In the Cash Receipts worksheet, freeze the top row so the headers remain on the screen as you scroll.
4. Make a copy of the Cash Receipts worksheet, and then rename the copied worksheet as **Feb Data**. (*Hint*: To make a copy of the worksheet, press and hold the Ctrl key as you drag the sheet tab to the right of the Cash Receipts sheet tab.)
5. In the Feb Data worksheet, unfreeze the top row.
6. Create an Excel table for the cash receipts data.
7. Format the Excel table with Table Style Medium 25, and then change the Amount field to the Accounting format with two decimal places.
8. Rename the Excel table as **FebruaryData**.
9. Make the following changes to the FebruaryData table:
   a. Add a record for **2/29/2016**, **Monday**, **10**, **Spec Drink**, **353.11**.
   b. Edit the record for Coffee on 2/27/2016 by changing the Amount from 219.71 to **269.71**.
   c. Delete any duplicate records.
10. Make a copy of the Feb Data worksheet, and then rename the copied worksheet as **Sort Trn Date**. In the Sort Trn Date worksheet, sort the cash receipts by Trn Date, displaying the newest receipts first, and then by Amount displaying the largest amounts first.
11. Make a copy of the Feb Data worksheet, and then rename the copied worksheet as **Sort By Day**. In the Sort By Day worksheet, sort the cash receipts by Day (use the custom list order of Sunday, Monday, …), then by Segment (A to Z), and then by Amount (smallest to largest).
12. Make a copy of the Feb Data worksheet, and then rename the copied worksheet as **Filter Omit Gifts**. In the Filter Omit Gifts worksheet, filter the FebruaryData table to display the cash receipts for all items except Gifts.
13. In the Filter Omit Gifts worksheet, insert the Total row to calculate the average amount of the cash receipts for the filtered data. Change the label in the Total row to **Average**. Sort the filtered data by descending order by Amount.
14. Split the Filter Omit Gifts worksheet into two panes above the last row of the table. Display the cash receipt records in the top pane, and display only the Total row in the bottom pane.
15. Make a copy of the Feb Data worksheet, and then rename the copied worksheet as **Filter By Day**. In the Filter By Day worksheet, insert a slicer for the Day column. Move the slicer to row 1. Format the slicer with Slicer Style Light 3. Change the slicer's width to 1.2" and its height to 2.5". Use the slicer to display cash receipts for Saturday and Sunday.
16. Make a copy of the Feb Data worksheet, and then rename the copied worksheet as **Subtotals**. In the Subtotals worksheet, convert the FebruaryData table to a range, and then sort the range by the Segment column.
17. In the Subtotals worksheet, use the Subtotal command to calculate the total cash receipts for each segment in the Amount column. Display only the subtotal results.
18. Based on the data in the Feb Data worksheet, create a PivotTable in a new worksheet that shows the total receipts by Day. Format the data area with the Currency format. Rename the worksheet with the PivotTable as **PivotTable By Day**.

19. In the PivotTable By Day worksheet, insert a Clustered Column PivotChart based on the PivotTable you created. Move the PivotChart to row 3. Remove the legend, and then change the PivotChart title to **Receipts by Day of Week**.

20. Based on the data in the Feb Data worksheet, create a PivotTable in a new worksheet that shows cash receipts by Trn Date. Add the Segment field to the FILTERS area. Format the PivotTable with Pivot Style Medium 4. Format the Amount field with the Accounting format with two decimal places. Rename the worksheet as **PivotTable By Trn Date**.

21. In the PivotTable By Trn Date worksheet, insert a slicer for the Segment field of the PivotTable. Change the slicer height to 1.6" and the width to 1.2". Format the slicer with Slicer Style Dark 3.

22. Use the slicer to filter the PivotTable by Trn Date to display only the Coffee and Spec Drink amounts.

23. Based on the data in the Feb Data worksheet, insert the Recommended PivotTable Sum of Amount By Week # and Segment PivotTable. Rename the worksheet as **Recommended PivotTable**.

24. Save the workbook, and then close it.

Case Problem 1

Data File needed for this Case Problem: Student.xlsx

College of Business Administration Peg Henderson is an assistant dean at the College of Business Administration (CBA). She uses Excel daily for a variety of tasks, including tracking student internships and alumni. For this project, Peg wants you to create an Excel table from information about current students and then analyze this data. Complete the following.

1. Open the **Student** workbook located in the Excel5 ▶ Case1 folder included with your Data Files, and then save the workbook as **Student Data**.
2. In the Documentation worksheet, enter your name and the date.
3. In the CBA Data worksheet, create an Excel table. Format the table with Table Style Medium 7, change the GPA data to the Number format showing two decimal places, and then change the Scholarships data to the Accounting format showing no decimal places. Rename the table as **StuData**.
4. Make a copy of the CBA Data worksheet, and then rename the copied worksheet as **Sort by Major**. (*Hint*: Press the Ctrl key as you drag and drop the sheet tab to the right of the CBA Data sheet tab to make a copy of the worksheet.)
5. Sort the data in the StuData table in ascending order by Major, and then in descending order by GPA.
6. Filter the StuData table to remove all undecided majors.
7. Insert a Total row in the StuData table that shows the number of students in the Last Name column, and the average GPA in the GPA column. Change the Total row label to **Average** and remove the entry in the Class column of the Total row.
8. Split the Sort by Major worksheet into two horizontal panes. Place the split bar two rows above the bottom row of the worksheet. In the top pane, display the student data. In the bottom pane, display only the Total row.
9. Make a copy of the CBA Data worksheet, and then rename the copied worksheet as **Filter by Class**. Filter the StuData table to display only those students who have a GPA greater than 3.00.
10. Insert a Class slicer to the right of the StuData table. Resize the slicer's height to 1.7" and its width to 1.2", and then format the slicer with the style that best matches the style of the Excel table.
11. Use the Class slicer to further filter the StuData table to display only Juniors and Seniors. Sort the filtered data in ascending order by Class and then in descending order by GPA.

12. Make a copy of the CBA Data worksheet, and then rename the copied worksheet as **Subtotals**. Convert the table to a normal range because the Subtotal command cannot be used with an Excel table. Use the Subtotal command to display the Average **GPA** for each Major in the GPA column.
13. Based on the data in the CBA Data worksheet, create a PivotTable in a new worksheet that counts the number of students in each class and major. In the Value Settings dialog box, change the Custom Name to Number. Apply Pivot Style Medium 14. Rename the worksheet as **PivotTable by Class and Major**.
14. In the PivotTable by Class and Major worksheet, insert a PivotChart with the Clustered Column chart type. Place the PivotChart to the right of the PivotTable. Filter the PivotChart to exclude the Freshman field. Insert a descriptive title. Remove the legend. Change the fill colors of the bars to match the PivotTable style.
15. Based on the data in the CBA Data worksheet, create a PivotTable that displays the average of GPA and number of students by Residence and Major in a new worksheet. Place Residence in the FILTERS area, and place Major in the ROWS area. Apply the Pivot Style Dark 7 to the PivotTable. Rename the worksheet as **PivotTable by Major**.
16. In the PivotTable, change the Residence filter to show In state students.
17. Save the workbook, and then close it.

Case Problem 2

Data File needed for this Case Problem: Players.xlsx

NBA Hoops Blog Jeff DeMarco is a sports enthusiast. Several years ago, he began writing a basketball blog called *NBA Hoops* that provides information, opinions, and analysis related to teams, players, and games in the National Basketball Association (NBA). To help him more easily respond to comments from his readers, he created an Excel table that tracks teams, positions, and salaries for each player in the league. He asks you to analyze this data. Complete the following:

1. Open the **Players** workbook located in the Excel5 ▸ Case2 folder included with your Data Files, and then save the workbook as **NBA Player Data**.
2. In the Documentation worksheet, enter your name and the date.
3. In the Players worksheet, create an Excel table named **NBAPlayers**. Format the Salary column with the Accounting format and no decimal places. Format the NBAPlayers table with the table style of your choice.
4. Make a copy of the Players worksheet, and then rename the copied worksheet as **Sort Position**. (*Hint*: Press the Ctrl key and drag the Players sheet tab to the right of the Players sheet tab to make a copy of the worksheet.) Sort the NBAPlayers table in ascending order by position, then in descending order by salary.
5. Use conditional formatting to apply a yellow fill with dark yellow text to highlight all players with a salary greater than $10,000,000.
6. Make a copy of the Players worksheet, and then rename the copied worksheet as **Filter Team**. Insert a slicer to filter by Team. Place the slicer to the right of the NBAPlayers table. Select a slicer style that matches the style you used to format the NBAPlayers table. Resize the slicer's height and width to improve its appearance.
7. Use the slicer to filter the NBAPlayers table to display all players on the NY Knicks and Miami Heat teams.
8. Expand the filter to display NY Knicks and Miami Heat players earning more than $5,000,000. Sort the filtered table in ascending order by salary.
9. Make a copy of the Players worksheet, and then rename the copied worksheet as **Filter Top 15%**. Filter the NBAPlayers table to display players whose salaries are in the top 15 percent. Sort the data by Salary in descending order.

10. Use the Total row to include the average salary at the bottom of the table, and then change the Total row label to **Average**. Add the Count of the Team column to the Total row. Remove the entry in the Division column of the Total row.
11. Make a copy of the Players worksheet, and then rename the copied worksheet as **Subtotals**. Use the Subtotal command to display the total salary for each team in the Salary column.
12. Based on the data in the Players worksheet, create a PivotTable in a new worksheet that totals salaries by team and position. Place the Position field in the COLUMNS area. Rename the worksheet as **PivotTable Team Position**. Format the salaries in the PivotTable with the Accounting format and no decimal places. Resize the columns as needed to display all the salaries.
13. Create a Division slicer for the PivotTable. Resize the slicer object and buttons as needed, and then select a slicer style that matches the PivotTable. Use the slicer to filter the PivotTable to display teams from the Atlantic, Central, and Southeast divisions.
14. Based on the data in the Player Salary worksheet, create a PivotTable that calculates the number and average salaries by position in a new worksheet. Format the average salaries, change the label above the average salaries to **Avg Salary**, and then change the label above the count to **Number**. Resize columns as needed to display all cell contents. Rename the worksheet as **PivotTable Avg Sal**.
15. Save the workbook, and then close it.

Case Problem 3

TROUBLESHOOT

Data File needed for this Case Problem: Cooking.xlsx

Healthy Cooking   Lian Michim started Healthy Cooking two years ago to provide prepared gourmet meals to retail food stores, living facilities for seniors, and businesses. Lian tracks orders using Excel. She has entered customer order data for the first half of the year in a worksheet, and wants to analyze the data in several ways. Complete the following:

1. Open the **Cooking** workbook located in the Excel5 ▸ Case3 folder included with your Data Files, and then save the workbook as **Healthy Cooking**.
2. In the Documentation sheet, enter your name and the date.
3. ⚙ **Troubleshoot** 3. Lian wants to view invoices with order amounts that are either less than $100 or greater than $5000. She tried filtering the orders in the Order Amount Filter worksheet, but it's not working as expected. Review the Order Amount Filter worksheet and fix the problem.
4. In the Orders worksheet, create an Excel table, and then rename the table as **CustOrders**.
5. In the CustOrders table, format the Order Amount, Discount, and Net Amount columns so that it is clear that these fields contain dollars.
6. Format the CustOrders table using the table style of your choice.
7. Make a copy of the Orders worksheet, and then rename the copied worksheet as **Sort**. (*Hint*: Press the Ctrl key and drag the sheet tab to the right of the current sheet tab to make a copy of the worksheet.) On the Sort worksheet, sort the data in ascending order by Customer Type, then in ascending order by Delivered To, and then in ascending order by Customer.
8. Using conditional formatting, highlight all orders in the sorted table that have a Net Amount greater than $4000 in the format of your choice.
9. Make a copy of the Orders worksheet, and then rename the copied worksheet as **Filter with Total Row**. Filter the CustOrders table to display all orders with an order date in June 2016 that included a discount.
10. Insert a Total row that calculates the totals for the Order Amount, Discount, and Net Amount columns for the filtered data.
11. ⚙ **Troubleshoot** 11. In the Customer Type Subtotal worksheet, Lian is trying to include the sum of the order amount for each Customer Type and the subtotals in the Order Amount field. However, the subtotal for each customer type appears more than once. Fix this report so it shows only one subtotal for each customer type.

12. In the Order Date column, insert a count of the number of orders for each customer type. This is in addition to the totals already in the worksheet. (*Hint*: Use the options at the bottom of the Subtotals dialog box.)
13. Based on the data in the Orders worksheet, create a PivotTable in a new worksheet that displays the number (Count) and average Order amount by Customer Type and Delivered To. Place the Customer Type and Delivered To fields in the ROWS area of the PivotTable. Apply the PivotTable style that matches the CustOrder table. Format the Average Order values using the Accounting format. Change the labels above the average orders to **Average Order**, and change the label above the count of orders to **Number**.
14. Use a slicer to filter the PivotTable to remove the Seniors customer type from the PivotTable. Format the slicer to match the PivotTable style. Rename the worksheet as **PivotTable**.
15. Based on the data in the Orders worksheet, create a PivotTable that shows the Total Order Amount by Customer in a new worksheet. Apply a PivotTable style to match the style of the CustOrder table. Format the Total Order Amount. Rename the worksheet as **Order Amount by Customers**.
16. Based on the PivotTable in the Order Amount by Customers worksheet, create a PivotChart using the Bar chart type. Move the PivotChart to row 3. Change the chart title to **Orders by Customers**. Change the axis to display units in thousands. Change the fill color of the bars to a color that matches the style in the PivotTable. Remove the legend.
17. Filter the PivotChart to remove the Corner Store and Drac Deli.
18. Save the workbook, and then close it.

Case Problem 4

Data File needed for this Case Problem: Benjis.xlsx

Benji's Department Stores Benji's Department Stores, with corporate headquarters in Colorado Springs, Colorado, operates department stores in midsize towns in selected areas of the West. The organization maintains a large database for its accounting operations; other departments often download data to complete additional analysis. Eve Darden, analyst for the corporate sales department, regularly creates reports based on her analysis of sales by product areas and regions. Right now, Eve is compiling and summarizing data about the best- and worst-performing product group and time period for certain regions and product groups. Complete the following:

1. Open the **Benjis** workbook located in the Excel5 ▸ Case4 folder included with your Data Files, and then save the workbook as **Benjis Stores**.
2. In the Documentation sheet, enter your name and the date.
3. In the Sales Data worksheet, create an Excel table. Rename the table as **ProductSales**. Format the Sales column in the Accounting format with no decimal places. Apply a table style of your choice.
4. Make a copy of the Sales Data worksheet, and then rename the copied worksheet as **Sort**. (*Hint*: Press the Ctrl key and drag the sheet tab to the right of the Sales Data sheet tab to make a copy of the worksheet.) Sort the table in ascending order by Product group, then in ascending order by Region, then in ascending order by Year, and then in chronological order by Month (Jan, Feb, Mar, ...).
5. Make a copy of the Sales Data worksheet, and then rename the copied worksheet as **Filter with Total Row**. Insert a slicer for the Product Group field. Move the slicer to row 1. Match the slicer style with the style you selected for the ProductSales table. Resize the slicer height and width to eliminate any excess space.
6. Display the records for Gardening and Sporting products in 2016, excluding sales in Utah. Sort this data in descending order of sales.
7. Add a Total row and calculate the average sales for the filtered data. Change the label in the Total row to **Average**.
8. Split the worksheet into two panes. In the top pane, display the table data. In the bottom pane, display the Total row. In the top pane, select cell A1.

9. Make a copy of the Sales Data worksheet, and then rename the copied worksheet as **Subtotals 2016**. Filter the list to display only data for 2016, and then include subtotals that calculate the total Sales by Region and Month. (*Hint*: You need two sets of subtotals.)

10. Make a copy of the Sales Data worksheet, and then rename the copied worksheet as **Bottom 15**. Display the 15 lowest periods based on sales (each row represents a period). Sort the sales so that the lowest sales appear first.

11. Based on the data in the Sales Data worksheet, create the PivotTable and PivotChart shown in Figure 5-49, summarizing sales by year and month. Rename the worksheet as **PivotChart**.

Figure 5-49 — PivotTable and PivotChart summarizing sales by year and month

	A	B
3		Sum of Sales
4	⊟ 2015	$ 8,463,036
5	Jan	$ 919,181
6	Feb	$ 645,049
7	Mar	$ 633,491
8	Apr	$ 707,317
9	May	$ 758,546
10	Jun	$ 806,661
11	Jul	$ 614,535
12	Aug	$ 467,779
13	Sep	$ 740,856
14	Oct	$ 804,503
15	Nov	$ 500,152
16	Dec	$ 864,966
17	⊟ 2016	$ 8,486,428
18	Jan	$ 770,256
19	Feb	$ 959,924
20	Mar	$ 431,734
21	Apr	$ 772,994
22	May	$ 744,420
23	Jun	$ 360,043
24	Jul	$ 704,907
25	Aug	$ 696,443
26	Sep	$ 403,160
27	Oct	$ 1,045,706
28	Nov	$ 925,298
29	Dec	$ 671,543
30	Grand Total	$16,949,464

12. Based on the data in the Sales Data worksheet, create the PivotTable shown in Figure 5-50 to calculate the sum, average, minimum, and maximum sales categorized by region and product group. Insert a Year slicer and use it to show sales in 2016. Rename the worksheet as **Region Statistics**.

Figure 5-50 PivotTable displaying sales categorized by region and product group

	A	B	C	D	E	F	G
2							
3	Row Labels	Sum of Sales	Average Sales	Minimum Sales	Maximum Sales		Year
4	⊟ Colorado	$ 3,330,178	$ 55,503	$ 7	$ 167,539		
5	Automotive	$ 564,908	$ 47,076	$ 7	$ 130,405		2015
6	Electronics	$ 499,670	$ 41,639	$ 1,738	$ 147,135		
7	Gardening	$ 782,519	$ 65,210	$ 5,607	$ 167,539		2016
8	Housewares	$ 788,597	$ 65,716	$ 21,017	$ 147,298		
9	Sporting	$ 694,484	$ 57,874	$ 2,522	$ 135,193		
10	⊟ Oklahoma	$ 2,636,197	$ 43,937	$ 175	$ 176,220		
11	Automotive	$ 916,489	$ 76,374	$ 969	$ 170,688		
12	Electronics	$ 452,901	$ 37,742	$ 1,154	$ 176,220		
13	Gardening	$ 405,111	$ 33,759	$ 175	$ 119,667		
14	Housewares	$ 333,699	$ 27,808	$ 1,176	$ 107,097		
15	Sporting	$ 527,997	$ 44,000	$ 5,441	$ 105,933		
16	⊟ Utah	$ 2,520,053	$ 42,001	$ 684	$ 168,339		
17	Automotive	$ 499,020	$ 41,585	$ 684	$ 168,220		
18	Electronics	$ 520,268	$ 43,356	$ 7,544	$ 145,865		
19	Gardening	$ 358,252	$ 29,854	$ 2,148	$ 78,942		
20	Housewares	$ 469,331	$ 39,111	$ 1,770	$ 127,490		
21	Sporting	$ 673,182	$ 56,099	$ 3,089	$ 168,339		

13. Based on the data in the Sales Data worksheet, create the PivotTable and slicers shown in Figure 5-51 displaying total sales by Year, Product Group, and Region. Include a second value calculation that displays each Product Group and Region as a percentage of the total company sales. (*Hint*: In Excel Help, read about how to calculate a percentage for subtotals in a PivotTable.) Rename the worksheet as **Percent of Company Sales**.

Figure 5-51 PivotTable displaying sales by Year, Product Group, and Region

	A	B	C	D	E	F	G	H
1	Year	(All)						
2								
3	Row Labels	Sales Total	% of Column Total		Year		Product Group	
4	⊟ Automotive	$ 3,678,817	21.7%					
5	Colorado	$ 950,869	5.6%		2015		Automotive	
6	Oklahoma	$ 1,496,198	8.8%		2016			
7	Utah	$ 1,231,750	7.3%				Electronics	
8	⊟ Electronics	$ 3,245,846	19.2%					
9	Colorado	$ 1,123,439	6.6%				Gardening	
10	Oklahoma	$ 1,057,029	6.2%				Housewares	
11	Utah	$ 1,065,378	6.3%					
12	⊟ Gardening	$ 3,174,345	18.7%				Sporting	
13	Colorado	$ 1,437,752	8.5%					
14	Oklahoma	$ 911,470	5.4%					
15	Utah	$ 825,123	4.9%					
16	⊟ Housewares	$ 3,109,955	18.3%					
17	Colorado	$ 1,430,658	8.4%					
18	Oklahoma	$ 867,120	5.1%					
19	Utah	$ 812,177	4.8%					
20	⊟ Sporting	$ 3,740,501	22.1%					
21	Colorado	$ 1,314,995	7.8%					

14. Format the PivotTable and slicers with matching styles, and adjust the height and width of the slicers as needed to improve their appearance.
15. Filter the Product Group to display sales in 2016 for the Automotive and Electronics product groups in all Regions except Utah.
16. Save the workbook, and then close it.

TUTORIAL 6

Managing Multiple Worksheets and Workbooks

Summarizing Recycling Data

OBJECTIVES

Session 6.1
- Create a worksheet group
- Format and edit multiple worksheets at once
- Create cell references to other worksheets
- Consolidate information from multiple worksheets using 3-D references
- Create and print a worksheet group

Session 6.2
- Create a link to data in another workbook
- Create a workbook reference
- Learn how to edit links

Session 6.3
- Insert a hyperlink in a cell
- Create a workbook based on an existing template
- Create a custom workbook template

Case | Better World Recycling

In 2010, Maria Guzman and Edward McKay, a couple of college friends, opened Better World Recycling, a collection site for recyclable plastics. Since then, they have expanded the business to accept other types of recyclable items, including paper, glass, metal, Styrofoam, and plastic. The company also expanded from the original location in Columbia, Kansas, to two additional locations—Richmond, Indiana, and Marion, Iowa. With the expansion, Maria assumed the duties and title of COO (Chief Operating Officer) and Edward became the CEO (Chief Executive Officer).

Maria, working in Columbia, is responsible for analyzing collections at all locations. Each recycling site tracks the amount of each material it collects during each quarter. Each site enters this information in a workbook, which is sent to Maria to consolidate and analyze. Maria has received the workbooks with the quarterly collections data for the past year from all three locations—Columbia, Richmond, and Marion. She wants you to create a worksheet in each workbook that summarizes the collection totals.

STARTING DATA FILES

Excel6 → Tutorial
Better World.xlsx
Kansas.xlsx
Marion.xlsx
Recycle Memo.docx
Richmond.xlsx

Review
BW.xlsx
Columbia KS.xlsx
Illinois.xlsx
Marion IA.xlsx
Paris Memo.docx
Richmond IN.xlsx

Case1
Cheese.xlsx

Case2
Eastern.xlsx
Internet.xlsx
Summary.xlsx
Western.xlsx

Case3
Clinic.xlsx

Case4
Ice Summary.xlsx
Ice Template.xltx
Midwest.xlsx

New Midwest.xlsx
Northeast.xlsx
Southeast.xlsx

Microsoft product screenshots used with permission from Microsoft Corporation.

EX 327

Excel | Tutorial 6 Managing Multiple Worksheets and Workbooks

Session 6.1 Visual Overview:

Anything you do in the active sheet—such as entering formulas, adding labels, and formatting—is automatically done to all sheets in the worksheet group, saving you time and ensuring consistency.

When worksheets are grouped, the workbook is in group-editing mode and "[Group]" appears in the title bar.

	A	B	C	D	E
1	Better World Recycling-Columbia				
2	Recycling Collection Data in Tons				
3	Quarter 1				
4					
5		January	February	March	Totals
6	Paper	506	420	385	1,311
7	Glass	430	256	205	891
8	Metal	302	385	402	1,089
9	Styrofoam	35	50	12	97
10	Plastic	125	175	136	436
11	Totals	1,398	1,286	1,140	3,824

You can click any tab outside the worksheet group to exit group-editing mode. In this case, clicking the Documentation sheet tab ungroups the worksheets.

A **worksheet group** is a collection of two or more selected worksheets. This worksheet group includes four worksheets.

The name of the active sheet in the worksheet group is in bold and a different color. In this worksheet group, Quarter 1 is the active sheet.

A worksheet group can contain adjacent or nonadjacent worksheets. This worksheet group contains adjacent worksheets.

© 2014 Cengage Learning

Tutorial 6 Managing Multiple Worksheets and Workbooks | Excel EX 329

Worksheet Groups and 3-D References

A **3-D reference** is a reference to the same cell or range in multiple worksheets in the same workbook. This 3-D reference refers to cell E10 in the Quarter 1, Quarter 2, Quarter 3, and Quarter 4 worksheets.

When two or more worksheets have identical row and column layouts, as the quarterly worksheets in this workbook do, you can enter formulas with 3-D references to summarize those worksheets in another worksheet.

F10 =SUM('Quarter 1:Quarter 4'!E10)

	A	B	C	D	E	F
1		Better World Recycling-Columbia Total				
2		Recycling Collection Data in Tons				
3	Fiscal Year - 2016					
4						
5		Quarter 1	Quarter 2	Quarter 3	Quarter 4	Totals
6	Paper	1,311	1,230	914	1,126	4,581
7	Glass	891	911	728	770	3,300
8	Metal	989	1,050	1,256	1,179	4,474
9	Styrofoam	97	195	197	287	776
10	Plastic	436	415	457	434	1,742
11	Totals	3,724	3,801	3,552	3,796	14,873

Quarter 1
='Quarter 1'!E6
='Quarter 1'!E7
='Quarter 1'!E8
='Quarter 1'!E9
='Quarter 1'!E10

Formulas can also reference cells and ranges in other worksheets. For example, the formula in cell B6 references cell E6 in the Quarter 1 worksheet.

The Summary worksheet uses 3-D references to summarize data from four worksheets—Quarter 1, Quarter 2, Quarter 3, and Quarter 4.

Single quotation marks surround a sheet name that includes spaces, as the Quarter 1 worksheet does in this formula.

The result displayed in cell F10 is the sum of values in cell E10 of the Quarter 1, Quarter 2, Quarter 3, and Quarter 4 worksheets.

© 2014 Cengage Learning

Grouping Worksheets

Workbook data is often placed in several worksheets. Using multiple worksheets makes it easier to group and summarize data. For example, a company such as Better World Recycling with branches in different geographic regions can place collection information for each region in separate worksheets. Rather than scrolling through one large and complex worksheet that contains data for all regions, users can access collection information for a specific region simply by clicking a sheet tab in the workbook.

Using multiple worksheets enables you to place summarized data first. Managers interested only in an overall picture can view the first worksheet of summary data without looking at the details available in the other worksheets. Others, of course, might want to view the supporting data in the individual worksheets that follow the summary worksheet. In the case of Better World Recycling, Maria used separate worksheets to summarize the amount of each item collected at the Columbia location for each quarter of the 2016 fiscal year.

You will open Maria's workbook and review the current information.

To open and review the Better World Recycling workbook:

1. Open the **Kansas** workbook located in the Excel6 ▸ Tutorial folder included with your Data Files, and then save the document as **Columbia** in the location specified by your instructor.

2. In the Documentation worksheet, enter your name and the date.

3. Go to the **Quarter 1** worksheet, and then view the recycling data for the first quarter of the year. See Figure 6-1.

Figure 6-1   Quarter 1 worksheet for Better World Recycling-Columbia

	A	B	C	D
1	Better World Recycling-Columbia			
2	Recycling Collection Data in Tons			
3	Quarter 1			
4				
5		January	February	March
6	Paper	506	420	385
7	Glass	430	256	205
8	Metal	302	385	402
9	Styrofoam	35	50	12
10	Plastic	125	175	136

data for each quarter is entered on its own worksheet

tons of recyclable items by month

Sheet tabs: Documentation | Quarter 1 | Quarter 2 | Quarter 3 | Quarter 4

4. Review the **Quarter 2**, **Quarter 3**, and **Quarter 4** worksheets. The layout for all four worksheets is identical.

Maria didn't enter any formulas in the workbook. You need to enter formulas to calculate the total number of tons of collected recyclables for each column (columns B through D) in all four worksheets. Rather than retyping the formulas in each worksheet, you can enter them all at once by creating a worksheet group. A worksheet group, like a range, can contain adjacent or nonadjacent worksheets. In group-editing mode, most editing tasks that you complete in the active worksheet also affect the other worksheets in the group. By forming a worksheet group, you can:

- **Enter or edit data and formulas.** Changes made to content in the active worksheet are also made in the same cells in all the worksheets in the group. You can also use the Find and Replace commands with a worksheet group.
- **Apply formatting.** Changes made to formatting in the active worksheet are also made to all the worksheets in the group, including changing row heights or column widths and applying conditional formatting.
- **Insert or delete rows and columns.** Changes made to the worksheet structure in the active worksheet are also made to all the worksheets in the group.
- **Set the page layout options.** Changes made to the page layout settings in one worksheet also apply to all the worksheets in the group, such as changing the orientation, scaling to fit, and inserting headers and footers.
- **Apply view options.** Changes made to the worksheet view such as zooming, showing and hiding worksheets, and so forth are also made to all the worksheets in the group.
- **Print all the worksheets.** You can print all of the worksheets in the worksheet group at the same time.

Worksheet groups save you time and help improve consistency among the worksheets because you can perform an action once, yet affect multiple worksheets.

REFERENCE

Grouping and Ungrouping Worksheets

- To select an adjacent group, click the sheet tab of the first worksheet in the group, press and hold the Shift key, click the sheet tab of the last worksheet in the group, and then release the Shift key.
- To select a nonadjacent group, click the sheet tab of one worksheet in the group, press and hold the Ctrl key, click the sheet tabs of the remaining worksheets in the group, and then release the Ctrl key.
- To ungroup the worksheets, click the sheet tab of a worksheet that is not in the group (or right-click the sheet tab of one worksheet in the group, and then click Ungroup Sheets on the shortcut menu).

In the Columbia workbook, you'll group an adjacent range of worksheets—the Quarter 1 worksheet through the Quarter 4 worksheet.

To group the quarterly worksheets:

1. Click the **Quarter 1** sheet tab to make the worksheet active. This is the first worksheet you want to include in the group.

2. Press and hold the **Shift** key, and then click the **Quarter 4** sheet tab. This is the last worksheet you want to include in the group.

3. Release the **Shift** key. The sheet tabs are white, the green border at the bottom of the sheet tab extends across all the tabs, and the sheet tab labels, Quarter 1 through Quarter 4, are in bold, indicating they are all selected. The text "[Group]" appears in the title bar to remind you that a worksheet group is selected in the workbook. See Figure 6-2.

TIP

If you cannot see the sheet tab of a worksheet you want to include in a group, use the sheet tab scroll buttons to display it.

Figure 6-2   **Grouped worksheets**

(Screenshot of Excel window titled "Columbia [Group] - Excel" showing the Home ribbon and a worksheet with the following content:)

Cell A1: Better World Recycling-Columbia
Cell A2: Recycling Collection Data in Tons
Cell A3: Quarter 1

	A	B	C	D
5		January	February	March
6	Paper	506	420	385
7	Glass	430	256	205
8	Metal	302	385	402
9	Styrofoam	35	50	12
10	Plastic	125	175	136

Sheet tabs: Documentation | Quarter 1 | Quarter 2 | Quarter 3 | Quarter 4

Callouts:
- indicates that worksheets are grouped
- worksheets in the group
- sheet tab scroll buttons
- active worksheet in the group

You can change which worksheet in a worksheet group is active. Just click the sheet tab of the worksheet you want to make active. If a worksheet group includes all the worksheets in a workbook, you cannot change which worksheet is the active sheet because clicking a sheet tab ungroups the worksheets.

> **To change the active sheet in the grouped quarterly worksheets:**
>
> 1. Click the **Quarter 2** sheet tab to make the worksheet active. The Quarter 2 worksheet is now the active worksheet in the group.
>
> 2. Click the **Quarter 4** sheet tab. The Quarter 4 worksheet is now the active worksheet in the group.

Entering Headings and Formulas in a Worksheet Group

When you enter a formula in the active worksheet (in this case, the Quarter 1 worksheet), the formula is entered in the same cells in all the worksheets in the group. The grouped worksheets must have the exact same organization and layout (rows and columns) in order for this to work. Otherwise, any formulas you enter in the active worksheet will be incorrect in the other worksheets in the group and could overwrite existing data.

With the quarterly worksheets grouped, you will enter the formulas to calculate the collection totals for each month.

To enter formulas to calculate the collection totals in the worksheet group:

1. Select cell **B11**. You want to enter the formula in cell B11 in each of the four worksheets in the group.

2. On the HOME tab, in the Editing group, click the **AutoSum** button, and then press the **Enter** key. The formula =SUM(B6:B10) is entered in cell B11 in each worksheet, adding the total tons of recyclable items collected at the Columbia site for the first month of the quarter. For Quarter 4, the October total of collected items shown in cell B11 is 1194.

3. Copy the formula in cell B11 to the range **C11:D11**. The formula calculates the total tons of recyclable items collected for the other months in the quarter. For Quarter 4, the other collection totals are 1209 tons in November and 1413 tons in December.

4. In cell **E6**, enter a formula with the SUM function to add the total tons of paper collected for each quarter at the Columbia site. The formula =SUM(B6:D6) adds the monthly totals of the tons of paper collected. In Quarter 4, 1126 tons of paper were collected.

5. Copy the formula in cell E6 to the range **E7:E11** to calculate the total tons of glass, metal, Styrofoam, and plastic, as well as the total tons of all recyclable items, collected at the Columbia site for each quarter. For Quarter 4, the Columbia site collected 770 tons of glass, 1179 tons of metal, 287 tons of Styrofoam, 454 tons of plastic, and 3816 tons of recyclables overall.

6. In cell **A11** and in cell **E5**, enter the label **Totals**.

7. Select cell **B11**. The formula =SUM(B6:B10) appears in the formula bar, and the formula result 1194 appears in the cell. See Figure 6-3.

Figure 6-3   **Formulas entered in all of the worksheets in the group**

	A	B	C	D	E
1	Better World Recycling-Columbia				
2	Recycling Collection Data in Tons				
3	Quarter 4				
4					
5		October	November	December	Totals
6	Paper	305	415	406	1126
7	Glass	215	225	330	770
8	Metal	452	325	402	1179
9	Styrofoam	120	42	125	287
10	Plastic	102	202	150	454
11	Totals	1194	1209	1413	3816

B11   fx   =SUM(B6:B10)

- formula in cell B11 is the same in all of the grouped worksheets
- Quarter 4 worksheet has the same layout as the Quarter 1, 2, and 3 worksheets
- formula result in cell B11 differs in each of the grouped worksheets
- active worksheet in the group

Sheet tabs: Documentation | Quarter 1 | Quarter 2 | Quarter 3 | **Quarter 4**

READY

The formulas and labels you entered in the Quarter 4 worksheet were entered in the Quarter 1, 2, and 3 worksheets at the same time.

8. Click the **Quarter 3** sheet tab, and then make sure that cell **B11** is the active cell. The formula =SUM(B6:B10), which adds the number of tons collected in Quarter 3, appears in the formula bar, and the formula result 1111 appears in the cell.

9. Click the **Quarter 2** sheet tab, and then make sure cell **B11** is the active cell. The formula =SUM(B6:B10), which adds the number of tons collected in Quarter 2, appears in the formula bar, and the formula result 1395 appears in the cell.

10. Click the **Quarter 1** sheet tab, and then make sure cell **B11** is the active cell. The formula =SUM(B6:B10), which adds the number of tons collected in Quarter 1, appears in the formula bar, and the formula result 1398 appears in the cell.

The grouped worksheets made it quick to enter the formulas needed to calculate the monthly and recyclable item totals for each quarter.

INSIGHT

Editing Grouped Worksheets

When you enter, edit, or format cells in a worksheet group, the changes you make to one worksheet are automatically applied to the other worksheets in the group. For example, if you delete a value from one cell, the content is also deleted from the same cell in all the worksheets in the group. Be cautious when editing a worksheet that is part of a group. If the layout and structure of the other grouped worksheets are not exactly the same, you might inadvertently overwrite data in some of the worksheets. Also, remember to ungroup the worksheet group after you finish entering data, formulas, and formatting. Otherwise, changes you intend to make in one worksheet will be made to all the worksheets in the group, potentially producing incorrect results.

Formatting a Worksheet Group

As when inserting formulas and text, any formatting changes you make to the active worksheet are applied to all worksheets in the group. You will format the quarterly worksheets, which are still grouped.

To apply formatting to the worksheet group:

1. Select cell **A1**, and then format the cell with the **Lucida Console** font, **bold**, and the **Olive Green, Accent 3, Darker 25%** font color. The company name is formatted to match the company name on the Documentation worksheet.

2. Increase the indent of cell **A11** by one. The label shifts to the right.

3. In the nonadjacent range **A2:A3;A6:A11;B5:E5**, bold the text in the headings.

4. Merge and center the range **A1:E1** and the range **A2:E2**.

5. In the range **B5:E5**, center the text.

6. In the range **B6:E11**, apply the **Comma Style** number format with no decimal places. No change is visible in any number that is less than 1000.

› 7. In the range **B5:E5** and the range **B10:E10**, add a bottom border.
› 8. Select cell **A1**. All the worksheets in the group are formatted.
› 9. Go to each worksheet in the group and review the formatting changes, and then go to the **Quarter 1** worksheet. See Figure 6-4.

Figure 6-4 Formatting applied to the worksheet group

Ungrouping Worksheets

When you ungroup the worksheets, each worksheet functions independently again. If you forget to ungroup the worksheets, any changes you make in one worksheet will be applied to all the worksheets in the group. So be sure to ungroup worksheets when you are finished making changes that apply to multiple worksheets. To ungroup worksheets, click the sheet tab of a worksheet that is not part of the group. If a worksheet group includes all of the sheets in a workbook, click any of the sheet tabs to ungroup the worksheets.

You will ungroup the quarterly worksheets so you can work in each worksheet separately.

To ungroup the quarterly worksheets:

1. Click the **Documentation** sheet tab. The worksheets are ungrouped because the Documentation worksheet was not part of the worksheet group. The text "[Group]" no longer appears in the Excel title bar.

2. Verify that the worksheets are ungrouped and the word "[Group]" no longer appears in the title bar.

Be sure to ungroup the worksheets; otherwise, any changes you make will affect all worksheets in the group.

Maria wants you to include a new Summary worksheet in the workbook. You'll start working on that next.

PROSKILLS

Written Communication: Using Multiple Worksheets with Identical Layouts

Using multiple worksheets to organize complex data can help make that data simpler to understand and analyze. It also makes it easier to navigate to specific data. For example, a workbook that contains data about a variety of products, stores, or regions could use a different worksheet for each product, store, or region. This arrangement provides a way to view discrete units of data that can be combined and summarized in another worksheet.

When you use multiple worksheets to organize similar types of data, the worksheets should have identical layouts. You can quickly group the worksheets with the identical layouts, and then enter the formulas, formatting, and labels in all of the grouped worksheets at once. This helps to ensure consistency and accuracy among the worksheets as well as make it faster to create the different worksheets needed.

Using multiple worksheets with identical layouts enables you to use 3-D references to quickly summarize the data in another worksheet. The summary worksheet provides an overall picture of the data that is detailed in the other worksheets. Often, managers are more interested in this big picture view. However, the supporting data is still available in the individual worksheets when a deeper analysis is needed.

So, when you are working with a large and complex worksheet filled with data, consider the different ways to organize it in multiple worksheets. Not only will you save time when entering and finding data, but also the data becomes more understandable, and connections and results become clearer.

Working with Multiple Worksheets

As you develop a workbook, you might need to add a worksheet that has the same setup as an existing worksheet. Rather than starting from scratch, you can copy that worksheet as a starting point. For example, Maria wants the workbook to include a Summary worksheet that adds the annual totals of tons of recyclable materials collected from quarterly worksheets. The formulas you create in the Summary worksheet will reference cells in each quarterly worksheet using 3-D references. You can then group the completed worksheets to develop a consistent page setup in all worksheets and then print them all at once.

Copying Worksheets

Often, after spending time developing a worksheet, you can use it as a starting point for creating another, saving you time and energy compared to developing a new worksheet from scratch. Copying a worksheet duplicates all the values, formulas, and formats into

Tutorial 6 Managing Multiple Worksheets and Workbooks | Excel EX 337

the new worksheet, leaving the original worksheet intact. You can then edit, reformat, and enter new content as needed to create the exact worksheet you need.

> **REFERENCE**
>
> ### Copying Worksheets
>
> - Select the sheet tabs of the worksheets you want to copy.
> - Right-click the sheet tabs, and then click Move or Copy on the shortcut menu.
> - Click the To book arrow, and then click the name of an existing workbook or click (new book) to create a new workbook for the worksheets.
> - In the Before sheet box, click the worksheet before which you want to insert the new worksheet.
> - Click the Create a copy check box to insert a checkmark to copy the worksheets.
> - Click the OK button.
>
> or
>
> - Select the sheet tabs of the worksheets you want to copy.
> - Press and hold the Ctrl key as you drag the selected sheet tabs to a new location in the sheet tabs, and then release the Ctrl key.

Maria wants you to create the Summary worksheet to provide an overall picture of the data in the detailed quarterly worksheets. The Summary worksheet needs the same formatting and structure as the quarterly worksheets. To ensure consistency among worksheets, you will copy the Quarter 1 worksheet to the beginning of the workbook, and then modify its contents.

To copy the Quarter 1 worksheet and create the Summary worksheet:

1. Click the **Quarter 1** sheet tab, and then press and hold the **Ctrl** key as you drag the worksheet to the left of the Documentation worksheet. The pointer changes to and a triangle indicates the drop location.

2. Release the mouse button, and then release the **Ctrl** key. An identical copy of the Quarter 1 worksheet appears in the new location. The sheet tab shows "Quarter 1 (2)" to indicate that this is the copied sheet.

3. Rename the Quarter 1 (2) worksheet as **Summary**.

4. Move the **Summary** worksheet between the Documentation worksheet and the Quarter 1 worksheet.

> **TIP**
>
> To move a worksheet or a worksheet group to another location in the same workbook, drag its sheet tab and drop it in its new location.

Maria wants the Summary worksheet to show the collection data for each product by quarter, and the total collections for each product and quarter. You will modify the Summary worksheet to do this now.

To modify the Summary worksheet:

1. Make sure the **Summary** worksheet is the active sheet.

2. In cell **A3**, enter **2016**. This is the year to which the summary refers.

3. In cell **A1**, enter **Better World Recycling–Columbia Total**. The new title reflects this worksheet's content. The formatting should remain intact.

4. Delete the collection data from the range **B6:E10**. The formatting remains intact. See Figure 6-5.

Figure 6-5 Summary worksheet created from the Quarter 1 worksheet

- headings changed to reflect the worksheet's content
- collection data cleared leaving the formatting and formulas intact
- copied and renamed worksheet

5. Insert a new **column C** into the worksheet. The column appears between the January and February labels with the same formatting as January.

6. In the range **B5:E5**, enter **Quarter 1**, **Quarter 2**, **Quarter 3**, and **Quarter 4** in each respective cell.

7. Copy the formula in cell B11 to cell **C11**. See Figure 6-6.

Figure 6-6 Summary worksheet modified

- headings reflect the collection periods
- new column C

Referencing Cells and Ranges in Other Worksheets

When you use multiple worksheets to organize related data, you can reference a cell or a range in another worksheet in the same workbook. For example, the Summary worksheet references cells in the four quarterly worksheets to calculate the total collections for the entire year. The syntax to reference a cell or a range in a different worksheet is

```
=SheetName!CellRange
```

where `SheetName` is the worksheet's name as listed on the sheet tab and `CellRange` is the reference for the cell or range in that worksheet. An exclamation mark (!) separates the worksheet reference from the cell or range reference. For example, you could enter the following formula in the Summary worksheet to reference cell D10 in the Quarter1 worksheet:

```
=Quarter1!D10
```

If the worksheet name contains spaces, you must enclose the name in single quotation marks. For example, the following formula references cell D10 in the Quarter 1 worksheet:

```
='Quarter 1'!D10
```

You can use these references to create formulas that reference cells in different locations in different worksheets. For example, to add collections from two worksheets—cell C9 in the Quarter 1 worksheet and cell C9 in the Quarter 2 worksheet—you would enter the following formula:

```
='Quarter 1'!C9+'Quarter 2'!C9
```

You could type the formula directly in the cell, but it is faster and more accurate to use your mouse to select cells to enter their references to other worksheets.

REFERENCE

Entering a Formula with References to Another Worksheet

- Select the cell where you want to enter the formula.
- Type = and begin entering the formula.
- To insert a reference from another worksheet, click the sheet tab for the worksheet, and then click the cell or select the range you want to reference.
- When the formula is complete, press the Enter key.

Maria wants you to enter a formula in cell A4 in each quarterly worksheet that displays the fiscal year entered in cell A3 in the Summary worksheet. All four quarterly worksheets will use the formula =Summary!A3 to reference the fiscal year in cell A3 of the Summary worksheet.

To enter the formula that references the Summary worksheet:

1. Click the **Quarter 1** sheet tab, press and hold the **Shift** key, and then click the **Quarter 4** worksheet. The Quarter 1 through Quarter 4 worksheets are grouped.

2. Select cell **A4**. This is the cell in which you want to enter the formula to display the fiscal year.

3. Type **=** to begin the formula, click the **Summary** sheet tab, and then click cell **A3**. The reference to cell A3 in the Summary worksheet is added to the formula in cell A4 in the grouped worksheets.

4. On the formula bar, click the **Enter** button ✓. The formula =Summary!A3 is entered in cell A4 in all the worksheets in the group. The formula appears in the formula bar and 2016 appears in cell A4. See Figure 6-7.

Figure 6-7   Formula with a worksheet reference

formula references cell A3 in the Summary worksheet

cell A4 displays the contents of cell A3 in the Summary worksheet

	A	B	C	D	E
1	Better World Recycling–Columbia				
2	Recycling Collection Data in Tons				
3	Quarter 1				
4	2016				
5		January	February	March	Totals
6	Paper	506	420	385	1,311
7	Glass	430	256	205	891

5. Go to each worksheet in the group and verify that the formula =Summary!A3 appears in the formula bar, and 2016 appears in cell A4.

6. Go to the **Summary** worksheet. The quarterly worksheets are ungrouped.

7. In cell **A3**, enter **Fiscal Year - 2016**. The descriptive label in cell A3 is entered in the Summary worksheet and is also displayed in the quarterly worksheets because of the formula you entered.

8. Go to the **Quarter 1** through **Quarter 4** worksheets and verify that the label "Fiscal Year - 2016" appears in cell A4 in each worksheet. See Figure 6-8.

Figure 6-8   Edited content displayed in the cell with the worksheet reference

formula remains unchanged

cell A4 in the Quarter 4 worksheet displays the updated contents of cell A3 in the Summary worksheet

	A	B	C	D	E
1	Better World Recycling–Columbia				
2	Recycling Collection Data in Tons				
3	Quarter 4				
4	Fiscal Year - 2016				
5		October	November	December	Totals
6	Paper	305	415	406	1,126
7	Glass	215	225	330	770

The Summary worksheet needs to include the quarterly totals for each category.

Tutorial 6 Managing Multiple Worksheets and Workbooks | Excel EX 341

To enter worksheet references for the quarterly totals:

1. In the Summary worksheet, select cell **B6**.

2. Type **=** to begin the formula.

3. Click the **Quarter 1** sheet tab, and then click cell **E6**. The cell is selected and added to the formula.

4. Click the **Enter** button ✓ on the formula bar to complete the formula and return to the Summary worksheet. Cell B6 remains selected, and the formula ='Quarter 1'!E6 appears in the formula bar. The formula result showing the total tons of paper collected in the first quarter of 2016—1,311—appears in cell B6.

5. Repeat Steps 2 through 4 to enter formulas with worksheet references in cells **C6**, **D6**, and **E6** that add the total tons of paper collected in Quarter 2 (**='Quarter 2'!E6**), Quarter 3 (**='Quarter 3'!E6**), and Quarter 4 (**='Quarter 4'!E6**). The quarterly totals are 1,230, 914, and 1,126 tons of paper, respectively.

6. Select the range **B6:E6**, and then drag the fill handle over the range **B7:E10**. The formulas with the worksheet references are copied to the rest of the item rows. The Auto Fill Options button appears below the copied range.

7. Click the **Auto Fill Options** button, and then click the **Fill Without Formatting** option button. You didn't copy the formatting in this case because you want to keep the bottom border formatting in the range B10:E10. The total values for the year appear in the range.

8. Click cell **B6** to deselect the range. The Summary worksheet now shows the 2016 total of each recyclable item collected in Columbia. The formula in cell F11 that was copied with the worksheet shows the total for all items collected in 2016. See Figure 6-9.

Figure 6-9 Recycling collection totals for Columbia in 2016

worksheet reference to cell E6 in the Quarter 1 worksheet added to the formula in the Summary worksheet

B6 — fx ='Quarter 1'!E6

	A	B	C	D	E	F
1	Better World Recycling-Columbia Total
2	Recycling Collection Data in Tons
3	Fiscal Year - 2016
4						
5		Quarter 1	Quarter 2	Quarter 3	Quarter 4	Totals
6	Paper	1,311	1,230	914	1,126	
7	Glass	891	911	728	770	
8	Metal	1,089	1,050	1,206	1,179	
9	Styrofoam	97	195	197	287	
10	Plastic	436	415	457	454	
11	Totals	3,824	3,801	3,502	3,816	14,943
12						

Quarter 1 paper total

Using 3-D References to Add Values Across Worksheets

Maria wants you to calculate the total tons of each material collected for the year and display the totals for the fiscal year in the Summary worksheet. To calculate the totals for the year, you can add the results from each quarterly worksheet and place the sum in the Summary worksheet. For example, in cell B6 of the Summary worksheet, you can enter the following formula:

```
='Quarter 1'!E6+'Quarter 2'!E6+'Quarter 3'!E6+'Quarter 4'!E6
```

This formula calculates the total amount of paper collected by adding the values in cell E6 in each of the quarterly worksheets. Continuing this approach for the entire worksheet would be time consuming and error prone.

Instead, when two or more worksheets have *identical* row and column layouts, as the quarterly worksheets in the Columbia workbook do, you can enter formulas with 3-D references to summarize those worksheets in another worksheet. The 3-D reference specifies not only the range of rows and columns, but also the range of worksheet names in which the cells appear. The general syntax of a 3-D reference is

WorksheetRange!*CellRange*

where *WorksheetRange* is the range of worksheets you want to reference and is entered as *FirstSheetName:LastSheetName* with a colon separating the first and last worksheets in the worksheet range. If the sheet names include spaces, they are surrounded by ' ' (single quotation marks). *CellRange* is the same cell or range in each of those worksheets that you want to reference. An exclamation mark (!) separates the worksheet range from the cell or range. For example, the following formula adds the values in cell D11 in the worksheets between Quarter1 and Quarter4, including Quarter1 and Quarter4:

```
=SUM(Quarter1:Quarter4!D11)
```

If worksheets named Quarter1, Quarter2, Quarter3, and Quarter4 are included in the workbook, the worksheet range Quarter1:Quarter4 references all four worksheets. Although the Quarter2 and Quarter3 worksheets aren't specifically mentioned in this 3-D reference, all worksheets positioned within the starting and ending names are included in the calculation.

INSIGHT

Managing 3-D References

The results of a formula using a 3-D reference reflect the current worksheets in the worksheet range. If you move a worksheet outside the referenced worksheet range or remove a worksheet from the workbook, the formula results will change. For example, consider a workbook with four worksheets named Quarter1, Quarter2, Quarter3, and Quarter4. If you move the Quarter3 worksheet after the Quarter4 worksheet, the worksheet range Quarter1:Quarter4 includes only the Quarter1, Quarter2, and Quarter4 worksheets. Similarly, if you insert a new worksheet or move an existing worksheet within the worksheet range, the formula results reflect the change. To continue the example, if you insert a Quarter5 worksheet before the Quarter4 worksheet, the 3-D reference Quarter1:Quarter4 includes the Quarter5 worksheet.

When you create a formula, make sure that the 3-D reference reflects the appropriate worksheets. Also, if you later insert or delete a worksheet within the 3-D reference, be aware of how the change will affect the formula results.

Tutorial 6 Managing Multiple Worksheets and Workbooks | Excel EX 343

3-D references are often used in formulas that contain Excel functions, including SUM, AVERAGE, COUNT, MAX, and MIN.

REFERENCE

Entering a Function That Contains a 3-D Reference
- Select the cell where you want to enter the formula.
- Type = to begin the formula, type the name of the function, and then type (to indicate the beginning of the argument.
- Click the sheet tab for the first worksheet in the worksheet range, press and hold the Shift key, and then click the tab for the last worksheet in the worksheet range.
- Select the cell or range to reference, and then press the Enter key.

In the Columbia workbook, Maria wants to use 3-D references in the Summary worksheet to add the total tons of each material collected for the year. You will begin by entering a formula to add the total tons collected for paper and glass in the first quarter. Then, you'll copy this formula to calculate the total tons of metal, Styrofoam, and plastic in the first quarter.

To use a 3-D reference to enter the total amount of paper collected:

1. In the Summary worksheet, select cell **F6**, and then type **=SUM(** to begin the formula.

2. Click the **Quarter 1** sheet tab, press and hold the **Shift** key, click the **Quarter 4** sheet tab, and then release the **Shift** key. The quarterly worksheets are grouped to create the worksheet range.

3. In the Quarter 1 worksheet, click cell **E6**. Cell E6 is selected in each quarterly worksheet and added to the function. Notice that the worksheet names are enclosed in single quotation marks because the worksheet names include spaces. See Figure 6-10.

Excel | Tutorial 6 Managing Multiple Worksheets and Workbooks

Figure 6-10   **3-D reference added to the SUM function**

3-D reference to cell E6 in the Quarter 1 through Quarter 4 worksheets

Formula bar: =SUM('Quarter 1:Quarter 4'!E6)

cell E6 selected in the Quarter 1 through Quarter 4 worksheets

	A	B	C	D	E	F
1		Better World Recycling–Columbia				
2		Recycling Collection Data in Tons				
3	Quarter 1					
4	Fiscal Year - 2016					
5		January	February	March	Totals	
6	Paper	506	420	385	1,311	
7	Glass	430	256	205	891	
8	Metal	302	385	402	1,089	
9	Styrofoam	35	50	12	97	
10	Plastic	125	175	136	436	
11	Totals	1,398	1,286	1,140	3,824	

worksheets grouped as you enter the formula (Quarter 1, Quarter 2, Quarter 3, Quarter 4)

Sheet tabs: Documentation | Summary | Quarter 1 | Quarter 2 | Quarter 3 | Quarter 4

POINT

- 4. Press the **Enter** key. The completed formula adds the total tons of paper collected in 2016.

- 5. In the Summary worksheet, select cell **F6**. The formula with the 3-D reference, =SUM('Quarter 1:Quarter 4'!E6), appears in the formula bar. The formula result—4,581—appears in the cell. See Figure 6-11.

Figure 6-11 — 3-D reference used in the SUM function

3-D reference to the Quarter 1, 2, 3, and 4 worksheets

Formula bar: `=SUM('Quarter 1:Quarter 4'!E6)`

totals tons of paper collected in 2016

	A	B	C	D	E	F
1		Better World Recycling–Columbia Total				
2		Recycling Collection Data in Tons				
3	Fiscal Year - 2016					
4						
5		Quarter 1	Quarter 2	Quarter 3	Quarter 4	Totals
6	Paper	1,311	1,230	914	1,126	4,581
7	Glass	891	911	728	770	
8	Metal	1,089	1,050	1,206	1,179	
9	Styrofoam	97	195	197	287	

The next formula will add the total tons of glass collected in the first quarter. It will also use a 3-D reference.

To use a 3-D reference to calculate the total glass collected:

1. In the Summary worksheet, click cell **F7**, and then type **=SUM(** to begin the formula.

2. Click the **Quarter 1** sheet tab, press and hold the **Shift** key, click the **Quarter 4** sheet tab, and then release the **Shift** key. The quarterly worksheets are grouped to create the worksheet range.

3. In the Quarter 1 worksheet, click cell **E7**. Cell E7 is selected in each quarterly worksheet and added to the function.

4. Press the **Enter** key to complete the formula that adds the total tons of glass collected in 2016.

5. In the Summary worksheet, click cell **F7**. The formula with the 3-D reference, =SUM('Quarter 1:Quarter 4'!E7), appears in the formula bar, and the formula result 3,300 appears in cell F7.

Instead of entering formulas with 3-D references to create the totals for the remaining recyclable materials, you can copy the formulas to the rest of the range. You copy formulas with 3-D references the same way you copy other formulas—using copy and paste or AutoFill.

Maria wants you to calculate the total tons of recyclable materials collected in 2016.

To copy the formulas with 3-D references:

1. In the Summary worksheet, make sure cell **F7** is selected. This cell contains the formula with the 3-D reference you already entered.

2. Drag the fill handle over the range **F8:F10**. The formulas are copied for the rest of the recyclable totals. The Auto Fill Options button appears below the copied range.

3. Click the **Auto Fill Options** button, and then click the **Fill Without Formatting** option button. You don't want to copy the formatting in this case because you want to keep the bottom border formatting in cell F10. The total values for the year appear in the range.

4. Select cell **B6** to deselect the range. The Summary worksheet now shows the totals for 2016 in Columbia for each recyclable material. See Figure 6-12.

Figure 6-12 Summary worksheet with the Columbia recycling collection totals

	A	B	C	D	E	F
1		Better World Recycling-Columbia Total				
2		Recycling Collection Data in Tons				
3	Fiscal Year - 2016					
4						
5		Quarter 1	Quarter 2	Quarter 3	Quarter 4	Totals
6	Paper	1,311	1,230	914	1,126	4,581
7	Glass	891	911	728	770	3,300
8	Metal	1,089	1,050	1,206	1,179	4,524
9	Styrofoam	97	195	197	287	776
10	Plastic	436	415	457	454	1,762
11	Totals	3,824	3,801	3,502	3,816	14,943

Cell B6 contains: ='Quarter 1'!E6

One benefit of summarizing data using formulas with 3-D references, like any other formula, is that if you change the value in one worksheet, the results of formulas that reference that cell reflect the change.

Maria has discovered an error in the collection data. The Columbia site collected 525 tons of metal in September (which is in Quarter 3), not 475. You will correct the tons of metal collected in September.

To change the tons of metal collected in the Quarter 3 worksheet:

1. In the Summary worksheet, note that 1,206 tons of metal were collected in Quarter 3.

2. Go to the **Quarter 3** worksheet.

3. In cell **D8**, enter **525**. The total tons collected for Quarter 3 is now 1,256.

   The results in the Summary worksheet are also updated because of the 3-D references in the formulas.

4. Go to the **Summary** worksheet. The total number of tons of metal collected in Quarter 3 is now 1,256. The Quarter 3 total is now 3,552, and the 2016 total is now 4,574. See Figure 6-13.

Tutorial 6 Managing Multiple Worksheets and Workbooks | Excel   EX 347

Figure 6-13   Summary worksheet with updated Quarter 3 metal data

	A	B	C	D	E	F
1	Better World Recycling-Columbia Total					
2	Recycling Collection Data in Tons					
3	Fiscal Year - 2016					
4						
5		Quarter 1	Quarter 2	Quarter 3	Quarter 4	Totals
6	Paper	1,311	1,230	914	1,126	4,581
7	Glass	891	911	728	770	3,300
8	Metal	1,089	1,050	1,256	1,179	4,574
9	Styrofoam	97	195	197	287	776
10	Plastic	436	415	457	454	1,762
11	Totals	3,824	3,801	3,552	3,816	14,993
12						

updated value → (D8)
updated totals → (row/column totals)

Cell D8 formula: ='Quarter 3'!E8

Printing a Worksheet Group

When you create a worksheet group, you apply the same page layout settings to all of the worksheets in the group at the same time. You can also print all of the worksheets in the group at once. The process for printing a worksheet group is the same as for printing a single worksheet, except that you must first group the worksheets you want to print.

Maria wants a printed copy of the five collection data worksheets to include in her report. Each page should have the same setup. Because the layout will be the same for all the quarterly worksheets in the Columbia workbook, you can speed the page layout setup by creating a worksheet group before selecting settings.

To preview the Summary and quarterly worksheets with a custom header and footer:

> Be sure to include all five worksheets in the group so you can apply page layout settings and print the worksheets at once.

1. Group the **Summary**, **Quarter 1**, **Quarter 2**, **Quarter 3**, and **Quarter 4** worksheets. The five worksheets are grouped.

2. On the ribbon, click the **PAGE LAYOUT** tab.

3. In the Page Setup group, click the **Dialog Box Launcher**. The Page Setup dialog box opens with the Page tab active.

4. Click the **Margins** tab, and then click the **Horizontally** check box in the Center on page section to insert a checkmark. The printed content will be centered horizontally on the page.

5. Click the **Header/Footer** tab, click the **Custom Header** button to open the Header dialog box, click in the **Center section** box, click the **Insert Sheet Name** button to add the &[Tab] code in the section box (which inserts the sheet tab name in the center section of the header), and then click the **OK** button. A preview of the header appears in the upper portion of the dialog box.

6. Click the **Custom Footer** button to open the Footer dialog box, type your name in the Left section box, click in the Right section box, click the **Insert Date** button to add the &[Date] code in the section box (which inserts the current date in the right section of the footer), and then click the **OK** button.

7. Click the **Print Preview** button. The preview of the Summary worksheet, the first worksheet in the group, appears on the Print screen in Backstage view. See Figure 6-14.

Figure 6-14   Preview of the worksheet group

8. Below the preview, click the **Next Page** button ▶ four times to view the other worksheets in the group. Each page has the same page layout but the header shows the sheet tab names.

   Trouble? If only one page appears in the preview, the worksheets are not grouped. Click the Back button to exit Backstage view, and then repeat Steps 1 through 8.

9. Click the **Back** button to exit Backstage view without printing the worksheet group.

10. Go to the **Documentation** worksheet to ungroup the worksheets, and then go to the **Summary** worksheet.

In this session, you consolidated the data in Better World Recycling's Columbia workbook into a Summary worksheet so that Maria can quickly see the collection totals for the recyclable items. In the next session, you will help Maria determine the annual totals for the other Better World Recycling collection sites—Richmond and Marion.

REVIEW

Session 6.1 Quick Check

1. What is a worksheet group?
2. How do you select an adjacent worksheet group? How do you select a nonadjacent worksheet group? How do you deselect a worksheet group?
3. What formula would you enter in the Summary worksheet to reference cell C8 in the Quarter 2 worksheet?
4. What is the 3-D reference to cell E6 in the adjacent Summary 1, Summary 2, and Summary 3 worksheets?
5. Explain what the formula =AVERAGE(Sheet1:Sheet4!B1) calculates.
6. If you insert a new worksheet named Sheet5 after Sheet4, how would you change the formula =MIN(Sheet1:Sheet4!B1) to include Sheet5 in the calculation?
7. If you insert a new worksheet named Sheet5 before Sheet4, how would you change the formula =SUM(Sheet1:Sheet4!B1) to include Sheet5 in the calculation?
8. How do you apply the same page layout to all of the worksheets in a workbook at one time?

Session 6.2 Visual Overview:

An **external reference** is a reference to cells or ranges in a worksheet from another workbook. For example, *[Columbia.xlsx]Summary!$B$6* references cell B6 in the Summary worksheet in the Columbia workbook.

When two workbooks are linked, the **destination file** (sometimes referred to as the dependent file) is the workbook that receives data from another workbook. In this case, Better World 2016 is the destination file.

A **link** is a connection between files that allows data to be transferred from one file to another.

The total value shown in the destination file is calculated from values in the three source files.

Better World 2016 - Excel

B6 =[Columbia.xlsx]Summary!$B$6+[Richmond.xlsx]Summary!$B$6+[Marion.xlsx]Summary!$B$6

	A	B	C	D
1		Better World Recycling-Summary Total		
2		Recycling Collection Data in Tons		
3	Fiscal Year - 2016			
4				
5		Quarter 1	Quarter 2	Quarter 3
6	Paper	3,651	3,756	2,764
7	Glass	3,435	2,634	2,175

Whenever a value in a source file changes, the destination is also updated to reflect the most recent information. For example, if the total glass collected in Columbia for Quarter 1 increased by 10, the change is also reflected in the Better World 2016 workbook.

Richmond - Excel

A1   Better World Recycling-Richmond

	A	B	C	D
1		Better World Recycling-Richmond Total		
2		Recycling Collection Data in Tons		
3	Fiscal Year - 2016			
4				
5		Quarter 1	Quarter 2	Quarter 3
6	Paper	1,445	1,274	950
7	Glass	1,494	803	665
8	Metal	828	1,120	1,067
9	Stryofoam	183	120	160

Tutorial 6 Managing Multiple Worksheets and Workbooks | Excel   EX 351

Links and External References

You can collapse the ribbon to make more space available for viewing the worksheet. This is helpful when you tile a workbook.

When the full ribbon cannot be displayed, the scroll button appears so you can shift the hidden tabs into view.

These windows are arranged in a tiled configuration. Other options are horizontal, vertical, and cascade.

When two or more workbooks are linked, the **source file** is a workbook that contains data to be used in the destination file. In this case, Columbia, Richmond, and Marion are source files.

The Switch Windows button lists each open workbook so you can change which workbook is active.

The Arrange All button displays all of the open workbooks in a tiled configuration within the program window.

Marion - Excel

	A	B	C	D
1	Better World Recycling–Marion Tota			
2	Recycling Collection Data in Tons			
3	Fiscal Year - 2016			
4				
5		Quarter 1	Quarter 2	Quarter 3
6	Paper	895	1,252	900
7	Glass	1,050	920	782
8	Metal	1,220	1,034	1,544
9	Styrofoam	100	162	143

Columbia - Excel

	A	B	C	D
2				
3	Fisc			
4				
5				
6	Paper	1,311	1,230	914
7	Glass	891	911	728
8	Metal	989	1,050	1,256
9	Styrofoam	97	195	197

Linking Workbooks

When creating formulas in a workbook, you can reference data in other workbooks. To do so, you must create a link between the workbooks. When two files are linked, the source file contains the data, and the destination file (sometimes called the dependent file) receives the data. For example, Maria wants to create a company-wide workbook that summarizes the annual totals from each of the three Better World collection sites. In this case, the Columbia, Marion, and Richmond workbooks are the source files because they contain the data from the three collection sites. The Better World 2016 workbook is the destination file because it receives the data from the three site workbooks to calculate the company totals for 2016. The Better World 2016 workbook will always have access to the most recent information in the site workbooks because it can be updated whenever any of the linked values change. See Figure 6-15.

Figure 6-15 Source and destination files

© 2014 Cengage Learning

To create the link between destination and source files, you need to insert a formula in the Better World 2016 workbook that references a specific cell or range in the three site workbooks. That reference, called an external reference, has the syntax

`[WorkbookName]WorksheetName!CellRange`

where `WorkbookName` is the filename of the workbook (including the file extension) enclosed in square brackets; `WorksheetName` is the name of the worksheet that contains the data followed by an exclamation mark; and `CellRange` is the cell or range that contains the data. For example, the following formula references cell B6 in the Summary worksheet of the Richmond.xlsx workbook:

`=[Richmond.xlsx]Summary!B6`

If the workbook name or the worksheet name contains one or more spaces, you must enclose the entire workbook name and worksheet name in single quotation marks. For example, the following formula references cell B6 in the Summary worksheet of the Columbia 2016.xlsx workbook:

`='[Columbia 2016.xlsx]Summary'!B6`

When the source and destination workbooks are stored in the same folder, you need to include only the workbook name in the external reference. However, when the source and destination workbooks are located in different folders, the workbook reference must include the file's complete location (also called the path). For example,

> **TIP**
> When you use the point-and-click method to build formulas with external references, Excel enters all of the required punctuation, including quotation marks.

if the destination file is stored in C:\Recycle Data and the source file is stored in C:\Recycle Data\Local Data, the complete reference in the destination file would be:

```
='C:\Recycle Data\Local Data\[Columbia.xlsx]Summary'!B6
```

The single quotation marks start at the beginning of the path and end immediately before the exclamation mark.

PROSKILLS

Decision Making: Understanding When to Link Workbooks

More than one person is usually involved in developing information that will be used in an organization's decision-making process. If each person has access to only part of the data, everyone's ability to see the whole picture and make good decisions is limited. Linking workbooks provides one way to pull together all of the data being compiled by different people or departments to support the decision-making process.

When deciding whether to link workbooks, consider the following questions:

- **Can separate workbooks have the same purpose and structure?** With linked workbooks, each workbook can focus on a different store, branch office, or department with the same products or expenditure types and reporting periods (such as weekly, monthly, and quarterly).
- **Is a large workbook too unwieldy to use?** A large workbook can be divided into smaller workbooks for each quarter, division, or product and then linked to provide the summary information.
- **Can information from different workbooks be summarized?** Linked workbooks provide a way to quickly and accurately consolidate information from multiple source workbooks, and the summary worksheet will always contain the most current information even when information is later updated.
- **Are source workbooks continually updated?** With linked workbooks, an outdated source workbook can be replaced and the destination workbook will then reflect the latest information.
- **Will the source workbooks be available to the destination workbook?** If the person who is working with the destination workbook cannot access the source workbooks, then the destination workbook cannot be updated.

If you can answer yes to these questions, then linked workbooks are the way to go. Creating linked workbooks can help you analyze data better, leading to better decision making. It also provides greater flexibility as data becomes more expansive and complex. However, keep in mind that workbooks with many links can take a long time to open and update.

Navigating Multiple Workbooks

When you create external reference formulas, you'll need to move between open workbooks. The Switch Windows button in the Window group on the VIEW tab lists each open workbook so you can change which workbook is active. Another method is to click the Excel button on the taskbar and then click the thumbnail of the workbook you want to make active.

Maria received workbooks from the Richmond and Marion managers that are similar to the one you helped prepare. These three collection data workbooks (named Columbia, Richmond, and Marion) contain the tons of recyclable materials collected in 2016. Maria wants to create a company-wide workbook that summarizes the annual totals from each site workbook. You'll combine the three site workbooks into one regional summary workbook. First you need to open the workbooks that you want to reference. Then you'll switch between them to make each Summary worksheet the active sheet in preparation for creating the external references.

To open the regional workbooks and switch between them:

1. If you took a break after the previous session, make sure the Columbia workbook is open and the Summary worksheet is active.

2. Open the **Better World** workbook located in the Excel6 ▸ Tutorial folder included with your Data Files, and then save the workbook as **Better World 2016** in the location specified by your instructor.

3. In the Documentation worksheet of the Better World 2016 workbook, enter your name and the date, and then make the **Summary** worksheet active.

4. Open the **Marion** and **Richmond** workbooks located in the Excel6 ▸ Tutorial folder included with your Data Files.

5. On the ribbon, click the **VIEW** tab.

6. In the Window group, click the **Switch Windows** button to display a list of all the workbooks that are currently open.

7. Click **Marion** to make it the active workbook, and then go to the **Summary** worksheet.

8. On the ribbon, click the **VIEW** tab.

9. In the Window group, click the **Switch Windows** button, click **Richmond** to make the Richmond workbook active, and then go to the **Summary** worksheet.

10. Make the **Better World 2016** workbook the active workbook. The Summary worksheet is the active sheet in each workbook.

Arranging Multiple Workbooks

Rather than continually switching between open workbooks, you can display all the open workbooks on your screen at the same time. This way, you can easily click among the open workbooks to create links as well as quickly compare the contents of worksheets in different workbooks. You can arrange workbooks in the following layouts:

- **Tiled**—divides the open workbooks evenly on the screen
- **Horizontal**—divides the open workbooks into horizontal bands
- **Vertical**—divides the open workbooks into vertical bands
- **Cascade**—layers the open workbooks on the screen

The layout you select will depend on the contents being displayed and your purpose.

REFERENCE

Arranging Workbooks

- On the VIEW tab, in the Window group, click the Arrange All button.
- Select the layout in which you want to arrange the open workbooks.
- When arranging multiple workbooks, uncheck the Windows of active workbook option. When arranging multiple worksheets within one workbook, check this option.
- Click the OK button.

Currently, the four workbooks are open but only one is visible. You'll arrange the workbooks using the tiled arrangement.

Tutorial 6 Managing Multiple Worksheets and Workbooks | Excel   EX 355

To tile the open workbooks:

1. On the VIEW tab, in the Window group, click the **Arrange All** button. The Arrange Windows dialog box opens so you can select the layout arrangement you want.

2. Click the **Tiled** option button, if necessary. The Tiled option arranges the four Better World Recycling workbooks evenly on the screen.

3. Click the **OK** button. The four open workbooks appear in a tiled layout.

4. Click in the **Better World 2016** workbook to make it the active workbook, if necessary. In the tiled layout, the active workbook contains the active cell.

   The ribbon appears in each window, taking up a lot of the workbook space. To see more of the worksheets, you will collapse the ribbon in each window to show only the ribbon tabs.

5. In each window, click the **Collapse the Ribbon** button in the lower-right corner of the ribbon (or press the **Ctrl+F1** keys). Only the ribbon tabs are visible in each window. If the ribbon includes more tabs than can be displayed, a ribbon scroll button appears to the right of the last visible tab, which you can click to display the other tabs. See Figure 6-16.

TIP

You can click the Windows of active workbook check box to tile the sheets in the current workbook on the screen.

Figure 6-16   Four workbooks arranged in a tiled layout

Creating Formulas with External References

A formula can include a reference to another workbook (called an external reference), which creates a set of linked workbooks. The process for entering a formula with an external reference is the same as for entering any other formula using references within the same worksheet or workbook. You can enter the formulas by typing them or using the point-and-click method. In most situations, you will use the point-and-click method to switch between the source files and the destination files so that Excel enters the references to the workbook, worksheet, and cell using the correct syntax.

You need to enter the external reference formulas in the Better World 2016 workbook to summarize the recycling center totals into one workbook for Maria. You'll start by creating the formula that adds the total tons of paper collected in Columbia, Marion, and Richmond for Quarter 1 of 2016. You cannot use the SUM function with 3-D references here because you are referencing multiple workbooks, and 3-D references can only be used to reference multiple worksheets in the same workbook.

To create the formula with external references to add the total tons of paper collected:

1. In the Better World 2016 workbook, in the Summary worksheet, select cell **B6**, and then type **=** to begin the formula.

2. Click anywhere in the **Columbia** workbook to make the Columbia workbook active and place the formula in its formula bar, and then click cell **B6** in the Summary worksheet. The external reference to cell B6 in the Summary worksheet of the Columbia workbook—'[Columbia.xlsx]Summary'!$B$6—is added to the formula in the Better World 2016 workbook. See Figure 6-17.

As you create the formula, be sure to verify each external reference before going to the next step.

Figure 6-17   Formula with an external cell reference

The reference created in a 3-D reference is an absolute cell reference, which does not change when the formula is copied. The formula remains in the formula bar of both the Better World 2016 and Columbia workbooks until you make another workbook active. At that time, the formula will appear in the Better World 2016 workbook and the active worksheet.

3. Type **+**. The Better World 2016 workbook becomes active and you can continue entering the formula. You need to create an external reference to the Richmond workbook.

4. Click anywhere in the **Richmond** workbook, click cell **B6** in the Summary worksheet, and then type **+**. The formula in the Better World 2016 workbook includes the external reference to the cell that contains the total tons of paper collected in Richmond during Quarter 1.

5. Click anywhere in the **Marion** workbook, click cell **B6** in the Summary worksheet, and then press the **Enter** key. The formula with three external references is entered in the Summary worksheet in the Better World 2016 workbook.

6. In the Better World 2016 workbook, in the Summary worksheet, click cell **B6**. The complete formula is too long to appear in the formula bar of the tiled window. You will expand the formula bar so that it can display the full formula.

7. At the right edge of the formula bar, click the **Expand Formula Bar** button (or press the **Ctrl+Shift+U** keys). The complete formula now is visible in the formula bar, and the Collapse Formula Bar button appears at the right edge of the formula bar, which you can click to return the formula bar to a single line. The formula results in cell B6 show that 3651 tons of paper were collected during Quarter 1 in the three recycling sites—1,311 in Columbia, 895 in Marion, and 1,445 in Richmond. See Figure 6-18.

Figure 6-18   Total paper collections from Columbia, Richmond, and Marion in Quarter 1

Trouble? If 3651 doesn't appear in cell B6 in the Summary worksheet in the Better World 2016 workbook, you might have clicked an incorrect cell for an external reference in the formula. Repeat Steps 1 through 6 to correct the formula.

You'll use the same process to enter the external reference formula for cells C6, D6, and E6, which contain the total tons of paper collected in Quarter 2, Quarter 3, and Quarter 4, respectively. These formulas will calculate the total collection amounts from all three locations.

To create the remaining external reference formulas:

1. In the Better World 2016 workbook, in the Summary worksheet, select cell **C6**, and then type **=** to begin the formula.

2. Click the **Columbia** workbook, click cell **C6** in the Summary worksheet, and then type **+**. The formula in the Better World 2016 workbook includes the external reference to cell C6 in the Summary worksheet in the Columbia workbook.

3. Click the **Richmond** workbook, click cell **C6** in the Summary worksheet, and then type **+**. The formula includes an external reference to cell C6 in the Summary worksheet in the Richmond workbook.

4. Click the **Marion** workbook, click cell **C6** in the Summary worksheet, and then press the **Enter** key. The external reference formula is complete.

5. In the Better World 2016 workbook, in the Summary worksheet, click cell **C6**. Cell C6 displays 3756, the total number of tons of paper collected in Quarter 2 in Columbia, Richmond, and Marion, and the following formula appears in the formula bar:
   =[Columbia.xlsx]Summary!$C$6+[Richmond.xlsx]Summary!$C$6
     +[Marion.xlsx]Summary!$C$6.

   Next, you'll enter the external reference formulas in cells D6 and E6 to add the total number of tons collected in Quarter 3 and Quarter 4.

6. Repeat Steps 1 through 4 to enter the formula from cell **D6** in the Summary worksheet in the Better World 2016 workbook. The formula result displayed in cell D6 is 2764—the total number of tons of paper collected during Quarter 3 in Columbia, Richmond, and Marion.

7. Repeat Steps 1 through 4 to enter the formula from cell **E6** in the Summary worksheet in the Better World 2016 workbook. The formula result displayed in cell E6 is 3648—the total number of tons of paper collected during Quarter 4 in Columbia, Richmond, and Marion.

You need to enter the remaining formulas for the other recyclable items. Rather than creating the rest of the external reference formulas manually, you can copy the formulas in row 6 and paste them in rows 7 through 10. The formulas created using the point-and-click method contain absolute references. Before you copy them to other cells, you need to change them to use mixed references because the rows in the formula need to change.

To edit the external reference formulas to use mixed references:

1. Maximize the Better World 2016 workbook, click the **Ribbon Display Options** button in the title bar, and then click **Show Tabs and Commands** (or press the **Ctrl+F1** keys) to pin the ribbon to show both the tabs and the commands. The other workbooks are still open but are not visible.

2. At the right edge of the formula bar, click the **Collapse Formula Bar** button (or press the **Ctrl+Shift+U** keys) to reduce the formula bar to one line.

Tutorial 6 Managing Multiple Worksheets and Workbooks | Excel   EX 359

3. In the Summary worksheet, double-click cell **B6** to enter Edit mode and display the formula in the cell.

TIP
You can also create the mixed reference by deleting the $ symbol from the row references in the formula.

4. Click in the first absolute reference in the formula, and then press the **F4** key twice to change the absolute reference $B$6 to the mixed reference $B6.

5. Edit the other two absolute references in the formula to be mixed references with absolute column references and relative row references.

6. Press the **Enter** key, and then select cell **B6**. The formula is updated to include mixed references, but the formula results aren't affected. Cell B6 still displays 3,651, which is correct. See Figure 6-19.

Figure 6-19   External reference formula with mixed references

7. Edit the formulas in cells **C6**, **D6**, and **E6** to change the absolute references to the mixed references **$C6**, **$D6**, and **$E6**, respectively. The formulas are updated, but the cells in the range C6:E6 still correctly display 3,756, 2,764, and 3,648, respectively.

With the formulas corrected to include mixed references, you can now copy the external reference formulas in the range B6:E6 to the other rows. Then you'll enter the SUM function to total the values in each row and column.

To copy and paste the external reference formulas:

1. Select the range **B6:E6**, and then drag the fill handle to select the range **B7:E10**. The formulas are copied to the range B7:E10 and the formula results appear in the cells. The Auto Fill Options button appears in the lower-right corner of the selected range, but you do not need to use it.

   Trouble? If all of the values in the range B7:E10 are the same as those in the range B6:E6, you didn't change the absolute cell references to mixed cell references in the formulas in the range B6:E6. Repeat Steps 3 through 7 in the previous set of steps, and then repeat Step 1 in this set of steps.

2. In cell **B11**, enter the SUM function to add the range **B6:B10**. A total of 12,439 tons of recyclable materials were collected in Quarter 1.

3. Copy the formula in cell B11 to the range **C11:E11**. The total recyclable materials collected were 11,401 tons in Quarter 2, 10,713 tons in Quarter 3, and 11,434 tons in Quarter 4.

EX 360 Excel | Tutorial 6 Managing Multiple Worksheets and Workbooks

4. In cell **F6**, enter the SUM function to add the range B6:E6. A total of 13,819 tons of paper were collected at all sites in 2016.

5. Copy the formula in cell F6 to the range **F7:F11**. The total recyclable materials collected in 2016 were 10,626 tons of glass, 13,430 tons of metal, 2,043 tons of Styrofoam, and 6,069 tons of plastic, with a grand total of 45,987 tons collected for the year.

6. Format the range B6:F11 with the **Comma style** and no decimal places.

7. Format the range B10:F10 with a **bottom border**, and then select cell **A1** to deselect the range. See Figure 6-20.

Figure 6-20 Completed summary of collection data

	A	B	C	D	E	F
1	Better World Recycling-Summary Total					
2	Recycling Collection Data in Tons					
3	Fiscal Year - 2016					
4						
5		Quarter 1	Quarter 2	Quarter 3	Quarter 4	Totals
6	Paper	3,651	3,756	2,764	3,648	13,819
7	Glass	3,435	2,634	2,175	2,382	10,626
8	Metal	3,137	3,204	3,867	3,222	13,430
9	Styrofoam	380	477	500	686	2,043
10	Plastic	1,836	1,330	1,407	1,496	6,069
11	Totals	12,439	11,401	10,713	11,434	45,987

Maria is pleased; the regional summary results match her expectations.

INSIGHT

Managing Linked Workbooks

As you work with a linked workbook, you might need to replace a source file or change where you stored the source and destination files. However, replacing or moving a file can affect the linked workbook. Keep in mind the following guidelines to manage your linked workbooks:

- If you rename a source file, the destination workbook won't be able to find it. A dialog box opens, indicating "This workbook contains one or more links that cannot be updated." Click the Continue button to open the workbook with the most recent values, or click the Change Source button in the Edit Links dialog box to specify the new name of that linked source file.
- If you move a source file to a different folder, the link breaks between the destination and source files. Click the Change Source button in the Edit Links dialog box to specify the new location of the linked workbook.
- If you receive a replacement source file, you can swap the original source file with the replacement file. No additional changes are needed.
- If you receive a destination workbook but the source files are not included, Excel will not be able to find the source files, and a dialog box opens with the message "This workbook contains one or more links that cannot be updated." Click the Continue button to open the workbook with the most recent values, or click the Break Link button in the Edit Links dialog box to replace the external references with the existing values.
- If you change the name of a destination file, you can open that renamed version destination file without affecting the source files or the original destination file.

Updating Linked Workbooks

When workbooks are linked, it is important that the data in the destination file accurately reflects the contents of the source file. When data in a source file changes, you want the destination file to reflect those changes. If both the source and destination files are open when you make a change, the destination file is updated automatically. If the destination file is closed when you make a change in a source file, you choose whether to update the link to display the current values, or continue to display the older values from the destination file when you open the destination file.

Updating a Destination Workbook with Source Workbooks Open

When both the destination and source workbooks are open, any changes you make in a source workbook automatically appear in the destination workbook. Maria tells you that Columbia actually collected 100 fewer tons of metal in March than was recorded. After you correct the March value in the Quarter 1 worksheet, the amount in the Summary worksheet of the Columbia workbook and the regional total in the Better World 2016 workbook will also change if both the source and destination files are open.

To update the source workbook with the destination file open:

▶ 1. Make the **Columbia** workbook active, and then go to the **Quarter 1** worksheet. You'll update the total for metal collected in March.

▶ 2. If the ribbon is still collapsed, pin the ribbon so you can see both the tabs and the groups.

3. In cell **D8**, enter **302**. Columbia's collection data is updated.

4. Go to the **Summary** worksheet in the Columbia workbook, and then verify that the total of metal collected in Quarter 1 (cell B8) is 989 tons, the total of recyclable materials collected in Quarter 1 (cell B11) is 3,724 tons, and the total of recyclable materials collected in 2016 (cell F11) is 14,893 tons. See Figure 6-21.

Figure 6-21 Summary worksheet in the Columbia workbook with the revised Quarter 1 data

	A	B	C	D	E	F
1		Better World Recycling-Columbia Total				
2		Recycling Collection Data in Tons				
3	Fiscal Year - 2016					
4						
5		Quarter 1	Quarter 2	Quarter 3	Quarter 4	Totals
6	Paper	1,311	1,230	914	1,126	4,581
7	Glass	891	911	728	770	3,300
8	Metal	989	1,050	1,256	1,179	4,474
9	Styrofoam	97	195	197	287	776
10	Plastic	436	415	457	454	1,762
11	Totals	3,724	3,801	3,552	3,816	14,893

B8 = 'Quarter 1'!E8

data reflects the new value in the Quarter 1 worksheet

5. Make the **Better World 2016** workbook active, and then verify in the Summary worksheet that the total of metal collected in Quarter 1 (cell B8) is 3,037 tons, the total of recyclable materials collected in Quarter 1 (cell B11) is 12,339 tons, and the total of recyclable materials collected in 2016 (cell F11) is 45,887 tons, reflecting the new value you entered in the Columbia workbook. Because both the destination and source files are open, Excel updated the destination file automatically. See Figure 6-22.

Figure 6-22 — Summary worksheet in the Better World 2016 workbook with the revised Quarter 1 data

reflects the new value in the Columbia workbook

	Quarter 1	Quarter 2	Quarter 3	Quarter 4	Totals
Paper	3,651	3,756	2,764	3,648	13,819
Glass	3,435	2,634	2,175	2,382	10,626
Metal	3,037	3,204	3,867	3,222	13,330
Styrofoam	380	477	500	686	2,043
Plastic	1,836	1,330	1,407	1,496	6,069
Totals	12,339	11,401	10,713	11,434	45,887

6. Save the Columbia and Better World 2016 workbooks, and then close the Marion, Richmond, and Better World 2016 workbooks. The Columbia workbook remains open.

Updating a Destination Workbook with Source Workbooks Closed

When you save a workbook that contains external reference formulas, such as the Better World 2016 workbook, Excel stores the most recent results of those formulas in the destination file. Source files, such as the Columbia, Richmond, and Marion workbooks, are often updated while the destination file is closed. In that case, the values in the destination file are not updated at the same time the source files are updated. The next time you open the destination file, the cells containing external reference formulas still display the old values. Therefore, some of the values in the edited source workbooks are different from the values in the destination workbook.

To update the destination workbook with the current data, you must specify that you want the update to occur. As part of the Excel security system that attempts to protect against malicious software, links to other workbooks are not updated without your permission. When you open a workbook with external reference formulas (the destination file), a dialog box appears, notifying you that the workbook contains links to an external source that could be unsafe. You then can choose to update the content, which allows the external reference formulas to function and updates the links in the destination workbook; or, you can choose not to update the links, which lets you continue working with the data you have. The old values in the destination workbook are displayed and the links to the source files have an unknown status.

Maria realizes that the Columbia workbook needs a second correction. In Quarter 4, the total plastic recycled in November was 182 tons, not 202 tons as currently entered in the Columbia workbook. She asks you to decrease the total tons of plastic collected in November by 20. As a result, the totals in the Summary worksheet of the Columbia workbook and the regional total in the Better World 2016 workbook will both decrease by 20. You'll edit the source file, the Columbia workbook, while the destination file is closed.

To update the source workbook with the destination file closed:

1. In the Columbia workbook, go to the **Quarter 4** worksheet.
2. In cell **C10**, enter **182**. The total tons of plastic collected in Quarter 4 decreases to 1,189.
3. Go to the **Summary** worksheet. The total of plastic collected for Quarter 4 (cell E10) is 434 tons, the total of plastic collected for 2016 (cell F10) is 1,742 tons, the total of recyclables collected for Quarter 4 (cell E11) is 3,796 tons, and the total of recyclables collected in 2016 (cell F11) is 14,873 tons. See Figure 6-23.

Figure 6-23 Revised plastic collections for Quarter 4 in the Columbia workbook

	A	B	C	D	E	F
1	Better World Recycling-Columbia Total					
2	Recycling Collection Data in Tons					
3	Fiscal Year - 2016					
4						
5		Quarter 1	Quarter 2	Quarter 3	Quarter 4	Totals
6	Paper	1,311	1,230	914	1,126	4,581
7	Glass	891	911	728	770	3,300
8	Metal	989	1,050	1,256	1,179	4,474
9	Styrofoam	97	195	197	287	776
10	Plastic	436	415	457	434	1,742
11	Totals	3,724	3,801	3,552	3,796	14,873
12						

reflects changes to plastic collected in Quarter 4

4. Save the Columbia workbook, and then close it.

Now you'll open the destination file (the Better World 2016 workbook). The total tons of recycling from the source workbooks won't be updated until you specify that they should. When the destination file is open and the source files are closed, the complete file path is included as part of the external reference formula that appears in the formula bar.

To open and update the destination workbook:

1. Open the **Better World 2016** workbook, and then go to the **Summary** worksheet, if necessary. The value in cell E10 has *not* changed; it is still 1,496. A dialog box appears, indicating that the workbook contains links to one or more external sources that could be unsafe. See Figure 6-24.

Tutorial 6 Managing Multiple Worksheets and Workbooks | Excel   EX 365

Figure 6-24   Dialog box warning of possible unsafe links

[Microsoft Excel dialog box: "This workbook contains links to one or more external sources that could be unsafe. If you trust the links, update them to get the latest data. Otherwise, you can keep working with the data you have." Buttons: Update | Don't Update | Help]

Trouble? If the Message Bar appears below the ribbon with the SECURITY WARNING Automatic update of links has been disabled, click the Enable Content button. The values in the destination workbook are updated. Continue with Step 3.

You want the current values in the source files to appear in the destination workbook.

▸ 2. In the dialog box, click the **Update** button. The values in the destination file are updated. The total amount of plastic collected in Quarter 4, shown in cell E10 of the Better World 2016 workbook, has decreased to 1,476 tons, the total plastic collected for 2016 (cell F10) is 6,049 tons, the total Quarter 4 recyclables (cell E11) is 11,414 tons, and the grand total of all recyclables collected by the company in 2016 (cell F11) decreased to 45,867 tons.

▸ 3. Select cell **E10**, and then look at the complete file path for each external reference in the formula. The full path appears because the source workbooks are closed. Note that the path you see will match the location where you save your workbooks.

▸ 4. Save the workbook.

Managing Links

When workbooks are linked, the Edit Links dialog box provides ways to manage the links. You can review the status of the links and update the data in the files. You can repair **broken links**, which are references to files that have been moved since the link was created. Broken links appear in the dialog box as having an unknown status. You can also open the source file and break the links, which converts all external reference formulas to their most recent values.

After the fiscal year audit is completed and the source workbooks are final, Maria will archive the summary workbook and move the files to an off-site storage location as part of her year-end backup process. You will save a copy of the Better World 2016 workbook and then break the links to the source files in the copy.

To save a copy of the Better World 2016 workbook and open the Edit Links dialog box:

▸ 1. Save the Better World 2016 workbook as **Better World 2016 Audited** in the location specified by your instructor. The Better World 2016 workbook closes, and the Better World 2016 Audited workbook remains open.

▸ 2. On the ribbon, click the **DATA** tab.

▸ 3. In the Connections group, click the **Edit Links** button. The Edit Links dialog box opens. Note that the path you see for source files will match the location where you save your workbooks. See Figure 6-25.

Figure 6-25 Edit Links dialog box

your paths will match the location where you save your workbooks

replaces the links to source files with the current values of the linked cells

updates the destination file with data from the latest saved version of the selected course file

The Edit Links dialog box lists all of the files to which the destination workbook is linked so that you can update, change, open, or remove the links. You can see that the destination workbook—Better World 2016 Audited—has links to the Richmond, Columbia, and Marion workbooks. The dialog box shows the following information about each link:

- **Source**—indicates the file to which the link points. The Better World 2016 Audited workbook contains three links pointing to the Columbia.xlsx, Richmond.xlsx, and Marion.xlsx workbooks.
- **Type**—identifies the type of each source file. In this case, the type is an Excel worksheet, but it could also be a Word document, a PowerPoint presentation, or some other type of file.
- **Update**—specifies the way values are updated from the source file. The letter *A* indicates the link is updated automatically when you open the workbook, or when both the source and destination files are open simultaneously. The letter *M* indicates the link must be updated manually by the user, which is useful when you want to see the older data values before updating to the new data. To manually update the link and see the new data values, click the Update Values button.
- **Status**—shows whether Excel successfully accessed the link and updated the values from the source document (status is OK), or Excel has not attempted to update the links in this session (status is Unknown). The status of the three links in the Better World 2016 Audited workbook is Unknown.

Maria wants you to break the links so that the Better World 2016 Audited workbook contains only the updated values (and is no longer affected by changes in the source files). Then she wants you to save the Better World 2016 Audited workbook for her to archive. This allows Maria to store a "snapshot" of the data at the end of the fiscal year.

TIP

You cannot undo the break link action. To restore the links, you must reenter the external reference formulas.

To convert all external reference formulas to their current values:

1. In the Edit Links dialog box, click the **Break Link** button. A dialog box opens, alerting you that breaking links in the workbook permanently converts formulas and external references to their existing values.
2. Click the **Break Links** button. No links appear in the Edit Links dialog box.
3. Click the **Close** button. The Better World 2016 Audited workbook now contains values instead of formulas with external references.
4. Select cell **B6**. The value 3,651 appears in the cell and the formula bar; the link (the external reference formula) was replaced with the data value. All of the cells in the range B6:E10 contain values rather than external reference formulas.

> **5.** Save the Better World 2016 Audited workbook, and then close it. The Better World 2016 workbook contains external reference formulas, and the Better World 2016 Audited workbook contains current values.

In this session, you worked with multiple worksheets and workbooks, summarizing data and linking workbooks. This ensures that the data in the summary workbook is accurate and remains updated with the latest data in the source files. In the next session, you will create templates and hyperlinks.

Session 6.2 Quick Check

1. What is the external reference to the range B6:F6 in the Grades worksheet in the Grade Book workbook located in the Course folder on drive D?
2. What is a source file?
3. What is a destination file?
4. How are linked workbooks updated when both the destination and source files are open?
5. How are linked workbooks updated when the source file is changed and the destination file is closed?
6. How would you determine to what workbooks a destination file is linked?
7. What are the layouts that you can use to arrange multiple workbooks?
8. When you have broken the links for a cell, what appears in the formula bar when you select that cell?

Session 6.3 Visual Overview:

This Weekly time sheet workbook was created from one of the templates available from Office.com. Microsoft provides many templates that you can download.

A template is a workbook with labels, formats, and formulas already built into it with data removed. In other words, a template includes everything but the variable data.

A template can use any Excel feature, including formatting, formulas, and charts. The template used to create this workbook includes labels, formatting, and formulas.

Variable data is entered in the workbook created from the template. In this workbook, employee data was entered to fill out the weekly time record.

These formulas to calculate the total hours worked were included in the template.

Tibbs Weekly Time Sheet

Better World Recycling

Weekly time record

Employee: Deborah Tibbs
Manager: Maria Guzman
Week ending: 12/10/2016

Employee phone:
Employee email:

Day		Regular Hours	Overtime	Sick	Vacation	Total
Monday	12/4/2016	8.00				
Tuesday	12/5/2016	8.00	2.00			
Wednesday	12/6/2016	8.00				
Thursday	12/7/2016	8.00				
Friday	12/8/2016	8.00	0.50			
Saturday	12/9/2016					
Sunday	12/10/2016					
Total hours		40.00	2.50			
Rate per hour		$8.50	$12.75			
Total pay		$340.00	$31.88			

Link to:
- Existing File or Web Page
- Place in This Document
- Create New Document
- E-mail Address

Tutorial 6 Managing Multiple Worksheets and Workbooks | Excel   EX 369

Templates and Hyperlinks

The Hyperlink button opens the Insert Hyperlink dialog box, which is used to create a hyperlink.

A **hyperlink** is a link in a file, such as a workbook, to information within that file or another file. In this case, the link opens a memo created in Word, which is supporting information for the workbook.

The Insert Hyperlink dialog box provides options to enter the hyperlink text, specify what the hyperlink links to, and set a custom ScreenTip.

This text appears in the cell that has the hyperlink.

Document that will open when the hyperlink is clicked.

Creating a Hyperlink

A hyperlink is a link in a file, such as a workbook, to information within that file or another file. Although hyperlinks are most often found on webpages, they can also be placed in a worksheet and used to quickly jump to a specific cell or range within the active worksheet, another worksheet, or another workbook. Hyperlinks can also be used to jump to other files, such as a Word document or a PowerPoint presentation, or sites on the web.

Inserting a Hyperlink

You can insert a hyperlink directly in a workbook file to link to information in that workbook, another workbook, or a file associated with another application on your computer, a shared file on a network, or a website. Hyperlinks are usually represented by words with colored letters and underlines or images. When you click a hyperlink, the computer switches to the file or portion of the file referenced by the hyperlink.

> **REFERENCE**
>
> *Inserting a Hyperlink*
>
> - Select the text, graphic, or cell in which you want to insert the hyperlink.
> - On the INSERT tab, in the Links group, click the Hyperlink button.
> - To link to a file or webpage, click Existing File or Web Page in the Link to list, and then select the file or webpage from the Look in box.
> - To link to a location in the current workbook, click Place in This Document in the Link to list, and then select the worksheet, cell, or range in the current workbook.
> - To link to a new document, click Create New Document in the Link to list, and then specify the filename and path of the new document.
> - To link to an email address, click E-mail Address in the Link to list, and then enter the email address of the recipient (such as name@example.com) and a subject line for the message.
> - Click the OK button.

Maria wrote a memo summarizing the collection results for Columbia, Marion, and Richmond in 2016. She wants the Better World 2016 workbook to include a link that points to the Recycle Memo Word document. You'll insert the hyperlink to the memo now.

To insert a hyperlink in the Better World 2016 workbook:

1. Open the **Better World 2016** workbook, but don't update the links.
2. Maximize the Better World 2016 worksheet window.
3. Go to the **Documentation** worksheet, and then select cell **A8**. You want to create the hyperlink in this cell.
4. On the ribbon, click the **INSERT** tab.
5. In the Links group, click the **Hyperlink** button. The Insert Hyperlink dialog box opens. You use this dialog box to define the hyperlink.
6. If necessary, click the **Existing File or Web Page** button in the Link to bar, and then click the **Current Folder** button in the Look in area. All the existing files and folders in the current folder are displayed. See Figure 6-26, which shows the Excel6 ▸ Tutorial folder included with your Data Files.

Tutorial 6 Managing Multiple Worksheets and Workbooks | Excel **EX 371**

Figure 6-26 | **Insert Hyperlink dialog box**

Word document to use as the file to link to (you may see additional files)

▶ 7. Click the **Text to display** box, and then type **Click here to read the Executive Memo**. This is the hyperlink text that will appear in cell A8 in the Documentation worksheet.

▶ 8. Click the **Recycle Memo** Word document in the list of files. This is the file you want to open when the hyperlink is clicked.

▶ 9. Click the **OK** button. The hyperlink text entered in cell A8 is underlined and in a blue font, indicating that the text within the cell is a hyperlink. See Figure 6-27.

Figure 6-27 | **Hyperlink to the Recycle Memo Word document**

hyperlink in cell A8

hyperlink won't work if you click text that flows into adjacent cells

You will test the hyperlink that you just created to ensure it works correctly. To use a hyperlink in a worksheet, you must click the text inside the cell that contains the link. If you click white space in the cell or any text that flows into an adjacent cell, the hyperlink does not work.

To test the hyperlink to the Recycle Memo:

1. Point to the text in cell **A8** so that the pointer changes to 👆, and then click the **Click here to read the Executive Memo** hyperlink. The Recycle Memo document opens in Word.

   Trouble? If the hyperlink doesn't work, you might have clicked the text that overflows cell A8. Point to the text within cell A8, and then click the hyperlink.

2. Close the Word document and Word. The Documentation worksheet in the Better World 2016 workbook is active. The hyperlink in cell A8 changed color to indicate that you used the link.

Editing a Hyperlink

TIP

To delete a hyperlink, right-click the hyperlink cell and then click Clear Contents. To delete the hyperlink but keep the text, right-click the hyperlink cell, and then click Remove Hyperlink.

You can modify an existing hyperlink by changing its target file or webpage, modifying the text that is displayed, or changing the ScreenTip for the hyperlink. ScreenTips, which appear whenever you place the pointer over a hyperlink, provide additional information about the target of the link. The default ScreenTip is the folder location and filename of the file you will link to, which isn't very helpful. You can insert a more descriptive ScreenTip when you create a hyperlink or edit an existing hyperlink.

Maria wants you to edit the hyperlink to the memo so that it has a more descriptive ScreenTip.

To edit the hyperlink:

1. In the Documentation worksheet, right-click cell **A8**, and then click **Edit Hyperlink** on the shortcut menu. The Edit Hyperlink dialog box opens; it has the same layout and information as the Insert Hyperlink dialog box.

2. Click the **ScreenTip** button. The Set Hyperlink ScreenTip dialog box opens.

3. In the ScreenTip text box, type **Click to view the Executive Summary for 2016**, and then click the **OK** button.

4. Click the **OK** button to close the Edit Hyperlink dialog box.

5. Point to the text in cell **A8** and confirm that the ScreenTip "Click to view the Executive Summary for 2016" appears just below the cell.

6. Save the Better World 2016 workbook, and then close it.

Using Templates

If you want to create a new workbook that has the same format as an existing workbook, you could save the existing workbook with a new name and replace the values with new data or blank cells. The potential drawback to this method is that you might forget to rename the original file and overwrite data you intended to keep. A better method is to create a template workbook that includes all the text (row and column labels), formatting, and formulas but does not contain any data. The template workbook is a model from which you create new workbooks. When you create a new workbook from a template, an unnamed copy of the template opens. You can then enter data as well as modify the existing content or structure as needed. Any changes or additions you make to the new workbook do not affect the template file; the next time you create a workbook based on the template, the original text, formatting, and formulas will be present.

Tutorial 6 Managing Multiple Worksheets and Workbooks | Excel **EX 373**

PROSKILLS

Teamwork: Using Excel Templates

A team working together will often need to create the same types of workbooks. Rather than each person or group designing a different workbook, each team member should create a workbook from the same template. The completed workbooks will then all have the same structure with identical formatting and formulas. Not only does this ensure consistency and accuracy, it also makes it easier to compile and summarize the results. Templates help teams work better together and avoid misunderstandings.

For example, a large organization may need to collect the same information from several regions. By creating and distributing a workbook template, each region knows what data to track and where to enter it. The template already includes the formulas, so the results are calculated consistently. If you want to review the formulas that are in the worksheet, you can display them using the Show Formula command in the Formula Auditing group on the FORMULAS tab or by pressing the Ctrl+` keys.

The following are just some of the advantages of using a template to create multiple workbooks with the same features:

- Templates save time and ensure consistency in the design and content of workbooks because all labels, formatting, and formulas are entered once.
- Templates ensure accuracy because formulas can be entered and verified once, and then used with confidence in all workbooks.
- Templates standardize the appearance and content of workbooks.
- Templates prevent data from being overwritten when an existing workbook is inadvertently saved with new data rather than saved as a new workbook.

If you are part of a team that needs to create the same type of workbook repeatedly, it's a good idea to use a template to both save time and ensure consistency in the design and content of the workbooks.

Creating a Workbook Based on an Existing Template

The Blank workbook template that you have used to create new, blank workbooks contains no text or formulas, but it includes formatting—General format applied to numbers, Calibri 11-point font, text left-aligned in cells, numbers and formula results right-aligned in cells, column widths set to 8.38 characters, one worksheet inserted in the workbook, and so forth.

Excel has many other templates available. Some are automatically installed on your hard drive when you install Excel. Other templates are available to download from the Office.com site or other sites that you can find by searching the web. These templates provide commonly used worksheet formats, saving you from "reinventing the wheel." Some of the task-specific templates available from the Office.com site include:

- **Family Monthly Budget Planner**—builds projections and actual expenditures for items such as housing, transportation, and insurance
- **Inventory List**—tracks the cost and quantity reorder levels of inventory
- **Team Roster**—organizes a list with each player's name, phone number, email address, and so forth
- **Time sheets**—creates an online time card to track employees' work hours
- **Expense Report**—creates an expense report to track employee expenses for reimbursement

Using a template to create a new workbook lets you focus on the unique content for that workbook.

Excel | Tutorial 6 Managing Multiple Worksheets and Workbooks

> **REFERENCE**
>
> **Creating a Workbook Based on a Template**
>
> - Click the FILE tab, and then click New in the navigation bar.
> - On the New screen, click a template category for the type of workbook you want to create (or type a keyword in the Search for online template box, and then press the Enter key).
> - Click the template you want to create.
> - Save the workbook based on the template with a new filename.

Deborah Tibbs works for Maria as the office receptionist. She uses the Weekly time sheet template to submit her work hours to Maria. You'll download the Weekly time sheet template and enter Deborah's most recent hours.

Note that you need an Internet connection to complete the following set of steps. If you don't have an Internet connection, you should read but not complete the steps involving creating and using the online template.

To create a workbook based on the Weekly time sheet template:

1. On the ribbon, click the **FILE** tab.

2. Click **New** in the navigation bar. The New screen in Backstage view shows the available templates on your computer and template categories on Office.com.

3. Click in the **Search for online templates** box, type **time sheets**, and then press the **Enter** key. All of the available time sheet templates are displayed. See Figure 6-28.

Figure 6-28   New screen with available time sheet templates

- templates found for time sheets (you may see different templates)
- type of template to find
- Weekly time sheet (8 1/2 x 11, portrait)
- available template categories

4. Click **Weekly time sheet (8 1/2 x 11, portrait)**. A preview of a worksheet based on the selected template appears in the center of the screen. If this is not the template you need, you can scroll through the time sheets by clicking the left or right arrow button. See Figure 6-29.

Tutorial 6 Managing Multiple Worksheets and Workbooks | Excel **EX 375**

Figure 6-29 | Weekly time record preview

- Back and Forward buttons appear so you can scroll through the available templates
- preview of the selected template
- button to create a workbook based on this template

5. Click the **Create** button. A new workbook based on the selected template opens. See Figure 6-30.

Figure 6-30 | Workbook created from the Weekly time sheet template

- labels and formatting are already in the workbook
- placeholder text
- cells contain formulas to calculate the total hours per day, though these aren't visible until you enter data
- filename shows this workbook was created from a template

A workbook based on a specific template always displays the name of the template followed by a sequential number. Just as a blank workbook that you open is named Book1, Book2, and so forth, the workbook based on the Weekly time sheet template is named "Weekly time sheet1" in the title bar, not "Weekly time sheet." Any changes or additions to data, formatting, or formulas that you make affect only this workbook and not the template (in this case, the Weekly time sheet template). When you save the workbook, the Save As screen opens so you can save the workbook with a new name and to the location you specify.

Look at the labels and formatting already included in the Weekly time sheet workbook. Some cells have descriptive labels, others are blank so you can enter data in them, and still other cells contain formulas where calculations for total hours worked each day and pay category will be automatically displayed as data is entered. The formulas aren't apparent unless you click in the cell and look at the cell contents in the formula bar, or you enter data and a calculation occurs.

Maria asks you to enter Deborah's data for the previous week in the Weekly time record worksheet based on the Weekly time sheet template.

To enter Deborah's data in the Weekly time sheet1 workbook:

1. In cell **B2**, enter **Better World Recycling** as the company name, and then format the text in **20** point font size.

2. In cell **C4**, enter **Deborah Tibbs** as the employee.

3. In cell **D10**, enter **8** for the regular hours Deborah worked on Monday. Totals appear in cells I10, D17, and I17 because formulas are already entered into these cells. Cell I10 shows the number of hours worked on Monday, cell D17 shows 8 regular hours worked that week, and cell I17 shows the total hours worked that week.

4. In cell **D11**, enter **8** for the regular hours Deborah worked on Tuesday.

5. In cell **E11**, enter **2** for the overtime hours Deborah worked on Tuesday. The totals are updated to 10 hours worked on Tuesday, 16 regular hours worked that week, 2 overtime hours worked that week, and 18 total hours worked that week.

6. Save the workbook as **Tibbs Weekly Time Sheet** in the location specified by your instructor. The Tibbs Weekly Time Sheet workbook, like any other workbook, is saved with the .xlsx file extension. It does not overwrite the template file.

7. Close the workbook.

Each day Deborah works at Better World Recycling, she or Maria can open the Tibbs Weekly Time Sheet workbook and enter the hours Deborah worked that day. The total hours are updated automatically. The template makes it fast and convenient to produce a weekly time sheet that contains all the necessary formulas and is fully formatted.

Creating a Custom Workbook Template

A **custom template** is a workbook template you create that is ready to run with the formulas for all calculations included as well as all formatting and labels. A template can use any Excel feature, including formulas and charts. To create a custom template, you build the workbook with all the necessary labels, formatting, and data, and then you save the workbook as a template. The template includes everything but the variable data. You can also create a template from a chart or chart sheet.

TIP

You can apply a fill color to cells in which users enter data to differentiate them from other cells in the worksheet.

Before you create a template from an existing workbook, you should make sure that all of the formulas work as intended, the numbers and text are entered correctly, and the worksheet is formatted appropriately. You should also remove any values and text that will change in each workbook created from the custom template. Be careful not to delete the formulas. When you are sure the workbook is complete and accurate, you save it as an Excel template file. You can store template files in any folder, but custom template files stored in the Templates folder are available on the New screen in Backstage view.

REFERENCE

Creating a Custom Template

- Prepare the workbook—enter values, text, and formulas as needed; apply formatting; and replace data values with zeros or blank cells.
- On the ribbon, click the FILE tab, and then click Save As in the navigation bar.
- Click the Browse button to open the Save As dialog box.
- In the File name box, enter the template name.
- Click the Save as type button, and then click Excel Template.
- If you don't want to save the template in the Custom Office Templates folder, select another folder in which to save the template file.
- Click the Save button.

or

- Create the chart you want to use for the template.
- Right-click the chart, and then click Save as Template.
- In the Save Chart Template dialog box, enter a filename, then select a folder in which to save the template file if you don't want to store it in the Charts subfolder of the Templates folder.
- Click the Save button.

The three collection workbooks for 2016 have the same format. Maria wants to use this workbook format for data collection and analysis for next year. She asks you to create a template from one of the recycling center workbooks. You'll use the Columbia workbook to build the custom template.

To prepare a custom template from the Columbia workbook:

1. Make sure that the latest version of the **Columbia** workbook is open.

2. Group the **Quarter 1** through **Quarter 4** worksheets. The worksheet group includes the four quarterly worksheets but not the Summary and Documentation worksheets.

3. Select the range **B6:D10**. This range includes the specific recycling data for each recycling site. You want to delete these values.

4. Right-click the selected range, and then click **Clear Contents** on the shortcut menu. The data values are cleared from the selected range in each of the quarterly worksheets, but the formulas and formatting remain intact. The cleared cells are blank. The ranges E6:E11 and B11:D11 display dashes, representing zeros, where there are formulas.

5. Change the fill color of the selected range to the standard **Orange** color. The orange fill color indicates where users should enter data for the tons of material collected in the quarterly worksheets.

6. In cell **A1**, enter **Better World Recycling**.

7. In cell **B3**, enter **[Site Name Here]**, and then merge and center the range **B3:C3**.

8. Go to the **Summary** worksheet. The quarterly worksheets are ungrouped, and dashes, representing zeros, appear in the cells in the ranges B6:F11, which contain formulas.

9. In cell **A1**, enter **Better World Recycling**. This text will remind users to enter the correct site name.

10. In cell **B3**, enter **[Site Name Here]**, and then merge and center **B3:C3**.

11. In cell **A3**, enter **[Enter Fiscal Year - yyyy]**. This text will remind users to enter the year.

12. Group the **Summary** through **Quarter 4** worksheets, and then increase the width of column A so you can see the entire contents of cell A3. See Figure 6-31.

Figure 6-31   **Worksheet modified to be used as the basis of a custom template**

text reminds users to enter data in this cell

range B6:F11 contains formulas and formatting but no values

13. Go to the **Documentation** worksheet, and then delete your name and the date from the range B3:B4.

14. In cell **A6**, enter **To compile the recycling collection data for:**.

15. In cell **B6**, enter **[Site Name Here]**, and then select cell **A1**. The Documentation worksheet is updated to reflect the purpose of the workbook.

    By default, Excel looks for template files in the Templates folder. This location opens when you save a workbook as a template and is where custom templates are often stored. However, you can change in which folder a template is saved. All template files have the .xltx file extension. This extension differentiates template files from workbook files, which have the .xlsx file extension. After you have saved a workbook in a template format, you can make the template accessible to other users.

    The Columbia workbook no longer contains any specific data, but the formulas and formatting will still be in effect when new data is entered. Maria asks you to save this workbook as a template.

Tutorial 6 Managing Multiple Worksheets and Workbooks | Excel   EX 379

To save the Columbia workbook as a template:

1. On the ribbon, click the **FILE** tab to open Backstage view, and then in the navigation bar, click **Save As**. The Save As screen appears.

2. Select the location where you are saving the files for this tutorial. If you are saving files to your hard drive, select **Computer**, and then click the **Browse** button. The Save As dialog box opens.

   Trouble? If you are saving your files in your SkyDrive, select **SkyDrive**, click **Sign In** to sign in to your account if necessary, and then follow the instructions for saving a document in SkyDrive.

3. In the File name box, type **Better World Recycling Template** as the template name.

4. Click the **Save as type** button, and then click **Excel Template**. The save location changes to the Custom Office Templates folder on your computer. You want to save the template in the same location as the other files you created in this tutorial.

5. Navigate to the location where you are storing the files you create in this tutorial.

6. Click the **Save** button. The Better World Recycling Template is saved in the location you specified.

7. Close the Better World Recycling Template workbook template.

> Make sure you change the save location so you can easily find and use the template file later in the next set of steps.

Maria will use the Better World Recycling Template file to create the workbooks to track next year's collections for each site, and then distribute the workbooks to each site manager. By basing these new workbooks on the template file, Maria has a standard workbook with identical formatting and formulas for each manager to use. She also avoids the risk of accidentally changing the workbook containing the 2016 data when preparing for 2017.

INSIGHT

Copying Styles from One Template to Another

Consistency is a hallmark of professional documents. If you have already created a template with a particular look, you can easily copy the styles from that template into a new template. This is much faster and more accurate than trying to recreate the same look by performing all of the steps you used originally. Copying styles from template to template guarantees uniformity. To copy styles from one template to another:

1. Open the template with the styles you want to copy.
2. Open the workbook or template in which you want to place the copied styles.
3. On the HOME tab, in the Styles group, click the Cell Styles button, and then click Merge Styles. The Merge Styles dialog box opens, listing the currently open workbooks and templates.
4. Select the workbook or template with the styles you want to copy, and then click the OK button to copy those styles into the current workbook or template.
5. If a dialog box opens, asking if you want to "Merge Styles that have the same names?", click the YES button.
6. Save the workbook with the new styles as the Excel Template file type.

Creating a New Workbook from a Template

A template file has special properties that allow you to open it, make changes, and save it in a new location. Only the data must be entered because the formulas are already in the template file. The original template file is not changed by this process. After you have saved a template, you can access the template from the New screen in Backstage view or in the location you saved it.

Maria wants all Better World Recycling locations to collect data in the same format and submit the workbooks to the central office for analysis. She wants you to create a workbook for fiscal year 2017 based on the Better World Recycling Template file. You will enter Columbia as the site name where indicated on all of the worksheets, and then enter test data for January.

TIP

To create a copy of workbook based on a template stored in the Custom Office Templates folder, click the FILE tab, click New in the navigation bar, click PERSONAL below the Search for online templates box, and then click the template.

To create a new workbook based on the Better World Recycling Template file:

1. On the taskbar, click the **File Explorer** button. The Libraries window opens.

2. Navigate to the location where you stored the template file.

3. Double-click the **Better World Recycling Template** file. A new workbook opens named "Better World Recycling Template1" to indicate this is the first copy of the Better World Recycling workbook created during the current Excel session.

4. Go to the **Summary** worksheet, enter **Columbia Total** in cell B3, and then enter **Fiscal Year - 2017** in cell A3.

5. Group the **Quarter 1** through **Quarter 4** worksheets, and then in cell **B3**, enter **Columbia** as the site name in the Site Name Here box.

6. Go to the **Documentation** worksheet to ungroup the worksheets.

7. In cell **B6**, enter **Columbia**.

8. Go to the **Quarter 1** worksheet. The text "Fiscal Year - 2017" appears in cell A4.

9. Enter the following test data in the range **B6:B10**, which has the orange fill color:

    cell B6: **150**

    cell B7: **50**

    cell B8: **123**

    cell B9: **45**

    cell B10: **23**

10. Review the totals in the range E6:E11 (the cells that contain formulas to sum each column). See Figure 6-32.

Tutorial 6 Managing Multiple Worksheets and Workbooks | Excel **EX 381**

| Figure 6-32 | New workbook based on the Better World Recycling Template file |

data you entered — range B6:B10 with values: Paper 150, Glass 50, Metal 123, Styrofoam 45, Plastic 23

formula in cell B11: =SUM(B6:B10)

Worksheet contents:
- A1: Better World Recycling
- A2: Recycling Collection Data in Tons
- A3: Quarter 1 C3: Columbia
- A4: Fiscal Year - 2017
- Row 5 headers: January, February, March, Totals
- Row 6: Paper 150 - - 150
- Row 7: Glass 50 - - 50
- Row 8: Metal 123 - - 123
- Row 9: Styrofoam 45 - - 45
- Row 10: Plastic 23 - - 23
- Row 11: Totals 391 - - 391

formulas in the workbook add the row and column totals

Sheet tabs: Documentation | Summary | **Quarter 1** | Quarter 2 | Quarter 3 | Quarter 4

READY

▶ 11. Go to the **Summary** worksheet. Totals appear in the ranges B6:B11 and F6:F11 as a result of the formulas in this worksheet. See Figure 6-33.

| Figure 6-33 | Summary worksheet with test data |

Title bar: Better World Recycling Template1 - Excel

filename shows this is the first copy of the template

Summary worksheet contents:
- A1: Better World Recycling
- A2: Recycling Collection Data in Tons
- A3: Fiscal Year 2017 C3: Columbia
- Row 5 headers: Quarter 1, Quarter 2, Quarter 3, Quarter 4, Totals
- Row 6: Paper 150 - - - 150
- Row 7: Glass 50 - - - 50
- Row 8: Metal 123 - - - 123
- Row 9: Styrofoam 45 - - - 45
- Row 10: Plastic 23 - - - 23
- Row 11: Totals 391 - - - 391

formulas show the new totals

▶ 12. Save the workbook as **Columbia 2017** in the location specified by your instructor. The copy of the template is saved as a workbook with the .xlsx file extension. The original template file is not changed.

You'll add data to the Quarter 2, Quarter 3, and Quarter 4 worksheets to verify that the Summary worksheet is correctly adding numbers from the four worksheets.

To test the Columbia 2017 workbook:

1. In the Columbia 2017 workbook, group the **Quarter 2**, **Quarter 3**, and **Quarter 4** worksheets. You did not include Quarter 1 in this group because you already entered test data in this worksheet.
2. In cell **C6**, enter **120**, and then in cell **D8**, enter **150**.
3. Go to the **Summary** worksheet. The total in cell F6 is 510 and the total in cell F8 is 573. The formulas in the Summary worksheet correctly add values from all the quarterly worksheets. The template workbook is functioning as intended.
4. Save the workbook, and then close it.

The templates you created will ensure that all recycling centers enter data consistently, making it simpler for Maria to add the total number of tons recycled by item and time period for Better World Recycling.

Session 6.3 Quick Check

1. How do you insert a hyperlink into a worksheet cell?
2. Why would you insert a hyperlink in a worksheet?
3. What is a template?
4. What is a custom template?
5. What is one advantage of using a custom template rather than simply using the original workbook file to create a new workbook?
6. What are some examples of task-specific templates available from the Office.com site?
7. How do you save a workbook as a template?
8. How do you create a workbook based on a template that is not saved in the Custom Office Templates folder?

Review Assignments

Data Files needed for the Review Assignments: Illinois.xlsx, Paris Memo.docx, BW.xlsx, Columbia KS.xlsx, Marion IA.xlsx, Richmond IN.xlsx

Based on its success in Columbia, Richmond, and Marion, Better World Recycling expanded to Paris, Illinois. The new site opened on January 1, 2016. Willa Jaworska, the manager of the Paris site, collected the center's recycling data in a workbook provided by Maria Guzman at the central office. Before Willa can send the completed workbook to Maria for the year-end reporting, she needs to summarize the results and format the worksheets. Complete the following:

1. Open the **Illinois** workbook located in the Excel6 ▸ Review folder included with your Data Files. Save the workbook as **Paris IL** in the location specified by your instructor.
2. In the Documentation worksheet, enter your name and the date, and then review the worksheets in the workbook.
3. Create a worksheet group that contains the Quarter 1 through Quarter 4 worksheets.
4. In the worksheet group, enter formulas in the range B11:D11 to total each column, and then enter formulas in the range E6:E11 to total each row.
5. Format the quarterly worksheets as specified below:
   a. In cell E5 and cell A11, enter **Totals**.
   b. In the range A2:A3;A6:A11;B5:E5, bold the text.
   c. Merge and center the range A1:E1 and the range A2:E2.
   d. In the range B5:E5, center the text.
   e. Add a bottom border to the range B5:E5 and the range B10:E10.
   f. Format the range B6:E11 with the Comma style and no decimal places.
6. Ungroup the worksheets, make a copy of the Quarter 1 worksheet, rename it as **Summary**, and then place it after the Documentation worksheet.
7. In the Summary worksheet, make the following changes:
   a. In cell A1, change the heading to **Better World Recycling - Paris Total**.
   b. Change cell A3 to **Fiscal Year - 2016**.
   c. Insert a column between columns B and C.
   d. In the range B5:E5, change the headings to **Quarter 1**, **Quarter 2**, **Quarter 3**, and **Quarter 4**, respectively.
   e. In the range B5:F5, center the text.
   f. Clear the data from the range B6:F11.
8. Complete the formulas in the Summary worksheet using the following steps. Remember to use the Fill Without Formatting so that you can keep the bottom border on the range B10:F10.
   a. Create formulas referencing cells in other worksheets to collect the quarterly totals for the recyclable products in the range B6:E10 in your Summary worksheet.
   b. Create 3-D cell references in the range F6:F10 to calculate totals for each type of recyclable product.
   c. Total the data in columns B through F using the SUM function.
9. The March collection total for metal should have been **164**. Make that correction, and then verify that the total metal collected in Quarter 1 in the Summary worksheet has changed to 384 tons, the total recyclables collected in Quarter 1 has changed to 2,065 tons, and the total metal collected in 2016 has changed to 2,111 tons.
10. Group the Quarter 1 through Quarter 4 worksheets, and then enter a formula in cell A4 to reference cell A3 in the Summary worksheet.
11. In cell A8 of the Documentation worksheet, insert a hyperlink pointing to the **Paris Memo** located in the Tutorial6 ▸ Review folder included with your Data Files. Make sure the text to display is **Click here to read Paris Executive Memo**.

12. Edit the hyperlink to use the ScreenTip **Paris Site Summary for 2016**.
13. Save the Paris IL workbook.
14. Open the **BW** workbook located in the Excel6 ▸ Review folder included with your Data Files. Save the workbook as **BW Totals** in the location specified by your instructor. In the Documentation worksheet enter your name and the date. Open the **Columbia KS**, **Marion IA**, and **Richmond IN** workbooks located in the Excel6 ▸ Review folder included with your Data Files.
15. In each workbook, make the maximum amount of data from the Summary worksheet viewable, make the BW Totals the active worksheet, and then tile the workbooks.
16. In the Summary worksheet, enter external reference formulas to create a set of linked workbooks to summarize the totals for Columbia KS, Marion IA, Paris IL, and Richmond IN, in the BW Totals workbook. Format the Summary worksheet in the BW Totals workbook making sure that the numbers are readable and the range B10:F10 has a bottom border. Save the BW totals workbook. Close the Columbia KS, Marion IA, and Richmond IN workbooks.
17. In the BW Totals workbook, break the links. Select some cells and notice that the formulas have been replaced with the values. Save the workbook as **BW Totals Audited**.
18. Prepare the Summary worksheet for printing. Display the name of the workbook and the name of the worksheet on separate lines in the right section of the header. Display your name and the date on separate lines in the right section of the footer. Save and close the BW Totals Audited workbook.
19. Save the Paris IL workbook as an Excel template with the filename **Paris IL Template** in the location specified by your instructor.
20. Create a new workbook based on the Paris IL Template. Save the workbook as **Paris IL 2017** in the location specified by your instructor. In the Documentation worksheet, enter your name and the date.
21. In the Summary worksheet, enter **2017** in cell A3. In the Quarter 1 worksheet, enter **1000** in each cell in the range B6:D10. In the Quarter 2 worksheet, enter **2000** in each cell in the range B6:D10. Confirm that the values entered in this step are correctly totaled in the Summary worksheet.
22. Save the Paris IL 2017 workbook, and then close it.

Case Problem 1

APPLY

Data File needed for this Case Problem: Cheese.xlsx

Cheese Plus Pizzeria Cheese Plus Pizzeria has three locations in Great Bend, Kansas—Downtown, East Side, and West Side. Mitch Samuels manages the three pizzerias. He uses Excel to summarize sales data from each location. He has compiled the year's data for each location in a workbook. He asks you to total the sales by type of service and location for each quarter, and then format each worksheet. Mitch also needs you to calculate sales for all of the locations and types of service. Complete the following:

1. Open the **Cheese** workbook located in the Excel6 ▸ Case1 folder included with your Data Files. Save the document as **Cheese Plus** in the location specified by your instructor.
2. In the Documentation worksheet, enter your name and the date.
3. Group the Downtown, East Side, and West Side worksheets.
4. In the grouped worksheets, calculate the quarterly totals in the range B7:E7 and the types of service totals in the range F4:F7.
5. Improve the look of the quarterly worksheets using the formatting of your choice. Ungroup the worksheets.
6. Place a copy of one of the location worksheets between the Documentation and Downtown worksheets, and then rename the new worksheet as **Summary Sales**.
7. Delete the values in the range B4:E6, and then change the label in cell A2 to **Summary Sales**.

8. In the range B4:E6, enter formulas that add the sales in the corresponding cells of the four quarterly worksheets. Use 3-D references to calculate the totals for each product group and location.
9. Set up the Summary Sales and the three location worksheets for printing. Each worksheet should be centered horizontally, fit on one page, display the name of the worksheet centered in the header, and display your name and the date on separate lines in the right section of the footer.
10. Save the Cheese Plus workbook, and then remove the sales data, but not the formulas, from each of the location worksheets.
11. Go to the Documentation worksheet, and then save the workbook as an Excel template with the name **Cheese Plus Template** in the location specified by your instructor.
12. Create a new workbook based on the Cheese Plus Template file. Save the workbook as **Cheese Plus 2016** in the location specified by your instructor.
13. In all three location worksheets, in the range B4:E6, enter **10**. Verify that the formulas in each worksheet summarize the data accurately.
14. Save and close the workbook.

Case Problem 2

Data Files needed for this Case Problem: Eastern.xlsx, Internet.xlsx, Western.xlsx, Summary.xlsx

Sweet Dreams Bakery Sweet Dreams Bakery opened its first retail location on June 1, 2000 in Jerome, Idaho, on the eastern side of town, with a dream and some great family dessert recipes. It opened a location on the western side of town three years later. In the past year, the bakery has developed a presence on the Internet. Each location tracks its sales by major categories—cupcakes, tarts, cookies, and pies. James Ray, the bakery manager, has asked the three locations to provide sales data for the past year. That data will be used at the next meeting of the senior managers to determine whether the bakery should expand to a fourth location. To analyze sales and service at each division, James wants you to prepare a report showing the sales of bakery items by quarter and location. Complete the following:

1. Open the **Eastern** workbook located in the Excel6 ▸ Case2 folder included with your Data Files, and then save the document as **Sweet Dreams Eastern** in the location specified by your instructor.
2. In the Documentation worksheet, enter your name and the date.
3. In the Eastern Sales worksheet, calculate the totals for each type of product in the range B8:E8, and the total for each quarter in the range F4:F8. Improve the look of the worksheet by using the formatting of your choice including a bottom underline in the range A7:F7.
4. Repeat Steps 1 through 3 for the **Internet** and **Western** workbooks, naming them **Sweet Dreams Internet** and **Sweet Dreams Western**, respectively.
5. Open the **Summary** workbook located in the Excel6 ▸ Case2 folder included with your Data Files, and then save the workbook as **Sweet Dreams Summary** in the location specified by your instructor.
6. In the Documentation worksheet, enter your name and the date.
7. Rename Sheet1 as **Summary**. In cell A2, enter **Summary Sales** as the new label.
8. **Troubleshoot** 8. The quarterly totals in the Sweet Dreams Summary worksheet are not displaying the correct results. Make any necessary corrections to the formulas so that they add the correct cells from the Sweet Dreams Eastern, Sweet Dreams Western, and Sweet Dreams Internet workbooks.
9. Insert formulas to calculate the totals for the range B4:E7.
10. **Troubleshoot** 10. The Documentation worksheet in the Sweet Dreams Summary workbook includes hyperlinks in the range A10:A12 for each region's corresponding workbook (Sweet Dreams Eastern, Sweet Dreams Internet, and Sweet Dreams Western located in the Excel6 ▸ Case2 folder). The hyperlink descriptions and source files are inconsistent. Check the hyperlinks and correct any links that have different descriptions and source files.
11. Add appropriate text for the ScreenTip to each hyperlink. Test each hyperlink.

12. Prepare each workbook for printing. For all worksheets except the Documentation worksheet, display the name of the workbook and the name of the worksheet on separate lines in the right section of the header and display your name and the date on separate lines in the right section of the footer.
13. Save and close all of the workbooks.

Case Problem 3

Data File needed for this Case Problem: Clinic.xlsx

C & M Veterinary Clinic C & M Veterinary Clinic has been treating small and medium-sized animals in the Marlow, Oklahoma, area for more than 10 years. The staff veterinarians perform all checkups and surgeries, and the staff technician handles all other visits. With the population explosion in the area, the clinic's patient list has increased beyond the current staff's capabilities. Bessie Neal, the manager of the clinic, has been tracking the clinic's activity by month for the past year. Before meeting with the clinic's veterinarians to discuss adding staff or facilities, she wants you to compile the data she has collected and create some preliminary charts. Complete the following:

1. Open the **Clinic** workbook located in the Excel6 ▸ Case3 folder included with your Data Files, and then save the workbook as **Vet Clinic** in the location specified by your instructor.
2. In the Documentation worksheet, enter your name and the date.
3. Group the 12 monthly worksheets to ensure consistency in headings and for ease in entering formulas. Enter the heading **Totals** in cells A11 and E4. For each month (January through December), enter formulas to calculate the total for each type of visit (the range B11:D11) and the total for each type of animal (the range E5:E11).
4. Improve the formatting of the monthly worksheets using the formatting of your choice. Make sure that you have included a lower border in the ranges A4:E4 and A10:E10. Ungroup the worksheets.
5. In the Service Analysis by Month worksheet, enter formulas with worksheet references in the range B5:B16. (=January!B11 through =December!B11) for the total checkup appointments for each month. Copy these formulas to the range C5:C16 (Surgery) and the range D5:D16 (Technician).
6. In cells A17 and E4, enter the label **Total**. Enter formulas to add the total by type of appointment (the range B17:E17) and total appointments each month (the range E5:E17). Bold the ranges A4:A17 and B4:E4. Center the range A4:E4. Place a bottom border in the ranges A4:E4 and A16:E16.
7. Create a bar or column chart to compare the type of service by month (the range A4:D16). Include an appropriate chart title and a legend. Make any formatting changes to the chart that you feel necessary to develop an attractive and effective chart. Position the chart below the data.
8. In the Service Analysis by Animal worksheet, create 3-D cell references to total the appointment type for each animal for each month of the year. Formulas for Small Dog would be Checkup =SUM(January:December!B5), Surgery =SUM(January:December!C5), and Technician =SUM(January:December!D5). These formulas can be copied down through all animal types (the range B5:D10).
9. In cells A11 and E4, enter the label **Total**. Enter formulas to add the total by type of appointment (the range B11:D11) and the total by type of animal (the range E5:E11). Bold the ranges A4:A11 and B4:E4. Center the range A4:E4. Place a bottom border in the ranges A4:E4 and A10:E10.
10. Create a pie chart based on the annual total for each type of animal. Include an appropriate chart title and a legend. Make any formatting changes to the chart that you feel necessary. Position the pie chart below the data in the Service Analysis by Animal worksheet.
11. Group all worksheets except Documentation. Prepare the workbook for printing with the name of the workbook and the name of the worksheet on separate lines in the right section of the header. Display your name and the date on separate lines in the right section of the footer.
12. Save and close the workbook.

Tutorial 6 Managing Multiple Worksheets and Workbooks | Excel **EX 387**

Case Problem 4

Data Files needed for this Case Problem: Midwest.xlsx, Northeast.xlsx, Southeast.xlsx, Ice Summary.xlsx, New Midwest.xlsx, Ice Template.xltx

Cubed Ice Sales Cubed Ice Sales manufactures and distributes ice products east of the Mississippi River. Located in Lancaster, Pennsylvania, it claims to make "everything ice," including ice cubes, ice blocks, and dry ice to name a few of its products. The chief financial analyst, Joni Snapp, asks you to prepare the annual sales and bonus summary based on workbooks from the Midwest, Northeast, and Southeast regions. In December, each salesperson establishes his or her monthly target sales and negotiates a bonus percentage for any sales over that amount. Each region submits a workbook that contains a worksheet for each salesperson in that region. The salesperson's worksheet contains his or her sales by month, monthly target sales, and bonus by percentage. Joni wants you to calculate the bonus for each month for each salesperson using the data he or she provided. She also wants you to summarize each workbook, reporting the quarterly gross sales, bonus sales, and bonus amount. After you have added this information to each workbook, Joni wants you to consolidate the information from the three regional workbooks into a single workbook. Complete the following:

1. Open the **Midwest** workbook located in the Excel6 ► Case4 folder included with your Data Files, and then save the workbook as **Cubed Ice Midwest** in the location specified by your instructor.
2. In the Documentation worksheet, enter your name and the date.
3. Repeat Steps 1 and 2, opening the **Northeast** and **Southeast** workbooks, and saving them as **Cubed Ice Northeast** and **Cubed Ice Southeast**, respectively.
4. Complete the salesperson worksheets in each region's workbook by doing the following:
   a. Group the Salesperson worksheets.
   b. Calculate the Bonus Sales for each month using the formula Gross Sales – Target. (A bonus will be paid only on sales over this amount.) If the salesperson did not sell more than the target, he or she receives no bonus. (*Hint*: Use an IF statement and absolute cell references.)
   c. Calculate the Bonus Amount using the formula Bonus Sales * Bonus Rate. (*Hint*: Remember to use absolute cell references.)
   d. Enter **Total** in cell A16. Total the Gross Sales, Bonus Sales, and Bonus Amount.
   e. Bold the ranges A4:A16 and B3:D3. Wrap the text and center the range B3:D3. Display all numbers with a comma and no decimal places. Display the total row values (the range B16:D16) with a dollar sign.
   f. Ungroup the worksheets.
5. In each of the regional workbooks, do the following:
   a. Make a copy of the first salesperson's worksheet. Rename it **Summary**, and then place it after the Documentation worksheet.
   b. Change the subheading (Salesperson name) to indicate that this is a summary worksheet. Clear the Gross Sales, Bonus Sales, and Bonus amounts, leaving the formulas for the totals.
   c. Clear the headings and data in the range A19:B20.
   d. Create 3-D reference formulas to calculate the totals by month for Gross Sales, Bonus Sales, and Bonus.
   e. Group all worksheets except the Documentation worksheet. Prepare the workbook for printing with the name of the workbook and the name of the worksheet on separate lines in the right section of the header. Display your name and the date on separate lines in the right section of the footer.
   f. Ungroup the worksheets and save the workbook.
6. Open the **Ice Summary** workbook located in the Excel6 ► Case4 folder included with your Data Files, and then save the workbook as **Cubed Ice Summary** in the location specified by your instructor.
7. Make sure all four of the Cubed Ice Workbooks are open and have the Summary worksheet as the active sheet.

8. Enter external reference formulas to create a set of linked workbooks to summarize Gross Sales, Bonus Sales, and Bonus Amount.

9. Enter **Total** in cell A16. Total the Gross Sales, Bonus Sales, and Bonus Amount. Bold the ranges A4:A16 and B3:D3. Wrap the text and center the range B3:D3. Display all numbers with a comma and no decimal places. Display the total row values (the range B16:D16) with a dollar sign.

10. Prepare the Summary worksheet for printing with the name of the workbook and the name of the worksheet on separate lines in the right section of the header. Display your name and the date on separate lines in the right section of the footer.

11. Save the Summary workbook.

Explore 12. The office manager for the Midwest Cubed Ice location found a newer workbook for that location's sales and commissions, and has submitted it to you. Close the Cubed Ice Midwest workbook that you have been working with, open the **New Midwest** workbook located in the Excel6 ▸ Case4 folder included with your Data Files, and then save the workbook as **New Midwest 2016** in the location specified by your instructor. Use Update Links to update the totals on the Summary worksheet in the Cubed Ice Summary workbook. The Totals before the update are Gross Sales $5,155,415; Bonus Sales $2,502,265; and Bonus Amount $125,133. The totals after the update are Gross Sales $5,155,415; Bonus Sales $2,502,265; and Bonus Amount $209,478.

13. Save and close all of the open workbooks for Cubed Ice.

Explore 14. Modify the template named **Ice Template** located in the Excel6 ▸ Case4 folder included with your Data Files. Make the following changes to the template, and then save the modified template as **Ice Template Revised**:

   a. Change the company name to **Ice Cubed**.

   b. Change the color of the company name to Dark Green.

15. Create a new workbook from the Ice Template Revised template. In the Documentation worksheet, enter your name and date.

16. Enter **10,000** for each month's sales, **1** for Bonus Rate, and **5000** for Target Sales. Verify that the formulas are working correctly.

17. Save the workbook as **Cubed Ice Test** in a location specified by your instructor, and then close it.

TUTORIAL 7

Developing an Excel Application
Creating a Receipt

OBJECTIVES

Session 7.1
- Create an application
- Create, edit, and delete defined names for cells and ranges
- Paste a list of defined names as documentation
- Use defined names in formulas
- Add defined names to existing formulas

Session 7.2
- Create validation rules for data entry
- Protect the contents of worksheets and workbooks
- Add, edit, and delete comments

Session 7.3
- Learn about macro viruses and Excel security features
- Add the DEVELOPER tab to the ribbon
- Create and run a macro
- Edit a macro using the Visual Basic Editor
- Assign a macro to a keyboard shortcut and a button
- Save and open a workbook in macro-enabled format

Case | Youth Soccer League

Sharon Hale, business manager for the Youth Soccer League in Oak Hill, West Virginia, is automating several processes for the league's business office. Each spring, the league mails a brochure to parents in the elementary schools in the area with information about the soccer league and a registration form. Then, parents complete the registration form and mail it in with their payment. Sharon wants to automate the process of creating the receipt, which will include capturing the data, calculating the charges, and printing a receipt. She also wants the process to collect the data for soccer clothing that registered students will require (soccer shirts and socks).

Many of these tasks can be accomplished in Excel. But without validating data entry, protecting cells with formulas from accidental deletion, and reducing repetitious keystrokes and mouse clicks, Sharon realizes too many opportunities for errors exist. In addition, as a nonprofit organization, the league relies on numerous volunteers who have varying degrees of computer experience and skill. To accommodate these varying skill levels and reduce potential errors, Sharon wants to create a custom interface for this project that does not rely exclusively on the ribbon, galleries, and so forth. You will help Sharon create a unique Excel application that can resolve these issues and help ensure accurate data entry.

STARTING DATA FILES

Excel7 → Tutorial
Soccer.xlsx

Review
TBall.xlsx

Case1
Study.xlsx

Case2
Cloggers.xlsm

Case3
Music.xlsx

Case4
(none)

Microsoft product screenshots used with permission from Microsoft Corporation.

Excel | Tutorial 7 Developing an Excel Application

Session 7.1 Visual Overview:

The Name box displays the cell reference or the defined name of the selected cell.

You can make the Name box longer so you can see the complete defined names by dragging its sizing handle.

An **Excel application** is a spreadsheet written or tailored to meet specific needs. It typically includes reports and charts, a data entry area, a custom interface, as well as instructions and documentation.

Click the Name box arrow to display a list of all of the defined names in the workbook.

An application includes an input area to enter and edit data. You can set what types of values can be entered and where the user can enter data.

© 2014 Cengage Learning

Tutorial 7 Developing an Excel Application | Excel   EX 391

Excel Application and Defined Names

A **defined name** (often called a **range name** is a word or string of characters assigned to a cell or range. The defined name Parent is assigned to cell B27.

The Defined Names group on the FORMULAS tab contains buttons to create, edit, delete, and manage defined names.

If a formula is too long to display in the formula bar, you can expand the formula bar so that the entire formula is visible.

Youth Soccer League
777 Main Street
Oak Hill, WV 25901

		Registration Date	12/1/2016
Parent	James Smith	Player Name	Sandy
Address	123 Main Street	Age Group	U5
City State Zip	Oak Hill, WV 25901	Shirt Size	SM
Telephone	304-555-1111	Sock Size	XSH

=Parent
=Address
=City_State_Zip
=Telephone

Season Fee		75
Discount Amount		5
Total	$	70

Defined names make entering formulas faster and make the formulas easier to understand.

An application often includes an area with formulas, labels, and so forth to generate output, such as a report or chart, that is based on the input data. Users cannot enter data into the output area.

You can click the Expand/Collapse Formula Bar button to expand or collapse the formula bar.

Planning an Excel Application

An Excel application is a spreadsheet written or tailored to meet specific needs, such as creating a receipt for Youth Soccer League registrations. Planning an Excel application includes designing how the worksheet(s) will be organized. You can include different areas for each function, depending on the complexity of the project. For example, an application often includes separate areas to:

- Enter and edit data (setting where and what types of data can be entered).
- Store data after it has been entered.
- Use formulas to manipulate and perform calculations on data.
- Display outputs, such as reports and charts.

Excel applications can be set up to help users understand how they will interact with the project. For example, you can have separate areas for inputting data and displaying outputs. You can create special buttons for performing specific tasks. You can also change the entire Excel interface by adding custom menus, toolbars, and commands.

An application often includes information about the workbook, such as its purpose, author, and date developed, in a Documentation worksheet as well as comments to explain cell contents and provide instructions. It can also include a set of clearly written instructions. All of these help you and others use the workbook correctly and accurately.

INSIGHT

Enhancing a Worksheet with WordArt

You can use WordArt to enhance any worksheet. **WordArt** is a text box in which you can enter stylized text. For example, the Youth Soccer League might use WordArt to create a special look for the organization's name or to add the word "PAID" angled across the receipt. WordArt is an object that is embedded in the worksheet the same way a chart is; it appears over the cells, covering any content they contain. After you insert the WordArt text box, you enter the text you want to display, and then you can format it by changing its font, color, size, and position—creating the exact look you want.

To add WordArt to a worksheet:

1. On the INSERT tab, in the Text group, click the Insert WordArt button. A gallery of WordArt styles opens.
2. Click the WordArt style you want to use. A text box appears on the worksheet with placeholder text selected, and the DRAWING TOOLS FORMAT tab appears on the ribbon.
3. Type the text you want to appear in the WordArt.
4. Drag a resize handle on the selection box to make the WordArt larger or smaller.
5. Drag the WordArt by its selection box to another location on the worksheet.
6. Use the options on the DRAWING TOOLS FORMAT tab to change the selected WordArt's shape, style, text, fill, size, and position.

Sharon wants to be able to easily print the receipt and transfer the data to another worksheet. In addition, she wants volunteers to be able to enter data for soccer registration in a specific area of the worksheet reserved for input. The application would use this data to automatically generate and print the receipt. To keep the process simple, she wants users to be able to click buttons to print a single receipt, print the entire worksheet, and transfer the data from one worksheet to another. You'll open the workbook Sharon created.

Tutorial 7 Developing an Excel Application | Excel   EX 393

To open and review the Soccer workbook:

1. Open the **Soccer** workbook located in the Excel7 ▶ Tutorial folder included with your Data Files, and then save the workbook as **Youth Soccer** in the location specified by your instructor.

2. In the Documentation worksheet, enter your name and the date.

3. Review the contents of each worksheet, and then go to the **Receipt** worksheet. See Figure 7-1.

Figure 7-1 Youth Soccer initial receipt worksheet – input area

input area for the registration data

	A	B		D	E	F
1						
2	Registration Data			Player Measurements		
3	Registration Date	12/1/2016		Age Group	Shirt Size	Sock Size
4	Player Name	Sandy		U4	XSM	XSH
5	Age Group	U5		U5	SM	SH
6	Shirt Size	SM		U6	M	M
7	Sock Size	SH		U7	L	T
8	Early Registration	Yes		U8	XL	XT
9	Parent	James Smith		U9		
10	Address	123 Main Street		U10		
11	City State Zip	Oak Hill, WV 25901				
12	Telephone	304-555-1111		Registration Fee/Discount		
13				Season Fee		75
14				Discount Amount		5
15						
16						

data about player measurements

data about early registration

> **TIP**
> Larger and more complex applications often place the input and output areas in separate worksheets.

In addition to the Documentation worksheet, the Youth Soccer workbook includes two other worksheets—Receipt and Registration Data. The Receipt worksheet contains input, output, and transfer areas. The input area is divided into the following three parts:

- Registration Data includes items that change for each registration, such as parent name, address, telephone, player name, age group, shirt size, sock size, and early registration discount.
- Player Measurements is the list of codes for the different age groups, shirt sizes, and sock sizes.
- Registration Fee/Discount includes costs that will not change during the upcoming season, such as season fee ($75/player) and early registration discount ($5/player).

The output section contains formulas and labels used to generate the receipt based on data in the input section. The receipt in the output section will be printed. The transfer section gathers selected data from the receipt in one area before the data is transferred to the Registration Data worksheet for storage. The transfer section makes it simpler and easier to identify the data to be moved to the Registration Data worksheet for storage and future analysis.

Naming Cells and Ranges

So far, you have referred to a cell or range by its address except when you entered formulas within an Excel table. Cell and range references do not indicate what data is stored in those cells. Instead, you can use a defined name to assign a meaningful, descriptive name to a cell or range. For example, if the range D1:D100 contains sales data for 100 transactions, you can use the defined name Sales to refer to the range of sales data.

A defined name enables you to quickly navigate within a workbook to the cell or range with the defined name. You can also use defined names to create more descriptive formulas. However, keep in mind that the defined name includes only the specified range. Any cells you insert within that range are then included with the defined name, but any cells you insert outside the range with the defined name are not included in the defined name.

In the Receipt worksheet, the range B3:B12 contains the data values for each soccer registration. As you can see, this range includes many variables. It will be simpler to remember where different data is stored by assigning a descriptive name to each cell or range rather than using its cell address. For example, the name PlayerName better identifies what is stored in the cell than cell B4.

PROSKILLS

Written Communication: Saving Time with Defined Names

Words can be more descriptive than numbers. This is especially true in cell references. Instead of using the letter and number references for cells, you can create defined names to provide more intuitive references. Defined names have several advantages over cell references, especially as a worksheet becomes longer and more complex. Some advantages include:

- Names, such as TaxRate and TotalSales, are more descriptive than cell references, making it easier to remember what a cell or range contains.
- Names can be used in formulas, making it easier for users to understand the calculations being performed. For example, =GrossPay–Deductions is more understandable than =C15–C16.
- When you move a named cell or range within a worksheet, its name moves with it. Any formulas that contain the name automatically reference the new location.
- In a formula, referencing a named cell or range is the same as referencing the cell or range's absolute reference. So, if you move a formula that includes a defined name, the reference remains pointed to the correct cell or range.

By using defined names, you'll often save time and everyone reviewing the worksheet will have a clearer understanding of what a formula is calculating.

Creating defined names for cells or ranges makes it easier to create and understand the formulas in a workbook. When you define a name for a cell or range, keep in mind the following rules:

- The name must begin with a letter or _ (an underscore).
- The name can include letters and numbers as well as periods and underscores, but not other symbols or spaces. To distinguish multiword names, use an underscore between the words or capitalize the first letter of each word. For example, the names Net_Income and NetIncome are valid, but Net Income and Net-Income are not.
- The name cannot be a valid cell address (such as FY2016), function name (such as Average), or reserved word (such as Print_Area).
- The name can include as many as 255 characters, although short, meaningful names of 5 to 15 characters are more practical.
- The name is not case sensitive. For example, both Sales and SALES refer to the same cell or range.

REFERENCE

Creating a Defined Name for a Cell or Range

- Select the cell or range to which you want to assign a name.
- Click in the Name box, type the name, and then press the Enter key (or on the FORMULAS tab, in the Defined Names group, click the Define Name button, type a name in the Name box, and then click the OK button).

or

- Select the range with labels to which you want to assign a name.
- On the FORMULAS tab, in the Defined Names group, click the Create from Selection button.
- Specify whether to create the ranges based on the top row, bottom row, left column, or right column in the list.
- Click the OK button.

Using the Name Box to Create Defined Names

The Name box is a quick way to create a defined name for a selected cell or range. Sharon wants you to create defined names for cells and ranges in the Receipt worksheet. You'll start by using the Name box to define some of these names.

To create defined names for the input area using the Name box:

1. Select cell **F13**, and then click the **Name box** to the left of the formula bar. The cell reference for the active cell, F13, is selected in the Name box.

2. Type **SeasonFee**, and then press the **Enter** key. Cell F13 remains active, and SeasonFee appears in the Name box instead of the cell reference. See Figure 7-2.

Figure 7-2   Defined name for cell F13

defined name for cell F13 → SeasonFee | 75

> **Trouble?** If SeasonFee appears in cell F13, you did not click the Name box before typing the name. On the Quick Access Toolbar, click the Undo button ↶, and then repeat Steps 1 and 2.

3. Select cell **F14**, click the **Name box** to select the cell reference, type **DiscountAmount**, and then press the **Enter** key. Cell F14 remains active, and DiscountAmount appears in the Name box instead of the cell reference.

4. Select the range **D2:F10**. The cell reference for the active cell in the range appears in the Name box.

5. Click the **Name box**, type **PlayerMeasurements**, and then press the **Enter** key. The name PlayerMeasurements is assigned to the range D2:F10.

6. Select the range **A40:F40**, click the **Name box**, type **TransferArea**, and then press the **Enter** key. The name TransferArea is assigned to the range A40:F40.

7. Select cell **E33**, click the **Name box** to select the cell reference, type **ReceiptSeasonFee**, and then press the **Enter** key. Cell E33 remains active, and ReceiptSeasonFee appears in the Name box instead of the cell reference.

8. Select cell **E34**, click the **Name box** to select the cell reference, type **ReceiptDiscountAmount**, and then press the **Enter** key. Cell E34 remains active, and ReceiptDiscountAmount appears in the Name box instead of the cell reference.

Selecting Cells and Ranges by Their Defined Names

The Name box displays all of the defined names in a workbook. You can click a name in the Name box list to quickly select the cell or range referenced by that name. Sharon wants you to verify that defined names are associated with the correct cell or range. You'll view the defined names you added to the workbook, and then use them to select cells and ranges.

To select cells and ranges with the Name box:

1. Click the **Name box arrow** to open a list of defined names in the workbook. Six names appear in the list. The names are longer than the Name box. You can make the Name box wider so that the full names are visible.

2. Press the **Esc** key to close the Name box.

3. On the right side of the Name box, drag the sizing handle (the three vertical dots) to the right until you can see the full names.

4. Click the **Name box arrow** to display the list of defined names. See Figure 7-3.

Tutorial 7 Developing an Excel Application | Excel   **EX 397**

Figure 7-3   Name box with the defined names in the workbook

all of the defined names in the workbook

5. Click **SeasonFee**. Cell F13 becomes the active cell.
6. Click the **Name box arrow**, and then click **PlayerMeasurements**. The range D2:F10 is selected in the worksheet.
7. Select the **DiscountAmount**, **ReceiptDiscountAmount**, **ReceiptSeasonFee**, and **TransferArea** defined names in the Name box to confirm that they select their associated cell or range.

Creating Defined Names by Selection

You can quickly define names without typing them if the data is organized as a structured range of data with labels in the first or last column, or in the top or bottom row. The defined names are based on the row or column labels. For example, the Registration Data area contains labels in column A that can be used as the defined names for the corresponding cells in column B. Any blank space or parenthesis in a label is changed to an underscore (_) in the defined name.

Sharon wants you to create names for each cell in the Registration Data area using the labels in the range A3:B12.

To create defined names by selection for the registration data:

1. Select the range **A3:B12**. Column A contains the labels you want to use as the defined names, and column B contains the cells you want to name.

Select only the range A3:B12; otherwise, formulas you create later in this tutorial will not work.

2. On the ribbon, click the **FORMULAS** tab.
3. In the Defined Names group, click the **Create from Selection** button. The Create Names from Selection dialog box opens. See Figure 7-4.

Figure 7-4   Create Names from Selection dialog box

left column of the selected range has the labels for the defined names of the adjacent cells

4. Make sure only the **Left column** check box contains a checkmark. The labels in the left column will be used to create the defined names.

5. Click the **OK** button. Each cell in the range B3:B12 is named based on its label in column A. For example, cell B3 is named Registration_Date based on the Registration Date label in cell A3.

6. Click the **Name box arrow** to see the 16 defined names in the list. Notice that underscores have replaced spaces in the names.

7. Press the **Esc** key to close the list of defined names.

Editing and Deleting Defined Names

Although you can use the Name box to verify that the names were created, the Name Manager dialog box lists all of the names currently defined in the workbook, including Excel table names. In addition to the name, it identifies the current value for that name as well as the worksheet and cell or range it references. You can use the Name Manager dialog box to create a new name, edit or delete existing names, and filter the list of names.

The names ReceiptSeasonFee and ReceiptDiscountAmount define the location of these two cells on the worksheet. Although the names are descriptive, they are also fairly long. Sharon wants you to use the shorter names ReceiptFee and ReceiptDiscount, respectively, which still reflect the stored data in each cell. Sharon also decides that the TransferArea and PlayerMeasurements defined names are not needed, so you will delete them.

To edit and delete defined names with the Name Manager dialog box:

1. On the FORMULAS tab, in the Defined Names group, click the **Name Manager** button (or press the **Ctrl+F3** keys). The Name Manager dialog box opens, listing the 16 defined names in the workbook. See Figure 7-5.

Figure 7-5   Name Manager dialog box

2. Click **ReceiptSeasonFee** in the Name list, and then click the **Edit** button. The Edit Name dialog box opens. You can change the name and its referenced cell or range in this dialog box. See Figure 7-6.

Figure 7-6 Edit Name dialog box

[Edit Name dialog box showing Name: ReceiptSeasonFee (type a new name), Scope: Workbook, Comment: (blank), Refers to: =Receipt!$E$33 (type or select a new cell or range), with OK and Cancel buttons]

3. In the Name box, type **ReceiptFee** to create a shorter defined name, and then click the **OK** button. The edited name appears in the list in the Name Manager dialog box.

4. Repeat Steps 2 and 3 to rename the ReceiptDiscountAmount defined name as **ReceiptDiscount**.

5. Scroll down to find the TransferArea name, click **TransferArea**, and then click the **Delete** button. A dialog box opens to confirm that you want to delete the selected name.

6. Click the **OK** button. The name is removed from the list.

7. Repeat Steps 5 and 6 to delete the **PlayerMeasurements** name.

8. Click the **Close** button. The Name Manager dialog box closes.

Using the Paste Names Command

When a workbook contains many defined names, it can be helpful to list all of the defined names and their corresponding cell addresses in the workbook's documentation. You can generate a list of names using the Paste Names command.

To create a list of the defined names in the Documentation worksheet:

1. Go to the **Documentation** worksheet.

2. In cell **B10**, enter **Defined Names**, and then format the label with bold.

3. Select cell **B11**. This is the upper-left cell of the range where you want to paste the list of defined names.

4. On the ribbon, click the **FORMULAS** tab, if necessary.

5. In the Defined Names group, click the **Use in Formula** button (or press the **F3** key). The list includes all of the defined names in the workbook followed by the Paste Names command.

6. Click **Paste Names**. The Paste Name dialog box opens. You can paste any selected name, or you can paste the entire list of names.

7. Click the **Paste List** button. The defined names and their associated cell references are pasted into the range B11:C24.

8. Deselect the range. See Figure 7-7. Only some names in the pasted list of defined names include underscores in place of spaces. The names with underscores were created using the Create from Selection button; you entered the names without underscores in the Name box.

Figure 7-7   Defined names in the Youth Soccer workbook

	A	B	C	D	E
7					
8					
9					
10		**Defined Names**			
11		Address	=Receipt!$B$10		
12		Age_Group	=Receipt!$B$5		
13		City_State_Zip	=Receipt!$B$11		
14		DiscountAmount	=Receipt!$F$14		
15		Early_Registration	=Receipt!$B$8		
16		Parent	=Receipt!$B$9		
17		Player_Name	=Receipt!$B$4		
18		ReceiptDiscount	=Receipt!$E$34		
19		ReceiptFee	=Receipt!$E$33		
20		Registration_Date	=Receipt!$B$3		
21		SeasonFee	=Receipt!$F$13		
22		Shirt_Size	=Receipt!$B$6		
23		Sock_Size	=Receipt!$B$7		
24		Telephone	=Receipt!$B$12		
25					

defined names used in the workbook — points to column B (Address … Telephone)

worksheet and cell or range reference for the location in the workbook — points to column C

Sheet tabs: Documentation | Receipt | Registration Data

If you edit a defined name or add a new defined name, the list of defined names and their addresses in the Documentation worksheet is not updated. You must paste the list again to update the names and locations. Usually, it is a good idea to wait until the workbook is complete before pasting defined names in the Documentation worksheet.

Using Defined Names in Formulas

You can create more descriptive formulas by using defined names instead of cell or range references in formulas. For example, in the following formulas, the defined name Sales replaces the range reference D1:D100 in a formula to calculate average sales:

Range reference	=AVERAGE(D1:D100)
Defined name	=AVERAGE(Sales)

Keep in mind that range references in formulas are not updated with their defined names. So, if you enter a range reference in a formula, its corresponding defined name does *not* automatically replace the range reference in the formula.

Sharon wants you to enter the formulas required to generate the receipt. You'll start by entering formulas to display the registration date, the parent's name, and the parent's address entered in the Registration Data area in the receipt.

Tutorial 7 Developing an Excel Application | Excel **EX 401**

To enter formulas to display the parent's name and address on the receipt:

1. Go to the **Receipt** worksheet.
2. In cell **B27**, enter **=B9**. James Smith, the parent's name, appears in the cell.
3. In cell **B28**, enter **=B10**. 123 Main Street, the parent's street address, appears in the cell.
4. In cell **B29**, enter **=B11**. The parent's city, state, and zip code—Oak Hill, WV 25901—appears in the cell.
5. Select cell **B29**. The formula =B11 appears in the formula bar. See Figure 7-8.

Figure 7-8 Formula to display the City, State, and Zip data

You entered these formulas using cell addresses rather than defined names. Although you defined names for cells B9, B10, and B11, the names do not automatically replace the cell addresses in the formula when you type the cell addresses.

Using Defined Names in Formulas

Defined names make formulas simpler to enter and understand. To use a defined name in a formula, you enter the formula as usual. As you type a defined name in a formula, the Formula AutoComplete box appears, listing functions and defined names that begin with the letters you typed. As you type additional letters, the list narrows. You can double-click the name you want in the Formula AutoComplete box or press the Tab key to enter the selected name. You can also just continue to type the rest of the name.

Sharon wants you to use named cells and ranges in the remaining formulas. You'll enter these now.

To type defined names in formulas:

1. In cell **B30**, type **=T** to display a list of functions and defined names that begin with the letter *T*.

2. Type **el** to narrow the list to the defined name =Telephone.

3. Press the **Tab** key to enter the defined name in the formula, and then press the **Enter** key. The parent's telephone number appears in the cell.

4. Select cell **B30**. The data from cell B12 appears in the cell, and the formula with the defined name =Telephone appears in the formula bar.

5. In cell **E25**, enter **=Reg** to list the defined name =Registration_Date, press the **Tab** key to insert the defined name in the formula, and then press the **Enter** key.

6. Select cell **E25**. The data from cell B3 appears in the cell, and the formula with the defined name =Registration_Date appears in the formula bar. See Figure 7-9.

Figure 7-9	Formula with a defined name

	A	B	C	D	E	F
19						
20						
21		Youth Soccer League				
22		777 Main Street				
23		Oak Hill, WV 25901				
24						
25			Registration Date		12/1/2016	
26						
27	Parent	James Smith	Player Name			
28	Address	123 Main Street	Age Group			
29	City State Zip	Oak Hill, WV 25901	Shirt Size			
30	Telephone	304-555-1111	Sock Size			
31						
32						
33			Season Fee			
34			Discount Amount			
35						
36			Total			
37						

Cell E25 formula bar shows: =Registration_Date — formula with defined name entered in cell E25. Data from cell B3 displayed in the receipt.

Trouble? If the date is displayed as an integer, you need to reformat the cell as a date. Format cell E25 in the Short Date format (*mm/dd/yyyy*) and then AutoFit column E so that the date is displayed.

You can also use the point-and-click method to create a formula with defined names. When you click a cell or select a range, Excel substitutes the defined name for the cell reference in the formula. You'll use this method to enter formulas that display the Player Name, Age Group, Shirt Size, and Sock Size from the Registration Data area in the Registration Receipt.

Tutorial 7 Developing an Excel Application | Excel **EX 403**

To enter formulas with defined names using the point-and-click method:

1. Select cell **E27**, type **=**, and then click cell **B4**. The formula uses the defined name Player_Name rather than the cell reference B4.

2. Press the **Enter** key. Sandy, which is the name of the player, appears in cell E27.

3. In cell **E28**, type **=**, and then click cell **B5**. The formula uses the defined name Age_Group rather than the cell reference B5.

4. Press the **Enter** key. The value is U5, indicating the age group U5, appears in cell E28.

5. In cell **E29**, type **=**, click cell **B6**, and then press the **Enter** key. The player's shirt size, SM, appears in cell E29, and the formula with the defined name =Shirt_Size appears in the formula bar.

6. In cell **E30**, type **=**, click cell **B7**, and then press the **Enter** key. The player's sock size, SH, appears in cell E30, and the formula with the defined name =Sock_Size appears in the formula bar.

7. In cell **E33**, type **=**, click cell **F13**, and then click the **Enter** button ✓ on the formula bar. The season fee, 75, appears in cell E33 and the formula with the defined name =SeasonFee appears in the formula bar. See Figure 7-10.

Figure 7-10   **SeasonFee formula**

formula with defined name entered in cell E33

results of formulas with defined names

	A	B	C	D	E	F
19						
20						
21			Youth Soccer League			
22			777 Main Street			
23			Oak Hill, WV 25901			
24						
25				Registration Date	12/1/2016	
26						
27	**Parent**	James Smith		**Player Name**	Sandy	
28	**Address**	123 Main Street		**Age Group**	U5	
29	**City State Zip**	Oak Hill, WV 25901		**Shirt Size**	SM	
30	**Telephone**	304-555-1111		**Sock Size**	SH	
31						
32						
33				**Season Fee**	75	
34				**Discount Amount**		
35						
36				**Total**		
37						

data from cell F13 displayed in the receipt

Documentation | **Receipt** | Registration Data

READY

Next, Sharon wants you to enter the formula to calculate the total registration paid based on the data in the Registration Fee/Discount area. All players pay the season fee ($75). Anyone who registers at least four weeks before the season starts receives a $5 discount. Because the formula results are based on the registration date, you need to use an IF function to determine whether the player will receive the $5 discount.

To enter the IF function to calculate the registration total:

1. Select cell **E34**. The defined name ReceiptDiscount appears in the Name box.

2. On the FORMULAS tab, in the Function Library group, click the **Logical** button, and then click **IF**. The Function Arguments dialog box opens.

3. In the Logical_test box, type **Early_Registration="Yes"**. This logical test evaluates whether the player qualifies for the early registration discount. If the value in cell B8 equals Yes, then the condition is true. TRUE appears to the right of the Logical_test box, indicating that this player qualifies for the early registration discount of $5.00.

   > **TIP**
   > Remember that the IF function uses quotation marks around text.

   Trouble? If an error value appears to the right of the Logical_test box, you probably mistyped the formula. If the error value is #NAME?, you mistyped the defined name or didn't include quotation marks around the word "Yes." If the error value is Invalid, you used single quotation marks ('') around the word "Yes." Edit the content in the Logical_test box as needed.

4. In the Value_if_true box, type **DiscountAmount**—the defined name for cell F14, which has the value 5. This discount amount will be added to the receipt if the logical test is true.

5. In the Value_if_false box, type **0** to indicate no discount will be applied if the value in cell B8 does not equal Yes. See Figure 7-11.

Figure 7-11   Completed IF Function Arguments dialog box

6. Click the **OK** button to enter the IF function in cell E34, which displays 5.

7. Select cell **E36**.

8. Enter the formula **=ReceiptFee-ReceiptDiscount** to calculate the registration total, which is $70. See Figure 7-12.

Figure 7-12   Receipt with all formulas entered

formula subtracts the discount amount from the season fee → `=ReceiptFee-ReceiptDiscount`

	A	B	C	D	E	F
19						
20						
21			Youth Soccer League			
22			777 Main Street			
23			Oak Hill, WV 25901			
24						
25				Registration Date	12/1/2016	
26						
27	**Parent**	James Smith		**Player Name**	Sandy	
28	**Address**	123 Main Street		**Age Group**	U5	
29	**City State Zip**	Oak Hill, WV 25901		**Shirt Size**	SM	
30	**Telephone**	304-555-1111		**Sock Size**	SH	
31						
32						
33				Season Fee	75	
34				Discount Amount	5	
35						
36				Total	$ 70	
37						

IF function displays discount for early registrations

total registration fee

Documentation | Receipt | Registration Data

Adding Defined Names to Existing Formulas

Sometimes you might name cells after creating formulas in the worksheet. Other times you might not use the defined names when you create formulas (as with the first three formulas you created in the receipt for the parent; parent address; and city, state, and zip). Because defined names are not automatically substituted for the cell addresses in a formula, you can replace cell addresses in existing formulas in the worksheet with their defined names to make the formulas more understandable.

REFERENCE

Adding Defined Names to Existing Formulas

- On the FORMULAS tab, in the Defined Names group, click the Define Name button arrow, and then click Apply Names (if the cell reference and defined name are in the same worksheet).
- In the Apply Names dialog box, select the names you want to apply.
- Click the OK button.

or

- Edit the formula by selecting the cell reference and typing the defined name or clicking the appropriate cell.

In the two formulas you created to display the parent's name and address in the receipt, Sharon wants you to use defined names instead of cell references. This will make the formulas much clearer to anyone who looks at the worksheet.

To add defined names to existing formulas in the receipt:

1. On the FORMULAS tab, in the Defined Names group, click the **Define Name button arrow**, and then click **Apply Names**. The Apply Names dialog box opens. See Figure 7-13.

Figure 7-13 | Apply Names dialog box

defined names in the workbook

You want to select only the names you need for the existing formulas with cell references.

2. If any name is selected in the Apply names list, click that name to deselect it.
3. In the Apply names list, click **Address**, **City_State_Zip**, and **Parent**. The three names you want to apply to the formulas are selected.
4. Make sure that the **Use row and column names** check box is unchecked. If you leave this checked, the formula will contain too many characters and return an error.
5. Click the **OK** button. The three selected names are applied to the formulas.
6. Click cell **B27** and verify that the formula changed to =Parent.
7. Click cell **B28** and verify that the formula changed to =Address.
8. Click cell **B29** and verify that the formula changed to =City_State_Zip. The formulas now use the defined names in the files.

> **TIP**
> You can also select a cell that contains a formula, click the Use in Formula button in the Defined Names group, click the name to replace the cell reference, and then press the Enter key.

Sharon wants to store the following items in the Registration Data worksheet—parent, telephone, player name, age group, shirt size, and sock size. Displaying this data in the Transfer Area enables you to copy and paste all of the items to the Registration Data worksheet at once. You'll enter formulas to display the appropriate items in this section of the worksheet.

To enter formulas to display data in the Transfer Area:

1. In cell **A40**, enter **=Parent**. The formula displays the parent name (James Smith).
2. In cell **B40**, enter **=Telephone**. The formula displays the telephone number (304-555-1111).

3. In cell **C40**, enter **=Player_Name**. The formula displays the name of the player (Sandy).
4. In cell **D40**, enter **=Age_Group**. The formula displays the age group of the player (U5).
5. In cell **E40**, enter **=Shirt_Size**. The formula displays the player shirt size (SM).
6. In cell **F40**, enter **=Sock_Size**. The formula displays the sock size (SH). See Figure 7-14.

Figure 7-14   **Formulas entered in the Transfer Area**

	Transfer Area					
39						
40	James Smith	304-555-1111	Sandy	U5	SM	SH
41						
42						
43						

Callouts: =Parent, =Telephone, =Player_Name, =Age_Group, =Shirt_Size, =Sock_Size

The worksheet contains all of the formulas required to create the receipt based on the registration data. Because Sharon relies on volunteers to enter registration data into the worksheet and print receipts, she wants to be sure the values entered are correct. You will continue to work on Sharon's application by creating validation checks, which are designed to prevent users from inserting incorrect data values. You will also protect cells so that volunteers cannot accidentally overwrite or delete the formulas. You'll complete both of these tasks in the next session.

Session 7.1 Quick Check

1. What is an Excel application?
2. What areas of a worksheet should you consider including in an Excel application?
3. What are two advantages of using defined names in workbooks?
4. What are three ways to create a defined name?
5. Is Annual Sales a valid defined name? Explain why or why not.
6. How do you select a cell or range using its defined name?
7. In the Report workbook, the defined name "Expenses" refers to a list of expenses in the range D2:D100. Currently, the total expenses are calculated by the formula =SUM(D2:D100). Change this formula to use the defined name.
8. How do you add defined names to existing formulas?

EX 408 Excel | Tutorial 7 Developing an Excel Application

Session 7.2 Visual Overview:

A red triangle indicates that the cell contains a comment. Point to the cell to display the comment box.

Cells for data entry must be unlocked before the worksheet is protected so that users can enter and edit data in these cells.

You can use **data validation** to create a set of rules that determine what users can enter in a specific cell or range. For example, Sock Size entries must match the sizes listed in the Player Measurements.

An **input message** appears when the cell becomes active, and can be used to specify the type of data the user should enter in that cell. This input message reminds users to select one of the sock sizes in the list.

When the arrow button is clicked, a list of the possible entries, as specified in the validation rule, appears. This list shows the sock sizes that users can select.

© Cengage Learning 2014

Tutorial 7 Developing an Excel Application | Excel **EX 409**

Data Validation and Protection

Worksheet protection limits users' ability to modify the worksheet's contents, structure, or formatting.

Workbook protection limits users' ability to make changes to the workbook's structure and windows.

A **comment** is a text box that is attached to a specific cell in a worksheet in which you can enter notes.

on Hale:
all data from the form into cells B3 gh B12.

	Shirt Size	Sock Size
U4	XSM	XSH
U5	SM	SH
U6	M	M
U7	L	T
U8	XL	XT
U9		
U10		

Measurements

Cells with data or formulas that you do not want to change are usually locked before the worksheet is protected so that users cannot accidentally overwrite it by entering new data in those cells.

Registration Fee/Discount	
Season Fee	75
Discount Amount	5

Invalid Sock Size

An invalid sock size has been entered. Click Cancel, and then use the arrow to select the sock size.

Retry   Cancel   Help

An **error alert** appears if a user tries to enter a value in a cell that does not meet the validation rule, as in the case when a user enters an invalid sock size.

Validating Data Entry

TIP
Each cell can have only one validation rule. Any subsequent validation rule replaces the existing rule.

When collecting data, accuracy is important. To ensure that correct data is entered and stored in a worksheet, you can use data validation. Each **validation rule** defines criteria for the data that can be entered and stored in a cell or range. You can also add input and error alert messages for the user to that cell or range. You specify the validation criteria, the input message, and the error alert for the active cell in the Data Validation dialog box.

> **REFERENCE**
>
> ### Validating Data
> - On the DATA tab, in the Data Tools group, click the Data Validation button.
> - Click the Settings tab.
> - Click the Allow arrow, click the type of data allowed in the cell, and then enter the validation criteria for that data.
> - Click the Input Message tab, and then enter a title and text for the input message.
> - Click the Error Alert tab, and then, if necessary, click the Show error alert after invalid data is entered check box to insert a checkmark.
> - Select an alert style, and then enter the title and text for the error alert message.
> - Click the OK button.

Specifying Validation Criteria

When you create a validation rule, you specify the type of data that is allowed as well as a list or range of acceptable values (called **validation criteria**). For example, you might specify integers between 1 and 100, or a list of codes such as Excellent, Good, Fair, and Poor. Figure 7-15 describes the types of data you can allow and the acceptable values for each type.

Figure 7-15   Allow options for validation

Type	Acceptable Values
Any value	Any number, text, or date; removes any existing data validation
Whole Number	Integers only; you can specify the range of acceptable integers
Decimal	Any type of number; you can specify the range of acceptable numbers
List	Any value in a range or entered in the Data validation dialog box separated by commas
Date	Dates only; you can specify the range of acceptable dates
Time	Times only; you can specify the range of acceptable times
Text Length	Text limited to a specified number of characters
Custom	Values based on the results of a logical formula

© 2014 Cengage Learning

Sharon wants you to add the following six validation rules to the workbook to help ensure that volunteers enter valid data in the Receipt worksheet:

- In cell B3, make sure a valid date is entered.
- In cell B4, specify an input message.
- In cell B5, make sure the value is one of the following age groups—U4, U5, U6, U7, U8, U9, or U10.
- In cell B6, make sure the value is one of the following shirt sizes—XSM, SM, M, L, or XL.
- In cell B7, make sure the value is one of the following sock sizes—XSH, SH, M, T, or XT.
- In cell B8, make sure the value is Yes or No.

Tutorial 7 Developing an Excel Application | Excel   EX 411

Cell B3, which contains the Registration Date, requires the current date. Sharon wants to be sure everyone enters a valid date in this cell. You will define the validation rule for the Registration Date.

To create the validation rule for the Registration Date cell:

1. If you took a break after the previous session, make sure the Youth Soccer workbook is open and the Receipt worksheet is active.

2. Select cell **B3**. You will enter a date validation rule to ensure that a valid date is entered in this cell.

3. On the ribbon, click the **DATA** tab.

4. In the Data Tools group, click the **Data Validation** button. The Data Validation dialog box opens with the Settings tab displayed. You use the Settings tab to enter the validation rule for the active cell.

5. On the Settings tab, click the **Allow** arrow, and then click **Date**. The Data Validation dialog box expands to display the options specific to dates.

6. Click the **Ignore blank** check box to deselect it. You want to ensure that cell B3 is not left blank, and require users to enter a date value in the cell.

7. If necessary, click the **Data** arrow, and then click **greater than or equal to**. The dialog box reflects the selected criteria.

8. Enter **1/1/2010** in the Start date box to provide an example of what to look for when checking the cell. You cannot use data validation to simply check for the presence of data. You must provide an example for checking. See Figure 7-16.

> **TIP**
> To apply a validation rule to all cells in an Excel table column, select the column of data, and then create the validation rule.

Figure 7-16   Settings tab in the Data Validation dialog box

[Data Validation dialog box screenshot showing:
- Settings tab selected
- Allow: Date (labeled "type of value to allow in the cell")
- Ignore blank checkbox checked (labeled "uncheck to apply the validation rule to empty cells (which means that the cell cannot be blank)")
- Data: less than or equal to (labeled "these options change to reflect the allowed value")
- End date: 1/12010]

If you wanted to create a validation rule that checks if the date is the current date, you would select "equal to" in the Data list and then enter =TODAY() in the Date box. Then, a user cannot enter any date other than the current date. Sharon wants to check only for the presence of a date because sometimes the registration form is completed on a different day than the data was received.

> **INSIGHT**
>
> ### Validating Existing Data
>
> Validation rules come into play only during data entry. If you add validation rules to a workbook that already contains data with erroneous values, Excel does not determine if any existing data is invalid. Instead, you can use the Circle Invalid Data command to help identify invalid data that is already in the workbook. (You'll learn about the Circle Invalid Data command in the Circle Invalid Data Command InSight box later in the tutorial.)

Creating an Error Alert Style and Message

An error alert determines what happens after a user tries to make an invalid entry in a cell that has a validation rule defined. The three error alert styles are Stop, Warning, and Information. The Stop alert prevents the entry from being stored in the cell. The Warning alert prevents the entry from being stored in the cell unless the user overrides the rejection and decides to continue using the data. The Information alert accepts the data value entered, but allows the user to choose to cancel the data entry.

Sharon wants to display an error alert if a volunteer enters data that violates the validation rule. Although the registration date is usually equal to the current date, a user might forget to enter the date. To account for this possibility, Sharon wants you to create a Warning error alert that appears when a user does not enter a registration date or enters a date prior to 1/1/2010. The user can then verify the date entered. If the entry is correct, the user can accept the entry. If the entry is incorrect, the user can reenter the correct date.

You'll create the Warning error alert for the Registration Date cell.

To create the Warning error alert for the Registration Date cell:

1. Make sure cell **B3** is still the active cell and the Data Validation dialog box is open.

2. In the Data Validation dialog box, click the **Error Alert** tab. You use this tab to select the type of error alert and enter the message you want to appear.

3. Make sure that the **Show error alert after invalid data is entered** check box is selected. If unchecked, the error alert won't appear when an invalid value is entered in the cell.

4. Click the **Style** arrow, and then click **Warning**. This style allows the user to accept the invalid value, return to the cell and reenter a valid value, or cancel the data entry and restore the previous value to the cell.

5. Click in the **Title** box, and then type **Invalid Registration Date**. This text will appear as the title of the error alert box.

6. Press the **Tab** key to move the insertion point to the Error message box, and then type **Invalid Registration Date. Enter a Registration Date after 1/1/2010. If the date you entered is correct, click Yes. If it is incorrect, click No. If you are not sure, click Cancel.** See Figure 7-17.

> **TIP**
>
> If only experienced users will enter data, you can hide the input and error alert messages by unchecking the Show check box. You can show them again if a new user will enter data.

Tutorial 7 Developing an Excel Application | Excel   EX 413

Figure 7-17   **Error Alert tab in the Data Validation dialog box**

- check so that the error alert is displayed
- type of error alert
- title of the error alert
- text of the error alert message

> 7. Click the **OK** button. The Data Validation dialog box closes.

Creating an Input Message

One way to reduce the chance of a data-entry error is to display an input message when a user makes the cell active. An input message provides additional information about the type of data allowed for that cell. Input messages appear as ScreenTips next to the cell when the cell is selected. You can add an input message to a cell even if you don't set up a rule to validate the data in that cell.

Sharon wants volunteers to see that they must enter a value for the player name in cell B4. An input message will minimize the chance of a volunteer skipping this cell, so you will create an input message for cell B4.

To create an input message for the Player Name cell:

> 1. Select cell **B4**. You will create an input message for this cell.

> 2. On the DATA tab, in the Data Tools group, click the **Data Validation** button. The Data Validation dialog box opens.

> 3. Click the **Input Message** tab. You enter the input message title and text on this tab.

> 4. Verify that the **Show input message when cell is selected** check box contains a checkmark. If you uncheck this option, you cannot enter a new input message and any existing input message will not be displayed when the selected cell becomes active.

TIP
The maximum number of characters allowed in the Title box is 32.

> 5. Click in the **Title** box, and then type **Player Name**. This title will appear in bold at the top of the ScreenTip above the text of the input message.

> 6. Press the **Tab** key to move the insertion point to the Input message box, and then type **Enter the Player's first name**. See Figure 7-18.

Figure 7-18 | Input Message tab in the Data Validation dialog box

- check so that the input message is displayed
- title of the input message
- text of the input message

7. Click the **OK** button. The Data Validation dialog box closes. The input message appears in a ScreenTip because the cell is active. See Figure 7-19.

Figure 7-19 | Input message for the Player Name cell

- input message appears when the cell is selected

Creating a List Validation Rule

You can use the data validation feature to restrict a cell to accept only entries that are on a list you create. You can create the list of valid entries in the Data Validation dialog box, or you can use a list of valid entries in a single column or row. Once you create a list validation rule for a cell, a list box with the possible values appears when the user selects the cell.

Sharon wants you to use list validation rules for the Age Group, Shirt Size, and Sock Size cells to ensure that users enter one of the correct values. The Age Group has seven possible values—U4, U5, U6, U7, U8, U9, and U10. You will create a validation rule so that users can enter only one of the seven possible values. You will also create an input message for the cell.

Tutorial 7 Developing an Excel Application | Excel **EX 415**

To create a validation rule and an input message for the Age Group cell:

1. Select cell **B5**. You will create a list validation rule for this cell.

2. On the DATA tab, in the Data Tools group, click the **Data Validation** button to open the Data Validation dialog box, and then click the **Settings** tab.

3. Click the **Allow** arrow, and then click **List**. The dialog box expands to display the Source box. You can enter values separated by commas directly in the Source box, or you can select a range of valid entries in the worksheet.

4. Next to the Source box, click the **Collapse** button so you can see the entire worksheet.

5. Select the range **D4:D10**, which contains the seven valid entry values, and then click the **Expand** button. The Data Validation dialog box returns to its full size and =$D$4:$D$10 appears in the Source box. See Figure 7-20.

Figure 7-20 | Settings tab in the Data Validation dialog box

type of data validation → List

range that contains the entry values → =$D$4:$D$10

Next, you'll create an input message and an error alert.

6. Click the **Input Message** tab, click in the **Title** box, and then type **Age Group** to enter the title of the input message.

7. Click in the **Input message** box, and then type **Click the arrow to select the player's age group.** to enter the text of the input message.

8. Click the **Error Alert** tab, and then make sure that **Stop** appears in the Style box. You want to prevent a user from entering a value that is not included in the list of values you specified.

9. In the Title text box, type **Invalid Age Group** to enter the title of the error alert.

10. In the Error message box, type **An invalid age group has been entered. Click Cancel, and then use the arrow to select a valid age group.** as the error message. See Figure 7-21.

EX 416 Excel | Tutorial 7 Developing an Excel Application

Figure 7-21   **Stop error alert for the Age Group cell**

Stop error alert prevents user from entering invalid values → Style: Stop

title of the error alert → Title: Invalid Age Group

text of the error message → Error message: An invalid age group has been entered. Click Cancel, and then use the arrow to select a valid age group.

▸ **11.** Click the **OK** button. The Data Validation dialog box closes, an arrow appears to the right of cell B5, and the input message appears in a ScreenTip.

▸ **12.** Click the **arrow** button ▼ to the right of cell B5 to view the list of valid age group entries. See Figure 7-22.

Figure 7-22   **List of valid age group entries**

	A	B	C	D	E	F
1						
2	Registration Data			Player Measurements		
3	Registration Date	12/1/2016		Age Group	Shirt Size	Sock Size
4	Player Name	Sandy		U4	XSM	XSH
5	Age Group	U5	▼	U5	SM	SH
6	Shirt Size	U4		U6	M	M
7	Sock Size	U5 / U6		U7	L	T
8	Early Registra	U7		U8	XL	XT
9	Parent	U8 / U9		U9		
10	Address	U10		U10		
11	City State Zip	Oak Hill, WV 25901				
12	Telephone	304-555-1111		Registration Fee/Discount		
13				Season Fee		75
14				Discount Amount		5

click the arrow button to display the list

valid data for the Age Group cell

values used in the list

Documentation | Receipt | Registration Data

▸ **13.** Press the **Esc** key to close the list.

Next, Sharon wants you to enter a list validation rule for cells B6 and B7, which specify the player's shirt size (XSM, SM, M, L, or XL) and sock size (XSH, SH, M, T, or XT), respectively. Both rules will include an error alert.

To create list validation rules for the Shirt Size and Sock Size cells:

1. Select cell **B6**. You will create a list validation rule for the Shirt Size cell.

2. On the DATA tab, in the Data Tools group, click the **Data Validation** button. The Data Validation dialog box opens.

3. Click the **Settings** tab, select **List** in the Allow box, click the **Source** box, and then select the range **E4:E8**. This range contains the five values you want to allow users to select for the shirt size.

4. Click the **Input Message** tab, type **Shirt Size** in the Title box, and then type **Click the arrow to select the shirt size.** in the Input message box.

5. Click the **Error Alert** tab, verify that **Stop** appears in the Style box, type **Invalid Shirt Size** in the Title box, and then type **An invalid shirt size has been entered. Click Cancel, and then use the arrow to select the shirt size.** in the Error message box.

6. Click the **OK** button. The dialog box closes, an arrow button appears to the right of cell B6, and the input message appears in a ScreenTip.

7. Select cell **B7** so you can create the validation rule for the Sock Size cell.

8. In the Data Tools group, click the **Data Validation** button to open the Data Validation dialog box, and then click the **Settings** tab.

9. Select **List** in the Allow box, click the **Source** box, and then select the range **F4:F8**. This range contains the five values you want to allow users to select for the sock size.

10. Click the **Input Message** tab, type **Sock Size** in the Title box, and then type **Click the arrow to select the sock size.** in the Input message box.

11. Click the **Error Alert** tab, make sure that **Stop** appears in the Style box, type **Invalid Sock Size** in the Title box, and then type **An invalid sock size has been entered. Click Cancel, and then use the arrow to select the sock size.** in the Error message box.

12. Click the **OK** button. An arrow button appears to the right of cell B7, and the input message appears in a ScreenTip.

Sharon also wants you to enter a validation rule for cell B8 to limit the Early Registration cell to either Yes or No. This rule will also include an input message and an error alert. To specify the entries that the list includes, you will type each entry separated by commas in the Source box on the Settings tab in the Data Validation dialog box.

To create a list validation rule for the Early Registration cell:

1. Select cell **B8** so you can create a validation rule for the Early Registration cell.

2. On the DATA tab, in the Data Tools group, click the **Data Validation** button. The Data Validation dialog box opens.

3. Click the **Settings** tab, select **List** in the Allow box, click the **Source** box, and then type **Yes, No** in the Source box. You typed the items for the list because they are not already contained in any range of the worksheet. See Figure 7-23.

Figure 7-23 Validation rule for the Early Registration cell

entries for the list are separated by commas → Source: Yes, No

4. Click the **Input Message** tab, type **Early Registration** in the Title box, and then type **Click the arrow to select the correct response.** in the Input message box.

5. Click the **Error Alert** tab, make sure that **Stop** appears in the Style box, type **Invalid Early Registration** in the Title box, and then type **An invalid response for Early Registration has been entered. Click Cancel, and then use the arrow to the right of cell B8 to select the response.** in the Error message box.

6. Click the **OK** button. An arrow button appears to the right of cell B8, and the input message appears in a ScreenTip.

You can edit an existing validation rule, input message, or error alert at any time by selecting the cell with the current validation rule and then opening the Data Validation dialog box. You can also add or remove an input message or error alert to an existing validation rule. Sharon notices that the Registration Date cell does not have an input message. For consistency, she wants you to add one now.

To create an input message for the Registration Date cell:

1. Select cell **B3**.
2. On the DATA tab, in the Data Tools group, click the **Data Validation** button.
3. Click the **Settings** tab. The validation rule you created earlier is displayed.
4. Click the **Input Message** tab, type **Registration Date** in the Title box, and then type **Enter the registration date.** in the Input message box.
5. Click the **OK** button. The input message is added to the Registration Date cell.

Testing Data Validation Rules

After you create validation rules, you should test them. You do this by entering incorrect values that violate the validation rules. Keep in mind that the only way an error occurs in cells that have a list validation is if an incorrect entry is typed or pasted in the cell. Entering invalid data will ensure that validation rules work as expected. Sharon asks you to test the validation rules you just created.

Tutorial 7 Developing an Excel Application | Excel   EX 419

To test the data validation rules:

1. Select cell **B3**, type **01/30/2004**, and then press the **Tab** key. The Invalid Registration Date message box opens, informing you that the value you entered might be incorrect. You'll enter a valid date.

2. Click the **No** button to return to cell B3, type the current date, and then press the **Enter** key. The date is entered in cell B3. Cell B4 is the active cell, and the input message for the Player Name cell appears.

3. In cell **B4**, type your name, and then press the **Enter** key. The value is accepted.

4. Select cell **B5** if necessary to display the list arrow, click the **arrow** to the right of cell B5, and then click **U6**. The value is accepted. The only way an error occurs in cells that have a list validation is if an incorrect entry is typed or copied in the cell. You'll try typing in cell B6.

5. In cell **B6**, enter **LG**. The Invalid Shirt Size message box opens.

6. Click the **Cancel** button to close the message box and return to the original value in the cell.

7. Click the **arrow** button to the right of cell B6, and then click **SM**.

8. In cell **B7**, enter **XSH**. An error alert does not appear because this is a valid entry. You could also have selected XSH from the validation list.

9. Select cell **B8**, click the **arrow** button to the right of cell B8, and then click **Yes** for Early Registration.

TIP

If you press the Retry button in the error alert dialog box, you must press the Esc key to return to the original cell value; otherwise, the error alert reappears when you click the arrow button.

The validation rules that you entered for cells B3 through B8 work as intended.

INSIGHT

Using the Circle Invalid Data Command

Validation rules come into play only during data entry. If you add validation rules to a workbook that already contains data with erroneous values, Excel does not determine if any existing data is invalid.

To ensure the entire workbook contains valid data, you need to also verify any data previously entered in the workbook. You can use the Circle Invalid Data command to find and mark cells that contain invalid data. Red circles appear around any data that does not meet the validation criteria, making it simple to scan a worksheet for errors. After you correct the data in a cell, the circle disappears.

To display circles around invalid data, perform the following steps:

1. Apply validation rules to an existing cell range.
2. On the DATA tab, in the Data Tools group, click the Data Validation button arrow, and then click Circle Invalid Data. Red circles appear around cells that contain invalid data.
3. To remove the circle from a single cell, enter valid data in the cell.
4. To hide all circles, on the DATA tab, in the Data Tools group, click the Data Validation button arrow, and then click Clear Validation Circles.

To ensure an error-free workbook, you should use the Circle Invalid Data command to verify data entered before you set up the validation criteria, or to verify data in a workbook you inherited from someone else, such as a coworker.

Protecting a Worksheet and a Workbook

Another way to minimize data-entry errors is to limit access to certain parts of the workbook. Worksheet protection prevents users from changing cell contents, such as editing formulas in a worksheet. Workbook protection also prevents users from changing the workbook's organization, such as inserting or deleting worksheets in the workbook. You can even keep users from viewing the formulas used in the workbook.

Sharon wants to protect the contents of the Receipt and Registration Data worksheets. She wants volunteers to have access only to the range B3:B12 in the Receipt worksheet, where new receipt data is entered. She also wants to prevent volunteers from editing the contents of any cells in the Registration Data worksheet.

Locking and Unlocking Cells

Every cell in a workbook has a **locked property** that determines whether changes can be made to that cell. The locked property has no impact as long as the worksheet is unprotected. However, after you protect a worksheet, the locked property controls whether the cell can be edited. You unlock a cell by turning off the locked property. By default, the locked property is turned on for each cell, and worksheet protection is turned off.

So, unless you unlock cells in a worksheet *before* protecting the worksheet, all of the cells in the worksheet will be locked, and you won't be able to make any changes in the worksheet. Usually, you will want to protect the worksheet but leave some cells unlocked. For example, you might want to lock cells that contain formulas and formatting so they cannot be changed, but unlock cells in which you want to enter data.

To protect some—but not all—cells in a worksheet, you first turn off the locked property of cells in which data can be entered. Then, you protect the worksheet to activate the locked property for the remaining cells.

In the Receipt worksheet, Sharon wants users to be able to enter data in the range B3:B12, but not in any other cell. To do this, you must unlock the cells in the range B3:B12.

To unlock the cells in the range B3:B12:

1. In the Receipt worksheet, select the range **B3:B12**. You want to unlock the cells in this range before you protect the worksheet.
2. On the ribbon, click the **HOME** tab.
3. In the Cells group, click the **Format** button, and then click **Format Cells** (or press the **Ctrl+1** keys). The Format Cells dialog box opens. The locked property is on the Protection tab.
4. Click the **Protection** tab, and then click the **Locked** check box to remove the checkmark. See Figure 7-24.

> **TIP**
>
> You can also click the Format button in the Cells group and then click Lock Cell to add or remove the locked property for the selected cells.

Figure 7-24   **Protection tab in the Format Cells dialog box**

Locked property is turned off for the selected cells

[Format Cells dialog box showing Protection tab with Locked checkbox unchecked and Hidden checkbox unchecked. Text reads: "Locking cells or hiding formulas has no effect until you protect the worksheet (Review tab, Changes group, Protect Sheet button)."]

▶ **5.** Click the **OK** button. The cells in the range B3:B12 are unlocked.

▶ **6.** Select cell **A1** to deselect the range.

Protecting a Worksheet

When you set up worksheet protection, you specify which actions are still available to users in the protected worksheet. For example, you can choose to allow users to insert new rows or columns, or to delete rows and columns. You can limit the user to selecting only unlocked cells, or allow the user to select any cell in the worksheet. These choices remain active as long as the worksheet is protected.

    A protected worksheet can always be unprotected. You can also add a password to the protected worksheet that users must enter in order to turn off the protection. Passwords are case sensitive, which means the uppercase and lowercase letters are considered different letters. If you are concerned that users will turn off protection and make changes to formulas, you should use a password; otherwise, it is probably best to not specify a password. Keep in mind that if you forget the password, it is very difficult to remove the worksheet protection.

REFERENCE

Protecting a Worksheet

- Select the cells and ranges to unlock so that users can enter data in them.
- On the HOME tab, in the Cells group, click the Format button, and then click Format Cells (or press the Ctrl+1 keys).
- In the Format Cells dialog box, click the Protection tab.
- Click the Locked check box to remove the checkmark, and then click the OK button.
- On the REVIEW tab, in the Changes group, click the Protect Sheet button.
- Enter a password (optional).
- Select all of the actions you want to allow users to take when the worksheet is protected.
- Click the OK button.

Sharon wants to protect the Receipt and Registration Data worksheets, but she doesn't want a password specified. You will enable worksheet protection that will allow users to select any cell in the worksheets, but enter data only in the unlocked cells.

To protect the Receipt worksheet:

1. On the ribbon, click the **REVIEW** tab.
2. In the Changes group, click the **Protect Sheet** button. The Protect Sheet dialog box opens. See Figure 7-25.

Figure 7-25 Protect Sheet dialog box

users will able to perform checked actions in the protected worksheet

You will leave the Password to unprotect sheet box blank because you do not want to use a password. By default, users can select both locked and unlocked cells, which constitute all of the cells in the worksheet, but they can enter or edit values only in unlocked cells.

3. Click the **OK** button. The Protect Sheet dialog box closes, and the Protect Sheet button changes to the Unprotect Sheet button.

TIP
Keep passwords in a safe place. Remember, passwords are case sensitive. If you forget the password, it is very difficult to remove the worksheet protection.

Any time you modify a worksheet, you should test the worksheet to ensure that changes work as intended. You'll test the protection you added to the Receipt worksheet by trying to edit a locked cell, and then trying to edit an unlocked cell.

Tutorial 7 Developing an Excel Application | Excel   EX 423

To test the Receipt worksheet protection:

▶ 1. Select cell **F13**, and then type **1**. As soon as you press any key, a dialog box opens, indicating that the cell is protected and cannot be modified. See Figure 7-26.

Figure 7-26   **Cell protection error message**

> Microsoft Excel
>
> ⚠ The cell or chart you're trying to change is on a protected sheet.
> To make changes, click Unprotect Sheet in the Review tab (you might need a password).
>
> OK

▶ 2. Click the **OK** button.

▶ 3. Click cell **B8**, type **No**, and then press the **Enter** key. The Early Registration cell is updated because you allowed editing in the range B3:B12. A user can enter and edit values in these cells. Although users can select any cell in the worksheet, they cannot make an entry in any other cell outside of that range.

▶ 4. On the Quick Access Toolbar, click the **Undo** button ↶ to return the Early Registration cell to Yes.

You will repeat this process to protect all of the cells in the Registration Data worksheet. Then you will test to see what would happen if someone tried to edit one of the cells. Because you did not unlock any cells in the Registration Data worksheet, no cells may be edited.

To protect and test the Registration Data worksheet:

▶ 1. Go to the **Registration Data** worksheet.

▶ 2. On the REVIEW tab, in the Changes group, click the **Protect Sheet** button. The Protect Sheet dialog box opens.

▶ 3. Click the **OK** button to accept the default set of user actions.

▶ 4. Select cell **A2**, and then type **B**. A dialog box opens, indicating that the cell is protected and cannot be modified. All of the cells in this worksheet are protected because no cells have been unlocked.

▶ 5. Click the **OK** button to close the dialog box.

Protecting a Workbook

Worksheet protection applies only to the contents of a worksheet, not to the worksheet itself. To keep a worksheet from being modified, you need to protect the workbook. You can protect both the structure and the windows of a workbook. Protecting the structure prevents users from renaming, deleting, hiding, or inserting worksheets. Protecting the windows prevents users from moving, resizing, closing, or hiding parts of the Excel window. The default is to protect only the structure of the workbook, not the windows used to display it.

You can also add a password to the workbook protection. However, the same guidelines apply as for protecting worksheets. Add a password only if you are concerned that others might unprotect the workbook and modify it. If you add a password, keep in mind that it is case sensitive and you cannot unprotect the workbook without it.

Excel | Tutorial 7 Developing an Excel Application

> **REFERENCE**
>
> ### Protecting a Workbook
>
> - On the REVIEW tab, in the Changes group, click the Protect Workbook button.
> - Click the check boxes to indicate whether you want to protect the workbook's structure, windows, or both.
> - Enter a password (optional).
> - Click the OK button.

The contents of the Receipt and Registration Data worksheets, with the exception of the range B3:B12 in the Receipt worksheet, cannot be changed. However, a volunteer could inadvertently rename or delete the protected worksheet. To keep the worksheets themselves from being modified, you will protect the workbook. Sharon doesn't want users to be able to change the structure of the workbook, so you will set workbook protection for the structure, but not the window.

To protect the Youth Soccer workbook:

1. On the REVIEW tab, in the Changes group, click the **Protect Workbook** button. The Protect Structure and Windows dialog box opens. See Figure 7-27.

Figure 7-27   Protect Structure and Windows dialog box

2. Make sure the **Structure** check box is checked and the **Password** box is blank. The Windows check box is unavailable and unchecked.
3. Click the **OK** button to protect the workbook without specifying a password.
4. Right-click the **Registration Data** sheet tab. On the shortcut menu, notice that the Insert, Delete, Rename, Move or Copy, Tab Color, Hide, and Unhide commands are gray. This indicates that the options for modifying the worksheets are no longer available for the Registration Data worksheet.
5. Press the **Esc** key to close the shortcut menu.

Unprotecting a Worksheet and a Workbook

You can turn off worksheet protection at any time. This is often referred to as *unprotecting* the worksheet. You must unprotect a worksheet to edit its contents. If you assigned a password when you protected the worksheet, you would need to enter the password to remove worksheet protection. Likewise, you can unprotect the workbook. If you need to insert a new worksheet or rename an existing worksheet, you can unprotect the protected workbook, make the changes to the structure, and then reapply workbook protection.

Tutorial 7 Developing an Excel Application | Excel **EX 425**

At this point, Sharon wants you to make additional changes to the Receipt worksheet, so you'll turn off worksheet protection in that worksheet. Later, when you've completed your modifications, Sharon can turn worksheet protection back on.

To turn off worksheet protection for the Receipt worksheet:

1. Go to the **Receipt** worksheet.

2. On the REVIEW tab, in the Changes group, click the **Unprotect Sheet** button. Worksheet protection is removed from the Receipt worksheet. The button changes back to the Protect Sheet button.

TIP
To remove workbook protection, click the Protect Workbook button in the Changes group on the REVIEW tab.

Inserting Comments

Comments are often used in workbooks to: (a) explain the contents of a particular cell, such as a complex formula; (b) provide instructions to users; and (c) share ideas and notes from several users collaborating on a project. The username for your installation of Excel appears in bold at the top of the comments box. If you collaborate on a workbook, the top of the comment boxes would show the name of each user who created that comment. A small red triangle appears in the upper-right corner of a cell with a comment. The comment box appears when you point to a cell with a comment.

REFERENCE

Inserting a Comment

- Select the cell to which you want to attach a comment.
- Right-click the selected cell, and then click Insert Comment on the shortcut menu (or press the Shift+F2 keys; or on the REVIEW tab, in the Comments group, click the New Comment button).
- Type the comment into the box.
- Click a cell to hide the comment.

Sharon wants you to insert a note in cell A2 about entering data from the order form into the input section, and a note in cell E34 explaining how the IF functions are used to determine whether to give the discount for early registration.

To insert comments in cells A2 and E34:

1. In the Receipt worksheet, select cell **A2**.

2. On the REVIEW tab, in the Comments group, click the **New Comment** button (or press the **Shift+F2** keys). A comment box opens to the right of cell A2. The username for your installation of Excel appears in bold at the top of the box. An arrow points from the box to the small red triangle that appears in the upper-right corner of the cell.

3. Type **Enter all data from the order form into cells B3 through B11.** in the box. A selection box with sizing handles appears around the comment box. If the box is too small or too large for the comment, you can drag a sizing handle to increase or decrease the size of the box. See Figure 7-28.

TIP
You can also add a comment by right-clicking the cell, and then clicking Insert Comment on the shortcut menu.

Excel | Tutorial 7 Developing an Excel Application

Figure 7-28   **Comment added to cell A2**

red triangle indicates this cell has a comment

username for your installation of Excel appears here

Sharon Hale:
Enter all data from the order form into cells B3 through B12.

drag a sizing handle to resize the box

	A	B	C	D	E	F
1						
2	Registration Data				er Measurements	
3	Registration Date	12/1/2016			Shirt Size	Sock Size
4	Player Name	Sandy		U4	XSM	XSH
5	Age Group	U6		U5	SM	SH
6	Shirt Size	SM		U6	M	M
7	Sock Size	XSH		U7	L	T
8	Early Registration	Yes		U8	XL	XT
9	Parent	James Smith		U9		
10	Address	123 Main Street		U10		
11	City State Zip	Oak Hill, WV 25901				
12	Telephone	304-555-1111		Registration Fee/Discount		
13				Season Fee		75

▶ 4. Click cell **B12** to hide the comment. The comment disappears. A small red triangle remains in the upper-right corner of cell A2 to indicate this cell contains a comment.

    Trouble? If the comment box did not disappear, comments are set to be displayed in the worksheet. On the REVIEW tab, in the Comments group, click the Show All Comments button to deselect it.

▶ 5. Move the pointer over cell **A2**. The comment appears.

▶ 6. Click cell **A2**.

▶ 7. In the Comments group, click the **Edit Comment** button. The comment appears with the insertion point at the end of the comment text, so you can edit the incorrect cell reference.

▶ 8. Select **B11** in the comment box, and then type **B12**. The comment in cell A2 now correctly references the range B3:B12.

> **TIP**
> To keep an active cell's comment displayed, click the Show/Hide Comment button in the Comments group on the REVIEW tab. Click the button again to hide the active cell's comment.

▶ 9. Select any other cell to hide the comment, and then point to cell **A2** to view the edited comment.

▶ 10. Click cell **E34**, and then on the REVIEW tab, in the Comments group, click the **New Comment** button. A comment box opens to the right of cell E34.

▶ 11. In the comment box, type **This IF function determines whether to allow the early registration discount.**

▶ 12. Select cell **E35** to hide the comment. A small red triangle remains in the upper-right corner of cell E34 to indicate it contains a comment.

▶ 13. Point to cell **E34** to see the comment.

    Sharon decides that the volunteers don't need to know how the early registration discount is calculated. You'll delete the comment in cell E34.

Tutorial 7 Developing an Excel Application | Excel   EX 427

> **14.** Select cell **E34**.
>
> **15.** In the Comments group, click the **Delete** button. The comment is deleted, and the red triangle in the upper-right corner of cell E34 is removed.

The comments provide helpful information for anyone using the Receipt worksheet.

PROSKILLS

Written Communication: Documenting a Spreadsheet

Providing documentation for a spreadsheet is important because it provides instructions on the spreadsheet's use, defines technical terms, explains complex formulas, and identifies assumptions. By documenting a spreadsheet, you help users work more effectively. In addition, documentation helps you recall what is in the spreadsheet that might otherwise be forgotten months or years from now. Furthermore, when someone else becomes responsible for modifying the spreadsheet in the future, the documentation will help that person get up to speed quickly.

You can create a Documentation worksheet to provide an overview, definitions, assumptions, and instructions on how to use various parts of a workbook. Excel also offers a variety of tools to help you document spreadsheets, including:

- Defined names and structured references to make formulas easier to create and understand
- Data validation including input messages specifying what to enter in a cell, and error messages providing instructions on what to do if the data entered is incorrect
- Cell comments to explain complex formulas, give reminders, and so on
- Formula mode to view all formulas in a worksheet at one time

Providing documentation will help users better understand the application, which will save time and minimize frustration.

In this session, you used data validation to help ensure that all values entered in the Receipt worksheet are valid. You created validation rules that included input messages and error alert messages. You learned how to protect and unprotect both the worksheet and the workbook. In addition, you used comments to add notes to specific cells. In the next session, you'll automate some of the steps in the application by recording macros.

REVIEW

Session 7.2 Quick Check

1. Why would you want to validate data?
2. What is the purpose of the input message in the Data Validation command?
3. Describe the three types of error alert messages Excel can display when a user violates a validation rule.
4. What is a locked cell? What are unlocked cells?
5. What is the difference between worksheet protection and workbook protection?
6. Can you rename a protected worksheet? Explain why or why not.
7. Give two reasons for adding a comment to a worksheet cell.

EX 428 Excel | Tutorial 7 Developing an Excel Application

Session 7.3 Visual Overview:

The Record Macro button opens the Record Macro dialog box, which you use to start recording a macro.

The Macros button opens the Macro dialog box, which you use to run or edit existing macros in the open workbook.

The macro security settings control what Excel will do about macros in a workbook when you open that workbook. You can set the level of macro security.

In the Record Macro dialog box, you specify a name, shortcut key, location, and description of the macro.

Record Macro

Macro name:
PDFReceipt

Shortcut key:
Ctrl+ r

Store macro in:
This Workbook

Description:
Created 12/1/2016. Save receipt area: range A18:F37 as a PDF file

OK   Cancel

A macro button runs the assigned macro when clicked. Placing a macro button on the worksheet makes it easier for a user to run the macro.

Create PDF Receipt   Transfer Data

The macro recorder, which you can turn on with this button, records keystrokes and mouse actions as you perform them.

Documentation | **Receipt** | Registration Data

READY

Working with Macros

You can customize the ribbon by showing or hiding tabs. You need to show the DEVELOPER tab to create macros.

To view the code of a macro, you need to open the **Visual Basic Editor (VBE)**, which is a separate application that works with Excel and all of the Office programs to view, debug, edit, and manage VBA code.

A **macro** is a series of stored commands that can be run whenever you need to perform the task. Commands can be viewed and edited in the Visual Basic Editor.

You can use a macro to automate any task you perform repeatedly, such as printing a receipt as a PDF.

When you run a macro, Excel performs each of the recorded actions in the same order as it was recorded. Macros perform repetitive tasks faster than you can.

```
Sub PDFReceipt()
'
' PDFReceipt Macro
' Created 12/1/2016. Save receipt area: range A18:F37 as PDF file.
'
' Keyboard Shortcut: Ctrl+r
'
    Range("A18:F37").Select
    ActiveSheet.PageSetup.PrintArea = "$A$18:$F$37"
    Application.PrintCommunication = False
    With ActiveSheet.PageSetup
        .PrintTitleRows = ""
        .PrintTitleColumns = ""
    End With
    Application.PrintCommunication = True
    ActiveSheet.PageSetup.PrintArea = "$A$18:$F$37"
    Application.PrintCommunication = False
    With ActiveSheet.PageSetup
        .LeftHeader = ""
        .CenterHeader = "Registration Receipt"
        .RightHeader = ""
        .LeftFooter = ""
        .CenterFooter = ""
        .RightFooter = ""
        .LeftMargin = Application.InchesToPoints(0.7)
        .RightMargin = Application.InchesToPoints(0.7)
        .TopMargin = Application.InchesToPoints(0.75)
        .BottomMargin = Application.InchesToPoints(0.75)
        .HeaderMargin = Application.InchesToPoints(0.3)
        .FooterMargin = Application.InchesToPoints(0.3)
        .PrintHeadings = False
        .PrintGridlines = False
        .PrintComments = xlPrintSheetEnd
        .PrintQuality = 600
        .CenterHorizontally = True
```

Automating Tasks with Macros

Using a macro, you can automate any task you perform repeatedly. For example, you can create a macro to print a worksheet, insert a set of dates and values, or import data from a text file and store it in Excel. Macros perform repetitive tasks consistently and faster than you can. And, after the macro is created and tested, you can be assured the tasks are done exactly the same way each time.

Sharon wants to save the receipt portion of the worksheet as a PDF file that she can send as an attachment to the parent along with an email confirming the registration. In addition, Sharon wants data from the receipt to be transferred to the Registration Data worksheet. Sharon wants to simplify these tasks so volunteers don't need to repeat the same actions for each registration, and also to reduce the possibility of errors being introduced during the repetitive process. You will create a macro for each action.

To create and run macros, you need to use the DEVELOPER tab. The DEVELOPER tab has five groups—one for code, one for add-ins, one for controls, one for XML, and one to modify document controls. You'll use the Code group when working with macros. By default, the DEVELOPER tab is not displayed on the ribbon, so you'll display it.

To display the DEVELOPER tab on the ribbon:

1. If you took a break after the previous session, make sure the Youth Soccer workbook is open and the Receipt worksheet is active.

2. Look for the **DEVELOPER** tab on the ribbon. If you do not see it, continue with Step 3; otherwise continue with Step 7.

3. On the ribbon, click the **FILE** tab to open Backstage view, and then click **Options** in the navigation bar. The Excel Options dialog box opens.

4. In the left pane, click **Customize Ribbon**. The different commands and tabs you can add and remove from the ribbon are displayed. See Figure 7-29.

TIP
You can also right-click the ribbon and click Customize the Ribbon on the shortcut menu to add a ribbon tab.

Figure 7-29 Customize the Ribbon options in the Excel Options dialog box

> **5.** In the right pane, click the **Developer** check box to insert a checkmark.
> **6.** Click the **OK** button. The DEVELOPER tab appears on the ribbon.
> **7.** On the ribbon, click the **DEVELOPER** tab. See Figure 7-30.

Figure 7-30	DEVELOPER tab on the ribbon

tab added to the ribbon

Protecting Against Macro Viruses

Viruses can be and have been attached as macros to files created in Excel and other Office programs. A **virus** is a computer program designed to copy itself into other programs with the intention of causing mischief or harm. When unsuspecting users open these infected workbooks, Excel automatically runs the attached virus-infected macro. **Macro viruses** are a type of virus that uses a program's own macro programming language to distribute the virus. Macro viruses can be destructive and can modify or delete files that may not be recoverable. Because it is possible for a macro to contain a virus, Microsoft Office 2013 provides several options from which you can choose to set a security level you feel comfortable with.

Macro Security Settings

The macro security settings control what Excel will do about macros in a workbook when you open that workbook. For example, one user may choose to run macros only if they are "digitally signed" by a developer who is on a list of trusted sources. Another user might want to disable all macros in workbooks and see a notification when a workbook contains macros. The user can then elect to enable the macros. Excel has four macro security settings, which are described in Figure 7-31.

Figure 7-31	Macro security settings

Setting	Description
Disable all macros without notification	All macros in all workbooks are disabled and no security alerts about macros are displayed. Use this setting if you don't want macros to run.
Disable all macros with notification	All macros in all workbooks are disabled, but security alerts appear when the workbook contains a macro. Use this default setting to choose on a case-by-case basis whether to run a macro.
Disable all macros except digitally signed macros	The same as the "Disable all macros with notification" setting except any macro signed by a trusted publisher runs if you have already trusted the publisher. Otherwise, security alerts appear when a workbook contains a macro.
Enable all macros	All macros in all workbooks run. Use this setting temporarily in such cases as when developing an application that contains macros. This setting is not recommended for regular use.

© 2014 Cengage Learning

Excel | Tutorial 7 Developing an Excel Application

You set macro security in the Trust Center. The **Trust Center** is a central location for all of the security settings in Office. By default, all potentially dangerous content, such as macros and workbooks with external links, is blocked without warning. If content is blocked, the Message Bar (also called the trust bar) opens below the ribbon, notifying you that some content was disabled. You can click the Message Bar to enable that content.

You can place files you consider trustworthy in locations you specify; the file paths of these locations are stored as Trusted Locations in the Trust Center. Any workbook opened from a trusted location is considered safe, and content such as macros will work without the user having to respond to additional security questions in order to use the workbook.

> **REFERENCE**
>
> ### Setting Macro Security in Excel
>
> - On the DEVELOPER tab, in the Code group, click the Macro Security button.
> - Click the option button for the macro setting you want.
> - Click the OK button.
>
> or
>
> - Click the FILE tab, and then click Options in the navigation bar (or right-click the ribbon, and then click Customize the Ribbon on the shortcut menu).
> - Click the Trust Center category, and then click the Trust Center Settings button.
> - Click the Macro Settings category, and then click the option button for a macro setting.
> - Click the OK button.

Sharon wants the workbook to have some protection against macro viruses, so she asks you to set the security level to "Disable all macros with notification." When you open a file with macros, this macro security level disables the macros and displays a security alert, allowing you to enable the macros if you believe the workbook comes from a trusted source. After the macros are enabled, you can run them.

To set the macro security level:

1. On the DEVELOPER tab, in the Code group, click the **Macro Security** button. The Trust Center dialog box opens with the Macro Settings category displayed.

2. In the Macro Settings section, click the **Disable all macros with notification** option button if it is not already selected. See Figure 7-32.

Figure 7-32 Macro Settings in the Trust Center dialog box

selected macro security level

Macro Settings selected

3. Click the **OK** button.

Each time you open a workbook that contains a macro detected by the Trust Center, the macro is disabled and a Message Bar containing the Security Warning that macros have been disabled appears below the ribbon. If you developed the workbook or trust the person who sent you the workbook, click the Enable Content button to run the macros in the workbook. If you do not click the Enable Content button, you cannot run the macros in the workbook, but you can use the rest of the workbook.

> **INSIGHT**
>
> ### Using Digital Signatures with Macros
>
> A **digital signature** is like a seal of approval. It is often used to identify the author of a workbook that contains macros. You add a digital signature as the last step before you distribute a file. Before you can add a digital signature to a workbook, you need to obtain a digital ID (also called a digital certificate) that proves your identity. Digital certificates are typically issued by a certificate authority. After you have a digital certificate, do the following to digitally sign a workbook:
>
> - On the ribbon, click the FILE tab, and then, in the navigation bar, click Info.
> - On the Info screen, click the Protect Workbook button, and then click Add a Digital Signature.
> - If a dialog box opens asking if you would like to get a digital ID from a Microsoft Partner, click the Yes button. Your browser opens to a website with information about digital signature providers and available digital IDs.
> - Read the information.
> - Select a provider and follow the steps to obtain a digital ID from that provider.
>
> By digitally signing a workbook that contains a macro you intend to publicly distribute, you assure others (1) of the identity of the creator of the macro; and (2) that the macro has not been altered since the digital signature was created. When you open a digitally signed file, you can see who the author is, and decide whether the information in the file is authentic and whether you trust that the macros in the workbook are safe to run.
>
> The digital signature is removed any time a file with a digital signature is saved. This ensures that no one (including the original workbook author) can open a digitally signed file, make changes to the workbook, save the workbook, and then send the file to another user with the digital signature intact.

Recording a Macro

You can create an Excel macro in one of two ways: You can use the macro recorder to record keystrokes and mouse actions as you perform them, or you can enter a series of commands in the **Visual Basic for Applications (VBA)** programming language. The macro recorder can record only those actions you perform with the keyboard or mouse. The macro recorder is a good choice for creating simple macros. For more sophisticated macros, you might need to write VBA code directly in the Visual Basic Editor (VBE).

For Sharon's application, the actions you need to perform can all be done with the keyboard and the mouse, so you will use the macro recorder to record the two macros. One macro will save the receipt as a PDF file, which is a file format created by Adobe Systems for document exchange. The second macro will transfer data from the Receipt worksheet to the Registration Data worksheet.

PROSKILLS

Decision Making: Planning and Recording a Macro

Advance planning and practice help to ensure you create an error-free macro. First, decide what you want to accomplish. Then, consider the best way to achieve those results. Next, practice the keystrokes and mouse actions before you actually record the macro. This may seem like extra work, but it reduces the chance of error when you actually record the macro. As you set up the macro, consider the following:

- Choose a descriptive name that helps you recognize the macro's purpose.
- Weigh the benefits of selecting a shortcut key against its drawbacks. Although a shortcut key is an easy way to run a macro, you are limited to one-letter shortcuts, which can make it difficult to remember the purpose of each shortcut key. In addition, the macro shortcut keys will override the standard Office shortcuts for the workbook.
- Store the macro with the current workbook unless the macro can be used with other workbooks.
- Include a description that provides an overview of the macro and perhaps your name and contact information.

Good decision making includes thinking about what to do and what not to do as you progress to your goals. This is true when developing a macro as well.

Each macro must have a unique name that begins with a letter. The macro name can contain up to 255 characters, including letters, numbers, and the underscore symbol. The macro name cannot include spaces or special characters. It is helpful to use a descriptive name that describes the macro's purpose.

Macro shortcut keys are used to run a macro directly from the keyboard. You can assign a shortcut key to run the macro by selecting the Ctrl key plus a letter or the Ctrl+Shift keys plus a letter. If you use the same set of shortcut keys that are already assigned to a default Excel shortcut, the new shortcut you create overrides the default Excel shortcut for the open workbook. For example, using the Ctrl+p keys to run a macro overrides the default Excel 2013 shortcut for opening the Print screen while the workbook containing the macro is open. Some people find macro shortcut keys a quick way to run a macro; others dislike them because they override the original function of the shortcut key. It's a personal preference.

A macro needs to be stored somewhere. By default, the macro is stored in the current workbook, making the macro available in only that workbook when it is open. Another option is to store the macro in the **Personal Macro workbook**, a hidden workbook named PERSONAL.xlsb that opens whenever you start Excel, making the macro available any time you use Excel. The Personal Macro workbook stores commonly used macros that apply to many workbooks. It is most convenient for users on stand-alone computers. Finally, you can store the macro in a new workbook. Keep in mind that the new workbook must be open in order to use the macro. For example, an accountant might store a set of macros that help with end-of-the-month tasks in a separate workbook.

You can also add a description of the macro to briefly explain what it does. The description can also include the name of the person to contact and the date it was created.

Tutorial 7 Developing an Excel Application | Excel   EX 435

REFERENCE

Recording a Macro

- On the DEVELOPER tab, in the Code group, click the Record Macro button.
- Enter a name for the macro.
- Specify a shortcut key (optional).
- Specify the location to store the macro.
- Enter a description of the macro (optional).
- Click the OK button to start the macro recorder.
- Perform the tasks you want to automate.
- Click the Stop Recording button.

Sharon provided you with the following outline of the actions needed for the macro to save the receipt as a PDF file:

1. Set the range A18:F37 as the print area for the Registration Receipt.
2. Create the custom header "Registration Receipt" centered horizontally on the page.
3. Create the PDF file and name it "Receipt."
4. Remove the custom header and horizontal centering from the page.
5. Remove the print area.
6. Make cell A1 the active cell.

You'll record the steps for this macro using a macro named PDFReceipt that is assigned a keyboard shortcut, has a description, and is stored in the Youth Soccer workbook. Practice these steps before recording the macro. Once you feel comfortable with the steps, you can start the macro recorder.

To start the macro recorder:

> Save the workbook before recording a macro in case you make a mistake and need to restart.

1. Save the Youth Soccer workbook. If you make a mistake when recording the macro, you can close the workbook without saving, reopen the workbook, and then record the macro again.

2. On the DEVELOPER tab, in the Code group, click the **Record Macro** button. The Record Macro dialog box opens. The Macro name box displays a default name for the macro that consists of the word "Macro" followed by a number that is one greater than the number of macros already recorded in the workbook during the current Excel session. See Figure 7-33.

Figure 7-33   Record Macro dialog box

- enter a descriptive macro name
- enter a shortcut key (optional)
- select the location to store the macro
- enter a description of the macro (optional)

3. In the Macro name box, type **PDFReceipt** to change the selected default name to a more descriptive one, and then press the **Tab** key.

4. In the Shortcut key box, type **r** to set the Ctrl+r keys as the shortcut to run the macro from the keyboard, and then press the **Tab** key.

5. Verify that the Store macro in box is set to **This Workbook** to store the macro in the Youth Soccer workbook, and then press the **Tab** key.

6. In the Description box, type **Created 12/1/2016. Save receipt area, range A18:F37, as PDF file.** to enter notes about the macro.

7. Click the **OK** button. The workbook enters macro record mode. The Record Macro button changes to the Stop Recording button, which also appears on the status bar.

From this point on, *every* mouse click and keystroke you perform will be recorded and stored as part of the PDFReceipt macro. For that reason, it is very important to follow the instructions in the next steps precisely. Take your time as you perform each step, reading the entire step carefully first. After you finish recording the keystrokes, click the Stop Recording button to turn off the macro recorder.

To record the PDFReceipt macro:

1. Select the range **A18:F37**. This range contains the receipt that you want to print.

2. On the ribbon, click the **PAGE LAYOUT** tab.

3. In the Page Setup group, click the **Print Area** button, and then click **Set Print Area**. The receipt is set as the print area. Next, you'll insert a custom header.

4. In the Page Setup group, click the **Dialog Box Launcher** to open the Page Setup dialog box.

5. Click the **Header/Footer** tab, and then click the **Custom Header** button to open the Header dialog box.

6. Click in the **Center section** box, type **Registration Receipt**, and then click the **OK** button to close the Header dialog box.

7. In the Page Setup dialog box, click the **Margins** tab, click the **Horizontally** check box to select it, and then click the **OK** button. The receipt is centered on the page.

8. On the ribbon, click the **FILE** tab to open Backstage view, and then click **Export** in the navigation bar.

9. On the Export screen, make sure **Create PDF/XPS Document** is selected in the left pane, and then click the **Create PDF/XPS** button in the right pane. The Publish as PDF or XPS dialog box opens, which is similar to the Save As dialog box.

10. In the File name box, type **Receipt** to replace the suggested filename.

11. Make sure the folder is set to the location specified by your instructor.

12. Click the **Publish** button. The receipt is saved as a PDF file, and automatically opens in Adobe Reader or Adobe Acrobat, depending on which program is installed on your computer.

Trouble? If the receipt doesn't open, you probably don't have Adobe Reader or Adobe Acrobat installed on your computer. Continue with Step 14.

Tutorial 7 Developing an Excel Application | Excel **EX 437**

> ▶ 13. Close the PDF file. You should now see the Receipt worksheet in the Youth Soccer workbook.
>
> ▶ 14. On the PAGE LAYOUT tab, in the Page Setup group, click the **Print Area** button, and then click **Clear Print Area**.
>
> ▶ 15. In the Page Setup group, click the **Dialog Box Launcher** to open the Page Setup dialog box, click the **Header/Footer** tab, and then click the **Custom Header** button to open the Header dialog box.
>
> ▶ 16. Click in the **Center section** box, delete the custom header, and then click the **OK** button to close the Header dialog box.
>
> ▶ 17. In the Page Setup dialog box, click the **Margins** tab, click the **Horizontally** check box so that the printout is no longer centered on the page, and then click the **OK** button.
>
> ▶ 18. In the Receipt worksheet, click cell **A1**.
>
> You have completed all of the steps in the PDFReceipt macro. You'll turn off the macro recorder.
>
> ▶ 19. Click the **Stop Recording** button ☐ on the status bar. The macro recorder turns off, and the button changes to the Record Macro button.
>
> **Trouble?** If you made a mistake while recording the macro, close the Youth Soccer workbook without saving. If you got past the creation of the Registration Receipt, you will need to delete the Receipt file that you created.
>
> Reopen the workbook, and then repeat all of the steps beginning with the "To start the macro recorder" steps.

Be sure to turn off the macro recorder; otherwise, you'll continue to record your keystrokes and mouse clicks, leading to unintended consequences.

Be aware that the process for saving a workbook that contains a macro is different from saving one that does not contain a macro. If you need to save the workbook before you complete this session, refer to the "Saving a Workbook with Macros" section later in this session.

Running a Macro

After you record a macro, you should run it to test whether it works as intended. Running a macro means Excel performs each of the steps in the same order as when it was recorded. To run the macro you created, you can either use the shortcut key you specified or select the macro in the Macro dialog box. The Macro dialog box lists all of the macros in the open workbooks. From this dialog box, you can select and run a macro, edit the macro with VBA, run the macro one step at a time so you can determine in which step an error occurs, or delete it.

REFERENCE

Running a Macro

- Press the shortcut key assigned to the macro.

or

- On the DEVELOPER tab, in the Code group, click the Macros button.
- Select the macro from the list of macros.
- Click the Run button.

You will test the PDFReceipt macro by running it.

To run the PDFReceipt macro:

1. On the ribbon, click the **DEVELOPER** tab.

2. In the Code group, click the **Macros** button. The Macro dialog box opens, listing all of the macros in the open workbooks. See Figure 7-34.

Figure 7-34   Macro dialog box

all macros in the workbooks open on your computer are listed

runs the selected macro

opens VBE so you can edit the selected macro

deletes the selected macro

3. Verify that **PDFReceipt** is selected in the Macro name box, and then click the **Run** button. The PDFReceipt macro runs. The receipt is saved as a PDF file and the file is opened in Adobe Reader or Adobe Acrobat.

4. Close Adobe Reader or Adobe Acrobat. No print area is selected, and cell A1 is the active cell in the Receipt worksheet.

   Trouble? If the PDFReceipt macro did not run properly, you might have made a mistake in the steps while recording the macro. On the DEVELOPER tab, in the Code group, click the Macros button. Select the PDFReceipt macro, and then click the Delete button. Click the OK button to confirm the deletion, and then repeat all of the steps beginning with the "To start the macro recorder" steps.

   Next, you will test the shortcut keys you used for the PDFReceipt macro.

5. Press the **Ctrl+r** keys. The PDFReceipt macro runs. The receipt is saved as a PDF file. No print area is selected, and cell A1 in the Receipt worksheet is the active cell.

6. Close Adobe Reader or Adobe Acrobat.

   Trouble? If your macro doesn't end on its own, you need to end it. Press the Ctrl+Break keys to stop the macro from running.

The macro works as expected, printing the receipt as a PDF file.

Tutorial 7 Developing an Excel Application | Excel   EX 439

> **INSIGHT**
>
> ### How Edits Can Affect Macros
>
> Be careful when making seemingly small changes to a workbook, as these can have a great impact on macros. If a run-time error (an error that occurs while running a macro) appears when you run a macro that has worked in the past, some part of the macro code no longer makes sense to Excel. For example, simply adding a space to a worksheet name can affect a macro that references the worksheet. If you recorded a macro that referenced a worksheet named RegistrationData (no spaces in the name) that you later changed to Registration Data (space added to the name), the macro no longer works because the RegistrationData worksheet no longer exists. You could record the macro again, or you could edit the macro in VBA by changing RegistrationData to Registration Data.

Creating the TransferData Macro

You need to record one more macro. The data you entered earlier in the input section of the Receipt worksheet was never added to the Registration Data worksheet. Sharon wants to add this data to the next available blank row in the Registration Data worksheet. You'll record another macro to do this. You may want to practice the following steps before recording the macro:

1. Go to the Registration Data worksheet.
2. Turn off worksheet protection in the Registration Data worksheet.
3. Switch to the Receipt worksheet.
4. Select and copy the Transfer Area to the Clipboard.
5. Go to the Registration Data worksheet.
6. Go to cell A1, and then go to the last row in the Registration Data area.
7. Turn on Use Relative References. The Use Relative Reference button controls how Excel records the act of selecting a range in the worksheet. By default, the macro will select the same cells regardless of which cell is first selected because the macro records a selection using absolute cell references. If you want a macro to select cells regardless of the position of the active cell when you run the macro, set the macro recorder to record relative cell references.
8. Move down one row.
9. Turn off Use Relative References.
10. Paste values to the Registration Data worksheet.
11. Go to cell A1.
12. Turn on worksheet protection.
13. Switch to the Receipt worksheet, and then make cell B3 the active cell.

You may want to practice these steps before recording the macro. Sharon wants you to name this new macro "TransferData" and assign the Ctrl+t keys as the shortcut.

To record the TransferData macro:

▶ 1. Click the **Record Macro** button 📇 on the status bar to open the Record Macro dialog box, type **TransferData** in the Macro name box, type **t** in the Shortcut key box, type **Created 12/1/2016. Copy values in the transfer area in the Receipt worksheet to the Registration Data worksheet.** in the Description box, and then click the **OK** button. The macro recorder is on.

▶ 2. Go to the **Registration Data** worksheet.

▶ 3. Click the **REVIEW** tab on the ribbon, and then click the **Unprotect Sheet** button in the Changes group to turn off protection.

4. Go to the **Receipt** worksheet, and then select the range **A40:F40** in the Transfer Area.

5. Click the **HOME** tab on the ribbon, and then click the **Copy** button in the Clipboard group.

6. Click the **Registration Data** sheet tab, click cell **A1**, and then press the **Ctrl+↓** keys to go to the last row with values.

7. Click the **DEVELOPER** tab on the ribbon.

8. In the Code group, click the **Use Relative References** button. Relative references ensure that the receipt data being transferred is inserted in the next blank row (in this case, row 3) and not always in row 3 in the Registration Data worksheet.

9. Press the ↓ key to move to the first blank cell in the worksheet.

10. On the DEVELOPER tab, in the Code group, click the **Use Relative References** button. The Use Relative References button is toggled off.

11. On the ribbon, click the **HOME** tab.

12. In the Clipboard group, click the **Paste button arrow**, and then click the **Values** button in the Paste Values section. This option pastes the values rather than the formulas from the Transfer Area.

    Trouble? If #REF! appears in row 3 of the Registration Data worksheet, you clicked the Paste button instead of the Paste Values button. Stop the macro recorder. Delete the macro and begin recording the macro again.

13. Click cell **A1**, and then click the **REVIEW** tab on the ribbon.

14. In the Changes group, click the **Protect Sheet** button. The Protect Sheet dialog box opens.

15. In the Protect Sheet dialog box, click the **OK** button.

16. Click the **Receipt** sheet tab, and then click cell **B3**.

17. Click the **Stop Recording** button on the status bar. The macro recorder turns off, and the button changes to the Record Macro button.

> **TIP**
> You can also turn off the macro recorder by clicking the Stop Recording button in the Code group on the DEVELOPER tab.

You have completed recording the TransferData macro. Next, you'll test whether it works. Sharon has a new registration to add to the worksheet. You'll enter this data as you test the TransferData macro.

To test the TransferData macro:

1. Enter the following data into the range B3:B12, pressing the **Enter** key after each entry:

   12/01/2016

   Jason

   U10

   XL

   XT

   No

   Sofia Kilmer

   294 Hott Street

Moorefield, WV 26836

304-555-3444

▶ 2. Press the **Ctrl+t** keys. The TransferData macro runs, and the data transfers to the Registration Data worksheet.

▶ 3. Go to the **Registration Data** worksheet, and then verify that the data for Sofia Kilmer appears in row 4.

▶ 4. Go to the **Receipt** worksheet.

The TransferData macro makes it easy for the entered data to be transferred to the Registration Data worksheet.

Fixing Macro Errors

If a macro does not work correctly, you can fix it. Sometimes you'll find a mistake when you test a macro you just created. Other times you might not discover that error until later. No matter when you find an error in a macro, you have the following options:

- Rerecord the macro using the same macro name.
- Delete the recorded macro, and then record the macro again.
- Run the macro one step at a time to locate the problem, and then use one of the previous methods to correct the problem.

You can delete or edit a macro by opening the Macro dialog box (shown earlier in Figure 7-34), selecting the macro from the list, and then clicking the appropriate button. To rerecord the macro, simply restart the macro recorder and enter the same macro name you used earlier. Excel overwrites the previous version of the macro.

Working with the Visual Basic Editor

To view the code of a macro, you need to open the Visual Basic Editor, which is a separate application that works with Excel and all of the Office programs to view, debug, edit, and manage VBA code. The VBE consists of several components, including the Code window that contains the VBA code, the Project Explorer window that displays a tree-like diagram consisting of every open workbook, and a menu bar with menus of commands you use to edit, debug, and run VBA statements. You can access the Visual Basic Editor through the Macro dialog box or the Visual Basic button in the Code group on the DEVELOPER tab.

REFERENCE

Editing a Macro

- On the DEVELOPER tab, in the Code group, click the Macros button, select the macro in the Macro name list, and then click the Edit button (or on the DEVELOPER tab, in the Code group, click the Visual Basic button).
- Use the Visual Basic Editor to edit the macro code.
- Click File on the menu bar, and then click Close and Return to Microsoft Excel.

Sharon wants the PDFReceipt macro to stop in cell B3 of the Receipt worksheet. Right now, the macro stops with cell A1 selected. Although you can delete the PDFReceipt macro and record it again, it is simpler to edit the existing macro. You will edit the VBA command in the macro.

EX 442 Excel | Tutorial 7 Developing an Excel Application

To view the code for the PDFReceipt macro:

1. On the ribbon, click the **DEVELOPER** tab.
2. In the Code group, click the **Macros** button. The Macro dialog box opens.
3. Click **PDFReceipt** in the Macro name list, and then click the **Edit** button. The Visual Basic Editor opens as a separate program, consisting of two windows—the Project Explorer and the Code window.
4. If the Code window is not maximized, click the **Maximize** button ☐ on the Code window title bar. The Code window contains the VBA code generated by the macro recorder. You will see the beginning of the PDFReceipt sub. See Figure 7-35 (your window may differ).

Figure 7-35 Visual Basic for Applications Editor window

Callouts:
- Code window for Module1
- Sub and the macro name indicate the first line of a macro
- command to select the range A18:F37
- command to set the center section of the header
- command to make cell A1 the active cell
- comments appear in green
- End of sub

```
Sub PDFReceipt()
'
' PDFReceipt Macro
' Created 12/1/2016. Save receipt area, range A18:F37, as PDF file.
'
' Keyboard Shortcut: Ctrl+r
'
    ActiveWindow.SmallScroll Down:=6
    Range("A18:F37").Select
    ActiveSheet.PageSetup.PrintArea = "$A$18:$F$37"
    Application.PrintCommunication = False
    With ActiveSheet.PageSetup
        .PrintTitleRows = ""
        .PrintTitleColumns = ""
    End With
    Application.PrintCommunication = True
    ActiveSheet.PageSetup.PrintArea = "$A$18:$F$37"
    Application.PrintCommunication = False
    With ActiveSheet.PageSetup
        .LeftHeader = ""
        .CenterHeader = "Registration Receipt"
        .RightHeader = ""
        .LeftFooter = ""
        .CenterFooter = ""
        .RightFooter = ""
        .LeftMargin = Application.InchesToPoints(0.7)
        .RightMargin = Application.InchesToPoints(0.7)
        .TopMargin = Application.InchesToPoints(0.75)
        .BottomMargin = Application.InchesToPoints(0.75)
        .HeaderMargin = Application.InchesToPoints(0.3)
        .FooterMargin = Application.InchesToPoints(0.3)
        .PrintHeadings = False
        .FirstPage.RightHeader.Text = ""
        .FirstPage.LeftFooter.Text = ""
        .FirstPage.CenterFooter.Text = ""
        .FirstPage.RightFooter.Text = ""
    End With
    Application.PrintCommunication = True
    ActiveWindow.SmallScroll Down:=-18
    Range("A1").Select
End Sub
Sub TransferData()
'
' TransferData Macro
' Recorded 12/1/2016. Copy values in the transfer area in the Receipt worksheet to the Registration Data worksheet
'
' Keyboard Shortcut: Ctrl+t
'
    Sheets("Registration Data").Select
    ActiveSheet.Unprotect
    Sheets("Receipt").Select
    ActiveWindow.SmallScroll Down:=24
    Range("A40:F40").Select
    Selection.Copy
```

Trouble? If you see a different number of windows in the Visual Basic Editor, your computer is configured differently. You will be working with the Code window, so you can ignore any other windows.

Understanding the Structure of Macros

The VBA code in the Code window lists all of the actions you performed when recording the PDFReceipt macro. In VBA, macros are called **sub procedures**. Each sub procedure begins with the keyword *Sub* followed by the name of the sub procedure and a set of parentheses. In the example in Figure 7-35, the code begins with

```
Sub PDFReceipt()
```

which provides the name of this sub procedure—PDFReceipt—the name you gave the macro. The parentheses are used to include any arguments in the procedure. These arguments pass information to the sub procedure and have roughly the same purpose as the arguments in an Excel function. If you write your own VBA code, sub procedure arguments are an important part of the programming process. However, they are not used when you create macros with the macro recorder.

Following the `Sub PDFReceipt()` statement are comments about the macro taken from the macro name, shortcut key, and description you entered in the Record Macro dialog box. Each line appears in green and is preceded by an apostrophe (*'*). The apostrophe indicates that the line is a comment and does not include any actions Excel needs to perform.

After the comments is the body of the macro, a listing of all of the commands performed by the PDFReceipt macro as written in the VBA language. Your list of commands might look slightly different, depending on the exact actions you performed when recording the macro. Even though you might not know VBA, some of the commands are easy to interpret. For example, near the top of the PDFReceipt macro, you should see the command:

```
Range("A18:F37").Select
```

which tells Excel to select the range A18:F37. Several lines below this command you see the following command, which sets the words "Registration Receipt" at the top of the print page in the center of the custom header:

```
.CenterHeader = "Registration Receipt"
```

At the bottom of the macro is the following statement, which indicates the end of the PDFReceipt sub procedure:

```
End Sub
```

A Code window can contain several sub procedures, with each procedure separated from the others by the `SubProcedureName()` statement at the beginning, and the End Sub statement at the end. Sub procedures are organized into **modules**. As was shown in Figure 7-35, all of the macros that have been recorded are stored in the Module1 module (your window may differ).

Editing a Macro Using the Visual Basic Editor

The Visual Basic Editor provides tools to assist you in writing error-free code. As you type a command, the editor will provide pop-up windows and text to help you insert the correct code.

Sharon wants you to edit the following command in the PDFReceipt sub procedure, which sets the active cell to cell A1:

```
Range("A1").Select
```

You'll change the command to

```
Range("B3").Select
```

to change the active cell from cell A1 to cell B3.

To edit a command in the macro:

1. Scroll down the Code window to the line immediately before `End Sub` in the PDFReceipt macro.

2. In the line with the command `Range("A1")`, select **A1**, and then type **B3**. The command in the macro is edited to select a different cell. See Figure 7-36.

Figure 7-36   **Edited Macro**

```
            .FirstPage.RightHeader.Text = ""
            .FirstPage.LeftFooter.Text = ""
            .FirstPage.CenterFooter.Text = ""
            .FirstPage.RightFooter.Text = ""
        End With
        Application.PrintCommunication = True
        ActiveWindow.SmallScroll Down:=-18
        Range("B3").Select
End Sub
Sub TransferData()
'
' TransferData Macro
' Recorded 12/1/2016. Copy values in the transfer area in the Receipt worksheet to the Registration
'
' Keyboard Shortcut: Ctrl+t
'
    Sheets("Registration Data").Select
    ActiveSheet.Unprotect
    Sheets("Receipt").Select
    ActiveWindow.SmallScroll Down:=24
    Range("A40:F40").Select
    Selection.Copy
```

cell reference changed from A1 to B3

3. On the menu bar, click **File**, and then click **Close and Return to Microsoft Excel**. The Visual Basic Editor closes, and the Youth Soccer workbook is displayed.

Sharon wants you to test the macro. You'll check to see whether cell B3 is the active cell once the macro has run.

To test the edited PDFReceipt macro:

1. Press the **Ctrl+r** keys. The PDFReceipt macro runs.

   Trouble? If a Microsoft Visual Basic message box appears with a run-time error, click the End button, click the Macros button, click PDFReceipt in the Macro name box, and then click the Edit button. In the Code window, find the line you edited (one line above End Sub), and then change it to `Range("B3").Select`. On the menu bar, click File, and then click Close and Return to Microsoft Excel.

2. Close Adobe Reader. Cell B3 is the active cell.

Creating Macro Buttons

Another way to run a macro is to assign it to a button placed directly in the worksheet. Macro buttons are often a better way to run macros than shortcut keys. Clicking a button (with a descriptive label) is often more intuitive and simpler for users than trying to remember different combinations of keystrokes.

Tutorial 7 Developing an Excel Application | Excel   EX 445

> **REFERENCE**
>
> **Creating a Macro Button**
>
> - On the DEVELOPER tab, in the Controls group, click the Insert button.
> - In the Form Controls section, click the Button (Form Control) button.
> - Click the worksheet where you want the macro button to be located, drag the pointer until the button is the size and shape you want, and then release the mouse button.
> - In the Assign Macro dialog box, select the macro you want to assign to the button.
> - With the button still selected, type a new label.

Sharon wants you to add two macro buttons to the Receipt worksheet—one for each of the macros you've created. You will create the macro buttons in the blank range A14:B16 so they don't obscure any existing data.

To insert a macro button in the worksheet:

1. Scroll so that the range **A14:B16** of the Receipt worksheet is completely visible.

2. On the DEVELOPER tab, in the Controls group, click the **Insert** button. The Form Controls appear, with a variety of objects that can be placed in the worksheet. You'll insert the Button form control. See Figure 7-37.

Figure 7-37   Form Controls

inserts a button on the worksheet

Trouble? If the Insert button is unavailable, the worksheet is protected. Click the REVIEW tab. In the Changes group, click the Unprotect Sheet button to unprotect the Receipt worksheet, and then repeat Step 2.

3. In the Form Controls section, click the **Button (Form Control)** button, and then point to cell **A14**. The pointer changes to ✚.

4. Click and drag the pointer over the range **A14:A16**, and then release the mouse button. A button appears on the worksheet. The Assign Macro dialog box opens with the button's default name in the Macro name box. See Figure 7-38.

Figure 7-38   **Assign Macro dialog box**

default macro name (yours might differ) → Button14_Click

select the macro you want to assign to this button → PDFReceipt

[Assign Macro dialog box showing Macro name: Button14_Click, with list containing PDFReceipt and TransferData; Macros in: All Open Workbooks; buttons New, Record, OK, Cancel]

From the Assign Macro dialog box, you can assign a macro to the button. After you assign a macro to the button, the button appears with a default label. You can change the default label to a descriptive one that will indicate which macro will run when the button is clicked.

Sharon wants you to assign the PDFReceipt macro to this new button, and then rename the button with a label that reflects the PDFReceipt macro.

To assign the PDFReceipt macro to the new button:

1. In the Macro name box, click **PDFReceipt**.
2. Click the **OK** button. The PDFReceipt macro is assigned to the selected button.
3. With the sizing handles still displayed around the button, type **Create PDF Receipt** (do not press the Enter key). The new label replaces the default label.

    Trouble? If no sizing handles appear around the button, the button is not selected. Right-click the button, click Edit Text to place the insertion point within the button, and then repeat Step 3.

    Trouble? If a new line appeared in the button, you pressed the Enter key after entering the label. Press the Backspace key to delete the line, and then continue with Step 4.

4. Click any cell in the worksheet to deselect the macro button.

At this point, if you click the Create PDF Receipt button, the PDFReceipt macro will run. Before you test the Create PDF Receipt button, you will add the other button.

To add another macro button to the Receipt worksheet:

1. On the DEVELOPER tab, in the Controls group, click the **Insert** button, and then click the **Button (Form Control)** button.

2. Drag the pointer over the range **B14:B16**.

3. In the Assign Macro dialog box, click **TransferData** in the Macro name box, and then click the **OK** button.

4. Type **Transfer Data** as the button label, and then click any cell in the worksheet to deselect the button. See Figure 7-39.

TIP
To move or resize a macro button, right-click it, press the Esc key, and then drag a sizing handle or the selection box.

Figure 7-39 Macro buttons on Receipt worksheet

			Age Group	Shirt Size	Sock Size
3	Registration Date	12/1/2016	U4	XSM	XSH
4	Player Name	Jason	U5	SM	SH
5	Age Group	U10	U6	M	M
6	Shirt Size	XL	U7	L	T
7	Sock Size	XT	U8	XL	XT
8	Early Registration	No	U9		
9	Parent	Sofia Kilmer	U10		
10	Address	294 Hott Street			
11	City State Zip	Moorefield, WV 26836			
12	Telephone	304-555-3444	Registration Fee/Discount		
13			Season Fee		75
14			Discount Amount		5
15	Create PDF Receipt	Transfer Data			
16					
17					
18					

macro buttons added to the worksheet

Trouble? If the macro buttons on your screen do not match the size and location of the buttons shown in the figure, right-click a button to select it, press the Esc key to close the shortcut menu, and then resize or reposition the button on the worksheet as needed.

You have completed the application, so you will reset worksheet protection.

5. On the ribbon, click the **REVIEW** tab.

6. In the Changes group, click the **Protect Sheet** button. The Protect Sheet dialog box opens.

7. Click the **OK** button to turn on worksheet protection.

You have completed the Create PDF Receipt and TransferData macro buttons.

INSIGHT

Creating a Macro Button with Pictures or Shapes

You are not restricted to using the control buttons on the DEVELOPER tab for macro buttons. A macro can also be assigned to a picture or shape. For example, sometimes you might want to assign to an arrow a macro that takes you to another worksheet.

1. On the INSERT tab, in the Illustrations group, click the button for the picture, online picture, or shape you want to use for a macro button.
2. Drag the pointer over the range where you want to insert the picture or shape on the worksheet.
3. Resize and position the picture or shape as needed.
4. Right-click the picture or shape, and then click Edit Text on the shortcut menu to add a name to the button.
5. Change the style, fill, and outline of the picture or shape as needed.
6. Right-click the picture or shape, and then click Assign Macro on the shortcut menu. The Assign Macro dialog box opens.
7. In the Macro name box, select the macro you want to assign to the button, and then click the OK button.

No matter what picture or shape you use for the macro button, the macro runs when the button is clicked.

Sharon has a new season registration to add to the worksheet. You'll enter this data and then test the Create PDF Receipt and TransferData macro buttons.

To test the macro buttons:

1. In the range **B3:B12**, enter the following subscriber order:

   12/2/2016

   Noah

   U8

   M

   M

   Yes

   Christopher Miller

   1231 Viking Avenue

   Wheeling, WV 26003

   304-555-8848

2. Click the **Create PDF Receipt** button to save the current receipt as a PDF file. See Figure 7-40.

Tutorial 7 Developing an Excel Application | Excel **EX 449**

| Figure 7-40 | PDF file created from the PDFReceipt macro |

Receipt.pdf - Adobe Reader

Registration Receipt

Youth Soccer League
777 Main Street
Oak Hill, WV 25901

		Registration Date	12/2/2016
Parent	Christopher Miller	**Player Name**	Noah
Address	1231 Viking Avenue	**Age Group**	U8
City State Zip	Wheeling, WV 26003	**Shirt Size**	M
Telephone	304-555-8848	**Sock Size**	M

Season Fee	75
Discount Amount	5
Total	**$ 70**

3. Close Adobe Reader to return to the Receipt worksheet.
4. Click the **Transfer Data** button to transfer data to the Registration Data worksheet. Excel inserts the new transaction in the table.
5. Go to the **Registration Data** worksheet and make sure the data was transferred. See Figure 7-41.

| Figure 7-41 | Data transferred to the Registration Data worksheet with the TransferData macro |

	A	B	C	D	E	F
1	Parent	Telephone	Player	Age Group	Shirt Size	Sock Size
2	Thomas Lincoln	304-555-2225	Patrick	U8	L	M
3	James Smith	304-555-1111	Sandy	U6	SM	XSH
4	Sofia Kilmer	304-555-3444	Jason	U10	XL	XT
5	Christopher Miller	304-555-8848	Noah	U8	M	M
6						

← new record inserted

The macro buttons make it simpler to create the receipt and transfer the data from the Receipt worksheet into the Registration Data worksheet.

INSIGHT

Making Data Entry Easier with a Data Form

When a lot of data needs to be entered, consider creating a data form. A data form is a dialog box that lists the labels and entry boxes from an Excel table or structured range of data in a worksheet. Data forms can be helpful when people who are unfamiliar with Excel need to enter the data. They can also be useful when a worksheet is very wide and requires repeated horizontal scrolling.

To create a data form, do the following:

1. Make sure each column in the structured range of data or the Excel table has column headers. These headers become the labels for each field on the form.
2. Add the Form button to the Quick Access Toolbar. Click the Customize Quick Access Toolbar button, and then click More Commands. In the Quick Access Toolbars options, click the Choose commands from arrow, click Commands Not in the Ribbon, click the Form button in the box, click the Add button, and then click the OK button. The Form button appears on the Quick Access Toolbar.
3. Select the range or table for which you want to create the data form.
4. On the Quick Access Toolbar, click the Form button. The data form opens with the selected fields ready for data entry.
5. Enter data in each box, and then click the New button to add the complete record to end of the range or table and create a new record.
6. Click the Close button to close the data form.

Saving a Workbook with Macros

When you save a workbook that contains macros, a dialog box opens indicating that the workbook you are trying to save contains features that cannot be saved in a macro-free workbook. The default Excel workbook does not allow macros to be stored as part of the file. If you want to save the workbook without the macros, click the Yes button. The workbook will be saved as a macro-free workbook, which means the macros you created will be lost. If you want to save the workbook with the macros, click the No button, and then save the workbook as a new file—one that allows macros to be saved as part of the file. The default Excel Workbook format, which is a macro-free workbook, has the .xlsx file extension. You need to change this to a macro-enabled workbook, which has the .xlsm file extension.

You have completed your work on the Excel application, so you will save and close the workbook and then exit Excel.

To save the workbook with macros:

1. On the Quick Access Toolbar, click the **Save** button 🖫. A dialog box opens indicating that the workbook you are trying to save contains features that cannot be saved in a macro-free workbook. See Figure 7-42.

Tutorial 7 Developing an Excel Application | Excel   **EX 451**

Figure 7-42   Macro warning dialog box

> Microsoft Excel
>
> The following features cannot be saved in macro-free workbooks:
>
> • VB project
>
> To save a file with these features, click No, and then choose a macro-enabled file type in the File Type list.
>
> To continue saving as a macro-free workbook, click Yes.
>
> [Yes]   [No]   [Help]

▶ 2. Click the **No** button. The Save As dialog box opens so you can save the workbook as a macro-enabled workbook.

▶ 3. In the File name box, type **Youth Soccer with Macros** so you can easily determine which workbook contains macros.

▶ 4. Click the **Save as type** button, and then click **Excel Macro-Enabled Workbook**.

▶ 5. Navigate to the location where you saved the files you created in this tutorial.

▶ 6. Click the **Save** button. The workbook is saved with the macros.

▶ 7. Close the workbook.

Opening a Workbook with Macros

TIP

After you enable the content, the filename is added to a list of trusted files and the Security Warning will not reappear as long as the workbook name or location is not changed.

When you open a file with macros, Excel checks the opening workbook to see if it contains any macros. The response you see is based on the security level set on the computer. Earlier, you disabled all macros with notification. Therefore, all of the macros will be disabled when the workbook opens. When the workbook opens the first time, a SECURITY WARNING appears in the Message Bar providing the option to enable the macros so they can be run, or to open the workbook with the macros disabled. If you know a workbook contains macros that you or a coworker created, you can enable them, which adds the filename to a list of trusted files so that you won't see the SECURITY WARNING when you open this file again. If you do not click the Enable Content button, the macros remain disabled and unavailable during the current session, but the other features of the workbook are still available.

You'll open the Youth Soccer with Macros workbook and enable the macros.

To open the Youth Soccer with Macros workbook and enable the macros:

▶ 1. Open the **Youth Soccer with Macros** workbook. The workbook opens, and "SECURITY WARNING Macros have been disabled." appears in the Message Bar below the ribbon. See Figure 7-43.

Figure 7-43   SECURITY WARNING in the Message Bar

SECURITY WARNING appears when opening a workbook that contains macros

2. In the Message Bar, click the **Enable Content** button. The macros in the workbook are available for use.

3. Go to the **Receipt** worksheet.

Removing a Tab from the Ribbon

If you decide you don't want a tab displayed on the ribbon, you can remove it. Now that the macros are completed, Sharon doesn't need the DEVELOPER tab to appear on the ribbon. You will remove it.

To remove the DEVELOPER tab from the ribbon:

1. Right-click any tab on the ribbon, and then click **Customize the Ribbon** on the shortcut menu. The Excel Options dialog box opens with the Customize Ribbon options displayed.

2. In the right box listing the Main Tabs, click the **Developer** check box to remove the checkmark.

3. Click the **OK** button. The DEVELOPER tab is removed from the ribbon.

4. Save the workbook, and then close it.

Sharon is pleased with your work on the Youth Soccer workbook. The workbook protection and macros will streamline the data entry process for volunteers.

Session 7.3 Quick Check

1. Which tab must be displayed on the ribbon in order to record a macro?
2. What types of actions should you record as a macro?
3. Describe two ways of creating a macro.
4. What are the three places in which you can store a macro?
5. Identify two ways to run a macro.
6. What are the steps to edit a macro?
7. How do you insert a macro button into a worksheet?
8. What happens when you save a workbook with the .xlsx extension and it contains a macro?

Review Assignments

PRACTICE

Data File needed for the Review Assignments: TBall.xlsx

You did such a good job helping Sharon with the Youth Soccer application that she recommended you to a friend, Terry Winkel, who has a similar project within the youth sports community. Terry wants to create a receipt system for the Youth T-Ball league. Complete the following:

1. Open the **TBall** workbook located in the Excel7 ► Review folder included with your Data Files, and then save the workbook as **Youth TBall** in the location specified by your instructor.
2. In the Documentation worksheet, enter your name and the date.
3. In the Receipt worksheet, do the following:
    a. Create defined names from selection using the range A3:B11 to name all of the input cells.
    b. Change the defined name Address to **Street_Address**.
    c. Use the Name box to create the defined name **Player_Sizes** for the range D2:E8.
    d. Paste the list of defined names in the Documentation worksheet.
4. Create the validation rules shown in Figure 7-44 for the range B5:B7.

Figure 7-44   Validation rules for cells B5, B6, and B7

Cell	Settings	Input Message	Error Alert
B5	List Source (4YO, 5-6YO)	Title: Age Group Message: Click arrow to select the player's age group.	Style: Stop Title: Invalid Age Group Message: Invalid Age Group. Use arrow to select Age Group.
B6	List Source (D4:D8)	Title: Shirt Size Message: Click arrow to select shirt size.	Style: Stop Title: Invalid Shirt Size Message: Invalid Shirt Size. Use arrow to select Shirt Size.
B7	List Source (D4:D7)	Title: Hat Size Message: Click arrow to select hat size.	Style: Stop Title: Invalid Hat Size Message: Invalid Hat Size. Use arrow to select Hat Size.

© 2014 Cengage Learning

5. In the range B3:B11, enter the data shown in Figure 7-45.

Figure 7-45   Registration Data

Registration Date	12/1/2016
Player Name	Nicole
Age Group	5-6YO
Shirt Size	SM
Hat Size	SM
Parent	Jason Headley
Address	1154 Wallenberg Place
City State Zip	Oak Hill, WV 25901
Telephone	304-555-3456

© 2014 Cengage Learning

6. Enter the following formulas for the transfer area in the specified cells using the defined names you created earlier:
   Cell A37: **=Parent**
   Cell B37: **=Telephone**
   Cell C37: **=Player_Name**
   Cell D37: **=Age_Group**
   Cell E27: **=Shirt_Size**
   Cell F27: **=Hat_Size**
7. Unlock the input cells on the Receipt worksheet so that the user can enter data only in the range B3:B11.
8. Enter the following formulas in the specified cells to add information to the registration receipt:
   Cell B26: **=Parent**
   Cell B27: **=Street_Address**
   Cell B28: **=City_State_Zip**
   Cell B29: **=Telephone**
   Cell E24: **=Registration_Date**
   Cell E26: **=Player_Name**
   Cell E27: **=Age_Group**
   Cell E28: **=Shirt_Size**
   Cell E29: **=Hat_Size**
9. In cell E33, enter a formula with an IF function. If the player is in the 4YO age group, the fee will be the value in cell E11; otherwise, it will be the value in cell E12.
10. Protect the Documentation and Registration Data worksheets so that the user cannot enter data. Do not use a password.
11. Add the DEVELOPER tab to the ribbon.
12. Save the workbook. If you have any trouble as you record the macros, you can close the workbook without saving, open the workbook that you saved, and start with Step 13.
13. Create a macro named **PDF_TBReceipt** with **Ctrl+r** as the shortcut key. Store the macro in the current workbook. Type **Created 12/1/2016. Save receipt area: range A17:F34 as PDF file.** as the description. Record the following steps to create the PDF_TBReceipt macro:
    a. Make the Receipt worksheet the active sheet.
    b. Select the range A17:F34 and set the range as the print area.
    c. Open the Page Setup dialog box.
    d. Type **T-Ball Registration Receipt** in the center pane of the custom header.
    e. Export the worksheet to create a PDF/XPS document with the filename **Receipt** saved to the location specified by your instructor.
    f. Close the PDF file.
    g. Clear the print area.
    h. In the Receipt worksheet, make cell B3 the active cell.
14. Remove worksheet protection from the Registration Data worksheet.
15. Create a macro named **TransferData** with **Ctrl+t** as the shortcut key. Store the macro in the current workbook. Type **Created 12/1/2016. Copy values in the transfer area of the Receipt worksheet to the Registration Data worksheet.** in the macro description. Record the following steps to create the TransferData macro:
    a. Make the Receipt worksheet the active worksheet.
    b. Select the transfer area and copy it to the Clipboard.

c. Go to the Registration Data worksheet.
   d. Click cell A1, and then go to the last row with values. (Hint: Press the Ctrl+↓ keys.)
   e. On the DEVELOPER tab, turn on Use Relative References located on the DEVELOPER tab.
   f. Move down one row.
   g. Turn off Use Relative References.
   h. Paste values in the Registration Data worksheet.
   i. Click cell A1.
   j. Turn on Use worksheet protection.
   k. Go to the Receipt worksheet, and then make cell B3 the active cell.
16. Create a macro named **ClearInput** with **Ctrl+i** as the shortcut key. Store the macro in the current workbook. Type **Created 12/1/2016. Clear the values in the input area, range B3:B11.** as the description. Record the following steps to create the ClearInput macro:
    a. In the Receipt worksheet, select the range B3:B11, and then delete the data from those cells.
    b. Make cell B3 the active cell.
17. Test each macro using the shortcut keys you assigned to it.
18. Create a macro button for each of the three macros, and place them between the Registration Data and the Receipt form on the Receipt worksheet. Assign the following labels to the macro buttons:
    a. **Print PDF Receipt** for the PDF_TBReceipt macro button
    b. **Transfer Data** for the TransferData macro button
    c. **Clear Input** for the ClearInput macro button
    (*Hint*: You may need to remove cell protection to create the buttons and then reset it.)
19. Remove the DEVELOPER tab from the ribbon.
20. Test the macro buttons. Save the workbook as **Youth TBall with Macros**, a macro-enabled workbook, and then close the workbook.

Case Problem 1

APPLY

Data File needed for this Case Problem: Study.xlsx

Greater Southern University The administration and faculty of Greater Southern University in Harrodsburg, Kentucky, have started a study abroad program and want to collect data from students who have completed this study. A group of volunteers will contact the students who participated in the program to get their information and impressions of the program. Adam Anderson, the dean of instruction, has started to design a form to enter this information, but he needs your help. He wants you to set up data validation rules and table lookups, and record macros to enter the data. Complete the following:

1. Open the **Study** workbook located in the Excel7 ▸ Case1 folder included with your Data Files, and then save the workbook as **Study Abroad** in the location specified by your instructor.
2. In the Documentation worksheet, enter your name and the date.
3. In the Input worksheet, create defined names from selection using the range A2:B9 to name all of the input cells.
4. On the Data Tables worksheet, paste the list of defined names.
5. Create the validation rules shown in Figure 7-46 for the range B4:B9.

Figure 7-46 Validation rules for the range B4:B9

Cell	Validation	Input Message	Error Alert
B4	List Source (A2:A10 on Data Tables worksheet)	Title: Major Message: Click arrow to select major.	Type: Stop Title: Invalid Major Message: Invalid Major. Use arrow to select Major.
B5	Must be greater than or equal to 2012	Title: Year of Study Message: Enter a year of study greater than or equal to 2012 (the starting year of the program).	Type: Stop Title: Invalid Year of Study Message: Invalid Year of Study. Enter a year of study greater than or equal to 2012 (the starting year of the program).
B6	List Source (FA, SP, SU)	Title: Semester of Study Message: Click arrow to select semester of study.	Type: Stop Title: Invalid Semester of Study Message: Invalid Semester of Study. Use arrow to select Semester of Study.
B7	List Source (C2:C11 on Data Tables worksheet)	Title: Country Message: Click arrow to select country.	Type: Stop Title: Invalid Country Message: Invalid Country. Use arrow to select Country.
B8	List Source (Yes, No)	Title: Completed Message: Click arrow to select response.	Type: Stop Title: Invalid Response Message: Invalid response. Use arrow to select response.
B9	Text input. Minimum of 0 characters, maximum of 1500 characters.	Title: Comments Message: Enter your comments. You will be limited to 1500 characters.	Type: Warning Title: Invalid Comments Message: Invalid comments. You have exceeded the limit of characters for comment. Those characters above the limit will be dropped.

© 2014 Cengage Learning

6. In the range B2:B8, enter the following data:
   Cell B2: **=12/1/2016**
   Cell B3: **=Otis Davidson**
   Cell B4: **=International Relations**
   Cell B5: **=2012**
   Cell B6: **=SP**
   Cell B7: **=Switzerland**
   Cell B8: **=Yes**
   Cell B9: **=I would LOVE to go back!**
7. Enter the following formulas for the specified cells in the transfer area:
   Cell A12: **=B2**
   Cell B12: **=B3**
   Cell C12: **=B4**
   Cell D12: **=B5**
   Cell E12: **=B6**
   Cell F12: **=B7**
   Cell G12: **=B8**
   Cell H12: **=B9**
8. Unlock the Input cells in the Input worksheet so that the user can enter data only in the range B2:B9.

9. Protect the Documentation, Data, and Data Tables worksheets so that the user cannot enter data. Do not use a password.
10. Add the DEVELOPER tab to the ribbon.
11. Save the workbook so that you can return to Step 12 and rerecord the macros if you have trouble.
12. Create a macro named **TransferData** with **Ctrl+t** as the shortcut key. Store the macro in the current workbook. Type **Created 12/1/2016. Copy values in the transfer area of the Input worksheet to the Data worksheet** as the description. Record the following steps to create the TransferData macro:
    a. Make the Input worksheet the active worksheet.
    b. Select the transfer area and then copy it to the Clipboard.
    c. Go to the Data worksheet and turn off the worksheet protection.
    d. Go to cell A1, and then go to the last row with values. (*Hint*: Press the Ctrl+↓ keys.)
    e. On the DEVELOPER tab, turn on Use Relative References.
    f. Move down one row.
    g. Turn off Use Relative References.
    h. Paste values to the Data worksheet.
    i. Go to cell A1.
    j. Turn on the worksheet protection.
    k. Go to the Input worksheet, and then make cell B2 the active cell.
13. Create a macro named **ClearInput** with **Ctrl+i** as the shortcut key. Store the macro in the current workbook. Type **Created 12/1/2016. Clear the values in the input area, range B2:B9.** in the macro description. Record the following steps to create the ClearInput macro:
    a. Select the range B2:B9 in the Input worksheet, and then delete the data from those cells.
    b. Make cell B3 the active cell.
14. Test the macros using the shortcut keys you assigned to each of them.
15. Create macro buttons for both macros to the right of the Study Abroad Input form. Enter labels that describe the corresponding macro. You will need to remove protection while creating the buttons. Be sure to reapply the cell protection once you have created the buttons.
16. Remove the DEVELOPER tab from the ribbon.
17. Test the macro buttons. Save your workbook as **Study Abroad with Macros**, a macro-enabled workbook, and then close the workbook.

Case Problem 2

Data File needed for this Case Problem: Cloggers.xlsm

OMG Cloggers OMG Cloggers is a group of traveling dancers based in Avon, Connecticut. The group goes from event to event demonstrating the techniques of clogging. It has been able to support its travels with a series of fundraisers. The most popular and profitable has been an annual fruit sale. The group sells cartons of various fresh fruits during the winter holidays. Armen Maslov, the director of the group, has started developing a workbook that will allow him to analyze the sales from the fruit fundraiser. He asks you to finish creating the application that would allow volunteers to enter order and sales data for any year and chart the profit. Complete the following:

1. Open the macro-enabled **Cloggers** workbook located in the Excel7 ▶ Case2 folder included with your Data Files, and then save the macro-enabled workbook as **OMG Fundraiser** in the location specified by your instructor.
2. In the Documentation worksheet, enter your name and the date. Review the formulas, defined names, and data validation information in the Fundraiser Data worksheet and the Fundraiser Chart worksheet.

   Troubleshoot 3. The profit calculation is not returning the correct results. Identify the error in the calculation and correct it.

⚙ **Troubleshoot** 4. In the Documentation worksheet, Armen pasted a list of defined names used in the workbook; but then he continued to modify the worksheet. Make sure all of the defined names are included in the list and are accurate. Fix any errors you find or replace the list.

5. Unlock the ranges B5:B9 and E5:E9 in the Fundraiser Data worksheet so that the user can enter data only in those cells.
6. Protect the Fundraiser Data worksheet. Do not use a password.
7. Make sure that the DEVELOPER tab is on the ribbon.
8. Save the workbook to back it up in case you have problems with your macros.

⚙ **Troubleshoot** 9. The macro ClearInput has already been recorded and saved with the Ctrl+i shortcut key. The macro should perform the following tasks, but is not working correctly. Edit the macro as needed to make it work as intended.
   a. Select the range B5:B9 and clear the contents.
   b. Select the range E5:E9 and clear the contents.
   c. Make cell A1 the active cell.

   Run the macro using the shortcut key. It does not perform all of the steps correctly. Locate the problem and correct it using the Visual Basic for Applications editor. If the macro still does not run correctly, close the workbook without saving your changes, reopen the workbook, and then edit the macro again.

10. Create a macro named **PrintChart** with the **Ctrl+c** shortcut key and an appropriate macro description that performs the following actions:
    a. Select the Fundraiser Chart worksheet.
    b. Export the Fundraiser Chart worksheet to a PDF named **Chart** in the location specified by your instructor.
    c. In the Fundraiser Data worksheet, make cell A1 the active cell.
11. Test the PrintChart macro. If the macro doesn't work, close the workbook without saving your changes, reopen the workbook, and record the macro again.
12. Create a button below the totals on the Fundraiser Data worksheet, and then assign the PrintChart macro to the button. Change the default label to a more descriptive one. Remember to remove cell protection while creating buttons. Make sure you reapply cell protection once you have finished creating your buttons.

⚙ **Troubleshoot** 13. The label is missing from the second button. Determine the name of the macro that is assigned to the button and correct the descriptive label. Remember to remove cell protection while modifying buttons. Make sure you reapply cell protection after you have finished editing the button.

14. Run the PrintChart and ClearInput macros to test the buttons and revise the macros if necessary.
15. Remove the DEVELOPER tab from the ribbon.
16. Save the workbook as **OMG Fundraiser with Macros**, a macro-enabled workbook, and then close the workbook.

CHALLENGE

Case Problem 3

Data File needed for this Case Problem: Music.xlsx

Music Inventory Christian Wirth has an extensive collection of music CDs. He wants to create a better way to organize the inventory of what he owns. Christian has started a workbook that he can use to enter each artist, CD, genre, and song in his collection. He asks you to finish it by incorporating input validation, cell protection, and macros to help ensure that the collected information is accurate. Complete the following:

1. Open the **Music** workbook located in the Excel7 ▸ Case3 folder included with your Data Files, and then save the workbook as **Music Inventory** in the location specified by your instructor.

2. In the Documentation sheet, enter your name and the date, and then review all of the worksheets in the workbook.
3. In the Music Entry worksheet, create appropriate defined names for each cell in the ranges A2:B4 and A12:B14.
4. Create the following validation rules:
   a. Genre (cell B4): The list of genres is in the range D2:D11. Enter an appropriate input message and error alert.
   b. Artist (cell B12): The list of artists are in the range A2:A3 on the CDs worksheet. Enter an appropriate input message and error alert.
   c. CD (cell B13): The list of CDs is in the range B2:B3 on the CDs worksheet. Enter an appropriate input message and error alert.
5. Test the validation rules for cells B4, B12, and B13 to ensure that the correct data appears in the validation lists.

   Explore 6. Insert a WordArt text box, and then enter **Music Inventory** as the text. Rotate the WordArt so that it is vertical in column E. Change the text fill to a color complementing the shade of green in the headings. (*Hint*: On the INSERT tab, click the Insert WordArt button. Then use the DRAWING TOOLS FORMAT tab to format the WordArt.)
7. Create the following formulas for the specified cells in the CD Transfer Area:
   Cell A22: **=Artist_Name**
   Cell B22: **=CD_Name**
   Cell C22: **=Genre**
8. Create the following formulas for the specified cells in the Song Transfer Area:
   Cell A25: **=Artist**
   Cell B5: **=CD**
   Cell C25: **=Song**
9. In the Music Entry worksheet, unlock the input cells, which are in the ranges B2:B4 and B12:B14.
10. Protect the Documentation, Music Entry, CDs, and Songs worksheets.
11. Enter the following data as a new CD:
    Artist_Name: **Sam Jones**
    CD Name: **Live Like You Were Having Fun**
    Genre: **Jazz**
12. Enter the following data as a new Song:
    Artist: **Josh Green**
    CD: **Darkness**
    Song: **Clouds of New York City**

    (*Hint*: The CD Darkness by Josh Green was entered earlier. In order to enter a new Song, the CD must have been already added.)
13. Save the workbook to back it up before recording macros.
14. Make sure that the DEVELOPER tab is displayed on the ribbon.
15. Create a macro named **AddCD** with the shortcut key **Ctrl+c** that performs the following actions:
    a. Go to the CDs worksheet, and then remove the cell protection.
    b. Insert a blank line above row 3, and then make the blank cell A3 the active cell.
    c. Make the Music Entry worksheet the active sheet.
    d. Select the CD Transfer Area and copy it to the Clipboard.
    e. Return to the CDs worksheet.
    f. In row 3, paste the values from the Clipboard.
    g. Select cell A1, and then turn on cell protection.
    h. Go to the Music Entry worksheet, and then make cell B2 the active cell.

16. Create a macro named **AddSong** with the shortcut key **Ctrl+s** that performs the following actions:
    a. Go to the Songs worksheet and remove the cell protection.
    b. Insert a blank line above row 3.
    c. Make the blank cell A3 the active cell.
    d. Make the Music Entry worksheet the active sheet.
    e. Select the Song Transfer Area and copy it to the Clipboard.
    f. Return to the Songs worksheet.
    g. In row 3, paste the values from the Clipboard.
    h. Select cell A1, and then turn on cell protection.
    i. Go to the Music Entry worksheet, and then make cell B2 the active cell.
17. Record a macro named **ClearCDInput** with no shortcut key to clear the range B2:B4 of the New CD input area. The last step should make cell B2 the active cell.
18. Record a macro named **ClearSongInput** with no shortcut key to clear the range B12:B14 of the New Song input area. The last step should make cell B2 the active cell.
19. Test all of the macros by selecting and running the macros on the DEVELOPER tab.
20. Explore Remove the cell protection on the Music Entry worksheet. Create macro buttons for all four macros using either clip art or shapes. Make sure that you have used descriptive labels for each macro button. Set cell protection again for the Music Entry worksheet.
21. Test all of the macro buttons. Check the CDs and Songs worksheets to see how and where new records were added.
22. Remove the DEVELOPER tab from the ribbon.
23. Save the workbook as **Music Inventory with Macros**, a macro-enabled workbook, and then close the workbook.

Case Problem 4

There are no Data Files needed for this Case Problem.

Trinette's Trilbies & Fedoras   Several years ago, Trinette Jalbert started making trilby hats (commonly called trilbies), which are narrow-brimmed fedora hats, for male family friends. As the requests started pouring in, she turned her hobby into a business. Her customers now include men and women, and she makes fedoras in addition to trilbies. Trinette wants a billing/invoicing system to expedite her work. You will create the finished application for her. Complete the following:

1. Open a new, blank workbook, and then save it as **Hats** in the location specified by your instructor.
2. Rename the sheet as **Documentation**, and then enter the company name, your name, the date, and a purpose statement. Insert two additional sheets, and then rename them as **Invoice** and **Product Information**.
3. In the Product Information worksheet, enter the data for the available colors, fabrics, sizes, hat types, standard hat price, surcharge, and shipping fee shown in Figure 7-47.

Figure 7-47 Input data for Trinette's Trilbies & Fedoras

	A	B	C	D	E	F	G	H
1	Color		Size		Hat Type		Shipping	
2	Dark Brown		XS		Trilby		15	
3	Navy Blue		S		Fedora			
4	Black		M					
5			L		Standard			
6	Fabric		XL				75	
7	Tweed		XXL					
8	Wool		XXXL		Surcharge			
9	Felt						15	
10								
11								

4. In the Invoice worksheet, create the invoice shown in Figure 7-48. Use defined names and structured references to assist in creating formulas. (*Hint*: Review the steps below before you begin to create the invoice.)

   a. Enter the labels as shown in Figure 7-48.
   b. Change the column widths and format the labels appropriately.
   c. Use a function to insert the current date.
   d. Insert a comment in the Sold To: cell with a reminder about what data should be entered in cells B10, B11, and B12.
   e. Use data validation rules to create lists of the different hat types, fabrics, colors, and sizes you entered on the Product Information worksheet. Use appropriate input messages and error alerts.
   f. Create defined names for the data on the invoice.
   g. For the unit price, enter a formula to display the standard price listed on the Product Information worksheet.
   h. Enter a formula to display for the fabric surcharge listed on the Product Information worksheet only when a customer purchases a hat with felt fabric. (*Hint*: You will need to use an IF function.)
   i. In the Subtotal cell, enter a formula that uses defined names to add the unit price and the surcharge.
   j. In the Sales Tax cell, enter a formula that uses a defined name to calculate 6.5% of the subtotal.
   k. In the Shipping cell, enter a formula to display the shipping fee listed on the Product Information worksheet.
   l. In the Total Due cell, enter a formula that sums the Subtotal, Sales Tax, and Shipping cells.
   m. Format the cells and add borders and shading where you feel they will make the invoice clearer to read.

Figure 7-48   Finished invoice for Trinette's Trilbies & Fedoras

	A	B	C	D	E	F	G	H	I
1									
2				Trinette's Trilbies & Fedoras					
3				56745 North Street					
4				Fredericktown, OH 43019					
5				740-555-6565					
6							Date		
7							7/19/2016		
8									
9		Sold To:							
10		Sam Smith							
11		123 Main Street							
12		Zanesville, OH 43701							
13									
14				Hat Information			Unit Price		
15		Hat Type	Trilby				$ 75.00		
16		Fabric	Tweed			Fabric Surcharge*	$ -		
17		Color	Navy Blue						
18		Size	M						
19									
20						Subtotal	$ 75.00		
21						Sales Tax	$ 4.88		
22						Shipping	$ 15.00		
23						Total Due	$ 94.88		
24		* Fabric Surcharge is on Felt only							
25									
26									

5. Protect the worksheet so a user can enter the Sold To: (cells B10, B11, and B12) and Hat Information (cells C15, C16, C17, and C18) data, but cannot enter data in any other cells. Do not use a password. Protect the entire Documentation and Product Information worksheets. Do not use a password.
6. Save the workbook.
7. Create a macro named **PrintInvoice** that prints the invoice. Assign a shortcut key and type an appropriate macro description as you begin recording this macro. Set the print area to the range A1:H25 and center the worksheet horizontally. The heading has the label I N V O I C E in the center of the page heading. Create a macro button on the Invoice worksheet, assign the PrintInvoice macro to the button, and then enter a descriptive label for the button.
8. Create a macro named **ClearInputs** that deletes the values from cells B10, B11, B12, C15, C16, C17, and C18. Assign a shortcut key and type an appropriate macro description as you begin recording this macro. Create a macro button on the Invoice worksheet, assign the ClearInputs macro to the button, and then enter a descriptive label for the button. (*Hint*: Use the Delete key to clear a value from a cell.)
9. Remove the cell protection from the Documentation worksheet. In the Documentation worksheet, paste a list of the defined names with their locations. Below this entry, type a list of the macro names and their shortcut keys. Reapply cell protection to the Documentation worksheet.
10. Test the worksheet by entering the data shown in Figure 7-47.
11. Use the PrintInvoice macro button to print the invoice for the data you entered in Step 10, and then use the ClearInputs macro button to remove the input data.
12. Remove the DEVELOPER tab from the ribbon.
13. Save the workbook as **Hats with Macros**, and then close the workbook.

TUTORIAL 8

Working with Advanced Functions

Calculating Employee Compensation and Benefits

OBJECTIVES

Session 8.1
- Use the IF function
- Use the AND function
- Use the OR function
- Use structured references in formulas

Session 8.2
- Nest the IF function
- Use the VLOOKUP function
- Use the HLOOKUP function
- Use the IFERROR function

Session 8.3
- Use conditional formatting to highlight duplicate values
- Summarize data using the COUNTIF, SUMIF, and AVERAGEIF functions

Case | Educational Video Games

Educational Video Games (EVG) is a software development company that develops and markets educational games for children in preschool through second grade. The business has expanded rapidly in the five years since it was founded and now has nearly 100 employees in four locations within the United States.

Patrick Yang, director of compensation and benefits, uses Excel to track basic employee information such as each employee's name, gender, birth date, hire date, medical and dental plans, job status, and current salary. Now he needs to track employee enrollment in and costs related to the compensation and benefit programs offered by the company, such as how much the company contributes to each employee's 401(k) retirement account and medical and dental plans. He also needs to calculate the amount EVG will spend on bonuses and salary increases for the next fiscal year. In addition, the human resources staff wants to send cards to each employee during her/his birthday month.

To provide Patrick with all this information, you'll use a variety of logical and lookup functions. After you calculate those values, you'll summarize information in the Employee Summary worksheet so Patrick can quickly see the impact of the compensation and benefits package on the company.

STARTING DATA FILES

Excel8 → Tutorial
EVG.xlsx

Review
Compensation.xlsx

Case1
Spirit.xlsx

Case2
Receivables.xlsx

Case3
Currency.xlsx

Case4
Instruments.xlsx

Microsoft product screenshots used with permission from Microsoft Corporation.

Session 8.1 Visual Overview:

When you create a formula that references all or parts of an Excel table, you can replace a specific cell or range address with a **structured reference**, which is the actual table name or column header.

The **IF function** is a logical function that evaluates a condition, and then returns one value if the condition is true and a different value if the condition is false.

A **logical condition** is an expression such as G2="FT" that returns either a TRUE value or a FALSE value.

The **AND function** is a logical function that returns a TRUE value if all of the logical conditions are true, and a FALSE value if any of the logical conditions are false.

The **OR function** is a logical function that returns a TRUE value if any of the logical conditions are true, and a FALSE value if none of the logical conditions are true.

P2: `=IF(OR([Location]="NY",[Location]`

`=IF(MONTH(D2)=$A`

`=IF(AND(G2="FT",`

`=IF(OR([Location]="NY",[Location]="SF"),[C`

Emp ID	Last Name	Birth Date	Location	Job Status	Current Salary
1002	Lowe	9/6/1966	NY	FT	$ 108,7
1006	Forbes	12/15/1985	SF	FT	$ 75,8
1010	Speulda	9/24/1968			
1014	Hunt	8/9/1959	NY	FT	$ 84,0
1018	Hanson	7/15/1950	NY		
1022	Philo	5/2/1958	SF		
1026	Stolt	12/7/1977	SF	FT	$ 101,8
1030	Akhalaghi	12/4/1961	NY	FT	$ 38,4
1034					
1038	McCorkle				
1042	Mattis	8/27/1989	AT	FT	$ 65,1
1046	Baker	1/6/1968	DA	FT	$ 71,0
1050	Vines	4/28/1958	AT	FT	$ 60,1
1054	Mittelman	10/4/1971	NY	FT	$ 64,8
1058	Coley	1/4/1960	AT	FT	$ 49,8
1062	Johnson	9/16/1970	NY	FT	$ 76,7
1066	Jackson	12/2/1985	AT	FT	$ 91,2

© 2014 Cengage Learning

Tutorial 8 Working with Advanced Functions | Excel EX 465

Logical Functions

In this formula, the structured reference [Current Salary] references the cells in column I of the Employee table.

When a formula is entered in a cell within an Excel table, the formula is automatically copied to all cells in that column. The column is referred to as a **calculated column**.

cation]="SF"),[Current Salary]*0.035,[Current Salary]*0.025)

Current Salary	Years Service	Birthday Month	401(k) Company Match	Salary Increase
08,706		Yes	$ 3,261.18	$ 3,804.71
75,818	2.3		$ 2,274.55	$ 2,653.64
=$AD$1,"Yes","")		es	$ 1,384.28	$ 1,614.99
84,036	2.5		$ 2,521.09	$ 2,941.27
ND(G2="FT",M2>=1),I2*0.03,0)			$ 2,054.11	$ 2,396.46
			$ 3,907.45	$ 4,558.69
01,822	3.8		$ 3,054.67	$ 3,563.78
38,421	1.1		$ 1,152.62	$ 1,344.72

),[Current Salary]*0.035,[Current Salary]*0.025)

609.33
629.53
775.51
503.25
269.60
245.80
684.73
281.00

To test two or more conditions and determine whether *all* conditions are true, you use the AND function as the logical test of the IF function.

To test two or more conditions and determine whether *any* condition is true, you use the OR function as the logical test of the IF function.

Function Arguments

IF
Logical_test   OR([Location]="NY",[Location]=   = TRUE
Value_if_true   [Current Salary]*0.035   = {3804.70588391606;2653.636681164...
Value_if_false [Current Salary]*0.025   = {2717.64705994004;1895.454772260...

= {3804.70588391606;2653.636681164...
Checks whether a condition is met, and returns one value if TRUE, and another value if FALSE.

Logical_test   is any value or expression that can be evaluated to TRUE or FALSE.

Formula result = $ 3,804.71

Help on this function   OK   Cancel

The Function Arguments dialog box makes it simpler to build an IF function with a nested AND function or a nested OR function (shown here) for the logical test.

120%

Working with Logical Functions

Logical functions such as IF, AND, and OR determine whether a condition is true or false. A condition uses one of the comparison operators <, <=, =, <>, >, or >= to compare two values. You can combine two or more functions in one formula, creating more complex conditions.

Patrick created a workbook that contains data for each EVG employee. He stored this information in an Excel table. The table includes each employee's ID, last name, hire date, birth date, gender, location, job status, performance rating, current salary, medical plan, dental plan, age, and years of service at EVG. Patrick wants you to determine if an employee birthday occurs in a specified month, calculate the 401(k) company cost, and calculate a proposed salary increase. You will use IF, AND, and OR functions to do this after you open Patrick's workbook and review the employee data.

To open and review the EVG workbook:

1. Open the **EVG** workbook located in the Excel8 ► Tutorial folder included with your Data Files, and then save the workbook as **EVG Employees** in the location specified by your instructor.

2. In the Documentation worksheet, enter your name and the date.

3. Go to the **Employee Data** worksheet. The worksheet contains an Excel table named Employee, which includes each employee's ID, last name, hire date, birth date, gender, location, job status, performance rating, current salary, medical plan, dental plan, age, and years of service at EVG. See Figure 8-1.

Figure 8-1   Employee Data worksheet

Emp ID	Last Name	Hire Date	Birth Date	Gender	Location	Job Status	Perf Rating	Current Salary	Medical Plan	Dental Plan	Age	Years Service
1002	Lowe	5/24/2010	9/6/1966	F	NY	FT	3	$108,706	SPOUSE2500	EMP+SPOUSE	49	6.6
1006	Forbes	8/28/2014	12/15/1985	F	SF	FT	2	$75,818	NONE	NONE	30	2.3
1010	Speulda	4/24/2015	9/24/1968	M	SF	FT	2	$46,143	FAMILY1000	EMP+FAMILY	47	1.7
1014	Hunt	7/18/2014	8/9/1959	M	NY	FT	3	$84,036	SPOUSE1000	NONE	56	2.5
1018	Hanson	8/21/2015	7/15/1950	F	NY	FT	1	$68,470	FAMILY1000	EMP+FAMILY	65	1.4
1022	Philo	3/5/2015	5/2/1958	F	SF	FT	2	$130,248	FAMILY1000	EMP+FAMILY	57	1.8
1026	Stolt	3/1/2013	12/7/1977	M	SF	FT	3	$101,822	FAMILY2500	NONE	38	3.8
1030	Akhalaghi	12/8/2015	12/4/1961	F	NY	FT	2	$38,421	SPOUSE1000	EMP+SPOUSE	54	1.1
1034	Vankeuren	8/11/2011	1/10/1959	F	NY	PT	3	$53,582	FAMILY1000	EMP+FAMILY	56	5.4
1038	Mccorkle	6/12/2009	1/30/1942	F	AT	FT	2	$24,373	FAMILY2500	EMP+FAMILY	73	7.6
1042	Mattis	5/4/2012	8/27/1989	M	AT	FT	2	$65,181	SINGLE1000	EMP	26	4.7
1046	Baker	12/18/2015	1/6/1968	F	DA	FT	3	$71,020	FAMILY2500	EMP+FAMILY	47	1.0
1050	Vines	5/4/2011	4/28/1958	M	AT	FT	2	$60,130	SINGLE1000	EMP	57	5.7
1054	Mittelman	11/26/2004	10/4/1971	M	NY	FT	2	$64,846	SPOUSE2500	EMP+SPOUSE	44	12.1
1058	Coley	2/22/2008	1/4/1960	F	AT	FT	1	$49,832	SINGLE1000	EMP	55	8.9
1062	Johnson	12/4/2015	9/16/1970	F	NY	FT	2	$76,707	FAMILY1000	EMP+FAMILY	45	1.1
1066	Jackson	10/12/2015	12/2/1985	F	AT	FT	3	$91,240	SINGLE2500	EMP	30	1.2

4. Scroll down and to the right. Although the column headers remain visible as you scroll down, the employee ID and name disappear as you scroll to the right.

5. Select cell **C2**, and then freeze the panes so columns A and B remain on the screen as you scroll across the screen.

Inserting Calculated Columns in an Excel Table

TIP

Calculated columns work only in Excel tables. In a range of data, you must copy and paste the formula or use the AutoFill feature.

An Excel table does not have a fixed structure. When you add a column to an Excel table, the table expands and the new column has the same table formatting style as the other columns. If you enter a formula in one cell of a column, the formula is automatically copied to all cells in that column. These calculated columns are helpful as you add formulas to an Excel table.

If you need to modify the formula in a calculated column, you edit the formula in any cell in the column and the formulas in all of the cells in that table column are also modified. If you want to edit only one cell in a calculated column, you need to enter a value or a formula that is different from all the others in that column. A green triangle appears in the upper-left corner of the cell with the custom formula in the calculated column, making the inconsistency easy to find. After a calculated column contains one inconsistent formula or value, any other edits you make to that column are no longer automatically copied to the rest of the cells in that column. Excel does not overwrite custom values.

PROSKILLS

Written Communication: Creating Excel Table Fields

Excel tables should be easy to use as well as understand. This requires labeling and entering data in a way that effectively communicates a table's content or purpose. If a field is entered in a way that is difficult to use and understand, it becomes more difficult to find and present data in a meaningful way.

To effectively communicate a table's function, keep the following guidelines in mind when creating fields in an Excel table:

- **Create fields that require the least maintenance.** For example, hire date and birth date require no maintenance after they are entered, unlike age and years of service, whose values change each year. If you need to know the specific age or years of service, use calculations to determine them based on values in the Hire Date and Birth Date columns.
- **Store the smallest unit of data possible in a field.** For example, use three separate fields for City, State, and Zip code rather than one field. Using separate fields for each unit of data enables you to sort or filter each field. If you want to display data from two or more fields in one column, you can use a formula to reference the City, State, and Zip code columns. For example, you can use the & operator to combine the city, state, and zip code in one cell as follows: `=C2&D2&E2`
- **Apply a text format to fields with numerical text data.** For example, formatting fields such as zip codes and Social Security numbers as text ensures that leading zeros are stored as part of the data. Otherwise, the zip code 02892 is stored as a number and displayed as 2892.

Using these guidelines means that you and others will spend less time interpreting data and more time analyzing results. This lets you more effectively communicate the data in an Excel table.

Using the IF Function

In many situations, the value you store in a cell depends on certain conditions. Consider the following examples:

- An employee's gross pay depends on whether that employee worked overtime.
- An income tax rate depends on the taxpayer's adjusted taxable income.
- A shipping charge depends on the dollar amount of an order.

To evaluate these types of conditions, you use the IF function. Recall that the IF function is a logical function that evaluates a condition, and then returns one value if the condition is true and another value if the condition is false. The value can be text, numbers, cell references, formulas, or functions. The IF function has the syntax

```
IF(logical_test, value_if_true, value_if_false)
```

where `logical_test` is a condition that is either true or false, `value_if_true` is the value returned by the function if the condition is true, and `value_if_false` is the value returned by the function if the condition is false. The IF function results in only one value—either the `value_if_true` or the `value_if_false`.

You will use an IF function to alert Patrick that an employee has a birthday during a specified month. EVG employees who have an upcoming birthday receive a birthday card. A Yes value in the Birthday Month column will indicate that an employee has a birthday during the specified month, and a blank cell will indicate that an employee does not have a birthday during the specified month.

The flowchart shown in Figure 8-2 illustrates Patrick's logic for determining whether a birthday occurs in a specified month. The flowchart shows that if an employee's birth month occurs in the specified month (*birth month = specified month* is True), "Yes" is entered in the cell. If the employee does not have a birthday in the specified month, the cell is left blank.

Figure 8-2   **Flowchart with logic to determine if an employee's birthday is in the specified month**

```
                    Employee's
         False    birth month =    True
                  specified month

   Birthday this month = " "        Birthday this month = Yes
```

© 2014 Cengage Learning

The Employee table doesn't include a column that lists only the birth month; this information is included as part of the employee's complete birth date, which is stored in column D. To extract the month portion of the employee's birth date, you will use the MONTH function. This function is a Date function that returns the month as a number from 1 (January) to 12 (December). The MONTH function has the syntax

```
MONTH(date)
```

where `date` is a date that includes the month you want to extract. Recall that Excel stores dates as a number equal to the number of days between January 1, 1900 and the specified date so they can be used in calculations. For example, January 1, 2016 is stored as the serial number 42370 because it occurs 42370 days since the start of Excel's calendar. The MONTH function determines the month number from the stored serial number. For example, the birth date of the employee in row 2 of the Employee table is 9/6/1966, which is stored in cell D2. The following MONTH function extracts the month portion of this stored date, which is 9:

```
=MONTH(D2)
```

You'll use the MONTH function in the logical test of the IF function, which will check whether the employee's birth month matches the month number entered in cell AD1 of the Employee Data worksheet. Patrick wants to know which employees have birthdays in September, so he entered 9 as the month number in cell AD1. The following formula includes the complete IF function to determine if an employee has a birthday in September:

```
=IF(MONTH(D2)=$AD$1,"Yes","")
```

The logical test MONTH(D2)=$AD$1 determines if the employee's birth month is equal to the birth month stored in cell AD1. If the condition is TRUE, Yes is displayed in the Birthday Month column; otherwise, the cell is left blank.

You'll add a column to the Employee table to display the results of the IF function that determines if an employee's birthday occurs in the specified month.

To determine which employees have birthdays in the specified month:

1. In cell **N1**, enter **Birthday Month**. The Excel table expands to include this column and applies the table formatting to all the rows in the new column.

2. Make sure cell **N2** is the active cell, and then click the **Insert Function** button f_x next to the formula bar. The Insert Function dialog box opens.

3. Click **Logical** in the Or select a category list, click **IF** in the Select a function box, and then click the **OK** button. The Function Arguments dialog box for the IF function opens.

4. In the Logical_test box, type **MONTH(D2)=$AD$1** and then press the **Tab** key. This condition tests whether the employee's birth month is equal to the month specified in cell AD1. The function MONTH returns the month number of the date specified in cell D2. TRUE appears to the right of the Logical_test argument box, indicating this employee has a birthday in the specified month.

5. In the Value_if_true box, type **Yes** and then press the **Tab** key. This argument specifies that if the condition is true (the employee's birth month matches the value in cell AD1), display Yes as the formula result. The value to the right of the Value_if_true argument box is Yes because the condition is true. Notice Excel inserts quotation marks around the text value because you did not include them.

6. In the Value_if_false box, type **""**. This argument specifies that if the condition is false (the employee's birth month does not match the value in cell AD1), display nothing in cell N2. The value to the right of the Value_if_false argument box is "", which indicates that cell N2 appears blank if the condition is false. See Figure 8-3.

Figure 8-3 Function Arguments dialog box for the IF function

function arguments applied to the employee in the current row of the table

7. Click the **OK** button. The formula =IF(MONTH(D2)=$AD$1,"Yes","") appears in the formula bar, and Yes appears in cell N2 because the condition is true. The formula is automatically copied to all cells in column N of the table. See Figure 8-4.

Figure 8-4 Birthday Month column added to the Employee table

Using the AND Function

The IF function evaluates a single condition. However, you often need to test two or more conditions and determine whether *all* conditions are true. You can do this with the AND function. The AND function is a logical function that returns the value TRUE if all of the logical conditions are true, and returns the value FALSE if any or all of the logical conditions are false. The syntax of the AND function is

```
AND(logical1[,logical2]...)
```

where `logical1` and `logical2` are conditions that can be either true or false. If all of the logical conditions are true, the AND function returns the logical value TRUE; otherwise, the function returns the logical value FALSE. You can include up to 255 logical conditions in an AND function. However, keep in mind that *all* of the logical conditions listed in the AND function must be true for the AND function to return a TRUE value.

Figure 8-5 illustrates how the AND function is used to determine student eligibility for the dean's list. In this scenario, when students have 12 or more credits (stored in cell B1) *and* their GPA is greater than 3.5 (stored in cell B2), they are placed on the dean's list. Both conditions must be true for the AND function to return the logical value TRUE.

Figure 8-5   AND function example

Purpose: To determine dean's list requirements

Logic Scenario: 12 or more semester credits and GPA above 3.5

Formula: AND function with two conditions
=AND(B1>=12,B2>3.5)

Data: cell B1 stores number of credits
cell B2 stores student's GPA

Example:

Data		Condition1	Condition2	Results
Cell B1	Cell B2	B1>=12	B2>3.5	(Dean's List?)
15	3.6	True	True	True
12	3.25	True	False	False
6	3.8	False	True	False
10	3.0	False	False	False

© 2014 Cengage Learning

Patrick wants you to use an AND function to determine employee eligibility for the company's 401(k) plan. EVG employees are eligible for the 401(k) benefit if they are full-time employees (FT in Job Status) *and* have worked for the company for one or more years (1 or greater in Years Service). As long as *both* conditions are true, the company contributes an amount equal to 3 percent of the employee's salary to the employee's 401(k). If neither condition is true or if only one condition is true, the employee is not eligible for the 401(k) benefit and the company's contribution is 0. Patrick outlined these eligibility conditions in the flowchart shown in Figure 8-6.

Figure 8-6   Flowchart illustrating AND logic for the 401(k) benefit

Full-Time Employee AND employed 1 or more years

One or more False → 401(k) Cost = 0

All True → 401(k) Cost = Current Salary X 3%

© 2014 Cengage Learning

To calculate the cost of the 401(k) plan for each employee, you need to use the AND function with the IF function. You use the AND function shown in the following formula as the logical test to evaluate whether each employee in the Employee table fulfills the eligibility requirements:

```
=AND(G2="FT",M2>=1)
```

This formula tests whether the value in cell G2 (the job status for the first employee) is equal to FT (an abbreviation for full time), and whether the value in cell M2 (the years of service for the first employee) is greater than or equal to 1 (indicating one or more years of employment at EVG). When an employee is a full-time employee (G2="FT") *and* has worked one or more years at EVG (M2>=1), the AND function returns the value TRUE; otherwise, the AND function returns the value FALSE. Figure 8-7 shows the result returned by the AND function for four different sets of employee values for job status and years of service.

Figure 8-7 AND function results for 401(k) plan eligibility

Purpose: To determine employee eligibility for the company's 401(k) plan

Logic Scenario: An employee is eligible for the 401(k) plan if the employee's status is full time (FT) AND the employee's years of service total one or more years.

Formula: AND function with two conditions
=AND(G2="FT",M2>=1)

Data: cell G2 stores Job Status
cell M2 stores Years Service

Example:

Data		Condition1	Condition2	Results
Cell G2	Cell M2	G2="FT"	M2>=1	(Eligible?)
FT	1	True	True	True
FT	0	True	False	False
PT	5	False	True	False
PT	0	False	False	False

© 2014 Cengage Learning

The AND function shows only whether an employee is eligible for the 401(k) plan. It does not calculate how much EVG will contribute to that employee's 401(k) plan if the employee is eligible. To determine whether an employee is eligible *and* to calculate the amount of the 401(k) contribution, you use this AND function within an IF function. When the results of one function are used as the argument of another function, the functions are *nested*. In the following formula, the AND function (shown in red) is nested within the IF function and is used as the logical test that determines whether the employee is eligible for a 401(k) contribution:

```
=IF(AND(G2="FT",M2>=1),I2*0.03,0)
```

If the employee is eligible, the AND function returns the logical value TRUE and the IF function multiplies the employee's current salary by 3 percent. If the AND function returns the logical value FALSE, the IF function displays the value 0.

Tutorial 8 Working with Advanced Functions | Excel EX 473

You'll insert a new column in the Employee table, and then enter the formula to calculate the 401(k) company match.

To calculate the 401(k) company match using the IF and AND functions:

1. In cell **O1**, enter **401(k) Company Match** as the column header. The Excel table expands to include the new column, and cell O2 is the active cell.

2. Make sure cell **O2** is the active cell, and then click the **Insert Function** button f_x next to the formula bar. The Insert Function dialog box opens.

3. Click **IF** in the Select a function box, and then click the **OK** button. The Function Arguments dialog box opens.

4. In the Logical_test box, type **AND(G2="FT",M2>=1)** and then press the **Tab** key. This logical test evaluates whether the employee is full time, indicated by FT in cell G2, *and* has worked at EVG for one year or more. TRUE appears to the right of the Logical_test box, indicating that the condition for the employee in row 2 is true. This employee is eligible for the 401(k) plan.

5. In the Value_if_true box, type **I2*0.03** and then press the **Tab** key. This argument specifies that if the condition is true (the employee is eligible for the 401(k) plan as determined by the AND function), the amount in the employee's salary cell is multiplied by 3 percent. The amount of the employer's 401(k) matching contribution, 3261.18, appears to the right of the Value_if_true box.

6. In the Value_if_false box, type **0**. This argument specifies that if the condition is false (the employee is not eligible for the 401(k) plan as determined by the AND function), the amount displayed in cell O2 is 0, which appears to the right of the Value_if_false box. See Figure 8-8.

Figure 8-8   Function Arguments dialog box for the IF function with the AND function

- AND function used as the logical test
- logical test is true for the employee in row 2
- result for the employee in row 2
- expression used if the logical test is false
- expression used if the logical test is true

7. Click the **OK** button. The formula with the IF function that you just created is entered in cell O2 and copied to all rows in column O of the table.

8. Position the pointer at the top of cell **O1** until the pointer changes to ⬇, click to select the 401(k) data values, format the range using the **Accounting** format, and then widen the column to display all values.

TIP
Double-click above the header row to select the column header and data.

EX 474 Excel | Tutorial 8 Working with Advanced Functions

9. Select cell **O2**. The formula =IF(AND(G2="FT",M2>=1),I2*0.03,0) appears in the formula bar and $3,261.18 appears in cell O2 because the condition is true. See Figure 8-9.

Figure 8-9   IF function with the AND function to calculate EVG's 401(k) contribution

formula in cell O2 uses the IF and AND functions

this part-time employee is not eligible for the 401(k) benefit

company 401(k) contributions for this employee is 0

O2: =IF(AND(G2="FT",M2>=1),I2*0.03,0)

	A	B	C	D	E	F	G	H	I	J	K	L	M	N	O
1	Emp ID	Last Name	Birth Date	Gender	Location	Job Status	Perf Rating	Current Salary	Medical Plan	Dental Plan	Age	Years Service	Birthday Month	401(k) Company Match
2	1002	Lowe	9/6/1966	F	NY	FT	3	$ 108,706	SPOUSE2500	EMP+SPOUSE	49	6.6	Yes	$ 3,261.18
3	1006	Forbes	12/15/1985	F	SF	FT	2	$ 75,818	NONE	NONE	30	2.3		$ 2,274.55
4	1010	Speulda	9/24/1968	M	SF	FT	2	$ 46,143	FAMILY1000	EMP+FAMILY	47	1.7	Yes	$ 1,384.28
5	1014	Hunt	8/9/1959	M	NY	FT	3	$ 84,036	SPOUSE1000	NONE	56	2.5		$ 2,521.09
6	1018	Hanson	7/15/1950	F	NY	FT	1	$ 68,470	FAMILY1000	EMP+FAMILY	65	1.4		$ 2,054.11
7	1022	Philo	5/2/1958	F	SF	FT	2	$ 130,248	FAMILY1000	EMP+FAMILY	57	1.8		$ 3,907.45
8	1026	Stolt	12/7/1977	M	SF	FT	3	$ 101,822	FAMILY2500	NONE	38	3.8		$ 3,054.67
9	1030	Akhalaghi	12/4/1961	F	NY	FT	2	$ 38,421	SPOUSE1000	EMP+SPOUSE	54	1.1		$ 1,152.62
10	1034	Vankeuren	1/10/1959	F	NY	PT	3	$ 53,582	FAMILY1000	EMP+FAMILY	56	5.4		$ -
11	1038	Mccorkle	1/30/1942	F	AT	FT	2	$ 24,373	FAMILY2500	EMP+FAMILY	73	7.6		$ 731.20
12	1042	Mattis	8/27/1989	M	AT	FT	2	$ 65,181	SINGLE1000	EMP	26	4.7		$ 1,955.43

The company match values are calculated for all employees.

INSIGHT

Using the DATEDIF Function to Calculate Employee Age

In the Employee table, the Age column was calculated using the DATEDIF function. The **DATEDIF function** calculates the difference between two dates and shows the result in months, days, or years. The syntax for the DATEDIF function is

    DATEDIF(*Date1*,*Date2*,*Interval*)

where *Date1* is the earliest date, *Date2* is the latest date, and *Interval* is the unit of time the DATEDIF function will use in the result. You specify the *Interval* with one of the following interval codes:

Interval Code	Meaning	Description
"m"	Months	The number of complete months between *Date1* and *Date2*
"d"	Days	The number of complete days between *Date1* and *Date2*
"y"	Years	The number of complete years between *Date1* and *Date2*

For example, the following formula calculates an employee's age in complete years:

    =DATEDIF(D2,$AF$1,"y")

The earliest date is located in cell D2, the birth date. The latest date is in cell $AF$1, which shows the date used to compare against the birth date—as of a cut-off date. The interval "y" indicates that you want to display the number of complete years between these two dates.

The DATEDIF function is undocumented in Excel, but it has been available since Excel 97. To learn more about this function, search the web using "DATEDIF function in Excel" as the search text in your favorite search engine.

Using the OR Function

The OR function is a logical function that returns a TRUE value if any of the logical conditions are true, and returns a FALSE value if all of the logical conditions are false. The syntax of the OR function is

OR(logical1[,logical2]...)

where `logical1` and `logical2` are conditions that can be either true or false. If any of the logical conditions are true, the OR function returns the logical value TRUE; otherwise, the function returns the logical value FALSE. You can include up to 255 logical conditions in the OR function. However, keep in mind that if *any* logical condition listed in the OR function is true, the OR function returns a TRUE value.

Figure 8-10 illustrates how the OR function is used to determine eligibility for a 10 percent discount. In this scenario, anyone who is 65 years or older (stored in cell B1) *or* anyone who is a college student (stored in cell B2) receives a 10 percent discount. At least one condition must be true for the OR function to return the logical value TRUE.

Figure 8-10   Example of the OR function

Purpose: To determine who is eligible for a discount

Logic Scenario: Discount is 10 percent for seniors (65 or older) or college students (Status =STU)

Formula: OR function with two conditions
=OR(B1>=65,B2="STU")

Data: cell B1 stores Age
cell B2 stores Status (STU, FAC, STF)

Example:

Data		Condition1	Condition2	Results
Cell B1	**Cell B2**	**B1>=65**	**B2="STU"**	**(Discount?)**
22	STU	False	True	True
67	FAC	True	False	True
65	STU	True	True	True
45	STF	False	False	False

© 2014 Cengage Learning

EVG is considering awarding a 3.5 percent raise to employees working in areas with a high cost of living, and a 2.5 percent raise for all other employees. The criteria for awarding a salary increase are based on location. If the employee is working in either New York (NY) or San Francisco (SF), the employee will receive the 3.5 percent raise. In other words, if either Location equals NY or Location equals SF is True, the condition is true and the employee will receive the 3.5 percent raise. If the condition is false— meaning the employee is located in a city other than New York or San Francisco—the employee receives a 2.5 percent raise. Patrick outlined the salary increase criteria in the flowchart shown in Figure 8-11.

Figure 8-11   Flowchart of the OR function to calculate salary increase

Flowchart:
- Decision: Location = "SF" OR Location = "NY"
- All False → Salary Increase = Current Salary X 2.5%
- At least one True → Salary Increase = Current Salary X 3.5%

© 2014 Cengage Learning

You need to use the OR function to test whether an employee meets the criteria for the 3.5 percent or 2.5 percent salary increase. The following formula uses the OR function to test whether the value in cell F2 (the work location for the first employee) is equal to NY *or* whether the value in cell F2 is equal to SF:

`=OR(F2="NY",F2="SF")`

If the employee works in New York (NY) *or* the employee works in San Francisco (SF), the OR function returns the value TRUE; otherwise, the OR function returns the value FALSE.

Figure 8-12 shows the results returned using the OR function for four different employee work locations—New York (NY), San Francisco (SF), Dallas (DA), and Atlanta (AT).

Figure 8-12   OR function results for four employee work locations

Purpose: To determine an employee's salary increase percentage

Logic Scenario: Proposed 3.5 percent salary increase to full-time (FT) employees located in NY or SF

Formula: OR function with two conditions
`=OR(F2="NY",F2="SF")`

Data: cell F2 stores Location

Example:

Data	Condition1	Condition1	Results
Cell F2	F2="NY"	F2="NY"	(OR function)
NY	True	True	True
SF	False	False	True
DA	False	False	False
AT	False	False	False

© 2014 Cengage Learning

The OR function only determines which raise an employee is eligible for. It does not calculate the amount of the salary increase. To determine the amount of the salary increase, the OR function must be nested within an IF function. In the formula

```
=IF(OR(F2="NY",F2="SF"),I2*0.035,I2*0.025)
```

the logical test of the IF function uses the OR function (shown in red) to determine whether an employee is either working in New York *or* working in San Francisco. If the OR function returns a TRUE value, the IF function multiplies the Current Salary by 3.5 percent. If the OR function returns a FALSE value, the IF function multiplies the Current Salary by 2.5 percent.

Using Structured References to Create Formulas in Excel Tables

When you create a formula that references all or parts of an Excel table, you can replace the specific cell or range address with a structured reference, the actual table name, or a column header. This makes the formula easier to create and understand. The default Excel table name is Table1, Table2, and so forth unless you entered a more descriptive table name, as Patrick did for the Employee table. Column headers provide a description of the data entered in each column. Structured references make it easier to create formulas that use portions or all of an Excel table because the names or headers are usually simpler to identify than cell addresses. For example, in the Employee table, the table name Employee refers to the range A2:O101, which is the range of data in the table excluding the header row and the Total row. When you want to reference an entire column of data in a table, you create a column qualifier, which has the syntax

```
Tablename[qualifier]
```

where *Tablename* is the name entered in the Table Name box in the Properties group on the TABLE TOOLS DESIGN tab, and *qualifier* is the column header enclosed in square brackets. For example, the following structured reference references the Current Salary data in the range I2:I101 of the Employee table (excluding the column header and total row, if any):

```
Employee[Current Salary]
```

You can use structured references in formulas. The following formula adds the Current Salary data in the range I2:I101 of the Employee table; in this case, [Current Salary] is the column qualifier:

```
=SUM(Employee[Current Salary])
```

When you create a calculated column, as you did to calculate the 401(k) contributions in the Employee table, you can use structured references in the formula. A formula that includes a structured reference can be fully qualified or unqualified. In a fully qualified structured reference, the table name precedes the column qualifier. In an unqualified structured reference, only the column qualifier (column header enclosed in square brackets) appears in the reference. For example, you could have used either of the following formulas with structured references to calculate the 401(k) company match in the calculated column you added to the Employee table:

Fully qualified
```
=IF(AND(Employee[Job Status]="FT",Employee[Years Service]>=1),
[Current Salary]*0.035,0)
```

Unqualified
```
=IF(AND([Job Status]="FT",[Years Service]>=1),
[Current Salary]*0.035,0)
```

If you are creating a calculated column or formula within an Excel table, you can use either the fully qualified structured reference or the unqualified structured reference in the formula. If you use a structured reference outside the table or in another worksheet to reference an Excel table or portion of the table, you must use a fully qualified reference.

You'll use structured references to calculate the salary increases for EVG employees.

To calculate the salary increase using the IF and OR functions:

1. In cell **P1**, enter **Salary Increase** as the column header. The Excel table expands to include the new column, and cell P2 is the active cell.

2. Make sure cell **P2** is the active cell, and then click the **Insert Function** button *fx* next to the formula bar. The Insert Function dialog box opens.

3. Click **IF** in the Select a function box, and then click the **OK** button. The Function Arguments dialog box opens.

4. In the Logical_test box, type **OR([Location]="NY",[Location]="SF")** to enter the OR function with structured references. This logical test evaluates whether the employee works in New York or works in San Francisco.

   > Be sure to type square brackets and use the exact spelling and location shown. Otherwise, the formula will return an error.

5. Click the **Collapse dialog box** button to so you can see the entire function in the Logical_test box. See Figure 8-13.

Figure 8-13   Logical_test argument for the OR function

- structured references
- Function Arguments
- OR([Location]="NY",[Location]="SF")
- first condition
- second condition

6. Click the **Expand dialog box** button, and then press the **Tab** key. TRUE appears to the right of the Logical_test box because the employee in the active row, row 2, is eligible for the 3.5 percent salary increase.

   Trouble? If Invalid appears instead of TRUE as the logical test results, you probably mistyped the logical test. Compare the function in your Logical_test box to the one shown in Figure 8-13, confirming that you used square brackets around the structured reference [Location] and typed all the text correctly.

Tutorial 8 Working with Advanced Functions | Excel **EX 479**

▶ **7.** In the Value_if_true box, type **[Current Salary]*0.035** and then press the **Tab** key. This argument specifies that if the logical test is true (the employee is eligible for the 3.5 percent increase), the amount in the employee's salary cell is multiplied by 3.5 percent. The salary increases for all employees, beginning in row 2, whose logical test is true appear to the right of the Value_if_true box.

▶ **8.** In the Value_if_false box, type **[Current Salary]*0.025**. This argument specifies that if the logical test is false (the employee is not eligible for the 3.5 percent salary increase), the amount in the employee's salary cell is multiplied by 2.5 percent. The salary increases for all employees, beginning in row 2, whose logical test is false appear to the right of the Value_if_false box. See Figure 8-14.

Figure 8-14	Function Arguments dialog box for the IF function with an OR function

▶ **9.** Click the **OK** button. The formula =IF(OR([Location]="NY",[Location]="SF"), [Current Salary]*0.035,[Current Salary]*0.025) appears in the formula bar, and the value 3804.705884 appears in cell P2 because the condition is true. The formula is automatically copied to all rows in column P of the table.

▶ **10.** Position the pointer at the top of cell **P1** until the pointer changes to ↓, and then click the left mouse button to select the Salary Increase data values.

▶ **11.** Format the range with the **Accounting** format, and then increase the column width to display all values.

EX 480 Excel | Tutorial 8 Working with Advanced Functions

12. Select cell **P2** to deselect the column. See Figure 8-15.

Figure 8-15 — IF function with the OR function calculates salary increase

formula uses structured references to calculate the salary increases

`=IF(OR([Location]="NY",[Location]="SF"),[Current Salary]*0.035,[Current Salary]*0.025)`

salary increase for employees

Emp ID	Last Name	Location	Job Status	Perf Rating	Current Salary	Medical Plan	Dental Plan	Age	Years Service	Birthday Month	401(k) Company Match	Salary Increase
1002	Lowe	NY	FT	3	$108,706	SPOUSE2500	EMP+SPOUSE	49	6.6	Yes	$3,261.18	$3,804.71
1006	Forbes	SF	FT	2	$75,818	NONE	NONE	30	2.3		$2,274.55	$2,653.64
1010	Speulda	SF	FT	2	$46,143	FAMILY1000	EMP+FAMILY	47	1.7	Yes	$1,384.28	$1,614.99
1014	Hunt	NY	FT	3	$84,036	SPOUSE1000	NONE	56	2.5		$2,521.09	$2,941.27
1018	Hanson	NY	FT	1	$68,470	FAMILY1000	EMP+FAMILY	65	1.4		$2,054.11	$2,396.46
1022	Philo	SF	FT	2	$130,248	FAMILY1000	EMP+FAMILY	57	1.8		$3,907.45	$4,558.69
1026	Stolt	SF	FT	3	$101,822	FAMILY2500	NONE	38	3.8		$3,054.67	$3,563.78
1030	Akhalaghi	NY	FT	2	$38,421	SPOUSE1000	EMP+SPOUSE	54	1.1		$1,152.62	$1,344.72
1034	Vankeuren	NY	PT	3	$53,582	FAMILY1000	EMP+FAMILY	56	5.4		$ -	$1,875.37
1038	Mccorkle	AT	FT	2	$24,373	FAMILY2500	EMP+FAMILY	73	7.6		$731.20	$609.33
1042	Mattis	AT	FT	2	$65,181	SINGLE1000	EMP	26	4.7		$1,955.43	$1,629.53
1046	Baker	DA	FT	3	$71,020	FAMILY2500	EMP+FAMILY	47	1.0		$2,130.61	$1,775.51
1050	Vines	AT	FT	2	$60,130	SINGLE1000	EMP	57	5.7		$1,803.90	$1,503.25
1054	Mittelman	NY	FT	2	$64,846	SPOUSE2500	EMP+SPOUSE	44	12.1		$1,945.37	$2,269.60
1058	Coley	AT	FT	1	$49,832	SINGLE1000	EMP	55	8.9		$1,494.96	$1,245.80
1062	Johnson	NY	FT	2	$76,707	FAMILY1000	EMP+FAMILY	45	1.1	Yes	$2,301.20	$2,684.73
1066	Jackson	AT	FT	3	$91,240	SINGLE2500	EMP	30	1.2		$2,737.20	$2,281.00

In this session, you used the IF, AND, and OR functions to determine if an employee's birth date occurs in a specified month, calculate 401(k) costs, and calculate next year's salary increases for EVG employees. Patrick still needs to calculate the employee bonuses, medical plan costs, dental plan costs, and the employee service award for each employee. In the next session, you will create formulas with functions to perform these calculations.

Session 8.1 Quick Check

REVIEW

1. What changes occur in the appearance and size of an Excel table after you enter a new column header named "Phone"?
2. Whenever you enter a formula in an empty column of an Excel table, Excel automatically fills the column with the same formula. What is this called?
3. If an Excel worksheet stores the cost per meal in cell Q5, the number of attendees in cell Q6, and the total cost of meals in cell Q7, what IF function would you enter in cell Q7 to calculate the total cost of meals (cost per meal times the number of attendees) with a minimum cost of $10,000?
4. When does the AND function return a TRUE value?
5. Write the formula that displays the label "Outstanding" in cell Y5 if the amount owed (cell X5) is greater than 0 and the transaction date (cell R5) is after 3/1/2016 (stored in cell R1), but otherwise leaves the cell blank.
6. When you create a formula that references all or parts of an Excel table, what can you use to replace the specific cell or range addresses with the actual table or column header names?
7. If the formula =IF(OR(B25="NY",B25="CA",B25="TX"),"Select","Ignore") is entered in cell B26, and "PA" is entered in cell B25, what is displayed in cell B26?
8. Write the OR function that represents the following rule—"A potential enlistee in the Army is not eligible to enlist if younger than 17 or older than 42." The age is stored in cell B25. Display "Eligible" if the potential enlistee can enlist, and display "Not Eligible" if the potential enlistee cannot enlist.

Session 8.2 Visual Overview:

A **nested IF function** is when one IF function is placed inside another IF function to test an additional condition, such as calculating employee bonuses based on three performance levels.

When the lookup value matches the first row of the lookup table, the corresponding value from the second row of the lookup table is returned to the cell with the HLOOKUP function.

This lookup table is organized horizontally and is used in the exact match HLOOKUP function to find the dental plan cost.

The invalid code in the Medical Plan column causes the IFERROR message to appear in the Medical Cost column.

The **IFERROR function** can determine if a cell contains an error value and then display the message you choose rather than the default error value.

EVG Employees - Excel

FILE | HOME | INSERT | PAGE LAYOUT | FORMULAS | DATA | REVIEW | VIEW

Q2 =IF([Perf Rating]=1,$X$2,IF([Perf Rat

	A	B	J	K	M
1	Emp ID	Last Name	Medical Plan	Dental Plan	Years Service
2	1002	Lowe	SPOUSE2500	EMP+SPOUSE	6.6
3	1006	Forbes	NONE	NONE	2.3
4	1010	Speulda	FAMILY		
5	1014	Hunt	SPOU		
6	1018	Hanson	FAMILY1000	EMP+FAMILY	1.4
7	1022	Philo	FAMILY2000	EMP+FAMILY	1.8
8	1026	Stolt	FAMILY2500	NONE	3.8
9	1030	Akhalaghi	SPOUSE1000	EMP+SPOUSE	
10	1034	Vankeuren	FAMILY1000	EM	=IFERROR(VLOOKU
11	1038	Mccorkle	FAMILY2500	EMP+FAMILY	7.6
12	1042	Mattis	SINGLE1000	EMP	4.7
13	1046	Baker	FAMIL		1.0
14	1050	Vines	SINGL		5.7
15	1054	Mittelman	SPOU		12.1
16	1058	Coley	SINGL		8.9
17	1062	Johnson	FAMIL		1.1
18	1066	Jackson	SINGL		1.2

Dental Plan Rates

Dental Plan Monthly Premium	EMP	EMP+SPOUSE	EMP+FAMI
	55	65	

Medical Plan Rates

Medical Plan	Monthly Premium
FAMILY1000	1400
FAMILY2500	1200
SPOUSE1000	1000
SPOUSE2500	950
SINGLE1000	600
SINGLE2500	425
NONE	0

Employee Data

READY

The **lookup value** is the value you are trying to find. In this case, the lookup value is the employee's years of service in the Years Service column, which is used to find the return value in the Service Award Payout table.

Tutorial 8 Working with Advanced Functions | Excel EX 483

Nested IFs and Lookup Tables

,IF([Perf Rating]=2,$X$3,$X$4))

Years Service	Bonus Amount	Medical Plan Cost	Service Award Payout	Dental Plan Cost
6.6	$ 7,500	$ 11,400	$ 250	$ 780
2.3	$ 2,750	$ -	$ 100	$ -
		=HLOOKUP(K2,DentalRates,2,FALSE)*12		
		$ 12,000	$ 100	$ -
1.4	$ -	$ 16,800	$ 100	$ 1,200
1.8	$ 2,750	Invalid Code	$ 100	$ 1,200
3.8	$ 7,500	$ 14,400	$ 100	$ -
			$ 100	$ 780

UP(J7,MedicalRates,2,FALSE)*12,"Invalid code")

				$ 1,200
7.6	$ 2,750	$ 14,400	$ 500	$ 1,200
4.7	$ 2,750	$ 7,200	$ 250	$ 660
1.	$ 7,500	$ 14,400	$ 100	$ 1,200
5.7	$ 2,750	$ 7,200	$ 250	660
12.1	$ 2,750	$ 11,400	$ 1,000	$ 780
8.9	$ -	=VLOOKUP([Years Service],Awards,2)		
1.1	$ 2,750	$ 16,800	$ 100	$ 1,200
1.2	$			$ 660

EMP+FAMILY NONE
100   0

Service Award Payout

Years of Service	Service Award
0	0
1	100
4	250
7	500
10	1000

The exact match **HLOOKUP function** (horizontal lookup function) searches across the first row of the lookup table until the lookup value exactly matches a value in the first row, and then retrieves the corresponding value from the second row of the lookup table.

The Invalid code error message appears in this cell because the lookup value Family2000 entered in the Medical Plan column is not found in the Medical Plan lookup table.

This approximate match VLOOKUP function looks up an employee's service award in the Service Award Payout table.

The values in the first column of this lookup table represent a range of values used with an approximate match VLOOKUP function. When the lookup value is less than or equal to the largest possible value in the first column of the lookup table, the corresponding value from the second column of the lookup table is returned to the cell with the VLOOKUP function.

Creating Nested IFs

The IF function can choose between only two outcomes. If you want it to choose from among three or more outcomes, you can nest IF functions. A nested IF function is when one IF function is placed inside another IF function to test an additional condition. You can nest more than one IF function to test for multiple outcomes.

Figure 8-16 illustrates how one nested IF function is used to determine among three outcomes—whether the home football team won, lost, or tied a game. The first IF function evaluates whether the home team score (stored in cell B1) is greater than the visiting team score (stored in cell B2). If the home team score is higher, Won appears in the cell. If not, the nested IF function evaluates whether the visiting team score is greater than the home team score. If the visiting team score is higher, Lost appears in the cell. Otherwise, Tie appears in the cell.

Figure 8-16 Example of nested IF functions

Purpose: To determine the outcome of football games for the home team

Logic Scenario: Display Won, Lost, or Tie based on home team and visitor team scores

Formula: Nested IF functions
=IF(B1>B2,"Won",IF(B2>B1,"Lost","Tie"))

Data: cell B1 stores the home team score
cell B2 stores the visitor team score

Example:

Data		Condition1	Condition2	Results
Cell B1	Cell B2	B1>B2	B2>B1	(Outcome)
21	18	True	Not evaluated	Won
17	24	False	True	Lost
9	9	False	False	Tie

© 2014 Cengage Learning

Figure 8-17 illustrates how nested IF functions are used to determine among four possible outcomes for a driver's license based on the applicant's age (stored in cell B1). The first IF function (highlighted in green) evaluates whether the applicant is less than 16 years old. If the applicant is younger than 16, Too Young appears in the cell. If not, the formula moves to the first nested IF function (highlighted in blue) and evaluates whether the applicant is 45 years old or younger. If so, 30 appears in the cell as the fee. If not, the second nested IF function (highlighted in red) evaluates whether the applicant is 60 years old or younger. If so, 25 appears in the cell as the fee. Otherwise, 20 appears in the cell as the fee.

Figure 8-17   Additional example of nested IF functions

Purpose:	To determine the fee for a driver's license
Logic Scenario:	Driver's license fee varies by age Below 16 "Too Young" 16–45 $30 46–60 $25 61 and older $20
Formula:	Nested IF functions =IF(B1<16,"Too Young",IF(B1<=45,30,IF(B1<=60,25,20)))
Data:	cell B1 stores the driver's age

Example:

Data	Condition1	Condition2	Condition3	Results
Cell B1	**B1<16**	**B1<=45**	**B1<=60**	**(Fee)**
15	True	Not evaluated	Not evaluated	Too Young
25	False	True	Not evaluated	30
55	False	False	True	25
65	False	False	False	20

© 2014 Cengage Learning

    You need to use nested IF functions to determine employee bonus amounts. EVG pays three levels of employee bonuses based on an employee's performance evaluation. EVG has three performance ratings (1=below average, 2=average, and 3=above average). Performance rating 1 has a bonus of $0, performance rating 2 has a bonus of $2,500, and performance rating 3 has a bonus of $7,500. In this case, you need to nest IF functions to calculate the different series of outcomes for the employee bonuses.

    Patrick created the flowchart shown in Figure 8-18 to illustrate the logic for determining bonus awards. He used different colors to identify each IF function. The flowchart shows that if an employee's pay performance rating equals 1, the bonus amount equals 0 and the IF function (shown in green) is finished. If the employee's performance rating does not equal 1, then the second IF function (shown in blue) is evaluated. If the employee's performance rating equals 2, then the bonus amount equals 2500 and the IF function is finished. If the employee's performance rating does not equal 2, then the bonus amount equals 7500.

Figure 8-18 — Flowchart of nested IF functions to determine the bonus amount

[Flowchart: Perf Rating = 1 → True: Bonus = 0; False → Perf Rating = 2 → True: Bonus = 2500; False: Bonus = 7500]

© 2014 Cengage Learning

The following formula converts Patrick's flowchart into a formula with nested IF functions:

```
=IF([Perf Rating]=1,0,IF([Perf Rating]=2,2500,7500))
```

The first IF function (shown in green) tests whether the value in the Perf Rating (performance rating) cell of the Employee table is equal to 1. If this condition ([Perf Rating]=1) is true, the formula returns 0 in the Bonus cell. If this condition is false (the performance rating cell is not equal to 1), the second IF function (shown in blue) is evaluated. The second IF function tests whether the value in the performance rating cell is equal to 2. If this condition ([Perf Rating]=2) is true, the formula returns 2500 in the Bonus cell. If this condition is false (the value in the current performance rating cell is not equal to 2), the formula returns 7500 in the Bonus cell.

PROSKILLS

Problem Solving: Finding and Fixing Errors in Formulas

If formulas in a worksheet are returning errors or not working as expected, you need to find and fix the problems. Two common categories of formula errors in Excel are syntax errors and logic errors. A syntax error is an error in a statement that violates the rules of Excel. A syntax error might occur due to unmatched parentheses or a required argument that is omitted in a function. Logic errors occur in formulas that work but return an incorrect result. Logic errors are often detected by the user because the results seem out of line. A logic error could occur because the formula uses the wrong calculation, the formula references the wrong cell, or the formula uses faulty reasoning, leading to incorrect results.

Some problem-solving approaches can help resolve these types of errors. First, examine the formulas in worksheet cells instead of the results by pressing the Ctrl+~ keys to display the formulas in each cell. Next, troubleshoot problem areas in the worksheet by pressing the F9 key to highlight part of a formula and temporarily display the actual value in the cell so you can check intermediate results. Press the Esc key to return the cell references. Finally, you can use the Formula Auditing tools on the FORMULAS tab to visually identify and trace cells used in a formula. This can help you locate and fix inaccurate cell references and faulty logic.

By carefully evaluating formulas and fixing any problems, you help to ensure that a worksheet is error-free and returns accurate results.

Patrick wants the Employee table to include a column that contains a formula to calculate the bonus amount. Patrick stored the three bonus amounts (0, 2500, and 7500) in the Employee worksheet. You will reference these cells in the formula to calculate the employee bonus. This approach enables you to quickly update the calculated bonus amounts in the Employee worksheet without having to edit the bonus formula.

To enter nested IFs to calculate employee bonuses:

▶ 1. If you took a break at the end of the previous session, make sure the EVG Employees workbook is open and the Employee Data worksheet is active.

▶ 2. In cell **Q1**, enter **Bonus Amount** as the column header. The Excel table expands to include the new column, and cell Q2 is the active cell.

▶ 3. Make sure cell **Q2** is the active cell, and then click the **Insert Function** button *fx* next to the formula bar. The Insert Function dialog box opens.

▶ 4. Click **IF** in the Select a function box, and then click the **OK** button. The Function Arguments dialog box opens.

▶ 5. In the Logical_test box, type **[Perf Rating]=1** and then press the **Tab** key to enter the logical test using a structured reference. This logical test evaluates whether the employee has a performance rating equal to 1. The values to the right of the Logical_test box are {False; False;... indicating that the performance ratings for the first few employees are false.

   Trouble? If the value to the right of the Logical_test box is Invalid, you probably mistyped the logical test. Select the text in the Logical_test box, and then repeat Step 5, typing the logical test exactly as shown, being sure to use square brackets around the structured reference.

▶ 6. In the Value_if_true box, type **$X$2** and then press the **Tab** key. The value to the right of the Value_if_true argument box is 0, which is the value in cell X2. This argument specifies that if the logical test is true (the performance rating cell is equal to 1), the value stored in cell X2 (the 0 bonus amount) is displayed. You used an absolute reference because you want the formula in each row to refer to cell X2, which contains the bonus amount. Note that a separate worksheet is often used to store values that change, such as the Bonus Amount values.

▶ 7. In the Value_if_false box, type **IF([Perf Rating]=2,$X$3,$X$4)** and then press the **Tab** key. This argument is a nested IF function that specifies if the logical condition is true (the performance rating cell is equal to 2), the value stored in cell X3 (the 2500 bonus amount) is displayed; otherwise, the value stored in cell X4 (the 7500 bonus amount) is displayed. Again, you used absolute references to ensure that the formula will always refer to cell X3 and cell X4, respectively. The values to the right of the Value_if_false box are {7500;2500;2500;... indicating the bonus amounts for the employees in the first few rows. See Figure 8-19.

> **TIP**
>
> If you type a formula directly in a cell, the available structured references appear when you type the opening bracket. Double-click the structured reference to add it to the formula, and then type the closing bracket.

EX 488 Excel | Tutorial 8 Working with Advanced Functions

Figure 8-19 **Function Arguments dialog box with a nested IF**

- structured references make the formula easier to write and understand
- use an absolute reference because this value is the same for all rows
- use a nested IF function to calculate the *value_if_false*

Function Arguments

- Logical_test: [Perf Rating]=1 = {FALSE;FALSE;FALSE;FALSE;TRUE;FALSE
- Value_if_true: $X$2 = 0
- Value_if_false: IF([Perf Rating]=2,$X$3,$X$4) = {7500;2500;2500;7500;7500;2500;7500;

= {7500;2500;2500;7500;0;2500;7500;250

Checks whether a condition is met, and returns one value if TRUE, and another value if FALSE.

Value_if_false is the value that is returned if Logical_test is FALSE. If omitted, FALSE is returned.

Formula result = 7500

Help on this function   OK   Cancel

▶ 8. Click the **OK** button. The formula =IF([Perf Rating]=1,$X$2,IF([Perf Rating]=2,$X$3,$X$4)) appears in the formula bar, and the value 7500 appears in cell Q2 because this employee has a performance rating of 3. The bonus formula is automatically copied to all other rows in the Bonus Amount column. The references to cells X2, X3, and X4 are absolute references and do not change from cell to cell in the Bonus Amount column.

▶ 9. Select the Bonus values, and then format the selected range using the **Accounting** format with no decimal places.

▶ 10. Select cell **Q2** to deselect the column. See Figure 8-20.

Figure 8-20 **Nested IF function calculating the employee bonus amounts**

- formula uses a nested IF function and structured references to calculate the bonus amount
- first IF function
- second (nested) IF function
- bonus amount based on each employee's Perf Rating

Q2 =IF([Perf Rating]=1,$X$2,IF([Perf Rating]=2,$X$3,$X$4))

	A	B	G	H	I	J	K	L	M	N	O	P	Q
1	Emp ID	Last Name	Job Status	Perf Rating	Current Salary	Medical Plan	Dental Plan	Age	Years Service	Birthday Month	401(k) Company Match	Salary Increase	Bonus Amount
2	1002	Lowe	FT	3	$108,706	SPOUSE2500	EMP+SPOUSE	49	6.6	Yes	$3,261.18	$3,804.71	$7,500
3	1006	Forbes	FT	2	$75,818	NONE	NONE	30	2.3		$2,274.55	$2,653.64	$2,500
4	1010	Speulda	FT	2	$46,143	FAMILY1000	EMP+FAMILY	47	1.7	Yes	$1,384.28	$1,614.99	$2,500
5	1014	Hunt	FT	3	$84,036	SPOUSE1000	NONE	56	2.5		$2,521.09	$2,941.27	$7,500
6	1018	Hanson	FT	1	$68,470	FAMILY1000	EMP+FAMILY	65	1.4		$2,054.11	$2,396.46	$ -
7	1022	Philo	FT	2	$130,248	FAMILY1000	EMP+FAMILY	57	1.8		$3,907.45	$4,558.69	$2,500
8	1026	Stolt	FT	3	$101,822	FAMILY2500	NONE	38	3.8		$3,054.67	$3,563.78	$7,500
9	1030	Akhalaghi	FT	2	$38,421	SPOUSE1000	EMP+SPOUSE	54	1.1		$1,152.62	$1,344.72	$2,500
10	1034	Vankeuren	PT	3	$53,582	FAMILY1000	EMP+FAMILY	56	5.4		$ -	$1,875.37	$7,500
11	1038	Mccorkle	FT	2	$24,373	FAMILY2500	EMP+FAMILY	73	7.6		$731.20	$609.33	$2,500
12	1042	Mattis	FT	2	$65,181	SINGLE1000	EMP	26	4.7		$1,955.43	$1,629.53	$2,500

The Bonus Amount column shows the bonuses for each employee.

INSIGHT

Checking Formulas for Matching Parentheses

A common problem when creating formulas is mismatched parentheses. As you write a formula, you should verify that you enclosed the correct argument, function, or term within the parentheses of the formula you are creating. This is especially important when you develop a complex formula that includes many parentheses, such as a nested IF function. Excel color-codes the parentheses as you build a formula so you can quickly determine whether the formula includes complete pairs of them. You can also verify that the formula includes matching pairs of parentheses by selecting the cell with the formula and then clicking in the formula bar. Press the → key to move the insertion point through the formula one character at a time. When the insertion point moves across one parenthesis, its matching parenthesis is also highlighted briefly. This color-coding helps you ensure that all parentheses in a formula are paired (opening and closing parentheses).

By using cell references to input values rather than including constants in formulas, you make a worksheet more flexible and easier to update. The executive team has increased the bonus for employees in performance rating 2 from $2,500 to $2,750. Patrick asks you to update this bonus amount so the employee bonuses will be current.

To update the bonus amount for performance rating 2:

1. In cell **X3**, enter **2750**.
2. Scroll to the **Bonus Amount** column and observe that all employees with a performance rating equal to 2 now have a bonus amount of $2,750.

Using LOOKUP Functions

Recall that lookup functions allow you to find values in a table of data and insert them in another worksheet location. For example, you might enter a product table in a worksheet that includes the product ID, product name, and price of all products a company sells. You could then use this product table to build an invoice in another worksheet by entering a product ID and having Excel look up the product name and price, and insert these values in the invoice. The table that stores the data you want to retrieve is called a lookup table.

Both the VLOOKUP and HLOOKUP functions are used to return a value from a lookup table. The VLOOKUP function always searches for a value in the first column of the lookup table. The HLOOKUP function always searches for a value in the first row of the lookup table. Both these functions can retrieve a value from lookup tables designed for *exact match* or *approximate match* lookups. Recall that an exact match lookup occurs when the lookup value must match one of the values in the first column (or row) of the lookup table. An approximate match lookup occurs when the lookup value is found within a range of numbers in the first column (or row) of the lookup table. Which function you use depends on how the data in the lookup table has been arranged. If the first column of the lookup table is searched, then use VLOOKUP; if the first row of the lookup table is searched, then use HLOOKUP.

At EVG, all employees are eligible for the company's medical plan. Employees can choose one of six plans—a family plan with either a $1000 or $2500 deductible (FAMILY1000 or FAMILY2500); an employee and spouse plan with either a $1000 or $2500 deductible (SPOUSE1000 or SPOUSE2500); and an employee plan with either a $1000 or $2500 deductible (SINGLE1000 or SINGLE2500). Each plan has a different cost, and EVG pays the entire amount. If an employee provides evidence of health coverage elsewhere, there is no medical plan cost (NONE). You could calculate the medical plan costs for each employee using several nested IF functions. However, a simpler approach is to use a lookup function.

You can use the Medical Plan Rates data shown in Figure 8-21 as an exact match lookup table. The lookup table includes the available plans and their corresponding monthly premiums. The medical plan cost for each eligible employee is based on the plan the employee selected. To retrieve the monthly cost for an employee, Excel moves down the first column in the Medical Plan Rates lookup table until it finds the medical plan code that matches the employee's medical plan. Then it moves to the second column in the lookup table to locate the monthly premium, which is then displayed in the cell where the lookup formula is entered or used as part of a calculation. If the employee's Medical Plan code doesn't match one of the values in the first column of the MedicalRates table (spelling or spaces are different), the #N/A error value is displayed. For example, to find the return value for the SPOUSE2500 lookup value, Excel searches the first column of the lookup table until the SPOUSE2500 entry is found. Then, Excel moves to the second column of the lookup table to locate the corresponding return value, which is 950, in this case.

Figure 8-21 MedicalRates lookup table used for an exact match lookup

Lookup Value = "SPOUSE2500"

search down the first column until the lookup value exactly matches the value in the first column

Medical Plan Rates

Medical Plan	Monthly Premium
FAMILY1000	1400
FAMILY2500	1200
SPOUSE1000	1000
SPOUSE2500	950
SINGLE1000	600
SINGLE2500	425
NONE	0

return the corresponding value from the second column of the lookup table

Return Value = 950

© 2014 Cengage Learning

Lookup tables can also be constructed as approximate match lookups. A discount based on the quantity of items purchased where each discount covers a range of units purchased is an example of an approximate match lookup. Figure 8-22 shows the approximate match lookup table for these quantity discounts. In this example, purchases of fewer than 25 units receive no discount, purchases of between 25 and 99 units receive a 2 percent discount, purchases of between 100 and 499 units receive a 3 percent discount, and purchases of 500 or more units receive a 4 percent discount. For example, to find the quantity discount for a purchase of 55 units, Excel searches the first column of the lookup table until the largest value that is less than or equal to 55 (the lookup value) is found, which is 25 in this example. Then, Excel moves to the second column of the lookup table and returns 2 percent as the quantity discount.

Tutorial 8 Working with Advanced Functions | Excel   EX 491

| Figure 8-22 | Approximate match lookup table |

Lookup Value = 55

search down the first column until the largest value less than or equal to the lookup value is found

Quantity	Discount Rate
0	0%
25	2%
100	3%
500	4%

return the corresponding value from the second column of the lookup table

Return Value = 2%

© 2014 Cengage Learning

Using the VLOOKUP Function to Find an Exact Match

To retrieve the correct value from the lookup table, you use the VLOOKUP function. Recall that the VLOOKUP function searches vertically down the first column of the lookup table for the value you entered, and then retrieves the corresponding value from another column of the table. The VLOOKUP function has the syntax

```
VLOOKUP(lookup_value,table_array,col_index_num[,range_lookup])
```

where *lookup_value* is the value, cell reference, a defined name, or a structured reference you want to search for in the first column of the lookup table; *table_array* is a range reference, a defined name, or the name of an Excel table that is the lookup table; *col_index_num* is the number of the column in the lookup table that contains the value you want to return; and *range_lookup* indicates whether the lookup table is an exact match (FALSE) or an approximate match (TRUE). The *range_lookup* argument is optional; if you don't include a *range_lookup* value, the value is considered TRUE (an approximate match).

You'll use the VLOOKUP function to calculate the annual medical plan cost for EVG because you want to search the values in the first column of the lookup table. You can use the range reference (the range A5:B11 on the Lookup Tables worksheet) or the defined name MedicalRates when you reference the lookup table in the VLOOKUP formula to determine the annual medical plan cost for an employee:

Range reference   =VLOOKUP(J2,'Lookup Tables'!$A$5:$B$11,2,FALSE)*12

Defined name   =VLOOKUP(J2,MedicalRates,2,FALSE)*12

Both of these formulas use the VLOOKUP function to search for the employee's Medical Plan code (column J) in the Employee table, in the first column of the Medical Rates lookup table (the range A5:B11 in the Lookup Tables worksheet), and then return the corresponding value from the second column of the lookup table, which shows the monthly cost. The formulas use FALSE as the *range_lookup* argument because you want the lookup value to exactly match a value in the first column of the lookup table.

Patrick wants you to enter the VLOOKUP function using the defined name to reference the lookup table in the VLOOKUP function so he can easily determine what's included in the function. This is also simpler than entering range references, and you don't need to change the reference to an absolute reference.

To find an exact match in the MedicalRates table using the VLOOKUP function:

1. In cell **R1**, enter **Medical Plan Cost**. The table expands to include the new column.

2. Make sure cell **R2** is the active cell, and then click the **Insert Function** button ƒx next to the formula bar. The Insert Function dialog box opens.

EX 492 Excel | Tutorial 8 Working with Advanced Functions

> 3. Click the **Or select a category** arrow, click **Lookup & Reference**, and then double-click **VLOOKUP** in the Select a function box. The Function Arguments dialog box opens.

> 4. Drag the Function Arguments dialog box below row 2 so you can see the column headers.

> 5. In the Lookup_value box, enter **J2** and then press the **Tab** key. The lookup value is the employee's medical plan code, which is located in column J.

> 6. In the Table_array box, type **MedicalRates** and then press the **Tab** key. MedicalRates is the defined name assigned to the range A5:B11 in the Lookup Tables worksheet. If the MedicalRates data was entered as a range rather than a defined name, the *table_array* argument would be entered as 'Lookup Tables'!A5:B11, and you would need to change the range to absolute references ('Lookup Tables'!$A$5:$B$11) so the formula would copy correctly to other cells.

> 7. In the Col_index_num box, type **2** and then press the **Tab** key. The number 2 indicates the monthly cost is stored in the second column of the MedicalRates lookup table.

> 8. In the Range_lookup box, type **FALSE**. This sets the function to find an exact match in the lookup table. See Figure 8-23.

For the col_index_num value, be sure to enter the number of the column's position in the table, not its column letter, to avoid receiving #NAME? or #VALUE! as the result.

Figure 8-23 Function Arguments dialog box for the VLOOKUP function

- defined name that references the data to look up
- the column in the MedicalRates table that stores the monthly cost
- cost of the medical plan for the employee in row 2 of the Employee table
- medical plan code for the employee in row 2
- FALSE makes the function an exact match lookup

VLOOKUP
- Lookup_value: J2 = "SPOUSE2500"
- Table_array: MedicalRates = {"FAMILY1000",1400;"FAMILY2500",120...
- Col_index_num: 2 = 2
- Range_lookup: FALSE = FALSE

= 950

Looks for a value in the leftmost column of a table, and then returns a value in the same row from a column you specify. By default, the table must be sorted in an ascending order.

Range_lookup is a logical value: to find the closest match in the first column (sorted in ascending order) = TRUE or omitted; find an exact match = FALSE.

Formula result = 950

> 9. Click the **OK** button. The dialog box closes, 950 appears in cell R2, and the formula =VLOOKUP(J2,MedicalRates,2,FALSE) appears in the formula bar. The remaining rows in the Medical Plan Cost column are filled with the VLOOKUP function. If the value in column J does not match a value in the first column of the MedicalRates table, an exact match does not exist and the function returns #N/A in the cell.

> 10. Select the Medical Plan Cost values, and then format the range using the **Accounting** format with no decimal places.

> 11. Select cell **R2** to deselect the column. See Figure 8-24.

Figure 8-24   Exact match VLOOKUP function calculating employee medical plan costs

Emp ID	Last Name	Perf Rating	Current Salary	Medical Plan	Dental Plan	Age	Years Service	Birthday Month	401(k) Company Match	Salary Increase	Bonus Amount	Medical Plan Cost
1002	Lowe	3	$108,706	SPOUSE2500	EMP+SPOUSE	49	6.6	Yes	$3,261.18	$3,804.71	7,500	$950
1006	Forbes	2	$75,818	NONE	NONE	30	2.3		$2,274.55	$2,653.64	2,750	$-
1010	Speulda	2	$46,143	FAMILY1000	EMP+FAMILY	47	1.7	Yes	$1,384.28	$1,614.99	2,750	$1,400
1014	Hunt	3	$84,036	SPOUSE1000	NONE	56	2.5		$2,521.09	$2,941.27	7,500	$1,000
1018	Hanson	1	$68,470	FAMILY1000	EMP+FAMILY	65	1.4		$2,054.11	$2,396.46	-	$1,400
1022	Philo	2	$130,248	FAMILY1000	EMP+FAMILY	57	1.8		$3,907.45	$4,558.69	2,750	$1,400
1026	Stolt	3	$101,822	FAMILY2500	NONE	38	3.8		$3,054.67	$3,563.78	7,500	$1,200

Callouts: VLOOKUP function; FALSE indicates this is an exact match lookup; employee medical plan costs based on the selected medical plan. Formula: =VLOOKUP(J2,MedicalRates,2,FALSE)

The medical plan costs in the Employee table are monthly amounts rather than annual amounts. Patrick wants you to modify the formula in the Medical Plan Cost column to reflect the annual amounts. Because the formula in the Excel table is a calculated column, you need to make the change in only one cell and the change will automatically be copied to all the cells in the column.

To modify the formula in the Medical Plan Cost column:

1. Double-click cell **R2** to enter Edit mode and display the formula in the cell.
2. Click at the end of the formula, type ***12** to multiply the monthly amount by 12, and then press the **Enter** key.
3. If necessary, increase the width of column R to display all the values in the Medical Plan Cost column.

The amount in cell R2 changes to $11,400, and all the other cells in the column are updated with the revised formula and display the annual cost.

Using the VLOOKUP Function to Find an Approximate Match

You can also use a VLOOKUP function to return a value from a lookup table that is based on an approximate match lookup. The previous lookup used the MedicalRates table to return a value only if Excel found an exact match in the first column of the lookup table. The values in the first column or row of a lookup table can also represent a range of values. Quantity discounts, shipping charges, and income tax rates are a few examples of approximate match lookups.

As part of EVG's 10-year anniversary, management plans to give employee-service awards based on the number of years employees have worked for EVG. Patrick developed the criteria shown in Figure 8-25 to summarize how the company plans to distribute the service awards.

Figure 8-25   Criteria for the Service Award Payout lookup table

Years of Service	Service Award
>=0 and <1	0
>=1 and <4	100
>=4 and <7	250
>=7 and <10	500
>=10	1000

© 2014 Cengage Learning

In the Service Award Payout table, you are not looking for an exact match for the lookup value. Instead, you need to use an approximate match lookup to determine which range of values the lookup value falls within. You want to use the lookup table to determine what years of service range an employee falls into, and then return the service award payout based on the appropriate row. To accomplish this, you must rearrange the first column of the lookup table so that each row in the table represents the *low end* of the years of service range, as shown in Figure 8-26.

Figure 8-26   Service Award Payout lookup table for an approximate match lookup

Lookup Value = 6

search down the first column until the largest value less than or equal to the lookup value is found

Service Award Payout

Years of Service	Service Award
0	0
1	100
4	250
7	500
10	1000

return the corresponding value from the second column of the lookup

Return Value = 250

© 2014 Cengage Learning

To determine whether a lookup value falls within a range of values in the lookup table, Excel searches the first column of the table until it locates the largest value that is less than or equal to the lookup value. Then Excel moves across the row in the table to retrieve the corresponding value. For example, for an employee working at EVG for six years, Excel would search the lookup table until the value in the first column is 4 (the largest value in the lookup table that is less than or equal to the lookup value) and retrieve 250 from column 2 of the corresponding row.

When a lookup table is used with a range of values (approximate match), the values in the first column must be sorted in low-to-high order. When the first column's values are arranged in a different order, Excel may not retrieve the correct value, leading to incorrect results. The setup of the lookup table in an approximate match is critical for a VLOOKUP formula to work properly.

Setting Up an Approximate Match Lookup Table

Approximate lookup tables are commonly used to find a taxpayer's tax rate in a tax table, find a shipping charge based on the weight of a package in a shipping charges table, or determine a student's letter grade from a table of grading criteria. Setting up the lookup tables for an approximate match lookup can be tricky. Consider the following example, in which an instructor uses Excel to calculate grades. The instructor assigns final grades based on the following grading policy table:

Score	Grade
90–100	A
80–89	B
70–79	C
60–69	D
0–59	F

To set up the lookup table so it works in Excel, the leftmost column in the lookup table must (1) represent the lower end of the range for each category; and (2) be sorted in ascending order based on the value in the first column. Otherwise, Excel cannot retrieve the correct result. Following this structure, the lookup table for the instructor's grading policy would be arranged as follows:

Score	Grade
0	F
60	D
70	C
80	B
90	A

In the Employee table, you will create the formula

```
=VLOOKUP([Years Service],Awards,2)
```

to determine the recognition award for each employee, where [Years Service] is the structured reference for the employee's years of service (the lookup value), Awards is the defined name that references the lookup table, and 2 specifies the column in the lookup table in which to find the service awards payout. The fourth argument is not needed because this is an approximate match lookup. You will use an approximate match VLOOKUP formula because each cell in the Years of Service column in the lookup table represents a range of values.

To insert the approximate match VLOOKUP formula:

1. In cell **S1**, enter **Service Award Payout**. A new column is added to the table, and cell S2 is the active cell.

2. Click the **Insert Function** button f_x next to the formula bar. The Insert Function dialog box opens with the Lookup & Reference category active.

3. In the Select a function box, double-click **VLOOKUP**. The Function Arguments dialog box opens.

4. In the Lookup_value box, type **[Years Service]** and then press the **Tab** key. The lookup value is entered using the column header (structured reference) for the employee's years of service, which is located in column M. You can also enter the lookup value as M2. The number 6.6 appears as the lookup value for the current row.

5. In the Table_array box, type **Awards** and then press the **Tab** key. Awards is the defined name assigned to the range D5:E9 in the Lookup Tables worksheet. If the Awards data was entered as a range reference, the *table_array* argument would be entered as 'Lookup Tables'!D5:E9, and you would need to change the range to absolute references ('Lookup Tables'!$D$5:$E$9) so that the formula would copy correctly to other cells.

6. In the Col_index_num box, type **2**. The number 2 indicates the column where the amount of the award is stored—the second column of the Awards table. See Figure 8-27. You do not need to enter the optional fourth argument in the VLOOKUP formula because Excel assumes the value to be TRUE and will use an approximate match table lookup.

Figure 8-27 **Function Arguments dialog box for the VLOOKUP function**

omitting the range_lookup entry is the same as entering TRUE and creates an approximate match lookup

7. Click the **OK** button. All the cells in the Service Award Payout calculated column are filled with the VLOOKUP formula and display the award amounts. The employee in row 2 has 6.6 years of service and will receive a service award of $250. This is a good illustration of the approximate match lookup because 6.6 does not equal a value in the first column of the lookup table. Instead, it falls between two values in the table.

8. Make sure that the values in the Service Award Payout column are formatted with the **Accounting** format and no decimal places.

9. Select cell **S2** to deselect the column. See Figure 8-28.

Figure 8-28 Approximate match VLOOKUP function for calculating the service award payout

approximate match VLOOKUP function formula without the fourth argument

each value falls between two values in the lookup table

service award payouts calculated for each employee

S2 =VLOOKUP([Years Service],Awards,2)

	A	B	J	K	L	M	N	O	P	Q	R	S
1	Emp ID	Last Name	Medical Plan	Dental Plan	Age	Years Service	Birthday Month	401(k) Company Match	Salary Increase	Bonus Amount	Medical Plan Cost	Service Award Payout
2	1002	Lowe	SPOUSE2500	EMP+SPOUSE	49	6.6	Yes	$ 3,261.18	$ 3,804.71	$ 7,500	$ 11,400	$ 250
3	1006	Forbes	NONE	NONE	30	2.3		$ 2,274.55	$ 2,653.64	$ 2,750	$ -	$ 100
4	1010	Speulda	FAMILY1000	EMP+FAMILY	47	1.7	Yes	$ 1,384.28	$ 1,614.99	$ 2,750	$ 16,800	$ 100
5	1014	Hunt	SPOUSE1000	NONE	56	2.5		$ 2,521.09	$ 2,941.27	$ 7,500	$ 12,000	$ 100
6	1018	Hanson	FAMILY1000	EMP+FAMILY	65	1.4		$ 2,054.11	$ 2,396.46	$ -	$ 16,800	$ 100
7	1022	Philo	FAMILY1000	EMP+FAMILY	57	1.8		$ 3,907.45	$ 4,558.69	$ 2,750	$ 16,800	$ 100
8	1026	Stolt	FAMILY2500	NONE	38	3.8		$ 3,054.67	$ 3,563.78	$ 7,500	$ 14,400	$ 100

Using the HLOOKUP Function to Find an Exact Match

The HLOOKUP function is very similar to the VLOOKUP function. The HLOOKUP function (horizontal lookup function) searches across the top row of the lookup table until the lookup value is found, and then retrieves the value from the same column in the lookup table. The HLOOKUP function has the syntax

```
HLOOKUP(lookup_value,table_array,row_index_num[,range_lookup])
```

where *lookup_value* is the value, cell reference, defined name, or structured reference you want to search for in the first row of the lookup table; *table_array* is the range reference, defined name, or Excel table name of the lookup table; *row_index_num* is the number of the row in the lookup table that contains the value you want to return; and *range_lookup* indicates whether the lookup table is an exact match (FALSE) or an approximate match (TRUE). The *range_lookup* argument is optional; if you don't include a *range_lookup* value, the value is considered TRUE (an approximate match).

The major difference between the HLOOKUP and VLOOKUP functions is the way the lookup tables are organized. Figure 8-29 shows how the MedicalRates and Awards tables would be arranged for a lookup using the HLOOKUP function.

Figure 8-29 Lookup tables for the HLOOKUP function

	B	C	D	E	F	G	H	I	J
4	Medical Plan	FAMILY1000	FAMILY2500	SPOUSE1000	SPOUSE2500	SINGLE1000	SINGLE2500	NONE	
5	Monthly Premium	1400	1200	1000	950	600	425	0	
6									
7									
8	Years of Service	0	1	4	7	10			
9	Service Award Payout	0	100	250	500	1000			

With the lookup tables arranged as shown in Figure 8-29, the exact match formula to calculate the annual medical plan cost is

```
=HLOOKUP(J2,MedicalRates,2,FALSE)*12
```

and the approximate match formula to calculate the service award payout is

```
=HLOOKUP(M2,Awards,2)
```

Patrick wants you to use the HLOOKUP function to calculate the cost of the dental plan for each employee. Figure 8-30 shows the DentalRates table in the Lookup Tables worksheet, which includes the different options available to EVG employees and the corresponding current monthly premium for each dental plan. The values in the first row of the horizontal lookup table are compared to the employee's dental plan code that you want to find (lookup value). When the match is found, the corresponding value in one of the rows in the lookup table is returned. For example, to find the return value for an employee with the EMP+FAMILY lookup value, Excel searches across the first row of the lookup table until it finds the EMP+FAMILY entry. Then Excel moves down to the second row to locate the corresponding return value, which is 100 in this case. The table in Figure 8-30 is an exact match lookup because if the employee's dental plan code does not match one of the values in the first row of the lookup table, the #N/A error value is returned.

Figure 8-30   DentalRates lookup table for an exact match lookup

Lookup Value = "EMP+FAMILY"

search across the first row until the lookup value exactly matches the value in the first row

Dental Plan Rates			
Dental Plan	EMP	EMP+SPOUSE	EMP+FAMILY	NONE
Monthly Premium	55	65	100	0

search begins with the first data value of the lookup table

return the corresponding value from the second column of the lookup table

Return Value = 100

© 2014 Cengage Learning

The following formula uses the employee's dental plan code and the DentalRates table to calculate the annual cost of the dental plan for each employee:

```
=HLOOKUP(K2,DentalRates,2,FALSE)*12
```

In this formula, K2 is the cell that stores the employee's dental plan in the Employee table, DentalRates is the defined name that references the lookup table, 2 specifies the row to find the monthly premium, and FALSE indicates that this is an exact match lookup. You will enter this formula to calculate the annual cost of the dental plan for each employee into the Employee table.

To find an exact match in the DentalRates table using the HLOOKUP function:

1. In cell **T1**, enter **Dental Plan Cost**. The table expands to include the new column.

2. Make sure cell **T2** is the active cell, and then click the **Insert Function** button *fx* in the formula bar. The Insert Function dialog box opens.

3. Click the **Or select a category** arrow and click **Lookup & Reference**, if necessary, and then double-click **HLOOKUP** in the Select a function box. The Function Arguments dialog box opens.

4. If necessary, drag the Function Arguments dialog box below row 2 so you can see the column headers.

5. In the Lookup_value box, enter **K2** and then press the **Tab** key. The lookup value is the employee's dental plan code, which is located in column K.

6. In the Table_array box, type the defined name **DentalRates** and then press the **Tab** key. DentalRates references the range H4:K5 in the Lookup Tables worksheet. If the defined name DentalRates was not defined, the table_array argument would be entered as 'Lookup Tables'!H4:K5, and you would need to change the range to absolute references ('Lookup Tables'!$H$4:$K$5) so the formula would copy correctly to other cells.

7. In the Row_index_num box, type **2** and then press the **Tab** key. The number 2 indicates the monthly cost is stored in the second row of the DentalRates lookup table.

8. In the Range_lookup box, type **FALSE**. This sets the function to find an exact match in the lookup table. See Figure 8-31.

| Figure 8-31 | Function Arguments dialog box for the HLOOKUP function |

9. Click the **OK** button. The dialog box closes, 65 appears in cell T2, and the formula =HLOOKUP(K2,DentalRates,2,FALSE) appears in the formula bar. The remaining rows in the Dental Plan Cost column are filled with the HLOOKUP function.

    Trouble? If #N/A appears in the Dental Plan Cost column, you may have used a VLOOKUP function. If necessary, edit the formula in cell T2 to use HLOOKUP instead of VLOOKUP.

10. Click at the end of the formula, type ***12** to multiply the monthly amount by 12, and then press the **Enter** key. The amount in cell T2 changes to $780, the annual amount, and all the other cells in the Dental Plan Cost column are updated.

11. Select the values in the Dental Plan Cost column, format the range in the **Accounting** format with no decimal places, and then widen the column width as needed to display all of the values.

12. Select cell **T2** to deselect the column. See Figure 8-32.

Figure 8-32   Exact match HLOOKUP function for calculating the dental plan cost

exact match HLOOKUP function formula → `=HLOOKUP(K2,DentalRates,2,FALSE)*12`

dental plan cost calculated for each employee based on the dental plan

	A	B	K	L	M	N	O	P	Q	R	S	T
1	Emp ID	Last Name	Dental Plan	Age	Years Service	Birthday Month	401(k) Company Match	Salary Increase	Bonus Amount	Medical Plan Cost	Service Award Payout	Dental Plan Cost
2	1002	Lowe	EMP+SPOUSE	49	6.6	Yes	$ 3,261.18	$ 3,804.71	$ 7,500	$ 11,400	$ 250	$ 780
3	1006	Forbes	NONE	30	2.3		$ 2,274.55	$ 2,653.64	$ 2,750	$ -	$ 100	$ -
4	1010	Speulda	EMP+FAMILY	47	1.7	Yes	$ 1,384.28	$ 1,614.99	$ 2,750	$ 16,800	$ 100	$ 1,200
5	1014	Hunt	NONE	56	2.5		$ 2,521.09	$ 2,941.27	$ 7,500	$ 12,000	$ 100	$ -
6	1018	Hanson	EMP+FAMILY	65	1.4		$ 2,054.11	$ 2,396.46	$ -	$ 16,800	$ 100	$ 1,200
7	1022	Philo	EMP+FAMILY	57	1.8		$ 3,907.45	$ 4,558.69	$ 2,750	$ 16,800	$ 100	$ 1,200
8	1026	Stolt	NONE	38	3.8		$ 3,054.67	$ 3,563.78	$ 7,500	$ 14,400	$ 100	$ -
9	1030	Akhalaghi	EMP+SPOUSE	54	1.1		$ 1,152.62	$ 1,344.72	$ 2,750	$ 12,000	$ 100	$ 780

Using the IFERROR Function

Error values indicate that some element in a formula or a cell referenced in a formula is preventing Excel from returning a calculated value. Recall that an error value begins with a number sign (#) followed by an error name that indicates the type of error. For instance, the error value #N/A appears in a Medical Plan Cost cell when the VLOOKUP function cannot find the medical plan code in the MedicalRates lookup table. This error value message is not particularly descriptive or helpful.

You can use the IFERROR function to display a more descriptive message that helps users fix the problem. The IFERROR function can determine if a cell contains an error value and then display the message you choose rather than the default error value; or if no error value exists in the formula, display the result of the formula. The IFERROR function has the syntax

```
IFERROR(expression,valueIfError)
```

where *expression* is the formula you want to check for an error, and *valueIfError* is the message you want displayed if Excel detects an error in the formula you are checking. If Excel does not detect an error, the result of the *expression* is displayed.

You can use the IFERROR function to find and handle formula errors. For example, you can enter the following formula to determine whether an invalid code was entered in the Medical Plan Cost column of the Employee table, and then display a more descriptive message if Excel detects an error:

```
=IFERROR(VLOOKUP(J2,MedicalRates,2,FALSE)*12,"Invalid code")
```

Based on this formula, if the value in cell J2 is SPOUSE2500, the result of the VLOOKUP formula is $950 (the corresponding value from the MedicalRates table), the first argument in the IFERROR function (shown in red) is executed, and the medical plan cost is displayed. On the other hand, if cell J2 has an invalid medical plan code, such as FAMILY1500, the VLOOKUP function returns the error value #N/A, the second argument in the IFERROR function (shown in blue) is executed, and Invalid code is displayed.

Patrick wants to verify that all employees have an amount assigned in the Medical Plan Cost column. You will check whether any cell in the Medical Plan Cost column contains an error value.

Tutorial 8 Working with Advanced Functions | Excel   EX 501

To check for an error value in the Medical Plan Cost column:

1. Scroll to row **54** in the Medical Plan Cost column, and notice the error value #N/A in cell R54.

2. Select cell **R54**. See Figure 8-33.

Figure 8-33   Error value in the Medical Plan Cost column

data entry error
VLOOKUP function cannot find FAMILY1500 in the MedicalRates lookup table
resulting error value

	Emp ID	Last Name	Medical Plan	Dental Plan	Age	Years Service	Birthday Month	401(k) Company Match	Salary Increase	Bonus Amount	Medical Plan Cost	Service Award Payout	Dent Pla Cos
48	1186	Greenwood	FAMILY2500	EMP+FAMILY	49	1.0		$ 4,827.90	$ 5,632.55	$ 2,750	$ 14,400	$ 100	$ 1,2
49	1190	Martuscelli	SPOUSE2500	EMP+SPOUSE	24	13.0		$ 3,730.37	$ 4,352.09	$ 2,750	$ 11,400	$ 1,000	$ 7
50	1194	Mcgovern	SPOUSE2500	EMP+SPOUSE	59	9.7		$ 4,213.23	$ 4,915.43	$ 2,750	$ 11,400	$ 500	$ 7
51	1198	Lapointe	FAMILY2500	EMP+FAMILY	65	9.6	Yes	$ 2,710.15	$ 3,161.84	$ 7,500	$ 14,400	$ 500	$ 1,2
52	1202	Sweet	FAMILY1000	EMP+FAMILY	62	6.6		$ 2,681.75	$ 3,128.71	$ 2,750	$ 16,800	$ 250	$ 1,2
53	1206	Boisclair	SPOUSE2500	EMP+SPOUSE	33	0.9		$ -	$ 1,902.88	$ 7,500	$ 11,400	$ -	$ 7
54	1210	Montagna	FAMILY1500	EMP+FAMILY	53	6.4		$ 1,100.16	$ 916.80	$ 2,7	#N/A	$ 250	$ 1,2
55	1214	Engstrume	SINGLE1000	EMP	41	1.3	Yes	$ 1,749.30	$ 2,040.85	$ 7,500	$ 7,200	$ 100	$ 6

3. In row 54, in the Medical Plan column, observe that the medical plan code is FAMILY1500, which is an invalid code.

Patrick asks you to modify the formulas in the Medical Plan Cost column so that the descriptive error message "Invalid code" appears rather than the error value. The IFERROR function will check for errors in the formula and display the error message you create rather than the error value if it finds an error.

You'll nest the VLOOKUP function within the IFERROR function to display "Invalid code" in the Medical Plan Cost column if Excel detects an error value.

To nest the VLOOKUP function within the IFERROR function:

1. Double-click cell **R54** to enter Edit mode. The formula =VLOOKUP(J54,MedicalRates,2,FALSE)*12 appears in the cell and the formula bar. You'll nest this formula within the IFERROR function.

2. Click to the right of **=** (the equal sign), and then type **IFERROR(** to begin entering the IFERROR function. The first argument in the IFERROR function is the formula you want to use if no error value is found; this is the VLOOKUP function already entered in the cell.

Be sure to type a comma before the error message.

3. Move the insertion point to the right of the entire formula, and then type **,"Invalid code")** to add the text you want to display if an error is found.

4. Press the **Enter** key. The error message "Invalid code" appears in cell R54, and the revised formula is automatically copied to all cells in the column. See Figure 8-34.

Figure 8-34   **Invalid code message in the Medical Plan Cost column**

IFERROR function used to check for error values

Formula bar: `=IFERROR(VLOOKUP(J55,MedicalRates,2,FALSE)*12,"Invalid code")`

descriptive error message

invalid medical plan

	A	B	J	K	L	M	N	O	P	Q	R	S	T
1	Emp ID	Last Name	Medical Plan	Dental Plan	Age	Years Service	Birthday Month	401(k) Company Match	Salary Increase	Bonus Amount	Medical Plan Cost	Service Award Payout	Dent Plan Cos
48	1186	Greenwood	FAMILY2500	EMP+FAMILY	49	1.0		$ 4,827.90	$ 5,632.55	$ 2,750	$ 14,400	$ 100	$ 1,2
49	1190	Martuscelli	SPOUSE2500	EMP+SPOUSE	24	13.0		$ 3,730.37	$ 4,352.09	$ 2,750	$ 11,400	$ 1,000	$ 7
50	1194	Mcgovern	SPOUSE2500	EMP+SPOUSE	59	9.7		$ 4,213.23	$ 4,915.43	$ 2,750	$ 11,400	$ 500	$ 7
51	1198	Lapointe	FAMILY2500	EMP+FAMILY	65	9.6	Yes	$ 2,710.15	$ 3,161.84	$ 7,500	$ 14,400	$ 500	$ 1,2
52	1202	Sweet	FAMILY1000	EMP+FAMILY	62	6.6		$ 2,681.75	$ 3,128.71	$ 2,750	$ 16,800	$ 250	$ 1,2
53	1206	Boisclair	SPOUSE2500	EMP+SPOUSE	33	0.9		$ -	$ 1,902.88	$ 7,500	$ 11,400	$ -	$ 7
54	1210	Montagna	FAMILY1500	EMP+FAMILY	53	6.4		$ 1,100.16	$ 916.80	$ 2,750	Invalid code	$ 250	$ 1,2
55	1214	Engstrume	SINGLE1000	EMP	41	1.3	Yes	$ 1,749.30	$ 2,040.85	$ 7,500	$ 7,200	$ 100	$ 6
56	1218	Travison	SPOUSE2500	EMP+SPOUSE	64	9.2		$ 1,112.71	$ 927.26	$ -	$ 11,400	$ 500	$ 7

Trouble? If the error #NAME? appears in cell R54, you may have omitted quotation marks around the "Invalid code" error message. Correct the formula, and then continue with Step 5.

▶ 5. In cell **J54**, enter **FAMILY2500**. The medical plan code you entered is valid, so the medical cost value $14,400 appears in cell R54.

▶ 6. Scroll to the top of the table, select cell **R2**, and then observe in the formula bar that the IFERROR formula was copied to this cell.

    In this session, you used nested IF functions to determine employee bonuses, you used the VLOOKUP function to calculate the medical plan cost, and you used the HLOOKUP function to calculate the dental plan cost and service award payouts. You also used the IFERROR function to display a descriptive message if invalid medical plan codes are entered in the Employee table. In the next session, you will use conditional formatting to identify duplicate records, and use the COUNTIF, SUMIF, and AVERAGEIF functions to report on employee salaries.

Session 8.2 Quick Check

1. What is a nested IF function?
2. If cell Y5 displays the value 35, cell Y6 displays the value 42, and cell Y7 contains the following formula, what is displayed in cell Y7?
   =IF(Y5>Y6,"Older",IF(Y5<Y6,"Younger","Same Age"))
3. Explain the difference between an exact match and an approximate match lookup.
4. A customer table includes columns for name, street address, city, state abbreviation, and zip code. A second table includes state abbreviations and state names from all 50 states (one state per row). You need to add a new column to the customer table with the state name. What is the most appropriate function to use to display the state name in this new column?
5. Convert the following criteria used to determine a student's level to a table that can be used in a VLOOKUP function to display the level of each student:

Earned Credits	Level
>=0 and <=30	Freshman
>=31 and <=60	Sophomore
>=61 and <=90	Junior
>=91	Senior

6. In cell X5, the error value #DIV/0! appears when you divide by 0. What IFERROR function can you use with the formula =W5/W25 so that instead of the error value #DIV/0! being displayed, the message "Dividing by zero" appears in the cell?
7. In cell X5, the formula =W5/W25 results in the error value #DIV/0! when W25 stores the value 0. Use the IF function to modify the formula =W5/W25 so that instead of the error value #DIV/0! being displayed when W25 stores 0, the message "Dividing by zero" appears in the cell.
8. Which function could be used with the following Sales Tax Rate table to display the sales tax rate for a customer in one of these four states?

State	CO	NM	OK	TX
Sales Tax Rate	10%	7%	9%	9.5%

Session 8.3 Visual Overview:

Highlighting duplicate values adds formatting to cells that have the same entry. In this instance, a gold fill highlights cells with the same employee ID.

The Conditional Formatting button provides access to the Duplicate Values conditional format and the Manage Rules option, which opens the Conditional Formatting Rules Manager dialog box.

You can edit existing conditional formatting rules from the Conditional Formatting Rules Manager dialog box. Click the Edit Rule button and make the appropriate changes.

Each time you apply a conditional format, you are defining a conditional formatting rule. You can also create a new rule from this dialog box by clicking the New Rule button.

A **conditional formatting rule** specifies the condition, the formatting, and the cell or range to apply the rule to. This rule highlights duplicate values with a gold fill in the range A1:A102.

Tutorial 8 Working with Advanced Functions | Excel EX 505

Conditional Formatting and Functions

These formulas use fully qualified structured references to make them easier to create and understand.

The **AVERAGEIF** function calculates the average of values in a range that match criteria you specify, such as calculating the average salary paid to employees in NY and SF.

D4: `=SUMIF(Employee[Location],B4,Employee[Current Salary])`

Location	Nbr Employees	Total Salary	Average Salary
NY	48	$ 3,987,083	$ 83,064
SF	18	$ 1,940,420	$ 107,801

Location Summary

`=AVERAGEIF(Employee[Location],B4,Employee[Current Salary])`

`=COUNTIF('Employee Data'!F2:F102,B4)`

`=SUMIF(Employee[Location],B4,Employee[Current Salary])`

The **COUNTIF** function calculates the number of cells in a range that match criteria you specify, such as counting the number of company employees located in NY.

The **SUMIF** function adds the values in a range that match criteria you specify, such as adding the total salary paid to NY employees.

Applying Conditional Formatting

Conditional formatting changes a cell's formatting when its contents match a specified condition. You have already used conditional formatting to highlight cells based on their values, and to add data bars that graph the relative values in a range. You can also use conditional formatting to highlight duplicate values in a column of data.

PROSKILLS

Decision Making: Using Conditional Formatting to Evaluate Data

Decisions are made by evaluating data. However, this becomes complex when large quantities of data or dynamic data are involved. In these instances, conditional formatting can be a useful tool to help with your decision making. Conditional formatting is designed to make searching a data range both simple and efficient. For instance, you can quickly find the latest market prices in a real-time stock quote spreadsheet by using conditional formatting to highlight them. You can use conditional formatting to find stocks whose price drops below the target buy price by highlighting the row of any stock that meets the buy criteria. You can use conditional formatting to quickly identify bank accounts with a bank balance that is overdrawn by highlighting accounts with a negative balance. Mastering the art of conditional formatting will help you make better decisions.

Highlighting Duplicate Values

Excel is often used to manage lists of data, such as employee information, inventory, or phone numbers. These types of lists often include data that repeats in different records, such as the employee's state in his or her mailing address, a warehouse location for inventory, or an area code for phone numbers. On the other hand, some of the data is usually unique for each record, such as an employee ID or a product number. As the list of data becomes more extensive, duplicate entries may inadvertently occur. One way to identify unintended duplicate entries is to use conditional formatting to highlight duplicate values in a range with a font and/or fill color. This color coding makes it easier to identify the duplicates so you can then determine whether an entry needs to be corrected. In addition to the colors provided, you can create a custom format for the highlighting.

REFERENCE

Highlighting Duplicate Values

- Select the range in which to highlight duplicate values.
- On the HOME tab, in the Styles group, click the Conditional Formatting button, point to Highlight Cells Rules, and then click Duplicate Values.
- Select the appropriate formatting option.
- Click the OK button.

Patrick wants you to use duplicate value highlighting to verify that each cell in the employee ID column has a unique entry. He believes the current employee ID data in the Employee table is accurate, but wants you to use conditional formatting to ensure that there are no duplicate entries.

To highlight duplicate employee IDs using conditional formatting:

1. If you took a break at the end of the previous session, make sure the EVG Employees workbook is open and the Employee Data worksheet is active.

2. Select the data in column A. Rows 2 through 101 in the Emp ID column are selected.

3. On the ribbon, click the **HOME** tab, if necessary.

4. In the Styles group, click the **Conditional Formatting** button, point to **Highlight Cells Rules**, and then click **Duplicate Values**. The Duplicate Values dialog box opens.

5. Click the **values with** arrow to display a list of formatting options, and then click **Custom Format** to create a format that is not in the list. The Format Cells dialog box opens. You'll change the background fill color to red.

6. Click the **Fill** tab, and then, in the Background Color palette, click **red** (the second color in the last row).

7. Click the **OK** button in the Format Cells dialog box, and then click the **OK** button in the Duplicate Values dialog box. Any duplicate values in the ID column appear in a red cell.

8. Scroll the table to ensure that no duplicate values are found, then select cell **A2**.

After you enter a formula, you should test all situations to verify how the formula performs in each case. In this case, you should test the column both with duplicate values and without duplicate values. No duplicate records appear in the Employee table, so you'll change the ID of the last record from 1398 to 1002, which is the ID of the first employee. The backgrounds of the cells with the duplicate IDs should turn red, which will confirm that the conditional formatting is working as intended. Then, you will return the ID to its original value and confirm that the duplicate value highlighting disappears.

To test the duplicate value conditional formatting:

1. Click in the **Name** box, and then enter **A101**. The active cell moves to the last row in the Employee table.

2. In cell **A101**, enter **1002**. The ID changes from 1398 to 1002, and cell A101 is filled with red because it contains a duplicate ID. See Figure 8-35.

Figure 8-35   **Duplicate record highlighted**

	A	B	C	D	E	F	G	H	I
1	Emp ID	Last Name	Hire Date	Birth Date	Gender	Location	Job Status	Perf Rating	Current Salary
95	1374	Wamsley	10/12/2013	1/17/1970	M	NY	PT	2	$ 49,599
96	1378	Anderson	2/12/2010	7/12/1974	F	NY	FT	1	$ 42,664
97	1382	Groneman	7/16/2011	6/11/1970	F	AT	FT	1	$ 55,551
98	1386	Johnson	10/2/2015	6/10/1968	F	DA	FT	2	$ 125,253
99	1390	Winters	2/14/2008	3/1/1953	M	AT	FT	2	$ 51,605
100	1394	Wang	8/24/2004	8/11/1966	M	NY	FT	2	$ 53,187
101	1002	Harrison	6/19/2015	11/25/1963	F	NY	FT	2	$ 63,491
102									

duplicate value is highlighted in red

3. Press the **Ctrl+Home** keys. Cell A2 has a red background fill because it contains the same ID that you entered in cell A101. The conditional formatting correctly identified the duplicate values.

Using the Conditional Formatting Rules Manager

Each time you apply a conditional format, you are defining a conditional formatting rule. A rule specifies the type of condition (such as formatting cells greater than a specified value), the type of formatting when that condition occurs (such as light red fill with dark red text), and the cell or range the formatting is applied to. You can edit existing conditional formatting rules from the Conditional Formatting Rules Manager dialog box.

REFERENCE

Editing a Conditional Formatting Rule

- Select the range with the conditional formatting you want to edit.
- On the HOME tab, in the Styles group, click the Conditional Formatting button, and then click Manage Rules.
- Select the rule you want to edit, and then click the Edit Rule button.
- In the Select a Rule Type box, click a rule type, and then make the appropriate changes in the Edit the Rule Description section.
- Click the OK button in each dialog box.

The red background fill makes the cell content difficult to read. Patrick asks you to use a gold fill color to better contrast with the black text. You'll use the Conditional Formatting Rules Manager dialog box to edit the rule that specifies the formatting applied to duplicate values in the ID column.

Tutorial 8 Working with Advanced Functions | Excel   EX 509

To change the duplicate values fill color using the Conditional Formatting Rules Manager:

1. On the HOME tab, in the Styles group, click the **Conditional Formatting** button, and then click **Manage Rules**. The Conditional Formatting Rules Manager dialog box opens, listing all the formatting rules for the current selection, which, in this case, is the Employee table.

2. Verify that the Show formatting rules for box shows **This Table**. All the rules currently in effect in the Employee table are displayed. You can add new rules and edit or delete existing rules. You also can control which formatting rules are displayed in the dialog box, such as all rules in a specific worksheet or table. See Figure 8-36.

Figure 8-36   Conditional Formatting Rules Manager dialog box

- rules displayed for the Employee table
- current rule formats cells with duplicate ID values with a red fill
- click to edit an existing rule

3. Click the **Edit Rule** button. The Edit Formatting Rule dialog box opens. See Figure 8-37.

Figure 8-37   Edit Formatting Rule dialog box

- selected rule type
- preview of the formatting for the selected rule type
- click to open the Format Cells dialog box

EX 510 Excel | Tutorial 8 Working with Advanced Functions

> **TIP**
> You can click a filter arrow, point to Filter by Color, and click a color to display only cells with that fill or click No Fill to display only cells without a fill.

4. Click the **Format** button. The Format Cells dialog box opens.

5. Click the **Fill** tab, if necessary, and then, in the Background Color palette, click **gold** (the third color in the last row).

6. Click the **OK** button in each dialog box. The duplicate records in the table are formatted with a gold background color. See Figure 8-38.

Figure 8-38 Edited conditional formatting for duplicate records

background color of duplicate value is gold

The cell text is easier to read on the gold background. Patrick wants you to correct the duplicate ID in cell A101 by entering the employee's actual ID number. The conditional format will remain active and apply to any new records that Patrick adds to the Employee table.

To correct the duplicate ID:

1. Make cell **A101** the active cell, and then enter **1398**. The employee's ID is updated and the conditional formatting disappears because the value in the ID column is no longer a duplicate.

2. Scroll to the top of the Employee table, and verify that the conditional formatting no longer appears in cell A2.

Keep in mind that the Duplicate Values rule enables you to verify that each entry in the ID column is unique, but it does not ensure that each unique value is accurate.

INSIGHT

Creating a Formula to Conditionally Format Cells

Sometimes the built-in conditional formatting rules do not apply the formatting you need. In these instances, you may be able to create a conditional formatting rule based on a formula that uses a logical expression to describe the condition you want. For example, you can create a formula that uses conditional formatting to compare cells in different columns or to highlight an entire row.

When you create the formula, keep in mind the following guidelines:

- The formula must start with an equal sign.
- The formula must be in the form of a logical test that results in a True or False value.
- In most cases, the formula should use relative references and point to the first row of data in the table. If the formula references a cell or range outside the table, use an absolute reference.
- After you create the formula, enter test values to ensure the conditional formatting works in all situations that you intended.

For example, to use conditional formatting to highlight whether the hire date entered in column C is less than the birth date entered in column D, you need to enter a formula that applies conditional formatting and compares cells in different columns of a table. The following steps describe how to create this formula:

1. Select the range you want to format (in this case, the Hire Date column).
2. On the HOME tab, in the Styles group, click the Conditional Formatting button, and then click New Rule.
3. In the Select a Rule Type box, click the "Use a formula to determine which cells to format" rule.
4. In the "Format values where this formula is true" box, enter the appropriate formula (in this case, =C2<D2).
5. Click the Format button to open the Format Cells dialog box, and then select the formatting you want to apply.
6. Click the OK button in each dialog box.

Another example is to highlight the entire row if an employee has 10 or more years of service. In this case, you would select the range of data, such as A2:T101, and then enter =$M2>=10 in the "Format values where this formula is true" box. The other steps remain the same.

Using Functions to Summarize Data Conditionally

The COUNT function tallies the number of data values in a range, the SUM function adds the values in a range, and the AVERAGE function calculates the average of the values in a range. However, sometimes you need to calculate a conditional count, sum, or average using only those cells that meet a particular condition. In those cases, you need to use the COUNTIF, SUMIF, and AVERAGEIF functions. For example, Patrick wants to create a report that shows the number, total, and average salaries for employees in New York and San Francisco. You will use the COUNTIF, SUMIF, and AVERAGEIF functions to do this.

Using the COUNTIF Function

You can calculate the number of cells in a range that match criteria you specify by using the COUNTIF function, which is sometimes referred to as a **conditional count**. The COUNTIF function has the syntax

```
COUNTIF(range, criteria)
```

where *range* is the range of cells you want to count, and *criteria* is a number, an expression, a cell reference, or text that defines which cells to count.

There are many ways to express the criteria in a COUNTIF function, as shown in Figure 8-39.

Figure 8-39 Examples of COUNTIF function criteria

Formula	Explanation of Formula	Result
=COUNTIF(F2:F101,"DA")	Number of employee in DA (Dallas)	13
=COUNTIF(F2:F101,F2)	Number of employees in cell F2 (NY)	48
=COUNTIF(I2:I101,"<50000")	Number of employees with salary <50000	22
=COUNTIF(I2:I101,">=" &I2)	Number of employees with salary >= value in cell I2 (108706)	24

© 2014 Cengage Learning

TIP
You can use structured references or cell and range addresses to reference cells within an Excel table.

Patrick wants to know how many employees are located in New York. You can use the COUNTIF function to find this answer because you want a conditional count (a count of employees who meet a specified criterion; in this case, employees located in New York). The location information is stored in column F of the Employee table. To count the number of employees in New York, you can use either one of the following formulas:

Range reference =COUNTIF('Employee Data'!F2:F101,"=NY")

Fully qualified structured reference =COUNTIF(Employee[Location],"=NY")

With either formula, Excel counts all of the cells in the Location column of the Employee table that contain the text equal to NY. Because NY is text, you must enclose it within quotation marks. It is not necessary to enclose numbers in quotation marks.

You will enter this formula using the COUNTIF function in the Employee Summary worksheet. You will use the Insert Function dialog box to help you build the formula using worksheet and range references to calculate the number of employees who work in New York.

To count employees located in New York using the COUNTIF function:

1. Go to the **Employee Summary** worksheet.
2. Select cell **C4**, and then click the **Insert Function** button next to the formula bar. The Insert Function dialog box opens.
3. Click the **Or select a category** arrow, and then click **Statistical**.
4. In the Select a function box, double-click **COUNTIF**. The Function Arguments dialog box opens.
5. In the Range box, type **'Employee Data'!F2:F101** to enter the range to search, and then press the **Tab** key. The range 'Employee Data'!F2:F101 refers to all data values in the range F2:F101 (Location column) in the Employee Data worksheet.

Tutorial 8 Working with Advanced Functions | Excel   EX 513

▸ **6.** In the Criteria box, type **B4**. Cell B4 contains NY, which is the criterion you want Excel to use to determine which employee records to count. See Figure 8-40. You could also have typed "=NY" or "NY" in the criteria box.

Figure 8-40   Function Arguments dialog box for the COUNTIF function

- reference to values in the Location column
- criterion to determine which employee records to count
- number of cells in the range that contain the criterion "NY"

Function Arguments — COUNTIF
- Range: 'Employee Data'!F2:F101 = {"NY";"SF";"SF";"NY";"NY";"SF";"SF";"NY";
- Criteria: B4 = "NY"
- = 48

Counts the number of cells within a range that meet the given condition.

Criteria is the condition in the form of a number, expression, or text that defines which cells will be counted.

Formula result = 48

▸ **7.** Click the **OK** button. Cell C4 remains active. The formula =COUNTIF('Employee Data'!F2:F101,B4) appears in the formula bar, and 48 appears in cell C4, indicating that the company has 48 employees in New York. See Figure 8-41.

Figure 8-41   Location Summary for NY employees

- completed COUNTIF function
- number of employees located in NY

C4 =COUNTIF('Employee Data'!F2:F101,B4)

	A	B	C	D	E
2			Location Summary		
3		Location	Nbr Employees	Total Salary	Average Salary
4		NY	48		
5		SF			

You will enter a similar formula to calculate the number of employees who work in San Francisco. This time, however, you will use structured references to specify the range to search.

To count the number of employees who work in San Francisco:

▸ **1.** Select cell **C5**, and then click the **Insert Function** button f_x next to the formula bar. The Insert Function dialog box opens with the Statistical category still selected.

2. In the Select a function box, double-click **COUNTIF**. The Function Arguments dialog box opens.

3. In the Range box, type **Employee[Location]** to enter the range to search, and then press the **Tab** key. The range Employee[Location] is a structured reference that refers to all data values in the Location column in the Employee table (the range F2:F101). The beginning values in the Location column appear to the right of the Range box.

4. In the Criteria box, type **B5**. Cell B5 contains SF (the value shown to the right of the Criteria box), which is the criterion Excel will use to determine which employee records to count.

5. Click the **OK** button. Cell C5 remains active. The formula =COUNTIF(Employee[Location],B5) appears in the formula bar and 17 appears in cell C5, indicating 17 employees work in San Francisco.

Using the SUMIF Function

The SUMIF function adds the values in a range that meet criteria you specify. The SUMIF function is also called a **conditional sum**. The syntax of the SUMIF function is

```
SUMIF(range, criteria[, sum_range])
```

where *range* is the range of cells you want to filter before calculating a sum; *criteria* is a number, an expression, a cell reference, or text that defines which cells to count; and *sum_range* is the range of cells to total. The *sum_range* is optional; if you omit it, Excel will total the values specified in the *range* argument. For example, if you want to total the salaries for all employees with salaries greater than $50,000 (">50000"), you do not use the optional third argument.

Patrick wants to compare the total salaries paid to employees in New York and San Francisco. You can use the SUMIF function to do this because Patrick wants to conditionally add salaries of employees at a specified location. Location is recorded in column F of the Employee Data worksheet, and the salary data is stored in column K. You can use either of the following formulas to calculate this value:

Range references
```
=SUMIF('Employee Data'!F2:F101,"NY",'Employee Data'!I2:I101)
```

Fully qualified structured references
```
=SUMIF(Employee[Location],"NY",Employee[Current Salary])
```

Both of these formulas state that the salary of any employee whose location is New York will be added to the total. Using the SUMIF function, you will insert the formula with structured references into the Employee Summary worksheet.

To sum employee salaries in the New York and San Francisco locations using the SUMIF function:

1. Select cell **D4**, and then click the **Insert Function** button f_x next to the formula bar. The Insert Function dialog box opens.

2. Click the **Or select a category** arrow, and then click **Math & Trig**.

3. In the Select a function box, double-click **SUMIF**. The Function Arguments dialog box opens.

Tutorial 8 Working with Advanced Functions | Excel **EX 515**

▶ 4. In the Range box, type **Employee[Location]** to specify the range of data to filter, and then press the **Tab** key. The range Employee[Location] is a structured reference that refers to all data values in the Location column in the Employee table (the range F2:F101).

▶ 5. In the Criteria box, type **B4** and then press the **Tab** key. Cell B4 contains "NY" (shown to the right of the Criteria box), which is the criterion Excel will use to determine which employee records to sum.

▶ 6. In the Sum_range box, type **Employee[Current Salary]** to indicate that the Current Salary column in the Employee table contains the data to sum in the filtered rows. The values to the right of the Sum_range box are the amounts in the filtered Current Salary column. See Figure 8-42.

Figure 8-42 Function Arguments dialog box for the SUMIF function

reference to values in the Location column using a structured reference

criterion to determine how to filter the employee records

total annual salary for NY employees

data to sum in the filtered records

▶ 7. Click the **OK** button. Cell D4 is active. The formula =SUMIF(Employee[Location],B4,Employee[Current Salary]) appears in the formula bar and $3,987,083 appears in cell D4, indicating the total annual salaries paid to New York employees.

Trouble? If Invalid appears in the cell or an error message appears, you probably mistyped some part of the formula. Review the SUMIF formula you entered and make sure it matches the formula =SUMIF(Employee[Location],B4, Employee[Current Salary]).

▶ 8. Copy the SUMIF formula in cell D4 to **D5**. The total Current Salary for employees working in San Francisco is $1,917,420.

Using the AVERAGEIF Function

The AVERAGEIF function is similar to the SUMIF function. You use the AVERAGEIF function to calculate the average of values in a range that meet criteria you specify. The syntax of the AVERAGEIF function is

```
AVERAGEIF(range, criteria[, average_range])
```

where *range* is the range of cells you want to filter before calculating the average, *criteria* is the condition used to filter the range, and *average_range* is the range of cells to average. The *average_range* is optional; if you omit it, Excel will average the values specified in the *range* argument.

Patrick also wants to compare the average salaries paid to employees in New York and San Francisco. Location is recorded in column F of the Employee Data worksheet, and the current salary data is stored in column I. The formulas to calculate this value are:

Range references
=AVERAGEIF('Employee Data'!F2:F101,"NY",'Employee Data'!I2:I101)

Fully qualified structured references
=AVERAGEIF(Employee[Location],"NY",Employee[Current Salary])

Both of these formulas state that the current salary of any employee whose location is New York will be included in the average. You will enter the formula into the Employee Summary worksheet using the AVERAGEIF function with structured references.

To average employee salaries in New York and San Francisco using the AVERAGEIF function:

1. Select cell **E4**, and then click the **Insert Function** button next to the formula bar. The Insert Function dialog box opens.

2. Click the **Or select a category** arrow, and then click **Statistical**.

3. In the Select a function box, double-click **AVERAGEIF**. The Function Arguments dialog box opens.

4. In the Range box, type the structured reference **Employee[Location]** to specify the range of data to filter, and then press the **Tab** key. The range Employee[Location] is a structured reference that refers to all data values in the Location column in the Employee table (the range F2:F101).

5. In the Criteria box, type **B4** and then press the **Tab** key. Cell B4 contains "NY" (shown to the right of the Criteria box), which is the criterion Excel will use to determine which employee records to average.

6. In the Average_range box, type **Employee[Current Salary]** to indicate that the Current Salary column in the Employee table contains the data to average in the filtered rows. See Figure 8-43.

Figure 8-43   Function Arguments dialog box for the AVERAGEIF function

7. Click the **OK** button. Cell E4 remains active. The formula =AVERAGEIF(Employee[Location],B4,Employee[Current Salary]) appears in the formula bar and $83,064 appears in cell E4, indicating the average salary paid to New York employees.

Tutorial 8 Working with Advanced Functions | Excel **EX 517**

8. Copy the formula in cell E4 to cell **E5**. EVG pays an average of $112,789 to employees working in San Francisco. See Figure 8-44.

Figure 8-44 | **Completed Location Analysis report**

completed AVERAGEIF function → `=AVERAGEIF(Employee[Location],B5,Employee[Current Salary])`

Location	Nbr Employees	Total Salary	Average Salary
NY	48	$ 3,987,083	$ 83,064
SF	17	$ 1,917,420	$ 112,789

average salary of employees located in SF

As Patrick enters new employees or edits the location or current salary values of current employees, the values in the Employee Summary worksheet will be automatically updated because the formulas reference the Employee table.

INSIGHT

Using the TRANSPOSE Function

The **TRANSPOSE function** is used to change the orientation of a range—that is, return a vertical range of cells as a horizontal range, or vice versa. The TRANSPOSE function has the syntax

`TRANSPOSE(array)`

where *array* is the range you want to convert from row data to column data (or vice versa). To use the TRANSPOSE function, complete the following steps:

1. Select the range where you want to place the transposed data. Be sure to select the opposite number of rows and columns as the original data. For example, if the range has five rows and three columns you would select a range that has three rows and five columns.
2. In the first cell of the selected range, type **=TRANSPOSE(** to begin the function.
3. Type the range reference of the original range of data.
4. Type **)** to complete the function.
5. Press the **Ctrl+Shift+Enter** keys to enter the function. (Note that pressing only the Enter key would create incorrect formula results.) Excel places curly brackets {} around the array formula and enters the formula in every cell of the selected range.

Keep in mind that the TRANSPOSE function only copies the data from the cells in the initial range. Any formatting applied to the original range must be reapplied to the new range. However, any changes made to the data in the original range are automatically made to the data in the transposed range. To delete the transposed range, select the entire range, and then press the Delete key.

Patrick has recently hired a new employee and he asks you to add the new record to the Excel table.

To add a record to the Employee table:

1. Go to the **Employee Data** worksheet, and then select cell **A102**. You will enter the new employee record in this row.

2. In the range **A102:K102**, enter **1402** for Emp ID, **Joplin** for Last Name, **4/1/2016** for Hire Date, **11/15/1970** for Birth Date, **M** for Gender, **SF** for Location, **PT** for Job Status, **3** for Perf Rating, **23000** for Current Salary, **None** for Medical Plan, and **None** for Dental Plan.

3. Select cell **A103**. The new employee record is added to the Employee table, and all values in the calculated columns are automatically updated.

4. Go to the **Employee Summary** worksheet. The Location Analysis report has been updated to reflect the new employee. The number of employees in San Francisco is 18 and the average salary is $107,801. See Figure 8-45.

Figure 8-45   Updated Location Analysis report

	Location	Nbr Employees	Total Salary	Average Salary
4	NY	48	$ 3,987,083	$ 83,064
5	SF	18	$ 1,940,420	$ 107,801

Formula in E5: =AVERAGEIF(Employee[Location],B5,Employee[Current Salary])

updated values in the SF row

5. Save the workbook, and then close it.

If the employee data had been stored as a range of data instead of an Excel table, the Location Analysis report would not have automatically updated. Instead, you would have had to modify all the formulas in the report to reflect the expanded range of employee data. Patrick is pleased with the formulas you added to the Employee Data and Employee Summary worksheets.

Session 8.3 Quick Check

1. Would you apply the duplicate value conditional formatting rule to a table column of last names? Why or why not?
2. If you receive a worksheet that includes conditional formatting, which dialog box would you use to find out what criteria were used for the formatting?
3. Explain what the following formula calculates:
   =COUNTIF(Employee[Gender],"=F")
4. Explain what the following formula calculates:
   =AVERAGEIF(Employee[Age],">50",Employee[Current Salary]) calculates.
5. Explain what the following formula calculates:
   =SUMIF(Employee[Job Status],"=FT",Employee[Current Salary])
6. Explain what the following formula calculates:
   =COUNTIF(Employee[Current Salary],">100000")
7. To display the number of employees working in Dallas (DA), which function would you use—the VLOOKUP, COUNTIF, IF, or COUNT function?
8. To identify duplicate values in a column of an Excel table, what Excel feature would you use?

Review Assignments

Data File needed for the Review Assignments: Compensation.xlsx

Patrick wants you to try using some alternative calculations for bonuses and benefits for EVG employees. Complete the following:

1. Open the **Compensation** workbook located in the Excel8 ▶ Review folder included with your Data Files, and then save the workbook as **Bonus and Benefits**.
2. In the Documentation worksheet, enter your name and the date.
3. In the Employee Data worksheet, rename the Excel table as **EmpData**.
4. Employees who are age 50 or older are allowed to contribute up to $22,000 during the year to their 401(k) plan; all employees under age 50 can contribute a maximum of $17,000 during the year. In the 401(k) Max Contrib column, use an IF function to determine the maximum 401(k) contribution for each employee.
5. Only full-time (Job Status) employees over the age of 30 (Age) with more than one year of service are eligible for the 401(k) benefit. In the 401(k) Company Match column, enter the IF and AND functions to calculate the 401(k) company match as a percentage of the employee's current salary; use a reference to cell X1 to obtain the 401(k) matching percent rate (3 percent). If the employee is not eligible, enter **0**.
6. All full-time (FT) employees are eligible for a bonus. Pay Grade A employees receive $3,000 (cell X2), Pay Grade B employees receive $6,000 (cell X3), and Pay Grade C employees receive $8,000 (cell X4). In the Bonus Amount column, enter nested IF functions to calculate the bonus. For employees not eligible for a bonus, display the text **NE**.
7. In the Eligible Salary Increase column, enter IF and OR functions to insert the text **Not Eligible** if the employee's pay grade is C or the employee's job status is a consultant (CN). Leave the cell blank if the individual is eligible for a salary increase.
8. In the Vision Plan Cost column, enter the HLOOKUP function to do an exact match lookup to calculate the annual vision plan cost. Use the VisionRates data (the range $H$3:$K$4 in the Lookup Tables worksheet), which contains the monthly vision rates. (*Hint*: The HLOOKUP function provides the monthly rate, which you will need to multiply by 12 to determine the annual rate.)
9. In the Years Service column, modify the formula to incorporate the IFERROR function and display the message **Invalid hire date** if an error value occurs. Test the modified formula by changing the date in cell C2 from 8/28/2014 to **18/28/2014**. Increase the column width as needed to display the entire message.
10. Edit the Duplicate Values conditional formatting rule applied to the Emp ID column so that the fill color of the duplicate value is formatted as light blue (the seventh color in the bottom row of the Background Color palette). Test this change by typing **1002** in cell A101.
11. In the Employee Summary worksheet, enter the COUNTIF function in cells C3 and C4 to count the number of female and male employees, respectively.
12. In cells D3 and D4, enter the AVERAGEIF function to calculate the average salary of female employees and the average salary of male employees, respectively. Format the average salary column using the Accounting format with two decimal places.
13. Save the workbook, and then close it.

Case Problem 1

Data File needed for this Case Problem: Spirit.xlsx

The Spirit Store Alice Meachen established The Spirit Store, which sells products to loyal alums of Central State College. Products offered by Alice on her website range from tee shirts and backpacks to mugs and blankets—and all feature the school's logo. Alice has a large, steady base of clients who find these uniquely designed products a great reminder of their college days. To ensure the timely receipt of payments, Alice wants you to use Excel to create an invoice she can use for each customer transaction. Complete the following:

1. Open the **Sprit** workbook located in the Excel8 ▸ Case1 folder included with your Data Files, and then save the workbook as **Spirit Store**.
2. In the Documentation worksheet, enter your name and the date.
3. In the Product Pricing and Shipping worksheet, assign the defined name **ShippingCost** to the data stored in the range D2:E7, which can be used for an approximate match lookup. (*Hint*: The lookup table includes only the values, not the descriptive labels.)
4. In the Invoice worksheet, use data validation to make it easier to enter ordered items in the range C16:C36 by creating a list of the different items in the Product Pricing table in the Product Pricing and Shipping worksheet. (*Hint*: Select the entire range before setting the validation rule.)
5. In the Per Unit column (the range G16:G36), use a VLOOKUP function to retrieve the per-unit price of each ordered product from the Product Pricing data in the range A3:B28 in the Product and Shipping worksheet. (*Hint*: Use the defined name ProductPrice that was assigned to the Product Pricing data.)
6. Modify the formula in the Per Unit column by combining the IFERROR function with the VLOOKUP function to display either the per-unit price or a blank cell if an error value occurs.
7. In the Total column (the range H16:H36), enter a formula to calculate the total charge for that row (Qty × Per Unit). Use the IFERROR function to display either the total charge or a blank cell if an error value occurs. Format the column appropriately.
8. In the Subtotal cell (cell H37), add a formula to sum the Total column. Use the IFERROR function to display either the subtotal or a blank cell if an error value occurs. Format this cell appropriately.
9. In the Sales Tax cell (cell H38), enter a formula with nested IF functions to calculate 8.25 percent of the subtotal (cell H37) if the customer's state (cell D12) is OH, or 8.75 percent if the state is MI; otherwise, use 0 percent for the sales tax. Format this cell appropriately. (*Hint*: The defined name Subtotl is assigned to cell H37. Note that the defined name "Subtotl" is intentionally not spelled as "Subtotal," which is the name of an Excel function. The defined name State is assigned to cell D12.)
10. In the Shipping cell (cell H39), enter a formula that looks up the shipping cost from the Shipping Cost table in the Product Pricing and Shipping worksheet based on the subtotal in cell H37. If the subtotal is 0, the shipping cost should display 0. Format this cell appropriately. (*Hint*: Use the defined name you created for the Shipping Cost table data.)
11. In the Total Due cell (cell H40), calculate the invoice total by entering a formula that adds the values in the Subtotal, Sales Tax, and Shipping cells. Format this cell appropriately.
12. Test the worksheet using the following data:
    Sold to: **Ellen Farmer**
                     222 Central Avenue
                     Arlington, MI 60005
    Date: **6/15/2016**
    Items ordered: **Blanket**, 2
                     Duffle Bag - Large, 1
                     Scarf, 2
13. Save the workbook, and then close it.

Case Problem 2

Data File needed for this Case Problem: Receivables.xlsx

Ward Consulting Doug Gold is an accountant for Ward Consulting, a firm that provides research services for various corporate and government agencies. Each month, Doug provides the controller with an analysis of the outstanding accounts. Doug uses Excel to track these accounts. He asks you to enter formulas to allow him to analyze the data. Complete the following:

1. Open the **Receivables** workbook located in the Excel8 ► Case2 folder included with your Data Files, and then save the workbook as **Receivables Overdue**.
2. In the Documentation worksheet, enter your name and the date.
3. In the Invoices worksheet, in cell B1, enter **7/1/2016** as the current date. Note the defined name CurrentDate has been assigned to cell B1.
4. **Troubleshoot** The sales rep commission rate varies for each sales rep. In column D, Doug used a VLOOKUP function to look up the commission rate for each sales rep, and then multiplied the commission rate by the invoice amount to calculate the commission. Although the first two rows in column D of the Excel table named Aging display the correct commission, all the other cells display #N/A. Find the problem with the formulas in the Commission column and fix it.
5. In column G, calculate the days past due. If the number of days since the invoice was sent (CurrentDate – Invoice Date) is greater than 30, calculate the days past due (Current Date – Invoice Date – 30); otherwise, enter 0.
6. Create the following formulas to assign the value in the Invoice Amount column to one of five columns—Current, 1–30 days, 31–60 days, 61–90 days, and Over 90 days:
   a. In the Current column, create a formula to display the invoice amount (column F) in the Current column if the number of days past due is 0.
   b. In the 1–30 days column, create a formula to display the invoice amount if the number of days past due is greater than or equal to 1 and less than or equal to 30.
   c. In the 31–60 days column, create a formula to display the invoice amount if the number of days past due is greater than or equal to 31 and less than or equal to 60.
   d. In the 61–90 days column, create a formula to display the invoice amount if the number of days past due is greater than or equal to 61 and less than or equal to 90.
   e. In the Over 90 days column, create a formula to display the invoice amount if the number of days past due is greater than or equal to 91 days.
   f. Format columns H through L in the Accounting format with two decimal places.
7. The invoice amount (column F) for each invoice can only appear once in columns H through L. In column N, do the following to create a formula to verify this rule.
   a. In cell N3, enter the label **Error Check**.
   b. In the range N4:N105, enter a formula using the IF and COUNT functions. The logical test of the IF function counts the number of cells that have an entry in columns H through L for each invoice. If the count is greater than one, the formula displays **Error**; otherwise, it leaves the cell blank.
8. Copy the Invoices worksheet to a new sheet and name it **Overdue Accts**. In the Overdue Accts worksheet, do the following:
   a. Filter the records so only invoices whose balance is past due are displayed.
   b. Sort the filtered data by invoice date (oldest first).
   c. Include a Total row in this table and display sums for columns I through L.
   d. Hide columns C, D, F, H, and N.
   e. Remove the filter buttons and gridlines from the table. (*Hint*: Use options on VIEW tab and the TABLE TOOLS DESIGN tab.)

Troubleshoot 9. In the Invoice Reports worksheet, Doug used the COUNTIF function to count the number of invoices for each sales rep. The formulas he created display only zeros. Fix the formulas in the range B3:B7 so that they display the number of invoices processed by each sales rep.

10. In the Invoice Reports worksheet, complete the Sales Rep Analysis report. In the Commission and Total Amount columns (columns C and D), use the SUMIF function to summarize commissions (column D in the Aging table in the Invoice worksheet) and the invoice amount (column F in the Aging table) for each sales rep. In row 7 of the report, calculate the totals. Format these columns appropriately.

11. In the Invoice Reports worksheet, complete the Accounts Receivable Aging report in the range F1:H8 by creating formulas that count the number of invoices for each group in the Invoices worksheet and sum the total amounts for those invoices.

12. In the Invoice Reports worksheet, in the range A12:B17, use the COUNTIF, SUMIF, and AVERAGEIF functions to complete the report. (*Hint*: The formulas will reference the Invoice Amount (column F) in the Invoices worksheet. Review Figure 8-39 to see various ways to enter criteria in the COUNTIF, SUMIF and AVERAGEIF functions.)

    a. In cell B15, use the COUNTIF function to count the number of invoices greater than the amount in cell B13.

    b. In cell B16, use the SUMIF function to add the total value of invoices greater than the amount in cell B13.

    c. In cell B17, use the AVERAGEIF function to calculate the average value of these invoices.

13. In cell B13, enter **1000** as the invoice amount above which invoices are included in the report.

14. Save the workbook, and then close it.

Case Problem 3

Data File needed for this Case Problem: Currency.xlsx

Convenient Currency Exchange Tourists about to travel from the United States to another country often need to obtain funds in the local currency of the country to which they are traveling. To satisfy this need, the Convenient Currency Exchange (CCE) set up kiosks at international airports around the country to provide currency exchange for a small fee. CCE's owner has asked you to complete the Excel workbook to simplify the calculation process. Complete the following:

1. Open the **Currency** workbook located in the Excel8 ▶ Case3 folder included with your Data Files, and then save the workbook as **Currency Calculator** in the location specified by your instructor.

2. In the Documentation worksheet, enter your name and the date.

3. In the Currency Calculator worksheet, in the range A3:D14, complete the Currency Conversion Table. Search the web to find the name of each country's currency (column B), its three-character currency code (column D), and what $1 (U.S.) equals in each country's currency (column C). As an example, the first row in the table has been completed for Australia. Be sure to update the $1 U.S. Equals cell for Australia to the current exchange rate.

4. In cell H4, create a data validation to create a list of countries in column A that users can select from to avoid data entry errors when entering the country name. (*Hint*: Use the defined name CountryList to reference countries.) Select Australia from the list.

5. In cell H5, enter **1000** as the U.S. dollars received.

6. In cell H6, enter a formula to calculate the conversion fee. If cell H5 is blank, cell H6 should also be blank. Otherwise, CCE charges a conversion fee of 3 percent (cell B17) of the total U.S. dollars received with a minimum charge of $5 (cell B18).

7. In cell H7, subtract the conversion fee (entered in cell H6) from the dollars received (in cell H5) to obtain the amount to be converted to the foreign currency.

8. In cell H9, use a VLOOKUP function to calculate the amount of foreign currency the traveler will receive. Multiply the amount being converted (in cell H7) by the correct exchange rate.
9. In cell G10, display the appropriate currency name of the country being visited. (*Hint*: Use a VLOOKUP function to retrieve the currency name. If cell H4 is blank, cell G10 should also be blank.)
10. In cell G12, look up and display the exchange rate for this transaction from the Currency Conversion Table.
11. In cell H12, lookup and display the currency code for this transaction from the Currency conversion table. If cell H4 is blank, cell G12 should also be blank.
12. In cell I12, enter the function that displays today's date.
13. Test the Currency Converter by deleting the country visiting (cell H4) and amount (cell H5) entries, and then modifying the formulas in any cell that displays an error value so that a blank cell is displayed instead of the error value.
14. Protect all cells except the cells into which you enter data (cells H4 and H5). Do not use a password.
15. Test the calculator by converting **500** U.S. dollars to Japanese yen.
16. Save the workbook, and then close it.

Case Problem 4

CHALLENGE

Data File needed for this Case Problem: **Instruments.xlsx**

Anthony's Music Store   Anthony Malone sells and rents musical instruments. One part of his business involves renting instruments to K–12 students who participate in school bands and orchestras. Instruments available for rent include flutes, clarinets, trombones, oboes, piccolos, saxophones, accordions, bassoons, and French horns. Anthony maintains an Excel worksheet to track instrument rentals that includes the following information:

- **Renter**—the name of the renter
- **Instrument**—the type of instrument rented
- **Rental Date**—the date the instrument was rented
- **Rental Period**—either 3 or 9 months, as shown in the Rental Period column; no other rental periods are allowed
- **Ins Cov**—indicates whether renters elected to purchase instrument insurance; if elected, Yes appears in the Ins Cov column; otherwise, No is entered
- **Shipping Code**—indicates whether the renter wants the instrument delivered directly to the school (either Ground or Rush), or the renter will pick up the instrument at the store (Pickup).

Anthony wants you to expand the information that is tracked. Complete the following:

1. Open the **Instruments** workbook located in the Excel8 ▸ Tutorial folder included with your Data Files, and then save the workbook as **Instrument Rentals** in the location specified by your instructor.
2. In the Documentation worksheet, enter your name and the date.
3. In the Rental Data worksheet, in column G, create a formula that uses the HLOOKUP function to assign a group code (A, B, C, D, or E) from the InstrumentGroups range in the Rental Information worksheet to the instrument listed in column B.

Explore 4. In column H, create a formula to determine the return date. Add the 3 or 9 month rental period (column D) to the rental date (column C) to calculate the return date. For example, if the rental date is 9/10/2016 and the rental period is 3 months, the return date is 12/10/2016. If the rental period is 9 months, then the return date is 6/10/2017. (*Hint*: Use the DATE function to calculate the return date. Use MONTH([Rental Date]), DAY([Rental Date]), and YEAR([Rental Date]) functions as arguments of the DATE function. Finally, add the rental period to the month argument.)

5. In column I, create a formula using the IF and VLOOKUP functions to calculate the rental charges for each instrument based on the instrument's group code, the rental period, and the Instrument Rental Charges table. (*Hint*: For the IF function arguments, use one VLOOKUP function for 3 months and another for 9 months. The defined name RentalCharges has been assigned to the Instrument Rental Charges table.)

6. In column J, enter a formula to calculate the insurance cost if the renter has elected insurance coverage (Yes in column E). Use the instrument's group code and the Monthly Insurance column in the RentalCharges table to look up the insurance cost. Remember to multiply the monthly insurance charge by the rental period. If the renter has not elected insurance, the cost is 0.

7. In column K, create a nested IF function to determine the shipping cost for each instrument. Use the shipping code (column F) and the shipping charge options Pickup (0), Ground ($25), and Rush ($50) to assign shipping costs to each rental instrument.

8. In column L, calculate the total cost, which is the sum of the rental charges, the insurance cost, and the shipping cost.

9. Format columns I through L with the Accounting format with no decimal places.

10. In the Rental Report worksheet, complete the Rental Summary report by creating formulas in the range C4:D5 using the COUNTIF and SUMIF functions.

11. In the Rental Data worksheet, enter the following new record:

    Renter: **Allen**
    Instrument: **Flute**
    Rental Date: **9/15/2016**
    Rental Period: **9**
    Ins Cov: **Yes**
    Shipping Code: **Rush**

Explore 12. Create the PivotTable shown in Figure 8-46 to display the number of rentals and rental $ by rental month. Rename the worksheet as **Monthly Rentals**. (*Hint*: Select any Rental Date in the PivotTable, and then on the PIVOTTABLE TOOLS ANALYZE tab, in the Group group, click the Group Field button to open the Grouping dialog box. Use Months as the grouping field.)

Figure 8-46   Monthly Rental Summary PivotTable

	# of Renters	Total Rental $
Jul	14	$ 2,262
Aug	16	$ 1,322
Sep	11	$ 1,494
Grand Total	**41**	**$ 5,078**

Explore 13. In the PivotTable, drill down to display the renters (all fields) in the source data that represent the 11 rentals in September. Rename the worksheet that is created as **SeptDetail**. (*Hint*: Double-click the appropriate cell in PivotTable to open a new worksheet with the supporting data.)

14. Save the workbook, and then close it.

Problem Solving

Solving a Problem Using an Excel Table

Problem solving is the ability to identify a gap between an existing state and a desired state of being. A problem can be a one-time issue such as which car to purchase, or a process-oriented dilemma such as how to track orders. The process of solving a problem follows a logical progression that consists of (1) recognizing and defining the problem; (2) determining feasible courses of action; (3) collecting information about those actions; and (4) evaluating the merits and drawbacks of each one in order to make a choice. Problem solving leads to decision making, and enables you to evaluate different courses of action and make an informed decision or select a good solution.

Recognize and Define the Problem

A problem is the gap between a desired state and reality. In order to recognize and define a problem, ask questions to determine the real issue and identify your ultimate goal. For example, ask such questions as: Why do I think there is a problem? Where is it occurring? When and how frequently is it occurring? What is causing the problem? Who is involved? Why is it occurring? The answers to these questions help you define the problem and determine what information you need in order to solve the problem. For instance, a company might want to make sure that employee benefits and overtime payments don't exceed a certain amount; therefore, it needs to track the cost of each employee's benefit package, salary, and overtime as well as determine that the total costs fall within the intended levels.

Determine Feasible Alternatives

With the problem defined, you can brainstorm possible solutions by collecting as many ideas as possible about how to correct the problem or achieve your goal. Write them all down. Don't discount any ideas as too radical, expensive, or impossible to achieve. Think creatively. Ask what-if questions, such as the following: What if we had unlimited resources? What if we had new skills? What if our competitors, suppliers, or customers acted in a certain way? What if I do nothing? For instance, a company might want to create a consistent way to track employee data—collecting the same data each time, categorizing the data by department or employee type, and then ensuring that paid benefits and overtime don't exceed a certain amount.

Collect Information Needed to Evaluate the Alternatives

Data is crucial to problem solving. Collect data and information related to each possible solution or alternative. This information can include data expressed as currency or numbers, as well as data that cannot be measured numerically. All collected data should be organized in a way that provides information for effective decision making and follow-up. For example, a business needs to collect data that enables it to write checks to employees, prepare reports about overtime, report payroll taxes to government agencies, provide premiums to health insurance companies, track Social Security payments, and so on. This requires an organized system to capture the appropriate data such as employee IDs, employee names, hours worked each day, salary or hourly rate, and insurance premium. You'll likely start to see relationships between the collected information that can provide insights into the feasibility of the possible solutions.

Evaluate and Choose an Alternative

Document both the benefits and costs of all alternatives, whether numerical (cost savings) or other (employee morale). Spreadsheet software often helps problem solvers track and quantify merits and drawbacks. Consider the resources required—financial, human, equipment, and so on. Are they affordable? Is there enough time to implement the different solutions? What risks are associated with an alternative? What consequences would result if the solution didn't work? The best choice is to go with the solution that offers the greatest reward for the least amount of risk. In some cases, the solution may require developing a "Plan B" to fall back on in case the chosen solution fails to solve the problem. For instance, when collecting payroll data, it may become apparent that insurance premiums constitute a higher percentage of payroll than previously thought, which requires further investigation and an alternative solution.

Don't try to select a solution that addresses every aspect of a problem, especially if it is complex. Solutions are rarely perfect. Instead, consider the overall effect each alternative may have. Will the resulting change generate positive results while solving the problem? Will the chosen alternative resolve the problem in the long term? Given the merits and drawbacks identified, what is realistic?

PROSKILLS

Develop an Excel Table

In daily life, you solve all sorts of problems, such as which car purchase makes the most economic sense when comparing purchase price, mileage, and maintenance, or which software package will help your biking club manage its funds, plan road trips, and keep memberships up to date. To solve these and other problems, you need to collect data that tracks the current situation, determine your ultimate goal, and then follow a logical progression to the best solution. Developing an Excel table can help you track the data you need to solve such problems.

In this exercise, you need to select an activity in which you participate or an organization to which you belong, and identify a one-time or process-oriented problem that needs to be solved. Then, create a worksheet and develop an Excel table to track relevant data and create a solution to the problem, using the Excel skills and features presented in Tutorials 5 through 8.

Note: Please be sure *not* to include any personal information of a sensitive nature in any worksheets you create to submit to your instructor. Later, you can update the worksheets with such information for your own personal use.

1. Identify a problem to solve. This can be a one-time problem, such as a car purchase, or a process-oriented problem, such as tracking membership data for a club to which you belong. Determine feasible alternatives to solve the problem, and then collect the data you need to evaluate these alternatives.
2. Plan the organization of your workbook and the Excel table you will develop based on how you will use the data. Consider the outputs you want to create, and the fields needed to produce those outputs. Decide what each record represents (such as data on a participant), and then identify the fields and field names (such as last name, first name, birth date, and so on) within each record. What calculations will you need to perform? How do you want to format the information?
3. Create a Documentation worksheet that includes your name, the date, and the purpose of your workbook. Include a data definition table to document the fields in each record. Format the worksheet appropriately.
4. Create an Excel table to track the data needed to solve the problem you identified. Enter an appropriate table name and column headers. Add one or more calculated columns to the table to perform calculations on the data that you will use to solve the problem.
5. Improve the appearance of the table by using appropriate formatting.
6. Apply validity checks to improve the accuracy of data entry.
7. Add records to the table.
8. Apply conditional formatting to at least one column in the table to visually highlight some aspect of the data that will help you evaluate and solve the problem.
9. Add a comment to the column with the conditional formatting to explain what the conditional formatting shows, and how it will help you to evaluate and solve the problem.
10. Insert a Total row in the table, and then make appropriate summary calculations that you can use to evaluate and solve the problem.
11. Divide the table into two horizontal panes—one for the data, and one for the Total row.
12. Sort the data in a logical way.
13. Use a filter to answer a question about the data to help you evaluate and solve the problem.

14. Create a PivotTable and a PivotChart to analyze the data. Format, filter, and sort the PivotTable appropriately.
15. In a Word document, explain the problem you solved, identify the alternatives you considered, document the data you collected to evaluate the alternatives, and then describe the results of your analysis. Include the PivotChart in the Word document.
16. In an appropriate worksheet, insert a hyperlink that links to the Word document you created.
17. Create at least one macro to automate a repetitive task you need to perform in the workbook, such as printing or saving a worksheet as a PDF file.
18. Prepare your workbook for printing. Include headers and footers that indicate the filename of your workbook, the workbook's author, and the date on which the report is printed. If a printed worksheet will extend across several pages, repeat appropriate print titles across all of the pages, and include page numbers and the total number of pages on each printed page.
19. Save the workbook.

TUTORIAL 9

Exploring Financial Tools and Functions

Analyzing a Business Plan

OBJECTIVES

Session 9.1
- Work with financial functions to analyze loans and investments
- Create an amortization schedule
- Calculate a conditional sum

Session 9.2
- Interpolate and extrapolate a series of values
- Calculate a depreciation schedule

Session 9.3
- Determine a payback period
- Calculate a net present value
- Calculate an internal rate of return
- Trace a formula error to its source

Case | Jerel's Restaurant

Jerel Troutman is a chef trained in the classical French tradition who has garnered acclaim in the Pacific Northwest for his delicious and imaginative menus. Jerel and his partner, Sylvia Lancaster, have decided to start a new restaurant in Gresham, Oregon. The restaurant, named Jerel's, will feature meals in the French brasserie style, fine wines and beers from an attached brewery, and live music. Jerel will focus his attention on developing the menus and running the kitchen. Sylvia will manage the business end of the restaurant.

Although Sylvia has lined up some financial backing, she also needs to find additional capital to launch the restaurant. To obtain funding and attract investors, Sylvia must present a detailed business plan that explores the different financial challenges the restaurant will face. The plan will include revenue and expense estimates for the restaurant's first five years of business. Investors will also want to know what return they will get from investing in this new business. Sylvia has created a workbook to analyze these financial issues, and she asks you to enter loan and investment functions, project income, and expense values; calculate depreciation; and calculate the return on the investment.

STARTING DATA FILES

Excel9 → Tutorial — Jerels.xlsx

Review — Restaurant.xlsx

Case1 — Digital.xlsx

Case2 — College.xlsx

Case3 — Red.xlsx

Case4 — Condo.xlsx

Microsoft product screenshots used with permission from Microsoft Corporation.

Session 9.1 Visual Overview:

The FV function calculates the future value of a loan or an investment.

A positive cash flow (or **cash inflow**) is a positive value that represents money coming to the investor.

The PV function calculates the present value of a loan or an investment.

The IPMT function calculates the amount of a loan payment that is used to repay the interest.

J8 =PMT(I8,G8,C8)

=FV(I9,G9,J9,C9)

Jerel's

Loan Analysis

	Financial Value	Business Loan (PV)	Future Value (FV)	Years	Payment
8	Quarterly Payment (PMT)	$ 400,000	$ -	5	
9	Future Value (FV)	$ 400,000	$ (210,387)	5	
10	Payments (NPER)	$ 400,000	$ -	9.06	
11	Business Loan (PV)	$ 301,552	$ -	5	

Annual Interest Rate: 7%

400000
=PV(I11,G11,J11)

=IPMT($I$8,D16,$G$8,$C$8)
=IPMT($I$8,D17,$G$8,$C$8)
=IPMT($I$8,D18,$G$8,$C$8)
=IPMT($I$8,D19,$G$8,$C$8)
=IPMT($I$8,D20,$G$8,$C$8)
=IPMT($I$8,D21,$G$8,$C$8)

Amortization Schedule

Remaining Principal	Interest Payment
400,000	$
383,124	$
365,952	$
348,479	$

READY

© 2014 Cengage Learning

Tutorial 9 Exploring Financial Tools and Functions | Excel   EX 531

Loan and Investment Functions

The **NPER function** calculates the number of payments required to repay a loan or reach an investment goal.

The **PMT function** calculates the payment in each period required to repay a loan or reach an investment goal.

=E9*F9
=NPER(I10,J10,C10)
=E11*F11

=PMT(I8,G8,C8)
-15000
-15000

Payments per Year	Payments (NPER)	Annual Rate	Rate per Quarter (RATE)	Quarterly Payments
4	20	7.00%	1.75%	$ (23,876)
4	20	7.00%	1.75%	$ (15,000)
4	36.23	7.00%	1.75%	$ (15,000)
4	20	7.00%	1.75%	$ (18,000)

A **negative cash flow** (or **cash outflow**) is a negative value that represents cash going *away* from the investor.

Schedule

Interest Payment	Principal Payment	Total Payment
(7,000)	$ (16,876)	$ (23,876)
(6,705)	$ (17,172)	$
(6,404)	$ (17,472)	$ (23,876)
(6,098)	$ (17,778)	$ (23,876)

Payment
=PPMT($I$8,D16,$G$8,$C$8)
=PPMT($I$8,D17,$G$8,$C$8)
=PPMT($I$8,D18,$G$8,$C$8)
=PPMT($I$8,D19,$G$8,$C$8)
=PPMT($I$8,D20,$G$8,$C$8)
=PPMT($I$8,D21,$G$8,$C$8)

An **amortization schedule** provides the schedule of payments used to repay a loan.

The **PPMT function** calculates the amount of a loan payment that is applied to the principal.

Calculating Borrowing Costs

Excel supports a multitude of functions to calculate the costs associated with borrowing money. Using these functions, you can determine the size of a loan, the number of payments needed to repay a loan, the size of each payment, and the amount left to be paid on a loan after a specified length of time has passed.

Sylvia has already lined up some of the financial backing needed to open Jerel's. However, she also needs to take out a business loan of $400,000 to cover the remaining costs for the first few years of business. She wants to know how much the payments would be if she repaid the loan in quarterly payments each year. You can calculate the payments with the PMT function.

> **REFERENCE**
>
> ### Working with Loans and Investments
>
> - To calculate the present value of a loan or an investment, use the PV function.
> - To calculate the future value of a loan or an investment, use the FV function.
> - To calculate the size of the monthly or quarterly payments required to repay a loan or meet an investment goal, use the PMT function.
> - To calculate the number of monthly or quarterly payments required to repay a loan or meet an investment goal, use the NPER function.
> - To calculate the interest on a loan or an investment, use the RATE function.

Calculating a Payment with the PMT Function

The PMT function is used to determine the size of payments made periodically to either repay a loan or reach an investment goal. The syntax of the PMT function is

```
PMT(rate, nper, pv[, fv=0][, type=0])
```

where `rate` is the interest rate per period, `nper` is the total number of payment periods, `pv` is the present value of the loan or investment, and `fv` is the future value of the loan or investment after all of the scheduled payments have been made. The optional `fv` argument has a default value of 0, which for loans means that the loan will be completely repaid. Finally, the optional `type` argument specifies whether payments are made at the end of each period (`type`=0) or at the beginning (`type`=1). The default is `type`=0.

For example, if Sylvia borrows $400,000 at 8 percent annual interest to be repaid quarterly over a five-year period, the value of the `rate` argument would be 8%/4, or 2 percent, because the 8 percent annual interest rate is divided into four quarters. The value of the `nper` argument is 4×5 (four payments per year for five years), which is 20 payments over the five-year period. The PMT function for this loan would be entered as

```
=PMT(2%, 20, 400000)
```

which returns –$24,463. This means that Sylvia would have to spend more than $24,400 each quarter to repay a $400,000 loan in five years at 8 percent annual interest. Note that 0 is assumed for the `fv` argument because the loan will be completely repaid.

Notice that the PMT function returns a negative value even though you entered a positive value for the `pv` argument. The PMT function, like many Excel financial functions, can be used with either loans or investments. The difference between a loan and an investment is based on cash flow.

> **TIP**
>
> The financial functions automatically format calculated values as currency; negative cash flows appear in a red font within parentheses.

Tutorial 9 Exploring Financial Tools and Functions | Excel   EX 533

Cash flow indicates the direction of money to and from an individual or a company. A positive cash flow represents money that is coming to the individual or received; a negative cash flow represents money that is leaving the individual or spent. For a loan, the *pv* argument is positive because it represents the amount of money being borrowed (coming *to* the individual), and the PMT function returns a negative value because it represents money being spent to repay the loan (going *away* from the individual). Conversely, the *pv* argument is negative when used with investments because it represents the initial amount of money being invested (or spent), and the PMT function returns a positive value because it represents returns from the investment coming back to the individual. Cash flow, whether positive or negative, has nothing to do with who owns the money. When Sylvia borrows money, that money still belongs to the lender even as it is being used to establish Jerel's.

Sylvia wants to know what would be the quarterly payment on a $400,000 loan at 7 percent interest to be completely repaid in five years. A good practice is to enter the loan conditions into separate cells rather than including them in the PMT function. This makes the loan conditions visible and allows them to be easily changed for what-if analyses. You'll enter the loan conditions in the workbook Sylvia created, and then use the PMT function to calculate the quarterly payment.

To calculate a quarterly payment with the PMT function:

1. Open the **Jerels** workbook located in the Excel9 ▸ Tutorial folder included with your Data Files, and then save the workbook as **Jerels Restaurant** in the location specified by your instructor.

2. In the Documentation worksheet, enter your name and the date.

3. Go to the **Loan Analysis** worksheet. Sylvia has already entered and formatted much of the content in this worksheet. In row 8, you will enter the parameters for the loan.

4. In cell **C8**, enter **400,000** for the amount of the loan.

5. In cell **D8**, enter **0** for the future value of the loan to specify that the loan will be completely repaid.

6. In cell **E8**, enter **5** for the length of the loan in years.

7. In cell **F8**, enter **4** for the number of payments per year, which is quarterly.

8. In cell **G8**, enter the formula **=E8*F8** to calculate the total number of payments, which is 20.

9. In cell **H8**, enter the formula **=$C$5** to reference the annual interest rate specified in cell C5, which is 7 percent. You used an absolute reference in this formula so that the argument continues to use the annual interest rate even if the formula is copied to other cells.

10. In cell **I8**, enter the formula **=H8/F8** to calculate the interest rate for each payment, which is 1.75 percent per quarter.

> **TIP**
> For monthly or quarterly payments, be sure to use the interest rate for that payment period rather than the annual interest rate.

11. In cell **J8**, enter the formula **=PMT(I8, G8, C8)** to calculate the payment due each quarter based on the *rate* value in cell I8, the *nper* value in cell G8, and the *pv* value in cell C8. The formula returns −$23,876, which means that Jerel's will have to make quarterly payments of nearly $24,000 to repay the loan in five years. See Figure 9-1.

Figure 9-1 Quarterly payment required to repay a loan

[Screenshot of Excel spreadsheet titled "Jerel's Loan Analysis" showing the PMT function `=PMT(I8,G8,C8)` in cell J8. Columns include: Financial Value, Business Loan (PV), Future Value (FV), Years, Payments per Year, Payments (NPER), Annual Rate, Rate per Quarter (RATE), Quarterly Payments (PMT). Row 8 Quarterly Payment (PMT): $400,000, -, 5, 4, 20, 7.00%, 1.75%, $(23,876). Callouts: "PMT function" pointing to formula bar; "future value is 0 (the loan will be repaid)"; "payments are made quarterly"; "amount to borrow"; "years to repay the loan"; "total number of loan payments"; "interest rate per quarter"; "amount of the quarterly payment".]

The $23,876 quarterly payments are higher than Sylvia anticipated. She was hoping for quarterly payments closer to $15,000. She asks to you determine how much of the loan would be unpaid after five years with $15,000 payments. You can calculate the amount left on the loan using the FV function.

Calculating a Future Value with the FV Function

So far, you have used the default value of 0 for the future value because the intent was to repay the loan completely. However, when a loan will not be completely repaid, you can use the FV function to calculate the loan's future value. The syntax of the FV function is

```
FV(rate, nper, pmt[, pv=0][, type=0])
```

where the *rate*, *nper*, *pmt*, and *type* arguments still represent the interest rate per period, the number of payments, the payment each period, and when the payment is due (beginning or end of the period). The *pv* argument is optional and represents the present value of the loan or investment, which is assumed to be 0 if no value is specified.

The FV function is often used with investments to calculate the future value of a series of payments. For example, if you deposit $100 per month in a new savings account that has a starting balance of $0 and pays 1 percent interest annually, the formula with the FV function to calculate the future value of that investment after 10 years or 120 months is

```
=FV(1%/12, 10*12, -100)
```

which returns $12,614.99. The extra $614.99, the amount above the $12,000 you deposited, is the interest earned from the money during that 10-year period. Note that the *pmt* value is –100 because it represents the monthly deposit (negative cash flow), and the value returned by the FV function is positive because it represents money earned (positive cash flow). The *pv* value in this example is assumed to be 0 because no money was in the savings account before the first deposit.

When used with a loan, a positive *pv* value is included as the present value of the loan. For example, if you borrow $1,200 at 8 percent annual interest and repay $100 each month, you would calculate the amount remaining on the loan after one year or 12 months using the formula

```
=FV(8%/12, 12, -100, 1200)
```

which returns –$54.61, indicating that you still must pay $54.61 to completely repay the loan.

Sylvia wants to know how much the restaurant would still owe after five years if it made quarterly payments of $15,000. You will use the FV function to calculate this future value.

To calculate the future value of the loan:

1. In cell **C9**, enter **400,000** as the size of the loan.
2. Copy the values and formulas from the range **E8:I8** to the range **E9:I9**.
3. In cell **J9**, enter **–15,000** as the size of the quarterly payments. Again, the value is negative because it represents money that the restaurant will spend (negative cash flow).
4. In cell **D9**, enter the formula **=FV(I9, G9, J9, C9)** to calculate the future value of the loan based on the *rate* value in cell I9, the *nper* value in cell G9, the *pmt* value in cell J9, and the *pv* value in cell C9. The formula returns –$210,387, indicating that the restaurant will still owe the lender more than $210,000 at the end of the five-year period. See Figure 9-2.

Figure 9-2   Future value of the loan

	A	B	C	D	E	F	G	H	I	J	K
5		Annual Interest Rate									
7		Financial Value	Business Loan (PV)	Future Value (FV)		Years	Payments per Year	Payments (NPER)	Annual Rate	Rate per Quarter (RATE)	Quarterly Payments (PMT)
8		Quarterly Payment (PMT)	$ 400,000	$ -		5	4	20	7.00%	1.75%	$ (23,876)
9		Future Value (FV)	$ 400,000	$ (210,387)		5	4	20	7.00%	1.75%	$ (15,000)
10		Payments (NPER)									
11		Business Loan (PV)									

- FV function (D9: =FV(I9,G9,J9,C9))
- loan amount
- amount owed on the loan after five years
- quarterly payments set to $15,000

At 7 percent interest, more than half of the original $400,000 loan will still need to be repaid at the end of five years if the quarterly payments are limited to $15,000. Sylvia wants to know how long it would take to repay the loan with those quarterly payments. You can calculate the length of the payment period using the NPER function.

INSIGHT

Calculating Inflation with the FV Function

You can use the FV function to calculate future costs assuming the effects of inflation. To project a future value of an item under inflation, use the formula

```
=FV(rate, years, 0, present)
```

where *rate* is the annual inflation rate, *years* is the number of years in the future for which you want to project the cost of the item, and *present* is the present day cost. For example, if an item currently costs $15,000 and the inflation rate is 3.2 percent, the cost of the item in eight years will be calculated as

```
=FV(3.2%, 8, 0, 15000)
```

which returns −$19,298.73. The negative value is based on how Excel handles the FV function with positive and negative cash flows. For the purposes of predicting an inflated value, you can ignore the minus sign and use a value of $19,298.73 as the future cost of the item. Notice that you enter 0 for the value of the *pmt* argument because you are not making payments toward inflation.

Calculating the Payment Period with the NPER Function

The NPER function calculates the number of payments required either to repay a loan or to reach an investment goal. The syntax of the NPER function is:

```
NPER(rate, pmt, pv [, fv=0] [, type=0])
```

where the *rate*, *pmt*, *pv*, *fv*, and *type* arguments are the same as described with the PMT and FV functions. For example, the following formula calculates the number of $50 monthly payments needed to repay a $1,000 loan at 8 percent annual interest:

```
=NPER(8%/12, -50, 1000)
```

The formula returns 21.537, indicating that the loan and the interest will be completely repaid in about 22 months.

To use the NPER function for investments, you define a future value of the investment along with the investment's present value and the periodic payments made to the investment. If you placed $200 per month in an account that pays 3 percent interest compounded monthly, the following formula calculates the number of payments required to reach $5,000:

```
=NPER(3%/12, -200, 0, 5000)
```

The formula returns 24.28, which is just over two years. Note that the *pv* value is set to 0 based on the assumption that no money was in the account before the first deposit.

Sylvia wants to know how long it will take to repay a $400,000 loan at 7 percent interest with quarterly payments of $15,000. You will use the NPER function to calculate the length of this loan in terms of the number of quarterly payments.

> **TIP**
> The NPER function returns the number of payments, not necessarily the number of years.

To calculate the length of a $400,000 loan at 7 percent interest with quarterly payments of $15,000:

1. In cell **C10**, enter **400,000** as the present value of the loan.
2. In cell **D10**, enter **0** to indicate that the loan will be completely repaid.
3. In cell **F10**, enter **4** to indicate that payments are made quarterly.
4. Copy the values and formulas in the range **H9:J9** to the range **H10:J10**.

TIP

If the NPER function returns #NUM!, the loan cannot be repaid because the monthly payments are less than the monthly interest due.

5. In cell **G10**, enter the formula **=NPER(I10, J10, C10)** to calculate the required number of payments based on the *rate* value in cell I10, the *pmt* value in cell J10, and the *pv* value in cell C10. The formula returns 36.23, indicating that about 37 payments are required to repay the loan.

6. In cell **E10**, enter the formula **=G10/F10** to divide the total number of payments by the payments per year, which determines the number of years to repay the loan. The formula returns 9.06, indicating that the loan will be repaid in a little more than nine years.

7. Select cell **G10**. See Figure 9-3.

Figure 9-3 Payments required to repay the loan

	B	C	D	E	F	G	H	I	J
4									
5	Annual Interest Rate								
6									
7	Financial Value	Business Loan (PV)	Future Value (FV)	Years	Payments per Year	Payments (NPER)	Annual Rate	Rate per Quarter (RATE)	Quarterly Payments (PMT)
8	Quarterly Payment (PMT)	$ 400,000	$ -	5	4	20	7.00%	1.75%	$ (23,876)
9	Future Value (FV)	$ 400,000	$ (210,387)	5	4	20	7.00%	1.75%	$ (15,000)
10	Payments (NPER)	$ 400,000	$ -	9.06	4	36.23	7.00%	1.75%	$ (15,000)
11	Business Loan (PV)								

Cell G10 formula bar: =NPER(I10,J10,C10) — NPER function

- loan amount
- loan will be repaid in more than nine years …
- … or in more than 36 quarterly payments
- amount of the quarterly payments

Sylvia doesn't want to take nine years to repay a business loan. Instead, she wants to know what size loan could be repaid within five years at $15,000 per quarter. You can determine that amount with the PV function.

Calculating the Present Value with the PV Function

The PV function calculates the present value of a loan or an investment. For a loan, the present value would be the size of the loan. For an investment, the present value is the amount of money initially placed in the investment account. The syntax of the PV function is

```
PV(rate, nper, pmt[, fv=0][, type=0])
```

where the *rate*, *nper*, *pmt*, *fv*, and *type* arguments have the same meanings they had for the other financial functions.

You can use the PV function to calculate the loan amount that you can afford given a set number of payments and an annual interest rate. For example, if you make $100 monthly payments at 8 percent annual interest for four years (or 48 months), the formula to calculate the largest loan you can afford is

`=PV(8%/12, 48, -100)`

which returns $4,096.19. Under these conditions, the largest loan you can afford is almost $4,100. Note that because you are paying $100 per month for 48 months, the total amount paid back to the lender is $4,800. The $703.81 difference between the total amount paid and the loan amount determined by the PV function ($4,800–$4,096.19 or $703.81) is the cost of the loan in terms of the total amount of interest paid.

With investments, the PV function calculates the initial investment amount required to reach a savings goal. For example, if you add $100 per month to a college savings account that grows at 4 percent annual interest and you want the account to reach a future value of $25,000 in 10 years (or 120 months), the following formula determines the initial investment:

`=PV(4%/12, 120, -100, 25000)`

The formula returns –$6,892.13, indicating you must start with almost $6,900 in the account to reach the $25,000 savings goal at the end of 10 years.

Sylvia wants to know what size loan the restaurant can afford if the loan is to be paid back in five years with $15,000 payments made each quarter at 7 percent annual interest. You will use the PV function to determine the size of the loan.

To calculate the size of the loan:

1. Copy the loan condition values and formulas in the range **D8:I8**, and then paste them in the range **D11:I11**.
2. In cell **J11**, enter **–15,000** as the quarterly payment amount.
3. In cell **C11**, enter **=PV(I11,G11,J11)** to calculate the size of the loan based on the *rate* value in cell I11, the *nper* value in cell G11, and the *pmt* value in cell J11. The formula results specify a loan amount of $251,293.

   Sylvia decides that a larger loan is needed to start Jerel's. She suggests increasing the quarterly payments to $18,000 over five years. You'll calculate how much of a loan the restaurant would get with those payments.

4. In cell **J11**, enter **–18,000** as the new quarterly payment amount. The loan amount increases to $301,552, which will be sufficient if Sylvia can find additional funding from other sources.
5. Select cell **C11**. See Figure 9-4.

Tutorial 9 Exploring Financial Tools and Functions | Excel **EX 539**

Figure 9-4   Present value of a loan

	Financial Value	Business Loan (PV)	Future Value (FV)	Years	Payments per Year	Payments (NPER)	Annual Rate	Rate per Quarter (RATE)	Quarterly Payments (PMT)
5	Annual Interest Rate	7%	*PV function*						
8	Quarterly Payment (PMT)	$ 400,000	$ —	5	4	20	7.00%	1.75%	$ (23,876)
9	Future Value (FV)	$ 400,000	$ (210,387)	5	4	20	7.00%	1.75%	$ (15,000)
10	Payments (NPER)	$ 400,000	$ —	9.06	4	36.23	7.00%	1.75%	$ (15,000)
11	Business Loan (PV)	$ 301,552	$ —	5	4	20	7.00%	1.75%	$ (18,000)

C11: =PV(I11,G11,J11)

loan amount

payments set at $18,000 per quarter

Sylvia has decided on a loan amount of $300,000 to be repaid at 7 percent interest in quarterly payments over the first five years of the restaurant's operation. You will enter this loan amount in the Startup worksheet, which Sylvia created to detail the restaurant's startup costs and assets.

To enter the loan amount:

1. Go to the **Startup** worksheet.
2. In cell **C29**, enter **300,000** as the loan amount.
3. Explore the rest of the Startup worksheet, noting the expenses and assets for starting up the restaurant as well as other sources of funding.

Sylvia wants to record more detailed information about the proposed business loan in the Loan Schedule worksheet. You'll start by entering the terms of the loan and calculate the exact value of each loan payment.

To calculate the size of the loan payments:

1. Go to the **Loan Schedule** worksheet.
2. Select cell **B6**, type **=** to begin the formula, go to the **Startup** worksheet, click cell **C29**, and then press the **Enter** key. The formula =Startup!C29 entered in cell B6 displays the loan amount of $300,000 from cell C29 in the Startup worksheet.
3. In cell **C6**, enter **7%** as the annual interest rate.
4. In cell **D6**, enter **4** as the number of payments per year (quarterly).
5. In cell **E6**, enter the formula **=C6/D6** to calculate the interest rate per quarter. The formula returns 1.75 percent.
6. In cell **F6**, enter **5** to indicate that the loan will be repaid in five years.

> 7. In cell **G6**, enter the formula **=D6*F6** to calculate the total number of payments, which is 20 payments in this instance.
>
> 8. In cell **H6**, enter the formula **=PMT(E6, G6, B6)** to calculate the size of each payment. The formula returns –$17,907, which is the exact amount the restaurant will have to spend per quarter to completely repay the $300,000 loan in five years.

Sylvia wants to examine how much of each $17,907 quarterly payment is spent on interest charged by the lender. To determine that value, you'll create an amortization schedule.

Creating an Amortization Schedule

An amortization schedule is a table that specifies how much of each loan payment is devoted toward interest and toward repaying the principal. The principal is the amount of the loan that is still unpaid. In most loans, the initial payments are usually directed toward interest charges. As more of the loan is repaid, the percentage of each payment devoted to interest decreases (because the interest is being applied to a smaller and smaller principal) until the last few payments are used almost entirely for repaying the principal. Figure 9-5 shows a typical relationship between the amount paid toward interest and the amount paid toward the principal plotted against the number of payments.

Figure 9-5 — Interest and principal payments

© 2014 Cengage Learning

Calculating Interest and Principal Payments

To calculate the amount of a loan payment devoted to interest and to principal, you use the IPMT and PPMT functions. The IPMT function returns the amount of a particular payment that is used to pay the interest on the loan. It has the syntax

```
=IPMT(rate, per, nper, pv[, fv=0][, type=0])
```

where the *rate*, *nper*, *pv*, *fv*, and *type* arguments have the same meaning as they do for the PMT and other financial functions. The *per* argument defines the period for which you want to calculate the interest due. For example, the following formula calculates how much interest is due in the fifth payment of the restaurant's $300,000 loan:

```
=IPMT(7%/4, 5, 20, 300000)
```

The formula returns –$4,340.45, indicating that the restaurant will spend $4,340.45 toward interest in the fifth payment.

The PPMT function calculates the amount used to repay the principal. The PPMT function has the following syntax, which is similar to the IPMT function:

```
=PPMT(rate, per, nper, pv[, fv=0][, type=0])
```

The following formula calculates the amount of the principal that is repaid with the fifth payment of the restaurant loan:

```
=PPMT(7%/4, 5, 20, 300000)
```

This formula returns –$13,566.91. Note that the sum of the interest payment and the principal payment is –$17,907.37, which is the same value returned by the PMT function earlier. The total amount paid to the bank each quarter doesn't change; only how that amount is allocated between paying interest and repaying the principal.

Sylvia asks you to create an amortization schedule for the restaurant's loan. You'll use the IPMT and PPMT functions to do this. The Loan Schedule worksheet already contains the table in which you'll enter the formulas to track the changing amounts spent on principal and interest over the next five years.

To create the amortization schedule for the restaurant's loan:

1. In cell **D10**, enter the formula **=B6** to display the initial principal of the loan.

2. In cell **E10**, enter the formula **=IPMT($E$6, C10, $G$6, $B$6)** to calculate the interest due for the first payment, with $E$6, $G$6, and $B$6 referencing the loan conditions specified in row 6 of the worksheet, and cell C10 referencing the number of the period. The formula returns –$5,250, which is the amount of interest paid with the first payment.

3. In cell **F10**, enter the formula **=PPMT($E$6, C10, $G$6, $B$6)** to calculate the principal payment in the first period. Excel returns the value –$12,657, which is the amount by which the principal is reduced after the first payment.

4. In cell **G10**, enter the formula **=E10+F10** to calculate the total payment for the first period of the loan. The formula returns –$17,907, matching the quarterly payment value in cell H6. See Figure 9-6.

> **TIP**
> Use absolute references for the loan conditions so the same values apply to every payment period when you copy the formulas to the rest of the amortization schedule.

Figure 9-6 | **Initial payment in the amortization schedule**

[Screenshot of Excel worksheet "Jerel's Loan Schedule" showing loan conditions: Loan (PV) $300,000, Annual Rate 7.00%, Payments per Year 4, Rate per Period (RATE) 1.75%, Years 5, Payments (NPER) 20, Payment (PMT) ($17,907) — labeled "loan conditions". Amortization Schedule row 10: Year 1, Period 1, Remaining Principal $300,000, Interest Payment (5,250), Principal Payment (12,657), Total Payment (17,907). Callouts: "interest due in the first quarter", "principal repaid in the first quarter", "sum of the interest and principal payments matches the PMT value".]

The formulas for the rest of the amortization schedule are similar to that for the first quarter except that the remaining principal in column D must be reduced by the amount paid toward the principal from the previous quarter. You will complete the amortization schedule.

To complete the amortization schedule:

1. In cell **D11**, enter the formula **=D10+F10** to add the remaining principal at the start of the first quarter to the first quarter principal payment. This calculates the principal remaining at the start of the second quarter of the loan, which is $287,343.

2. Copy the formulas in the range **E10:G10** to the range **E11:G11** to calculate the interest, principal, and total payment for the second quarter. The interest payment is $5,028, the principal payment is $12,879, and the total payment remains $17,907. The interest due for the second quarter is less than for the first quarter because the remaining principal is lower. As a result, more of the total payment for this quarter is used to reduce the principal.

3. Use the fill handle to copy the formulas in the range **D11:G11** to the range **D12:G29**. The formulas are copied into the rest of the rows of the amortization schedule to calculate the remaining principal, interest payment, principal payment, and total payment for each of the remaining 18 quarters of the loan.

4. Click the **Auto Fill Options** button, and then click the **Fill Without Formatting** option button. The formulas are entered without overwriting the existing worksheet formatting. Notice that in the last quarterly payment at the end of the fifth year, only $308 of the $17,907 payment is used to pay the interest on the loan. The remaining $17,599 is used to repay the principal.

5. In cell **D30**, enter the formula **=D29+F29** to calculate the final balance of the loan after the final payment. The final balance is 0, verifying that the loan is completely repaid at the end of the five-year period. See Figure 9-7.

Figure 9-7 Completed amortization schedule

total payment remains constant at $17,907 per quarter

remaining principal on the loan steadily decreases

final balance is 0 after the last payment

	A	B	C	D	E	F	G
14		2	5	248,026	(4,340)	(13,567)	(17,907)
15		2	6	234,459	(4,103)	(13,804)	(17,907)
16		2	7	220,655	(3,861)	(14,046)	(17,907)
17		2	8	206,609	(3,616)	(14,292)	(17,907)
18		3	9	192,317	(3,366)	(14,542)	(17,907)
19		3	10	177,775	(3,111)	(14,796)	(17,907)
20		3	11	162,979	(2,852)	(15,055)	(17,907)
21		3	12	147,924	(2,589)	(15,319)	(17,907)
22		4	13	132,605	(2,321)	(15,587)	(17,907)
23		4	14	117,018	(2,048)	(15,860)	(17,907)
24		4	15	101,159	(1,770)	(16,137)	(17,907)
25		4	16	85,022	(1,488)	(16,419)	(17,907)
26		5	17	68,602	(1,201)	(16,707)	(17,907)
27		5	18	51,895	(908)	(16,999)	(17,907)
28		5	19	34,896	(611)	(17,297)	(17,907)
29		5	20	17,599	(308)	(17,599)	(17,907)
30			Final Balance	$0.00			

interest payments steadily decrease each period

principal payments steadily increase each period

Sylvia finds it helpful to see how much interest the restaurant is paying each quarter. However, many financial statements also show the amount paid toward interest and principal over the whole year. This information is used when creating annual budgets and calculating taxes.

Calculating Cumulative Interest and Principal Payments

Cumulative totals of interest and principal payments can be calculated using the CUMIPMT and CUMPRINC functions. The CUMIPMT function calculates the sum of several interest payments and has the syntax

```
CUMIPMT(rate, nper, pv, start, end, type)
```

where *start* is the starting payment period for the interval you want to sum and *end* is the ending payment period. This function has no *fv* argument; the assumption is that loans are always completely repaid. Also, note that the *type* argument is not optional. You must specify whether the payments are made at the start of the period (*type*=0) or at the end (*type*=1). For example, to calculate the total interest paid in the second year of the restaurant's loan (payments 5 through 8), you would enter the formula

```
=CUMIPMT(7%/4, 20, 300000, 5, 8, 0)
```

which returns −15,920.60 as the total spent on interest in the second year of the loan.

To calculate the cumulative total of payments made toward the principal, you use the CUMPRINC function, which has the syntax

```
CUMPRINC(rate, nper, pv, start, end, type)
```

where the *rate*, *nper*, *pv*, *start*, *end*, and *type* arguments have the same meaning as they do for the CUMIPMT function. The formula

```
=CUMPRINC(7%/4, 20, 300000, 5, 8, 0)
```

calculates the total amount spent on reducing the principal in the second year and returns −$55,708.87, indicating that the amount remaining on the loan is reduced by almost $56,000 during the second year.

Sylvia wants you to add the total interest and principal payments for the loan for each of the five years in the amortization schedule. You'll use the CUMIPMT and CUMPRINC functions to calculate these values. The table at the bottom of the Loan Schedule worksheet already has the starting and ending quarters for each year of the loan, which you'll reference in the functions.

To calculate the cumulative interest and principal payments:

1. In cell **C37**, enter the formula **=CUMIPMT($E$6, $G$6, $B$6, C35, C36, 0)** to calculate the cumulative interest payments for the first year. The formula returns −19,655, which is the amount spent on interest the first year. Notice that the formula uses absolute references to cells E6, G6, and B6 for the *rate*, *nper*, and *pv* arguments so that these arguments always reference the loan conditions at the top of the worksheet, which don't change throughout the loan schedule. The references to cells C35 and C36 for the *start* and *end* arguments are relative because they change based on the time period over which the payments are made.

   Next you'll calculate the cumulative payments made toward the principal.

2. In cell **C38**, enter the formula **=CUMPRINC($E$6, $G$6, $B$6, C35, C36, 0)** to calculate the principal payments in the first year. The formula returns −$51,974, which is the amount by which the principal will be reduced the first year.

3. Copy the formulas in the range **C37:C38** to the range **D37:G38** to calculate the cumulative interest and principal payments for each of the next four years.

   Each year, more money is spent reducing the principal. For example, in Year 5, the restaurant will spend $3,027 on interest payments and will reduce the loan principal by $68,602. See Figure 9-8.

Figure 9-8   Annual interest and principal payments

		Year 1	Year 2	Year 3	Year 4	Year 5
	Quarters	1	5	9	13	17
		4	8	12	16	20
Interest		($19,655)	($15,921)	($11,917)	($7,627)	($3,027)
Principal		($51,974)	($55,709)	($59,712)	($64,003)	($68,602)
Principal Remaining						

Cumulative Interest and Principal Payments per Year

Formula bar: =CUMIPMT($E$6,$G$6,$B$6,C35,C36,0) — CUMIPMT function

cumulative interest payments for Year 1 through Year 5

cumulative principal payments for Year 1 through Year 5

4. Select the range **H37:H38**.

5. On the HOME tab, in the Editing group, click the **AutoSum** button ∑ to calculate the total interest and principal payments over the five years of the loan, which are –$58,147 and –$300,000, respectively.

Finally, you will calculate the principal remaining at the end of each year.

6. In cell **C39**, enter the formula **=$B$6+C38** to add the cumulative principal payment to the initial amount of the loan in cell B6. The formula returns $248,026, which is the amount of the loan remaining to be paid after the first year.

7. In cell **D39**, enter the formula **=C39+D38** to calculate the remaining principal at the end of Year 2 by adding the Year 1 principal to the Year 2 principal payments. The formula returns $192,317.

8. Copy the formula in cell **D39** to the range **E39:G39**, calculating the remaining principal at the end of each of the next three years.

9. Select cell **B32** to deselect the table. Figure 9-9 shows the final table of cumulative interest and principal payments.

Figure 9-9 — Total loan payments

		Year 1	Year 2	Year 3	Year 4	Year 5	
	Quarters	1	5	9	13	17	
		4	8	12	16	20	Total
Interest		($19,655)	($15,921)	($11,917)	($7,627)	($3,027)	($58,147)
Principal		($51,974)	($55,709)	($59,712)	($64,003)	($68,602)	($300,000)
Principal Remaining		$248,026	$192,317	$132,605	$68,602	$0	

Cumulative Interest and Principal Payments per Year

- total interest on the loan
- total principal matches the loan amount
- principal remaining at the end of each year

The Loan Schedule worksheet shows that the restaurant will spend $58,147 on interest. The total principal payment is $300,000 because the loan will be repaid in full. Calculating the total principal payment lets you verify that the loan conditions are set up correctly. If the total does not match the initial amount of the loan, there must be a mistake in the calculations used in the loan schedule.

PROSKILLS

Written Communication: Writing a Financial Workbook

The goal of all writing is communication. A properly written financial workbook should be simple for others to read and understand. It should also be easily edited to allow exploration of what-if scenarios needed to analyze the impact of different financial conditions on the bottom line.

To help ensure that any financial workbook you create meets these goals, keep in mind the following principles:

- Place all important financial variables at or near the top of a worksheet so that they can be easily read by others. For example, place the interest rate you use in calculations in a well-labeled worksheet cell.
- Use defined names with the financial variables to make it easier to apply them in formulas and functions.
- Clearly identify the direction of the cash flow in all of your financial calculations. Most Excel financial functions require a particular direction to the cash flow to return the correct value. Using the wrong sign will turn the calculation of a loan payment into an investment deposit or vice versa.
- Place argument values in worksheet cells where they can be viewed and easily changed. Never place these values directly into a financial formula.
- When values are used in more than one calculation, enter them in a cell that you can reference in all formulas rather than repeating the same value throughout the workbook.
- Use the same unit of time for all the arguments in a financial function. For example, when using the PMT function to calculate monthly loan payments, the interest rate and the number of payments should be based on the interest rate per month and the total months to repay the loan.

A financial workbook that is easy to read and understand is more useful to yourself and others when making business decisions.

You have finished analyzing the conditions for the restaurant's business loan. In the next session, you'll make projections about the company's future earnings by developing an income statement for the first five years of the restaurant's operation.

Session 9.1 Quick Check

REVIEW

1. Explain the difference between positive and negative cash flow. If you borrow $10,000 from a bank, is that a positive or negative cash flow? Justify your answer.
2. What is the formula to calculate how much a savings account would be worth if the initial balance is $500 with monthly deposits of $50 for 10 years at 5.8 percent annual interest compounded monthly? What is the formula result?
3. You want a savings account to grow from $1,000 to $3,000 within two years. Assume the bank provides a 5.2 percent annual interest rate compounded monthly. What is the formula to calculate how much you must deposit each month to meet your savings goal? What is the formula result?
4. You want to take out a loan for $200,000 at 7 percent interest compounded monthly. If you can afford to make monthly payments of only $1,500 on the loan, what is the formula to calculate the number of months required to repay the loan completely? What is the formula result?
5. Rerun your calculations from Question 4 assuming that you can afford only a $1,000 monthly payment. What are the revised formula and resulting value? How do you explain the result?
6. You take out a 10-year loan for $150,000 at 6.3 percent interest compounded monthly. What are the formula to calculate the monthly payment and the resulting value?
7. For the loan conditions specified in Question 6, what are the formulas to calculate the amount of the first payment used for interest and the amount of the first payment used to repay the principal? What are the resulting values?
8. For the loan conditions specified in Question 6, what are the formulas to calculate how much interest you will pay in the first year and how much you will repay toward the principal? What are the resulting values?

Session 9.2 Visual Overview:

Interpolation is used to fill in a series when you know the starting and ending values of that series.

An **income statement** (also called a **profit and loss statement**) displays how much money a person or business makes or loses over a specified period of time.

Cost of sales (also known as **cost of goods sold**) consists of expenses directly related to production.

General expenses or **fixed expenses** are expenses not directly related to production.

Depreciation is the process of allocating the original cost of an asset over the lifetime of the asset.

G30 =DB(180000, 60000,15,5)

	A	B	C	D	E
7		Income	Year 1	Year 2	Year 3
8		Food	$ 800,000	$ 885,346	$ 979,7
9		Bar/Beverages	300,000	322,371	346,4
10		Total Revenue	1,100,000	1,207,717	1,326,2
11		Direct Cost of Food	280,000	309,871	342,9
12		Direct Cost of Bar/Beverages	105,000	112,830	121,2
13		Total Cost of Sales	385,000	422,701	464,1
14					
15		GROSS PROFIT	715,000	785,016	862,0
16					
17		Expenses	Year 1	Year 2	Year 3
18		Payroll	$ 400,000	$ 420,000	$ 441,0
19		Utilities	60,000	63,000	66,1
20		Marketing	30,000	31,500	33,0
21		Occupancy Costs	90,000	94,500	99,2
22		Fees and Banking	35,000	36,750	38,5
23		Insurance	20,000	21,000	22,0
24		Leased Equipment	15,000	15,750	16,5
25		Music & Entertainment	9,000	9,450	9,9
26		TOTAL GENERAL EXPENSES	659,000	691,950	726,5
27					
28		Earnings	Year 1	Year 2	Year 3
29		Earnings before Depreciation,	$ 56,000	$ 93,066	$ 135,4
30		Depreciation	12,780	11,873	11,0
31		Operating Profit	43,220	81,193	124,4

Income Statement | Balance Sheet | Cash Flow | Loan Ana...

READY

Tutorial 9 Exploring Financial Tools and Functions | Excel   EX 549

Income Statement and Depreciation

A **linear trend** changes values by a constant amount.

A **growth trend** changes values by a constant percentage.

Extrapolation is used to extend a series from a single value or a few values to project future values.

The **DB function** calculates the declining balance depreciation in which the asset depreciates by a constant percentage each time period.

E	F	G	H	I	J
Year 3	Year 4	Year 5			
979,796	$ 1,084,322	$ 1,200,000			
346,410	372,242	400,000			
326,206	1,456,564	1,600,000			
342,929	379,513	420,000			
121,244	130,285	140,000		Linear	Growth
464,172	509,798	560,000		1	1.0
				12	1.7
862,034	946,767	1,040,000		23	2.8
				34	4.6
Year 3	Year 4	Year 5		45	7.7
441,000	$ 463,050	$ 486,203		56	12.9
66,150	69,458	72,930		67	21.5
33,075	34,729	36,465		78	35.9
99,225	104,186	109,396		89	59.9
38,588	40,517	42,543		100	100.0
22,050	23,153	24,310			
16,538	17,364	18,233			
9,923	10,419	10,940			
726,548	762,875	801,019			
Year 3	Year 4	Year 5		Year 5	
135,486	$ 183,892	$ 238,981		=G15-G26	
11,030	10,247	9,519		=DB(180000, 60000,15,5)	
124,457	173,645	229,462		=G29-G30	

Projecting Future Income and Expenses

A key business report is the income statement, also known as a profit and loss statement, which shows a business's income and expenses over a specified period of time. Income statements are often created monthly, semiannually, or annually.

Sylvia created the Income Statement worksheet to project the restaurant's income and expenses for its first five years of operation. This income statement is divided into three main sections. The Income section projects the restaurant's income from sales of food and beverages as well as the cost of supplying those items. The Expenses section projects the general expenses incurred by restaurant operations. The Earnings section estimates the restaurant's net profit and tax liability. You'll open and review this worksheet.

To view the Income Statement worksheet:

1. If you took a break after the previous session, make sure the Jerels Restaurant workbook is open.

2. Go to the **Income Statement** worksheet and review the three main sections—Income, Expenses, and Earnings. See Figure 9-10.

Figure 9-10   Income Statement worksheet

Exploring Linear and Growth Trends

TIP

A growth trend is also called exponential growth in the fields of science, economics, and statistics.

Sylvia foresees two possibilities for the restaurant's income in its first five years—(1) revenue will grow by a constant amount from one year to the next; or (2) revenue will grow by a constant percentage each year. The first scenario, in which revenue changes by a constant amount, is an example of a linear trend. When plotted, a linear trend appears as a straight line. The second possibility, in which revenue changes by a constant percentage rather than a constant amount, is an example of a growth trend. For example, each value in a growth trend might be 15 percent higher than the previous year's value. When plotted, a growth trend appears as a curve with the greatest increases occurring near the end of the series.

Figure 9-11 shows a linear trend and a growth trend for revenue that starts at $300,000 in Year 1 and increases to $1,200,000 by Year 5. The growth trend lags behind the linear trend in the early stages but reaches the same stopping value at the end of the time period.

Figure 9-11   **Linear and growth trends**

Chart showing Linear Trend and Growth Trend from Year 1 to Year 5. Linear trends increase by a constant amount; growth trends increase by a constant percentage.

© 2014 Cengage Learning

Interpolating from a Starting Value to an Ending Value

Interpolation is the process that estimates values that fall between a starting point and an ending point. You can use AutoFill to interpolate values for both linear and growth trends. Sylvia wants you to estimate revenues for the first five years of the proposed restaurant. She projects that the food revenue will grow from $800,000 in Year 1 to $1,200,000 in Year 5, and that beverage revenue will increase from $300,000 to $400,000 in the same period. She first wants to determine how much revenue will be generated if it grows by a constant amount each year. You'll interpolate the restaurant's revenue for Year 2 through Year 4 using a linear trend.

To project the food and beverage revenues based on a linear trend:

1. In cell **C8**, enter **800,000** as the starting revenue for food, and then in cell **C9**, enter **300,000** as the starting revenue for beverages.

2. In cell **G8**, enter **1,200,000** as the ending revenue for food, and then in cell **G9**, enter **400,000** as the ending revenue for beverages.

3. Select the range **C8:G9**, which includes the starting and ending revenues for both food and beverages.

4. On the HOME tab, in the Editing group, click the **Fill** button, and then click **Series**. The Series dialog box opens.

TIP

To interpolate a series, the cells between the first and last cells in the series must be blank.

5. Verify that the **Rows** option button and the **Linear** option button are selected. Excel will fill the series within the same rows using a linear trend.

6. Click the **Trend** check box to insert a checkmark. This applies a trend to interpolate the values between the starting and ending values. See Figure 9-12.

Figure 9-12   **Series dialog box for interpolation**

- fills the series within the same row
- applies a trend to interpolate the values between the starting and ending values
- fills the series by a constant amount
- fills the series by a constant percentage

7. Click the **OK** button. The values inserted in the range D8:G9 show the restaurant's projected revenue based on a linear trend. The food revenue increases by $100,000 each year and the beverage revenue increases by $25,000. See Figure 9-13.

Figure 9-13   **Linear trend values**

- food revenue increases by $100,000 per year
- interpolated values
- beverage revenue increases by $25,000 per year

Next, you'll fill in the revenue values in Year 2 through Year 4 assuming a growth trend. To interpolate the growth trend correctly, you first must remove the Year 2 through Year 4 values, leaving those cells blank.

To project the food and beverage revenues based on a growth trend:

1. On the Quick Access Toolbar, click the **Undo** button to remove the interpolated values.

2. On the HOME tab, in the Editing group, click the **Fill** button, and then click **Series**. The Series dialog box opens.

3. In the Type section, click the **Growth** option button, and then click the **Trend** check box to insert a checkmark. This applies a growth trend to interpolate the values between the starting and ending values.

4. Click **OK**. The Year 1 through Year 5 revenue projections are now based on a growth trend. The largest revenue increases occur near the end of the five-year period. For example, food revenue grows by about $85,000 from Year 1 to Year 2, but by about $115,000 from Year 4 to Year 5.

5. Select the range **C10:G10**. You will add the total food and beverage revenues in these cells.

6. In the Editing group, click the **AutoSum** button to add the total food and beverage revenues for each year based on a growth trend. See Figure 9-14.

Figure 9-14 Growth trend values

	A	B	C	D	E	F	G
6							
7		Income	Year 1	Year 2	Year 3	Year 4	Year 5
8		Food	$ 800,000	$ 885,346	$ 979,796	$ 1,084,322	$ 1,200,000
9		Beverages	300,000	322,371	346,410	372,242	400,000
10		Total Revenue	1,100,000	1,207,717	1,326,206	1,456,564	1,600,000
11		Direct Cost of Food					
12		Direct Cost of Beverages					
13		Total Cost of Sales					
14							

filled-in values

increase in food and beverage revenues follow a growth trend

total revenues from food and beverages

TIP
You can calculate the percent change by dividing one year's value by the previous year's value.

By calculating the percentage change in revenue from year to year under the growth trend projection rather than the absolute change in dollars, you determined that the projected revenue increase is about 10.7 percent for food and 7.5 percent for beverages.

Calculating the Cost of Sales

The next part of the income statement displays the cost of sales, also known as the cost of goods sold. The restaurant needs to purchase the ingredients to produce its food and beverage items. The more meals and drinks the restaurant serves, the higher that cost will be. Based on industry standards, Sylvia calculates that for every dollar of sales revenue from food and beverages, the restaurant needs to spend 35 cents to cover the production costs. In other words, the cost of sales is about 35 percent of the revenue generated. The difference between the company's sales revenue and the cost of goods sold is the company's **gross profit**.

Sylvia wants to project the cost of sales and the restaurant's gross profit for each of the next five years. You'll add these calculations to the income statement.

To project the cost of sales and the gross profit:

1. In cell **G4**, enter **35%** as the cost of goods percentage.
2. In cell **C11**, enter the formula **=C8*$G$4** to multiply the food revenue for Year 1 by the cost of goods percentage. The cost of food for the first year of business is $280,000.
3. In cell **C12**, enter the formula **=C9*$G$4** to multiply the beverage revenue for Year 1 by the cost of goods percentage. The cost of beverages for the first year is $105,000.
4. In cell **C13**, enter the formula **=C11+C12** to add the total cost of food and the total cost of beverages for Year 1. The total cost of sales, which is the total amount the restaurant will spend on food and drinks for the first year, is $385,000.
5. In cell **C15**, enter the formula **=C10–C13** to subtract the total cost of sales from the total revenue for Year 1. The gross profit for the first year is $715,000.
6. Copy the formulas in the range **C11:C15** to the range **D11:G15** to calculate the cost of food and beverages, the total cost of sales, and the gross profits for the remaining four years on the income statement.
7. Select cell **C16**. See Figure 9-15.

Figure 9-15 Cost of sales and gross profit

	A	B	C	D	E	F	G
3		Pro Forma Income Statement					
4						Percent Cost of Sales	35%
5						Assumed Tax Rate	
6							
7		Income	Year 1	Year 2	Year 3	Year 4	Year 5
8		Food	$ 800,000	$ 885,346	$ 979,796	$ 1,084,322	$ 1,200,000
9		Beverages	300,000	322,371	346,410	372,242	400,000
10		Total Revenue	1,100,000	1,207,717	1,326,206	1,456,564	1,600,000
11		Direct Cost of Food	280,000	309,871	342,929	379,513	420,000
12		Direct Cost of Beverages	105,000	112,830	121,244	130,285	140,000
13		Total Cost of Sales	385,000	422,701	464,172	509,798	560,000
14							
15		GROSS PROFIT	715,000	785,016	862,034	946,767	1,040,000
16							
17		Expenses	Year 1	Year 2	Year 3	Year 4	Year 5
18		Payroll					
19		Utilities					
20		Marketing					
21		Occupancy Costs					

- cost of sales assumed to be 35 percent of revenue
- gross profit equals total revenue minus total cost of sales

Based on these calculations, the restaurant's gross profit is projected to increase from $715,000 in Year 1 to $1,040,000 in Year 5.

Tutorial 9 Exploring Financial Tools and Functions | Excel   EX 555

REFERENCE

Interpolating and Extrapolating a Series

To interpolate a series of values between starting and ending values:

- Select the range with the first cell containing the starting value, blank cells for middle values, and the last cell containing the ending value.
- On the HOME tab, in the Editing group, click the Fill button, and then click Series.
- Select whether the series is organized in rows or columns, select the type of series to interpolate, and then check the Trend check box.
- Click the OK button.

To extrapolate a series from a starting value:

- Select a range with the first cell containing the starting value followed by blank cells to store the extrapolated values.
- On the HOME tab, in the Editing group, click the Fill button, and then click Series.
- Select whether the series is organized in rows or columns, select the type of series to extrapolate, and then enter the step value in the Step value box.
- Click the OK button.

The next section of the income statement contains the projected general expenses for the restaurant. These expenses are not directly related to production. For example, the restaurant must purchase insurance, provide for general maintenance, and pay for advertising regardless of the number of customers it serves. Sylvia has estimated the Year 1 general expenses. You will add these to the income statement.

To enter the Year 1 expenses:

1. In cell **C18**, enter **400,000** as the payroll expense.
2. In cell **C19**, enter **60,000** as the utilities expense.
3. In cell **C20**, enter **30,000** as the marketing expense.
4. In cell **C21**, enter **90,000** as the occupancy costs expense.
5. In cell **C22**, enter **35,000** as the fees and banking expense.
6. In cell **C23**, enter **20,000** as the insurance expense.
7. In cell **C24**, enter **15,000** as the leased equipment expense.
8. In cell **C25**, enter **9,000** as the music and entertainment expense.
9. Select cell **C26**, and then use **AutoSum** to calculate the total estimated general expenses for Year 1, which is $659,000.

Next, you'll project these initial expenses over the succeeding four years. To do that, you'll extrapolate a trend from the Year 1 values.

Extrapolating from a Series of Values

Extrapolation differs from interpolation in that only a starting value is provided; the succeeding values are estimated by assuming that the values follow a trend. As with interpolation, Excel can extrapolate a data series based on either a linear trend or a growth trend. With a linear trend, the data values are assumed to change by a constant amount. With a growth trend, they are assumed to change by a constant percentage. To extrapolate a data series, you must provide a step value representing the amount by which each value is changed as the series is extended. You do not have to specify a stopping value.

Sylvia estimates that general expenses will increase by about 5 percent per year. This is equivalent to multiplying each year's expenses by 1.05 to project the next year's expenses. Rather than writing a formula to perform this multiplication, you'll extrapolate the expenses using the Fill command.

To extrapolate the Year 1 expenses through the next four years:

1. Select the range **C18:G25**, which contains the general expenses; be sure not to select the total general expenses in cell C26.

2. On the HOME tab, in the Editing group, click the **Fill** button, and then click **Series**. The Series dialog box opens.

3. Click the **Rows** option button to create a series of values in the rows of the selected range.

> Select the Rows option button so the series values fill the row, not the column.

4. Click the **Growth** option button, and then type **1.05** in the Step value box to specify the growth trend percentage. See Figure 9-16.

Figure 9-16 Series dialog box for extrapolation

- fills the series within the same row
- multiplies each value in the series by 1.05 to extrapolate the next value
- increases the starting value by a constant value
- increases the starting value by a constant percentage
- identifies the value where the extrapolation stops

TIP

To extrapolate a decreasing trend, use a negative step value for a linear trend, and use a step value between 0 and 1 for a growth trend.

5. Click the **OK** button. The expense values from Year 1 are extrapolated into the Year 2 through Year 5 columns.

6. Copy the formula in cell **C26** to the range **D26:G26** to calculate the total general expenses for the company for each of the five years. These calculations show that the projected general expenses will rise from $659,000 in Year 1 to $801,019 by the end of Year 5.

Next, you want to calculate the company's earnings during each of the next five years. The initial earnings estimate is equal to the company's gross profit minus the total general expenses.

To calculate the company's initial earnings:

1. In cell **C29**, enter the formula **=C15–C26** to subtract the total general expenses from the gross profit for Year 1. The estimate of earnings for the first year is $56,000.

2. Copy the formula in cell **C29** to the range **D29:G29** to project yearly earnings through Year 5. These calculations project that the restaurant's earnings will increase from $56,000 in Year 1 to $238,981 in Year 5.

3. Select cell **C30**. See Figure 9-17.

Figure 9-17 Projected general expenses and earnings

	A	B	C	D	E	F	G
16							
17		**Expenses**	Year 1	Year 2	Year 3	Year 4	Year 5
18		Payroll	$ 400,000	$ 420,000	$ 441,000	$ 463,050	$ 486,203
19		Utilities	60,000	63,000	66,150	69,458	72,930
20		Marketing	30,000	31,500	33,075	34,729	36,465
21		Occupancy Costs	90,000	94,500	99,225	104,186	109,396
22		Fees and Banking	35,000	36,750	38,588	40,517	42,543
23		Insurance	20,000	21,000	22,050	23,153	24,310
24		Leased Equipment	15,000	15,750	16,538	17,364	18,233
25		Music & Entertainment	9,000	9,450	9,923	10,419	10,940
26		TOTAL GENERAL EXPENSES	659,000	691,950	726,548	762,875	801,019
27							
28		**Earnings**	Year 1	Year 2	Year 3	Year 4	Year 5
29		Initial Earnings	$ 56,000	$ 93,066	$ 135,486	$ 183,892	$ 238,981
30		Depreciation					
31		Operating Profit					
32							
33		Interest Expense					
34		Pretax Profit					

expenses are assumed to increase 5 percent per year from the Year 1 values

initial earnings equal to the gross profit minus total general expenses

Calculating Depreciation of Assets

The financial status of a company is not determined solely by its revenue and expenses. Its wealth also includes non-cash assets such as equipment, land, buildings, and vehicles. These assets are known as **tangible assets** because they are long-lasting material assets not intended for sale but for use only by the company. Not all material assets are tangible assets. For example, assets such as the ingredients the restaurant uses when preparing its dishes are not considered tangible assets because although they are used in the cooking process, they are sold indirectly to the consumer in the form of a finished meal. However, items such as the cooking stove, refrigeration units, deep fryers, and so forth are tangible assets.

Tangible assets wear down over time and lose their value. Because this reduces the company's wealth, tax laws allow companies to deduct this loss of value from reported earnings on the company's income statement, reducing the company's tax liability. The loss of the asset's original value doesn't usually happen all at once, but is instead spread out over several years in a process known as depreciation. For example, an asset whose original value is $200,000 might be depreciated to $100,000 after 10 years of use. Different types of tangible assets have different rates of depreciation. Some items depreciate faster than others, which maintain their value for longer periods. In general, to calculate the depreciation of an asset, you need to know the following:

- The asset's original cost
- The length of the asset's useful life
- The asset's **salvage value**, which is the asset's value at the end of its useful life
- The rate at which the asset is depreciated over time

There are several ways to depreciate an asset. This tutorial focuses on straight-line depreciation and declining balance depreciation.

Straight-Line Depreciation

With **straight-line depreciation**, the asset loses value by equal amounts each year until it reaches the salvage value at the end of its useful life. You can calculate the straight-line depreciation value using the SLN function, which has the syntax

```
SLN(cost, salvage, life)
```

where *cost* is the initial cost or value of the asset, *salvage* is the salvage value of the asset at the end of its useful life, and *life* is the number of periods over which the asset will be depreciated. In most cases, *life* is expressed in terms of years. For example, to calculate the yearly depreciation of an asset with an initial value of $200,000 and a salvage value of $50,000 after 10 years, you would enter the formula

```
=SLN(200000, 50000, 10)
```

which returns $15,000, indicating that the asset will decline $15,000 every year from its initial value until it reaches its salvage value.

Declining Balance Depreciation

Under **declining balance depreciation**, the asset depreciates by a constant percentage each year rather than a constant amount. The depreciation is highest early in the asset's lifetime and steadily decreases as the asset itself loses value. Figure 9-18 compares the yearly straight-line and declining balance depreciation over a 20-year lifetime as an asset declines from its initial value of $100,000 to $20,000.

Figure 9-18 Straight-line and declining balance depreciation

© 2014 Cengage Learning

An asset shows a greater initial decline under declining balance depreciation than under straight-line depreciation. Declining balance depreciation is another example of a negative growth trend in which the asset decreases in value by a constant percentage rather than by a constant amount, as is the case with straight-line depreciation.

You can use the DB function to calculate the declining balance depreciation. The DB function has the syntax

```
DB(cost, salvage, life, period[, month=12])
```

where *cost*, *salvage*, and *life* are again the initial cost, salvage cost, and lifetime of the asset, respectively, and *period* is the period for which you want to calculate the depreciation. If you are calculating depreciation on a yearly basis, then *period* would contain the year value of the depreciation. For example, to calculate the fourth year of depreciation of a $200,000 asset that declines to a salvage value of $50,000 after 10 years, you would enter the formula

```
=DB(200000, 50000, 10, 4)
```

which returns $17,048.03, indicating that the asset declines in value more than $17,000 during its fourth year of use. By contrast, the asset's depreciation in its fifth year is calculated with the formula

```
=DB(200000, 50000, 10, 5)
```

which returns $14,848.83. The depreciation is smaller in the fifth year because the asset has a lower value.

The DB function also supports an optional *month* argument, which is needed when the asset is used for only part of the first year. For example, if you are depreciating the $200,000 asset after using it for only two months in Year 1, you would calculate its depreciation in the fifth year as

```
=DB(200000, 50000, 10, 5, 2)
```

which returns $16,681.50. This is a higher depreciation value because the asset has not been subjected to wear and tear for a full five years, making it more valuable going into Year 5.

As part of the restaurant startup, Jerel will supply cooking equipment valued at $180,000. The useful life of this cooking equipment is about 15 years. After 15 years, the restaurant will replace those items with new equipment. The projected salvage value of the old equipment after 15 years is about one-third of its initial value, or $60,000. You will calculate the depreciation of this asset over the restaurant's first five years of operation in the Depreciation worksheet.

To specify the values of the tangible assets:

1. Go to the **Startup** worksheet.

2. In cell **C15**, enter **180,000** as the value of the long-term assets.

3. Go to the **Depreciation** worksheet.

4. In cell **C5**, type **=** to begin the formula, go to the **Startup** worksheet, click cell **C15**, and then press the **Enter** key. The formula =Startup!C15 is entered in cell C5, which displays the $180,000 long-term assets value from the Startup worksheet.

5. In cell **C6**, enter **60,000** as the asset's estimated salvage value.

6. In cell **C7**, enter **15** as the useful life of the asset.

Next, you'll calculate the depreciation of the restaurant equipment using straight-line depreciation.

To calculate the straight-line depreciation:

1. In cell **C11**, enter the formula **=SLN($C$5, $C$6, $C$7)** to calculate the straight-line depreciation in Year 1 based on the *cost* value in cell C5, the *salvage* value in cell C6, and the *life* value in cell C7. The formula returns a depreciation value of $8,000, indicating the asset will decline in value by $8,000 in Year 1.

2. Copy the formula in cell **C11** to the range **D11:G11** to calculate the straight-line depreciation for the remaining years. Because the straight-line depreciation is a constant amount every year, the formula returns a depreciation value of $8,000 for Year 2 through Year 5.

   Next, you'll calculate the cumulative depreciation of the asset from Year 1 through Year 5.

3. In cell **C12**, enter the formula **=C11** to display the depreciation for the first year.

4. In cell **D12**, enter the formula **=C12+D11** to add the Year 2 depreciation to the depreciation from Year 1. The total depreciation through the first two years is $16,000.

5. Copy the formula in cell **D12** to the range **E12:G12** to calculate cumulative depreciation through the first five years. By Year 5, the asset's value will have declined by $40,000.

6. In cell **C13**, enter the formula **=$C$5–C12** to calculate the depreciated asset's value after the first year. The asset's value is $172,000.

7. Copy the formula in cell **C13** to the range **D13:G13**. By Year 5, the asset's value has been reduced to $140,000.

8. Select cell **C11**. See Figure 9-19.

Figure 9-19 | **Straight-line depreciation of the asset**

Sylvia also wants to explore the depreciation of the restaurant equipment under the declining balance depreciation method. You'll calculate these values in the Depreciation worksheet.

To calculate the declining balance depreciation:

1. In cell **C17**, enter the formula **=DB($C$5, $C$6, $C$7, C16)** to calculate the declining balance depreciation for Year 1 based on the initial *cost* of the asset in cell $C$5, the *salvage* value in cell $C$6, the *life* of the asset in cell $C$7, and the current *period* (or year) in cell C16. The formula returns $12,780, which is the amount that the assets will depreciate in Year 1.

2. Copy the formula in cell **C17** to the range **D17:G17** to calculate the depreciation in each of the remaining four years. The depreciation amount decreases each year under the declining balance schedule, reaching a value of $9,519 in Year 5.

3. Copy the formulas in the range **C12:G13** to the range **C18:G19** to calculate the cumulative depreciation and depreciated value of the asset. Based on the declining balance depreciation method, the value of the asset declines to $124,552 by the end of Year 5.

4. Select cell **C17**. Figure 9-20 shows the depreciation, cumulative depreciation, and depreciated value for Years 1 through 5 under declining balance depreciation.

Figure 9-20 | Declining balance depreciation of the asset

Excel supports several other depreciation functions to satisfy specialized accounting needs. Figure 9-21 summarizes all of the Excel depreciation functions.

Figure 9-21   **Depreciation functions**

Function	Description
SLN(cost, salvage, life)	Returns the straight-line depreciation in which the asset declines by a constant amount each year, where cost is the initial cost of the asset, salvage is the salvage value, and life is the useful lifetime of the asset.
DB(cost, salvage, life, period [, month])	Returns the declining balance depreciation in which the asset declines by a constant percentage each year, where period is the year of the depreciation and month is an optional argument that defines the number of months that the asset was owned during Year 1.
SYD(cost, salvage, life, period)	Returns the sum-of-years' digit depreciation that results in a more accelerated depreciation than straight-line depreciation, but a less accelerated depreciation than declining balance depreciation.
DDB(cost, salvage, life, period [, factor=2])	Returns the double-declining balance depreciation that doubles the depreciation under the straight-line method and applies that accelerated rate to the original asset value minus the cumulative depreciation. The factor argument specifies the factor by which the straight-line depreciation is multiplied. If no factor is specified, a factor of 2 (for doubling) is assumed.
VDB(cost, salvage, life, start, end[, factor=2] [, no_switch=FALSE])	Returns a variable declining depreciation for any specified period using any specified depreciation method, where start is the starting period of the depreciation, end is the ending period, factor is the rate at which the depreciation declines, and no_switch specifies whether to switch to the straight-line method when the depreciation falls below the estimate given by the declining balance method.

© 2014 Cengage Learning

Decision Making: Choosing a Depreciation Schedule

How do you decide which method of depreciation is the most appropriate? The answer depends on the type of asset being depreciated. Tax laws allow different depreciation methods for different kinds of assets and different situations. In general, you want to choose the depreciation method that most accurately describes the true value of the asset and its impact on the company's financial status. In tax statements, depreciation appears as an expense that is subtracted from the company's earnings. So, if you accelerate the depreciation of an asset in the early years of its use, you might be underestimating the company's profits, making it appear that the company is less profitable than it actually is. On the other hand, depreciating an asset slowly could make it appear that the company is more profitable than it really is. For this reason, the choice of a depreciation method is best made in consultation with a tax accountant who is fully aware of the financial issues and the tax laws involved.

Adding Depreciation to an Income Statement

Depreciation is part of a company's income statement because even though the company is not losing actual revenue, it is losing worth as its tangible assets decline in value, and that reduces its tax liability. Sylvia wants to add the declining balance depreciation figures from the Depreciation worksheet to the projected income statement to project the restaurant's operating profit, which represents the restaurant's profits before calculating its tax liability.

To add depreciation to the income statement:

1. Go to the **Income Statement** worksheet.
2. In cell **C30**, type **=** to begin the formula, go to the **Depreciation** worksheet, click cell **C17**, and then press the **Enter** key. The formula in cell C30 of the Income Statement worksheet displays a depreciation of $12,780.
3. Copy the formula in cell **C30** to the range **D30:G30** to show the annual depreciation for Year 2 through Year 5.
4. In cell **C31**, enter the formula **=C29−C30** to subtract the depreciation from the company's earnings. The restaurant's operating profit is $43,220.
5. Copy the formula in cell **C31** to the range **D31:G31** to calculate the operating profit for Year 2 through Year 5.

When depreciation is included, the restaurant's operating profit in Year 1 is $43,220 and increases to $229,462 by the end of Year 5.

Adding Taxes and Interest Expenses to an Income Statement

Interest expenses are also part of a company's income statement. You have already projected the annual interest payments the restaurant will have to make on its $300,000 loan (shown earlier in row 37 of Figure 9-9). Rather than reenter these values, you can reference the calculated values from that worksheet in the income statement. Because those values were displayed as negative numbers, you'll change the sign to match the format of the Income Statement worksheet.

To include the interest expense in the income statement:

1. In cell **C33**, type **=−** (an equal sign followed by a minus sign) to begin the formula.
2. Go to the **Loan Schedule** worksheet, click cell **C37**, which contains the total interest payments in Year 1, and then press the **Enter** key. The formula in cell C33 of the Income Statement worksheet displays the interest expense as the positive value 19,655.
3. In cell **C34**, enter the formula **=C31−C33** to subtract the interest expense from the operating profit for Year 1. The restaurant's pretax profit after paying interest on its loan for the first year is 23,565.

4. Copy the formulas in the range **C33:C34** to the range **D33:G34** to calculate the interest payments and pretax profits for the remaining years. When interest is considered, the restaurant's projected profit ranges from $23,565 in Year 1 to $226,435 by the end of Year 5.

Finally, you need to account for the taxes that the restaurant will pay on the money it makes. Sylvia estimates that the restaurant will be subject to a 31 percent tax rate on its pretax income. You will add this tax rate to the Income Statement worksheet and then calculate the restaurant's tax liability. The restaurant will only pay taxes if it makes money, so you will use an IF function to test whether the pretax income is positive. If it is, the pretax income will be multiplied by the value in cell G5; otherwise, the formula will return the value 0.

To calculate the restaurant's tax liability:

1. In cell **G5**, enter **31%** as the tax rate.

2. In cell **C36**, enter the formula **=IF(C34>0, C34*$G$5, 0)** to first test whether the pretax income in Year 1 is greater than 0. If it is, then the pretax income will be multiplied by the tax rate in cell G5. Otherwise, the formula will return 0. Because the pretax income for the first year is positive (greater than 0), the pretax income is multiplied by 31 percent, returning a tax liability of $7,305 for the first year.

3. In cell **C37**, enter the formula **=C34−C36** to subtract the taxes owed for Year 1 from the pretax income. The restaurant's after-tax profit for the first year is $16,260.

4. Copy the formulas in the range **C36:C37** to the range **D36:G37** to calculate the tax liability and after-tax profit for the remaining years. After accounting for taxes, profit from the restaurant will range from $16,260 in Year 1 to $156,240 in Year 5.

5. Select cell **C36** to deselect the range. See Figure 9-22.

Figure 9-22   Revised income statement

	A	B	C	D	E	F	G
28		Earnings	Year 1	Year 2	Year 3	Year 4	Year 5
29		Initial Earnings	$ 56,000	$ 93,066	$ 135,486	$ 183,892	$ 238,981
30		Depreciation	12,780	11,873	11,030	10,247	9,519
31		Operating Profit	43,220	81,193	124,457	173,645	229,462
32							
33		Interest Expense	19,655	15,921	11,917	7,627	3,027
34		Pretax Profit	23,565	65,273	112,539	166,019	226,435
35							
36		Taxes Liability	7,305	20,234	34,887	51,466	70,195
37		After-Tax Profit	$ 16,260	$ 45,038	$ 77,652	$ 114,553	$ 156,240

Cell C36: =IF(C34>0, C34*$G$5, 0)

- IF function calculates tax liability
- the restaurant's operating profit after accounting for depreciation of its assets
- profit after accounting for interest expense
- profit after accounting for tax liability

Tutorial 9 Exploring Financial Tools and Functions | Excel

With much of the financial planning complete, the restaurant needs to attract some investors. In the next session, you will evaluate the return on investment that the restaurant will be able to offer investors, and the impact it will have on the restaurant's profitability.

Session 9.2 Quick Check

1. The first value in a linear trend is 1000 and the fifth value is 4000. What are the values of the second, third, and fourth items?
2. The first value in a growth trend is 1000 and the fifth value is 4000. What are the values of the second, third, and fourth items?
3. The first value in a series is 1000. Extrapolate the next four values assuming a linear trend with a step size of 500.
4. The first value in a series is 1000. Extrapolate the next four values assuming a growth trend step size of 15 percent.
5. A new business buys $25,000 worth of computer equipment. If the useful life of the equipment is five years with a salvage value of $2,000, what is the formula to determine the depreciation during the first year assuming straight-line depreciation? What is the formula result?
6. Assume a declining balance depreciation for the computer equipment described in Question 5. What are the formula and the result?
7. Write the formula to calculate how much the computer equipment described in Question 5 would depreciate in the first year assuming double-declining balance depreciation with a factor of 2. What is the result?

Session 9.3 Visual Overview:

The **payback period** is the length of time before an investment recovers its initial cost, which occurs when the values change from negative to positive.

The **rate of return** (or **discount rate**) is an interest rate that compares the value of current dollars to future dollars from a series of cash flows.

The **net present value** is the difference between the present value of an investment and the initial expenditure on that investment.

The **internal rate of return (IRR)** is the return rate for a series of future cash flows that will result in a net present value of 0.

The **NPV function** calculates the present value of a series of future cash flows.

Cell D29 formula: `=IRR(C19:C24)`

Return on the Investment

		Payments	Net Cash Flow
19	Startup	$ (200,000)	$ (200,000)
20	Year 1	45,000	(155,000)
21	Year 2	50,000	(105,000)
22	Year 3	55,000	(50,000)
23	Year 4	60,000	10,000
24	Year 5	70,000	80,000

Desired Rate of Return		10%
Present Value (NPV)		$207,999
Net Present Value		7,999
Internal Rate of Return (IRR)		11.44%

0.1
=NPV(D26,C20:C24)
=C19+D27
=IRR(C19:C24)

NPV and IRR Functions and Auditing

Tutorial 9 Exploring Financial Tools and Functions | Excel EX 567

The Formula Auditing group includes commands to fix formula errors and trace formulas to their roots.

```
45000
5
=RATE(G20,G19,G18)
```

	Investment (PV)	$ (200,000)
	Yearly Payments (PMT)	45,000
	Payments (NPER)	5
	Interest Rate (RATE)	4.06%

The RATE function calculates the per-period interest rate required to repay a loan or reach an investment goal.

	Total Income	45,000
	Accounting	10,000
	Advertising	14,000
	Insurance	9,000
	Total Expenses	#NAME?
	Earnings	#NAME?

Tracer arrows track errors to their source by pointing from the precedent cell to the dependent cell.

Tracer arrows identify **precedent cells**, which supply data values to the active cell, and **dependent cells**, which depend on the value in the active cell for their result.

Red tracer arrows indicate an error in the value being received from the precedent cell or passed to the dependent cell.

The IRR function calculates the internal rate of return for an investment.

Calculating Interest Rates with the RATE function

When you evaluated potential loans in the first session, you may have noticed that the *pmt*, *fv*, *nper*, and *pv* arguments corresponded to Excel functions of the same name. The *rate* argument also has a corresponding RATE function that calculates the interest rate based on the values of the other financial arguments. The RATE function is used primarily to evaluate the return from investments (because borrowers rarely set the interest rates of their loans) when you know the *pv*, *fv*, *pmt*, and *nper* values. The syntax of the RATE function is

```
RATE(nper, pmt, pv[, fv=0][, type=0][, guess=0.1])
```

where *nper* is the number of payments, *pmt* is the amount of each payment, *pv* is the loan or investment's present value, *fv* is the future value, and *type* defines when the payments are made. The optional *guess* argument is used when the RATE function cannot calculate the interest rate value and needs an initial guess to arrive at a solution.

For example, if you invest $14,000 in a company and then receive $150 per month for the next 10 years (or 120 months) for a total of $18,000, you can calculate the interest rate from that investment using the formula

```
=RATE(120, 150, -14000)
```

which returns an interest rate of 0.43 percent per month or 5.2 percent annually. Note that the *pmt* value is positive because this is an investment and the payments are coming to you (positive cash flow), but the present value –14,000 is negative because that is money you spent investing in the company (negative cash flow). The future value is 0 by default because once you have been completely repaid for your investment, there are no funds left.

With loans, the positive and negative signs of the *pmt* and *pv* values are switched. For example, if you can borrow $14,000 and repay it by making payments of $150 per month over the next 10 years, you can calculate the monthly interest rate using the formula

```
=RATE(120, -150, 14000)
```

which again returns 0.43 percent per month or 5.2 percent annually. Notice that the payment value is negative and the present value is positive.

Not every combination of payments and present value will result in a viable interest rate. For example, if you try to calculate the interest rate for a $14,000 loan that is repaid with payments of $100 per month for 120 months, the formula

```
=RATE(120, -100, 14000)
```

returns an interest rate of –0.25 percent per month or –3.0 percent annually. The interest rate is negative because you cannot repay a $14,000 loan within 10 years by paying only $100 per month. The total payments would amount to only $12,000.

The restaurant needs another $200,000 in startup capital. Sylvia is considering repaying the investors $45,000 per year for the first five years of the restaurant's operation, which would total $225,000. She wants to know the annual interest rate that this repayment schedule would represent. You will use the RATE function to find out.

> **TIP**
> Always multiply the RATE function results by the number of payments per year. For monthly payments, multiply the rate value by 12.

To calculate the interest rate of an investment:

1. If you took a break after the previous session, make sure the Jerels Restaurant workbook is open.

2. Go to the **Startup** worksheet, and then in cell **C34**, enter **200,000** as the amount contributed by investors.

Tutorial 9 Exploring Financial Tools and Functions | Excel   EX 569

▶ 3. Go to the **Investment Analysis** worksheet.

▶ 4. In cell **C7**, type **=−** (an equal sign followed by a minus sign), go to the **Startup** worksheet, click cell **C34**, and then press the **Enter** key. The formula displays −$200,000 in the cell. You want to use a negative value because you are examining this investment from the point of view of the investors, who are making an initial payment of $200,000 to the restaurant (a negative cash flow).

▶ 5. In cell **C8**, enter **45,000** as the annual payment. The value is positive because this money is being repaid to the investors each year (a positive cash flow from their point of view).

▶ 6. In cell **C9**, enter **5** as the total number of payments made to the investors.

▶ 7. In cell **C10**, enter the formula **=RATE(C9, C8, C7)** to calculate the interest rate of this repayment schedule based on the *nper* value in cell C9, the *pmt* value in cell C8, and the *pv* value in cell C7. The annual interest rate to the investors for this repayment schedule is 4.06 percent.

▶ 8. Select cell **C10**. See Figure 9-23.

Figure 9-23   Interest rate of the repayment schedule

	B	C
1	Jerel's	
3	Investment Analysis	
5	Proposed Repayment Schedule to Investors	
7	Investment (PV)	$ (200,000)
8	Yearly Payments (PMT)	45,000
9	Payments (NPER)	5
10	Interest Rate (RATE)	4.06%

- initial investment made by investors
- annual repayment to the investors
- interest rate from the annual repayment schedule
- RATE function: =RATE(C9,C8,C7)

The interest rate is one way of measuring the value of an investment. Investors are also interested in knowing how long they will have to wait to recoup their investment. You can determine this result by examining the payback period.

Viewing the Payback Period of an Investment

One simple measure of the return from an investment is the payback period, which is the length of time required for an investment to recover its initial cost. For example, a $300,000 investment that returns $25,000 per year would take 12 years to repay the initial cost of the investment.

Sylvia isn't sure she can attract investors with a 4.06 percent annual interest rate. Another possibility is to pay the investors dividends taken from the restaurant's annual profits. Because the restaurant will not show much profit initially, leaving less cash to pay dividends, Sylvia is considering the following schedule of dividend payments: Year 1—$0; Year 2—$5,000; Year 3—$10,000; Year 4—$15,000; and Year 5—$25,000.

Sylvia wants you to add these dividends to the repayment of the investors' original $200,000 investment, and then calculate the payback period.

To determine the payback period for the investment:

1. In cell **C13**, enter the formula **=$C$8** to reference the annual loan repayment to the investors.

2. Copy the formula in cell **C13** to the range **D13:G13** to apply the same loan repayment to each year.

3. In the range **C14:G14**, enter the dividend payments of **0** in cell C14 for Year 1, **5,000** in cell D14 for Year 2, **10,000** in cell E14 for Year 3, **15,000** in cell F14 for Year 4, and **25,000** in cell G14 for Year 5.

4. Select the range **C15:G15**, and then use AutoSum to calculate the total reimbursement to the investors for each of the first five years. The total values range from $45,000 in Year 1 to $70,000 by the end of Year 5.

Next, you'll add these totals to the initial investment to view the cumulative total payments made to the investors.

5. In cell **C19**, enter the formula **=C7** to reference the initial investment value.

6. In the range **C20:C24**, enter the following formulas to reference the annual payments made to the investors: **=C15** in cell C20 for the Year 1 repayment, **=D15** in cell C21 for the Year 2 repayment, **=E15** in cell C22 for the Year 3 repayment, **=F15** in cell C23 for the Year 4 repayment, and **=G15** in cell C24 for the Year 5 repayment.

7. Select the range **C19:C24**, click the **Quick Analysis** button, click **TOTALS**, scroll right to the end of the TOTALS tools, and then click **Running Total** to calculate a column of running totals for the net cash flow to investors. See Figure 9-24.

Figure 9-24   Payback period of the investment

Based on these calculations, the investors will be repaid for their investments during the fourth year (when the value of the cumulative net cash flow changes from negative to positive). By the end of the fifth year, investors will see a profit of $80,000 on their original investments.

Calculating Net Present Value

The payback period is a quick method of assessing the long-term value of an investment. The major drawback of the payback period is that it does not take into account the time value of money. To understand why, you must explore how time impacts financial decisions.

The Time Value of Money

The **time value of money** is based on the observation that money received today is worth more than the same amount received later. One reason for this is that you can invest the money you receive today and earn interest on that investment. The time value of money can be expressed in terms of what represents a fair exchange between current dollars and future dollars.

For example, is it better to get $100 today or $105 one year from now? The answer depends on what you could do with that $100 during the year. If you could invest it in an account that pays 6 percent interest per year, the $100 would turn into $106 in one year, making it better to receive the $100 now. But, if you could only earn 4 percent interest on the $100, it would be better to wait a year and receive the $105.

The interest rate you assume for the present value of your investment is known as the rate of return or the discount rate. It defines the time value of money by providing a way to measure future value in terms of current value.

You can use the PV function to calculate the time value of money under different rates of return. For example, to determine the present value of receiving $100 per year for the next five years at a 6 percent annual rate of return, you would enter the formula

```
=PV(6%, 5, 100)
```

which returns –$421.24, indicating that it would be a fair exchange to spend $421.24 today in order to receive $100 per year for each of the next five years. In other words, $421.24 today is worth the same as $500 given in $100 annual payments over the next five years if the rate of return is 6 percent.

For investments that pay off at the end of the investment period without any intermediate payments, you enter 0 for the *pmt* value and enter the amount returned by the investment for the *fv* value. So, to calculate the present value of receiving $500 at the end of five years at a 6 percent rate of return, you enter the formula

```
=PV(6%, 5, 0, 500)
```

which returns –$373.63, indicating that it would be a fair exchange to spend $373.63 today to receive $500 five years from now.

You also can use the FV function to estimate how much a dollar amount today is worth in terms of future dollars. For example, to determine the future value of $100 in two years when the rate of return is 5 percent, you would enter the formula =FV(5%, 2, 0, –100). This formula returns $110.25, which is a positive cash flow indicating that spending $100 today is a fair exchange for receiving $110.25 two years from now.

Using the NPV Function

The PV function assumes that all future payments are equal. If the future payments are not equal, you must use the NPV (net present value) function to determine what would be a fair exchange. The syntax of the NPV function is

```
NPV(rate, value1[, value2, value3, ...])
```

where `rate` is the rate of return, and `value1`, `value2`, `value3`, and so on are the values of future payments from the investment. The NPV function assumes that payments occur at the end of each payment period and that the payment periods are evenly spaced.

For example, to calculate the present value of a three-year investment that pays $100 at the end of the first year, $200 at the end of the second year, and $500 at the end of the third year with a 6 percent annual rate of return, you would enter the formula

```
=NPV(6%, 100, 200, 500)
```

which returns $692.15, indicating that the investment's value is equal to receiving $692.15 today.

Unlike the PV function, which returns a negative value for the investment's present value, the NPV function returns a positive value. This occurs because the PV function returns a cash flow value that indicates how much you need to invest now (a negative cash flow) to receive money later (a positive cash flow); whereas the NPV function calculates the value of those payments in today's dollars based on your chosen rate of return.

You can receive some surprising results when you take into account the time value of money. Consider an investment that has a rate of return with the following transactions: Year 1—Investor receives $250; Year 2—Investor receives $150; Year 3—Investor receives $100; Year 4—Investor pays $150; and Year 5—Investor pays $400.

At first glance, this seems to be a bad investment. The investor receives a total of $500 in the first three years but spends $550 in Year 4 and Year 5, yielding an apparent net loss of $50. However, this doesn't take into account the time value of money. When the present value of this transaction is calculated using the NPV function

```
=NPV(6%, 250, 150, 100, -150, -400)
```

the value of the investment in current dollars is equal to $35.59, a positive result. The investment is actually profitable because the returns come early, but the payments are made later, paid in dollars of lesser value.

Choosing a Rate of Return

Choosing an appropriate rate of return is related to the concept of **risk**—the possibility that the entire transaction will fail, resulting in a loss of the initial investment. Investments with higher risks generally should have higher rates of return. If investors invest $200,000 in a simple bank account (a low-risk venture), they would not expect a high rate of return; on the other hand, investing the $200,000 in a new restaurant is riskier and merits a higher rate of return.

After discussing the issue with financial analysts, Sylvia has settled on a 10 percent rate of return. This means she believes that their restaurant will return to the investors at least as much as they would get if they had invested $200,000 in an account paying 10 percent annual interest. You'll use that rate of return in the NPV function as you calculate the net present value of Sylvia's proposal.

To calculate the net present value of the investment:

1. In cell **D26**, enter **10%** as the desired rate of return.
2. In cell **D27**, enter the formula **=NPV(D26, C20:C24)** to calculate the net present value of the investment based on the rate value in cell D26 and the return paid to the investors for Year 1 through Year 5 in the range C20:C24. The formula returns $207,999, indicating that the present value of the investment is almost $208,000.

3. In cell **D28**, enter the formula **=C19+D27** to combine the present value with the initial investment of $200,000. The net present value is $7,999.
4. Select cell **D27**. See Figure 9-25.

Figure 9-25   Net present value of the investment

	A	B	C	D	E	F
				=NPV(D26, C20:C24) ← NPV function		
17		Return on the Investment				
18			Payments	Net Cash Flow		
19		Startup	$ (200,000)	$ (200,000)		
20		Year 1	45,000	(155,000)		
21		Year 2	50,000	(105,000)		
22		Year 3	55,000	(50,000)		
23		Year 4	60,000	10,000		
24		Year 5	70,000	80,000		
25						
26		Desired Rate of Return		10%		
27		Present Value (NPV)		$207,999		
28		Net Present Value		7,999		
29		Internal Rate of Return (IRR)				

According to these results, the $200,000 investment is worth about $8,000 more than the payout obtained by placing the same amount in a savings account that pays 10 percent annual interest.

INSIGHT

Understanding Net Present Value and the NPV Function

The financial definition of net present value is the difference between the present value of a series of future cash flows and the current value of the initial investment. One source of confusion for Excel users is that despite its name, the NPV function does *not* return the net present value of an investment. Instead, it returns the investment's present value based on the returns that the investment will provide in the future.

To calculate the net present value in Excel, the cost of the initial investment must be added to the value returned by the NPV function using the formula

```
=initial investment + NPV value
```

where `initial investment` is the initial cost of the investment and `NPV value` is the value returned by the NPV function. The `initial investment` is assumed to have a negative cash flow because that investment is being purchased.

The only exception to this rule is when the initial investment also takes place in the future. For example, if the initial investment takes place in one year and the returns occur annually after that, then the NPV function will return the net present value without having to be adjusted because the initial investment is also paid with discounted dollars.

Sylvia mentions that in any financial analysis, it is a good idea to test other values to see how they impact your conclusions. You will rerun the analysis using return rates of 5 percent, 11 percent, and 12 percent.

> **To view the impact of different rates of return:**
>
> 1. In cell **D26**, change the value to **5%** to decrease the desired rate of return. The net present value in cell D28 increases to $39,929. The investment is almost $40,000 more profitable than what could be achieved by an account bearing 5 percent annual interest.
>
> 2. In cell **D26**, change the value to **11%**, increasing the desired rate of return. Now the net present value of the investment declines to $2,403. This is still profitable, but not as profitable as an investment promising an 11 percent annual interest rate.
>
> 3. In cell **D26**, change the value to **12%**. The net present value of the investment is –$2,963. Investing the $200,000 in the restaurant would be less profitable than investing the same amount in another investment promising a 12 percent annual interest rate.
>
> 4. In cell **D26**, change the value back to **10%**.

At higher rates of return, the net present value of the restaurant investment decreases. That's not surprising when you realize the restaurant project is being compared with investments that offer higher and higher returns.

Calculating the Internal Rate of Return

Your analysis of different rates of return for the restaurant illustrates an important principle: At some rate of return, the net present value of an investment will change from a positive value to a negative value. Figure 9-26 shows the change in net present value for a sample investment using different rates of return.

Figure 9-26   Net present value and internal rate of return

© 2014 Cengage Learning

The point at which the net present value of an investment equals 0 is the internal rate of return (IRR) of the investment. The internal rate of return is another popular measure of the value of an investment because it provides a basis of comparison between one investment and another. Investments with higher internal rates of return are usually preferred to those with lower IRRs.

Using the IRR Function

The IRR function calculates the internal rate of return for an investment. The IRR function has the syntax

```
IRR(values[, guess=0.1])
```

where values are the cash flow values from the investment, and guess is an optional argument in which you provide a guess for the IRR value. A guess is needed for financial transactions that have several possible internal rates of return, such as investments that require the investor to make multiple future payments rather than a single initial payment. For those types of transactions, an initial guess helps Excel locate the final value for the IRR. Without the guess, Excel might not be able to calculate the IRR. If you don't include a guess, Excel will use an initial guess of 10 percent for the IRR and proceed from there to determine the answer.

For example, the internal rate of return for a $500 investment that pays $100 in the first year, $150 in the second and third years, and $200 in the fourth year is calculated using the formula

```
=IRR({-500, 100, 150, 150, 200})
```

giving a value of 6.96 percent. This indicates that the return for this investment is as profitable as an account that pays 6.96 percent annual interest.

The order of payments affects the internal rate of return. In the above example, the total amount of money paid back on the investment is $600. However, if the payments were made in the opposite order—$200, $150, $150, and $100—the internal rate of return would be calculated as

```
=IRR({-500, 200, 150, 150, 100})
```

giving a value of 8.64 percent. The increased rate of return is due to the larger payments made earlier with dollars of greater value.

The list of values in the IRR function must include at least one positive cash flow and one negative cash flow, and the order of the values must reflect the order in which the payments are made and the payoffs are received. Like the NPV function, the IRR function assumes that the payments and payoffs occur at evenly spaced intervals. Unlike the NPV function, you include the initial cost of the investment in the values list.

> **TIP**
> When you enter values directly in the IRR function, you must enclose them within curly braces. This is not necessary if the values are expressed as cell references.

REFERENCE

Calculating the Value of an Investment

- To calculate the net present value when the initial investment is made immediately, use the NPV function with the discount rate and the series of cash returns from the investment. Add the cost of the initial investment (negative cash flow) to the value returned by the NPV function.
- To calculate the net present value when the initial investment is made at the end of the first payment period, use the NPV function with the discount rate and the series of cash returns from the investment. Include the initial cost of the investment as the first value in the series.
- To calculate the internal rate of return, use the IRR function with the cost of the initial investment as the first cash flow value in the series. For investments that have several positive and negative cash flow values, include a guess to aid Excel in finding a reasonable internal rate of return value.

You'll use the IRR function to calculate the internal rate of return from the investment in the restaurant.

To calculate the internal rate of return for the restaurant investment:

1. In cell **D29**, enter the formula **=IRR(C19:C24)**, where the range C19:C24 contains the initial investment and the returns that investors can expect. The internal rate of return is 11.44 percent.

2. Select cell **D29**. See Figure 9-27.

Figure 9-27 — Internal rate of return for the investment

	A	B	C	D
17		Return on the Investment		
18			Payments	Net Cash Flow
19		Startup	$ (200,000)	$ (200,000)
20		Year 1	45,000	(155,000)
21		Year 2	50,000	(105,000)
22		Year 3	55,000	(50,000)
23		Year 4	60,000	10,000
24		Year 5	70,000	80,000
25				
26		Desired Rate of Return		10%
27		Present Value (NPV)		$207,999
28		Net Present Value		7,999
29		Internal Rate of Return (IRR)		11.44%

- IRR function: =IRR(C19:C24)
- cash flow values used to calculate the internal rate of return
- return rate that investors can expect from the restaurant

Based on the IRR calculation, Sylvia will be able to tell potential restaurant investors that they will receive an 11.44 percent return on their investments. If this analysis is correct, that would seem like a worthwhile return compared to other competing investments.

Decision Making: Using Net Present Value and Internal Rate of Return to Compare Investments

Businesses often must choose from several possible investment options. In general, they want only investments that have positive net present values or internal rates of return that are higher than a specified rate. In comparing two investments, businesses usually want to select the investment with the higher net present value or the higher internal rate of return.

If they rely on the net present value, they can receive contradictory results depending on the value specified for the desired rate of return. For example, consider the following two returns from an initial investment of $1,000. Option 1 has a higher net present value when discount rates are greater than 9 percent, while Option 2 has a higher net present value when the discount rate is 9 percent or less.

Options	Investment	Year 1	Year 2	Year 3	Year 4
Option 1	−$1,000	$350	$350	$350	$350
Option 2	−$1,000	0	0	0	$1,600

Using the internal rate of return instead of the net present value can also lead to contradictory results. This often occurs when an investment includes several switches between positive and negative cash flows during its history. In those situations, more than one internal rate of return value could fit the data.

To choose between two or more investments, it is a good idea to graph the net present value for each investment against different possible rates of return. By comparing the graphs, you can reach a decision about which investment is the most profitable and under what conditions. This helps you make the best decision about which investment to select.

Exploring the XNPV and XIRR Functions

Both the NPV and IRR functions assume that the cash flows occur at evenly spaced intervals such as annual payments in which the cash receipts from an investment are returned at the end of the financial year. For cash flows that appear at unevenly spaced intervals, you use the XNPV and XIRR functions.

The XNPV function, which calculates the net present value of a series of cash flows at specified dates, has the syntax

```
XNPV(rate, values, dates)
```

where *rate* is the desired rate of return, *values* is the list of cash flows, and *dates* is the dates associated with each cash flow. The series of values must contain at least one positive and one negative value. The cash flow values are discounted starting after the first date in the list, with the first value not discounted at all. Figure 9-28 shows an investment in which the initial deposit of $300,000 on September 1 is returned with eight payments spaced at irregular intervals over the next two years for a total of $350,000. The net present value of this investment is $25,667 based on a 5 percent rate of return. Note that the net present value is not $50,000 (the difference between the deposit and the total payments) because the investment is paid back over time with dollars of lesser value.

Figure 9-28 Net present value calculated over irregular time intervals

	A	B	C
1	Rate of Return	5%	← discount rate (B1)
2			
3	Date	Cash Flow	
4	September 1, 2014	$ (300,000)	
5	December 3, 2014	10,000	
6	February 24, 2015	15,000	
7	June 1, 2015	25,000	
8	September 5, 2015	35,000	← investment transactions (range B4:B12)
9	December 10, 2015	45,000	
10	March 4, 2016	60,000	
11	June 15, 2016	75,000	
12	September 14, 2016	85,000	
13			
14	XNPV	$ 25,667	← XNPV =XNPV(B1,B4:B12,A4:A12)

transaction dates (range A4:A12)

net present value of the investment is $25,667

© 2014 Cengage Learning

Likewise, the XIRR function calculates the internal rate of return for a series of cash flows made at specified dates. It has the syntax

`XIRR(values, dates[, guess=0.1])`

where *values* is the list of cash flow values, *dates* are the dates of each cash flow, and *guess* is an optional argument to help Excel arrive at an answer. Figure 9-29 shows the internal rate of return for the transaction presented in Figure 9-28. After an initial deposit of $300,000, the investment returns a total of $350,000. This investment's rate of return is 11.06 percent, which means that it performs a bit better than an account yielding 11 percent annual interest over the same time period.

Figure 9-29 Internal rate of return calculated over irregular time intervals

	A	B	C
1	Date	Cash Flow	
2	September 1, 2014	$ (300,000)	
3	December 3, 2014	10,000	
4	February 24, 2015	15,000	
5	June 1, 2015	25,000	
6	September 5, 2015	35,000	← investment transactions (range B2:B10)
7	December 10, 2015	45,000	
8	March 4, 2016	60,000	
9	June 15, 2016	75,000	
10	September 14, 2016	85,000	
11			
12	XIRR	11.06%	← RR =XIRR(B2:B10,A2:A10)
13			

transaction dates (range A2:A10)

rate of return from the investment is 11.06 percent

© 2014 Cengage Learning

In Sylvia's business plan, all of the payments to the investors are to be made at regular intervals, at the end of the upcoming fiscal years, so you do not need to use either the XNPV or the XIRR function.

To complete the income statement, Sylvia wants you to project the restaurant's retained earnings, which is the money that the restaurant will make after accounting for depreciation, interest expenses, taxes, and dividends to shareholders. You will enter the dividend payments and calculate the retained earnings in the Income Statement worksheet.

To enter the dividend payments and calculate the retained earnings in the income statement:

1. Go to the **Income Statement** worksheet.

2. In cell **C39**, type **=** to begin the formula, go to the **Investment Analysis** worksheet, click cell **C14**, and then press the **Enter** key. The formula ='Investment Analysis'!C14 is entered in cell C39 of the Income Statement worksheet.

3. Copy the formula in cell **C39** to the range **D39:G39** to display the dividend payments for Year 1 through Year 5.

4. In cell **C41**, enter the formula **=C37–C39** to calculate the retained earnings for the first year. The Year 1 retained earnings are $16,260.

5. Copy the formula in cell **C41** to the range **D41:G41** to calculate the retained earnings for the next four years.

6. Select cell **C42**. Figure 9-30 shows the retained earnings for the restaurant for its first five years of operation.

Figure 9-30   Final income statement

A	B	C	D	E	F	G
28	**Earnings**	Year 1	Year 2	Year 3	Year 4	Year 5
29	Initial Earnings	$ 56,000	$ 93,066	$ 135,486	$ 183,892	$ 238,981
30	Depreciation	12,780	11,873	11,030	10,247	9,519
31	Operating Profit	43,220	81,193	124,457	173,645	229,462
32						
33	Interest Expense	19,655	15,921	11,917	7,627	3,027
34	Pretax Profit	23,565	65,273	112,539	166,019	226,435
35						
36	Taxes Liability	7,305	20,234	34,887	51,466	70,195
37	After-Tax Profit	$ 16,260	$ 45,038	$ 77,652	$ 114,553	$ 156,240
38						
39	Dividends to Shareholders	-	5,000	10,000	15,000	25,000
40						
41	Retained Earnings	$ 16,260	$ 40,038	$ 67,652	$ 99,553	$ 131,240

dividends paid to shareholders

retained earnings after accounting for dividends

Based on these calculations, the retained earnings of the restaurant will grow from $16,260 in Year 1 to $131,240 by the end of Year 5. After the fifth year, the restaurant will have completely repaid the $300,000 business loan and the $200,000 contributed by investors.

Auditing a Workbook

One challenge with large and complex workbooks is that the cell values and formulas are interconnected. Changing the value of one cell can alter the value returned by a formula located in a completely different part of the workbook.

The Jerel's Restaurant workbook combines information from several worksheets covering startup costs, loan schedules, interest rates, depreciation, and investor dividends. The workbook also contains a balance sheet and a cash flow schedule. The Balance Sheet worksheet projects the company's expected assets, liabilities, and equity for the next five years. This sheet provides a picture of what a business owns in both cash and tangible assets, and what it owes to banks and investors. The Cash Flow worksheet projects the amount of cash that the restaurant will generate and use in its first five years of operation.

Unfortunately, these worksheets contain errors. Sylvia has asked you to locate the source of those errors and fix them. You'll start by reviewing the Balance Sheet worksheet to see if you can locate the errors.

To review the Balance Sheet worksheet:

1. Go to the **Balance Sheet** worksheet. Several cells display the #NAME? error value. See Figure 9-31.

Figure 9-31   Error values in the Balance Sheet worksheet

	A	B	C	D	E	F	G
1		Jerel's					
3		Pro Forma Balance Sheet					
5		Assets	Year 1	Year 2	Year 3	Year 4	Year 5
6		Current Assets					
7		Cash	#NAME?	#NAME?	#NAME?	#NAME?	#NAME?
8		Accounts Receivable	-	-	-	-	-
9		Inventory	-	-	-	-	-
10		Total Current Assets	#NAME?	#NAME?	#NAME?	#NAME?	#NAME?
12		Property and Equipment					
13		Property	30,000	30,000	30,000	30,000	30,000
14		Miscellaneous Assets	40,000	40,000	40,000	40,000	40,000
15		Long-Term Assets	180,000	180,000	180,000	180,000	180,000
16		Less Accumulated Depreciation	(12,780)	(24,653)	(35,682)	(45,929)	(55,448)
17		Net Property & Equipment	237,220	225,347	214,318	204,071	194,552

← error values

2. Go to the **Cash Flow** worksheet and observe that several cells in this sheet also display the #NAME? error value.

The source of the error is unclear at first glance. Is the mistake in the Balance Sheet worksheet or is it located elsewhere? Are there multiple errors or is one error the source for different formulas scattered throughout the workbook? Tracing an error back to its source can be a daunting task that grows more difficult as the number of worksheets and formulas increases. For this reason, Excel includes several auditing tools to help you explore the interconnectedness of the cells and formulas in a workbook.

Tracing an Error

When an error occurs in a cell, you need to determine where the error originates. The error could be located in the cell containing the error value. Or it could be in a dependent cell or a precedent cell. A dependent cell is one whose value depends on the values of other cells in the workbook; a precedent cell is one whose value is referenced by other cells. A cell can be both a dependent cell and a precedent cell. For example, if cell C15 contains the formula =C13+C14, then cells C13 and C14 are precedent cells for cell C15, and cell C15 is dependent on cells C13 and C14. This means that any error values in cell C13 or cell C14 would also cause an error in cell C15. If cell C16 contains the formula =C15/10, then cell C15 acts a precedent for that cell, and errors in cell C13 or cell C14 would also affect cell C16.

To locate the source of an error value, you select any cell containing the error value and trace its precedent cells. If any of the precedent cells displays an error value, you need to trace that cell's precedents and so on until you reach an error cell that has no precedents. That cell is the source of the error values in all of its dependent cells. After correcting the error, if other errors still exist, select another cell containing an error and repeat the process until you have removed all of the errors from the workbook.

REFERENCE

Tracing Error Values

- Select the cell containing an error value.
- On the FORMULAS tab, in the Formula Auditing group, click the Error Checking button arrow, and then click Trace Error.
- Follow the tracer arrows to a precedent cell containing an error value.
- If the tracer arrow is connected to a worksheet icon, double-click the tracer arrow and open the cell references in the worksheet.
- Continue to trace the error value to its precedent cells until you locate a cell containing an error value that has no precedent cells with errors.

You will trace the #NAME? error values to their source or sources, and then correct the error.

To trace an error in the Jerel's Restaurant workbook:

1. Go back to the **Balance Sheet** worksheet, and then select cell **G10**. You'll start tracing the error from this cell.

2. On the ribbon, click the **FORMULAS** tab.

3. In the Formula Auditing group, click the **Error Checking button arrow**, and then click **Trace Error**. A tracer arrow is attached to cell G10. See Figure 9-32.

Figure 9-32   Error value being traced in the worksheet

[Screenshot of Excel worksheet showing Jerel's Pro Forma Balance Sheet with #NAME? errors. Callouts indicate: "icon indicates that the precedent cell is located on another worksheet", "Error Checking button arrow", "precedent cell" (pointing to G7), and "dependent cell" (pointing to G10).]

The tracer arrow provides a visual clue to the source of the error. A blue tracer arrow indicates that no error has been received or passed. A red tracer arrow indicates that an error has been received from the precedent cell or passed to the dependent cell. In this case, a red tracer arrow points from cell G7 to cell G10, indicating that cell G7 is the source of the error in cell G10. However, cell G7 also has a precedent cell. A black dashed tracer arrow points from a worksheet icon, indicating that the precedent cell for the value in cell G7 is in another worksheet in the workbook. You'll follow the tracer arrow to that sheet.

To continue tracing the error to its source:

1. Double-click the **tracer arrow** that connects the worksheet icon to cell G7. The Go To dialog box opens, listing a reference to cell G22 in the Cash Flow worksheet.

2. In the Go to box, click the reference to cell **G22**, and then click the **OK** button. Cell G22 in the Cash Flow worksheet is now the active cell. Notice that the #NAME? error appears throughout this worksheet, too.

3. On the FORMULAS tab, in the Formula Auditing group, click the **Error Checking button arrow**, and then click **Trace Error** to trace the source of the error in cell G22.

    The tracer arrows pass through several cells in row 22 before going to cell C21 and settling on cell C19. Cell C19 has a single precedent indicated by the blue arrow and the blue box, which surrounds the range that is the precedent to the formula in cell C19. Because blue is used to identify precedent cells that are error free, the source of the error must be in cell C19 of the Cash Flow worksheet, which is selected.

4. Review the formula for cell C19 in the formula bar. Notice that the function name in the formula was entered incorrectly as SUMM, which is why the #NAME? error code is displayed in cell C19. See Figure 9-33.

Tutorial 9 Exploring Financial Tools and Functions | Excel   EX 583

Figure 9-33   Source of the error value

[Screenshot of Excel worksheet with annotations:
- "SUM function name is misspelled" pointing to formula bar showing =SUMM(C14:C18)
- "blue tracer arrow indicates the precedent cell or range has no errors"
- "precedent ranges are outlined"
- "source of the error"
- "red tracer arrows trace the error back to its source"

Visible data:
	Year 1	Year 2	Year 3	Year 4	Year 5
	45,000	45,000	45,000	45,000	45,000
	-	5,000	10,000	15,000	25,000
	7,305	20,234	34,887	51,466	70,195
	19,655	15,921	11,917	7,627	3,027
18 Debt Payment	51,974	55,709	59,712	64,003	68,602
19 TOT	#NAME?	$ 141,864	$ 161,517	$ 183,095	$ 211,824
21 NET CASH FLOW	#NAME?	$ (48,798)	$ (26,030)	$ 797	$ 27,157
22 CASH BALANCE	#NAME?	#NAME?	#NAME?	#NAME?	#NAME? |]

5. In cell **C19**, change the formula to **=SUM(C14:C18)**. After you edit the formula, the #NAME? error values disappear from the worksheet. Also, the color of the tracer arrows changes from red to blue because they no longer connect to cells containing errors.

   Trouble? If the tracer arrows already disappeared from your workbook, it's not a problem. Excel removes tracer arrows automatically. Continue with Step 6.

6. On the FORMULAS tab, in the Formula Auditing group, click the **Remove Arrows** button to remove all of the tracer arrows from the worksheet.

7. Go to the **Balance Sheet** worksheet and verify that no errors appear on that sheet.

TIP

To restore the tracer arrows that have disappeared, retrace the formulas in the workbook.

You have located the source of the #NAME? error. Note that you can use the auditing tools to track any cell formula whether or not it contains an error. To trace the precedents of the active cell, click the Trace Precedents button in the Formula Auditing group on the FORMULAS tab. To locate cells that are dependent upon the active cell, click the Trace Dependents button.

Evaluating a Formula

One drawback to using tracer arrows is that they can clutter a worksheet. Sometimes you want to trace only a single formula to its roots. Another way to explore the relationship between cells in a workbook is by evaluating formulas. From the Evaluate Formula dialog box, you can display the value of different parts of the formula or "drill down" through the cell references in the formula to discover the source of the formula's value. This is helpful for worksheet errors that are not easily seen and fixed.

On a balance sheet, the value of the company's total assets should equal the value of the total liabilities and equity. Checking that these totals match is a basic step in auditing any financial report. In the Balance Sheet worksheet, the values match for Year 1 through Year 4, but not for Year 5. In Year 5, the restaurant's total assets value reported in cell G19 is $239,743 but the total liabilities and equity value reported in cell G35 is $308,345. Because the values differ, an error must occur somewhere in the workbook. Although you could use the tracer arrows to trace the precedents of cells G19 and G35, you'll instead evaluate the formula in cell G35 to see if you can locate the source of the error that way.

To evaluate the formula in cell G35 of the Balance Sheet worksheet:

1. Select cell **G35**, which contains the total liabilities and equity value for Year 5.

2. On the FORMULAS tab, in the Formula Auditing group, click the **Evaluate Formula** button. The Evaluate Formula dialog box opens with the formula in cell G35 displayed. See Figure 9-34.

Figure 9-34   Evaluate Formula dialog box

displays the formula in the underlined cell

displays the value of the underlined cell reference

formula in cell G35

From this dialog box, you can evaluate each component of the formula in cell G35. To display the value of the underlined cell reference, click the Evaluate button. If the underlined part of the formula is a reference to another formula located elsewhere in the workbook, click the Step In button to display the other formula. Likewise, the Step Out button hides the nested formula.

3. Click the **Evaluate** button. The selected cell reference G23 is replaced with its value. Cell G23 contains the current liabilities for Year 5. Because there are none, the value displayed is 0. Cell G26 is now the underlined reference.

4. Click the **Step In** button to view the formula in cell G26. The formula ='Loan Schedule'!F39 appears below the original formula, indicating that cell G26 gets its value from cell F39 in the Loan Schedule worksheet. See Figure 9-35.

Figure 9-35   Stepping into a formula

formula in the selected cell

click to step out of the selected cell back to the previous formula

selected cell reference

5. Click the **Step In** button to evaluate the formula in cell F39 of the Loan Schedule worksheet. As shown in Figure 9-36, cell F39 in the Loan Schedule worksheet is the Principal Remaining value for Year 4 of the loan payment schedule. However, it should be pointing to cell G39, which contains the Year 5 value, because you are examining liabilities and assets for Year 5.

Figure 9-36 Finding the source of the error

[Screenshot of Excel Evaluate Formula dialog showing:]

	A	B	C	D	E	F
29		5	20	17,599	(308)	(17,599)
30			Final Balance	$0.00		
33	**Cumulative Interest and Principal Payments per Year**					
34			Year 1	Year 2	Year 3	Year 4
35		Quarters	1	5	9	13
36			4	8	12	16
37		Interest	($19,655)	($15,921)	($11,917)	($7,627)
38		Principal	($51,974)	($55,709)	($59,712)	($64,003)
39		Principal Remaining	$248,026	$192,317	$132,605	$68,602

- formula points to the principal payment in Year 4 instead of Year 5
- formula in cell F39 of the Loan Schedule worksheet

▶ 6. Click the **Step Out** button to hide the nested formula and redisplay the Balance Sheet worksheet.

▶ 7. Click the **Close** button to close the Evaluate Formula dialog box and return to the Balance Sheet worksheet with cell G26 selected.

▶ 8. In cell **G26**, change the formula from ='Loan Schedule'!F39 to **='Loan Schedule'!G39**.

The total liabilities and equity value in cell G35 changes to $239,743, matching the assets value in cell G19. The balance sheet is in balance again.

Using the Watch Window

Workbooks can contain dozens of worksheets with interconnected formulas. When you change a value in one worksheet, you may want to view the impact of that change on cell values in other worksheets. Moving back and forth among worksheets can be time consuming and clumsy if the workbook contains many worksheets and the values you want to follow are spread across several of them. Rather than jumping to different worksheets, you can create a **Watch Window**, which is a window that displays values of cells located throughout the workbook. When you change a cell's value, a Watch Window allows you to view the impact of the change on widely scattered dependent cells. The window also displays the workbook, worksheet, defined name, cell value, and formula of each cell being watched.

Sylvia wants to examine some of the underlying assumptions in the restaurant venture. When you worked on the income statement, you assumed a 31 percent income tax rate. She wants to know what would happen if the federal government increased taxes in the next five years from 31 percent to 35 percent. You'll create a Watch Window to display the restaurant's Year 5 retained earnings from the Income Statement worksheet, the Year 5 net worth value from the Balance Sheet worksheet, and the Year 5 cash balance value from the Cash Flow worksheet.

Excel | Tutorial 9 Exploring Financial Tools and Functions

To use the Watch Window to display values from multiple cells:

1. Go to the **Income Statement** worksheet and scroll to the top of the sheet.

2. On the FORMULAS tab, in the Formula Auditing group, click the **Watch Window** button. The Watch Window opens.

3. Click the **Add Watch** button to open the Add Watch dialog box.

4. Click cell **G41** in the Income Statement worksheet, and then click the **Add** button. The Year 5 retained earnings value in cell G41 of the Income Statement worksheet is added to the Watch Window.

5. Click the **Add Watch** button, click cell **G37** in the Balance Sheet worksheet, and then click the **Add** button. The Year 5 net worth value in cell G37 of the Balance Sheet worksheet is added to the Watch Window.

6. Click the **Add Watch** button, click cell **G22** in the Cash Flow worksheet, and then click the **Add** button. The Year 5 cash balance in cell G22 of the Cash Flow worksheet is added to the Watch Window.

Now you can see the impact on these three values when the tax rate changes from 31 percent to 35 percent.

7. At the top of the Income Statement worksheet, in cell **G5**, change the assumed tax rate value from 31% to **35%**. The Watch Window shows the impact of increasing the tax rate. The Year 5 retained earnings amount changes from $131,240 to $122,183—a drop of almost $10,000. The Year 5 net worth changes from $239,743 to $215,990—a drop of about $24,000. Finally, the Year 5 cash balance changes from $45,191 to $21,438—also a drop of about $24,000. See Figure 9-37.

> **TIP**
> You can assign defined names to watched cells to make the Watch Window easier to interpret.

Figure 9-37   Watch Window shows the impact of a tax increase to a 35 percent rate

Book	Sheet	Name	Cell	Value	Formula
Jerels ...	Incom...		G41	$122,183	=G37-G39
Jerels ...	Balan...		G37	215,990	=G19-G26
Jerels ...	Cash ...		G22	$21,438	=F22+G21

- retained earnings in Year 5 (G41)
- net worth in Year 5 (G37)
- cash balance in Year 5 (G22)

8. In cell **G5**, change the assumed tax rate value back to **31%**, and then close the Watch Window.

9. Save the workbook, and then close it.

If the tax rate is increased from 31 percent to 35 percent, it will cost the restaurant about $10,000 in income, the restaurant will lose about $24,000 in cash over the next five years, and the restaurant's net worth will drop by $24,000. With operating margins so tight in the restaurant business, any increase in the tax rate and the resulting losses are a great concern. Sylvia will study this more closely and perhaps revise the business plan to deal with this possibility.

Session 9.3 Quick Check

1. If you take out a loan for $200,000 that must be repaid in 10 years with quarterly payments of $7,200, what is the formula to calculate the annual interest rate of the loan? What is the result?
2. If the annual rate of return is 5 percent, is $95 today worth more than, less than, or the same as $100 a year from now? Show the formula and formula results you used to answer this question.
3. You receive $50 at the end of Year 1 from an investment, $75 at the end of Year 2, and $100 at the end of Year 3. If the rate of return is 6 percent, what is the present value of this investment? Show the formula and formula results you used to answer this question.
4. You spend $350 on an investment that pays $75 per year for the next six years. If you make the investment immediately, what is the net present value of the investment? Assume a 6 percent rate of return. Show the formula and formula results you used to answer this question.
5. Suppose that instead of spending $350 immediately on an investment, you spend $350 one year from now and then receive $75 per year for the next six years after that. What is the net present value assuming a 6 percent rate of return? Show the formula and formula results you used to answer this question.
6. Calculate the internal rate of return for the investment in Question 4. If another investment is available that pays a 7.3 percent rate of return, should you take it? Show the formula and formula results you used to answer this question.
7. What do red tracer arrows indicate?
8. What is the purpose of the Watch Window?

ASSESS

SAM Projects

Put your skills into practice with SAM Projects! SAM Projects for this tutorial can be found online. If you have a SAM account, go to www.cengage.com/sam2013 to download the most recent Project Instructions and Start Files.

PRACTICE

Review Assignments

Data File needed for the Review Assignments: Restaurant.xlsx

Sylvia has some new figures for the business plan for Jerel's. She has received slightly better conditions on the business loan, which means that she needs less money from investors to fund the restaurant. She has also modified the depreciation schedule for the restaurant's tangible assets. She wants you to make the necessary changes in the workbook to calculate the restaurant's financial data for the next five years. Complete the following:

1. Open the **Restaurant** workbook located in the Excel9 ▸ Review folder included with your Data Files, and then save the workbook as **Restaurant Plan** in the location specified by your instructor.
2. In the Documentation worksheet, enter your name and the date.
3. In the Loan Analysis worksheet, in cell C5, enter the **6.85%** annual interest rate that the restaurant has secured for a business loan.
4. In rows 8 through 11, calculate the following possible loan scenarios:
   a. In row 8, for a $450,000 business loan that is repaid in 10 years at a 6.85 percent interest rate with quarterly payments, use the PMT function to calculate the quarterly payments.
   b. In row 9, for a $450,000 loan at a 6.85 percent interest rate with quarterly payments of $12,000 made over 10 years, use the FV function to calculate the principal at the end of 10 years.
   c. In row 10, for a $450,000 loan at a 6.85 percent interest rate that is completely repaid with quarterly payments of $12,000, use the NPER function to calculate the number of quarterly payment periods and then calculate the number of years required to repay the loan.
   d. In row 11, with quarterly payments of $18,000 for 10 years at a 6.85 percent interest rate, use the PV function to calculate the largest loan the restaurant could completely repay in 10 years.
5. In the Startup Plan worksheet, in cell C26, enter a business loan amount of **$400,000**.
6. In the Amortization Schedule worksheet, in the range B6:G6, enter the conditions for a $400,000 loan at a 6.85 percent interest rate with quarterly payments to be repaid in 10 years. Reference the loan value from cell C26 in the Startup Plan worksheet. In cell H6, use the PMT function to calculate the amount of the quarterly payments required to repay the loan.
7. In the range D10:G49, complete the amortization schedule using absolute references to the loan conditions in row 6 of the worksheet. Use the PPMT function to calculate the principal payment for each quarter, and use the IPMT function to calculate the interest payment for each quarter. Reduce the principal owed for each new quarter by the amount paid in the previous quarter. Verify that the loan is completely repaid by displaying the sum of the remaining principal and the last principal payment in cell D50.
8. In the range C55:G59, calculate the cumulative interest and principal payments per year as follows:
   a. In the range C57:G57, use the CUMPRINC function to calculate the cumulative principal payments in each of the first five years of the loan. Include absolute references to the loan conditions in row 6 as part of your calculations.
   b. In the range C58:G58, use the CUMIPMT function to calculate the cumulative interest payments in each of the first five years of the loan.

c. In cells H57 and H58, calculate the total principal payments and interest payments in the first five years of the loan.
   d. In the range C59:G59, calculate the remaining principal at the end of each of the first five years of the loan.
9. In the Income Statement worksheet, in the range D8:F9, interpolate the Year 2 through Year 4 food and beverage revenue values assuming a growth trend. In the range C10:G10, calculate the total revenue for each year.
10. In cell G4, enter **37%** as the Percent Cost of Sales for the restaurant products.
11. In the range D18:G25, extrapolate the general expenses from the provided Year 1 through Year 5 values assuming a 4 percent growth trend. In the range C26:G26, calculate the total expenses for each year.
12. In the range C29:G29, calculate the restaurant's initial earnings for each year, which is equal to the gross profit minus the total general expenses.
13. In the Startup Plan worksheet, in cell C12, enter **$240,000** as the long-term tangible assets that will need to be depreciated.
14. In the Depreciation Schedule worksheet, in cell C5, reference the tangible assets' value from cell C12 in the Startup Plan worksheet. In cell C6, enter **120,000** as the assets' salvage value. In cell C7, enter **20** as the useful lifetime of the assets.
15. In the range C11:G11, calculate the yearly straight-line depreciation of the long-term assets using the SLN function. In the range C12:G12, calculate the cumulative depreciation through the first five years. In the range C13:G13, calculate the depreciated value of the assets at the end of each of the first five years.
16. In the range C17:G17, use the DB function to calculate the yearly declining balance of the assets. In the range C18:G18, calculate the cumulative depreciation of the assets. In the range C19:G19, calculate the depreciated value of the assets at the end of each year.
17. In the Income Statement worksheet, in the range C30:G30, enter formulas to reference the declining balance depreciation values in the range C17:G17 of the Depreciation Schedule worksheet. Calculate the restaurant's operating profit by subtracting the yearly depreciation from the yearly initial earnings.
18. In the range C33:G33, enter formulas for the yearly interest expenses that reference the cumulative interest payments in the range C58:G58 of the Amortization Schedule worksheet. Enter the interest expenses as positive values. In the range C34:G34, calculate the restaurant's pretax profit by subtracting the interest expenses from the operating profit.
19. In cell G5, enter **32%** as the assumed tax rate.
20. In the range C36:G36, use an IF statement to calculate the restaurant's tax liability for each of the first five years assuming a 32 percent tax rate. If the restaurant's pretax profit is negative, set the tax burden to **$0**. In the range C37:G37, calculate the restaurant's after-tax profit by subtracting the taxes owed from the pretax profit.
21. In the Startup Plan worksheet, in cell C31, enter **$150,000** as the amount Sylvia hopes to attract from investors.
22. In the Investment Proposal worksheet, in cell C7, enter a reference to cell C31 in the Startup Plan worksheet as a negative cash flow. Sylvia proposes that the restaurant repay the investors $35,000 per year for five years. Enter these values into cells C8 and C9. In cell C10, use the RATE function to calculate the interest of the proposed repayment schedule.
23. Investors will be repaid with a combination of yearly payments and dividends.
    a. In the range C13:G13, enter a reference to the value in cell C8 to display $35,000.
    b. In the range C14:G14, enter the following dividend schedule: **$0** in Year 1, **$5,000** in Year 2, **$10,000** in Year 3 and Year 4, and **$15,000** in Year 5.
    c. In the range C15:G15, use the SUM function to calculate the total money investors will receive in Years 1 through 5.
24. In the range C19:D24, determine the payback period and calculate the net cash flow to the investors.

25. In cell D26, enter **12%** as the desired rate of return. In cell D27, use the NPV function to calculate the present value of the payments made to the investors from the range C20:C24 using the desired rate of return specified in cell D26. In cell D28, enter a formula to calculate the net present value of their investment in the restaurant given their initial payment of $150,000.
26. In cell D29, use the IRR function to calculate the internal rate of return of their investment.
27. In the Income Statement worksheet, in the range C39:G39, enter a reference to the yearly dividend values paid to the shareholders as specified in the range C14:G14 of the Investment Proposal worksheet. In the range C41:G41, calculate the restaurant's retained earnings by subtracting the dividends from the after-tax profit.
28. In the Balance Sheet worksheet, starting with cell G17, trace the #REF error in the workbook back to its source and correct it.
29. Save the workbook, and then close it.

Case Problem 1

Data File needed for this Case Problem: Digital.xlsx

Digital Frames Linda Pfeltz is a videographer and owner of Digital Frames, a company in Hickory, North Carolina, that records and edits videos for businesses, families, weddings, and special events. Linda wants to upgrade the company's computer system and is evaluating whether to buy new equipment or to lease it. She has asked you to complete an Excel workbook that compares the costs of owning versus leasing. Complete the following:

1. Open the **Digital** workbook located in the Excel9 ▶ Case1 folder included with your Data Files, and then save the workbook as **Digital Frames** in the location specified by your instructor.
2. In the Documentation worksheet, enter your name and the current date.
3. Linda can upgrade the computer system by purchasing equipment for $18,000. She would also want to buy a 36-month service contract at the time of the purchase for $540. Linda anticipates that she would be able to sell the system for $12,000 after three years, when it will be time for her next upgrade. Enter these values in the Buy vs. Lease worksheet in the range B4:B6.
4. Under the lease option, Linda will be able to lease the equipment for $325 per month for the next 36 months. She will also have to pay a $1,000 security deposit at the time of the purchase. She won't need to buy a service contract because the company provides service on the computers it leases. Enter these values in the Buy vs. Lease worksheet under the Lease Conditions section in cells B9 and B10.
5. In the range E2:F2, enter the initial investment for each option. For the Buy Option, Linda will have to initially pay for the computer system and the service deposit. Under the Lease Option, Linda will have to initially pay for the security contract. (*Hint*: Enter these initial expenditures as negative cash flows.)
6. In the range E3:E38, for Month 1 through Month 36, enter **0** to indicate that Linda will not make monthly payments once she has bought the computer equipment.
7. In the range F3:F38, enter the amount Linda would have to spend under the Lease Option each month as a negative cash flow.
8. In the range E39:F39, enter formulas that reference the revenue Linda will earn from selling the computer system under the Buy Option, and the revenue she will receive under the Lease Option when her security deposit is returned. These values should be entered as positive cash flows.
9. In cell B12, enter an annual discount rate of **9.6%**. In cell B14, enter a formula to calculate the monthly discount rate.
10. In cell B15, enter a formula to calculate the net present value of buying the computer system by adding the initial investment in cell E2 to the present value of the cash flows in the range E3:E39. Use the NPV function with the monthly discount rate in cell B14 as the rate of return to calculate the ultimate cost of the computer system if Linda buys it.

11. In cell B16, enter a formula to calculate the net present value of leasing by adding the initial investment from cell F2 to the present value of the cash flows in the range F3:F39. Again, use cell B14 as the rate of return and calculate the ultimate cost to lease the computer equipment.
12. Save the workbook.
13. Use Goal Seek to determine the monthly payment from leasing that will cause the net present value of leasing to exactly match the net present value of buying. (*Hint*: You must explicitly enter the net present value of the buy option in the Goal Seek dialog box.)
14. Save the workbook as **Digital Frames 2**.
15. Return the monthly payment under leasing to its original value of **$325**.
16. Linda might not be able to sell the computer system for $12,000. Use Goal Seek to determine the resale value for the computer system after 36 months that will cause the net present value of buying to exactly match the net present value of leasing.
17. Save the workbook as **Digital Frames 3**, and then close it.

Case Problem 2

Data File needed for this Case Problem: College.xlsx

College Savers Eric Hoiland is a financial consultant at College Savers who works with families with young children to help them save for the rising cost of college. Currently, he is helping Jaime and Lucia Juarez develop a savings plan for their daughter, Adelita, who is 9. The couple's goal is to save enough money over the next 10 years to fund Adelita's four years of college. They plan to make annual deposits into their savings fund starting immediately and continue them through Adelita's college years. When Adelita begins college, they'll withdraw money at the beginning of each term to cover much of the cost of tuition, room, and board. They have several options for the amount to deposit. Eric has asked you to help set up an Excel workbook to determine whether different savings plans will cover the cost of Adelita's college education. Complete the following:

1. Open the **College** workbook located in the Excel9 ▸ Case2 folder included with your Data Files, and then save the workbook as **College Savers** in the location specified by your instructor.
2. In the Documentation worksheet, enter your name and the current date.
3. In the Savings Plan worksheet, enter **Adelita Juarez** as the student name in cell B4, her age of **9** in cell B5, her years until starting college as **10** in cell B6, and her parents **Jaime and Lucia Juarez** in cell B7.
4. Based on current data, the one-year cost of college is $21,000. Enter this value in cell B10.
5. College costs are projected to increase at an annual rate of 6.25 percent. Enter this value in cell B11.
6. The savings portfolio Eric devised has a historic rate of return of 4.70 percent. Enter this value in cell B15.
7. Adelita's parents plan to make an initial investment of $18,000 into the fund. Enter this value as a positive cash flow in cell B16.
8. After their initial investment, they plan to make a deposit of $10,000 every year on December 1. Enter this positive cash flow value in cell B17.
9. Adelita's grandmother has pledged to make a contribution of $150 every year on Adelita's birthday (July 17) and on Christmas. Enter this positive cash flow value in cell B18.
10. In the range H5:H45, enter the deposits made to the savings fund based on the dates specified in the previous step. Use cell references to the values you entered in column B of the worksheet. The initial investment occurs on March 1 of Year 0. Note that Adelita's parents and her grandmother will continue to make contributions even as Adelita is attending college.
11. Adelita's grandmother plans to make a special gift of $750 on Adelita's 18th birthday. Enter this value in cell H30 as a positive cash flow in place of the usual $150 contribution.
12. College tuition is projected to be due on August 15 of each year. In cell H34, calculate the value of the first year of college under the inflation rate suggested in cell B11, the year value in cell E33, and the current one-year cost in cell B10. The value should appear as a negative cash flow.

13. Repeat Step 12 for cells H38, H42, and H46 to calculate the future cost of Adelita's sophomore, junior, and senior years.
14. In the range I5:I46, calculate the net cash flow of the deposits to the savings fund and the withdrawals to pay for Adelita's education. Note that the final cash flow is negative, indicating that there might not be enough money for college but that this analysis does not take into account the interest that would be earned by the savings fund.
15. In cell B12, calculate the total cost of four years of college by adding the values you calculated in cells H34, H38, H42, and H46.
16. In cell B19, use a SUMIF function to calculate the sum of positive cash flows in the range H5:H46. This will represent the total deposits made by the family.
17. **Explore** In cell B22, calculate the net present value of the proposed savings plan in current dollars. Use the XNPV function with the rate of return in cell B15, the cash flow values in the range H5:H46, and the date values in the range G5:G46.
18. In cell B23, use an IF function to display **YES** if the net present value is greater than or equal to 0 (meaning that the savings plan will cover college costs) and **NO** if otherwise.
19. Apply conditional formatting to the value in cell B23 to display YES values in dark green on a light green background and NO values in dark red on a light red background.
20. Save the workbook.
21. Use Goal Seek to determine the size of the initial investment that will result in a net present value of 0 for the savings plan (covering the cost of college).
22. Save the workbook as **College Savers 2**.
23. Restore cell B16 to its original value of **$18,000**. Use Goal Seek to determine the size of the annual deposit that will result in a net present value of 0 for the savings fund.
24. Save the workbook as **College Savers 3**, and then close it.

Case Problem 3

CHALLENGE

Data File needed for this Case Problem: Red.xlsx

Red Stone Rocks Stephen Rawlings is an accounts manager at Red Stone Rocks, a quarry located near Castle Rock, Colorado. He is currently analyzing a proposal for excavating a new site in the area that is believed to have a rich vein of Colorado red stone that, according to recent estimates, will be able to support a new dig for the next 20 years.

Starting a new quarry requires substantial startup costs, and it will be a few years before the quarry is profitable. The quarry will also face substantial costs when shutting down because environmental regulations require that the area be returned to a pristine state. The quarry will be most profitable in its early and middle stages of development, but will lose profitability in its later stages as it becomes more difficult to extract the remaining red stone deposits. Stephen asks you to do a quick estimate of the site's profitability over the next 20 years. He will conduct a more thorough analysis later. Complete the following:

1. Open the **Red** workbook located in the Excel9 ▸ Case3 folder included with your Data Files, and then save the workbook as **Red Stone Rocks** in the location specified by your instructor.
2. In the Documentation worksheet, enter your name and the current date.
3. In the Investment Analysis worksheet, enter **0** as the quarry's startup income, and then enter **5.1** (for $5.1 million) for the startup expenses. Note that income and expense values will be entered in terms of millions of dollars.
4. During the early phase (Year 1 through Year 10), estimate that the income from the quarry will start at $0.35 million in Year 1 and increase to $3 million in Year 10. Interpolate the intervening income values using a linear trend.
5. During the middle phase (Year 10 through Year 17), estimate that the income in Year 10 will grow at a 3 percent rate each year through Year 17. Use extrapolation to determine the Year 11 through Year 17 values.

Tutorial 9 Exploring Financial Tools and Functions | Excel   EX 593

Explore 6. During the late phase (Year 17 through Year 25), estimate that the income will decline following a linear trend starting from the Year 17 value and declining to $0.25 million in Year 25. Find the intervening values using interpolation.

7. Enter the estimated Year 1 expenses as **$0.92** million. Extrapolate a growth trend from that value through Year 25 with a growth rate of 3 percent per year.

8. During the shut-down phase, enter the estimated shut-down income as **$0** and the shut-down expense for clean-up as **$14.8** million.

9. In the range D4:D30, enter formulas to calculate the profit from the startup phase through the shut-down phase. Apply conditional formatting to the profit values so that years in which the quarry loses money will appear in a red font on a red background.

10. In the range F4:F18, enter **1%** to **15%** in steps of 1 percent as the possible discount rates in the Red Stone Rocks investment.

11. In the range G4:G18, calculate the net present value of the Red Stone Rocks investment based on the present value of the cash flows in the range D5:D30 and the discount rates in the range F4:F18, and then add that present value to the initial investment in cell D4. Apply conditional formatting to net present values so that negative values appear in a red font on a light red background.

12. In cell G20, calculate the internal rate of return of the Red Stone Rocks investment using the cash flows in the range D4:D30.

13. In the range I3:N12, insert a line chart of the income values in the range A3:B30. Format the chart as you wish to make it easy to read and interpret.

14. In the range I14:N24, insert a clustered column chart of the income and expenses in the range A3:C30. Format the chart to make it easy to read and interpret.

15. Save the workbook.

16. New environmental regulations will make the project more expensive to the company. Change the estimate of the startup phase expenses from $5.1 million to **$5.9** million, and change the shut-down phase expenses from $14.8 million to **$17.2** million.

Explore 17. Because the cash flow values in the range D4:D30 change between positive to negative several times, more than one internal rate of return will match the investment data. Enter **3%** in cell F23 and enter **9%** in cell F24. In cell G23, calculate the internal rate of return of the cash flow values in the range D4:D30 using the guess entered in cell F23. In cell G24, calculate the internal rate of return for the investment cash flows using the guess in cell F24. Note that the two values for the internal rate of return don't match.

Explore 18. The different internal rates of return can be explained by charting the net present value for different discount rates. The internal rate of return equals the discount rate where the net present value is 0. In the range I26:N36, create an area chart of Net Present Values vs. Discount Rate from the range F3:G18. Format the chart to make the content easy to read and interpret.

19. Save the workbook as **Red Stone Rocks 2**, and then close it.

Case Problem 4

Data File needed for this Case Problem: Condo.xlsx

Mountain View Condos Gary Douglas owns and operates Mountain View Condos, a real estate company in Orem, Utah. Gary is examining the financial details involved with purchasing a large condo outside of the village. Mountain View Condos will retain the condominium for the next 10 years, receiving yearly income from rentals that will cover the expenses and will eventually repay the cost of the initial investment. Gary wants you to calculate the return from this investment. His assistant created a workbook to perform the financial analysis, but several errors have crept into the workbook. You will use auditing tools to locate and fix the errors.

Complete the following:

1. Open the **Condo** workbook located in the Excel9 ▶ Case4 folder included with your Data Files, and then save the workbook as **Condo Investment** in the location specified by your instructor.

2. In the Documentation worksheet, enter your name and the current date.

⚙ **Troubleshoot** 3. The Rental Income worksheet includes errors. Trace the error in cell K23 back to its origin and fix it. Remove the arrows when you are finished.

⚙ **Troubleshoot** 4. The Rental Income worksheet still has an error in cell K23. Fix and locate the source of the error. Remove the arrows when you are finished.

⚙ **Troubleshoot** 5. Trace and fix the remaining three errors in the workbook.

6. In the Real Estate Data worksheet, enter the following data about the condo that Gary wants to purchase:
   - The assessed value of the condo is **$315,000**.
   - The inflation rate is **4.8%**.
   - Gary wants to retain the condo for **10** years.
   - The property tax rate in Orem is **1.5%**.

7. In cell B10, calculate the future value of the property in 10 years based on the assessed value, the inflation rate, and the years to hold values. Express your answer as a positive cash flow.

8. In the Depreciation worksheet, enter the initial investment value of the condo that Gary wants to purchase by inserting a reference to cell B5 in the Real Estate Data worksheet. Set the salvage value of the condo to **$160,000** after 10 years have passed.

9. In the Rental Income worksheet, project the income and expenses associated with owning the condo. In cell B6, enter the Year 1 rental income as equal to 1/12 of the assessed value of the condo from the Real Estate Data worksheet.

10. Extrapolate the rental income for Year 2 through Year 10 by assuming a growth trend of 4 percent per year.

11. In the range B7:K7, enter formulas that reference each corresponding value in the range B6:K6.

12. In cell B10, enter a formula to calculate the Year 1 property taxes by multiplying the assessed value of the condo in the Real Estate Data worksheet by the property tax rate in the Real Estate Data worksheet. Extrapolate the property tax values for Year 2 through Year 10 by assuming a 4 percent growth rate from the Year 1 property tax value.

13. In cell B11, enter **1000** as the Year 1 miscellaneous expense. Extrapolate the miscellaneous expenses for the remaining years by assuming a 4 percent growth rate.

14. In cell K3, enter a tax rate of **31%** on rental income.

15. At the end of 10 years, Gary will sell the condo at its future value. Calculate the tax on the sale in the Resale Tax Calculator worksheet. Enter a tax rate of **33%** on the sale. The other values are referenced from values located elsewhere in the workbook.

16. In the Investment Cash Flow worksheet, calculate the profitability of the condo investment. The worksheet shows the net cash flow from the initial investment through the 10 years of owning the condo. Gary wants his investment to have a 7 percent rate of return. Enter this value in cell B9.

17. In cell B10, enter a formula to calculate the net present value of the condo investment by determining the present value of the investment based on the discount rate and the cash flow values in the range B6:K6, and then adding the cost of the investment in cell A6.

18. In cell B11, enter a formula to calculate the internal rate of return of this investment based on the cash flow values from the range A6:K6.

19. Save the workbook, and then close it.

TUTORIAL 10

Performing What-If Analyses

Analyzing Financial Data to Maximize Profits

OBJECTIVES

Session 10.1
- Explore the principles of cost-volume-profit relationships
- Create a one-variable data table
- Create a two-variable data table

Session 10.2
- Create and apply different Excel scenarios with the Scenario Manager
- Generate a scenario summary report
- Generate a scenario PivotTable report

Session 10.3
- Explore the principles of a product mix
- Run Solver to calculate optimal solutions
- Create and apply constraints to a Solver model
- Save and load a Solver model

Case | Cycle Green

Gianna Bartoli is a production manager at Cycle Green, a small shop in Bowling Green, Kentucky, that creates handcrafted bicycles and bicycle frames. Gianna wants to use Excel to analyze the company's financial status. She wants to know in general how many bikes the company must sell to remain profitable. She is also interested in whether the company can increase its net income by reducing the sales price of its bikes as long as it increases sales volume.

Your analysis for Gianna will focus on the four most popular models the company sells. As part of your analysis, you will also study whether the company can increase its profits by promoting one model over another. In the process, you'll try to find the best product mix—one that maximizes profits subject to the limitations of available parts and manufacturing capability.

STARTING DATA FILES

Excel10 →
- Tutorial: Cycle.xlsx
- Review: Mountain.xlsx
- Case1: Loan.xlsx
- Case2: English.xlsx
- Case3: Optimal.xlsx
- Case4: Employee.xlsx

Microsoft product screenshots used with permission from Microsoft Corporation.

EX 595

Session 10.1 Visual Overview:

A one-variable data table performs several what-if analyses by specifying one input cell and several result cells.

Input cells are the cells that contain values that are used in formulas of a what-if analysis.

Input values are values in a data table that are based on input cells in the worksheet. The values in the range D5:D13 are based on the value in input cell B4.

Result values are values in a data table that come from formulas applied to one or more input values. The values in the range E4:G13 are calculated from the result cells in the range B24:B26.

Result cells are the cells that contain the outcome of formulas involving input cells.

Cell D4 = =B4

CYCLE GREEN

Income Statement

	A	B	C	D	E	F
1	**CYCLE GREEN**					
2	Income Statement				Break-Even Analysis	
3	Revenue			Units Sold	Revenue	Expenses
4	Units Sold	570		570	$1,197,000.00	1,072,000.00
5	Average Price per Unit	2,100.00		300	630,000.00	775,000.00
6	Total Revenue	$1,197,000.00		350	735,000.00	830,000.00
7				400	840,000.00	885,000.00
8	Variable Expenses			450	945,000.00	940,000.00
9	Units Produced	570		500	1,050,000.00	995,000.00
10	Average Material Cost per Unit	950.00		550	1,155,000.00	1,050,000.00
11	Total Material Cost	541,500.00		600	1,260,000.00	1,105,000.00
12	Average Manufacturing Cost per Unit	150.00		650	1,365,000.00	1,160,000.00
13	Total Manufacturing Cost	85,500.00		700	1,470,000.00	1,215,000.00
14	Total Variable Expenses	$627,000.00				
15						
16	Fixed Expenses					
17	Salaries and Benefits	325,000.00				
18	Advertising	25,000.00				
19	Administrative	45,000.00				
20	Miscellaneous	50,000.00				
21	Total Fixed Expenses	$445,000.00				
22						
23	Summary					
24	Total Revenue	1,197,000.00				
25	Total Expenses	1,072,000.00				
26	Net Income	$125,000.00				

EX 596 Excel | Tutorial 10 Performing What-If Analyses

© 2014 Cengage Learning

Tutorial 10 Performing What-If Analyses | Excel   EX 597

Data Tables and What-If Analysis

A two-variable data table includes a reference to the result cell at the intersection of the first row and column.

A two-variable data table performs several what-if analyses by specifying two input cells and one result cell.

Net Income Analysis

Average Price per Unit

Units Sold	$1,900	$2,000	$2,100	$2,200
300	(205,000.00)	(175,000.00)	(145,000.00)	(115,000.00)
350	(165,000.00)	(130,000.00)	(95,000.00)	(60,000.00)
400	(125,000.00)	(85,000.00)	(45,000.00)	(5,000.00)
450	(85,000.00)	(40,000.00)	5,000.00	50,000.00
500	(45,000.00)	5,000.00	55,000.00	105,000.00
550	(5,000.00)	50,000.00	105,000.00	160,000.00
600	35,000.00	95,000.00	155,000.00	215,000.00
650	75,000.00	140,000.00	205,000.00	270,000.00
700	115,000.00	185,000.00	255,000.00	325,000.00

The formula =B26 is displayed.

You can use a custom format to display a label rather than a numeric value. This cell's underlying value is the formula =B26, which would show the net income.

The point where total revenue equals total expenses is called the **break-even point**.

Understanding Cost-Volume Relationships

Cost-volume-profit (CVP) analysis is a branch of financial analysis that studies the relationship between expenses, sales volume, and profitability. CVP analysis is an important business decision-making tool because it can help predict the effect of cutting overhead or raising prices on a company's net income. For example, Gianna needs to determine a reasonable price to charge for Cycle Green's line of bicycles. She needs to know how much to charge to break even, and how much added profit Cycle Green could realize by increasing (or even decreasing) the sales price.

Comparing Expenses and Revenue

The first component of CVP analysis is cost, or expense. There are three types of expenses—variable, fixed, and mixed. **Variable expenses** change in proportion to the volume of production. For each additional bike that the company produces, it spends more on parts, labor, raw materials, and other expenses associated with manufacturing that bike. On average, each bike produced by the company costs $950 in materials and $150 in manufacturing, for a total average cost of $1,100 per bike. The company's total variable expenses are equal to the cost of producing each bike multiplied by the total number of bikes produced. Figure 10-1 shows a line graph of the total variable expenses based on the production volume. Based on this graph, Cycle Green will incur about $900,000 in variable expenses to produce 800 bikes.

Figure 10-1   Chart of variable expenses

© 2014 Cengage Learning

On average, Cycle Green charges $2,100 per bike, which is $1,000 more than the variable expense for producing each bike. At first glance, it might seem that Cycle Green earns a $1,000 profit on each sale, but that is not exactly correct. The sales price also must cover Cycle Green's fixed expenses. A **fixed expense** is an expense that must be paid regardless of sales volume. For example, Cycle Green must pay salaries and benefits for its employees as well as insurance, maintenance fees, and administrative overhead. Gianna tells you that Cycle Green has $445,000 in fixed expenses, which must be paid even if the company doesn't produce or sell a single bike.

You can estimate Cycle Green's total expense for its line of bikes by adding the company's variable and fixed expenses. The graph in Figure 10-2 shows the company's total expenses for a given number of bikes produced each year. As you can see, if the company produces 500 bikes each year, its total expense would be about $1,000,000. Of this, $445,000 represents fixed expenses and about $555,000 represents variable expenses related to the actual production of the bikes.

Figure 10-2 Chart of total expense

[Chart showing total expenses vs bikes produced. Callout: "the total expense for producing 500 bicycles is $1,000,000". Callout: "the company has $445,000 in fixed expenses"]

© 2014 Cengage Learning

A third type of expense is a **mixed expense**, which is an expense that is part variable and part fixed. For example, if the salespeople at Cycle Green receive bonuses based on sales volume, their compensation would be an example of a mixed expense to the company. Each salesperson would have a fixed salary with extra income as the volume of sales increases. In this analysis, you will not consider any mixed expenses.

Cycle Green is selling most of what it produces, so the company should bring in more revenue as it increases production. Figure 10-3 shows the increase in revenue in relation to the increase in sales volume. For example, selling 800 bikes at an average price of $2,100 per bike would generate about $1,700,000 in revenue.

Figure 10-3 Chart of revenue

selling 800 bicycles brings in about $1,700,000 in revenue

© 2014 Cengage Learning

Exploring the Break-Even Point

The point where total revenue equals total expenses is called the break-even point. For this reason, CVP analysis is sometimes called **break-even analysis**. The more bikes Cycle Green sells above the break-even point, the greater its profit. Conversely, when sales levels fall below the break-even point, the company loses money.

You can illustrate the break-even point by graphing revenue and total expenses against sales volume. The break-even point occurs where the two lines cross. This type of chart is called a **cost-volume-profit (CVP) chart**. As shown in Figure 10-4, a CVP chart shows the relationship between total expenses and total revenue.

Figure 10-4 Typical CVP chart

© 2014 Cengage Learning

Gianna has prepared an income statement for Cycle Green that includes projected revenue, variable expenses, and fixed expenses based on the previous year's sales. You'll review the worksheet with this data. Later, you will use this data to calculate the company's break-even point.

To review the income statement for Cycle Green:

1. Open the **Cycle** workbook located in the Excel10 ▸ Tutorial folder included with your Data Files, and then save the workbook as **Cycle Green** in the location specified by your instructor.

2. In the Documentation worksheet, enter your name and the date.

3. Go to the **Income Statement** worksheet and review its contents and formulas. See Figure 10-5.

Figure 10-5   Cycle Green's income statement

	A	B
2	Income Statement	
3	Revenue	
4	Units Sold	570
5	Average Price per Unit	2,100.00
6	Total Revenue	$1,197,000.00
7		
8	Variable Expenses	
9	Units Produced	570
10	Average Material Cost per Unit	950.00
11	Total Material Cost	541,500.00
12	Average Manufacturing Cost per Unit	150.00
13	Total Manufacturing Cost	85,500.00
14	Total Variable Expenses	$627,000.00
15		
16	Fixed Expenses	
17	Salaries and Benefits	325,000.00
18	Advertising	25,000.00
19	Administrative	45,000.00
20	Miscellaneous	50,000.00
21	Total Fixed Expenses	$445,000.00
22		
23	Summary	
24	Total Revenue	1,197,000.00
25	Total Expenses	1,072,000.00
26	Net Income	$125,000.00

- revenue from selling 570 bikes at an average of $2,100 per bike
- variable expenses directly related to the cost of producing 570 bikes
- fixed expenses regardless of how many bikes are actually produced
- net income calculated by subtracting the company's total expenses from its revenue

As itemized in the Income Statement worksheet, the company projects that it will sell 570 bikes at an average price of $2,100 per bike, generating $1,197,000 in revenue. The variable expenses involved in producing 570 bikes are $627,000. The company's fixed expenses are $445,000. Based on this revenue, variable expenses, and fixed expenses, Cycle Green's net income is projected to be $125,000.

Finding the Break-Even Point with What-If Analysis

What-if analysis lets you explore the impact of changing different values in a worksheet. You can use what-if analysis to explore the impact of changing financial conditions on a company's profitability. Gianna wants to know what the impact would be if the number of bikes Cycle Green produced and sold fell to 500 or rose to 600.

To perform what-if analysis for different sales volumes:

1. In cell **B4**, enter **500** to change the units sold value. When the number of units sold drops from 570 to 500, the net income shown in cell B26 drops to $55,000—a $70,000 decline in profits.

2. In cell **B4**, enter **600**. When the number of units sold increases to 600, the net income increases to $155,000—a $30,000 increase in profits over the current projections.

3. In cell **B4**, enter **570** to return to the original units sold projection.

Gianna wants to know how low can sales go and still maintain a profit. In other words, what is the sales volume for the break-even point? One way of finding the break-even point is to use Goal Seek. Recall that Goal Seek is a what-if analysis tool that can be used to find the input value needed for an Excel formula to match a specified value. In this case, you'll find out how many bikes must be sold to set the net income to $0.

To use Goal Seek to find the break-even point:

1. On the ribbon, click the **DATA** tab. In the Data Tools group, click the **What-If Analysis** button, and then click **Goal Seek**. The Goal Seek dialog box opens. The cell reference in the Set cell box is selected.

2. In the Income Statement worksheet, click cell **B26** to replace the selected cell reference in the Set cell box with $B$26. The absolute reference specifies the Net Income cell as the cell whose value you want to set.

3. Press the **Tab** key to move the insertion point to the To value box, and then type **0**. This specifies that the goal is to set the net income value in cell B26 to 0.

4. Press the **Tab** key to move the insertion point to the By changing cell box, and then click cell **B4** in the Income Statement worksheet to enter the cell reference $B$4. The absolute reference specifies that you want to reach the goal of setting the net income to 0 by changing the units sold value in cell B4.

5. Click the **OK** button. The Goal Seek Status dialog box opens once Excel finds a solution.

6. Click the **OK** button to return to the worksheet. The value 445 appears in cell B4, indicating that the company must produce and sell 445 bikes in order to break even. See Figure 10-6.

Figure 10-6 — Annual sales required to break even

	A	B
2	**Income Statement**	
3	Revenue	
4	Units Sold	445
5	Average Price per Unit	2,100.00
6	Total Revenue	$934,500.00
7		
8	**Variable Expenses**	
9	Units Produced	445
10	Average Material Cost per Unit	950.00
11	Total Material Cost	422,750.00
12	Average Manufacturing Cost per Unit	150.00
13	Total Manufacturing Cost	66,750.00
14	Total Variable Expenses	$489,500.00
15		
16	**Fixed Expenses**	
17	Salaries and Benefits	325,000.00
18	Advertising	25,000.00
19	Administrative	45,000.00
20	Miscellaneous	50,000.00
21	Total Fixed Expenses	$445,000.00
22		
23	**Summary**	
24	Total Revenue	934,500.00
25	Total Expenses	934,500.00
26	Net Income	$0.00

selling 445 bikes results in a net income of $0

▶ **7.** In cell **B4**, enter **570** to return to the original units sold projection.

Gianna wants to continue to analyze the company's net income under different sales assumptions. For example, what would the company's net income be if sales increased to 700 bikes? How much would the company lose if the number of sales fell to 400 bikes? How many bikes must the company sell to reach a net income of exactly $75,000? You could continue to use Goal Seek to answer these questions, but a more efficient approach is to use a data table.

Working with Data Tables

A data table is an Excel table that displays the results from several what-if analyses. The table consists of input cells and result cells. The input cells are the cells whose value would be changed in a what-if analysis. The result cells are cells whose values are impacted by the changing input values. In Excel, you can use one-variable data tables and two-variable data tables.

Creating a One-Variable Data Table

In a one-variable data table, you specify one input cell and any number of result cells. The range of possible values for the input cell is entered in the first row or column of the data table, and the corresponding result values appear in the subsequent rows or columns. One-variable data tables are particularly useful in business to explore how changing a single input value can impact several financial results.

Figure 10-7 shows a one-variable data table that is used to determine the impact of different interest rates on a loan's monthly payment, total payments, and cost. In this worksheet, cell B3 containing the interest rate is the input cell, and the cells in the range B8:B10 are the result cells. Possible input values for cell B3, ranging from a 4 percent interest rate to an 8 percent rate, are entered in the first column of the data table. The next three columns of the table show the result values based on these interest rates. Using the table, you can quickly see that a 7 percent interest rate results in a $1,663.26 monthly payment, total payments of $598,772.25, and a loan cost of $348,772.25. You can also observe how quickly the loan cost rises with an increasing interest rate. For example, when the annual interest rate increases two percentage points from 6 percent to 8 percent, the total cost of the loan increases by more than $120,000.

Figure 10-7 One-variable data table example

	A	B	C	D	E	F	G
1	Loan Conditions				One-Variable Data Table		
2	Loan Amount (PV)	$250,000.00		Rates	Monthly Payments	Total Payments	Cost of the Loan
3	Annual Interest Rate	6.00%		6.00%	($1,498.88)	($539,595.47)	($289,595.47)
4	Monthly Rate (RATE)	0.50%		4.00%	($1,193.54)	($429,673.77)	($179,673.77)
5	Years	30		4.50%	($1,266.71)	($456,016.78)	($206,016.78)
6	Number of Monthly Payments	360		5.00%	($1,342.05)	($483,139.46)	($233,139.46)
7				5.50%	($1,419.47)	($511,010.10)	($261,010.10)
8	Monthly Payment	($1,498.88)		6.00%	($1,498.88)	($539,595.47)	($289,595.47)
9	Total Payments	($539,595.47)		6.50%	($1,580.17)	($568,861.22)	($318,861.22)
10	Cost of the Loan	($289,595.47)		7.00%	($1,663.26)	($598,772.25)	($348,772.25)
11				7.50%	($1,748.04)	($629,293.06)	($379,293.06)
12				8.00%	($1,834.41)	($660,388.12)	($410,388.12)

- input cell (B3)
- result cells
- input values
- result values

REFERENCE

Creating a One-Variable Data Table

- In the upper-left cell of the table, enter a formula that references the input cell.
- In either the first row or the first column of the table, enter input values.
- For input values in the first row, enter formulas referencing result cells in the table's first column; for input values in the first column, enter formulas referencing result cells in the table's first row.
- Select the table (excluding any row or column headings).
- On the DATA tab, in the Data Tools group, click the What-If Analysis button, and then click Data Table.
- If the input values are in the first row, enter the cell reference to the input cell in the Row input cell box; if the input values are in the first column, enter the cell reference to the input cell in the Column input cell box.
- Click the OK button.

Gianna wants to examine the impact of changing sales volume on the company's revenue, total expenses, and net income. You'll create a one-variable data table to do this. The first step is to set up the data table so that the first row of the table starts with a reference to the input cell in the worksheet, followed by references to one or more result cells.

To set up the one-variable data table to examine the impact of changing sales volume:

1. In cell **D2**, enter **Break-Even Analysis**, merge and center the range **D2:G2**, and then format the text with the **Heading 2** cell style.

2. In the range **D3:G3**, enter the labels **Units Sold**, **Revenue**, **Expenses**, and **Net Income**, respectively.

3. In the range **D3:G3**, change the fill color to **Blue, Accent 1, Lighter 60%** and center the text within the cells.

4. In cell **D4**, enter the formula **=B4** to create a reference to the input cell to be used in the data table.

5. In cell **E4**, enter the formula **=B24** to reference the result cell that displays the company's expected revenue.

6. In cell **F4**, enter the formula **=B25** to reference the company's expenses.

7. In cell **G4**, enter the formula **=B26** to reference the company's net income.

8. In the range **D4:G4**, change the fill color to **Gold, Accent 4, Lighter 80%** and add a bottom border.

9. In cell **D5**, enter **300**, and then in cell **D6**, enter **350** to specify the input values.

10. Select the range **D5:D6**, drag the fill handle to cell **D13**, and then fill the series to enter the remaining input values. The units sold values range from 300 to 700 in 50-unit increments.

11. Select cell **D4**. See Figure 10-8.

Figure 10-8 Setup for the one-variable data table

Next, you'll fill the table with the result values. To do this, you must identify the row input cell or the column input cell. Both reference the input cell from the worksheet; the difference between them is based on where the input values are placed in the data table. The **row input cell** is used when the input values have been placed in the first row of the data table, and the **column input cell** is used when the input values are placed in the data table's first column. In the Income Statement worksheet, the input values are in the first column, so you'll use the column input cell option. If you had oriented the table so that the input values were in the first row, you would use the row input cell option.

To complete the one-variable data table:

1. Select the range **D4:G13**. This is the range of the data table.
2. On the DATA tab, in the Data Tools group, click the **What-If Analysis** button, and then click **Data Table**. The Data Table dialog box opens.
3. Press the **Tab** key to move the insertion point to the Column input cell box, and then click cell **B4** in the Income Statement worksheet. The absolute reference specifies the Units Sold cell in the Income Statement worksheet. See Figure 10-9.

Figure 10-9   Data Table dialog box

input cell for the values in the first column of the data table

4. Click the **OK** button. Excel completes the data table by entering the revenue, expenses, and net income for each units sold value specified in column D.
5. Use the Format Painter to copy the format from cell **B24** and apply it to the result values in the range **E5:G13**.
6. Select cell **D14**. See Figure 10-10.

Figure 10-10   Completed one-variable data table

	A	B	C	D	E	F	G
1	**CYCLE GREEN**						
2	Income Statement				Break-Even Analysis		
3	Revenue			Units Sold	Revenue	Expenses	Net Income
4	Units Sold	570		570	1,197,000.00	1,072,000.00	$125,000.00
5	Average Price per Unit	2,100.00		300	630,000.00	775,000.00	(145,000.00)
6	Total Revenue	$1,197,000.00		350	735,000.00	830,000.00	(95,000.00)
7				400	840,000.00	885,000.00	(45,000.00)
8	Variable Expenses			450	945,000.00	940,000.00	5,000.00
9	Units Produced	570		500	1,050,000.00	995,000.00	55,000.00
10	Average Material Cost per Unit	950.00		550	1,155,000.00	1,050,000.00	105,000.00
11	Total Material Cost	541,500.00		600	1,260,000.00	1,105,000.00	155,000.00
12	Average Manufacturing Cost per Unit	150.00		650	1,365,000.00	1,160,000.00	205,000.00
13	Total Manufacturing Cost	85,500.00		700	1,470,000.00	1,215,000.00	255,000.00
14	Total Variable Expenses	$627,000.00					
15							
16	Fixed Expenses						
17	Salaries and Benefits	325,000.00					

break-even point

result values

The data table shows the results of several what-if analyses simultaneously. For example, if annual sales increase to 700 units, the company's revenue will be $1,470,000, but the total expenses will be $1,215,000, yielding a net income of $255,000.

Charting a One-Variable Data Table

The data table provides the results of several what-if analyses, but the results are often clearer if you include a CVP chart along with the table. The chart gives a better picture of the relationship between sales volume, revenue, and expenses.

You'll use a scatter chart to map out the revenue and total expenses against the total number of units sold.

To create the CVP chart of the data table:

1. Select the range **D3:F13**, which contains the data you want to chart.
2. On the ribbon, click the **INSERT** tab.
3. In the Charts group, click the **Insert Scatter (X, Y) or Bubble Chart** button, and then click **Scatter with Straight Lines** (the second option in the second row of the Scatter section). Each point in the data table is plotted on the chart and connected with a line. The blue line represents revenue; the red line represents expenses. The break-even point occurs where the two lines cross.
4. Move and resize the chart so that it covers the range **D14:G26**.
5. Remove the chart title.
6. Change the scale of the horizontal axis to **300** to **700**, and then change the scale of the vertical axis to **600,000** to **1,600,000**.
7. Change the fill color of the chart area to **Gray - 25%, Background 2**, and then change the fill color of the plot area to **white**.
8. Select cell **D27** to deselect the chart, and then close the Format pane. The data table and CVP chart provide a comprehensive picture of the impact of sales volume on total expenses and revenue. See Figure 10-11.

Figure 10-11 Completed CVP chart

Modifying a Data Table

Because data tables are dynamic, changes in the worksheet are automatically reflected in the data table values. This includes changes to cells that are not part of the data table but are involved in the values displayed in the result cells. Cycle Green is considering lowering its prices to be more competitive with other manufacturers. Gianna asks you to perform another what-if analysis using an average sales price of $1800. Changing the value in the Income Statement worksheet will affect other results in the sheet, including the what-if analysis displayed in the one-variable data table and the break-even chart.

To view the impact of changing the sales price:

1. In cell **B5**, enter **1800** to change the average price per unit from $2,100 to $1,800. At this lower sales price, the break-even point moves to somewhere between 600 and 650 units. You can see this in both the data table and the CVP chart. See Figure 10-12.

Figure 10-12   Data table for $1800 sales price

	A	B	C	D	E	F	G
3	Revenue			Units Sold	Revenue	Expenses	Net Income
4	Units Sold	570		570	1,026,000.00	1,072,000.00	($46,000.00)
5	Average Price per Unit	1,800.00		300	540,000.00	775,000.00	(235,000.00)
6	Total Revenue	$1,026,000.00		350	630,000.00	830,000.00	(200,000.00)
7				400	720,000.00	885,000.00	(165,000.00)
8	Variable Expenses			450	810,000.00	940,000.00	(130,000.00)
9	Units Produced			500	900,000.00	995,000.00	(95,000.00)
10	Average Material Cost per Unit	950.00		550	990,000.00	1,050,000.00	(60,000.00)
11	Total Material Cost	541,500.00		600	1,080,000.00	1,105,000.00	(25,000.00)
12	Average Manufacturing Cost per Unit	150.00		650	1,170,000.00	1,160,000.00	10,000.00
13	Total Manufacturing Cost	85,500.00		700	1,260,000.00	1,215,000.00	45,000.00
14	Total Variable Expenses	$627,000.00					
15							
16	Fixed Expenses						
17	Salaries and Benefits	325,000.00					
18	Advertising	25,000.00					
19	Administrative	45,000.00					
20	Miscellaneous	50,000.00					
21	Total Fixed Expenses	$445,000.00					

average price dropped

break-even point increases to between 600 and 650 units

break-even point

2. In cell **B5**, enter **2100** to return the price to its original value.

This analysis indicates that Cycle Green will need to sell about 200 more bikes to break even at the lower sales price. You could continue to perform what-if analyses with different sales prices to find the amount that best fits Gianna's plan for Cycle Green, but another approach is to create a two-variable data table.

INSIGHT

Directly Calculating the Break-Even Point

A CVP chart is a useful visual tool for displaying the break-even point. You can also calculate the break-even point directly by using the following formula:

$$\text{break-even point} = \frac{\text{fixed expenses}}{\text{sales price per unit} - \text{variable expenses per unit}}$$

For example, with a sales price of $2,100, fixed expenses of $445,000, and variable expenses of $1,100 per unit, the break-even point of 445 units is calculated as follows:

$$\text{break-even point} = \frac{445{,}000}{2100 - 1100} = 445$$

Creating a Two-Variable Data Table

A two-variable data table lets you view the relationship between two input cells, such as price and units sold. Unlike a one-variable data table, a two-variable data table can display only a single result value, such as net income. Figure 10-13 shows a two-variable data table that examines the impact of the interest rate and the length of the mortgage on the monthly payment. The two input cells are cell B3 and cell B6, which show the interest rate and the number of months before the loan is repaid, respectively. The first column of the data table displays a range of interest values for the first input cell, and the first row of the data table shows a range of possible numbers of payments for the second input cell. The result cell in this what-if analysis is cell B8—the monthly payment. The data table is set up to display a reference to the result cell in the upper-left corner of the table. A result value is displayed at the intersection of each input value. For example, a 240-month loan at 7.5 percent interest would require a monthly payment of $2,013.98 (cell G11). This two-variable data table quickly shows the results of 36 what-if analyses on different loan conditions.

Figure 10-13 Two-variable data table example

	A	B	C	D	E	F	G	H
1	Loan Conditions				Two-Variable Data Table			
2	Loan Amount (PV)	$250,000.00			Number of Monthly Payments			
3	Annual Interest Rate	6.00%		($1,498.88)	120	180	240	360
4	Monthly Rate (RATE)	0.50%		4.00%	($2,531.13)	($1,849.22)	($1,514.95)	($1,193.54)
5	Years	30		4.50%	($2,590.96)	($1,912.48)	($1,581.62)	($1,266.71)
6	Number of Monthly Payments	360		5.00%	($2,651.64)	($1,976.98)	($1,649.89)	($1,342.05)
7				5.50%	($2,713.16)	($2,042.71)	($1,719.72)	($1,419.47)
8	Monthly Payment	($1,498.88)		6.00%	($2,775.51)	($2,109.64)	($1,791.08)	($1,498.88)
9	Total Payments	($539,595.47)		6.50%	($2,838.70)	($2,177.77)	($1,863.93)	($1,580.17)
10	Cost of the Loan	($289,595.47)		7.00%	($2,902.71)	($2,247.07)	($1,938.25)	($1,663.26)
11				7.50%	($2,967.54)	($2,317.53)	($2,013.98)	($1,748.04)
12				8.00%	($3,033.19)	($2,389.13)	($2,091.10)	($1,834.41)

Callouts: input cells → B3, B6; reference to the result cell → D3; input values → E3:H3 and D4:D12; result values → E4:H12; result cell → B8; input values → D4:D12

> **REFERENCE**
>
> **Creating a Two-Variable Data Table**
>
> - In the upper-left cell of the table, enter a formula that references the result cell.
> - In the first row and first column of the table, enter input values.
> - Select the table (excluding any row or column headings).
> - On the DATA tab, in the Data Tools group, click the What-If Analysis button, and then click Data Table.
> - Enter the cell reference to the first row input values in the Row input cell box; enter the cell reference to the first column input values in the Column input cell box.
> - Click the OK button.

Gianna wants you to examine the impact of the sales price and the yearly sales volume on Cycle Green's net income. You'll create a two-variable data table to do this.

To set up the two-variable data table:

▶ 1. In cell **I2**, enter **Net Income Analysis**, merge and center the range **I2:N2**, and then apply the **Heading 2** cell style to the merged range.

2. In cell **I3**, enter **Average Price per Unit**, and then merge the range **I3:N3**.
3. Copy the values in the range **D5:D13** and paste them into the range **I5:I13**.
4. In the range **J4:N4**, enter **$1900** through **$2300** in increments of **$100**. The prices are entered in the range.
5. Select the nonadjacent range **I5:I13;J4:N4**, and then change the fill color to **Gold, Accent 4, Lighter 80%**.
6. Add a right border to the range **I5:I13** and a bottom border to the range **J4:N4**.

   In two-variable data tables, the reference to the result cell is placed in the upper-left corner of the table at the intersection of the row and column input values. In this case, you'll enter a formula in cell I4 that references the company's net income.

7. In cell **I4**, enter the formula **=B26**. The current net income value $125,000 is displayed in cell I4. See Figure 10-14.

Figure 10-14 Setup for the two-variable data table

(Screenshot showing Excel spreadsheet with Net Income Analysis table. Callouts indicate: "reference to the result cell" pointing to $125,000.00 in cell I4; "input values in the first column" pointing to the column of values 300–700; "input values in the first row" pointing to the row $1,900–$2,300.)

Formatting the Result Cell

The reference to the result cell in the table's upper-left corner might confuse some users. To prevent that, you can hide the cell value using the custom format "text", where text is the text you want to display in place of the cell value. In this case, you'll use a custom format to display "Units Sold" instead of the value in cell I4.

To apply a custom format to cell I4:

1. Right-click cell **I4**, and then click **Format Cells** on the shortcut menu (or press the **Ctrl+1** keys) to open the Format Cells dialog box.
2. If necessary, click the **Number** tab.

Tutorial 10 Performing What-If Analyses | Excel **EX 611**

> Be sure to use opening and closing quotation marks around the custom text.

3. In the Category box, click **Custom**.

4. In the Type box, select any text, and then type **"Units Sold"** (including the quotation marks) as the custom text to display in the cell. See Figure 10-15.

Figure 10-15 Format Cells dialog box

custom format to display the text "Units Sold" in the cell

> **TIP**
> You can also hide the reference to the result cell by applying the same font and fill color to the cell.

5. Click the **OK** button. The text "Units Sold" appears in cell I4 even though the cell's underlying content is the formula =B26.

    Trouble? If "Units Sold" does not appear in cell I4, you probably didn't include the quotation marks in the custom format. Repeat Steps 1 through 5, making sure that you include both opening and closing quotation marks.

6. In cell I4, change the fill color to **Gold, Accent 4, Lighter 80%**.

Gianna wants you to complete the two-variable table by identifying the two input cells, which will display the net income for each combination of price and units sold. Because this is a two-variable data table, you'll specify both the row input cell (matching the input values from the table's first row) and the column input cell (matching the values from the first column).

To complete the two-variable data table:

1. Select the range **I4:N13**. This range includes input values from the table's first row and first column and the hidden reference to the result cell (cell I4).

2. On the ribbon, click the **DATA** tab. In the Data Tools group, click the **What-If Analysis** button, and then click **Data Table**. The Data Table dialog box opens.

3. In the Row input cell box, type **B5** to reference the price per unit value from the income statement.

4. In the Column input cell box, type **B4** to reference the number of units sold value from the income statement.

5. Click the **OK** button. The data table values are filled in.
6. Use the Format Painter to copy the formatting from cell **G5** to the range **J5:N13**.
7. Select cell **I4** to deselect the range. See Figure 10-16.

Figure 10-16 Completed two-variable data table

custom text label appears in place of the cell value

break-even point

Units Sold	$1,900	$2,000	$2,100	$2,200	$2,300
300	(205,000.00)	(175,000.00)	(145,000.00)	(115,000.00)	(85,000.00)
350	(165,000.00)	(130,000.00)	(95,000.00)	(60,000.00)	(25,000.00)
400	(125,000.00)	(85,000.00)	(45,000.00)	(5,000.00)	35,000.00
450	(85,000.00)	(40,000.00)	5,000.00	50,000.00	95,000.00
500	(45,000.00)	5,000.00	55,000.00	105,000.00	155,000.00
550	(5,000.00)	50,000.00	105,000.00	160,000.00	215,000.00
600	35,000.00	95,000.00	155,000.00	215,000.00	275,000.00
650	75,000.00	140,000.00	205,000.00	270,000.00	335,000.00
700	115,000.00	185,000.00	255,000.00	325,000.00	395,000.00

Net Income Analysis — Average Price per Unit

result values show the net income for each combination of units sold and average price per unit

The break-even points for different combinations of price and units sold are easy to track because negative net income values are displayed in red and positive net income values are displayed in black. For example, if the average price per unit is set to $2,000, Cycle Green must sell between 450 and 500 bikes to break even. If the price is increased to $2,300, the break-even point falls between 350 and 400 bikes.

Charting a Two-Variable Data Table

You can chart the values from a two-variable data table using lines to represent the different columns of the table. Gianna wants you to create a scatter chart based on the two-variable data table you just created.

To create a chart of the two-variable data table:

1. Select the range **I5:N13**. You'll plot this range on a scatter chart. You did not select the unit prices in row 4 because Excel would interpret these values as data values to be charted, not as labels.
2. On the ribbon, click the **INSERT** tab. In the Charts group, click the **Insert Scatter (X, Y) or Bubble Chart** button, and then click the **Scatter with Straight Lines** chart subtype (the second option in the second row of the Scatter section).
3. Move and resize the chart so that it covers the range **I14:N26**.

4. Remove the chart title, and then position the chart legend to the right of the chart.

5. Change the fill color of the chart area to **Gray - 25%, Background 2**, and then change the fill color of the plot area to **white**.

6. Change the scale of the horizontal axis to range from **300** to **700** units, and then close the Format pane. The initial appearance of the chart is shown in Figure 10-17.

Figure 10-17   Two-variable data table chart

a break-even point occurs when a net income line crosses the horizontal axis

The chart shows a different trend line for each of the five possible values for unit price. However, the prices are not listed in the chart, and Excel uses generic series names (Series1, Series2, Series3, Series4, and Series5). To use the unit prices rather than the generic names in the chart, you must edit the name property of each series.

To edit the chart series names:

1. On the CHART TOOLS DESIGN tab, in the Data group, click the **Select Data** button. The Select Data Source dialog box opens.

2. In the Legend Entries (Series) box, click **Series1**, and then click the **Edit** button. The Edit Series dialog box opens with the insertion point in the Series name box.

3. In the Income Statement worksheet, click cell **J4** to insert the reference to that cell in the Series name box, and then click the **OK** button. The Select Data Source dialog box reappears with the Series1 name changed to $1,900. See Figure 10-18.

Figure 10-18 Select Data Source dialog box

- click to edit the data source of the selected series
- revised series name (taken from cell J4)
- generic series names

4. Repeat Steps 2 and 3 to edit **Series2** to use cell **K4** as the series name, edit **Series3** to use cell **L4** as the series name, edit **Series4** to use cell **M4** as the series name, and edit **Series5** to use cell **N4** as the series name. All of the chart series in the chart are renamed.

5. Click the **OK** button. The legend shows the renamed series.

You'll complete the chart by changing the line colors to shades of green, reflecting the increasing value of the unit price.

6. On the CHART TOOLS DESIGN tab, in the Chart Styles group, click the **Change Colors** button, and then click **Color 17** (the last entry in the gallery of color choices). See Figure 10-19.

Figure 10-19 Final chart of net income values

- click to change the color scheme
- revised series names appear in the legend
- lines are different shades of green

7. Save the workbook.

The chart shows how different unit prices will affect the relationship between sales volume and net income. The horizontal axis represents the break-even point. For example, the $2,000 line (the second from the bottom) crosses the horizontal axis near 500, indicating that with an average cost of $2,000, the company will have to sell about 500 bikes to break even. At that same sales volume of 500 bikes but with an average sales price of $2,200, the company will generate a net profit of about $100,000.

INSIGHT

Data Tables and Arrays

If you examine the cells in the two-variable data table you just created, you can see that every cell displays a different value even though it has the same formula: {=TABLE(B5, B4)}. This formula is an **array formula**, which performs multiple calculations in a single step, returning either a single value to one cell or multiple values to several cells. Array formulas are always enclosed within curly braces.

One example of an array formula that returns a single value is {=SUM(B1:B10*C1:C10)}. This formula multiplies each cell in the range B1:B10 by the matching cell in the same row of the range C1:C10. The sum of those 10 products is then calculated and returned. To create this array formula, enter the formula =SUM(B1:B10*C1:C10) and then press the Ctrl+Shift+Enter keys. Excel treats the formula as an array formula, adding the curly braces for you.

The **TABLE function** is an array function that returns multiple values to multiple cells. Other such functions include the TREND, MINVERSE, MMULT, and TRANSPOSE functions. To calculate multiple cell values, select the range, type the array formula, and then press the Ctrl+Shift+Enter keys to enter the formula. Excel applies the array formula to all of the selected cells.

Array formulas are a powerful feature of Excel. If used properly, they help you perform complex calculations within a single formula and extend a single formula over a range of cells. Use Excel Help to learn more about array formulas and the functions that support them.

So far, you have used what-if analysis with Goal Seek and data tables to analyze how much Cycle Green can charge for its bikes and what impact sales volume has on the company's profitability. In the next session, you will use other what-if analysis tools to examine the impact of more than two factors on a financial outcome.

REVIEW

Session 10.1 Quick Check

1. Describe the difference between a what-if analysis and Goal Seek.
2. Name the three components of the Goal Seek command.
3. What is a data table? What is an input cell? What is a result cell?
4. What is a one-variable data table? What is a two-variable data table?
5. How many result cells can you display with a one-variable data table? How many result cells can you display with a two-variable data table?
6. Cell E5 contains the formula =B10. You want to display the text "Profits" instead of the formula's value. What custom format would you use?
7. What is an array formula?

Session 10.2 Visual Overview:

The **Scenario Manager** enables you to create as many scenarios as you want and switch among them to display the results of several what-if analyses within the worksheet.

A **scenario** is a defined collection of input values used to perform a what-if analysis.

Expanded Operations scenario

Reduced Operations scenario

Tutorial 10 Performing What-If Analyses | Excel   EX 617

What-If Scenarios

The scenario summary report lists the values for the changing cells and result cells under each scenario.

Scenario Summary

	Current Values:	Expanded Operations	Reduced Operations
Changing Cells:			
Units_Sold	570	600	500
Average_Price_per_Unit	2,100.00	2,300.00	2,000.00
Salaries_and_Benefits	325,000.00	450,000.00	275,000.00
Advertising	25,000.00	50,000.00	30,000.00
Administrative	45,000.00	60,000.00	35,000.00
Miscellaneous	50,000.00	50,000.00	30,000.00
Result Cells:			
Total_Revenue	1,197,000.00	1,380,000.00	1,000,000.00
Total_Expenses	1,072,000.00	1,270,000.00	920,000.00
Net_Income	$125,000.00	$110,000.00	$80,000.00

Input cells whose values you will change within each scenario are called **changing cells**.

The scenario PivotTable report displays the scenario changing and result values in an Excel PivotTable.

	A	B	C	D
1	$B$4:$B$5,$B$17:$B$20 by	(All)		
2				
3	Row Labels	Total_Revenue	Total_Expenses	Net_Income
4	Expanded Operations	$1,380,000.00	$1,270,000.00	$110,000.00
5	Reduced Operations	$1,000,000.00	$920,000.00	$80,000.00

The values of result cells are displayed in the scenario summary and scenario PivotTable reports.

Developing Financial Scenarios with the Scenario Manager

Many financial analyses explore the impact of several input values on several different results. Because data tables are limited to two input cells, you must create a scenario to perform a what-if analysis with more than two input cells. A scenario is a defined set of values for different cells grouped under a common name.

Gianna wants to explore other ways of increasing Cycle Green's profitability. She has developed the four scenarios listed in Figure 10-20. The Status Quo scenario assumes that everything remains the same for the upcoming year. All of the fixed expenses, units sold, and unit prices are unchanged. The Expanded Operations scenario assumes that the company will expand its production and marketing. Under this proposal, the company will hire additional workers, greatly expand its advertising budget, and spend more on administrative and miscellaneous expenses hoping that bike sales will increase. The Reduced Operations scenario foresees a downturn in the economy that forces the company to reduce its costs in an attempt to become more efficient. This scenario also assumes that Cycle Green's sales price will drop to attract more buyers, and that overall sales will be slightly reduced even with the lower sales price. Finally, the Spring Sale scenario proposes a large decrease in the sales price of the bikes with a corresponding large increase in sales partly due to expanded advertising and marketing.

Figure 10-20 — What-if scenarios

Input Cells	Status Quo	Expanded Operations	Reduced Operations	Spring Sale
Units Sold (cell B4)	570	675	500	750
Average Price per Unit (cell B5)	$2,100	$2,300	$2,000	$1,800
Salaries and Benefits (cell B17)	$325,000	$450,000	$275,000	$350,000
Advertising (cell B18)	$25,000	$50,000	$30,000	$70,000
Administrative (cell B19)	$45,000	$60,000	$35,000	$30,000
Miscellaneous (cell B20)	$50,000	$50,000	$30,000	$25,000

© 2014 Cengage Learning

You cannot generate this report using a data table because you need six input cells. Instead, you will create scenarios using the Scenario Manager. Rather than manually changing every input cell value, the Scenario Manager lets you define those input values within a named scenario and quickly switch from one scenario to another. The Scenario Manager can also be used to create reports that summarize the key differences in how the various scenarios impact result cells in the financial worksheet.

Before using the Scenario Manager, you should define names for all the input and result cells that you intend to use in the what-if analysis. As you'll see later in this tutorial, the defined names appear in the reports generated by the Scenario Manager. Although not a requirement, using defined names makes it easier to work with scenarios and for other people to understand the scenario reports.

Gianna asks you to define names for the income statement values that will be used in the various scenarios.

To define names for the income statement values:

▶ 1. If you took a break after the previous session, make sure the Cycle Green workbook is open, and the Income Statement worksheet is the active sheet.

Tutorial 10 Performing What-If Analyses | Excel   EX 619

- **2.** In the Income Statement worksheet, select the nonadjacent range **A4:B5;A17:B20;A24:B26**. You'll define names for each of these cells.
- **3.** On the ribbon, click the **FORMULAS** tab. In the Defined Names group, click the **Create from Selection** button. The Create Names from Selection dialog box opens.
- **4.** Click the **Left column** check box to insert a checkmark, if necessary, and then click any other check boxes that have a checkmark to deselect them.
- **5.** Click the **OK** button. The selected cells in column B are named using the labels in the corresponding cells in column A.
- **6.** Select cell **A1** to deselect the range.

Defining a Scenario

You use the Scenario Manager to define the scenarios. Each scenario includes a scenario name, input or changing cells, and the values of each input cell. The number of scenarios you can create is limited only by your computer's memory.

REFERENCE

Defining a Scenario

- Enter the data values in the worksheet for the scenario.
- On the DATA tab, in the Data Tools group, click the What-If Analysis button, and then click Scenario Manager.
- Click the Add button in the Scenario Manager dialog box.
- In the Scenario name box, type a name for the scenario.
- In the Changing cells box, specify the changing cells.
- Click the OK button.
- In the Scenario Values dialog box, specify values for each input cell, and then click the Add button.
- Click the OK button.

You'll start by creating the Status Quo scenario, whose values match those currently entered in the workbook.

To add the Status Quo scenario:

- **1.** On the ribbon, click the **DATA** tab. In the Data Tools group, click the **What-If Analysis** button, and then click **Scenario Manager**. The Scenario Manager dialog box opens. No scenarios are defined yet.
- **2.** Click the **Add** button. The Add Scenario dialog box opens.
- **3.** In the Scenario name box, type **Status Quo**, and then press the **Tab** key. The range in the Changing cells box is selected.

TIP
Scenarios are limited to a maximum of 32 changing cells.

The Scenario Manager refers to input cells as "changing cells" because these worksheet cells contain values that are changed under the scenario. Changing cells can be located anywhere in the worksheet. You can type the range names or locations of changing cells, but it's faster and more accurate to select them with the mouse. To select nonadjacent changing cells, press and hold the Ctrl key as you click each cell.

The changing cells for each of the four scenarios are:

- Cell B4: Units Sold
- Cell B5: Average Price per Unit
- Cell B17: Salaries and Benefits
- Cell B18: Advertising
- Cell B19: Administrative
- Cell B20: Miscellaneous

You'll specify the changing cells for the Status Quo scenario.

To specify the changing cells for the Status Quo scenario:

1. With the Changing Cells box still active, select the nonadjacent range **B4:B5;B17:B20**. The range appears in the Changing cells box. These are the input cells.

2. Press the **Tab** key to select the default text in the Comment box, and then type **Scenario assuming current values.** in the Comment box. See Figure 10-21.

Figure 10-21   Edit Scenario dialog box

- scenario name
- input cells in the scenario
- description of the scenario
- select to prevent changes to this scenario
- select to hide the scenario in a protected worksheet

3. Click the **OK** button. The Scenario Values dialog box opens so you can specify values for each input cell you entered in the Changing cells box in the Edit Scenario dialog box. Because the Status Quo scenario values are the current values in the workbook, you can accept the values displayed in the Scenario Values dialog box. See Figure 10-22.

Figure 10-22   Scenario Values dialog box

- defined names of the scenario's input cells
- input values for the scenario

Tutorial 10 Performing What-If Analyses | Excel EX 621

4. Click the **OK** button. The Scenario Manager dialog box reopens with the Status Quo scenario listed in the Scenarios box as shown in Figure 10-23.

Figure 10-23 | **Scenario Manager dialog box**

- Status Quo scenario added to the workbook
- click to add, edit, or delete scenarios
- click to create a summary report comparing the scenarios
- click to merge scenarios from different worksheets or workbooks
- click to show the selected scenario in the workbook

Changing cells: $B$4:$B$5,$B$17:$B$20
Comment: Scenario assuming current values.

You'll use the same process to add the remaining three scenarios that Gianna is interested in—Expanded Operations, Reduced Operations, and Spring Sale.

To add the remaining scenarios:

1. Click the **Add** button. The Add Scenario dialog box opens. You need to enter the scenario name.

2. In the Scenario name box, type **Expanded Operations**, and then press the **Tab** key. The nonadjacent range you selected for the Status Quo scenario is selected in the Changing cells box. Because you want to use the same set of changing cells, you won't make any edits to the range. You will enter a new scenario comment.

3. Press the **Tab** key to select the text in the Comment box, type **Scenario assuming expanded operations.** in the Comment box, and then click the **OK** button. The Scenario Values dialog box opens. This scenario uses different values for the changing cells, which you'll enter now.

4. Enter **675** for Units_Sold, **2300** for Average_Price_per_Unit, **450,000** for Salaries_and_Benefits, **50,000** for Advertising, **60,000** for Administrative, and **50,000** for Miscellaneous, pressing the **Tab** key to move from one input box to the next.

   Trouble? If the Scenario Manager dialog box reopens, you probably pressed the Enter key instead of the Tab key. Make sure that the Expanded Operations scenario is selected in the Scenarios box, click the Edit button, and then click the OK button to return to the Scenario Values dialog box. Enter the remaining values in the scenario, being sure to press the Tab key to move to the next input box.

5. Click the **Add** button. The Add Scenario dialog box reopens. You'll create the third scenario now. As with the second scenario, you need to enter a new name and comment. The changing cells are the same.

   Trouble? If the Scenario Manager dialog box reopens, you clicked the OK button instead of the Add button. Click the Add button in the Scenario Manager dialog box to return to the Add Scenario dialog box, and then continue with Step 6.

6. Type **Reduced Operations** in the Scenario name box, press the **Tab** key twice, type **Scenario assuming reduced operations.** in the Comment box, and then click the **OK** button.

7. Enter **500** for Units_Sold, **2000** for Average_Price_per_Unit, **275,000** for Salaries_and_Benefits, **30,000** for Advertising, **35,000** for Administrative, and **30,000** for Miscellaneous.

8. Click the **Add** button to add the Reduced Operations scenario to the Scenario Manager.

9. Type **Spring Sale** in the Scenario name box, press the **Tab** key twice, type **Scenario assuming a sale.** in the Comment box, and then click the **OK** button.

10. Enter **750** for Units_Sold, **1800** for Average_Price_per_Unit, **350,000** for Salaries_and_Benefits, **70,000** for Advertising, **30,000** for Administrative, and **25,000** for Miscellaneous.

11. Click the **OK** button to add the Spring Sale scenario and return to the Scenario Manager.

Viewing Scenarios

You can view the effect of each scenario by selecting the scenario in the Scenario Manager dialog box. You switch from one scenario to another by clicking the Show button in the Scenario Manager dialog box. You do not have to close the dialog box to switch scenarios.

You'll start by viewing the impact of the Expanded Operations scenario on the company's income statement.

To view the impact of the Expanded Operations scenario:

1. In the Scenario Manager dialog box, click **Expanded Operations** in the list of scenarios. The changing cells and the comment for the selected scenario appear at the bottom of the Scenario Manager dialog box.

2. Click the **Show** button. The values in the Income Statement worksheet change to reflect the scenario.

3. Click the **Close** button. The Scenario Manager dialog box closes. The income statement for Cycle Green is updated to show expanded operations with increased fixed expenses. See Figure 10-24.

TIP

You can also double-click a scenario name in the Scenarios box in the Scenario Manager dialog box to view that scenario.

Figure 10-24 | Income statement under the Expanded Operations scenario

	A	B
2	**Income Statement**	
3	Revenue	
4	Units Sold	675
5	Average Price per Unit	2,300.00
6	Total Revenue	$1,552,500.00
7		
8	Variable Expenses	
9	Units Produced	675
10	Average Material Cost per Unit	950.00
11	Total Material Cost	641,250.00
12	Average Manufacturing Cost per Unit	150.00
13	Total Manufacturing Cost	101,250.00
14	Total Variable Expenses	$742,500.00
15		
16	Fixed Expenses	
17	Salaries and Benefits	450,000.00
18	Advertising	50,000.00
19	Administrative	60,000.00
20	Miscellaneous	50,000.00
21	Total Fixed Expenses	$610,000.00
22		
23	Summary	
24	Total Revenue	1,552,500.00
25	Total Expenses	1,352,500.00
26	Net Income	$200,000.00

Rows 4, 5, 10, 12, 17, 18 — input values under the Expanded Operations scenario

Rows 24, 25, 26 — result values under the Expanded Operations scenario

Trouble? If the values in your income statement do not match those in the figure, you might have entered the values for the scenario incorrectly. You'll learn how to edit a scenario shortly.

Excel automatically changes the values of the six input cells to match the scenario. Under the Expanded Operations scenario, the company's net income increases from the current value of $125,000 to $200,000. You'll review the other scenarios.

To view the impact of the remaining scenarios:

1. On the DATA tab, in the Data Tools group, click the **What-If Analysis** button, and then click **Scenario Manager** to reopen the Scenario Manager dialog box.

2. In the Scenarios box, double-click **Reduced Operations** to update the worksheet, and then click the **Close** button to close the Scenario Manager dialog box. Under the Reduced Operations scenario, the net income value shown in cell B26 drops to $80,000.

3. Repeat Steps 1 and 2 to update the worksheet with the **Spring Sale** scenario. Under the Spring Sale scenario, with the reduced unit price of each bike, the company would generate a net income of $50,000. Figure 10-25 shows the income statements for the Reduced Operations and Spring Sale scenarios.

Figure 10-25 Income statements for the Reduced Operations and Spring Sale scenarios

	A	B
2	Income Statement	
3	Revenue	
4	Units Sold	500
5	Average Price per Unit	2,000.00
6	Total Revenue	$1,000,000.00
7		
8	Variable Expenses	
9	Units Produced	500
10	Average Material Cost per Unit	950.00
11	Total Material Cost	475,000.00
12	Average Manufacturing Cost per Unit	150.00
13	Total Manufacturing Cost	75,000.00
14	Total Variable Expenses	$550,000.00
15		
16	Fixed Expenses	
17	Salaries and Benefits	275,000.00
18	Advertising	30,000.00
19	Administrative	35,000.00
20	Miscellaneous	30,000.00
21	Total Fixed Expenses	$370,000.00
22		
23	Summary	
24	Total Revenue	1,000,000.00
25	Total Expenses	920,000.00
26	Net Income	$80,000.00

Reduced Operations scenario

	A	B
2	Income Statement	
3	Revenue	
4	Units Sold	750
5	Average Price per Unit	1,800.00
6	Total Revenue	$1,350,000.00
7		
8	Variable Expenses	
9	Units Produced	750
10	Average Material Cost per Unit	950.00
11	Total Material Cost	712,500.00
12	Average Manufacturing Cost per Unit	150.00
13	Total Manufacturing Cost	112,500.00
14	Total Variable Expenses	$825,000.00
15		
16	Fixed Expenses	
17	Salaries and Benefits	350,000.00
18	Advertising	70,000.00
19	Administrative	30,000.00
20	Miscellaneous	25,000.00
21	Total Fixed Expenses	$475,000.00
22		
23	Summary	
24	Total Revenue	1,350,000.00
25	Total Expenses	1,300,000.00
26	Net Income	$50,000.00

Spring Sale scenario

Notice that when you substitute a new scenario for the Status Quo scenario, all worksheet values and charts are automatically updated. For example, under the Spring Sale scenario, the one-variable and two-variable data tables changed to reflect the new values of the input and result cells. The break-even point for the Spring Sale scenario is between 650 and 700 units. The company will have to sell almost 700 bikes just to break even under this scenario, so the sale had better be successful.

Editing a Scenario

After you create a scenario, you can edit its assumptions to view other possible outcomes. When you edit a scenario, the worksheet calculations are automatically updated to reflect the new scenario.

The most profitable scenario, the Expanded Operations scenario, relies on the company selling 675 bikes at an average price of $2,300. Gianna is unsure whether the company can meet that sales goal at that sales price. She asks you to modify the Expanded Operations scenario, reducing the total sales to 600 units to see how this impacts the company's profitability.

To edit the Expanded Operations scenario:

1. On the DATA tab, in the Data Tools group, click the **What-If Analysis** button, and then click **Scenario Manager**. The Scenario Manager dialog box opens.

2. In the Scenarios box, click **Expanded Operations**, and then click the **Edit** button. The Edit Scenario dialog box opens with the entries you made for the Expanded Operations scenario. You don't need to make any changes in this dialog box.

3. Click the **OK** button. The Scenario Values dialog box opens.

▶ **4.** Change the Units_Sold value from 675 to **600**, and then click the **OK** button to return to the Scenario Manager dialog box.

▶ **5.** Click the **Show** button followed by the **Close** button. The Income Statement worksheet updates to reflect the revised scenario, which results in net income decreasing from $200,000 to $110,000. See Figure 10-26.

Figure 10-26 Revised Expanded Operations scenario

	A	B
2	Income Statement	
3	Revenue	
4	Units Sold	600
5	Average Price per Unit	2,300.00
6	Total Revenue	$1,380,000.00
7		
8	Variable Expenses	
9	Units Produced	600
10	Average Material Cost per Unit	950.00
11	Total Material Cost	570,000.00
12	Average Manufacturing Cost per Unit	150.00
13	Total Manufacturing Cost	90,000.00
14	Total Variable Expenses	$660,000.00
15		
16	Fixed Expenses	
17	Salaries and Benefits	450,000.00
18	Advertising	50,000.00
19	Administrative	60,000.00
20	Miscellaneous	50,000.00
21	Total Fixed Expenses	$610,000.00
22		
23	Summary	
24	Total Revenue	1,380,000.00
25	Total Expenses	1,270,000.00
26	Net Income	$110,000.00

projected sales units decrease to 600 units

net income decreases from $200,000 to $110,000

▶ **6.** Open the Scenario Manager dialog box, and then double-click **Status Quo** in the Scenarios box. The income statement displays the original values. You'll leave the Scenario Manager dialog box open.

Creating Scenario Summary Reports

Although scenarios can help you make important business decisions, repeatedly switching scenarios can become time consuming. To compare the results from multiple scenarios on a single worksheet, you can create a report either as an Excel table or as an Excel PivotTable. Gianna wants you to create both types of reports with the four scenarios you generated for Cycle Green, starting with a summary report that appears in the form of an Excel table.

REFERENCE

Creating a Scenario Summary Report or a Scenario PivotTable Report

- On the DATA tab, in the Data Tools group, click the What-If Analysis button, and then click Scenario Manager.
- Click the Summary button.
- Click the Scenario summary or Scenario PivotTable report option button.
- Select the result cells to display in the report.
- Click the OK button.

EX 626 Excel | Tutorial 10 Performing What-If Analyses

To create a scenario summary report, you must identify which result cells you want to include in the report. Gianna is interested in the following result cells—cell B24 (Total Revenue), cell B25 (Total Expenses), and cell B26 (Net Income). You'll display these values along with the values of the input cell defined by the scenario in your report.

To create the scenario summary report:

1. In the Scenario Manager dialog box, click the **Summary** button. The Scenario Summary dialog box opens, allowing you to create a scenario summary report or a scenario PivotTable report. You want to create a scenario summary report.

2. Verify that the **Scenario summary** option button is selected.

3. Make sure that the Result cells box is active, and then select the range **B24:B26**. This range references the result cells you want to display in the report.

4. Click the **OK** button. The scenario summary report is inserted in the workbook.

5. Move the **Scenario Summary** worksheet to the end of the workbook. See Figure 10-27.

Figure 10-27 Scenario summary report

	Current Values:	Status Quo	Expanded Operations	Reduced Operations	Spring Sale
Changing Cells:					
Units_Sold	570	570	600	500	750
Average_Price_per_Unit	2,100.00	2,100.00	2,300.00	2,000.00	1,800.00
Salaries_and_Benefits	325,000.00	325,000.00	450,000.00	275,000.00	350,000.00
Advertising	25,000.00	25,000.00	50,000.00	30,000.00	70,000.00
Administrative	45,000.00	45,000.00	60,000.00	35,000.00	30,000.00
Miscellaneous	50,000.00	50,000.00	50,000.00	30,000.00	25,000.00
Result Cells:					
Total_Revenue	1,197,000.00	1,197,000.00	1,380,000.00	1,000,000.00	1,350,000.00
Total_Expenses	1,072,000.00	1,072,000.00	1,270,000.00	920,000.00	1,300,000.00
Net_Income	$125,000.00	$125,000.00	$110,000.00	$80,000.00	$50,000.00

Notes: Current Values column represents values of changing cells at time Scenario Summary Report was created. Changing cells for each scenario are highlighted in gray.

TIP
Use the outline tools to hide and expand different parts of the scenario summary report.

The scenario summary report displays the values of the input cells and result cells under each scenario. Each scenario is listed by name, and the current worksheet values are also displayed. Note that the report uses the defined names you created earlier to identify the changing and result cells. The defined names make the report simpler to interpret.

Next, Gianna wants you to compare the scenarios using a PivotTable report. As the name implies, a Scenario PivotTable report displays the results from each scenario as a PivotTable field in a PivotTable. Scenario PivotTable reports are created through the same Scenario Manager used to create a summary report.

Tutorial 10 Performing What-If Analyses | Excel   EX 627

To create the Scenario PivotTable report:

1. Return to the **Income Statement** worksheet.

2. Open the Scenario Manager dialog box, click the **Summary** button to reopen the Scenario Summary dialog box, and then click the **Scenario PivotTable report** option button.

3. Click the **OK** button. The Scenario PivotTable sheet is inserted in the workbook and contains the scenario values in a PivotTable.

4. Move the **Scenario PivotTable** worksheet to the end of the workbook, and then increase the magnification of the worksheet to **120%**. See Figure 10-28.

Figure 10-28   Scenario PivotTable report

Row Labels	Total_Revenue	Total_Expenses	Net_Income
Expanded Operations	1380000	1270000	110000
Reduced Operations	1000000	920000	80000
Spring Sale	1350000	1300000	50000
Status Quo	1197000	1072000	125000

scenarios → ← *result values*

Gianna wants you to edit the scenario PivotTable to make it easier to read, but not filter it. Then, she wants you to generate a PivotChart of revenue, expenses, and net income under each scenario.

To edit and format the PivotTable report:

1. In the PivotTable Fields pane, in the VALUES box, click the **Total_Revenue** button, and then click **Value Field Settings**. The Value Field Settings dialog box opens.

2. Click the **Number Format** button to open the Format Cells dialog box, click **Currency** in the Category box, and then click the last entry **($1,234.10)** in the Negative numbers box to display negative currency values in a red font enclosed in parentheses.

3. Click the **OK** button in the Format Cells dialog box, and then click the **OK** button in the Value Field Settings dialog box. The number format is applied to the Total_Revenue cells.

4. Repeat Steps 1 through 3 for the **Total_Expenses** and the **Net_Income** buttons in the Values box to apply the same number format.

5. In the PivotTable Fields pane, in the FILTERS box, click the **$B$4:$B$5,$...** button, and then click **Remove Field**. You do not need to filter the PivotTable.

6. In cell **A1**, enter **Scenario PivotTable**, and then format the text with the **Title** cell style. See Figure 10-29.

Figure 10-29   Formatted scenario PivotTable

	A	B	C	D
1	Scenario PivotTable			
2				
3	Row Labels	Total_Revenue	Total_Expenses	Net_Income
4	Expanded Operations	$1,380,000.00	$1,270,000.00	$110,000.00
5	Reduced Operations	$1,000,000.00	$920,000.00	$80,000.00
6	Spring Sale	$1,350,000.00	$1,300,000.00	$50,000.00
7	Status Quo	$1,197,000.00	$1,072,000.00	$125,000.00

PivotTable report

Gianna wants you to display the results of this table in a PivotChart. You'll do this from the PIVOTTABLE TOOLS ANALYZE tab.

To create the PivotChart with the scenario results:

1. Select cell **A3** to select the PivotTable.

2. On the ribbon, click the **PIVOTTABLE TOOLS ANALYZE** tab. In the Tools group, click the **PivotChart** button. The Insert Chart dialog box opens.

3. If it is not already selected, click the **Clustered Column** chart type (the first chart subtype in the Column section), and then click the **OK** button.

4. Move and resize the embedded chart so that it covers the range **A8:E19**.

5. On the ribbon, click the **PIVOTCHART TOOLS ANALYZE** tab. In the Show/Hide group, click the **Field Buttons** to hide the field buttons in the chart. See Figure 10-30.

Figure 10-30   Scenario PivotChart

PivotTable

PivotChart

6. Save the workbook.

Based on the income statements from the different scenarios, Gianna can expect a net income for the company that ranges from $50,000 to $125,000 per year.

PROSKILLS

Teamwork: Merging Scenarios

In a business, several workbooks often track the same set of figures and evaluate the same set of scenarios. Colleagues can share scenarios by merging the scenarios from multiple workbooks into one workbook. The Scenario Manager dialog box includes a Merge button that you can use to merge scenarios from different workbooks. The scenarios merge into the active sheet. It's easier to merge scenarios if all of the what-if analyses on the different worksheets and workbooks are identical. All of the changing cells from the merged scenario must correspond to changing cells in the active workbook and worksheet. By sharing scenarios, a team can more easily explore the impact of different financial situations, ensuring that the entire team is always working from a common set of assumptions and goals.

In this session, you examined the impact of different financial scenarios on the profitability of Cycle Green's operations. In the next session, you'll explore how changing the types of items the company produces and sells can impact its profitability.

REVIEW

Session 10.2 Quick Check

1. What is one advantage of scenarios over data tables?
2. What should you do before creating a scenario report to make the entries on the report easier to interpret?
3. What are changing cells?
4. What are result cells?
5. Where do you define result cells in the Scenario Manager?
6. How do you display a scenario in the active worksheet?
7. How do you create a scenario PivotTable report?

Excel | Tutorial 10 Performing What-If Analyses

Session 10.3 Visual Overview:

Product mix is the combination of different products offered by a company for sale to the consumer.

Variable cells are input cells that contain values that will be changed to reach an optimal solution. In this worksheet, the range B4:E5 contains variable cells.

Solver models can be saved to cells in the worksheet to be reloaded and used later.

The **objective cell** is a result cell that contains a value to maximize, minimize, or set to a specific value. In this worksheet, cell B18 is the objective cell.

B18 =B14-(B15+B16+B17)

CYCLE GREEN

	A	B	C	D
3	Product Mix Analysis	K100	K95	K85
4	Optimal Product Mix	118	154	123
5	Current Product Mix	159	118	140
6	Change	-41	36	-17
7	Sales Price per Model	$1,000.00	$1,800.00	$2,400.00
8	Revenue per Model (Optimal)	$118,000.00	$277,200.00	$295,200.00
9	Material Cost per Model	$498.00	$667.00	$1,009.00
10	Manufacturing Cost per Model	$131.00	$150.00	$153.00
11				
12	Summary	Optimal	Current	Change
13	Units Sold	570	570	0
14	Total Revenue	1,250,400.00	1,197,000.00	53,400.00
15	Total Material Cost	562,789.00	541,500.00	21,289.00
16	Total Manufacturing Cost	86,602.00	85,500.00	1,102.00
17	Total Fixed Expenses	445,000.00	445,000.00	0.00
18	Net Income	$156,009.00	$125,000.00	$31,009.00
19				
20	Maximum Net Income Model			
21		$156,009.00		
22		4		

Documentation | Income Statement | **Product Mix** | Scenario S

Tutorial 10 Performing What-If Analyses | Excel   EX 631

Optimal Solutions with Solver

Solver is an Excel add-in that searches for the optimal solution to a problem involving several variables.

Solver sets an objective cell to a specified value, or finds the maximum or minimum possible value for a cell.

Solver Parameters

Set Objective: $B$18

To: ● Max ○ Min ○ Value Of: 0

By Changing Variable Cells:
$B$4:$E$4

Subject to the Constraints:
$B$4:$E$4 = integer
$B$13 = 570
$B$4:$E$4 >= 115
$J$21:$J$34 >= 0

Solver changes the value of one or more variable cells to reach a solution for the objective cell.

Solver can use **constraints** to limit the solution to a set of possible values.

☑ Make Unconstrained Variables Non-Negative

Select a Solving Method: GRG Nonlinear

Solving Method
Select the GRG Nonlinear engine for Solver Problems that are smooth nonlinear. Select the LP Simplex engine for linear Solver Problems, and select the Evolutionary engine for Solver problems that are non-smooth.

Help   Solve   Close

You can use the Load/Save button in the Solver Parameters dialog box to save the Solver model to the current worksheet.

Superlight aluminum frame	321	272
Carbon fiber frame	298	298

Introducing Product Mix

The combination of products offered by a company is known as the company's product mix. Not all products are alike; one product may differ from another in its sales price, its production costs, and its attractiveness to the consumer. Because of this, a company might find that it is more profitable to devote more of its resources to selling one product over another. For example, Cycle Green might make a larger profit off of each high-end bike it sells compared to its profit margin on less expensive bikes.

The challenge for the company is to maximize its profits while still meeting the demands of the market. So even though Cycle Green might make more money off of each high-end bike it sells, the demand for those kinds of bikes is smaller than the demand for a more entry-level bicycle. In general, companies want their product mix to cover the widest possible range of consumer needs. For that reason, Cycle Green produces and sells four models of road bikes of increasing quality and performance—K100, K95, K85, and K5. Each lower-end K100 bike sells for $1,000 but costs $629 to manufacture. By contrast, each K95 bike costs $817 to manufacture and sells for $1,800, each K85 bike costs $1,162 to manufacture and sells for $2,400, and finally each high-end K5 bike costs $1,751 to manufacture and sells for $3,200.

Gianna estimates the company can sell 570 road bikes consisting of 159 K100 bikes, 118 K95s, 140 K85s, and 153 high-end K5s. She has estimated that this current product mix will produce a net income of $125,000 for the company. However, Gianna wants to find the **optimal product mix**, which is the product mix that will result in the most profit for the company (assuming the company can sell every bike it produces).

Gianna has listed the sales price, costs, and variable expenses for each model in the Product Mix worksheet. She asks you to find a more profitable product mix by entering new sales numbers in row 4, which contains the optimal product mix estimates.

To find the optimal product mix by trial and error:

1. If you took a break after the previous session, make sure the Cycle Green workbook is open.
2. Go to the **Product Mix** worksheet. See Figure 10-31.

Figure 10-31 Product Mix worksheet

	A	B	C	D	E
1	CYCLE GREEN				
2					
3	Product Mix Analysis	K100	K95	K85	K5
4	Optimal Product Mix	159	118	140	153
5	Current Product Mix	159	118	140	153
6	Change	0	0	0	0
7	Sales Price per Model	$1,000.00	$1,800.00	$2,400.00	$3,200.00
8	Revenue per Model (Optimal)	$159,000.00	$212,400.00	$336,000.00	$489,600.00
9	Material Cost per Model	$498.00	$667.00	$1,009.00	$1,584.00
10	Manufacturing Cost per Model	$131.00	$150.00	$153.00	$167.00
11					
12	Summary	Optimal	Current	Change	
13	Units Sold	570	570	0	
14	Total Revenue	1,197,000.00	1,197,000.00	0.00	
15	Total Material Cost	541,500.00	541,500.00	0.00	
16	Total Manufacturing Cost	85,500.00	85,500.00	0.00	
17	Total Fixed Expenses	445,000.00	445,000.00	0.00	
18	Net Income	$125,000.00	$125,000.00	$0.00	

- road bike models
- number of bikes produced and sold by model
- price of each model
- variable expenses associated with each model
- net change between the optimal and current product mixes

3. In cell **C4**, enter **130** to increase the sales estimates for the K95 bike by 12 units.

4. In cell **D4**, enter **128** to decrease the sales estimates for the K85 bike by 12 units. The overall sales number remains at 570 bikes, but this new product mix drops the company's net income by $3,060 to a new total of $121,940. See Figure 10-32.

Figure 10-32 Changed product mix

	A	B	C	D	E
1	CYCLE GREEN				
2					
3	Product Mix Analysis	K100	K95	K85	K5
4	Optimal Product Mix	159	130	128	153
5	Current Product Mix	159	118	140	153
6	Change	0	12	-12	0
7	Sales Price per Model	$1,000.00	$1,800.00	$2,400.00	$3,200.00
8	Revenue per Model (Optimal)	$159,000.00	$234,000.00	$307,200.00	$489,600.00
9	Material Cost per Model	$498.00	$667.00	$1,009.00	$1,584.00
10	Manufacturing Cost per Model	$131.00	$150.00	$153.00	$167.00
11					
12	Summary	Optimal	Current	Change	
13	Units Sold	570	570	0	
14	Total Revenue	1,189,800.00	1,197,000.00	(7,200.00)	
15	Total Material Cost	537,396.00	541,500.00	(4,104.00)	
16	Total Manufacturing Cost	85,464.00	85,500.00	(36.00)	
17	Total Fixed Expenses	445,000.00	445,000.00	0.00	
18	Net Income	$121,940.00	$125,000.00	($3,060.00)	

- 12 more K95 bikes are produced and sold
- 12 fewer K85 bikes are produced and sold
- total number of bikes remains at 570
- net income decreased by $3,060
- net income under this product mix drops to $121,940

Next, you'll try a different product mix to see if that mix increases the company's net income. You'll use the original units for the K95 and K85 models, but change the units for the K100 and K5 models.

5. In the range **B4:E4**, enter **144**, **118**, **140**, and **168**, respectively. When 15 fewer K100 bikes and 15 more K5 bikes are produced and sold, the total number of bikes sold remains at 570, but the company's net income increases by $16,170 to a total of $141,170. This product mix is more profitable to the company.

6. In cell **B4**, enter **159**, and in cell **E4**, enter **153**. The optimal product mix matches the original product mix.

Different product mixes result in lower or higher profit for the company, and the best way to find the optimal product mix usually isn't obvious. There are just too many possible combinations. To find the one product mix that results in the maximum net profit for the company, you can use Solver.

Finding an Optimal Solution Using Solver

Solver finds the numeric solution to a problem involving several input values. For example, Solver can be used to find the combination of input values that maximizes profits. It also can be used to find a set of input values that minimizes costs, or it can act like Goal Seek and find the input values required to match a given result.

Activating Solver

Solver is an **add-in**, which is a program that adds customized commands and features to Microsoft Office programs such as Excel. You might need to activate Solver before you can use it.

> **REFERENCE**
>
> ### Activating Solver
>
> - On the DATA tab, in the Analysis group, confirm whether Solver appears. If it appears, Solver is already active. If it does not appear, continue with the rest of these steps.
> - Click the FILE tab, and then click the Options button in the navigation bar.
> - Click Add-Ins in the left pane, click the arrow next to the Manage box, and then click Excel Add-ins.
> - Click the Go button to open the Add-Ins dialog box.
> - Click the Solver Add-in check box, and then click the OK button.
> - Follow the remaining prompts to install Solver, if it is not already installed.

You will check whether Solver is already active on your version of Excel. If the Solver button does not appear on the DATA tab, the Solver add-in needs to be activated. If you are working on a network, you might need your instructor or network administrator to activate Solver for you. If you are working on a stand-alone PC, you can activate Solver yourself.

To activate the Solver add-in:

1. On the ribbon, click the **DATA** tab, and then look for the Analysis group and the Solver button. If you see the Solver button, as shown in Figure 10-33, Solver is active and you should read but not perform the rest of the steps in this section. If you don't see the Solver button, continue with Step 2.

Figure 10-33   Solver button in the Analysis group on the DATA tab

Solver button indicates that Solver is installed and active

> **TIP**
>
> You can also open the Excel Options dialog box by right-clicking the ribbon, and then clicking Customize the Ribbon on the shortcut menu.

2. Click the **FILE** tab, and then click the **Options** button in the navigation bar to open the Excel Options dialog box.

3. In the left pane, click **Add-Ins**. Information about all of the add-ins currently installed within Excel appears in the right pane.

4. If necessary, click the **Manage box arrow** at the bottom of the dialog box, and then click **Excel Add-ins**.

5. Click the **Go** button. The Add-Ins dialog box opens and displays a list of all of the available Excel add-ins. These add-ins may be available but they might not have been activated.

6. Click the **Solver Add-in** check box to insert a checkmark.

Tutorial 10 Performing What-If Analyses | Excel **EX 635**

> **Trouble?** If you don't see Solver in the list of available add-ins, you may have to reinstall Excel on your computer. See your instructor or technical resource person for help.
>
> 7. Click the **OK** button. Solver is activated and its button is added to the DATA tab in the Analysis group.

Now that Solver is activated, you are ready to use it to find the optimal product mix.

INSIGHT

Excel Add-Ins

Solver is only one of the available Excel add-ins. Other add-ins provide the ability to perform statistical analyses, generate business reports, and retrieve financial data from the Internet. You can also create your own add-in using the Visual Basic for Applications (VBA) macro language. The process for activating add-ins is the same as the process you used to activate the Solver add-in. Most third-party add-ins provide detailed instructions for their installation and use.

Setting the Objective Cell and Variable Cells

Every Solver model needs an objective cell and one or more variable cells. An objective cell is a result cell that is maximized, minimized, or set to a specific value. A variable cell is an input cell that changes so that the objective cell can meet its defined goal.

In the Product Mix worksheet, cell B18, which displays the optimal net income, is the objective cell whose value you want to maximize. The cells in the range B4:E4, which contains the number of bikes produced and sold by the company under the optimal product mix, are the variable cells whose values you want Solver to change.

REFERENCE

Setting Solver's Objective and Variable Cells

- On the DATA tab, in the Analysis group, click the Solver button.
- In the Set Objective box, specify the cell whose value you want to set to match a specific objective.
- Click the Max, Min, or Value Of option buttons to maximize the objective cell, minimize the objective cell, or set the objective cell to a specified value, respectively.
- In the By Changing Variable Cells input box, specify the changing cells.

You will start Solver now and define the objective cell and the variable cells.

To set up the Solver model:

1. On the DATA tab, in the Analysis group, click the **Solver** button. The Solver Parameters dialog box opens with the insertion point in the Set Objective box.

2. Click cell **B18** in the Product Mix worksheet.

3. Verify that the **Max** option button is selected. This option tells Solver to find the maximum net income value possible for cell B18.

EX 636 Excel | Tutorial 10 Performing What-If Analyses

4. Click the **By Changing Variable Cells** box, and then select the range **B4:E4** in the Product Mix worksheet. The absolute reference to this range tells Solver to use the product mix values stored in these cells in order to maximize the value in cell B18. See Figure 10-34.

Figure 10-34 Solver Parameters dialog box

finds the maximum value of cell B18
variable cells
click to find the maximum value

Solver Parameters dialog:
- Set Objective: $B$18 — *objective cell*
- To: ● Max ○ Min ○ Value Of: 0
- By Changing Variable Cells: $B$4:$E$4
- Subject to the Constraints: (empty)
- Buttons: Add, Change, Delete, Reset All, Load/Save
- ✔ Make Unconstrained Variables Non-Negative
- Select a Solving Method: GRG Nonlinear
- Options
- Solving Method: Select the GRG Nonlinear engine for Solver Problems that are smooth nonlinear. Select the LP Simplex engine for linear Solver Problems, and select the Evolutionary engine for Solver problems that are non-smooth.
- Help, Solve, Close

5. Click the **Solve** button. Solver finds the maximum net income and the optimal product mix by evaluating different product mix combinations. The Solver Results dialog box opens, showing the results. See Figure 10-35.

Figure 10-35 Solver results

	A	B	C	D
1	CYCLE GREEN			
3	Product Mix Analysis	K100	K95	K85
4	Optimal Product Mix	2271319546	3314573064	5876067387
5	Current Product Mix	159	118	140
6	Change	2271319387	3314572946	5876067247
7	Sales Price per Model	$1,000.00	$1,800.00	$2,400.00
8	Revenue per Model (Optimal)	########	########	########
9	Material Cost per Model			
10	Manufacturing Cost per Model			
12	Summary	Optimal	Current	Change
13	Units Sold	19676085104	570	19676084534
14	Total Revenue	########	1,197,000.00	########
15	Total Material Cost	########	541,500.00	########
16	Total Manufacturing Cost	########	85,500.00	########
17	Total Fixed Expenses	445,000.00	445,000.00	0.00
18	Net Income	########	$125,000.00	########

Solver Results dialog:
- The Objective Cell values do not converge.
- ● Keep Solver Solution
- ○ Restore Original Values
- ☐ Return to Solver Parameters Dialog
- Reports: ☐ Outline Reports
- OK, Cancel, Save Scenario...
- ⚠ The Objective Cell values do not converge. Solver can make the Objective Cell as large (or small when minimizing) as it wants.

Solver finds unrealistically high numbers of bikes
choose to either keep the Solver solution or restore the original values from before Solver was run
select to return to Solver to try another model

The Solver results show that Cycle Green should produce and sell billions of bikes to maximize its net income—a nice idea, but hardly practical.

6. Click the **Restore Original Values** option button to reset the original product mix numbers.

7. Click the **Return to Solver Parameters Dialog** check box, and then click the **OK** button. The Product Mix worksheet returns to the original values for the optimal product mix cell, and the Solver Parameters dialog box reappears for another attempt.

The initial Solver model had no limits on the solution. Therefore, Solver kept increasing the number of bikes produced and sold to find the maximum net income because selling more bikes means more profit. To fix this problem, you must add constraints to the model.

Adding Constraints to Solver

Almost every Solver model needs one or more constraints. A constraint is a limit that is placed on the solution. Solver applies constraints to different result cells found within the worksheet. Solver supports the six types of constraints described in Figure 10-36.

Figure 10-36   **Constraint types**

Constraint	Description
<= , = , >=	Constrains the cell to be less than or equal to a defined value, equal to a defined value, or greater than or equal to a defined value
int	Constrains the cell to contain only integer values
bin	Constrains the cell to contain only binary values (0 or 1)
dif	Constrains the values in a cell range to be all different

© 2014 Cengage Learning

For example, you can use the <= constraint to limit the total number of bikes produced and sold to a reasonable number, or you can use the = constraint to ensure that a specific number of bikes are produced and sold, but no more and no less.

REFERENCE

Setting Constraints on the Solver Solution

- In the Solver Parameters dialog box, click the Add button.
- Enter the cell reference of the cell or cells containing the constraint.
- Select the constraint type (<=, =, >=, int, bin, or dif).
- Enter the constraint value in the Constraint box.
- Click the OK button to add the constraint and return to the Solver Parameters dialog box.
- Repeat for each constraint you want to add.

Gianna wants to limit the total number of bikes sold to exactly 570 so that she can compare the optimal product mix results to the results of the current product mix, which produces and sells 570 bikes. You will add an = constraint to Solver.

Excel | Tutorial 10 Performing What-If Analyses

To add the units sold constraint to Solver:

1. In the Solver Parameters dialog box, click the **Add** button. The Add Constraint dialog box opens with the insertion point in the Cell Reference box.

2. Click cell **B13** in the Product Mix worksheet to enter the absolute cell reference to the Optimal Units Sold value.

3. Click the **arrow** next to the constraint type box (the center box), and then click **=** in the list to specify an equal to constraint.

4. In the Constraint box, type **570**. The constraint limits cell B13 to be equal to 570. See Figure 10-37.

> **TIP**
> Constraints can be applied only to adjacent ranges. For a nonadjacent range, you need to apply separate constraints to each separate part of the range.

Figure 10-37 Add Constraint dialog box

constrains the total number of bikes to exactly 570

Cell Reference: $B$13 = Constraint: 570

5. Click the **OK** button. The Solver Parameters dialog box reappears with the constraint $B$13=570 added to the Solver model.

6. Click the **Solve** button. The Solver Results dialog box opens, indicating that the solution that Solver found satisfies the objective and constraints. Solver's solution, shown in the Product Mix worksheet, is that the company should produce only K5 road bikes and no other model. See Figure 10-38.

Figure 10-38 Solver results with one constraint

the most profitable model is the K5 road bike

total units sold fixed at 570 bikes

	A	B	C	D	E
1	**CYCLE GREEN**				
2					
3	Product Mix Analysis	K100	K95	K85	K5
4	Optimal Product Mix	0	0	0	570.0000058
5	Current Product Mix	159	118	140	153
6	Change	-159	-118	-140	417.0000058
7	Sales Price per Model	$1,000.00	$1,800.00	$2,400.00	$3,200.00
8	Revenue per Model (Optimal)	$0.00	$0.00	$0.00	$1,824,000.02
9	Material Cost per Model	$498.00	$667.00	$1,009.00	$1,584.00
10	Manufacturing Cost per Model	$131.00	$150.00	$153.00	$167.00
11					
12	Summary	Optimal	Current	Change	
13	Units Sold	570	570	0	
14	Total Revenue	1,824,000.02	1,197,000.00	627,000.02	
15	Total Material Cost	902,880.01	541,500.00	361,380.01	
16	Total Manufacturing Cost	95,190.00	85,500.00	9,690.00	
17	Total Fixed Expenses	445,000.00	445,000.00	0.00	
18	Net Income	$380,930.01	$125,000.00	$255,930.01	

Gianna has several problems with this solution. First, Cycle Green cannot limit its production to only the K5 bike because there is not enough demand for only that model. Second, Cycle Green wants to diversify its offerings by producing and selling a variety of bicycle models to attract a wide range of customers. Finally, the value in cell E4 is not an integer; Cycle Green cannot produce and sell fractions of a bike.

To fix these problems, you will add two more constraints to the Solver model—(1) The company must produce at least 115 units of each model; and (2) the number of bikes produced and sold must be an integer value.

To apply additional constraints to the model:

1. Click the **Restore Original Values** option button, verify that the **Return to Solver Parameters Dialog** check box is selected, and then click the **OK** button to return to the Solver Parameters dialog box.

2. Click the **Add** button. The Add Constraint dialog box opens with the insertion point in the Cell Reference box.

3. Select the range **B4:E4** in the Product Mix worksheet, select **>=** as the constraint type, and then enter **115** in the Constraint box. This specifies that each value in the range B4:E4 must be greater than or equal to 115.

4. Click the **Add** button to add the constraint to the Solver model. The Add Constraint dialog box remains open so you can add another constraint.

5. Select the range **B4:E4** in the Product Mix worksheet, and then select **int** as the constraint type. The word "integer" is added to the Constraint box. This constraint specifies that each value in the range B4:E4 must be an integer.

6. Click the **OK** button to add the constraint to the model and return to the Solver Parameters dialog box.

7. Click the **Solve** button. The Solver results appear in the Product Mix worksheet. See Figure 10-39.

Figure 10-39 Solver model with added constraints

	A	B	C	D	E
1	CYCLE GREEN				
2					
3	Product Mix Analysis	K100	K95	K85	K5
4	Optimal Product Mix	115	115	115	225
5	Current Product Mix	159	118	140	153
6	Change	-44	-3	-25	72
7	Sales Price per Model	$1,000.00	$1,800.00	$2,400.00	$3,200.00
8	Revenue per Model (Optimal)	$115,000.00	$207,000.00	$276,000.00	$720,000.00
9	Material Cost per Model	$498.00	$667.00	$1,009.00	$1,584.00
10	Manufacturing Cost per Model	$131.00	$150.00	$153.00	$167.00
11					
12	Summary	Optimal	Current	Change	
13	Units Sold	570	570	0	
14	Total Revenue	1,318,000.00	1,197,000.00	121,000.00	
15	Total Material Cost	606,410.00	541,500.00	64,910.00	
16	Total Manufacturing Cost	87,485.00	85,500.00	1,985.00	
17	Total Fixed Expenses	445,000.00	445,000.00	0.00	
18	Net Income	$179,105.00	$125,000.00	$54,105.00	

- the company must produce at least 115 units of each model
- net income increases by $54,105 under this product mix

> 8. Click the **Return to Solver Parameters Dialog** check box to deselect it.
>
> 9. Click the **OK** button to keep the Solver solution.

As you can see in the Product Mix worksheet, Solver's solution is a product mix in which Cycle Green produces and sells 225 K5 bikes and 115 of each of the other three models. With this product mix, the company will show a net income of $179,105, which is an increase of $54,105 over the current product mix.

Although this product mix is the most profitable to the company, production is limited by the number of available parts. In the Product Mix worksheet, Gianna included a table that tracks the number of parts each model requires, the quantity of each part currently available, and the number of parts remaining after the proposed production run. Figure 10-40 shows the parts usage under the optimal product mix you just found using Solver.

Figure 10-40   Parts remaining after the production run for the proposed product mix

	F	G	H	I	J	K	L	M	N
19		Parts Available							
20		Part	Available	Used	Remaining				
21		Superlight aluminum frame	321	230	91				
22		Carbon fiber frame	298	340	(42)				
23		Standard performance fork	311	230	81				
24		Road endurance fork	181	115	66				
25		Carbon fiber control fork	175	225	(50)				
26		CC drive train	175	115	60		the proposed product mix requires more parts than are currently available		
27		CC extended drive train	277	230	47				
28		CC wireless drive train	182	225	(43)				
29		CC standard brake system	463	345	118				
30		CC extended brake system	205	225	(20)				
31		CC commuter bars	163	115	48				
32		CC road bars	301	230	71				
33		CC triathlon bars	215	225	(10)				
34		Installation kit	703	570	133				

Cycle Green cannot manufacture the bikes in the proposed product mix because it lacks enough carbon fiber frames, carbon fiber control forks, wireless drive trains, extended brake systems, and triathlon bars. Gianna asks you to add one more constraint that limits the company to produce a bike only when it has all of the required parts.

To add a constraint limiting the product mix to the available parts:

> 1. On the DATA tab, in the Analysis group, click the **Solver** button. The Solver Parameters dialog box opens showing the current Solver model.
>
> 2. Click the **Add** button. The Add Constraint dialog box opens.
>
> 3. Select the range **J21:J34**, which contains the number of parts remaining after the production run, select **>=** as the constraint type, and then type **0** in the Constraint box to force all of the values in the range J21:J34 to be greater than or equal to 0. Solver will use parts as needed until none are remaining.
>
> 4. Click the **OK** button. See Figure 10-41.

Tutorial 10 Performing What-If Analyses | Excel   EX 641

Figure 10-41   Final Solver model

Solver Parameters dialog box

- Set Objective: $B$18
- To: ● Max   ○ Min   ○ Value Of: 0
- By Changing Variable Cells: $B$4:$E$4
- Subject to the Constraints:
  - $B$13 = 570
  - $B$4:$E$4 = integer
  - $B$4:$E$4 >= 115
  - $J$21:$J$34 >= 0

Callouts:
- four constraints
- click to add a new constraint (Add)
- click to change a selected constraint (Change)
- click to delete a selected constraint (Delete)
- click to reset the Solver model (Reset All)
- Load/Save

☑ Make Unconstrained Variables Non-Negative

Select a Solving Method: GRG Nonlinear   Options

Solving Method
Select the GRG Nonlinear engine for Solver Problems that are smooth nonlinear. Select the LP Simplex engine for linear Solver Problems, and select the Evolutionary engine for Solver problems that are non-smooth.

Help   Solve   Close

▶ 5. Scroll to the top of the Product Mix worksheet so you'll see the Solver results.
▶ 6. Click the **Solve** button. Solver displays the solution it found. See Figure 10-42.

Figure 10-42   Final Solver solution

optimal product mix that satisfies all four constraints

CYCLE GREEN

	A	B	C	D	E
3	Product Mix Analysis	K100	K95	K85	K5
4	Optimal Product Mix	118	154	123	175
5	Current Product Mix	159	118	140	153
6	Change	-41	36	-17	22
7	Sales Price per Model	$1,000.00	$1,800.00	$2,400.00	$3,200.00
8	Revenue per Model (Optimal)	$118,000.00	$277,200.00	$295,200.00	$560,000.00
9	Material Cost per Model	$498.00	$667.00	$1,009.00	$1,584.00
10	Manufacturing Cost per Model	$131.00	$150.00	$153.00	$167.00

	A	B Optimal	C Current	D Change
12	Summary			
13	Units Sold	570	570	0
14	Total Revenue	1,250,400.00	1,197,000.00	53,400.00
15	Total Material Cost	562,789.00	541,500.00	21,289.00
16	Total Manufacturing Cost	86,602.00	85,500.00	1,102.00
17	Total Fixed Expenses	445,000.00	445,000.00	0.00
18	Net Income	$156,009.00	$125,000.00	$31,009.00

optimal product mix increases net income by $31,009

net income under the optimal product mix

... | Income Statement | **Product Mix** | Scenario Summary | Scenario PivotTable | ⊕

READY

▶ 7. Click the **OK** button in the Solver Results dialog box, and then click the **Close** button in the Solver Parameters dialog box to accept the Solver solution.

▶ 8. Scroll through the worksheet to verify that all four constraints have been met, including the constraint that manufacturing the bikes in the proposed product mix will not exceed the number of available parts.

These results show that if Cycle Green can produce and sell 118 K100 bikes, 154 K95 bikes, 123 K85 bikes, and 175 K5 bikes, the company will generate a net income of $156,009, which is an increase of $31,009 over the current product mix. Gianna will share these figures with Cycle Green's marketing team to determine whether there is sufficient demand to support this product mix.

INSIGHT

Understanding the Iterative Process

Solver arrives at optimal solutions through an **iterative procedure**, in which Solver starts with an initial solution (usually the current values from the worksheet) and uses that as a basis to calculate a new set of values. If those values improve the value of the objective cell, the new values are used as a basis to generate the next set of values. If they don't improve the solution, Solver tries a different set of values. Each step, or iteration, in this process improves the solution until Solver reaches the point where the new solutions are not significantly better than the solution from the previous step. At that point, Solver will stop and indicate that it has found an answer.

What does "significantly better" mean? The default convergence value is 0.001, which means that if the change in the value of the objective cell between the current solution and the previous solution is less than or equal to 0.001, Solver stops the iterative process and reports the current solution.

Solver will also stop if it is not making progress toward a solution. The default length of time that Solver will spend on the iterative process is 100 seconds or 100 total iterations (whichever comes first). If 100 seconds or 100 iterations have passed and Solver has not found a solution, it will report this fact. At that point, you can have Solver continue the iterative process or stop the process without finding a solution. If Solver is taking too long to find a solution, you can halt the program at any time by pressing the Esc key. If you want to see the iterative process in action, click the Show Iteration Results check box in the Options dialog box, and Excel will pause after each iteration and show the intermediate solution.

Creating a Solver Answer Report

TIP
You cannot display sensitivity and limits reports when the Solver model contains integer constraints.

Solver can create three different reports—an answer report, a sensitivity report, and a limits report—that you can use to evaluate the solution that Solver produced. The **answer report** is probably the most useful because it summarizes the results of a successful solution by displaying information about the objective cell, changing cells, and constraints. This report includes the original and final values for the objective and changing cells, as well as the constraint formulas. The **sensitivity report** and **limits report** are often used in science and engineering to investigate the mathematical aspects of the Solver solution. These reports allow you to quantify the reliability of the solution.

Tutorial 10 Performing What-If Analyses | Excel   EX 643

Gianna wants you to create an answer report, which will provide information on the process used to determine the optimal product mix. To ensure that the answer report includes information on the entire process, you'll set the quantities back to their original values, and then you will run the Solver model again.

To create an answer report for the optimal product mix:

1. In the range **B4:E4**, enter **159**, **118**, **140**, and **175**, respectively, to return to the original product mix.

2. On the DATA tab, in the Analysis group, click the **Solver** button to open the Solver Parameters dialog box, and then click the **Solve** button to run Solver.

3. In the Solver Results dialog box, click **Answer** in the Reports box, and then verify that the **Keep Solver Solution** option button is selected.

4. Click the **Outline Reports** check box so that Solver returns its report using Excel's outline tools. See Figure 10-43.

Figure 10-43   Solver Results dialog box with answer report

select to display an answer report summarizing the results

select to display the answer report with Excel's outline buttons

click to save the Solver solution as a scenario

TIP
Answer reports are named Answer Report 1, Answer Report 2, and so forth, with the newest report assigned the next highest available number.

5. Click the **OK** button to accept the solution and generate the answer report in a separate sheet called Answer Report 1.

6. Click the **Close** button to close the Solver Parameters dialog box.

7. Drag the **Answer Report 1** worksheet to the end of the workbook, and then rename the worksheet **Optimal Product Mix**.

The answer report is long. With the outline tools turned on, some of the report is hidden.

8. Click the last three **expand outline buttons** + to view more detailed information about the variable cells and the constraints used in the solution. See Figure 10-44.

Figure 10-44 Solver Answer report

answer report titles and technical information about the solution

	A	B	C	D	E	F	G
1	Microsoft Excel 15.0 Answer Report						
2	Worksheet: [Cycle Green.xlsx]Product Mix						
3	Report Created: 6/10/2016 11:38:16 AM						
4	Result: Solver found a solution. All Constraints and optimality conditions are satisfied.						
5	Solver Engine						
9	Solver Options						
13							

information about the objective cell

14	Objective Cell (Max)					
15	Cell	Name		Original Value	Final Value	
16	$B$18	Net Income Optimal		$125,000.00	$156,009.00	

information about the variable cells

19	Variable Cells					
20	Cell	Name		Original Value	Final Value	Integer
21	$B$4:$E$4					
22	$B$4	Optimal Product Mix K100		159	118	Integer
23	$C$4	Optimal Product Mix K95		118	154	Integer
24	$D$4	Optimal Product Mix K85		140	123	Integer
25	$E$4	Optimal Product Mix K5		153	175	Integer

information about the impact of the constraints on the solution

29	Constraints					
30	Cell	Name	Cell Value	Formula	Status	Slack
31	$B$13	Units Sold Optimal	570	$B$13=570	Binding	0
32	$J$21:$J$34 >= 0					
33	$J$21	Superlight aluminum frame Remaining	49	$J$21>=0	Not Binding	49
34	$J$22	Carbon fiber frame Remaining	0	$J$22>=0	Binding	0
35	$J$23	Standard performance fork Remaining	39	$J$23>=0	Not Binding	39
36	$J$24	Road endurance fork Remaining	58	$J$24>=0	Not Binding	58

The answer report is divided into the following sections:

- The Title section identifies the worksheet containing the Solver model, the date on which the report was created, and whether Solver found a solution.
- The Solver Engine section provides technical information about how long Solver took to find a solution.
- The Solver Options section lists the technical options used by Solver in arriving at a solution.
- The Object Cell section provides the original and final value of the objective cell.
- The Variable Cells section lists the original and final values of the variable cells used in the solution.
- The Constraints section lists the constraints imposed on the solution by Solver.

The status of each constraint is listed as either Binding or Not Binding. A **binding constraint** is a constraint that must be included in the Solver model, and is a limiting factor in arriving at the solution. The other possibility is a **nonbinding constraint**, which is a constraint that did not need to be included as part of the Solver model. For example, the constraint that the number of units produced and sold be equal to 570 is a binding constraint that limited the solutions available to Solver. On the other hand, the constraint in the range B4:E4 that the company produce and sell at least 115 of each model turned out to be nonbinding. Once Cycle Green was limited to producing exactly 570 bikes and was limited by the available parts on hand to manufacture those bikes, the optimal product mix would have resulted in the company producing at least 115 of each bike model anyway.

The last column in the Constraints section shows the slack for each constraint. The **slack** is the difference between the value in the cell and the value at the limit of the constraint. A binding constraint always shows a slack of 0, while nonbinding constraints show a non-zero value. For example, the slack for cell J21, the number of aluminum frames remaining in stock, is 49. This indicates that when Solver found the optimal product mix, there were still 49 aluminum frames in stock, ready to be used. As a result, the availability of aluminum frames was not a limiting factor in the solution.

Decision Making: Choosing a What-If Analysis Tool

Part of performing an effective what-if analysis is deciding which what-if analysis tool to use. Each tool has its own set of advantages and disadvantages. Data tables are best used when you want to perform several what-if analyses involving one or two input cells and you need to display the analysis in a tabular format. Data tables can also be easily displayed as charts, providing a visual picture of the relationship between your input values and the result values.

For what-if analyses involving more than two input cells, you must create a scenario. Scenario summary tables and scenario PivotTables can be used to obtain a quick snapshot of several possible outcomes, and scenarios can be merged and shared among several workbooks.

Data tables and scenarios can provide a lot of information, but they cannot easily deliver a single solution or "best outcome." If you need to maximize or minimize a value, you must use Solver. You can also use Solver to set a calculated cell to a specific value. However, if you don't need to specify any constraints on your solution, it is generally quicker and easier to use Goal Seek.

Saving and Loading Solver Models

Sometimes you might want to apply several Solver models to the same data. For example, in addition to knowing what product mix maximizes the company's net income, Gianna wants to know what product mix minimizes the company's total cost spent on materials. To determine this, you would use another Solver model. However, creating another Solver model in the worksheet overwrites the previous model. If you later wanted to rerun the first model, you would have to reenter its parameters. Instead, you can store the Solver parameters for a model in worksheet cells that you can later retrieve and use to rerun that Solver model.

Saving and Loading a Solver Model

To save a Solver model:
- Open the Solver dialog box.
- Click the Load/Save button, and then select an empty range containing the number of cells specified in the dialog box.
- Click the Save button.

To load a Solver model:
- Open the Solver dialog box.
- Click the Load/Save button, and then select the range containing the saved model.
- Click the Load button.

Before running the second Solver problem for Gianna, you'll store the parameters of the current model that maximizes the company's net income.

To save the current model:

1. Go to the **Product Mix** worksheet.
2. On the DATA tab, in the Analysis group, click the **Solver** button. The Solver Parameters dialog box opens.
3. Click the **Load/Save** button. The Load/Save dialog box opens, specifying that you need to select an empty range with eight cells to store the model.
4. Select the range **A21:A28** in the Product Mix worksheet. You'll store the Solver parameters in this range.
5. Click the **Save** button. The information about the Solver model is entered in the range A21:A28 and the Solver Parameters dialog box reappears.
6. Click the **Close** button to close the Solver Parameters dialog box.
7. In cell **A20**, enter **Maximum Net Income Model**, and then format the text with the **40% - Accent6** cell style. See Figure 10-45.

Figure 10-45 Saved Solver model

	A	B	C	D	E	F
12	Summary	Optimal	Current	Change		CC standa
13	Units Sold	570	570	0		CC extend
14	Total Revenue	1,250,400.00	1,197,000.00	53,400.00		CC comm
15	Total Material Cost	562,789.00	541,500.00	21,289.00		CC road b
16	Total Manufacturing Cost	86,602.00	85,500.00	1,102.00		CC triathl
17	Total Fixed Expenses	445,000.00	445,000.00	0.00		Installatio
18	Net Income	$156,009.00	$125,000.00	$31,009.00		
19						Parts Ava
20	Maximum Net Income Model					Part
21	$156,009.00					Superlight
22	4					Carbon fil
23	TRUE					Standard
24	TRUE					Road end
25	TRUE					Carbon fil
26	TRUE					CC drive t
27	32767					CC extend
28	0					CC wirele
29						CC standa
30						CC extend

- current value of the objective cell → $156,009.00
- logical values indicate whether the four constraints are currently met in the worksheet → TRUE values
- number of changing cells in the model → 4
- Solver options saved as an array of numbers → 32767, 0

The first parameter in cell A21 displays $156,009, which is the value of the objective cell under this model. The second parameter in cell A22 displays 4, indicating the number of variable cells in the model. The next four cells display TRUE, which correspond to the constraints in the model. TRUE indicates that the values currently in the worksheet satisfy the constraints. If you later change some of the worksheet data so that it violates a constraint, the Solver parameter cells will display FALSE. The cells provide a quick visual check that all of the model's conditions are still being met as the worksheet is modified. The final two cells, cells A27 and A28, are used to store the technical options for the iterative process by which Solver arrives at a solution (refer to the InSight box "Understanding the Iterative Process").

Now that you have saved this Solver model, you can create a second model to determine the product mix that minimizes the material cost for Cycle Green. Gianna wants to know what product mix would result in the lowest material cost given that the company still wants to produce 570 bikes and still wants to make at least 115 of each model. The objective cell for this model is cell B15 instead of cell B18.

To determine the product mix that minimizes the total material cost:

1. On the ribbon, click the **DATA** tab. In the Analysis group, click the **Solver** button. The Solver Parameters dialog box opens. The cell reference in the Set Objective box is selected.

2. Click cell **B15** in the Product Mix worksheet. The objective cell changes to $B$15, which is the absolute reference to cell B15, which contains the optimal total material cost.

3. Click the **Min** option button. You want Solver to find the minimum value for cell B15. The changing cells and constraints you used to find the maximum net income remain unchanged for this model.

4. Click the **Solve** button. Solver finds the product mix that minimizes the total material cost. See Figure 10-46.

Figure 10-46 Solver solution for minimizing the total material cost

	A	B	C	D	E
1	CYCLE GREEN				
2					
3	Product Mix Analysis	K100	K95	K85	K5
4	Optimal Product Mix	163	148	129	130
5	Current Product Mix	159	118	140	153
6	Change	4	30	-11	-23
7	Sales Price per Model	$1,000.00	$1,800.00	$2,400.00	$3,200.00
8	Revenue per Model (Optimal)	$163,000.00	$266,400.00	$309,600.00	$416,000.00
9	Material Cost per Model	$498.00	$667.00	$1,009.00	$1,584.00
10	Manufacturing Cost per Model	$131.00	$150.00	$153.00	$167.00
11					
12	Summary	Optimal	Current	Change	
13	Units Sold	570	570	0	
14	Total Revenue	1,155,000.00	1,197,000.00	(42,000.00)	
15	Total Material Cost	515,971.00	541,500.00	(25,529.00)	
16	Total Manufacturing Cost	85,000.00	85,500.00	(500.00)	
17	Total Fixed Expenses	445,000.00	445,000.00	0.00	
18	Net Income	$109,029.00	$125,000.00	($15,971.00)	

- product mix to minimize the total material cost
- minimum material cost based on the constraints
- optimal material cost is $25,529 less than the current material cost

5. Click the **OK** button to close the Solver Results dialog box.

The minimum material cost to the company is $515,971 which is $25,529 less than the material cost under the current product mix. This is the optimal solution based on the constraints that the company must produce exactly 570 bikes, produce at least 115 units of each model, and not exceed the available parts. You will save this model in the Product Mix worksheet.

To save the model to minimize material costs:

1. In cell **A30**, enter **Minimum Material Cost Model**, and then format the text with the **40% - Accent6** cell style.

2. Reopen Solver, and then in the Solver Parameters dialog box, click the **Load/Save** button. The Load/Save Model dialog box opens.

3. Select the range **A31:A38** in the Product Mix worksheet to specify the eight cells in which to save the model.

4. Click the **Save** button. The current Solver model is saved in the Product Mix worksheet.

You have two Solver models saved in the Product Mix worksheet—the Maximum Net Income model and the Minimum Material Cost model. You can quickly reload each of these Solver models in the worksheet from the Solver Parameters dialog box.

Gianna wants the worksheet to display the Solver model that maximizes net income for the company. You'll load and run the Maximum Net Income model.

To load the Maximum Net Income model and run it:

1. In the Solver Parameters dialog box, click the **Load/Save** button. The Load/Save Model dialog box opens.

2. Select the range **A21:A28** in the Product Mix worksheet. This range contains the parameters of the Maximum Net Income model.

3. Click the **Load** button to load the Solver parameters from the worksheet. The Load Model dialog box opens, asking whether you want to replace the current model or merge the new model with the current model. You want to replace the current model.

> **TIP**
> To combine the Solver model with the model currently used in the worksheet, click the Merge button.

4. Click the **Replace** button. The Solver Parameters dialog box reappears. The parameters for the Maximum Net Income model have replaced the parameters for the Minimum Material Cost model.

5. Click the **Solve** button. Solver runs the Maximum Net Income model, and then the Solver Results dialog box opens.

6. Click the **OK** button to keep the Solver solution.

7. Save the Cycle Green workbook, and then close it.

By saving the Solver model parameters to cells on the worksheet, you can create as many models as you need to effectively analyze the data. You can then load and apply these different models to your analysis as new data is entered.

You have finished analyzing how Cycle Green can maximize its profits by modifying its product mix. Through the use of data tables, Excel scenarios, and Solver models, you provided Gianna with several pricing and production options to increase the company's net income for the upcoming year.

Session 10.3 Quick Check

1. What is an add-in?
2. What are three options for the objective cell using Solver?
3. What is an objective cell? What is a variable cell?
4. What are the six types of constraints you can put on a cell in a Solver model?
5. What is the difference between a binding constraint and a nonbinding constraint?
6. In the Solver report, what is meant by the term "slack"?
7. How do you save several Solver models on a single worksheet?
8. What is an iterative procedure?

SAM Projects

Put your skills into practice with SAM Projects! SAM Projects for this tutorial can be found online. If you have a SAM account, go to www.cengage.com/sam2013 to download the most recent Project Instructions and Start Files.

Review Assignments

Data File needed for the Review Assignments: **Mountain.xlsx**

Cycle Green is expanding its product mix into a new line of mountain bikes. Gianna has created a workbook with an income statement detailing the revenue and expenses associated with this new lineup. She wants you to perform what-if analyses of the data and determine the optimal product mix. Complete the following:

1. Open the **Mountain** workbook located in the Excel10 ▸ Review folder included with your Data Files, and then save the workbook as **Mountain Bikes** in the location specified by your instructor.
2. In the Documentation worksheet, enter your name and the date.
3. In the Income Statement worksheet, in cell D4, enter a formula that references cell B4. In cell E4 through cell G4, enter formulas that reference cell B24 through cell B26, respectively.
4. In the range D5:D13, enter bikes sold values of **100** up to **900** in increments of 100.
5. In the range D4:G13, create a one-variable data table using **$B$4** as the column input cell to explore the impact of different sales volumes on revenue, expenses, and net income.
6. Create a cost-volume-profit chart as a scatter chart in the range B14:G26. Format the chart appropriately.
7. Complete the following steps to create a two-variable data table to analyze the impact of price and sales volume on net income:
   a. In cell I4, enter a formula using a defined name to reference cell B26.
   b. Format cell I4 so that it displays the text **Bikes Sold**.
   c. In the range I5:I13, enter sales volume values of **100** up to **900** in increments of 100.
   d. In the range J4:N4, enter average bike prices of **$600** up to **$1,000** in increments of $100.
   e. In the range I4:N13, insert a two-variable data table using **$B$5** as the row input cell and **$B$4** as the column input cell.
8. In the range I14:N26, create a scatter chart of the net income values from the two-variable data table, displaying each average sales price as a different line in the chart. Format the chart appropriately; make sure that the chart legend identifies each line by the average sales price value listed in row 4.
9. Use the Scenario Manager to analyze the financial impact of the different scenarios listed in Figure 10-47.

Figure 10-47 What-if scenarios for mountain bikes

Input Cells	Status Quo	Increased Production	Reduced Production	Spring Sale
Units Sold (cell B4)	330	500	250	600
Average Price per Unit (cell B5)	$890	$820	$800	$775
Salaries and Benefits (cell B17)	$150,000	$200,000	$100,000	$175,000
Advertising (cell B18)	$10,000	$30,000	$5,000	$40,000
Administrative (cell B19)	$15,000	$30,000	$5,000	$25,000
Miscellaneous (cell B20)	$5,000	$10,000	$5,000	$10,000

© 2014 Cengage Learning

10. Create a scenario summary report of the four scenarios proposed by Gianna, displaying the total revenue, total expenses, and net income under each scenario. Move the worksheet to the end of the workbook. Add a comment to the workbook noting the highest net income to the company.

11. Based on the values in the Income Statement worksheet, create a Scenario PivotTable report of the four scenarios displaying the total revenue, total expenses, and net income under each scenario. Move the Scenario PivotTable to the end of the worksheet.

12. Format the Scenario PivotTable worksheet as follows:
    a. Remove the filter from the PivotTable.
    b. In cell A1, enter **Scenario Report** and format the text using the Title cell style.
    c. Format the revenue, expense, and net income values using the Currency format with negative numbers displayed in red and enclosed within parentheses.
    d. Add a PivotChart of the PivotTable displaying the data as a clustered column chart positioned over the range A8:E21. Format the chart to make it easy to read and interpret.

13. The Product Mix worksheet lists four mountain bike models produced by Cycle Green. Use Solver to find the product mix that maximizes the value in cell B18 by changing the values in the range B4:E4.

14. Apply the following constraints to your model:
    - The total bikes produced and sold as indicated in cell B13 must be 330.
    - Only integer numbers of each bike model indicated in the range B4:E4 can be produced and sold.
    - At least 50 units of each bike model must be produced and sold.
    - The number of parts remaining, as indicated in the range J21:J34, after the production run must be greater than or equal to 0.

15. Run Solver and note how much net income increases under the Solver model.

16. Save the parameters of the Solver model to the range A21:A28 in the Product Mix worksheet. Enter the text **Maximum Net Income Model** in cell A20.

17. Restore the values in the range B4:E4 to their current product mix value, and then rerun Solver. Create an answer report detailing the Solver solution, and then move the Answer Report 1 worksheet to the end of the workbook.

18. In the Product Mix worksheet, change the Solver model so that it minimizes the total material cost in cell B15. Save the parameters of this model to the range A31:A38, and then enter the text **Minimum Material Expenses** in cell A30.

19. Reload the Maximum Net Income Model into Solver and run Solver to display the product mix that results in the maximum net income.

20. Save the workbook, and then close it.

Case Problem 1

Data File needed for this Case Problem: Loan.xlsx

Stewart Financial Diane Haas, a financial officer at Stewart Financial located in Gulfport, Mississippi, needs to analyze loans with different interest rates. She wants to use one-variable and two-variable data tables that explore how modifying the interest rate and length of the loan affects the cost of the loan. She also wants to create scenarios based on the current interest rates for 10-year, 15-year, 20-year, and 30-year fixed loans. She has asked you to help develop the workbook. Complete the following:

1. Open the **Loan** workbook located in the Excel10 ▸ Case1 folder included with your Data Files, and then save the workbook as **Loan Analysis** in the location specified by your instructor.

2. In the Documentation worksheet, enter your name and the current date.

3. In the Loan Analysis worksheet, in the range B3:B5, enter the conditions for a $250,000 loan at an annual interest rate of 3.6 percent, with 12 monthly payments per year.

4. In the range B6:B8, calculate the interest rate per month, enter **30** for the total number of years on the loan, and calculate the total number of payments over those 30 years.
5. In the range B10:B12, use the PMT function to calculate the total monthly payment, calculate the total of all monthly payments over the 30-year loan, and calculate the cost of the loan (equal to the loan amount plus the total payments).
6. In the range D3:G25, complete the following steps to create a one-variable data table that shows the financial values for different annual interest rates:
   a. In row 4, enter references to the loan's annual interest rate, monthly payment, total payments, and cost of the loan.
   b. In the range D5:D25, enter interest rates from **2%** up to **4.5%** in increments of **0.125%**.
   c. In the range E5:G25, create a one-variable data table to calculate the financial values in the table.
7. In the range I4:M25, complete the following steps to create a two-variable data table that shows the total cost of the loan for different combinations of interest rates and years until repayment:
   a. In the range I5:I25, enter interest rates from **2%** up to **4.5%** in increments of **0.125%**.
   b. In the range J4:M4, enter the year values **10**, **15**, **20**, and **30**.
   c. In cell I4, enter a reference to cell B12 containing the cost of the loan.
   d. In the range J5:M25, create a two-variable data table to display the total loan cost in the table.
8. Apply a custom format to cell I4 to display **Interest Rate** instead of the value in cell I4.
9. Create a Scatter with Straight Lines chart of the data in the two-variable data table in the range I5:M25. Use the Select Data command to name the four data series based on the Year values in the range J4:M4.
10. Move and resize the chart to cover the range A14:B25. Format the chart to make the content easily visible and understandable.
11. The more time given to repay a loan, the more the loan costs. But shorter loans usually have lower interest rates. Use the Scenario Manager to create the scenarios outlined in Figure 10-48 based on the current interest rates for 10-year, 15-year, 20-year, and 30-year mortgages. Add appropriate comments to each scenario.

Figure 10-48 Interest rate scenarios

Scenario	Interest Rate	Years	Loan
30 Year Fixed	3.625%	30	$250,000
20 Year Fixed	3.250%	20	$250,000
15 Year Fixed	2.625%	15	$250,000
10 Year Fixed	2.375%	10	$250,000

© 2014 Cengage Learning

12. Generate a scenario summary report that shows the values of the monthly payment, total payments, and cost of the loan under each scenario. Move the worksheet to the end of the workbook.
13. Create a Scenario PivotTable report showing only the cost of the loan under the four scenarios. Format the values using the Currency format with negative values displayed in red and enclosed in parentheses. Remove any filters from the PivotTable. In cell A1 of the Scenario PivotTable worksheet, enter **Scenario PivotTable**, and then format the cell with the Title cell style.
14. Add a PivotChart to the report displaying the cost of the loan as a clustered column chart. Format the chart appropriately to make the information clear and legible.
15. Move the Scenario PivotTable worksheet to the end of the workbook.
16. Save the workbook, and then close it.

Case Problem 2

Data File needed for this Case Problem: English.xlsx

English 117 Professor David Warren is the instructor of English 117 at Youngdale College in Danville, Virginia. Professor Warren and his teaching assistants have recently graded the semester final exam for the 140 students in the class. He needs to use Excel to determine an appropriate grading curve. Professor Warren wants roughly the top 15 percent of his students to receive an A, the next 45 percent to receive a B, the next 30 percent to receive a C, and the bottom 10 percent to receive a D. The professor has already created a workbook that contains the student scores and the start of a grading scale. He wants you to use the Scenario Manager and Solver to determine appropriate cutoff points for each grade. Complete the following:

1. Open the **English** workbook located in the Excel10 ▸ Case2 folder included with your Data Files, and then save the workbook as **English Grades** in the location specified by your instructor.
2. In the Documentation worksheet, enter your name and the current date.
3. In the Final Grades worksheet, the range E5:F8 will contain the lower and upper range for each grade, as follows:
   a. In the range E5:E8, enter the values **0**, **70**, **80**, and **90** to indicate that the lowest value Ds, Cs, Bs, and As are 0, 70, 80, and 90 points, respectively.
   b. In the range F5:F7, calculate the upper limit for each grade by entering a formula that returns a value 1 point less than the lowest value for the next grade. For example, the formula in cell F5 is **=E6–1**.
   c. In cell F8, enter **100** as the upper limit for an A.
4. In the range C5:C144, calculate each student's grade with the VLOOKUP function, using the final score in column B as the lookup value, the range E5:G8 as the lookup table, and the third column of that table as the return value. Use an approximate match to perform the lookup.
5. In the range H5:H8, use the COUNTIF function to count the number of students in the range C5:C144 who fall within each of the four possible class grades, using the letter grades in the range G5:G8 as the criteria.
6. In cell H9, calculate the total number of grades given.
7. In the range I5:I8, calculate the percentage of the students who received each grade.
8. In cell I9, calculate the total percentage given to four possible grades, confirming that the total percentage adds up to 100 percent.
9. The range K5:K8 uses the ABS function to calculate the absolute value of the difference between the percentages in column I and the percentage goals in column J. In cell K9, calculate the sum of the values in the range K5:K8. This represents the total difference between the observed distribution of grades and the curve that Professor Warren wants.
10. Use the Scenario Manager to enter the three grading scenarios outlined in Figure 10-49. Add appropriate comments to each scenario.

Figure 10-49   Possible grading scales

Input Cells	Standard Scale	Curved Scale	Highly Curved Scale
Lower Range for C	70	65	60
Lower Range for B	80	75	70
Lower Range for A	90	85	80

© 2014 Cengage Learning

11. Create a scenario summary report using the range E5:F8;K9 as the result cells. Mark the scenario that results in the smallest value for cell K9 with a comment indicating that it is the closest to Professor Warren's grading curve goal.

12. Show the best scenario in the workbook. Using that scale as a starting point, use Solver to find the grading scale that results in a minimum value for cell K9 by changing the lower range values in the range E6:E8 based on the following constraints:
    - Each value in the range E6:E8 must be an integer.
    - The value of cell E6 must be less than or equal to cell E7.
    - Cell E7 must be less than or equal to cell E8.
    - Cell E8 must be less than or equal to 100.
13. Run Solver to find the optimal solution that minimizes the total absolute difference.
14. Save the grading scale that Solver found as a fourth scenario named **Optimal Scale**. Add appropriate comments describing the grading scale.
15. Create a second scenario summary report in a worksheet named **Final Scenario Summary**. Move the Scenario Summary worksheet to the end of the workbook.
16. Save the workbook, and then close it.

Case Problem 3

Data File needed for this Case Problem: Optimal.xlsx

CyberBugs   Kerstin Nilsson is the business manager at CyberBugs, a toy company in Columbia, Missouri, that sells small robotic toys that mimic the appearance and actions of insects. Kerstin wants to create an income statement for the Basic CyberBugs kit. She wants to find the optimal price for selling the kit. From her market research, Kerstin projects that the company can sell 12,000 kits at $21 per kit.

Kerstin wants to know if the company's profits would increase if the sales price increased. Obviously, the higher the sales price, the higher the profit per kit; but the company might also sell fewer kits at the higher price, resulting in an overall loss of profit. The optimal price point occurs when the company can sell the most units possible at the highest price without hurting sales.

To calculate the optimal price point, you need to take into account the price elasticity of demand, which measures the response of sales volume to changes in price. From her research, Kerstin has determined a price elasticity value of 1.6 for CyberBugs products, which basically means that a 10 percent increase in prices will cause a 16 percent decline in sales. Taking this information into account, Kerstin asks you to determine the price that results in the highest net income. Complete the following:

1. Open the **Optimal** workbook located in the Excel10 ▸ Case3 folder included with your Data Files, and then save the workbook as **Optimal Price Point** in the location specified by your instructor.
2. In the Documentation worksheet, enter your name and the current date.
3. In the Income Statement worksheet, in cell C10, enter **21** as the price per CyberBug kit. Kerstin has already inserted the basic information about the Price Elasticity of Demand. Based on her calculations in cell C11, the company can sell 12,000 kits if the price per kit is $21.
4. In cell C12, calculate the projected revenue by multiplying the price per kit by the number of kits produced.
5. The company plans to manufacture about 3 percent more kits than it sells. In cell C15, calculate the kits produced by multiplying the value in C11 by 1.03.
6. In cell C16, enter a material cost per kit of **$7.20**, and in cell C17, calculate the total material cost by multiplying the material per kit by the number of kits produced.
7. In cell C18, enter a manufacturing cost per kit of **$4.80**, and in cell C19, calculate the total manufacturing cost for all of the kits produced.
8. In cell C20, calculate the total variable expenses by adding the total material cost and the total manufacturing cost for all of the kits produced by the company.
9. In the range C23:C25, enter fixed expenses of **$15,000** for advertising, **$35,000** for administration, and **$15,000** for miscellaneous expenses. In cell C26, calculate the total fixed expenses.

10. In cell C29, reference the total revenue from cell C12. In cell C30, calculate the sum of the variable and fixed expenses. In cell C31, calculate the net income (revenue minus total expenses).
11. In the range E5:I36, set up a one-variable data table that tracks the effect of changing price on kits sold, total revenue, total expenses, and net income. In cell E5, reference the price per kit from cell C10. In cell F5, reference the kits sold from cell C11. In the range G5:I5, reference the total revenue, total expenses, and net income from the range C29:C31. In the range E6:E36, enter price values from **$15** up to **$30** in increments of $0.50.
12. Complete the one-variable data table by calculating the remaining values in the range F6:I36.
13. Create a scatter chart with smooth lines, plotting net income versus price per unit using the values in the ranges I6:I36 and E6:E36, respectively. Move and resize the chart to cover the range K4:P17, and format it appropriately to make the chart easy to read and interpret.
14. Use Solver to find the sales price in cell C10 that maximizes the company's net income. The company has a contract with a building shop and must manufacture at least 8000 kits; however, Kerstin does not feel the company should manufacture more than 12,000 kits at this time. Add those two constraints to your model.

Explore 15. Kerstin wants you to track Solver as it iterates toward a solution. Within Solver, click the Options button to open the Options dialog box. On the All Methods tab, click the Show Iteration Results check box to view the intermediate results as Solver approaches a solution. Run Solver with cell C10 in view, and then click the Continue button to move from one iteration to the next. Note the intermediate results for cell C10 and include them in a comment attached to cell C10 on the worksheet once Solver is done.

Explore 16. Create answer and limits reports for the Solver solution, and then move the report sheets to the end of the workbook.

17. Go to the answer report and add a comment indicating whether the constraints on the number of kits to be produced were binding on the Solver solution.

Explore 18. Go to the limits report. The limits report provides information on the upper and lower limits of the variable or changing cell given the constraints of the model. In this case, you can view the sales price and net income when the production run is at 8000 units and at 12,000 units. Add a comment to cell F14 indicating that this is the sales price and the net income when the production run is exactly 12,000 units. Add a comment to cell I14 indicating that this is the sales price and net income when the production run is exactly 8000 units.

19. Save the Solver model to the range K20:K25 on the Income Statement worksheet. In cell K19, enter **Solver Model** and format the label with the **Accent3** cell style.
20. Save the workbook, and then close it.

Case Problem 4

Data File needed for this Case Problem: Employee.xlsx

Sheffield Museum of Art   Brian Lewis is the personnel director at the Sheffield Museum of Art in Tempe, Arizona. One of his jobs is to create the work schedule for the museum attendants. The museum employs 16 attendants—14 are full-time and two are part-time. The museum needs eight attendants to work at the museum each weekday, 11 on Saturday, and nine on Sunday. Brian is currently working on the attendant schedule for the second week in June. Because it's summer, many employees are making vacation plans and have requested time off. Brian tries to accommodate all time-off requests while maintaining the required staff. It's an arduous task to arrange a schedule that pleases everyone. Brian has been developing a workbook to automatically generate the work schedule. The workbook already contains the names of the attendants and their time-off requests. He asks you to determine which attendants will be working which days. Complete the following:

1. Open the **Employee** workbook located in the Excel10 ▸ Case4 folder included with your Data Files, and then save the workbook as **Employee Schedule** in the location specified by your instructor.
2. In the Documentation worksheet, enter your name and the current date.

3. In the Schedule worksheet, you will indicate what shifts each employee is working by entering a 0 or a 1 in the range D5:J19. For example, a 1 in cell D5 would indicate that Kevin Adler is scheduled to work a shift that Monday, while a 0 would indicate that he is not working that day. In the range D5:J19, enter **0** in each cell to indicate that you have not yet scheduled any shift for any employee.
4. In the range K5:K19, enter formulas to calculate the total number of shifts for each employee.
5. In the range L5:L19, calculate the total number of hours worked by each employee. Each shift is eight hours.
6. In the range D21:J21, enter the number of shifts required per day. The museum requires eight shifts on weekdays, 11 shifts on Saturday, and nine shifts on Sunday.
7. In the range D22:J22, enter a formula that calculates the total number of shifts actually worked by the employees on each day.
8. In the range D23:J23, enter a formula to subtract the attendants required value from the attendants actually scheduled value. A negative number indicates that not enough employees have been scheduled to cover the day's shifts.
9. In cell D25, calculate the total shortfall in shifts by entering a formula to total the values in the range D23:J23.

Explore 10. Create a Solver model that sets the value of cell D25 to 0 by changing the values in the range D5:J19.

Explore 11. Add the following constraints to the model:
   a. Add a binary constraint to the Solver model to force every value in the range D5:J19 to be either a 0 or a 1.
   b. Add a constraint to limit the total hours worked by each full-time employee to less than or equal to 40.
   c. Add a constraint to limit the total hours worked by each part-time employee to less than or equal to 24.
   d. Add a constraint to require that the difference values in the range D23:J23 all equal 0.
   e. Based on the entries in the Notes column, add constraints to the Solver model so that employees are not scheduled to work shifts on days when they are unavailable to work.

12. Run the Solver model. Confirm that the schedule generated by Solver fulfills all of the requirements—all shifts are covered each day, no employee works more hours than allowed by his or her full- or part-time status, and no employee works on a requested day off.
13. Create a Solver answer report detailing the results of your model, and then move the Answer Report 1 worksheet to the end of the workbook.
14. Save the workbook, but do not close it.

Explore 15. Brian just learned that the museum will be having a special event during the opening of the Vatican Frescoes exhibit on Sunday. The museum director wants 10 attendants working on that day instead of nine. Revise the work schedule information, set the values in the range D5:J19 to **0**, and then rerun Solver to determine whether the schedule can be revised to accommodate the director's request. Write your analysis of the Solver results as a comment in cell D25 of the Schedule worksheet.

16. Save the revised workbook as **Employee Schedule 2**, and then close it.

TUTORIAL 11

Connecting to External Data

Building a Financial Report from Several Data Sources

OBJECTIVES

Session 11.1
- Import data from a text file
- Work with connections and external data ranges
- Define a trusted location

Session 11.2
- Understand databases and queries
- Use the Query Wizard to import data from several tables
- Edit a query
- Import tables from Access for use with a PivotTable
- Manage table relationships with PowerPivot

Session 11.3
- Create a web query
- Retrieve financial data using an Office app
- Access data from an XML document
- Work with XML data maps

Case | Chesterton Financial

Chesterton Financial is a brokerage firm in Burlington, Vermont. As part of its investment services business, the company advises clients on their investment portfolios. The investment counselors at the company need current financial data and reports, but they also must examine information on long-term trends in the market.

Some of this information comes from Excel workbooks, but other information is stored in specialized financial packages and statistical programs. In addition, the company maintains a database with detailed financial information about a variety of stocks, bonds, and funds. Company employees also use the Internet to receive up-to-the-minute market reports. Because much of the information that the counselors need comes from outside the company, they must retrieve information to analyze it and make decisions.

Rafael Garcia is an investment counselor at Chesterton Financial. He wants you to help him manage the different types of data available as he works on the Chalcedony Fund, one of the company's most important stock portfolios. You'll retrieve sample data from different sources and include them in a workbook.

STARTING DATA FILES

Excel11

Tutorial
Chalcedony.accdb
Chalcedony.xlsx
CHHistory.txt
chldfunds.htm
Documentation.xml
Rules.xsd

Review
Crystal.xlsx
Crystal Data.accdb
Crystal Docs.xml
Crystal History.txt
crystalweb.htm
Schema.xsd

Case1
Lighthouse.xlsx
Lighthouse Data.accdb

Case2
Eggert.xlsx
Home Data.txt
Price List.txt

Case3
Climate.xlsx
US Weather.accdb

Case4
Flower.xlsx
Flower Data.accdb
Flower Sales.xlsx

Microsoft product screenshots used with permission from Microsoft Corporation.

Excel | Tutorial 11 Connecting to External Data

Session 11.1 Visual Overview:

The DATA tab contains commands for retrieving and refreshing data from external sources.

A **stock chart** displays the high, low, and closing values of a stock.

A **text file** contains only text and numbers without any formulas, graphics, special fonts, or formatted text.

Text files can be stored as **delimited text** in which a special character such as a space, comma, or tab marks the beginning of each column.

	A	B	C	D
1	Chalcedony Fund			
2	Fund History			
3				
4	Date	High	Low	Close
5	4/1/2013	44.86	42.3	42.33
6	4/2/2013	42.36	41.67	41.89
7	4/3/2013	44.15	39.59	42.21
8	4/4/2013	45.49	40.17	42.93
9	4/5/2013	44.4	42.18	43.52
10	4/8/2013	46.39	42.59	44.29
11	4/9/2013	45.14	43.37	44.13
12	4/10/2013	45.51	42.35	44.35
13	4/11/2013	46.29	43.55	44.54
14	4/12/2013	44.63	41.12	44.47
15	4/15/2013	47.62	43.15	44.69
16	4/16/2013	47.16	43.62	44.05
17	4/17/2013	46.6	43.54	44.25
18	4/18/2013	47.92	44.49	45.25
19	4/19/2013	48.69	44.73	45.53
20	4/22/2013	48.5	43.21	46.27
21	4/23/2013	47.33	44.52	46.67

```
Chesterton Financial. Annual Repo
Chalcedony Funds History
Daily Values: 2013-2016
================================
Date        High        Low        Cl
20130401    45.23       42.30
20130402    42.36       41.67
20130403    44.15       39.59
20130404    45.49       40.17
20130405    44.40       42.18
20130408    46.39       42.59
20130409    45.14       43.37
20130410    45.51       42.35
20130411    46.29       43.55
```

© 2014 Cengage Learning

Tutorial 11 Connecting to External Data | Excel   EX 659

Retrieving Text Data

Workbook Connections

Name	Description	Last Refreshed
CHHistory		

Add...
Remove
Properties...
Refresh
Manage Sets...

Locations where connections are used in this workbook

Sheet	Name	Location	Value	Formula
Fund History	Chalcedony Fund History: 2013 - 2016	$A$4:$D$785		

Close

> The Workbook Connections dialog box lists all of the connections in the workbook.

> A **connection** is a defined process for retrieving data from an external file.

Connection Properties

Connection name: CHHistory
Description:

Usage | Definition

Refresh control
Last Refreshed:
☐ Prompt for file name on refresh
☐ Refresh every [60] minutes
☑ Refresh data when opening the file
  ☐ Remove data from the external data range before saving the workbook
☑ Refresh this connection on Refresh All

OLAP Server Formatting
Retrieve the following formats from the server when using this connection:
☐ Number Format   ☐ Fill Color
☐ Font Style   ☐ Text Color

OLAP Drill Through
Maximum number of records to retrieve: [   ]

Language
☐ Retrieve data and errors in the Office display language when available

OK   Cancel

> The Connection Properties dialog box defines how and when connections to external data sources are retrieved and updated.

Date

Information   4/1/2016
       -- Rafael Garcia
================================
       Open
42.33   44.06
41.89   42.33
42.21   41.89
42.93   42.21
43.52   42.93
44.29   43.52
44.13   44.29
44.35   44.13
44.54   44.35

> A text file can also be stored in a **fixed-width format** in which each column starts at the same location in the text file.

Exploring External Data Sources

Many Excel projects involve working with data that is stored in locations other than the Excel workbook. These other locations are data files, known as **data sources**, that can be saved in a wide variety of formats. Learning how to retrieve and analyze data from different kinds of data sources is a key skill for any Excel user.

As an investment counselor, Rafael helps his clients plan their investment strategies. To do his job well, Rafael must look at the market from a variety of angles. He examines long-term trends so that his clients understand the benefits of creating long-term investment strategies. He tracks market performance in recent months to analyze current trends, and he also assesses the daily mood of the market by regularly viewing up-to-the-minute reports.

The information that Rafael needs comes from many data sources. As shown in Figure 11-1, long-term and historical stock information from the company's old record-keeping system has been retrieved from financial software packages and placed in text files that all counselors can use. Chesterton Financial stores its current market information in databases, which is where Rafael finds information on recent trends. Rafael can also access current market reports electronically from data sources located on the Internet.

Figure 11-1   Data sources for the Chalcedony Fund

© 2014 Cengage Learning

Rafael's current project is to track the performance of the Chalcedony Fund, one of Chesterton Financial's oldest and most successful funds. The fund is composed of several stocks on the New York Stock Exchange (NYSE). He wants to develop a workbook that summarizes essential information from only a few stocks in the fund. Rafael wants the workbook to connect to sources containing (1) the fund's performance over the past few years; (2) more recent information on the fund's performance in the last year as well as the last few days; and (3) up-to-the-minute reports on the fund's current status. Figure 11-2 shows Rafael's strategy for the workbook he wants you to create.

Figure 11-2   Data plan for the Chalcedony Fund workbook

1. **Documentation sheet** describing the workbook's contents and the source of the data used in the workbook

2. **Long-term historical reports** detailing the history and long-term performance of the fund

3. **Short-term historical reports** describing the recent performance of the fund in the past year and over the past few days

4. **Current reports** containing reports on the fund's current performance, updated hourly from the Internet

© 2014 Cengage Learning

To gather this data, you'll need to connect the workbook to several external data sources. First, you'll create a connection to the Chalcedony Fund's historical data. The daily values for the fund during the previous three years are stored in a text file, which you'll import directly into Excel.

Importing Data from Text Files

A text file contains only text and numbers without any formulas, graphics, special fonts, or formatted text. The text file is one of the simplest and most widely used formats for storing data because most software programs can save and retrieve data in this format. For example, Excel can open a text file in a worksheet, where you can format it as you would any data. Excel can also save a workbook as a text file, preserving only the data values without any of its formats. In addition, many types of computers can read text files. So, although text files contain only raw, unformatted data, they are very useful when you want to share data across a wide variety of software programs and computer systems.

REFERENCE

Connecting to a Text File

- On the DATA tab, in the Get External Data group, click the From Text button, and then select the text file containing the data.
- In the first step of the Text Import Wizard, choose how the data is organized, and then specify the row in which to start the import.
- In the second step, in the Data preview box, click to insert a column break, double-click a column break to delete it, and drag a column break to a new location.
- In the third step, click each column and select the appropriate data format option button or click the Do not import (skip) option button.
- Click the Finish button.
- Specify where to insert the imported text, and then click the OK button.

Understanding Text File Formats

Because a text file doesn't contain formatting codes to give it structure, a program needs another way to understand the file contents. If a text file contains only numbers, the importing program needs to know where one group of values ends and another begins. One way to distinguish data that is organized within a text file is to use a **delimiter**, which is a symbol—usually a space, a comma, or a tab—that separates one column of data from another.

Figure 11-3 shows the same four columns of stock market data delimited by spaces, commas, and tabs. Columns in delimited text files are not always vertically aligned as they would be in a spreadsheet, but this is not a problem for a program that recognizes the delimiter. A tab delimiter is often the best way to separate text columns because tab-delimited text can include spaces or commas within each column.

Figure 11-3   Delimited text files

Space-Delimited Text	Comma-Delimited Text	Tab-Delimited Text
Symbol High Low Yield	Symbol,High,Low,Yield	Symbol → High → Low → Yield
AA 10.24 7.97 1.44	AA,10.24,7.97,1.44	AA → 10.24 → 7.97 → 1.44
AEP 49.99 37.09 3.8	AEP,49.99,37.09,3.8	AEP → 49.99 → 37.09 → 3.8
BA 88.56 66.62 2.3	BA,88.56,66.62,2.3	BA → 88.56 → 66.62 → 2.3
CNI 103.7 77.78 1.7	CNI,103.7,77.78,1.7	CNI → 103.7 → 77.78 → 1.7

© 2014 Cengage Learning

- a single space separates one column from another
- a comma separates columns
- a tab separates columns

The other way to organize data is in a fixed-width text file in which each column starts at the same location in the file. For example, the first column starts at the first space in the file, the second column starts at the tenth space, and so forth. Figure 11-4 shows columns arranged in a fixed-width text file. In this example, all the columns line up visually because each one must start at the same location.

Figure 11-4   Fixed-width text file

each column begins at the same point in the text file

Fixed-Width Text			
Symbol	High	Low	Yield
AA	10.24	7.97	1.44
AEP	49.99	37.09	3.8
BA	88.56	66.62	2.3
CNI	103.7	77.78	1.7

© 2014 Cengage Learning

Tutorial 11 Connecting to External Data | Excel   EX 663

Starting the Text Import Wizard

When you use Excel to connect to a text file, the Text Import Wizard determines whether the data is stored in a delimited text file or a fixed-width text file—and if it's delimited, what delimiter is used. You can also tell Excel how to interpret the text file.

The text that Rafael wants you to import into Excel is stored in the file named CHHistory.txt. The file extension .txt identifies it as a text file. (Other common text file extensions are .dat, .prn, and .csv.) Although you know nothing about the file's structure, you can easily determine how the data is arranged by using the Text Import Wizard. You'll begin by creating a connection to the text file.

To create a connection to the CHHistory text file:

1. Open the **Chalcedony** workbook located in the Excel11 ▸ Tutorial folder included with your Data Files, and then save the workbook as **Chalcedony Fund** in the location specified by your instructor.

2. Go to the **Fund History** worksheet.

3. On the ribbon, click the **DATA** tab. In the Get External Data group, click the **From Text** button. The Import Text File dialog box opens.

4. Click the **CHHistory** text file located in the Excel11 ▸ Tutorial folder included with your Data Files, and then click the **Import** button. The Text Import Wizard - Step 1 of 3 dialog box opens. In the Original data type section, the Fixed width option button is already selected, indicating that the Text Import Wizard has determined that the data is in a fixed-width text file. See Figure 11-5.

> **TIP**
> You can also open a text file by using the Open dialog box. When Excel detects the data in the text file, the Text Import Wizard opens.

Figure 11-5 Text Import Wizard - Step 1 of 3

- available text file types (the Text Import Wizard detects the file type)
- specifies the first row to import
- select if the first row contains column labels or headers
- contents of the text file

5. Scroll the preview box to view the data in the text file. The column labels for the data are in row 5, and the data list begins in row 6.

Specifying the Starting Row

By default, the Text Import Wizard starts importing text at the first row of the file. You can specify a different starting row if you want to skip those initial lines of text. In this case, Rafael wants the Text Import Wizard to skip the first four lines of the file, which contain titles and a description of the text file's contents. Because he is interested only in the data, he wants you to start importing at row 5, which contains the labels for each column of numbers—Date, High, Low, Close, and Open—that correspond to the date, the fund's high and low values on that date, and the fund's opening and closing values, respectively.

To specify row 5 as the starting row:

1. Click the **Start import at row up arrow** to change the value to **5**.
2. Click the **My data has headers**. check box to insert a checkmark. This specifies that the first row to be imported contains the column labels or headers.
3. Click the **Next** button to display the second step of the Text Import Wizard.
4. Scroll the Data preview box down four rows. The data to import from the text file starts with the column labels. See Figure 11-6.

Figure 11-6 Text Import Wizard - Step 2 of 3

Editing Column Breaks

To correctly import a fixed-width text file, the Text Import Wizard needs to know where each column begins and ends. The point at which one column ends and another begins is called a **column break**. In a delimited file, the delimiter determines the column breaks. In a fixed-width file, the wizard guesses the locations of the column breaks. Sometimes, the wizard incorrectly defines the number and location of columns, so you should always check the Data preview box and edit the columns as needed.

You insert a new column break by clicking the position in the Data preview box where you want the break to appear. If a break is in the wrong location, you click and drag the break line to a new location in the Data preview box. You can delete an extra column break by double-clicking its break. Rafael wants you to make sure the column breaks in the CHHistory text file are accurate. You'll edit them to make sure the data is split into columns correctly.

To edit the column breaks in the CHHistory text file:

1. Drag the first break line directly after the column of dates.

2. Drag the second break line to the right directly after the values in the High column.

3. Drag the third break line to the right directly after the values in the Low column.

4. Drag the fourth break line to the right directly after the values in the Close column.

5. Double-click the last break line to remove it from the Data preview window. See Figure 11-7.

Make sure the column breaks do not intersect the data values in the column.

Figure 11-7   **Revised column breaks**

new layout of the column breaks

6. Click the **Next** button to move to the third step of the Text Import Wizard.

Formatting and Trimming Incoming Data

In the third and final step of the Text Import Wizard, you format the data in each column. Unless you specify a format, the General format is applied to all of the columns. To specify a format, you select a column in the Data preview box, and then click the appropriate option button in the Column data format section. You can also indicate whether a column should not be imported. Eliminating columns is useful when you want to import only a few items from a large text file containing many columns.

The values from the Date column display each date with no separators between the four-digit year value and the month and day values. This is not a common date format. Rafael wants to make sure that the Text Import Wizard correctly interprets these values, so you'll change the General format style to a date format. He also wants to minimize the amount of data in the workbook, so you'll import only the date and the high, low, and closing values of the fund for each day, and not the fund's daily opening value, which is the same as its closing value from the previous day.

To specify a date format and remove the Open column:

1. If the first column is not selected in the Data preview box, click anywhere within the column to select it.

2. In the Column data format section, click the **Date** option button. The first column heading changes from General to MDY.

3. Click the **Date** box arrow to display a list of date formats, and then click **YMD**. The column heading for the first column changes to YMD, indicating the values in this column will be interpreted as dates formatted with the year followed by the month and the day.

4. In the Data preview box, click anywhere within the **Open** column to select it, and then click the **Do not import column (skip)** option button. The column heading for the Open column changes from General to Skip Column, indicating the data from this column will not be imported into the worksheet. See Figure 11-8.

TIP
For international data, click the Advanced button to that has a different number format.

Figure 11-8 Text Import Wizard - Step 3 of 3

5. Click the **Finish** button. The Import Data dialog box opens so you can specify where to place the imported data in the worksheet. Note that if you used the Open dialog box to access the text file, its contents will be placed in the worksheet starting with cell A1.

6. Select cell **A4** in the Sheet1 worksheet, and then click the **OK** button. The data appears in the worksheet in the range A4:D785. Excel assigns the range a defined name that matches the name of the text file. See Figure 11-9.

Tutorial 11 Connecting to External Data | Excel EX 667

Figure 11-9 Data imported into the Fund History worksheet

possible connections to external data

data imported from a text file

	A	B	C	D
1	Chalcedony Fund			
2	Fund History			
3				
4	Date	High	Low	Close
5	4/1/2013	44.86	42.3	42.33
6	4/2/2013	42.36	41.67	41.89
7	4/3/2013	44.15	39.59	42.21
8	4/4/2013	45.49	40.17	42.93
9	4/5/2013	44.4	42.18	43.52
10	4/8/2013	46.39	42.59	44.29
11	4/9/2013	45.14	43.37	44.13
12	4/10/2013	45.51	42.35	44.35
13	4/11/2013	46.29	43.55	44.54
14	4/12/2013	44.63	41.12	44.47
15	4/15/2013	47.62	43.15	44.69
16	4/16/2013	47.16	43.62	44.05
17	4/17/2013	46.6	43.54	44.25
18	4/18/2013	47.92	44.49	45.25
19	4/19/2013	48.69	44.73	45.53

In addition to the fund values themselves, Rafael wants you to include a chart in the workbook displaying the fund's recent history. You will use a High-Low-Close chart designed to compare the high, low, and closing prices of a stock.

To create a High-Low-Close chart for the fund data:

1. Make sure cell **A4** is selected, and then press the **Ctrl+Shift+End** keys to select the range A4:D785. All of the fund data is selected.

2. Scroll to the top of the worksheet without deselecting the range.

3. On the ribbon, click the **INSERT** tab. In the Charts group, click the **Insert Stock, Surface or Radar Chart** button, and then click **High-Low-Close** (the first chart in the gallery).

4. Resize the chart so that it covers the range **F2:M16**.

5. Change the chart title to **Historical Trends**, and then remove the legend.

6. Add Primary Major Vertical gridlines to the chart, and then change the minimum value of the vertical axis from its default value of 0 to **40**.

7. Add the Primary Vertical axis title **Fund Value**, and then add the horizontal axis title **Date**.

8. Close the Format pane, and then select cell **A3**. See Figure 11-10.

Figure 11-10   **High-Low-Close chart**

	A	B	C	D
1	Chalcedony Fund			
2	Fund History			
3				
4	Date	High	Low	Close
5	4/1/2013	44.86	42.3	42.33
6	4/2/2013	42.36	41.67	41.89
7	4/3/2013	44.15	39.59	42.21
8	4/4/2013	45.49	40.17	42.93
9	4/5/2013	44.4	42.18	43.52
10	4/8/2013	46.39	42.59	44.29
11	4/9/2013	45.14	43.37	44.13
12	4/10/2013	45.51	42.35	44.35
13	4/11/2013	46.29	43.55	44.54
14	4/12/2013	44.63	41.12	44.47
15	4/15/2013	47.62	43.15	44.69
16	4/16/2013	47.16	43.62	44.05
17	4/17/2013	46.6	43.54	44.25
18	4/18/2013	47.92	44.49	45.25
19	4/19/2013	48.69	44.73	45.53

history of the Chalcedony Fund displayed in a High-Low-Close chart

Exploring External Data Ranges and Data Connections

When data is imported into a worksheet, it is stored within an **external data range**. Excel automatically assigns this data range a defined name based on the filename of the data source. You can change this to a more descriptive name that will help you and other users understand the purpose and content of the data stored in the external data range.

REFERENCE

Editing the Properties of an External Data Range

- Click any cell in the range containing the external data.
- On the DATA tab, in the Connections group, click the Properties button.
- To define a name for the data range, enter the name in the Name box.
- To specify how the external data is refreshed in the workbook, check the appropriate check boxes in the External Data Range Properties dialog box.
- Click the OK button.

The external data range in the range A4:D785 of the Fund History worksheet is named CHHistory, which was the filename of the original text file. Rafael wants you to change this name to something more descriptive. You'll edit the properties of the external data range.

To edit the properties of the CHHistory external data range:

1. Select cell **A4** to make the CHHistory external data range active.
2. On the DATA tab, in the Connections group, click the **Properties** button. The External Data Range Properties dialog box opens for the active external data range.

3. In the Name box, select **CHHistory**, and then type **Chalcedony Fund History: 2013 - 2016**. See Figure 11-11.

Figure 11-11 | External Data Range Properties dialog box

External Data Range Properties dialog box showing:
- Name: Chalcedony Fund History: 2013 - 2016 ← external data range name
- Query definition: ✓ Save query definition; ☐ Save password
- Refresh control: ✓ Prompt for file name on refresh ← check to prompt for the data filename on every refresh of the data range
- ☐ Refresh every 60 minutes
- ☐ Refresh data when opening the file ← check to refresh the data range when the workbook is initially opened
  - ☐ Remove external data from worksheet before closing
- Data formatting and layout: ✓ Include field names; ☐ Preserve column sort/filter/layout; ☐ Include row numbers; ✓ Preserve cell formatting; ✓ Adjust column width ← options to control how the refreshed data range is formatted within the workbook
- If the number of rows in the data range changes upon refresh:
  - ● Insert cells for new data, delete unused cells
  - ○ Insert entire rows for new data, clear unused cells
  - ○ Overwrite existing cells with new data, clear unused cells
- ☐ Fill down formulas in columns adjacent to data
- [OK] [Cancel]

4. Click the **OK** button. The external data range is renamed.

Excel supports other properties for external data ranges, which include:

- Keep the contents of the external data range current by having Excel reimport or refresh the data from the external file when the workbook is opened or at specific intervals when the workbook is in use.
- Require the user to enter a password before data is refreshed, preventing other users from updating the data without permission.
- Define whether the refreshed external data range retains the formatting and layout you've already defined for those cells, or replaces the current format and layout based on the content of the new data.
- Define whether Excel inserts or overwrites cells when new rows are added to the data range.

Although you can change the properties of a data range, it is often more efficient to set the properties of the data connection from where the range gets its data.

Viewing a Data Connection

A data connection is like a pipeline from a data source to one or more locations in the workbook. The same data connection can link multiple data ranges, PivotTables, or PivotCharts. When you imported the contents of the CHHistory text file, Excel established a connection between a data range and that data source. To see where a data connection is being used, you can view that connection's properties.

Rafael wants you to review the data connections that are established in the Chalcedony Fund workbook. You'll do that from the Workbook Connections dialog box.

EX 670 Excel | Tutorial 11 Connecting to External Data

To view the Chalcedony Fund workbook connections:

> **TIP**
> To delete a connection and separate the data from its source, select the connection in the Workbook Connections dialog box, and then click the Remove button.

1. On the ribbon, click the **DATA** tab. In the Connections group, click the **Connections** button. The Workbook Connections dialog box opens, listing all of the connections in the workbook. Only one connection is listed—the one linked to the CHHistory text file.

2. Click the **Click here to see where the selected connections are used** link. The Workbook Connections dialog box shows that the connection to the CHHistory text file is used in only one location. See Figure 11-12.

Figure 11-12 Workbook Connections dialog box

[Screenshot of the Workbook Connections dialog box with callouts:]
- click to set the properties of the data connection
- click to remove the data connection
- connections to external data in the workbook → CHHistory
- worksheet containing the external data range → Fund History
- name of the external data range → Chalcedony Fund History: 2013 - 2016
- cell reference of the imported data → $A$4:$D$785
- click to refresh the data connection

3. Click the **Close** button to close the dialog box.

Modifying Data Connection Properties

After a data connection has been established, you can modify its properties including how often the connection is refreshed or updated by the workbook. For example, you can set the connection to be refreshed whenever the workbook is reopened. In that case, every value in the workbook that relies on that data connection will also be refreshed.

REFERENCE

Refreshing External Data

- On the DATA tab, in the Connections group, click the Refresh All button.

or

- On the DATA tab, in the Connections group, click the Connections button.
- Select the connection, and then click the Refresh button.

or

- On the DATA tab, in the Connections group, click the Connections button.
- Select the connection, and then click the Properties button.
- Click the Refresh data when opening the file check box, click OK, and then click Close.

Tutorial 11 Connecting to External Data | Excel   EX 671

Rafael wants to automatically refresh the data connection to the CHHistory text file whenever the workbook is reopened. He also wants this data connection to have a more useful name and provide a description about the data source itself. You'll modify the properties of the CHHistory data connection to make these changes.

To modify the properties of a data connection:

1. On the DATA tab, in the Connections group, click the **Connections** button. The Workbook Connections dialog box opens, again listing all of the data connections currently in the workbook.

2. Click the **CHHistory** connection, if necessary, and then click the **Properties** button. The Connection Properties dialog box opens.

3. In the Connection name box, type **Chalcedony Fund History** as a more descriptive name, and then press the **Tab** key.

4. In the Description box, type **Daily values imported from the CHHistory.txt text file**.

> **TIP**
> To reduce the workbook's size when it is not in use, select the Remove data from the external data range before saving the workbook check box.

5. Click the **Prompt for file name on refresh** check box to remove the checkmark. Excel will not always prompt you for the filename when refreshing the data.

6. Click the **Refresh data when opening the file** check box to insert a checkmark. Now the connection to the CHHistory text file will be updated whenever the workbook is opened. See Figure 11-13.

Figure 11-13   Connection Properties dialog box

7. Click the **OK** button to close the Connection Properties dialog box, and then click the **Close** button to close the Workbook Connections dialog box.

Rafael discovered an error in the CHHistory text file. The first value in the High column was entered incorrectly. You'll fix the error and verify that the workbook will be automatically updated to reflect the edit when it is reopened.

To edit the text file and refresh external data:

1. Save and close the Chalcedony Fund workbook.
2. In Notepad or another text editor, open the **CHHistory** text file located in the Excel11 ▸ Tutorial folder included with your Data Files.
3. Change the High value in the first row from 44.86 to **45.23**. See Figure 11-14.

Figure 11-14 Revised CHHistory text file

```
                          CHHistory - Notepad              _ □ ×
File  Edit  Format  View  Help
Chesterton Financial. Annual Report Information      4/1/2016
Chalcedony Funds History                        -- Rafael Garcia
Daily Values: 2013-2016
================================================================
Date      High     Low      Close     Open
20130401  45.23    42.30    42.33     44.06
20130402  42.36    41.67    41.89     42.33
20130403  44.15    39.59    42.21     41.89
20130404  45.49    40.17    42.93     42.21
20130405  44.40    42.18    43.52     42.93
20130408  46.39    42.59    44.29     43.52
20130409  45.14    43.37    44.13     44.29
20130410  45.51    42.35    44.35     44.13
20130411  46.29    43.55    44.54     44.35
20130412  44.63    41.12    44.47     44.54
20130415  47.62    43.15    44.69     44.47
20130416  47.16    43.62    44.05     44.69
20130417  46.60    43.54    44.25     44.05
20130418  47.92    44.49    45.25     44.25
20130419  48.69    44.73    45.53     45.25
```

High value changed from 44.86 to 45.23

4. Save the CHHistory text file, and then close the file and the text editor.
5. In Excel, open the **Chalcedony Fund** workbook. A security warning appears in the Message Bar below the ribbon, indicating that the external data connections have been disabled. Notice that the value in cell B5 has not yet been updated and still displays the original High value of 44.86. Disabling the connection is a security feature designed to prevent users from inadvertently opening workbooks infected with connections to invalid data sources.
6. In the Message Bar, click the **Enable Content** button.
7. If the Security Warning dialog box opens, prompting you to make this file a trusted document, click the **Yes** button. Excel refreshes the connection to the CHHistory text file, and the value in cell B5 changes from 44.86 to 45.23.

After opening the workbook, you can refresh external data manually by clicking the Refresh All button in the Connections group on the DATA tab. The Refresh All button provides two options—Refresh All refreshes all of the data connections in the workbook, and Refresh refreshes only the currently selected external data range.

Tutorial 11 Connecting to External Data | Excel   EX 673

PROSKILLS

Teamwork: Maintaining Data Security

Data security is essential for any business to maintain the integrity of its data and retain the trust of its colleagues and customers. It is critical to secure data to prevent lapses in security. If your Excel workbooks are connected to external data sources, keep in mind the following tips:

- **Apply data security controls.** Make sure your data files are set up with password controls to prohibit unauthorized access.
- **Keep software updated.** Be sure to diligently update the software that stores your data with the latest security patches.
- **Closely monitor data copying.** Have only one source of your data. When multiple copies of the data are allowed, data security, consistency, and integrity are compromised.
- **Encrypt data.** Use data encryption to prevent hackers from gaining unauthorized access to sensitive information.

Maintaining data security requires that everyone with access to your data files knows how to retrieve and process that data appropriately. In the end, your data will only be as secure as the work habits of the people who access it.

Defining a Trusted Location

Excel helps to maintain data security by using trusted locations. A **trusted location** is a data location that Excel will access without prompting you to confirm that the connection is secure. Any location that is not specifically identified as trusted requires users to accept it before proceeding to access the data. A trusted location is defined in the Trust Center from the Excel Options dialog box.

REFERENCE

Defining a Trusted Location

- On the ribbon, click the FILE tab, and then click Options in the navigation bar.
- Click Trust Center in the Excel Options list, and then click the Trust Center Settings button.
- Click Trusted Locations in the Trust Center list, and then click the Add new location button.
- Click the Browse button to locate the trusted location, and then specify whether to include subfolders.
- Click the OK button in each dialog box.

Rafael is concerned about Excel automatically disabling external data and forcing the user to enable it before the data can be refreshed. He asks you to override the default settings so that it always enables his data sources without prompting. You do this by defining all of the subfolders in the Excel11 folder as trusted locations.

To set up the Excel11 folder as a trusted location:

1. On the ribbon, click the **FILE** tab, and then click **Options** in the navigation bar. The Excel Options dialog box opens.

2. Click **Trust Center** in the left pane, and then click the **Trust Center Settings** button in the right pane. The Trust Center dialog box opens.

3. Click **Trusted Locations** in the left pane to display the list of locations that are trusted by Microsoft Office.

4. Only if your data files are located in a network folder, click the **Allow Trusted Locations on my network** check box.

5. Click the **Add new location** button. The Microsoft Office Trusted Location dialog box opens.

6. Click the **Browse** button, and then navigate to the **Excel11** folder included with your Data Files.

7. Double-click the **Excel11** folder icon to open it, and then click the **OK** button to return to the Microsoft Office Trusted Location dialog box.

8. Click the **Subfolders of this location are also trusted** check box to insert a checkmark. This option allows all of the subfolders in the Excel11 folder to be trusted.

9. In the Description box, type **Data sources for Tutorial 11**. See Figure 11-15.

Figure 11-15 Microsoft Office Trusted Location dialog box

path to trusted location (your path will differ)

check to trust files in the specified folder and its subfolders

description of the trusted location

10. Click the **OK** button in each of the three dialog boxes to return to the workbook. Excel now trusts your data source from the Excel11 folder and will refresh the data from those sources without prompting.

11. Save and close the **Chalcedony Fund** workbook, and then reopen the workbook, verifying that you are not prompted to enable the data connections in the workbook when you reopen it.

By setting the Excel11 folder as a trusted location, Rafael will save time as he works with the Chalcedony Fund workbook.

INSIGHT

Moving a Data Source

When an Excel project is copied to another computer or when a data source is moved to a new folder, the path names to the external data sources might change and become unusable. To fix this problem, you must modify the properties of the connections established in the workbook. When you move or copy a workbook that is connected to external data, you must change the path to the external data. To update the connection, you modify the path on the Definition tab in the Connection Properties dialog box, which you open by clicking the Connections button in the Connections group on the DATA tab, selecting the connection, and then clicking the Properties button. With a revised definition established for the connection, other users can access and refresh the data from its new location.

You have set up the connection from the Chalcedony Fund workbook to the CHHistory text file. In the process, you've worked with connections, external data ranges, and trusted locations. In the next session, you'll learn about databases and how to connect an Excel workbook to a database.

REVIEW

Session 11.1 Quick Check

1. What is the difference between a fixed-width text file and a delimited text file?
2. Name three delimiters that can be used to separate data in a delimited text file.
3. How do you insert column breaks when importing a text file using the Text Import Wizard?
4. What is the relationship between a connection and an external data range?
5. Name two ways in which Excel automatically refreshes a connection.
6. What is a trusted location?
7. Describe how to reestablish a data connection when the data source is moved to a new location.

Session 11.2 Visual Overview:

Data in a database is stored in **tables** arranged in column (fields) and rows (records).

A **record** displays a collection of characteristics of a particular person, place, or thing. This record stores all the characteristics about Boeing Company.

A **database** is a collection of data values organized in such a way that they can be easily retrieved and manipulated by the end user.

In a **relational database**, tables are joined by common fields—Ticker Symbol, in these tables—that indicate the relationship between one table and another.

Chalcedony Fund Portfolio

	A	B
3	Ticker Symbol	Company
4	HPQ	Hewlett-Packard Company
5	BA	Boeing Company
6	MPC	Marathon Petroleum Corporation
7	CVX	Chevron Texaco Corporation
8	T	AT&T Corporation
9	AA	Aluminum Company of America
10	DAL	Delta Air Lines Incorporated
11	R	Ryder System, Incorporated
12	CNI	Canadian National Railway Company
13	UNP	Union Pacific Corporation
14	LUV	Southwest Airlines Corporation
15	ED	Consolidated Edison Company of New York, Inc.
16	PPL	P P & L Resources Incorporated
17	AEP	American Electric Power Company, Incorporated
18	WEC	Wisconsin Energy Corporation

Recent Performance
- Ticker Symbol
- Date
- Volume
- High
- Low

Company
- Ticker Symbol
- Title
- Category
- Industry Code
- Industry Description

Portfolio_Table
- Ticker Symbol
- Title
- Portfolio Percent
- Year High
- Year Low

© 2014 Cengage Learning

Tutorial 11 Connecting to External Data | Excel   EX 677

Excel Databases and Queries

A **field** stores information about a specific characteristic of a person, place, or thing. This field stores information about the portfolio percentage.

Database tables can be used as the data source for PivotCharts and PivotTables.

Microsoft Query is an application that creates queries to retrieve data from multiple database tables and stores the data in a workbook.

A **query** is a set of guidelines that specify what values to retrieve from a database and in what order the values should be retrieved.

An Introduction to Databases

A database is a highly structured collection of data values organized to be easily retrieved and examined by the end user. Databases are commonly used as the data sources for Excel workbooks. A database is divided into separate tables. Each table is arranged in columns and rows, which are also referred to as fields and records. A field stores information about a specific characteristic of a person, place, or thing such as an individual's last name, a company address, or a stock value. A record is a collection of these fields. For example, a single record might contain a complete profile of an individual or a company, providing important information to the user. Excel can retrieve data directly from most database programs, including Microsoft Access, the database program that is part of Microsoft Office.

Analysts at Chesterton Financial store information about the Chalcedony Fund in an Access database named Chalcedony. Figure 11-16 shows the Company table, which contains fields—including the Ticker Symbol, Title, and Category fields shown in Figure 11-16—and records for 15 stocks that Rafael included in this sample database. Each stock is stored as a separate record in the table. For example, the first record in the Company table displays information for the Aluminum Company of America, which has the ticker symbol AA and is an industrial stock.

Figure 11-16 Company table in the Chalcedony database

columns of fields

Ticker Symbol	Title	Category
AA	Aluminum Company of America	INDUSTRIALS
AEP	American Electric Power Company, Incorporated	UTILITIES
BA	Boeing Company	INDUSTRIALS
CNI	Canadian National Railway Company	TRANSPORTATIC
CVX	Chevron Texaco Corporation	INDUSTRIALS
DAL	Delta Air Lines Incorporated	TRANSPORTATIC
ED	Consolidated Edison Company of New York, Inc.	UTILITIES
HPQ	Hewlett-Packard Company	INDUSTRIALS
LUV	Southwest Airlines Corporation	TRANSPORTATIC
MPC	Marathon Petroleum Corporation	INDUSTRIALS
PPL	P P & L Resources Incorporated	UTILITIES
R	Ryder System, Incorporated	TRANSPORTATIC
T	AT&T Corporation	INDUSTRIALS
UNP	Union Pacific Corporation	TRANSPORTATIC
WEC	Wisconsin Energy Corporation	UTILITIES

rows of records

Record: 16 of 16 No Filter Search

The Chalcedony database has four tables—Company, Long-Term Performance, Recent Performance, and Stock Info. Figure 11-17 describes the contents of each table.

Figure 11-17 Chalcedony database tables

Table Name	Description
Company	Includes data about each company in the fund and the percentage of the fund that is allocated to purchasing stocks for that company
Long-Term Performance	Summarizes the performance over the last 52 weeks for each stock, recording the high and low values over that period of time, and its standard deviation
Recent Performance	Daily high, low, closing, and volume values for each stock in the portfolio over the last five days
Stock Info	Description of each stock, including the yield, dividend amount and date, earnings per share, and average trading volume

© 2014 Cengage Learning

Different tables are connected through **database relationships** in which fields common to each table are used to match a record from one table to a record from another table. As shown in Figure 11-18, the Company table and the Stock Info table are related through the Ticker Symbol field. By matching the values of the Ticker Symbol field, information from both tables can be combined into a single data structure. This type of relationship is known as a **one-to-one relationship** because one record from the first table is matched to exactly one record from the second table. Another important relationship is the **one-to-many relationship** in which one record is matched to one or more records in the second table. A one-to-many relationship could be used in a customer orders database that matches a single customer record to a table describing the multiple orders made by that customer, for example.

Figure 11-18 Relating two tables based on a common field

Company table

Stock Info table

combined data

© 2014 Cengage Learning

Databases in which tables can be joined through the use of common fields are known as **relational databases**. Relational databases are extremely useful in that they allow similar pieces of information to be grouped in smaller, more manageable tables. Because the tables can be joined through a common field, it is unnecessary to duplicate the same piece of information across multiple tables. For example, a customer's name or address need only be entered in one table rather than several tables. By removing duplication, relational databases make it easier to manage large data sets and thus improve data quality and integrity.

Retrieving Data with Microsoft Query

Because a large database can contain dozens or hundreds of tables, and each table can have several fields and thousands of records, you need a way to retrieve only the information that you most want to see. To extract specific information from a database, you create a query. A **query** contains a set of criteria that specify what values to retrieve from a database and in what order the values should be retrieved. In the case of the Chalcedony database, Rafael might create a query to retrieve the ticker symbol, company title, and annual yield from the top-10 performing industrial stocks in the database. The query could further specify that any retrieved records be sorted alphabetically by company title.

Queries are written in a language called **SQL** or **Structured Query Language**. Writing a SQL query is beyond the scope of this tutorial, but you can create SQL-based queries using Microsoft Query, a program supplied with Microsoft Office and accessible from within Excel. Like the Text Import Wizard you used in the previous session, Microsoft Query uses a wizard containing a collection of dialog boxes that guide you through the entire query process.

Rafael wants the workbook to list the stocks in the Chalcedony Fund and describe their performance over the last year. According to the worksheet plan (refer back to Figure 11-2), you can extract this information from the Chalcedony database. You'll use the Microsoft Query Wizard to define your query.

To start the Microsoft Query Wizard:

1. If you took a break at the end of the previous session, make sure the Chalcedony Fund workbook is open.
2. Go to the **Portfolio** worksheet.
3. On the ribbon, click the **DATA** tab. In the Get External Data group, click the **From Other Sources** button, and then click **From Microsoft Query**. The Choose Data Source dialog box opens. See Figure 11-19.

Figure 11-19 Choose Data Source dialog box

available data sources (your list might differ)

Tutorial 11 Connecting to External Data | Excel EX 681

Connecting to a Data Source

In the first step of the wizard, you select the data source. The Choose Data Source dialog box lists several types of data sources from which you can retrieve data. You can also define your own data source by clicking <New Data Source> in the list of databases. In this case, Rafael wants you to connect to a Microsoft Access database, so you'll use the MS Access Database data source and connect to the Chalcedony database.

To connect to an Access data source:

▶ 1. Click **MS Access Database*** in the list of data sources.

▶ 2. Verify that the **Use the Query Wizard to create/edit queries** check box is checked, and then click the **OK** button. The Select Database dialog box opens.

▶ 3. Navigate to the **Excel11 ▶ Tutorial** folder included with your Data Files, and then click the **Chalcedony** Access database file.

   Trouble? Microsoft Query does not reference network folders. If your data source is located on a network folder, you must map the folder to a drive letter. To do so, click the Network button in the Select Database dialog box to open the Map Network Drive dialog box.

▶ 4. Click the **OK** button. Microsoft Query connects to the Chalcedony database file and opens the Query Wizard - Choose Columns dialog box. See Figure 11-20.

Figure 11-20 Query Wizard - Choose Columns dialog box

click to display the fields in the table

tables in the Chalcedony database

Choosing Tables and Fields

The next step in retrieving data from a database is to choose the table and fields to include in the query. You'll start by examining the fields in the Company table.

To view a list of fields in the Company table:

▶ 1. In the Available tables and columns box, click the **Expand** button [+] next to Company.

▶ 2. Verify that the columns (or fields) in the Company table are displayed in the Available tables and columns list box. See Figure 11-21.

Figure 11-21 Fields in the Company table

click to include the selected field in the query

table name

field names

Because the Chalcedony database is relational, each of the tables listed by the Query Wizard is related by a common field, which in this case is the Ticker Symbol field. This means you can select fields from multiple tables and the Query Wizard will match records based on the Ticker Symbol value. Rafael's query will extract the ticker symbol, the company title, and the portfolio percent from the Company table. The portfolio percent is the percentage of the portfolio that is invested in each stock. The query will also include the Year High and Year Low fields from the Long-Term Performance table so that Rafael can identify the high and low market values from the previous year.

To select the fields to include in the query:

1. Click **Ticker Symbol** in the Available tables and columns box, and then click the **Select Field** button **>** to move it to the Columns in your query box.

2. In the Available tables and columns box, double-click **Title**, and then double-click **Portfolio Percent**. These fields now appear in the Columns in your query box. Note that the order the fields are listed is the order they are retrieved and displayed within the workbook. You can reorder the fields if needed.

3. Click the **Expand** button **+** next to Long-Term Performance to display the list of columns in that table.

4. Double-click the **Year High** and **Year Low** column names. The five fields that Rafael wants to include in the query are selected. See Figure 11-22.

TIP
You can preview the selected field by clicking the Preview Now button.

Figure 11-22 Fields selected for the query

fields to include in the query

moves the selected field within the query

Filtering and Sorting Data

In the next step of the Query Wizard, you provide criteria to filter the records returned by the query. When you filter data, you specify which records you want to retrieve using specific criteria. For example, you can filter the data so that only a few specified stocks are retrieved, or limit the query to stocks that are bought and sold above a specified value.

You can include multiple filters in a query. To add another filter, you would fill in the next row of filter boxes in the dialog box. Select the And option button if all of the filter conditions must be matched to retrieve the record. Select the Or option button if a record will be retrieved if any of the filter conditions is met. Although the Query Wizard - Filter Data dialog box shows only three rows of criteria, the dialog box expands to provide additional rows as you specify requirements for your filter.

Rafael wants you to filter the query so that it retrieves information on stocks that constitute 7 percent or more of the Chalcedony Fund portfolio. To do this, you create a filter that returns records for stocks where the value of the Portfolio Percent field is 0.07 or greater.

To add a query to the filter:

1. Click the **Next** button to go to the Query Wizard - Filter Data dialog box.
2. In the Column to filter box, click **Portfolio Percent**, and then press the **Tab** key.
3. In the Only include rows where section, click the **arrow** button in the left column of the first row, and then click **is greater than or equal to** in order to select the type of comparison.
4. Press the **Tab** key to move to the next box, and then type **0.07**. See Figure 11-23.

Figure 11-23 Query Wizard - Filter Data dialog box

5. Click the **Next** button.

The last part of the Query Wizard lets you specify how to sort the data. You select the sort field and then specify either ascending or descending order. Microsoft Query allows you to specify up to three sort fields.

Rafael wants to display the portfolio information showing the stocks in which the Chalcedony Fund has the largest capital investment, and then showing the stocks with the smallest capital investment. Because the Portfolio Percent field tells you how much of the fund is invested in each stock, you'll sort the data by the values in that field in descending order (from highest percentage to lowest).

To sort the data in the query:

1. Click the **Sort by** arrow, and then click **Portfolio Percent** to select the sort field.
2. Click the **Descending** option button to sort the values from highest percentage to lowest percentage. See Figure 11-24.

Figure 11-24   **Query Wizard - Sort Order dialog box**

records will be sorted in descending order of the Portfolio Percent field values

3. Click the **Next** button to go to the final Query Wizard dialog box.

The Query Wizard - Finish dialog box provides three options. You can return (import) the data into the Excel workbook; you can display the results of the query in Microsoft Query, where you can further edit the data and the query definition; or you can save the query to a file. Saving the query to a file creates a text file containing the query's definition in SQL code. Because you don't need to refine the query at this point or save it to a file, you'll simply import the data into the Chalcedony Fund workbook. With Microsoft Query, you can import the query data in the form of an Excel table, a PivotTable, or a PivotTable and PivotChart, or you can simply create the connection to the query without actually importing the data. Rafael wants you to import the query data into an Excel table.

To import the query data into an Excel table:

1. Make sure the **Return Data to Microsoft Excel** option button is selected, and then click the **Finish** button. The Import Data dialog box opens so you can select where to insert the imported data.

Be sure to select that the data should be imported into the workbook as an Excel table.

2. Verify that the **Table** option button is selected so that the data is stored as an Excel table.
3. Click cell **A4** in the Portfolio worksheet to specify the location to create the Excel table. See Figure 11-25.

Tutorial 11 Connecting to External Data | Excel   EX 685

Figure 11-25   Import Data dialog box

- saves the data in an Excel table
- creates the data connection but doesn't display the data
- click to set the properties of the data connection
- location of the imported data

4. Click the **OK** button. The data from the query is imported into the Portfolio worksheet at cell A4.

5. In the range **C5:C13**, format the data using the **Percentage** format with two decimal places, and then in the range **D5:E13**, format the data using the **Number** format.

6. Select cell **A4**. See Figure 11-26.

Figure 11-26   Data imported into an Excel table

- query data imported into an Excel table
- records limited to Portfolio Percent values of 7 percent or greater
- data sorted in descending order of Portfolio Percent

	A	B	C	D	E
1	Chalcedony Fund				
2	Portfolio				
3					
4	Ticker Symbol	Title	Portfolio Percent	Year High	Year Low
5	HPQ	Hewlett-Packard Company	9.50%	25.40	11.35
6	DAL	Delta Air Lines Incorporated	9.20%	17.25	8.42
7	ED	Consolidated Edison Company of New York, Inc.	8.50%	65.98	53.63
8	PPL	P P & L Resources Incorporated	8.30%	31.91	26.68
9	AEP	American Electric Power Company, Incorporated	8.20%	49.99	37.09
10	R	Ryder System, Incorporated	7.50%	61.73	32.76
11	CNI	Canadian National Railway Company	7.50%	103.70	77.78
12	UNP	Union Pacific Corporation	7.20%	143.00	140.49
13	WEC	Wisconsin Energy Corporation	7.10%	43.32	42.99

According to the retrieved data, 9.50 percent of the Chalcedony Fund is invested in Hewlett-Packard Company, and the value of that stock has ranged from a high of 25.40 points to a low of 11.35 points over the previous year. The table is sorted in descending order by the percentage of each stock in the portfolio, placing the most heavily invested stocks at the top of the list. The table shows only the nine stocks that constitute 7 percent or more of the total Chalcedony fund. After seeing these results, Rafael wants you to revise the query to show information about all of the stocks in the Chalcedony fund.

Editing a Query

By editing a query, you can add new columns to a worksheet, change the sort order options, or revise any filters. You edit a query by editing the definition of the connection. When you edit the connection, Excel recognizes that the Query Wizard was used to define the parameters of the connection and restarts the Query Wizard. You can then walk through the steps of the wizard, modifying the query definition as you go.

REFERENCE

Editing a Database Query

- On the DATA tab, in the Connections group, click the Connections button.
- Select the connection used by the database query, and then click the Properties button.
- Click the Definition tab, and then click the Edit Query button.
- Change the query definition using the dialog boxes provided by the Query Wizard.

Rafael wants you to remove the filter that limited the query to stocks with 7 percent or more of the portfolio, and he wants you to add the Category field to the query so that he can see each stock category (Industrials, Transportation, or Utilities). He also wants you to change the sort order so that the Excel table is sorted by Category field first, and then by descending order of the Portfolio Percent field within each category. You'll edit the query now.

To edit the query:

1. On the DATA tab, in the Connections group, click the **Connections** button. The Workbook Connections dialog box opens.

2. Click the **Query from MS Access Database** connection, and then click the **Properties** button. The Connection Properties dialog box opens.

3. Click the **Definition** tab. From this tab, you can view the current definition of the Chalcedony Portfolio query. You can also edit the query.

4. Click the **Edit Query** button. The Query Wizard - Choose Columns dialog box reopens.

5. In the Available tables and column box, click the **Expand** button [+] next to the Company table entry, and then double-click the **Category** field. "Category" is added to the end of the list of columns in the query.

6. Click the **Next** button to go to the Query Wizard - Filter Data dialog box.

7. Select **Portfolio Percent** from the list of fields, click the first box arrow in the Only include rows where box, and then select the blank entry at the top of the list of comparison options. The Portfolio Percent filter is removed.

8. Click the **Next** button to go to the Query Wizard - Sort Order dialog box.

9. Click the **Sort by** arrow, click **Category**, and then click the **Ascending** option button. The sort order for the query is modified to first sort in ascending order by Category.

10. Click the **Then by** arrow, click **Portfolio Percent**, and then click the **Descending** option button. In each category, the records will be sorted in descending order by Portfolio Percent. See Figure 11-27.

> **TIP**
> You can view and edit the SQL code associated with the query by working with the contents of the Command text input box.

Figure 11-27 Modified sort order for the query

query will be sorted by Category and then by Portfolio Percent

[Query Wizard - Sort Order dialog box: Sort by Category (Ascending); Then by Portfolio Percent (Descending); Then by (blank)]

- 11. Click the **Next** button, and then click the **Finish** button to close the Query Wizard.
- 12. Click the **OK** button in the Connection Properties dialog box, and then click the **Close** button in the Workbook Connections dialog box to return to the Portfolio worksheet. See Figure 11-28.

Figure 11-28 Revised Portfolio table

Category field added to the query results

data sorted by the Category field and Portfolio Percent field

	A	B	C	D	E	F
1	Chalcedony Fund					
2	Portfolio					
3						
4	Ticker Symbol	Title	Portfolio Percent	Year High	Year Low	Category
5	HPQ	Hewlett-Packard Company	9.50%	25.40	11.35	INDUSTRIALS
6	BA	Boeing Company	5.50%	88.56	66.82	INDUSTRIALS
7	MPC	Marathon Petroleum Corporation	5.10%	75.38	52.63	INDUSTRIALS
8	CVX	Chevron Texaco Corporation	4.20%	121.56	95.73	INDUSTRIALS
9	T	AT&T Corporation	3.80%	38.80	30.50	INDUSTRIALS
10	AA	Aluminum Company of America	3.50%	10.24	7.97	INDUSTRIALS
11	DAL	Delta Air Lines Incorporated	9.20%	17.25	8.42	TRANSPORTATION
12	R	Ryder System, Incorporated	7.50%	61.73	32.76	TRANSPORTATION
13	CNI	Canadian National Railway Company	7.50%	103.70	77.78	TRANSPORTATION
14	UNP	Union Pacific Corporation	7.20%	143.00	140.49	TRANSPORTATION
15	LUV	Southwest Airlines Corporation	4.90%	13.58	7.76	TRANSPORTATION
16	ED	Consolidated Edison Company of New York, Inc.	8.50%	65.98	53.63	UTILITIES
17	PPL	P P & L Resources Incorporated	8.30%	31.91	26.68	UTILITIES
18	AEP	American Electric Power Company, Incorporated	8.20%	49.99	37.09	UTILITIES
19	WEC	Wisconsin Energy Corporation	7.10%	43.32	42.99	UTILITIES

The fund is composed of 15 stocks—with six industrial stocks, five transportation stocks, and four utility stocks. The most heavily invested stocks within each category are Hewlett-Packard Company, an industrial stock with 9.50 percent of the portfolio; Delta Air Lines Inc., a transportation stock with 9.20 percent of the portfolio; and Consolidated Edison Company of New York, Inc., a utility stock with 8.50 percent of the portfolio.

Excel has assigned the name Table_Query_from_MS_Access_Database to the Portfolio table containing the data imported from the Microsoft Query. The name reflects the fact that the data has been imported into a table using the Query from MS Access Database connection. Rafael wants you to change the table name to better describe the table's contents.

To rename the table:

1. On the ribbon, click the **TABLE TOOLS DESIGN** tab. In the Properties group, in the Table Name box, select the table name.
2. Type **Portfolio_Table** as the new table name, and then press the **Enter** key.

As you did with the data connection to the CHHistory text file, Rafael wants you to modify the properties of this data connection to give it a useful description and to have Excel automatically refresh the data whenever the workbook is reopened.

To edit the properties of the connection to the Chalcedony database:

1. On the ribbon, click the **DATA** tab. In the Connections group, click the **Connections** button. The Workbook Connections dialog box opens, listing the two data connections in the workbook.
2. Click **Query from MS Access Database** in the list, and then click the **Properties** button. The Connection Properties dialog box opens.
3. In the Connection name box, type **Chalcedony Portfolio Query**.
4. In the Description box, type **Stock data imported from the Chalcedony database using Microsoft Query**.
5. Click the **Refresh data when opening the file** check box to insert a checkmark.
6. Click the **OK** button to close the Connection Properties dialog box, and then click the **Close** button to close the Workbook Connections dialog box.

TIP
To disconnect an Excel table from its data source, click the Unlink button in the External Table Data group on the TABLE TOOLS DESIGN tab.

You are finished working with the query for the portfolio table. Next, Rafael wants you to directly connect Excel to an Access database.

INSIGHT

Saving a Data Connection

You can save the definition of a data connection as a permanent file in either the Office Data Connection (ODC) format or the Universal Data Connection (UDC) format. Connection files are used to share connections with other individuals, or to create a library of connection files for use with large database structures.

To manually save a connection to an ODC file, use the Export Connection File button on the Definition tab in the Connection Properties dialog box to specify the name and location of your Office Data Connection file. The default location for ODC files is the My Data Sources subfolder of your Documents folder. ODC files are added to the My Data Sources subfolder whenever you create a connection to an Access database table. UDC files are not created within Excel. To create a UDC file, you can use Microsoft InfoPath for creating and designing XML-based data entry forms for businesses.

To access a saved connection file, click the Existing Connections button in the Get External Data group on the Data tab to select the connection file from your workbook, your network, or your computer.

Tutorial 11 Connecting to External Data | Excel EX 689

Importing Data from Multiple Tables into a PivotTable

You can import multiple tables from a database directly into Excel without using Microsoft Query. If the tables are related through a common field, Excel will automatically include the relationship between the tables as part of the data import. This method does not include defining a query, so the entire tables will be imported into the workbook.

Rafael wants to include an analysis of the most recent performance of each stock in the Chalcedony Fund. To do this, he wants to import the Company table and the Recent Performance table shown in Figure 11-29. The tables share a one-to-many relationship because one record from the Company table will be matched to many records (in this case, five records) in the Recent Performance table.

Figure 11-29 Relationship between the Company and Recent Performance tables

one-to-many relationship between the Company table and the Recent Performance table

© 2014 Cengage Learning

You'll import these two tables now.

To import the Company and Recent Performance tables:

1. Go to the **5-Day Report** worksheet.

2. On the ribbon, click the **DATA** tab. In the Get External Data group, click the **From Access** button. The Select Data Source dialog box opens.

3. Select the **Chalcedony** database file located in the Excel11 ▸ Tutorial folder included with your Data Files, and then click the **Open** button.

   Depending on your system, the Data Link Properties dialog box might open with information about the link to this data source.

4. If the Data Link dialog box opens, click the **OK** button twice to open the Select Table dialog box.

5. Click the **Enable selection of multiple tables** check box so you can select more than one table from the database.

6. Click the **Company** and **Recent Performance** check boxes to select the two tables in the Chalcedony database. See Figure 11-30.

Figure 11-30 Select Table dialog box

select to import more than one database table

the Company and Recent Performance tables selected for importing

> 7. Click the **OK** button. The Import Data dialog box reappears.

Rafael wants the data to appear in an interactive report so that he can select the name of a company from the Chalcedony Fund and view the closing value and shares traded over the last five days. You'll import the data into a PivotTable report that summarizes each stock's activity. You will also change the properties of this data connection so that the data is automatically refreshed when the workbook is opened.

To import the Chalcedony database data into a PivotTable report:

1. In the Import Data dialog box, verify that the **PivotTable Report** option button is selected.

2. Click in the **Existing worksheet** box, and then click cell **D4** in the Recent Performance worksheet. This is the cell where you want to place the PivotTable.

3. Click the **Properties** button. The Connection Properties dialog box opens.

4. In the Connection name box, type **5-Day Performance Data**.

5. In the Description box, type **Data from the Company and Recent Performance tables in the Chalcedony database**.

6. Click the **Refresh data when opening the file** check box. Excel will refresh the data in this connection whenever the workbook is opened.

7. Click the **OK** button. The Import Data dialog box reappears.

8. Click the **OK** button. The data is imported, the PivotTable is inserted into cell D4, and the fields from the Company and Recent Performance tables are displayed in the PivotTable Fields pane organized by table.

> **TIP**
> The Table option creates multiple worksheets, and each sheet contains an Excel table with the complete contents of one of the selected database tables.

Rafael wants the PivotTable to display the dates, closing value, and volume of shares traded for each of the stocks in the Chalcedony fund. He wants the company titles to appear in a slicer next to the PivotTable. You will create and format the PivotTable and slicer now.

To set up and format the PivotTable and slicer:

1. In the PivotTable Fields pane, scroll down to the list of fields in the Recent Performance table.

2. Drag the **Date** field to the Rows area. The list of five dates is displayed in the range E5:E9 in the worksheet.

3. From the list of fields in the Recent Performance table, drag the **Volume** field to the VALUES area, and then drag the **Closing** fields to the VALUES area.

   The column labels include "Sum of" before the names of the Volume and Closing fields. This label is misleading because only one value will appear for these items for each stock on each day, so the PivotTable shows a "sum" of only one record. You'll revise the column labels to better reflect their contents.

4. In the range **D4:F4**, enter the following labels: **Date**, **Shares Traded**, and **Closing Value**.

5. In the range **E5:E9**, format the Volume values using the **Comma Style** with no decimal places.

6. In the range **F5:F9**, format the Closing values using the **Number** format with two decimal places.

7. On the PIVOTTABLE TOOLS DESIGN tab, in the Layout group, click the **Grand Totals** button, and then click **Off for Rows and Columns**. The Grand Totals are removed from the PivotTable because Rafael doesn't need to see grand totals for the five-day history.

   Next, you'll add a slicer containing the Title field from the Company table.

8. On the ribbon, click the **PIVOTTABLE TOOLS ANALYZE** tab. In the Filter group, click the **Insert slicer** button. The Insert slicers dialog box opens.

9. From the list of fields in the Company table, select the **Title** field, and then the **OK** button.

10. Move and resize the Title slicer so that it covers the range A4:C20.

11. In the Title slicer, click **Aluminum Company of America** from the list of company titles. The five most recent shares traded and closing values for that stock are displayed in the PivotTable. See Figure 11-31.

Figure 11-31   Formatted PivotTable and slicer

[Screenshot of Excel worksheet showing the Chalcedony Fund 5-Day Report with a PivotTable and slicer. Callouts indicate: revised column labels; fields in the Recent Performance table; recent performance of the Aluminum Company of America stock; slicer filtering the PivotTable by values of the Title field. Data shown includes:

Date	Shares Traded	Closing Value
4/11/2016	41,561,330	8.39
4/12/2016	40,913,710	8.39
4/13/2016	24,233,610	8.24
4/14/2016	18,809,240	8.22
4/15/2016	17,495,780	8.30

Title slicer entries: Aluminum Company of America, American Electric Power Compa..., AT&T Corporation, Boeing Company, Canadian National Railway Com..., Chevron Texaco Corporation, Consolidated Edison Company o..., Delta Air Lines Incorporated, Hewlett-Packard Company, Marathon Petroleum Corporation.]

Rafael can use the PivotTable and slicer to quickly view the five-day history for each stock in the portfolio. As new data is added to the Chalcedony database, Rafael can refresh the data connection to view the results on the 5-Day Report worksheet.

Rafael wants to compare the recent values of the stocks in the Chalcedony Fun with their highest and lowest values from the previous year. He suggests that you add the Year High and Year Low values from the Portfolio worksheet (shown in Figure 11-28) to the PivotTable report. This requires joining the data in the Portfolio worksheet with the data from the Company and Recent Performance tables. You can do this with the data model.

> ### INSIGHT
>
> ### Opening Non-Native Files in Excel
>
> Often, you can simplify the process of connecting to data sources by opening the data source files directly in Excel. You do this from the Open screen in Backstage view. If Excel supports the file format, it will open the appropriate dialog boxes to import the data into the Excel workbook. For example, opening a text file from the Open screen will launch the Text Import wizard. Opening an Access database will display a dialog box from which you can select one or more tables from the database. To choose other file formats in the Open dialog box, click the button directly above the Open button and choose the file format you want to display.

Exploring the Data Model and PowerPivot

The **data model** is a database built into Excel that provides many of the same tools found in database programs such as Access. Because the data model database is part of the Excel workbook, its contents are immediately available to PivotTables, PivotCharts, and other Excel features used for analyzing data.

The data model is constructed from different tables related by common fields. A table becomes part of the data model database when it is imported from an external database file like the Chalcedony database. When you imported the Company and Recent Performance tables, their data was added to the data model along with information about the relationship between the two tables. Excel tables can also be added to the data model, allowing database tools to be used to combine, analyze, and create queries among different Excel tables, or among Excel tables and tables imported from external database files.

Installing the PowerPivot Add-In

You interact with the data model using **PowerPivot**, which is an add-in for Excel 2013 that provides the tools for performing more advanced data analysis and modeling. With PowerPivot, you can:

- Apply filters to tables stored in the data model.
- Rename tables and fields within the data model.
- Define and manage the relationships among data tables joined by common fields.
- Format data values that will be used in PivotTables and other Excel reports.
- Create calculated fields based on data fields from multiple data sources.
- Create advanced data structures and models.

Note that the PowerPivot add-in is not available for Microsoft Office running on tablet devices. Rafael wants you to view the data model that is part of the Chalcedony Fund workbook. You will install the PowerPivot add-in.

To install the PowerPivot add-in:

1. On the ribbon, look for the **POWERPIVOT** tab. If it appears on the ribbon, skip the rest of these steps because the PowerPivot add-in is already installed. If it doesn't appear on the ribbon, continue with Step 2.

2. On the ribbon, click the **FILE** tab, and then click **Options** in the navigation bar. The Excel Options dialog box opens.

3. In the Excel Options categories, click **Add-Ins**.

4. Click the **Manage** box arrow, click **COM Add-ins**, and then click the **Go** button. The COM Add-Ins dialog box opens.

5. In the list of available add-ins, click the **Microsoft Office PowerPivot for Excel 2013** check box.

6. Click the **OK** button. The POWERPIVOT tab is added to the ribbon.

Adding a Table to the Data Model

The POWERPIVOT tab contains the commands for working with the data model. You use the Add to Data Model command to add Excel tables to the data model. PowerPivot displays the contents of the data model in a separate window from the Excel workbook window.

Rafael wants you to add the Excel table from the Portfolio worksheet to the data model so that it can be joined with the data imported from the Recent Performance and Company tables.

To add an Excel table to the data model:

1. Go to the **Portfolio** worksheet, and then select cell **A4** to make the Excel table active in the worksheet.

2. On the ribbon, click the **POWERPIVOT** tab. The PowerPivot commands are displayed on the ribbon.

EX 694 Excel | Tutorial 11 Connecting to External Data

3. In the Tables group, click the **Add to Data Model** button. The Portfolio table is added to the data model. See Figure 11-32.

Figure 11-32 Data view of the tables in the data model

contents of the Portfolio table are added to the data model

database tables appear on separate tabs

Viewing the Data Model

You can view the contents of a data model in Data view and in Diagram view. Data view shows the contents of each database table in the data model on a separate tab. Diagram view shows each table as an icon, and relationships between tables are indicated by connecting arrows. To see which field joins the two tables, you click the arrow connecting the tables.

The data model currently includes three tables—the Company and the Recent Performance tables, whose data was imported from the Chalcedony database, and the Portfolio table you just added. You'll review the contents of each table in Data view, and then switch to Diagram view and review the relationship among the tables.

To view the data model in Data view and Diagram view:

1. In the PowerPivot for Excel window, click the **Company** tab. The contents of the Company table are displayed.

2. Click the **Recent Performance** tab to view contents of that table.

3. Click the **Portfolio_Table** tab to return to the Portfolio table.

4. On the Home tab, in the View group, click the **Diagram View** button. The tables and relationships within the data model are displayed graphically in the PowerPivot window. An arrow connects the Company and Recent Performance tables, indicating that those two tables are related by a common field.

5. Click the arrow connecting the Company table and the Recent Performance table. The Ticker Symbol field is highlighted, indicating that it is the common field joining the two tables. See Figure 11-33.

Figure 11-33   Diagram view of the tables in the data model

Managing Relationships in the Data Model

When no arrow connects a table to any of the other tables in the data model, there is no way to match the records of that table with the other tables. To fix this, you can create a relationship between tables. When creating a relationship, you need to identify a field in each table that will be used to match the table records.

Because no arrow is connecting the Portfolio table to another table in the data model, the records of the Portfolio table cannot be matched with the records of the two other tables. Rafael wants you to establish a relationship between the Portfolio table and the Company table using the Ticker Symbol field, which is the common field in all of the tables.

Excel | Tutorial 11 Connecting to External Data

> **TIP**
> To define a relationship from within Excel, on the DATA tab, in the Data Tools group, click the Relationships button, and then click the New button in the Manage Relationships dialog box.

To create a relationship between two tables:

1. On the ribbon, click the **Design** tab. In the Relationships group, click the **Create Relationship** button. The Create Relationship dialog box opens.

2. Click the **Table** arrow, and then click **Portfolio_Table**. This identifies one of the tables you want to use to create a relationship.

3. Click the **Column** arrow, and then click **Ticker Symbol**. This identifies the field you want to use to create the relationship.

4. Click the **Related Lookup Table** arrow, and then click **Company**. This identifies the other table you want to use to create a relationship. Ticker Symbol is selected in the Related Lookup Column box, identifying the corresponding field in the Company table. See Figure 11-34.

Figure 11-34 Create Relationship dialog box

[Create Relationship dialog box showing Table: Portfolio_Table, Column: Ticker Symbol, Related Lookup Table: Company, Related Lookup Column: Ticker Symbol, with Create and Cancel buttons. Callouts: "tables to create a relationship between" and "common field between the two tables"]

5. Click the **Create** button. An arrow appears linking the Portfolio table to the Company table.

   You don't need to create a relationship between the Portfolio and Recent Performance tables because they are related via the Company table.

6. On the ribbon, click the **File** tab, and then click **Close**. The PowerPivot window closes, and you return to the Excel workbook.

Rafael wants you to add the Year High and Year Low fields to the PivotTable to display the high and low values for each stock from the previous year. Because you established a relationship between the Portfolio table and the Company table, you can add the information in the Portfolio table to the PivotTable report.

To add the Year High and Year Low fields to the PivotTable:

1. Go to the **5-Day Report** worksheet, and then click cell **D4**, if necessary, to display the PivotTable Fields pane.

2. Click **ALL** from the PivotTable Fields menu to display all of the tables accessible to this PivotTable report. Verify that Portfolio_Table is listed between the Company and Recent Performance tables.

Tutorial 11 Connecting to External Data | Excel   EX 697

3. In the PivotTable Fields pane, click **Portfolio_Table** in the list of tables. The list of fields in that table is displayed.

4. Right-click the **Year High** field, and then click **Add to Values** on the shortcut menu. The Year High field is added to the PivotTable.

5. Right-click the **Year Low** field, and then click **Add to Value** on the shortcut menu. The Year Low field is added to the PivotTable. A Message Bar appears, indicating that relationships between tables may be needed. You can ignore this warning because you have already defined the table relationship.

6. In the range **G5:H9**, format the values with the **Number** format.

7. In cell **G4**, change the column label to **Previous High**, and in cell **H4**, change the column label to **Previous Low**. See Figure 11-35.

Figure 11-35 PivotTable with the Previous High and Previous Low values added

	A	B	C	D	E	F	G	H
1	Chalcedony Fund							
2	5-Day Report							
3								
4	Title			Date	Shares Traded	Closing Value	Previous High	Previous Low
5				4/11/2016	41,561,330	8.39	10.24	7.97
6	Aluminum Company of America			4/12/2016	40,913,710	8.39	10.24	7.97
7	American Electric Power Compa...			4/13/2016	24,233,610	8.24	10.24	7.97
8	AT&T Corporation			4/14/2016	18,809,240	8.22	10.24	7.97
9	Boeing Company			4/15/2016	17,495,780	8.30	10.24	7.97
10	Canadian National Railway Com...							
11	Chevron Texaco Corporation							
12	Consolidated Edison Company o...							
13	Delta Air Lines Incorporated							
14	Hewlett-Packard Company							
15	Marathon Petroleum Corporation							

(values of the Year High and Year Low fields; fields from the Portfolio table)

PivotTable Fields — ACTIVE | ALL
- Title
- Portfolio Percent
- ☑ Year High
- ☑ Year Low

ROWS: Date
VALUES: Shares Tra..., Closing Va...

With the addition of the Year High and Year Low fields, Rafael can quickly compare the most recent values of the stock to the annual high and low values. For example, the most recent values of the Aluminum Company of America stock appear in the middle of the range of the low and high values from the previous year. To visualize this relationship, Rafael wants you to add a PivotChart to the worksheet displaying the values from the PivotTable. You'll create a combo chart with the Shares Traded values displayed as a column chart, and the Closing, Previous High, and Previous Low values displayed as a line chart on the secondary axis.

To add and format a PivotChart based on the PivotTable:

1. On the ribbon, click the **PIVOTTABLE TOOLS ANALYZE** tab. In the Tools group, click the **PivotChart** button.

2. Select **Combo** from the list of chart groups.

3. Select **Line** for the Closing Value, Previous High, and Previous Low data series, and then click the **Secondary Axis** button for each of those series.

4. Click the **OK** button.

5. Move and resize the PivotChart so that it covers the range **D10:H20**.

6. On the ribbon, click the **PIVOTCHART TOOLS ANALYZE** tab. In the Show/Hide group, click the **Field Buttons** button. The field button is no longer displayed on the PivotChart.

7. Position the chart legend at the top of the PivotChart.

8. In the Title slicer, click each company name to display information about that company in the PivotTable and PivotChart, and then click **Union Pacific Corporation** to see the PivotTable and PivotChart for the recent performance of the Union Pacific Corporation stock. See Figure 11-36.

Figure 11-36 PivotChart of recent performance data

Date	Shares Traded	Closing Value	Previous High	Previous Low
4/11/2016	1,714,000	141.30	143.00	140.49
4/12/2016	1,343,700	139.73	143.00	140.49
4/13/2016	1,261,100	139.62	143.00	140.49
4/14/2016	1,930,600	138.54	143.00	140.49
4/15/2016	2,626,500	138.46	143.00	140.49

Title slicer companies:
- Chevron Texaco Corporation
- Consolidated Edison Company o...
- Delta Air Lines Incorporated
- Hewlett-Packard Company
- Marathon Petroleum Corporation
- P P & L Resources Incorporated
- Ryder System, Incorporated
- Southwest Airlines Corporation
- Union Pacific Corporation (selected company in the Title slicer)
- Wisconsin Energy Corporation

combo PivotChart

recent stock values have fallen below the lowest value of the previous year

9. Save the workbook.

The PivotChart makes it easy to identify stocks that have fallen below or risen above the annual benchmarks. For example, the PivotChart for the Union Pacific Corporation shown in Figure 11-36 makes it clear that the stock's value in the recent week has fallen below the previous year's low point. Rafael may want to investigate this issue further.

PROSKILLS

Written Communication: Designing a Database

When creating a database within either the Excel data model or Microsoft Access, keep in mind the following common, yet important, principles:

- **Split data into multiple tables.** Keep each table focused on a specific topical area. Link the tables through one or more common fields.
- **Avoid redundant data.** Key pieces of information, such as a customer's address or phone number, should be entered in only one place in your database.
- **Use understandable field names.** Avoid using acronyms or abbreviations that may confuse your users.
- **Maintain consistency in data entry.** For example, if you abbreviate titles (such as Mr. instead of Mister), include validation rules that ensure this rule is always followed.
- **Test the database on a small subset of data before committing all of the data.** The more errors you weed out early, the easier it will be to manage your database.

Databases are great tools to organize information, track statistics, and generate reports. When used in conjunction with Excel, a properly designed database can provide valuable information and help you make informed financial decisions. However, like any tool, databases must be used correctly. A badly designed or improperly used database will end up creating more problems rather than solving them.

This session only scratched the surface of what can be accomplished using database queries and the Excel data model. Databases are a powerful addition to any workbook, and Excel is an effective tool for analyzing and reporting on that data. Rafael is pleased with your progress and wants to examine other data sources that he can use in the workbook. In the next session, you'll explore how to integrate Rafael's workbook with data from the Internet.

REVIEW

Session 11.2 Quick Check

1. Define the following terms: (a) database, (b) table, (c) field, (d) record, (e) common field.
2. What is a relational database?
3. What is a query?
4. In database design, what is a one-to-one relationship? What is a one-to-many relationship?
5. What is SQL?
6. What is the Excel data model?
7. Name two sources for the data tables that can be added to the Excel data model.
8. What is PowerPivot?

Session 11.3 Visual Overview:

A **web query** specifies which data should be retrieved from different sections of a webpage.

Web queries can apply the formatting from the webpage to the cells, such as the table format applied here.

The **URL (Uniform Resource Locator)** provides the location of a webpage.

You create a web query by specifying the URL and using Excel Web Query to select the portions of the Web page to import, such as the Fees and Expenses table.

Tutorial 11 Connecting to External Data | Excel — EX 701

Web and XML Connections

Dragging an element from the data map to a cell binds that XML value to the cell.

An **XML data map** shows the structure of an XML document in a schematic diagram.

XML Source
XML maps in this workbook:
document_Map
- document
  - Title
  - Fund_Manager
  - Manager_Tenure
  - Inception_Date
  - Net_Assets
  - Yield

Extensible Markup Language (XML) structures data in text files that can be read by a wide variety of programs, including Excel.

Title	Descriptive Information
Fund_Manager	Domestic/Hybrid
Manager_Tenure	5
Inception_Date	6/1/2008
Net_Assets	$470.2M
Yield	3.85%

```xml
<?xml version="1.0" ?>
<document>
    <Title>Descriptive Information</Title>
    <Fund_Manager>Domestic/Hybrid</Fund_Manager>
    <Manager_Tenure>5</Manager_Tenure>
    <Inception_Date>6/1/2008</Inception_Date>
    <Net_Assets>$470.2M</Net_Assets>
    <Yield>3.85%</Yield>
</document>
```

Each piece of data in an XML document is contained within an **element**, which includes an opening tag, the element content, and a closing tag, such as the Yield element.

```xml
    Manager_Tenure
    <Inception_Date>6/1/
    <Net_Assets>$470.2M</N
    <Yield>3.85%</Yield>
</document>
```

The **opening tag** marks the beginning of the data value.

The **element content** is the actual data.

The **closing tag** marks the end of the data value.

Creating a Web Query

Chesterton Financial often stores corporate information on its web server to be displayed on the company webpage. To keep his Excel workbooks in sync with the data stored on the company's website, Rafael wants to create a query that retrieves data from the company webpage. The Chesterton Financial website includes pages that describe the various funds the company supports. The Chalcedony Fund webpage shown in Figure 11-37 provides descriptive information about the fund, such as the name of the fund manager and the fund's inception date.

Figure 11-37   Webpage about the Chalcedony Fund

Chesterton Financial

Chalcedony Fund

Descriptive Information	
Category	Domestic/Hybrid
Fund Manager	Garcia/Calley
Manager Tenure	8
Inception Date	6/1/2011
Net Assets	$711.5 mil
Yield	2.75%

Fees and Expenses	
Expense Ratio	0.74%
Front Load	5%
Deferred Sales Charge	0%
Redemption Fee	0%
12b-1 Fee	0%
Purchase Constraints	None
Minimum Initial Purchase	$5,000 (reg), $0 (IRA)
Minimum Subsequent Purchase	$300 (reg), $0 (IRA)

Projected Expenses for $1,000 Purchase	
3-year	$96
5-year	$126
10-year	$212
Redemption Fee	0%

three tables describing the fund

You could copy and paste the data from the webpage into the workbook, but Rafael wants to create a query between the webpage and the workbook so that the workbook always matches the material on the company's website. To create this web query, you need to know the URL of the page you are accessing. A copy of the Chalcedony Fund's information webpage, chldfunds.htm, is included with your Data Files. If the file is stored on a web server, the URL would follow the format

```
http://server/path/filename
```

where *server* is the name of the computer or web server storing the page, *path* is the path to the folder on the server in which the page is stored, and *filename* is the name of the webpage file. The following is an example of a URL in this format:

```
http://www.example.net/docs/chldfunds.htm
```

When a file is stored locally and not on a web server, the URL follows the format

```
file:///drive:/path/filename
```

where *drive* is the letter of the drive containing the file, *path* is the full path name of the folder containing the file, and *filename* is the filename of the webpage.

TIP
If you don't know the complete path to a webpage, open the page in your web browser and copy the path from the browser's Address box.

Tutorial 11 Connecting to External Data | Excel   EX 703

For example, if the Data Files are on drive Z and chldfunds.htm is located in the Excel11 ► Tutorial folder, the URL is as follows:

```
file:///Z:/Excel11/Tutorial/chldfunds.htm
```

If you don't include the `file:` prefix for the URL, your computer will attempt to locate the file on the web and not in a folder stored locally on your computer. If you don't want to enter this long string of text, you can also enter the path to the folder and webpage file in the following form, which is more standard:

```
Z:\Excel11\Tutorial\chldfunds.htm
```

The web query will replace this text with the URL form.

REFERENCE

Working with Web Queries

To create a web query:
- On the DATA tab, in the Get External Data group, click the From Web button.
- In the Address box, enter the URL of the website or the folder path to a local file.
- Click the selection arrows for the parts of the webpage you want to retrieve.
- Click the Import button.

To set the web query format options:
- Open the Connection Properties dialog box for the query.
- On the Definition tab, click the Edit Query button.
- Click the Options button, select format options, and then click the OK button.

To save a web query:
- Open the Connection Properties dialog box for the query.
- On the Definition tab, click the Edit Query button.
- Click the Save Query button, specify the filename and location, and then click the Save button.

You'll create a web connection to the Chalcedony Web page using the chldfunds.htm file included with your Data Files.

To create a web query to import the Chalcedony webpage:

1. If you took a break at the end of the previous session, make sure the Chalcedony Fund workbook is open. If a dialog box opens, prompting you to enter a password for the 5-Day Performance Data connection, click the Cancel button to proceed to the workbook.

2. Go to the **Summary** worksheet.

3. On the ribbon, click the **DATA** tab. In the Get External Data group, click the **From Web** button. The New Web Query dialog box opens.

   Trouble? If a Security Alert dialog box opens, click the No button in that and each subsequent dialog box to proceed to the New Web Query dialog box.

4. In the Address box, enter the path to the **chldfunds.htm** file located in the Excel11 ► Tutorial folder included with your Data Files. For example, if the file is located in the Documents\Data\Excel11\Tutorial folder of drive E, you would enter E:\Documents\Data\Excel11\Tutorial\chldfunds.htm.

   Make sure you enter the complete path to the webpage file and not simply its filename.

5. Press the **Enter** key. The contents of the chldfunds webpage appear in the dialog box. See Figure 11-38.

Figure 11-38   New Web Query dialog box

click the selection arrow to select the table for importing

▶ 6. Click the **selection** arrow next to the Descriptive Information table. The selection arrow changes to a green checkmark to indicate that this table is selected.

▶ 7. Scroll down, click the **selection** arrow next to the Fees and Expenses table, and then click the **selection** arrow next to the Projected Expenses for $1,000 Purchase table. The tables are selected.

▶ 8. Click the **Import** button. The Import Data dialog box opens.

▶ 9. Click cell **A1** in the Summary worksheet, and then click the **OK** button. The webpage content is imported into the Summary worksheet. See Figure 11-39.

Figure 11-39   Worksheet with imported webpage data

unformatted data from the chldfunds.htm file

	A	B
1	Chalcedony Fund	
2	Summary	
3		
4	Descriptive Information	
5	Category	Domestic/Hybrid
6	Fund Manager	Garcia/Calley
7	Manager Tenure	8
8	Inception Date	6/1/2011
9	Net Assets	$711.5 mil
10	Yield	2.75%
11		
12	Fees and Expenses	
13	Expense Ratio	0.74%
14	Front Load	5%
15	Deferred Sales Charge	0%
16	Redemption Fee	0%
17	12b-1 Fee	0%
18	Purchase Constraints	None
19	Minimum Initial Purchase	$5,000 (reg), $0 (IRA)

Summary | Portfolio | Current Values | 5-Day Report | Fund History

READY

Formatting a Web Query

The text from the web query was placed in the worksheet as unformatted text. If you format this text, the formatting is preserved when Excel refreshes the data later. Another option is to retrieve both the webpage data and the styles used on the webpage.

You can retrieve the webpage format using None, Rich text formatting only, or Full HTML formatting. None, which is the default, imports the text but not the formatting. **Rich Text Format (RTF)** is a file format that allows for text formatting styles including boldface, italic, and color, but not advanced features such as hyperlinks or complicated table structures. The Full HTML formatting option retrieves all simple as well as advanced HTML formatting features, including hyperlinks. Full HTML formatting results in imported data that most closely resembles the appearance of the webpage.

Rafael wants the text on this page to resemble the webpage. You'll format the web query you just created to use full HTML formatting by modifying the connection properties.

To format the web query:

1. On the DATA tab, in the Connections group, click the **Connections** button. The Workbook Connections dialog box opens.

2. Click **Connection** in the Name column, and then click the **Properties** button. The Connection Properties dialog box opens.

3. Type **Chalcedony Fund webpage** in the Connection name box, type **Data from the Chalcedony Fund webpage** in the Description box, and then click the **Refresh data when opening the file** check box.

4. Click the **Definition** tab, and then click the **Edit Query** button. The Edit Web Query dialog box opens and displays the contents of the Chalcedony HTML file.

5. On the Edit Web Query toolbar, click the **Options** button. The Web Query Options dialog box opens.

6. Click the **Full HTML formatting** option button to specify that this web query should retrieve the HTML formatting along with the webpage text, and then click the **OK** button.

7. Click the **Import** button in the Edit Web Query dialog box, and then click the **OK** button in the Connection Properties dialog box. The Workbook Connections dialog box reappears.

8. Make sure the Chalcedony Fund webpage is still selected, click the **Refresh** button, and then click the **Close** button. The Workbook Connections dialog box closes. The worksheet is updated, reflecting the full HTML formatting of the original webpage. See Figure 11-40.

Figure 11-40 | **Formatted web data**

	A	B	C	D	E	F	G
1	Chalcedony Fund						
2	Summary						
3							
4	**Descriptive Information**						
5	Category	Domestic/Hybrid					
6	Fund Manager	Garcia/Calley					
7	Manager Tenure	8					
8	Inception Date	6/1/2011					
9	Net Assets	$711.5 mil					
10	Yield	2.75%					
11							
12	**Fees and Expenses**						
13	Expense Ratio	0.74%					
14	Front Load	5%					
15	Deferred Sales Charge	0%					
16	Redemption Fee	0%					
17	12b-1 Fee	0%					
18	Purchase Constraints	None					

◀ ... **Summary** | Portfolio | Current Values | 5-Day Report | Fund History | ⊕

data displayed with the webpage formatting

Saving a Web Query

You can save the web query to a permanent file that you share among other Office documents. The saved connection file can then be loaded in any Office program. For example, after saving the Chalcedony Fund webpage web query, Rafael can retrieve the contents of the Chalcedony Fund webpage and display them in a Word document. Because Rafael wants to place the Chalcedony Fund information in other workbooks, you'll save the Chalcedony Fund webpage web query in a permanent file.

To save the Chalcedony Fund webpage web query:

1. On the DATA tab, in the Connections group, click the **Connections** button. The Workbook Connections dialog box opens.

2. Click **Chalcedony Fund webpage** in the Name column, and then click the **Properties** button. The Connection Properties dialog box opens.

3. Click the **Definition** tab, and then click the **Edit Query** button. The Edit Web Query dialog box opens.

4. On the Edit Web Query toolbar, click the **Save Query** button 📇. The Save Workspace dialog box opens, displaying the contents of the Microsoft ▸ Queries folder. You'll save the query file in the location specified by your instructor.

5. Navigate to the location specified by your instructor, type **Chalcedony Web Query** in the File name box, and then click the **Save** button.

6. Click the **Import** button in the Edit Web Query dialog box, click the **OK** button in the Connection Properties dialog box, and then click the **Close** button in the Workbook Connections dialog box to return to the workbook.

> **TIP**
> You can view and edit web query files in Notepad. Using web query language, you can create sophisticated programs to retrieve and process web data.

Tutorial 11 Connecting to External Data | Excel **EX 707**

Retrieving Data Using Office Apps

Excel can be used with **Office apps**, which are small, specialized programs that enhance the features of Excel, Word, PowerPoint, and other programs in the Office suite. Microsoft includes Office apps for a variety of tasks including retrieving articles from online encyclopedias such as Wikipedia, inserting maps whose contents can be linked with locations listed in the worksheet, and retrieving timely stock quotes and financial information for specified companies.

Rafael often needs to know how the stocks in the Chalcedony Fund portfolio are performing at each moment. To retrieve up-to-the-minute reports on each stock's trading value, you will use an Office app.

Inserting an Office App

Apps are downloaded from the Microsoft Office Store. Most apps are free. To download and use Office apps, you need an account with Microsoft Office. The account is free, requiring only a username and password to set up.

Rafael wants you to use the Bing Finance app to display information on the stocks in the Chalcedony Fund. You'll download and install this app from the Microsoft Office Store. First, you must add this app to your Office account. If you don't have an Office account, you'll need to sign up for one before you can complete the steps in this section. Otherwise, read but do not complete the steps in this section.

To add the Bing Finance app to your Office account:

1. On the ribbon, click the **INSERT** tab. In the Apps group, click the **Apps for Office** button. The Apps for Office window opens, showing any apps in your Office account. See Figure 11-41, which shows an account with no apps added.

Figure 11-41   Apps for Office window

Apps for Office
MY APPS | FEATURED APPS   Refresh

No Apps
Add apps to your account at the Office Store.

Office Store

- click to view a list of your active Office apps
- click to view a list of featured Office apps
- click to refresh the list of available apps
- click to access the Microsoft Office Store for apps and programs

Trouble? If you see "You need a Microsoft account to use apps from the Office Store. Sign In.," click the Sign In link, type your email address, click the Next button, type your password, and then click the Sign in button.

2. Check whether the **Bing Finance** app is listed. If it is, the app has already been added to your Office account and you can skip these steps. Otherwise, continue with Step 3.

3. Click the **FEATURED APPS** link. A list of recently added and highly rated apps appears in the window.

4. Click in the **Search for apps on the Office Store** box near the upper-right corner of the window, type **Bing Finance**, and then press the **Enter** key. The Office Store website opens in your web browser and displays a list of finance apps.

5. Click **Bing Finance** in the list of apps. A webpage displays information about the Bing Finance app.

   Trouble? If you don't see Bing Finance, scroll down the list to locate the Bing Finance app. If you still can't locate the app, its name might have changed. Ask your instructor or technical resource person for help.

6. Click the **Add** button to add the app to your Microsoft Office account.

7. If you are prompted to sign in to your Office account, enter your username and password, and then click the **Sign in** button. If you do not have an Office account, click the **Sign up now** link to set up your free account, and then return to the Office Store to add the Bing Finance app.

8. Click the **Continue** button to confirm that you want to add the Bing Finance app to your Office account.

Once an app has been added to your account, you need to insert it into Excel to make it available for use with your workbooks. You'll insert the Bing Finance app now.

To insert the Bing Finance app into Excel:

1. Close your web browser and return to Excel.

2. On the INSERT tab, in the Apps group, click the **Apps for Office** button. The Apps for Office window opens.

3. In the upper-left corner, click the **MY APPS** link to display a list of apps added to your Office account.

4. Click **Bing Finance**, and then click the **Insert** button. The Bing Finance pane opens on the right side of the Excel window.

Retrieving Stock Market Data

Now that you've added and activated the Bing Finance app, you can use it to import current stock market data into your workbook. The Bing Finance app provides current price quotes and news on stocks. You specify the stock by entering the stock's ticker

Tutorial 11 Connecting to External Data | Excel EX 709

symbol (an abbreviation for a stock name) or its name. The app searches through its database and lists the stocks that match your search criteria. You select a stock from that list, and then add its information to an Excel table or display it in the Bing Finance pane.

Rafael wants you to display information on the Hewlett-Packard stock. You'll place this information in the Current Values worksheet.

To retrieve current price data and news using Bing Finance:

1. Go to the **Current Values** worksheet, and then select cell **A4**.

2. If necessary, in the Bing Finance pane, click **PORTFOLIO**.

3. Click the **Enter security symbol or name** box, type **HPQ** (the ticker symbol for the Hewlett-Packard stock), and then press the **Enter** key.

4. Click **HPQ-Exchange: NYS** from the search list to retrieve current price quotes for Hewlett-Packard stock on the New York Stock Exchange.

5. In the Bing Finance pane, click the **Insert New Table** box. A table of current stock values is inserted into an Excel table in the worksheet.

6. Set the width of column B to **22** characters so that you can view the complete name of the stock, set the width of columns C through E to **18** characters, and then select cell **A5**. See Figure 11-42.

Figure 11-42 NEWS pivot in the Bing Finance app

TIP

You can view detailed stories about the stock by scrolling down and clicking the links below the NEWS pivot in the Bing Finance pane.

The app shows the current price of the stock as well as the change in price since the market opened expressed in the stock value and as a percentage of the stock's opening value. For example, as you can see in Figure 11-42, the Hewlett-Packard stock has declined in value by 0.1 percent since the market closed the previous day. Also note that in the Bing Finance pane, NEWS displays a line chart of stock activity during the current day, the current month, a one-year period, a five-year period, or the entire history of the stock.

By default, the Excel table shows the symbol, company name, current price, change in price, percent change in price, quantity, and total for the current stock. You can change what values are included in the Excel table to highlight other stock information. Rafael is not interested in the Quantity and Total columns, but he wants the table to display the volume of shares traded.

To display different stock data in the Excel table:

1. Delete columns F and G from the Excel table.
2. In the Bing Finance pane, click **PORTFOLIO**, and then scroll down to see the list of selected and available data columns.
3. Drag the **Volume** box from the AVAILABLE column to the bottom of the SELECTED column. The volume data is added to the Excel table.
4. Increase the width of column F to **12** characters.
5. In the Bing Finance pane, click **PORTFOLIO** to redisplay the list of data columns. See Figure 11-43.

Figure 11-43 Selected columns for the finance table

You can add additional rows to the table for other stocks by entering their ticker symbols in the first column. The Bing Finance app will automatically retrieve and insert the current stock prices for each row. Be aware that stock quotes from the free Bing Finance app are delayed by 15 minutes. To obtain the most current stock quotes, you must purchase an app from the Office Store.

Rafael wants you to add the rest of the stocks that make up the Chalcedony Fund. Rather than looking up and typing each stock symbol, you can copy them from the information you imported into the Portfolio worksheet.

Tutorial 11 Connecting to External Data | Excel   EX 711

To add the rest of the Chalcedony Fund stocks to the table:

1. Go to the **Portfolio** worksheet, and then copy the range **A6:A19**.

2. Go to the **Current Values** worksheet, and then paste the ticker symbol but not the formats in the range **A6:A19** of that worksheet.

3. In the Bing Finance pane, click the **Refresh** button to refresh the stock market data in the Excel table. The current price and volume data on all 15 stocks are displayed in the table. See Figure 11-44 (your data will differ).

Figure 11-44 Quotes for all of the stocks in the Chalcedony fund

Symbol	Company Name	Current Price	Change in Price	% Change in Price	Volume
HPQ	Hewlett-Packard Co	26.42	0.04	0.13%	8.33M
BA	Boeing Co	104.25	-1.41	-1.33%	5.21M
MPC	Marathon Petroleum	70.07	-3.04	-4.15%	4.44M
CVX	Chevron	124.06	-0.63	-0.50%	3.1M
T	AT&T	35.84	0.29	0.82%	14.39M
AA	Alcoa Inc	8.1	-0.07	-0.86%	8.62M
DAL	Delta Air Lines	19.28	-0.16	-0.82%	4.52M
R	Ryder System Inc	60.39	-0.98	-1.60%	583.1K
CNI	Canadian National Railwa	100.71	-0.27	-0.27%	279.84K
UNP	Union Pacific Corp	159.23	-0.57	-0.36%	1.15M
LUV	Southwest Airlines Co	13.42	-0.06	-0.45%	3.1M
ED	Consolidated Edison Inc	59.8	-0.25	-0.42%	1.12M
PPL	PPL Corp	30.82	-0.07	-0.22%	2.73M
AEP	American Electric Power (	47.22	-0.28	-0.59%	2.13M
WEC	Wisconsin Energy Corp	42.83	-0.27	-0.63%	1.22M

- ticker symbols pasted into the table
- current price and volume data

You can view detailed information about any particular stock in the Bing Finance pane by selecting its ticker symbol in the table.

4. Select cell **A6**, which contains the ticker symbol for Boeing Company. Detailed information about the Boeing stock appears in the Bing Finance pane.

5. Explore the current values for the other stocks in the portfolio. Close the Bing Finance pane when you are finished.

Importing Data from XML

Another important data source for Excel workbooks is XML documents. XML (the Extensible Markup Language) is a language used to create structured documents using only text. Because an XML document is a simple text file, a wide variety of programs and applications can read it. In fact, the internal code for Microsoft Office documents is saved in an XML format called the Office Open XML. XML documents are also easy to transfer over the Internet, which makes them ideal for web-based applications. Figure 11-45 shows an example of an XML document named Documentation created by a programmer at Chesterton Financial.

Figure 11-45 Contents of the Documentation XML file

root element →

```xml
<?xml version="1.0" encoding="UTF-8" standalone="yes"?>
<document xmlns:xsi="http://www.w3.org/2001/XMLSchema-instance"
          xsi:noNamespaceSchemaLocation="Rules.xsd">

    <title>Chesterton Financial</title>
    <subtitle>Chalcedony Funds Report</subtitle>
    <date>2016-04-15</date>
    <author>Rafael Garcia</author>
    <filename>Chalcedony Report.xlsx</filename>
    <notes>1) Chalcedony Funds information comes from the Web page, chldfunds.htm</notes>
    <notes>2) Portfolio data comes from the Access database, Chalcedony Data.accdb</notes>
    <notes>3) Current Values data comes from the NYSE Web site</notes>
    <notes>4) Recent Results data comes from the Access database, Chalcedony Data.accdb</notes>
    <notes>5) Fund History data comes from the CHHistory.txt file</notes>

</document>
```

opening tag | element content | closing tag

Each piece of data in an XML document is contained within an element. The data is marked by an opening and closing tag. For example, the following code shows the author element, Rafael Garcia, contained within an opening (`<author>`) and closing (`</author>`) tag:

`<author>Rafael Garcia</author>`

The opening and closing tags in Figure 11-45 are black and the data content is red to make it easier to differentiate the tags from the information they contain.

An XML document is structured like a tree in which elements are placed within one another, descending from a common **root element**. The structure of the document is displayed in a data map. The data map associated with the Documentation XML file is shown in Figure 11-46. Under this structure, the root element, `document`, contains six elements named `title`, `subtitle`, `date`, `author`, `filename`, and `notes`.

Figure 11-46 Data map of the Documentation XML file

root element → document
- title
- subtitle ← optional element
- date
- author
- filename
- notes ← notes element allows for multiple values

required elements →

One advantage of XML is that the document author can create rules specifying which elements are required and what types of values are allowed within each element. These rules are stored in a second document called the **schema**. Schemas are not required, but they are useful in ensuring the integrity and validity of XML data. Rules from the schema also appear in the data map. For example, required elements are marked with a red star. The required elements in the Documentation XML file are `document`, `title`, `date`, `author`, and `filename`. Elements that can contain multiple values are identified in the data map by a document icon with an arrow. In Figure 11-46, only the `notes` element allows multiple values.

Editing an XML File

Before you import the data from the Documentation XML file, you'll edit it by inserting your own name in the author element.

To edit the Documentation XML document:

▶ 1. Start Notepad or another text editor, and then open the **Documentation** XML file located in the Excel11 ▶ Tutorial folder included with your Data Files.

▶ 2. Select the author name **Rafael Garcia** located between the <author> and </author> tags, and then type your name. Do not delete the tags when you replace the name.

▶ 3. Save the file, and then close it.

▶ 4. Return to the **Chalcedony Fund** workbook in Excel.

The first step in connecting a workbook to an XML document is to generate the data map. After Excel has generated a data map, you can use it to place XML content anywhere within the workbook.

Loading an XML Data Map

The commands to access the data map of an XML document are part of the Excel Developer tools. To work with an XML data map, you must show the DEVELOPER tab on the ribbon. If the XML document has a schema file attached to it, you can load a data map without actually importing the data into the Excel workbook.

REFERENCE

Loading an XML Data Map

- On the DEVELOPER tab, in the XML group, click the Source button.
- In the XML Source task pane, click the XML Maps button.
- Locate and select the XML document file.
- In the XML Maps dialog box, click the Rename button to define a name for the map.

Rafael wants you to load the Documentation XML document and generate a data map for the workbook.

To generate an XML data map:

▶ 1. If the DEVELOPER tab does not appear on the ribbon, right-click the ribbon, click **Customize the Ribbon** on the shortcut menu, click the **Developer** check box in the Customize the Ribbon box, and then click the **OK** button.

▶ 2. Go to the **Documentation** worksheet.

▶ 3. On the ribbon, click the **DEVELOPER** tab. In the XML group, click the **Source** button. The XML Source pane opens on the right side of the workbook window. From this pane, you can generate the data map for the Documentation.xml file.

4. Click the **XML Maps** button at the bottom of the XML Source pane. The XML Maps dialog box opens so you can add an XML data map to the workbook.

5. Click the **Add** button. The Select XML Source dialog box opens.

6. Click the **Documentation** XML file located in the Excel11 ▸ Tutorial folder included with your Data Files, and then click the **Open** button. The document map for the Documentation XML file is added to the list of XML maps in the current workbook and assigned the name document_Map.

7. Click the **Rename** button, type **Documentation information**, and then press the **Enter** key to give the data map a more descriptive name.

8. Click the **OK** button. The Documentation information data map is loaded into Excel and appears in the XML Source pane. See Figure 11-47.

Figure 11-47   XML Source pane

XML Source pane showing:
- XML maps in this workbook: Documentation information
- data map for the Documentation XML file: document > title, subtitle, date, author, filename, notes
- click to set display options for the data map: Options
- click to add a new data map: XML Maps...
- Verify Map for Export...
- Tips for mapping XML

Binding XML Elements to a Worksheet

One advantage of using XML as a data source is that you can attach or **bind** elements to specific cells in the workbook, providing greater freedom in laying out the data. To bind an element to a cell, you drag the element name from the data map and drop it into the cell. After you drop the element, you can place the element name above or to the right of the cell (if those locations are available). If a Header Options button appears next to a cell, you can click the button to define where you want to place an element's name (if you want it displayed at all). The Header Options button does not appear for elements you place in the leftmost column of the worksheet because no room is available to place the element name to the left of or above the element data.

Rafael wants you to bind the elements of the Documentation XML file to cells in the Documentation worksheet.

Tutorial 11 Connecting to External Data | Excel   EX 715

To bind elements from the data map to the workbook:

TIP
To map an entire XML document into an Excel table, click the From Other Sources button in the Get External Data group on the DATA tab, and then click From XML Data Import.

1. In the XML Source pane, click **author** in the Documentation information data map and drag it to cell **B4** in the Documentation worksheet. No data appears in the cell because you have not actually imported the contents of the Documentation XML file. You've only defined where you want to bind the contents of the author element.

2. Click the **Header Options** button located to the right of cell B4 and click the **Place XML Heading to Left** option button. The author element name appears in cell A4.

3. Repeat Steps 1 and 2 to bind the **date** and **filename** elements in cells **B5** and **B6**, respectively.

4. Drag the **notes** element from the data map to cell **B8**. Because this element can contain multiple values, Excel places it into the cell as an Excel table. The element name is placed above the table in cell B8. See Figure 11-48.

Figure 11-48   XML elements bound to the worksheet

- element content highlighted with a blue box
- element names
- notes element displayed as an Excel table

Importing XML Data

By using XML and the data map, you placed the elements in specific locations in the Documentation worksheet. Because these cells are now bound with elements from the XML file, you can import the XML data directly into the worksheet cells. To retrieve the XML data, you refresh the connection to the data source. Excel will automatically place the data in the correct worksheet cells.

Rafael wants you to import the data from the Documentation XML file into the Documentation worksheet.

To import data from the Documentation XML file:

1. In the Documentation worksheet, select cell **B4**. The active cell could be any of the cells in which an XML element is bound—in this case, cell B4, cell B5, cell B6, or cell B8.

2. On the ribbon, click the **DATA** tab. In the Connections group, click the **Refresh All button arrow**, and then click **Refresh**. Excel retrieves the XML data and places it in the workbook. See Figure 11-49.

Figure 11-49   XML data imported into the worksheet

your name and the current date appear here

You will complete the XML data connection by defining the connection properties.

3. In the Connections group, click the **Connections** button. The Workbook Connections dialog box opens.

4. Click **Documentation** in the list of workbook connections, and then click the **Properties** button.

5. Type **Report Documentation** in the Connection name box, and then type **Retrieves information about the Chalcedony Fund Report from the Documentation.xml file** in the Description box to provide descriptive information about the connection established to the Documentation XML file.

6. Click the **OK** button to close the Connection Properties dialog box, and then click the **Close** button to close the Workbook Connections dialog box.

7. Remove the **DEVELOPER** tab from the ribbon.

As with database and webpage queries, you can automatically update the XML data in a workbook to reflect changes to the source XML document.

> ### INSIGHT
>
> ### Consolidating Data
>
> When a workbook contains many data sources, you will often want to consolidate that information in one simple report. You can summarize or consolidate data from several data sources by doing any of the following:
>
> - Create a PivotTable report. This method is extremely flexible in terms of choosing the data sources, calculating summary statistics, and laying out the appearance of the summary report and accompanying charts.
> - Write formulas that include 3-D references to summarize data drawn from several worksheets or workbooks. This approach requires more work because you must lay out the report from scratch, but it can result in creative and visually appealing summary reports.
> - Use the Consolidate button in the Data Tools group on the DATA tab to create a master worksheet that summarizes data from multiple worksheets within the same workbook. You can display the sum, count, average, or other summary statistics of data values from the worksheets.
>
> The Consolidate command can be applied in two ways. One way is to consolidate by position, which requires data to be laid out exactly the same way and in the same ranges on all the worksheets. The second way is to consolidate by category, which uses labels in the top row or first column of the data ranges on the different worksheets to identify the categories to be summarized. This means that the data can be laid out differently on each worksheet as long as the worksheets use the same row and column labels. You can use Excel Help to learn more about the Consolidate command.

Using Real-Time Data Acquisition

For Rafael's workbook, you imported data from four sources—simple text files, databases, webpages, and XML documents. Scientists and researchers have a fifth possible data source—**real-time data acquisition** in which data values are retrieved from measuring devices and scientific equipment connected to a computer. For example, a climate researcher might connect a laptop to a temperature sensor and import temperature values at one-minute intervals directly into a workbook. To use real-time data acquisition, you usually need to purchase an add-in that manages the communication stream between Excel and the measuring device. To facilitate real-time data acquisition, Excel provides the RTD (real-time data) function. The syntax of the RTD function is

```
RTD(ProgID, server, topic1[, topic2][, topic3]...)
```

where `ProgID` is the program ID of the add-in that has been installed on the computer to manage the communication stream, `server` is the name of the server where the add-in is run (leave `server` blank if the add-in is being run on your computer), and `topic1`, `topic2`, and so forth are names assigned to the real-time data values. You can insert up to 28 different topics. After you insert the RTD function into a cell, the value of the cell displays the latest value retrieved from the measuring device. You can also write a VBA macro to run the RTD function in a range of cells, recording the last several values from the measuring device.

By using the RTD function along with an add-in program, the scientist or researcher can save hours of data entry time and concentrate on analysis.

PROSKILLS

Problem Solving: Best Practices for Data Storage

In the past, it was generally accepted that the solution to the ever-increasing need for data was to simply increase the amount of data storage. However, this is no longer the case as the cost of managing the stored data is outstripping the cost of purchasing and upgrading the physical data storage medium. In order to reduce costs and improve data quality, many information managers are looking at different ways to improve their data storage practices. Whether you are storing data in text files, databases, web servers, or XML documents, keep in mind the following practices:

- Maintain an inventory of your data, including where it is located and how it is stored. Know what you have and make that information available for others.
- Develop a system that searches for and removes duplicated data.
- Develop a policy for handling stale data. Many businesses will regularly purge records that are more than five years old or move them to offsite storage.

By developing a data storage policy, you can help ensure that the data you want to analyze can be easily retrieved and imported into your Excel workbooks. It also ensures that more of your time is spent understanding the data rather than trying to locate it.

The Chalcedony Fund workbook is complete. By tapping into a variety of data sources, you have created a file that Rafael can use to get current information on the fund as well as examine long-term and short-term data to look for important trends. He expects to find many ways to incorporate this new information into his daily work as an investment counselor at Chesterton Financial.

REVIEW

Session 11.3 Quick Check

1. Describe how to import data from a webpage into a workbook.
2. What are the three options for retaining the format styles found within an imported webpage?
3. Describe how to insert an Office app into an Excel workbook.
4. How would you import the most current stock market data into a workbook?
5. What is XML?
6. What is an XML data map?
7. What Excel function would you use to retrieve real-time data from a measuring device connected to your computer?

Tutorial 11 Connecting to External Data | Excel   EX 719

SAM Projects

Put your skills into practice with SAM Projects! SAM Projects for this tutorial can be found online. If you have a SAM account, go to www.cengage.com/sam2013 to download the most recent Project Instructions and Start Files.

Review Assignments

Data Files needed for the Review Assignments: Crystal.xlsx, Crystal History.txt, Crystal Data.accdb, Crystal Docs.xml, crystalweb.htm, Schema.xsd

Rafael has another fund he wants you to analyze. The Crystal Fund is based on dozens of stocks with information stored in text files, Access databases, webpages, and XML files. Current stock values can also be downloaded from the web using an Office app. Rafael wants you to create a workbook based on all of those data sources, displaying historic, short-term, and current information on the fund. Complete the following:

1. Open the **Crystal** workbook located in the Excel11 ▸ Review folder included with your Data Files, and then save the workbook as **Crystal Fund** in the location specified by your instructor.
2. In the Historic Record worksheet, retrieve 10 years of data on the fund by importing the contents of the **Crystal History** text file located in the Tutorial11 ▸ Review folder. Start the import from row 6 of the text file where the column labels are placed. The text uses a tab delimiter to separate one column from another. Format the Date column with the MDY date format, and format the Close column with the General format. Do not import the Open, High, and Low columns. Import the data into the Historic Record worksheet starting at cell A4.
3. Change the connection properties. Rename the data connection **Crystal Fund historical records**. Add the description **Data imported from the Crystal History.txt file**. Set the data to refresh whenever the workbook is opened, but do not have Excel prompt for the filename.
4. Create a line chart of the data you just imported. Move the chart to cover the range D4:K18. Add descriptive titles to the chart. Format the chart appropriately to best convey the data.
5. In the Stock Summary worksheet, use Microsoft Query to import data from the **Crystal Data** Access database located in the Excel11 ▸ Review folder. From the Profile table, include the Symbol, Name, and Sector fields. From the Summary table, include the Year High, Year Low, PE, EPS, Dividends, and Yield fields. From the Financial table, include the Profit Margin field.
6. Add a query to sort the data by ascending order of the Name field.
7. Import the selected data into cell A4 of the Stock Summary worksheet as an Excel table. Name the table **Stock_Summary**.
8. Rename the data connection **Crystal Fund Stocks**, and enter the description **Data retrieved from the Crystal Data Access database**. Refresh the data whenever the workbook is opened.
9. Import the Profile and Recent History tables from the Crystal Data Access database into Excel. Place the imported tables into a PivotTable report located in cell E4 of the Stock Performance worksheet.
10. Format the PivotTable report displaying the recent history of the stocks in the Crystal Fund with the following content:
    a. Place the Date field in the ROWS section of the PivotTable. Place the Volume and Close fields in the VALUE section of the table.
    b. Rename cells E4, F4, and G4 as **Date**, **Shares Traded**, and **Closing Value**, respectively.
    c. Format the closing values using the Comma style with no decimal places. Format the closing values with the Number format with two decimal places. Resize the columns to fit the column labels.

d. Remove the grand totals from the PivotTable.
e. In the range A4:D14, add a PivotTable slicer that contains the Name field.
11. Add the Stock_Summary Excel table displayed in the Stock Summary worksheet to the data model.
12. Use PowerPivot to create a relationship connecting the Recent History table to the Profile table using the Symbol field as the common field. Create another relationship that connects the Stock_Summary table to the Profile table using Symbol as the common field.
13. In the Stock Performance worksheet, add the Year High and Year Low fields to the VALUE section of the PivotTable. Change the column labels for the two fields to **Previous High** and **Previous Low**, respectively.
14. Add a Combo PivotChart to the A15:D26 range with the Shares Traded value displayed as a Column chart, and the Closing, Previous High, and Previous Low values displayed in the Line chart on the secondary axis. Format the chart as you wish to make the data easy to read and interpret.
15. Click different company names in the slicer and verify that you can view the recent history of each stock in the Crystal Fund.
16. Add a new sheet named **Fund Summary** and move it to be the first worksheet in the workbook. In cell A1, enter **Crystal Fund** and format it with the Title cell style. In cell A2, enter **Fund Summary** and format it with the Heading 4 cell style.
17. In the Fund Summary worksheet, import data from the **crystalweb** HTML file located in the Tutorial11 ▶ Review folder. Select the contents of the Fund Overview, Performance Overview, and Sector Weightings tables. Import the webpage data into cell A4 using full HTML formatting.
18. Name the connection to the webpage **Crystal Fund webpage** with the description **Data retrieved from the webpage**. Set the connection to be refreshed when the workbook is opened.
19. In the Current Values worksheet, starting from cell A4, use the Bing Finance app to insert an Excel table containing columns for Symbol, Company Name, Current Price, % Change in Price, and Previous Close for the American Water Works Company using the stock symbol AWK.
20. In the Current Values worksheet, in the range A6:A19, add the symbols from the remaining stocks in the Crystal Fund to the values, and then format the Excel table so that the values are easy to read.
21. Save the workbook, and then close it.
22. Open the **Crystal Docs** XML file located in the Tutorial11 ▶ Review folder using your text editor. Replace the name **Rafael Garcia** located in the author element with your name, and then save and close the file.
23. Reopen the **Crystal Fund** workbook. In the Documentation worksheet, load the XML data map for the **Crystal Docs** XML file located in the Tutorial11 ▶ Review folder.
24. Display the author element in cell B4 with the XML heading placed to the left, display the date element in cell B5 with the XML heading placed to the left, and then place the notes element in cell B6.
25. Refresh the XML data so that the documentation values appear in the worksheet.
26. Modify the connection properties for the Crystal Docs connection, changing the connection name to **Crystal Fund Documentation** and the description to **Documentation from the Crystal Docs.xml file**.
27. Save the workbook, and then close it.

Case Problem 1

Data Files needed for this Case Problem: Lighthouse.xlsx, Lighthouse Data.accdb

The Lighthouse Alicia Whitmore is the developmental director at The Lighthouse, a charitable organization in central Kentucky that works with poor and underprivileged youth. Data on donors and their contributions has been saved to an Access database. Alicia wants you to create a report that displays the total contributions from each donor.

Complete the following:

1. Open the **Lighthouse** workbook located in the Excel11 ▸ Case1 folder included with your Data Files, and then save the workbook as **Lighthouse Donor Report** in the location specified by your instructor.
2. In the Documentation worksheet, enter your name and the date.
3. Directly import the contents of the Contacts and Contributions tables from the **Lighthouse Data** Access database located in the Tutorial11 ▸ Case1 folder. Do not use Microsoft Query. Import the tables into Excel tables.
4. Name the worksheet containing the Excel table with the donor list **Donors**, and name the worksheet containing the list of contributions **Donations**.
5. Change the properties of the Lighthouse Data connection to **Lighthouse Donors and Donations** and enter the description **Data retrieved from the Contacts and Contributions tables in the Lighthouse Data.accdb file**. Refresh the connection whenever the workbook is reopened.
6. Open the data model using PowerPivot. Create a relationship from the Contributions table to the Contacts table using ID as the common field.
7. In the Donor Report worksheet, in cell A3, insert a PivotTable report using the PivotTable button located in the Tables group on the INSERT tab. In the Create PivotTable dialog box, specify the Lighthouse Donors and Donations connections as the external data source.
8. From the Contacts table, add the Last Name, First Name, Address, City, State, and Postal Code to the ROWS section of the PivotTable in that order.
9. From the Contributions table, add the Date and Amount fields to the VALUES section of the PivotTable in that order.
10. On the PIVOTTABLE TOOLS DESIGN tab, in the Layout group, click the Report Layout button, and then click the Show in Tabular Form option. The PivotTable is displayed in a table format.
11. On the PIVOTTABLE TOOLS DESIGN tab, in the Layout group, click the Subtotals button, and then click the Do Not Show Subtotals option.
12. In cell G3, change the Count of Date label to **Donations**.
13. In cell H3, change the Sum of Amount label to **Total Contributions**. Display the contribution amounts in the range H4:H38 in the Currency format.
14. Save the workbook, and then close it.

Case Problem 2

APPLY

Data Files needed for this Case Problem: Eggert.xlsx, Price List.txt, Home Data.txt

Eggert Realty David Eggert is the owner of Eggert Realty, a large real-estate agency in New Braunfels, Texas. David wants to create an Excel workbook analyzing sales prices for homes in the area. He wants to import data from two text files. The Price List text file contains a list of home prices in the area and information about whether an offer is pending on a home. The Home Data text file contains information about each listed home including the size of the home, its age, its features, its location, whether it is located on a corner lot, and the annual property tax. The text files use a delimited format in which one column is separated from another using the forward slash (/) character. You'll import the data from these text files, and then use that data to create a PivotTable comparing homes of different ages and sizes. Complete the following:

1. Open the **Eggert** workbook located in the Excel11 ▸ Case2 folder included with your Data Files, and then save the workbook as **Eggert Realty** in the location specified by your instructor.
2. In the Documentation worksheet, enter your name and the date.
3. In the Home Listings worksheet, import the contents of the **Price List** text file located in the Excel11 ▸ Case2 folder starting at row 7. Use / as the delimiter character. Insert the contents starting at cell A4 in the Home Listings worksheet and add the data to the data model.

4. Add the description **Data retrieved from the Price List.txt file** to the Price List connection. Refresh the data when the workbook is reopened, but do not prompt for the filename when the data is refreshed.
5. In the Home Data worksheet, import the contents of the **Home Data** text file located in the Excel11 ▸ Case2 folder. Again, start at row 7 and use / as the delimiter character. Insert the contents starting at cell A4 in the Home Data worksheet and add the data to the data model.
6. Add the description **Data retrieved from the Home Data.txt file** to the Home Data connection. Again, refresh the data when the workbook is reopened, but do not prompt for the filename when the data is refreshed.
7. Open PowerPivot and establish a one-to-one relationship between the Price List and Home Data tables using Listing ID as the common field.
8. In the Housing Summary worksheet, insert a PivotTable. Use an external data source for the PivotTable connection selecting the two Tables in the Workbook Data Model by clicking the tables in the Tables tag of the Existing Connections dialog box.
9. Place the PivotTable report in cell A4 of the Housing Summary worksheet.
10. David wants to compare housing prices based on the size of the house in square feet, its age, and its location. Place the Square Feet field from the Home Data table in the ROWS section of the table. Place the Age field in the COLUMNS section and the Price field in the VALUES section.
11. Change the value field settings of the Price field to display the average price value in the PivotTable.
12. In cell A5, change the Row Labels text to **Square Feet**. In cell B4, change the Column Labels text to **Age Category**. In cell A4, change the label to **Average Price**. In cell E5 and cell A19, change the labels from Grand Total to **Overall Average**.
13. Format the PivotTable to make the content easy to read and understand.
14. Add a PivotTable slicer containing the NE Sector field to the range F4:J8.
15. Create a PivotChart of the PivotTable data using the Clustered Bar chart type with the Age field as the legend category. Place the chart to cover the range F9:J19. Format the chart so that it is easy to read and interpret.
16. Save the workbook, and then close it.

Case Problem 3

Data Files needed for this Case Problem: Climate.xlsx, US Weather.accdb

Climate Report   Monica Brecht is a professor of meteorology at Lake Academy in Lancaster, Pennsylvania. For an upcoming lecture, she wants to create a workbook that provides weather statistics for major U.S. cities. This data is stored in an Access database, which she wants you to import into Excel. She also wants you to create maps that graphically display the temperature, precipitation, and snowfall for regions across the United States. To do this, you'll use an Office app that maps data values. Complete the following:

1. Open the **Climate** workbook located in the Excel11 ▸ Case3 folder included with your Data Files, and then save the workbook as **Climate Report** in the location specified by your instructor.
2. In the Documentation worksheet, enter your name and the date.
3. In the Temperature worksheet, use Microsoft Query to import the City and Temperature fields from the US Cities table in the **US Weather** Access database file located in the Tutorial11 ▸ Case3 folder. Import the data as an Excel table into cell A4.
4. Name the data connection **Temperature data** and add the description **Data retrieved from the US Weather.accdb file using MS Query**. Refresh the data connection when the workbook is opened.
5. Download and install the Bing Maps Office app from the Office Store.

Tutorial 11 Connecting to External Data | Excel **EX 723**

Explore 6. Start the Bing Maps app to display a map app on the workbook. Select the range A4:B104, and then click the Plot Locations icon at the top of the map. After several seconds, the app will map circles for each of the cities listed in the Excel table with the size of each circle proportional to the average annual temperature of each city in the selected range. (*Hint*: Because the Bing Maps app must download location data from the Internet, you will need an Internet connection to map the temperature values. If the app is temporarily unable to retrieve the location data for some of the cities, it might show an undefined warning message. You can reload the temperature data to try to show the location plots.)

7. Resize the map so that it covers the range D1:L30 in the worksheet. Zoom the map to display the continental United States, if necessary.

8. In the Precipitation worksheet, repeat Steps 3 through 7, importing the City and Annual Precipitation fields from the database. Plot the annual precipitation for each city on the map over the range D1:L30. Name the data connection **Precipitation Data**, add the description **Data retrieved from the US Weather.accdb file using MS Query**, and then refresh the data when the workbook is reopened.

9. In the Snowfall worksheet, repeat Steps 3 through 7 with the City and Annual Snowfall fields. Plot the annual snowfall in inches for each city in the map over the range D1:L30. Name the data connection **Snowfall Data** and use the same description you used for the first two data connections. Refresh the connection automatically when the workbook is reopened.

10. In the Rain Days worksheet, use Microsoft Query to retrieve the City, Precipitation Days, and Nonprecipitation Days fields from the US Cities database. Import the data into cell A4 of the worksheet.

11. Name the connection **Rainfall Days** and add the description **Data retrieved from the US Weather.accdb file using MS Query**. Refresh the connection automatically when the workbook is reopened.

Explore 12. Select the range A4:C104 and plot the selected data values on the map as pie charts.

13. Save the workbook, and then close it.

Case Problem 4

Data Files needed for this Case Problem: Flower.xlsx, Flower Data.accdb, Flower Sales.xlsx

Flower Pocket Chris Barnes is the owner of Flower Pocket, an online company that sells and delivers flowers and gift baskets. Chris has been storing orders in an Access database and wants to import a subset of this data into an Excel worksheet. The database, named Flower Data, contains five tables. The Customers table lists the names and contact information for customers who have ordered during the past several weeks. The Orders table lists each order and the date it was submitted. The Products table lists products sold by Flower Pocket. The Customers_Orders table matches each order with the customer who ordered it. Finally, the Orders_Products table matches each order with the products in the order. You'll import the data from the Customers and Products tables into separate worksheets. You'll also create a PivotTable that displays details on each order. Complete the following:

1. Open the **Flower** workbook located in the Excel11 ▸ Case4 folder included with your Data Files, and then save the workbook as **Flower Pocket** in the location specified by your instructor.

2. In the Documentation worksheet, enter your name and the date.

3. In the Customers worksheet, import the Customers table from the **Flower Data** Access database located in the Excel11 ▸ Case4 folder. Import the data as an Excel table in cell A4 of the worksheet.

4. Edit the connection properties. Name the connection **Customer List** and add the description **Data retrieved from the Customers table in the Flower Data database**. Refresh the connection whenever the workbook is opened.

5. In the Products worksheet, import the Products table from the **Flower Data** Access database located in the Excel11 ▸ Case4 folder. Import the data as an Excel table starting in cell A4 of the worksheet. Format the Price values in column C with the Currency format.

6. Edit the connection properties. Name the connection **Product List** and enter the description **Data retrieved from the Products table in the Flower Data database**. Refresh the connection whenever the workbook is opened.
7. In the Order Report worksheet, use Microsoft Query to create a query based on the tables in the Flower Data database. The query should extract the fields in the following tables:
   - Customers—Name, Street, City, and State
   - Customers_Orders—CID and OID
   - Orders—Date
   - Orders_Products—PID
   - Products—Product and Price
8. Import the data from the query as a PivotTable Report into cell A5 of the Order Report worksheet.
9. Place the Name, Street, City, State, Date, and Product fields in the ROWS section of the PivotTable.
10. Place the Price field in the VALUES section of the table, showing the sum of the prices for the products ordered by customers.
11. Place the Name, Date, and Product fields as row labels in the PivotTable. Display the sum of the Price field in the Values section of the table. Format the Sum of Price values using the Currency format.
12. On the PIVOTTABLE TOOLS DESIGN tab, in the Layout group, use the Report Layout button to change the layout of the PivotTable to a tabular form.
13. Do not display any subtotals in the PivotTable.
14. Change the column label for the Price field to **Order Price**, and then format the appearance of the table so that it is easy to read.
15. Name the connection for the PivotTable **Product Orders** with the description **Retrieves product orders from the Flower Data database**. Refresh the connection whenever the workbook opens.

Explore 16. Chris wants to save the connections you created as Office Data Connection (ODC) files for use in other projects. To save the connections as permanent files, open the Connection Properties dialog box for each of the three connections you have created, and then click the Export Connection File button on the Definition tab. Save the ODC files as **Customer List**, **Product List**, and **Product Orders** in the location specified by your instructor.

17. Save the Flower Pocket workbook, and then close it.
18. Chris wants an analysis of the most popular products sold by Flower Pocket. Open the **Flower Sales** workbook located in the Excel11 ► Case4 folder included with your Data Files, and then save the workbook as **Flower Sales Report** in the location specified by your instructor.

Explore 19. Test the connection files you created in Step 16. Click the Connections button in the Connections group on the DATA tab, and then click the Add button. Click the Browse for More button in the Existing Connections dialog box, and then locate and open the **Product Orders** ODC file you created in Step 16.

20. In the Sales Report worksheet, create a PivotTable report that lists each product retrieved from the Product Orders connection with the number of times the product was purchased by the customer and the amount of revenue generated by each product (in terms of the Price field). The layout of the PivotTable is up to you.
21. Save the workbook, and then close it.

TUTORIAL 12

Collaborating on a Shared Workbook

Working with Others to Create a Stockholder's Report

OBJECTIVES

Session 12.1
- Share a workbook with multiple users
- Track changes made to a workbook
- Accept and reject workbook edits
- Merge multiple workbooks into a single file
- Save and share workbooks on the cloud

Session 12.2
- Set workbook properties and tags
- Encrypt a document file
- Mark a workbook as final
- Link and embed an Office document
- Customize the Excel working environment
- Save a workbook as a PDF file

Case | Plush Pets

Plush Pets, which is based in Athens, Georgia, sells stuffed animals and toys that young children design and build themselves in one of the many Plush Pets stores across the country. Each year the company publishes a financial report for its stockholders. Chayla Sastry and her team in the financial department are responsible for creating and publishing the year-end financial report as an Excel document. In the process of developing this report, different employees will review and edit the workbook's content, which will go through several drafts and revisions. Chayla asks you to help manage this collaborative process of development from initial draft to final form. The finished report will be distributed to the rest of the company and presented to the stockholders in time for the annual meeting. As part of the finished report, you will integrate the Excel workbook with other Office documents.

STARTING DATA FILES

Excel12 →

Tutorial
Financial.xlsx
Greer Edits.xlsx
Hughes.docx
Income.xlsx
Paris.xlsx
Plush.xlsx
Team.xlsx

Review
Brussels.xlsx
Cash.xlsx
Cash Flow.xlsx
Group.xlsx
Notes.docx
Projected.xlsx
Sanders Edits.xlsx

Case1
Pizza.xlsx
Store1.xlsx
Store2.xlsx
Store3.xlsx
Store4.xlsx

Case2
Building.docx
Donor.xlsx

Case3
Healthy.xlsx
Review.docx

Case4
Larson.xlsx
Tufte.xlsx
Wilkes.xlsx

Microsoft product screenshots used with permission from Microsoft Corporation.

EX 726 Excel | Tutorial 12 Collaborating on a Shared Workbook

Session 12.1 Visual Overview:

A **shared workbook** is a workbook that can be edited by more than one user at the same time.

Cells with changes listed in the tracking log are marked with a color border.

The highlighted change is displayed in a comment box labeled with the name of the person who made the edit, the date and time of the edit, and a description of the edit.

Each comment in a shared workbook is labeled with the name of the person who made the comment.

A list of the changes made to the shared workbook is stored in a **tracking log**, which can be displayed in a History worksheet.

Team Edits [Share…

FILE HOME INSERT PAGE LAYOUT FORMULAS DATA REVIEW

Spelling Research Thesaurus | Translate | New Comment | Delete Previous Next | Show/Hide Com… Show All Comme… Show Ink

Proofing | Language | Comments

B9 fx ='Income Statement'!B16

	A	B	C
7	Cash and cash equivalents at beginning of year	2,582	1,3
8	Cash and cash equivalents at end of year	5,268	3,9
9	Net income	8,545	4,0
10	Net cash provided by operating activities	12,634	8,9
11	**At Year End**		
12	Marketable assets	5,078	5,0
13	Current assets	18,468	14,1
14	Total assets	28,200	23,2
15	Current liabilities	3,163	3,3
16	Long-term liabilities	10,273	7,7
17	Total liabilities	6,718	11,1
18	Stockholders' equity	21,482	17,7
19	Working capital	15,305	10,7
20			
21	Full-time staff		
22			
23	**Common Stock Data**		
24	Shares		
25	Net income per share		

Linda Thorpe, 2/16/2017 1:4
Changed cell A21 from 'Full-time
'Full-time staff'.

[Cell Comment]
Joshua Allen:
Do these numbers include part-tir
and contract workers?
Kevin Leland:
No. I'll edit the text to make this

Documentation | **Financial Summary** | History

Cell A21 commented by Joshua Allen

Collaborating on a Workbook

The Share Workbook button lets you turn workbook sharing on or off and see who has the shared workbook open.

The Track Changes button contains the Highlight Changes command that turns on track changes in a shared workbook, and the Accept/Reject command that you use to review tracked changes in the workbook.

To view the edits stored in the tracking log, you choose when, by whom, and where the edits were made.

Each edit is stored in the tracking log, where you can see conflicting changes and accept the one you want.

Click to accept the highlighted edit.

Click to reject all of the edits in the workbook.

Sharing a Workbook Among Multiple Users

Many documents are the combined efforts of multiple authors. For example, in the workplace, several people might collaborate on a workbook, with each person providing input and content from his or her area of expertise. Excel facilitates such collaboration through the use of shared workbooks, which can be created and edited by several users.

Team members can work on the same document either simultaneously or sequentially, where the next person continues working on the document after the previous person has finished his or her tasks. A shared Excel workbook tracks the changes made by different people so everyone can examine when and where each change was made.

There are limits to what can be performed when working on a shared workbook. You can enter numbers and text, edit cells, move data, insert new rows and columns, and perform other usual editing tasks. However, you cannot delete worksheets and ranges, insert ranges, merge and split cells, edit charts, or use drawing tools. In general, you can do anything in a shared workbook that does not drastically change the layout or content to such an extent that Excel can no longer reconcile your edits with the edits made by other users.

Shared workbooks are usually stored in shared folders located on either a local network or the Internet. This location on the Internet is also referred to as the **cloud**. These secure locations are established to prevent unauthorized users from viewing the document's contents.

Setting Privacy Options

Once you have saved your workbook in a secure location, you can begin the process of sharing it. Excel workbooks are not shared by default. When a workbook includes review comments, hidden cells or worksheets, or document properties containing descriptive information about the file that are likely to contain personal information, you cannot share the workbook unless you change the workbook's privacy options. Note that privacy options are set for the active workbook, not for all Excel workbooks. So you need to reset the privacy options in each workbook you want to share.

Chayla saved the first draft of the financial report in an Excel workbook. The workbook contains worksheets describing the company's financial status during the previous three years. Chayla wants to share this workbook with her colleagues. You'll reset the privacy options to allow Excel to save and share the workbook with other users.

To enable sharing for the Plush Pets workbook:

▶ 1. Open the **Plush** workbook located in the Excel12 ▸ Tutorial folder included with your Data Files, and then save the workbook as **Plush Pets** in the location specified by your instructor.

▶ 2. In the Documentation worksheet, enter your name and the date.

▶ 3. On the ribbon, click the **FILE** tab, and then click **Options** in the navigation bar. The Excel Options dialog box opens.

▶ 4. In the left pane, click **Trust Center**, and then in the right pane, click the **Trust Center Settings** button. The Trust Center dialog box opens.

▶ 5. In the left pane, click **Privacy Options**.

▶ 6. In the Document-specific settings section, click the **Remove personal information from file properties on save** check box to remove the checkmark. Excel will share and save the workbook without having to remove any personal information.

▶ 7. Click the **OK** button in each dialog box to return to the workbook. The privacy options are reset for the workbook.

Tutorial 12 Collaborating on a Shared Workbook | Excel   EX 729

Enable Workbook Sharing

To make it possible for other users to access and edit the same data simultaneously, you need to share a workbook. This is done from the Share Workbook dialog box. You can also use this dialog box to monitor who has access to the shared workbook. For example, after sharing the Financial Report workbook and placing it in a network folder, both Chayla and her colleague Joshua Allen can open the workbook at the same time. As shown in Figure 12-1, the Share Workbook dialog box tells both Chayla and Joshua who is currently working on the document and when they first started editing the file.

Figure 12-1   Share Workbook dialog box

- check to allow simultaneous editing of the workbook
- list of users currently editing the workbook
- click to stop sharing the workbook with the selected user

You can also restrict editing to specific ranges in a workbook and limit the editors who have access to those ranges by assigning permissions and then protecting the sheet. To do so, click the Allow Users to Edit Ranges button in the Changes group on the REVIEW tab.

Chayla wants to share the Plush Pets workbook with other employees. You'll turn on workbook sharing so she can do this.

To share the Plush Pets workbook:

1. On the ribbon, click the **REVIEW** tab. In the Changes group, click the **Share Workbook** button. The Share Workbook dialog box opens with the Editing tab active.

2. Click the **Allow changes by more than one user at the same time.** check box to insert a checkmark. This allows others to access and edit this workbook. Notice that your name appears as the exclusive user in the Who has this workbook open now box.

3. Click the **OK** button. A dialog box opens indicating the workbook will be saved.

4. Click the **OK** button. The workbook is saved, and "[Shared]" appears on the title bar next to the workbook name.

5. Close the workbook.

> **TIP**
> To password protect and share a workbook, click the Protect and Share Workbook button in the Changes group on the REVIEW tab.

Now that the workbook has been shared, you'll explore how Excel manages several users editing the same workbook.

Tracking Changes in a Workbook

Excel tracks the changes made to a shared workbook, recording the name of the user who made the changes and when the changes were saved. In some cases, two or more people edit the same workbook simultaneously. In that situation, when a current user saves the workbook, Excel notifies that user of any conflicting edits made by other users. Consider the situation shown in Figure 12-2, in which Chayla Sastry and Joshua Allen are editing the same workbook at the same time. Joshua changes the value in cell B5, and then saves the workbook. When Chayla saves the workbook a little later, Joshua's edit appears as a comment attached to the changed cell notifying Chayla about what Joshua did. Excel removes these comments automatically when the workbook is reopened at a later date. However, the edit history will be saved for 30 days in case further review is needed.

Figure 12-2   Two users simultaneously edit a shared workbook

Chayla Sastry and Joshua Allen edit the same document simultaneously.

	A	B	C	D	E
1	Plush Pets				
2	Income Statement				
3			(in thousands, except per share data)		
4	Period Ending	Dec 30, 2016	Dec 31, 2015	Dec 31, 2014	
5	Revenue	$ 38,508	$ 30,856	$ 24,834	
6	Cost and expenses				
7	Cost of goods sold	3,818	3,567	3,211	
8	Marketing and selling	13,028	11,855	9,997	
9	Research and development	7,140	6,122	4,685	
10	General and administrative	6,370	5,554	3,951	
11	Total cost and expenses	30,356	27,098	21,844	

Joshua enters a new value in cell B5 and then saves his workbook.

	A	B	C	D	E
1	Plush Pets				
2	Income Statement				
3			(in thousands, except per share data)		
4	Period Ending	Dec 30, 2016	Dec 31, 2015	Dec 31, 2014	
5	Revenue	$ 36,150	$ 30,856	$ 24,834	
6	Cost and expenses				
7	Cost of goods sold	3,818	3,567	3,211	
8	Marketing and selling	13,028	11,855	9,997	
9	Research and development	7,140	6,122	4,685	
10	General and administrative	6,370	5,554	3,951	
11	Total cost and expenses	30,356	27,098	21,844	

When Chayla saves her workbook, a comment notifies her of Joshua's edit.

	A	B	C	D	E
1	Plush Pets				
2	Income Statement				
3			(in thousands, except per share data)		
4	Period Ending	Dec 30, 2016			
5	Revenue	$ 36,150	Joshua Allen, 2/17/2017 1:49 PM: Changed cell B5 from ' $38,508.00 ' to ' $36,150.00 '.		
6	Cost and expenses				
7	Cost of goods sold	3,818			
8	Marketing and selling	13,028			
9	Research and development	7,140	6,122	4,685	
10	General and administrative	6,370	5,554	3,951	
11	Total cost and expenses	30,356	27,098	21,844	

© 2014 Cengage Learning

Conflicts occur when users try to save different values in the same cell. Suppose Joshua saves his workbook first and enters $36,150 in cell B5, but then Chayla, unaware of Joshua's edit, enters $37,248 in the same cell. When she saves the workbook, the Resolve Conflicts dialog box opens, flagging the conflict between her edit and Joshua's earlier edit in cell B5 (see Figure 12-3). From this dialog box,

Chayla can resolve the conflict by choosing which value to accept. Note that the Resolve Conflicts dialog box opens only when users edit the same cell while working on the document simultaneously. It will not appear if one user edits a cell and the other user leaves that cell unchanged. All users have equal authority to resolve conflicts, but only the person who first saves the document when there is a conflict sees the Resolve Conflicts dialog box.

Figure 12-3   **Resolve Conflicts dialog box**

Chayla's edit to cell B5
Joshua Allen's simultaneous edit to cell B5
click to accept your change
click to accept all of your changes
click to accept everyone else's changes
click to accept the conflicting change

Since sharing the Plush Pets workbook, Chayla distributed the workbook to her colleagues to review. You'll open their edited version of Chayla's original workbook.

To open the shared workbook:

▶ 1. Open the **Team** workbook located in the Excel12 ▶ Tutorial folder included with your Data Files.

▶ 2. In the Documentation worksheet, replace the author and date with your name and the current date. These edits are saved in the tracking log.

▶ 3. Save the workbook as **Team Edits** in the location specified by your instructor.

Trouble? If Excel reports that the file is locked, click the Notify button, wait until Excel notifies you that the file is no longer locked for editing, and then click the Read/Write button in the next dialog box that opens.

Reviewing Comments in a Shared Workbook

Comments are a powerful collaboration tool, giving team members the ability to offer insights and make suggestions about the workbook and its content. The running conversation among users about a cell is displayed within a single comment box connected to that cell. Each comment in the comment box is identified by the user who entered it.

Joshua Allen, Kevin Leland, and Linda Thorpe all added comments about how to improve Chayla's workbook. You'll review their suggestions.

To review comments in the shared workbook:

1. On the ribbon, click the **REVIEW** tab. In the Comments group, click the **Next** button. The next—or, in this case, the first—comment in cell D4 of the Financial Summary worksheet is selected. It contains responses to Chayla's query about whether to expand the report scope to five years. Joshua and Linda suggest leaving the report as is; Kevin prefers the five-year report. See Figure 12-4.

Figure 12-4 User comments for cell D4 in the shared workbook

2. Click the **Next** button again. Excel moves through the workbook, searching within each sheet from left to right and then top to bottom, starting from the first sheet and continuing through the last. The next comment appears in cell A21, which is selected. In this comment, Joshua asked whether the number of employees reported in the worksheet includes part-time employees. Kevin responded that it doesn't, and then he changed the label.

3. Click the **Next** button again. Linda's comment in cell B25 regarding the Net income per share value is displayed along with Joshua's response.

4. Click the **Next** button again. A dialog box opens, indicating that you have reached the end of the workbook, and asking whether you want to return to the beginning of the workbook to continue reviewing comments.

5. Click the **Cancel** button to end the comment review.

Usually, the document owner will delete comments that have been addressed, leaving only the ones that still need follow-up. You have reviewed all of the comments in the workbook, and none require additional changes. Chayla wants you to remove the comments from the document.

To delete the comments from the shared workbook:

1. In the Financial Summary worksheet, select cell **A1**. You want to review the comments, starting at the beginning of the worksheet.

2. On the REVIEW tab, in the Comments group, click the **Next** button to go to the first comment in the workbook located in cell D4.

Tutorial 12 Collaborating on a Shared Workbook | Excel   EX 733

> 3. In the Comments group, click the **Delete** button. The list of comments attached to cell D4 is deleted.
>
> 4. Repeat Steps 2 and 3 for the other two comments in the workbook. When no comments remain in the workbook, the Delete, Previous, and Next buttons in the Comments group are grayed out.
>
> 5. Select cell **A1** to return to the beginning of the report.

Now that you have reviewed the comments, you'll examine what changes Chayla's colleagues have made to the workbook.

Reviewing Changes Using the Tracking Log

TIP

To change the length of the tracking log history, specify a new length in days on the Advanced tab in the Share Workbook dialog box.

In a shared workbook, all edits are stored in a tracking log for 30 days. The tracking log includes edits such as changes to cell values or worksheet names, but inserted or deleted worksheets, comments, and style changes are not recorded. Also, once the workbook is no longer shared, the tracking log is erased. Because the edit history can become very long and cumbersome to review, you can filter the tracking log based on when the edits were made, who made the edits, and where they appear in the workbook.

The contents of the tracking log can be reviewed either in the form of comments attached to the edited cells, or within a list displayed in a separate worksheet. In both methods, each edit is accompanied by text describing the edit, the name of the author who made the edit, and the date and time of the edit. Edited cells are also highlighted by a colored border.

REFERENCE

Reviewing Tracked Changes in a Shared Workbook

- On the REVIEW tab, in the Changes group, click the Track Changes button, and then click Highlight Changes.
- Specify when, who, and where in the Highlight which changes section.
- Click the Highlight changes on screen check box to see edits in comments.
- Click the List changes on a new sheet check box to view the tracking log.
- Click the OK button.
- Point to the highlighted cells to see the edits and/or view the tracking log in the History worksheet.

Chayla wants you to highlight and review the edits in the Team Edits workbook as comments attached to the changed cells.

To highlight and review the changes to the shared workbook:

> 1. On the REVIEW tab, in the Changes group, click the **Track Changes** button, and then click **Highlight Changes**. The Highlight Changes dialog box opens. You'll review all the changes made by everyone but yourself.
>
> 2. Click the **When** arrow, and then click **All**. This specifies that you'll review changes made at any time in the workbook.
>
> 3. Click the **Who** arrow, and then click **Everyone but Me**. This limits your review only to edits made by other people.

4. If necessary, click the **Highlight changes on screen** check box to insert a checkmark, and then click the **List changes on a new sheet** check box to remove the checkmark. The changes will be displayed in comments in the worksheets. See Figure 12-5.

Figure 12-5   **Highlight Changes dialog box**

- highlights all edits made at any time in the tracking log
- highlights edited cells using comments
- highlights edits by everyone but the current author

5. Click the **OK** button. A color border with a marker in the upper-left corner appears around each cell that was changed.

6. In the Financial Summary worksheet, point to cell **A12**. A comment box appears with a description of the change made to the cell, including the author and the date and time of the change. See Figure 12-6.

Figure 12-6   **Highlighted change**

- click to track changes in the document made by others
- comment describes the nature, author, and time of the change

Joshua Allen, 2/16/2017 4:06 PM:
Changed cell A12 from 'Marketable securities' to 'Marketable assets'.

Examining all the sheets in a workbook to locate the highlighted changes can be time consuming, especially in workbooks with many worksheets. A quicker approach is to review the list of all changes from the tracking log in a separate worksheet. Chayla wants you to display the contents of the tracking log. You'll list these changes on a new worksheet.

Tutorial 12 Collaborating on a Shared Workbook | Excel   **EX 735**

To list the edits on a separate worksheet:

▶ 1. On the REVIEW tab, in the Changes group, click the **Track Changes** button, and then click **Highlight Changes**. The Highlight Changes dialog box opens.

▶ 2. Click the **List changes on a new sheet** check box to insert a checkmark.

▶ 3. Click the **OK** button. The History worksheet is added to the end of the workbook, detailing the history of the six changes made to the document in chronological order along with who made each change, where it was made, and what kind of change it was. See Figure 12-7.

Figure 12-7   Tracking log in the History worksheet

Action Number	Date	Time	Who	Change	Sheet	Range	New Value	Old Value
1	2/15/2017	3:04 PM	Joshua Allen	Cell Change	Income Statement	B7	3,818.00	3,418.00
2	2/16/2017	8:25 AM	Kevin Leland	Cell Change	Financial Summary	A21	Full-time employees	Number of employees
3	2/16/2017	8:25 AM	Kevin Leland	Worksheet Rename	Financial Summary		Financial Summary	Financial Data
4	2/16/2017	1:42 PM	Linda Thorpe	Cell Change	Income Statement	B18	2,250.00	2,330.00
5	2/16/2017	1:42 PM	Linda Thorpe	Cell Change	Financial Summary	A21	Full-time staff	Full-time employees
6	2/16/2017	4:06 PM	Joshua Allen	Cell Change	Financial Summary	A12	Marketable assets	Marketable securities

The history ends with the changes saved on 2/16/2017 at 4:06 PM.

- author of the edit
- date and time of the edit
- type of edit
- location of the edit
- description of the edit

From the History worksheet, you can see that a total of six edits were made to the workbook by various users. Five edits have changed cell values, and one edit, made by Kevin Leland, changed the second worksheet name from Financial Data to Financial Summary. Joshua Allen made the last edit at 4:06 PM. Note that the History worksheet exists only for the current Excel session. It is automatically deleted when the workbook is closed, or when you start rejecting or accepting the changes from the tracking log.

Accepting and Rejecting Edits

Ultimately, someone must decide which edits to use in the workbook. You can accept an edit to keep its new value, or you can reject an edit to return to the original value. Before you start, you specify which changes you want to examine for accepting and rejecting using the same options as with tracking changes. The changes are reviewed in chronological order, just as they appeared in the tracking log.

REFERENCE

Accepting and Rejecting Edits

- On the REVIEW tab, in the Changes group, click the Track Changes button, and then click Accept/Reject Changes.
- Specify when, by whom, and where changes are to be reviewed.
- Click the OK button.
- Click the Accept, Reject, Accept All, or Reject All button to accept and reject changes.
- Click the Close button.

Chayla wants to keep some edits but not others. You'll accept and reject edits based on her preferences.

To accept or reject edits in the workbook:

1. On the REVIEW tab, in the Changes group, click the **Track Changes** button, and then click **Accept/Reject Changes**. The Select Changes to Accept or Reject dialog box opens.

2. Make sure **Not yet reviewed** appears in the When box and **Everyone but Me** appears in the Who box. See Figure 12-8.

Figure 12-8   Select Changes to Accept or Reject dialog box

- displays edits not previously reviewed
- displays edits made by everyone except the current user

3. Click the **OK** button. The Accept or Reject Changes dialog box opens, listing the first of six edits made in the workbook. The first edit is in cell B7 of the Income Statement worksheet. Joshua Allen changed the cell value from 3,418.00 to 3,818.00. See Figure 12-9.

Figure 12-9   Accept or Reject Changes dialog box

- author of the edit, and the date and time the edit was made
- description of the edit
- click to accept or reject the current edit
- click to accept or reject all edits in the workbook

TIP
You can accept or reject all the changes to the workbook at one time by clicking the Accept All or Reject All button.

4. Click the **Accept** button. The edit is accepted, and the dialog box lists the next change—cell A21 in the Financial Summary worksheet contains two conflicting edits. See Figure 12-10.

Tutorial 12 Collaborating on a Shared Workbook | Excel   EX 737

Figure 12-10   **Multiple edits to the same cell**

original cell value and subsequent edits to the cell → Accept or Reject Changes dialog box:
Select a value for cell A21:
- Number of employees (Original Value)
- Full-time employees (Kevin Leland 2/16/2017 8:25)
- Full-time staff (Linda Thorpe 2/16/2017 13:42)

select the value to use and click the Accept button → Accept

click to accept all of the changes dated last in the tracking log → Accept All

click to reject all of the workbook changes → Reject All

Close

▶ **5.** In the Select a value for cell A21 box, click **Full-time employees**, and then click the **Accept** button. This accepts Kevin Leland's edit and rejects the original text and Linda Thorpe's later edit. The dialog box lists the next edit, in which the name of a worksheet was changed from "Financial Data" to "Financial Summary."

▶ **6.** Click the **Accept** button. Kevin Leland's edit to rename the worksheet is accepted, and the next change is listed in the dialog box. In the fifth edit, Linda Thorpe changed cell B18 from 2,330 to 2,250.

▶ **7.** Click the **Accept** button. The change is accepted, and the dialog box lists the sixth and last edit occurring in cell A12, in which Joshua Allen changed the text of the cell from "Marketable securities" to "Marketable assets."

▶ **8.** Click the **Reject** button. The edit is rejected and the original text is restored to the cell.

▶ **9.** Save the Team Edits workbook, and then close it.

The choices you make regarding conflicting edits become part of the tracking log, and are displayed in the Action Type and Losing Action columns of the History worksheet. When two edits conflict, the Action Type column will display "Won" for the edit that is kept and "Undo" or "Result of rejected action" for rejected edits. The row numbers in the Losing Action column identify the rows in the History worksheet containing information about the edits that weren't kept, including any deleted data. This way, you can always view not only the edits that have been made to the workbook, but also how conflicting edits were resolved.

Merge and Compare Workbooks

Another way to collaborate on a document is to provide a separate copy of the same shared file to multiple users. Each user works on his or her copy, and then returns the edited workbook. The different versions of the workbook can then be merged so that the changes in the copies can be compared and conflicting edits can be resolved. The following conditions must be met to merge two or more workbooks:

- The copies must originate from the same shared file.
- The copies must have different filenames.
- The copies must either have the same password or not be password-protected.

- The Track Changes feature must be turned on for all copies.
- The length of time spent editing the copies cannot exceed the length of the tracking history (30 days by default), or important changes might be lost.

> **REFERENCE**
>
> ### Merging Workbooks
>
> - Customize the Quick Access Toolbar to display the Compare and Merge Workbooks button.
> - Open the workbook into which you want to merge the workbooks.
> - Click the Compare and Merge Workbooks button on the Quick Access Toolbar.
> - Select the workbook that you want to merge into the current document, and then click the OK button.

The Compare and Merge Workbooks button does not appear on the ribbon. Before you can compare and merge two workbooks, you will add the Compare and Merge Workbooks button to the Quick Access Toolbar.

To add the Compare and Merge Workbooks button to the Quick Access Toolbar:

1. On the Quick Access Toolbar, click the **Customize Quick Access Toolbar** button, and then click **More Commands**. The Excel Options dialog box opens with the options to customize the Quick Access Toolbar displayed.

2. Click the **Choose commands from** arrow, and then click **Commands Not in the Ribbon**. The box displays an alphabetical list of all the commands that do not appear on the ribbon.

3. Click **Compare and Merge Workbooks** from the list of commands, and then click the **Add** button. The Compare and Merge Workbooks command button is added as the last command in the Customize Quick Access Toolbar box.

4. Click the **OK** button. The Compare and Merge Workbooks button appears on the Quick Access Toolbar.

Chayla's supervisor, Anne Greer, was at a conference and could not access the shared file on the company network. Instead, she edited a copy of the workbook and emailed her edited version to Chayla. Chayla wants to include Anne's edits in the report, so you'll merge and compare Chayla's and Anne's workbooks. First, you open the workbook into which you want to place the result of merging the two documents, which in this case is Chayla's workbook. Then, you use the Compare and Merge Workbooks button to open Anne's workbook and merge it with Chayla's file.

To merge Chayla's workbook with Anne's workbook:

1. Open the **Financial** workbook located in the Excel12 ▸ Tutorial folder included with your Data Files, and then save it as **Financial Report**. This is Chayla's version of the report with all of the latest edits included.

   Trouble? If a dialog box opens indicating that the file is locked for editing, click the Notify button, proceed to the workbook, and then click the Read/Write button in the next dialog box that opens.

2. In the Documentation worksheet, enter your name and the date.

3. On the Quick Access Toolbar, click the **Compare and Merge Workbooks** button. A dialog box opens indicating the workbook will be saved.

4. Click the **OK** button to save the current workbook. The Select Files to Merge Into Current Workbook dialog box opens.

5. Select the **Greer Edits** workbook located in the Excel12 ▸ Tutorial folder included with your Data Files.

6. Click the **OK** button. The two workbooks are merged, and all of the edits and comments from both workbooks appear in the Financial Report file.

7. Go to the **Financial Summary** worksheet, and then select cell **A2**. The comment that Anne added to that cell is displayed. Anne thinks the workbook is in good shape, and she only made a few minor edits.

8. On the ribbon, click the **REVIEW** tab, if necessary. In the Comments group, click the **Delete** button. The comment in cell A2 is deleted. The workbook contains no other comments.

Next, you'll review the edits in the merged workbook. You have already reviewed the changes in Chayla's workbook, so you need to review only the changes that Anne made in her copy of the workbook.

To review Anne's changes in the merged workbook:

1. On the REVIEW tab, in the Changes group, click the **Track Changes** button, and then click **Accept/Reject Changes**. The Select Changes to Accept or Reject dialog box opens.

2. Click the **Who** arrow, and then click **Anne Greer**. Only the changes that Anne made will be displayed.

3. Click the **OK** button. Anne made nine changes, all dealing with the text labels of items in the workbook. The first change listed is in cell A7 of the Cash Flow worksheet, where Anne changed the capitalization used in the cell.

4. Click the **Accept** button to accept the change. You could continue to review each change one at a time, or you could accept or reject all of the changes. Chayla wants you to accept all of Anne's edits.

5. Click the **Accept All** button. All of Anne's edits are accepted, and the dialog box closes.

Now that you have reviewed and accepted Anne's edits and have finished the process of accepting or rejecting edits from other users, you can remove workbook sharing. Before removing workbook sharing, be sure that you are finished collaborating with others. Once workbook sharing is removed, the contents of the tracking log are erased, and there is no way to retrieve the history of edits made to the document.

To turn off workbook sharing:

1. On the REVIEW tab, in the Changes group, click the **Share Workbook** button. The Share Workbook dialog box opens.

2. On the Editing tab, click the **Allow changes by more than one user at the same time** check box to remove the checkmark.

▶ 3. Click the **OK** button in the Share Workbook dialog box. A dialog box opens, warning that the workbook will no longer be shared, the change history will be erased, and anyone else editing the workbook will not be able to save his or her changes.

▶ 4. Click the **Yes** button. Workbook sharing is turned off, and the workbook is once again exclusive to the current user.

Next, you'll remove the Compare and Merge Workbooks button from the Quick Access Toolbar.

▶ 5. On the Quick Access Toolbar, right-click the **Compare and Merge Workbooks** button, and then click **Remove from Quick Access Toolbar** in the shortcut menu. The button no longer appears on the Quick Access Toolbar.

Collaborating on the Web

Colleagues and clients can be located almost anywhere in the world. In such cases, it is often more convenient to use the Internet to share work rather than a local network. The Internet supports a wide collection of file hosting sites that allow document sharing. Among the most popular are Dropbox, Google Docs, Amazon Cloud Drive, and iCloud.

The Microsoft file hosting service offers 7 gigabytes of free storage for new users with the option to purchase additional storage space. One advantage of using the Microsoft file hosting service is that its tools and features are integrated into Microsoft Office applications. You can sign up for the Microsoft file hosting service when you install Windows 8 or Microsoft Office.

With the Plush Pets franchise expanding across the country, and with plans to introduce stores into other countries and regions, Chayla will use a file hosting service to share her workbooks with colleagues and clients located across the country and across the world.

Saving a Workbook to a File Hosting Service

Once you have subscribed to a file hosting service, you can save files to that account using the same process as for saving files to your computer or local network folder. Many hosting services include folders for private and publically shared files and you can usually create your own folders.

To save a workbook to a file hosting service, you perform the following general steps:

1. Sign in to your Microsoft account.
2. On the ribbon, click the FILE tab, and then click Save As in the navigation bar.
3. On the Save As screen, select the file hosting service you want to use.
4. Navigate to the folder on the file hosting service in which you want to save the workbook.
5. Click the Save button.

Other file hosting services require different methods to save and access files. In most cases, you access your folders using a program supplied by the file hosting service, which makes those folders appear as local folders installed on your computer.

Editing a Shared Workbook

Once a workbook has been saved to the Microsoft file hosting service, you can access the workbook either from within Excel (as you would if the workbook had been saved locally) or through the Microsoft Excel web app using your web browser. You can then edit the workbook as usual. Figure 12-11 shows how the Financial Report workbook that you have been developing for Chayla would appear in the Excel web app. Keep in mind that the web is a dynamic medium whose content is constantly being updated and changed. So, the most current version of the Excel web app might differ from that shown in the figure.

Figure 12-11 Financial Report workbook in the Excel web app

The Excel web app includes most of the tools for editing a workbook that are in the Excel desktop application such as the ribbon, sheet tabs, and command buttons. For example, you can rename and reorder worksheets, format cells, and enter formulas into existing cells. If you need more editing tools than the Excel web app provides, you can simply reopen and edit the workbook in the Excel desktop application. Programs like the Excel web app make it simple for users to view and edit workbooks while traveling using laptops or tablets.

Sharing Workbooks on the Cloud

Most file hosting services make it easy to share documents with others, providing them with different levels of access to the document content. For example, you might give some users only the ability to view a workbook but give other users the ability to view, edit, and create new content within the workbook. You should avoid storing personal or confidential information in a file that you save in a publically accessible folder because then anyone can access your data.

You can share workbooks you store on the cloud with other users by performing the following steps in Excel:

1. Save your workbook to the Microsoft file hosting service.
2. On the ribbon, click the FILE tab, and then click Share in the navigation bar.
3. On the Share screen, do one of the following:
   - Click Invite People to send an email message to access the shared workbook.
   - Click Get a Sharing Link to send a link to the shared workbook.
   - Click Post to Social Networks to post an invitation to colleagues and friends on a social network such as Facebook or Google+.
   - Click Email to send a workbook as an attachment to an email message.

Figure 12-12 shows how Chayla might use the Share screen to send an invitation to a colleague to access her workbook stored on Microsoft's file hosting service. The email message her colleague receives will include a link to the shared workbook on the file hosting service. Any sharing privileges are applied only to that workbook and not to other files or folders.

Figure 12-12   **Share screen**

[Screenshot of Excel Share screen with callouts:
- click to invite users to access the shared workbook via an email message
- enter the recipient's email address
- select the access level; this recipient will be able to edit the workbook
- click to send a link to the shared workbook
- click to share the workbook
- email message inviting the user to share the workbook
- click to send the workbook as an attachment to an email message
- click to post an invitation on a social media site like Facebook]

You can remove sharing from your workbook at any time by reopening the Share screen and editing the list of recipients, removing users who should no longer have access to the file.

PROSKILLS

Teamwork: Improving the Collaborative Process

The collaborative tools in Excel make it simpler for groups to share the work of writing, editing, and finishing a financial report. But no tool, however useful, can overcome problems associated with colleagues who cannot work together effectively. Keep in mind the following to improve the collaborative process:

- Project goals should be stated in advance, with all team members clearly understanding what is expected of them. Team members should feel comfortable requesting clarification of those goals at any time in the process.
- Identify the strengths and weaknesses of each team member and adjust the project accordingly.
- Start work on the project at the earliest possible date.
- Constantly monitor the progress of the project, staying up to date on what has been done and what needs to be done. Communicate the status of the project with progress reports to each team member.
- Make it easy for team members to suggest new ideas and voice objections.
- Finish your tasks on time and meet your project goals.
- Treat each team member with respect. Do not allow personal grudges or differences to influence the successful completion of the project.

By successfully managing the group dynamic, you can make Excel's collaborative tools even more effective and useful.

Chayla's supervisor has no additional edits to make to the workbook. You have completed the process of sharing Chayla's workbook with her colleagues, merging her workbook with another file, and making the workbook available on SkyDrive. In the next session, you'll finalize the financial report so that it can eventually be distributed to Plush Pets stockholders.

REVIEW

Session 12.1 Quick Check

1. What is a shared workbook?
2. How does Excel resolve two different edits made to the same worksheet cell simultaneously?
3. How long does Excel store edits in the tracking log?
4. What are the two ways you can review the contents of the tracking log?
5. What are some edits that are not included in a tracking log?
6. Can any two workbooks be merged together? Explain why or why not.
7. List two advantages of saving workbooks to a file hosting service.
8. What is the advantage of using the Microsoft hosting service?

excel | Tutorial 12 Collaborating on a Shared Workbook

Session 12.2 Visual Overview:

The Info screen provides information about the current workbook.

Click the Protect Workbook button to mark the workbook as final and to password-protect the workbook.

Click the Check for Issues button to run the Document Inspector, run the Compatibility Checker, and run the Accessibility Checker to verify that the workbook is accessible to users with special needs.

The **Document Inspector** checks the workbook for hidden properties or personal information.

You can use the Document Inspector to remove the issues it finds.

Financial Report Final [Read

Info
New
Open
Save
Save As
Print
Share
Export
Close
Account
Options

Info

Financial Report Final

Protect Workbook
This workbook has been marked as final to dis
A password is required to open this workbook.

Inspect Workbook
Before publishing this file, be aware that it contains
- Document properties, author's name and abso

Versions
There are no previous versions of file.

Manage Versions

Document Inspector

Review the inspection results.

✓ Comments and Annotations
   No items were found.

! Document Properties and Personal Information   [Remove All]
   The following document information was found:
   * Document properties
   * Author
   * Absolute path to the workbook

✓ Data Model
   No embedded data found in the Data Model.

✓ Content Apps
   We did not find any Content apps for Office.

✓ Task Pane Apps
   We did not find any Task Pane apps for Office.

✓ Custom XML Data
   No custom XML data was found.

✓ Headers and Footers
   No headers or footers were found.

⚠ Note: Some changes cannot be undone.

[Reinspect] [Close]

Options
when this workbook is

Microsoft
The following versions of E opening this this workbo

Select versions t

Summary

Minor loss of fid
Some cells or st formatting that selected file for converted to th

☐ Check compat

[Copy to New Sh

© 2014 Cengage Learning

Tutorial 12 Collaborating on a Shared Workbook | Excel   EX 745

Finalizing a Workbook

...ort Final [Read-Only] - Excel

Chayla Sastry

A workbook that is marked as final is changed to read-only to discourage future edits.

You can click Properties and then click Advanced Properties to add custom properties to the workbook.

...d as final to discourage editing.
...this workbook.

Properties ▼

Size	36.5KB
Title	Annual Financial Rep...
Tags	stockholders; yearly ...
Categories	Financial statements

Document properties or **metadata** are the descriptive details about a workbook, including its author, title, and subject.

Related Dates

Last Modified	Today, 11:09 AM
Created	2/17/2017 1:28 PM
Last Printed	

...that it contains:
...name and absolute path

Related People

Author   Chayla Sastry

Last Modified By   Chayla Sastry

...of this file.

Related Documents

Open File Location

Show All Properties

...orkbook is viewed on the Web.

You can click the Show All Properties link to display additional workbook properties on the Info screen.

Microsoft Excel - Compatibility Checker

...e following features in this workbook are not supported by earlier
...rsions of Excel. These features may be lost or degraded when
...ening this workbook in an earlier version of Excel or if you save
...s workbook in an earlier file format.

...versions to show ▼

...ry   Occurrences

loss of fidelity

...e cells or styles in this workbook contain   24
...atting that is not supported by the   Help
...ted file format. These formats will be   Excel 97-2003
...erted to the closest format available.

The Compatibility Checker flags parts of the workbook that might be incompatible with earlier versions of Excel.

...ck compatibility when saving this workbook.

...to New Sheet   OK

Preparing the Final Workbook Version

After a workbook has been reviewed and revised to the author's satisfaction, the finished workbook can be modified to create a final version. Although what constitutes a final workbook can vary from organization to organization, the following general steps are usually part of the process of finalizing a document:

1. Add descriptive keywords and tags to the file to make it easier to locate the file within the company library.
2. Inspect the workbook to ensure that any personal information has been removed and that the workbook conforms to authoring standards.
3. Protect the workbook from unauthorized viewing and editing.
4. Mark the workbook as final to avoid confusion with earlier drafts.
5. Sign off on the workbook to ensure that the saved file represents the final version as intended by the author.

Chayla has a finished version of the Financial Report workbook that she wants you to prepare as the final workbook. You'll complete these five steps to create the final workbook.

Setting Document Properties

Document properties or metadata are the descriptive details about a workbook. The document properties are organized into the following categories:

- **Standard properties** are properties associated with all Office files and include the author, title, and subject.
- **Automatically updated properties** are properties usually associated with the actual file, such as the file size or the date the file was last edited. You cannot modify the automatically updated properties.
- **Custom properties** are properties you define and create specifically for a workbook.
- **Organization properties** are properties created for organizations to use in designing and distributing electronic forms.
- **Document library properties** are properties associated with documents in a document library on a website or in a public network folder.

Users can search for files that contain these document properties without having to open the actual files. For example, in a network folder with hundreds of files, Chayla's colleagues can quickly locate the workbooks she authored or workbooks about a specific topic, such as the stockholders' meeting.

Chayla wants you to add a title, tag, comment, status and other details to the workbook. You'll add these as document properties.

To add document properties to the workbook:

▶ 1. Open the **Financial Report** workbook you saved in the previous session.

▶ 2. On the ribbon, click the **FILE** tab, and then click **Info** in the navigation bar, if necessary. The Info screen displays information about the workbook.

▶ 3. At the bottom of the right pane, click the **Show All Properties** link. All of the document properties appear in the right pane.

▶ 4. In the Properties section, next to the Title property, click **Add a title**, and then type **Annual Financial Report**.

▶ 5. Next to the Tags property, click **Add a tag**, and then type **stockholders; yearly meeting**. Notice that you typed a semicolon to separate the two tags.

Tutorial 12 Collaborating on a Shared Workbook | Excel **EX 747**

6. Next to the Comments property, click **Add comments**, and then type **Final draft of the annual report to be presented at the April meeting in New Orleans**.

7. Next to the Status property, click **Add text**, and then type **Final draft**.

TIP

You can display the document properties above the workbook window by clicking the Properties button and then clicking Show Document Panel.

8. Next to the Categories property, click **Add a category**, and then type **Financial statements**.

9. Next to the Subject property, click **Specify the subject**, and then type **Plush Pets financial report**.

10. Next to the Company property, click **Specify the company**, and then type **Plush Pets**. See Figure 12-13.

Figure 12-13   Info screen showing all of the document properties

11. In the Related People section, next to the Author property, click **Add an author**, and then type your name.

If none of the listed properties fits your needs, you can create a custom property. You can either select custom properties from a list of property names or provide your own name. The value associated with the property can be text, a date, a number, or Yes or No. Chayla wants to identify the department that created this workbook. Because no department tag appears in the document properties list, you'll add a custom property.

To add a custom Department property:

1. On the Info screen, at the top of the right pane, click the **Properties** button, and then click **Advanced Properties**. The Financial Report Properties dialog box opens.

2. Click the **Custom** tab. You enter the custom properties for the workbook here. The Name box includes some common properties that you might want to add to a workbook.

3. In the Name box, click **Department**. The Department property is selected, and the data type is set as Text. You do not need to change this.

4. In the Value box, type **Finance** as the property value.

5. Click the **Add** button. The Department property is added to the Properties box. See Figure 12-14.

Figure 12-14   Custom tab in the Financial Report Properties dialog box

list of custom properties

custom property value

6. Click the **OK** button to close the dialog box and return to the Info screen.

Although the Department property is not listed on the Info screen, it is still part of the document properties. After you save and close a workbook, its properties are available to other programs, including the Windows operating system, to be used in file searches.

Inspecting a Workbook

The next step in finalizing a workbook is to review its contents for sensitive or personal information that you don't want distributed to other users. Personal information can appear in comments and annotations, document properties and metadata attached to the workbook, headers and footers, or hidden worksheets and cells. To determine whether a workbook contains sensitive or personal information, you use the Document Inspector to search the workbook to locate data and text that you may want removed.

Chayla asks you to use the Document Inspector to inspect the workbook and remove any personal information.

To inspect the Financial Report workbook:

1. On the Info screen, click the **Check for Issues** button, and then click **Inspect Document**. A dialog box opens reminding you to save the workbook.
2. Click the **Yes** button. The Document Inspector dialog box opens.
3. Make sure all of the check boxes are selected, and then click the **Inspect** button. The Document Inspector checks the content of the workbook for hidden properties or personal information in all of the selected categories. The inspection results appear in the dialog box. See Figure 12-15.

Figure 12-15 Document Inspector dialog box

Document Inspector dialog box showing:
- Comments and Annotations: No items were found.
- Document Properties and Personal Information — The following document information was found:
  * Document properties
  * Author
  * Related dates
  * Absolute path to the workbook
  * Printer properties (e.g. printer path, secure print passcode, etc.)
- Data Model: No embedded data found in the Data Model.
- Content Apps: We did not find any Content apps for Office.
- Task Pane Apps: We did not find any Task Pane apps for Office.
- Custom XML Data: No custom XML data was found.

Note: Some changes cannot be undone.

Callouts: workbook properties that might contain personal information you want to remove; click to remove all personal information from the workbook (Remove All button).

The Document Inspector located two instances where personal or sensitive information might appear in the workbook. The first relates to issues with document properties and personal information, including the names of the document authors. The second is a hidden worksheet. Chayla is fine with releasing the workbook with the list of the document authors, but she uses hidden worksheets to conceal source data and documentation that is useful to her but could be irrelevant or confusing to others. Before Chayla distributes the workbook, you'll find out what the hidden sheet contains and remove it.

To review the hidden worksheet, and then remove it:

1. Click the **Close** button to close the Document Inspector dialog box.
2. Right-click any sheet tab in the workbook, and then click **Unhide** on the shortcut menu. The Unhide dialog box opens, displaying a list of all the hidden sheets in the workbook. In this case, the only hidden sheet is the Notes worksheet.

3. With the Notes sheet name selected, click the **OK** button. The Notes worksheet appears between the Financial Summary and Income Statement worksheets. The worksheet contains Chayla's to-do list for the project, which is not relevant for colleagues and does not need to be part of the final report.

   Rather than just deleting the Notes worksheet, you'll hide it again, and then delete it using the Document Inspector.

4. Right-click the **Notes** sheet tab, and then click **Hide** on the shortcut menu. The worksheet is again hidden from view.

5. On the ribbon, click the **FILE** tab, and then, if necessary, click **Info** in the navigation bar.

6. On the Info screen, click the **Check for Issues** button, and then click **Inspect Document**. A dialog box opens, prompting you to save the workbook.

7. Click the **Yes** button. The Document Inspector dialog box opens with all the categories selected.

8. Click the **Inspect** button to rerun the Document Inspector.

9. Scroll down to the Hidden Worksheets section, and then click the **Remove All** button. The hidden worksheet is deleted from the workbook.

10. Click the **Close** button to close the Document Inspector.

> **TIP**
> Use caution when you remove information and data from a workbook with the Document Inspector because you cannot undo the removal.

Note that the Document Inspector will not remove comments, annotations, document properties, and personal information from a shared workbook. If you need to remove this information, run the Document Inspector before sharing the workbook.

INSIGHT

Using the Document Inspector to Detect Viruses

In addition to ensuring that no personal or inappropriate information is included in the final version of a workbook, the Document Inspector can be used to verify that the workbook has not been corrupted by a malicious program. Workbook viruses are often signaled by a hidden worksheet or hidden code attached to the XML code in the file. One way of detecting such viruses is to use the Document Inspector on any workbook you receive from an unknown source.

Another concern when finalizing a workbook is whether anyone working with an earlier version of Excel will have trouble reading the workbook contents. To determine whether a workbook is compatible with those older versions, you can inspect the document for compatibility. The Compatibility Checker flags any content, formatting, or element in the workbook that cannot be transferred to earlier versions of Excel, indicating the severity of the problem. The most serious differences between Excel 2013 and older versions of Excel include:

- **Worksheet size**—Excel versions 2007, 2010, and 2013 support worksheets that are 16,384 columns by 1,048,576 rows; earlier versions of Excel have a maximum worksheet size of 256 columns by 65,536 rows.
- **International dates**—Excel versions 2007, 2010, and 2013 support international date formats such as Hebrew Lunar, Japanese Lunar, and Chinese; earlier versions do not.
- **Sparklines**—Versions of Excel from 2010 forward support sparklines; earlier versions of Excel do not.

Tutorial 12 Collaborating on a Shared Workbook | Excel   EX 751

In addition to these differences, more minor issues might involve the font formats and color styles used in older Excel versions. In those cases, Excel will attempt to duplicate the formats as closely as possible when saving a new file to an older Excel version.

Chayla wants to know whether the Financial Report workbook will be compatible with older versions of Excel. You'll use the Compatibility Checker to determine this.

To run the Compatibility Checker on the Financial Report workbook:

TIP
To save the compatibility report to a worksheet, click the Copy to New Sheet button.

1. On the ribbon, click the **FILE** tab to return to the Info screen.

2. Click the **Check for Issues** button, and then click **Check Compatibility**. The Compatibility Checker dialog box opens, displaying the results of the compatibility test. See Figure 12-16.

Figure 12-16   Microsoft Excel - Compatibility Checker dialog box

- click to choose the Excel version to test for compatibility
- some minor format changes will be made when the document is opened in Excel 97 through 2003
- select to automatically check for compatibility issues when the document is saved
- click to copy the compatibility report to a new sheet in the workbook
- Excel versions with compatibility issue

The Compatibility Checker finds only a minor issue involving formatting changes between the current document and versions of Excel 97, 2000, 2002, and 2003. Chayla does not see a need to make changes to the workbook at this time.

3. Click the **OK** button to close the Compatibility Checker.

You can have Excel automatically check the compatibility of the workbook each time you save by clicking the Check compatibility when saving this workbook check box in the Compatibility Checker dialog box.

PROSKILLS

Written Communication: Making Your Workbook Accessible

The workplace should be an inclusive environment regardless of each employee's disabilities and special needs. One way of testing whether your workbooks meet this goal is the Accessibility Checker. To run the Accessibility Checker, click the Check for Issues button on the Info screen, and then click Check Accessibility. Excel will review the contents of your workbook and flag any issues that might prove challenging to users with disabilities. Many of these issues are focused on users with visual impairments who may need to use a screen reader to interpret the content of your workbook aurally. Issues that are flagged by the Accessibility Checker include:

- Embedded clip art and images without alternate text
- Embedded video clips without closed captioning
- Data tables without a header row, making it difficult to interpret the table contents
- Hypertext links lacking meaningful text and ScreenTips
- Complicated table structures involving multiple cases of merged cells and nested tables
- Tables with blank rows or columns that can mislead users with screen readers into thinking that the end of the table has been reached
- Worksheets using the default names of Sheet1, Sheet2, etc. that provide no useful information for people with disabilities in navigating through the workbook

By following the suggestions made by the Accessibility Checker, you can make your workbooks more accessible to colleagues who might otherwise be unable to contribute to the final product.

Protecting a Workbook

Excel workbooks often contain confidential financial data that needs to be secured. One way of increasing the security of your financial documents is with file encryption. **Encryption** is the process by which a file is encoded so that it cannot be opened without the proper password. The encryption password is different from the passwords that prevent users from editing a worksheet or the entire workbook. An encryption password prevents unauthorized users from even opening the file. Passwords can be up to 255 characters and can include numbers, symbols, uppercase letters, and lowercase letters.

Chayla wants to protect the final version of the Financial Report workbook before sending it to the Plush Pets department heads to ensure that only authorized users can view the data. You'll do this by encrypting the workbook.

To encrypt the workbook:

1. Save the workbook as **Financial Report Final** in the location specified by your instructor.

2. On the ribbon, click the **FILE** tab, and then click **Info** in the navigation bar, if necessary.

3. Click the **Protect Workbook** button, and then click the **Encrypt with Password** button.

4. In the Password box, type **plushpets** (in all lowercase letters), and then click the **OK** button.

Type the password carefully to avoid a misspelling, which will make the file difficult or impossible to reopen.

Tutorial 12 Collaborating on a Shared Workbook | Excel **EX 753**

> 5. In the Reenter password box, type **plushpets**, and then click the **OK** button. A password is now required to open this workbook.
>
> 6. Save and close the workbook, and then reopen it. The Password dialog box opens, preventing the workbook from opening without the correct password.
>
> 7. In the Password box, type **plushpets**, and then click the **OK** button. The workbook opens.
>
>   **Trouble?** If the workbook doesn't open, you might have mistyped the password. Repeat Step 7. If the workbook still doesn't open, you might have mistyped the password in Steps 4 and 5. There is no simple way to recover a mistyped password from an encrypted document. Open the Financial Report workbook, and then repeat Steps 1 through 7 to resave the Financial Report Final workbook with the correct password.

Marking a Workbook as Final

Marking a workbook as final makes the workbook read-only, discouraging a user from making any changes to it. A workbook marked as final has the editing, typing, and proofing commands turned off. As a result, a user can only view the contents of the file, and cannot modify it unless he or she removes the final status from the document.

Even though Chayla's workbook has been encrypted, it can still be edited by anyone who knows the password. Chayla wants to discourage this from happening. You'll mark the workbook as the final version of the report.

> **To mark Chayla's workbook as final:**
>
> 1. On the ribbon, click the **FILE** tab, and then click **Info** in the navigation bar, if necessary.
>
> 2. Click the **Protect Workbook** button, and then click **Mark as Final**. A dialog box opens indicating that the workbook will be marked as final and then saved.
>
> 3. Click the **OK** button. A second dialog box opens indicating that the file has been marked as final and its status property is now Final.
>
> 4. Click the **OK** button. A read-only version of the workbook is opened, as indicated by "[Read-Only]" in the title bar. The Message Bar also indicates that the workbook has been marked as final.
>
> 5. Click a blank cell in the active worksheet and try to enter some text to confirm that you cannot edit the workbook.
>
> 6. Close the workbook.

TIP

Excel saves versions of your workbook as you work. If Excel closes unexpectedly, you can recover unsaved workbooks by clicking the Manage Versions button on the Info screen.

Marking a workbook as final does not completely prevent anyone from editing the document. Depending on your Excel setup, the Message Bar might include an Edit Anyway button, which a user can click to edit the workbook despite its final status. You can also remove the final status by clicking the Protect Workbook button on the Info screen, and then clicking Mark as Final to deselect the command.

Signing Off on a Workbook

A final way to ensure that a document has not been changed by an unauthorized user is with a digital signature, which can be thought of as an electronic version of a written signature. Digital signatures provide a way for the author to authenticate the document by "signing off" on it. Because a workbook marked with a digital signature cannot be altered without removing the signature, the presence of a digital signature lets users know that the workbook comes from a trusted source and has not been altered since it was originally signed.

To add a digital signature to a document, you need a **digital ID** or **digital certificate**, which is an attachment to a document that authenticates the source of the signature. If you do not have a digital certificate, you can get one from a third-party source known as a **certificate authority (CA)**. The CA acts like a notary public, verifying signatures and tracking those that have expired or been revoked.

Chayla will work with the company's IT department to obtain a digital certificate and then finalize the Financial Report workbook herself at a later date. Once she has obtained a digital certificate, the digital signature can be either inserted directly into the workbook where it's visible to other users or added as an invisible signature that can only be viewed through the Info page or on the workbook's status bar.

To create a visible signature, select a cell in the workbook, and then click the Add a Signature Line button in the Text group on the INSERT tab. The Signature Setup dialog box shown in Figure 12-17 opens so you can enter the name of the signer, the signer's work title and email address, and instructions to the signer.

Figure 12-17 Signature Setup dialog box

TIP
If you don't want a signature line in the document, you can create an invisible signature by clicking the Protect Workbook button on the Info page and clicking Add a Digital Signature.

Once the signature has been defined, Excel displays a visible representation of the signature line. To sign off on the document, double-click the signature line and type a name in the signature box. If you have a touch device, you can sign the box or insert an image of the signature. Click the Sign button to display the signature in the document. See Figure 12-18.

Tutorial 12 Collaborating on a Shared Workbook | Excel **EX 755**

Figure 12-18 Workbook being signed

a signed workbook is marked as final

visible signature in the workbook certifies the document

digital signature

After the document has been signed, it will be marked as final and further editing will be discouraged. If additional edits are made to the document, the digital signature is no longer valid and this fact is noted on the workbook's Info screen. By creating and signing off with a digital signature, Chayla lets other users know that she has signed off on and supports this workbook and that subsequent changes to her workbook by other users will not be attributed to her.

INSIGHT

Creating Digital Certificates

If you cannot obtain a digital certificate from a third party, you can create your own **self-signed certificate**, which is a certificate created and signed by the person it certifies. Because a self-signed certificate is not created and maintained by a trusted authority, it lacks the safeguards associated with third-party certificates. For example, you would never use a self-signed certificate on an e-commerce site or with any transaction that involves personal information such as credit card or Social Security numbers.

Self-signed certificates are useful for developers who create sample documents and applications, and don't want to pay hundreds of dollars a year for a third-party certificate. They can also be used with projects that don't involve personal or confidential information in which all of the parties involved are well known to each other.

To create a self-signed certificate with Microsoft Office, go to the Program Files ▶ Microsoft Office ▶ Office15 folder and run the selfcert.exe program. You will be asked to provide a name for the certificate (usually your own name). The certificate will then be available to your Excel workbooks for digital signing. Note that a self-signed certificate authenticates the document only for the local computer and not for other computers or networks.

If you want to remove or edit your certificate, use the Windows Certification Manager by running the certmgr.msc program from the Windows run command. The Certification Manager will list all of the third-party and self-signed certificates installed on your computer, and provide commands to edit or remove them.

Now that Chayla has completed the process of reviewing and editing the financial report, she will begin distributing that data among the wider group of Plush Pets employees. Some of these users do not work with Excel and instead prefer to receive this type of information within Word documents or PowerPoint slides. So, you'll need to make her workbook available in other programs.

Integrating Excel with Other Office Applications

With Microsoft Office, you can create a document that combines objects from several different programs. An **object** is anything that appears on your screen that can be selected and manipulated, such as a table, a picture, a chart, a cell, a worksheet, or even Excel itself. For example, it's very common to create a Microsoft Word document that contains an Excel table or chart, or a PowerPoint slide show that displays part of a Word document or an Excel workbook. These documents involve source files and destination files. A **source file** contains the object that is displayed in the **destination file**. Integrated documents are easy to create in Office because all Office programs share a common interface and can read each other's file formats. Figure 12-19 describes the three ways to integrate a document—copying and pasting, linking, and embedding. Each method has advantages and disadvantages.

Figure 12-19   Integration methods

Method	Description	When to Use
Copying and pasting	Inserts an object into a file	You want to exchange the data between the two files only once. If the source file changes, that change is not reflected in the destination file.
Linking	Displays an object in the destination file, but only stores the location of the source file	You need to ensure that the data will be current and identical in both the source and destination files. Any changes made to the source file will be reflected in the destination file.
Embedding	Displays and stores an object within the destination file	You want the object to become a part of the destination file. Any changes made in the source file are not reflected in the object.

© 2014 Cengage Learning

Copying and Pasting Data

You can copy text, values, cells and ranges, and even charts and graphics from one program and paste them in another program using the Windows copy and paste features. When you paste an object from the source file, it becomes part of the destination file but the pasted object is static, having no connection to the source file. If you want to change the pasted object, you must do so within the destination file. For example, an Excel table pasted into a Word document can be edited only within the Word document. Any changes made in the original Excel workbook have no impact on the Word document. For this reason, pasting is used only for one-time exchanges of information.

Object Linking and Embedding

If you want to create a live connection between the source file and the destination file, you must use object linking and embedding. **Object linking and embedding (OLE)** refers to the technology that allows one to copy and paste objects, such as graphics files, cells and ranges, and charts, so that information about the program that created the object is included with the object itself.

The objects are inserted into the destination file as either linked objects or embedded objects. A **linked object** is stored within the destination file and remains connected to the source file. If you make a change to the source file, that change will be reflected in the destination file. On the other hand, an **embedded object** is stored within the destination file and is no longer part of the source file. In the case of an embedded chart, the destination file will store not only the chart image but also any data values on which the chart is based. Figure 12-20 illustrates the difference between linking and embedding.

Figure 12-20 Embedding contrasted with linking

© 2014 Cengage Learning

When you paste an object into an Office document, you have the choice of either keeping the formatting applied in the source document, or using the formatting styles defined in the destination document. Figure 12-21 summarizes some of the different paste options available in Microsoft Office.

Figure 12-21 Paste options

Icon	Paste Option
	Keep the formatting applied to the object in the source file
	Use the styles used in the destination file
	Link to the source file and keep the formatting from the source file
	Link to the source file and keep the styles used in the destination file
	Paste the object as a graphic image
	Paste only the text from the object

© 2014 Cengage Learning

INSIGHT

Inserting a Screenshot

Another way to share content between files is by taking a screenshot of the open file. Microsoft Office includes a built-in tool to capture and insert images from your computer screen. To capture a screen image, click the INSERT tab on the ribbon, and then click the Screenshot button in the Illustrations group. A gallery opens displaying thumbnails of all the open windows on your desktop. You can choose to take a screenshot of one of these open windows, or you can click the Screen Clipping button to select a portion of an open window for the screenshot.

Unlike linking and embedding, inserting a screenshot does not insert the actual data from the document. Instead, it inserts only the image of that document as a picture. Therefore, screenshots are best used for content that is not going to change. For data that will be edited or to allow users to access Microsoft Office tools to manipulate the data, choose linking or embedding the data rather than inserting a screenshot.

Chayla wants you to insert part of the financial summary from the Financial Report workbook into a staff memo she's preparing for Gary Hughes, who is coordinating the documents for the annual stockholders meeting. Rather than pasting the data each time she modifies the report, she wants you to create a link between her Excel workbook and a Word document so that any subsequent edits she makes to the workbook are automatically reflected in the document. You will open both files, copy the Excel data, and then paste the data as a link in the Word document.

To link the Word document to the table in the Excel workbook:

1. Open the **Hughes** Word document located in the Excel12 ► Tutorial folder, and then save the document as **Hughes Memo** in the location specified by your instructor.

2. At the top of the page, enter your name in the From line and enter the date in the Date line.

Tutorial 12 Collaborating on a Shared Workbook | Excel   EX 759

3. Open the **Income** workbook located in the Excel12 ▸ Tutorial folder included with your Data Files, and then save the workbook as **Income Report** in the location specified by your instructor.

4. In the Documentation worksheet, enter your name and the date.

5. Go to the **Income Statement** worksheet, and then copy the range **A3:D16**.

6. Return to the **Hughes Memo** Word document, and then click to the left of the paragraph mark below the letter's second paragraph.

   Trouble? If you do not see paragraph marks at the end of each paragraph, you need to show the nonprinting characters. On the HOME tab, in the Paragraph group, click the Show/Hide ¶ button.

7. On the HOME tab, in the Clipboard group, click the **Paste button arrow** to display the list of paste options.

8. Point to the **Link & Keep Source Formatting (F)** button. Note that the pasted table maintains the formatting styles used in the Income Report workbook. See Figure 12-22.

Figure 12-22   Excel table linked to the Word document

- click to link to the Excel workbook and keep the source file styles
- table uses the formatting styles from the source file
- table is linked to worksheet cells in the source file

TIP
You can click Paste Special on the Paste button menu to better control the format of the pasted worksheet cells.

9. Point to the other paste options to see a Live Preview of the table as it would appear using the styles in the Hughes Memo document, as a graphic image, or as text.

10. Click the **Link & Keep Source Formatting (F)** button to paste the Excel table using the source formatting with the values and text linked to the Income Report workbook.

Word updates a linked object every time you open the Word document or any time the Excel source file changes while the Word document is open. Chayla wants to edit one of the cell titles in the Income Statement worksheet. You'll make her suggested edit and confirm that the table in the Hughes Memo document changes to match.

To update the linked object:

1. Go to the **Income Report** workbook, and then press the **Esc** key to deselect the range A3:D16.
2. In cell **A14**, type **Pretax income**, and then press the **Enter** key.
3. Save the workbook.
4. Return to the **Hughes Memo** document, right-click the table, and then click **Update Link** on the shortcut menu. Notice that the text linked to cell A14 of the source file changes to "Pretax income."

Chayla also wants her memo to include the pie chart from the Income Report workbook that details the source of the company's costs and expenses. She is confident that the pie chart is accurate, so you will embed the chart in the memo. Embedding is done with the same tools used to paste a link to the source object. However, the pie chart and the data it is based on are both stored in the destination document, so changes to the embedded chart will not affect the original chart in the workbook. You'll embed the pie chart from the Income Report workbook now.

To embed the pie chart from the Income Report workbook in the Hughes Memo document:

1. Return to the **Income Report** workbook, click the pie chart to select it, and then copy it.
2. Return to the **Hughes Memo** document, and then click to the left of the paragraph mark above the next-to-last paragraph in the memo (above the sentence that begins "Please let me know…").
3. On the HOME tab, in the Clipboard group, click the **Paste button arrow**, and then click the **Keep Source Formatting & Embed Workbook (K)** button. A copy of the chart is embedded as an object in the document.
4. Click the chart to select it, and then drag the resizing handles to resize the chart so that it fits on the first page. See Figure 12-23.

Tutorial 12 Collaborating on a Shared Workbook | Excel **EX 761**

| Figure 12-23 | Excel pie chart embedded in Word document |

- CHART TOOLS tabs appear when the chart is selected
- click to specify how the chart is laid out on the page
- pie chart embedded within the memo
- Office chart tools

All of the chart tools that are available within Excel are also available with a linked chart or an embedded chart. You'll use the chart tools to change the style of the chart.

To change the chart style:

1. With the embedded chart still selected, click the **Chart Styles** button to the right of the chart.
2. Click the **Style 3** pie chart style from the style gallery. Word applies the style to the chart. See Figure 12-24.

Figure 12-24   Chart style being changed

[Screenshot of Hughes Memo - Word document showing a pie chart titled "Cost and expenses" with segments: Cost of goods sold (43%), Marketing and selling (23%), Research and development (21%), General and administrative (13%). A Style gallery is shown on the right with "Style 3 chart style" highlighted. Callout points to the chart labeled "revised chart appearance".]

▶ 3. Return to the **Income Report** workbook, verify that the appearance of the chart is unaffected, and then return to the **Hughes Memo** document.

Changing the style of the pie chart has no impact on the chart in the source file because both the embedded chart and the data that it's based on are stored within the memo document. You can view and edit the underlying data to alter the chart's appearance.

To view the data embedded within the Hughes Memo document:

▶ 1. Right-click the pie chart, and then click **Edit Data** on the shortcut menu. A spreadsheet window containing the entire contents of the embedded window opens. Notice that even those cells and worksheets that are not used in the chart are still embedded in the document. See Figure 12-25.

Tutorial 12 Collaborating on a Shared Workbook | Excel   **EX 763**

Figure 12-25   **Embedded workbook data**

workbook embedded in the document

the embedded workbook contains all of the cells and sheets found in the source file

2. In cell **B7**, enter **5,818** to change the embedded data from 3,818. The percentage of the cost of goods sold changes from 13% to 18%.

3. In cell **B7**, change the value back to its original **3,818**.

4. Close the spreadsheet window.

5. Save the Hughes Memo document, and then close Microsoft Word.

An embedded object such as a chart includes not only the chart sheet but also the other worksheets in the workbook. One disadvantage of embedded objects is that they tend to greatly increase the size of the destination file. You should embed an object only when file size is not an issue, and when you need the object's entire contents to be embedded in the destination file.

INSIGHT

Inserting Objects

Another way of embedding one Office object inside another that doesn't involve linking to a source file is to click the Object button in Text group on the INSERT tab in any Office program. Office will display a list of objects that can be embedded within the document, including Excel worksheets, Word documents, and PowerPoint slides and presentations. Once embedded within the document, all of the tools and commands associated with the object are available for use.

The advantage of directly embedding the object is that you do not have to maintain two separate files. However, files with several embedded objects are much larger in size and may work more slowly.

Customizing Excel for Your Working Preferences

Although it is common to collaborate on documents and reports, everyone has his or her own working style. Excel provides options for customizing the Excel environment to meet your own needs and preferences. You have already seen some of these choices in the Excel Options dialog box. You'll examine some of the other customization features of Excel now.

Excel screen elements fall into three general categories—(1) elements that are part of the Excel program; (2) elements that are part of the Excel workbook window; and (3) elements that are part of the Excel worksheet. The difference between these categories is important because it affects under what conditions those elements can be modified. For example, any modifications to the elements that are part of the workbook window are applied to any open workbook. Screen elements that are part of the worksheet are modified only in that worksheet and not in other worksheets and workbooks. Finally, screen elements that are part of the Excel program will be modified across all open workbooks and worksheets. Figure 12-26 lists the screen elements you can customize and the category to which they belong.

Figure 12-26 — Excel screen elements

Display Location	Screen Element
Excel window	Formula bar
	ScreenTips
	Chart element names on hover
Workbook	Horizontal scroll bar
	Vertical scroll bar
	Sheet tabs
Worksheet	Row and column headers
	Gridlines

© 2014 Cengage Learning

Sometimes when Chayla presents her workbooks at conferences and talks, she wants to limit the view to only the workbook or worksheet contents to avoid filling the screen with distractions. She asks you to temporarily hide those distracting elements from the viewer. You'll make this change by customizing the Excel display options.

To hide Excel screen elements:

1. Return to the **Income Report** workbook in Excel.
2. On the ribbon, click the **FILE** tab, and then click **Options** in the navigation bar. The Excel Options dialog box opens.
3. In the left pane, click **Advanced**.
4. Scroll down to the Display section, and then click the **Show formula bar** check box to remove the checkmark.

Tutorial 12 Collaborating on a Shared Workbook | Excel **EX 765**

▶ 5. Scroll down to the Display options for this workbook section, and make sure that **Income Report** appears in the box.

▶ 6. Click the **Show horizontal scroll bar**, **Show vertical scroll bar**, and **Show sheet tabs** check boxes to remove the checkmarks.

▶ 7. Go to the Display options for this worksheet section, and make sure that the **Income Statement** worksheet appears in the box.

▶ 8. Click the **Show row and column headers** and **Show gridlines** check boxes to remove the checkmarks. See Figure 12-27.

Figure 12-27	Advanced Excel options

- uncheck to hide the formula bar
- advanced Excel options
- uncheck to hide the scroll bars for the Income Report workbook
- uncheck to hide the sheet tabs for the Income Report workbook
- uncheck to hide the row and column headers in the Income Statement worksheet
- uncheck to hide the gridlines in the Income Statement worksheet

▶ 9. Click the **OK** button to apply the new options and close the dialog box. The contents of the Income Statement worksheet appear with many Excel screen elements hidden from view. See Figure 12-28.

Figure 12-28 Hidden screen elements

[Screenshot of Excel window showing the Income Report with callouts labeling: formula bar hidden, row and column headings hidden, sheet tabs hidden, worksheet gridlines removed, and scroll bars hidden. The worksheet displays Plush Pets Income Statement data for Dec 30, 2016; Dec 31, 2015; and Dec 31, 2014, alongside a "COST AND EXPENSES" pie chart.]

To redisplay the hidden screen elements, simply return to the Excel Options dialog box and click the check boxes for those elements.

To redisplay the workbook and worksheet screen elements:

1. On the ribbon, click the **FILE** tab, and then click **Options** in the navigation bar to reopen the Excel Options dialog box.
2. In the left pane, click **Advanced**.
3. Click the **Show formula bar**, **Show horizontal scroll bar**, **Show vertical scroll bar**, **Show sheet tabs**, **Show row and column headers**, and **Show gridlines** check boxes to insert checkmarks and redisplay those screen elements.
4. Click the **OK** button. The workbook window returns to its default view with all screen elements displayed.
5. Save and close the Income Report workbook, but keep Excel open.

The Excel Options dialog box provides many customization options for controlling how Excel works on your computer. For example, you can change the default font setting, which is 11-point Calibri. Or you can change the default number of worksheets in new workbooks from one to another number. Figure 12-29 lists other features you can customize.

Figure 12-29 Excel customization options

Excel Options	Customization Option
Formulas options	Turn on and off Formula AutoComplete
Save options	Select the default file format for saving workbooks
	Set the length of time in minutes to create an Auto Recover file
	Set the default location for Excel workbook files
Advanced options, Display section	Set the number of recent documents to show in the Office menu
	Show all workbook windows as separate icons on the Windows taskbar
Advanced options, Editing options section	Automatically format percent values in the Percent style
	Turn on or off AutoComplete for cell values
	Change the behavior of the Enter key

© 2014 Cengage Learning

INSIGHT

Controlling How Excel Recalculates Formulas

Excel automatically recalculates any formula when the input cells to that formula are changed. This process works seamlessly when the workbook is small and few formulas are involved. However, when the workbook increases in size—think several worksheets with thousands of rows with multiple formulas for each row—this process slows noticeably as Excel recalculates tens of thousands of formulas. One way to solve this problem is to change how Excel handles recalculation. You can choose from the following options:

- **Automatic**—All dependent formulas are recalculated every time a change is made to their input cells.
- **Automatic except for data tables**—Automatic recalculation is done for all dependent formulas except for formulas within data tables created with the Data Tables feature.
- **Manual**—No recalculation is done except when manually requested by the user.

To manually recalculate the contents of the workbook, press the F9 key or click the Calculate Now button in the Calculation group on the FORMULAS tab. You can define calculation options on the Formulas tab in the Excel Options dialog box, or by clicking the Calculation Options button in the Calculation group on the FORMULAS tab.

Another way to speed up a large workbook is to reduce the number of iterative calculations used in performing what-if analyses involving goal seeking. You can set this value using the Enable iterative calculation check box on the Formulas tab in the Excel Options dialog box.

Plush Pets is going international with a few stores already operating in Europe, and several more on the way in Asia and South America. Chayla wants you to examine how Excel could be customized to help her collaborate with colleagues and clients in different countries.

Developing a Workbook for International Clients

Businesses increasingly need their employees to develop reports and analysis for international customers. If you are creating a workbook that will be viewed by clients in another country, you may need to check on the standards for rendering times, dates, currency, and numbers for use in the country of interest. For example, countries differ in terms of how they use blank spaces, commas, and periods to mark decimal places and number groups. Figure 12-30 shows how the same number will be represented in several different countries.

Figure 12-30 International number formats

Style	Description	Supported In
5,308,421.64	Thousands grouped by a comma, decimals marked with a period	English Canada, China, Ireland, Israel, Japan, Korea, Malaysia, New Zealand, Taiwan, Thailand, United Kingdom, United States
5 308 421,64	Thousands grouped by a space, decimals marked with a comma	Albania, Belgium, Brazil, Denmark, France, French Canada, Finland, Germany, Greece, Italy, Netherlands, Poland, Portugal, Romania, Sweden, Switzerland
5.308.421,64	Thousands grouped by a period, decimals marked with a comma	Brazil, Denmark, Germany, Greece Italy, Netherlands, Portugal, Romania, Spain, Sweden
53,08,421.64	Thousands above 9,999 marked in two-digit groups with a comma, decimals marked with a period	India
5'308'421.64	Thousands grouped with an apostrophe, decimals marked with a period	Switzerland
5'308'421,64	Thousands grouped with an apostrophe, decimals marked with a comma	Germany, Greece, Italy, Romania

© 2014 Cengage Learning

The number format used by Excel is set by the computer's operating system. If you are running Windows, you can use the Language section of the Control Panel to change the symbols used for the thousands separator and decimal marks, as well as set the parameters for other number formats. However, in some cases, you might want to only temporarily change the number format for a particular workbook. You can make such a change using the advanced Excel options.

Chayla has an income statement for the new Plush Pets store in Paris. She wants to change the number format to match the format used in France.

To change the number format style used by Excel:

1. Open the **Paris** workbook located in the Excel12 ▸ Tutorial folder included with your Data Files, and then save the file as **Paris Income** in the location specified by your instructor.

2. In the Documentation worksheet, enter your name and the date.

Tutorial 12 Collaborating on a Shared Workbook | Excel   EX 769

3. Go to the **Income Statement** worksheet. Note that all of the numbers are expressed using the default number formats set in your operating system. For this data, Chayla wants to replace the thousands separator with a period and the decimal mark with a comma.

> **TIP**
> You can set the language Excel uses for grammar, spell checking, and sorting in the Language options in the Excel Options dialog box.

4. On the ribbon, click the **FILE** tab, and then click **Options** in the navigation bar to open the Excel Options dialog box.

5. In the left pane, click **Advanced**.

6. Click the **Use system separators** check box to remove the checkmark so that Excel does not use the number format defined by the operating system.

7. Select the symbol in the **Decimal separator** box, and then type **,** (a comma).

8. Select the symbol in the **Thousands separator** box, and then type **.** (a period). See Figure 12-31.

Figure 12-31   New decimal and thousands separators

[Excel Options dialog box showing Advanced pane with Editing options. Callouts indicate:
- "select to use the number format defined by the operating system" pointing to the Use system separators check box
- "enter symbols used for the decimal and thousands separators" pointing to the Decimal separator and Thousands separator fields]

9. Click the **OK** button. A period is now used for the thousands separator and a comma is used for the decimal separator. See Figure 12-32.

Figure 12-32 Numbers displayed in a European format

	A	B
1	Plush Pets	
2	Paris Store Income Statement	
3		(currency values in euros)
4	Period Ending	Dec 30, 2016
5	Revenue	44.318,38
6	Cost of Goods Sold	15.740,21
7	Gross Margin	28.578,17
8		
9	Operating Expenses	
10	Payroll	13.819,88
11	Depreciation	750,00
12	Advertising	1.578,38
13	Rent	2.148,73
14	Insurance	477,25
15	Total	18.774,24
16		
17	Profit before Interest and Taxes	9.803,93
18	Interest Expense	411,39
19	Pretax Profit	9.392,54

numbers use a period for the thousands separator and a comma for the decimal separator

Chayla also wants to be clear that the currency values in the Income Statement are expressed in euros, not dollars. You'll make this formatting change to the revenue and net profit values in the worksheet.

To express the currency values in euros:

1. Select the nonadjacent range **B5;B22**.

2. On the HOME tab, in the Number group, click the **Accounting Number Format button arrow** $, and then click **Euro**. The euro symbol appears with the values in cells B5 and B22. See Figure 12-33.

Figure 12-33   **Euro currency values**

[Screenshot of Excel showing Paris Income workbook with the Home ribbon. Cell B22 is selected with formula =B19-B21. The worksheet contains:]

	A	B
1	Plush Pets	
2	Paris Store Income Statement	
3		(currency values in euros)
4	Period Ending	Dec 30, 2016
5	Revenue	€ 44.318,38
6	Cost of Goods Sold	15.740,21
7	Gross Margin	28.578,17

Callouts:
- currency values with the euro symbol
- click to select the euro accounting symbol

3. Save the workbook.

Excel also includes currency symbols for the English pound (£) and Chinese yuan (¥), which you can select by clicking the Account Number Format button arrow.

> ### INSIGHT
> ### Utilizing International Symbols
>
> If you are creating a document for an international audience, you might need to insert international symbols into the text. One way of quickly doing this is with the Symbol dialog box. To open the Symbol dialog box, click the Symbol button Ω in the Symbols group on the INSERT tab. Microsoft Office organizes symbols into different topical categories. For example, you can click the Subset list box to display a gallery of currency symbols from across the world. European characters that include accent or tilde marks such as è and õ can be found within the Latin Extended-A or Latin Extended-B subset of characters.
>
> Many keyboard shortcuts exist for inserting international characters. One form of the keyboard shortcut involves holding down the Alt key and typing the character code using your numeric keypad. This character code is usually written as
>
>   Alt+*character_code*
>
> where *character_code* is an ASCII code that identifies the character you wish to insert. For example, the keyboard shortcut Alt+0232 will insert the è character. You can view the codes associated with each character in the Symbol dialog box.
>
> A more extensive list of characters is provided using the Unicode character set; however, these characters can only be inserted using the Symbol dialog box. Excel does not support keyboard shortcuts for these characters.

The Excel option to set the symbol for the decimal and thousands separator applies to the entire Excel working environment. This means that *any workbook* will now show numbers in the French number format until you change the Excel options back to the default operating system settings. Chayla doesn't want to change her number formats permanently. Instead, she wants only a hard-copy version of this data using the euro currency and number formatting. She asks you to save a version of this file as a PDF.

Saving a Worksheet as a PDF File

PDF (Portable Document Format) is a file format developed by Adobe Systems for displaying formatted documents containing text, graphics, and complicated layouts. PDFs are often used for collaborative work because Adobe Reader software is free and available on a wide variety of devices and operating systems.

Excel provides two options for publishing workbooks as PDFs. The Standard option optimizes the PDF for use with online publishing and printing. The Minimum size option is used strictly for online publishing, but not for printing. Chayla asks you to save the contents of the Income Statement worksheet as a PDF using the Standard option so that she can share the document with users who do not have Excel.

To save the Income Statement worksheet as a PDF file:

1. On the ribbon, click the **FILE** tab, and then click **Save As** in the navigation bar.
2. Click the **Excel12 ▸ Tutorial** folder from the list of recent folders to open the Save As dialog box.
3. In the File name box, type **Paris Income Statement**.
4. Click the **Save as type** box, and then click **PDF** in the list of file types.
5. Verify that the **Standard** option button is selected, and then click the **Save** button. The worksheet is saved as a PDF file and opens a PDF reader to view the file contents. See Figure 12-34.

Tutorial 12 Collaborating on a Shared Workbook | Excel **EX 773**

Figure 12-34 PDF version of the Paris report

Plush Pets
Paris Store Income Statement

(currency values in euros)

Period Ending		Dec 30, 2016
Revenue	€	44.318,38
Cost of Goods Sold		15.740,21
Gross Margin		28.578,17
Operating Expenses		
Payroll		13.819,88
Depreciation		750,00
Advertising		1.578,38
Rent		2.148,73
Insurance		477,25
Total		18.774,24
Profit before Interest and Taxes		9.803,93
Interest Expense		411,39
Pretax Profit		9.392,54
Taxes Incurred		4.414,81
Net Profit	€	**4.977,73**

© 2014 Cengage Learning

Trouble? If you don't have Adobe Reader, you can download a free version from the Adobe website at www.adobe.com.

▶ **6.** Close the PDF reader and return to the Excel workbook.

Before finishing your work, Chayla wants you to change the numeric formats back to their default operating system settings.

To restore the number format to the system settings:

1. On the ribbon, click the **FILE** tab, and then click **Options** in the navigation bar. The Excel Options dialog box reopens.
2. In the left pane, click **Advanced**.
3. In the Editing options section, click the **Use system separators** check box.
4. Click the **OK** button.
5. Save the Paris Income workbook, and then close Excel.

You have finished creating collaborative documents in Excel for Chayla and the Plush Pets company. In the process, you learned several ways that information can be shared among a team of employees working together to create a final, polished document that can be read by different devices and programs, and can be used by international customers and colleagues.

Session 12.2 Quick Check

1. What are document properties?
2. How do you add multiple values to a document tag?
3. How can you determine whether a workbook contains sensitive or personal information?
4. Why should you not use the default Sheet1, Sheet2 worksheet names supplied by Excel?
5. What is workbook encryption?
6. What happens to a workbook that is edited after it is digitally signed?
7. What is the difference between linking and embedding?
8. How do you override the default number format used by Excel that is set by the computer's operating system?

SAM Projects

Put your skills into practice with SAM Projects! SAM Projects for this tutorial can be found online. If you have a SAM account, go to www.cengage.com/sam2013 to download the most recent Project Instructions and Start Files.

Review Assignments

Data Files needed for the Review Assignments: Projected.xlsx, Group.xlsx, Cash.xlsx, Sanders Edits.xlsx, Cash Flow.xlsx, Notes.docx, Brussels.xlsx

Chayla needs to provide a projected income statement and projected cash flow schedule for the coming year for the stockholders' meeting. She created the initial workbook, but she wants you to send it out for review and then reconcile the edits made by her colleagues. After Chayla has a final draft, she wants you to add document properties, encrypt the workbook, and mark it as final. Complete the following:

1. Open the **Projected** workbook located in the Excel12 ▸ Review folder included with your Data Files, and then save the workbook as **Projected Statements** in the location specified by your instructor. In the Documentation worksheet, enter your name and the date.

2. In the Projected Income worksheet, add the following comment to cell B5: **Do you think that $40,000,000 is a reasonable estimate for next year's revenue?**

3. Share the workbook, enabling changes by more than one user at a time, and then save and close the workbook.

4. Open the **Group** workbook located in the Excel12 ▸ Review folder, and then save the workbook as **Group Edits** in the location specified by your instructor. In the Documentation worksheet, enter your name and the date.

5. In the Projected Income Statement worksheet, delete the comments that were added to cell B5.

6. Review the changes in the workbook by everyone but you, accepting or rejecting the changes as follows:

    a. In cell B5, accept Linda Thorpe's recommended projection for the coming year's net revenue of $41,000,000.

    b. In cell B7, accept Joshua Allen's edit that set the cost of goods sold to $4,000,000.

    c. In cell B10, accept Joshua Allen's edit that set the general and administrative costs to $6,600,000.

    d. Accept Joshua Allen's renaming of the cash flow sheet to "Cash Flow Projections," and accept his renaming of the income statement sheet to "Income Projections."

    e. In cell B15, reject Kevin Leland's edit.

    f. Reject Joshua Allen's last two edits to the worksheet names.

7. Display the contents of the tracking log for everyone's changes to the workbook but yours. Print the History worksheet on a single page.

8. Save and close the Group Edits workbook.

9. Open the **Cash** workbook located in the Excel12 ▸ Review folder, and then save the workbook as **Cash and Income Report** in the location specified by your instructor. In the Documentation worksheet, enter your name and the date.

10. Add the Compare and Merge Workbooks button to the Quick Access Toolbar, and then use it to merge the contents of the current workbook with the **Sanders Edits** workbook located in the Excel12 ▸ Review folder to incorporate the edits and comments from Neil Sanders. Delete Neil's comment from the workbook, and then accept all of his changes to the workbook.

11. Save the Cash and Income Report workbook.

12. Save the workbook again as **Cash and Income Report Final**, and then remove the workbook from shared use.
13. On the Info screen, show all properties, and then add the following document properties to the workbook:
    - Title: **Financial Projections**
    - Tags: **projections; stockholders**
    - Comments: **Financial projections for the stockholders' conference**
    - Status: **Final Draft**
    - Categories: **Conference Reports**
    - Subject: **Stockholders' Report**
    - Author: your name
14. Insert the Department custom property using Text as the type and **Finance** as the value.
15. Encrypt the document using the password **plushpets**.
16. Mark the document as final, and then close the workbook.
17. Open the **Cash Flow** workbook located in the Excel12 ▸ Review folder, enter your name and the date in the Documentation worksheet, and then save the workbook as **Cash Flow Data** in the location specified by your instructor.
18. Using Microsoft Word, open the **Notes** document located in the Excel12 ▸ Review folder included with your Data Files, enter your name on the From line and the date on the Date line, and then save the document as **Notes on Cash Flow**.
19. Copy the range A4:E37 from the Cash Flow Projections worksheet in the Cash Flow Data workbook, and then paste a link in the blank line after the opening paragraph in the Notes on Cash Flow document. Use the formatting from the source file—the Cash Flow Data workbook.
20. Save and close the Cash Flow Data workbook and the linked Notes on Cash Flow document.
21. Open the **Brussels** workbook located in the Excel12 ▸ Review folder included with your Data Files, and then save the workbook as **Brussels Income** in the location specified by your instructor. In the Documentation worksheet, enter your name and the date.
22. In the Income Statement worksheet, format the currency values in cells B5 and B22 with the euro currency symbol.
23. Set the Excel options to use a blank space as the thousands separator and a comma as the decimal separator.
24. Save the Income Statement worksheet as a Standard PDF file with the filename **Brussels Income Statement**.
25. Save the Brussels Income workbook, and then close it.
26. Restore the Excel options to use the operating system settings for number formats.

Case Problem 1

Data Files needed for this Case Problem: Pizza.xlsx, Store1.xlsx, Store2.xlsx, Store3.xlsx, Store4.xlsx

Bandoni's Take 'n' Bake Brenda Giles is the financial manager at Bandoni's Take 'n' Bake, a new pizza franchise in Colorado. Currently, the company has four restaurants—two are located in Fort Collins, one is in Longmont, and the fourth is in Greeley. Each month, Brenda compiles the income statistics from the four stores based on the sales figures that each store manager has sent. Brenda has received the latest month's sales results that need to be merged and compared within a single workbook. Complete the following:

1. Open the **Pizza** workbook located in the Excel12 ▸ Case1 folder included with your Data Files, and then save the file as **Pizza Sales** in the location specified by your instructor.
2. In the Documentation worksheet, enter your name and the date.

3. From the Income Statements worksheet, merge the contents of the **Store1.xlsx**, **Store2.xlsx**, **Store3.xlsx**, and **Store4.xlsx** workbooks located in the Excel12 ▶ Case1 folder into the Pizza Sales workbook. You can select all four workbooks in the Select Files to Merge Into Current Workbook dialog box.
4. In the Income Statements worksheet, enter the following formulas:
   a. In the range B6:E6, enter the sales for each store.
   b. In the range B9:E9, enter the cost of sales for each store.
   c. In the range B10:E10, calculate the gross profit (Total Sales − Total Cost of Sales).
   d. In the range B33:E33, calculate the total expenses for each store.
   e. In the range B35:E35, calculate the net operating income (Gross Profit − Total Expenses).
   f. In column F, calculate the total values of each category in the income statement across all four stores.
5. In the Income Statements worksheet, in cell A1, add the following comment: **Data compiled from workbooks provided by Anne Faulkner, Robert Sanchez, Stefan Statz, and Carol Munoz**.
6. Remove the document from shared use.
7. Add the following names to the list of document authors—your name, **Anne Faulkner**, **Robert Sanchez**, **Stefan Statz**, and **Carol Munoz**.
8. Add the following properties to the workbook—**Monthly Income** as the title; **income statement** as the tag; **Data compiled from the four stores in the Northern Colorado region** as the comment; **Final** as the status; and **Bandoni's Take 'n' Bake** as the company.
9. Add the custom Checked by property to the workbook using your name as the property value.
10. Add the custom Date completed property to the workbook using the current date as the property value. Set the data type of the property value to Date.
11. Encrypt the workbook with the password **pizza** and mark it as final.
12. Save the Income Statements worksheet as a PDF file with the filename **Pizza Sales Report** to the location specified by your instructor.
13. Close any open files.

Case Problem 2

APPLY

Data Files needed for this Case Problem: Donor.xlsx, Building.docx

Lakeside College Karen Dale is in charge of fund-raising efforts for the building fund at Lakeside College in Madison, Wisconsin. As the college's fund-raising drive approaches, Karen needs to compile a mailing list of past contributors. She created a workbook with names and addresses, and had her assistants review the workbook and correct errors they found. You'll review her shared workbook and reconcile the edits made by her assistants. Karen will send a final draft of the workbook to other members of the fund-raising team who are creating the form letters and mailing labels. Complete the following:

1. Open the **Donor** workbook located in the Excel12 ▶ Case2 folder included with your Data Files, and then save the workbook as **Donor List** in the location specified by your instructor.
2. In the Documentation worksheet, enter your name and the date.
3. Display the tracking log for all edits made to the workbook except yours in a new sheet. Print the History worksheet with the tracking log in landscape orientation scaled to fit on a single page.
4. Review the changes made by Karen's assistants. Accept all of the edits except for Patrick Ihm's edit of cell B52 in the Donor List worksheet. In cell B14, accept Enitan Nwosu's edit over those made by Patrick Ihm and Michael Rodman.
5. Remove the workbook from shared use.
6. Add the following names as the workbook authors—your name, **Patrick Ihm**, **Enitan Nwosu**, and **Michael Rodman**.

7. Add the following document properties to the workbook—**Lakeside College** as the title; **Donor list for the building fund** as the comment; **Final** as the status; **fundraiser** as the category; and **Donor list** as the subject.
8. In the custom properties, add the Checked by property using Text as the type and **Karen Dale; Patrick Ihm; Enitan Nwosu; Michael Rodman** as the value.
9. Add the Date completed property, use Date as the value type, and then enter the current date as the value.
10. Create a new custom property named **Approved** with the value type set to Yes or no. Enter the value **Yes**.
11. Run the Compatibility Checker on the workbook to find any issues that Karen's colleagues will encounter if they are running older versions of Excel. Copy the report results to a new worksheet.
12. Start Word and open the **Building** document located in the Excel12 ▸ Case2 folder included with your Data Files, and then save the document as **Building Fund** in the location specified by your instructor.
13. In the From: and Date: lines of the memo, enter your name and the date.
14. In the Donor List workbook, in the Donor List worksheet, copy the range A4:F14, which contains the list of the top 10 donors.
15. Paste the selected range at the bottom of the Building Fund document using the Link & Keep Source Formatting (F) option.
16. In the Donor List workbook, in the Donor List worksheet, change the value in cell B12 from Brown to **Browne**.
17. Encrypt the workbook with the password **lakeside**.
18. Mark the Donor List workbook as final, and then close it.
19. In the Building Fund document, right-click anywhere in the linked table, and then click Update Link on the shortcut menu. Enter the password to the Donor List document when prompted. Notice that the donor's name changed from "Brown" to "Browne," reflecting the edits you made in the workbook.
20. Save and close the Building Fund document.

Case Problem 3

Data Files needed for this Case Problem: Healthy.xlsx, Review.docx

Healthy Meals Jacque Duvall runs a website called Healthy Meals that displays information about restaurant menus. The review displays both the price and calories for each menu item. Jacque works with several colleagues on reviewing and updating the menu information. He has stored menu data about the French restaurant La Petite Bistro in a workbook. He wants your help with reconciling the different edits to that workbook by his colleagues. He also wants you to link the workbook to a Word document containing a full review of La Petite Bistro. Complete the following:

1. Open the **Healthy** workbook located in the Excel12 ▸ Case3 folder included with your Data Files, and then save the workbook as **Healthy Meals** in the location specified by your instructor.
2. In the Documentation worksheet, enter your name and the date.
3. Review the edits made by Sean Moore and Brian Drew, accepting their edits. In case of a conflict, accept Sean Moore's edits over Brian Drew's and the original cell value.
4. Save the Healthy Meals workbook.
5. Display the contents of the tracking log on the History worksheet, showing everyone's edits, including your edits, and showing your own actions accepting or rejecting the other edits made to the document. Print the log on a single sheet in landscape orientation.
6. Remove sharing from the workbook.

Tutorial 12 Collaborating on a Shared Workbook | Excel **EX 779**

Explore 7. To be spelled correctly, several menu items should contain international symbols. Using the Symbol dialog box, make the following edits:

  a. In cell A6, change "Crudites" to **Crudités**.
  b. In cell A8, change "Pate" to **Pâté**.
  c. In cell A18, change "bearnaise" to **béarnaise**.
  d. In cells A26 and A28, change "Creme" to **Crème**.
  e. In cell A28, change "brulee" to **brûlée**.

8. Display the price values in column B as currency using the euro currency symbol.

9. Add the following properties to the document—your name as an author; **La Petite Bistro Review** as the title; and **Healthy Meals** as the company.

10. Add the custom property Checked by with the value **Sean Moore; Brian Drew**. Add the custom property Date completed using the Date value type and the current date as the value.

Explore 11. Jacque saved a review of the restaurant as a Word document and he wants it linked to the file. On the INSERT tab, in the Text group, use the Object button to open the Object dialog box. On the Create from File tab, create an object from the **Review.docx** file located in the Excel12 ▸ Case3 folder included with your Data Files, and then click the Link to file check box. Place the Word document object in the Menu worksheet with its upper-left corner in cell E3.

12. Use the Compatibility Checker to check the workbook for compatibility with earlier versions of Excel. Copy the results of the report to a new sheet in the workbook.

Explore 13. Run the Accessibility Checker to check for issues that might affect users with special needs. The Accessibility Checker will return one issue related to inserting an object (in this case, the linked Word document) without also providing alternate text. Follow the instructions from the Accessibility Checker pane to add the text of the first paragraph of the review as alternate text for the Word document object.

14. Run the Accessibility Checker again to verify that no accessibility issues occur in the workbook.

15. Mark the workbook as final, and then save and close the workbook.

Case Problem 4

CHALLENGE

Data Files needed for this Case Problem: Tufte.xlsx, Larson.xlsx, Wilkes.xlsx

Tufte Financial Jeri Paulson works for Tufte Financial, an investment firm in Seattle, Washington. She is currently developing a financial portfolio for one of her clients. She developed the basic template for the workbook but asked her colleagues to fill in the data for this portfolio. Her assistant, Andrew Larson, supplied the information about the financial value of the stocks in the portfolio while another assistant, Amanda Wilkes, provided background information on the stocks. You need to merge the workbooks into a single file. Jeri also wants you to sign off on the final product using a self-signed digital signature. Because all of this work is being done in-house, she does not need a third-party digital certificate. Complete the following:

1. Open the **Tufte** workbook located in the Excel12 ▸ Case4 folder included with your Data Files, and then save the workbook as **Tufte Financial** in the location specified by your instructor.

2. In the Documentation worksheet, enter your name and the date.

3. In the Portfolio worksheet, merge the current workbook with the contents of the **Larson** and **Wilkes** workbooks located in the Excel12 ▸ Case4 folder included with your Data Files.

4. Remove sharing from the workbook.

5. The charts in the Portfolio worksheet are based on data from the PivotTables in the PivotTables worksheet. On the DATA tab, in the Connections group, use the Refresh All button to refresh all of the data in the workbook and regenerate the two pie charts and the bar chart in the workbook.

6. Add the following properties to the document—your name, **Andrew Larson**, and **Amanda Wilkes** as the document authors; **Investment Portfolio** as the title; **In progress** as the status; **Tufte Financial** as the company.

7. Add the custom property Date completed to the document using the current date as the date value.

Explore 8. Go to the Program Files ► Microsoft Office ► Office15 folder and run the selfcert.exe program to create your own self-signed certificate. Use your name as the certificate name. (If you have trouble accessing this program, ask your instructor or technical resource person about creating your own digital certificate.)

Explore 9. In the Tufte Financial workbook, in the Documentation worksheet, select cell A7. On the INSERT tab, in the Text group, use the Add a Signature Line button to insert a digital signature. Use your name as the suggested signer, **Financial analyst** as the suggested signer's title, and your email address as the suggested signer's email address. Click the OK button to close the dialog box.

Explore 10. Double-click the signature line in the Documentation worksheet, type your name as the signer, and then click the Sign button. Click the Yes button if you are prompted to use the certificate even though it cannot be verified. Click the OK button to confirm that the digital signature is saved with the document. Notice that the signed document is automatically marked as final and changed to a read-only document.

11. Save the workbook, and then close it.

Teamwork

Working in a Team to Analyze Data

Teamwork is a collaborative process by which managers and non-managers work together to achieve a common goal or outcome. Teamwork usually involves setting aside individual success for the greater good of the team's collective work. It might also involve collaboration with customers, suppliers, or other organizations.

Characteristics of Teams

Team members get to know how their teammates work so each member can make contributions where they will count most. For example, on a football team, not everyone plays the role of quarterback; the team needs other positions working with him to score touchdowns. However, before the first play is ever made, members bring their skills to the group and spend time learning each others' moves. The best teams have members whose background, skills, and abilities complement each other.

Team Diversity

Team diversity comes in a variety of forms. Gender, race, ethnicity, and age are certainly part of it. But diversity can also be expressed in terms of experience, culture, and personality. A team that is too homogenous might lead to average solutions. A team that is too diverse might require extra effort just to get everyone heading in the same direction. But a good mix can lead to greater performance and creativity.

Roles You Might Play

If a team is to be successful for any length of time, members must see the value in both their contribution and what the team gets out of it. This means meeting two important requirements—task performance and social satisfaction. Task performance is usually handled by one or more members who are specialists. Task specialists spend a lot of time and effort ensuring that the team achieves its goals. Often, they initiate ideas, give opinions, gather information, sort and cull details, and provide the spark that keeps the team on track. The socioemotional role is handled by people who strengthen the team's social bonds. This is often done through encouragement, empathy, conflict resolution, compromise, and tension reduction. In a group that has conflict, the person who steps in to tell a joke or soften the blow of criticism holds the socioemotional role.

Most teams will have other roles as well, including team leaders, work coordinators, idea people, and critics. These roles are not mutually exclusive. On a team, no single role is more or less important than the others. The progress and results the team achieves depend on how well the roles mesh in getting the work done.

Develop a Financial Report

Excel is a powerful program for analyzing financial data, projecting future income and expenses, and organizing information from a wide variety of sources. With the Excel support for Visual Basic for Applications, experienced users and programmers can expand Excel's capability to accommodate a wide range of problems and challenges. In this exercise, you will work with a team to prepare a financial report. Your team should talk to instructors, colleagues, and business leaders about obtaining some real-world financial data, if possible. You'll want to obtain accounting data that you can use to perform a financial analysis, including a balance sheet, an income statement, a cash flow report, and sales data for a product or service that indicates the level of sales volume for a given price or fee. Your team will then use Excel to create a workbook that contains the information of your choice, using the

Excel skills and features presented in Tutorials 9 through 12. **Note:** Please be sure *not* to include any personal information of a sensitive nature in the workbooks you create to submit to your instructor. Later, you can update the worksheets with such information for your personal use.

1. Prepare a working schedule and a list of responsibilities for your team. Select an individual to act as the team leader who will coordinate the efforts of the members.
2. One or more team members should work on assembling the financial data in external data files. Those members should be ready to consolidate several sources of data from text files and databases to web queries and other workbooks.
3. The team should develop a new workbook to contain the business information the group intends to collect. Use the first worksheet to document the scope and purpose of the workbook, including a listing of all data sources you intend to use and a description of the team members and their responsibilities.
4. The workbook should contain connections to the financial data you have accumulated and stored in external files.
5. On the next several sheets in the workbook, use the connections in the workbook to import and display the data. Format the data so it is easy to read and interpret. If your team has collected financial reports from a company, examine how the reports interrelate. Replace the data values with formulas whenever possible.
6. Assign a team member to perform a what-if analysis on your financial data. He or she should determine what would happen to the company's balance sheets, cash flow, or net income if certain key variables were changed.
7. The workbook should contain a worksheet with either a one- or a two-variable table. Use the data table to explore the financial impact of several what-if analyses.
8. Extrapolate the company's income and expenses three years into the future assuming first a linear trend and then a growth trend. Discuss with your colleagues and advisors what would constitute a realistic trend line.
9. Include charts and tables in the financial report that clearly explain the projections and assumptions the team made.
10. Add document properties to the workbook file including a list of the document's authors, the document title, comments, tags, and subject matter.
11. Mark the workbook as final when you have completed all of your analysis.
12. Save the workbook, and then close it.

ADDITIONAL CASE 1

Creating a Grading Workbook

OBJECTIVES

- Create a connection to a text file
- Create defined names
- Apply data validation based on a list of values
- Use the VLOOKUP function to retrieve data from a list
- Use the SUMPRODUCT function to calculate the sum from multiplying two lists of numbers
- Use the COUNTIF function to count totals corresponding to a query
- Display data values using data bars
- Display an array of data values with freeze panes
- Save a workbook as a template file

Case | Country Day School

Robert James teaches senior math at Country Day School in Grand Forks, North Dakota. He's been developing a grading workbook to calculate final grades based on a weighted average of homework, projects, quizzes, and exams. It also contains worksheets for entering absences and tardiness as well as any notes about student progress and behavior. The school uses a special database system in which homework, quiz, and exam scores are entered automatically during class, and then exported to text files. The workbook must connect to these text files and extract the student scores. You'll finish the workbook, and then save it as a template file. Complete the following:

1. Open the **Grading** workbook located in the AddCases ► Case1 folder included with your Data Files, and then save it as **Grading Book** in the location specified by your instructor.
2. In the Documentation sheet, enter your name and the date.
3. In the Class Summary worksheet, enter **Calculus** for the course title, **Robert James** for the instructor, and **IV** for the quarter. Assign the following weights to the grading components: **25%** for Homework, **45%** for Quizzes, and **30%** for Exams.
4. In the Class Summary sheet, assign the defined name **Grade_Scale** to the range B13:C26.
5. In the Student List worksheet, create a connection to the student list stored in the tab-delimited **Student List** text file located in the AddCases ► Case1 folder. Import the data starting at row 7. Set the import properties so that Excel does not adjust the column width when importing the data. Place the imported data in the range B6:C25.
6. Assign the defined name **Student_List** to the range B6:B25 of the Student List worksheet.
7. In the Student Notes worksheet, add data validation to the Student column (the range B5:B40), limiting entries to the list of students from the Student_List range. In the Resolved? column (the range E5:E40), limit entries to either Yes or No.

STARTING DATA FILES

AddCases → Case1

Exam Grades.txt
Grading.xlsx
Homework Grades.txt
Quiz Grades.txt
Student List.txt

ADD 1

8. Add the following notes to the worksheet:
   Boyd, Jason   4/12/2016   Missing homework   Yes
   Walton, Marie   4/13/2016   Talking in class, disruptive behavior   No
9. In the Attendance worksheet, limit the entries in the Student column to the student names from the Student_List range. Limit the entries in the Attendance Issue column to either Absent or Tardy. Limit the entries in the Excused? column to either Yes or No.
10. Add the following attendance issues to the worksheet:
    Singleton, Ryan   4/13/2016   Absent   Yes
    Singleton, Ryan   4/14/2016   Absent   Yes
    Biggs, Sheila   4/15/2016   Tardy   No
11. In the Homework worksheet, insert references in the range A9:A28 to the names in the Student List worksheet.
12. Create a connection to the homework scores from the **Homework Grades** text file AddCases ▶ Case1 folder. Import the data starting at row 6, excluding the first column. Set the import properties so that Excel does not adjust the column width when importing the data. Import the data into the range B9:O28 in the Homework worksheet.
13. In the Homework worksheet, freeze panes at cell B9.
14. Repeat Steps 11 through 13 for the Quizzes worksheet. In Step 12, import the grades from the **Quiz Grades** text file in to the range B9:E28 in the Quizzes worksheet.
15. Repeat Steps 11 through 13 for the Exams worksheet. In Step 12, import the grades from the **Exam Grades** text file into the range B9:C28 in the Exams worksheet.
16. In the Grades worksheet, which will calculate each student's final grade, insert references in the range B6:D6 to the three grading component percentages in the Class Summary worksheet in the range C9:C11. In cell E6, calculate the total of the percentages and verify that the sum of the percentages is 100%.
17. In the range A7:A26, insert references to the student names in the Student List worksheet.
18. In cell B7, enter a formula to calculate the first student's homework percentage score by adding all the values in that student's row in the Homework worksheet and then dividing the sum by the total number of homework points in row 7 of the Homework worksheet. Fill the formula into the rest of the column to calculate each student's percentage.
19. Repeat Step 18 to calculate each student's quiz percentage in column C based on values in the Quizzes worksheet, and to calculate each student's exam percentage in column D based on values in the Exam worksheet.
20. In cell E7, use the SUMPRODUCT function to calculate the weighted percentage of each component score multiplied by the weight assigned to that component. Copy the formula into the rest of the column to calculate each student's final overall grade percentage.
21. In cell F7, calculate the student's final grade using the VLOOKUP function based on the total percentage. Use an approximate match to the scores in the Grade_Scale range.
22. In the Student List worksheet, insert references to the Grades worksheet to display each student's weighted average score and grade.
23. In the Class Summary sheet, in the range D14:D26, use the COUNTIF function with the grades in the Student List worksheet to calculate the total number of each grade in the class.
24. In the range D14:D26, add green data bars to indicate the frequency of each grade in the class. Save the workbook.
25. In the Class Summary worksheet, delete the class data from the range C4:C6;C9:C11. In the Student List worksheet, delete the student name data from the range B6:C25, but do not delete the query. In the Student Notes and Attendance worksheets, delete the student notes data and the attendance data.
26. In the Homework worksheet, delete the homework descriptions in row 5, the homework points in row 7, and the homework scores in the range B9:O28. Do not delete the query.
27. Repeat Step 26 for the quiz and exam data in the Quizzes and Exams worksheets.
28. Save the workbook as a template file named **Grading Template**. Do not have Excel automatically refresh the external data before saving the workbook nor when the workbook is opened.

ADDITIONAL CASE 2

Finding an Optimal Product Mix

OBJECTIVES

- Merge several workbooks into a single document
- Use the SUMPRODUCT function to sum the products of two ranges
- Use the IF function to return text
- Create scenarios using the Scenario Manager
- Maximize net income using Solver
- Create a scenario summary report
- Add document properties to the workbook file
- Format the printed output
- Mark a workbook as final

Case | *Advantage Cookware*

Karen Drexel is a financial analyst for Advantage Cookware, a manufacturer of quality cooking products based in Helena, Montana. She has been asked to develop a product mix for Advantage Cookware's line of food processors that optimizes the company's profits. To do this analysis, she will collaborate with two colleagues to obtain information about the parts used in each model of food processor and the revenue and expenses associated with the production. Complete the following:

1. Open the **Advantage** workbook located in the AddCases ► Case2 folder included with your Data Files, and then save the workbook as **Advantage Cookware** in the location specified by your instructor.
2. In the Documentation worksheet, enter your name and the date.
3. Pete Bradshaw, who manages production at the manufacturing facility, has stored information about the parts used in creating the four models of food processors and the productions costs involved. Yolanda Anderson has information on the company's revenue and expenses from this line of products. Merge the Advantage Cookware workbook with **Bradshaw.xlsx** and **Anderson.xlsx files** located in the AddCases ► Case2 folder.
4. Remove sharing from the workbook but leave any comments in the workbook.
5. In the Product Mix worksheet, AutoFit the contents of column G and column M.
6. In the range B7:E7, calculate the total revenue from each of the four food processors.

STARTING DATA FILES

AddCases → Case2

Advantage.xlsx
Anderson.xlsx
Bradshaw.xlsx

7. In cell B10, calculate the material cost of the Prep 1000 food processor using the SUMPRODUCT function based on the range H4:H23 that contains a list of the Prep 1000 parts and the range L4:L23 that contains the cost of each part. In the range C10: E10, use the same function to calculate the material cost of the other three food processors.
8. In the range B12:E12, calculate the total cost per unit of each food processor by adding the material and manufacturing costs.
9. In the range B13:E13, calculate the total variable expenses of producing the food processors by multiplying the per unit cost by the number of units produced and sold.
10. In cell B21, calculate the total revenue generated from all four models. In cell B22, calculate the total variable expenses. In cell B23, calculate the total fixed expenses. In cell B24, calculate the net income from this line of food processors by subtracting the total variable and fixed expenses from the total revenue.
11. The current workbook has the company producing 3000 units of each model. To determine how many parts that would involve, enter **Parts Used** in cell N3, and then use the SUMPRODUCT function in cell N4 to multiply the number of models produced and sold in the range B5:E5 by the parts required for each product in the range H4:K4. (Use an absolute reference to the range B5:E5.) Copy the formula to the range N5:N23 to calculate the number of each part that will be used in the production run.
12. To determine the number of each part remaining, enter **Remaining** in cell O3, and then in the range O4:O23, calculate the parts remaining by subtracting the Parts Used value from the Parts In Stock value.
13. Copy the format from the range M4:M23 and apply it to the range N4:O23.
14. In the range O4:O23, apply conditional formatting so that any value less than zero appears in a bold red font.
15. In cell A26, enter **Production Status**. In cell B26, enter an IF statement that tests whether the minimum value in the range O4:O23 is less than zero. If it is, display **Not Enough Parts**; otherwise, display **Parts OK**.
16. Use the Scenario Manager to create the following scenarios that Karen wants to investigate for production:
    - **Base** scenario with the company producing and selling 3000 units of every model.
    - **Expanded** scenario with the company producing and selling 5000 units of every model.
    - **High End** scenario with the company producing and selling 2000 units each of the Prep 1000 and Prep 1200 models and 5000 units each of the Prep 2000 and Elite Prep models.
    - **Low End** scenario with the company producing and selling 5000 units each of the Prep 1000 and Prep 1200 models and 2000 units each of the Prep 2000 and Elite Prep models.
17. Use Solver to find the optimal product mix by maximizing the net income value by changing the number of each model produced and sold, subject to the following constraints
    - The number of each model produced and sold is an integer.
    - At least 3000 of each food processor model is produced.
    - The number of each part remaining after the production run is greater than or equal to zero.
18. Save the resulting Solver solution as a scenario under the name **Optimal**.
19. Create defined names for the production values in the range B5:E5 using the labels in the range B4:E4. Create defined names for the revenue, expense, and net income values in the range B21:B24 using the labels from the range A21:A24. Create a defined name for cell B26 using the label in cell A26.

20. Create a scenario summary report for the five scenarios using the range B21:B24;B26 as the result cells. Add the comment **Invalid Scenario** to any scenario in which there are not enough parts to complete this order. Move the Scenario Summary worksheet to the end of the workbook.
21. Modify the following document properties of the workbook:
    - Add your name as an author
    - Set the Title property as **Optimal Product Mix**
    - Set the Tags property as **food processors; product mix**
    - Set the Categories property as **food processors**
    - Set the Company property as **Advantage Cookware**
22. Create the custom Department property with the value **Financial Analysis**, and then create the custom Checked by property with your name as the value.
23. Modify the page layout so that all pages are printed in landscape orientation and scaled so that each worksheet fits on a single page.
24. Create a footer for each page that displays the filename in the left section, the sheet name in the right section, and the page number in the center section. Create a header for each page that displays your name in the right section.
25. Display the results of the Optimal scenario in the Product Mix worksheet, and then print all of the worksheets in the workbook.
26. Mark the workbook as Final, and then close it.

ADDITIONAL CASE 3

Creating an Interactive Order Form

OBJECTIVES

- Import data from an Excel table
- Use exact and approximate matches to a vertical lookup table
- Use the IFERROR function to hide Excel error values
- Apply data validation to cell values
- Apply data validation to text lengths
- Calculate the next working date after a given number of days
- Record a macro and assign it to a macro button
- Unlock worksheet cells and protect the worksheet
- Save a workbook as a macro-enabled template

Case | *The Sauce Shoppe*

Helen Jankowski works at the Sauce Shoppe, an online store based in Rock Hill, South Carolina, that sells a wide variety of hot sauces and dips. She wants to develop a workbook to process online orders. The workbook will calculate the shipping costs of the order and use that information to calculate the overall cost of the order including sales tax. Helen has stored a list of Sauce Shoppe products in an Access database table. You'll import the database table as part of the order form and set the properties of the data connection. Complete the following:

1. Open the **Sauce** workbook located in the AddCases ▶ Case3 folder included with your Data Files, and then save the workbook as **Sauce Shoppe** as a macro-enabled workbook in the location specified by your instructor.
2. In the Documentation worksheet, enter your name and the date.
3. In the Product List worksheet, import the Product List table from the **Sauce Shoppe Products** database located in the AddCases ▶ Case3 folder into cell A4 of the worksheet.
4. Add the description **Product list imported from the Product List table in the Sauce Shoppe Products database** to the data connection for the product data. Have Excel refresh this data whenever the workbook is reopened.
5. Name the Excel table containing the product data **Product_List**.
6. Change the table style to **Table Style Medium 6**.
7. In the Order Form worksheet, in cell B26, enter a formula that returns the current date.
8. In cell B27, add a data validation to limit the possible type of delivery values in the cell to Standard, 3 Day, 2 Day, or Overnight based on the values in the range A14:A17 of the Delivery Calculator worksheet.

STARTING DATA FILES

AddCases → Case3

Sauces.xlsx
Sauce Shop Products.accdb

9. In cell B28, calculate the number of workdays to deliver the order based on the lookup table in the range A14:C17 of the Deliver Calculator worksheet and using the value of cell B27 as the lookup value. If the formula returns an error value, display no text in the cell.
10. In cell B29, calculate the estimated delivery day, assuming that deliveries are only made on the weekdays, using the value in cell B28 to estimate the number of workdays that have passed from the current date in cell B26. Have the estimated delivery date skip holidays using the list of holiday dates in the range A20:A75 of the Delivery Calculator worksheet. If the formula returns an error value, display no text in the cell.
11. In the range A32:A41, add data validation to limit the product ID of items ordered by the customer to the list of product IDs in the range A5:A70 of the Product List worksheet.
12. In the range B32:C41, use the Product_List table as a lookup table to retrieve the name of the product ordered by the customer. Use the corresponding Product ID in column A as the lookup value. If the formula returns an error value, display no text in the cell.
13. In the range D32:D41, use the Product_List table as a lookup table to retrieve the price of the product ordered by the customer. Use the corresponding value in column A as the lookup value. If no Product ID is entered in the corresponding cell in column A, display no text in the cell.
14. In the range F32:F41, calculate the charge for the item ordered by multiplying the price of the item by the quantity ordered. If the formula returns an error value, display no text in the cell.
15. In cell F43, calculate the subtotal of the charges for the items ordered by the customer.
16. In cell F44, calculate the sales tax on the order using the tax rate quoted in cell H33.
17. In cell F45, calculate the total cost of shipping and handling based on the following rules:
    - Calculate the initial shipping charge by looking up the shipping fee in the table in the range A6:B11 of the Delivery Calculator worksheet using cell F43 as the lookup value.
    - Any merchandise subtotal greater than $100 receives free shipping.
    - Add a surcharge based on the type of delivery by looking up the surcharge from the range A14:C17 on the Delivery Calculator worksheet and the type of delivery specified in cell B27.
    - If the formula returns an error value, display no text in the cell.
18. In cell F47, calculate the total bill by adding the subtotal, sales tax, and shipping & handling fee. If the formula returns an error value, display no text in the cell.
19. Use data validation to limit the value in cell E26 to either VISA or MasterCard, which are the credit cards that The Sauce Shoppe accepts.
20. VISA and MasterCard credit card numbers are 16 digits. Add data validation to limit the text in cell E27 to 16 characters. Apply the Number format with no decimal places to the value in the cell.
21. Cell H27 is used for storing a three-digit security code. Add data validation to set the length of the text in the cell to three characters.
22. In cell E28, add data validation to verify that the expiration date entered in the cell is past the date specified in cell B26 (the date of the order).
23. Record a macro named **Copy_Address** that performs the following steps:
    - Select and copy the range B8:B13.
    - Paste the copied cells into the range B19:B24.
    - Select cell B26.
24. Assign the Copy_Address macro to the macro button, "Copy Shipping Address --->"
25. Unlock all of the cells in the worksheet except those containing formulas (indicated by the light green fill).

26. Protect the Order Form worksheet from being changed. Do not specify a password for the sheet protection.
27. Enter the customer information listed below. Use the macro button to copy the shipping address into the billing address.
    Customer: **Jaime Kingsolver**
    Order No.: **OR1284**
    Address 1: **414 Jefferson Lane**
    City: **Newberry**
    State: **South Carolina**
    ZIP: **29108**
    Phone: **(803) 555-1021**
28. Choose **Standard** shipping for the order.
29. Add the following items to the order and calculate the total bill: **3** of item **FM008**, **1** of item **EX012**, and **1** of item **HVM015**.
30. Enter the following VISA credit card number for the customer: **4123456789012340** with the security code **999**. Enter **3/1/2016** as the expiration date and **Jaime Kingsolver** as the cardholder's name.
31. Print the order form on a single sheet of paper in portrait orientation.
32. Save the workbook.
33. Delete all of the customer- and order-specific information from the Order Form worksheet. Save the file as **Order Form** in Excel Macro-Enabled Template format in the location specified by your instructor. Do not have Excel clear the external data before saving the template.

ADDITIONAL CASE 4

Analyzing a Sales Database

OBJECTIVES

- Import data from several database tables
- Add Excel tables to the Excel data model
- Establish relationships between tables using a common field
- Insert tables into a PivotTable report
- Display PivotTable in a tabular format
- Add a PivotTable slicer
- Sort and filter a PivotTable based on a value field
- Install an app from the Office Store
- Display data values on a map using the Bing Maps app

Case | Yogaland

Shannon Goodwin is a sales manager at Yogaland, an online seller of yoga products and accessories based in Lafayette, Indiana. Shannon wants to analyze recent sales data for the company. She needs to retrieve data from an Access database and add that data to the Excel data model. She also needs to establish the relationships between the tables. Once the data has been imported into Excel, she wants to summarize the data using PivotTables. Finally, Shannon wants a list of the customers and the items they ordered, a list of the most popular Yogaland products, and a map of the locations of Yogaland customers. Complete the following:

1. Open the **Yogaland** workbook located in the AddCases ▶ Case4 folder included with your Data Files, and then save the workbook as **Yogaland Sales** in the location specified by your instructor.
2. In the Documentation worksheet, enter your name and the date.
3. In the Sales worksheet, starting from cell A4, import the contents of the Sales table from the **Market** database file located in the AddCases ▶ Case4 folder into an Excel table.
4. Rename the Excel table as **Sales_Data** and change the table style to Table Style Medium 5.
5. Change the name of the data connection to **Sales Data**. Add the description **Data retrieved from the Sales table in the Market database**. Have Excel refresh the data connection when the workbook is reopened.
6. In the Products worksheet, import the Products table from the Market database into cell A4. Rename the Excel table **Product_Data** and change the table style to Table Style Medium 5. Change the name of the data connection to **Product Data**. Add the description **Data retrieved from the Products table in the Market database**. Have Excel refresh the data connection when the workbook is reopened.
7. In the Customers worksheet, import the Customers table from the Market database into cell A4. Rename the Excel table

STARTING DATA FILES

AddCases ▶ Case4

Market.accdb
Yogaland.xlsx

Customer_Data and change the table style to Table Style Medium 5. Change the name of the data connection to **Customer Data**. Add the description **Data retrieved from the Customers table in the Market database**. Have Excel refresh the data connection when the workbook is reopened.
8. Add the Sales_Table, Product_Data, and Customer_Data tables to the Excel data model.
9. Open the Excel data model using PowerPivot. Create a relationship linking the Sales_Data table to the Product_Data table through the Product ID field.
10. Create a relationship linking the Sales_Data table to the Customer_Data table through the Customer ID field.
11. In the Customer Report worksheet, create a list of the products ordered by each customer by inserting a PivotTable report into cell A4 that connects to the Sales_Data, Product_Table, and Customer_Data tables in the data model.
12. Add the Last, First, and Product Name fields to the ROWS section of the PivotTable. Add the Quantity field to the VALUES section.
13. Change the layout of the PivotTable to tabular format. Do not display any subtotals in the PivotTable. Format the table and its labels to make the data easy to read.
14. In the Product Report worksheet, insert a PivotTable report into cell A4 using the Sales_Data, Product_Table, and Customer_Table as the data source. Add the Product Name field to the ROWS section of the PivotTable. Add the Quantity field to the VALUES section to create a report showing Yogaland's best-selling products.
15. Change the layout to tabular format. Do not show any subtotals in the table.
16. In the PivotTable, click the Product Name filter button, and then use the More Sort Options command to open the Sort dialog box. Sort the PivotTable by descending order of the Sum of Quantity column.
17. Click the Product Name filter button again, and then use the Value Filters command to filter the PivotTable so that it shows only the top 10 products sold by the company.
18. Add a PivotTable slicer that displays the different values in the Category field.
19. Format the table and rename the columns to make the content easier to read.
20. In the Sales Locations worksheet, insert a PivotTable into cell A4 using the fields from the Sales_Table, Product_Table, and Customer_Table tables from the data model.
21. Add the City and State field from the Customer_Data table to the ROWS section of the table. Add the Quantity field to the VALUES section.
22. Format the PivotTable to make the data easy to read and interpret.
23. Download and install the free Bing Map app from the Microsoft Office Store.
24. Start the Bing Maps app to display a map app on the workbook. Select columns A and B from the PivotTable and click the Plot Locations icon located at the top of the map app. After several seconds, the app will add circles proportionally sized to the quantity of sales at each city listed in the PivotTable.
25. Save the workbook, and then close it.

APPENDIX A

Working with Text Functions and Creating Custom Formats

Cleaning Data in a Spreadsheet

OBJECTIVES

- Open a workbook in Compatibility Mode
- Use the LEN function
- Use the LEFT function
- Apply the Paste Values command
- Use the PROPER function
- Use the CONCATENATE function
- Apply the Text to Columns command
- Use the UPPER function
- Use the SUBSTITUTE function
- Apply a special format to phone numbers
- Create custom formats for numbers and dates
- Use the Compatibility Checker

Case | Sharp Blades Hockey Club

The town of Drumright, Oklahoma, started the Sharp Blades Hockey Club in 2010. The adult division of the club has members from the towns in the area, and the average age of the members is 42. They have elected officers for president, secretary, and treasurer. James Perez has been elected secretary, and part of his job is to keep the records for the club. The officers of the club would like to know more about the players and the prospects for the growth of the club.

The club has a spreadsheet containing data about the current players, but the data was compiled by volunteers and is not organized for any kind of analysis. Before James begins his analysis, he needs to "clean" the data, and he has asked for your help.

STARTING DATA FILES

ExcelA

- Tutorial — Hockey.xls
- Review — Early.xlxs
- Case1 — Golf.xlxs
- Case2 — Lawn.xlxs

Microsoft product screenshots used with permission from Microsoft Corporation.

Opening and Saving Workbooks Created in Earlier Versions of Excel

When you open a workbook that was created in Excel 2003 or earlier, it opens in Compatibility Mode. **Compatibility Mode** keeps the workbook in the older file format with the .xls file extension, making the workbook accessible for users who do not have the current version of Excel installed. The words "[Compatibility Mode]" appear in the title bar, indicating the file is not in the latest Excel format. You can work in Compatibility Mode. However, to have access to all the latest features and tools in Excel 2013, you must convert the workbook to the current file format, which has the .xlsx file extension. This is the file format you have used to save workbooks in the tutorials.

The workbook James received from the previous secretary was created in Excel 2003. James wants you to convert the workbook to the current format.

To save the workbook in the current Excel file format:

1. Open the **Hockey** workbook located in the ExcelA ▶ Tutorial folder included with your Data Files. The workbook opens in Compatibility Mode because the workbook was created in an earlier version of Excel. See Figure A-1.

Figure A-1 Workbook in Compatibility Mode

2. On the ribbon, click the **FILE** tab to open Backstage view, and then click the **Save As** command in the navigation bar.

3. Click the **Browse** button to open the Save As dialog box.

4. In the File name box, type **Sharp Blades**. The Save as type box shows that the current file format is Excel 97-2003 Workbook, which is the earlier file format. You'll change this to the latest file format.

5. Click the **Save as type** button, and then click **Excel Workbook**. This is the file format for Excel 2007, 2010, and 2013.

6. Click the **Save** button. The workbook is saved with the new name and file type.

As you can see from the title bar, the workbook remains in Compatibility Mode. You can continue to work in Compatibility Mode, or you can close the workbook and then reopen it in the new file format. You will open the workbook in the current file format.

Appendix A Working with Text Functions and Creating Custom Formats | Excel   EX A3

To open the Sharp Blades workbook in the current file format:

1. Close the Sharp Blades workbook.
2. Open the **Sharp Blades** workbook. The text "[Compatibility Mode]" no longer appears in the title bar, indicating that the workbook is in the current version file format of Excel.
3. In the Documentation worksheet, enter your name and the date.

The Players worksheet contains data about the club members. Before working with this data, James wants you to convert it to an Excel table.

To create an Excel table from the list of player information:

1. Go to the **Players** worksheet.
2. On the ribbon, click the **INSERT** tab.
3. In the Tables group, click the **Table** button. The Create Table dialog box opens with the range $A$1:$G$45 selected, and the My table has headers box is checked.
4. Click the **OK** button to create the Excel table. Note that filter arrows appear in the column heading cells.
5. On the TABLE TOOLS DESIGN tab, in the Properties group, enter **Player** in the Table Name box to rename the table.
6. On the ribbon, click the **DATA** tab.
7. Select any cell in the Excel table.

Using Text Functions

If you receive a workbook from a coworker or obtain data from other software packages, you often have to edit (sometimes referred to as *clean* or *scrub*) and manipulate the data before it is ready to use. To help users edit and correct the text values in their workbooks, Excel provides Text functions. Text, also referred to as a *text string* or *string*, contains one or more characters and can include spaces, symbols, and numbers as well as uppercase and lowercase letters. You can use Text functions to return the number of characters in a string, remove extra spaces, and change the case of text strings. Figure A-2 reviews some of the common Text functions available in Excel.

Figure A-2: Text functions

Function	Syntax	Description	Example
LEFT	=LEFT(*text, nbr chars*)	Returns a specified number of characters at the left of the string	=LEFT("Michael",3) returns Mic
RIGHT	=RIGHT(*text, nbr chars*)	Returns a specified number of characters at the right of the string	=RIGHT("Michael",3) returns ael
MID	=MID(*text, start nbr, nbr chars*)	Returns a specified number of characters from a string, starting at a position you specify	=MID("Net Income",5,3) returns Inc
UPPER	=UPPER(*text*)	Converts all lowercase characters in a string to uppercase	=UPPER("kim") returns KIM
LOWER	=LOWER(*text*)	Converts all uppercase characters in a string to lowercase	=LOWER("KIM") returns kim
PROPER	=PROPER(*text*)	Capitalizes the first letter of each word in a string	=PROPER("JASON BAKER") returns Jason Baker
LEN	=LEN(*text*)	Returns the number of characters in a string	=LEN("Judith Tinker") returns 13
SEARCH	=SEARCH(*find_text, within_text, start_nbr*)	Returns the number of the character at which the find_text is first found reading from left to right	=SEARCH("Main","1234 Main St.",1) returns 6
TEXT	=TEXT(*value, format_text_code*)	Formats numbers within text using a specific number format	=TEXT(SUM(D5:D75), "$#,0.00") returns $1,052.00
TRIM	=TRIM(*text*)	Removes all spaces from a string except for single spaces between words	=TRIM(" Mariah Ells") returns Mariah Ells

© 2014 Cengage Learning

Using the LEN and LEFT Functions

The Zip column in the Players worksheet includes zip codes in both five-digit and 10-digit formats. James wants only the five-digit component of the zip code. You can use the LEN and LEFT functions nested in an IF function to convert all of the zip codes to the shorter form. The IF function uses the LEN function to test whether the zip code has 10 digits. If true (the zip code is 10 digits), the LEFT function displays the first five digits in the cell. If false (the code is not 10 digits), all the digits in the cell are displayed.

The **LEN function** returns the number of characters (length) of the specified string. Cell C6 stores the text "Cushing, ok" so the formula =LEN(C6) returns 11, which is the number of characters, including spaces, in "Cushing, ok." You will use the LEN function to determine how many characters are in each cell of the Zip column.

The **LEFT function** returns a specified number of characters from the beginning of the string. To extract the five-digit zip code from the zip code 74079-1236 stored in cell D3, you use the formula =LEFT(D3,5) to return 74079.

The following formula shows the LEN and LEFT functions nested in an IF function to display a five-digit zip code—=IF(LEN([Zip])=10,LEFT([Zip],5),[Zip]).

Before you enter the IF function to extract the five-digit zip code, you need to prepare the worksheet. First, you need to insert a new column to the left of the Phone # column. Then, you will copy the zip code data into the new column, pasting the data as values so you can use the data in a formula. The results of the formula will appear in the new column as well.

Appendix A Working with Text Functions and Creating Custom Formats | Excel EX A5

To extract the five-digit zip code from the Zip column:

1. Select cell **E2**. You'll insert the table column to the left of this column.

2. On the ribbon, click the **HOME** tab.

3. In the Cells group, click the **Insert button arrow**, and then click **Insert Table Columns to the Left**. A new column named Column1 is inserted with the Text number format, which is the same format as the Zip column (column D). The columns in the worksheet automatically adjust as you add new columns. For example, the phone number in cell F2 changed to 9.186E+09. You will adjust column widths later, so you don't need to be concerned about these automatic adjustments.

4. Select the range **E2:E45**. Because the range is formatted as Text, you cannot enter a formula in a cell. You need to change the formatting of the selected range.

5. On the HOME tab, in the Number group, click the **Dialog Box Launcher**. The Format Cells dialog box opens with the Number tab displayed.

6. In the Category box, click **General**, then click the **OK** button. Now, you can enter the formula in cell E2.

7. Select cell **E2**, and then click the **Insert Function** button f_x next to the formula bar. The Insert Function dialog box opens.

8. Click **Logical** in the Or select a category list, click **IF** in the Select a function box, and then click the **OK** button. The Function Arguments dialog box opens.

9. In the Logical_test box, type **LEN([Zip])=10**. The logical test tests whether the number of characters in the current cell of the Zip column equals 10.

10. In the Value_if_true box, type **LEFT([Zip],5)**. This argument specifies that if the condition is true, the first five characters from the cell are displayed.

11. In the Value_if_false box, type **[Zip]**. This argument specifies that if the condition is false, all the characters from the cell are displayed. See Figure A-3.

Figure A-3	IF function with LEN and LEFT functions

Function Arguments

IF
Logical_test   LEN([Zip])=10   = {FALSE;FALSE;FALSE;TRUE;FALSE;FALSE
Value_if_true   LEFT([Zip],5)   = {"74079";"74079";"74030";"74010";"74...
Value_if_false   [Zip]   = {74079;"74079";74030;"74010-0999";...

= {74079;"74079";74030;"74010";74079...
Checks whether a condition is met, and returns one value if TRUE, and another value if FALSE.

Value_if_false is the value that is returned if Logical_test is FALSE. If omitted, FALSE is returned.

Formula result = 74079

Help on this function   OK   Cancel

12. Click the **OK** button. The formula =IF(LEN([Zip])=10,LEFT([Zip],5),[Zip]) appears in the formula bar, and the value 74079 appears in cell E2 because the condition is false. The results are automatically copied to all rows in column E of the table. Each cell in column E displays the five-digit zip code. See Figure A-4.

Figure A-4   Table column with five-digit zip codes

formula to display five-digit zip codes: `=IF(LEN([Zip])=10,LEFT([Zip],5),[Zip])`

five- and 10-digit zip codes (column D) / *five-digit zip codes appear in the new column* (column E)

	A	B	C	D	E	F	G
1	Last Name	First Name	City State	Zip	Column1	Phone #	Joined
2	WHITNEY	Natalie	Stroud, ok	74079	74079	9.186E+09	1/5/2010
3	SWIFT	Stephen	Stroud, ok	74079	74079	9.188E+09	1/8/2010
4	ROSE	Nancy	Drumright, ok	74030	74030		
5	PROVOST	Robert	Bristow, ok	74010-0999	74010		
6	TEMKIN	William	Cushing, ok	74079	74079		
7	PISANI	Yong	Drumright, ok	74030	74030		
8	UHLIG	Roxana	Cushing, ok	74023	74023	9.186E+09	3/8/2010
9	ROBERTSON	Jayne	Drumright, ok	74030-4444	74030	9.184E+09	3/11/2010
10	JENISON	Jeffrey	Bristow, ok	74010	74010	9.182E+09	3/19/2010

▶ **13.** If necessary, left-align the data in the new zip column.

Using the Paste Values Command

You now have two columns with zip codes (columns D and E). You need to keep only the column that displays the five-digit zip code. However, the data in column E is dependent on column D. If you delete column D, column E will display the #REF! error value. Therefore, before you delete column D, you need to convert the data in column E, which is based on a formula, to values. The easiest way to do that is to copy and paste the formula results, but not the actual formula, in the same column using the Paste Values command. Then, you can delete column D.

To convert the five-digit zip code formula results to values:

▶ **1.** Select the range **E2:E45**, which contains the formula results you want to convert to values.

▶ **2.** On the HOME tab, in the Clipboard group, click the **Copy** button, and then select cell **E2**.

▶ **3.** In the Clipboard group, click the **Paste button arrow**, and then click the **Values** button. The values are pasted over the original formulas, replacing them.

▶ **4.** Select the range **E2:E45**. You need to format these values as text, in case any zip codes start with zeros.

▶ **5.** In the Number group, click the **Number Format box arrow**, and then click **Text**.

▶ **6.** Select column **D**, right-click the selected column, and then click **Delete** on the shortcut menu. The column is removed.

7. In cell **D1**, enter **Zip**. Column D, which stores the five-digit zip code values, now has a descriptive column header.

8. Autofit the Zip column to fit the five-digit zip codes.

Using the PROPER Function and the CONCATENATE Function

The **PROPER function** converts the first letter of each word to uppercase, capitalizes any letter that does not follow another letter, and changes all other letters to lowercase. The formula =PROPER("WHITNEY") changes the word "WHITNEY" to "Whitney." You will first use the PROPER function to convert the last name so that the first letter is capitalized.

The **CONCATENATE function** joins, or concatenates, two or more text values. The syntax of the CONCATENATE function is

=CONCATENATE(*text1*,*text2*,...)

where *text1*, *text2*, etc., are constants or cells storing text or numbers. The CONCATENATE function joins these values to produce a single string. For example, if the last name "WHITNEY" is in cell A2 and the first name "Natalie" is in cell B2, you can use the formula =CONCATENATE(A2,B2) to join the contents of the two cells (last name and first name) to display the full name in cell C2. However, this formula returns "WHITNEYNatalie" in cell C2. To include a comma and a space between the two names, you must change the formula to =CONCATENATE(PROPER(A2),", ",B2), which uses a function, two values, and a string constant (a comma and a space enclosed in quotation marks) to display "Whitney, Natalie" in the cell.

James wants to combine the Last Name and First Name columns into one column and use standard capitalization for the names. You will use a formula that includes the PROPER function and the CONCATENATION function to do this.

To combine the names in one column with standard capitalization:

1. Select cell **C2**, and then insert a table column to the left. A new column named Column1 is inserted to the left of the City State column.

2. In cell **C2**, type **=CONCATENATE(PROPER([Last Name]),", ",[First Name])** and then press the **Enter** key. The formula is entered for every record in column C, and displays the player's last name and first name with standard capitalization separated by a comma.

3. AutoFit column C to accommodate the longest entry. Each cell in column C displays the player's name in the form *Last name, First name* with the first letter of each name capitalized. Notice that the Joined column is no longer wide enough to display some of the entries; you will resize the column later. See Figure A-5.

Figure A-5 — Player's name displayed in one column

CONCATENATE function joins two or more text values

PROPER function converts the first letter of each word to uppercase

full names listed Last name, First name in one column

Now that the players' name data is stored in column C, you no longer need the data in column A (Last Name) and column B (First Name). Because the results in column C are based on a formula, you need to convert the formula in column C to values before you delete the other columns.

To paste the formula results as values and delete the original data:

1. Select the range **C2:C45**, and then copy the range to the Clipboard.
2. Select cell **C2**, and then paste the values from the Clipboard to column C.
3. Press the **Esc** key, and then AutoFit column C so you can see the players' full names.
4. In cell **C1**, enter **Player** as the column header.
5. Delete columns **A** and **B**. The Player column remains in the Excel table.

Applying the Text to Columns Command

When multiple pieces of data are stored in one cell, you can separate each piece of data into a different column by using the Text to Columns command. This command starts the Convert Text to Column Wizard. You specify how to split the data based on how the data is stored. You can select what **delimits**, or separates, the data, such as a tab, a semicolon, a comma, or a space. For fixed-width data, you specify break locations. For example, you might need to specify a break location in a string where the first character identifies the warehouse location, characters 2 through 4 identify the aisle, and characters 5 through 8 identify the actual location on the shelf. Each entry in a fixed-width field is the same length no matter how many characters are entered in the field.

The Players worksheet has the city and state separated by a comma delimiter. James wants you to split the city and state data into different columns.

Appendix A Working with Text Functions and Creating Custom Formats | Excel   EX A9

To split the city and state data into separate columns:

1. Select cell **C2**, and then insert a table column to the left. A new column named Column1 is inserted to the left of the Zip column.
2. Select the range **B2:B45**. These cells contain the values you want to split.
3. On the ribbon, click the **DATA** tab.
4. In the Data Tools group, click the **Text to Columns** button. The Convert Text to Columns Wizard - Step 1 of 3 dialog box opens. You select how the data is organized in this step—delimited or a fixed width.
5. In the Original data type area, verify that the **Delimited** option button is selected, and then click the **Next** button. The Convert Text to Columns Wizard - Step 2 of 3 dialog box opens. You select the delimiter character in this step. The data in the City State column is separated by a comma.
6. Click any check box with a checkmark in the Delimiters section to remove the checkmark, and then click the **Comma** check box to insert a checkmark. The Data preview box shows the City and State data in separate columns. See Figure A-6.

Figure A-6   **Convert Text to Columns Wizard - Step 2 of 3 dialog box**

7. Click the **Next** button. The Convert Text to Columns Wizard - Step 3 of 3 dialog box opens so you can set the data format for each column. The Data preview box shows that each column is set to the General number format, which is what you want.
8. Click the **Finish** button. Cities remain in column B; states move to column C.
9. In cell **B1**, enter **City** and then in cell **C1**, enter **State**.
10. AutoFit the widths of columns B and C. See Figure A-7.

Figure A-7   **City and State displayed in separate columns**

state data moved to column C

city data remains in column B

Text to Columns button

Using the UPPER Function to Convert Case

The **UPPER function** converts all letters of each word in a text string to uppercase. For example, the formula =UPPER("ri") returns RI. James wants you to change state abbreviations in column D from lowercase to uppercase. You'll use the UPPER function to do this.

To use the UPPER function to capitalize the state abbreviations:

1. Select cell **D2**, and then insert a table column to the left. A new column named Column1 is inserted to the left of the Zip column.

2. In cell **D2**, type **=U** and then double-click the **UPPER** function in the list. The beginning of the formula =UPPER(is in the cell and the formula bar.

3. Type **[** to begin the column specifier, double-click **State** in the list of column qualifiers, type **]** to end the column specifier, and then type **)**. The formula =UPPER([State]) appears in the formula bar.

4. Press the **Enter** key. The state abbreviation appears in all uppercase letters in column E. See Figure A-8.

Figure A-8 UPPER function converted state abbreviations to uppercase

UPPER function formula converts cell contents to uppercase → formula bar shows `=UPPER([State])`

state abbreviations are capitalized → column D values

	A	B	C	D	E	F	G	H
1	Player	City	State	Column1	Zip	Phone #	Joined	Equip F
2	Whitney, Natalie	Stroud	ok	OK	74079	9.2E+09	1/5/2010	550
3	Swift, Stephen	Stroud	ok	OK	74079	9.2E+09	1/8/2010	330
4	Rose, Nancy	Drumright	ok	OK	74030	9.2E+09	#######	529
5	Provost, Robert	Bristow	ok	OK	74010	02675615	#######	430
6	Temkin, William	Cushing	ok	OK	74079	9.2E+09	#######	511
7	Pisani, Yong	Drumright	ok	OK	74030	9.2E+09	#######	391
8	Uhlig, Roxana	Cushing	ok	OK	74023	9.2E+09	3/8/2010	342
9	Robertson, Jayne	Drumright	ok	OK	74030	9.2E+09	#######	323
10	Jenison, Jeffrey	Bristow	ok	OK	74010	9.2E+09	#######	535
11	Coulahan, Linda	Drumright	ok	OK	74030	4.1E+09	#######	348
12	Dimond, Pamela	Bristow	ok	OK	74010	9.2E+09	#######	298
13	Forrester, Dolores	Drumright	ok	OK	74030	4.1E+09	#######	260
14	Gordon, Jon	Cushing	ok	OK	74023	5.8E+09	#######	256

You want to keep only the data in column D. Because the results of column D are based on a formula, you again will convert the formula in column D to values before you delete column C.

To paste the state abbreviations as values:

1. Select the range **D2:D45**, and then copy the range to the Clipboard.
2. Select cell **D2**, and then paste the values from the Clipboard. Verify that the formula bar displays a value and not a formula.
3. Press the **Esc** key.
4. Delete column **C**.
5. In cell **C1**, enter **State**. The column is renamed with a more descriptive header.

Using the SUBSTITUTE Function

The **SUBSTITUTE function** replaces existing text with new text. The SUBSTITUTE function has the syntax

    SUBSTITUTE(text,old_text,new_text,instance_num)

where *text* is a string constant or reference to a cell containing text you want to replace, *old_text* is the existing text you want to replace, *new_text* is the text you want to replace *old_text* with, and *instance_num* specifies which occurrence of *old_text* you want to replace. If you omit *instance_num*, every instance of *old_text* is replaced. The formula

    =SUBSTITUTE("164-45-890","-","")

returns 16445890.

The entries for the phone numbers in column E are inconsistent. Sometimes they are an eight-digit value, and other times they are preceded with 1- (which James wants you to remove from the Phone # column). You'll enter a formula with the SUBSTITUTE function to remove the preceding 1- from this data.

Excel | Appendix A Working with Text Functions and Creating Custom Formats

To remove the preceding 1- from the phone number data and paste the values:

1. Select cell **F2**, and then insert a table column to the left. A new column named Column1 is inserted to the left of the Joined column.
2. AutoFit column E (Phone # column) so you can see that some phone numbers are preceded by 1-.
3. Click the **Insert Function** button f_x next to the formula bar. The Insert Function dialog box opens.
4. Click the **Or select a category** arrow, click **Text** to display the Text functions, and then scroll down to and double-click **SUBSTITUTE** in the Select a function box. The Function Arguments dialog box opens.
5. In the Text box, type **E2**. The text in cell E2 is displayed.
6. In the Old_text box, type **"1-"**. The text you want to remove is enclosed in quotation marks.
7. In the New_text box, type **""**. You want to replace the old text with nothing. You do not need to enter anything in the Instance_num box because you want to replace every instance of 1-.
8. Click the **OK** button. All of the phone numbers are changed to 10-digit numbers, and wherever necessary, the preceding 1- is replaced with an empty string (a blank, or nothing).
9. AutoFit column F, and then select cell **F2**. See Figure A-9.

Figure A-9 SUBSTITUTE function removed 1- from the phone numbers

SUBSTITUTE function replaces 1- with an empty string, converting the phone number to 10 digits

some phone numbers have a preceding 1-

10. Select the range **F2:F45**, and then copy this range to the Clipboard.
11. Select cell **F2**, paste the values from the Clipboard, and then press the **Esc** key.
12. Delete column **E**.
13. In cell **E1**, enter **Phone #** to identify the data in the column.
14. AutoFit the columns as needed to display their entire contents.

Using Special Formats

Four commonly used formats, referred to as special formats, are available—two zip code formats (five-digit and 10-digit), a phone number format (with the area code in parentheses and a hyphen between the prefix and the last four digits), and a Social Security number format (a nine-digit number with hyphens after the third and fifth digits). Using these special formats allows you to type a number without punctuation, yet still display that number in its common format.

James wants you to display the phone number using the common format of area code in parentheses and a hyphen between the prefix and the last four digits.

To format the phone numbers with the Phone Number format:

1. Select the range **E2:E45**. Notice the green triangle in the upper-left corner for the cells in this range.

2. Point to any triangle to display the Error Alert button, click the **Error Alert button arrow**, and then click **Convert to Number** in the list of options.

3. With the range E2:E45 still selected, on the HOME tab, in the Number group, click the **Dialog Box Launcher**. The Format Cells dialog box opens with the Number tab active.

4. In the Category box, click **Special**. Four special formats appear in the Type list—Zip Code, Zip Code + 4, Phone Number, and Social Security Number.

5. In the Type box, click **Phone Number**. See Figure A-10.

Figure A-10   Special category on the Number tab

6. Click the **OK** button. The phone numbers are formatted in a standard telephone format.

Creating Custom Formats

> **TIP**
> Any custom format you create is stored only in the workbook in which it was created. To use it in another workbook, you must reenter it.

Excel supplies a generous collection of formats and styles to improve the appearance and readability of worksheets. However, sometimes you will need a format and style to accommodate a specific requirement. In these cases, you can create your own formats, called **custom formats**. Custom formats use **format codes**, a series of symbols, to describe exactly how Excel should display a number, date, time, or text string. You can use format codes to display text strings and spaces, and determine how many decimal places to display in a cell.

Creating a Custom Number Format

Each number is composed of digits. In displaying these digits, Excel makes special note of **insignificant zeros**, which are zeros whose omission from the number does not change the number's value. For example, the number 0.1 is displayed in the General number format, but changes to 0.10 when the cell is formatted as a number. To format a value, Excel uses the **placeholders** shown in Figure A-11 to represent individual digits.

Figure A-11 — Description of digit placeholders

Placeholder	Description
#	Displays only significant digits; insignificant zeros are omitted
0 (zero)	Displays significant digits as well as insignificant zeros
?	Replaces insignificant zeros with spaces on either side of the decimal point so that decimal points align when formatted with a fixed-width font, such as Courier

© 2014 Cengage Learning

A custom format can use combinations of these placeholders. For example, the custom format #.00 displays the value 8.9 as 8.90. If a value has more digits than placeholders in the custom format, Excel rounds the value to match the number of placeholders. Thus, the value 8.938 formatted with the custom format #.## is displayed as 8.94. Figure A-12 shows how the same series of numbers appears with different custom number formats.

Figure A-12 — Examples of digit placeholders

Cell Value	#.##	0	?.??	#.#0
0.57	0.57	0.57	0.57	0.57
123.4	123.4	123.4	123.4	123.4
3.45	3.45	3.45	3.45	3.45

(Custom Formats)

© 2014 Cengage Learning

Number formats also include the decimal point separator (.), the thousands separator (,), and the fraction separator (/). You can use the thousands separator to separate a number in groups of 1,000 or to scale a number by a multiple of 1,000.

The fraction separator displays decimal values as fractions. The general syntax is *placeholder/placeholder*, where *placeholder* is one or more of the custom format placeholders. Excel displays the fraction that best approximates the decimal value. You can also specify the denominator for the fraction to convert the decimals to halves, quarters, and so forth. Figure A-13 provides examples of the thousands and fraction separators.

Appendix A Working with Text Functions and Creating Custom Formats | Excel EX A15

Figure A-13 Examples of thousands and fraction separators

Value	Custom Format	Appearance
12000	#,###	12,000
12000	#,	12
12200000	0.0,,	12.2
5.4	# #/#	5 2/5

© 2014 Cengage Learning

You can combine all of the numeric format codes in a single custom format. If you don't specify a numeric code for data values, Excel uses the General format code, which hides all insignificant zeros.

James wants equipment rentals displayed as a number with two decimal positions followed by the letter "p" to indicate paid. You'll create a custom format for the equipment rental.

To create a custom format for the equipment rentals:

1. Select the range **G2:G45**.
2. On the HOME tab, in the Number group, click the **Dialog Box Launcher**. The Format Cells dialog box opens with the Number tab displayed.
3. In the Category box, click **Custom**. You will enter a custom format to display the numbers to the nearest thousand.
4. In the Type box, double-click **General** to select it, and then type **.00?p?** as the custom format code. See Figure A-14.

Figure A-14 Custom category on the Number tab

Trouble? If you return to the worksheet, you double-clicked General in the list of custom formats. Repeat Step 4, making sure you double-click General in the Type box.

> 5. Click the **OK** button. The equipment rentals are displayed as a number with two decimal positions followed by the letter "p" to indicate paid. Because you used the custom format, this text is treated as a number even though it has a letter character (the character is ignored).

Creating a Custom Date Format

When you have dates, times, or both in a workbook, you can use a predefined date and time format to display this information in a readable format. Although the predefined time and date formats are usually fine, you can also create your own custom date formats. Figure A-15 describes the format codes used for dates and times.

Figure A-15 Date and Time format codes

Code	Displays
m	Months as 1 through 12
mm	Months as 01 through 12
mmm	Months as Jan through Dec
mmmm	Months as January through December
d	Days as 1 through 31
dd	Days as 01 through 31
ddd	Days as Sun through Sat
dddd	Days as Sunday through Saturday
yy	Years as 00 through 99
yyyy	Years as 1900 through 9999
h	Hours as 1 through 24
mm	Minutes as 01 through 60 (when immediately following h, mm signifies minutes; otherwise, months)
ss	Seconds as 01 through 60

© 2014 Cengage Learning

James wants the date values in the Joined column to show the name of the month followed by the year (for example, 7/22/2016 should be displayed as July 2016). You need to apply the custom format code *mmmm yyyy* to do this.

To apply a custom date format to the Joined dates:

> 1. Select the range **F2:F45**.
> 2. On the HOME tab, in the Number group, click the **Dialog Box Launcher**. The Format Cells dialog box opens with the Number tab active.
> 3. In the Category box, click **Custom**.
> 4. In the Type box, select the current format, and then type **mmmm yyyy**. The Sample box shows an example of the custom format you entered.
> 5. Click the **OK** button, and then click cell **A1** to deselect the range. See Figure A-16.

Appendix A Working with Text Functions and Creating Custom Formats | Excel   EX A17

Figure A-16   **Final formatted workbook**

	A	B	C	D	E	F	G
1	Player	City	State	Zip	Phone #	Joined	Equip R
2	Whitney, Natalie	Stroud	OK	74079	(918) 580-9520	January 2010	550.00 p
3	Swift, Stephen	Stroud	OK	74079	(918) 783-8810	January 2010	330.00 p
4	Rose, Nancy	Drumright	OK	74030	(918) 486-3933	January 2010	529.00 p
5	Provost, Robert	Bristow	OK	74010	(580) 267-5615	January 2010	430.00 p
6	Temkin, William	Cushing	OK	74079	(918) 732-3349	February 2010	511.00 p
7	Pisani, Yong	Drumright	OK	74030	(918) 364-6833	February 2010	391.00 p
8	Uhlig, Roxana	Cushing	OK	74023	(918) 580-9520	March 2010	342.00 p
9	Robertson, Jayne	Drumright	OK	74030	(918) 364-6832	March 2010	323.00 p
10	Jenison, Jeffrey	Bristow	OK	74010	(918) 183-5703	March 2010	535.00 p
11	Coulahan, Linda	Drumright	OK	74030	(405) 483-4659	April 2010	348.00 p

dates with custom formats

▶ **6.** Save the workbook.

Using the Compatibility Checker

When you save an Excel 2007, 2010, or 2013 workbook in an earlier format, the **Compatibility Checker** alerts you to any features that are not supported by earlier versions of Excel. You can click the Cancel button and redo the worksheet using a different approach, or you can click the Continue button to save the workbook in the earlier format. If you save the workbook in an earlier format, unsupported features will be lost.

You'll save a copy of the workbook in the Excel 2003 format.

To convert the workbook to the Excel 2003 file format:

▶ **1.** On the ribbon, click the **FILE** tab to open Backstage view, and then click **Save As** in the navigation bar. The Save As screen appears.

▶ **2.** Click the **Browse** button to open the Save As dialog box, navigate to the location specified by your instructor, and then change the filename to **Sharp Blades 2003**.

▶ **3.** Click the **Save as type** button, and then click **Excel 97-2003 Workbook**. This is the earlier Excel file format you want to use.

▶ **4.** Click the **Save** button. The Compatibility Checker dialog box opens, alerting you to features not supported by earlier versions of Excel. See Figure A-17.

Figure A-17   **Compatibility Checker with error message**

Excel tables are not supported in Excel 97-2003

number of times this problem occurs in the workbook

5. Read the message, and then click the **Continue** button. The workbook is saved in the earlier file format with the .xls file extension. Close the workbook.

The workbook data is clean and the workbook is formatted as James requested. He'll be able to analyze this data for the club.

Appendix A Working with Text Functions and Creating Custom Formats | Excel   EX A19

PRACTICE

Review Assignments

Data File needed for the Review Assignments: Early.xlsx

The Sharp Blades Hockey Club also has a youth division for players from 6 to 18 years of age. James has a second workbook to store the information that has been collected for these players. James asks you to clean and format the data. Complete the following:

1. Open the **Early** workbook located in the ExcelA ▶ Review folder included with your Data Files, and then save the workbook in Excel Workbook format as **Sharp Youth** in the location specified by your instructor.
2. In the Documentation worksheet, enter your name and the date.
3. In the Youth Players worksheet, create an Excel table for the data in the range A1:F40. Name the table **Youth**. (*Hint*: Remember to remove the filter arrows.)
4. Insert a blank column to the left of column B to store the first name, and leave the last name in column A.
5. Use the Text to Columns command to split the Player column into two columns named **Last Name** and **First Name**.
6. In cell H1, enter **Status** as the column header. In cell H2, use the IF and LEFT functions to display the word **Discard** if the address begins with PO; otherwise, leave the cell blank.
7. In cell I1, enter **Addr** as the column header. In cell I2, enter a formula to trim the extra spaces from the address.
8. In cell J1, enter **Twn** as the column header. In cell J2, enter a formula to convert the data in the Town column to proper case.
9. In cell K1, enter **St** as the column header. In column K, enter a formula to convert the data in the State column to uppercase.
10. In cell L1, enter **Town State** as the column header. In column L, combine the town and state data from columns J and K into one column using the format *town, state*.
11. Format the data in the Phone column (column F) with the Phone Number format.
12. Save the workbook, and then close it.

APPLY

Case Problem 1

Data File needed for this Case Problem: Golf.xlsx

Early Bird Golf Group   Camilla Cortez, organizer of the Early Bird Golf Group, has begun compiling a list of the group's members. She has asked you to clean and format the data in the worksheet before she continues working on the project. Complete the following:

1. Open the **Golf** workbook located in the ExcelA ▶ Case1 folder and save the workbook in the Excel Workbook format as **Early Bird** in the location specified by your instructor.
2. In the Documentation worksheet, enter your name and the date.
3. In the Members worksheet, create an Excel table for the data. Name the table **Golf**.
4. Apply the Phone Number format to the data in the Telephone column.
5. Split the data in the Name column into two columns. Store the first names in column B and the last names in column C. Change the column headers to **First Name** and **Last Name**, respectively.
6. In the Member Since column, apply a custom format that displays only the year.
7. Split the City, State Zip column into three columns named **City**, **State**, and **Zip**, respectively. (*Hint*: Repeat the split twice. The second split is a fixed width.)
8. The locker numbers were entered from an old system. The only characters that are important are the three numbers after the letter. Use the MID function in column I (name it **L Number**) to separate those numbers.

9. The last number in the locker number is the actual row that the locker is in. Use the RIGHT function in column J (name it **L Row**) to separate that value.
10. Save the workbook, and then close it.

Case Problem 2

APPLY

Data File needed for this Case Problem: Lawn.xlsx

Dianna's Lawncare   Every two weeks, Dianna Turley collects payroll information for the employees who work for her at her lawncare business. The worksheet with the information is sent to a payroll service that generates the paychecks. Dianna has started to collect the information, but she needs you to clean up the data before it is sent. Complete the following:

1. Open the **Lawn** workbook located in the ExcelA ▶ Case2 folder included with your Data Files, and then save the workbook in the Excel Workbook format as **Lawncare** in the location specified by your instructor.
2. In the Documentation worksheet, enter your name and the date.
3. In the Employee Hours worksheet, create an Excel table named **Hours** with a blue table style.
4. Split the data in the Name column into two columns. Store the first name data in column A and the last name data in column B. Change the column headers to **First Name** and **Last Name**, respectively.
5. Split the data in the City, State Zip column into three columns. Store the city data in column D, the state data in column E, and the zip codes in column F. (*Hint*: Repeat the split twice.) Change the column headers to **City**, **State**, and **Zip**, respectively.
6. Use functions as needed to change the data in the City and State columns to use standard capitalization. (*Hint*: Remember to copy the data as values and remove any unnecessary columns.)
7. Apply the Social Security Number format to the data in the SS Number column.
8. Use a function to change the data in the Type of Work column so that it is all lowercase. (*Hint*: Remember to copy the data as values and remove any unnecessary columns.)
9. Apply a custom format to the data in the Hourly Rate column that shows two decimal places.
10. Apply a custom format to the data in the Overtime Hours column so that full hours display only significant digits and partial hours display two digits whether significant or insignificant. (*Hint*: Refer to Figure A-11 to see a description of the digit placeholders used in custom formats for values.)
11. Save the workbook, and then close it.

APPENDIX B

OBJECTIVES

- Use advanced filters
- Create a criteria range
- Use Database functions
- Summarize data using the COUNTIFS, SUMIFS, and AVERAGEIFS functions

Advanced Filters, Database Functions, and Summary IFS Functions

Filtering and Summarizing Database Information

Case | *E-Quip Tools*

E-Quip Tools, a tool supplier in Bethel, Alaska, has been tracking the computer equipment at its main location on Tundra Way and its secondary location at Chief Eddie Hoffman Highway. Recognizing the need to keep current with ever-changing technology, Patricia Koon, the IT manager for both locations, has developed a replacement plan for the company's technology equipment. She has established the following criteria to plan the technology-related equipment replacement:

- Equipment with no service agreement should be replaced at "end of life," which is today, 12/31/2016.
- Equipment under service agreement with a value less than $600 and with an "end-of-life" date one year after today's date (12/31/2017). This would allow enough time to acquire budget to replace the equipment before "end-of-life" is reached.

In addition to identifying equipment eligible for replacement, Patricia wants to know the average value of the company's inventory, and to review a summary of the equipment's lifetime as well as its total and average values. She asks you to use advanced filters to generate the list of equipment that is eligible for replacement, and then to use Database functions and other Excel functions to calculate the summary information.

STARTING DATA FILES

ExcelB →

Tutorial
Tools.xlsx

Review
Tools Review.xlsx

Case1
Donations.xlsx

Case2
House.xlsx

Microsoft product screenshots used with permission from Microsoft Corporation.

Using Advanced Filters

Advanced filtering displays a subset of the rows in an Excel table or a range of data that match the criteria you specify. With advanced filtering, you specify the filter criteria in a separate range. Advanced filtering enables you to perform Or conditions across multiple fields, such as the criteria Patricia wants you to use to find eligible equipment for replacement within E-Quip Tools. You can also use advanced filtering to create complex criteria using functions and formulas. For example, Patricia could use advanced filtering to find all equipment with no service agreement at the end of life.

Patricia created a workbook that contains an Excel table named Equipment to store the data for all of the equipment. For each piece of equipment, Patricia has listed the Date Acquired, Life (Years), and End of Life, which is calculated using the Date Acquired and Life data. You will open Patricia's workbook and filter the inventory data to identify equipment eligible for replacement.

To open and review Patricia's workbook:

1. Open the **Tools** workbook located in the ExcelB ▸ Tutorial folder included with your Data Files, and then save the workbook as **E-Quip** in the location specified by your instructor.
2. In the Documentation worksheet, enter your name and the date.
3. Go to the **Equipment Inventory** worksheet, and then review the Equipment table. See Figure B-1.

Figure B-1   Equipment table in the Equipment Inventory worksheet

	A	B	C	D	E	F	G	H	I
6	ID	Description	Date Acquired	Life	End of Life	Location	Status	Service	Value
7	1064	Tower	1/8/2014	5	1/7/2019	Tundra	R	Y	$ 350
8	1025	Server	5/24/2009	8	5/22/2017	Hoffman	A	Y	$12,000
9	1026	Keyboard	11/26/2014	2	11/25/2016	Hoffman	A	N	$ 60
10	1024	Tower	11/26/2014	5	11/25/2019	Tundra	A	Y	$ 475
11	1027	Tower	11/26/2014	5	11/25/2019	Tundra	A	Y	$ 475
12	1029	Keyboard	11/26/2014	2	11/25/2016	Hoffman	A	N	$ 60
13	1028	Tower	11/26/2014	5	11/25/2019	Tundra	A	Y	$ 475
14	1030	Tower	11/26/2014	5	11/25/2019	Hoffman	A	Y	$ 500
15	1032	Keyboard	8/28/2016	2	8/28/2018	Hoffman	R	N	$ 55
16	1033	Monitor	11/26/2014	5	11/25/2019	Hoffman	A	N	$ 150
17	1034	Monitor	11/26/2014	5	11/25/2019	Tundra	A	N	$ 120
18	1031	Tower	11/26/2014	5	11/25/2019	Hoffman	A	Y	$ 500
19	1036	Monitor	5/4/2016	5	5/3/2021	Tundra	R	N	$ 495
20	1042	Tower	11/26/2014	5	11/25/2019	Tundra	A	Y	$ 475
21	1038	Monitor	11/26/2016	5	11/25/2021	Hoffman	A	N	$ 150
22	1043	Tower	11/26/2014	5	11/25/2019	Hoffman	A	Y	$ 500
23	1040	Keyboard	11/26/2014	2	11/25/2016	Tundra	A	N	$ 90

Documentation | **Equipment Inventory** | Inventory Summary

READY

Appendix B Advanced Filters, Database Functions, and Summary IFS Functions | Excel   EX B3

Understanding the Criteria Range

The **criteria range** is an area in a worksheet, separate from a range of data or an Excel table, used to specify the criteria for the data to be displayed after the filter is applied to the range or Excel table. The criteria range consists of a header row that lists field names from the table's header row, and at least one row with the specific filtering criteria for each field. The criteria range specifies which records from the data range will be included in the filtered data.

Criteria placed on the same row are considered to be connected with the logical operator And. That means all criteria in the same row must be met before a record is included in the filtered data. Figure B-2 shows an And criteria range filter to retrieve all equipment not under service agreements at end of life on or before December 31, 2016.

Figure B-2 And filter specified in a criteria range

all criteria in a row must be met for a record to be retrieved (And condition)

	A	B	C	D	E	F	G	H
1	ID	Description	Date Acquired	Life	End of Life	Location	Status	Service
2					<=12/31/2016			N
3								
4								
5								
6	ID	Description	Date Acquired	Life	End of Life	Location	Status	Service
7	1064	Tower	1/8/2014	5	1/7			$
8	1025	Server	5/24/2009	8	5/22			$1
9	1026	Keyboard	11/26/2014	2	11/25			$
10	1024	Tower	11/26/2014	5	11/25			$
11	1027	Tower	11/26/2014	5	11/25/2019	Tundra	A	Y	$
12	1029	Keyboard	11/26/2014	2	11/25/2016	Hoffman	A	N	$
13	1028	Tower	11/26/2014	5	11/25/2019	Tundra	A	Y	$
14	1030	Tower	11/26/2014	5	11/25/2019	Hoffman	A	Y	$
15	1032	Keyboard	8/28/2016	2	8/28/2018	Hoffman	R	N	$
16	1033	Monitor	11/26/2014	5	11/25/2019	Hoffman	A	N	$
17	1034	Monitor	11/26/2014	5	11/25/2019	Tundra	A	N	$
18	1031	Tower	11/26/2014	5	11/25/2019	Hoffman	A	Y	$
19	1036	Monitor	5/4/2016	5	5/3/2021	Tundra	R	N	$
20	1042	Tower	11/26/2014	5	11/25/2019	Tundra	A	Y	$

retrieves all equipment not under service agreements and at end of life on December 31, 2016

Criteria placed on separate rows of the criteria range are treated as being connected by the logical operator Or. That means records that meet all the criteria on either row in the criteria range will be displayed. Figure B-3 shows an example of the Or filter to retrieve all equipment not under service agreements at end of life on December 31, 2016 or equipment in the Hoffman location.

Figure B-3 — Or filter specified in a criteria range

criteria for the Or condition are entered on different rows

retrieves all equipment not under service agreements and at end of life on December 31, 2016 or in the Hoffman location

To specify criteria between a range of values in the same field, you use the same field name repeated in separate cells within the same row to match a range of values (Between criteria). Figure B-4 shows a criteria range to retrieve all equipment at end of life between January 1, 2016 and December 31, 2016.

Appendix B Advanced Filters, Database Functions, and Summary IFS Functions | Excel   EX B5

Figure B-4 Between filter specified in a criteria range

	A	B	C	D	E	F	G	H
1	ID	Description	Date Acquired	Life	End of Life	End of Life	Status	Service
2					>=01/01/2016	<=12/31/2016		
3								
4								
5								
6	ID	Description	Date Acquired	Life	End of Life	Location	Status	Service
7	1064	Tower	1/8/2014	5			R	Y
8	1025	Server	5/24/2009	8	retrieves all equipment at end of life between January 1, 2016 and December 31, 2016		A	Y
9	1026	Keyboard	11/26/2014	2			A	N
10	1024	Tower	11/26/2014	5			A	Y
11	1027	Tower	11/26/2014	5	11/25/2019	Tundra	A	Y
12	1029	Keyboard	11/26/2014	2	11/25/2016	Hoffman	A	N
13	1028	Tower	11/26/2014	5	11/25/2019	Tundra	A	Y
14	1030	Tower	11/26/2014	5	11/25/2019	Hoffman	A	Y
15	1032	Keyboard	8/28/2016	2	8/28/2018	Hoffman	R	N
16	1033	Monitor	11/26/2014	5	11/25/2019	Hoffman	A	N
17	1034	Monitor	11/26/2014	5	11/25/2019	Tundra	A	N
18	1031	Tower	11/26/2014	5	11/25/2019	Hoffman	A	Y
19	1036	Monitor	5/4/2016	5	5/3/2021	Tundra	R	N
20	1042	Tower	11/26/2014	5	11/25/2019	Tundra	A	Y

Creating a Criteria Range

Typically, you place a criteria range above the data range to keep it separate from the data. If you place a criteria range next to the data range, the criteria might be hidden when the advanced filtering causes rows to be hidden. You can also place a criteria range in a separate worksheet, particularly if you need to use several criteria ranges in different cells to perform calculations based on various sets of filtered records.

You will place the criteria range in rows 1 through 4 of the Equipment Inventory worksheet to make it easier to locate. Because the field names in the criteria range must exactly match the field names in the Excel table or range except for capitalization, you should copy and paste the field names instead of retyping them. In row 2, you will enter an And criteria range with the criteria for equipment with no service agreement at end of life. In row 3, you will enter the criteria for equipment under service agreement with a value of less than $600 and an end of life one year before today's date.

To create the criteria range to find equipment with or without service agreements:

1. Point to the left side of cell **A6** until the pointer changes to ➡, and then click the mouse button. The column headers in row 6 are selected.

2. Copy the field names to the Clipboard.

3. Select cell **A1**, and then paste the field names. The field names for the criteria range appear in row 1.

4. Press the **Esc** key to remove the copied data from the Clipboard.

   Now, you will enter the first set of criteria.

5. In cell **E2**, enter **<=12/31/2016**. This condition retrieves all equipment with an end of life equivalent to today's date (12/31/2016).

6. In cell **H2**, enter **N**. This condition retrieves equipment with no service agreement.

   Next, you will enter the second set of criteria.

TIP
Text entered in the criteria range is not case sensitive.

7. In cell **E3**, enter **<=12/31/2017**. The condition retrieves all equipment with an end of life that is one year after today's date (12/31/2016).

8. In cell **H3**, enter **Y**. This condition retrieves all equipment with a service agreement.

9. In cell **I3**, enter **<600**. This condition retrieves all equipment with a value of less than $600. The criteria in row 3 retrieve equipment with a service agreement that has a value of less than $600 and is within a year of its end of life. See Figure B-5.

Figure B-5   Criteria range to filter records

all criteria in a row must be met for a record to be retrieved (And condition)

Now that the criteria range is established, you can use the Advanced Filter command to filter the Equipment table. You can filter the records in their current location by hiding rows that don't match your criteria, as you have done with the Filter command. Or, you can copy the records that match your criteria to another location in the worksheet. Patricia wants you to filter the records in their current location.

To filter the Equipment table in its current location:

▶ 1. Select any cell in the Equipment table to make the table active.

▶ 2. On the ribbon, click the **DATA** tab.

▶ 3. In the Sort & Filter group, click the **Advanced** button. The Advanced Filter dialog box opens.

▶ 4. Make sure the **Filter the list, in-place** option button is selected and the range **$A$6:$I$79** appears in the List range box. The range $A$6:$I$79 is the current location of the Equipment table, which is the table you want to filter.

▶ 5. Make sure the Criteria range box displays **$A$1:$I$3**. This range references the criteria range, which includes the field names.

▶ 6. Make sure the **Unique records only** option box is unchecked. Every record in the Equipment table is unique. You would check this option if the table contained duplicate records that you did not want to display. See Figure B-6.

Figure B-6 | Advanced Filter dialog box

▶ 7. Click the **OK** button, and then scroll through the worksheet. The list is filtered in its current location, and 15 equipment records (as shown in the status bar) match the criteria. See Figure B-7.

Figure B-7 Filtered equipment inventory data

	A	B	C	D	E	F	G	H	I
6	ID	Description	Date Acquired	Life	End of Life	Location	Status	Service	Value
9	1026	Keyboard	11/26/2014	2	11/25/2016	Hoffman	A	N	$ 60
12	1029	Keyboard	11/26/2014	2	11/25/2016	Hoffman	A	N	$ 60
23	1040	Keyboard	11/26/2014	2	11/25/2016	Tundra	A	N	$ 90
24	1041	Keyboard	11/26/2014	2	11/25/2016	Tundra	A	N	$ 90
34	1051	Keyboard	11/26/2014	2	11/25/2016	Hoffman	A	N	$ 60
38	1055	Keyboard	11/26/2014	2	11/25/2016	Tundra	A	N	$ 90
45	1062	Keyboard	11/26/2014	2	11/25/2016	Tundra	A	N	$ 90
46	1063	Keyboard	11/26/2014	2	11/25/2016	Tundra	A	N	$ 90
47	1090	Tower	12/11/2012	5	12/10/2017	Hoffman	R	Y	$ 450
48	1035	Tower	8/28/2012	5	8/27/2017	Tundra	A	Y	$ 450
49	1066	Keyboard	9/7/2014	2	9/6/2016	Tundra	R	N	$ 85
52	1069	Keyboard	11/26/2014	2	11/25/2016	Hoffman	A	N	$ 60
53	1070	Keyboard	11/26/2014	2	11/25/2016	Hoffman	A	N	$ 60
64	1081	Keyboard	11/26/2014	2	11/25/2016	Hoffman	A	N	$ 60
77	1094	Keyboard	11/26/2014	2	11/25/2016	Tundra	A	N	$ 90

- equipment eligible for replacement
- number of records that match the criteria (15 OF 73 RECORDS FOUND)

Trouble? If all of the data in the table is filtered, the list range or criteria range might be incorrect. Click the Clear button in the Sort & Filter group on the DATA tab, and then repeat Steps 1 through 6, making sure the list range is $A$6:$I$79 and the criteria range is $A$1:$I$3 in the Advanced Filter dialog box.

After providing the list of eligible equipment to Patricia, she asks you to remove the filter to display all of the records in the Equipment table.

To show all of the records in the table:

1. On the DATA tab, in the Sort & Filter group, click the **Clear** button. All of the records in the Equipment table are redisplayed.

Using Database Functions to Summarize Data

Database functions (or **Dfunctions**) perform summary data analysis, such as sum, average, and count, on an Excel table or data range based on criteria specified in a criteria range. Figure B-8 lists the Database functions. Although you can often use the SUMIF, AVERAGEIF, and COUNTIF functions; the Total row of an Excel table; and PivotTables to achieve the same results as Database functions, some situations require Database functions. For example, the type of summary analysis, the placement of the summary results, or the complexity of the criteria might require using Database functions.

Figure B-8 Database functions

Function	Description
DAVERAGE	Returns the average of the values that meet specified criteria
DCOUNT	Returns the number of cells containing numbers that meet specified criteria
DCOUNTA	Returns the number of nonblank cells that meet specified criteria
DMAX	Returns the maximum value in the search column that meets specified criteria
DMIN	Returns the minimum value in the search column that meets specified criteria
DSTDEV	Returns the estimate of standard deviation based on a sample of entries that meet the specified criteria
DSUM	Returns the sum of the values in the summary column that meet specified criteria

© 2014 Cengage Learning

Patricia needs to know the average value of the equipment by location and by status. The status of the equipment indicates whether or not it is in use (active), or whether it is not in use but available if needed (reserve). To generate this information, you must set up a criteria range to retrieve the appropriate records for each calculation. Consequently, a Database function is a good approach.

Database functions use a criteria range to specify the records to summarize. In a Database function, the criteria range is used as one of the arguments of the function. The general syntax for any Database function is

```
DatabaseFunctionName(table range, column to summarize,
criteria range)
```

where *table range* refers to the cells where the data to summarize is located, including the column header; *column to summarize* is the column name of the field to summarize entered within quotation marks; and *criteria range* is the range where the criteria that determine which records are used in the calculation are specified.

You will use Database functions to summarize the average inventory for each location by status. First, you will set up a criteria range. Although the criteria range often includes all fields from the table, even those not needed to select records, you do not have to include all field names from the table when setting up a criteria range. In this case, you will use only the fields needed to specify the criteria.

You will create two criteria ranges to complete the Average Inventory section in the Inventory Summary sheet.

To create criteria ranges for the active and reserve equipment for the Tundra and Hoffman locations:

1. Go to the **Inventory Summary** worksheet. The column headers for the criteria range have already been copied from the Equipment Inventory worksheet.

2. In cell **G6**, enter **Tundra** and then in cell **H6**, enter **A**. These are the criteria to find all active equipment at the Tundra location.

3. In cell **J6**, enter **Tundra** and then in cell **K6**, enter **R**. These are the criteria to find all reserve equipment at the Tundra location.

4. In cell **G10**, enter **Hoffman** and then in cell **H10**, enter **A**. These are the criteria to find all active equipment at the Hoffman location.

5. In cell **J10**, enter **Hoffman** and then in cell **K10**, enter **R**. These are the criteria to find all reserve equipment at the Hoffman location. See Figure B-9.

Figure B-9 Criteria ranges for the active and reserve equipment in both locations

The criteria ranges are complete, so you can use the DAVERAGE function to calculate the average value of active equipment by location. The first two arguments are the same for each location. The third argument, the criteria range, is different for each location so you can average a different subset of each location inventory.

To find the average value of the active equipment for the Tundra and Hoffman locations:

1. Select cell **C5**, and then click the **Insert Function** button next to the formula bar. The Insert Function dialog box opens.

2. Click the **Or select a category** arrow, and then click **Database** in the list of functions.

3. In the Select a function box, select **DAVERAGE**, if necessary, and then click the **OK** button. The Function Arguments dialog box opens.

Appendix B Advanced Filters, Database Functions, and Summary IFS Functions | Excel   EX B11

TIP

You could use the Equipment table reference in the Database box named Equipment to reference all of the equipment.

4. In the Database box, type **'Equipment Inventory'!$A$6:$I$79** to enter the range to search, and then press the **Tab** key. In this case, 'Equipment Inventory'!$A$6:$I$79 refers to all data values in the range A6:I79 of the Equipment Inventory worksheet.

   Trouble? If the error "Invalid" appears to the right of the Database box, you probably mistyped the range to search. Make sure you typed apostrophes (') and not quotation marks (") around the Equipment Inventory worksheet name, included a space in the Equipment Inventory worksheet name, and typed ! (an exclamation mark) before the criteria range.

5. In the Field box, type **"Value"** and then press the **Tab** key. The field specifies the table column that contains the data to be averaged.

6. In the Criteria box, type **G5:H6** to specify the criteria for active equipment in the Tundra location. See Figure B-10.

Figure B-10 DAVERAGE Function Arguments dialog box

7. Click the **OK** button. The formula =DAVERAGE('Equipment Inventory'!$A$6:$I$79,"Value",G5:H6) appears in the formula bar, and $1,065 appears in cell C5, indicating the average value of the active equipment in the Tundra location. See Figure B-11.

Figure B-11 Average value of the active equipment in the Tundra location

8. Select cell **C6**, and then click the **Insert Function** button next to the formula bar.

9. Repeat Step 3 to open the DAVERAGE Function Arguments dialog box, and then repeat Steps 4 and 5 to enter the first two arguments for the DAVERAGE function, specifying all data values in the Equipment table and the field name.

10. In the Criteria box, type **G9:H10** to specify the active equipment in the Hoffman location.

11. Click the **OK** button. The formula =DAVERAGE ('Equipment Inventory' !$A$6:$I$79,"Value",G9:H10) appears in the formula bar, and $827 appears in cell C6, indicating the average value of the active equipment in the Hoffman location.

To calculate the average inventory value for the reserve equipment in the Tundra and Hoffman locations, you will copy the formulas in the range C5:C6 to cells D5 and D6, and then edit the third argument.

To find the average inventory value for reserve equipment for the Tundra and Hoffman locations:

1. Copy the formula in cell **C5** to cell **D5**.

2. Select cell **D5**, and then change the criteria range (the third argument) from H5:I6 to **J5:K6**. The formula =DAVERAGE('Equipment Inventory'!$A$6:$I$79,"Value",J5:K6) appears in the formula bar, and $2,816 appears in cell D5, indicating the average value of the reserve equipment in the Tundra location.

3. Copy the formula from cell **C6** to cell **D6**.

4. Select cell **D6**, and then change the criteria range (the third argument) from K5:L6 to **J9:K10**. The formula =DAVERAGE('Equipment Inventory'!$A$6:$I$79, "Value",J9:K10) appears in the formula bar, and $2,151 appears in cell D6, indicating the average value of the reserve equipment in the Hoffman location. See Figure B-12.

Figure B-12 Average inventory values

	A	B	C	D	E	F	G	H	I	J	K
1											
2											
3			Average Inventory				Criteria				
4			Active	Reserve			Active Equipment			Reserve Equipment	
5		Tundra	$ 1,065	$ 2,816			Location	Status		Location	Status
6		Hoffman	$ 827	$ 2,151			Tundra	A		Tundra	R
7											
8							Active Equipment			Reserve Equipment	
9							Location	Status		Location	Status
10							Hoffman	A		Hoffman	R
11											

Summarizing Data Using the COUNTIFS, SUMIFS, and AVERAGEIFS Functions

Patricia wants you to summarize the years of service for the company's inventory. She needs to know the total and average values of the active equipment based on the life of the equipment.

The COUNTIFS, SUMIFS, and AVERAGEIFS functions are similar to the COUNTIF, SUMIF, and AVERAGEIF functions except the latter functions enable you to specify only one condition to summarize the data, whereas the former functions enable you to summarize the data using several conditions.

The **COUNTIFS function** counts the number of cells within a range that meet multiple criteria. Its syntax is

```
COUNTIFS(criteria_range1,criteria1[,criteria_range2,criteria2,…])
```

where *criteria_range1*, *criteria_range2*, and so on represent up to 127 ranges (columns of data) in which to evaluate the associated criteria; and *criteria1*, *criteria2*, and so on represent up to 127 criteria in the form of a number, an expression, a cell reference, or text that define which cells will be counted. Criteria can be expressed as a number such as 50 to find a number equal to 50; an expression such as ">10000" to find an amount greater than 10,000; text such as "A" to find a text value equal to A; or a cell reference such as B4 to find the value equal to the value stored in cell B4. Each cell in a range is counted only if all of the corresponding criteria specified in the COUNTIFS function are true.

To count the number of pieces of Active (A) equipment in the Tundra location (Tundra) and with a value more than $500, you can use the COUNTIFS function.

```
=COUNTIFS(Equipment[Status],"A",Equipment[Location],"Tundra",
Equipment[Value],">500")
```

The criteria are treated as if they are connected by an AND function, so all conditions must be true for a record to be counted.

The SUMIFS and AVERAGEIFS functions have a slightly different syntax. The **SUMIFS function** adds values in a range that meet multiple criteria using the syntax

```
SUMIFS(sum_range,criteria_range1,criteria1[,criteria_range2,
criteria2,…])
```

where *sum_range* is the range you want to add; *criteria_range1*, *criteria_range2*, and so on represent up to 127 ranges (columns of data) in which to evaluate the associated criteria; and *criteria1*, *criteria2*, and so on represent up to 127 criteria in the form of a number, an expression, a cell reference, or text that define which cells will be added.

To calculate the total value of active equipment acquired after 2016 in the Tundra location, you can use the following SUMIFS function to add the values (Equipment[Value]) of the equipment located in Tundra (Equipment[Location],"Tundra") that was acquired on or later than 1/1/2016 (Equipment[Date Acquired],">=1/1/2016") and has an active status (Equipment[Status],"A"):

```
=SUMIFS(Equipment[Value],Equipment[Location],"Tundra",
Equipment[Date Acquired],">=1/1/2016",Equipment[Status],"A")
```

The **AVERAGEIFS function** calculates the average of values within a range of cells that meet multiple conditions. Its syntax is

```
AVERAGEIFS(average_range,criteria_range1,criteria1
[,criteria_range2, criteria2,…])
```

where `average_range` is the range to average; `criteria_range1, criteria_range2`, and so on represent up to 127 ranges in which to evaluate the associated criteria; and `criteria1, criteria2`, and so on represent up to 127 criteria in the form of a number, an expression, a cell reference, or text that define which cells will be averaged.

To calculate the value of active equipment that has a two-year lifetime, you can use the following AVERAGEIFS function to average the values (Equipment[Value]) of active equipment (Equipment[Status],"A") having two years of life (Equipment[Life],"2"):

```
=AVERAGEIFS(Equipment[Value],Equipment[Status],"A",
Equipment[Life],"2")
```

One of the first items you need for the Years' Service Summary report is a count of equipment with a two-year lifetime. You will use the COUNTIFS function to compute statistical information for the active equipment in both locations.

To calculate the total amount of active equipment with lifetimes of two, five, and greater than five years:

1. Select cell **C16**, and then click the **Insert Function** button f_x next to the formula bar. The Insert Function dialog box opens.

2. Click the **Or select a category** arrow, and then click **Statistical**.

3. In the Select a function box, click **COUNTIFS**, and then click the **OK** button. The Function Arguments dialog box opens.

4. In the Criteria_range1 box, enter **Equipment[Status]** and then press the **Tab** key. This criterion selects all of the equipment in the Equipment table that is in active use.

5. In the Criteria1 box, type **"A"** to specify active equipment, and then press the **Tab** key. The first condition is complete, and 60 appears as the total count in the middle of the Function Arguments dialog box.

6. In the Criteria_range2 box, enter **Equipment[Life]** and then press the **Tab** key. This criterion selects equipment that will have a lifetime of two years.

7. In the Criteria2 box, type **"2"** to select equipment with a lifetime of two years, and then press the **Tab** key. The second condition is complete, and 17 appears as the total count. See Figure B-13.

> **TIP**
> You could also use the worksheet reference 'Equipment Inventory'!G7:G79 to reference all of the equipment.

Figure B-13   **COUNTIFS Function Arguments box**

Appendix B Advanced Filters, Database Functions, and Summary IFS Functions | Excel   EX B15

8. Click the **OK** button. The formula =COUNTIFS(Equipment[Status],"A", Equipment[Life],"2") appears in the formula bar, and the value 17 appears in cell C16. See Figure B-14.

Figure B-14 Summary of the equipment with a two-year lifetime

COUNTIFS function calculates the number of items that have a life of two years

number of items that have a life of two years

9. Copy the formula from cell **C16** to the range **C17:C18**.

10. In cell **C17**, change the second criteria argument from "2" to **"5"**. The criteria specify a lifetime of five years. The formula =COUNTIFS(Equipment[Status], "A",Equipment[Life],"5") appears in the formula bar, and 40 appears in cell C17.

11. In cell **C18**, change the second criteria argument from 2 to **">5"**. The criteria specify a lifetime of greater than five years. The formula =COUNTIFS(Equipment[Status],"A",Equipment[Life],">5") appears in the formula bar, and 3 appears in cell C18.

Next, you will calculate the total value of the active equipment based on the life of the equipment. To do this, you will use the SUMIFS function.

To calculate the total value of active equipment based on the life of the equipment:

1. Select cell **D16**, and then click the **Insert Function** button f_x next to the formula bar. The Insert Function dialog box opens.

2. Click the **Or select a category** arrow, and then click **Math & Trig**.

3. In the Select a function box, click **SUMIFS**, and then click the **OK** button. The Function Arguments dialog box opens.

4. In the Sum_range box, type **Equipment[Value]** to enter the range of data to sum, and then press the **Tab** key.

5. In the Criteria_range1 box, enter **Equipment[Status]** and then press the **Tab** key.

6. In the Criteria1 box, type **"A"** to specify active equipment, and then press the **Tab** key. The first condition is complete. See Figure B-15.

Figure B-15	SUMIFS Function Arguments dialog box

first criteria specifies active items

column to sum

enter additional criteria here

Function Arguments

SUMIFS
- Sum_range: Equipment[Value] = {350;12000;60;475;475;60;475;500;55;1
- Criteria_range1: Equipment[Status] = {"R";"A";"A";"A";"A";"A";"A";"A";"R";"A";"A
- Criteria1: "A" = "A"
- Criteria_range2: = reference

= 58885

Adds the cells specified by a given set of conditions or criteria.

Criteria1: is the condition or criteria in the form of a number, expression, or text that defines which cells will be added.

Formula result = $ 58,885

Help on this function OK Cancel

7. In the Criteria_range2 box, enter **Equipment[Life]** for the range referencing the life of the equipment, and then press the **Tab** key.

8. In the Criteria2 box, type **"2"** to specify the lifetime of the equipment, and then press the **Tab** key.

9. Click the **OK** button. The formula =SUMIFS(Equipment[Value], Equipment[Status],"A",Equipment[Life],"2") appears in the formula bar, and $1,325 appears in cell D16.

10. Copy the formula from cell **D16** to the range **D17:D18**.

11. In cell **D17**, change the second criteria argument from "2" to **"5"**. The formula =SUMIFS(Equipment[Value],Equipment[Status],"A", Equipment[Life],"5") appears in the formula bar, and $25,560 appears in cell D17.

12. In cell **D18**, change the second criteria argument to **">5"**. The formula =SUMIFS(Equipment[Value],Equipment[Status],"A",Equipment[Life],">5") appears in the formula bar, and $32,000 appears in cell D18.

Next, you will calculate the average value of active equipment based on the life of the equipment. You will use the AVERAGEIFS function to do this.

To calculate the average value of active equipment based on the life of the equipment:

1. Select cell **E16**, and then click the **Insert Function** button f_x next to the formula bar. The Insert Function dialog box opens.
2. Click the **Or select a category** arrow, and then click **Statistical**.
3. In the Select a function box, click **AVERAGEIFS**, and then click the **OK** button. The Function Arguments dialog box opens.
4. In the Average_range box, type **Equipment[Value]** to enter the range to be averaged, and then press the **Tab** key.
5. In the Criteria_range1 box, enter **Equipment[Status]** and then press the **Tab** key.
6. In the Criteria1 box, type **"A"** to specify active equipment, and then press the **Tab** key. The first condition is complete.
7. In the Criteria_range2 box, enter **Equipment[Life]** for the range referencing the life of the equipment, and then press the **Tab** key.
8. In the Criteria2 box, type **"2"** to specify a lifetime of two years for the equipment, and then press the **Tab** key.
9. Click the **OK** button. The formula =AVERAGEIFS(Equipment[Value], Equipment[Status],"A",Equipment[Life],"2") appears in the formula bar, and $78 appears in cell E16.
10. Copy the formula from cell E16 to the range **E17:E18**.
11. In cell **E17**, change the second criteria argument from "2" to **"5"**. The formula =AVERAGEIFS(Equipment[Value],Equipment[Status],"A", Equipment[Life],"5") appears in the formula bar, and $639 appears in cell E17.
12. In cell **E18**, change the second criteria argument to **">5"**. The formula =AVERAGEIFS(Equipment[Value],Equipment[Status],"A", Equipment[Life],">5" appears in the formula bar, and $10,667 appears in cell E18.
13. Select cell **E18**. See Figure B-16.

Figure B-16 — Equipment Life Summary report

AVERAGEIFS function calculates the average value of active equipment with a lifetime greater than five years

Formula in E18: `=AVERAGEIFS(Equipment[Value],Equipment[Status],"A",Equipment[Life],">5")`

- "lifetime greater than five years" → `Equipment[Life],">5"`
- "equipment with an active status" → `Equipment[Status],"A"`
- "average value of active equipment with a lifetime greater than five years" → cell E18

Equipment Life Summary*

Life	Number/Items	Total Value	Average Value
2	17	$1,325	$78
5	40	$25,560	$639
>5	3	$32,000	$10,667

* Excluding Reserve Equipment

14. Save the workbook, and then close it.

The Inventory Summary worksheet is complete. In this appendix, you used advanced filtering techniques to evaluate the equipment inventory. You also used the DAVERAGE and AVERAGEIFS functions to calculate the average value of inventory broken down by location and status.

Review Assignments

Data File needed for the Review Assignments: Tools Review.xlsx

Patricia wants you to perform advanced filtering tasks that focus on items with service contracts in the Hoffman location. Complete the following:

1. Open the **Tools Review** workbook located in the ExcelB ▸ Review folder included in your Data Files, and then save the workbook as **Tools Update** in the location specified by your instructor.
2. In the Documentation worksheet, enter your name and the date.
3. Place the criteria range in rows 1 to 4 of the Equipment Inventory worksheet. Enter the And criteria to select items at the Hoffman location with a service contract (Y in column H). Then, enter the Or criteria to select items with a value of >1000. Filter the data. (*Hint*: Watch the criteria range to make sure that the proper range is selected.)
4. Use the DAVERAGE function on the Inventory Summary worksheet to calculate the average value of equipment with and without service agreements at the Tundra and Hoffman locations:
   a. Enter criteria in the criteria ranges G5:H6, G9:H10, J5:K6, and J9:K10.
   b. Enter the DAVERAGE formulas in the range C5:D6 using the criteria you entered in the criteria ranges.
5. Complete the Equipment Summary for each type of item (Description). The summary should only include active items. Complete the summary using the following:
   a. Use COUNTIFS for the range C16:C18.
   b. Use SUMIFS for the range D16:D18.
   c. Use AVERAGEIFS for the range E16:E18.
6. Save the workbook, and then close it.

Case Problem 1

Data File needed for this Case Problem: Donations.xlsx

Personal Donations Bradley Cassidy wants to analyze the donations and monetary gifts he has made over the past few years. Complete the following:

1. Open the **Donations** workbook located in the ExcelB ▸ Case1 folder included with your Data Files, and then save the workbook as **Bradley Gifts** in the location specified by your instructor.
2. In the Documentation worksheet, enter your name and the date.
3. Make a copy of the Gifts worksheet and rename the copied sheet as **Q4**. Format the data on each sheet as a table; name the table on the Gifts worksheet **Gifts** and name the table on the Q4 sheet **Gifts4**.
4. In the Q4 worksheet, use advanced filtering to display donations in 2016 that were greater than $25. Sort the filtered data in the Amount column from highest to lowest, and format the Amount column appropriately.
5. In the Summary worksheet, complete the following gift analysis:
   a. Total tax deductions and non-tax deductions by year
   b. Total count by gift type by year
6. Save the workbook, and then close it.

Case Problem 2

Data File needed for this Case Problem: House.xlsx

Tea House   Linda Hill is analyzing sales orders from salespeople in several European countries. Complete the following:

1. Open the **House** workbook located in the ExcelB ▸ Case2 folder included with your Data Files, and then save the workbook as **Tea House** in the location specified by your instructor.
2. In the Documentation worksheet, enter your name and the date.
3. Make a copy of the Orders worksheet, and then rename the copied worksheet as **March**. In the March worksheet, use advanced filtering to display all sales in Sweden and all sales for Janet Leverling.
4. Make a copy of the Orders worksheet, and then rename the copied worksheet as **Sept**. In the Sept worksheet, use advanced filtering to display all records for Laura Callahan with sales greater than $1,500 in September.
5. In the Summary worksheet, complete the summary analysis for France. Use the DAVERAGE and DSUM functions to enter formulas in row 11 to average and sum the orders in March for France. Format the range B11:C11 with the Accounting format and no decimal places. Set up an appropriate criteria range in rows 1 and 2.
6. In the Summary worksheet, complete the summary analysis for the United Kingdom (UK). Use the AVERAGEIFS and SUMIFS functions to enter formulas in row 12 to average and sum the orders in March in the U.K. Format the range B12:C12 with the Accounting format and no decimal places.
7. Save the workbook, and then close it.

APPENDIX C

Enhancing Excel with Visual Basic for Applications

Designing a Stock Report Application

OBJECTIVES

- Create a macro using the macro recorder
- Work with the Project Explorer and Properties window in the VBA Editor
- Edit a sub procedure
- Run a sub procedure
- Work with VBA objects, properties, and methods
- Work with VBA variables
- Explore conditional statements
- Explore custom functions

Case | Coolidge Financial

Michael Evans is a financial analyst at Coolidge Financial, a small investment firm located in Rockford, Illinois. Michael wants to create a stock report application in Excel that he can supply to his clients. The report will display charts and statistics for a selected stock from the current week, month, quarter and year. Because users of the application might not have experience with Excel, Michael wants to automate the process of switching between various reports and charts using Excel's macro tools. To create the macros needed for the application, you will work with Visual Basic for Applications, which is the programming language for Office macros.

STARTING DATA FILES

ExcelC

- Tutorial — Stock.xlsx
- Review — Interactive.xlsm
- Case1 — Maxwell.xlsm
- Case2 — Red.xlsm, Stores.xlsx

Microsoft product screenshots used with permission from Microsoft Corporation.

Developing an Excel Application

An Excel application uses Excel commands, tools, and functions to perform an action. The application itself is stored as an Excel file and can only be opened from within Excel. Michael wants you to create an Excel application based on a workbook that contains stock values for a selected stock from the current year. The Report worksheet has the five macro buttons shown in Figure C-1. The first four buttons—Statistics, Line Chart, Stock Chart, and Stock History—will be used to display the corresponding worksheets in the workbook. The Statistics worksheet contains summary statistics for the price of the stock and the volume of shares traded over the past year. The Line Chart worksheet displays the closing value and volumes of shares traded over that same time interval. The Stock Chart worksheet provides an Open-High-Low-Close chart showing the stock's opening, high, low, and closing values for each day of the reporting interval. Finally, the Stock History chart provides a table showing the stock's daily values and volume of shares traded over the past year. The fifth button—Apply the Time Window—will be used to change the time interval displayed in the report. Michael wants users to choose between displaying reports for the current week, month, quarter, and year. The Statistics, Line Chart, Stock Chart, and Stock History worksheets each have a macro button—Return to Report Control—to return to the Report worksheet.

Figure C-1   Proposed stock reporter application

© 2014 Cengage Learning

The fastest way to create macros is to use the Excel macro recorder. After recording a macro, you can edit it as needed for more specific tasks. Michael wants you to record a macro to display the contents of the Statistics worksheet. You'll save the file as a macro-enabled workbook, and then record the Statistics macro.

To record the Statistics macro:

1. Open the **Stock** workbook located in the ExcelC ▸ Tutorial folder included with your Data Files, and then save it as a macro-enabled workbook named **Stock Report** in the location specified by your instructor.

Appendix C Enhancing Excel with Visual Basic for Applications | Excel   EX C3

> 2. In the Documentation worksheet, enter your name and the date.
> 3. Display the **DEVELOPER** tab on the ribbon, if necessary, and then click the **DEVELOPER** tab.
> 4. Go to the **Report** worksheet.
> 5. In the Code group, click the **Record Macro** button. The Record Macro dialog box opens.
> 6. Create a macro named **Statistics** stored in **This Workbook** with **This macro displays the contents of the Statistics worksheet.** as the description, and then click the **OK** button. The dialog box closes, and you can begin to record the macro.
> 7. Click the **Statistics** sheet tab, and then press the **Ctrl+Home** keys to select cell A1 (even if cell A1 is already selected).
>
>   *This ensures that the macro will select cell A1 no matter what cell in the worksheet is active.*
>
> 8. In the Code group, click the **Stop Recording** button. The Statistics macro is complete.
>
>   You'll run the Statistics macro to verify that it makes the Statistics worksheet active.
>
> 9. In the Statistics worksheet, click cell **C2** to make it the active cell, and then go to the **Report** worksheet.
> 10. In the Code group, click the **Macros** button to open the Macro dialog box, click **Statistics** in the Macro name box if necessary, and then click the **Run** button. The Statistics worksheet becomes active and cell A1 is selected.
>
>   **Trouble?** If a different worksheet is active or another cell is selected in the Statistics worksheet, you need to re-record the Statistics macro. Open the Macro dialog box, click Statistics in the Macro name box, and then click the Delete button to delete the macro. Repeat Steps 4 through 10 to record and test the macro again.
>
> 11. Save the workbook.

Working with the Visual Basic Editor

After you have recorded a macro, you can edit the macro code in the Visual Basic Editor. The Visual Basic Editor has three windows you can use to examine the structure and content of workbooks as well as macros. The **Project Explorer** displays a hierarchical list of all of the macros, worksheets, data-entry forms, and other items that make up a custom Office application. The **Properties window** lists the properties and values associated with each object in the Project Explorer. Finally, the **Code window** displays the VBA code associated with the selected item in the Project Explorer. You might see other windows, depending on how the Editor was installed on your system.

Michael wants you to review and edit the Statistics macro. You'll do this using the Visual Basic Editor.

To start the Visual Basic Editor:

> 1. On the DEVELOPER tab, in the Code group, click the **Macros** button.
> 2. In the Macro name box, click **Statistics**, if necessary, and then click the **Edit** button. The Visual Basic Editor opens. See Figure C-2.

TIP

You can also display the Visual Basic Editor by pressing the Alt+F11 keys.

EX C4 Excel | Appendix C Enhancing Excel with Visual Basic for Applications

Figure C-2   **Visual Basic Editor**

- Code window
- Project Explorer
- Properties window
- VBA code

Trouble? If the Project Explorer, Properties window, or the Code window is not visible, you need to display it. On the menu bar, click View, and then Project Explorer, Properties Window, or Code.

Examining Project Explorer

One important use of the Visual Basic Editor is to manage projects. A **project** is a collection of macros, worksheets, data-entry forms, and other items that make up a customized application. The Project Explorer contains a hierarchical list of all of these objects, as shown in Figure C-3. At the top of the hierarchy is the project itself. Each project is identified by a project icon, followed by the project name, and then the filename in parentheses—in this case, VBAProject (Stock Report.xlsm). You might see other projects listed in Project Explorer, including projects for Excel add-ins such as Solver. Within each project are various objects, including each worksheet in the workbook and the `ThisWorkbook` object which references the open workbook—in this case, the Stock Report workbook.

Figure C-3   **Project Explorer contents**

- VBA project
- project name
- objects in the project
- Modules folder contains modules for storing macros

Appendix C Enhancing Excel with Visual Basic for Applications | Excel   EX C5

VBA projects organize macros within modules. A project can contain more than one module, and each module can contain related macros. For example, you might group all macros that handle printing tasks in one module and group all macros that format worksheets in another. The Statistics macro you created using the Macro Recorder was automatically inserted into the Module1 module. The VBA code stored within a module can all be viewed within the Code window, as was shown in Figure C-2.

Modifying a Project's Properties

All objects within an Excel project have **properties** that define their characteristics, such as the object's name, content or location within the project. The project itself is an object with the default name `VBAProject`. To help you manage and organize projects, you can rename the project with a meaningful and easily recognized name and include a description to provide others with a clear understanding of the project.

Michael wants you to change the default project name, `VBAProject`, to a more informative name and enter a description of the project. You'll modify these properties in the Project Properties dialog box.

To rename the project and add a description:

1. On the menu bar, click **Tools**, and then click **VBAProject Properties**. The VBAProject – Project Properties dialog box opens with the General tab displayed and the project name selected.

2. In the Project Name box, type **Stock_Reporter**, and then press the **Tab** key.

3. In the Project Description box, type **Application to report stock values and statistics.**

4. Click the **OK** button.

5. In Project Explorer, scroll up. The project name in the first line is now Stock_Reporter.

TIP
Project names cannot include spaces; use underscores (_) to separate the words in a name.

You can also use the Properties window view and edit the properties of any object in the current project, including objects found within the workbook. You'll explore how to work with the Properties window by using it to change the name of the Report worksheet. You could do this in Excel, but changing the name from within VBA will give you practice with Project Explorer and the Properties window. Although the different worksheets have object names with consecutive numbers (`Sheet1`, `Sheet2`, and so forth), these names correspond to the order in which the worksheets were created, not to their location in the workbook.

To rename the Report worksheet from the Properties window:

1. In the Project Explorer window, Click **Sheet2 (Report)**. The Properties window lists all the properties associated with the Report worksheet. The left column contains the name of the property and the right column contains the property value.

2. In the Properties window, click the **Alphabetic** tab, if necessary, to list the properties in alphabetical order rather than by category.

3. In the left column, click the **Name** property, and then press the **Tab** key. The property value, Report, is selected in the right column.

4. Type **Report Control** as the property value, and then press the **Enter** key. The worksheet is renamed as shown in Figure C-4.

TIP
To learn about a property, select its name and press the F1 key.

Figure C-4   **Name property for the selected Sheet2 object**

(figure showing the VBA Project window for Stock_Reporter with Sheet2 selected, and the Properties - Sheet2 panel with the Name property highlighted showing "Report Control"; callouts: "selected sheet in the workbook", "properties associated with the Sheet2 object", "value of the Name property", "Name property")

5. Return to Excel. Notice that the worksheet name has been changed from Report to Report Control.
6. Press the **Alt+F11** keys to return to the VBA Editor.

Working with Sub Procedures

VBA code is stored within **procedures**. There are there are three kinds of procedures—sub procedures, function procedures, and property procedures. A sub procedure performs an action on your project or workbook, such as formatting a cell or displaying a chart. You created a sub procedure when you recorded the Statistics macro. A **function procedure** returns a value and is used to create custom functions that can be used within your worksheet. A **property procedure** is used to create custom properties for the objects in your project. In this appendix, you'll only be working with sub procedures.

Recall that all sub procedures use the general syntax

```
Sub Procedure_Name(arguments)
    VBA commands and comments
End Sub
```

where `Procedure_Name` is the name of the procedure (or macro), and `arguments` pass information to the sub procedure and have roughly the same purpose as the arguments in an Excel function.

Appendix C Enhancing Excel with Visual Basic for Applications | Excel   EX C7

Figure C-5 shows the code the Statistics sub procedure created using the macro recorder. Although the Statistics sub procedure has no arguments, the parentheses are still required. After the name of the sub procedure, the description you entered in the Record Macro dialog box appears as a comment. A **VBA comment** is a statement that describes the behavior or purpose of commands in the VBA code but doesn't perform any action. VBA comments begin with an apostrophe (') and appear in green to distinguish them from other statements. After the VBA comments are the commands to select the Statistics worksheet and to select cell A1 on that worksheet. The `End Sub` line signals the end of the Statistics sub procedure.

Figure C-5 Statistics sub procedure

```
Sub Statistics()
'
' Statistics Macro
' This macro displays the contents of the Statistics worksheet.
'
'
    Sheets("Statistics").Select
    Range("A1").Select
End Sub
```

- name of the sub procedure
- VBA comments
- VBA commands
- end of the sub procedure

INSIGHT

Private and Public Sub Procedures

Sub procedures can be public or private. A **public sub procedure** is available to other modules in the project. A **private sub procedure** is hidden from other modules and is limited to the VBA code within its module. All sub procedures are public unless they are identified as "Private" by selecting the Private option button in the Add Procedure dialog box.

Copying and Pasting a Sub Procedure

One way to generate code quickly is to copy the code from an existing procedure. You can then edit the code, making minor changes for each new procedure. For example, the Statistics sub procedure you created displays the Statistics worksheet. Michael wants you to create additional procedures to display the other worksheets in the workbook. Because the code to display the other worksheets will be very similar to the Statistics sub procedure, you can simply copy and paste that code and then edit it for the other procedures.

To copy and paste the Statistics sub procedure:

1. Click the title bar of the Code window to make it the active window.
2. On the menu bar, click **Insert**, and then click **Procedure**. The Add Procedure dialog box opens.
3. In the Name box, type **Line_Chart** as the title for the new sub procedure.
4. Verify that the **Sub** and **Public** option buttons are selected to create a public sub procedure. See Figure C-6.

Figure C-6　Add Procedure dialog box

- sub procedure name
- type of procedure
- scope of procedure

> 5. Click the **OK** button. The beginning and ending lines of the new sub procedure are added to the Code window below a horizontal line that separates the new procedure from the Statistics sub procedure.

You add, delete, and replace text in the Code window the same way you do in any text editor. You could type the entire code for the new macro. But because you already recorded the Statistics macro, you can copy and paste the code of the Statistics procedure.

To copy the VBA code from the Statistics sub procedure:

> 1. Select all the comment lines and VBA commands from the Statistics sub procedure, beginning with the first apostrophe directly below the `Sub Statistics()` line and ending with the `Range("A1").Select` line. Do not select either the `Sub Statistics()` or the `End Sub` line.
>
> 2. On the Standard toolbar, click the **Copy** button (or press the **Ctrl+C** keys). The selected code is copied to the Clipboard.
>
> 3. In the Code window, click the blank line below the `Public Sub Line_Chart()` command line.
>
> 4. On the Standard toolbar, click the **Paste** button (or press the **Ctrl+V** keys). The Statistics sub procedure code is pasted into the Line_Chart sub procedure.

You need to edit the pasted code. You could type individual changes in the code or you can use the Replace dialog box to replace multiple instances of text in the code. You can choose to replace the text throughout the current procedure, the current module (across several procedures), or the current project (across several modules) by clicking the corresponding option button in the Replace dialog box.

Michael wants you to edit the code to create a macro that selects cell A1 in the Line Chart worksheet. You'll replace all occurrences of "Statistics" with "Line Chart."

To replace text in the Line_Chart sub procedure:

> 1. Click in the Line_Chart sub procedure, if necessary.

Appendix C Enhancing Excel with Visual Basic for Applications | Excel   EX C9

> 2. On the menu bar, click **Edit**, and then click **Replace** (or press the **Ctrl+H** keys). The Replace dialog box opens.
> 3. In the Find What box, type **Statistics**, and then press the **Tab** key.
> 4. In the Replace With box, type **Line Chart**.
> 5. In the Search section, click the **Current Procedure** option button to specify that text is replaced only within the current procedure—in this case, the Line_Chart procedure. See Figure C-7.

Figure C-7 Replace dialog box to edit the Line_Chart sub procedure

- text to be replaced
- replacement text
- limits the search and replace to the current sub procedure

> 6. Click the **Replace All** button. A dialog box indicates that three replacements of the Statistics text were made.
> 7. Click the **OK** button, and then click the **Cancel** button to close the Replace dialog box. The Line_Chart sub procedure is edited.

Running a Sub Procedure

After creating a procedure, you should test it to ensure that it works as intended. You can test a macro by running it from the workbook or from the Visual Basic Editor. Michael wants you to run the Line_Chart sub procedure to verify that it opens the Line Chart worksheet. You'll do this from the Visual Basic Editor.

To run the Line_Chart sub procedure in the Visual Basic Editor:

> 1. Make sure the insertion point is still within the Line_Chart sub procedure.
> 2. On the menu bar, click **Run**, and then click **Run Sub/UserForm** (or press the **F5** key). The Visual Basic Editor runs the sub procedure selected in the Code window—in this case, the Line_Chart sub procedure.
>
>   **Trouble?** If the Visual Basic Editor displays an error message, you probably made a mistake while creating the Line_Chart sub procedure. Click the End button in the dialog box, make sure Line Chart is spelled correctly in all three instances, correct any errors you find, and then repeat Steps 1 and 2.
>
> 3. Return to Microsoft Excel, and verify that the Line Chart worksheet is now the active sheet in the workbook.
> 4. Save the workbook, and then press the **Alt+F11** keys to return to the Visual Basic Editor.

You'll use the same process to create macros that display the remaining worksheets in the Tornado Analysis workbook. You'll copy and edit the sub procedure to display the contents of the Stock Chart, Stock History, and Report Control worksheets.

To create the remaining sub procedures:

1. Make sure the Code window in the Visual Basic Editor is active.
2. On the menu bar, click **Insert**, and then click **Procedure**. The Add Procedure dialog box opens.
3. Type **Stock_Chart** in the Name box, verify that the **Sub** and **Public** option buttons are selected, and then click the **OK** button.
4. On the Standard toolbar, click the **Paste** button (or press the **Ctrl+V** keys). The lines of code you copied from the Statistics sub procedure are pasted into the new sub procedure.
5. On the menu bar Click **Edit**, and then click **Replace** (or press the **Ctrl+H** keys). The Replace dialog box opens.
6. Click the **Find What** arrow, click **Statistics**, type **Stock Chart** in the Replace With box, verify that the **Current Procedure** option button is selected, and then click the **Replace All** button.
7. Click the **OK** button to confirm that three replacements were made, and then click the **Cancel** button to close the Replace dialog box.
8. Repeat Steps 2 through 7 to create a sub procedure named **Stock_History**, replacing Statistics with **Stock History** in the pasted program code.
9. Repeat Steps 2 through 7 to create a sub procedure named **Report_Control**, replacing Statistics with **Report Control** in the pasted program code. Figure C-8 show the code for the three sub procedures you just created. You'll need to scroll the Code window to see all of the code.

Figure C-8   Stock_Chart, Stock_History, and Report_Control sub procedures

```
Public Sub Stock_Chart()
'
' Stock Chart Macro
' This macro displays the contents of the Stock Chart worksheet.
'

    Sheets("Stock Chart").Select
    Range("A1").Select

End Sub

Public Sub Stock_History()
'
' Stock History Macro
' This macro displays the contents of the Stock History worksheet.
'


    Sheets("Stock History").Select
    Range("A1").Select

End Sub

Public Sub Report_Control()
'
' Report Control Macro
' This macro displays the contents of the Report Control worksheet.
'


    Sheets("Report Control").Select
    Range("A1").Select

End Sub
```

Appendix C Enhancing Excel with Visual Basic for Applications | Excel EX C11

Assigning a Sub Procedure to a Macro Button

You have created five sub procedures to display each worksheet in the Stock Report workbook. You'll return to Excel and assign those sub procedures to macro buttons.

To assign the sub procedures to macro buttons:

1. Return to Excel, and go to the **Report Control** worksheet.
2. Right-click the **Statistics** macro button and then click **Assign Macro**. The Assign Macro dialog box opens.
3. In the Macro name box, click **Statistics** and then click the **OK** button. The Statistics macro is assigned to the Statistics macro button.
4. Press the **Esc** key, and then click the **Statistics** button. The Statistics worksheet becomes the active sheet in the workbook with cell A1 selected.

   Trouble? If the worksheet doesn't open, the macro button might be selected (indicated by selection handles around the button). If the button is selected, press the Esc key, and then click the button again.

5. Right-click the **Return to Report Control** macro button, click **Assign Macro** to open the Assign Macro dialog box, select **Report Control** as the macro name, and then click the **OK** button. The Report Control macro is assigned to the button.
6. Press the **Esc** key, and then click the **Return to Report Control** button. The Report Control worksheet becomes the active sheet in the workbook.
7. Repeat Steps 2 through 6 to assign the appropriate macros to the Line Chart, Stock Chart, and Stock History buttons on the Report Control worksheet to open the Line Chart, Stock Chart and Stock History worksheets.
8. On the Line Chart, Stock Chart and Stock History worksheets, repeat Steps 2 through 6 to assign a macro to the Return to Report Control button to return the user to the Report Control worksheet.
9. Save the workbook.

Now that you have created a few sub procedures using the Visual Basic Editor, you'll examine the VBA commands in those procedures.

PROSKILLS

Problem Solving: Learning VBA

The best way to learn VBA is by doing. Start with the macro recorder to generate VBA code. The code is guaranteed to be free of syntax errors, so you can identify the key elements of the VBA language. However, the macro recorder does not write the most efficient code. It also records commands and actions that you might not want or need in a finished project. Experienced programmers might use the macro recorder as a starting point, but then edit the generated code to remove the extraneous material.

Another good source of information is the Microsoft Visual Basic for Applications Help. Help contains descriptions of all of the VBA commands and operations. It also includes code samples you can often apply to your own projects.

Next, try writing some code. The interactive tools guide you to use the correct syntax by identifying syntax errors as you type them.

Finally, examine what other programmers are doing. In many cases, program code is password-protected. You can learn from others' techniques, and the web is a great source of VBA code samples. However, if you do use code from another programmer, be sure to obtain permission and to cite the programmer's work in any publication.

An Introduction to Visual Basic for Applications

VBA is an **object-oriented programming language**, in which tasks are performed by manipulating objects. Almost anything in Excel—from a single cell, to an entire worksheet, to the Excel application itself—is considered a Visual Basic object. You can perform any task on these objects that you can perform in Excel, such as creating charts, moving worksheets, or entering formulas into cells. Figure C-9 describes some of the common Excel objects used in many VBA programs.

Figure C-9   VBA objects in Excel

Excel Object	Description
`Range`	A range in a worksheet
`Name`	A defined name in a workbook
`Chart`	A chart in a workbook (either embedded within a worksheet or stored as a chart sheet)
`ChartObject`	A chart embedded within a worksheet
`Worksheet`	A worksheet in a workbook
`Workbook`	An Excel workbook
`VBAProject`	A VBA project
`Application`	The Excel program itself

© 2014 Cengage Learning

Objects are often grouped into **collection objects**, which are themselves objects. For example, a sheet is an object, but the collection of all the sheets in a workbook is also an object. To refer to a specific object in a collection, use the object reference

`object_collection(id)`

where `object_collection` is the name of the object collection and `id` is either a name or number that identifies an object in the collection. For example, the object collection `Sheets` refers to all of the sheets in a particular workbook. The reference to the Statistics worksheet out of that collection is

`Sheets("Statistics")`

You could also use the object reference `Sheets(6)` because the Statistics worksheet is the sixth object in the collection of worksheets. Note that the number does not indicate the sheet's location in the workbook. For example, the Statistics worksheet is the sixth worksheet in the collection, but it might be moved to any location in the workbook. Figure C-10 provides other examples of references to objects within collections.

Figure C-10   Object collection examples

Object Collection	Description
`Range("A1:B10")`	The collection of cells in the range A1:B10
`Names("StockDates")`	The range name StockDates within the collection of all defined names
`ChartObjects(3)`	The third embedded chart in a worksheet
`Charts(3)`	The third chart sheet in a workbook
`Sheets("Statistics")`	The Statistics worksheet
`Workbooks("Stock Report")`	The Stock Report workbook
`Windows(2)`	The second open Excel workbook window

© 2014 Cengage Learning

VBA organizes objects and object collections in a hierarchy with the Excel application at the top and the individual cells of a workbook at the bottom. This hierarchy is often referred to as the **Excel Object Model**. The general syntax for referencing an object's location within this hierarchy is

```
object1.object2.object3
```

where `object1` is an object at the upper level of the hierarchy, `object2` is the object at the next lower level in the hierarchy, `object3` is the next lower-level object, and so forth. For example, the complete object reference to cell A1 in the Info worksheet of the Stocks workbook within the Excel application is:

```
Application.Workbooks("Stocks").Sheets("Info").Range("A1")
```

If you don't include the complete object hierarchy, the object is assumed to be based in the active application, workbook, and worksheet. For example, the following object reference refers to cell A1 of the Info worksheet, and the workbook is assumed to be the active workbook within the Excel application:

```
Sheets("Info").Range("A1")
```

Similarly, the following object reference refers to cell A1 of the active sheet in the active workbook:

```
Range("A1")
```

To help you work with the hierarchy of objects in the Excel Object Model, VBA provides special object names to refer directly to certain objects. Figure C-11 describes some of these special object names.

Figure C-11   Special object names in VBA

Object Name	Description
`ActiveCell`	The currently selected cell
`ActiveChart`	The currently selected chart
`ActiveSheet`	The currently selected sheet
`ActiveWindow`	The currently selected window
`ActiveWorkbook`	The current workbook
`ThisCell`	The cell from which a custom function is being run
`ThisWorkbook`	The workbook containing the macro code that is currently running

© 2014 Cengage Learning

In VBA, the following two references are equivalent because they reference cell A1 of the active sheet and workbook:

```
Range("A1")
ActiveWorkbook.ActiveSheet.Range("A1")
```

The `ActiveWorkbook` refers to the workbook in which the macro is running; the `ThisWorkbook` object refers to the workbook in which the macro code has been stored.

Modifying Properties

The VBA language alters objects by modifying the object's properties. For example, a worksheet cell supports several properties, such as the value or formula contained in the cell, the formatting applied to the cell's appearance, and the text of the comment that might be attached to the cell. Figure C-12 describes some Excel objects and the properties associated with them. Note that some properties are themselves objects.

Figure C-12 Objects and their properties

Object	Property	Description
Range	`Address`	The cell reference of the range
	`Comment`	A comment attached to the cell
	`Formula`	The formula entered into the cell
	`Value`	The value of the cell
Name	`RefersTo`	The cell(s) that the defined name refers to
	`Value`	The value of the cell referred to by the defined name
Worksheet	`Name`	The name of the worksheet
	`Visible`	Whether the worksheet is visible or hidden
Chart	`ChartTitle`	The text of the chart's title
	`ChartType`	The type of the chart
	`HasLegend`	Whether the chart has a legend
Workbook	`HasPassword`	Whether the workbook has a password
	`Name`	The name of the workbook
	`Path`	The folder and drive in which the workbook is stored
	`Saved`	Whether the workbook has been saved

© 2014 Cengage Learning

This is only a small sample of the objects and properties available in VBA programs. Literally everything in Excel can be expressed in terms of an object or a property.

Object properties can be changed using the VBA statement

> **TIP**
> Property values that are text or formulas must be placed within quotation marks; numbers and true or false values do not.

`object.property = expression`

where `object` is a reference to an object, `property` is the name of the object's property, and `expression` is a value that you want to assign to the property. For example, the following command changes the value of cell A2 in the active sheet to 395:

`Range("A2").Value = 395`

Figure C-13 shows other VBA statements that change the property value of Excel objects.

Figure C-13 Examples of changing a property's value

VBA Code	Description
`ActiveCell.Value = 23`	Changes the value of the active cell to 23
`Sheets("Table").Range("A3").Value = Sheets("History").Range("B3").Value`	Set the value of cell A3 in the Table worksheet equal to the value of cell B3 in the History worksheet
`Range("A5").Font.Italic = true`	Displays the text of cell A5 in an italic font
`Worksheets("Raw Data").Name = "Table"`	Changes the name of the Raw Data worksheet to Table
`ActiveWorkbook.Password = "stocks"`	Changes the password of the current workbook to stocks
`Application.StatusBar = "Running macro"`	Changes the status bar text to "Running macro"
`Application.StatusBar = false`	Resets the status bar text to its default value
`Application.ScreenUpdating = false`	Turns off screen updating within Excel
`Application.ScreenUpdating = true`	Turns on screen updating within Excel

© 2014 Cengage Learning

You can also use an object property statement to turn a property on or off. The following VBA command hides the Documentation worksheet from the user by setting the sheet's `Visible` property to `false`; to make the worksheet visible again, you switch the value to `true`:

```
Sheets("Documentation").Visible = false
```

Applying Methods

A **method** is an action that can be performed on an object, such as closing a workbook or printing the contents of a worksheet. The syntax to apply a method is

```
object.method
```

where `object` references an Excel object and `method` is the name of the VBA method that can be applied to the object. For example, the following commands from the Stock_Chart sub procedure use the `Select` method to select the Stock Chart worksheet from the `Sheets` collection and then select cell A1 in that worksheet:

```
Sheets("Statistics").Select
Range("A1").Select
```

Figure C-14 describes some of the other methods associated with different VBA objects.

Figure C-14   Objects and their methods

Object	Method	Description
Range	ClearContents	Clears all formulas and values in the range
	Copy	Copies the values in the range to the Clipboard
	Merge	Merges the cells in the range
Worksheet	Delete	Deletes the worksheet
	Select	Selects (and displays) the worksheet
Workbook	Close	Closes the workbook
	Protect	Protects the workbook
	Save	Saves the workbook
Chart	Copy	Copies the chart to the Clipboard
	Select	Selects the chart
	Delete	Deletes the chart
Charts	Select	Selects the chart sheets in the workbook
Worksheets	Select	Selects the worksheets in the workbook

© 2014 Cengage Learning

Methods often have parameters that govern how they are applied. For example, the workbook object has the `SaveAs` method for saving the workbook to a file. But to apply the `SaveAs` method, you need to supply a filename. The syntax to apply parameter values to a method is

```
object.method parameter1:=value1 parameter2:=value2...
```

where `parameter1` and `parameter2` are the names of parameters associated with `method`, and `value1` and `value2` are the values assigned to those parameters. So, the following VBA command saves the active workbook using the filename Budget.xlsx:

```
ActiveWorkbook.SaveAs Filename:="Budget.xlsx"
```

Figure C-15 describes other ways of applying methods with parameter values to an object.

Figure C-15 — Code to apply a method to an Excel object

VBA Code	Description
`Range("A1").Copy Destination:=Range("A5")`	Copies the contents of cell A1 into cell A5
`Sheets("Orders").Range("C5:C10, E10:E11").ClearContents`	Clear the contents of cells C5:C10 and E10:E11 in the Orders worksheet
`Sheets("Sheet1").Move After:=Sheets("Sheet3")`	Moves the Sheet1 worksheet after the Sheet3 worksheet
`ActiveWorkbook.SaveAs Filename:="Stocks"`	Saves the active workbook with the filename "Stocks"
`ActiveSheet.Protect Password:="penguin"`	Protects the active worksheet using the password "penguin"
`ActiveSheet.Unprotect Password:="penguin"`	Unprotects the active sheet using the password "penguin"
`Workbooks.Open Filename:="Budget.xlsx"`	Opens the Budget.xlsx file, adding it to the collection of open workbooks

© 2014 Cengage Learning

Another way of entering an object method is to use the following syntax, which requires that the parameter values be entered in a specific order as determined by the syntax for the method that is being applied:

object.*method*(*value1*, *value2*, ...)

However, you must know exactly what parameters are required for the method and in what order they need to be entered. Thus, to save the active workbook in the Budget.xlsx file, you could run the following VBA command:

`ActiveWorkbook.SaveAs("Budget.xlsx")`

Which syntax you use is often a matter of personal preference.

Writing a Visual Basic Sub Procedure

Once you've learned the basic concepts of the VBA programming language, it is often more efficient to write your own sub procedures rather than using the macro recorder.

Michael wants you to write a sub procedure that displays results for different time windows in the stock report application. To create this program, you first must understand how Michael organized the data in the Stock Report workbook. Michael defined range names for the data columns in the Stock History worksheet. Figure C-16 lists the defined names that track the stock values throughout the current year.

Figure C-16 — Defined range names for stock values over the year

Defined Name	Definition	Refers to
`YearDates`	`='Stock History'!$B$5:$B$255`	Dates on which stock values were recorded throughout the year
`YearOpen`	`='Stock History'!$C$5:$C$255`	Daily opening values
`YearHigh`	`='Stock History'!$D$5:$D$255`	Daily high values
`YearLow`	`='Stock History'!$E$5:$E$255`	Daily low values
`YearClose`	`='Stock History'!$F$5:$F$255`	Daily closing values
`YearVolume`	`='Stock History'!$G$5:$G$255`	Daily volume of shares traded

© 2014 Cengage Learning

Michael also defined names for the current week, month, and quarter. For example, the stock dates for the current week are referenced with the defined name WeekDates while the opening values from the current week are referenced with the defined name WeekOpen. The month values are referenced with MonthDates and MonthOpen, while the quarter values are referenced with QuarterDates and QuarterOpen. The other columns are similarly named.

To create the charts and table of statistics, Michael uses the defined names listed in Figure C-17. For example, the formula to calculate the highest stock value for the current time period is:

    =MAX(StockHigh)

Because the defined name StockHigh currently has the value =YearHigh, this formula returns the highest stock value for the current year. To change the time period displayed in the charts and statistics, Michael simply changes the definition of the defined names in Figure C-17. For example, to create charts and statistics for the current week, the definition of the StockDates range name changes from =YearDates to =WeekDates, the definition of StockOpen changes from =YearOpen to =WeekOpen, and so forth. All of the charts and statistics will automatically reflect the new time period under the revised values of the Stock range names.

Figure C-17 Defined names for stock statistics

Defined Name	Definition	Refers to
StockDates	=YearDates	Dates displayed in the stock report's charts and statistics
StockOpen	=YearOpen	Daily opening values
StockHigh	=YearHigh	Daily high values
StockLow	=YearLow	Daily low values
StockClose	=YearClose	Daily closing values
StockVolume	=YearVolume	Daily volume of shares traded

© 2014 Cengage Learning

To see this in action, you could use the Name Manager dialog box in Excel. Instead, you'll write a sub procedure to change the time window from its current one-year window to one week. This sub procedure will use the Names object collection along with the Value property to change the value of each range name. So, to change the value of the StockDates range name to =WeekDates and StockOpen to =WeekOpen, you would run the following commands:

    Names("StockDates").Value="=WeekDates"
    Names("StockOpen").Value="=WeekOpen"

Commands to change the values of the StockHigh, StockLow, StockClose, and StockVolume range names are similar.

The stock report application also identifies the size of the time window in cell C5 of the Report Control worksheet. Currently, that cell has the value YEAR because the current workbook is showing stock information for the entire year. To change the value of this cell to WEEK, you would use the following object hierarchy to point to cell C5 in the Report Control worksheet, changing its value using the Value property

    Sheets("Report Control").Range("C5").Value = "WEEK"

Michael wants you to use these commands to write the new sub procedure.

To write a sub procedure to change the range name values:

1. Press the **Alt+F11** keys to return to the Visual Basic Editor.
2. On the menu bar, click **Insert**, and then click **Procedure**. The Add Procedure dialog box opens.
3. Type **Change_Time** in the Name box, verify that the **Sub** and **Public** option buttons are selected, and click the **OK** button. The Change_Time sub procedure is added to the Code window.
4. Type the following lines of code, pressing the **Tab** key at the beginning of each line to make the code easier to read:

   Sheets("Report Control").Range("C5").Value = "WEEK"

   Names("StockDates").Value = "=WeekDates"
   Names("StockOpen").Value = "=WeekOpen"
   Names("StockHigh").Value = "=WeekHigh"
   Names("StockLow").Value = "=WeekLow"
   Names("StockClose").Value = "=WeekClose"
   Names("StockVolume").Value = "=WeekVolume"

Figure C-18 shows the code of the Change_Time sub procedure.

Figure C-18   Initial Change_Time sub procedure

- changes the value of cell C5 in the Report Control worksheet to "WEEK"
- changes the values of names in the Names object collection

```
Public Sub Change_Time()
    Sheets("Report Control").Range("C5").Value = "WEEK"
    
    Names("StockDates").Value = "=WeekDates"
    Names("StockOpen").Value = "=WeekOpen"
    Names("StockHigh").Value = "=WeekHigh"
    Names("StockLow").Value = "=WeekLow"
    Names("StockClose").Value = "=WeekClose"
    Names("StockVolume").Value = "=WeekVolume"
End Sub
```

Next, you'll test your code to verify that the charts and statistics in the Stock Report workbook change to reflect the new time window.

To test the Change_Time sub procedure:

1. Verify that the insertion point is still within the Change_Time sub procedure, and then press the **F5** key to run the code.

   Trouble? If an error message appears, check your code against the code shown in Figure C-18. Common errors include not enclosing values within quotation marks or not adding the = symbol within the defined name value.

2. Return to Excel, and then go to the **Report Control** worksheet. Notice that the word WEEK appears in cell C5.

Appendix C Enhancing Excel with Visual Basic for Applications | Excel   **EX C19**

▶ **3.** Click the **Line Chart** macro button to go to the Line Chart worksheet. The chart displays the closing values and volume for the week. See Figure C-19.

Figure C-19	Line Chart worksheet showing values from the current week

▶ **4.** Go to the other sheets in the workbook and confirm that the Statistics and Stock Chart worksheets summarize the values for the current week.

The Change_Time sub procedure works effectively to show the stock values for the current week, but Michael wants a more general macro that will work with other time intervals. You can create such a macro using variables.

> **INSIGHT**
>
> ### Using the Immediate Window
>
> As you work in VBA, you might want to see the effects of a single command rather than an entire sub procedure. You can run single command lines in the Visual Basic Editor Immediate window. To open the Immediate window, click View on the VBA menu bar, and then click Immediate Window (or press the Ctrl+G keys). The Immediate window opens and you can then type your VBA commands directly into this window. Every time you reach the end of a command and press the Enter key, the command runs and you obtain immediate feedback on the effects of the command.

Working with Variables and Values

So far, you have written code for tasks that you could have done directly within Excel using your mouse and keyboard. The power of VBA really begins when you start using variables. A **variable** is a named element in a program used to store data. For example, you could create a variable named time_window and use it to store the time window that is displayed in the stock report. Variable names are case sensitive, so VBA treats the time_window and Time_Window variables names as two distinct variables.

Declaring a Variable

Variables are declared using the command

```
Dim variable
```

where *variable* is the variable name. The `Dim` in this command is short for "dimensioning," which refers to the process of allocating memory space for the variable. Variables can store a wide variety of data from text to numbers to objects. You specify the type of data stored in the variable using the command

```
Dim variable as type
```

where *type* is the data type. For example, a variable containing text is declared using the statement

```
Dim SheetName as String
```

where `String` is the data type for text values. Other data types include `Date` for date values, `Integer` for integers, `Decimal` for whole or decimal numbers, and `Object` for Excel objects such as workbooks, worksheets, or cells. You can learn more about data types in Excel Help.

INSIGHT

Determining a Data Type

It is not strictly required to specify a data type or declare a variable in Visual Basic. If you don't specify a data type, Excel determines the data type by what is stored in the variable. Likewise, if you don't declare a variable, Excel creates the variable when you first attempt to store data in it. However, good programming practice is to declare variables and their data types as a way of catching errors that might creep into the code.

Assigning a Value to a Variable

After you declare a variable, you store data in it using the command

```
Variable = expression
```

where *expression* is the initial value or text that is assigned to the variable. For example, the following command stores the text "Budget" in the variable `SheetName`. If you have not declared the `SheetName` variable beforehand, this command also declares the variable:

```
SheetName = "Budget"
```

Because variables can also store objects such as worksheets, workbooks, or ranges, the command

```
Set variable = object
```

stores an object in a variable, where *object* is an Excel object. For example, the following command stores a reference to the Statistics worksheet object in the `StatsSheet` variable.

```
Set StatsSheet = Sheets("Statistics")
```

One advantage of using object variables is that you can take a long extended object reference and reduce it to a compact variable name. Figure C-20 shows VBA statements in which variables are assigned values or are used to store objects.

Appendix C Enhancing Excel with Visual Basic for Applications | Excel   EX C21

Figure C-20 Code to set the value of a variable

VBA Code	Description
`Year = 2016`	Stores the value 2016 in the Year variable
`time_window = "MONTH"`	Stores the text string "MONTH" in the time_window variable
`time_window = Range("C5").Value`	Stores the value entered in cell C5 of the active worksheet in the time_window variable
`Set WSheet = Sheets("Statistics")`	References the Statistics worksheet using the WSheet variable
`Set WBook = Workbooks("Stock Report")`	References the Stock Report workbook using the WBook variable

© 2014 Cengage Learning

Michael wants you to create a variable named time_window for the Change_Time sub procedure that uses whatever text is entered into cell C5 of the Report worksheet as the value of this variable. You'll declare the time_window variable and set its initial value now.

To create the time_window variable:

1. Press the **Alt+F11** keys to return to the Visual Basic Editor.
2. In the Code window, click the end of the Public Sub Change_Time() line, and then press the **Enter** key to insert a new blank line.
3. Press the **Tab** key to indent the line, type **Dim time_window**, and then press the **Enter** key.
4. Type **time_window = Sheets("Report Control").Range("C5").Value** and then press the **Enter** key. See Figure C-21.

Figure C-21 Code window with the time_window variable

declares the time_window variable

sets the value of the time_window variable to the value of cell C5 in the Report Control worksheet

```
Public Sub Change_Time()
    Dim time_window
    time_window = Sheets("Report Control").Range("C5").Value
    
    Sheets("Report Control").Range("C5").Value = "WEEK"
    
    Names("StockDates").Value = "=WeekDates"
    Names("StockOpen").Value = "=WeekOpen"
    Names("StockHigh").Value = "=WeekHigh"
    Names("StockLow").Value = "=WeekLow"
    Names("StockClose").Value = "=WeekClose"
    Names("StockVolume").Value = "=WeekVolume"
End Sub
```

Next, you will use the variable that you declared as part of the Change_Time sub procedure.

> ### Problem Solving: Common Sources of Program Errors
>
> VBA programs can lead to three types of errors:
>
> - **Syntax errors** occur when a line of VBA code is entered improperly. The Visual Basic Editor catches such errors before you get a chance to run the program and usually provides ScreenTips to help you fix the error.
> - **Run-time errors** occur when the program is running. At that point, the code has no known syntax errors, but something in the code keeps it from running successfully. For example, Excel does not recognize a mistyped worksheet name as a programming error, but the code will fail when it cannot locate the sheet object the program references. You can use the Visual Basic Editor to run the program up to a certain spot in the code. By running only part of the code, you can quickly locate the command line that is causing the program to fail. After you identify the command, you can use Excel Help to determine the reason for the error.
> - **Logical errors** can be the most difficult to resolve. With these errors, the program is free of syntax errors and it runs without failing, but the results are incorrect. To fix a logical error, run the program one line at a time, confirming the accuracy of each operation until you find the command that results in an incorrect value or operation. If you still cannot find the source of the error, consider a different approach to solving the problem. VBA often provides several different ways of performing the same task.

Referencing a Variable

Once a variable has been declared and assigned a value you can use it with any for VBA command. For example, if you set the `TitleText` variable to reference cell A1 in the Statistics worksheet

```
Set TitleText = Sheets("Statistics").Range("A1")
```

both of the following commands will change the value stored in that cell to "Statistics Report":

```
Sheets("Statistics").Range("A1").Value = "Statistics Report"
TitleText.Value = "Statistics Report"
```

In the following example, the initial_number variable is set to 100. When this is referenced in the second command, 150 is stored in the next_number variable:

```
initial_number = 100
next_number = initial_number + 50
```

Finally, you can combine variables that contain text using the ampersand (&) character. The following VBA commands combine the text "Coolidge", a space, and the text "Financial." The result is that the Title_Line variable contains the text "Coolidge Financial."

```
Word1 = "Coolidge"
Word2 = "Financial"
Title_Line = Word1 & " " & Word2
```

Michael wants to use the ampersand character along with the time_window variable to set the value of the different Stock names in the workbook. For example, instead of writing the command

```
Names("StockDates").Value = "=WeekDates"
```

you'll use:

```
Names("StockDates").Value = "=" & time_window & "Dates"
```

Appendix C Enhancing Excel with Visual Basic for Applications | Excel **EX C23**

where the time_window variable will contain the text string "WEEK", "MONTH", "QUARTER" or "YEAR". You'll revise the Change_Time sub procedure to use the time_window variable to set the values of the different Stock range names in the workbook.

To reference the time_window variable:

1. Select the line `Sheets("Report Control").Range("C5").Value = "WEEK"` and then press the **Delete** key. You no longer need this line in the function.
2. On the menu bar, click **Edit**, and then click **Replace** (or press the **Ctrl+H** keys). The Replace dialog box opens.
3. In the Find What box, type **"=Week** and then press the **Tab** key.
4. In the Replace With box, type **"=" & time_window & "**.
5. Make sure that the **Current Procedure** option button is selected. See Figure C-22.

Figure C-22 Replace dialog box

- text to be replaced
- replacement text
- limit to the current sub procedure

6. Click the **Replace All** button. All occurrences of "=Week are replaced in the Change_Time sub procedure.
7. Click the **OK** button to confirm that six replacements were made, and then click the **Cancel** button to return to the Code window. See Figure C-23.

Figure C-23 Final Change_Time sub procedure

```
Public Sub Change_Time()
    Dim time_window
    time_window = Sheets("Report Control").Range("C5").Value

    Names("StockDates").Value = "=" & time_window & "Dates"
    Names("StockOpen").Value = "=" & time_window & "Open"
    Names("StockHigh").Value = "=" & time_window & "High"
    Names("StockLow").Value = "=" & time_window & "Low"
    Names("StockClose").Value = "=" & time_window & "Close"
    Names("StockVolume").Value = "=" & time_window & "Volume"
End Sub
```

- reference to the time_window variable

The Change_Time sub procedure is complete. Michael wants you to assign the sub procedure to a macro button and then test it to ensure that you can display weekly, monthly, quarterly, and yearly stock reports.

To assign the Change_Time macro and test it:

1. On the menu bar, click **File**, and then click **Close and Return to Microsoft Excel** (or press the **Alt+Q** keys).
2. Go to the **Report Control** worksheet, right-click the **Apply the Time Window** macro button, and then click **Assign Macro** on the shortcut menu.
3. In the Macro name box, click **Change_Time**, and then click the **OK** button.
4. Press the **Esc** key to deselect the macro button.
5. In cell **C5**, select **MONTH** from the list of possible values.
6. Click the **Apply the Time Window** macro button. The worksheets in the Statistics, Line Chart, and Stock Chart worksheets now show the month results.
7. Click the **Line Chart** macro button to go to the Line Chart worksheet. The chart shows the closing values and volume of the current month. See Figure C-24.

Figure C-24 Line Chart worksheet for the current month

8. View the **Stock Chart** and **Statistics** worksheets, and verify that they summarize the stock values for the current month.

    Next you'll switch the time window to the current quarter.

9. Go to the **Report Control** worksheet, select **QUARTER** in cell C5, and then click the **Apply the Time Window** button to generate the quarterly reports.
10. Go to the **Statistics**, **Line Chart**, and **Stock Chart** worksheets and verify that their content changed to show the quarterly data.
11. Save the workbook, and then close it.

The Stock Report workbook is complete. Using the Visual Basic Editor, you created macros so that users can easily switch between worksheets and change the time window.

> **INSIGHT**
>
> ### Sharing Macros between Workbooks
>
> If you need to use the same macro for different workbooks, you can save time by sharing the macro in a special workbook containing your personal macros. The personal macro workbook has the filename Personal.xlsb and is stored in the C:\Users*username*\AppData\Roaming\Microsoft\Excel\XLSTART folder where *username* is your user name. This is a hidden folder. To access it directly, you must set Windows to display hidden files and folders. You do not need to do so because Excel will automatically open the Personal.xlsb file each time you start Excel, making all the macros stored in that file available to any open workbooks.
>
> To record a personal macro and create the Personal.xlsb file if it is not already created, use the macro recorder and choose Personal Macro Workbook from the Store macro list box in the Record Macro dialog box, and then record the macro steps. After you have created one macro in the Personal.xlsb file, you can use the Visual Basic Editor to revise the macro and create other sub procedures. You can also copy the Personal.xlsb file from one computer to another to share your macros with other users.

Exploring Conditional Statements

VBA programs often need to run one set of commands if a certain condition is present and another set of commands for a different set of conditions. For example, a bank might use an Excel sub procedure to track information on a loan, running different commands based on the size and payment schedule of the loan. Commands that run only when specified conditions are met are called **conditional statements**.

Using the If Statement

The most basic way to run a VBA command in response to a particular condition is the `If` statement. The `If` statement has the general syntax:

```
If Condition Then Command
```

where `Condition` is a VBA expression that is either true or false, and `Command` is a command that the macro will run if the condition is true. For example, the following statement sets the value of cell B10 to "Loan Approved" if the `Savings` variable has a value greater than 20,000:

```
If Savings > 20000 Then Range("B10").Value = "Loan Approved"
```

If the value of the `Savings` variable is 20,000 or less, nothing changes in cell B10, which retains whatever value it had before the statement was run.

Testing for Multiple Conditions

A macro requires an `If-Then-Else` statement to run an alternate command when the condition is false. In an `If-Then-Else` statement, one set of commands is run if the condition is true and a different set of commands is run if the condition is false. The If-Then-Else control statement has the syntax

```
If Condition Then
   Commands if Condition is true
Else
   Commands if Condition is false
End If
```

where `Condition` is a VBA expression that is either true or false. If the condition is true, then the first set of commands is run; otherwise, the second set of commands is run. For example, the following code sets the value of cell B10 to "Loan Approved" if the value of the `Savings` variable is greater than 20,000 and sets the value to "Loan Denied" if otherwise.

```
If Savings > 20000 Then
   Range("B10").Value = "Loan Approved"
Else
   Range("B10").Value = "Loan Denied"
End If
```

If you have several conditions, you need to use an `If-Then-ElseIf` statement to run commands in response to each condition. This general syntax is:

```
If Condition1 Then
   Commands if Condition1 is true
ElseIf Condition2 Then
   Commands if Condition2 is true
ElseIf Condition3 Then
   Commands if Condition3 is true
Else
   Commands if none of the previous conditions are true
End If
```

where `Condition1`, `Condition2`, `Condition3`, and so forth are expressions that represent distinct conditions. You can specify an unlimited number of conditions. VBA analyzes the conditions in sequence, bypassing any remaining conditions when it finds a condition that is true. There should be no overlap between the conditions so that one, and only one, condition is true for any If statement.

For example, the following code applies tests for three conditions: (1) the person applying for the loan could have more than $20,000 in savings; (2) the person could have between $15,000 and $20,000; or (3) the person could have less than $15,000. Based on which condition is true, the text Loan Approved, Loan Pending, or Loan Denied is entered into cell B10.

```
If Savings > 20000 Then
     Range("B10").Value = "Loan Approved"
ElseIf Savings > 15000 Then
     Range("B10").Value = "Loan Pending"
Else
     Range("B10").Value = "Loan Denied"
End If
```

Using Comparison and Logical Operators

To determine whether the expression used in a condition is true or false, the expression must contain a comparison operator. Recall that a comparison operator is a symbol used to compare one value with another, such as <, >, =, <=, >=, and <>. Another common comparison operator—is—tests whether one object is the same as another.

As you write conditions for various conditional statements, you'll also use logical operators. **Logical operators** combine expressions within a condition. The most common logical operators are the `And` operator and the `Or` operator. The `And` operator requires both expressions to be true before the procedure acts on them; the `Or` operator requires only one expression to be true. For example, the following conditional statements test whether the value of the `Savings` variable is greater than 20,000 and the value of the `Credit` variable is "Good". If both those conditions are met, the loan is approved, otherwise it is denied.

```
If Savings > 20000 And Credit = "Good" Then
     Range("B10").Value = "Loan Approved"
Else
     Range("B10").Value = "Loan Denied"
End If
```

The following set of statements uses the `Or` logical operator to approve a loan if either the `Savings` variable is greater than 20,000 or the value of the `Equity` variable is greater than or equal to 10,000.

```
If Savings > 20000 Or Equity >= 10000 Then
     Range("B10").Value = "Loan Approved"
Else
     Range("B10").Value = "Loan Denied"
End If
```

VBA supports other types of conditional statements. These include the `For-Next` conditional statement to repeat a series of commands a set number of times, and the `Do-While` conditional statement to repeat a series of commands as long as a particular condition is true. Finally, the `Do-Until` conditional statement repeats a series of commands until a particular condition is true.

An Introduction to Custom Functions

Another type of VBA procedure is the function procedure used to create custom functions that can be used within a worksheet. Function procedures have the general syntax

```
Function function_name(parameters)
     VBA commands
     function_name = expression
End Function
```

where *function_name* is the name of the custom function, and *parameters* is a list of parameters (separated by commas) required by the function. Note that *function_name* is listed twice—once in the `Function` statement that starts the function procedure, and again in the last statement of the function procedure in which a value is assigned to the function. It is this last value that is returned by VBA to Excel.

The following `TaxesDue` function has two parameters—`income` and `taxrate`—and returns the amount of taxes due by multiplying the `income` value by the `taxrate` value (`taxrate` is assumed to be a percentage):

```
Function TaxesDue(income, taxrate)
     TaxesDue = income * taxrate
End Function
```

Once added to a workbook, the `TaxesDue` function can be run just like any of the Excel built-in functions. For example, to calculate the taxes due for an income of $45,000 at a 33% tax rate, you would enter the formula `=TaxesDue(45000, 33%)` into a cell. The formula results in 14850 or $14,850.

The following is a slightly more complex custom function that uses an If-Then statement to apply one of two tax rates, depending on whether the value of the `income` parameter is less than 30,000:

```
Function TaxesDue(income, lowtax, hightax)
   If income < 30000 Then
      TaxesDue = income * lowtax
   Else
      TaxesDue = income * hightax
   End If
End Function
```

Using this custom function, the formula `=TaxesDue(45000, 20%, 33%)` would return 14,850 (using the higher tax rate), whereas the formula `=TaxesDue(25000, 20%, 33%)` would return 5000 (using the lower tax rate).

> **INSIGHT**
>
> ### Turning a Workbook into an Add-In
>
> You can store favorite macros and custom functions in an add-in file, which makes them available to other workbooks. To convert an Excel workbook into an add-in file, save the workbook in the Excel Add-In file format. If you need to support earlier versions of Excel, save it in the Excel 97-2003 Add-In file format. You can view the contents of add-in files only in the Visual Basic Editor.
>
> To load a customized add-in, open the Excel Options dialog box, click Add-Ins, and then click the Go button to manage your Excel add-ins. In the Add-Ins dialog box, click the Browse button and then locate and select the add-in file. The selected add-in will be available to all of the tasks you perform in Excel.

You have finished creating the Excel application that Michael will distribute to his clients. He is pleased with the completed workbook.

Appendix C Enhancing Excel with Visual Basic for Applications | Excel   EX C29

Review Assignments

Data File needed for the Review Assignments: Interactive.xlsm

Michael is developing a new stock reporting application so that users can select a stock ticker symbol and display a line chart, statistics, and a table of values for the selected stock. To create this application, you'll work with the Visual Basic Editor to develop sub procedures that jump the user to different worksheets and to change the appearance of a stock market chart. Complete the following:

1. Open the **Interactive** workbook located in the ExcelC ▸ Review folder included with your Data Files, and then save the workbook as **Interactive Report** in the location specified by your instructor.
2. In the Documentation worksheet, enter your name and the date.
3. Use the macro recorder to create the **Control_Jump** macro that first goes to the Control worksheet and then selects cell H2.
4. Assign the Control_Jump macro to the Return to Control Page macro button on every worksheet. Test each macro button to ensure that it returns you to the Control worksheet.
5. From the Documentation worksheet, record a macro named **Summary_Jump** that first goes to the AMZN Summary worksheet and then selects cell A1.
6. Go to the Visual Basic Editor and open the Code window for the Module1 module.
7. Edit the Summary_Jump procedure as follows:
   a. Directly below the opening comments declare the `Ticker` variable.
   b. Set the value of the `Ticker` variable to the value of cell H2 in the Control worksheet.
   c. Change the name of worksheet to be selected from "AMZN Summary" to `Ticker & "Summary"` where `Ticker` is the value of the `Ticker` variable.
8. Copy the Summary_Jump procedure to a new procedure named **History_Jump**.
9. Edit the History_Jump procedure so that the procedure opens the worksheet with the name equal to the value of the `Ticker` variable.
10. Return to Excel, assign the Summary_Jump procedure to the View Summary macro button on the Control worksheet, and then assign the History_Jump procedure to the View History macro button.
11. Test the macros and verify that they jump to the Summary and History worksheets for the stock symbol specified in cell H2.
12. Save the workbook, and then return to Visual Basic Editor.
13. Insert a new sub procedure named **Change_Stock**, and then do the following:
    a. Declare the `Ticker` variable setting its value equal to the value of cell H2 on the Control worksheet.
    b. Change the value of the Closing range name to `TickerClosing` where `Ticker` is the value of the `Ticker` variable.
    c. Change the value of Volume range name to `TickerVolume`.
14. Return to Excel, and assign the Change_Stock macro to the Apply Symbol button on the Control worksheet.
15. In cell H2, select a different symbol in the Control worksheet, and then test that clicking the Apply Symbol button changes the stock chart on the worksheet to display values for the selected stock.
16. Save the workbook, and then close it.

Case Problem 1

Data File needed for this Case Problem: Maxwell.xlsm

Maxwell Scientific   Helen Minikin works at Maxwell Scientific, a small science supply store for elementary schools and high schools. She is creating an Excel workbook for entering customer orders. The workbook includes an order form to enter each item ordered, an inventory that updates the amount of items left in inventory after each order, and an order history that will present a log of all of the customer orders. You'll help her develop the Excel application using VBA to automate the process of copying the order information from the order form into the order history log. Complete the following:

1. Open the **Maxwell** workbook located in the ExcelC ▶ Case1 folder included with your Data Files, and then save the workbook as **Maxwell Scientific** in the location specified by your instructor.
2. In the Documentation worksheet, enter your name and the date.
3. In the Order Form worksheet, record a macro named **Add_Order** that performs the following actions so that a new row in the Order History worksheet will store orders entered from the Order Form:
   a. Select the Order History worksheet.
   b. Select the entire fifth row of the worksheet.
   c. Insert a new sheet row into the worksheet.
   d. Using the Format Options button, apply the Format Same as Below option so that the new row adopts the same format as the row below it.
   e. Select the Order Form worksheet.
   f. Click cell C5 in the Order Form worksheet.
4. In the Visual Basic Editor, change the name of the VBA Project to **Customer_Orders.**
5. In the Add_Order sub procedure, directly above the closing `End Sub` line, insert the following VBA commands:
   a. Set the value of cell A5 in the Order History worksheet equal to the value of cell C5 in the Order Form sheet.
   b. Set the value of cell B5 in the Order History worksheet equal to the value of cell C6 in the Order Form worksheet.
   c. Continue to set the value of the cells in the fifth row of the Order History equal to their corresponding entries in the Order Form worksheet. Your last command should set the value of cell N5 in the Order History sheet equal to cell F10 in the Order Form sheet.
6. **Explore**   After an order is submitted and stored in the Order History log, it should be cleared from the Order Form sheet. Using the `ClearContents` method of the `Range` object, add a VBA command to the Add_Order procedure to clear the contents of the previous order using the parameter value "C5:C6, C9, F5:F10".
7. In the Excel workbook, delete the blank fifth row in the Order History worksheet.
8. Save the workbook.
9. Assign the Add_Order macro to the Submit Order button on the Order Form worksheet.
10. Use the macro you wrote to add the orders shown in Figure C-25 to the Order History worksheet. Verify that the Order Form is cleared after each order is submitted.

Appendix C Enhancing Excel with Visual Basic for Applications | Excel   EX C31

Figure C-25 Sample orders for Maxwell Scientific

Order Form Items	Order 1	Order 2
Order ID	R3	R4
Stock ID	E1027	O1000
Items to Order	20	15
Name	Robert Blaska	Linda Nuland
School Name	Elmwood High School	Country Day
Street	100 North Avenue	45 Ridge Lane
City	Nampa	Woodburn
State	ID	OR
ZIP Code	83686	97071

© 2014 Cengage Learning

11. Check the Order History sheet and verify that the orders were inserted at the top of the history log. If the macro didn't work, close the workbook without saving it, and then start again from Step 9.
12. Unlock the cells in the range C5:C6, cell C9, and the range F5:F10 in the Order Form worksheet and then protect the sheet so that only those unlocked cells can be edited.
13. Save the workbook, and then close it.

Case Problem 2

Data File needed for this Case Problem: Red.xslm, Stores.xlsx

Red Hot Ribs   Amanda Gard is a sales manager for Red Hot Ribs, a popular chain of restaurants in the Midwest. One of her duties is to tracks sales figures from the 21 stores. The past year's sales data for these stores is in a workbook named Stores. Each store's information is in a separate worksheet numbered as Store 1, Store 2, and so forth through Store 21.

Because navigating 21 worksheets is cumbersome, Amanda created a second workbook to display summary information for a single store. All of the sales values in this workbook are linked to source data in the Stores workbook. Currently, the workbook displays information about the first store. To display the information for a different store, Amanda had to replace the store number in a selected range with the store number she wants to view. The formulas are then updated to display information about the specified store.

To automate this process, Amanda created a data validation rule so she can select a store from a list of the 21 stores. She wants Excel to automatically replace the data in the worksheet with data from the store selected in the list. To do this, you'll need to use the `Replace` method of the `Range` object, which has the syntax

```
Range.Replace OldText, NewText
```

where `Range` is an object reference to a cell range, `OldText` is text within that range to be replaced, and `NewText` is the new text you want to substitute for the old text. For example, the statement

```
Range("A1:A10").Replace "red", "hot"
```

replaces every occurrences of "red" with "hot" in the range A1:A10. Complete the following:

1. Open the **Red** workbook located in the ExcelC ► Case2 folder included with your Data Files, and then save the workbook as **Red Hot Ribs** in the location specified by your instructor.
2. In the Documentation worksheet, enter your name and the date.

3. Review the formulas and contents of the Sales Report worksheet. Note that all of the data values in the range B6:B7;B9:B21 are formulas linked to cells in the Stores workbook. For example, cell B6 is linked to cell B3 in the Store 1 worksheet of the Stores workbook.
4. Unlock cell B4, which contains the list of stores that Amanda can choose from, and then protect the Sales Report worksheet using the password **redhot** so that the only cell in this worksheet that users will be able to change is cell B4.
5. In the Visual Basic Editor, in the Module1 module, insert a new sub procedure named **Retrieve_Sales**.
6. In the Retrieve_Sales sub procedure, declare the following variables: `OldStore` with the `String` data type and `NewStore` with the `String` data type.
7. Set `OldStore` equal to the value of cell D7. Set `NewStore` equal to the value of cell B4.

Explore 8. Insert a VBA command to unprotect the Sales Report worksheet using the `Unprotect` method with the password **redhot**.

Explore 9. Use the `Replace` method of the `Range` object to replace all occurrences of `OldStore` with `NewStore` in the range B6:B21, where `OldStore` is the value of the `OldStore` variable and `NewStore` is the value of the `NewStore` variable.

10. Use the `Replace` method to replace the occurrence of `OldStore` with `NewStore` in cell D7.

Explore 11. Use the `Protect` method to protect the Sales Report worksheet using the password **redhot**.

12. Close the Visual Basic Editor and return to the Red Hot Ribs workbook.
13. Unprotect the Sales Report worksheet, assign the Go macro button to the Retrieve_Sales macro, and then protect the worksheet with the password **redhot**.
14. Save the workbook, and then close it.

APPENDIX D

Working with Enhanced Formatting Tools

Formatting a Chemistry Report

OBJECTIVES

- Create a custom cell style
- Create a custom table style
- Create a conditional format to highlight cells
- Create a color scale conditional format
- Create an icon set conditional format
- Insert and modify a SmartArt graphic
- Modify the image properties of a picture
- Create and save a theme

Case | Online Interactive Chemistry

Dr. Charles Scott is an award-winning high school chemistry teacher with 30 years of teaching experience. In recent years, he has turned his attention to creating a collection of interactive chemistry tutorials called Online Interactive Chemistry (OIC). Charles knows from his classroom experience and discussions with other professionals that Excel is a useful tool for recording and analyzing chemistry experiments. He wants to create a series of Excel chemistry workbooks to allow students to work with chemical concepts, perform what-if analyses, and generate reports.

The first set of workbooks he wants to create is based on the chemical properties described in the periodic table. Rather than provide students with raw data values, he wants the periodic table to present these values graphically with custom symbols and colors. You'll help him develop the first prototypes for his project.

STARTING DATA FILES

ExcelD →

Tutorial
Dalton.jpg
Democritus.jpg
Mendeleev.jpg
Periodic.xlsx

Review
Elements.xlsx
Table1.jpg
Table2.jpg
Table3.jpg
Table4.jpg

Case1
Big.xlsx
Water.jpg

Case2
FPS.xlsx

Microsoft product screenshots used with permission from Microsoft Corporation.

Creating a Custom Cell Style

A **custom cell style** is a cell style created by a user that can be applied to cells in the workbook. Custom cell styles are created using the same formatting tools that you have used with individual cells. After a cell contains all the formatting you want to include in the custom cell style, you save the cell style with a new name. This name will appear in the Cell Styles gallery alongside the built-in styles.

REFERENCE

Creating a Cell Style

- Select a cell that contains the formatting you want to use in the custom cell style.
- On the HOME tab, in the Styles group, click the Cell Styles button, and then click New Cell Style.
- In the Style name box, type a name for the style.
- In the Style Includes (By Example) section, check the style elements that you want to be part of the custom style.
- Click the Format button, and then select any other formatting options you want to include in the custom style.
- Click the OK button in each dialog box to add the custom cell style to the Cell Styles gallery.

Charles wants to use custom styles to create a unifying look for his workbook describing the periodic table. The workbook contains four worksheets in addition to the Documentation worksheet. The Element Families worksheet displays the periodic table with each element labeled according to its element family. The Ionization Energy worksheet contains the periodic table listing each element's ionization energy. The Radioactive Elements worksheet contains the periodic table identifying radioactive elements. The Element Data worksheet contains the raw data about each element from which the other worksheets draw their information. You'll create a custom cell style named PTitle that will format the title from the four worksheets in a large bold font centered over a double bottom border.

To create the PTitle cell style:

1. Open the **Periodic** workbook located in the ExcelD ▸ Tutorial folder included with your Data Files, and then save the workbook as **Periodic Table** in the location specified by your instructor.

2. In the Documentation worksheet, enter your name and the date.

3. Go to the **Element Families** worksheet, and then select cell **B4**.

4. On the HOME tab, in the Styles group, click the **Cell Styles** button to open the Cell Styles gallery, and then click **New Cell Style**. The Style dialog box opens.

5. In the Style name box, type **PTitle**.

6. Click the **Number**, **Fill**, and **Protection** check boxes to remove the checkmarks, leaving the Alignment, Font, and Border style elements checked. The checked items are included in the custom style. See Figure D-1.

Appendix D Working with Enhanced Formatting Tools | Excel   EX D3

Figure D-1   Style dialog box with the PTitle custom cell style

- click to add other formatting to the style
- name of the custom cell style
- checked items are included in the custom cell style
- description of the included alignment, font, and border formats

Style dialog box:
- Style name: PTitle
- Format...
- Style Includes (By Example)
  - ☐ Number
  - ☑ Alignment — General, Bottom Aligned
  - ☑ Font — Calibri (Body) 11, Text 1
  - ☑ Border — No Borders
  - ☐ Fill
  - ☐ Protection

▸ 7. Click the **Format** button. The Format Cells dialog box opens.

▸ 8. Click the **Alignment** tab, click the **Horizontal** arrow, and then click **Center**.

▸ 9. Click the **Font** tab, click **Bold** in the Font style box, and then click **20** in the Size box.

▸ 10. Click the **Border** tab, click the **double line** in the Style box, and then click the **bottom border** of the Border preview.

▸ 11. Click the **OK** button in each dialog box to create the custom style and return to the workbook.

Custom styles appear at the top of the Cell Styles gallery. You will use the Cell Style gallery to apply the PTitle cell style to the active cell, which is cell B4.

To apply the PTitle cell style:

▸ 1. On the HOME tab, in the Styles group, click the **Cell Styles** button to open the Cell Styles gallery.

▸ 2. In the Custom section, click **PTitle**. The custom style is applied to the selected cell, cell B4.

▸ 3. Select cell **A1** to deselect the cell with the formatted title. See Figure D-2.

Figure D-2   **PTitle cell style applied to cell B4**

[Screenshot of Excel showing the PTitle cell style applied to cell B4, with "OIC" and "Online Interactive Chemistry" text, and "Element Families" label. A callout points to the cell formatted with the PTitle cell style.]

4. Apply the **PTitle** cell style to cell **B4** in the Ionization Energy, Radioactive Elements, and Element Data worksheets.
5. Return to the **Element Families** worksheet.

Modifying a cell style changes the appearance of any cell formatted with that style. You can use styles to make global changes to the workbook's appearance without having to select and reformat individual cells. Charles wants you to modify the PTitle cell style, changing the font color to a dark olive green.

To modify the PTitle cell style:

1. On the HOME tab, in the Styles group, click the **Cell Styles** button. The Cell Styles gallery opens.
2. In the Custom section, right-click **PTitle**, and then click **Modify** on the shortcut menu. The Style dialog box for the PTitle cell style opens.
3. Click the **Format** button. The Format Cells dialog box opens.
4. Click the **Font** tab, click the **Color** arrow, and then, click **Olive Green, Accent 3, Darker 50%** (the last color in the sixth column) in the Theme Colors section of the color palette.
5. Click the **OK** button in each dialog box. The PTitle cell style is updated, and the font color in cell B4 of each worksheet is now dark olive green.

Creating a Custom Table Style

You can also create custom table styles. A **table style** is a style definition that describes the appearance of different elements of an Excel table. To create a table style, you specify the format for the 13 table elements, including the header row, the first and last columns, the first and last rows, and the stripes used in banded rows or columns. Any element left unformatted in a custom table style uses its default style.

Charles wants you to format the data in the Element Data worksheet as an Excel table.

Appendix D Working with Enhanced Formatting Tools | Excel **EX D5**

To apply a table style to the elements list in the Element Data worksheet:

1. Go to the **Element Data** worksheet, select cell **B6**, and then press the **Ctrl+Shift+End** keys. The entire range of the elements list is selected.

2. Without deselecting the range, scroll back to the top of the worksheet.

3. On the HOME tab, in the Styles group, click the **Format as Table** button to open the gallery, and then click **Table Style Medium 4** (the fourth table style in the first row) in the Medium section. The Format As Table dialog box opens.

4. Make sure the range **$B$6:$I$124** is specified as the data for your table and that the My table has headers check box is checked, and then click the **OK** button. The selected range is converted to an Excel table with the table style applied.

5. On the TABLE TOOLS DESIGN tab, in the Table Style Options group, click the **First Column** check box to insert a checkmark. The first column of the table (in column B) is formatted with bold and other elements of the table are formatted. See Figure D-3.

Figure D-3   Element Data table formatted with a default table style

Charles wants you to format the Excel table in the Element Data worksheet so that table headers have a dark green fill, banded rows fill color with white and not light green, and the first column has a dark green fill. You'll make these changes to the table style, save them as a custom style, and then apply the custom style to the Element Data table.

To create and apply the custom table style:

1. On the ribbon, click the **HOME** tab. In the Styles group, click the **Format as Table** button, and then click **New Table Style**. The New Table Style dialog box opens. The Table Element box lists the 13 table elements you can format. The Preview box shows the formatted table.

2. In the Name box, type **ElemTable** as the name of the custom table style.

3. In the Table Element box, click **Header Row**, and then click the **Format** button. The Format Cells dialog box opens.

4. Click the **Fill** tab, and then in the Background Color palette, click **dark green** (the seventh color in the sixth row).

5. Click the **Font** tab, click the **Color** arrow, and then click **White, Background 1** (the first color in the first row) in the Theme Colors section of the palette.

6. Click the **OK** button to return to the New Table Style dialog box. You can see the header row formatting in the Preview box.

7. In the Table Element box, click **First Row Stripe**, verify that **1** is entered in the Stripe Size box, and then click the **Format** button.

8. Click the **Fill** tab, click **white** (the first color in the first row) in the Background Color palette, and then click the **OK** button. The first color used in the banded rows will be white.

9. In the Table Element box, click **Second Row Stripe**, and then verify that **1** is entered in the Stripe Size box.

10. Click the **Format** button, click **light orange** (the last color in the third row) in the Background Color palette on the Fill tab, and then click the **OK** button. The second color used in the banded rows will be light orange.

11. In the Table Element box, click **First Column**, click the **Format** button, and then click **orange** (the last color in the fifth row) in the Background Color palette on the Fill tab.

12. Click the **Font** tab, click the **Color** arrow, click **White, Background 1** (the first color in the first row) in the Theme Colors section of the palette, and then click the **OK** button. The first row is formatted with white font on an orange fill. See Figure D-4.

> **TIP**
> You can create banded rows that cover more than one row with a color by increasing the value in the Stripe Size box.

Figure D-4 — Modify Table Style dialog box

- custom table style name
- bolded table elements have custom formatting
- preview of the custom table style

13. Click the **OK** button. The ElemTable style is added to the Table Styles gallery.

14. With the Element Data table still selected, click the **Format as Table** button, and then click the **ElemTable** table style in the Custom section. The table is formatted with the custom table style.

> **TIP**
> To make a table style available in every workbook, create the style in a blank workbook named book.xltx in the XLSTART folder.

Working with Conditional Formats

Charles wants to present the information in the three periodic table worksheets in a visually interesting and informative way. The periodic table in the Element Families worksheet lists each element along with its atomic number and family. All of this information is stored in the Element Data worksheet.

Highlighting Cells

Charles added a legend to the worksheet that indicates how he wants the different cells colored. Although you could edit the fill colors of selected cells to match the legend, it is more efficient to highlight the cells using conditional formatting. Charles defined a name for the periodic table cells, which you can use with the highlight cells rules to quickly format them.

To highlight the non-metals element family:

1. Go to the **Element Families** worksheet, click the **Name Box** arrow, and then click **Family_Data**. All of the cells in the periodic table containing the element names are selected.

2. On the HOME tab, in the Styles group, click the **Conditional Formatting** button, point to **Highlight Cells Rules**, and then click **Equal To**. The Equal To dialog box opens. Instead of typing text, you'll use the element family entry from the legend.

3. Click cell **H6**, click the **with** box, and then click **Custom Format**. The Format Cells dialog box opens.

4. Click the **Fill** tab, click **light orange** (the last color in the second row) in the Background Color palette, and then click the **OK** button to return to the Equal To dialog box.

5. Click the **OK** button to create the cell highlighting rule.

6. Select cell **A1**, and then scroll the worksheet to verify that the only cells with a light orange fill are Hydrogen (H1), Carbon (C6), Nitrogen (N7), Oxygen (O8), Phosphorus (P15), Sulfur (S16), and Selenium (Se34). The background color of the other cells remains white. See Figure D-5.

Figure D-5   Custom conditional formatting applied to non-metals

To highlight the other eight element families, you'll repeat this process for the remaining entries in the legend.

To highlight the remaining element families:

1. Click the **Name Box** arrow, and then click **Family_Data** to select all of the elements in the periodic table.

2. On the HOME tab, in the Styles group, click the **Conditional Formatting** button, point to **Highlight Cells Rules**, and then click **Equal To**. The Equal To dialog box opens.

3. Click cell **N6**, click the **with** box, and then click **Custom Format**. The Format Cells dialog box opens.

4. On the Fill tab, click **light blue** (the ninth color in the second row) in the Background Color palette, and then click the **OK** button in each dialog box.

5. Repeat Steps 2 through 4 for the remaining legend entries, using the following cell references and colors:

   cell **T6** (Halogens): **light purple** (eighth color in the second row)

   cell **H8** (Alkali Metals): **blue** (fifth color in the fourth row)

   cell **N8** (Earth Metals): **rose** (sixth color in the fourth row)

   cell **T8** (Metalloids): **medium orange** (last color in the fourth row)

   cell **H10** (Other Metals): **gray** (first color in the fourth row)

   cell **N10** (Metals): **tan** (third color in the second row)

   cell **T10** (Rare Earth Metals): **medium tan** (third color in the fourth row)

6. Select cell **A1** to deselect the range and reduce the zoom level to **90%** so you can see more of the table. See Figure D-6.

Figure D-6   Custom conditional formatting applied to each element family

fill colors match the colors in the legend

Charles wants you to hide the element family names to make the periodic table easier to read. Instead of changing the font color to match the background color to hide the text, you'll apply a custom format that prevents Excel from displaying a cell's value.

Appendix D Working with Enhanced Formatting Tools | Excel EX D9

To hide the element family names in the periodic table:

1. Click the **Name Box** arrow, and then click **Family_Data** to select all of the elements in the periodic table.

2. On the HOME tab, in the Number group, click the **Dialog Box Launcher**. The Format Cells dialog box opens with the Number tab displayed.

3. In the Category box, click **Custom**, type **;;;** (three semicolons) in the Type box, and then click the **OK** button. All of the family names are hidden.

Modifying a Conditional Formatting Rule

As with cell styles, you can modify a conditional formatting rule to change the look of cells formatted with that rule. Charles wants you to change the color of the Metals family elements to a dark red fill color.

To modify a conditional formatting rule:

1. On the HOME tab, in the Styles group, click the **Conditional Formatting** button, and then click **Manage Rules**. The Conditional Formatting Rules Manager dialog box opens. Current Selection appears in the Show formatting rules for box because the Family_Data range is selected.

2. In the Rule list, click **Cell Value = $N$10** to select the rule for the Metals family elements, and then click the **Edit Rule** button. The Edit Formatting Rule dialog box opens.

3. Click the **Format** button to open the Format Cells dialog box, click the **Fill** tab, and then click **dark red** (the sixth color in the fifth row) in the Background Color palette.

4. Click the **OK** button in each dialog box to return to the worksheet.

5. Select cell **M10** to select the Metals legend entry, and then change its fill color to **Red, Accent 2, Darker 25%** in the Theme Colors section of the palette. See Figure D-7.

> **TIP**
> To delete a rule, select the rule in the Rule list, and then click the Delete Rule button.

Figure D-7 Final periodic table of element families

Metals family highlight color changed to red

family names are hidden

The highlight cells rule you created changes the fill color when cells have a specific value. You can also create an arrow of fill colors based on a range of possible cell values.

Working with Color Scales

A **color scale** is a conditional format in which the fill color is based on a range of cell values where larger values have progressively darker or lighter shades of color. You'll create a color scale for the Ionization Energy worksheet.

Ionization energy is the energy required to remove an electron from an element, indicating the element's ability to form bonds with other elements. The higher the ionization energy, the more difficult it is for the element to bond. For example, noble gases (Helium, Argon, Neon, Krypton, etc.) have the highest ionization energy and are the most difficult to bond with other elements.

To illustrate this concept clearly in the Ionization Energy worksheet, Charles wants to base the fill color of each element on its ionization energy. The color shade should grow increasingly darker as the ionization energy increases. Elements with the lowest ionization energy will have the lightest fill and elements with the highest ionization energy will have the darkest fill.

To apply a color scale to the ionization energy periodic table:

1. Go to the **Ionization Energy** worksheet, click the **Name Box** arrow, and then click **Ionization_Data** to select the cells with the ionization data values.

2. On the HOME tab, in the Styles group, click the **Conditional Formatting** button, point to **Color Scales**, and then click **Green – Yellow – Red Color Scale** (the first color scale in the first row). The color scale is applied to the ionization data values.

3. Select cell **A1**, and change the zoom level to **90%** so you can see more of the periodic table. See Figure D-8.

Figure D-8   Color scale added to the ionization energy data values

The color scale displays cells with the highest values in dark green, the lowest values in dark red, and the middle values in orange and yellow. The cells that remain white are unstable synthetic elements that do not exist long enough to have their ionization energies determined. Charles entered a period (.) for these values that cannot be placed on a color scale.

Appendix D Working with Enhanced Formatting Tools | Excel   EX D11

Charles doesn't think the default color scale presents the data clearly. He wants all of the cells to be orange, growing increasingly darker for higher ionization values. To do this, you'll change the conditional formatting rule for the color scale.

To modify the color scale:

1. On the HOME tab, in the Styles group, click the **Conditional Formatting** button, and then click **Manage Rules**. The Conditional Formatting Rules Manager dialog box opens.

2. Click the **Show formatting rules for** box, and then click **This Worksheet** to display all of the conditional formatting rules for the current worksheet.

3. In the Rule list, click **Graded Color Scale**, and then click the **Edit Rule** button. The Edit Formatting Rule dialog box opens, showing the three colors used in the color scale and a Preview box with the color gradation.

4. Click the **Minimum Color** arrow, and then click **Orange, Accent 6, Lighter 80%** in the Theme Colors section of the color palette.

5. Click the **Midpoint Color** arrow, and then click **Orange, Accent 6, Lighter 40%** in the Theme Colors section of the color palette.

6. Click the **Maximum Color** arrow, and then click **Orange, Accent 6, Darker 50%** in the Theme Colors section of the color palette. See Figure D-9.

Figure D-9   Edit Formatting Rule dialog box

7. Click the **OK** button in each dialog box to return to the worksheet. The revised color scale is applied to the periodic table. The highest ionization values have the darkest shades of orange.

The revised color scale more clearly shows how the ionization energies generally increase as you move across the table to the right, and the highest values occur for elements of the Noble Gases family. You'll add a legend to the worksheet to make this interpretation clear to the reader.

To add a color scale legend:

1. Zoom the worksheet to **120%** and scroll to the top of the worksheet.
2. Merge and center the range **G10:X10**.
3. Right-click the merged cell, click **Format Cells** on the shortcut menu to open the Format Cells dialog box, click the **Fill** tab, and then click the **Fill Effects** button. The Fill Effects dialog box opens.
4. In the Colors section, click the **Color 1** arrow, and then click **Orange, Accent 6, Lighter 80%** in the Theme Colors section of the color palette.
5. Click the **Color 2** arrow, and then click **Orange, Accent 6, Darker 50%** in the Theme Colors section of the color palette.
6. In the Shading styles box, click the **Vertical** option button.
7. In the Variants box, click the **first color variant** in the first row, in which the color shades darken from left to right. See Figure D-10.

Figure D-10   Fill Effects dialog box

8. Click the **OK** button in each dialog box to return to the worksheet. The vertical gradient fill effect appears in the merged cell G10.
9. In cell **G11**, enter **lower energy** and then top-align the text.
10. In cell **X11**, enter **higher energy** and then right-align and top-align the text.
11. Select cell **A1**, and then scroll up to row **5**. See Figure D-11.

Appendix D Working with Enhanced Formatting Tools | Excel   EX D13

Figure D-11   Color scale legend

legend shows the color scale gradation

Working with Icon Sets

An **icon set** is a conditional format in which different icons are displayed in a cell based on the cell's value. Icon sets are useful for identifying extreme values or tracking changing values. For example, up and down arrow icons can be used to mark rising and falling stock prices.

You'll use icon sets for the Radioactive Elements worksheet, which lists elements that are considered radioactive. In the periodic table on this sheet, radioactive elements have the value 1.0; nonradioactive elements have a period (.) as their value. Charles wants you to use icon sets to replace the 1.0 values with a red circle indicating a radioactive element.

To apply and modify the icon set in the Radioactive Elements worksheet:

1. Go to the **Radioactive Elements** worksheet, click the **Name Box** arrow, and then click **Radioactivity_Data** to select the periodic table on the sheet.

2. On the HOME tab, in the Styles group, click the **Conditional Formatting** button, point to **Icon Sets**, and then click **3 Traffic Lights (Rimmed)**, the second icon set in the Shapes section.

3. Scroll down the worksheet so that you see green traffic lights in all cells in the periodic table that have the value 1.0.

4. In the Styles group, click the **Conditional Formatting** button, and then click **Manage Rules**. The Conditional Formatting Rules Manager dialog box opens.

5. Verify that **Current Selection** is listed in the Show formatting rules for box.

6. In the Rule list, click **Icon Set**, and then click the **Edit Rule** button. The Edit Formatting Rule dialog box opens.

According to the rule description, the green traffic light icon appears in cells with a value greater than or equal to 67%. The yellow traffic light icon appears in cells with a value less than 67% but greater than or equal to 33%. The red traffic light icon appears in all other cells in the range. In this case, you want to display a red traffic light icon for cells with a value equal to 1.0.

7. Click the **Reverse Icon Order** button. The red icon is now first and the green icon is now last.

8. In the red icon row, click the **Type arrow**, click **Number**, and then type **1** in the Value box.

9. In the yellow icon row, click the **Type arrow**, and then click **Number**. The value changes to 0 and the types are consistent, although it has no effect in this case.

10. Click the **Show Icon Only** check box to insert a checkmark, which hides the cell values. See Figure D-12.

Figure D-12 — Edited icon set rule

red traffic light icon is displayed in cells whose value is greater than or equal to 1

11. Click the **OK** button in each dialog box to return to the worksheet and verify that the red traffic light icon appears in the radioactive elements. The nonradioactive elements still show periods because the icon set rule applies only to numeric values.

TIP
When possible, use one conditional formatting rule for the legend and the cell values so any edits you make affect both.

Charles wants you to add a legend to this table, making it clear that the red traffic light icon identifies the radioactive elements. You'll create the legend by editing the conditional formatting rule you used in the table to include the legend text. This ensures that if you change the icon style in the icon set rule, both the periodic table and the legend are automatically updated.

To create a legend for the icon set:

1. In cell **J10**, enter **1** and then horizontally center and vertically middle-align the value.

2. On the HOME tab, in the Styles group, click the **Conditional Formatting** button, and then click **Manage Rules**. The Conditional Formatting Rules Manager opens.

3. Click the Show formatting rules for arrow, and then click **This Worksheet**.

4. Click after = (the equal sign) in the Applies to box, click cell **J10** in the worksheet to insert an absolute reference to the legend cell, and then type **,** (a comma). The range =$J$10,$H$24:$AK$24,$H$22:$AK$2 is visible in the Applies to box.

5. Click the **OK** button. The red traffic light icon appears in cell J10, matching the icon for radioactive elements in the periodic table.

6. In cell **K10**, enter **Radioactive Element** and then middle-align the text.

7. Select cell **A1**, and then change the zoom level to **60%** to see the entire periodic table. See Figure D-13.

Figure D-13 Final radioactive element periodic table

legend shows the icon used in the table

Using Formulas to Apply Conditional Formatting

All of the conditional formats you have used so far are based on the cell's value. You can also base the format on a function of the cell's value. For example, you can highlight cells with dates that fall on a weekend differently from cells with dates that fall on a weekday. To highlight a cell based on a formula, click the Conditional Formatting button in the Styles group on the HOME tab, click New Rule to open the New Formatting Rule dialog box, and then click "Use a formula to determine which cells to format" in the Select a Rule Type box. In the Edit the Rule Description section of the dialog box, enter a formula that begins with an equal sign and uses a logical function that returns a true or false value. If the formula's value is true, the conditional formatting is applied; if its value is false, the formatting is not applied. For example, the following formula will format the cell only if the value in cell A3 is less than the value in cell A4:

```
=IF(A3<A4, true, false)
```

A more compact way of writing the same formula is:

    =A3<A4

Conditional formatting formulas can use relative, absolute, and mixed references. When applying a conditional format formula to a range of cells, write the formula for the active cell in the selected range. Excel will modify the references to match the new location of each cell in the range.

You can use formulas when defining conditional formatting rules for data bars, color scales, and icon sets. Enter the formula as a function of the selected cell using a logical function. For example, to display different icons based on the cell's value relative to the average value in the range A1:A10, enter the following formula in the Value box for the conditional formatting rule:

    =AVERAGE(A1:A10)

As with formulas stored within cells, Excel will adjust the relative references as the format is copied across the selected range.

Working with Pictures and SmartArt Graphics

SmartArt graphics are professionally-designed business graphics included with Microsoft Office. For example, you can use SmartArt graphics to create flow charts, organization charts, and production cycle charts, as well as other illustrations. Charles wants you to use SmartArt graphics to create a logo for Online Interactive Chemistry based on the idea he sketched in Figure D-14.

Figure D-14 Charles' proposed logo

© 2014 Cengage Learning

You'll insert a SmartArt graphic in the Documentation worksheet to create the logo.

To insert the SmartArt graphic logo:

1. Go to the **Documentation** worksheet.

2. On the ribbon, click the **INSERT** tab. In the Illustrations group, click the **SmartArt** button. The Choose a SmartArt Graphic dialog box opens.

3. Click **Cycle** in the left pane, and then click **Gear** in the center pane. See Figure D-15.

Appendix D Working with Enhanced Formatting Tools | Excel **EX D17**

Figure D-15 | Choose a SmartArt Graphic dialog box

- SmartArt categories
- selected SmartArt graphic
- description of the selected SmartArt graphic

4. Click the **OK** button. The gear SmartArt graphic is inserted in the Documentation worksheet. The Text pane is displayed along its left side, and the SMARTART TOOLS contextual tabs appear on the ribbon. See Figure D-16.

Figure D-16 | SmartArt graphic inserted into the worksheet

- tools to format the appearance of the SmartArt graphic
- Text pane
- text labels for the SmartArt graphic
- gear graphic

Trouble? If you do not see the Text pane, you need to display it. Click the Text Pane button in the Create Graphic group on the SMARTART TOOLS DESIGN tab.

You can modify the SmartArt graphic in a variety of ways.

> ### INSIGHT
>
> ### Inserting Images and Shapes
>
> If you don't want to use SmartArt graphics, you can also insert graphics from image files saved on your computer or the web. To insert an image, click the Pictures or Online Pictures button in the Illustrations group on the INSERT tab. Select the image you want to use and insert it into the worksheet. You can then use the sizing handles to set the image size. Excel has drawing tools to modify the image's brightness, contrast, sharpness, and softness. You can also modify the image's color and create transparent sections of the image.
>
> You can also insert ready-made shapes such as circles, squares, and arrows. Click the Shapes button in the Illustrations group, and then select the shape you want to use. You can format a shape by modifying its line and fill colors and adding special visual effects such as drop shadows.

Adding Text Labels to SmartArt Graphics

You enter or edit text for each element of the SmartArt graphic in the Text pane. Most SmartArt graphics support several levels of text. The gear graphic has three rows of text by default. The first level of text will appear in the largest gear, in the lower-right corner of the graphic. As you type the text, the font size changes so that the label fits within its graphic element. Font sizes also increase or decrease as needed when the SmartArt graphic is resized. The Text pane uses the following rules for editing the SmartArt graphic text:

- Press the Enter key to add a new row of text to the Text pane and a new element to the SmartArt graphic.
- Press the Tab key to demote the text to the next lower level.
- Press the Backspace key to promote the text to the next higher level.
- Hold down the Shift key as you press the Enter key to insert text on a new line at the same level.
- Press the ↑ and ↓ keys to move between the entries in the Text pane without inserting new text.

Charles wants you to insert the label "Online Interactive Chemistry" in the SmartArt graphic. Because the most prominent and largest gear is listed first in the Text pane but appears as the last graphic, you'll enter the label text in reverse order so that it reads correctly on the screen.

> **To enter text into the gear SmartArt graphic:**
>
> 1. With the first entry selected in the Text pane, type **Chemistry** as the text label, and then click the second text label entry.
> 2. Type **Interactive** for the second text label, and then click the third text label entry.
> 3. Type **Online** for the third text label. The three text labels appear in the gear graphic.

Appendix D Working with Enhanced Formatting Tools | Excel   EX D19

Applying SmartArt Styles

You can format a SmartArt graphic to achieve a unique look that fits the workbook's purpose. As with other Excel elements, you can use a style to format the SmartArt graphic. A **SmartArt style** is a collection of formats you can use to change a SmartArt graphic's appearance. You can also apply formatting to change the color and outline style of the graphic. You can rotate the graphic elements to give them a 3-D look. Charles wants the SmartArt graphic to have a "chiseled" 3-D look, and the gear color to match the olive green color used elsewhere in the workbook. You'll format the gear SmartArt graphic.

TIP
To restore a SmartArt graphic to its original appearance, click the Reset Graphic button in the Reset group on the SMARTART TOOLS DESIGN tab.

To format the SmartArt graphic:

1. On the SMARTART TOOLS DESIGN tab, in the SmartArt Styles group, click the **More** button, and then click the **Inset** style (in the first row and second column) in the 3-D section of the gallery. The style is applied to the gear graphic.

2. In the SmartArt Styles group, click the **Change Colors** button, and then click **Gradient Loop – Accent 3** (the fourth option) in the Accent 3 section. The graphic color changes to shades of olive green. See Figure D-17.

Figure D-17   Formatted SmartArt graphic

Inserting and Editing a Picture

Pictures or other images can enhance a worksheet or object such as a SmartArt graphic. Charles has images of three famous chemists—Democritus, the Greek philosopher who first proposed that all matter is composed of atoms; John Dalton, the English chemist and physicist who proposed a modern interpretation of the atomic theory; and Dmitri Mendeleev, the Russian chemist who was the primary creator of the first periodic table of elements. Charles wants you to insert these images into the three gears of the logo.

Excel | Appendix D Working with Enhanced Formatting Tools

To fill the gear elements of the logo with images:

1. In the SmartArt graphic, click the **Chemistry gear**. A selection box appears around the selected gear element.

    Trouble? If the selection box is dotted, only the Chemistry label is selected. Click the gear element but not its label to select the entire gear element.

2. On the ribbon, click the **SMARTART TOOLS FORMAT** tab. In the Shape Styles group, click the **Shape Fill button** arrow, and then click **Picture**. The Insert Picture window opens.

3. Click the **From a file** button to open the Insert Picture dialog box, click the **Mendeleev** image file located in the ExcelD ▶ Tutorial folder included with your Data Files, and then click the **Insert** button. The Chemistry gear is filled with a portion of the Mendeleev image. However, the Chemistry label is now difficult to read.

4. On the ribbon, click the **HOME** tab, and then change the font to **bold** and change the font color to the **Yellow** standard color. The Chemistry label is now bold yellow.

5. In the SmartArt graphic, click the **Interactive gear**, repeat Steps 2 and 3 to fill the background with the **Dalton** image file, and then repeat Step 4 to change the Interactive label to **bold yellow**.

6. In the SmartArt graphic, click the **Online** gear, repeat Steps 2 and 3 to fill the background with the **Democritus** image file, and then repeat Step 4 to change the Online label to **bold yellow**. See Figure D-18.

Figure D-18   Gear SmartArt graphic with pictures as the shape fill

- click to format the background pictures
- pictures as shape fill
- labels are a bold yellow font

Photographs are Public Domain

Appendix D Working with Enhanced Formatting Tools | Excel EX D21

Imaging tools enable you to modify the appearance of pictures in a workbook. You can recolor pictures and change the picture's contrast and brightness level. For pictures inserted into a workbook as separate graphic objects (as opposed to fills), you can change the picture's shape, add a graphical border, and apply special effects such as rotating the picture in three dimensions and adding a drop shadow.

REFERENCE

Editing a Picture

- Select the picture image, and then click the PICTURE TOOLS FORMAT tab on the ribbon.
- To change the color tint, brightness, or contrast of the picture, click the Color button or the Corrections button in the Adjust group.
- To add an artistic effect to the picture, click the Artistic Effects button in the Adjust group.
- To apply a style to the picture, select an effect in the Styles gallery in the Picture Styles group.
- To add a graphical border or a special effect, click the Picture Border or Picture Effects button, respectively, in the Pictures Styles group.
- To crop or resize the picture, click the Crop button or enter values in the Size boxes in the Size group.
- To restore the picture to its original appearance, click the Reset Picture button in the Adjust group.

The yellow labels on the images are still difficult to read. Charles wants you to recolor the graphic images to make them darker, which would make the labels more readable. You'll also give the Mendeleev image a green tint, the Dalton image a red tint, and the Democritus image a purple tint, and then increase the contrast to make the labels stand out better.

To edit the pictures:

1. Click the **Mendeleev** image in the Chemistry gear to select it.

2. On the ribbon, click the **PICTURE TOOLS FORMAT** tab. In the Adjust group, click the **Color** button, and then in the Recolor section, click the **Olive Green, Accent color 3 Dark** color (in the second row and fourth column) to change the gear color to olive green.

3. In the Adjust group, click the **Corrections** button, and then in the Brightness and Contrast section, click **Brightness: -20% Contrast: 0% (Normal)** in the third row and second column.

4. Click the **Dalton** image in the Interactive gear to select it, repeat Step 2 to change the gear color to **Red, Accent color 2 Dark** (in the second row and third column), and then repeat Step 3 to select the **Brightness: -40% Contrast: +40%** (in the fifth row and first column) correction.

5. Click the **Democritus** image in the Online gear to select it, repeat Step 2 to change the gear color to **Purple Accent color 4 Dark** (in the second row and fifth column), and then repeat Step 3 to adjust the **Brightness: -40% Contrast: 0% (Normal)** (in the third row and first column). See Figure D-19.

EX D22 Excel | Appendix D Working with Enhanced Formatting Tools

Figure D-19   **Edited SmartArt graphic**

- click to recolor the image
- click to change the brightness, contrast, and sharpness of the image
- background images recolored and corrected for brightness and contrast

Photographs are Public Domain

6. Select cell **A1** to deselect the SmartArt graphic.

The logo labels are much easier to read with the pictures adjusted for color, brightness, and contrast.

> **INSIGHT**
>
> ### Creating Text Boxes
>
> Excel worksheets are not always a good document format for inserting a lot of text. Although you can merge cells to create big text blocks, that might not work well with other rows and columns in the worksheet. Another option is to insert a text box. Text boxes are objects in which you can type that are placed on top of the worksheet and can be sized to any width or height. You create a text box using the Text Box button in the Text group on the INSERT tab. You can format the content of text boxes using the font and alignment tools on the HOME tab. You can also format the border and fill color of the text box itself using the tools on the DRAWING TOOLS FORMAT tab. Text boxes can be oriented horizontally on the page, or you can rotate it so that the text is at right angles to the rest of the worksheet content.

Appendix D Working with Enhanced Formatting Tools | Excel   EX D23

Positioning a SmartArt Graphic

You can reposition an object in the worksheet by dragging it to a new location. You can fine-tune the position of selected objects in the worksheet by pressing the arrow keys to move the object a few pixels in that direction. Objects, such as SmartArt graphics and pictures, are moved and resized along with the worksheet cells. So, if you insert a cell, column, or row within the object, the object will be repositioned to the right or down to compensate for the new worksheet content. You can change this default behavior by right-clicking the object, clicking Size and Properties on the shortcut menu, and then choosing one of the following options in the PROPERTIES section of the Format Shape pane: (a) move and size the object with the worksheet cells, (b) move but don't resize with the cells, or (c) don't move and don't resize the object with the cells.

Charles wants you to reposition the SmartArt graphic so that it is closer to column F.

To reposition the SmartArt graphic:

1. Select the SmartArt graphic, and then point to the border of the SmartArt graphic until the pointer changes to ✥.
2. Drag the image to the left until the arrows in the upper-left corner of the SmartArt graphic surround the lower-right corner of the merged cell C6.
3. Select cell **A1** to deselect the SmartArt graphic. See Figure D-20.

TIP
To convert a SmartArt graphic to a shape, click the Convert to Shape button in the Reset group on the PICTURE TOOLS FORMAT tab.

Figure D-20 Final placement of the SmartArt graphic

Photographs are Public Domain

Charles is pleased with the final version of the logo that you created.

PROSKILLS

Decision Making: Choosing a Graphic Image Type

Excel supports most graphic file formats, so you have a choice of formats for the pictures you import into workbooks. The most common picture format is the **Joint Photographic Experts Group** format, commonly known as **JPEG**. JPEGs are produced by most digital cameras and can support up to 16.7 million colors (which is more colors than the human eye can distinguish). JPEGs can also be compressed to save file space without greatly affecting image quality. You will most often use JPEGs with photo images.

Another popular format is the **Portable Network Graphics** format, or **PNG**. Like JPEGs, PNG graphics allow for picture compression for smaller file sizes. PNG is a better choice than JPEG for storing images that contain line art or text. PNG also supports transparency, allowing graphic images in which sections of the background will appear through the graphic. You will use PNGs for photo images, line art images, and images that require the use of transparency.

For better quality photos, choose the **Tagged Image File Format**, or **TIFF**. Although TIFFs provide higher quality photos, the image files tend to be much larger as well, which increases the workbook's size.

Finally, you can also import logos and formatted documents in **Encapsulated PostScript** format, or **EPS**. Written in the PostScript language, EPS files provide perhaps the highest quality format for clip art files, but require access to a PostScript printer to view the results; otherwise, EPS files are not viewable.

Working with Themes

To quickly change the appearance of a workbook, you can change its theme. Office supports a large library of built-in themes. If a workbook uses only theme colors and fonts, you can switch between themes without editing the styles of individual cells and ranges. Charles wants you to use a different theme for the Periodic Table workbook.

To apply a different theme:

1. On the ribbon, click the **PAGE LAYOUT** tab. In the Themes group, click the **Themes** button to open the Themes gallery, and then click **Organic**. The workbook's theme changes from the default Office theme to the Organic theme.

2. View each worksheet in the workbook to see the impact of the Organic theme on the workbook, and note that the fonts and colors changed to reflect the Organic theme.

3. Go to the **Element Families** worksheet and change the zoom level to **60%** so you can view the entire periodic table. See Figure D-21.

Figure D-21 Element Families worksheet with the Organic theme

colors used for the element families are now based on the Organic theme colors

Modifying a Theme's Fonts and Colors

If the built-in themes do not meet your needs, you can create a custom theme by selecting different fonts, colors, and effects. You can choose from a list of built-in theme fonts, colors, and effects, or you can create your own collection.

Creating and Saving a Theme

- On the PAGE LAYOUT tab, in the Themes group, click the Themes button, and then click a theme to apply it.
- In the Themes group, click the Fonts button, the Colors button, or the Effects button, and then click the theme fonts, colors, or effects you want to use in the custom theme.
- In the Themes group, click the Themes button arrow, and then click Save Current Theme.
- Type a filename in the File name box, and then click the Save button.

A font can be defined for either the theme's heading text or for the body text. The default font under the Organic theme is Garamond for both the heading and body text. Charles likes the Organic theme's effects, but not its fonts or colors. You'll change the heading font to Impact and the body font to Times New Roman.

To change the heading and body font:

1. On the PAGE LAYOUT tab, in the Themes group, click the **Fonts** button. The Fonts gallery lists heading/body font options. Instead of selecting one of these options, you'll create a custom set of fonts.
2. Click **Customize Fonts**. The Create New Theme Fonts dialog box opens.
3. Click the **Heading font** arrow, and then click **Impact** to select the Heading font for the theme.
4. Click the **Body font** arrow, and then click **Times New Roman** to select the Body font for the theme.
5. In the Name box, type **Chemistry Fonts** as the name for the custom theme font choices. See Figure D-22.

Figure D-22   Create New Theme Fonts dialog box

6. Click the **Save** button. Chemistry Fonts is added as a font option for heading and body text and applied to the workbook.

The heading text in cell A1 changes to the Impact font and the body text located everywhere else in the worksheet changes to the Times New Roman font. You can also change the theme colors used in the workbook. Charles wants you to select a different set of theme colors for Periodic Table workbook.

To select different theme colors for the workbook:

1. On the PAGE LAYOUT tab, in the Themes group, click the **Colors** button. The Colors gallery shows the color options available for the current theme.
2. Click **Red Orange**. The workbook changes to the new theme colors. See Figure D-23.

TIP

You can click Customize Colors in the Colors gallery to select custom colors in the Create New Theme Colors dialog box.

Appendix D Working with Enhanced Formatting Tools | Excel   EX D27

Figure D-23   Element Families worksheet with custom theme fonts and colors

- click to select theme colors
- click to select heading and body fonts for the theme
- heading text is the Impact font
- body text is the Times New Roman font

Saving a Custom Theme

When you are satisfied with the look of the custom theme, you can save it as a permanent file to be used in formatting other workbooks. You can save theme files in the default theme folders on your computer or in another folder you choose. Files stored in the default theme folders appear in the Themes gallery, which is not the case when you save the theme file elsewhere. All theme files have the .thmx file extension.

To save the current theme:

1. On the PAGE LAYOUT tab, in the Themes group, click the **Themes** button, and then click **Save Current Theme**. The Save Current Theme dialog box opens, displaying the default Office theme folders.

2. Save the custom theme with the filename **OIC** in the location specified by your instructor.

   You no longer need the Chemistry Fonts because you saved the OIC theme. You can delete these theme fonts.

3. In the Themes group, click the **Fonts** button.

4. In the Custom section of the Fonts gallery, right-click the **Chemistry Fonts** entry, and then click **Delete** on the shortcut menu. A dialog box opens to confirm that you want to delete these theme fonts.

5. Click the **Yes** button to confirm the deletion. The theme fonts are deleted.

6. Save the Periodic Table workbook, and then close it.

Word and PowerPoint use the same file format for theme files, so you can share custom themes that you create in Excel with other Office files. For example, Charles could create a consistent look and feel for all of his Office files by designing a theme with the fonts, colors, and effects he wants. If Charles later modifies and resaves the custom theme file, the changes will be automatically reflected in every Excel, PowerPoint, and Word document that uses the theme.

The Periodic Table workbook is complete. Charles is pleased with the design and graphic elements you added. He plans to produce other workbooks for students to use in their explorations of chemistry concepts.

Review Assignments

Data Files needed for the Review Assignments: Elements.xlsx, Table1.jpg, Table2.jpg, Table3.jpg, Table4.jpg

Charles created another workbook of chemistry information based on the periodic table. This workbook contains charts of the periodic table describing the orbital group of each element, each element's melting and boiling point, and a list of the elements present in the human body. He wants you to add graphical elements to the workbook and create a unified design theme. Complete the following:

1. Open the **Elements** workbook located in the ExcelD ▶ Review folder included with your Data Files, and then save the workbook as **Elements Table** in the location specified by your instructor.
2. In the Documentation worksheet, enter your name and the date.
3. Create a new custom cell style named **ETitle** with the following formatting:
   - Font size of 18-point bold with the Olive Green, Accent 3, Darker 50% theme color
   - Text centered horizontally
   - Single thick bottom border in Olive Green, Accent 3, Darker 50% theme color
4. Apply the ETitle cell style to cell B4 in the last five worksheets of the workbook.
5. In the Data worksheet, create a custom table style named **ETable** with the following formatting:
   - A header row with white text on a dark olive background (use the theme color) and a double bottom border
   - Banded rows five stripes high—the first set of stripes has a light green background fill (using the theme colors); the next set of stripes has a white background
6. Apply the ETable table style to the Element Data table in the Data worksheet. Display the filter buttons in the header row.
7. Switch to the Sub-Orbital Blocks worksheet, which indicates to which of four electron sub-orbital groups each element belongs: S, D, P, and F. The defined name Sub_Orbital_Blocks_Data references all of the data in the table and the entries in the legend. Create the following conditional formatting rules to highlight the values in this range:
   - Highlight cells that contain the "S" character with a medium orange fill color (the tenth theme color).
   - Highlight cells that contain the "D" character with a medium turquoise fill color (the ninth theme color).
   - Highlight cells that contain the "P" character with a medium lavender fill color (the eighth theme color).
   - Highlight cells that contain the "F" character with a medium olive green fill color (the seventh theme color).
8. Hide the cell text of all values in the Sub_Orbital_Blocks_Data table.
9. In the Melting Point worksheet, which contains the melting points of the elements from the periodic table, use the defined name **Melting_Point** to select the data values in the table, and then display the values from this table using a color scale ranging from a light red theme color for the lowest melting points to a dark red theme color for the highest melting points.
10. Use a gradient fill in cell H9 to indicate the range of colors used in the table.
11. In the Boiling Point worksheet, repeat Steps 9 and 10, using the orange theme color to indicate low to high boiling points.
12. In the Human Body worksheet, create a conditional formatting rule that displays a green circle with a white checkmark for all cells in the table and a legend in place of the value 1. Use the Human_Body_Data defined name to select the appropriate cells in the worksheet.

13. In the Documentation worksheet, insert the Picture Caption List SmartArt graphic (located in the first row and third column of the List category). Add the text labels **Sub-Orbital Blocks**, **Melting Point**, **Boiling Point**, and **Human Body** to the four blocks in the list.
14. Apply the Brick Scene SmartArt style to the SmartArt graphic.
15. Insert the graphic image files **Table1.jpg**, **Table2.jpg**, **Table3.jpg**, and **Table4.jpg** located in the ExcelD ▶ Review folder included with your Data Files into the four blocks from the SmartArt graphic.
16. Apply the Slice theme to the workbook.
17. Modify the theme to use the Garamond font for text headings and the Trebuchet MS font for body text.
18. Change the themes to the Median theme colors.
19. Save the revised workbook theme as **ETheme** in the location specified by your instructor.
20. Change the color of the four graphic images in the SmartArt graphic on the Documentation worksheet as follows:
    - Recolor the Sub-Orbital Blocks picture with the Gold, Accent color 4 Dark color.
    - Recolor the Melting Point picture with the Ice Blue Accent color 1 Dark color.
    - Recolor the Boiling Point picture with the Orange Accent color 2 Dark color.
    - Recolor the Human Body picture with the Brown Text color 2 Dark color.
21. Save the workbook, and then close it.

Case Problem 1

Data Files needed for this Case Problem: Big.xlsx, Water.jpg

Big Wave Water Park Robert Tru is an operations manager at Big Wave Water Park, a popular indoor/outdoor water park located outside of Greenville, South Carolina. He is preparing an annual report that contains the daily attendance figures at the park and compares the total annual attendance to that of previous years. He wants you to format the workbook. Complete the following:

1. Open the **Big** workbook located in the ExcelD ▶ Case1 folder included with your Data Files, and then save the workbook as **Big Wave** in the location specified by your instructor.
2. In the Documentation worksheet, enter your name and the date.
3. In the 2016 Attendance worksheet, create a color scale for the daily attendance figures in the range C7:AG18 that displays the days of lowest attendance with a light blue fill and the days of highest attendance with a dark blue fill.
4. Add conditional formatting to the daily attendance figures that highlights the day of highest attendance with a bold yellow font and a solid yellow border.
5. Add a color scale to the monthly totals in the range AH7:AH18 that displays the months of lowest attendance with a light green fill and the months of highest attendance with a dark green fill.
6. Add conditional formatting to the monthly attendance figures that highlights the month of highest attendance with a bold yellow font and a solid yellow border.
7. In the Yearly Attendance worksheet, replace the values in the change column with an icon set that displays a green up arrow for years the attendance increased compared to the previous year, a yellow horizontal arrow when the attendance was unchanged, and a red down arrow for years the attendance decreased. Center the arrows in the cells both horizontally and vertically. (*Hint*: Edit the rule to show the icon only.)

Appendix D Working with Enhanced Formatting Tools | Excel   EX D31

8. Create a new table style named **Attendance**. The header row should be displayed in a white font on a dark blue background with a double bottom border. The contents of the table should be displayed in banded rows, starting with a light blue fill color on the first row and alternating with rows with a white fill color.

9. Apply the Attendance table style to the Yearly Attendance table. Do not display filter buttons in the header row of the table.

Explore 10. Insert the picture file **Water.jpg** located in the ExcelD ▶ Case1 folder included with your Data Files next to the yearly attendance table. Make the following edits to the picture:
- Change the picture size to 2.67 inches high by 4 inches wide.
- Recolor the picture with the Blue, Accent color 1 Light color.
- Apply the Reflected Rounded Rectangle picture style (located in the first row and fifth column of the Pictures Styles gallery) to the graphic.

11. Save the workbook, and then close it.

Case Problem 2

CHALLENGE

Data File needed for this Case Problem: FPS.xlsx

FPS Productions   Linda Thomas owns FPS Productions, a video production company located in St. Charles, Missouri, that specializes in creating short videos for local businesses and government agencies. The company just received a contract to create a promotional video for the St. Charles Civic Center. The video must be ready for distribution in four weeks. To keep the project on schedule, Linda wants to create a Gantt chart (a graphical representation of a project with each phase represented as a horizontal bar, with vertical lines often superimposed to indicate the current date to show the progress of the project versus time). Linda asks you to create the Gantt chart. Complete the following:

1. Open the **FPS** workbook located in the ExcelD ▶ Case2 folder included with your Data Files, and then save the workbook as **FPS Productions** in the location specified by your instructor.

2. In the Documentation worksheet, enter your name and the date.

3. In the Production Schedule worksheet, you'll create the Gantt chart. Linda already entered the start and stop dates of the eight tasks involved in producing the video. In the range B7:B14, enter formulas to calculate the percentage of each task that has been completed given the task's start and stop dates and the current date in cell E5. (*Hint*: The percentage equals the number of days from the current date shown in cell E5 to the task's start date in column D divided by the number of days allotted to complete each task.)

Explore 4. Replace the percentages in the range B7:B14 with the 5 Quarters icon set. Modify the icon set to display the full circle when the cell's value is greater than or equal to 1; display the three-quarter circle when the cell's value is from 0.75 up to 1; display the half circle when the cell's value is from 0.5 up to 0.75; display the quarter circle when the cell's value is from 0.25 up to 0.5; and display an empty circle when the cell's value is less than 0.25.

Explore 5. Create a conditional formatting rule that places a red right border in the Gantt chart cells that fall on the current date as specified in cell E5. To create the rule, select the range F7:AG14 and create a highlight rule for the cells in the range using a formula. The formula should use the IF function to test whether the value in the cell F$4 (a date from the Gantt chart) is equal to the value in cell $E$5 (the current date). If the function returns the value true, the cell should display a red right border.

Explore 6. Create another conditional formatting rule that highlights the cells in the Gantt chart corresponding to the dates in which the task is performed. To create this rule, add a second highlight rule for the cells in the range F7:AG14 using another formula. The formula should use the IF function to test whether the value in cell F$4 is greater than or equal to the value in cell $D7 (the start date), and whether the value in cell F$4 is less than or equal to the value in cell $E7 (the stop date). If the formula returns a value of true, the cell should have a horizontal gradient fill starting with a white color at the top and ending with a purple color at the bottom. (*Hint*: Use the IF function and the AND function in the formula.)

7. In the Production Tasks worksheet, insert the Continuous Block Process SmartArt graphic located in the Process category, and then type the eight task names from the Production Schedule worksheet into the eight blocks on the SmartArt graphic.

8. Format the SmartArt graphic by setting its size to 3.75 inches high by 7 inches wide, changing its color to Colored Fill - Accent 4, and applying the Cartoon style located in the 3-D section of the SmartArt Styles gallery.

9. Move the SmartArt graphic under the Civic Center Promotional Video Task List title so that it covers column A through column I.

10. Save the workbook, and then close it.

Microsoft Excel 2013, Comprehensive   REF 1

GLOSSARY/INDEX

SPECIAL CHARACTERS
\ (backslash), FM 11
< (left angle bracket), EX 172
> (right angle bracket), EX 172
(pound sign), EX 24, EX 84, EX 150
* (asterisk), EX 32
+ (plus sign), EX 32
- (minus sign), EX 32
/ (forward slash), EX 32
= (equal sign), EX 30, EX 172
^ (caret), EX 32
_ (underscore), EX 397
. (dot), FM 16

A

absolute reference A cell reference that remains fixed when the cell formula is copied to a new location. EX 133, EX 154, EX 159

Accept or Reject Changes dialog box, EX 736

accepting an edit, EX 735–737

Accounting format The number format that places a currency symbol at the left edge of the column, adds a thousands separator to the value, and shows two decimal places; lines up numbers within a column by their currency symbols and decimal points; negative numbers are enclosed in parentheses. EX 68, EX 82–84

active cell The cell currently selected in the active worksheet. EX 2
    changing, EX 10

active sheet The sheet currently displayed in the workbook window. EX 2
    changing, EX 8–9

ActiveCell object, EX C13

ActiveChart object, EX C13

ActiveSheet object, EX C13

ActiveWindow object, EX C13

ActiveWorkbook object, EX C13

Add Chart Element button, EX 203

Add Constrain dialog box, EX 638

Add Procedure dialog box, EX C8

add-in A program that adds customized commands and features to Microsoft Office programs such as Excel. EX 634. *See also* Solver
    turning a workbook into, EX C28

addition operator (+), EX 32

advanced filtering A filter that displays a subset of the rows in an Excel table or range of data that match the criteria specified in the criteria range. EX B2–B8
    criteria range, EX B3–B8

Align Left button, EX 87

Align Right button, EX 87

aligning cell content, EX 87

alignment button, EX 87

amortization schedule A table that provides the schedule of payments used to repay a loan. EX 531, EX 540–547
    calculating cumulative interest and principal payments, EX 543–545
    calculating interest and principal payments, EX 541–543

AND function A logical function that returns a TRUE value if all of the logical conditions are true, and a FALSE value if any or all of the logical conditions are false. EX 464, EX 470–474

answer report A report created by Solver that summarizes the results of a successful solution by displaying information about the objective cell, changing cells, and constraints. EX 642–645

application. *See* Excel application; Visual Basic for Applications (VBA)

Application object, EX C12

Apply Names dialog box, EX 406

approximate match lookup A lookup where the lookup value falls within a range of numbers in the compare values in the lookup table. EX 176

Apps for Office window, EX 707

archive A special type of folder containing compressed files. FM 26

area chart, EX 199

argument The numbers, text, or cell references used by the function to return a value. EX 36, EX 133, EX 141

arithmetic operator An operator that performs addition, subtraction, multiplication, division, or exponentiation. EX 32–33

Arrange All button, EX 351

array formula A formula that performs multiple calculations in a single step, returning either a single value to one cell or multiple values to several cells. EX 615

arrow button, FM 2, FM 3, FM 11

ascending order The arrangement of text alphabetically from A to Z, numbers from smallest to largest, and dates from oldest to newest. EX 271

Assign Macro dialog box, EX 445–446

asterisk, (*) multiplication operator, EX 32

auditing a workbook, EX 580–586
    evaluating formulas, EX 583–585
    tracing errors, EX 581–583
    Watch Window, EX 585–586

AutoComplete The feature that displays text that begins with the same letters as a previous entry in the same column to help make entering repetitive text easier. EX 20

AutoFill A feature that copies content (text, values, or formulas) and formats from a cell or range into an adjacent cell or range. EX 162–166
    AutoFill Options button, EX 163
    fill handle, EX 162–163
    filling a series, EX 164–166

AutoFill Options button, EX 163

AutoFit The feature that changes the column width or row height to display longest or tallest entry within the column or row. EX 27

automatic page break A page break Excel sets automatically when the page of the printout is full. EX 97

automatic recalculation, EX 767

AutoSum The button that inserts functions to sum, average, or count values in a range, or find the minimum or maximum value in a range. EX 31, EX 36–39

AVERAGE function An Excel function that calculates the average value from a collection or numbers. EX 98–99, EX 141

AVERAGEIF function A function that calculates the average of values in a range that match criteria you specify. EX 504, EX 515–518

AVERAGEIFS function A function that calculates the average of values within a range that meet multiple criteria. EX B13–14, EX B16–B18

axis
    horizontal, EX 191
    primary, EX 222, EX 232–234
    secondary, EX 222, EX 232–234
    unit labels, EX 223
    vertical, EX 190

axis title Descriptive text that appears next to an axis. EX 219

B

background image, EX 77–78

backslash (\ ), file path, FM 11

Backstage view The FILE tab of the ribbon, which provides access to various screens that allow you to manage files and Excel options. EX 4

backup A duplicate copy of a file. FM 25

bar chart A column chart turned on its side so that the length of each bar is proportional to its value. EX 199, EX 200, EX 211

bind The process by which an XML element is attached to a specific cell in the workbook. EX 714–715

binding constraint A constraint that must be included in the Solver model, and is a limiting factor in arriving at the solution. EX 644

border A line you can add along an edge of cell that prints. EX 30
    cells, EX 88–90

borrowing cost, calculating with PMT function, EX 532–534

Bottom Align button, EX 87

break-even analysis Another term for cost-volume-profit (CVP) analysis, a branch of financial analysis that studies the relationship between expenses, sales volume, and profitability. EX 600–603

break-even point The point where total revenue equals total expenses. EX 597, EX 600–603
    directly calculating, EX 608
    finding with what-if analysis, EX 601–603

broken link A reference to a file that has been moved since the link was created. EX 365

C

CA. *See* certificate authority

calculated column A column in an Excel table in which a formula entered or edited in one cell of the column is automatically copied into to all cells in that column. EX 465
    inserting in Excel tables, EX 467

calculated field, PivotTable reports, EX 316

caret (^), exponentiation operator, EX 32

cash flow An indicator of the direction of money to and from an individual or company. EX 533

cash inflow Another term for positive cash flow, where a positive value represents money coming to the investor. EX 530

cash outflow Another term for negative cash flow, where a negative value represents money going away from the investor. EX 531

category axis. *See* horizontal axis

Category field A field that groups the values in a PivotTable; appears in a PivotTable as a row label, a column label, and a report filter. EX 298

category value The group or category that a series values belong to. EX 190

cell The intersection of a row and a column. EX 3
    content. *See* cell content
    copying, EX 40–41
    defined names. *See* defined name
    formatting. *See* formatting worksheet cells
    formatting text, EX 70–75
    highlighting. *See* highlighting cells
    locking and unlocking, EX 420–421
    moving, EX 40–41
    in other worksheets, referencing, EX 339–341
    styles, EX 99–101

cell border, worksheets, EX 50

cell content
    editing, EX 19–20
    formatting, EX 71

cell highlighting A conditional format that changes a cell's font color or fill color based on the cell's value. EX 97, EX 108–113, EX D7–9
    based on values, EX 109–110
    with top/bottom rule, EX 110–112

cell range (range) A group of cells in a rectangular block.
    copying, EX 40–42
    defined names. *See* defined name
    deleting, EX 46–48
    inserting, EX 46–48
    moving, EX 40–42
    in other worksheets, referencing, EX 339–341
    selecting, EX 11–13

cell reference The column and row location that identifies a cell within a worksheet. EX 9, EX 152–159
    absolute, EX 133, EX 154, EX 159
    changing in formulas, EX 156–157
    external, EX 350
    mixed, EX 154–155, EX 159
    planning which to use in a formula, EX 157–159
    relative, EX 133, EX 152–153, EX 159

cell style Predefined formatting options that you can apply to cells in a worksheet. EX 97
    custom, EX D2–4

Center button, EX 87

certificate authority (CA) A third-party source from which you can obtain a digital certificate; the CA verifies signatures and tracks those that have expired or been revoked. EX 754

Change your view button, FM 2

changing cell An input cell whose value is changed within each scenario. EX 617

Charms bar, FM 4

chart (graph) A visual representation of a set of data values. EX 190
    axes. *See* axis
    changing and formatting title, EX 214–215
    changing type, EX 214
    chart design theory, EX 245
    colors, EX 208
    columns. *See* chart column
    communicating effectively using, EX 217

    copying and pasting formats, EX 234
    creating, EX 197–203
    data markers. *See* data marker
    editing scale of vertical axis, EX 222–223
    elements. *See* chart element
    embedded, EX 190
    formatting labels, EX 207–208
    formatting legend, EX 205–206
    gridlines, EX 223–224
    inserting with Quick Analysis tool, EX 200–202
    moving and resizing, EX 202–203
    moving to different worksheet, EX 214
    selecting data source, EX 198
    styles, EX 204–205
    types and subtypes, EX 199–200, EX 237
    what-if-analysis using, EX 210–211

chart animation A slowed down effect of changing data source values, making it easier to see how changing one value affects the chart. EX 210

chart area The chart and all of the other chart elements. EX 190
    formatting, EX 209–210

chart column, width, EX 224–225

chart element An individual part of a chart, such as the title or the legend. EX 191
    overlaying, EX 229

Chart object, EX C12
    methods, EX C15
    properties, EX C14

chart sheet A sheet that contains only a chart that provides a visual representation of worksheet data. EX 7

Chart Styles gallery, EX 204

chart subtype A variation of a chart type. EX 199–200

chart title A descriptive label or name for the chart area. EX 191
    changing and formatting, EX 214–215

CHART TOOLS DESIGN tab
    Add Chart Element button, EX 203
    Chart Styles gallery, EX 204
    Move Chart button, EX 197
    Select Data button, EX 237

CHART TOOLS FORMAT tab
    Chart Elements tab, EX 209
    Size group, EX 214

CHART TOOLS tab, EX 191, EX 202
    formatting buttons, EX 207

ChartObject object, EX C12

Charts object, method, EX C15

Check for Issues button, EX 741–743

Choose a SmartArt Graphic dialog box, EX D16–17

Circle Invalid Data command, EX 419

clearing To remove the data from a row or column but leave the blank row or column in the worksheet; also to remove, such as a filter. EX 45, EX 281
    conditional formats, EX 112

Clipboard A temporary storage area for files and information that you have copied or moved from one place and plan to use somewhere else. EX 35, FM 21
    moving files, FM 22–23

closing a workbook, EX 13

closing tag The XML tag that marks the end of a data value. EX 701

cloud Folders located on the Internet. EX 728
    sharing workbooks on, EX 741–743

clustered column chart A column chart that displays the data values in separate columns side-by-side. EX 212–124

Code window The window in the Visual Basic Editor that displays the VBA macro code associated with the selected item in Project Explorer. EX C3

collection object An object that contains a collection of Excel objects. EX C12

color
    custom, EX 74
    enhancing workbooks, EX 76
    fill, changing, EX 76–77
    fonts, EX 73–74
    pie chart slices, EX 208
    standard, EX 73
    themes, EX 73, EX D25–27

color scale A conditional format in which the fill color is based on a range of cell values where larger values have progressively darker or lighter shades of color. EX D10–13

column break The point at which one column ends and another begins. EX 664
    editing, EX 664–665

column chart A chart that displays data values as columns with the height of each column proportional to its value. EX 199, EX 200, EX 211–216
    changing and formatting title, EX 214–215
    clustered, EX 212–214
    moving to different worksheet, EX 214
    100% stacked, EX 212
    stacked, EX 212, EX 215–217
    subtypes, EX 212

column header A unique label that describes the contents of the data in a column; also called a field name. EX 259

column heading The letter along the top of the worksheet window that identifies the different columns in the worksheet. EX 3

column input cell The cell that references the input cell when the input values are placed in the first column of a data table. EX 605

COLUMNS area, PivotTables, EX 303

combination chart A chart that combines two or more Excel chart types into a single graph. EX 219
    creating, EX 230–234

combo chart, EX 199

Comma style The number format that adds a thousands separator to numbers, adds two decimal places, and lines up values within a column by their decimal points. EX 69, EX 84–85

comment A text box that is attached to a specific cell in a worksheet in which you can enter notes. EX 409, EX 425–427
    shared workbooks, reviewing, EX 731–733
    VBA, EX C7

compare values The categories used for matching to a specified lookup value in a lookup table. EX 160

comparing workbooks, EX 737–740

comparison operator A symbol that indicates the relationship between two values. EX 172, EX C26

Compatibility Checker A dialog box that alerts you to any features that are not supported by earlier versions of Excel when you save a workbook in an earlier format. EX 745, EX A17–A18

Compatibility Mode The mode that keeps a workbook in the older file format, which has the .xls file extension, making the workbook accessible for users who do not have the current version of Excel installed. EX A2

compressed file, FM 26–28
    compressing files and folders, FM 26, 27
    extracting, FM 26, FM 27–28
compressed folder A folder that stores files in a format that requires less disk space. FM 2
Computer icon, FM 3
CONCATENATE function A text function that joins, or concatenates, two or more text values. EX A7–A8
conditional count A function that calculates the number of cells in a range that match criteria you specify. EX 504, EX 512–514
conditional format Formatting applied to a cell when its value meets a specified condition. EX 108, EX 506–511, EX D7–16
    applying using formulas, EX D15–16
    clearing, EX 112
    color scales, EX D10–13
    creating a formula to conditionally format cells, EX 511
    effective use, EX 113
    evaluating data, EX 506
    highlighting cells, EX 108–113, EX D7–9
    highlighting duplicate values, EX 506–508
    icon sets, EX D13–15
    legend, EX 112–113
    modifying conditional formatting rules, EX D9–10
conditional formatting rule A rule that specifies the condition, the formatting, and the cell or range to apply the rule to. EX 504
    editing, EX 508–510
Conditional Formatting Rules Manager dialog box, EX 508–510
conditional statement A command that runs only when specified conditions are met. EX C25–27
conditional sum A function that adds the values in a range that match criteria you specify. EX 504, EX 514–515
connecting to a text file, EX 661
connection A defined process for retrieving data from an external file. EX 659
Connection properties dialog box, EX 671
consolidating data, EX 717
constant A value in a formula that doesn't change. EX 135–138
    deciding where to place, EX 136
constraint A limit that is placed on the solution to a set of possible values. EX 631
    adding to Solver, EX 637–642
Convert Text to Columns Wizard, EX A8–A10
Copy command, FM 21
Copy to button, FM 21
copying
    cells, EX 40–41
    formats. See copying formats
    formulas, EX 35–36
    ranges, EX 40–42
    styles, from one template to another, EX 379
    worksheets, EX 336–338
copying (file) To place a file in a new location that you specify without removing it from its current location. FM 20
    in File Explorer, FM 20–21, FM 24–25
copying and pasting
    chart formats, EX 234
    data, EX 756
    external reference formulas, EX 359–360
    sub procedures, EX C7–9

copying formats
    Format Painter, EX 101–103
    Paste Options button, EX 103–104
    Paste Special, EX 104
cost of goods sold. See cost of sales
cost of sales Any expenses directly related to production; also referred to as cost of goods sold. EX 548
    calculating, EX 553–555
cost-volume-profit (CVP) analysis A branch of financial analysis that studies the relationship between expenses, sales volume, and profitability; sometimes called break-even analysis. EX 598–603
    break-even point, EX 600–603
    comparing expenses and revenue, EX 598–600
cost-volume-profit (CVP) chart A chart that graphs revenue and total expenses against sales volume; the point where the two lines cross is the break-even point. EX 600
    one-variable data table, EX 607
    two-variable data table, EX 612–615
COUNT function The Excel function that tallies how many cells in specified range contain numbers or dates. EX 42–43, EX 141, EX 160
COUNTA function A function that tallies how many cells in specified range are not blank (contain numbers, dates, or text). EX 141, EX 160, EX 170–172
COUNTIF function (conditional count) A function that calculates the number of cells in a range that match criteria you specify. EX 504, EX 512–514
COUNTIFS function A function that counts the number of cells within a range that meet multiple criteria. EX B13, EX B14–B15
Create New Theme Fonts dialog box, EX D26
Create PivotTable dialog box, EX 301–302
Create Relationship dialog box, EX 696
criteria filter Conditions you specify for a filter. EX 282–285
criteria range An area in a worksheet, separate from a range of data or an Excel table, used to specify the criteria for the data to be displayed after a filter is applied to the range or Excel table. EX B3–B8
Cube function, EX 140
Currency format The number format that places a currency symbol directly to the left of the first digit of the currency value, adds a thousands separator to the value, and shows two decimal places; lines up numbers within a column by their decimal points; negative numbers are displayed with a negative sign. EX 82
Custom AutoFilter dialog box, EX 283–284
custom cell style A cell style created by the user that can be applied to cells in the workbook. EX D2–4
custom color, EX 74
custom format A format and style you create to accommodate a specific requirement. EX A14–A17
    dates, EX A16–A17
    numbers, EX A14–A16
custom function, EX C27–28
custom list The sequence you specify to sort data. EX 274–275
Custom Lists dialog box, EX 274–275
custom template A workbook template you create that is ready to run with the formulas for all calculations included as well as all formatting and labels. EX 376–379
custom theme, saving, EX D27–28
Cut command, FM 21
CVP. See cost-volume-profit analysis; cost-volume-profit chart

D
data
    existing, validating, EX 412
    structured range, EX 260–262
data bar A conditional format that adds a horizontal bar to the background of a cell proportional in length to the cell's value. EX 218
    creating, EX 242–244
    modifying data bar rules, EX 243–244
data callout A data label that appears as a callout bubble pointing to a data marker. EX 219
data connection, EX 669–673
    modifying properties, EX 670–673
    saving, EX 688
    viewing, EX 669–670
data definition table Documentation that lists the fields to be maintained for each record, a description of the information each field will include, and the type of data stored in each field. EX 261
data form, data entry, EX 450
data label Text associated with an individual data marker. EX 190
    formatting, EX 207–208
data marker A graphical representation of a value in a chart, such as a column or pie slice. EX 191
    formatting, EX 225–227
data model A database built into Excel that provides many of the same tools found in database programs such as Access. EX 692–699
    adding tables, EX 693–694
    managing relationships, EX 695–699
    viewing, EX 694–695
data security, EX 673
data series The range that contains the values plotted on a chart. EX 190
data source A range that contains the data displayed in a chart, or any file that contains the data you want to retrieve. EX 190, EX 660–661
    connecting to, EX 681
    editing, EX 234–237
    moving, EX 675
    PivotTable cells, displaying, EX 312
    selecting, EX 198
data storage, EX 718
data table. See one-variable data table; two-variable data table
Data Table dialog box, EX 606
data type, determining, EX C28
data validation A set of rules that determine what users can enter in a specific cell or range. EX 408–419
    Circle Invalid Data command, EX 419
    error alert style and message, EX 412–413
    input messages, EX 413–414
    list validation rules, EX 414–418
    specifying validation criteria, EX 410–412
    testing data validation rules, EX 418–419
Data Validation dialog box, EX 411, EX 412–414, EX 415–416, EX 417–418
database A file that stores a collection of data values organized in a way that they can be easily retrieved and manipulated. EX 676–699
    data model. See data model
    designing, EX 699
    queries. See query
    relational, EX 676, EX 680
    tables. See table

Database function (Dfunction) A function that performs summary data analysis, such as sum, average, or count, on an Excel table or data range based on criteria specified in a criteria range. EX 140, EX B9–B12

database relationship A connection between different tables that is made when fields common to each table are used to match a record from one table to a record from another table. EX 679
  managing, EX 695–699

date, formatting, EX 86
  custom formats, EX A16–A17

Date & Time function, EX 140

date data A value in a recognized date format. EX 17
  entering, EX 17, EX 22–24
  international date formats, EX 23

DATE function, EX 167

date function A function that inserts or calculates dates and times. EX 166–169

DATEDIF function A function that calculates the difference between two dates and shows the result in months, days, or years. EX 474

DAVERAGE function, EX B9, EX B10–B12

DAY function, EX 167

DB function The financial function to calculate the declining balance depreciation in which the asset depreciates by a constant percentage. EX 549, EX 559, EX 562

DCOUNT function, EX B9

DCOUNTA function, EX B9

DDB function, EX 562

declining balance depreciation The depreciation of an asset by a constant percentage each year rather than a constant amount. EX 558–562

Decrease Indent button, EX 87

defined name (range name) A word or string of characters assigned to a cell or range. EX 391, EX 394–401
  creating by selection, EX 397–398
  creating using Name box, EX 395–396
  deleting, EX 398–399
  editing, EX 398–399
  formulas, EX 400–407
  Paste Names command, EX 399–400
  selecting cells and ranges by, EX 396–397

deleting. *See also* removing
  defined names, EX 398–399
  files and folders, FM 25
  ranges, EX 46–48
  records in tables, EX 270
  worksheets, EX 17

deleting To remove the data from a row or column as well as the row or column itself. EX 45
  columns, EX 44, EX 45
  rows, EX 44, EX 45

delimit To separate; for example, data with a character such as a tab, a semicolon, a column, or a space. EX *–A10

delimited text A text file in which a special character such as a space, comma, or tab marks the beginning of each column. EX 658

delimiter A symbol-usually a space, a comma, or a tab-that separates one column of data from another in a text file. EX 662

dependent cell A cell whose value depends on the value in the active cell for its result. EX 567

depreciation The process of allocating the original cost of an asset over the lifetime of the asset. EX 548, EX 557–563
  adding to income statement, EX 563
  choosing method, EX 562
  declining balance, EX 558–562
  straight-line, EX 558

descending order The arrangement of text in reverse alphabetical order from Z to A, numbers from largest to smallest, and dates from newest to oldest. EX 271

DESIGN tab, EX 202

desktop, Windows 8 and Windows 7 compared, FM 4

destination file The file that displays data from a source file, such as the workbook that receives data from another workbook when two workbooks are linked; sometimes referred to as the dependent file. EX 350, EX 756
  updating with source workbook closed, EX 363–364
  updating with source workbook open, EX 361–362

Details pane The pane in Windows Explorer that displays the characteristics of the folder or selected object. FM 2

Dfunction A function that performs summary data analysis, such as sum, average, or count, on an Excel table or data range based on criteria specified in a criteria range. EX 140, EX B9–B12

digital certificate An attachment to a document that authenticates the source of a digital signature. EX 754–756

digital ID. *See* digital certificate

digital signature An electronic version of a signature that provides a way to authenticate a workbook; also called a digital certificate. EX 433

discount rate Another term for rate of return, an interest rate that compares the value of current dollars to future dollars from a series of cash flows. EX 566

disk A computer device for storing data. FM 5

displaying. *See also* viewing
  data source for a PivotTable cell, EX 312

#DIV/0! error value, EX 151

division operator (/), EX 32

DMAX function, EX B9

DMIN function, EX B9

Document Inspector A feature that checks a workbook for hidden properties or personal information and then removes them, if necessary. EX 744, EX 748–752

document property Descriptive detail about a workbook, including its author, title, and subject; also called metadata. EX 745
  setting, EX 746–748

documenting
  formulas, EX 135
  spreadsheets, EX 427

dot (.), filenames, FM 16

drag and drop The technique to move a cell or range by selecting it, dragging the selection by its bottom border to a new location, and then releasing the mouse button to drop the selection in the new location. EX 40–41

dragging, moving files, FM 21–22

drive A computer device that can retrieve and sometimes record data on a disk. FM 6

DSTDEV function, EX B9

DSUM function, EX B9

duplicate values, highlighting, EX 506–508

E

Edit Formatting Rule dialog box, EX 244, EX 509, EX D11

Edit Links dialog box, EX 365–366

Edit mode The mode in which you can edit cell contents. EX 19–20

Edit Name dialog box, EX 399

editing
  accepting and rejecting edits in shared workbooks, EX 735–737
  cell content, EX 19–20
  chart data sources, EX 234–37
  column breaks, EX 664–665
  defined names, EX 398–399
  effects on macros, EX 439
  external data range properties, EX 668–669
  external reference formulas, EX 358–359
  grouped worksheets, EX 334
  macros, EX 441, EX 443–444
  pictures, EX D21–22
  queries, EX 686–688
  records in tables, EX 269
  scale of vertical axis, EX 222–223
  shared workbooks, EX 741
  sparklines, EX 239
  stacked column charts, EX 216
  XML files, EX 713

element The unit that stores a piece of data in an XML document. EX 701

embedded chart A chart object placed in a worksheet. EX 190

embedded object An object that is stored within the destination file. EX 757

embedding Excel objects in other Office applications, EX 760–763

Encapsulated PostScript (EPS) Written in the PostScript language, provide perhaps the highest quality format for clip art files, but require access to a PostScript printer to view the results. EX D24

encryption The process by which a file is encoded so that it cannot be opened without the proper password. EX 752
  workbooks, EX 752–753

Engineering function, EX 140

EPS. *See* Encapsulated PostScript

equal sign (=)
  comparison operators, EX 172
  formulas, EX 30

error
  formulas, finding and fixing, EX 486
  logical, EX C22
  macros, fixing, EX 441
  run-time, EX C22
  syntax, EX C22
  tracing, EX 581–583

error alert A message that appears if a user tries to enter a value in a cell that does not meet the validation rule. EX 409
  style and message, creating, EX 412–413

error value A message in a cell that indicates some part of a formula is preventing Excel from returning a calculated value. EX 150–152
  deciding when to correct, EX 151

Evaluate Formula dialog box, EX 584

exact match lookup A lookup where the lookup value must match one of the compare values in the lookup table. EX 176

Excel. *See* Microsoft Excel 2013

Excel add-in, EX 635. *See also* Solver

Excel application A spreadsheet written or tailored to meet specific needs; typically includes reports and charts, a data entry area, a custom interface, as well as instructions and documentation. EX 389–452
    data validation. *See* data validation
    defined names in formulas, EX 400–407
    macros. *See* macro
    naming cells and ranges, EX 394–400
    planning, EX 392–394
    protection. *See* workbook protection; worksheet protection

Excel Help, EX 6

Excel Object Model The hierarchy that VBA uses to organize objects and object collections, with the Excel application at the top and the individual cells of a workbook at the bottom. EX C13

Excel Options dialog box, EX 430–431

Excel table A range of related data that is managed independently from other data in the worksheet. EX 258–275
    adding records, EX 268–269
    calculated columns, EX 467
    creating, EX 264–266
    creating fields, EX 467
    creating formulas using structured references, EX 477–480
    deleting records, EX 270
    editing records, EX 269
    filtering. *See* filter
    filtering data. *See* filter
    finding records, EX 269
    modifying, EX 266–267
    renaming, EX 266
    saving time using, EX 264
    sorting data, EX 271–275
    structured range of data, EX 260–262

expense
    fixed, EX 549, EX 599
    mixed, EX 599–600
    variable, EX 598

exploded pie chart A pie chart that moves one slice away from the others as if someone were taking the piece away from the pie. EX 209

exponentiation operator (^), EX 32

Extensible Markup Language (XML) A language that structures data in text files that can be read by a wide variety of programs, including Excel. EX 701
    importing data from. *See* importing data from XML
    XML data map, EX 701

extension The three of four characters that follow the dot in a filename and identify the file's type. FM 16

external data, refreshing, EX 670

external data range A cell range containing data retrieved from an external data source. EX 668–673
    data connections, EX 669–673
    editing properties, EX 668–669

external data source, EX 660–661

external reference A reference to cells or ranges in a worksheet from another workbook. EX 350
    formulas, creating, EX 355–360

extract To create an uncompressed copy of a compressed file in a folder you specify. FM 26, FM 27–28

extrapolation The process used to extend series from a single value or a few values to project future values. EX 549, EX 555–557

F

field A single piece of data that describes a characteristic of a person, place, or thing (such as a last name, a city, or a project); each column in an Excel table or structured range of data represents a field. EX 259
    adding to FILTERS area, EX 308–309
    adding to PivotTables, EX 303–305
    calculated, adding to PivotTable reports, EX 316
    choosing for query, EX 681–682
    Excel tables, creating, EX 467
    PivotTable, filtering, EX 309–310

field Information about a specific characteristic of a person, place, or thing. EX 677

field name A unique label that describes the contents of the data in a column; also called a column header. EX 259

file A collection of data that has a name and is stored on a computer. FM 5
    backup copy, FM 25
    compressed, FM 2, FM 26–28
    copying, FM 20–21, FM 24–25
    deleting, FM 25
    determining where to store, FM 8
    moving, FM 20–24
    multiple, selecting, FM 24
    opening, FM 15–16
    organizing files, FM 6–8
    saving, FM 16–18

File Explorer A Windows 8 tool that displays the contents of your computer and uses icons to represent drives, folders, and files. FM 3, FM 8–14
    changing views, FM 12–13
    compressed files, FM 26–28
    copying files and folders, FM 20–21, FM 24–25
    creating folders, FM 19–20
    deleting files and folders, FM 25
    expanding ribbon, FM 13–14
    moving files and folders, FM 20–24
    navigating to data files, FM 10–12
    opening, FM 10
    opening files, FM 15–16
    panes, FM 8
    renaming files, FM 26
    saving files, FM 16–18

file icon An icon that indicates a file's type. FM 3

file path A notation that indicates a file's location. FM 2, FM 3, FM 10–12

file system An operating system's hierarchy of folders and files, which ensures system stability and enables Windows to find files quickly. FM 6, FM 7

filename The name of a file; provides important information about the file, including its contents and purpose. FM 3, FM 16–17

fill color A background color that can be added to cells to help differentiate parts of a worksheet or highlight data. EX 69
    changing, EX 76–77

Fill Effects dialog box, EX D12

fill handle A small black square in the lower-right corner of a selected cell or range that you drag over an adjacent cell or range to copy the original content and formatting into the selected range. EX 162–163

filter The process of displaying a subset of rows in an Excel table or structured range of data that meets the specified criteria. EX 210, EX 276–297
    clearing filters, EX 281
    criteria filters, EX 282–285
    date filters, EX 282
    finding appropriate data, EX 283
    number filters, EX 282
    PivotTables, EX 308–312
    queries, EX 683–685
    selecting multiple filter items, EX 281–282
    slicers, EX 285–287
    text filters, EX 280, EX 282
    using multiple columns, EX 280–281
    using one column, EX 278–280

FILTERS area
    adding fields, EX 308–309
    PivotTables, EX 303

financial function, EX 140, EX 192–197. *See also specific functions*

Find and Replace dialog box, EX 104–106

Find command, EX 97

finding
    matches. *See* HLOOKUP function; lookup function; VLOOKUP function
    records in tables, EX 269

finding and replacing text and formats, EX 104–106

fixed expense An expense not directly related to production that must be paid regardless of sales volume; another term for general expense. EX 548, EX 599

fixed-width format A text file in which each column starts at the same location in the file. EX 659, EX 662

Flash Fill The feature that enters text based on patterns it finds in the data. EX 48–49

folder A container for files and subfolders. FM 5
    backup copy, FM 25
    copying, FM 20–21, FM 24–25
    creating, FM 19–20
    deleting, FM 25
    moving, FM 20–24
    multiple, selecting, FM 24
    organizing folders, FM 6–8

font A set of characters that employ the same typeface, such as Arial, Times New Roman, and Courier. EX 68
    color, EX 73–74
    non-theme, EX 71
    sans serif, EX 71
    serif, EX 71
    themes, EX 71, EX D25–27

font size The size of text. EX 30
    changing, EX 51

font style Formats that can applied to a font such as italic, bold, bold italic, underline, strikethrough, and color. EX 68

footer Information that appears at the bottom of each printed page. EX 119–121

Footer dialog box, EX 121

format, numbers, international, EX 768–770

Format button, EX 48

Format Cells dialog box, EX 92–95, EX 420–421, EX 611

format code A series of symbols used to describe exactly how Excel should display a number, date, time, or text string. EX 14, EX 16

Format Painter A feature that copies and pastes formatting from one cell or range to another without duplicating any data. EX 96, EX 101–103

Format pane An area that provides a collection of commands to format the selected chart element. EX 191

FORMAT tab, EX 202
    formatting buttons, EX 207

formatting Changes to a worksheet's appearance to make its content easier to read. EX 49, EX D1–28
    cell content, EX 71
    cell text, EX 70–75
    cells. *See* formatting worksheet cells
    chart area, EX 209–210
    chart columns, EX 224–225
    chart legends, EX 205–206
    chart titles, EX 214–215
    conditional. *See* conditional format; conditional formatting rule
    copying and pasting chart formats, EX 234
    copying formats. *See* copying formats
    custom cell styles, EX D2–4
    custom formats. *See* custom format
    custom table styles, EX D4–6
    data labels, EX 207–208
    data markers, EX 225–227
    finding and replacing formats, EX 104–106
    incoming data from text files, EX 665–668
    monetary values, EX 83
    numbers, EX 82–86
    percentages, EX 85–86
    PivotTables, EX 306–308
    for printing. *See* formatting worksheets for printing
    SmartArt graphics. *See* SmartArt graphics
    sparkline axes, EX 240
    special, EX A13
    text selections, EX 75
    themes. *See* theme
    workbooks, EX 70
    worksheet cells. *See* formatting worksheet cells
    worksheet groups, EX 334–335
    worksheets, EX 49–51. *See also* formatting worksheets for printing

formatting worksheet cells, EX 87–92
    adding borders, EX 88–90
    aligning cell content, EX 87
    indenting cell content, EX 88
    merging cells, EX 90–91
    rotating cell contents, EX 91–92

formatting worksheets for printing, EX 114–122
    adding print titles, EX 117–119
    defining print area, EX 115–116
    headers and footers, EX 119–121
    inserting page breaks, EX 116–117
    Page Break Preview, EX 114–115
    setting page margins, EX 121–122

formula A mathematical expression that returns a value. EX 31
    applying conditional formatting using, EX D15–16
    calculating sales data, EX 78–82
    checking for matching parentheses, EX 489
    constants, EX 135–138
    copying and pasting, EX 35–36
    creating, to conditionally format cells, EX 511
    creating using structured references, EX 477–480

    defined names, EX 400–407
    documenting, EX 135
    entering, EX 32–34
    evaluating, EX 583–585
    external references, EX 355–360
    finding and fixing errors, EX 486
    operators, EX 32–33
    recalculation options, EX 767
    with references to another worksheet, EX 339–340
    referencing function results, EX 149–150
    simplifying with functions, EX 36–40
    with 3-D references, copying, EX 345–346
    viewing, EX 56–57
    worksheet groups, EX 332–334

formula bar The bar located below the ribbon that displays the value or formula entered in the active cell. EX 2

forward slash (/), division operator, EX 32

freeze The process of keeping rows and/or columns you select visible as you scroll the worksheet. EX 262–263

function A named operation that replaces the action of an arithmetic expression in a formula. EX 31, EX 36–40, EX 132, EX 140–150. *See also specific functions*
    calculating sales data, EX 78–82
    categories, EX 140
    custom, EX C27–28
    effective, EX 40
    entering with AutoSum, EX 36–39
    entering with Insert Function dialog box, EX 145–149
    entering with Quick Analysis tool, EX 142–145
    financial, EX 140, EX 192–197. *See also specific functions*
    lookup. *See* HLOOKUP function; lookup function; VLOOKUP function
    referencing results in formulas, EX 149–150
    summarizing data conditionally, EX 511–518
    syntax, EX 36, EX 141–142
    Text, EX 140, EX A3–A13

Function Arguments dialog box, EX 132, EX 133, EX 146–147, EX 168–169, EX 174, EX 178, EX 194–195
    AVERAGEIF function, EX 516–518
    COUNTIF function, EX 513
    COUNTIFS function, EX B14–B15
    DAVERAGE function, EX B11
    AND function, EX 473
    IF function, EX 465, EX 469–470, EX 473, EX 479
    nested IF functions, EX 488
    OR function, EX 479
    SUMIF function, EX 515
    SUMIFS function, EX B16

function procedure A procedure that returns a value and is used to create custom functions that can be used within a worksheet. EX C6

future value, calculating with FV function, EX 534–536

FV function The financial function to calculate the future value of a loan or an investment. EX 192, EX 197, EX 530, EX 534–536

G

gallery A menu or grid that shows a visual representation of the options available or the selected button. EX 70

GB. *See* gigabyte

general expense An expense that is not directly related to production; also called fixed expense. EX 548

General format The number format that, for the most part, displays values exactly as they are typed. EX 82

gesture, FM 4–5

gigabyte (GB) 1 billion bytes of data. FM 6

Go To dialog box, EX 10–11

Goal Seek A feature that automates the trial-and-error method by allowing you to specify a value for the calculated item, which Excel uses to determine the input value needed to reach that goal. EX 180–181

graph. *See* chart

gridline A line that extends the value of a major or minor tick mark across the plot area of a chart. EX 30, EX 219
    adding to charts, EX 223–224

gross profit The difference between a company's sales revenue and the cost of goods sold. EX 553–554

group A collection of buttons for related commands on a ribbon tab. EX 3

Group button, EX 241

grouped sparklines A set of sparklines that share a common format. EX 219, EX 240–242

grouping worksheets. *See* worksheet; worksheet group

growth trend A series in which values change by a constant percentage. EX 549, EX 550–551, EX 552–553

H

hard disk A storage device permanently housed inside the computer case. FM 6

header Information that appears at the top of each printed page. EX 119–121

Header dialog box, EX 120

header row The first row of the range or Excel table that contains field names. EX 258

heading, worksheet groups, EX 332–334

hiding To make a row, column, or worksheet not visible. EX 48

Highlight Changes dialog box, EX 734

highlighting
    cells. *See* cell highlighting
    duplicate values, EX 506–508

HLOOKUP function A lookup function that searches across the first row of the lookup table until the lookup value exactly matches a value in the first row, and then retrieves the corresponding value from the second row of the lookup table. EX 483, EX 489
    finding exact matches, EX 497–500

HOME tab
    Cell Styles button, EX 108
    Format button, EX 48
    formatting buttons, EX 207

horizontal axis (category axis) The axis that displays the category values from each data series. EX 191

hyperlink A link in a file, such as a workbook, to information within that file or another file. EX 368–372
    editing, EX 372
    hyperlinks, EX 372
    inserting, EX 370–372

I

icon, Windows 8 and Windows 7 compared, FM 4

icon set A conditional format in which different icons are displayed in a cell based on the cell's value. EX D13–15

IF function The logical function that tests a condition and then returns one value if the condition is true and another value if the condition is false. EX 161, EX 172–176, EX 467–470

IF Function Arguments dialog box, EX 404

IFERROR function A function that can determine if a cell contains an error value and then display the message you choose rather than the default error value. EX 482, EX 500–502

image
    background, EX 77–78
    inserting from image files, EX D18
    SmartArt. *See* SmartArt graphic

Immediate window, EX C19

Import Data dialog box, EX 684–685

importing data from multiple tables into a PivotTable, EX 689–692

importing data from text files, EX 661–668
    connecting to text files, EX 661
    editing column breaks, EX 664–665
    formatting and trimming incoming data, EX 665–668
    specifying starting row, EX 664
    starting Text Import Wizard, EX 663
    text file formats, EX 662

importing data from XML, EX 711–717
    binding XML elements to a worksheet, EX 714–715
    editing XML files, EX 713
    loading XML data maps, EX 713–714

income statement A document that shows how much money a person or business makes or loses over a specified period of time; also called a profit and loss statement. EX 548, EX 550
    adding depreciation, EX 563
    adding taxes and interest expenses, EX 563–565

Increase Indent button, EX 87

indenting cell content, EX 88

inflation, calculating with FV function, EX 536

Information function, EX 140

input cell A cell that contains a value that is used in a formula of a what-if analysis. EX 596

input message A message that appears when the cell becomes active; can be used to specify the type of data the user should enter in that cell. EX 408
    creating, EX 413–414

input value A value in a data table that is based on input cells. EX 596

Insert Chart dialog box, EX 213

Insert Function button, EX 132

Insert Function dialog box, entering functions, EX 145–149

Insert Hyperlink dialog box, EX 368, EX 370–371

INSERT tab
    Charts group, EX 200
    Recommended Chart button, EX 197

inserting
    hyperlinks, EX 370–372
    objects, EX 763
    page breaks, EX 116–117
    screenshots, EX 758
    worksheet columns, EX 43–45
    worksheet rows, EX 43–45
    worksheets, EX 16

insignificant zero A zero whose omission from a number does not change the number's value. EX A14

INT function, EX 141

integrating Excel with other Office applications, EX 756–763
    copying and pasting data, EX 756
    inserting objects, EX 763
    object linking and embedding, EX 757–763

interest The amount added to the principal by the lender. EX 192
    adding to income statement, EX 563–565
    amortization schedule, EX 540–545

interest rate, calculating with RATE function, EX 568–569

internal rate of return (IRR) The return rate for a series of future cash flows that will result in a net present value of 0. EX 566, EX 574–579
    comparing investments, EX 577
    IRR function, EX 575–576

international client, workbook for, EX 768–772

international date format, EX 23

international symbol, EX 771

interpolation The process used to fill in a series when you know the starting and ending values of that series. EX 548, EX 555
    from starting value to ending value, EX 551–553

investment
    calculating borrowing costs with PMT function, EX 532–534
    calculating future value with FV function, EX 534–536
    calculating payment period with NPER function, EX 536–537
    calculating value, EX 575
    comparing using net present value and internal rate of return, EX 577
    payback period, EX 566, EX 569–571
    present value. *See* PV function

IPMT function The financial function to calculate the amount of a loan payment that is used to repay the interest. EX 192, EX 197, EX 530

IRR. *See* internal rate of return

IRR function The financial function to calculate the internal rate of return for an investment. EX 567, EX 575–576

iterative procedure The approach by which Solver starts with an initial solution (usually the current values from the worksheet) and uses that as a basis to calculate a new set of values to arrive at an optimal solution. EX 642

J

Joint Photographic Experts Group (JPEG) The most common picture format; can support up to 16.7 million colors and can be compressed to save file space without greatly affecting image quality. EX D24

K

Key Tip Label that appears over each tab and command on the ribbon when you press the Alt key that specifies the key or keys to click to access that tab, button, or command. EX 6

keyboard, Windows 8 and Windows 7 compared, FM 4

keyboard shortcut A key or combination of keys that you press to access a feature or perform a command. EX 6

L

landscape orientation The page orientation where the page is wider than it is tall. EX 53

Large icons view button, FM 3

layout
    PivotTables, EX 305–306
    reports, EX 306

leader line A line that connects a data label to its corresponding data marker. EX 207

left angle bracket (<), comparison operators, EX 172

LEFT function A text function that returns a specified number of characters from the beginning of a specified string. EX A4–A6

legend A key that identifies the colors or the shapes used in a worksheet or a chart. EX 112, EX 191
    conditional formatting, EX 112–113

LEN function A text function that returns the number of characters (length) of a specified string. EX A4–A6

library In File Explorer, a container for folders and files that organize files by category-documents, music, pictures, and videos, no matter where these files are stored, such as your hard disk, removable drives, and network. FM 2, FM 3

limits report A report created by Solver that is often used in science and engineering to investigate the mathematical aspects of the Solver solution. EX 642

line chart A chart that displays data values using a connected line rather than columns or bars. EX 199, EX 200, EX 219
    creating, EX 220–222, EX 235
    scatter charts compared, EX 221

linear trend A series in which values change by a constant amount. EX 549, EX 550–551, EX 552

link A connection between files that allows data to be transferred from one file to another. EX 350
    broken, EX 365
    linking workbooks, EX 352–361
    managing, EX 365–367

linked object An object that is stored within the destination file and remains connected to the source file. EX 757

linking Excel and otehr Office applications, EX 758–760

list, custom, EX 274–275

list validation rule, EX 414–418

Live Preview A preview of how a workbook would be affected by an option in a gallery. EX 70

loading
    Solver models, EX 645–648
    XML data maps, EX 713–714

loan
    amortization schgedule. *See* amortization schedule
    calculating borrowing costs with PMT function, EX 532–534
    calculating future value with FV function, EX 534–536
    calculating payment period with NPER function, EX 536–537
    present value. *See* PV function

locked property A setting that determines whether changes can be made to a cell. EX 420–421

logical condition An expression that returns either a TRUE value or a FALSE value. EX 464

logical error A programming error that occurs when a program is free of syntax errors and runs without failing, but produces results that are incorrect. EX C22

logical function A function that works with statements that are either true or false. EX 140, EX 161, EX 172–176, EX 464–481. *See also* AND function; IF function; OR function
    DATEDIF function, EX 474
    inserting calculated columns in Excel tables, EX 467

logical operator An operator that combines expressions within a condition. EX C27

Long Date format A format for dates that displays the day of the week and the full month in addition to the day of the month and the year. EX 86

Lookup & Reference function, EX 140

lookup function A function that finds a value in a table of data and inserts it in another location in the worksheet, such as a cell or in a formula. EX 160, EX 176–179, EX 489–500. *See also* HLOOKUP function; VLOOKUP function

lookup table A table that stores the data you want to retrieve with a lookup function in categories. EX 160

lookup value The category you want to find in a lookup table. EX 160

LOWER function, EX A4

M

macro A series of stored commands that can be run whenever you need to perform that task. EX 428–452
    automating tasks, EX 430–431
    creating, EX 439–441
    creating macro buttons, EX 444–450
    digital signature, EX 433
    editing, EX 441, EX 443–444
    effect of edits, EX 439
    fixing errors, EX 441
    opening workbooks with, EX 451–452
    planning, EX 434
    recording, EX 433–437
    running, EX 437–438
    saving workbooks with, EX 450–451
    security settings, EX 431–433
    sharing between workbooks, EX C25
    structure, EX 443
    Visual Basic Editor, EX 441–444

macro button, EX 428
    assigning sub procedures to, EX C11
    creating, EX 444–450
    pictures or shapes, EX 448

Macro dialog box, EX 428, EX 438

macro recorder, EX 428

macro security settings The settings that controls what Excel will do about macros in a workbook when you open that workbook. EX 428

macro virus A type of virus that uses a program's own macro programming language to distribute the virus. EX 431
    protecting against, EX 431–433

major tick mark Line that identifies the main units on a chart axis. EX 222

manual page break A page break you insert to indicate where a new page of the printout should start. EX 96

manual recalculation, EX 767

margin The space between the page content and the edges of the page. EX 121
    setting, EX 121–122

match, finding. *See* HLOOKUP function; lookup function; VLOOKUP function

Math & Trig function, EX 140

MAX function The function that displays the maximum value in a range. EX 132, EX 141

Maximize button The button that expands a window to fill the screen. EX 3

median The middle value in data. EX 145

MEDIAN function The function that determines the middle value in a range. EX 132, EX 141

Merge & Center button, EX 87

merging To combine, such as several cells into one cell. EX 68, EX 90–91
    workbooks, EX 737–740

metadata. *See* document property

method An action that can be performed on an object, such as closing a workbook or printing the contents of a worksheet. EX C15–16

Microsoft Excel 2013 (Excel) An application used to enter, analyze, and present quantitative data. EX 1
    compatibility of versions, EX A17–A18
    customizing, EX 764–767
    Excel applications. *See* Excel application
    integrating with other Office applications. *See* integrating Excel with other Office applications
    screen elements, EX 764–766
    starting, EX 4
    tables. *See* Excel table

Microsoft Excel - Compatibility Checker dialog box, EX 751

Microsoft Office Trusted Location dialog box, EX 674

Microsoft Query An application that creates queries to retrieve data from multiple database tables and stores the data values in an Excel workbook. EX 677, EX 680–688
    choosing tables and fields, EX 681–682
    connecting to data source, EX 681
    starting, EX 680

MID function, EX A4

Middle Align button, EX 87

MIN function The function that displays the minimum value in the range. EX 132, EX 141

Mini toolbar A toolbar that contains buttons to perform common formatting options for a selection. EX 75

Minimize button The button that hides a window so that only its program button is visible on the taskbar. EX 3

minor tick mark Line that identifies the smaller intervals between major tick marks on a chart axis. EX 222

minus sign (-), subtraction operator, EX 32

mixed expense An expense that is part variable and part fixed. EX 599

mixed reference A cell reference that contains both relative and absolute references; for example, the mixed reference for cell D2 can have an absolute row (such as $D$6) or an absolute column (such as $D$6). EX 154–155

Modify Table Style dialog box, EX D6

module In VBA, a collection of sub procedures. EX 443

monetary value, formatting, EX 83

MONTH function, EX 167

mouse interaction, FM 4–5

move (file) To remove a file from its current location and place it in a new location. FM 20
    in File Explorer, FM 20–24

Move Chart button, EX 197

Move to button, FM 21, FM 23–24

moving
    cells, EX 40–41
    charts, EX 202–203
    charts to different worksheet, EX 214
    data sources, EX 675
    ranges, EX 40–42
    SmartArt graphics, EX D23
    worksheets, EX 16
    multiple worksheets, EX 336–347
    copying worksheets, EX 336–338
    referencing cells and ranges in other worksheets, EX 339–341

multiplication operator (*), EX 32

N

#N/A error value, EX 151

Name box The box located at the left side of the formula bar that displays the cell reference of the active cell. EX 2

Name box, creating defined names, EX 395–396

#NAME? error value, EX 151

Name object, EX C12
    properties, EX C14

navigating
    to data files in File Explorer, FM 10–12
    multiple workbooks, EX 353–354
    worksheets, EX 9–11

navigation pane The left pane of the File Explorer window that provides access to resources and locations on your computer. FM 2, FM 3, FM 9

negative cash flow A negative value that represents money going away from the investor; also called cash outflow. EX 531

nested IF function One IF function placed inside another IF function to test an additional condition. EX 482, EX 484–489

nesting To place one thing inside another, such as a function inside another function. EX 142, EX 173

net present value The difference between the present value of an investment and the initial expenditure on that investment. EX 566, EX 571–574
    comparing investments, EX 577
    NPV function, EX 571–574
    rate of return, EX 572–574
    time value of money, EX 571

NETWORKDAYS function, EX 167

New Web Query dialog box, EX 703–704

nonadjacent range A collection of separate ranges. EX 2

nonbinding constraint A constraint that did not need to be included as part of the Solver model. EX 644

non-native file, importing in Excel, EX 692

non-theme font A font that is not associated with a particular theme; non-theme fonts retain their appearance no matter what theme is used with the workbook. EX 71

Normal view The Excel view that shows the contents of the active sheet in the workbook window. EX 31

NOW function, EX 167

NPER function The financial function to calculate the number of payments required to repay a loan or reach an investment goal. EX 192, EX 197, EX 531, EX 536–537

NPV function The financial function to calculate the present value of a series of future cash flows. EX 566, EX 571–574

#NULL! error value, EX 151

#NUM! error value, EX 151

number
    custom formats, EX A14–A16
    international formats, EX 768–770

numeric data Any number that can be used in a mathematical calculation. EX 17
    displaying as text, EX 21–22
    entering, EX 24–25
    formatting, EX 82–86

O

object Anything that appears on your screen that can be selected and manipulated, such as a table, a picture, a chart, a cell, a worksheet, or even Excel itself. EX 756
    collection, EX C12

embedded, EX 757
inserting, EX 763
linked, EX 757
properties. *See* property
special object names, EX C13
VBA, EX C12–13

Object linking and embedding (OLE) The technology used to copy and paste objects, such as graphic files, cell and ranges, or charts, so that information about the program that created the object is included with the object itself. EX 757–763

objective cell A result cell that Solver sets to a specified value or sets to its maximum or minimum possible value. EX 630, EX 635

object-oriented programming language A programming language, such as VBA, in which tasks are performed by manipulating objects. EX C12

Office app A small, specialized program that enhances the features of Excel, Word, PowerPoint, and other programs in the Office suite. EX 707–711
inserting, EX 707–708
retrieving data, EX 708–711

OLE. *See* Object linking and embedding

100% stacked column chart A column chart that places the data series values within combined columns showing what percentage is contributed by each series. EX 212

one-to-many relationship A connection between two database tables in which one record from the first table is matched to one or more records from the second table. EX 679

one-to-one relationship A connection between two database tables in which one record from the first table is matched to exactly one record from the second table. EX 679

one-variable data table A data table used to perform several what-if analyses by specifying one input cell and several result cells. EX 596
charting, EX 607
creating, EX 603–606
modifying, EX 607–608

Open command, FM 15

opening
File Explorer, FM 10
files, FM 15–16
non-native files in Excel, EX 692
workbooks, EX 4–7, EX 71
workbooks with macros, EX 451–452

opening tag The XML tag that marks the beginning of a data value. EX 701

operator A mathematical symbol used in a formula to combine different values, resulting in a single value that is displayed within the cell. EX 32

optimal product mix The product mix that will result in the most profit for the company (assuming that the company can sell every item it produces). EX 632–633

optional argument An argument that is not required for the function to return a value. EX 133

OR function A logical function that returns a TRUE value if any of the logical conditions are true, and a FALSE value if none of the logical conditions are true. EX 464, EX 475–477

order of operations A set of predefined rules used to determine the sequence in which operators are applied in a calculation. EX 32–34

Orientation button, EX 87

Outline view, subtotals, EX 295–297

overlaying chart elements, EX 229

P

page break
automatic, EX 97
inserting, EX 116–117
manual, EX 96
Page Break Preview, EX 114–115
removing, EX 116, EX 117

Page Break Preview The Excel view that shows the location of page breaks in the printed sheet. EX 31, EX 97, EX 114–115

PAGE LAYOUT tab, EX 30, EX 96
Themes button, EX 108

Page Layout view The Excel view that shows how the sheet will appear when printed. EX 31

page orientation, worksheets, EX 53

Page Setup dialog box, EX 118, EX 120, EX 122

pane A section of a window; In Excel, you can split the worksheet window into two or four resizable panes. EX 277, EX 290–292
Windows Explorer, FM 8

parentheses, matching, checking formulas for, EX 489

Paste Names command, EX 399–400

paste options, list, EX 758

Paste Options button, EX 103–104

Paste Special, EX 104

Paste Values command, EX A6–A7

pasting formulas, EX 35–36

payback period The length of time before an investment recovers its initial cost. EX 566, EX 569–571

payment period
calculating with NPER function, EX 536–537

PDF (Portable Document Format) A file format developed by Adobe Systems for displaying formatted documents containing text, graphics, and complicated layouts. EX 772
saving worksheets as, EX 772–774

Percent style The number format for percentages that adds the % symbol after the number and no decimal places. EX 68

percentage, formatting, EX 85–86

personal finances, managing with financial functions, EX 197

Personal Macro workbook A hidden workbook named PERSONAL.xlsb that opens whenever you start Excel, making the macros you stored there available any time you use Excel. EX 434

pie chart A chart in the shape of a circle divided into slices like a pie that show data values as a percentage of the whole. EX 199, EX 200, EX 212
exploding, EX 209
filtered, EX 210–211
formatting data labels, EX 207–208
formatting legend, EX 205, EX 206
inserting with Quick Analysis tool, EX 200–202
selecting colors for slices, EX 208

PivotChart A graphical representation of the data in a PivotTable. EX 298, EX 299
creating, EX 317–318

PivotTable An interactive table used to group and summarize either a range of data or an Excel table into a concise, tabular format for reporting and analysis. EX 298–316
adding fields, EX 303–305
analyzing data, EX 300
calculated fields, EX 316
cell, displaying data source, EX 312
creating, EX 300–308

filtering, EX 308–312
formatting, EX 306–308
importing data from multiple tables into, EX 689–692
layout, EX 305–306
layout areas, EX 303
recommended, EX 314–315
refreshing, EX 312–313
types, EX 313

PivotTable report
adding calculated fields, EX 316
layouts, EX 306

pixel A single point on a computer monitor or printout. EX 25

placeholder A special character used to represent individual digits. EX A14

planning
Excel applications, EX 392–394
importance, EX 261
macros, EX 434
structured range of data, EX 260–262
workbooks, EX 13–14

planning analysis sheet A series of questions that help you think about a workbook's purpose and how to achieve your desired results. EX 13

plot area The part of a chart that contains the graphical representation of the data series. EX 219
formatting, EX 227–229
plot area, EX 227–229

plus sign (+), addition operator, EX 32

PMT function The financial function that calculates the payment schedule required to repay a loan. EX 192, EX 193–197, EX 532–534, EX C531

PNG. *See* Portable Network Graphics

point A unit of measure equal to approximately 1/72 of an inch. EX 29

Portable Document Format. *See* PDF

Portable Network Graphics (PNG) A popular picture format that allows for picture compression for smaller file sizes. EX D24

portrait orientation The page orientation where the page is taller than it is wide. EX 53

positive cash flow A positive value that represents money coming to the investor; also called cash inflow. EX 530

pound sign (#)
error values, EX 150
numbers exceeding cell size, EX 24, EX 84

PowerPivot An add-in for Excel 2013 that provides the tools for performing more advanced data analysis and modeling. EX 693–699
installing, EX 693

PPMT function The financial function to calculate the amount of a loan payment that is applied to the principal. EX 192, EX 197, EX 531

precedent cell A cell that supplies a data value to the active cell. EX 567

present value. *See* PV function

primary axis The axis against which data series in a chart is plotted; usually appears along the left side of a chart. EX 222, EX 232–234

primary sort field The first sort field. EX 272

principal The amount of money being loaned. EX 192
amortization schedule, EX 540–545

print area The range or ranges in a worksheet that you specify to be printed. EX 97
defining, EX 115–116

print title Information that appears on every printed page; specified as rows or columns to repeat on the top or left of each page. EX 96, EX 117–119

printing
    formatting worksheets for. *See* formatting worksheets for printing
    workbooks, EX 61–56
    worksheet groups, EX 347–348

privacy, shared workbooks, EX 728

private sub procedure A procedure that is hidden from other modules in a project and is limited to the VBA code within its module. EX C7

procedure The location where VBA code is stored. EX C6
    function, EX C6
    property, EX C6
    sub procedures. *See* sub procedure

product mix The combination of different products offered by a company for sale to the consumer. EX 630, EX 632–633
    optimal, EX 632–633

profit and loss statement Another term for an income statement, a document that shows how much money a person or business makes or loses over a specified period of time.. *See* income statement

project A collection of macros, worksheets, data-entry forms, and other items that make up a customized application. EX C4–6
    modifying properties, EX C5–6

Project Explorer The window in the Visual Basic Editor that displays a hierarchical list of all the macros, worksheets, data-entry forms, and other items that make up a custom Office application. EX C3, EX C4–5

PROPER function A text function that converts the first letter of each word to uppercase, capitalizes any letter that does not follow another letter, and changes all other letters to lowercase. EX A4, EX A7–A8

Properties window The window in the Visual Basic Editor that lists the properties and values associated with each object in the Project Explorer. EX C3

property An attribute of an object that defines one of its characteristics, such as its name, size, color, or location; all objects in an Excel project have properties. EX C5
    modifying, EX C5–6, EX C13–15

property procedure A procedure that is used to create custom properties for the objects in a project. EX C6

Protect Sheet dialog box, EX 422

Protect Structure and Windows dialog box, EX 41_

Protect Workbook button, EX 741–743

public sub procedure A procedure that is available to other modules in a project. EX C7

PV function The financial function to calculate the present value of a loan or an investment. EX 192, EX 197, EX 530, EX 537–540

Q

query A set of guidelines that specify what values to retrieve from a database and in what order the values should be retrieved. EX 677
    choosing tables and files, EX 681–682
    editing, EX 686–688
    filtering and sorting data, EX 683–685

Query Wizard - Sort dialog box, EX 684

Quick Access toolbar A row of buttons on a program's title bar that give you one-click access to frequently used commands. FM 3

Quick Analysis tool A button that appears whenever you select a range of cells, providing access to the most common tools for data analysis and formatting for the selected range. EX 110–112
    entering functions, EX 142–145
    inserting pie charts, EX 200–202

R

radar chart, EX 199

RAND function, EX 141

range. *See* cell range

range name. *See* defined name

Range object, EX C12
    methods, EX C15
    properties, EX C14

range reference The cell reference of the upper-left cell in the range and the cell reference of the lower-right cell separated by a colon that identifies the range. EX 11–13

RATE function The financial function to calculate the per-period interest rate required to repay a loan or reach an investment goal. EX 192, EX 567, EX 568–569

rate of return An interest rate that compares the value of current dollars to future dollars from a series of cash flows, also known as the discount rate. EX 566
    choosing, EX 572–574

real-time data acquisition A data source in which data values are retrieved from measuring devices and scientific equipment connected to a computer. EX 717–718

recalculation options, EX 767

Recommended Chart button, EX 197

Recommended PivotTable dialog box, EX 314–315

record A group of related fields that displays a collection of characteristics of a particular person, place, or thing; each row in an Excel table or structured range of data represents a record. EX 258, EX 676
    adding to tables, EX 268–269
    deleting, EX 270
    editing, EX 269
    finding, EX 269
    sorting. *See* sort

Record Macro button, EX 428

Record Macro dialog box, EX 435–436

recording a macro, EX 433–437

Recycle Bin, FM 25

redoing actions, EX 19

#REF! error value, EX 151

referencing a variable, EX C22–25

refresh To update. EX 312
    PivotTables, EX 312–313

rejecting an edit, EX 735–737

relational database A database in which tables are joined by common fields that indicate the relationship between one table and another. EX 676, EX 680

relative reference A cell reference that is interpreted in relation to the location of the cell containing the formula. EX 133, EX 152–153

Remove Duplicates dialog box, EX 270

removing. *See also* deleting
    page breaks, EX 116, EX 117

Rename command, FM 26

renaming worksheets, EX 16

Replace command, EX 97

Replace dialog box, EX C8–9, EX C23

required argument An argument that is needed for the function to return a value. EX 132

resizing charts, EX 202–203

Resolve Conflicts dialog box, EX 731

Restore Down button The button that returns a window to its previous size. EX 3

result cell A cell that contains the outcome of a formula involving input cells. EX 596
    two-variable data table, formatting, EX 610–612

result value A value in a data table that comes from a formula applied to one or more input value. EX 596

return values The data values you want to retrieve from a lookup table. EX 160

RGB Color model A format used to create custom colors by specifying varying intensities of red, green, and blue. EX 74

ribbon The main set of commands organized into tabs and groups with buttons that you click to execute commands. EX 2, FM 3
    expanding, FM 13–14
    removing tabs, EX 452

Ribbon Display Options button, EX 3

Rich Text Format (RTF) A file format that allows text formatting styles including boldface, italic, and color, but not advanced features such as hyperlinks or complicated table structures. EX 705

right angle bracket (>), comparison operators, EX 172

RIGHT function, EX A4

risk The possibility that an entire transaction will fail, resulting in a loss of the initial investment. EX 572
    rate of return, EX 572–574

root directory The location at the top of the file system hierarchy where Windows stores folders and important files that it needs when you turn on the computer. FM 6, FM 7

root element The common element on which an XML document is structured and which contains all other XML elements. EX 712

rotating cell contents, EX 91–92

ROUND function, EX 141, EX 142

row heading The numbers along the left side of the workbook window that identify the different rows of the worksheet. EX 2

row input cell The cell that references the input cell when the input values are placed in the first row of a data table. EX 605

ROWS area, PivotTables, EX 303

RTF. *See* Rich Text Format

running
    macros, EX 437–438
    sub procedures, EX C9–10

run-time error A programming error that occurs when something in the code keeps the program from running successfully. EX C22

S

sales data calculating, EX 78–82

salvage value The value of an asset at the end of its useful life. EX 557

sans serif font A font that does not include extra strokes, such as Arial. EX 71

Save As dialog box, FM 17, FM 18

Save Current Theme dialog box, EX 108

saving
  data connections, EX 688
  files, FM 16–18
  Solver models, EX 645–648
  themes, EX D25, EX D27–28
  web queries, EX 703, EX 706
  workbooks, with new name, EX 57–58
  workbooks to file hosting services, EX 740
  workbooks with macros, EX 450–451
  worksheets, EX 17
  worksheets as PDF files, EX 772–774

scale The range of values displayed on a chart axis. EX 54, EX 222
  vertical axis, editing, EX 222–223

scaling To change the size of the worksheet on the printed page. EX 54

scatter chart. *See* XY scatter chart

scenario A defined collection of input values used to perform a what-if analysis. EX 616
  merging scenarios, EX 629

Scenario Manager An Excel feature used create as many scenarios as you want and switch between them to display the results of several what-if analyses within a worksheet. EX 616–629
  defining scenarios, EX 619–622
  editing scenarios, EX 624–625
  summary reports, EX 617, EX 625–629
  viewing scenarios, EX 622–624

scenario PivotTable report A PivotTable report generated by the Scenario Manager that displays the scenario changing and result values in an Excel PivotTable. EX 617, EX 625, EX 627–628

scenario summary report A report generated by the Scenario Manager that lists the values for the changing cells and result cells under each scenario. EX 617, EX 625–629

schema A document that stores the rules about which elements in an XML document are required and what types of values are allowed within each element. EX 712

screenshot, inserting, EX 758

ScreenTip A box with descriptive text about a command that appears when you point to a button on the ribbon. EX 6

scrolling Windows 8 and Windows 7 compared, FM 4

Search box, FM 2

SEARCH function, EX A4

secondary axis An alternate axis in a chart against which other data series with a different scale is plotted; usually appears on the right side of a chart. EX 222, EX 232–234

secondary sort field The second sort field. EX 272

security, data, EX 673

security setting, macros, EX 431–433

Select Changes to Accept or Reject dialog box, EX 736

Select Data button, EX 237

Select Data Source dialog box, EX 614

Select table dialog box, EX 689–690

selecting
  cells and ranges by their defined names, EX 396–397
  multiple files or folders, FM 24
  multiple filter items, EX 281–282

selection box A box surrounding an object such as a chart that is used to move or resize the object. EX 202

self-signed certificate A digital certificate that is created and signed by the person it certifies. EX 755

sensitivity report A report created by Solver that is often used in science and engineering to investigate the mathematical aspects of the Solver solution. EX 642

series, filling, EX 164–166

Series dialog box, EX 165–166, EX 552, EX 556

serif font A font that has extra strokes at the end of each character, such as Times New Roman. EX 71

Share Workbook button, EX 726

Share Workbook dialog box, EX 729

shared workbook A workbook that can be edited simultaneously by more than one user at the same time. EX 725–756
  collaborating on the web. *See* collaborating on the web
  comparing workbooks, EX 738–740
  editing, EX 741
  enabling sharing, EX 729
  inspecting, EX 748–752
  marking as final, EX 753
  merging workbooks, EX 737–740
  privacy options, EX 728–729
  protecting, EX 752–753
  setting document properties, EX 746–748
  sharing workbooks on the cloud, EX 741–743
  signing off on, EX 754–756
  tracking changes. *See* tracking changes in a shared workbook

sharing styles and themes, EX 108

sheet A page included in a workbook; can be a worksheet or a chart sheet. EX 2

sheet tab The area at the bottom of the worksheet that identifies the sheet by name. EX 2

Short Date format An abbreviated format for dates in the format mm/dd/yyyy. EX 86

shortcut menu A list of commands related to a selection that opens when you click the right mouse button. EX 17

Signature Setup dialog box, EX 754

significant digit The number of digits that should be displayed for a calculation; they indicate the accuracy of the measured and calculated values. EX 140

sizing handle A square or dot on the edge of a selection box that is used to change the object's width and height. EX 202

SkyDrive A Microsoft service that provides online storage space for your files. FM 17

slack The difference between the value in the cell and the value at the limit of the constraint. EX 644–645

slicer An object used to filter an Excel table, a PivotTable, or a PivotChart. EX 277, EX 285–287
  filtering PivotTables, EX 310–312

SLN function, EX 562

SmartArt graphic A professionally designed business diagram, such as a flow chart, organization chart, or production cycle chart, included with Microsoft Office. EX D16–24
  inserting and editing, EX D19–22
  positioning, EX D23
  styles, EX D19
  text labels, EX D18

SmartArt style A collection of formats you use to change a SmartArt graphic's appearance. EX D19

Solver An Excel add-in that searches for the optimal solution to a problem involving several variables. EX 631, EX 633–648
  activating, EX 634–635
  adding constraints, EX 637–642
  answer reports, EX 642–645
  iterative procedure, EX 642

  saving and loading models, EX 645–648
  setting objective cell and variable cells, EX 635–637

Solver Parameters dialog box, EX 636

Solver Results dialog box, EX 643

sort To list files and folders in a particular order, such as alphabetically by name or type or chronologically by their modification date. FM 14

sort (Excel) The process of rearranging data such as the records in an Excel table or range based on one or more fields; data can be sorted in ascending or descending order. EX 258
  custom list, EX 274–275
  Excel tables, EX 271–275
  multiple columns, EX 272–274
  queries, EX 683–685
  single column, EX 271

Sort button, sorting single column, EX 271

Sort dialog box, sorting multiple columns, EX 272–274

sort field A field that you use to order data. EX 258
  sorting multiple columns, EX 272–274

source file A file that contains the data that are displayed within the destination file, such as a workbook that contains data to be used in the destination file when two or more workbooks are linked. EX 351, EX 756
  closed, updating destination workbook with, EX 363–364
  open, updating destination workbook with, EX 361–362

sparkline A chart that is displayed entirely within a worksheet cell. EX 218
  creating, EX 228–242
  editing, EX 239
  formatting axis, EX 240
  grouped, EX 219, EX 240–242

SPARKLINE TOOLS DESIGN tab, EX 218
  Group button, EX 241

special format, EX A13

split bar A moveable bar that indicates the division between panes and that can be dragged to resize the panes. EX 277

spreadsheet A grouping of text and numbers in a rectangular grid or table. EX 4. *See also* worksheet
  documentation, EX 427

SQL (Structured Query Language) The language in which queries are written. EX 680

stacked column chart A column chart that places the data series values within combined columns showing how much is contributed by each series. EX 212
  creating, EX 215–216
  editing, EX 216

standard color The 10 colors-dark red, red, orange, yellow, light green, green, light blue, blue, dark blue, and purple-that are always available regardless of the workbook's theme. EX 73

Start menu, Windows 8 and Windows 7 compared, FM 4

starting
  Excel, EX 4
  macro recorder, EX 435–436
  Text Import Wizard, EX 663
  VBE, EX C3–4

Statistical function, EX 140

status bar An area at the bottom of the Excel window that provides information about the workbook. EX 2

stock chart A chart that displays the high, low, and closing value of a stock. EX 199, EX 658

storage
    data, EX 718
    files, determining location, FM 8
    Windows 8 and Windows 7 compared, FM 4
straight-line depreciation The depreciation of an asset by equal amounts each year until it reaches the salvage value at the end of its useful life. EX 558
Structured Query Language. *See* SQL
structured reference The Excel table name or column header that you can use in a formula in place of its cell or range reference. EX 464
    creating formulas in Excel tables, EX 477–480
style A collection of formatting options that include a specified font, font size, font style, font color, fill color, and borders. EX 99–101
    charts, EX 204–205
    copying from one template to another, EX 379
    sharing, EX 108
    SmartArt, EX D19
Style dialog box, EX D2–3
sub procedure In VBA, all of the actions performed in a macro. EX 443, EX C6–11
    assigning to macro buttons, EX C11
    copying and pasting, EX C7–9
    running, EX C9–10
    writing, EX C16–19
subfolder A folder contained within another folder. FM 6, FM 7
    viewing in File Explorer, FM 9
SUBSTITUTE function A text function that replaces existing text with new text. EX A11–A12
subtotal
    inserting, EX 292–297
    Outline view, EX 295–297
subtraction operator (-), EX 32
SUM function The function that adds values in a specified range. EX 31, EX 132, EX 141
SUMIF function (conditional sum) A function that adds the values in a range that match criteria you specify. EX 504, EX 514–515
SUMIFS function A function that adds values in a range that meet multiple criteria. EX B13, EX B15–B16
summarizing using PivotTables. *See* PivotTable
summary statistics, calculating with Total row, EX 276, EX 287–290
surface chart, EX 199
Switch Windows button, EX 351
SYD function, EX 562
symbol, international, EX 771
syntax A set of rules that specifies how a function should be written. EX 36, EX 141–142
syntax error A programming error that occurs when a line of code is entered improperly. EX C22

T

tab The part of the ribbon that includes commands related to particular activities or tasks. EX 2
    removing from ribbon, EX 452
table A collection of data values arranged in columns (fields) and rows (records) in a database. EX 676. *See also* Excel table
    adding to data model, EX 693–694
    choosing for query, EX 681–682
    importing data from multiple tables into a PivotTable, EX 689–692
table column
    calculated. *See* calculated column
    multiple, filtering using, EX 280–281
    multiple, sorting, EX 272–274
    single, filtering using, EX 278–280
    single, sorting, EX 271
TABLE function An array function that returns multiple values to multiple cells. EX 615
table style A preset style that describes the appearance of different elements of an Excel table and is used to quickly format an entire table. EX 259
    custom, EX D4–6
Tagged Image File Format (TIFF) A picture format that provides higher quality photos, but much larger image files, increasing the workbook's size. EX D24
tangible asset A long-lasting material asset not intended for sale but for use only by the company. EX 557
    depreciation. *See* depreciation
taxes, adding to income statement, EX 563–565
template A preformatted workbook with many design features and some content already filled in. EX 4, EX 372–382
    copying styles from one template to another, EX 379
    creating new workbook from, EX 380–382
    creating workbooks based on, EX 373–376
    custom, EX 376–379
text
    finding and replacing formats, EX 104–106
    formatting selections, EX 75
    wrapping within cells, EX 28
text box, EX D22
text data Any combination of letters, numbers, and symbols. EX 17
    displaying numbers as text, EX 21–22
    entering, EX 18–21
text file A file type that contains only text and numbers without any formulas, graphics, special fonts, or formatted text. EX 658
    importing data from. *See* importing data from text files
TEXT function, EX A4
Text function, EX 140, EX A3–A13
Text Import Wizard, EX 663–668
    starting, EX 663
text label, SmartArt graphics, EX D18
text string A series of text characters. EX 17
Text to Columns command, EX A8–A10
theme A collection of formatting for text, colors, images, and graphical effects that are applied throughout a workbook to create a specific look and feel. EX 70, EX 106–108, EX D24–28
    modifying fonts and colors, EX D25–27
    saving, EX D25, EX D27–28
    sharing, EX 108
theme color The 12 colors that belong to the workbook's theme. EX 73
theme font A font associated with a particular theme and used for headings and body text in the workbook; theme fonts change automatically when you change the theme applied to the workbook. EX 71
This Workbook object, EX C13
ThisCell object, EX C13
3-D reference A reference to the same cell or range in multiple worksheets in the same workbook. EX 329
    adding values across worksheets, EX 342–347
    managing, EX 342
thumbnail image, FM 2, FM 3
tick mark A line that identifies the units at regular intervals on a chart axis. EX 222
TIFF. *See* Tagged Image File Format
tile, FM 4
tiling multiple workbooks, EX 354–355
time, formatting, EX 86
time data A value in a recognized time format. EX 17
time value of money The observation that money received today is worth more than the same amount received later. EX 571
TODAY function The date function that displays the current date. EX 167
toolbar A set of buttons for completing current tasks. FM 2
Top Align button, EX 87
Total row A row at the end of an Excel table that is used to calculate summary statistics (such as sum, average, count, maximum, and minimum) for each column in the Excel table. EX 276, EX 287–290
touch interaction, FM 4–5
Touch Mode The mode for use with a touchscreen; changes the ribbon to make it easier to use a finger or a stylus to tap a button. EX 6–7
tracer arrow An arrow used to track an error to its source by pointing from the precedent cell to the dependent cell. EX 567
Track Changes button, EX 726
tracking changes in a shared workbook, EX 730–737
    accepting and rejecting edits, EX 735–737
    reviewing changes using tracking log, EX 733–735
    reviewing comments, EX 731–733
tracking log A list of the changes made to a shared workbook. EX 726
    reviewing changes, EX 733–735
TRANSPOSE function A function that changes the orientation of a range-that is, return a vertical range of cells as a horizontal range, or vice versa. EX 517
trial-and-error method A way to perform what-if analysis by changing one or more of the input values to a value you estimate to see how it impacts the calculated results. EX 179–180
TRIM function, EX A4
trimming incoming data from text files, EX 665–668
Trust Center A central location for all of the security settings in Office. EX 432
Trust Center dialog box, EX 432
trusted location A data location that Excel will access without prompting you to confirm that the connection is secure. EX 673–675
Tufte, Edward, EX 245
two-variable data table A data table used to perform several what-if analyses by specifying two input cells and one result cell. EX 597, EX 609–615
    charting, EX 612–615
    creating, EX 609–610
    formatting result cell, EX 610–612

U

underscore (_), defined names, EX 397
undoing an action, EX 19
ungrouped sparklines A set of sparklines that can be formatted individually. EX 219
ungrouping worksheets, EX 331, EX 335–336
unhiding To redisplay a hidden row, column, or worksheet. EX 48
Uniform Resource Locator (URL) The location of a webpage. EX 700
unit labels, chart axes, EX 223
unprotecting a workbook or worksheet, EX 424–425
updating linked workbooks, EX 361–367
UPPER function A text function that converts all letters of each word in a text string to uppercase. EX A4, EX A10–A11
uppercase
    converting all letters to, EX A10–11
    converting first letter of each word to, EX A7–A8
URL. *See* Uniform Resource Locator
USB drive A removable disk you can plug into your computer and use to store files. FM 6

V

validation criteria The type of data as well as a list or range of acceptable values specified for a validation rule. EX 410–412
validation rule A statement that defines criteria for the data that can be entered and stored in a cell or range. EX 410
    list, EX 414–418
    testing, EX 418–419
value, assigning to variables, EX C20–22
value axis. *See* vertical axis
#VALUE! error value, EX 151
Value field A field that contains summary data in a PivotTable. EX 298
Value Field Settings dialog box, EX 307
VALUES area, PivotTables, EX 303
variable A named element in a program that is used to store data. EX C19–25
    assigning values, EX C20–22
    declaring, EX C20
    referencing, EX C22–25
variable cell An input cell whose values Solver changes in order to reach a solution for the objective cell. EX 630, EX 635
variable expense An expense that changes in proportion to the volume of production. EX 598
VBA. *See* Visual Basic for Applications
VBA comment A statement that describes the behavior or purpose of commands in the BVA code but does not perform any action. EX C7
VBAProject object, EX C12
VBE. *See* Visual Basic Editor
VDB function, EX 562
vertical axis (value axis) The axis that displays the series values from the data series. EX 190
    editing scale, EX 222–223
view, changing in File Explorer, FM 12–13

View tab A tab on the File Explorer window's ribbon that contains options for specifying the view of the window. FM 3
viewing. *See also* displaying
    data connections, EX 669–670
    data model, EX 694–695
    files in File Explorer, FM 9
    formulas, EX 56–57
virus A computer program designed to copy itself into other programs with the intention of causing mischief or harm. EX 431
    detecting with Document Inspector, EX 750
    macro, protecting against, EX 431–433
Visual Basic Editor (VBE) An application that works with Excel and all of the Office programs to view, debug, edit, and manage VBA code. EX 429, EX 441–444, EX C3–6
    editing macros, EX 443–444
    modifying a project's properties, EX C5–6
    Project Explorer, EX C3, EX C4–5
    starting, EX C3–4
Visual Basic for Applications (VBA) A programming language. EX 433, EX C1–28
    conditional statements. *See* conditional statement
    custom functions, EX C27–28
    developing applications, EX C2–3
    Excel Object Model, EX C13
    learning, EX C11
    methods, EX C15–16
    modifying an object's properties, EX C13–15
    modules, EX 443
    objects, EX C12–16EX C12–13
    sub procedures, EX 443. *See* sub procedure
    variables. *See* variable
    VBE. *See* Visual Basic Editor (VBE)
VLOOKUP function The function that returns values from a vertical lookup table. EX 160, EX 483, EX 489
    finding approximate matches, EX 493–497
    finding exact matches, EX 177–179, EX 491–493

W

Watch Window A window that displays values of cells located throughout the workbook so the user can view the impact of changing a cell's value on widely scattered dependent cells. EX 585–586
watermark Text or an image that appears in the background of each page behind other content. EX 245–247
web, collaborating on, EX 740–743
Web function, EX 140
web query A set of guidelines that specifies which data should be retrieved from different sections of a webpage. EX 700
    creating, EX 702–706
    formatting, EX 705–706
    saving, EX 703, EX 706
    setting format options, EX 703
    web queries, EX 705–706
what-if analysis A way to explore the impact that changing input values has on the calculated values in a workbook. EX 179–182
    choosing tools, EX 645
    finding break-even point, EX 601–603
    Goal Seek, EX 180–181
    performing with charts, EX 210–211
    scenarios. *See* scenario; Scenario Manager
    trial-and-error method, EX 179–180

Windows 8, Windows 7 compared, FM 4–5
Windows Explorer A Windows 7 tool that displays the contents of your computer and uses icons to represent drives, folders, and files. FM 2
WordArt A text box in which you can enter stylized text. EX 392
workbook An Excel file that stores a spreadsheet; contains a collection of worksheets and chart sheets. EX 2
    auditing. *See* auditing a workbook
    encryption, EX 752–753
    enhancing with color, EX 76
    existing, opening, EX 4–5
    formatting, EX 70
    inspecting, EX 748–752
    for international clients, EX 768–772
    linked, managing, EX 361
    linked, updating, EX 361–367
    linking, EX 352–361
    macros. *See* macro
    opening, EX 71
    printing, EX 51–56
    saving to file hosting service, EX 740
    saving with new name, EX 57–58
    sharing macros between, EX C25
    themes, EX 106–108
    turning into an add-in, EX C28
    unprotecting, EX 424–425
    user-friendly, EX 134–140
    writing, EX 546
Workbook object, EX C12
    methods, EX C15
    properties, EX C14
workbook protection A setting that limits users' ability to make changes to the workbook's structure and windows. EX 409, EX 423–424
workbook window The area of the Excel window that displays the contents of the workbook. EX 3
WORKDAY function The function that displays the date of a weekday that is specified number of weekdays past a starting date. EX 161, EX 167, EX 168–169
worksheet A grid of rows and columns in which content is entered. EX 3
    AutoComplete, EX 20–21
    background images, EX 77–78
    binding XML elements to, EX 714–715
    cells. *See* formatting worksheet cells; worksheet cell
    changing active sheet, EX 8–9
    changing font size, EX 51
    changing views, EX 51–53
    closing, EX 13
    columns. *See* worksheet column
    deleting, EX 17
    displaying numbers as text, EX 21–22
    effective, EX 14
    entering dates, EX 22–24
    entering numbers, EX 24–25
    entering text, EX 18–21
    formatting cells. *See* formatting worksheet cells
    formatting for printing. *See* formatting worksheets for printing
    formulas. *See* formula
    grouping, EX 330–336. *See also* worksheet group
    hiding and unhiding, EX 48
    identifying notes, input values, and calculated values, EX 138–139

inserting, EX 16
moving, EX 16
moving charts between, EX 214
multiple, EX 336–347
navigating within, EX 9–11
new, creating, EX 15–17
page orientation, EX 53
planning, EX 13–14
redoing actions, EX 19
renaming, EX 16
row. *See* worksheet row
saving, EX 17
saving as PDF file, EX 772–774
scaling, EX EX 43
3-D references to add values across, EX 342–347
undoing and actions, EX 19
unprotecting, EX 424–425
WordArt, EX 392
worksheet cell
   borders, EX 50
   editing content, EX 19–20
   formatting. *See* formatting worksheet cells
   selecting cell ranges, EX 11–13
worksheet column
   changing width, EX 25–27
   deleting, EX 44, EX 45

freezing, EX 262–263
hiding and unhiding, EX 48
inserting, EX 43–45
wrapping text within cells, EX 25–27
worksheet group A collection of two or more selected worksheets. EX 328
   editing, EX 334
   formatting, EX 334–335
   formulas, EX 332–334
   headings, EX 332–334
   printing, EX 347–348
   ungrouping, EX 331, EX 335–336
Worksheet object, EX C12
   methods, EX C15
   properties, EX C14
worksheet protection A setting that limits users' ability to modify the worksheet's contents, structure, or formatting. EX 420–422
   locking and unlocking cells, EX 420–421
worksheet row
   changing height, EX 29
   deleting, EX 44, EX 45
   freezing, EX 262–263
   hiding and unhiding, EX 48
   inserting, EX 43–45

worksheet window, splitting into panes, EX 290–292
Worksheets object, method, EX C15
Wrap Text button, EX 87

X

XIRR function, EX 577–579

XML. *See* Extensible Markup Language

XML data map A schematic diagram that shows the structure of an XML document. EX 701, EX 712
   loading, EX 713–714

XNPV function, EX 577–579

XY scatter chart A chart that shows the pattern or relationship between two or more sets of values. EX 199, EX 237
   line charts compared, EX 221

Y

YEAR function, EX 167

Z

Zoom control Control that increases or decreases the magnification of the worksheet content. EX 3

TASK REFERENCE

Microsoft Excel 2013, Comprehensive

TASK	PAGE #	RECOMMENDED METHOD
3-D reference, use	EX 343	*See* Reference box: Entering a Function That Contains a 3-D Reference
Absolute reference, create	EX 154	Type a $ before both the row and column references
Action, undo or redo	EX 19	Click or on the Quick Access Toolbar
Advanced filter, clear	EX B8	On the DATA tab, in the Sort & Filter group, click the Clear button
Advanced filter, create	EX B5	On the DATA tab, in the Sort & Filter group, click the Advanced button, set filter options, data, and criteria ranges, click OK
AutoSum feature, enter function with	EX 37	Click a cell, click AutoSum in the Editing group on the HOME tab, click a function, verify the range, press Enter
Border, add to cells	EX 50	Select a range, click in the Font group on the HOME tab, click a border
Cell, change fill color	EX 76	Click in the Font group on the HOME tab, click a color
Cell, clear contents of	EX 58	Select a cell, press Delete
Cell, delete	EX 46	Select a cell, range, column, or row; click Delete button in the Cells group on the HOME tab
Cell, edit	EX 19	Double-click a cell, enter changes
Cell, go to	EX 10	Click Find & Select button in the Editing group on the HOME tab, click Go To
Cell contents, align within a cell	EX 87	Click , , or in the Alignment group on the HOME tab
Cell contents, change indent of	EX 88	Click or in the Alignment group on the HOME tab
Cell contents, rotate	EX 91	Click in the Alignment group on the HOME tab, click angle
Cell or range, select by its defined name	EX 396	Click the Name box arrow, click a defined name
Cell style, create a custom	EX D2	*See* Reference box: Creating a Cell Style
Cells, lock or unlock	EX 420	Select a cell or range, on the HOME tab, in the Cells group, click the Format button, click Format Cells (or press Ctrl+1), click then Protection tab, check or uncheck the Locked check box, click OK
Cells, merge and center	EX 90	Select adjacent cells, click in the Alignment group on the HOME tab
Cells, reference in other worksheets	EX 339	Enter a reference in the format =*SheetName*!*CellRange*
Chart, choose style	EX 204	Select the chart, click , select a chart style
Chart, create	EX 197	*See* Reference box: Creating a Chart
Chart, resize	EX 202	Select the chart, drag the sizing handle
Chart element, format	EX 205	Double-click the chart element, make changes in the Format pane
Chart type, change	EX 214	Select the chart, click the Change Chart Type button in the Type group on the CHART TOOLS DESIGN tab, click a new chart type
Color scale, apply	EX D10	On the HOME tab, in the Styles group, click the Conditional Formatting button, point to Color Scales, click a color scale
Column, change width	EX 25	Drag the right border of the column heading left or right
Column, select	EX 26	Click the column heading

TASK	PAGE #	RECOMMENDED METHOD
Comment, delete	EX 427	Click a cell with a comment, on the REVIEW tab, in the Comments group, click the Delete button
Comment, edit	EX 426	Click a cell with a comment, on the REVIEW tab, in the Comments group, click the Edit Comment button, edit comment text as needed
Comment, insert	EX 425	See Reference box: Inserting a Comment
Comment, show or hide	EX 426	Click a cell with a comment, the Show/Hide Comment button
Comments, review next	EX 731	On the REVIEW tab, in the Comments group, click the Next button
Compressed folder, extract all files and folders from	FM 27	Click the compressed folder, click the Compressed Folder Tools Extract tab, click the Extract all button
Compressed folder, open	FM 27	Double-click the compressed folder
Conditional format, apply	EX 108	See Reference box: Highlighting a Cell with a Conditional Format
Conditional formatting rule, edit	EX 508	See Reference box: Editing a Conditional Formatting Rule
Custom format, create	EX A15	Select a range, on the HOME tab, in the Number group, click the Dialog Box Launcher, click Number tab, click Custom in the Category box, enter the format codes in the Type box, click OK
Custom format, hide a cell's value with	EX D9	On the HOME tab, in the Number group, click the Dialog Box Launcher, click Custom, type ;;; (three semicolons) in the Type box, click OK
Data, consolidate	EX 717	On the DATA tab, in the Data Tools group, click the Consolidate button, select whether to consolidate the data by position or by category
Data, split from one column into separate columns	EX A9	Select the range, on the DATA tab, in the Data Tools group, click the Text to Columns button, complete the wizard
Data bars, create	EX 242	See Reference Box: Creating Data Bars
Data connection, set properties for	EX 671	On the DATA tab, in the Connections group, click the Connections button, select the data connection, click the Properties button
Data Model, display in Data View or Diagram view	EX 694	On the POWERPIVOT tab, in the Data Model group, click the Manage button, on the Home tab, in the View group, click the Data View button or the Diagram View button
Database query, edit	EX 686	See Reference box: Editing a Database Query
Database tables, import from Access	EX 689	On the DATA tab, in the Get External Data group, click the From Access button, select the Access database file, click the Enable selection of multiple tables checkbox in the Select Tables dialog box, select the tables to import, click OK
Date, enter into a cell	EX 23	Click a cell, type the date, press Enter or Tab
Date, insert the current	EX 167	Enter TODAY() or NOW() function in cell
Defined name, create	EX 395	See Reference box: Creating a Defined Name for a Cell or Range
Defined name, edit or delete	EX 398	On the FORMULAS tab, in the Defined Names group, click the Name Manager button (or press Ctrl+F3), select a name, click Edit and modify or click Delete, click OK, click Close
Defined names, add to existing formulas	EX 405	See Reference Window: Adding Defined Names to Existing Formulas
Defined names, paste list in worksheet	EX 399	Click the upper-left cell of the range for the list, on the FORMULAS tab, in the Defined Names group, click the Use in Formula button (or press F3), click Paste Names, click the Paste List button

Microsoft Excel 2013, Comprehensive   REF 17

TASK	PAGE #	RECOMMENDED METHOD
Developer tab, display or hide on the ribbon	EX 430	Click the FILE tab, click Options in the navigation pane, click Customize Ribbon, check or uncheck Developer check box, click OK
Document properties, add	EX 746	Click the FILE tab, click Info, click the Show All Properties link, enter values for each propery
Document properties, add custom	EX 747	Click the FILE tab, click Info, click the Properties button, click Advanced Properties, click the Custom tab, select a custom property in the Name box, enter a value in the Values box, click Add, click OK
Documents library, open	FM 10	In File Explorer, click ▷ next to Libraries, click ▷ next to Documents
Duplicate values, highlight	EX 506	See Reference box: Highlighting Duplicate Values
Edits, accept or reject	EX 735	See Reference box: Accepting and Rejecting Edits
Error, trace to its source	EX 581	See Reference box: Tracing Error Values
Error alert message, create	EX 410	See Reference box: Validating Data
Excel, start	EX 4	Click the Excel 2013 tile on the Start screen
Excel table, add a record	EX 268	Click the row below the Excel table, type values for the new record, pressing Tab to move from field to field
Excel table, add to Data Model	EX 693	Select a cell in the Excel table, click the POWERPIVOT tab, in the Tables group, click the Add to Data Model button
Excel table, apply a style	EX 267	On the TABLE TOOLS DESIGN tab, in the Table Styles group, click the More button, click a table style
Excel table, create	EX 264	On the INSERT tab, in the Tables group, click the Table button, verify the range of data, click OK
Excel table, delete a record	EX 270	Select a record, on the HOME tab, in the Cells group, click the Delete button arrow, click Delete Table Rows
Excel table, filter using a slicer	EX 286	Click a slicer button on the slicer
Excel table, find and replace a record	EX 269	Click in the Excel table, on the HOME tab, in the Editing group, click the Find & Select button, click Find, use the Find and Replace dialog box
Excel table, modify	EX 267	On TABLE TOOLS DESIGN tab, in the Table Style Options group, check or uncheck options
Excel table, remove duplicate records	EX 270	Click in the Excel table, on the TABLE TOOLS DESIGN tab, in the Tools group, click Remove Duplicates button, use Remove Duplicates dialog box to select columns to find duplicate records, click OK
Excel table, rename	EX 266	Click in the Excel table, on the TABLE TOOLS DESIGN tab, in the Properties group, select the name in the Table Name box, type a name, press Enter
External data range, refresh	EX 670	See Reference box: Refreshing External Data
External data range, set properties for	EX 668	See Reference box: Editing the Properties of an External Data Range
Extrapolated values, calculate	EX 555	See Reference box: Interpolating and Extrapolating a Series
File, copy	FM 24	Right-click the file, click Copy, right-click destination, click Paste
File, delete	FM 25	Right-click the file, click Delete
File, move	FM 21	Drag the file to the folder
File, open from File Explorer	FM 15	Right-click the file, point to Open with, click an application
File, rename	FM 26	Right-click the file, click Rename, type the new filename, press Enter
File, save with new name in WordPad	FM 18	Click the File tab, click Save as, enter the filename, click Save

TASK	PAGE #	RECOMMENDED METHOD
File Explorer, open	FM 10	Click [icon] on the taskbar
File Explorer, return to a previous location	FM 22	Click [icon]
File list, sort	FM 14	Click the column heading button
Files, select multiple	FM 24	Press and hold the Ctrl key and click the files
Files, view in Large Icons view	FM 13	Click the View tab, click [icon] in the Layout group
Files and folders, compress	FM 27	Select the files to compress, click the Share tab, click the Zip button in the Send group
Fill handle, use	EX 162	*See Reference box: Copying Formulas and Formats with AutoFill*
Filter, clear from a column	EX 281	Click the filter button, click Clear Filter From "*column*"
Filter, clear from an Excel table	EX 285	On the DATA tab, in the Sort & Filter group, click the Clear button
Filter, select multiple items	EX 282	Click the filter button, check two or more items, click OK
Filter, specify complex criteria	EX 283	Click the filter button, point to Number Filters, Text Filters, or Date Filters, specify the filter criteria, click OK
Filter, use multiple columns	EX 280	Filter for one column, repeat to filter for additional columns
Filter, use one column	EX 278	Click a filter button, deselect the (Select All) check box, click the item to filter by, click OK
Filter buttons, display or hide	EX 278	On the DATA tab, in the Sort & Filter group, click the Filter button
Find and replace, text or format	EX 104	Click Find & Select in the Editing group on the HOME tab, click Replace
Flash Fill, apply	EX 49	Type a few entries in a column to establish a pattern, Flash Fill adds the remaining entries
Folder, create	FM 19	Click the New folder button in the New group on the Home tab
Font, change color	EX 74	Click [A] in the Font group on the HOME tab, click a color
Font, change size	EX 72	Click the Font Size arrow in the Font group on the HOME tab, click a point size
Font, change style	EX 72	Click [B], [I], or [U] in the Font group on the HOME tab
Font, change typeface	EX 71	Click the Font arrow in the Font group on the HOME tab, click a font
Fonts, manage multiple options for +Body and +Heading	EX D26	On the PAGE LAYOUT tab, in the Themes group, click the Fonts button, click Customize Fonts, select fonts, type a name, click Save
Formula, enter	EX 32	Click the cell, type = and then a formula, press Enter or Tab
Formula, evaluate	EX 584	Select the cell with the formula, on the FORMULAS tab, in the Formula Auditing group, click the Evaluate Formula button, click the Evaluate button
Formula, reference another worksheet	EX 339	*See Reference box: Entering a Formula with References to Another Worksheet*
Formula results, copy and paste as values	EX A6	Copy the range with formula results, click the first cell in the paste location, on the HOME tab, in the Clipboard group, click the Paste button arrow, click the Values button [icon]
Formula with an external reference, create	EX 356	Click a cell in the destination file, type =, click a cell in the source file, complete the formula as usual
Formulas, display in a worksheet	EX 56	Press Ctrl+`

TASK	PAGE #	RECOMMENDED METHOD
Formulas, watch	EX 586	On the FORMULAS tab, in the Formula Auditing group, click the Watch Window button
Function, insert	EX 145	Click a function category in the Function Library group on the FORMULAS tab, click a function, enter arguments, click OK
Goal seek, perform	EX 180	See Reference box: Performing What-if Analysis and Goal Seek
Hyperlink, create	EX 370	See Reference box: Inserting a Hyperlink
Hyperlink, edit	EX 372	Right-click the cell with the hyperlink, click Edit Hyperlink, make edits in the Edit Hyperlink dialog box, click OK
Icon set, apply	EX D14	On the HOME tab, in the Styles group, click the Conditional Formatting button, point to Icon Sets, click an icon set
Input message, create	EX 410	See Reference box: Validating Data
International numbering, apply	EX 769	Click the FILE tab, click Options, click Advanced, deselect the Use system separators check box, enter symbols in the Decimal separator box and the Thousands separator box, click OK
Interpolated values, calculate	EX 555	See Reference box: Interpolating and Extrapolating a Series
Invalid data, circle	EX 419	On the DATA tab, in the Data Tools group, click the Data Validation button arrow, click Circle Invalid Data
Investment value, calculate	EX 575	See Reference box: Calculating the Value of an Investment
Link, embed	EX 760	Copy a range or a chart, go to the destination file, on the HOME tab, in the Clipboard group, click the Paste button arrow, click the Keep Source Formatting & Embed Workbook (K) button
Link, paste	EX 759	Copy a range or a chart, go to the destination file, on the HOME tab in the Clipboard group, click the Paste button arrow, click the Link & Keep Source Formatting (F) button
Link, update	EX 760	Right-click the linked object, click Update Link
Linked workbooks, update	EX 361	Click in the source file, edit as usual
Links, manage	EX 365	On the DATA tab, in the Connections group, click the Edit Links button, select an option, click OK
Loans and investments, calculate	EX 532	See Reference box: Working with Loans and Investments
Macro, edit	EX 441	See Reference box: Editing a Macro
Macro, record	EX 435	See Reference box: Recording a Macro
Macro, run	EX 437	See Reference box: Running a Macro
Macro, set security level for	EX 432	See Reference box: Setting Macro Security in Excel
Macro, view code	EX 441	See Reference box: Editing a Macro
Macro button, create	EX 445	See Reference box: Creating a Macro Button
Macro button, move or resize	EX 447	Right-click the macro button, press Esc, drag the button by its selection box to new location or drag a sizing handle
Margins, set	EX 121	Click the Margins button in the Page Setup group on the PAGE LAYOUT tab, select a margin size
Mixed reference, create	EX 154	Type $ before either the row or column reference
My Documents folder, open	FM 10	In File Explorer, click ▷ next to Libraries, click ▷ next to Documents, click My Documents
Non-native file, open in Excel	EX 692	Click the FILE tab, click Open, select the file format, click the Open button

TASK	PAGE #	RECOMMENDED METHOD
Number, enter as text	EX 21	Type ' and then type the number
Number format, apply	EX 84	Click $, %, ,, or the Number Format arrow in the Number group on the HOME tab
Object, insert	EX 763	On the INSERT tab, in the Text group, click the Object button, select an object type on the Create New tab or insert a file on the Create from File tab
Office App, insert	EX 707	On the INSERT tab, in the Apps group, click the Apps for Office button, click the Office Store button, select an app to install, click Add
One-variable data table, create	EX 604	See Reference box: Creating a One-Variable Data Table
Page break, insert or remove	EX 116	See Reference box: Inserting and Removing Page Breaks
Picture, edit	EX D21	See Reference box: Editing a Picture
Picture, insert	EX D18	On the INSERT tab, in the Illustrations group, click the Pictures or Online Pictures button and select the clip art image to insert
PivotChart, create	EX 316	On the PIVOTTABLE TOOLS ANALYZE tab, in the Tools group, click the PivotChart button, select a chart, click OK
PivotTable, create	EX 301	See Reference box: Creating a PivotTable
PivotTable, create recommended	EX 314	Click in an Excel table, on the INSERT tab, in the Tables group, click the Recommended PivotTables button, select a PivotTable, click OK
PivotTable, filter using slicer	EX 311	Click a slicer button
PivotTable, rearrange	EX 306	In the PivotTable Fields pane, drag field buttons between the ROWS, COLUMNS and FILTERS areas
PivotTable, refresh	EX 312	On the PIVOTTABLE TOOLS ANALYZE tab, in the Data group, click the Refresh button
PivotTable field, filter	EX 309	Click a filter arrow, click a filter item, click OK
PivotTable Fields pane, show or hide	EX 311	Click in the PivotTable, on the PIVOTTABLE TOOLS ANALYZE tab, in the Show group, click the Field List button
PivotTable report, filter	EX 308	Drag a field button from PivotTable Fields pane to FILTERS area or drag a field button from ROWS or COLUMNS area to FILTERS area
PivotTable Row and Column field items, filter	EX 309	In the PivotTable, click the Column Labels or Row Labels filter button, check or uncheck items, click OK
PivotTable style, apply	EX 307	On the PIVOTTABLE TOOLS DESIGN tab, in the PivotTable Styles group, click the More button, click a style
PivotTable value fields, format	EX 307	In the VALUES area of the PivotTable Fields pane, click the button, click the Value Field Settings button, click the Number Format button, select a format, click OK
PowerPivot, install	EX 693	Click the FILE tab, click Options, click Add-Ins, click the Manage box arrow, click COM Add-ins, click the Go button, select the Microsoft Office PowerPivot for Excel 2013 check box, click OK
Print area, set	EX 115	Select a range, click the Print Area button in the Page Setup group on PAGE LAYOUT tab, click Set Print Area
Print titles, add	EX 118	Click the Print Titles button in the Page Setup group on the PAGE LAYOUT tab, click Rows to repeat at top, select a range, click OK
Query Wizard, start	EX 680	On the DATA tab, in the Get External Data group, click the From Other Sources button, click From Microsoft Query
Range, select adjacent	EX 11	Click a cell, drag the pointer from the selected cell to the cell in the lower-right corner of the range

Microsoft Excel 2013, Comprehensive   REF 21

TASK	PAGE #	RECOMMENDED METHOD
Range, select nonadjacent	EX 12	Select a cell or an adjacent range, press the Ctrl key as you select additional cells or adjacent ranges
Relationships, manage within Excel	EX 696	On the DATA tab, in the Data Tools group, click the Relationships button, click the New button
Relationships, manage within PowerPivot	EX 696	In the PowerPivot window, on the Design tab, in the Relationships group, click the Manage Relationships button
Relative reference, create	EX 152	Type the cell reference as it appears in the worksheet
Ribbon, expand in File Explorer	FM 13	Click ∨
Row, change height	EX 29	Drag the bottom border of the row heading up or down
Row, select	EX 44	Click the row heading
Row(s) and column(s), freeze	EX 263	Click the cell below and to the right of row(s) and column(s) to freeze, on the VIEW tab, in the Window group, click the Freeze Panes button, click an option
Row(s) and column(s), unfreeze	EX 263	On the VIEW tab, in the Window group, click the Freeze Panes button, click Unfreeze Panes
Rows, repeat in printout	EX 118	Click the Print Titles button in the Page Setup group on the PAGE LAYOUT tab, click Rows to repeat at top, select range, click OK
Scenario, define	EX 619	See Reference box: Defining a Scenario
Scenario, edit	EX 624	Open the Scenario Manager, select a scenario from the list of scenarios, click the Edit button
Scenario, view	EX 622	Open the Scenario Manager, select a scenario from the list of scenarios, click the Show button
Scenario Manager, open	EX 619	On the DATA tab, in the Data Tools group, click the What-If Analysis button, and then click Scenario Manager
Scenario PivotTable Report, create	EX 625	See Reference box: Creating a Scenario Summary Report or a Scenario PivotTable Report
Scenario Summary Report, create	EX 625	See Reference box: Creating a Scenario Summary Report or a Scenario PivotTable Report
Screenshot, insert	EX 758	On the INSERT tab, in the Illustrations group, click the Screenshot button, select a screenshot or click the Screen Clipping button
Series, create with AutoFill	EX 164	Enter the first few entries in a series, drag the fill handle over the adjacent range
Slicer, create for a PivotTable	EX 310	On the PIVOTTABLE TOOLS ANALYZE tab, in the Filter group, click the Insert Slicer button, click a field check box, click OK
Slicer, create for an Excel table	EX 285	On the TABLE TOOLS DESIGN tab, in the Tools group, click the Insert Slicker button, select one or more field check boxes, click OK
Slicer, format	EX 285	On the SLICER TOOLS OPTONS tab, set the slicer's size and style
SmartArt graphic, insert	EX D17	On the INSERT tab, in the Illustrations group, click the SmartArt button, select a graphic
Solver, activate	EX 634	See Reference box: Activating Solver
Solver, add constraints to	EX 637	See Reference box: Setting Constraints on the Solver Solution
Solver, set objective	EX 635	See Reference box: Setting Solver's Objective and Variable Cells
Solver, set variable cells	EX 635	See Reference box: Setting Solver's Objective and Variable Cells
Solver Answer Report, create	EX 643	In the Solver Results dialog box, click Answer in the Reports box, and then click OK

TASK	PAGE #	RECOMMENDED METHOD
Solver model, load	EX 645	See Reference box: Saving and Loading a Solver Model
Solver model, save	EX 645	See Reference box: Saving and Loading a Solver Model
Sort, multiple columns	EX 272	See Reference box: Sorting Data Using Multiple Sort Fields
Sort, one column	EX 271	Click in the column to sort, on the DATA tab, in the Sort & Filter group, click A↓ or Z↓
Sort, with a custom list	EX 274	See Reference box: Sorting Using a Custom List
Sparklines, create	EX 239	See Reference box: Creating and Editing Sparklines
Special format, apply to data	EX A13	Select a range, on the HOME tab, in the Number group, click the Dialog Box Launcher, click Number tab, click Special in the Category box, click a format, click OK
Structured reference, create for Excel table	EX 477	Use the format Tablename[qualifier]
Subtotal Outline view, use	EX 295	Click an outline button to show or hide the selected outline level
Subtotals, insert	EX 293	See Reference box: Calculating Subtotals for a Range of Data
Subtotals, remove	EX 296	On the DATA tab, in the Outline group, click the Subtotal button, click the Remove All button
Table style, create a custom	EX D5	Select the Excel table, on the HOME tab, in the Styles group, click the Format as Table button, click New Table Style; type a name, select each table element and click the Format button, click OK
Template, create a custom	EX 377	See Reference box: Creating a Custom Template
Text, enter into a cell	EX 18	Click cell, type entry, press Enter or Tab
Text, enter multiple lines in a cell	EX 28	Type the first line of the entry, press Alt+Enter, type the next line
Text, wrap within a cell	EX 28	Select the cell, click [icon] in the Alignment group on the HOME tab
Text box, insert	EX D22	On the INSERT tab, in the Text group, click the Text Box button, enter text
Text file, import	EX 661	See Reference box: Connecting to a Text File
Text Import Wizard, start	EX 663	On to the DATA tab, in the Get External Data group, click the From Text button
Theme, change for workbook	EX 107	Click the Themes button in the Themes group on the PAGE LAYOUT tab, click a theme
Theme, create and save	EX D25	See Reference box: Creating and Saving a Theme
Total row, add or remove from an Excel table	EX 288	On the TABLE TOOLS DESIGN tab, in the Table Style Options group, click the Total Row check box
Total row, select a summary statistics	EX 288	In the Total row cell, click the arrow button, click a summary function
Tracked changes, review	EX 733	See Reference box: Reviewing Changes in a Shared Workbook
Tracked changes, view in History worksheet	EX 735	On the REVIEW tab, in the Changes group, click the Track Changes button, click Highlight Changes, click the List changes on a new sheet check box, click OK
Trust Center, set privacy options for	EX 728	Click the FILE tab, click Options, click Trust Center; click the Trust Center Settings button, click Privacy Options; specify the privacy option, click OK in each dialog box
Trusted location, define	EX 673	See Reference box: Defining a Trusted Location
Two-variable data table, create	EX 609	See Reference box: Creating a Two-Variable Data Table
Validation circle, clear from a cell	EX 419	Enter valid data in the circled cell

TASK	PAGE #	RECOMMENDED METHOD
Validation circles, clear all	EX 419	On the DATA tab, in the Data Tools group, click the Data Validation button arrow, click Clear Validation Circles
Validation rule, create	EX 410	See Reference box: Validating Data
VBA code, view	EX 441	See Reference box: Editing a Macro
VBA project, rename	EX C5	Select the project in the Visual Basic Editor, click Tools on the menu bar, click the VBA project; enter a name and description, click OK
VBA sub procedure, insert public	EX C7	In the Visual Basic Editor click Insert on the menu bar, click Procedure, type a the name, click the Public option button, click OK
VBA sub procedure, run	EX C9	Click in the sub procedure code, click Run on the menu bar, and then click Run Sub/UserForm (or press the F5 key)
View, change in File Explorer	FM 12	See Reference box: Changing the View in File Explorer
Visual Basic Editor, display	EX C4	On the DEVELOPER tab, in the Code group, click the Visual Basic button (or press the Alt+F11 keys)
Visual Basic Editor, open or close	EX 441	See Reference box: Editing a Macro
Web query, create, format, or save	EX 703	See Reference box: Working with Web Queries
Workbook, check for accessibility	EX 752	Click the FILE tab, click Info, click the Check for Issues button, click Check Accessibility
Workbook, check for compatibility	EX 751	Click the FILE tab, click Info, click the Check for Issues button, click Check Compatibility, click OK
Workbook, close	EX 13	Click the FILE tab, click Close
Workbook, create a new	EX 15	Click the FILE tab, click New
Workbook, create from an existing template	EX 374	See Reference box: Creating a Workbook Based on a Template
Workbook, enable sharing	EX 729	On the REVIEW tab, in the Changes group, click the Share Workbook button, click the Allow changes by more than one user at the same time check box, click OK, click OK
Workbook, encrypt	EX 752	Click the FILE tab, click Info, click the Protect Workbook button, click Encrypt with Password button, enter and reenter the password, click OK
Workbook, inspect	EX 749	Click the FILE tab, click Info, click the Check for Issues button, click Inspect Document, click Inspect
Workbook, mark as final	EX 753	Click the FILE tab, click Info, click the Protect Workbook button, click Mark as Final, click OK, click OK
Workbook, open an existing	EX 4	Click Open Other Workbooks link on the Recent screen (or click the FILE tab, click Open), select the workbook file
Workbook, preview and print	EX 55	Click the FILE tab, click Print
Workbook, protect	EX 424	See Reference box: Protecting a Workbook
Workbook, save	EX 17	Click 💾 on the Quick Access Toolbar
Workbook, save as PDF	EX 772	Click the FILE tab, click Save As, select PDF as the file type, click Save
Workbook, save earlier Excel file format in current format	EX A2	Click the FILE tab, click the Save As in the navigation bar, click Browse button, type filename, click the Save as type button, click Excel Workbook, click Save
Workbook, save in the Excel 2003 file format	EX A17	Click the FILE tab, click the Save As command, click the Browse button, click the Save as type button, click Excel 97-2003 Workbook, click Save, click Continue

TASK	PAGE #	RECOMMENDED METHOD
Workbook, save with macros	EX 450	On the Quick Access Toolbar, click 💾, click No, select the save location, enter the filename, click the Save as type button, click Excel Macro-Enabled Workbook, click Save
Workbook sharing, turn off	EX 739	On the REVIEW tab, in the Changes group, click the Share Workbook button, and uncheck the Allow changes by more than one user at the same time check box, click OK, click Yes
Workbooks, arrange	EX 354	See Reference box: Arranging Workbooks
Workbooks, link	EX 352	Enter a formula in the format =[WorkbookName]WorksheetName!CellRange
Workbooks, merge and compare	EX 738	See Reference box: Merging Workbooks
Workbooks, switch between	EX 354	On the VIEW tab, in the Window group, click the Switch Windows button, click the workbook to make active
Worksheet, change orientation	EX 53	Click the Orientation button in the Page Setup group on the PAGE LAYOUT tab, click Landscape or Portrait
Worksheet, change view	EX 52	Click 🔳, 🔲, or 🔳 on the status bar
Worksheet, copy	EX 16	Hold down Ctrl and drag a sheet tab to a new location
Worksheet, delete	EX 17	Right-click a sheet tab, click Delete
Worksheet, insert	EX 16	Click ⊕
Worksheet, move	EX 16	Drag the sheet tab to a new location
Worksheet, protect	EX 422	See Reference box: Protecting a Worksheet
Worksheet, rename	EX 16	Double-click the sheet tab, type a new name, press Enter
Worksheet, scale for printing	EX 54	Set the width and height in the Scale to Fit group on the PAGE LAYOUT tab
Worksheet, unprotect	EX 425	Go to the worksheet, on the REVIEW tab, in the Changes group, click the Unprotect Sheet button
Worksheet group, print	EX 347	Create a worksheet group, apply page layout settings, click the FILE tab, click Print
Worksheet window, split into panes or remove split	EX 290	On the VIEW tab, in the Window group, click the Split button
Worksheets, copy to another workbook	EX 337	See Reference box: Copying Worksheets
Worksheets, group or ungroup	EX 331	See Reference box: Grouping and Ungrouping Worksheets
Worksheets, move between	EX 8	Click a sheet tab or click a tab scrolling button and then click a sheet tab
XML data, bind to worksheet	EX 715	Drag XML elements from the XML Source pane to cells in the worksheet
XML data map, load	EX 713	See Reference box: Loading an XML Data Map

NEW PERSPECTIVES ON
Microsoft® Access® 2013

COMPREHENSIVE

Joseph J. Adamski
Grand Valley State University

Kathleen T. Finnegan

Sharon Scollard
Mohawk College

CENGAGE Learning

Australia • Brazil • Japan • Korea • Mexico • Singapore • Spain • United Kingdom • United States

Microsoft Access 2013, Comprehensive

BRIEF CONTENTS

ACCESS

Tutorial 1 Creating a Database. . . . . AC 1
Tracking Patient, Visit, and Billing Data

Tutorial 2 Building a Database and Defining Table Relationships . . . . . AC 51
Creating the Billing and Patient Tables

Tutorial 3 Maintaining and Querying a Database. . . . . AC 115
Updating and Retrieving Information About Patients, Visits, and Invoices

Tutorial 5 Creating Advanced Queries and Enhancing Table Design . . . AC 233
Making the Clinic Database Easier to Use

Tutorial 8 Sharing, Integrating, and Analyzing Data. . . . . AC 443
Importing, Exporting, Linking, and Analyzing Data in the Clinic Database

Glossary/Index   **REF 1**

New Perspectives Series

TABLE OF CONTENTS

Tutorial 1 Creating a Database
Tracking Patient, Visit, and Billing Data . . . . **AC 1**

Session 1.1 Visual Overview: The Access Window . . . . AC 2

Introduction to Database Concepts . . . . AC 4

    Organizing Data . . . . AC 4

    Databases and Relationships . . . . AC 4

    Relational Database Management Systems . . . AC 6

Starting Access and Creating a Database. . . . . . . AC 7

    Working in Touch Mode . . . . AC 9

Creating a Table in Datasheet View . . . . AC 11

    Renaming the Default Primary Key Field . . . . AC 12

    Changing the Data Type of the Default Primary Key Field . . . . AC 13

    Adding New Fields . . . . AC 14

    Entering Records. . . . . AC 16

    Saving a Table . . . . AC 19

    Opening a Table . . . . AC 22

Closing a Table and Exiting Access. . . . . AC 22

Session 1.1 Quick Check . . . . AC 23

Session 1.2 Visual Overview: The CREATE Tab Options . . . . AC 24

Copying Records from Another Access Database . . . . AC 26

Navigating a Datasheet . . . . AC 29

Creating a Simple Query . . . . AC 30

Creating a Simple Form. . . . . AC 33

Creating a Simple Report . . . . AC 35

    Printing a Report. . . . . AC 39

Viewing Objects in the Navigation Pane. . . . . . . AC 40

Using Microsoft Access Help. . . . . AC 40

Managing a Database . . . . AC 41

    Compacting and Repairing a Database . . . . . AC 42

    Backing Up and Restoring a Database . . . . . . AC 43

Session 1.2 Quick Check . . . . AC 44

Review Assignments . . . . AC 45

Case Problems. . . . . AC 46

Tutorial 2 Building a Database and Defining Table Relationships
Creating the Billing and Patient Tables . . . . **AC 51**

Session 2.1 Visual Overview: Table Window in Design View. . . . . AC 52

Guidelines for Designing Databases. . . . . AC 54

Guidelines for Setting Field Properties. . . . . AC 56

    Naming Fields and Objects . . . . AC 56

    Assigning Field Data Types. . . . . AC 56

    Setting Field Sizes. . . . . AC 57

    Setting the Caption Property for Fields . . . . . AC 58

Creating a Table in Design View . . . . AC 59
    Defining Fields . . . . AC 59
    Specifying the Primary Key. . . . . AC 67
    Saving the Table Structure . . . . AC 68

Modifying the Structure of an Access Table . . . . AC 68
    Moving a Field in Design View . . . . AC 69
    Adding a Field in Design View . . . . AC 69

Modifying Field Properties . . . . AC 71
    Changing the Format Property in Datasheet View. . . . . AC 71
    Changing Properties in Design View . . . . AC 73

Session 2.1 Quick Check . . . . AC 75

Session 2.2 Visual Overview: Understanding Table Relationships . . . . AC 76

Adding Records to a New Table . . . . AC 78

Importing Data from an Excel Worksheet. . . . . . AC 80

Creating a Table by Importing an Existing Table Structure . . . . AC 83

Adding Fields to a Table Using the Data Type Gallery. . . . . AC 86

Modifying the Imported Table . . . . AC 87
    Deleting Fields from a Table Structure. . . . . . AC 87
    Renaming Fields in Design View. . . . . AC 89
    Changing the Data Type for a Field in Design View . . . . AC 90

Setting the Default Value Property for a Field . . . AC 93

Adding Data to a Table by Importing a Text File . . . . AC 95

Defining Table Relationships. . . . . AC 98
    One-to-Many Relationships . . . . AC 98
    Referential Integrity . . . . AC 99
    Defining a Relationship Between Two Tables . . . . AC 100

Session 2.2 Quick Check. . . . . AC 104

Review Assignments . . . . AC 105

Case Problems. . . . . AC 107

Tutorial 3 Maintaining and Querying a Database
Updating and Retrieving Information About Patients, Visits, and Invoices . . . . **AC 115**

Session 3.1 Visual Overview: Query Window in Design View. . . . . AC 116

Updating a Database. . . . . AC 118
    Modifying Records . . . . AC 118
    Hiding and Unhiding Fields. . . . . AC 119
    Finding Data in a Table. . . . . AC 121
    Deleting Records. . . . . AC 122

Introduction to Queries. . . . . AC 124

Creating and Running a Query . . . . AC 125

Updating Data Using a Query. . . . . AC 128

Creating a Multitable Query . . . . AC 129

Sorting Data in a Query . . . . AC 131
    Using an AutoFilter to Sort Data . . . . AC 132
    Sorting on Multiple Fields in Design View. . . AC 133

Filtering Data. . . . . AC 136

Session 3.1 Quick Check . . . . AC 139

Session 3.2 Visual Overview: Selection Criteria
in Queries . . . . AC 140

Defining Record Selection Criteria for
Queries . . . . AC 142

    Specifying an Exact Match . . . . AC 142

    Modifying a Query . . . . AC 144

    Using a Comparison Operator to Match a
    Range of Values. . . . . AC 147

Defining Multiple Selection Criteria for
Queries. . . . . AC 149

    The And Logical Operator . . . . AC 150

    The Or Logical Operator . . . . AC 151

Changing a Datasheet's Appearance . . . . AC 154

    Modifying the Font Size . . . . AC 154

    Changing the Alternate Row Color in a
    Datasheet . . . . AC 154

Creating a Calculated Field. . . . . AC 156

    Formatting a Calculated Field . . . . AC 160

Using Aggregate Functions. . . . . AC 161

    Working with Aggregate Functions Using
    the Total Row . . . . AC 162

    Creating Queries with Aggregate
    Functions. . . . . AC 163

    Using Record Group Calculations. . . . . AC 166

Working with the Navigation Pane . . . . AC 167

Session 3.2 Quick Check . . . . AC 170

Review Assignments . . . . AC 171

Case Problems. . . . . AC 172

Tutorial 5 Creating Advanced Queries and Enhancing Table Design
Making the Clinic Database Easier to Use . . . . **AC 233**

Session 5.1 Visual Overview: Calculated Field . . . . AC 234

Reviewing the Clinic Database . . . . AC 236

Using a Pattern Match in a Query . . . . AC 237

Using a List-of-Values Match in a Query . . . . . . AC 240

Using the Not Logical Operator in a Query . . . AC 241

    Using an AutoFilter to Filter Data . . . . AC 242

Assigning a Conditional Value to a Calculated Field . . . . AC 245

Creating a Parameter Query . . . . AC 249

    Creating a More Flexible Parameter Query . . . . AC 251

Session 5.1 Quick Check . . . . AC 253

Session 5.2 Visual Overview: Advanced Query Wizards . . . . AC 254

Creating a Crosstab Query . . . . AC 256

Creating a Find Duplicates Query . . . . AC 262

Creating a Find Unmatched Query . . . . AC 264

Creating a Top Values Query . . . . AC 267

Session 5.2 Quick Check . . . . AC 269

Session 5.3 Visual Overview: Lookup Fields and Input Masks . . . . AC 270

Creating a Lookup Field . . . . AC 272

Using the Input Mask Wizard . . . . AC 276

Identifying Object Dependencies . . . . AC 282

Defining Data Validation Rules . . . . AC 283

    Defining Field Validation Rules . . . . AC 284

    Defining Table Validation Rules . . . . AC 286

Working with Long Text Fields . . . . AC 287

Designating a Trusted Folder . . . . AC 290

Session 5.3 Quick Check . . . . AC 293

Review Assignments . . . . AC 294

Case Problems . . . . AC 295

Tutorial 8 Sharing, Integrating, and Analyzing Data
Importing, Exporting, Linking, and Analyzing Data in the Clinic Database .... **AC 443**

Session 8.1 Visual Overview: Exporting data to XML and HTML .... AC 444

Exporting an Access Query to an HTML Document .... AC 446

    Viewing an HTML Document Using Internet Explorer............................. AC 448

Importing a CSV File as an Access Table ..... AC 449

    Analyzing a Table with the Table Analyzer... AC 452

Importing a table from an Access Database... AC 454

Using XML .... AC 456

    Importing Data from an XML File.......... AC 456

    Saving and Running Import Specifications... AC 457

    Exporting an Access Table as an XML File... AC 460

    Saving and Running Export Specifications... AC 463

Session 8.1 Quick Check .... AC

Session 8.2 Visual Overview: Tabbed Control with a Chart................................. AC

Creating a Tabbed Form Using a Tab Control................................... AC

Integrating Access with Other Programs ..... AC

Embedding a Chart in a Form.............. AC

Using Templates and Application Parts ......AC

Exporting a Report to a PDF File .... AC

Linking Data from an Excel Worksheet....... AC

Session 8.2 Quick Check .... AC

Review Assignments .... AC

Case Problems........................... AC

ProSkills Exercise: Decision Making .... AC

Glossary/Index......................... RE

TUTORIAL 1

Creating a Database
Tracking Patient, Visit, and Billing Data

OBJECTIVES

Session 1.1
- Learn basic database concepts and terms
- Start and exit Access
- Explore the Microsoft Access window and Backstage view
- Create a blank database
- Create and save a table in Datasheet view
- Enter field names and records in a table datasheet
- Open a table using the Navigation Pane

Session 1.2
- Open an Access database
- Copy and paste records from another Access database
- Navigate a table datasheet
- Create and navigate a simple query
- Create and navigate a simple form
- Create, preview, navigate, and print a simple report
- Use Help in Access
- Learn how to compact, back up, and restore a database

Case | Chatham Community Health Services

Chatham Community Health Services, a nonprofit health clinic located in Hartford, Connecticut, provides a range of medical services to patients of all ages. The clinic specializes in the areas of pulmonology, cardiac care, and chronic disease management. Cindi Rodriguez, the office manager for Chatham Community Health Services, oversees a small staff and is responsible for maintaining the medical records of the clinic's patients.

In order to best manage the clinic, Cindi and her staff rely on electronic medical records for patient information, billing, inventory control, purchasing, and accounts payable. Several months ago, the clinic upgraded to **Microsoft Access 2013** (or simply **Access**), a computer program used to enter, maintain, and retrieve related data in a format known as a database. Cindi and her staff want to use Access to store information about patients, billing, vendors, and products. She asks for your help in creating the necessary Access database.

STARTING DATA FILES

Access1 → Tutorial
Cindi.accdb

Review
Company.accdb

Case1
Program.accdb

Case2
Consulting.accdb

Case3
Animal.accdb

Case4
Tour.accdb

Microsoft product screenshots used with permission from Microsoft Corporation.

AC 1

AC 2 Access | Tutorial 1 Creating a Database

Session 1.1 Visual Overview:

The **Quick Access Toolbar** provides one-click access to commonly used commands, such as Save.

The **Shutter Bar Open/Close Button** allows you to close and open the Navigation Pane; you might want to close the pane so that you have more room on the screen to view the object's contents.

Access assigns the default name "Table1" to the first new table you create. When you save the table, you can give it a more meaningful name.

By default, Access creates the **ID field** as the primary key field for all new tables.

The **Click to Add column** provides another way for you to add new fields to a table.

The **Add & Delete group** contains options for adding different types of fields, including Short Text and Number, to a table.

The **FIELDS tab** provides options for adding, removing, and formatting the fields in a table.

The **Navigation Pane** lists all the objects (tables, reports, and so on) in the database, and it is the main control center for opening and working with database objects.

Datasheet view shows the table's contents as a datasheet.

Tutorial 1 Creating a Database | Access   AC 3

The Access Window

The **Access window** is the program window that appears when you create a new database or open an existing database.

You use the window buttons to minimize, maximize, and close the Access window.

The **Sign in link** lets you sign into your Office account. If you have already signed in, your name might appear here instead of this link.

The **ribbon** provides the main Access commands organized by task into tabs and groups.

The **title bar** displays the name of the open file and the program.

The **status bar** provides information about the program or open file, as well as buttons for working with the file. At the far left, the status bar indicates the current view, in this case, Datasheet view.

A **datasheet** displays the table's contents in rows and columns, similar to a table that you create in a Word document or an Excel spreadsheet. Each row will be a separate record in the table, and each column will contain the field values for one field in the table.

Introduction to Database Concepts

Before you begin using Access to create the database for Cindi, you need to understand a few key terms and concepts associated with databases.

Organizing Data

Data is a valuable resource to any business. At Chatham Community Health Services, for example, important data includes patients' names and addresses, visit dates, and billing information. Organizing, storing, maintaining, retrieving, and sorting this type of data are critical activities that enable a business to find and use information effectively. Before storing data on a computer, however, you must organize the data.

Your first step in organizing data is to identify the individual fields. A **field** is a single characteristic or attribute of a person, place, object, event, or idea. For example, some of the many fields that Chatham Community Health Services tracks are patient ID, first name, last name, address, phone number, visit date, reason for visit, and invoice amount.

Next, you group related fields together into tables. A **table** is a collection of fields that describes a person, place, object, event, or idea. Figure 1-1 shows an example of a Patient table that contains the following four fields: PatientID, FirstName, LastName, and Phone. Each field is a column in the table, with the field name displayed as the column heading.

Figure 1-1   Data organization for a table of patients

Patient table

PatientID	FirstName	LastName	Phone
22501	Edward	Darcy	860-305-3985
22504	Lilian	Aguilar	860-374-5724
22510	Thomas	Booker	860-661-2539
22512	Lisa	Chang	860-226-6034
22529	Robert	Goldberg	860-552-2873
22537	Amrita	Mehta	860-552-0375

© 2014 Cengage Learning

The specific content of a field is called the **field value**. In Figure 1-1, the first set of field values for PatientID, FirstName, LastName, and Phone are, respectively: 22501; Edward; Darcy; and 860-305-3985. This set of field values is called a **record**. In the Patient table, the data for each patient is stored as a separate record. Figure 1-1 shows six records; each row of field values in the table is a record.

Databases and Relationships

A collection of related tables is called a **database**, or a **relational database**. In this tutorial, you will create the database for Chatham Community Health Services, and within that database, you'll create a table named Visit to store data about patient visits. Later on, you'll create two more tables, named Patient and Billing, to store related information about patients and their invoices.

As Cindi and her staff use the database that you will create, they will need to access information about patients and their visits. To obtain this information, you must have a way to connect records in the Patient table to records in the Visit table. You connect the records in the separate tables through a **common field** that appears in both tables.

In the sample database shown in Figure 1-2, each record in the Patient table has a field named PatientID, which is also a field in the Visit table. For example, Robert Goldberg is the fifth patient in the Patient table and has a PatientID field value of 22529. This same PatientID field value, 22529, appears in two records in the Visit table. Therefore, Robert Goldberg is the patient who made these two visits.

Figure 1-2   Database relationship between tables for patients and visits

Patient table

PatientID	FirstName	LastName	Phone
22501	Edward	Darcy	860-305-3985
22504	Lilian	Aguilar	860-374-5724
22510	Thomas	Booker	860-661-2539
22512	Lisa	Chang	860-226-6034
22529	Robert	Goldberg	860-552-2873
22537	Amrita	Mehta	860-552-0375

Visit table

VisitID	PatientID	VisitDate	Reason
1539	22504	11/18/2015	Annual wellness visit
1549	22501	11/30/2015	Influenza
1564	22512	1/5/2016	Annual wellness visit
1610	22529	2/9/2016	Sinusitis
1613	22510	2/11/2016	Hypertension
1688	22529	4/12/2016	Annual wellness visit
1690	22537	4/13/2016	Varicella

© 2014 Cengage Learning

Each PatientID value in the Patient table must be unique so that you can distinguish one patient from another. These unique PatientID values also identify each patient's specific visits in the Visit table. The PatientID field is referred to as the primary key of the Patient table. A **primary key** is a field, or a collection of fields, whose values uniquely identify each record in a table. No two records can contain the same value for the primary key field. In the Visit table, the VisitID field is the primary key because Chatham Community Health Services assigns each visit a unique identification number.

When you include the primary key from one table as a field in a second table to form a relationship between the two tables, it is called a **foreign key** in the second table, as shown in Figure 1-2. For example, PatientID is the primary key in the Patient table and a foreign key in the Visit table. The PatientID field must have the same characteristics in both tables. Although the primary key PatientID contains unique values in the Patient table, the same field as a foreign key in the Visit table does not necessarily contain unique values. The PatientID value 22529, for example, appears two times in the Visit table because Robert Goldberg made two visits to the clinic. Each foreign key value, however, must match one of the field values for the primary key in the other table. In the example shown in Figure 1-2, each PatientID value in the Visit table must match a PatientID value in the Patient table. The two tables are related, enabling users to connect the facts about patients with the facts about their visits to the clinic.

Storing Data in Separate Tables

When you create a database, you must create separate tables that contain only fields that are directly related to each other. For example, in the Chatham database, the patient and visit data should not be stored in the same table because doing so would make the data difficult to update and prone to errors. Consider the patient Robert Goldberg and his visits to the clinic, and assume that he has many more than just two visits. If all the patient and visit data were stored in the same table, so that each record (row) contained all the information about each visit and the patient, the patient data would appear multiple times in the table. This causes problems when the data changes. For example, if Robert Goldberg's phone number changed, you would have to update the multiple occurrences of the phone number throughout the table. Not only would this be time-consuming, it would increase the likelihood of errors or inconsistent data.

Relational Database Management Systems

To manage its databases, a company uses a database management system. A **database management system (DBMS)** is a software program that lets you create databases and then manipulate the data they contain. Most of today's database management systems, including Access, are called relational database management systems. In a **relational database management system**, data is organized as a collection of tables. As stated earlier, a relationship between two tables in a relational DBMS is formed through a common field.

A relational DBMS controls the storage of databases and facilitates the creation, manipulation, and reporting of data, as illustrated in Figure 1-3.

Figure 1-3 Relational database management system

© 2014 Cengage Learning

Specifically, a relational DBMS provides the following functions:

- It allows you to create database structures containing fields, tables, and table relationships.
- It lets you easily add new records, change field values in existing records, and delete records.
- It contains a built-in query language, which lets you obtain immediate answers to the questions (or queries) you ask about your data.
- It contains a built-in report generator, which lets you produce professional-looking, formatted reports from your data.
- It protects databases through security, control, and recovery facilities.

An organization such as Chatham Community Health Services benefits from a relational DBMS because it allows users working in different groups to share the same data. More than one user can enter data into a database, and more than one user can retrieve and analyze data that other users have entered. For example, the database for Chatham Community Health Services will contain only one copy of the Visit table, and all employees will use it to access visit information.

Finally, unlike other software programs, such as spreadsheet programs, a DBMS can handle massive amounts of data and can be used to create relationships among multiple tables. Each Access database, for example, can be up to two gigabytes in size, can contain up to 32,768 objects (tables, reports, and so on), and can have up to 255 people using the database at the same time. For instructional purposes, the databases you will create and work with throughout this text contain a relatively small number of records compared to databases you would encounter outside the classroom, which would likely contain tables with very large numbers of records.

Starting Access and Creating a Database

Now that you've learned some database terms and concepts, you're ready to start Access and create the Chatham database for Cindi.

To start Access:

1. Display the Windows Start screen, if necessary.

   Using Windows 7? To complete Step 1, click the Start button on the taskbar.

2. Click the **Access 2013** tile. Access starts and displays the Recent screen in Backstage view. See Figure 1-4.

Figure 1-4 Recent screen in Backstage view

- option for searching for a template online
- option for creating a new, blank database
- a list of recently opened databases might appear here
- option for opening an existing database
- options for creating a new database using a template

Trouble? If you don't see the Access 2013 tile on your Start screen, type Access to display the Apps screen with the Access 2013 tile highlighted, and then click the tile.

Using Windows 7? To complete Step 2, point to All Programs on the Start menu, click Microsoft Office 2013, and then click Access 2013.

When you start Access, the first screen that appears is Backstage view, which is the starting place for your work in Access. **Backstage view** contains commands that allow you to manage Access files and options. The Recent screen in Backstage view provides options for you to create a new database or open an existing database. To create a new database that does not contain any data or objects, you use the Blank desktop database option. If the database you need to create contains objects that match those found in common databases, such as databases that store data about contacts or tasks, you can use one of the templates provided with Access. A **template** is a predesigned database that includes professionally designed tables, reports, and other database objects that can make it quick and easy for you to create a database. You can also search for a template online using the Search box.

In this case, the templates provided do not match Cindi's needs for the clinic's database, so you need to create a new, blank database from scratch.

To create the new Chatham database:

1. Make sure you have the Access starting Data Files on your computer.

   Trouble? If you don't have the starting Data Files, you need to get them before you can proceed. Your instructor will either give you the Data Files or ask you to obtain them from a specified location (such as a network drive). If you have any questions about the Data Files, see your instructor or technical support person for assistance.

Tutorial 1 Creating a Database | Access   AC 9

> **Be sure to type Chatham or you'll create a database named Database1.**

2. Click the **Blank desktop database** option (see Figure 1-4). The Blank desktop database screen opens.

3. In the File Name box, type **Chatham** to replace the selected database name provided by Access, Database1. Next you need to specify the location for the file.

4. Click the **Browse** button to the right of the File Name box. The File New Database dialog box opens.

5. Navigate to the drive and folder where you are storing your files, as specified by your instructor.

6. Make sure the "Save as type" box displays "Microsoft Access 2007 – 2013 Databases."

   Trouble? If your computer is set up to show filename extensions, you will see the Access filename extension ".accdb" in the File name box.

> **TIP**
> If you don't type the filename extension, Access adds it automatically.

7. Click the **OK** button. You return to the Blank desktop database screen, and the File Name box now shows the name Chatham.accdb. The filename extension ".accdb" identifies the file as an Access 2007 - 2013 database.

8. Click the **Create** button. Access creates the new database, saves it to the specified location, and then opens an empty table named Table1.

   Trouble? If you see only ribbon tab names and no buttons, click the HOME tab to expand the ribbon, and then in the bottom-right corner of the ribbon, click the Pin the ribbon button.

Refer back to the Session 1.1 Visual Overview and spend some time becoming familiar with the components of the Access window.

INSIGHT

Understanding the Database File Type

Access 2013 uses the .accdb file extension, which is the same file extension used for databases created with Microsoft Access 2007 and 2010. To ensure compatibility between these earlier versions and the Access 2013 software, new databases created using Access 2013 have the same file extension and file format as Access 2007 and Access 2010 databases. This is why the File New Database dialog box provides the Microsoft Access 2007 - 2013 Databases option in the "Save as type" box. In addition, the notation "(Access 2007 - 2013 file format)" appears in the title bar next to the name of an open database in Access 2013, confirming that database files with the .accdb extension can be used in Access 2007, Access 2010, and Access 2013.

Working in Touch Mode

> **TIP**
> On a touch device, you *tap* instead of *click*.

If you are working on a touch device, such as a tablet, you can switch to Touch Mode in Access to make it easier for you to tap buttons on the ribbon and perform other touch actions. Your screens will not match those shown in the book exactly, but this will not cause any problems.

Note: The following steps assume that you are using a mouse. If you are instead using a touch device, please read these steps but don't complete them, so that you remain working in Touch Mode.

To switch to Touch Mode:

1. On the Quick Access Toolbar, click the **Customize Quick Access Toolbar** button. A menu opens listing buttons you can add to the Quick Access Toolbar as well as other options for customizing the toolbar.

   Trouble? If the Touch/Mouse Mode command on the menu has a checkmark next to it, press the Esc key to close the menu, and then skip to Step 3.

2. Click **Touch/Mouse Mode**. The Quick Access Toolbar now contains the Touch/Mouse Mode button, which you can use to switch between Mouse Mode, the default display, and Touch Mode.

3. On the Quick Access Toolbar, click the **Touch/Mouse Mode** button. A menu opens with two commands: Mouse, which shows the ribbon in the standard display and is optimized for use with the mouse; and Touch, which provides more space between the buttons and commands on the ribbon and is optimized for use with touch devices. The icon next to Mouse is shaded red to indicate that it is selected.

   Trouble? If the icon next to Touch is shaded red, press the Esc key to close the menu and skip to Step 5.

4. Click **Touch**. The display switches to Touch Mode with more space between the commands and buttons on the ribbon. See Figure 1-5.

Figure 1-5   **Ribbon displayed in Touch Mode**

Touch/Mouse Mode button on Quick Access Toolbar

ribbon includes more space around buttons and options

The figures in this text show the standard Mouse Mode display, and the instructions assume you are using a mouse to click and select options, so you'll switch back to Mouse Mode.

Trouble? If you are using a touch device and want to remain in Touch Mode, skip Steps 5 and 6.

5. On the Quick Access Toolbar, click the **Touch/Mouse Mode** button, and then click **Mouse**. The ribbon returns to the standard display, as shown in the Session 1.1 Visual Overview.

6. On the Quick Access Toolbar, click the **Customize Quick Access Toolbar** button, and then click **Touch/Mouse Mode** to deselect it. The Touch/Mouse Mode button is removed from the Quick Access Toolbar.

Creating a Table in Datasheet View

Tables contain all the data in a database and are the fundamental objects for your work in Access. There are different ways to create a table in Access, including entering the fields and records for the table directly in Datasheet view.

> **REFERENCE**
>
> **Creating a Table in Datasheet View**
>
> - On the ribbon, click the CREATE tab.
> - In the Tables group, click the Table button.
> - Rename the default ID primary key field and change its data type, if necessary; or accept the default ID field with the AutoNumber data type.
> - In the Add & Delete group on the FIELDS tab, click the button for the type of field you want to add to the table (for example, click the Short Text button), and then type the field name; or, in the table datasheet, click the Click to Add column heading, click the type of field you want to add from the list that opens, and then press the Tab or Enter key to move to the next column in the datasheet. Repeat this step to add all the necessary fields to the table.
> - In the first row below the field names, enter the value for each field in the first record, pressing the Tab or Enter key to move from one field to the next.
> - After entering the value for the last field in the first record, press the Tab or Enter key to move to the next row, and then enter the values for the next record. Continue this process until you have entered all the records for the table.
> - On the Quick Access Toolbar, click the Save button, enter a name for the table, and then click the OK button.

For Chatham Community Health Services, Cindi needs to track information about each patient visit at the clinic. She asks you to create the Visit table according to the plan shown in Figure 1-6.

Figure 1-6   Plan for the Visit table

Field	Purpose
VisitID	Unique number assigned to each visit; will serve as the table's primary key
PatientID	Unique number assigned to each patient; common field that will be a foreign key to connect to the Patient table
VisitDate	Date on which the patient visited the clinic
Reason	Reason/diagnosis for the patient visit
WalkIn	Whether the patient visit was a walk-in or a scheduled appointment

© 2014 Cengage Learning

As shown in Cindi's plan, she wants to store data about visits in five fields, including fields to contain the date of each visit, the reason for the visit, and if the visit was a walk-in or scheduled appointment. These are the most important aspects of a visit and, therefore, must be tracked. Also, notice that the VisitID field will be the primary key for the table; each visit at Chatham Community Health Services has a unique number assigned to it, so this field is the logical choice for the primary key. Finally, the PatientID field is needed in the Visit table as a foreign key to connect the information about visits to patients. The data about patients and their bills will be stored in separate tables, which you will create later.

Notice the name of each field in Figure 1-6. You need to name each field, table, and other object in an Access database.

PROSKILLS

Decision Making: Naming Fields in Access Tables

One of the most important tasks in creating a table is deciding what names to specify for the table's fields. Keep the following guidelines in mind when you assign field names:

- A field name can consist of up to 64 characters, including letters, numbers, spaces, and special characters, except for the period (.), exclamation mark (!), grave accent (`), and square brackets ([ ]).
- A field name cannot begin with a space.
- Capitalize the first letter of each word in a field name that combines multiple words, for example VisitDate.
- Use concise field names that are easy to remember and reference, and that won't take up a lot of space in the table datasheet.
- Use standard abbreviations, such as Num for Number, Amt for Amount, and Qty for Quantity, and use them consistently throughout the database. For example, if you use Num for Number in one field name, do not use the number sign (#) for Number in another.
- Give fields descriptive names so that you can easily identify them when you view or edit records.
- Although Access supports the use of spaces in field names (and in other object names), experienced database developers avoid using spaces because they can cause errors when the objects are involved in programming tasks.

By spending time obtaining and analyzing information about the fields in a table, and understanding the rules for naming Access fields, you can create a well-designed table that will be easy for others to use.

Renaming the Default Primary Key Field

As noted earlier, Access provides the ID field as the default primary key for a new table you create in Datasheet view. Recall that a primary key is a field, or a collection of fields, whose values uniquely identify each record in a table. However, according to Cindi's plan, the VisitID field should be the primary key for the Visit table. You'll begin by renaming the default ID field to create the VisitID field.

To rename the ID field to the VisitID field:

TIP

A **shortcut menu** opens when you right-click an object and provides options for working with that object.

1. Right-click the **ID** column heading to open the shortcut menu, and then click **Rename Field**. The column heading ID is selected, so that whatever text you type next will replace it.

2. Type **VisitID** and then click the row below the heading. The column heading changes to VisitID, and the insertion point moves to the row below the heading. See Figure 1-7.

   Trouble? If you make a mistake while typing the field name, use the Backspace key to delete characters to the left of the insertion point or the Delete key to delete characters to the right of the insertion point. Then type the correct text. To correct a field name by replacing it entirely, press the Esc key, and then type the correct text.

Tutorial 1 Creating a Database | Access   AC 13

Figure 1-7   **ID field renamed to VisitID**

TABLE TOOLS contextual tab is active

AutoNumber data type assigned to the default primary key field (ID)

VisitID field name entered in the column heading

option for specifying the data type for a field

The **insertion point** is a flashing cursor that shows where text you type will be inserted. In this case, it is hidden within the selected field value (New).

Notice that the TABLE TOOLS tab is active on the ribbon. This is an example of a **contextual tab**, which is a tab that appears and provides options for working with a specific object that is selected—in this case, the table you are creating. As you work with other objects in the database, other contextual tabs will appear with commands and options related to each selected object.

Buttons and Labels on the Ribbon

INSIGHT

Depending on the size of the monitor you are using and your screen resolution settings, you might see more or fewer buttons on the ribbon, and you might not see labels next to certain buttons. The screenshots in these tutorials were created using a screen resolution setting of 1366 x 768 with the program window maximized. If you are using a smaller monitor or a lower screen resolution, some buttons will appear only as icons, with no labels next to them, because there is not enough room on the ribbon to display the labels.

You have renamed the default primary key field, ID, to VisitID. However, the VisitID field still retains the characteristics of the ID field, including its data type. Your next task is to change the data type of this field.

Changing the Data Type of the Default Primary Key Field

Notice the Formatting group on the FIELDS tab. One of the options available in this group is the Data Type option (see Figure 1-7). Each field in an Access table must be assigned a data type. The **data type** determines what field values you can enter for the field. In this case, the AutoNumber data type is displayed. Access assigns the AutoNumber data type to the default ID primary key field because the **AutoNumber** data type automatically inserts a unique number in this field for every record, beginning with the number 1 for the first record, the number 2 for the second record, and so on. Therefore, a field using the AutoNumber data type can serve as the primary key for any table you create.

Visit numbers at Chatham Community Health Services are specific, four-digit numbers, so the AutoNumber data type is not appropriate for the VisitID field, which is the primary key field in the table you are creating. A better choice is the **Short Text** data type, which allows field values containing letters, digits, and other characters, and which is appropriate for identifying numbers, such as visit numbers, that are never used in calculations. So, Cindi asks you to change the data type for the VisitID field from AutoNumber to Short Text.

To change the data type for the VisitID field:

1. Make sure that the VisitID column is selected. A column is selected when you click a field value, in which case the background color of the column heading changes to orange (the default color) and the insertion point appears in the field value. You can also click the column heading to select a column, in which case the background color of both the column heading and the field value changes (the default colors are gray and blue, respectively).

2. In the Formatting group on the FIELDS tab, click the **Data Type arrow**, and then click **Short Text**. The VisitID field is now a Short Text field. See Figure 1-8.

Figure 1-8   Short Text data type assigned to the VisitID field

Note the Unique check box in the Field Validation group. This check box is selected because the VisitID field assumed the characteristics of the default primary key field, ID, including the fact that each value in the field must be unique. Because this check box is selected, no two records in the Visit table will be allowed to have the same value in the VisitID field.

With the VisitID field created and established as the primary key, you can now enter the rest of the fields in the Visit table.

Adding New Fields

When you create a table in Datasheet view, you can use the options in the Add & Delete group on the FIELDS tab to add fields to your table. You can also use the Click to Add column in the table datasheet to add new fields. (See Figure 1-8.) You'll use both methods to add the four remaining fields to the Visit table. The next field you need to add is the PatientID field. Similar to the VisitID field, the PatientID field will contain numbers that will not be used in calculations, so it should be a Short Text field.

Tutorial 1 Creating a Database | Access   AC 15

To add the rest of the fields to the Visit table:

1. In the Add & Delete group on the FIELDS tab, click the **Short Text** button. Access adds a new field named "Field1" to the right of the VisitID field. See Figure 1-9.

Figure 1-9   New Short Text field added to the table

[Screenshot showing Access table with annotations: "new field added as the second field in the table", "indicates the data type of the new field", and "default name highlighted in the new field"]

The text "Field1" is selected, so you can simply type the new field name to replace it.

2. Type **PatientID**. The second field is added to the table. Next, you'll add the VisitDate field. Because this field will contain date values, you'll add a field with the **Date/Time** data type, which allows field values in a variety of date and time formats.

3. In the Add & Delete group, click the **Date & Time** button. Access adds a third field to the table, this time with the Date/Time data type.

4. Type **VisitDate** to replace the highlighted name "Field1." The fourth field in the Visit table is the Reason field, which will contain brief descriptions of the reason for the visit to the clinic. You'll add another Short Text field—this time using the Click to Add column.

5. Click the **Click to Add** column heading. Access displays a list of available data types from which you can choose the data type for the new field you're adding.

6. Click **Short Text** in the list. Access adds a fourth field to the table.

7. Type **Reason** to replace the highlighted name "Field1," and then press the **Enter** key. The Click to Add column becomes active and displays the list of field data types.

The fifth and final field in the Visit table is the WalkIn field, which will indicate whether or not the visit was a walk-in (that is, the patient did not have a scheduled appointment). The **Yes/No** data type is suitable for this field because it is used to define fields that store values representing one of two options—true/false, yes/no, or on/off.

TIP
You can also type the first letter of a data type to select it and close the Click to Add list.

8. Click **Yes/No** in the list, and then type **WalkIn** to replace the highlighted name "Field1."

   Trouble? If you pressed the Tab or Enter key after typing the WalkIn field name, press the Esc key to close the Click to Add list.

9. Click in the row below the VisitID column heading. All five fields are now entered for the Visit table. See Figure 1-10.

Figure 1-10   **Table with all fields entered**

- five fields entered
- record (row) selector
- field (column) selector
- values for first record will go in this row

The table contains three Short Text fields (VisitID, PatientID, and Reason), one Date/Time field (VisitDate), and one Yes/No field (WalkIn). You'll learn more about field data types in the next tutorial.

As noted earlier, Datasheet view shows a table's contents in rows (records) and columns (fields). Each column is headed by a field name inside a field selector, and each row has a record selector to its left (see Figure 1-10). Clicking a **field selector** or a **record selector** selects that entire column or row (respectively), which you then can manipulate. A field selector is also called a **column selector**, and a record selector is also called a **row selector**.

Entering Records

With the fields in place for the table, you can now enter the field values for each record. Cindi requests that you enter eight records in the Visit table, as shown in Figure 1-11.

Figure 1-11   **Visit table records**

VisitID	PatientID	VisitDate	Reason	WalkIn
1550	22549	12/1/2015	Influenza	Yes
1527	22522	11/9/2015	Allergies - environmental	Yes
1555	22520	12/7/2015	Annual wellness visit	No
1542	22537	11/24/2015	Influenza	Yes
1530	22510	11/10/2015	Seborrheic dermatitis	No
1564	22512	1/5/2016	Annual wellness visit	No
1575	22513	1/13/2016	Broken leg	Yes
1538	22500	11/17/2015	Migraine	Yes

© 2014 Cengage Learning

To enter records in a table datasheet, you type the field values below the column headings for the fields. The first record you enter will go in the first row (see Figure 1-10).

Tutorial 1 Creating a Database | Access   **AC 17**

To enter the first record for the Visit table:

> Be sure to type the numbers "0" and "1" and not the letters "O" and "I" in the field value.

1. In the first row for the VisitID field, type **1550** (the VisitID field value for the first record), and then press the **Tab** key. Access adds the field value and moves the insertion point to the right, into the PatientID column. See Figure 1-12.

Figure 1-12   **First field value entered**

[Screenshot showing Access Table1 in datasheet view with callouts: "pencil symbol", "star symbol", "first VisitID field value entered" (1550), and "insertion point positioned in the PatientID field"]

   Trouble? If you make a mistake when typing a value, use the Backspace key to delete characters to the left of the insertion point or the Delete key to delete characters to the right of the insertion point. Then type the correct value. To correct a value by replacing it entirely, press the Esc key, and then type the correct value.

   Notice the pencil symbol that appears in the row selector for the new record. The **pencil symbol** indicates that the record is being edited. Also notice the star symbol that appears in the row selector for the second row. The **star symbol** identifies the second row as the next row available for a new record.

2. Type **22549** (the PatientID field value for the first record), and then press the **Tab** key. Access enters the field value and moves the insertion point to the VisitDate column.

3. Type **12/1/15** (the VisitDate field value for the first record), and then press the **Tab** key. Access displays the year as "2015" even though you entered only the final two digits of the year. This is because the VisitDate field has the Date/Time data type, which automatically formats dates with four-digit years.

   Trouble? Depending on your Windows date setting, your VisitDate field values might be displayed in a different format. This difference will not cause any problems.

4. Type **Influenza** (the Reason field value for the first record), and then press the **Tab** key to move to the WalkIn column.

   Recall that the WalkIn field is a Yes/No field. Notice the check box displayed in the WalkIn column. By default, the value for any Yes/No field is "No"; therefore, the check box is initially empty. For Yes/No fields with check boxes, you press the Tab key to leave the check box unchecked, or you press the spacebar to insert a checkmark in the check box. The record you are entering in the table is for a walk-in visit, so you need to insert a checkmark in the check box to indicate "Yes."

TIP

You can also click a check box in a Yes/No field to insert or remove a checkmark.

5. Press the **spacebar** to insert a checkmark, and then press the **Tab** key. The first record is entered into the table, and the insertion point is positioned in the VisitID field for the second record. The pencil symbol is removed from the first row because the record in that row is no longer being edited. The table is now ready for you to enter the second record. See Figure 1-13.

Figure 1-13   **Datasheet with first record entered**

next row available for a new record

field values for the first record entered

value displayed with a four-digit year

Now you can enter the remaining seven records in the Visit table.

To enter the remaining records in the Visit table:

TIP

You can also press the Enter key instead of the Tab key to move from one field to another, and to the next row.

1. Referring to Figure 1-11, enter the values for records 2 through 8, pressing the **Tab** key to move from field to field and to the next row for a new record. Keep in mind that you do not have to type all four digits of the year in the VisitDate field values; you can enter only the final two digits and Access will display all four. Also, for any WalkIn field values of "No," be sure to press the Tab key to leave the check box empty.

   Trouble? If you enter a value in the wrong field by mistake, such as entering a Reason field value in the VisitDate field, a menu might open with options for addressing the problem. If this happens, click the "Enter new value" option in the menu. You'll return to the field with the incorrect value highlighted, which you can then replace by typing the correct value.

   Notice that not all of the Reason field values are fully displayed. To see more of the table datasheet and the full field values, you'll close the Navigation Pane and resize the Reason column.

2. At the top of the Navigation Pane, click the **Shutter Bar Open/Close Button** «. The Navigation Pane closes, and only the complete table datasheet is displayed.

3. Place the pointer on the vertical line to the right of the Reason field name until the pointer changes to a ↔ shape, and then double-click the vertical line. All the Reason field values are now fully displayed. See Figure 1-14.

Figure 1-14   **Datasheet with eight records entered**

Navigation Pane is closed

VisitID	PatientID	VisitDate	Reason	WalkIn
1550	22549	12/1/2015	Influenza	✓
1527	22522	11/9/2015	Allergies - environmental	✓
1555	22520	12/7/2015	Annual wellness visit	
1542	22537	11/24/2015	Influenza	✓
1530	22510	11/10/2015	Seborrheic dermatitis	
1564	22512	1/5/2016	Annual wellness visit	
1575	22513	1/13/2016	Broken leg	✓
1538	22500	11/17/2015	Migraine	✓

field values are completely visible

When you resize a datasheet column by double-clicking the column dividing line, you are sizing the column to its **best fit**—that is, so the column is just wide enough to display the longest visible value in the column, including the field name.

> *Carefully compare your VisitID and PatientID values with those in the figure, and correct any errors before continuing.*

4. Compare your table to the one in Figure 1-14. If any of the field values in your table do not match those shown in the figure, you can correct a field value by clicking to position the insertion point in the value, and then using the Backspace key or Delete key to delete incorrect text. Then type the correct text and press the Enter key. To correct a value in the WalkIn field, simply click the check box to add or remove the checkmark as appropriate. Also, be sure the spelling and capitalization of field names in your table match those shown in the figure exactly, and that there are no spaces between words. To correct a field name, double-click it to select it, and then type the correct name; or use the Rename Field option on the shortcut menu to rename a field with the correct name.

Saving a Table

The records you enter are immediately stored in the database as soon as you enter them; however, the table's design—the field names and characteristics of the fields themselves, plus any layout changes to the datasheet—are not saved until you save the table. When you save a new table for the first time, you should give it a name that best identifies the information it contains. Like a field name, a table name can contain up to 64 characters, including spaces.

REFERENCE

Saving a Table

- Make sure the table you want to save is open.
- On the Quick Access Toolbar, click the Save button. The Save As dialog box opens.
- In the Table Name box, type the name for the table.
- Click the OK button.

According to Cindi's plan, you need to save the table with the name "Visit."

To save and name the Visit table:

1. On the Quick Access Toolbar, click the **Save** button. The Save As dialog box opens.

2. With the default name Table1 selected in the Table Name box, type **Visit**, and then click the **OK** button. The tab for the table now displays the name "Visit," and the Visit table design is saved in the Chatham database.

> **TIP**
> You can also use the Save command in Backstage view to save and name a new table.

Notice that after you saved and named the Visit table, Access sorted and displayed the records in order by the values in the VisitID field because it is the primary key. If you compare your screen to Figure 1-11, which shows the records in the order you entered them, you'll see that the current screen shows the records in order by the VisitID field values.

Cindi asks you to add two more records to the Visit table. When you add a record to an existing table, you must enter the new record in the next row available for a new record; you cannot insert a row between existing records for the new record. In a table with just a few records, such as the Visit table, the next available row is visible on the screen. However, in a table with hundreds of records, you would need to scroll the datasheet to see the next row available. The easiest way to add a new record to a table is to use the New button, which scrolls the datasheet to the next row available so you can enter the new record.

To enter additional records in the Visit table:

1. If necessary, click the first record's VisitID field value (**1527**) to make it the current record.

2. On the ribbon, click the **HOME** tab.

3. In the Records group, click the **New** button. The insertion point is positioned in the next row available for a new record, which in this case is row 9. See Figure 1-15.

Figure 1-15   Entering a new record

4. With the insertion point in the VisitID field for the new record, type **1548** and then press the **Tab** key.

5. Complete the entry of this record by entering each value shown below, pressing the **Tab** key to move from field to field:

   PatientID = **22519**

   VisitDate = **11/30/2015**

   Reason = **Hypertension**

   WalkIn = **No (unchecked)**

6. Enter the values for the next new record, as follows, and then press the **Tab** key after entering the WalkIn field value:

   VisitID = **1560**

   PatientID = **22514**

   VisitDate = **12/15/2015**

   Reason = **Influenza**

   WalkIn = **Yes (checked)**

   Your datasheet should now look like the one shown in Figure 1-16.

Figure 1-16 Datasheet with additional records entered

[Screenshot of Access datasheet showing the Visit table with records. Annotations point to "button for closing the Visit table" (X on object tab) and "two new records added at the end of the table" (records 1548 and 1560).]

Records shown in table:
VisitID	PatientID	VisitDate	Reason	WalkIn
1527	22522	11/9/2015	Allergies - environmental	✓
1530	22510	11/10/2015	Seborrheic dermatitis	
1538	22500	11/17/2015	Migraine	✓
1542	22537	11/24/2015	Influenza	✓
1550	22549	12/1/2015	Influenza	✓
1555	22520	12/7/2015	Annual wellness visit	
1564	22512	1/5/2016	Annual wellness visit	
1575	22513	1/13/2016	Broken leg	✓
1548	22519	11/30/2015	Hypertension	
1560	22514	12/15/2015	Influenza	✓

The new records you added appear at the end of the table, and are not sorted in order by the primary key field values. For example, VisitID 1548 should be the fifth record in the table, placed between VisitID 1542 and VisitID 1550. When you add records to a table datasheet, they appear at the end of the table. The records are not displayed in primary key order until you either close and reopen the table or switch between views.

7. Click the **Close** button ⓧ on the object tab (see Figure 1-16 for the location of this button). The Visit table closes, and the main portion of the Access window is now blank because no database object is currently open. The Chatham database file is still open, as indicated by the filename in the Access window title bar.

Opening a Table

The tables in a database are listed in the Navigation Pane. You open a table, or any Access object, by double-clicking the object name in the Navigation Pane. Next, you'll open the Visit table so you can see the order of all the records you've entered.

To open the Visit table:

1. On the Navigation Pane, click the **Shutter Bar Open/Close Button** ≫ to open the pane. Note that the Visit table is listed.
2. Double-click **Visit** to open the table in Datasheet view. See Figure 1-17.

Figure 1-17   Table with 10 records entered and displayed in primary key order

- Visit table object in the Chatham database
- two records added now appear in primary key order
- records listed in order by the values in the primary key field
- Current Record box indicates the table contains 10 records

VisitID	PatientID	VisitDate	Reason	WalkIn
1527	22522	11/9/2015	Allergies - environmental	✓
1530	22510	11/10/2015	Seborrheic dermatitis	
1538	22500	11/17/2015	Migraine	✓
1542	22537	11/24/2015	Influenza	✓
1548	22519	11/30/2015	Hypertension	
1550	22549	12/1/2015	Influenza	✓
1555	22520	12/7/2015	Annual wellness visit	
1560	22514	12/15/2015	Influenza	✓
1564	22512	1/5/2016	Annual wellness visit	
1575	22513	1/13/2016	Broken leg	✓

The two records you added, with VisitID field values of 1548 and 1560, now appear in the correct primary key order. The table now contains a total of 10 records, as indicated by the Current Record box at the bottom of the datasheet. The **Current Record box** displays the number of the current record as well as the total number of records in the table.

Each record contains a unique VisitID value because this field is the primary key. Other fields, however, can contain the same value in multiple records; for example, note the three values of "Influenza" in the Reason field.

Closing a Table and Exiting Access

When you are finished working in an Access table, it's a good idea to close the table so that you do not make unintended changes to the table data. You can close a table by clicking its Close button on the object tab, as you did earlier. Or, if you want to close the Access program as well, you can click the program's Close button. When you do, any open tables are closed, the active database is closed, and you exit the Access program.

TIP

To close a database without exiting Access, click the FILE tab to display Backstage view, and then click Close.

To close the Visit table and exit Access:

1. Click the **Close** button ☒ on the program window title bar. Access closes the Visit table and the Chatham database, and then the Access program closes.

> **INSIGHT**
>
> ### Saving a Database
>
> Unlike the Save buttons in other Office programs, the Save button on the Quick Access Toolbar in Access does not save the active document (database). Instead, you use the Save button to save the design of an Access object, such as a table (as you saw earlier), or to save datasheet format changes, such as resizing columns. Access does not have a button or option you can use to save the active database.
>
> Access saves changes to the active database automatically when you change or add a record or close the database. If your database is stored on a removable medium, such as a USB drive, you should never remove the drive while the database file is open. If you do, Access will encounter problems when it tries to save the database, which might damage the database. Make sure you close the database first before removing the drive.

Now that you've become familiar with database concepts and Access, and created the Chatham database and the Visit table, Cindi wants you to add more records to the table and work with the data stored in it to create database objects including a query, form, and report. You'll complete these tasks in the next session.

Session 1.1 Quick Check

REVIEW

1. A(n) _____ is a single characteristic of a person, place, object, event, or idea.
2. You connect the records in two separate tables through a(n) _____ that appears in both tables.
3. The _____, whose values uniquely identify each record in a table, is called a(n) _____ when it is placed in a second table to form a relationship between the two tables.
4. The _____ is the area of the Access window that lists all the objects in a database, and it is the main control center for opening and working with database objects.
5. What is the name of the field that Access creates, by default, as the primary key field for a new table in Datasheet view?
6. Which group on the FIELDS tab contains the options you use to add new fields to a table?
7. What does a pencil symbol at the beginning of a record represent? What does a star symbol represent?
8. Explain how the saving process in Access is different from saving in other Office programs.

Session 1.2 Visual Overview:

The CREATE tab provides options for creating various database objects, including tables, forms, and reports. The options appear on the tab grouped by object type.

The Query Wizard button opens a dialog box with different types of wizards that guide you through the steps to create a query. One of these, the **Simple Query Wizard**, allows you to select records and fields quickly to display in the query results.

You use the options in the Tables group to create a table in Datasheet view or in Design view.

The Forms group contains options for creating a **form**, which is a database object you use to enter, edit, and view records in a database.

Chatham : Database- E:\Access1\Tutorial\Chatham.accd

FILE | HOME | CREATE | EXTERNAL DATA | DATABASE TOOLS

Application Parts — Templates | Table, Table Design, SharePoint Lists — Tables | Query Wizard, Query Design — Queries | Form, Form Design, Blank Form — Forms | Form Wizard, Navigation, More Forms

The **Form tool** quickly creates a form containing all the fields in the table (or query) on which you're basing the form.

The **Form Wizard** guides you through the process of creating a form.

The Queries group contains options for creating a **query**, which is a question you ask about the data stored in a database. In response to a query, Access displays the specific records and fields that answer your question.

Navigation Pane

Ready

Tutorial 1 Creating a Database | Access AC 25

The CREATE Tab Options

The Reports group contains options for creating a **report**, which is a formatted printout (or screen display) of the contents of one or more tables (or queries) in a database.

The Microsoft Access Help button opens the **Access Help** window, where you can find information about Access commands and features as well as instructions for using them.

atham.accdb (Access 2007 - 2013 file format) - Access

Sign in

Form Wizard
Navigation
More Forms

Report | Report Design | Blank Report | Report Wizard | Labels

Macro | Module | Class Module | Visual Basic

Reports   Macros & Code

The **Report tool** places all the fields from a selected table (or query) on a report, making it the quickest way to create a report.

The **Report Wizard** guides you through the process of creating a report.

You can enter words or phrases in the search box and the Access Help system will search online to find related topics.

Access Help

Search online help

Popular searches

Criteria	Format	Input mask
Query	Filter	Sum
Date	Like	Relationships

Get started more

What's new in Access
Access keyboard shortcuts
Make the switch to Access 2013

Basics and beyond more

Basic tasks for an Access 2013 desktop database
Introduction to tables
Introduction to queries
Create an Access form

The Popular searches section provides links to commonly searched Access Help topics.

Because the Access online Help system is a dynamic environment and subject to change, your Help screen might look slightly different from this one.

Copying Records from Another Access Database

When you created the Visit table, you entered records directly into the table datasheet. There are many other ways to enter records in a table, including copying and pasting records from a table into the same database or into a different database. To use this method, however, the two tables must have the same structure—that is, the tables must contain the same fields, with the same design, in the same order.

Cindi has already created a table named Appointment that contains additional records with visit data. The Appointment table is contained in a database named Cindi located in the Access1 ▸ Tutorial folder included with your Data Files. The Appointment table has the same table structure as the Visit table you created.

REFERENCE

Opening a Database

- Start Access and display the Recent screen in Backstage view.
- Click the name of the database you want to open in the list of recently opened databases.

or

- Start Access and display the Recent screen in Backstage view.
- In the navigation bar, click Open Other Files to display the Open screen.
- Click Computer, click the Browse button, and then navigate to the drive and folder containing the database file you want to open.
- Click the name of the database file you want to open, and then click the Open button.

Your next task is to copy the records from the Appointment table and paste them into your Visit table. To do so, you need to open the Cindi database.

To copy the records from the Appointment table:

1. Display the Windows Start screen, if necessary.

   Using Windows 7? To complete Step 1, click the Start button on the taskbar.

2. Click the **Access 2013** tile. Access starts and displays the Recent screen in Backstage view.

   Using Windows 7? To complete Step 2, click All Programs on the Start menu, click Microsoft Office 2013, and then click Access 2013.

3. Click **Open Other Files** to display the Open screen in Backstage view.

4. On the Open screen, click **Computer**. The right side of the screen now shows folder information for your computer.

   Trouble? If you are storing your files on SkyDrive, click SkyDrive, and then log in if necessary.

5. Click the **Browse** button, and then navigate to the drive that contains your Data Files.

6. Navigate to the **Access1 ▸ Tutorial** folder, click the database file named **Cindi**, and then click the **Open** button. The Cindi database opens in the Access program window. Note that the database contains only one object, the Appointment table.

Tutorial 1 Creating a Database | Access   AC 27

Trouble? If a security warning appears below the ribbon indicating that some active content has been disabled, click the Enable Content button next to the warning. Access provides this warning because some databases might contain content that could harm your computer. Because the Cindi database does not contain objects that could be harmful, you can open it safely. If you are accessing the file over a network, you might also see a dialog box asking if you want to make the file a trusted document; click Yes.

▶ **7.** In the Navigation Pane, double-click **Appointment** to open the Appointment table in Datasheet view. The table contains 76 records and the same five fields, with the same characteristics, as the fields in the Visit table. See Figure 1-18.

Figure 1-18 Appointment table in the Cindi database

same fields as in the Visit table

click the datasheet selector to select all the records in the table

table contains a total of 76 records

VisitID	PatientID	VisitDate	Reason	Walkin
1528	22507	11/9/2015	Diabetes mellitus Type 2 - initial diagnosis	☑
1535	22546	11/12/2015	Transverse fracture of left ulna	☑
1536	22526	11/17/2015	Gastroenteritis	☐
1539	22504	11/18/2015	Annual wellness visit	☐
1541	22526	11/24/2015	Gastroenteritis - follow up	☐
1544	22560	11/25/2015	Influenza	☑
1549	22501	11/30/2015	Influenza	☑
1552	22511	12/3/2015	Annual wellness visit	☐
1557	22526	12/10/2015	Annual wellness visit	☐
1562	22516	12/22/2015	COPD management visit	☐
1563	22546	1/4/2016	Follow-up - cast removal	☐
1567	22519	1/8/2016	Hypertension monitoring	☐
1569	22558	1/11/2016	COPD management visit	☐
1570	22561	1/11/2016	Nasopharyngitis	☑
1572	22560	1/13/2016	Acute sinusitis	☑
1573	22511	1/13/2016	Cardiac monitoring	☐
1576	22514	1/14/2016	Hypertension monitoring	☐
1580	22552	1/15/2016	Annual wellness visit	☐
1583	22560	1/22/2016	Acute sinusitis follow-up	☐
1585	22555	1/25/2016	Acute viral rhinopharyngitis	☑
1586	22523	1/25/2016	Nasopharyngitis	☑
1588	22535	1/25/2016	Hypertension	☐
1590	22505	1/26/2016	Annual wellness visit	☐
1591	22544	1/26/2016	Acute viral rhinopharyngitis	☑
1594	22533	1/28/2016	Nasopharyngitis	☑

Cindi wants you to copy all the records in the Appointment table. You can select all the records by clicking the **datasheet selector**, which is the box to the left of the first field name in the table datasheet (see Figure 1-18).

▶ **8.** Click the **datasheet selector** to the left of the VisitID field, as shown in Figure 1-18. Access selects all the records in the table.

▶ **9.** In the Clipboard group on the HOME tab, click the **Copy** button. All the records are copied to the Clipboard.

▶ **10.** Click the **Close 'Appointment'** button ☒ on the object tab. A dialog box opens asking if you want to save the data you copied to the Clipboard. This dialog box opens only when you copy a large amount of data to the Clipboard.

▶ **11.** Click the **Yes** button. The dialog box closes, and then the Appointment table closes.

With the records copied to the Clipboard, you can now paste them into the Visit table. First you need to close the Cindi database while still keeping the Access program open, and then open the Chatham database.

To close the Cindi database and then paste the records into the Visit table:

1. Click the **FILE** tab to display Backstage view, and then click **Close** in the navigation bar to close the Cindi database. You return to the HOME tab in the Access program window.

2. Click the **FILE** tab to return to Backstage view, and then click **Open** in the navigation bar. The Recent section of the Open screen shows a list of the recently opened database files. This list should include the Chatham database.

3. In the Recent section of the screen, click **Chatham** to open the Chatham database file.

    Trouble? If the Chatham database file is not listed in the Recent section on your computer, click Computer, and then click Browse. In the Open dialog box, navigate to the drive and folder where you are storing your files, and then open the Chatham database file.

    Trouble? If the security warning appears below the ribbon, click the Enable Content button, and then, if necessary, click Yes to make the file a trusted document.

4. In the Navigation Pane, double-click **Visit** to open the Visit table in Datasheet view.

5. On the Navigation Pane, click the **Shutter Bar Open/Close Button** to close the pane.

6. Position the pointer on the star symbol in the row selector for row 11 (the next row available for a new record) until the pointer changes to a ➡ shape, and then click to select the row.

7. In the Clipboard group on the HOME tab, click the **Paste** button. The pasted records are added to the table, and a dialog box opens asking you to confirm that you want to paste all the records (76 total).

    Trouble? If the Paste button isn't active, click the ➡ pointer on the row selector for row 11, making sure the entire row is selected, and then repeat Step 7.

8. Click the **Yes** button. The dialog box closes, and the pasted records are highlighted. See Figure 1-19. Notice that the table now contains a total of 86 records—10 records that you entered and 76 records that you copied and pasted.

Figure 1-19 Visit table after copying and pasting records

(Screenshot of Visit table datasheet showing original records (10), pasted records (76), table now contains 86 records, scroll box, scroll bars, and navigation buttons.)

Not all the Reason field values are completely visible, so you need to resize this column to its best fit.

9. Place the pointer on the vertical line to the right of the Reason field name until the pointer changes to a ↔ shape, and then double-click the vertical line. The Reason field values are now fully displayed.

Navigating a Datasheet

The Visit table now contains 86 records, but only some of the records are visible on the screen. To view fields or records not currently visible on the screen, you can use the horizontal and vertical scroll bars shown in Figure 1-19 to navigate the data. The **navigation buttons**, shown in Figure 1-19 and also described in Figure 1-20, provide another way to move vertically through the records. The Current Record box appears between the two sets of navigation buttons and displays the number of the current record as well as the total number of records in the table. Figure 1-20 shows which record becomes the current record when you click each navigation button. Note the New (blank) record button, which works in the same way as the New button on the HOME tab you used earlier to enter a new record in the table.

Figure 1-20 Navigation buttons

Navigation Button	Record Selected	Navigation Button	Record Selected
◀|	First record	▶|	Last record
◀	Previous record	▶*	New (blank) record
▶	Next record		

© 2014 Cengage Learning

Cindi suggests that you use the various navigation techniques to move through the Visit table and become familiar with its contents.

To navigate the Visit datasheet:

TIP
You can make a field the current field by clicking anywhere within the column for that field.

1. Click the first record's VisitID field value (**1527**). The Current Record box shows that record 1 is the current record.

2. Click the **Next record** navigation button. The second record is now highlighted, which identifies it as the current record. Also, notice that the second record's value for the VisitID field is selected, and the Current Record box displays "2 of 86" to indicate that the second record is the current record.

3. Click the **Last record** navigation button. The last record in the table, record 86, is now the current record.

4. Drag the scroll box in the vertical scroll bar (see Figure 1-19) up to the top of the bar. Notice that record 86 is still the current record, as indicated in the Current Record box. Dragging the scroll box changes the display of the table datasheet, but does not change the current record.

5. Drag the scroll box in the vertical scroll bar back down until you can see the end of the table and the current record (record 86).

6. Click the **Previous record** navigation button. Record 85 is now the current record.

7. Click the **First record** navigation button. The first record is now the current record and is visible on the screen.

   As you moved through the datasheet, you might have noticed that not all the Reason field values are fully displayed. When you resize a column to its best fit, the column expands to fully display only the field values that are visible on the screen at that time. To make sure all field values are displayed for the entire table, you need to scroll through the datasheet and repeat the resizing process.

8. Drag the scroll box down to display more of the table, until you see other Reason field values that are not fully displayed. Then use the pointer to resize the field.

9. Repeat Step 8, as necessary, until you reach the bottom of the table and have resized all the Reason field values, and then drag the scroll box back up to display the beginning of the table.

The Visit table now contains all the data about patient visits for Chatham Community Health Services. To better understand how to work with this data, Cindi asks you to create simple objects for the other main types of database objects—queries, forms, and reports.

Creating a Simple Query

As noted earlier, a query is a question you ask about the data stored in a database. When you create a query, you tell Access which fields you need and what criteria it should use to select the records that will answer your question. Then Access displays only the information you want, so you don't have to navigate through the entire database for the information. In the Visit table, for example, Cindi might create a query to display only those records for visits that occurred in a specific month. Even though a query can display table information in a different way, the information still exists in the table as it was originally entered.

Cindi wants to see a list of all the visit dates and reasons for visits in the Visit table. She doesn't want the list to include all the fields in the table, such as PatientID and WalkIn. To produce this list for Cindi, you'll use the Simple Query Wizard to create a query based on the Visit table.

To start the Simple Query Wizard:

▶ 1. On the ribbon, click the **CREATE** tab.

▶ 2. In the Queries group on the CREATE tab, click the **Query Wizard** button. The New Query dialog box opens.

▶ 3. Make sure **Simple Query Wizard** is selected, and then click the **OK** button. The first Simple Query Wizard dialog box opens. See Figure 1-21.

Figure 1-21   **First Simple Query Wizard dialog box**

[Dialog box showing Simple Query Wizard with callouts:
- default source for the query → Tables/Queries: Table: Visit
- moves all available fields to the Selected Fields box → >> button
- removes a selected field → < button
- moves the selected (highlighted) field to the Selected Fields box → > button
- removes all fields from the Selected Fields box → << button
Available Fields list: VisitID, PatientID, VisitDate, Reason, WalkIn]

Because the Visit table is the only object in the Chatham database, it is listed in the Tables/Queries box by default. If the database contained more objects, you could click the Tables/Queries arrow and choose another table or a query as the basis for the new query you are creating. The Available Fields box lists all the fields in the Visit table.

You need to select fields from the Available Fields box to include them in the query. To select fields one at a time, click a field and then click the > button. The selected (highlighted) field moves from the Available Fields box on the left to the Selected Fields box on the right. To select all the fields, click the >> button. If you change your mind or make a mistake, you can remove a field by clicking it in the Selected Fields box and then clicking the < button. To remove all fields from the Selected Fields box, click the << button.

Each Simple Query Wizard dialog box contains buttons on the bottom that allow you to move to the previous dialog box (Back button), move to the next dialog box (Next button), or cancel the creation process (Cancel button). You can also finish creating the object (Finish button) and accept the wizard's defaults for the remaining options.

Cindi wants her list to include data from only the following fields: VisitID, VisitDate, and Reason. You need to select these fields to include them in the query.

To create the query using the Simple Query Wizard:

> **TIP**
> You can also double-click a field to move it from the Available Fields box to the Selected Fields box.

1. Click **VisitID** in the Available Fields box to select the field (if necessary), and then click the `>` button. The VisitID field moves to the Selected Fields box.

2. Repeat Step 1 for the fields **VisitDate** and **Reason**, and then click the **Next** button. The second, and final, Simple Query Wizard dialog box opens and asks you to choose a name (title) for your query. Access suggests the name "Visit Query" because the query you are creating is based on the Visit table. You'll change the suggested name to "VisitList."

3. Click at the end of the suggested name, use the **Backspace** key to delete the word "Query" and the space, and then type **List**. Now you can view the query results.

4. Click the **Finish** button to complete the query. Access displays the query results in Datasheet view, on a new tab named "VisitList." A query datasheet is similar to a table datasheet, showing fields in columns and records in rows—but only for those fields and records you want to see, as determined by the query specifications you select.

5. Place the pointer on the vertical line to the right of the Reason field name until the pointer changes to a ↔ shape, and then double-click the vertical line to resize the Reason field. See Figure 1-22.

Figure 1-22   **Query results**

- only the three selected fields are displayed in the query datasheet

VisitID	VisitDate	Reason
1527	11/9/2015	Allergies - environmental
1528	11/9/2015	Diabetes mellitus Type 2 - initial diagnosis
1530	11/10/2015	Seborrheic dermatitis
1535	11/12/2015	Transverse fracture of left ulna
1536	11/17/2015	Gastroenteritis
1538	11/17/2015	Migraine
1539	11/18/2015	Annual wellness visit
1541	11/24/2015	Gastroenteritis - follow up
1542	11/24/2015	Influenza
1544	11/25/2015	Influenza
1548	11/30/2015	Hypertension
1549	11/30/2015	Influenza
1550	12/1/2015	Influenza
1552	12/3/2015	Annual wellness visit
1555	12/7/2015	Annual wellness visit
1557	12/10/2015	Annual wellness visit
1560	12/15/2015	Influenza
1562	12/22/2015	COPD management visit
1563	1/4/2016	Follow-up - cast removal
1564	1/5/2016	Annual wellness visit
1567	1/8/2016	Hypertension monitoring
1569	1/11/2016	COPD management visit
1570	1/11/2016	Nasopharyngitis
1572	1/13/2016	Acute sinusitis
1573	1/13/2016	Cardiac monitoring

Record: 1 of 86

- all 86 records are included in the results

The VisitList query datasheet displays the three selected fields for each record in the Visit table. The fields are shown in the order you selected them in the Simple Query Wizard, from left to right. The records are listed in order by the primary key field, VisitID. Even though the query datasheet displays only the three fields you chose for the query, the Visit table still includes all the fields for all records.

Notice that the navigation buttons are located at the bottom of the window. You navigate a query datasheet in the same way that you navigate a table datasheet.

6. Click the **Last record** navigation button. The last record in the query datasheet is now the current record.

7. Click the **Previous record** navigation button. Record 85 in the query datasheet is now the current record.

8. Click the **First record** navigation button. The first record is now the current record.

9. Click the **Close 'VisitList'** button on the object tab. A dialog box opens asking if you want to save the changes to the layout of the query. This dialog box opens because you resized the Reason column.

10. Click the **Yes** button to save the query layout changes and close the query.

The query results are not stored in the database; however, the query design is stored as part of the database with the name you specified. You can re-create the query results at any time by opening the query again. When you open the query at a later date, the results displayed will reflect up-to-date information to include any new records entered in the Visit table.

Next, Cindi asks you to create a form for the Visit table so that Chatham Community Health Services employees can use the form to enter and work with data in the table easily.

Creating a Simple Form

As noted earlier, you use a form to enter, edit, and view records in a database. Although you can perform these same functions with tables and queries, forms can present data in many customized and useful ways.

Cindi wants a form for the Visit table that shows all the fields for one record at a time, with fields listed one below another in a column. This type of form will make it easier for her staff to focus on all the data for a particular visit. You'll use the Form tool to create this form quickly and easily.

To create the form using the Form tool:

1. Make sure the Visit table is still open in Datasheet view. The table or other database object you're using as the basis for the form must either be open or selected in the Navigation Pane when you use the Form tool.

   Trouble? If the Visit table is not open, click the Shutter Bar Open/Close Button to open the Navigation Pane. Then double-click Visit to open the Visit table in Datasheet view. Click the Shutter Bar Open/Close Button to close the pane.

2. Make sure the CREATE tab is displayed.

3. In the Forms group, click the **Form** button. The Form tool creates a simple form showing every field in the Visit table and places it on a tab named "Visit." Access assigns this name because the form is based on the Visit table. See Figure 1-23.

Figure 1-23   **Form created by the Form tool**

[Screenshot of Access Form in Layout view with the following callouts: "form graphic identifies the object as a form"; "new tab for the form"; "field values for the first record displayed"; "depending on your computer's settings, your field value boxes might be a different width"; "form displayed in Layout view"; "record 1 of 86 total records". Visible field values: VisitID 1527, PatientID 22522, VisitDate 11/9/2015, Reason Allergies - environmental, Walkin checked.]

Trouble? Depending on the size of your monitor and your screen resolution settings, the fields in your form might appear in multiple columns instead of a single column. This difference will not present any problems.

The form displays one record at a time in the Visit table, providing another view of the data that is stored in the table and allowing you to focus on the values for one record. Access displays the field values for the first record in the table and selects the first field value (VisitID) by placing a border around the value. Each field name appears on a separate line and on the same line as its field value, which appears in a box to the right. Depending on your computer's settings, the field value boxes in your form might be wider or narrower than those shown in the figure. As indicated in the status bar, the form is displayed in Layout view. In **Layout view**, you can make design changes to the form while it is displaying data, so that you can see the effects of the changes you make immediately.

To view, enter, and maintain data using a form, you must know how to move from field to field and from record to record. Notice that the form contains navigation buttons, similar to those available in Datasheet view, which you can use to display different records in the form. You'll use these now to navigate the form; then you'll save and close the form.

To navigate, save, and close the form:

1. Click the **Next record** navigation button ▶. The form now displays the values for the second record in the Visit table.

2. Click the **Last record** navigation button ▶| to move to the last record in the table. The form displays the information for VisitID 1700.

3. Click the **Previous record** navigation button ◀ to move to record 85.

4. Click the **First record** navigation button to return to the first record in the Visit table.

   Next, you'll save the form with the name "VisitData" in the Chatham database. Then the form will be available for later use.

5. On the Quick Access Toolbar, click the **Save** button. The Save As dialog box opens.

6. In the Form Name box, click at the end of the highlighted word "Visit," type **Data**, and then press the **Enter** key. Access saves the form as VisitData in the Chatham database and closes the dialog box. The tab containing the form now displays the name VisitData.

7. Click the **Close 'VisitData'** button on the object tab to close the form.

INSIGHT

Saving Database Objects

In general, it is best to save a database object—query, form, or report—only if you anticipate using the object frequently or if it is time consuming to create, because all objects use storage space and increase the size of the database file. For example, you most likely would not save a form you created with the Form tool because you can re-create it easily with one mouse click. (However, for the purposes of this text, you usually need to save the objects you create.)

After attending a staff meeting, Cindi returns with another request. She would like to see the information in the Visit table presented in a more readable and professional format. You'll help Cindi by creating a report.

Creating a Simple Report

As noted earlier, a report is a formatted printout (or screen display) of the contents of one or more tables or queries. You'll use the Report tool to quickly produce a report based on the Visit table for Cindi. The Report tool creates a report based on the selected table or query.

To create the report using the Report tool:

1. With the Visit table open in Datasheet view, click the **CREATE** tab on the ribbon.

2. In the Reports group, click the **Report** button. The Report tool creates a simple report showing every field in the Visit table and places it on a tab named "Visit." Again, Access assigns this name because the object you created (the report) is based on the Visit table. See Figure 1-24.

Figure 1-24 Report created by the Report tool

[Screenshot of Access report in Layout view with callouts:]
- report graphic
- column headings appear in a different font color
- current day, date, and time displayed (yours might differ)
- dashed lines show the page edges
- borders around field values
- report displayed in Layout view

Trouble? The records in your report might appear in a different order from the records shown in Figure 1-24. This difference will not cause any problems.

The report shows each field in a column, with the field values for each record in a row, similar to a table or query datasheet. However, the report offers a more visually appealing format for the data, with the column headings in a different color, borders around each field value, a graphic of a report at the top left, and the current day, date, and time at the top right. Also notice the dashed horizontal and vertical lines on the top and right, respectively; these lines mark the edges of the page and show where text will print on the page.

The report needs some design changes to better display the data. The columns are much wider than necessary for the VisitID and PatientID fields, and the Reason and WalkIn field values and borders are not completely displayed within the page area defined by the dashed lines, which means they would not appear on the same page as the rest of the fields in the printed report. You can resize the columns easily in Layout view.

To resize the VisitID and PatientID columns:

1. Position the pointer on the right border of any field value in the VisitID column until the pointer changes to a ↔ shape.

2. Click and drag the mouse to the left; dark outlines surround the field name and each field value to show the column width as you change it. Drag to the left until the column is slightly wider than the VisitID field name.

3. Release the mouse button. The VisitID column is now narrower, and the other four columns have shifted to the left. The Reason and WalkIn fields, values, and borders are now completely within the page area. See Figure 1-25.

Tutorial 1 Creating a Database | Access **AC 37**

Figure 1-25   Report after resizing the VisitID column

- field values and borders are now within the area marked by the dashed lines
- column is now narrower

4. Click the first field value for PatientID to establish the field as the current field.

5. Position the pointer on the right border of the first value in the PatientID column until the pointer changes to ↔, click and drag to the left until the column is slightly wider than its field name, and then release the mouse button.

6. Drag the scroll box on the vertical scroll bar all the way down to the bottom of the report to check its entire layout.

   The Report tool displays the number "86" at the bottom left of the report, showing the total number of records in the report and the table on which it is based—the Visit table. The Report tool also displays the page number at the bottom right, but the text "Page 1 of 1" appears cut off through the vertical dashed line. This will cause a problem when you print the report, so you need to move this text to the left.

7. Click anywhere on the words **Page 1 of 1**. An orange outline appears around the text, indicating it is selected. See Figure 1-26.

Figure 1-26   Report page number selected

- text to the right of this dashed line would print on its own page
- text is selected and can be moved to the left
- shows total number of records in the report

With the text selected, you can use the keyboard arrow keys to move it.

TIP

You can also use the mouse to drag the selected page number, but the arrow key is more precise.

8. Press the ← key repeatedly until the selected box containing the page number is to the left of the vertical dashed line (roughly 35 times). The page number text is now completely within the page area and will print on the same page as the rest of the report.

9. Drag the scroll box back up to redisplay the top of the report.

The report is displayed in Layout view, which doesn't show how many pages there are in the report. To see this, you need to switch to Print Preview.

To view the report in Print Preview:

1. In the Views group on the DESIGN tab, click the **View button arrow**, and then click **Print Preview**. The first page of the report is displayed in Print Preview. See Figure 1-27.

Figure 1-27   First page of the report in Print Preview

Print Preview shows exactly how the report will look when printed. Notice that Print Preview provides page navigation buttons at the bottom of the window, similar to the navigation buttons you've used to move through records in a table, query, and form.

2. Click the **Next Page** navigation button. The second page of the report is displayed in Print Preview.

3. Click the **Last Page** navigation button to move to the last page of the report.

4. Drag the scroll box in the vertical scroll bar (see Figure 1-27) down until the bottom of the report page is displayed. The notation "Page 3 of 3" appears at the bottom of the page, indicating that you are on page 3 out of a total of 3 pages in the report.

Trouble? Depending on the printer you are using, your report might have more or fewer pages, and some of the pages might be blank. If so, don't worry. Different printers format reports in different ways, sometimes affecting the total number of pages and the number of records printed per page.

5. Click the **First Page** navigation button to return to the first page of the report, and then drag the scroll box in the vertical scroll bar back up so that the top of the report is displayed.

Next you'll save the report as VisitDetails, and then print it.

6. On the Quick Access Toolbar, click the **Save** button. The Save As dialog box opens.

7. In the Report Name box, click at the end of the highlighted word "Visit," type **Details,** and then press the **Enter** key. Access saves the report as VisitDetails in the Chatham database and closes the dialog box. The tab containing the report now displays the name "VisitDetails."

Printing a Report

After creating a report, you might need to print it to distribute it to others who need to view the report's contents. You can print a report without changing any print settings, or display the Print dialog box and select options for printing.

REFERENCE

Printing a Report

- Open the report in any view, or select the report in the Navigation Pane.
- Click the FILE tab to display Backstage view, click Print, and then click Quick Print to print the report with the default print settings.

or

- Open the report in any view, or select the report in the Navigation Pane.
- Click the FILE tab, click Print, and then click Print (or, if the report is displayed in Print Preview, click the Print button in the Print group on the PRINT PREVIEW tab). The Print dialog box opens, in which you can select the options you want for printing the report.

Cindi asks you to print the entire report with the default settings, so you'll use the Quick Print option in Backstage view.

Note: To complete the following steps, your computer must be connected to a printer. Check with your instructor first to see if you should print the report.

To print the report and then close it:

1. On the ribbon, click the **FILE** tab to display Backstage view.

2. In the navigation bar, click **Print**, and then click **Quick Print**. The report prints with the default print settings, and you return to the report in Print Preview.

   Trouble? If your report did not print, make sure that your computer is connected to a printer, and that the printer is turned on and ready to print. Then repeat Steps 1 and 2.

3. Click the **Close 'VisitDetails'** button on the object tab to close the report.

4. Click the **Close 'Visit'** button on the object tab to close the Visit table.

   Trouble? If you are asked to save changes to the layout of the table, click Yes.

You can also use the Print dialog box to print other database objects, such as table and query datasheets. Most often, these objects are used for viewing and entering data, and reports are used for printing the data in a database.

Viewing Objects in the Navigation Pane

The Chatham database now contains four objects—the Visit table, the VisitList query, the VisitData form, and the VisitDetails report. When you work with the database file—such as closing it, opening it, or distributing it to others—the file includes all the objects you created and saved in the database. You can view and work with these objects in the Navigation Pane.

To view the objects in the Chatham database:

1. On the Navigation Pane, click the **Shutter Bar Open/Close Button** » to open the pane. See Figure 1-28.

Figure 1-28   Chatham database objects displayed in the Navigation Pane

- specifies that all objects in the database are displayed
- displays a menu with options for grouping objects in the Navigation Pane
- table icon
- query icon
- form icon
- report icon
- enter text here to find objects in the database containing the search text

The Navigation Pane currently displays the default category, **All Access Objects**, which lists all the database objects in the pane. Each object type (Tables, Queries, Forms, and Reports) appears in its own group. Each database object (the Visit table, the VisitList query, the VisitData form, and the VisitDetails report) has a unique icon to its left to indicate the type of object. This makes it easy for you to identify the objects and choose which one you want to open and work with.

The arrow on the All Access Objects bar displays a menu with options for various ways to group and display objects in the Navigation Pane. The Search box enables you to enter text for Access to find; for example, you could search for all objects that contain the word "Visit" in their names. Note that Access searches for objects only in the categories and groups currently displayed in the Navigation Pane.

As you continue to build the Chatham database and add more objects to it in later tutorials, you'll use the options in the Navigation Pane to manage those objects.

Using Microsoft Access Help

The Access program provides a Help system you can use to search for information about specific Access features. You start Help by clicking the Microsoft Access Help button in the top right of the Access window, or by pressing the F1 key. You'll use Help now to learn more about the Navigation Pane.

To search for information about the Navigation Pane in Help:

1. Click the **Microsoft Access Help** button ? on the title bar. The Access Help window opens, as shown earlier in the Session 1.2 Visual Overview.
2. Click in the search box, type **Navigation Pane**, and then press the **Enter** key. The Access Help window displays a list of topics related to the Navigation Pane.
3. Click the topic **Manage database objects in the Navigation Pane**. The Access Help window displays the article you selected. See Figure 1-29.

Figure 1-29 Article displayed in the Access Help window

search text entered

selected article is displayed

drag the scroll box to scroll through and read the article

Access Help

Navigation Pane

Manage database objects in the Navigation Pane

TIP Press F11 to display or hide the Navigation Pane.

All the objects in a database are listed in the Navigation Pane, a feature introduced in Access 2007. The Database window of earlier versions is not available.

You can customize the categories and groups of objects in the Navigation Pane. You can also hide objects, groups, or even the entire Navigation Pane. Access provides several categories that you can use right away, and you can also create custom categories and groups.

NOTE The Navigation Pane is not available when you use an Access app or a web database in a browser. Although you can use the Navigation Pane in an Access app opened in Access, it has a limited feature set: display, sort, and search for database objects.

In this article
↓ Overview
↓ Select a category
↓ Display and sort objects

Trouble? If the article on managing database objects is not listed in your Help window, choose another article related to the Navigation Pane to read.

4. Scroll through the article to read detailed information about working with the Navigation Pane.
5. When finished, click the **Close** button ✕ on the Access Help window to close it.

The Access Help system is an important reference tool for you to use if you need additional information about databases in general, details about specific Access features, or support with problems you might encounter.

Managing a Database

One of the main tasks involved in working with database software is managing your databases and the data they contain. Some of the activities involved in database management include compacting and repairing a database and backing up and restoring a database. By managing your databases, you can ensure that they operate in the most efficient way, that the data they contain is secure, and that you can work with the data effectively.

Compacting and Repairing a Database

Whenever you open an Access database and work in it, the size of the database increases. Further, when you delete records or when you delete or replace database objects—such as queries, forms, and reports—the storage space that had been occupied by the deleted or replaced records or objects does not automatically become available for other records or objects. To make the space available, and also to increase the speed of data retrieval, you must compact the database. **Compacting** a database rearranges the data and objects in a database to decrease its file size, thereby making more storage space available and enhancing the performance of the database. Figure 1-30 illustrates the compacting process.

Figure 1-30 Compacting a database

© 2014 Cengage Learning

When you compact a database, Access repairs the database at the same time, if necessary. In some cases, Access detects that a database is damaged when you try to open it and gives you the option to compact and repair it at that time. For example, the data in your database might become damaged, or corrupted, if you exit the Access program suddenly by turning off your computer. If you think your database might be damaged because it is behaving unpredictably, you can use the Compact & Repair Database option to fix it.

REFERENCE

Compacting and Repairing a Database

- Make sure the database file you want to compact and repair is open.
- Click the FILE tab to display the Info screen in Backstage view.
- Click the Compact & Repair Database button.

Access also allows you to set an option to compact and repair a database file automatically every time you close it. The Compact on Close option is available in the Current Database section of the Access Options dialog box, which you open from

Backstage view by clicking the Options command in the navigation bar. By default, the Compact on Close option is turned off.

Next, you'll compact the Chatham database manually using the Compact & Repair Database option. This will make the database smaller and allow you to work with it more efficiently. After compacting the database, you'll close it.

To compact and repair the Chatham database:

1. On the ribbon, click the **FILE** tab to display the Info screen in Backstage view.
2. Click the **Compact & Repair Database** button. Access closes Backstage view and returns to the HOME tab. Although nothing visible happens on the screen, Access compacts the Chatham database, making it smaller, and repairs it at the same time.
3. Click the **FILE** tab to return to the Info screen, and then click **Close** in the navigation bar. Access closes the Chatham database.

Backing Up and Restoring a Database

Backing up a database is the process of making a copy of the database file to protect your database against loss or damage. The Back Up Database command enables you to back up your database file from within the Access program, while you are working on your database. To use this option, click the FILE tab to display the Info screen in Backstage view, click Save As in the navigation bar, click Back Up Database in the Advanced section of the Save Database As pane, and then click the Save As button. In the Save As dialog box that opens, Access provides a default filename for the backup copy that consists of the same filename as the database you are backing up (for example, "Chatham"), and an underscore character, plus the current date. This filenaming system makes it easy for you to keep track of your database backups and when they were created. To restore a backup database file, you simply copy the backup from the location where it is stored to your hard drive, or whatever device you use to work in Access, and start working with the restored database file. (You will not actually back up the Chatham database in this tutorial unless directed by your instructor to do so.)

INSIGHT

Planning and Performing Database Backups

Experienced database users make it a habit to back up a database before they work with it for the first time, keeping the original data intact. They also make frequent backups while continuing to work with a database; these backups are generally on flash drives, recordable CDs or DVDs, external or network hard drives, or cloud-based storage (such as SkyDrive). Also, it is recommended to store the backup copy in a different location from the original. For example, if the original database is stored on a flash drive, you should not store the backup copy on the same flash drive. If you lose the drive or the drive is damaged, you would lose both the original database and its backup copy.

If the original database file and the backup copy have the same name, restoring the backup copy might replace the original. If you want to save the original file, rename it before you restore the backup copy. To ensure that the restored database has the most current data, you should update the restored database with any changes made to the original between the time you created the backup copy and the time the original database became damaged or lost.

By properly planning for and performing backups, you can avoid losing data and prevent the time-consuming effort required to rebuild a lost or damaged database.

In the following tutorials, you'll help Cindi complete and maintain the Chatham database, and you'll use it to meet the specific information needs of the clinic's employees.

PROSKILLS

Decision Making: When to Use Access vs. Excel

Using a spreadsheet application like Microsoft Excel to manage lists or tables of information works well when the data is simple, such as a list of contacts or tasks. As soon as the data becomes complex enough to separate into tables that need to be related, you start to see the limitations of using a spreadsheet application. The strength of a database application such as Access is in its ability to easily relate one table of information to another. Consider a table of contacts that includes home addresses, with a separate row for each person living at the same address. When an address changes, it's too easy to make a mistake and not update the home address for each person who lives there. To ensure you have the most accurate data at all times, it's important to have only one instance of each piece of data. By creating separate tables that are related, and keeping only one instance of each piece of data, you'll ensure the integrity of the data. Trying to accomplish this in Excel is a complex process, whereas Access is specifically designed for this functionality.

Another limitation of using Excel instead of Access to manage data has to do with the volume of data. Although a spreadsheet can hold thousands of records, a database can hold millions. A spreadsheet containing thousands of pieces of information is cumbersome to use. Think of large-scale commercial applications such as enrollment at a college or tracking customers for a large company. It's hard to imagine managing such information in an Excel spreadsheet. Instead, you'd use a database. Finally, with an Access database, multiple users can access the information it contains at the same time. Although an Excel spreadsheet can be shared, there can be problems when users try to open and edit the same spreadsheet at the same time.

When you're trying to decide whether to use Excel or Access, ask yourself the following questions.

1. Do you need to store data in separate tables that are related to each other?
2. Do you have a very large amount of data to store?
3. Will more than one person need to access the data at the same time?

If you answer "yes" to any of these questions, an Access database is most likely the appropriate application to use.

REVIEW

Session 1.2 Quick Check

1. To copy the records from a table in one database to another table in a different database, the two tables must have the same _____.
2. A(n) _____ is a question you ask about the data stored in a database.
3. The quickest way to create a form is to use the _____.
4. Which view enables you to see the total number of pages in a report and navigate through the report pages?
5. In the Navigation Pane, each database object has a unique _____ to its left that identifies the object's type.
6. _____ a database rearranges the data and objects in a database to decrease its file size and enhance the speed and performance of the database.
7. _____ a database is the process of making a copy of the database file to protect the database against loss or damage.

SAM Projects

Put your skills into practice with SAM Projects! SAM Projects for this tutorial can be found online. If you have a SAM account, go to www.cengage.com/sam2013 to download the most recent Project Instructions and Start Files.

Review Assignments

Data File needed for the Review Assignments: Company.accdb

For Chatham Community Health Services, Cindi asks you to create a new database to contain information about the vendors that the clinic works with to obtain medical supplies and equipment for the clinic, and the vendors who service and maintain the equipment. Complete the following steps:

1. Create a new, blank database named **Vendor** and save it in the folder where you are storing your files, as specified by your instructor.
2. In Datasheet view for the Table1 table, rename the default ID primary key field to **SupplierID**. Change the data type of the SupplierID field to Short Text.
3. Add the following 10 fields to the new table in the order shown; all of them are Short Text fields *except* InitialContact, which is a Date/Time field: **Company**, **Category**, **Address**, **City**, **State**, **Zip**, **Phone**, **ContactFirst**, **ContactLast**, and **InitialContact**. Resize the columns as necessary so that the complete field names are displayed. Save the table as **Supplier**.
4. Enter the records shown in Figure 1-31 in the Supplier table. For the first record, be sure to enter your first name in the ContactFirst field and your last name in the ContactLast field.

   Note: When entering field values that are shown on multiple lines in the figure, do not try to enter the values on multiple lines. The values are shown on multiple lines in the figure for page spacing purposes only.

Figure 1-31 Supplier table records

SupplierID	Company	Category	Address	City	State	Zip	Phone	ContactFirst	ContactLast	InitialContact
ARE318	Aresco Surgical, Inc.	Supplies	48 Vienna St	Bridgeport	CT	06601	203-774-3048	Student First	Student Last	9/2/2015
GRE364	Greinke Labs, Inc.	Supplies	451 Summit Dr	Tiverton	RI	02878	401-208-9823	Evan	Brighton	1/12/2016
DUR368	Durasurg Equipment, Inc.	Equipment	74 Jessie St	Roanoke	VA	24036	540-340-3829	Kristin	Taylor	12/1/2015
STE472	Sterile Labs of CT, Inc.	Service	938 Gormley Ave	North Branford	CT	06517	203-537-5940	Carmine	San Marcos	11/3/2015
GSE420	GSE Medical, Inc.	Equipment	583 Renovo Dr	Claremont	NH	03743	603-202-4951	John	Vereen	9/10/2015

© 2014 Cengage Learning

5. Cindi created a database named Company that contains a Business table with supplier data. The Supplier table you created has the same design as the Business table. Copy all the records from the **Business** table in the **Company** database (located in the Access1 ► Review folder provided with your Data Files) and then paste them at the end of the Supplier table in the Vendor database.

6. Resize all datasheet columns to their best fit, and then save the Supplier table.
7. Close the Supplier table, and then use the Navigation Pane to reopen it. Note that the records are displayed in primary key order by the values in the SupplierID field.
8. Use the Simple Query Wizard to create a query that includes the Company, Category, ContactFirst, ContactLast, and Phone fields (in that order) from the Supplier table. Name the query **SupplierList**, and then close the query.
9. Use the Form tool to create a form for the Supplier table. Save the form as **SupplierInfo**, and then close it.
10. Use the Report tool to create a report based on the Supplier table. In Layout view, resize all fields except the Company field, so that each field is slightly wider than the longest entry (either the field name itself or an entry in the field). Display the report in Print Preview and verify that all the fields fit across two pages in the report. Save the report as **SupplierDetails**, and then close it.
11. Close the Supplier table, and then compact and repair the Vendor database.
12. Close the Vendor database.

Case Problem 1

Data File needed for this Case Problem: Program.accdb

GoGopher! Amol Mehta, a recent college graduate living in Boulder, Colorado, spent months earning money by running errands and completing basic chores for family members and acquaintances, while looking for full-time employment. As his list of customers needing such services continued to grow, Amol decided to start his own business called GoGopher! The business, which Amol operates completely online from his home, offers customers a variety of services—from grocery shopping and household chores to yard work and pet care—on a subscription basis. Clients become members of GoGopher! by choosing the plan that best suits their needs. Each plan provides a certain number of tasks per month to members, for a specified period of time. Amol wants to use Access to maintain information about the members who have joined GoGopher! and the types of plans offered. He needs your help in creating this database. Complete the following:

1. Create a new, blank database named **Gopher** and save it in the folder where you are storing your files, as specified by your instructor.
2. In Datasheet view for the Table1 table, rename the default primary key ID field to **PlanID**. Change the data type of the PlanID field to Short Text.
3. Add the following three fields to the new table in the order shown: **PlanDescription** (a Short Text field), **PlanCost** (a Currency field), and **FeeWaived** (a Yes/No field). Save the table as **Plan**.
4. Enter the records shown in Figure 1-32 in the Plan table. Note: When entering the PlanCost field values, you do not have to type the dollar signs, commas, or decimal places; Access will enter them automatically.

Figure 1-32   Plan table records

PlanID	PlanDescription	PlanCost	FeeWaived
301	20 tasks per month for 12 months	$6,000.00	Yes
311	10 tasks per month for 3 months	$750.00	No
304	10 tasks per month for 12 months	$3,000.00	Yes
303	15 tasks per month for 12 months	$4,500.00	Yes
312	8 tasks per month for 3 months	$600.00	No

when entering currency values, you do not have to type the dollar signs, commas, or decimal places

© 2014 Cengage Learning

5. Amol created a database named Program that contains a Service table with plan data. The Plan table you created has the same design as the Service table. Copy all the records from the **Service** table in the **Program** database (located in the Access1 ▸ Case1 folder provided with your Data Files) and then paste them at the end of the Plan table in the Gopher database.

6. Resize all datasheet columns to their best fit, and then save the Plan table.
7. Close the Plan table, and then use the Navigation Pane to reopen it. Note that the records are displayed in primary key order by the values in the PlanID field.
8. Use the Simple Query Wizard to create a query that includes the PlanID, PlanDescription, and PlanCost fields from the Plan table. In the second Simple Query Wizard dialog box, select the Detail option. (This option appears because the query includes a Currency field.) Save the query as **PlanData**, and then close the query.
9. Use the Form tool to create a form for the Plan table. Save the form as **PlanInfo**, and then close it.
10. Use the Report tool to create a report based on the Plan table. In Layout view, resize the PlanID field so it is slightly wider than the longest entry, which is the field name in this case. Also, resize the box containing the total amount that appears below the PlanCost column by clicking the box and then dragging its bottom border down so that the amount is fully displayed. (The Report Tool calculated this total automatically.) Display the report in Print Preview; then verify that all the fields are within the page area and all field values are fully displayed. Save the report as **PlanList**, print the report (only if asked by your instructor to do so), and then close it.
11. Close the Plan table, and then compact and repair the Gopher database.
12. Close the Gopher database.

Case Problem 2

Data File needed for this Case Problem: Consulting.accdb

O'Brien Educational Services After teaching English in a public high school for 15 years, Karen O'Brien decided to channel her experience in education in a new direction and founded O'Brien Educational Services, a small educational consulting company located in South Bend, Indiana. The company offers tutoring services to high school students to help prepare them for standardized tests, such as the SAT and the ACT. The company provides group, private, and semi-private tutoring sessions to best meet the needs of its students. As her business continues to expand, Karen wants to use Access to maintain information about the tutors who work for her, the students who sign up for tutoring, and the contracts they sign. She needs your help in creating this database. Complete the following steps:

1. Create a new, blank database named **OBrien** and save it in the folder where you are storing your files, as specified by your instructor.
2. In Datasheet view for the Table1 table, rename the default primary key ID field to **TutorID**. Change the data type of the TutorID field to Short Text.
3. Add the following five fields to the new table in the order shown; all of them are Short Text fields *except* HireDate, which is a Date/Time field: **FirstName**, **LastName**, **Degree**, **School**, and **HireDate**. Resize the columns, if necessary, so that the complete field names are displayed. Save the table as **Tutor**.
4. Enter the records shown in Figure 1-33 in the Tutor table. For the first record, be sure to enter your first name in the FirstName field and your last name in the LastName field.

Figure 1-33 Tutor table records

TutorID	FirstName	LastName	Degree	School	HireDate
31-1200	Student First	Student Last	BA	Pierre University	8/2/2015
68-8234	Caitlin	Shea	MS	Towns University	1/5/2016
55-1234	Samuel	Glick	BA	Manoog College	7/23/2016
69-2254	Sachi	Hatanaka	MA	Wyman College	3/23/2015
71-1698	Richard	Keating	Ph.D	Hobert University	5/3/2015

© 2014 Cengage Learning

5. Karen created a database named Consulting that contains an Instructor table with tutor data. The Tutor table you created has the same design as the Instructor table. Copy all the records from the **Instructor** table in the **Consulting** database (located in the Access1 ▸ Case2 folder provided with your Data Files) and then paste them at the end of the Tutor table in the OBrien database.
6. Resize all datasheet columns to their best fit, and then save the Tutor table.
7. Close the Tutor table, and then use the Navigation Pane to reopen it. Note that the records are displayed in primary key order by the values in the TutorID field.
8. Use the Simple Query Wizard to create a query that includes the FirstName, LastName, and HireDate fields from the Tutor table. Save the query as **StartDate**, and then close the query.
9. Use the Form tool to create a form for the Tutor table. Save the form as **TutorInfo**, and then close it.
10. Use the Report tool to create a report based on the Tutor table. In Layout view, resize the TutorID, FirstName, LastName, and Degree fields so they are slightly wider than the longest entry (either the field name itself or an entry in the field). All six fields should fit within the page area after you resize the specified fields. At the bottom of the report, move the text "Page 1 of 1" to the left so it is within the page area. Display the report in Print Preview; then verify that the fields and page number fit within the page area, and that all field values are fully displayed. Save the report as **TutorList**, print the report (only if asked by your instructor to do so), and then close it.
11. Close the Tutor table, and then compact and repair the OBrien database.
12. Close the OBrien database.

Case Problem 3

Data File needed for this Case Problem: Animal.accdb

Rosemary Animal Shelter Ryan Lang is the director of the Rosemary Animal Shelter in Cobb County, Georgia. The main goals of the shelter, which has several locations in the county, are to rescue dogs and cats and to find people who will adopt them. The shelter was established by Rosemary Hanson, who dedicated her life to rescuing pets and finding good homes for them. Residents of Cobb County generously donate money, food, and equipment in support of the shelter. Some of these patrons also adopt animals from the shelter. Ryan has asked you to create an Access database to manage information about the animals, patrons, and donations. Complete the following steps:

1. Create a new, blank database named **Shelter** and save it in the folder where you are storing your files, as specified by your instructor.
2. In Datasheet view for the Table1 table, rename the default primary key ID field to **PatronID**. Change the data type of the PatronID field to Short Text.
3. Add the following four Short Text fields to the new table in the order shown: **Title**, **FirstName**, **LastName**, and **Phone**. Save the table as **Patron**.
4. Enter the records shown in Figure 1-34 in the Patron table. For the first record, be sure to enter your title in the Title field, your first name in the FirstName field, and your last name in the LastName field.

Figure 1-34   Patron table records

PatronID	Title	FirstName	LastName	Phone
30405	*Student Title*	*Student First*	*Student Last*	770-427-9300
33287	Dr.	Ali	Haddad	770-528-8973
32189	Mrs.	Gini	Smith	770-499-2775
36028	Mr.	Michael	Carlucci	678-283-6334
30753	Ms.	Cynthia	Crosby	678-444-2676

© 2014 Cengage Learning

5. Ryan created a database named Animal that contains a Donor table with data about patrons. The Patron table you created has the same design as the Donor table. Copy all the records from the **Donor** table in the **Animal** database (located in the Access1 ▸ Case3 folder provided with your Data Files) and then paste them at the end of the Patron table in the Shelter database.
6. Resize all datasheet columns to their best fit, and then save the Patron table.
7. Close the Patron table, and then use the Navigation Pane to reopen it. Note that the records are displayed in primary key order by the values in the PatronID field.

⊕ **Explore** 8. Use the Simple Query Wizard to create a query that includes all the fields in the Patron table *except* the Title field. (*Hint*: Use the >> and < buttons to select the necessary fields.) Save the query using the name **PatronPhoneList**.

⊕ **Explore** 9. The query results are displayed in order by the PatronID field values. You can specify a different order by sorting the query. Display the HOME tab. Then, click the insertion point anywhere in the LastName column to make it the current field. In the Sort & Filter group on the HOME tab, click the Ascending button. The records are now listed in order by the values in the LastName field. Save and close the query.

⊕ **Explore** 10. Use the Form tool to create a form for the Patron table. In the new form, navigate to record 15 (the record with PatronID 33765), and then print the form *for the current record only*. (*Hint*: You must use the Print dialog box in order to print only the current record. Go to Backstage view, click Print in the navigation bar, and then click Print to open the Print dialog box. Click the Selected Record(s) option button and then click the OK button to print the current record.) Save the form as **PatronInfo**, and then close it.

11. Use the Report tool to create a report based on the Patron table. In Layout view, resize each field so it is slightly wider than the longest entry (either the field name itself or an entry in the field). All five fields should fit within the page area after resizing. At the bottom of the report, move the text "Page 1 of 1" to the left so it is within the page area. Display the report in Print Preview, then verify that the fields and page number fit within the page area and that all field values are fully displayed. Save the report as **PatronList**. Print the report (only if asked by your instructor to do so), and then close it.
12. Close the Patron table, and then compact and repair the Shelter database.
13. Close the Shelter database.

Case Problem 4

Data File needed for this Case Problem: Tour.accdb

Stanley EcoTours Janice and Bill Stanley live in Pocatello, Idaho, and are the proud owners and operators of Stanley EcoTours. Their passion is to encourage people to visit natural areas around the world in a responsible manner that does not harm the environment. Their advertising has drawn clients from Idaho, Wyoming, Montana, and Canada. As the interest in ecotourism grows, Janice and Bill's business is also expanding to include more tours in Africa and South America. Because of the growth in business that they anticipate, Janice and Bill realize their current recordkeeping system is inadequate. They would like you to build an Access database to manage information about guests, tours, and reservations. Complete the following:

1. Create a new, blank database named **Stanley** and save it in the folder where you are storing your files, as specified by your instructor.
2. In Datasheet view for the Table1 table, rename the default primary key ID field to **GuestID**. Change the data type of the GuestID field to Short Text.
3. Add the following eight Short Text fields to the new table in the order shown: **GuestFirst**, **GuestLast**, **Address**, **City**, **State/Prov**, **PostalCode**, **Country**, and **Phone**. Save the table as **Guest**.

4. Enter the records shown in Figure 1-35 in the Guest table. For the first record, be sure to enter your first name in the GuestFirst field and your last name in the GuestLast field.

Figure 1-35   Guest table records

GuestID	GuestFirst	GuestLast	Address	City	State/Prov	PostalCode	Country	Phone
401	Student First	Student Last	10 Winter Ave	Boise	ID	83702	USA	208-344-0975
417	Isabelle	Rouy	227 Front Ln	Calgary	AB	T1Y 2N7	Canada	403-226-0065
403	Brian	Anderson	5003 Grant Blvd	Great Falls	MT	59401	USA	406-761-4515
425	Kelly	Skolnik	15 Tobin Dr	Red Deer	AB	T4N 3D5	Canada	403-755-1597
420	Alberto	Lopez	991 Crestview Dr	Butte	MT	59701	USA	406-782-1183

© 2014 Cengage Learning

5. Bill created a database named Tour that contains a Customer table with data about guests. The Guest table you created has the same design as the Customer table. Copy all the records from the **Customer** table in the **Tour** database (located in the Access1 ▸ Case4 folder provided with your Data Files) and then paste them at the end of the Guest table in the Stanley database.

6. Resize all datasheet columns to their best fit, and then save the Guest table.

7. Close the Guest table, and then use the Navigation Pane to reopen it. Note that the records are displayed in primary key order.

8. Use the Simple Query Wizard to create a query that includes the following fields from the Guest table, in the order shown: GuestID, GuestLast, GuestFirst, State/Prov, and Phone. Name the query **GuestData**.

Explore 9. The query results are displayed in order by the GuestID field values. You can specify a different order by sorting the query. Display the HOME tab. Then, click the insertion point anywhere in the State/Prov column to make it the current field. In the Sort & Filter group on the HOME tab, click the Ascending button. The records are now listed in order by the values in the State/Prov field. Save and close the query.

Explore 10. Use the Form tool to create a form for the Guest table. In the new form, navigate to record 10 (the record with GuestID 412), and then print the form *for the current record only*. (*Hint*: You must use the Print dialog box in order to print only the current record. Go to Backstage view, click Print in the navigation bar, and then click Print to open the Print dialog box. Click the Selected Record(s) option button and then click the OK button to print the current record.) Save the form as **GuestInfo**, and then close it.

11. Use the Report tool to create a report based on the Guest table. In Layout view, resize each field so it is slightly wider than the longest entry (either the field name itself or an entry in the field). At the bottom of the report, move the text "Page 1 of 1" to the left so it is within the page area on the report's first page. Display the report in Print Preview and notice that the columns of the report are still spread across two pages, even after resizing the fields. Save the report as **GuestList**.

Explore 12. In the Close Preview group, click the Close Print Preview button to return to the report in Layout view. To make more room on the first page, you'll delete the Address, PostalCode, and Country columns from the report. Click anywhere in the Address column to make it active. Click the ARRANGE tab (one of the REPORT LAYOUT TOOLS contextual tabs), and then click the Select Column button in the Rows & Columns group. Click the HOME tab, and then click the Delete button in the Records group to delete the selected column from the report. Repeat this process to delete the PostalCode and Country columns. The remaining six fields should now all fit on the report's first page.

13. Display the report in Print Preview again, then verify that the fields and page number fit within the page area and that all field values are fully displayed.

14. Save the report, print it (only if asked by your instructor to do so), and then close it.

15. Close the Guest table, and then compact and repair the Stanley database.

16. Close the Stanley database.

TUTORIAL 2

Building a Database and Defining Table Relationships

Creating the Billing and Patient Tables

OBJECTIVES

Session 2.1
- Learn the guidelines for designing databases and setting field properties
- Create a table in Design view
- Define fields, set field properties, and specify a table's primary key
- Modify the structure of a table
- Change the order of fields in Design view
- Add new fields in Design view
- Change the Format property for a field in Datasheet view
- Modify field properties in Design view

Session 2.2
- Import data from an Excel worksheet
- Create a table by importing an existing table structure
- Add fields to a table with the Data Type gallery
- Delete and rename fields
- Change the data type for a field in Design view
- Set the Default Value property for a field
- Add data to a table by importing a text file
- Define a relationship between two tables

Case | Chatham Community Health Services

The Chatham database currently contains one table, the Visit table. Cindi Rodriguez also wants to track information about the clinic's patients and the invoices sent to them for services provided by Chatham Community Health Services. This information includes such items as each patient's name and address, and the amount and billing date for each invoice.

In this tutorial, you'll create two new tables in the Chatham database—named Billing and Patient—to contain the additional data Cindi wants to track. You will use two different methods for creating the tables, and learn how to modify the fields. After adding records to the tables, you will define the necessary relationships between the tables in the Chatham database to relate the tables, enabling Cindi and her staff to work with the data more efficiently.

STARTING DATA FILES

Access1 → Tutorial
Chatham.accdb *(cont.)*
Invoices.xlsx
Kelly.accdb
Patient.txt

Review
Supplies.xlsx
Vendor.accdb *(cont.)*

Case1
Customers.txt
Gopher.accdb *(cont.)*

Case2
Agreements.xlsx
Client.accdb
OBrien.accdb *(cont.)*
Students.txt

Case3
Animals.txt
Donations.xlsx
Shelter.accdb *(cont.)*

Case4
Bookings.txt
Stanley.accdb *(cont.)*
Travel.accdb

Microsoft product screenshots used with permission from Microsoft Corporation.

Session 2.1 Visual Overview:

Design view allows you to define or modify a table structure or the properties of the fields in a table.

The default name for a new table you create in Design view is Table1. This name appears on the tab for the new table.

The top portion of the Table window in Design view is called the **Table Design grid**. Here, you enter values for the Field Name, Data Type, and Description field properties.

In the Field Name column, you enter the name for each new field in the table. When you first open a new Table window in Design view, Field Name is the current property.

In the Data Type column, you select the appropriate data type for each new field in the table. The data type determines what field values you can enter for a field and what other properties the field will have. The default data type for a new field is Short Text.

After you assign a data type to a field, the General tab displays additional field properties for that data type. Initially, most field properties are assigned default values.

When defining the fields in a table, you can move from the Table Design grid to the Field Properties pane by pressing the **F6 key**.

Table Window in Design View

Chatham : Database- E:\Access1\Tutorial\Chatham.accdb (Access...

Rename/Delete Macro
d & Table Events

Relationships

Object Dependencies

Relationships

Description (Optional)

Properties

A field name can be up to 64 characters long, including spaces. Press F1 for help on field names.

You can use the **Description property** to enter an optional description for a field to explain its purpose or usage. A field's Description property can be up to 255 characters long, and its value appears on the status bar when you view the table datasheet.

The bottom portion of the Table window in Design view is called the **Field Properties pane**. Here, you select values for all other field properties, most of which are optional.

The purpose or characteristics of the current property (Field Name, in this case) appear in this section of the Field Properties pane.

You can display more complete Help information about the current property by pressing the **F1 key**.

Guidelines for Designing Databases

A database management system can be a useful tool, but only if you first carefully design the database so that it meets the needs of its users. In database design, you determine the fields, tables, and relationships needed to satisfy the data and processing requirements. When you design a database, you should follow these guidelines:

- **Identify all the fields needed to produce the required information.** For example, Cindi needs information about patients, visits, and invoices. Figure 2-1 shows the fields that satisfy these information requirements.

Figure 2-1   Cindi's data requirements

VisitID	InvoiceDate
PatientID	Reason
InvoiceAmt	Phone
FirstName	WalkIn
LastName	Email
Address	VisitDate
City	InvoiceNum
State	InvoicePaid
Zip	BirthDate

© 2014 Cengage Learning

- **Organize each piece of data into its smallest useful part.** For example, Cindi could store each patient's complete name in one field called PatientName instead of using two fields called FirstName and LastName, as shown in Figure 2-1. However, doing so would make it more difficult to work with the data. If Cindi wanted to view the records in alphabetical order by last name, she wouldn't be able to do so with field values such as "Ben Li" and "Amanda Fox" stored in a PatientName field. She could do so with field values such as "Li" and "Fox" stored separately in a LastName field.
- **Group related fields into tables.** For example, Cindi grouped the fields related to visits into the Visit table, which you created in Tutorial 1. The fields related to invoices are grouped into the Billing table, and the fields related to patients are grouped into the Patient table. Figure 2-2 shows the fields grouped into all three tables for the Chatham database.

Figure 2-2   Cindi's fields grouped into tables

Visit table	Billing table	Patient table
VisitID	InvoiceNum	PatientID
PatientID	VisitID	LastName
VisitDate	InvoiceDate	FirstName
Reason	InvoiceAmt	BirthDate
WalkIn	InvoicePaid	Phone
		Address
		City
		State
		Zip
		Email

© 2014 Cengage Learning

- **Determine each table's primary key.** Recall that a primary key uniquely identifies each record in a table. For some tables, one of the fields, such as a credit card number, naturally serves the function of a primary key. For other tables, two or more fields might be needed to function as the primary key. In these cases, the primary key is called a **composite key**. For example, a school grade table would use a combination of student number, term, and course code to serve as the primary key. For a third category of tables, no single field or combination of fields can uniquely identify a record in a table. In these cases, you need to add a field whose sole purpose is to serve as the table's primary key. For Cindi's tables, VisitID is the primary key for the Visit table, InvoiceNum is the primary key for the Billing table, and PatientID is the primary key for the Patient table.
- **Include a common field in related tables.** You use the common field to connect one table logically with another table. For example, Cindi's Visit and Patient tables include the PatientID field as a common field. Recall that when you include the primary key from one table as a field in a second table to form a relationship, the field in the second table is called a foreign key; therefore, the PatientID field is a foreign key in the Visit table. With this common field, Cindi can find all visits to the clinic made by a particular patient; she can use the PatientID value for a patient and search the Visit table for all records with that PatientID value. Likewise, she can determine which patient made a particular visit by searching the Patient table to find the one record with the same PatientID value as the corresponding value in the Visit table. Similarly, the VisitID field is a common field, serving as the primary key in the Visit table and a foreign key in the Billing table.
- **Avoid data redundancy.** When you store the same data in more than one place, **data redundancy** occurs. With the exception of common fields to connect tables, you should avoid data redundancy because it wastes storage space and can cause inconsistencies. An inconsistency would exist, for example, if you type a field value one way in one table and a different way in the same table or in a second table. Figure 2-3, which contains portions of potential data stored in the Patient and Visit tables, shows an example of incorrect database design that has data redundancy in the Visit table. In Figure 2-3, the LastName field in the Visit table is redundant, and one value for this field was entered incorrectly, in three different ways.

Figure 2-3 Incorrect database design with data redundancy

Patient table

PatientID	Last Name	FirstName	Address
22542	Diaz	Anna	93 Gates Ln
22544	Sutherland	Max	48 Vine St
22546	Ingram	Julia	834 Kiefer Rd
22560	Lewis	Patrice	15 Prince Rd
22561	Shaw	Daniel	33 Agnes Ct

Visit table

VisitID	PatientID	Last Name	VisitDate	WalkIn
1535	22546	Ingraham	11/12/2015	Yes
1570	22561	Shaw	1/11/2016	Yes
1571	22546	Ingrams	1/15/2016	No
1591	22544	Sutherland	1/26/2016	Yes
1601	22542	Diaz	2/2/2016	No
1620	22546	Engram	3/7/2016	No
1638	22560	Lewis	3/11/2016	Yes

© 2014 Cengage Learning

- **Determine the properties of each field.** You need to identify the **properties**, or characteristics, of each field so that the DBMS knows how to store, display, and process the field values. These properties include the field's name, data type, maximum number of characters or digits, description, valid values, and other field characteristics. You will learn more about field properties later in this tutorial.

The Billing and Patient tables you need to create will contain the fields shown in Figure 2-2. Before creating these new tables in the Chatham database, you first need to learn some guidelines for setting field properties.

Guidelines for Setting Field Properties

As just noted, the last step of database design is to determine which values to assign to the properties, such as the name and data type, of each field. When you select or enter a value for a property, you **set** the property. Access has rules for naming fields and objects, assigning data types, and setting other field properties.

Naming Fields and Objects

You must name each field, table, and other object in an Access database. Access stores these items in the database, using the names you supply. It's best to choose a field or object name that describes the purpose or contents of the field or object so that later you can easily remember what the name represents. For example, the three tables in the Chatham database are named Visit, Billing, and Patient because these names suggest their contents. Note that a table or query name must be unique within a database. A field name must be unique within a table, but it can be used again in another table.

Assigning Field Data Types

Each field must have a data type, which is either assigned automatically by Access or specifically by the table designer. The data type determines what field values you can enter for the field and what other properties the field will have. For example, the Billing table will include an InvoiceDate field, which will store date values, so you will assign the Date/Time data type to this field. Then Access will allow you to enter and manipulate only dates or times as values in the InvoiceDate field.

Figure 2-4 lists the most commonly used data types in Access, describes the field values allowed for each data type, explains when you should use each data type, and indicates the field size of each data type. You can find more complete information about all available data types in Access Help.

| Figure 2-4 | Common data types |

Data Type	Description	Field Size
Short Text	Allows field values containing letters, digits, spaces, and special characters. Use for names, addresses, descriptions, and fields containing digits that are *not used in calculations*.	0 to 255 characters; default is 255
Long Text	Allows field values containing letters, digits, spaces, and special characters. Use for long comments and explanations.	1 to 65,535 characters; exact size is determined by entry
Number	Allows positive and negative numbers as field values. A number can contain digits, a decimal point, commas, a plus sign, and a minus sign. Use for fields that will be used in calculations, except those involving money.	1 to 15 digits
Date/Time	Allows field values containing valid dates and times from January 1, 100 to December 31, 9999. Dates can be entered in month/day/year format, several other date formats, or a variety of time formats, such as 10:35 PM. You can perform calculations on dates and times, and you can sort them. For example, you can determine the number of days between two dates.	8 bytes
Currency	Allows field values similar to those for the Number data type, but is used for storing monetary values. Unlike calculations with Number data type decimal values, calculations performed with the Currency data type are not subject to round-off error.	Accurate to 15 digits on the left side of the decimal point and to 4 digits on the right side
AutoNumber	Consists of integer values created automatically by Access each time you create a new record. You can specify sequential numbering or random numbering, which guarantees a unique field value, so that such a field can serve as a table's primary key.	9 digits
Yes/No	Limits field values to yes and no, on and off, or true and false. Use for fields that indicate the presence or absence of a condition, such as whether an order has been filled or whether an invoice has been paid.	1 character
Hyperlink	Consists of text used as a hyperlink address, which can have up to four parts: the text that appears in a field or control; the path to a file or page; a location within the file or page; and text displayed as a ScreenTip.	Up to 65,535 characters total for the four parts of the hyperlink

© 2014 Cengage Learning

Setting Field Sizes

The **Field Size property** defines a field value's maximum storage size for Short Text, Number, and AutoNumber fields only. The other data types have no Field Size property because their storage size is either a fixed, predetermined amount or is determined automatically by the field value itself, as shown in Figure 2-4. A Short Text field has a default field size of 255 characters; you can also set its field size by entering a number from 0 to 255. For example, the FirstName and LastName fields in the Patient table will be Short Text fields with sizes of 20 characters and 25 characters, respectively. These field sizes will accommodate the values that will be entered in each of these fields.

PROSKILLS

Decision Making: Specifying the Field Size Property for Number Fields

When you use the Number data type to define a field, you need to decide what the Field Size setting should be for the field. You should set the Field Size property based on the largest value that you expect to store in that field. Access processes smaller data sizes faster, using less memory, so you can optimize your database's performance and its storage space by selecting the correct field size for each field. Field Size property settings for Number fields are as follows:

- **Byte**: Stores whole numbers (numbers with no fractions) from 0 to 255 in one byte
- **Integer**: Stores whole numbers from –32,768 to 32,767 in two bytes
- **Long Integer** (default): Stores whole numbers from –2,147,483,648 to 2,147,483,647 in four bytes
- **Single**: Stores positive and negative numbers to precisely seven decimal places in four bytes
- **Double**: Stores positive and negative numbers to precisely 15 decimal places in eight bytes
- **Replication ID**: Establishes a unique identifier for replication of tables, records, and other objects in databases created using Access 2003 and earlier versions in 16 bytes
- **Decimal**: Stores positive and negative numbers to precisely 28 decimal places in 12 bytes

Choosing an appropriate field size is important to optimize efficiency. For example, it would be wasteful to use the Long Integer field size for a Number field that will store only whole numbers ranging from 0 to 255 because the Long Integer field size uses four bytes of storage space. A better choice would be the Byte field size, which uses one byte of storage space to store the same values. By first gathering and analyzing information about the number values that will be stored in a Number field, you can make the best decision for the field's Field Size property and ensure the most efficient user experience for the database.

Setting the Caption Property for Fields

The **Caption property** for a field specifies how the field name is displayed in database objects, including table and query datasheets, forms, and reports. If you don't set the Caption property, Access displays the field name as the column heading or label for a field. For example, field names such as InvoiceAmt and InvoiceDate in the Billing table can be difficult to read. Setting the Caption property for these fields to "Invoice Amt" and "Invoice Date" would make it easier for users to read the field names and work with the database.

INSIGHT

Setting the Caption Property vs. Naming Fields

Although Access allows you to include spaces in field names, this practice is not recommended because the spaces cause problems when you try to perform more complex tasks with the data in your database. Setting the Caption property allows you to follow best practices for naming fields, such as not including spaces in field names, while still providing users with more readable field names in datasheets, forms, and reports.

In Tutorial 1, you created the Chatham database file and, within that file, you created the Visit table working in Datasheet view. According to her plan for the Chatham database, Cindi also wants to track information about the invoices the clinic sends to its patients. Next, you'll create the Billing table for Cindi—this time, working in Design view.

Tutorial 2 Building a Database and Defining Table Relationships | Access | AC 59

Creating a Table in Design View

Creating a table in Design view involves entering the field names and defining the properties for the fields, specifying a primary key for the table, and then saving the table structure. Cindi documented the design for the new Billing table by listing each field's name and data type; each field's size and description (if applicable); and any other properties to be set for each field. See Figure 2-5.

Figure 2-5   Design for the Billing table

Field Name	Data Type	Field Size	Description	Other
InvoiceNum	Short Text	5	Primary key	Caption = Invoice Num
VisitID	Short Text	4	Foreign key	Caption = Visit ID
InvoiceAmt	Currency			Format = Currency
				Decimal Places = 2
				Caption = Invoice Amt
InvoiceDate	Date/Time			Format = mm/dd/yyyy
				Caption = Invoice Date
InvoicePaid	Yes/No			Caption = Invoice Paid

© 2014 Cengage Learning

You'll use Cindi's design as a guide for creating the Billing table in the Chatham database.

To begin creating the Billing table:

1. Start Access and open the **Chatham** database you created in Tutorial 1.

    Trouble? If the security warning is displayed below the ribbon, click the Enable Content button.

2. If the Navigation Pane is open, click the **Shutter Bar Open/Close Button** to close it.

3. On the ribbon, click the **CREATE** tab.

4. In the Tables group, click the **Table Design** button. A new table named Table1 opens in Design view. Refer to the Session 2.1 Visual Overview for a complete description of the Table window in Design view.

Defining Fields

When you first create a table in Design view, the insertion point is located in the first row's Field Name box, ready for you to begin defining the first field in the table. You enter values for the Field Name, Data Type, and Description field properties, and then select values for all other field properties in the Field Properties pane. These other properties will appear when you move to the first row's Data Type box.

REFERENCE

Defining a Field in Design View

- In the Field Name box, type the name for the field, and then press the Tab key.
- Accept the default Short Text data type, or click the arrow and select a different data type for the field. Press the Tab key.
- Enter an optional description for the field, if necessary.
- Use the Field Properties pane to type or select other field properties, as appropriate.

The first field you need to define is the InvoiceNum field. This field will be the primary key for the Billing table. Each invoice at Chatham Community Health Services is assigned a specific five-digit number. Although the InvoiceNum field will contain these number values, the numbers will never be used in calculations; therefore, you'll assign the Short Text data type to this field. Any time a field contains number values that will not be used in calculations—such as phone numbers, zip codes, and so on—you should use the Short Text data type instead of the Number data type.

To define the InvoiceNum field:

TIP
You can also press the Enter key to move from one property to the next in the Table Design grid.

1. Type **InvoiceNum** in the first row's Field Name box, and then press the **Tab** key to advance to the Data Type box. The default data type, Short Text, appears highlighted in the Data Type box, which now also contains an arrow, and the field properties for a Short Text field appear in the Field Properties pane. See Figure 2-6.

Figure 2-6   Table window after entering the first field name

Notice that the right side of the Field Properties pane now provides an explanation for the current property, Data Type.

Trouble? If you make a typing error, you can correct it by clicking to position the insertion point, and then using either the Backspace key to delete characters to the left of the insertion point or the Delete key to delete characters to the right of the insertion point. Then type the correct text.

Because the InvoiceNum field values will not be used in calculations, you will accept the default Short Text data type for the field.

2. Press the **Tab** key to accept Short Text as the data type and to advance to the Description (Optional) box.

Tutorial 2 Building a Database and Defining Table Relationships | Access   AC 61

Next you'll enter the Description property value as "Primary key." The value you enter for the Description property will appear on the status bar when you view the table datasheet. Note that specifying "Primary key" for the Description property does *not* establish the current field as the primary key; you use a button on the ribbon to specify the primary key in Design view, which you will do later in this session.

3. Type **Primary key** in the Description (Optional) box.

   Notice the Field Size property for the field. The default setting of 255 for Short Text fields is displayed. You need to change this number to 5 because all invoice numbers at Chatham Community Health Services contain only five digits.

4. Double-click the number **255** in the Field Size property box to select it, and then type **5**.

   Finally, you need to set the Caption property for the field so that its name appears with a space, as "Invoice Num."

5. Click the **Caption** property box, and then type **Invoice Num**. The definition of the first field is complete. See Figure 2-7.

Figure 2-7 InvoiceNum field defined

Field Name	Data Type	
InvoiceNum	Short Text	Primary key

- Short Text data type is selected
- Description property entered
- Field Size property set

Field Properties

General | Lookup

Field Size	5
Format	
Input Mask	
Caption	Invoice Num
Default Value	
Validation Rule	
Validation Text	
Required	No
Allow Zero Length	Yes
Indexed	Yes (Duplicates OK)
Unicode Compression	Yes
IME Mode	No Control
IME Sentence Mode	None
Text Align	General

- Caption property set

Design view. F6 = Switch panes. F1 = Help.

Cindi's Billing table design (Figure 2-5) shows VisitID as the second field. Because Cindi and other staff members need to relate information about invoices to the visit data in the Visit table, the Billing table must include the VisitID field, which is the Visit table's primary key. Recall that when you include the primary key from one table as a field in a second table to connect the two tables, the field is a foreign key in the second table. The field must be defined in the same way in both tables—that is, the field properties, including field size and data type, must match exactly.

Next, you will define VisitID as a Short Text field with a field size of 4. Later in this session, you'll change the Field Size property for the VisitID field in the Visit table to 4 so that the field definition is the same in both tables.

To define the VisitID field:

1. In the Table Design grid, click the second row's Field Name box, type **VisitID** in the box, and then press the **Tab** key to advance to the Data Type box.

2. Press the **Tab** key to accept Short Text as the field's data type. Because the VisitID field is a foreign key to the Visit table, you'll enter "Foreign key" in the Description (Optional) box to help users of the database understand the purpose of this field.

3. Type **Foreign key** in the Description (Optional) box. Next, you'll change the Field Size property to 4.

4. Press the **F6** key to move to the Field Properties pane. The current entry for the Field Size property, 255, is highlighted.

5. Type **4** to set the Field Size property. Finally, you need to set the Caption property for this field.

6. Press the **Tab** key until the insertion point is in the Caption box, and then type **Visit ID** (be sure to include a space between the two words). You have completed the definition of the second field.

TIP
The quickest way to move back to the Table Design grid is to use the mouse.

The third field in the Billing table is the InvoiceAmt field, which will display the dollar amount of each invoice the clinic sends to its patients. Cindi wants the values to appear with two decimal places because invoice amounts include cents. She also wants the values to include dollar signs, so that the values will be formatted as currency when they are printed in bills sent to patients. The Currency data type is the appropriate choice for this field.

To define the InvoiceAmt field:

1. Click the third row's Field Name box, type **InvoiceAmt** in the box, and then press the **Tab** key to advance to the Data Type box.

2. Click the **Data Type** arrow, click **Currency** in the list, and then press the **Tab** key to advance to the Description (Optional) box.

   According to Cindi's design (Figure 2-5), you do not need to enter a description for this field. If you've assigned a descriptive field name and the field does not fulfill a special function (such as primary key), you usually do not enter a value for the optional Description property. InvoiceAmt is a field that does not require a value for its Description property.

   Cindi wants the InvoiceAmt field values to be displayed with two decimal places. The **Decimal Places property** specifies the number of decimal places that are displayed to the right of the decimal point.

Tutorial 2 Building a Database and Defining Table Relationships | Access AC 63

> **TIP**
> You can display the arrow and the list simultaneously by clicking the right side of a box.

3. In the Field Properties pane, click the **Decimal Places** box to position the insertion point there. An arrow appears on the right side of the Decimal Places box. When you position the insertion point or select text in many boxes, Access displays an arrow, which you can click to display a list with options.

4. Click the **Decimal Places** arrow, and then click **2** in the list to specify two decimal places for the InvoiceAmt field values.

5. Press the **Tab** key until the insertion point is in the Caption box, and then type **Invoice Amt**. The definition of the third field is now complete. See Figure 2-8.

Figure 2-8 Table window after defining the first three fields

Field Name	Data Type	
InvoiceNum	Short Text	Primary key
VisitID	Short Text	Foreign key
InvoiceAmt ← current field	Currency	

General | Lookup

Format	Currency
Decimal Places	2
Input Mask	
Caption	Invoice Amt
Default Value	0
Validation Rule	
Validation Text	
Required	No
Indexed	No
Text Align	General

(property values set for the current field)

Notice that the Format property is set to "Currency," which formats the values with dollar signs.

The fourth field in the Billing table is the InvoiceDate field. This field will contain the dates on which invoices are generated for the clinic's patients. You'll define the InvoiceDate field using the Date/Time data type. Also, according to Cindi's design (Figure 2-5), the date values should be displayed in the format mm/dd/yyyy, which is a two-digit month, a two-digit day, and a four-digit year.

To define the InvoiceDate field:

1. Click the fourth row's Field Name box, type **InvoiceDate**, and then press the **Tab** key to advance to the Data Type box.

    You can select a value from the Data Type list as you did for the InvoiceAmt field. Alternately, you can type the property value in the box or type just the first character of the property value.

2. Type **d**. The value in the fourth row's Data Type box changes to "date/Time," with the letters "ate/Time" highlighted. See Figure 2-9.

Figure 2-9 — Selecting a value for the Data Type property

"d" typed
"ate/Time" highlighted

Field Name	Data Type	
InvoiceNum	Short Text	Primary key
VisitID	Short Text	Foreign key
InvoiceAmt	Currency	
InvoiceDate	date/Time	

3. Press the **Tab** key to advance to the Description (Optional) box. Note that Access changes the value for the Data Type property to "Date/Time."

    Cindi wants the values in the InvoiceDate field to be displayed in a format showing the month, the day, and a four-digit year, as in the following example: 03/11/2016. You use the Format property to control the display of a field value.

4. In the Field Properties pane, click the right side of the **Format** box to display the list of predefined formats for Date/Time fields. See Figure 2-10.

Figure 2-10 — Displaying available formats for Date/Time fields

Field Properties

General	Lookup		
Format			
Input Mask	General Date	11/12/2015 5:34:23 PM	
Caption	Long Date	Thursday, November 12, 2015	
Default Value	Medium Date	12-Nov-15	
Validation Rule	Short Date	11/12/2015	
Validation Text	Long Time	5:34:23 PM	
Required	Medium Time	5:34 PM	
Indexed	Short Time	17:34	
IME Mode	No Control		
IME Sentence Mode	None		
Text Align	General		
Show Date Picker	For dates		

formats for Date/Time fields

The display layout for the field. Select a predefined format or enter a custom format. Press F1 for help on formats.

click to display a list of predefined formats

Design view. F6 = Switch panes. F1 = Help.

Trouble? If you see an arrow instead of a list of predefined formats, click the arrow to display the list.

Tutorial 2 Building a Database and Defining Table Relationships | Access   AC 65

As noted in the right side of the Field Properties pane, you can either choose a predefined format or enter a custom format. Even though the Short Date format seems to match the format Cindi wants, it displays only one digit for months that contain only one digit. For example, it would display the month of March with only the digit "3"—as in 3/11/2016—instead of displaying the month with two digits, as in 03/11/2016.

Because none of the predefined formats matches the exact layout Cindi wants for the InvoiceDate values, you need to create a custom date format. Figure 2-11 shows some of the symbols available for custom date and time formats.

Figure 2-11   **Symbols for some custom date formats**

Symbol	Description
/	date separator
d	day of the month in one or two numeric digits, as needed (1 to 31)
dd	day of the month in two numeric digits (01 to 31)
ddd	first three letters of the weekday (Sun to Sat)
dddd	full name of the weekday (Sunday to Saturday)
w	day of the week (1 to 7)
ww	week of the year (1 to 53)
m	month of the year in one or two numeric digits, as needed (1 to 12)
mm	month of the year in two numeric digits (01 to 12)
mmm	first three letters of the month (Jan to Dec)
mmmm	full name of the month (January to December)
yy	last two digits of the year (01 to 99)
yyyy	full year (0100 to 9999)

© 2014 Cengage Learning

Cindi wants the dates to be displayed with a two-digit month (mm), a two-digit day (dd), and a four-digit year (yyyy). You'll enter this custom format now.

5. Click the **Format** arrow to close the list of predefined formats, and then type **mm/dd/yyyy** in the Format box.

6. Press the **Tab** key until the insertion point is in the Caption box, and then type **Invoice Date**. See Figure 2-12.

Figure 2-12   Specifying the custom date format

[Figure showing Table1 in Design view with fields: InvoiceNum (Short Text, Primary key), VisitID (Short Text, Foreign key), InvoiceAmt (Currency), InvoiceDate (Date/Time) — labeled as "current field". Field Properties pane shows Format: mm/dd/yyyy (labeled "custom date format entered"), Caption: Invoice Date (labeled "Caption property entered"), Required: No, Indexed: No, IME Mode: No Control, IME Sentence Mode: None, Text Align: General, Show Date Picker: For dates.]

The fifth, and final, field to be defined in the Billing table is InvoicePaid. This field will be a Yes/No field to indicate the payment status of each invoice record stored in the Billing table. Recall that the Yes/No data type is used to define fields that store true/false, yes/no, and on/off field values. When you create a Yes/No field in a table, the default Format property is set to Yes/No.

To define the InvoicePaid field:

1. Click the fifth row's Field Name box, type **InvoicePaid**, and then press the **Tab** key to advance to the Data Type box.

2. Type **y**. Access completes the data type as "yes/No."

3. Press the **Tab** key to select the Yes/No data type and move to the Description (Optional) box. In the Field Properties pane, note that the default format of "Yes/No" is selected, so you do not have to change this property.

4. In the Field Properties pane, click the Caption box, and then type **Invoice Paid**.

You've finished defining the fields for the Billing table. Next, you need to specify the primary key for the table.

Tutorial 2 Building a Database and Defining Table Relationships | Access   AC 67

Specifying the Primary Key

As you learned earlier, the primary key for a table uniquely identifies each record in the table.

> **REFERENCE**
>
> ### Specifying a Primary Key in Design View
>
> - Display the table in Design view.
> - Click in the row for the field you've chosen to be the primary key to make it the active field. If the primary key will consist of two or more fields, click the row selector for the first field, press and hold down the Ctrl key, and then click the row selector for each additional primary key field.
> - In the Tools group on the DESIGN tab, click the Primary Key button.

According to Cindi's design, you need to specify InvoiceNum as the primary key for the Billing table. You can do so while the table is in Design view.

To specify InvoiceNum as the primary key:

1. Click in the row for the InvoiceNum field to make it the current field.

2. In the Tools group on the DESIGN tab, click the **Primary Key** button. The Primary Key button in the Tools group is now highlighted, and a key symbol appears in the row selector for the first row, indicating that the InvoiceNum field is the table's primary key. See Figure 2-13.

TIP
This button is a toggle; you can click it to remove the key symbol.

Figure 2-13   InvoiceNum field selected as the primary key

INSIGHT

Understanding the Importance of the Primary Key

Although Access does not require a table to have a primary key, including a primary key offers several advantages:

- A primary key uniquely identifies each record in a table.
- Access does not allow duplicate values in the primary key field. For example, if a record already exists in the Visit table with a VisitID value of 1550, Access prevents you from adding another record with this same value in the VisitID field. Preventing duplicate values ensures the uniqueness of the primary key field.
- When a primary key has been specified, Access forces you to enter a value for the primary key field in every record in the table. This is known as **entity integrity**. If you do not enter a value for a field, you have actually given the field a **null value**. You cannot give a null value to the primary key field because entity integrity prevents Access from accepting and processing that record.
- You can enter records in any order, but Access displays them by default in order of the primary key's field values. If you enter records in no specific order, you are ensured that you will later be able to work with them in a more meaningful, primary key sequence.
- Access responds faster to your requests for specific records based on the primary key.

Saving the Table Structure

The last step in creating a table is to name the table and save the table's structure. When you save a table structure, the table is stored in the database file (in this case, the Chatham database file). Once the table is saved, you can enter data into it. According to Cindi's plan, you need to save the table you've defined as "Billing."

To name and save the Billing table:

1. On the Quick Access Toolbar, click the **Save** button 🖫. The Save As dialog box opens.
2. Type **Billing** in the Table Name box, and then press the **Enter** key. Access saves the Billing table in the Chatham database. Notice that the tab for the table now displays the name "Billing" instead of "Table1."

Modifying the Structure of an Access Table

Even a well-designed table might need to be modified. Some changes that you can make to a table's structure in Design view include changing the order of fields and adding new fields.

After meeting with her assistant, Kelly Schwarz, and reviewing the structure of the Billing table, Cindi has changes she wants you to make to the table. First, she wants the InvoiceAmt field to be moved so that it appears right before the InvoicePaid field. Then, she wants you to add a new Short Text field named InvoiceItem to the table to include information about what the invoice is for, such as office visits, lab work, and so on. Cindi would like the InvoiceItem field to be inserted between the InvoiceDate and InvoiceAmt fields.

Moving a Field in Design View

To move a field, you use the mouse to drag it to a new location in the Table Design grid. Although you can move a field in Datasheet view by dragging its column heading to a new location, doing so rearranges only the *display* of the table's fields; the table structure is not changed. To move a field permanently, you must move the field in Design view.

Next, you'll move the InvoiceAmt field so that it is before the InvoicePaid field in the Billing table.

To move the InvoiceAmt field:

1. Position the pointer on the row selector for the InvoiceAmt field until the pointer changes to a ➡ shape.

2. Click the **row selector** to select the entire InvoiceAmt row.

3. Place the pointer on the row selector for the InvoiceAmt field until the pointer changes to ▷, and then click and drag to the row selector for the InvoicePaid field. Notice that as you drag, the pointer changes to ▷. See Figure 2-14.

Figure 2-14   Moving the InvoiceAmt field in the table structure

4. Release the mouse button. The InvoiceAmt field now appears between the InvoiceDate and InvoicePaid fields in the table structure.

   Trouble? If the InvoiceAmt field did not move, repeat Steps 1 through 4, making sure you hold down the mouse button during the drag operation.

Adding a Field in Design View

To add a new field between existing fields, you must insert a row. You begin by selecting the row below where you want the new field to be inserted.

REFERENCE

Adding a Field Between Two Existing Fields

- In the Table window in Design view, select the row below where you want the new field to be inserted.
- In the Tools group on the DESIGN tab, click the Insert Rows button.
- Define the new field by entering the field name, data type, optional description, and any property specifications.

Next, you need to add the InvoiceItem field to the Billing table structure between the InvoiceAmt and InvoicePaid fields.

To add the InvoiceItem field to the Billing table:

1. Click the **InvoicePaid** Field Name box. You need to establish this field as the current field so that the row for the new record will be inserted above this field.

2. In the Tools group on the DESIGN tab, click the **Insert Rows** button. Access adds a new, blank row between the InvoiceAmt and InvoicePaid fields. The insertion point is positioned in the Field Name box for the new row, ready for you to type the name for the new field. See Figure 2-15.

Figure 2-15   Table structure after inserting a row

new, blank row inserted

Field Name	Data Type	
InvoiceNum	Short Text	Primary key
VisitID	Short Text	Foreign key
InvoiceDate	Date/Time	
InvoiceAmt	Currency	
InvoicePaid	Yes/No	

Trouble? If you selected the InvoicePaid field's row selector and then inserted the new row, you need to click the new row's Field Name box to position the insertion point in it.

You'll define the InvoiceItem field in the new row of the Billing table. This field will be a Short Text field with a field size of 40, and you need to set the Caption property to include a space between the words in the field name.

3. Type **InvoiceItem**, press the **Tab** key to move to the Data Type property, and then press the **Tab** key again to accept the default Short Text data type.

4. Press the **F6** key to move to the Field Size box and to select the default field size, and then type **40**.

5. Press the **Tab** key until the insertion point is in the Caption box, and then type **Invoice Item**. The definition of the new field is complete. See Figure 2-16.

Tutorial 2 Building a Database and Defining Table Relationships | Access   AC 71

| Figure 2-16 | InvoiceItem field added to the Billing table |

Billing table shown in Design view with the following fields:

Field Name	Data Type	
InvoiceNum	Short Text	Primary key
VisitID	Short Text	Foreign key
InvoiceDate	Date/Time	
InvoiceAmt	Currency	
InvoiceItem ← new field	Short Text	
InvoicePaid	Yes/No	

Field Properties (General tab):
- Field Size: 40 *(Field Size property set to 40)*
- Format:
- Input Mask:
- Caption: Invoice Item *(Caption property set)*
- Default Value:
- Validation Rule:
- Validation Text:
- Required: No
- Allow Zero Length: Yes
- Indexed: No
- Unicode Compression: Yes
- IME Mode: No Control
- IME Sentence Mode: None
- Text Align: General

6. On the Quick Access Toolbar, click the **Save** button to save the changes to the Billing table structure.

7. Click the **Close 'Billing'** button on the object tab to close the Billing table.

Modifying Field Properties

With the Billing table design complete, you can now go back and modify the properties of the fields in the Visit table you created in Tutorial 1, as necessary. You can make some changes to properties in Datasheet view; for others, you'll work in Design view.

Changing the Format Property in Datasheet View

The Formatting group on the FIELDS tab in Datasheet view allows you to modify some formatting for certain field types. When you format a field, you change the way data is displayed, but not the actual values stored in the table.

Next, you'll check the properties of the VisitDate field in the Visit table to see if any changes are needed to improve the display of the date values.

To modify the VisitDate field's Format property:

1. On the Navigation Pane, click the **Shutter Bar Open/Close Button** » to open the pane. Notice that the Billing table is listed above the Visit table in the Tables section. By default, objects are listed in the pane in alphabetical order.

2. Double-click **Visit** to open the Visit table in Datasheet view.

3. On the Navigation Pane, click the **Shutter Bar Open/Close Button** « to close the pane. See Figure 2-17.

Figure 2-17   Visit table datasheet

- Short Text field values are left-aligned
- check boxes for Yes/No field are centered
- Date/Time field values are right-aligned

Notice that the values in the three Short Text fields—VisitID, PatientID, and Reason—appear left-aligned within their boxes, and the values in the Date/Time field (VisitDate) appear right-aligned. In Access, values for Short Text fields are left-aligned, and values for Number, Date/Time, and Currency fields are right-aligned. The WalkIn field is a Yes/No field, so its values appear in check boxes that are centered within the column.

4. On the ribbon, click the **FIELDS** tab.

5. Click the first field value in the VisitDate column. The Data Type option shows that this field is a Date/Time field.

   By default, Access assigns the General Date format to Date/Time fields. Note the Format option in the Formatting group; this is the same as the Format property in the Field Properties pane in Design view. Even though the Format box is empty, the VisitDate field has the General Date format applied to it. The General Date format includes settings for date or time values, or a combination of date and time values. However, Cindi wants *only date values* to be displayed in the VisitDate field, so she asks you to specify the Short Date format for the field.

6. In the Formatting group, click the **Format arrow**, and then click **Short Date**. See Figure 2-18.

Figure 2-18   VisitDate field after modifying the format

- date picker
- field values appear unchanged, but the format is applied
- Short Date format specified

TIP
When working with date values, you can type dates directly or click the date picker shown in Figure 2-18 to select a date from an interactive calendar.

Although no change is apparent in the worksheet—the VisitDate field values already appear with the Short Date setting (for example, 11/9/2015), as part of the default General Date format—the field now has the Short Date format applied to it. This ensures that only date field values, and not time or date/time values, are allowed in the field.

Changing Properties in Design View

Recall that each of the Short Text fields in the Visit table—VisitID, PatientID, and Reason—still has the default field size of 255, which is too large for the data contained in these fields. Also, the VisitID and PatientID fields need descriptions to identify them as the primary and foreign keys, respectively, in the table. Finally, each of these fields needs a caption either to include a space between the words in the field name or to make the name more descriptive. You can make all of these property changes more easily in Design view.

To modify the Field Size, Description, and Caption field properties:

1. In the Views group on the FIELDS tab, click the **View** button. The table is displayed in Design view with the VisitID field selected. You need to enter a Description property value for this field, the primary key in the table, and change its Field Size property to 4 because each visit number at Chatham Community Health Services consists of four digits.

TIP
You can also click the Design View button in the far right of the status bar to switch to Design view.

2. Press the **Tab** key until the insertion point is in the Description (Optional) box, and then type **Primary key**.

3. Press the **F6** key to move to and select the default setting of 255 for the Field Size property, and then type **4**. Next you need to set the Caption property for this field.

4. Press the **Tab** key until the insertion point is in the Caption box, and then type **Visit ID**.

    Next you need to enter a Description property value for the PatientID field, a foreign key in the table, and set its Field Size property to 5 because each PatientID number at Chatham Community Health Services consists of five digits. You also need to set this field's Caption property.

5. Click the **Description (Optional)** box for the PatientID field, and then type **Foreign key**.

6. Press the **F6** key, type **5**, press the **Tab** key until the insertion point is in the Caption box, and then type **Patient ID**.

   Next you'll set the Caption property for the VisitDate field.

7. Click the **VisitDate** Field Name box, click the **Caption** box, and then type **Date of Visit**.

   For the Reason field, you will set the Field Size property to 60. This size can accommodate the longer values in the Reason field. You'll also set this field's Caption property to provide a more descriptive name.

8. Click the **Reason** Field Name box, press the **F6** key, type **60**, press the **Tab** key until the insertion point is in the Caption box, and then type **Reason/Diagnosis**.

   Finally, you'll set the Caption property for the WalkIn field.

9. Click the **WalkIn** Field Name box, click the **Caption** box, and then type **Walk-in?** See Figure 2-19.

Figure 2-19   Visit table after modifying field properties

[Screenshot of the Visit table in Design view showing fields VisitID (Short Text, Primary key), PatientID (Short Text, Foreign key), VisitDate (Date/Time), Reason (Short Text), WalkIn (Yes/No). Callouts: "Description property values entered", "Caption property set for each field", "Field Size property set for each Short Text field", "Caption property for current field" (Walk-in?), "Default Value property for current field" (No).]

Notice that the WalkIn field's Default Value property is automatically set to "No," which means the check box for this field will be empty for each new record. This is the default for this property for any Yes/No field. You can set the Default Value property for other types of fields to make data entry easier. You'll learn more about setting this property in the next session.

The changes to the Visit table's properties are now complete, so you can save the table and view the results of your changes in Datasheet view.

Tutorial 2 Building a Database and Defining Table Relationships | Access AC 75

To save and view the modified Visit table:

1. On the Quick Access Toolbar, click the **Save** button to save the modified table. A dialog box opens informing you that some data may be lost because you decreased the field sizes. Because all of the values in the VisitID, PatientID, and Reason fields contain the same number of or fewer characters than the new Field Size properties you set for each field, you can ignore this message.

2. Click the **Yes** button.

3. In the Views group on the DESIGN tab, click the **View** button to display the Visit table in Datasheet view. Notice that each column (field) heading now displays the text you specified in the Caption property for that field. See Figure 2-20.

Figure 2-20 Modified Visit table in Datasheet view

column headings display Caption property values

Visit ID	Patient ID	Date of Visit	Reason/Diagnosis	Walk-in?
1527	22522	11/9/2015	Allergies - environmental	✓
1528	22507	11/9/2015	Diabetes mellitus Type 2 - initial diagnosis	✓
1530	22510	11/10/2015	Seborrheic dermatitis	
1535	22546	11/12/2015	Transverse fracture of left ulna	✓
1536	22526	11/17/2015	Gastroenteritis	
1538	22500	11/17/2015	Migraine	✓
1539	22504	11/18/2015	Annual wellness visit	
1541	22526	11/24/2015	Gastroenteritis - follow up	
1542	22537	11/24/2015	Influenza	✓
1544	22560	11/25/2015	Influenza	✓

4. Click the **Close 'Visit'** button on the object tab to close the Visit table.

5. If you are not continuing to Session 2.2, click the **FILE** tab, and then click **Close** in the navigation bar to close the Chatham database.

You have created the Billing table and made modifications to its design. In the next session, you'll add records to the Billing table and create the Patient table in the Chatham database.

Session 2.1 Quick Check

REVIEW

1. What guidelines should you follow when designing a database?
2. What is the purpose of the Data Type property for a field?
3. The _____ property specifies how a field's name is displayed in database objects, including table and query datasheets, forms, and reports.
4. For which three types of fields can you assign a field size?
5. The default Field Size property setting for a Short Text field is _____.
6. In Design view, which key do you press to move from the Table Design grid to the Field Properties pane?
7. List three reasons why you should specify a primary key for an Access table.

Session 2.2 Visual Overview:

Click the Close button to close the Relationships window.

You click the Show Table button to open the Show Table dialog box. From there, you can choose a table to add to the Relationships window.

The Relationships window illustrates the relationships among a database's tables. Using this window, you can view or change existing relationships, define new relationships between tables, and rearrange the layout of the tables in the window.

The key symbol next to a field name indicates that the field is the table's primary key. For example, PatientID is the primary key for the Patient table.

A one-to-many relationship exists between two tables when one record in the first table matches zero, one, or many records in the second table, and when one record in the second table matches at most one record in the first table. Here, the Patient and Visit tables have a one-to-many relationship because a patient can have many visits, and each visit is associated with only one patient. The two tables are still separate tables, but because they are joined, you can use the data in them as if they were one table.

Tutorial 2 Building a Database and Defining Table Relationships | Access   AC 77

Understanding Table Relationships

The "one" side of a one-to-many relationship is represented by the digit 1 at the end of the join line.

The "many" side of a one-to-many relationship is represented by the infinity symbol at the end of the join line.

Visit
- VisitID
- PatientID
- VisitDate
- Reason
- WalkIn

Billing
- InvoiceNum
- VisitID
- InvoiceDate
- InvoiceAmt
- InvoiceItem
- InvoicePaid

When you add a table to the Relationships window, the fields in the table appear in a field list.
Here, the window contains three field lists, one for each table: Patient, Visit, and Billing.

The join line connects the common field used to create the relationship between two tables. Here, the common field VisitID is used to create the one-to-many relationship between the Visit and Billing tables.

The primary table is the "one" table in a one-to-many relationship. Here, Visit is the primary table because there is at most one visit for each invoice.

The related table is the "many" table in a one-to-many relationship. Here, Billing is the related table because there can be more than one invoice generated as a result of each visit.

AC 78 Access | Tutorial 2 Building a Database and Defining Table Relationships

Adding Records to a New Table

Before you can begin to define the table relationships illustrated in the Session 2.2 Visual Overview, you need to finish creating the tables in the Chatham database.

The Billing table design is complete. Now, Cindi would like you to add records to the table so it will contain the invoice data for Chatham Community Health Services. As you learned earlier, you add records to a table in Datasheet view by typing the field values in the rows below the column headings for the fields. You'll begin by entering the records shown in Figure 2-21.

Figure 2-21   **Records to be added to the Billing table**

Invoice Num	Visit ID	Invoice Date	Invoice Amt	Invoice Item	Invoice Paid
35801	1527	11/10/2015	$100.00	Office visit	Yes
35818	1536	11/18/2015	$100.00	Office visit	Yes
35885	1570	01/12/2016	$85.00	Pharmacy	No
35851	1550	12/02/2015	$85.00	Pharmacy	No

© 2014 Cengage Learning

To add the first record to the Billing table:

1. If you took a break after the previous session, make sure the Chatham database is open and the Navigation Pane is open.

2. In the Tables section of the Navigation Pane, double-click **Billing** to open the Billing table in Datasheet view.

3. Close the Navigation Pane, and then use the ↔ pointer to resize columns, as necessary, so that the field names are completely visible.

4. In the Invoice Num column, type **35801**, press the **Tab** key, type **1527** in the Visit ID column, and then press the **Tab** key.

   > Be sure to type the numbers "0" and "1" and *not* the letters "O" and "I" in the field values.

   Next you need to enter the invoice date. Recall that you specified a custom date format, mm/dd/yyyy, for the InvoiceDate field. You do not need to type each digit; for example, you can type just "3" instead of "03" for the month, and you can type "16" instead of "2016" for the year. Access will display the full value according to the custom date format.

5. Type **11/10/15** and then press the **Tab** key. Notice that Access displays the date "11/10/2015" in the Invoice Date column.

   Next you need to enter the invoice amount for the first record. This is a Currency field with the Currency format and two decimal places specified. Because of the field's properties, you do not need to type the dollar sign, comma, or zeroes for the decimal places; Access will display these items automatically for you.

6. Type **100** and then press the **Tab** key. Access displays the value as "$100.00."

7. In the Invoice Item column, type **Office visit** and then press the **Tab** key.

   The last field in the table, InvoicePaid, is a Yes/No field. Recall that the default value for any Yes/No field is "No"; therefore, the check box is initially empty. For the record you are entering in the Billing table, the invoice has been paid, so you need to insert a checkmark in the check box.

8. Press the **spacebar** to insert a checkmark, and then press the **Tab** key. The values for the first record are entered. See Figure 2-22.

Tutorial 2 Building a Database and Defining Table Relationships | Access   AC 79

Figure 2-22   First record entered in the Billing table

field value displayed in the Currency format with two decimal places

field value displayed according to the custom date format

checkmark indicates a "Yes" value for the field

Now you can add the remaining three records. As you do, you'll learn a keyboard shortcut for inserting the value from the same field in the previous record. A **keyboard shortcut** is a key or combination of keys you press to complete an action more efficiently.

To add the next three records to the Billing table:

1. Refer to Figure 2-21 and enter the values in the second record's Invoice Num, Visit ID, and Invoice Date columns.

   Notice that the value in the second record's Invoice Amt column is $100.00. This value is the exact same value as in the first record. You can quickly insert the value from the same column in the previous record using the **Ctrl + '** (apostrophe) keyboard shortcut. To use this shortcut, you press and hold down the Ctrl key, press the ' key once, and then release both keys. (The plus sign in the keyboard shortcut indicates you're pressing two keys at once; you do not press the + key.)

2. With the insertion point in the Invoice Amt column, press the **Ctrl + '** keys. Access inserts the value "$100.00" in the Invoice Amt column for the second record.

3. Press the **Tab** key to move to the Invoice Item column. Again, the value you need to enter in this column—Office visit—is the same as the value for this column in the previous record. So, you can use the keyboard shortcut again.

4. With the insertion point in the Invoice Item column, press the **Ctrl + '** keys. Access inserts the value "Office visit" in the Invoice Item column for the second record.

5. Press the **Tab** key to move to the Invoice Paid column, press the **spacebar** to insert a checkmark in the check box, and then press the **Tab** key. The second record is entered in the Billing table.

6. Refer to Figure 2-21 to enter the values for the third and fourth records, using the Ctrl + ' keys to enter the values in the fourth record's Invoice Amt and Invoice Item columns. Also, for both records, the invoices have not been paid. Therefore, be sure to press the Tab key to leave the Invoice Paid column values unchecked (signifying "No"). Your table should look like the one in Figure 2-23.

Figure 2-23   Billing table with four records added

Invoice Num	Visit ID	Invoice Date	Invoice Amt	Invoice Item	Invoice Paid
35801	1527	11/10/2015	$100.00	Office visit	✓
35818	1536	11/18/2015	$100.00	Office visit	✓
35885	1570	01/12/2016	$85.00	Pharmacy	☐
35851	1550	12/02/2015	$85.00	Pharmacy	☐
*			$0.00		☐

"Yes" values ← (first two Invoice Paid checkboxes)
"No" values ← (last two Invoice Paid checkboxes)

To finish entering records in the Billing table, you'll use a method that allows you to import the data.

Importing Data from an Excel Worksheet

Often, the data you want to add to an Access table exists in another file, such as a Word document or an Excel workbook. You can bring the data from other files into Access in different ways. For example, you can copy and paste the data from an open file, or you can **import** the data, which is a process that allows you to copy the data from a source without having to open the source file.

Cindi had been using Excel to track invoice data for Chatham Community Health Services and already created a worksheet, named "Invoices," containing this data. You'll import this Excel worksheet into your Billing table to complete the entry of data in the table. To use the import method, the columns in the Excel worksheet must match the names and data types of the fields in the Access table.

INSIGHT

Caption Property Values and the Import Process

When you import data from an Excel worksheet into an Access table, any Caption property values set for the fields in the table are not considered in the import process. For example, your Access table could have fields such as InvoiceDate and InvoiceAmt with Caption property values of Invoice Date and Invoice Amt, respectively. If the Excel worksheet you are importing has the column headings Invoice Date and Invoice Amt, you might think that the data matches and you can proceed with the import. However, if the underlying field names in the Access table do not match the Excel worksheet column headings exactly, the import process will fail. It's a good idea to double-check to make sure that the actual Access field names—and not just the column headings displayed in a table datasheet (as specified by the Caption property)—match the Excel worksheet column headings. If there are differences, you can change the column headings in the Excel worksheet to match the Access table field names before you import the data, ensuring that the process will work correctly.

The Invoices worksheet contains the following columns: InvoiceNum, VisitID, InvoiceDate, InvoiceAmt, InvoiceItem, and InvoicePaid. These column headings match the field names in the Billing table exactly, so you can import the data. Before you import data into a table, you need to close the table.

Tutorial 2 Building a Database and Defining Table Relationships | Access   AC 81

To import the Invoices worksheet into the Billing table:

1. Click the **Close 'Billing'** button ☒ on the object tab to close the Billing table. A dialog box opens asking if you want to save the changes to the table layout. This dialog box opens because you resized the table columns.
2. Click the **Yes** button in the dialog box.
3. On the ribbon, click the **EXTERNAL DATA** tab.
4. In the Import & Link group on the EXTERNAL DATA tab, click the **Excel** button. The Get External Data - Excel Spreadsheet dialog box opens. See Figure 2-24.

Figure 2-24   **Get External Data - Excel Spreadsheet dialog box**

click to find the Excel workbook containing the data you want to import

you might see a different path here

option for adding records to an existing table

Trouble? If the Export - Excel Spreadsheet dialog box opens instead of the dialog box shown in Figure 2-24, you probably clicked the Excel button in the Export group. If so, click the Cancel button in the dialog box, and then repeat Step 4, being sure to click the Excel button in the Import & Link group.

The dialog box provides options for importing the entire worksheet as a new table in the current database, adding the data from the worksheet to an existing table, or linking the data in the worksheet to the table. You need to add, or append, the worksheet data to the Billing table.

5. Click the **Browse** button. The File Open dialog box opens. The Excel workbook file is named "Invoices" and is located in the Access1 ▸ Tutorial folder provided with your Data Files.
6. Navigate to the **Access1 ▸ Tutorial** folder, where your starting Data Files are stored, and then double-click the **Invoices** Excel file. You return to the dialog box.
7. Click the **Append a copy of the records to the table** option button. The box to the right of this option becomes active and displays the Billing table name, because it is the first table listed in the Navigation Pane.

   Trouble? If another table name appears in this box, click the arrow on the box, and then click Billing.

8. Click the **OK** button. The first Import Spreadsheet Wizard dialog box opens. See Figure 2-25.

Figure 2-25   **First Import Spreadsheet Wizard dialog box**

- selected check box confirms that the first row contains column headings
- data from the worksheet to be imported

The dialog box confirms that the first row of the worksheet you are importing contains column headings. The bottom section of the dialog box displays some of the data contained in the worksheet.

TIP

Carefully check the data to make sure it should be imported into the selected table.

9. Click the **Next** button. The second, and final, Import Spreadsheet Wizard dialog box opens. Notice that the Import to Table box shows that the data from the spreadsheet will be imported into the Billing table.

10. Click the **Finish** button. A dialog box opens asking if you want to save the import steps. If you needed to repeat this same import procedure many times, it would be a good idea to save the steps for the procedure. However, you don't need to save these steps because you'll be importing the data only one time. Once the data is in the Billing table, Cindi will no longer use Excel to track invoice data.

11. Click the **Close** button in the dialog box to close it without saving the steps.

The data from the Invoices worksheet has been added to the Billing table. Next, you'll open the table to view the new records.

To open the Billing table and view the imported data:

1. Open the Navigation Pane, and then double-click **Billing** in the Tables section to open the table in Datasheet view.

2. Resize the Invoice Item column to its best fit, scrolling the worksheet and resizing, as necessary.

Tutorial 2 Building a Database and Defining Table Relationships | Access AC 83

3. Press the **Ctrl + Home** keys to scroll to the top of the datasheet. Notice that the table now contains a total of 204 records—four records you entered plus 200 records imported from the Invoices worksheet. The records are displayed in primary key order by the values in the Invoice Num column. See Figure 2-26.

Figure 2-26 Billing table after importing data from Excel

records displayed in order by the values in the Invoice Num column

table contains a total of 204 records

4. Save and close the Billing table, and then close the Navigation Pane.

Two of the tables—Visit and Billing—are now complete. According to Cindi's plan for the Chatham database, you need to create a third table, named "Patient," to track data about the clinic's patients. You'll use a different method to create this table.

Creating a Table by Importing an Existing Table Structure

If another Access database contains a table—or even just the design, or structure, of a table—that you want to include in your database, you can import the table and any records it contains or import only the table structure into your database.

Cindi documented the design for the new Patient table by listing each field's name and data type, as well as any applicable field size, description, and caption property values, as shown in Figure 2-27. Note that each field in the Patient table, except BirthDate, will be a Short Text field, and the PatientID field will be the table's primary key.

Figure 2-27 Design for the Patient table

Field Name	Data Type	Field Size	Description	Caption
PatientID	Short Text	5	Primary key	Patient ID
LastName	Short Text	25		Last Name
FirstName	Short Text	20		First Name
BirthDate	Date/Time			Date of Birth
Phone	Short Text	14		
Address	Short Text	35		
City	Short Text	25		
State	Short Text	2		
Zip	Short Text	10		
Email	Short Text	50		

© 2014 Cengage Learning

Cindi's assistant Kelly already created an Access database containing a Patient table design. She never entered any records into the table because she wasn't sure if the table design was complete or correct. After reviewing the table design, both Kelly and Cindi agree that it contains some of the fields they want to track, but that some changes are needed. So, you can import the table structure in Kelly's database to create the Patient table in the Chatham database, and then modify the imported table to produce the final table structure according to Cindi's design.

To create the Patient table by importing the structure of another table:

1. Make sure the EXTERNAL DATA tab is the active tab on the ribbon.

2. In the Import & Link group, click the **Access** button. The Get External Data - Access Database dialog box opens. This dialog box is similar to the one you used earlier when importing the Excel spreadsheet.

3. Click the **Browse** button. The File Open dialog box opens. The Access database file from which you need to import the table structure is named "Kelly" and is located in the Access1 ▸ Tutorial folder provided with your Data Files.

4. Navigate to the **Access1 ▸ Tutorial** folder, where your starting Data Files are stored, and then double-click the **Kelly** database file. You return to the dialog box.

5. Make sure the **Import tables, queries, forms, reports, macros, and modules into the current database** option button is selected, and then click the **OK** button. The Import Objects dialog box opens. The dialog box contains tabs for importing all the different types of Access database objects—tables, queries, forms, and so on. The Tables tab is the current tab.

6. Click the **Options** button in the dialog box to see all the options for importing tables. See Figure 2-28.

Tutorial 2 Building a Database and Defining Table Relationships | Access   AC 85

Figure 2-28 **Import Objects dialog box**

- tabs for importing other types of database objects
- table object to be imported
- options for importing the table data and/or the table definition

Note the Import Tables section of the dialog box, which contains options for importing the definition and data—that is, the structure of the table and any records contained in the table—or the definition (structure) only. You need to import only the structure of the Patient table Kelly created.

▸ **7.** On the Tables tab, click **Patient** to select this table.

▸ **8.** In the Import Tables section of the dialog box, click the **Definition Only** option button, and then click the **OK** button. Access creates the Patient table in the Chatham database using the structure of the Patient table in the Kelly database, and opens a dialog box asking if you want to save the import steps.

▸ **9.** Click the **Close** button to close the dialog box without saving the import steps.

▸ **10.** Open the Navigation Pane and note that the Patient table is listed in the Tables section.

▸ **11.** Double-click **Patient** to open the table, and then close the Navigation Pane. The Patient table opens in Datasheet view. The table contains no records. See Figure 2-29.

Figure 2-29 **Imported Patient table in Datasheet view**

The table structure you imported contains some of the fields Cindi wants, but not all (see Figure 2-27); it also contains some fields Cindi does not want in the Patient table. You can add the missing fields using the Data Type gallery.

Adding Fields to a Table Using the Data Type Gallery

The **Data Type gallery**, available in the Add & Delete group on the FIELDS tab, allows you to add a group of related fields to a table at the same time, rather than adding each field to the table individually. The group of fields you add is called a **Quick Start selection**. For example, the **Address Quick Start selection** adds a collection of fields related to an address, such as Address, City, State, and so on, to the table at one time. When you use a Quick Start selection, the fields added already have properties set. However, you need to review and possibly modify the properties to ensure the fields match your design needs for the database.

Next, you'll use the Data Type gallery to add the missing fields to the Patient table.

To add fields to the Patient table using the Data Type gallery:

1. On the ribbon, click the **FIELDS** tab.

   Note the More Fields button in the Add & Delete group; this button allows you to display the Data Type gallery. Before inserting fields from the Data Type gallery, you need to place the insertion point in the field to the right of where you want to insert the new fields. According to Cindi's design, the Address field should come after the Phone field, so you need to make the next field, Email, the active field.

   Make sure the correct field is active before adding new fields.

2. Click the first row in the **Email** field to make it the active field.

3. In the Add & Delete group, click the **More Fields** button. The Data Type gallery opens and displays options for different types of fields you can add to your table.

4. Scroll the gallery down so the Quick Start section is visible. See Figure 2-30.

Figure 2-30   Patient table with the Data Type gallery displayed

Tutorial 2 Building a Database and Defining Table Relationships | Access   AC 87

The Quick Start section provides options that will add multiple, related fields to the table at one time. The new fields will be inserted to the left of the current field.

5. In the Quick Start section, click **Address**. Access adds five fields to the table: Address, City, State Province, ZIP Postal, and Country Region. See Figure 2-31.

Figure 2-31 Patient table after adding fields from the Data Type gallery

five fields added with Address Quick Start selection

Modifying the Imported Table

Refer back to Cindi's design for the Patient table (Figure 2-27). To finalize the table design, you need to modify the imported table by deleting fields, renaming fields, and changing field data types. You'll begin by deleting fields.

Deleting Fields from a Table Structure

After you've created a table, you might need to delete one or more fields. When you delete a field, you also delete all the values for that field from the table. So, before you delete a field, you should make sure that you want to do so and that you choose the correct field to delete. You can delete fields in either Datasheet view or Design view.

REFERENCE

Deleting a Field from a Table Structure

- In Datasheet view, click anywhere in the column for the field you want to delete.
- In the Add & Delete group on the FIELDS tab, click the Delete button.

or

- In Design view, click the Field Name box for the field you want to delete.
- In the Tools group on the DESIGN tab, click the Delete Rows button.

The Address Quick Start selection added a field named "Country Region" to the Patient table. Cindi doesn't need a field to store country data because all Chatham Community Health Services patients are located in the United States. You'll begin to modify the Patient table structure by deleting the Country Region field.

AC 88 Access | Tutorial 2 Building a Database and Defining Table Relationships

To delete the Country Region field from the table in Datasheet view:

1. Click the first row in the **Country Region** field (if necessary).
2. In the Add & Delete group on the FIELDS tab, click the **Delete** button. The Country Region field is removed and the first field, PatientID, is now the active field.

You can also delete fields from a table structure in Design view. You'll switch to Design view to delete the other unnecessary fields.

To delete the fields in Design view:

1. In the Views group on the FIELDS tab, click the **View** button. The Patient table opens in Design view. See Figure 2-32.

Figure 2-32   Patient table in Design view

click to delete the current field

fields to be deleted (including Notes field, which is not visible)

2. Click the **Title** Field Name box to make it the current field.
3. In the Tools group on the DESIGN tab, click the **Delete Rows** button. The Title field is removed from the Patient table structure.

    You'll delete the Fax, County, and Notes fields next. Instead of deleting these fields individually, you'll select and delete them at the same time.

4. Click and hold down the mouse button on the row selector for the **Fax** field, and then drag the mouse to select the **County** and **Notes** fields.
5. Release the mouse button. The rows for the three fields are outlined in a red box, meaning all three fields are selected.

Tutorial 2 Building a Database and Defining Table Relationships | Access   AC 89

6. In the Tools group, click the **Delete Rows** button. See Figure 2-33.

Figure 2-33   **Patient table after deleting fields**

fields to be renamed

Field Name	Data Type
PatientID	Short Text
LastName	Short Text
FirstName	Short Text
BirthDate	Date/Time
Phone	Number
Address	Short Text
City	Short Text
StateProvince	Short Text
ZIPPostal	Short Text
Email	Short Text

Renaming Fields in Design View

To match Cindi's design for the Patient table, you need to rename the StateProvince and ZIPPostal fields. In Tutorial 1, you renamed the default primary key field (ID) in Datasheet view. You can also rename fields in Design view by simply editing the names in the Table Design grid.

To rename the fields in Design view:

1. Click to position the insertion point to the right of the word **StateProvince** in the eighth row's Field Name box, and then press the **Backspace** key eight times to delete the word "Province." The name of the eighth field is now State.

   You can also select an entire field name and then type new text to replace it.

2. In the ninth row's Field Name box, drag to select the text **ZIPPostal**, and then type **Zip**. The text you type replaces the original text. See Figure 2-34.

Figure 2-34   **Patient table after renaming fields**

(Screenshot of Access Design view showing Patient table with fields: PatientID, LastName, FirstName, BirthDate, Phone, Address, City, State, Zip, Email. Callouts: "renamed fields" pointing to the field list; "data type to be changed" pointing to the Number data type of the Phone field.)

Changing the Data Type for a Field in Design View

According to Cindi's plan, all of the fields in the Patient table, except BirthDate, should be Short Text fields. The table structure you imported specifies the Number data type for the Phone field; you need to change this to Short Text. In Tutorial 1, you used an option in Datasheet view to change a field's data type. You can also change the data type for a field in Design view.

To change the data type of the Phone field in Design view:

1. Click the right side of the **Data Type** box for the Phone field to display the list of data types.

2. Click **Short Text** in the list. The Phone field is now a Short Text field. Note that, by default, the Field Size property is set to 255. According to Cindi's plan, the Phone field should have a Field Size property of 14. You'll make this change next.

3. Press the **F6** key to move to and select the default Field Size property, and then type **14**.

Each of the remaining fields you added using the Address Quick Start selection—Address, City, State, and Zip—also has the default field size of 255. You need to change the Field Size property for these fields to match Cindi's design. You'll also delete any Caption property values for these fields because the field names match how Cindi wants them displayed, so captions are unnecessary.

Tutorial 2 Building a Database and Defining Table Relationships | Access   AC 91

To change the Field Size and Caption properties for the fields:

1. Click the **Address** Field Name box to make it the current field.

2. Press the **F6** key to move to and select the default Field Size property, and then type **35**.

   Note that the Caption property setting for this field is the same as the field name. This field doesn't need a caption, so you can delete this value.

3. Press the **Tab** key until the the word Address is selected in the Caption box, and then press the **Delete** key. The Caption property value is removed.

4. Repeat Steps 1 through 3 to change the Field Size property for the City field to **25** and to delete its Caption property value.

5. Change the Field Size property for the State field to **2**, and then delete its Caption property value.

6. Change the Field Size property for the Zip field to **10**, and then delete its Caption property value.

7. On the Quick Access Toolbar, click the **Save** button to save your changes to the Patient table.

Finally, Cindi would like you to set the Description property for the Patient ID field and the Caption property for the PatientID, LastName, FirstName, and BirthDate fields. You'll make these changes now.

To enter the Description and Caption property values:

1. Click the **Description (Optional)** box for the PatientID field, and then type **Primary key**.

2. In the Field Properties pane, click the **Caption** box.

   After you leave the Description (Optional) box, the Property Update Options button appears below this box for the PatientID field. When you change a field's property in Design view, you can use this button to update the corresponding property on forms and reports that include the modified field. For example, if the Chatham database included a form that contained the PatientID field, you could choose to **propagate**, or update, the modified Description property in the form by clicking the Property Update Options button, and then choosing the option to make the update everywhere the field is used. The text on the Property Update Options button varies depending on the task; in this case, if you click the button, the option is "Update Status Bar Text everywhere PatientID is used."

   Because the Chatham database does not include any forms or reports that are based on the Patient table, you do not need to update the properties, so you can ignore the button for now. In most cases, however, it is a good idea to perform the update.

3. In the Caption box for the PatientID field, type **Patient ID**.

4. Click the **LastName** Field Name box to make it the current field.

5. Click the **Caption** box, and then type **Last Name**.

6. Click the **FirstName** Field Name box to make it the current field, click the **Caption** box, and then type **First Name**.

7. Click the **BirthDate** Field Name box to make it the current field, click the **Caption** box, and then type **Date of Birth**. See Figure 2-35.

Figure 2-35 Patient table after entering description and captions

[Screenshot of the Patient table in Design view showing fields: PatientID (Short Text, Primary key — Description property value entered), LastName (Short Text), FirstName (Short Text), BirthDate (Date/Time), Phone (Short Text — data type changed to Short Text), Address (Short Text), City (Short Text), State (Short Text), Zip (Short Text), Email (Short Text). Field Properties pane shows: Format: Short Date; Caption: Date of Birth (Caption property entered); Required: No; Indexed: No; IME Mode: No Control; IME Sentence Mode: None; Text Align: General; Show Date Picker: For dates.]

8. On the Quick Access Toolbar, click the **Save** button 💾 to save your changes to the Patient table.

9. In the Views group on the DESIGN tab, click the **View** button to display the table in Datasheet view.

Tutorial 2 Building a Database and Defining Table Relationships | Access AC 93

10. Resize each column to its best fit, and then click in the first row for the **Patient ID** column. See Figure 2-36.

Figure 2-36 | **Modified Patient table in Datasheet view**

After viewing the Patient table datasheet, both Cindi and Kelly agree that data entry would be made easier if the State field value of "CT" was automatically filled in for each new record added to the table, because all of the clinic's patients live in Connecticut. You can accomplish this by setting the Default Value property for the field.

Setting the Default Value Property for a Field

The **Default Value property** for a field specifies what value will appear, by default, for the field in each new record you add to a table. Recall the InvoicePaid field in the Billing table; this is a Yes/No field, which automatically includes a Default Value property setting of "No." That's why the check box for the InvoicePaid field is initially empty for a new record in the Billing table.

Because all the patients at Chatham Community Health Services live in Connecticut, you'll specify a default value of "CT" for the State field in the Patient table. With this setting, each new record in the Patient table will have the correct State field value entered automatically.

To set the Default Value property for the State field:

1. In the Views group on the HOME tab, click the **View** button to display the Patient table in Design view.

2. Click the **State** Field Name box to make it the current field.

3. In the Field Properties pane, click the **Default Value** box, type **CT** and then press the Tab key. See Figure 2-37.

Figure 2-37   Specifying the Default Value property for the State field

State field is current → (points to State field row in table design)

Default Value property entered and enclosed within quotation marks → (points to Default Value: "CT")

Note that a text entry in the Default Value property must be enclosed within quotation marks. If you do not type the quotation marks, Access adds them for you. However, for some entries, you would receive an error message indicating invalid syntax if you omitted the quotation marks. In such cases, you have to enter the quotation marks yourself.

4. On the Quick Access Toolbar, click the **Save** button to save your changes to the Patient table.

TIP
You can change the value in a record from the default value to another value, if necessary.

5. In the Views group on the DESIGN tab, click the **View** button to display the table in Datasheet view. Note that the State field for the first row now displays the default value "CT" as specified by the Default Value property. Each new record entered in the table will automatically have this State field value entered.

With the Patient table design set, you can now enter records in it. You'll begin by entering two records, and then you'll use a different method to add the remaining records.

Note: *Be sure to enter your last name and first name where indicated.*

To add two records to the Patient table:

1. Enter the following values in the columns in the first record; note that you can press Tab to move past the default State field value:

   Patient ID = **22500**

   Last Name = *[student's last name]*

   First Name = *[student's first name]*

   Date of Birth = **2/28/1994**

   Phone = **860-938-2822**

   Address = **501 Perkins Dr**

   City = **Hartford**

   State = **CT**

   Zip = **06120**

   Email = **student1@example.edu**

2. Enter the following values in the columns in the second record:

   Patient ID = **22533**

   Last Name = **Rowe**

   First Name = **Christina**

   Date of Birth = **12/5/1941**

   Phone = **860-552-5920**

   Address = **27 Tracey Ct**

   City = **Windsor**

   State = **CT**

   Zip = **06095**

   Email = **c.rowe@example.com**

3. Resize columns to their best fit, as necessary, and then save and close the Patient table.

Before Cindi decided to store data using Access, Kelly managed the clinic's patient data in a different system. She exported that data into a text file and now asks you to import it into the new Patient table. You can import the data contained in this text file to add the remaining records to the Patient table.

Adding Data to a Table by Importing a Text File

There are many ways to import data into an Access database. So far, you've learned how to add data to an Access table by importing an Excel spreadsheet, and you've created a new table by importing the structure of an existing table. You can also import data contained in text files.

To complete the entry of records in the Patient table, you'll import the data contained in Kelly's text file. The file is named "Patient" and is located in the Access1 ▶ Tutorial folder provided with your Data Files.

To import the data contained in the Patient text file:

1. On the ribbon, click the **EXTERNAL DATA** tab.

2. In the Import & Link group, click the **Text File** button. The Get External Data - Text File dialog box opens. This dialog box is similar to the one you used earlier when importing the Excel spreadsheet and the Access table structure.

3. Click the **Browse** button. The File Open dialog box opens.

4. Navigate to the Access1 ▶ Tutorial folder, where your starting Data Files are stored, and then double-click the **Patient** file. You return to the dialog box.

5. Click the **Append a copy of the records to the table** option button. The box to the right of this option becomes active. Next, you need to select the table to which you want to add the data.

6. Click the arrow on the box, and then click **Patient**.

7. Click the **OK** button. The first Import Text Wizard dialog box opens. The dialog box indicates that the data to be imported is in a delimited format. A **delimited text file** is one in which fields of data are separated by a character such as a comma or a tab. In this case, the dialog box shows that data is separated by the comma character in the text file.

8. Make sure the **Delimited** option button is selected in the dialog box, and then click the **Next** button. The second Import Text Wizard dialog box opens. See Figure 2-38.

Figure 2-38   Second Import Text Wizard dialog box

- fields in the text file are separated by commas
- preview of the data being imported

TIP

Carefully check the data to make sure it should be imported into the selected table.

This dialog box asks you to confirm the delimiter character that separates the fields in the text file you're importing. Access detects that the comma character is used in the Patient text file and selects this option. The bottom area of the dialog box provides a preview of the data you're importing.

9. Make sure the **Comma** option button is selected, and then click the **Next** button. The third, and final, Import Text Wizard dialog box opens. Notice that the Import to Table box shows that the data will be imported into the Patient table.

Tutorial 2 Building a Database and Defining Table Relationships | Access AC 97

> 10. Click the **Finish** button. A dialog box opens asking if you want to save the import steps. You'll only import the patient data once, so you can close the dialog box without saving the import steps.

> 11. Click the **Close** button in the dialog box to close it without saving the import steps.

Cindi asks you to open the Patient table in Datasheet view so she can see the results of importing the text file.

To view the Patient table datasheet:

> 1. Open the Navigation Pane, and then double-click **Patient** to open the Patient table in Datasheet view. The Patient table contains a total of 51 records.

> 2. Close the Navigation Pane.

> 3. Resize columns to their best fit, scrolling the table datasheet as necessary, so that all field values are displayed. When finished, scroll back to display the first fields in the table, and then click the first row's Patient ID field. See Figure 2-39.

Figure 2-39   Patient table after importing data from the text file

Patient ID	Last Name	First Name	Date of Birth	Phone	Address	City	State	Zip	Email
22500	Student Last	Student First	2/28/1994	860-938-2822	501 Perkins Dr	Hartford	CT	06120	student1@example.edu
22501	Darcy	Edward	7/15/1986	860-305-3985	723 Oxford Ave	Bloomfield	CT	06002	edarcy@example.org
22502	Mendez	Andreas	3/1/1934	860-552-6893	57 Wallace Rd	Windsor	CT	06095	a.mendez@example.org
22504	Aguilar	Lilian	8/16/1938	860-374-5724	329 Fairchild Ave	Hartford	CT	06114	laguilar@example.com
22505	Finnerty	Amber	5/7/1946	860-226-4930	37 Noyes Ct	Hartford	CT	06112	a.finnerty@example.com
22506	Gorski	Drea	2/19/2005	860-305-8394	83 Everett Ln	Bloomfield	CT	06002	
22507	Weiss	Matthew	6/7/1997	860-426-7492	38 German St	Hartford	CT	06106	matt.weiss@example.org
22509	Kervin	Steve	4/6/1993	860-938-0025	49 Davenport St	Hartford	CT	06120	skervin@example.edu
22510	Booker	Thomas	8/25/1966	860-661-2539	59 Nicola Ave	Hartford	CT	06105	
22511	Castro	Daniel	9/23/1933	860-637-0430	61 Osmond Way	West Hartford	CT	06117	d_castro@example.com
22512	Chang	Lisa	10/5/1955	860-226-6034	731 Macon Rd	Hartford	CT	06112	lchang@example.com
22513	Smith	Troy	1/31/1996	860-305-0384	16 Ravine Rd	Bloomfield	CT	06002	t_smith@example.edu
22514	Parker	Ian	6/3/1953	860-938-1873	12 Adelbert St	Hartford	CT	06120	ian_parker@example.org
22516	King	Susan	12/7/1963	860-661-9347	48 Fenton St	Hartford	CT	06105	susan.king@example.edu
22517	O'Brien	Henry	12/10/1940	860-637-9203	58 Redmond Dr	West Hartford	CT	06117	h.obrien32@example.com
22518	Torres	Sera	4/9/2008	860-938-2098	27 Reno Dr	Hartford	CT	06120	
22519	Belanger	Malcolm	10/17/1950	860-637-3927	723 Nicola Ave	West Hartford	CT	06117	
22520	Hallick	Davis	3/26/1944	860-552-4495	84 Churchill Pl	Windsor	CT	06095	dhallick@example.com
22521	Engber	Cathy	4/7/2006	860-305-3048	58 Deering Pl	Bloomfield	CT	06002	
22522	Li	Siyang	7/25/1986	860-305-6548	225 Krauss Rd	Bloomfield	CT	06002	li.siyang@example.org
22523	Fraser	Nancy	11/8/1977	860-552-7392	7 Quinn Dr	Windsor	CT	06095	
22525	Rodriguez	Maria	2/11/1936	860-552-9023	624 Noyes St	Windsor	CT	06095	m.rodriguez@example.com
22526	Swenson	Lucia	5/1/1943	860-226-0293	83 Osage Ave	Hartford	CT	06112	
22527	Lee	Hwan	8/25/1987	860-661 3974	153 Agnes Ct	Hartford	CT	06105	hwan.lee@example.com
22529	Goldberg	Robert	5/30/1961	860-552-2873	92 Gaston Ave	Windsor	CT	06095	

> 4. Save and close the Patient table, and then open the Navigation Pane.

The Chatham database now contains three tables—Patient, Visit, and Billing—and the tables contain all the necessary records. Your final task is to complete the database design by defining the necessary relationships between its tables.

Defining Table Relationships

One of the most powerful features of a relational database management system is its ability to define relationships between tables. You use a common field to relate one table to another. The process of relating tables is often called performing a **join**. When you join tables that have a common field, you can extract data from them as if they were one larger table. For example, you can join the Patient and Visit tables by using the PatientID field in both tables as the common field. Then you can use a query, form, or report to extract selected data from each table, even though the data is contained in two separate tables, as shown in Figure 2-40. The PatientVisits query shown in Figure 2-40 includes the PatientID, LastName, and FirstName fields from the Patient table, and the VisitDate and Reason fields from the Visit table. The joining of records is based on the common field of PatientID. The Patient and Visit tables have a type of relationship called a one-to-many relationship.

Figure 2-40 — One-to-many relationship and sample query

Patient (primary table)

Patient ID	Last Name	First Name	Date of Birth	Phone
22506	Gorski	Drea	2/19/2005	860-305-8394
22507	Weiss	Matthew	6/7/1997	860-426-7492
22509	Kervin	Steve	4/6/1993	860-938-0025
22510	Booker	Thomas	8/25/1966	860-661-2539
22511	Castro	Daniel	9/23/1933	860-637-0430
22512	Chang	Lisa	10/5/1955	860-226-6034
22513	Smith	Troy	1/31/1996	860-305-0384

two visits for patient 22506 — common field

Visit (related table)

Visit ID	Patient ID	Date of Visit	Reason/Diagnosis
1667	22506	4/1/2016	Fifth Disease
1670	22509	4/4/2016	Tinea pedis
1672	22525	4/6/2016	Wound care for patellar abrasion
1673	22549	4/6/2016	Pertussis
1675	22507	4/7/2016	Diabetes mellitis Type 2 - serum glucose check
1679	22557	4/8/2016	Hypertension monitoring
1680	22536	4/8/2016	Laceration of left eyelid -sutured
1682	22518	4/8/2016	Conjunctivitis follow-up
1683	22506	4/8/2016	Fifth Disease follow-up
1685	22517	4/11/2016	Idiopathic abdominal pain

PatientVisits — query that joins fields from the Patient and Visit tables (fields from the Patient table / fields from the Visit table)

Patient ID	Last Name	First Name	Date of Visit	Reason/Diagnosis
22501	Darcy	Edward	11/30/2015	Influenza
22502	Mendez	Andreas	3/30/2016	Annual wellness visit
22504	Aguilar	Lilian	11/18/2015	Annual wellness visit
22505	Finnerty	Amber	1/26/2016	Annual wellness visit
22506	Gorski	Drea	4/1/2016	Fifth Disease
22506	Gorski	Drea	4/8/2016	Fifth Disease follow-up
22507	Weiss	Matthew	11/9/2015	Diabetes mellitis Type 2 - initial diagnosis
22507	Weiss	Matthew	2/9/2016	Diabetes mellitis Type 2 - serum glucose check

One-to-Many Relationships

As shown earlier in the Session 2.2 Visual Overview, a one-to-many relationship exists between two tables when one record in the first table matches zero, one, or many records in the second table, and when one record in the second table matches at most one record in the first table. For example, as shown in Figure 2-40, patient 22506 has two visits in the Visit table. Other patients have one or more visits. Every visit has a single matching patient.

Access refers to the two tables that form a relationship as the primary table and the related table. The primary table is the "one" table in a one-to-many relationship; in Figure 2-40, the Patient table is the primary table because there is only one patient for each visit. The related table is the "many" table; in Figure 2-40, the Visit table is the related table because a patient can have zero, one, or many visits.

Because related data is stored in two tables, inconsistencies between the tables can occur. Referring to Figure 2-40, consider the following three scenarios:

- Cindi adds a record to the Visit table for a new patient, Jack Perry, using PatientID 22570. She did not first add the new patient's information to the Patient table, so this visit does not have a matching record in the Patient table. The data is inconsistent, and the visit record is considered to be an **orphaned record**.
- In another situation, Cindi changes the PatientID in the Patient table for Drea Gorski from 22506 to 22601. Because there is no longer a patient with the PatientID 22506 in the Patient table, this change creates two orphaned records in the Visit table, and the database is inconsistent.
- In a third scenario, Cindi deletes the record for Drea Gorski, patient 22506, from the Patient table because this patient moved and no longer receives medical services from Chatham Community Health Services. The database is again inconsistent; two records for patient 22506 in the Visit table have no matching record in the Patient table.

You can avoid these types of problems and avoid having inconsistent data in your database by specifying referential integrity between tables when you define their relationships.

Referential Integrity

Referential integrity is a set of rules that Access enforces to maintain consistency between related tables when you update data in a database. Specifically, the referential integrity rules are as follows:

- When you add a record to a related table, a matching record must already exist in the primary table, thereby preventing the possibility of orphaned records.
- If you attempt to change the value of the primary key in the primary table, Access prevents this change if matching records exist in a related table. However, if you choose the **Cascade Update Related Fields option**, Access permits the change in value to the primary key and changes the appropriate foreign key values in the related table, thereby eliminating the possibility of inconsistent data.
- When you attempt to delete a record in the primary table, Access prevents the deletion if matching records exist in a related table. However, if you choose the **Cascade Delete Related Records option**, Access deletes the record in the primary table and also deletes all records in related tables that have matching foreign key values.

INSIGHT

Understanding the Cascade Delete Related Records Option

Although there are advantages to using the Cascade Delete Related Records option for enforcing referential integrity, its use does present risks as well. You should rarely select the Cascade Delete Related Records option because doing so might cause you to inadvertently delete records you did not intend to delete. It is best to use other methods for deleting records that give you more control over the deletion process.

Defining a Relationship Between Two Tables

When two tables have a common field, you can define a relationship between them in the Relationships window (see the Session 2.2 Visual Overview). Next, you need to define a one-to-many relationship between the Patient and Visit tables, with Patient as the primary table and Visit as the related table, and with PatientID as the common field (the primary key in the Patient table and a foreign key in the Visit table). You'll also define a one-to-many relationship between the Visit and Billing tables, with Visit as the primary table and Billing as the related table, and with VisitID as the common field (the primary key in the Visit table and a foreign key in the Billing table).

To define the one-to-many relationship between the Patient and Visit tables:

1. On the ribbon, click the **DATABASE TOOLS** tab.

2. In the Relationships group, click the **Relationships** button. The Show Table dialog box opens. See Figure 2-41.

Figure 2-41   Show Table dialog box

add these two tables to the Relationships window

You must add each table participating in a relationship to the Relationships window. Because the Patient table is the primary table in the relationship, you'll add it first.

TIP
You can also double-click a table in the Show Table dialog box to add it to the Relationships window.

3. Click **Patient**, and then click the **Add** button. The Patient table's field list is added to the Relationships window.

    Trouble? If you add the same table more than once to the Relationships window, click the Close button in the Show Table box, right-click the field list for the duplicate table, and then click Hide Table. Then in the Relationships group on the DESIGN tab, click the Show Table button to reopen the Show Table dialog box.

4. Click **Visit**, and then click the **Add** button. The Visit table's field list is added to the Relationships window.

5. Click the **Close** button in the Show Table dialog box to close it.

So that you can view all the fields and complete field names, you'll resize the Patient table field list.

▶ 6. Use the ⇕ pointer to drag the bottom of the Patient table field list to lengthen it until the vertical scroll bar disappears and all the fields are visible.

To form the relationship between the two tables, you drag the common field of PatientID from the primary table to the related table. Then Access opens the Edit Relationships dialog box, in which you select the relationship options for the two tables.

▶ 7. Click **PatientID** in the Patient field list, and then drag it to **PatientID** in the Visit field list. When you release the mouse button, the Edit Relationships dialog box opens. See Figure 2-42.

Figure 2-42   **Edit Relationships dialog box**

The primary table, related table, common field, and relationship type (One-To-Many) appear in the dialog box. Note that Access correctly identifies the "One" side of the relationship and places the primary table Patient in the Table/Query section of the dialog box; similarly, Access correctly identifies the "Many" side of the relationship and places the related table Visit in the Related Table/Query section of the dialog box.

▶ 8. Click the **Enforce Referential Integrity** check box.

After you click the Enforce Referential Integrity check box, the two cascade options become available. If you select the Cascade Update Related Fields option, Access will update the appropriate foreign key values in the related table when you change a primary key value in the primary table. You will *not* select the Cascade Delete Related Records option because doing so could cause you to delete records that you do not want to delete; this option is rarely selected.

▶ 9. Click the **Cascade Update Related Fields** check box.

▶ 10. Click the **Create** button to define the one-to-many relationship between the two tables and to close the dialog box. The completed relationship appears in the Relationships window, with the join line connecting the common field of PatientID in each table. See Figure 2-43.

Figure 2-43 | **Defined relationship in the Relationships window**

"one" side of the relationship represented by the digit 1

"many" side of the relationship represented by the infinity symbol

join line

Trouble? If a dialog box opens indicating a problem that prevents you from creating the relationship, you most likely made a typing error when entering the two records in the Patient table. If so, click the OK button in the dialog box and then click the Cancel button in the Edit Relationships dialog box. Refer back to the earlier steps instructing you to enter the two records in the Patient table and carefully compare your entries with those shown in the text, especially the PatientID field values. Make any necessary corrections to the data in the Patient table, and then repeat Steps 7 through 10. If you still receive an error message, ask your instructor for assistance.

Now you need to define the one-to-many relationship between the Visit and Billing tables. In this relationship, Visit is the primary ("one") table because there is at most one visit for each invoice. Billing is the related ("many") table because there are zero, one, or many invoices that are generated for each patient visit. For example, some visits require lab work or pharmacy charges, which are invoiced separately.

To define the relationship between the Visit and Billing tables:

1. In the Relationships group on the DESIGN tab, click the **Show Table** button. The Show Table dialog box opens.

2. Make sure the **Billing** table is selected on the Tables tab, click the **Add** button, and then click the **Close** button to close the Show Table dialog box. The Billing table's field list appears in the Relationships window to the right of the Visit table's field list.

3. Use the ↕ pointer to drag the bottom of the Billing table field list to lengthen it until the vertical scroll bar disappears.

   Because the Visit table is the primary table in this relationship, you need to drag the VisitID field from the Visit field list to the Billing field list.

4. Click and drag the **VisitID** field in the Visit field list to the **VisitID** field in the Billing field list. When you release the mouse button, the Edit Relationships dialog box opens.

5. Click the **Enforce Referential Integrity** check box, and then click the **Cascade Update Related Fields** check box.

TIP

You can also use the mouse to drag a table from the Navigation Pane to add it to the Relationships window.

Tutorial 2 Building a Database and Defining Table Relationships | Access   AC 103

6. Click the **Create** button to define the one-to-many relationship between the two tables and to close the dialog box. The completed relationship appears in the Relationships window. See Figure 2-44.

Figure 2-44   **Both relationships defined**

[Screenshot of the Relationships window in Access showing the Patient, Visit, and Billing tables connected with one-to-many relationships. The Navigation Pane on the left shows All Access Objects including Tables (Billing, Patient, Visit), Queries (VisitList), Forms (VisitData), and Reports (VisitDetails). The Patient table shows fields: PatientID, LastName, FirstName, BirthDate, Phone, Address, City, State, Zip, Email. The Visit table shows: VisitID, PatientID, VisitDate, Reason, WalkIn. The Billing table shows: InvoiceNum, VisitID, InvoiceDate, InvoiceAmt, InvoiceItem, InvoicePaid.]

Trouble? If a dialog box opens indicating a problem that prevents you from creating the relationship, you most likely made a typing error when entering the two records in the Visit table. If so, click the OK button in the dialog box and then click the Cancel button in the Edit Relationships dialog box. Refer back to the steps in Tutorial 1 instructing you to enter the records in the Visit table and carefully compare your entries with those shown in the text, especially the VisitID field values. Make any necessary corrections to the data in the Visit table, and then repeat Steps 4 through 6. If you still receive an error message, ask your instructor for assistance.

With both relationships defined, you have connected the data among the three tables in the Chatham database.

7. On the Quick Access Toolbar, click the **Save** button to save the layout in the Relationships window.

8. In the Relationships group on the DESIGN tab, click the **Close** button to close the Relationships window.

9. Click the **FILE** tab on the ribbon to display Backstage view.

10. Click the **Compact & Repair Database** button. Access compacts and repairs the Chatham database.

11. Click the **FILE** tab, and then click **Close** to close the Chatham database.

PROSKILLS

Problem Solving: Creating a Larger Database

When you create a small database that contains only a few tables, and the data and the reports you want to generate from it are fairly simple, you could follow the process outlined in this text: create the tables, populate them, and then define the necessary relationships between tables. This method, however, would not be suitable for creating a larger database. A larger database would most likely have many more tables and different types of relationships that can be quite complex. When creating a large database, a standard process to follow would include these steps:

1. Talk to people who will be using the data, and gather as much documentation as possible to try to understand how the data will be used. Gather sample reports, and ask the users to describe the data they require.
2. Gather some representative sample data, if possible.
3. Plan the tables, fields, data types, other properties, and the relationships between the tables.
4. Create the tables and define the relationships between them.
5. Populate the tables with sample data.
6. Design some queries, forms, and reports that will be needed, and then test them.
7. Modify the database structure, if necessary, based on the results of your tests.
8. Enter the actual data into the database tables.

Testing is critical at every stage of creating a database. Once the database is finalized and implemented, it's not actually finished. The design of a database evolves as new functionality is required and as the data that is gathered changes.

REVIEW

Session 2.2 Quick Check

1. What is the keyboard shortcut for inserting the value from the same field in the previous record into the current record?
2. _____ data is a process that allows you to copy the data from a source without having to open the source file.
3. The _____ gallery allows you to add a group of related fields to a table at the same time, rather than adding each field to the table individually.
4. What is the effect of deleting a field from a table structure?
5. A(n) _____ text file is one in which fields of data are separated by a character such as a comma or a tab.
6. The _____ is the "one" table in a one-to-many relationship, and the _____ is the "many" table in the relationship.
7. _____ is a set of rules that Access enforces to maintain consistency between related tables when you update data in a database.

SAM Projects

Put your skills into practice with SAM Projects! SAM Projects for this tutorial can be found online. If you have a SAM account, go to www.cengage.com/sam2013 to download the most recent Project Instructions and Start Files.

Review Assignments

Data Files needed for the Review Assignments: Vendor.accdb *(cont. from Tutorial 1)* and Supplies.xlsx

In addition to tracking information about the vendors Chatham Community Health Services works with, Cindi also wants to track information about their products and services. First, Cindi asks you to modify the necessary properties in the existing Supplier table in the Vendor database; then she wants you to create a new table in the Vendor database to contain product data. Complete the following:

1. Open the **Vendor** database you created in Tutorial 1.
2. Open the **Supplier** table in Design view, and set the field properties as shown in Figure 2-45.

Figure 2-45   Field properties for the Supplier table

Field Name	Data Type	Description	Field Size	Other
SupplierID	Short Text	Primary key	6	Caption = Supplier ID
Company	Short Text		50	
Category	Short Text		15	
Address	Short Text		35	
City	Short Text		25	
State	Short Text		2	
Zip	Short Text		10	
Phone	Short Text		14	Caption = Contact Phone
ContactFirst	Short Text		20	Caption = Contact First Name
ContactLast	Short Text		25	Caption = Contact Last Name
InitialContact	Date/Time			Format = Short Date
				Caption = Initial Contact

© 2014 Cengage Learning

3. Save the Supplier table. Click the Yes button when a message appears indicating some data might be lost. Switch to Datasheet view and resize columns, as necessary, to their best fit. Then save and close the Supplier table.
4. Create a new table in Design view, using the table design shown in Figure 2-46.

Figure 2-46   Design for the Product table

Field Name	Data Type	Description	Field Size	Other
ProductID	Short Text	Primary key	5	Caption = Product ID
SupplierID	Short Text	Foreign key	6	Caption = Supplier ID
ProductName	Short Text		75	Caption = Product Name
Price	Currency			Format = Standard Decimal Places = 2
TempControl	Yes/No			Caption = Temp Controlled?
Sterile	Yes/No			Caption = Sterile?
Units	Number		Integer	Decimal Places = 0 Caption = Units/Case Default Value = [no entry]

© 2014 Cengage Learning

5. Specify ProductID as the primary key, and then save the table as **Product**.
6. Modify the table structure by adding a new field named **Weight** (data type: **Number**; field size: **Single**; Decimal Places: **2**; Caption: **Weight in Lbs**; Default Value: [no entry]) between the Price and TempControl fields. Then move the **Units** field so that it is positioned between the Price and Weight fields.
7. Enter the records shown in Figure 2-47 in the Product table. Resize all datasheet columns to their best fit. When finished, save and close the Product table.

Figure 2-47   Records for the Product table

Product ID	Supplier ID	Product Name	Price	Units/Case	Weight in Lbs	Temp Controlled?	Sterile?
SS582	DUR368	Stethoscopes	65.00	1	1	No	No
AL487	COU392	Alcohol wipes	15.00	1000	12	Yes	Yes

© 2014 Cengage Learning

8. Use the Import Spreadsheet Wizard to add data to the Product table. The data you need to import is contained in the Supplies workbook, which is an Excel file located in the Access1 ► Review folder provided with your Data Files.
   a. Specify the Supplies workbook as the source of the data.
   b. Select the option for appending the data.
   c. Select Product as the table.
   d. In the Import Spreadsheet Wizard dialog boxes, make sure Access confirms that the first row contains column headings, and import to the Product table. Do not save the import steps.
9. Open the **Product** table in Datasheet view and resize columns to their best fit, as necessary. Then save and close the Product table.
10. Define a one-to-many relationship between the primary Supplier table and the related Product table. Resize the table field lists so that all field names are visible. Select the referential integrity option and the cascade updates option for the relationship.
11. Save the changes to the Relationships window and close it, compact and repair the Vendor database, and then close the database.

Case Problem 1

Data Files needed for this Case Problem: Gopher.accdb *(cont. from Tutorial 1)* **and Customers.txt**

GoGopher! Amol Mehta wants to use the Gopher database to track information about members who join his online business, which provides a variety of services on a subscription basis, and the plans in which members are enrolled. He asks you to help maintain this database. Complete the following:

1. Open the **Gopher** database you created in Tutorial 1.
2. Open the **Plan** table in Design view, and change the following field properties:
   a. PlanID: Enter **Primary key** for the description, change the field size to **3**, and enter **Plan ID** for the caption.
   b. PlanDescription: Change the field size to **40** and enter **Plan Description** for the caption.
   c. PlanCost: Change the format to **Standard**, specify **0** decimal places, and enter **Plan Cost** for the caption.
   d. FeeWaived: Enter **Fee Waived** for the caption.
3. Save and close the Plan table. Click the Yes button when a message appears indicating some data might be lost.
4. Create a new table in Design view, using the table design shown in Figure 2-48.

Figure 2-48   Design for the Member table

Field Name	Data Type	Description	Field Size	Other
MemberID	Short Text	Primary key	4	Caption = Member ID
PlanID	Short Text	Foreign key	3	Caption = Plan ID
FirstName	Short Text		20	Caption = First Name
LastName	Short Text		25	Caption = Last Name
Phone	Short Text		14	
Expiration	Date/Time	Date when membership expires		Format = Short Date Caption = Expiration Date

© 2014 Cengage Learning

5. Specify MemberID as the primary key, and then save the table as **Member**.
6. Use the Address Quick Start selection in the Data Type gallery to add five fields between the LastName and Phone fields.
7. Switch to Design view, and then make the following changes to the Member table design:
   a. Address field: Change the name of this field to **Street**, change the field size to **40**, and delete the entry for the caption.
   b. City field: Change the field size to **25** and delete the entry for the caption.
   c. StateProvince field: Change the name of this field to **State**, change the field size to **2**, delete the entry for the caption, and enter **CO** for the default value.
   d. ZIPPostal field: Change the name of this field to **Zip**, change the field size to **10**, and delete the entry for the caption.
   e. Delete the **CountryRegion** field from the Member table structure.
   f. Add a new field named **DateJoined** (data type: **Date/Time**; format: **Short Date**; Caption: **Date Joined**) between the Phone and Expiration fields.
8. Enter the records shown in Figure 2-49 in the Member table. Be sure to enter your first and last names in the appropriate fields for the first new record. Resize all datasheet columns to their best fit. When finished, save and close the Member table.

Figure 2-49   Records for the Member table

Member ID	Plan ID	First Name	Last Name	Street	City	State	Zip	Phone	Date Joined	Expiration Date
1200	311	*Student First*	*Student Last*	45 Lakeview Dr	Boulder	CO	80301	303-559-1238	11/1/2015	2/1/2016
1210	312	Todd	Grant	6 Rosebriar Rd	Erie	CO	80516	303-674-2140	1/20/2016	4/20/2016

© 2014 Cengage Learning

9. Use the Import Text File Wizard to add data to the Member table. The data you need to import is contained in the Customers text file, which is located in the Access1 ▸ Case1 folder provided with your Data Files.
    a. Specify the Customers text file as the source of the data.
    b. Select the option for appending the data.
    c. Select Member as the table.
    d. In the Import Text File Wizard dialog boxes, choose the options to import delimited data, to use a comma delimiter, and to import the data into the Member table. Do not save the import steps.
10. Open the **Member** table in Datasheet view and resize columns to their best fit, as necessary. Then save and close the Member table.
11. Define a one-to-many relationship between the primary Plan table and the related Member table. Resize the Member table field list so that all field names are visible. Select the referential integrity option and the cascade updates option for this relationship.
12. Save the changes to the Relationships window and close it, compact and repair the Gopher database, and then close the database.

Case Problem 2

APPLY

Data Files needed for this Case Problem: OBrien.accdb *(cont. from Tutorial 1)*, **Client.accdb, Students.txt, and Agreements.xlsx**

O'Brien Educational Services   Karen O'Brien plans to use the OBrien database to maintain information about the students, tutors, and contracts for her educational services company. Karen asks you to help her build the database by updating one table and creating two new tables in the database. Complete the following:

1. Open the **OBrien** database you created in Tutorial 1.
2. Open the **Tutor** table in Design view, and set the field properties as shown in Figure 2-50.

Figure 2-50   Field properties for the Tutor table

Field Name	Data Type	Description	Field Size	Other
TutorID	Short Text	Primary key	7	Caption = Tutor ID
FirstName	Short Text		20	Caption = First Name
LastName	Short Text		25	Caption = Last Name
Degree	Short Text		7	
School	Short Text		50	
HireDate	Date/Time			Format = Short Date
				Caption = Hire Date

© 2014 Cengage Learning

3. Add a new field as the last field in the Tutor table with the field name **Groups**, the **Yes/No** data type, and the caption **Groups Only**.
4. Save the Tutor table. Click the Yes button when a message appears indicating some data might be lost.

5. In the table datasheet, specify that the following tutors conduct group tutoring sessions only: Student First/Student Last (i.e., your name), Amy Hawkins, Lori Burns, Samuel Glick, and Caitlin Shea. Close the Tutor table.
6. Karen created a table named Student in the Client database that is located in the Access1 ▸ Case2 folder provided with your Data Files. Import the structure of the Student table in the Client database into a new table named Student in the OBrien database. Do not save the import steps.
7. Open the **Student** table in Datasheet view, and then add the following two fields to the end of the table: **BirthDate** (Date/Time field) and **Gender** (Short Text field).
8. Use the Phone Quick Start selection in the Data Type gallery to add four fields related to phone numbers between the Zip and BirthDate fields. (*Hint:* Be sure to make the BirthDate field the active field before adding the new fields.)
9. Display the Student table in Design view, delete the BusinessPhone and FaxNumber fields, and then save and close the Student table.
10. Reopen the Student table and modify its design so that it matches the design in Figure 2-51, *including the revised field names and data types*.
    Note: You must type the quotation marks around the Default Property value for the State field.

Figure 2-51 — Field properties for the Student table

Field Name	Data Type	Description	Field Size	Other
StudentID	Short Text	Primary key	7	Caption = Student ID
LastName	Short Text		25	Caption = Last Name
FirstName	Short Text		20	Caption = First Name
Address	Short Text		35	
City	Short Text		25	
State	Short Text		2	Default Value = "IN"
Zip	Short Text		10	
HomePhone	Short Text		14	
CellPhone	Short Text		14	Caption = Cell Phone
BirthDate	Date/Time			Format = Short Date
				Caption = Date of Birth
Gender	Short Text	F(emale), M(ale)	1	

© 2014 Cengage Learning

you must type the quotation marks for this Default Value property

11. Move the LastName field so it follows the FirstName field.
12. Save your changes to the table design, and then add the records shown in Figure 2-52 to the Student table.

Figure 2-52 — Records for the Student table

Student ID	First Name	Last Name	Address	City	State	Zip	Home Phone	Cell Phone	Date of Birth	Gender
TUR8005	Lynne	Turner	6 Crowell Ct	South Bend	IN	46614	574-245-2125	574-245-8842	7/24/2002	F
CHA8034	Henry	Chang	1401 Lauren Dr	Oscela	IN	46561	574-607-3045	574-674-2410	10/5/1999	M

© 2014 Cengage Learning

13. Resize the fields to their best fit, and then save and close the Student table.
14. Use the Import Text File Wizard to add data to the Student table. The data you need to import is contained in the Students text file, which is located in the Access1 ▸ Case2 folder provided with your Data Files.
    a. Specify the Students text file as the source of the data.
    b. Select the option for appending the data.

c. Select Student as the table.

d. In the Import Text File Wizard dialog boxes, choose the options to import delimited data, to use a comma delimiter, and to import the data into the Student table. Do not save the import steps.

15. Open the **Student** table in Datasheet view, resize columns in the datasheet to their best fit (as necessary), and then save and close the table.

16. Create a new table in Design view, using the table design shown in Figure 2-53.

Figure 2-53   **Design for the Contract table**

Field Name	Data Type	Description	Field Size	Other
ContractID	Short Text	Primary key	4	Caption = Contract ID
StudentID	Short Text	Foreign key	7	Caption = Student ID
TutorID	Short Text	Foreign key	7	Caption = Tutor ID
SessionType	Short Text		15	Caption = Session Type
Length	Number		Integer	Decimal Places = 0 Caption = Length (Hrs) Default Value = [no entry]
NumSessions	Number		Integer	Decimal Places = 0 Caption = Number of Sessions Default Value = [no entry]
Cost	Currency			Format = Currency Decimal Places = 0 Default Value = [no entry]
Assessment	Yes/No	Pre-assessment exam complete		Caption = Assessment Complete

© 2014 Cengage Learning

17. Specify ContractID as the primary key, and then save the table using the name **Contract**.

18. Add a new field to the Contract table, between the TutorID and SessionType fields, with the field name **ContractDate**, the **Date/Time** data type, the description **Date contract is signed**, the **Short Date** format, and the caption **Contract Date**. Save and close the Contract table.

19. Use the Import Spreadsheet Wizard to add data to the Contract table. The data you need to import is contained in the Agreements workbook, which is an Excel file located in the Access1 ▸ Case2 folder provided with your Data Files.

a. Specify the Agreements workbook as the source of the data.

b. Select the option for appending the data to the table.

c. Select Contract as the table.

d. In the Import Spreadsheet Wizard dialog boxes, choose the Agreements worksheet, make sure Access confirms that the first row contains column headings, and import to the Contract table. Do not save the import steps.

20. Open the **Contract** table and add the records shown in Figure 2-54. (*Hint*: Use the New (blank) record button in the navigation buttons to add a new record.)

Figure 2-54   **Records for the Contract table**

Contract ID	Student ID	Tutor ID	Contract Date	Session Type	Length (Hrs)	Number of Sessions	Cost	Assessment Complete
5168	LUF8037	68-8234	8/30/2016	Group	3	12	$1,440	Yes
5172	GOS8029	71-1698	9/7/2016	Private	2	6	$720	Yes

© 2014 Cengage Learning

21. Resize columns in the datasheet to their best fit (as necessary), and then save and close the Contract table.

22. Define the one-to-many relationships between the database tables as follows: between the primary Student table and the related Contract table, and between the primary Tutor table and the related Contract table. Resize the table field lists so that all field names are visible. Select the referential integrity option and the cascade updates option for each relationship.
23. Save the changes to the Relationships window and close it, compact and repair the OBrien database, and then close the database.

Case Problem 3

Data Files needed for this Case Problem: Shelter.accdb *(cont. from Tutorial 1)*, **Donations.xlsx, and Animals.txt**

Rosemary Animal Shelter Ryan Lang wants to use the Shelter database to maintain information about the patrons, animals, and donations for his not-for-profit agency. Ryan asks you to help him maintain the database by updating one table and creating two new ones. Complete the following:

1. Open the **Shelter** database you created in Tutorial 1.
2. Open the **Patron** table in Design view, and then change the following field properties:
    a. PatronID: Enter **Primary key** for the description, change the field size to **5**, and enter **Patron ID** for the caption.
    b. Title: Change the field size to **4**.
    c. FirstName: Change the field size to **20** and enter **First Name** for the caption.
    d. LastName: Change the field size to **25** and enter **Last Name** for the caption.
    e. Phone: Change the field size to **14**.
3. Save and close the Patron table. Click the Yes button when a message appears indicating some data might be lost.

Explore 4. Use the Import Spreadsheet Wizard to create a table in the Shelter database. As the source of the data, specify the Donations workbook, which is located in the Access1 ▶ Case3 folder provided with your Data Files. Select the option to import the source data into a new table in the database.

Explore 5. Complete the Import Spreadsheet Wizard dialog boxes as follows:
    a. Select Donation as the worksheet you want to import.
    b. Specify that the first row contains column headings.
    c. Accept the field options suggested by the wizard, and do not skip any fields.
    d. Choose DonationID as your own primary key.
    e. Import the data to a table named **Donation**, and do not save the import steps.

6. Open the Donation table in Datasheet view, and then delete the Requires Pickup field.
7. Open the Donation table in Design view, and then modify the table so it matches the design shown in Figure 2-55, including changes to data types, field name, and field position. For the Short Text fields, delete any formats specified in the Format property boxes.

Figure 2-55   Design for the Donation table

Field Name	Data Type	Description	Field Size	Other
DonationID	Short Text	Primary key	4	Caption = Donation ID
PatronID	Short Text	Foreign key	5	Caption = Patron ID
DonationDate	Date/Time			Format = mm/dd/yyyy
				Caption = Donation Date
Description	Short Text		30	
DonationValue	Currency	Dollar amount or estimated value		Format = Currency
				Decimal Places = 2
				Caption = Donation Value
				Default Value = [no entry]

© 2014 Cengage Learning

8. Save your changes to the table design, click Yes for the message about lost data, and then switch to Datasheet view.
9. Resize the columns in the Donation datasheet to their best fit.

Explore 10. Ryan decides that the values in the Donation Value column would look better without the two decimal places. Make this field the current field in the datasheet. Then, in the Formatting group on the FIELDS tab, use the Decrease Decimals button to remove the two decimal places and the period from these values. Switch back to Design view, and note that the Decimal Places property for the DonationValue field is now set to 0.

11. Save and close the Donation table.
12. Use Design view to create a table using the table design shown in Figure 2-56.

Figure 2-56   **Design for the Animal table**

Field Name	Data Type	Description	Field Size	Other
AnimalID	Short Text	Primary key	3	Caption = Animal ID
AnimalName	Short Text		15	Caption = Animal Name
Age	Short Text		2	Caption = Age at Arrival
Gender	Short Text		6	
AnimalType	Short Text		5	Caption = Animal Type
Description	Short Text		60	
ArrivalDate	Date/Time			Format = Short Date
				Caption = Arrival Date
AdoptionDate	Date/Time			Format = Short Date
				Caption = Adoption Date
Adopted	Yes/No			
PatronID	Short Text		5	Caption = Patron ID

© 2014 Cengage Learning

13. Specify AnimalID as the primary key, save the table as **Animal**, and then close the table.
14. Use the Import Text File Wizard to add data to the Animal table. The data you need to import is contained in the Animals text file, which is located in the Access1 ▶ Case3 folder provided with your Data Files.
    a. Specify the Animals text file as the source of the data.
    b. Select the option for appending the data.
    c. Select Animal as the table.
    d. In the Import Text File Wizard dialog boxes, choose the options to import delimited data, to use a comma delimiter, and to import the data into the Animal table. Do not save the import steps.
15. Open the Animal table in Datasheet view, and resize all columns to their best fit.
16. Display the Animal table in Design view. Move the PatronID field to make it the second field in the table, and enter the description **Foreign key** for the PatronID field. Then move the Adopted field so it is positioned between the ArrivalDate and AdoptionDate fields. Save the modified Animal table design.
17. Switch to Datasheet view, and then add the records shown in Figure 2-57 to the Animal table. (*Hint*: Use the New (blank) record button in the navigation buttons to add a new record.) Close the table when finished.

Figure 2-57   **Records for the Animal table**

Animal ID	Patron ID	Animal Name	Age at Arrival	Gender	Animal Type	Description	Arrival Date	Adopted	Adoption Date
B45		Gizmo	12	Male	Dog	Hound mix	3/6/2016	No	
R39	38398	Simba	3	Female	Cat	Siamese	4/12/2016	Yes	5/14/2016

© 2014 Cengage Learning

Tutorial 2 Building a Database and Defining Table Relationships | Access   AC 113

18. Define the one-to-many relationships between the database tables as follows: between the primary Patron table and the related Animal table, and between the primary Patron table and the related Donation table. (*Hint:* Place the Patron table as the middle table in the Relationships window to make it easier to join the tables.) Resize the Animal field list so that all field names are visible. Select the referential integrity option and the cascade updates option for each relationship.
19. Save the changes to the Relationships window and close it, compact and repair the Shelter database, and then close the database.

Case Problem 4

CHALLENGE

Data Files needed for this Case Problem: Stanley.accdb (*cont. from Tutorial 1*), Travel.accdb, and Bookings.txt

Stanley EcoTours   Janice and Bill Stanley use the Stanley database to track the data about the tours they offer to clients of their ecotourism business. They ask you to help them maintain this database. Complete the following:

1. Open the **Stanley** database you created in Tutorial 1.
2. Open the **Guest** table in Design view and change the following field properties:
   a. GuestID: Enter **Primary key** for the description, change the field size to **3**, and enter **Guest ID** for the caption.
   b. GuestFirst: Change the field size to **20** and enter **Guest First Name** for the caption.
   c. GuestLast: Change the field size to **25** and enter **Guest Last Name** for the caption.
   d. Address: Change the field size to **35**.
   e. City: Change the field size to **25**.
   f. State/Prov: Change the field size to **2**.
   g. PostalCode: Change the field size to **10** and enter **Postal Code** for the caption.
   h. Country: Change the field size to **15**.
   i. Phone: Change the field size to **14**.
3. Save the Guest table, click the Yes button when a message appears indicating some data might be lost, resize the Guest First Name and Guest Last Name columns in Datasheet view to their best fit, and then save and close the table.

Explore 4. In addition to importing the structure of an existing Access table, you can also import both the structure *and* the data contained in a table to create a new table. Import the **Trip** table structure and data from the **Travel** database into a new table in the **Stanley** database as follows:
   a. Start the process for importing an Access table structure.
   b. As the source of the data, specify the Travel database, which is located in the Access1 ▶ Case4 folder provided with your Data Files.
   c. Select the option button to import tables, queries, forms, reports, macros, and modules into the current database.
   d. In the Import Objects dialog box, select the Trip table, click the Options button, and then make sure that the correct option is selected to import the table's data and structure (definition).
   e. Do not save your import steps.

Explore 5. Using a shortcut menu in the Navigation Pane, rename the Trip table as **Tour** to give this name to the new table in the Stanley database.

6. Open the **Tour** table in Design view, delete the VIPDiscount field, and then move the PricePerPerson field so that it appears between the Country and SingleSupplement fields.

7. Change the following properties:
    a. TourID: Enter the description **Primary key**, change the field size to **4**, and enter **Tour ID** for the caption.
    b. TourName: Enter **Tour Name** for the caption.
    c. PricePerPerson: Enter **Price Per Person** for the caption.
    d. SingleSupplement: Enter the description **Additional charge for single accommodation**, and enter **Single Supplement** for the caption.
    e. TourType: Change the field size to **15**, and enter **Tour Type** for the caption.
    f. Nights: Enter **Num of Nights** for the caption.
8. Save the modified table, click the Yes button when a message appears indicating some data might be lost, and then display the table in Datasheet view. Resize all datasheet columns to their best fit, and then save and close the table.
9. In Design view, create a table using the table design shown in Figure 2-58.

Figure 2-58   Design for the Reservation table

Field Name	Data Type	Description	Field Size	Other
ReservationID	Short Text	Primary key	3	Caption = Reservation ID
GuestID	Short Text	Foreign key	3	Caption = Guest ID
TourID	Short Text	Foreign key	4	Caption = Tour ID
StartDate	Date/Time			Caption = Start Date
People	Number	Number of people in the party	Integer	Decimal Places = 0 Default Value = [no entry]

© 2014 Cengage Learning

10. Specify ReservationID as the primary key, and then save the table as **Reservation**.
11. **Explore** Refer back to Figure 2-11 to review the custom date formats. Change the Format property of the StartDate field to a custom format that displays dates in a format similar to 05/25/16. Save and close the Reservation table.
12. Use the Import Text File Wizard to add data to the Reservation table. The data you need to import is contained in the Bookings text file, which is located in the Access1 ▶ Case4 folder provided with your Data Files.
    a. Specify the Bookings text file as the source of the data.
    b. Select the option for appending the data.
    c. Select Reservation as the table.
    d. In the Import Text File Wizard dialog boxes, choose the options to import delimited data, to use a comma delimiter, and to import the data into the Reservation table. Do not save the import steps.
13. Resize columns in the **Reservation** table datasheet to their best fit (as necessary), verify that the date values in the StartDate field are displayed correctly according to the custom format, and then save and close the table.
14. Define the one-to-many relationships between the database tables as follows: between the primary Guest table and the related Reservation table, and between the primary Tour table and the related Reservation table. (*Hint:* Place the Reservation table as the middle table in the Relationships window to make it easier to join the tables.) Resize the Guest and Tour field lists so that all field names are visible. Select the referential integrity option and the cascade updates option for each relationship.
15. Save the changes to the Relationships window and close it, compact and repair the Stanley database, and then close the database.

TUTORIAL 3

Maintaining and Querying a Database

Updating and Retrieving Information About Patients, Visits, and Invoices

OBJECTIVES

Session 3.1
- Find, modify, and delete records in a table
- Hide and unhide fields in a datasheet
- Work in the Query window in Design view
- Create, run, and save queries
- Update data using a query datasheet
- Create a query based on multiple tables
- Sort data in a query
- Filter data in a query

Session 3.2
- Specify an exact match condition in a query
- Use a comparison operator in a query to match a range of values
- Use the And and Or logical operators in queries
- Change the font size and alternate row color in a datasheet
- Create and format a calculated field in a query
- Perform calculations in a query using aggregate functions and record group calculations
- Change the display of database objects in the Navigation Pane

Case | Chatham Community Health Services

At a recent meeting, Cindi Rodriguez and her staff discussed the importance of maintaining accurate information about the clinic's patients, visits, and invoices, and regularly monitoring the business activities of Chatham Community Health Services. For example, Kelly Schwarz, Cindi's assistant, needs to make sure she has up-to-date contact information, such as phone numbers and email addresses, for all the clinic's patients. The office staff also must monitor billing activity to ensure that invoices are paid on time and in full. Ethan Ward, a staff member who handles marketing and community outreach efforts for the clinic, tracks patient activity to develop new strategies for promoting services provided by the clinic. In addition, Cindi is interested in analyzing other aspects of the business related to patient visits and finances. You can satisfy all these informational needs for Chatham Community Health Services by updating data in the Chatham database and by creating and using queries that retrieve information from the database.

STARTING DATA FILES

Access1 → Tutorial
Chatham.accdb *(cont.)*

Review
Vendor.accdb *(cont.)*

Case1
Gopher.accdb *(cont.)*

Case2
OBrien.accdb *(cont.)*

Case3
Shelter.accdb *(cont.)*

Case4
Stanley.accdb *(cont.)*
Tour.accdb

Microsoft product screenshots used with permission from Microsoft Corporation.

Session 3.1 Visual Overview:

When you are constructing a query, you can see the results at any time by clicking the View button or the Run button. In response, Access displays the query datasheet, which contains the set of fields and records that results from answering, or **running**, the query.

The top portion of the Query window in Design view contains the field list (or lists) for the table(s) used in the query.

The default query name, Query1, is displayed on the tab for the query. You change the default query name to a more meaningful one when you save the query.

The bottom portion of the Query window in Design view contains the design grid. In the **design grid**, you include the fields and record selection criteria for the information you want to see.

In the Query Type group, the active Select button indicates that you are creating a select query, which is the default type of query. A **select query** is one in which you specify the fields and records you want Access to select.

Each **field list** contains the fields for the table(s) you are querying. The table name appears at the top of the field list, and the fields are listed in the order in which they appear in the table. Notice that the primary key for the table is identified by the key symbol.

You can scroll the field list to see more fields, or you can expand the field list box by dragging its borders to display all the fields and the complete field names. When all the field names are displayed, the scroll bar disappears.

Tutorial 3 Maintaining and Querying a Database | Access   AC 117

Query Window in Design View

Chatham : Database- E:\Access1\Tutorial\Chatham.accdb (Acces...

Insert Rows | Insert Columns | Totals | Parameters | Property Sheet | Table Names
Delete Rows | Delete Columns
Builder | Return: All

Query Setup | Show/Hide

The ribbon displays the QUERY TOOLS DESIGN tab with options for creating and running queries. Note the Query Type group on the DESIGN tab; it provides buttons you can click to create various types of queries.

In Design view, you specify the data you want to view by constructing a query by example. When you use **query by example (QBE)**, you give Access an example of the information you are requesting. Access then retrieves the information that precisely matches your example.

Each column in the design grid contains specifications about a field you will use in the query. You can choose a single field for your query by double-clicking its name in the field list to place the field in the next available design grid column.

The view buttons on the status bar allow you to change to different views; for example, you can click the Datasheet View button to run the query and display the results in Datasheet view.

Updating a Database

Updating, or **maintaining**, a database is the process of adding, modifying, and deleting records in database tables to keep them current and accurate. After reviewing the data in the Chatham database, Kelly identified some changes that need to be made to the data. She would like you to update the field values in one record in the Patient table, correct an error in one record in the Visit table, and then delete a record in the Visit table.

Modifying Records

To modify the field values in a record, you must first make the record the current record. Then you position the insertion point in the field value to make minor changes, or select the field value to replace it entirely. In Tutorial 1, you used the mouse with the scroll bars and the navigation buttons to navigate the records in a datasheet. You can also use keyboard shortcuts and the F2 key to navigate a datasheet and to select field values. The **F2 key** is a toggle that you use to switch between navigation mode and editing mode:

- In **navigation mode**, Access selects an entire field value. If you type while you are in navigation mode, your typed entry replaces the highlighted field value.
- In **editing mode**, you can insert or delete characters in a field value based on the location of the insertion point.

Figure 3-1 shows some of the navigation mode and editing mode keyboard shortcuts.

Figure 3-1 Navigation mode and editing mode keyboard shortcuts

Press	To Move the Selection in Navigation Mode	To Move the Insertion Point in Editing Mode
←	Left one field value at a time	Left one character at a time
→	Right one field value at a time	Right one character at a time
Home	Left to the first field value in the record	To the left of the first character in the field value
End	Right to the last field value in the record	To the right of the last character in the field value
↑ or ↓	Up or down one record at a time	Up or down one record at a time and switch to navigation mode
Tab or Enter	Right one field value at a time	Right one field value at a time and switch to navigation mode
Ctrl + Home	To the first field value in the first record	To the left of the first character in the field value
Ctrl + End	To the last field value in the last record	To the right of the last character in the field value

© 2014 Cengage Learning

The Patient table record Kelly wants you to change is for Patrice Lewis. This patient recently moved to another location in Windsor and also changed her email address, so you need to update the Patient table record with the new street address and email address.

Tutorial 3 Maintaining and Querying a Database | Access   AC 119

To open the Patient table in the Chatham database:

1. Start Access and open the **Chatham** database you created and worked with in Tutorials 1 and 2.

   Trouble? If the security warning is displayed below the ribbon, click the Enable Content button.

2. Open the **Patient** table in Datasheet view.

The Patient table contains many fields. Sometimes, when updating data in a table, it can be helpful to remove the display of some fields on the screen.

Hiding and Unhiding Fields

TIP

Hiding a field removes it from the datasheet display *only*; the field and its contents are still part of the table.

When you are viewing a table or query datasheet in Datasheet view, you might want to temporarily remove certain fields from the displayed datasheet, making it easier to focus on the data you're interested in viewing. The **Hide Fields** command allows you to remove the display of one or more fields, and the **Unhide Fields** command allows you to redisplay any hidden fields. Hiding fields can be especially useful in a table with many fields.

To make it easier to modify the patient record, you'll first hide a couple of fields in the Patient table.

To hide fields in the Patient table and modify the patient record:

1. Right-click the **Date of Birth** field name to display the shortcut menu, and then click **Hide Fields** on the shortcut menu. The Date of Birth column is removed from the datasheet display.

2. Right-click the **Phone** field name, and then click **Hide Fields** on the shortcut menu. The Phone column is removed from the datasheet display.

   With the fields hidden, you can now update the patient record. The record you need to modify is near the end of the table and has a PatientID field value of 22560.

3. Drag the vertical scroll box down until you see the last records in the table.

4. Click the PatientID field value **22560**, for Patrice Lewis. The field value is not selected, indicating you are in editing mode.

5. Press the **Tab** key to move to the Last Name field value, Lewis. The field value is selected, indicating you are in navigation mode.

6. Press the **Tab** key twice to move to the Address field and select its field value, type **83 Highland St**, press the **Tab** key four times to move to the Email field, type **plewis5@example.org**, and then press the **Tab** key. The changes to the record are complete. See Figure 3-2.

Figure 3-2   Table after changing field values in a record

	22555	Phillips	Aquon	632 Perkins Dr	Hartford	CT	06120	
	22556	Grus	Mateo	18 Norman Rd	Hartford	CT	06112	m.grus@example.com
	22557	Kirk	Isobel	48 Grafton St	Bloomfield	CT	06002	
	22558	Ropiak	Jane	637 Filbert St	Hartford	CT	06120	jropiak@example.edu
	22559	Morales	Jose	251 Lilac St	West Hartford	CT	06117	j.morales@example.org
	22560	Lewis	Patrice	83 Highland St	Windsor	CT	06095	plewis5@example.org
	22561	Shaw	Daniel	33 Agnes Ct	West Hartford	CT	06117	dshaw@example.com
*						CT		

field values changed

Access saves changes to field values when you move to a new field or another record, or when you close the table. You don't have to click the Save button to save changes to field values or records.

Note that the PatientID field value for the last record in the table is selected, indicating you are in navigation mode.

7. Press the **Ctrl+Home** keys to move to the first field value in the first record.

   With the changes to the record complete, you can unhide the hidden fields.

8. Right-click any field name to display the shortcut menu, and then click **Unhide Fields**. The Unhide Columns dialog box opens. See Figure 3-3.

Figure 3-3   Unhide Columns dialog box

All currently displayed fields are checked in this dialog box, and all hidden fields are unchecked. To redisplay them, you simply click their check boxes to select them.

9. In the Unhide Columns dialog box, click the **Date of Birth** check box to select it, click the **Phone** check box to select it, and then click the **Close** button to close the dialog box. The two hidden fields are now displayed in the datasheet.

10. Close the Patient table. A dialog box opens asking if you want to save changes to the layout of the Patient table. This box appears because you hid fields and redisplayed them.

    In this case, you can click either the Yes button or the No button, because no changes were actually made to the table layout or design.

11. Click the **No** button to close the dialog box.

Next you need to correct an error in the Visit table for a visit made by Jane Ropiak, Patient ID 22558. A staff member incorrectly entered "COPD management visit" as the reason for the visit, when the patient actually came to the clinic that day suffering from influenza. Ensuring the accuracy of the data in a database is an important maintenance task.

To correct the record in the Visit table:

1. Open the **Visit** table in Datasheet view. The record containing the error is for Visit ID 1635.

Tutorial 3 Maintaining and Querying a Database | Access   AC 121

> 2. Scroll down the Visit table until you locate Visit ID **1635**, and then click at the end of the **Reason** field value for this record. Because the field value is not selected, you are in editing mode.
>
> 3. Press the **Backspace** key until the current entry for the Reason field is deleted, type **Influenza**, and then press the **Enter** key twice. The record now contains the correct value in the Reason field, and Access saves this change automatically in the Visit table.

The next update Kelly asks you to make is to delete a record in the Visit table. One of the clinic's patients, Robert Goldberg, recently notified Kelly that he received an invoice for an annual wellness visit, but that he had cancelled this scheduled appointment to the clinic. Because this patient visit did not take place, the record for this visit needs to be deleted from the Visit table. Rather than scrolling through the table to locate the record to delete, you can have Access find the data for you.

Finding Data in a Table

Access provides options you can use to locate specific field values in a table. Instead of scrolling the Visit table datasheet to find the visit that you need to delete—the record for Visit ID 1688—you can use the Find command to find the record. The **Find command** allows you to search a table or query datasheet, or a form, to locate a specific field value or part of a field value. This feature is particularly useful when searching a table that contains a large number of records.

To search for the record in the Visit table:

TIP
You can click any value in the column containing the field you want to search to make the field current.

> 1. Make sure the VisitID field value **1638** is still selected. You need to search the VisitID field to find the record containing the value 1688, so the insertion point is already correctly positioned in the field you want to search.
>
> 2. Make sure the **HOME** tab is displayed on the ribbon.
>
> 3. In the Find group, click the **Find** button. The Find and Replace dialog box opens. See Figure 3-4.

Figure 3-4   **Find and Replace dialog box**

- specifies that the current field will be searched
- specifies that Access will search for a match to the entire field value
- value selected in the table datasheet
- specifies that all records in the table will be searched

The field value 1638 appears in the Find What box because this value is selected in the table datasheet. The Look In box indicates that the current field will be searched for the value. The Match box indicates that the Find command will match the whole field value, which is correct for your search. You also can choose to search for only part of a field value, such as when you need to find all Visit IDs that start with a certain value. The Search box indicates that all the records in the table will be searched for the value you want to find. You also can choose to search up or down from the currently selected record.

> **Trouble?** Some of the settings in your dialog box might be different from those shown in Figure 3-4 depending on the last search performed on the computer you're using. If so, change the settings so that they match those in the figure.
>
> 4. Make sure the value 1638 is selected in the Find What box, type **1688** to replace the selected value, and then click the **Find Next** button. Access scrolls the datasheet to record 81 and selects the field value you specified.
>
> 5. Click the **Cancel** button to close the Find and Replace dialog box.

Deleting Records

To delete a record, you need to select the record in Datasheet view, and then delete it using the Delete button in the Records group on the HOME tab or the Delete Record option on the shortcut menu.

> **REFERENCE**
>
> ### Deleting a Record
>
> - With the table open in Datasheet view, click the row selector for the record you want to delete.
> - In the Records group on the HOME tab, click the Delete button (or right-click the row selector for the record, and then click Delete Record on the shortcut menu).
> - In the dialog box asking you to confirm the deletion, click the Yes button.

Now that you have found the record with Visit ID 1688, you can delete it. To delete a record, you must first select the entire row for the record.

> **To delete the record:**
>
> 1. Click the row selector for the record containing the VisitID field value **1688**, which should still be highlighted. The entire row is selected.
>
> 2. In the Records group on the HOME tab, click the **Delete** button. A dialog box opens and indicates that you cannot delete the record because the Billing table contains records that are related to VisitID 1688. Recall that you defined a one-to-many relationship between the Visit and Billing tables and you enforced referential integrity. When you try to delete a record in the primary table (Visit), Access prevents the deletion if matching records exist in the related table (Billing). This protection helps to maintain the integrity of the data in the database.
>
>   To delete the record in the Visit table, you first must delete the related records in the Billing table.
>
> 3. Click the **OK** button in the dialog box to close it. Notice the plus sign that appears at the beginning of each record in the Visit table. The **plus sign** indicates that the Visit table is the primary table related to another table—in this case, the Billing table.
>
> 4. Scroll the datasheet down until you see the rest of the records in the table, so that you have room to view the related records for the visit record.

Tutorial 3 Maintaining and Querying a Database | Access   AC 123

5. Click the **plus sign** next to VisitID 1688. Access displays the one related record from the Billing table for this visit. See Figure 3-5.

Figure 3-5   Related record from the Billing table in the subdatasheet

minus sign appears when related records are displayed

subdatasheet with related record from the Billing table

plus signs indicate records have related records in another table

TIP

The plus sign changes to a minus sign for the current record when its related records are displayed.

The related record from the Billing table is displayed in a **subdatasheet**. When you first open a table that is the primary table in a one-to-many relationship, the subdatasheet containing the records from the related table is not displayed. You need to click the plus sign, also called the **expand indicator**, to display the related records in the subdatasheet. When the subdatasheet is open, you can navigate and update it, just as you can using a table datasheet.

You need to delete the record in the Billing table that is related to Visit ID 1688 before you can delete this visit record. The record is for the invoice that was mistakenly sent to the patient, Robert Goldberg, who had cancelled his annual wellness visit at the clinic. You could open the Billing table and find the related record. However, an easier way is to delete the record right in the subdatasheet. The record will be deleted from the Billing table automatically.

6. In the Billing table subdatasheet, click the row selector for invoice number **36087**. The entire row is selected.

7. In the Records group on the HOME tab, click the **Delete** button. Access opens a dialog box asking you to confirm the deletion of one record. Because the deletion of a record is permanent and cannot be undone, Access prompts you to make sure that you want to delete the record.

8. Click the **Yes** button to confirm the deletion and close the dialog box. The record is removed from the Billing table, and the subdatasheet is now empty.

9. Click the **minus sign** next to VisitID 1688 to close the subdatasheet.

Now that you have deleted the related record in the Billing table, you can delete the record for Visit ID 1688. You'll use the shortcut menu to do so.

Be sure to select the correct record before deleting it.

10. Right-click the row selector for the record for Visit ID **1688**. Access selects the record and displays the shortcut menu.

11. Click **Delete Record** on the shortcut menu, and then click the **Yes** button in the dialog box to confirm the deletion. The record is deleted from the Visit table.

12. Close the Visit table.

> **INSIGHT**
>
> ### Process for Deleting Records
>
> When working with more complex databases that are managed by a database administrator, you typically need special permission to delete records from a table. Many companies also follow the practice of archiving records before deleting them so that the information is still available but not part of the active database.

You have finished updating the Chatham database by modifying and deleting records. Next, you'll retrieve specific data from the database to meet various requests for information about Chatham Community Health Services.

Introduction to Queries

As you learned in Tutorial 1, a query is a question you ask about data stored in a database. For example, Cindi might create a query to find records in the Patient table for only those patients located in a specific city. When you create a query, you tell Access which fields you need and what criteria Access should use to select the records. Access provides powerful query capabilities that allow you to do the following:

- Display selected fields and records from a table
- Sort records
- Perform calculations
- Generate data for forms, reports, and other queries
- Update data in the tables in a database
- Find and display data from two or more tables

Most questions about data are generalized queries in which you specify the fields and records you want Access to select. These common requests for information, such as "Which patients are located in Bloomfield?" or "How many invoices have been paid?" are select queries. The answer to a select query is returned in the form of a datasheet. The result of a query is also referred to as a **recordset** because the query produces a set of records that answers your question.

> **INSIGHT**
>
> ### Designing Queries vs. Using a Query Wizard
>
> More specialized, technical queries, such as finding duplicate records in a table, are best formulated using a Query Wizard. A **Query Wizard** prompts you for information by asking a series of questions and then creates the appropriate query based on your answers. In Tutorial 1, you used the Simple Query Wizard to display only some of the fields in the Visit table; Access provides other Query Wizards for more complex queries. For common, informational queries, designing your own query is more efficient than using a Query Wizard.

Ethan wants you to create a query to display the patient ID, last name, first name, city, and email address for each record in the Patient table. He needs this information to complete an email campaign advertising a special blood pressure screening being offered to patients of Chatham Community Health Services. You'll open the Query window in Design view to create the query for Ethan.

Tutorial 3 Maintaining and Querying a Database | Access   AC 125

To open the Query window in Design view:

1. Close the Navigation Pane so that more of the workspace is displayed.
2. On the ribbon, click the **CREATE** tab. Access displays the options for creating different database objects.
3. In the Queries group, click the **Query Design** button. The Show Table dialog box opens on the Query window in Design view. See Figure 3-6.

Figure 3-6   **Show Table dialog box**

[Show Table dialog box image: Tables/Queries/Both tabs with list showing Billing, Patient, Visit; Add and Close buttons]

- tabs for selecting the source of the query
- list of tables in the database

The Show Table dialog box lists all the tables in the Chatham database. You can choose to base a query on one or more tables, on other queries, or on a combination of tables and queries. The query you are creating will retrieve data from the Patient table, so you need to add this table to the Query window.

4. Click **Patient** in the Tables list, click the **Add** button, and then click the **Close** button. Access places the Patient table's field list in the Query window and closes the Show Table dialog box. Refer to the Session 3.1 Visual Overview to familiarize yourself with the Query window in Design view.

   Trouble? If you add the wrong table to the Query window, right-click the bar at the top of the field list containing the table name, and then click Remove Table on the shortcut menu. To add the correct table to the Query window, click the Show Table button in the Query Setup group on the DESIGN tab to redisplay the Show Table dialog box, and then repeat Step 4.

Now you'll create and run Ethan's query to display selected fields from the Patient table.

Creating and Running a Query

The default table datasheet displays all the fields in the table in the same order as they appear in the table. In contrast, a query datasheet can display selected fields from a table, and the order of the fields can be different from that of the table, enabling those viewing the query results to see only the information they need and in the order they want.

Ethan wants the PatientID, LastName, FirstName, City, and Email fields from the Patient table to appear in the query results. You'll add each of these fields to the design grid. First you'll resize the Patient table field list to display all of the fields.

To select the fields for the query, and then run the query:

1. Position the pointer on the bottom border of the Patient field list until the pointer changes to a ↕ shape, and then click and drag the pointer down until the vertical scroll bar in the field list disappears and all fields in the Patient table are displayed in the list.

   Note that it's not necessary to resize the field list in order to create the query, but doing so enables you to see all the fields in the list, making it easier to select fields to include in the query.

2. In the Patient field list, double-click **PatientID** to place the field in the design grid's first column Field box. See Figure 3-7.

Figure 3-7   **Field added to the design grid**

- field list resized to display all the fields in the table
- field added from field list to the first column in the design grid
- specifies the field is in the Patient table
- indicates that the field will appear in the query datasheet

In the design grid's first column, the field name PatientID appears in the Field box, the table name Patient appears in the Table box, and the checkmark in the Show check box indicates that the field will be displayed in the datasheet when you run the query. Sometimes you might not want to display a field and its values in the query results. For example, if you are creating a query to list all patients located in Windsor, and you assign the name "WindsorPatients" to the query, you do not need to include the City field value for each record in the query results—the query design only lists patients with the City field value of "Windsor." Even if you choose not to display a field in the query results, you can still use the field as part of the query to select specific records or to specify a particular sequence for the records in the datasheet.

Tutorial 3 Maintaining and Querying a Database | Access   AC 127

You can also add a field to the design grid using the arrow on the Field box; this arrow appears when you click the right side of an empty Field box.

TIP
You can also use the mouse to drag a field from the field list to a column in the design grid.

3. In the design grid, click the right side of the second column's Field box to display a menu listing all the fields in the Patient table, and then click **LastName**. Access adds this field to the second column in the design grid.

4. Use the method you prefer to add the **FirstName**, **City**, and **Email** fields to the design grid in that order.

   Trouble? If you accidentally add the wrong field to the design grid, you can remove the field from the grid. Select the field's column by clicking the pointer ↓ on the field selector, which is the thin bar above the Field box, for the field you want to delete, and then press the Delete key (or in the Query Setup group on the DESIGN tab, click the Delete Columns button).

   Having selected the five fields for Ethan's query, you can now run the query.

5. In the Results group on the DESIGN tab, click the **Run** button. Access runs the query and displays the results in Datasheet view. See Figure 3-8.

Figure 3-8   Datasheet displayed after running the query

Patient ID	Last Name	First Name	City	Email
22500	Student Last	Student First	Hartford	student1@example.edu
22501	Darcy	Edward	Bloomfield	edarcy@example.org
22502	Mendez	Andreas	Windsor	a.mendez@example.org
22504	Aguilar	Lilian	Hartford	laguilar@example.com
22505	Finnerty	Amber	Hartford	a.finnerty@example.com
22506	Gorski	Drea	Bloomfield	
22507	Weiss	Matthew	Hartford	matt.weiss@example.org

selected fields displayed

The five fields you added to the design grid appear in the datasheet in the same order as they appear in the design grid. The records are displayed in primary key sequence by PatientID. Access selected all 51 records from the Patient table for display in the query datasheet. Ethan asks you to save the query as "PatientEmail" so that he can easily retrieve the same data again.

6. On the Quick Access Toolbar, click the **Save** button 💾. The Save As dialog box opens.

7. In the Query Name box, type **PatientEmail** and then press the **Enter** key. Access saves the query with the specified name in the Chatham database and displays the name on the tab for the query.

PROSKILLS

Decision Making: Comparing Methods for Adding All Fields to the Design Grid

If the query you are creating includes every field from the specified table, you can use one of the following three methods to transfer all the fields from the field list to the design grid:

- Double-click (or click and drag) each field individually from the field list to the design grid. Use this method if you want the fields in your query to appear in an order that is different from the order in the field list.
- Double-click the asterisk at the top of the field list. Access places the table name followed by a period and an asterisk (as in "Patient.*") in the Field box of the first column in the design grid, which signifies that the order of the fields is the same in the query as it is in the field list. Use this method if you don't need to sort the query or specify conditions based on the fields in the table you added in this way (for example, in a query based on more than one table). The advantage of using this method is that you do not need to change the query if you add or delete fields from the underlying table structure. Such changes are reflected automatically in the query.
- Double-click the field list title bar to highlight all the fields, and then click and drag one of the highlighted fields to the first column in the design grid. Access places each field in a separate column and arranges the fields in the order in which they appear in the field list. Use this method when you need to sort your query or include record selection criteria.

By choosing the most appropriate method to add all the table fields to the query design grid, you can work more efficiently and ensure that the query produces the results you want.

When viewing the query results, Ethan noticed that the record for one of the patients contains information that is not up to date. This patient, Nancy Fraser, had informed the clinic that she was recently married and changed her last name; she also provided a new email address. So Ethan asks you to update the record with the new last name and email address for this patient.

Updating Data Using a Query

A query datasheet is temporary and its contents are based on the criteria in the query design grid; however, you can still update the data in a table using a query datasheet. In this case, Ethan has changes he wants you to make to a record in the Patient table. Instead of making the changes in the table datasheet, you can make them in the PatientEmail query datasheet because the query is based on the Patient table. The underlying Patient table will be updated with the changes you make.

To update data using the PatientEmail query datasheet:

1. Locate the record with PatientID 22523, Nancy Fraser (record 21 in the query datasheet).
2. In the Last Name column for this record, double-click **Fraser** to select the name, and then type **Bennett**.
3. Press the **Tab** key three times to move to the Email column, type **n.bennett@example.com** and then press the **Tab** key.
4. Close the PatientEmail query, and then open the Navigation Pane. Note that the PatientEmail query is listed in the Queries section of the Navigation Pane.

Tutorial 3 Maintaining and Querying a Database | Access   AC 129

Now you'll check the Patient table to verify that the changes you made in the query datasheet are reflected in the Patient table.

5. Open the **Patient** table in Datasheet view, and then close the Navigation Pane.
6. Locate the record for PatientID 22523 (record 21). Notice that the changes you made in the query datasheet to the Last Name and Email field values were made to the record in the Patient table.
7. Close the Patient table.

INSIGHT

Query Datasheet vs. Table Datasheet

Although a query datasheet looks just like a table datasheet and appears in Datasheet view, the contents of a query datasheet are temporary and are based on the criteria you establish in the design grid. Whenever you run a query, the results displayed reflect the current data in the underlying table. In contrast, a table datasheet shows the permanent data in a table. However, you can update data while viewing a query datasheet, just as you can when working in a table datasheet or form.

Kelly also wants to view specific information in the Chatham database. She would like to review the visit data for patients while also viewing certain contact information for them. So, she needs to see data from both the Patient table and the Visit table at the same time.

Creating a Multitable Query

A multitable query is a query based on more than one table. If you want to create a query that retrieves data from multiple tables, the tables must have a common field. In Tutorial 2, you established a relationship between the Patient (primary) and Visit (related) tables based on the common PatientID field that exists in both tables, so you can now create a query to display data from both tables at the same time. Specifically, Kelly wants to view the values in the City, FirstName, and LastName fields from the Patient table and the VisitDate and Reason fields from the Visit table.

To create the query using the Patient and Visit tables:

1. On the ribbon, click the **CREATE** tab.
2. In the Queries group, click the **Query Design** button. Access opens the Show Table dialog box. You need to add the Patient and Visit tables to the Query window.
3. Click **Patient** in the Tables list, click the **Add** button, click **Visit**, click the **Add** button, and then click the **Close** button. The Patient and Visit field lists appear in the Query window, and the Show Table dialog box closes.
4. Use the ↕ pointer to resize the Patient and Visit field lists so that all the fields in each list are displayed and the vertical scroll bars disappear.

   The one-to-many relationship between the two tables is shown in the Query window in the same way that Access indicates a relationship between two tables in the Relationships window. Note that the join line is thick at both ends; this signifies that you selected the option to enforce referential integrity. If you had not selected this option, the join line would be thin at both ends and neither the "1" nor the infinity symbol would appear, even though the tables have a one-to-many relationship.

You need to place the City, FirstName, and LastName fields (in that order) from the Patient field list into the design grid, and then place the VisitDate and Reason fields from the Visit field list into the design grid. This is the order in which Kelly wants to view the fields in the query results.

▶ 5. In the Patient field list, double-click **City** to place this field in the design grid's first column Field box.

▶ 6. Repeat Step 5 to add the **FirstName** and **LastName** fields from the Patient table to the second and third columns of the design grid.

▶ 7. Repeat Step 5 to add the **VisitDate** and **Reason** fields (in that order) from the Visit table to the fourth and fifth columns of the design grid. The query specifications are complete, so you can now run the query.

▶ 8. In the Results group on the DESIGN tab, click the **Run** button. Access runs the query and displays the results in Datasheet view. See Figure 3-9.

Figure 3-9 — Datasheet for query based on the Patient and Visit tables

fields from the Patient table *fields from the Visit table*

City	First Name	Last Name	Date of Visit	Reason/Diagnosis
Hartford	Student First	Student Last	11/17/2015	Migraine
Bloomfield	Edward	Darcy	11/30/2015	Influenza
Windsor	Andreas	Mendez	3/30/2016	Annual wellness visit
Hartford	Lilian	Aguilar	11/18/2015	Annual wellness visit
Hartford	Amber	Finnerty	1/26/2016	Annual wellness visit
Bloomfield	Drea	Gorski	4/1/2016	Fifth Disease
Bloomfield	Drea	Gorski	4/8/2016	Fifth Disease follow-up
Hartford	Matthew	Weiss	11/9/2015	Diabetes mellitus Type 2 - initial diagnosis
Hartford	Matthew	Weiss	2/9/2016	Diabetes mellitus Type 2 - serum glucose check
Hartford	Matthew	Weiss	4/7/2016	Diabetes mellitus Type 2 - serum glucose check
Hartford	Steve	Kervin	4/4/2016	Tinea pedis
Hartford	Steve	Kervin	4/18/2016	Tinea pedis follow-up
Hartford	Thomas	Booker	11/10/2015	Seborrheic dermatitis
Hartford	Thomas	Booker	3/1/2016	Seborrheic dermatitis follow-up
West Hartford	Daniel	Castro	12/3/2015	Annual wellness visit
West Hartford	Daniel	Castro	1/13/2016	Cardiac monitoring
Hartford	Lisa	Chang	1/5/2016	Annual wellness visit
Bloomfield	Troy	Smith	1/13/2016	Broken leg
Bloomfield	Troy	Smith	2/24/2016	Follow-up - cast removal
Hartford	Ian	Parker	12/15/2015	Influenza
Hartford	Ian	Parker	1/14/2016	Hypertension monitoring
Hartford	Susan	King	12/22/2015	COPD management visit
West Hartford	Henry	O'Brien	2/1/2016	Annual wellness visit
West Hartford	Henry	O'Brien	4/11/2016	Idiopathic abdominal pain
Hartford	Sera	Torres	4/1/2016	Conjunctivitis

Only the five selected fields from the Patient and Visit tables appear in the datasheet. The records are displayed in order according to the values in the PatientID field because it is the primary key field in the primary table, even though this field is not included in the query datasheet.

Tutorial 3 Maintaining and Querying a Database | Access   AC 131

> Kelly plans on frequently tracking the data retrieved by the query, so she asks you to save it as "PatientVisits."
>
> ▶ 9. On the Quick Access Toolbar, click the **Save** button 💾. The Save As dialog box opens.
>
> ▶ 10. In the Query Name box, type **PatientVisits** and then press the **Enter** key. Access saves the query and displays its name on the object tab.

Kelly decides she wants the records displayed in alphabetical order by city. Because the query displays data in order by the field values in the PatientID field, which is the primary key for the Patient table, you need to sort the records by the City field to display the data in the order Kelly wants.

Sorting Data in a Query

Sorting is the process of rearranging records in a specified order or sequence. Sometimes you might need to sort data before displaying or printing it to meet a specific request. For example, Kelly might want to review visit information arranged by the VisitDate field because she needs to know which months are the busiest for Chatham Community Health Services in terms of patient visits. Cindi might want to view billing information arranged by the InvoiceAmt field because she monitors the finances of the clinic.

When you sort data in a query, you do not change the sequence of the records in the underlying tables. Only the records in the query datasheet are rearranged according to your specifications.

To sort records, you must select the **sort field**, which is the field used to determine the order of records in the datasheet. In this case, Kelly wants the data sorted alphabetically by city, so you need to specify City as the sort field. Sort fields can be Short Text, Number, Date/Time, Currency, AutoNumber, or Yes/No fields, but not Long Text, Hyperlink, or Attachment fields. You sort records in either ascending (increasing) or descending (decreasing) order. Figure 3-10 shows the results of each type of sort for these data types.

| Figure 3-10 | Sorting results for different data types |

Data Type	Ascending Sort Results	Descending Sort Results
Short Text	A to Z (alphabetical)	Z to A (reverse alphabetical)
Number	lowest to highest numeric value	highest to lowest numeric value
Date/Time	oldest to most recent date	most recent to oldest date
Currency	lowest to highest numeric value	highest to lowest numeric value
AutoNumber	lowest to highest numeric value	highest to lowest numeric value
Yes/No	yes (checkmark in check box) then no values	no then yes values

© 2014 Cengage Learning

Access provides several methods for sorting data in a table or query datasheet and in a form. One of the easiest ways is to use the AutoFilter feature for a field.

Using an AutoFilter to Sort Data

TIP
You can also use the Ascending and Descending buttons in the Sort & Filter group on the HOME tab to quickly sort records based on the currently selected field in a datasheet.

As you've probably noticed when working in Datasheet view for a table or query, each column heading has an arrow to the right of the field name. This arrow gives you access to the **AutoFilter** feature, which enables you to quickly sort and display field values in various ways. When you click this arrow, a menu opens with options for sorting and displaying field values. The first two options on the menu enable you to sort the values in the current field in ascending or descending order. Unless you save the datasheet or form after you've sorted the records, the rearrangement of records is temporary.

Next, you'll use an AutoFilter to sort the PatientVisits query results by the City field.

To sort the records using an AutoFilter:

1. Click the **arrow** on the City column heading to display the AutoFilter menu. See Figure 3-11.

Figure 3-11   Using AutoFilter to sort records in the datasheet

- sort buttons on the ribbon
- choose to specify an ascending sort order
- City field will be sorted
- menu displayed with AutoFilter options

Kelly wants the data sorted in ascending (alphabetical) order by the values in the City field, so you need to select the first option in the menu.

2. Click **Sort A to Z**. The records are rearranged in ascending alphabetical order by city. A small, upward-pointing arrow appears on the right side of the City column heading. This arrow indicates that the values in the field have been sorted in ascending order. If you used the same method to sort the field values in descending order, a small downward-pointing arrow would appear there instead.

After viewing the query results, Kelly decides that she would also like to see the records arranged by the values in the VisitDate field, so that the data is presented in chronological order. She still wants the records to be arranged by the City field values as well. To produce the results Kelly wants, you need to sort using two fields.

Sorting on Multiple Fields in Design View

Sort fields can be unique or nonunique. A sort field is **unique** if the value in the sort field for each record is different. The PatientID field in the Patient table is an example of a unique sort field because each patient record has a different value in this primary key field. A sort field is **nonunique** if more than one record can have the same value for the sort field. For example, the City field in the Patient table is a nonunique sort field because more than one record can have the same City value.

When the sort field is nonunique, records with the same sort field value are grouped together, but they are not sorted in a specific order within the group. To arrange these grouped records in a specific order, you can specify a **secondary sort field**, which is a second field that determines the order of records that are already sorted by the **primary sort field** (the first sort field specified).

Access lets you select up to 10 different sort fields. When you use the buttons on the ribbon to sort by more than one field, the sort fields must be in adjacent columns in the datasheet. (Note that you cannot use an AutoFilter to sort on more than one field. This method works for a single field only.) You can specify only one type of sort—either ascending or descending—for the selected columns in the datasheet. You highlight the adjacent columns, and Access sorts first by the first column and then by each remaining highlighted column in order from left to right.

Kelly wants the records sorted first by the City field values, as they currently are, and then by the VisitDate values. The two fields are in the correct left-to-right order in the query datasheet, but they are not adjacent, so you cannot use the Ascending and Descending buttons on the ribbon to sort them. You could move the City field to the left of the VisitDate field in the query datasheet, but both columns would have to be sorted with the same sort order. This is not what Kelly wants—she wants the City field values sorted in ascending order so that they are in the correct alphabetical order, for ease of reference; and she wants the VisitDate field values to be sorted in descending order, so that she can focus on the most recent patient visits first. To sort the City and VisitDate fields with different sort orders, you must specify the sort fields in Design view.

In the Query window in Design view, Access first uses the sort field that is leftmost in the design grid. Therefore, you must arrange the fields you want to sort from left to right in the design grid, with the primary sort field being the leftmost. In Design view, multiple sort fields do not have to be adjacent to each other, as they do in Datasheet view; however, they must be in the correct left-to-right order.

> **TIP**
> The primary sort field is *not* the same as a table's primary key. A table has at most one primary key, which must be unique, whereas any field in a table can serve as a primary sort field.

REFERENCE

Sorting a Query Datasheet

- In the query datasheet, click the arrow on the column heading for the field you want to sort.
- In the menu that opens, click Sort A to Z for an ascending sort, or click Sort Z to A for a descending sort.

or

- In the query datasheet, select the column or adjacent columns on which you want to sort.
- In the Sort & Filter group on the HOME tab, click the Ascending button or the Descending button.

or

- In Design view, position the fields serving as sort fields from left to right.
- Click the right side of the Sort box for each field you want to sort, and then click Ascending or Descending for the sort order.

Access | Tutorial 3 Maintaining and Querying a Database

To achieve the results Kelly wants, you need to modify the query in Design view to specify the sort order for the two fields.

To select the two sort fields in Design view:

1. In the Views group on the HOME tab, click the **View** button to open the query in Design view. The fields are currently in the correct left-to-right order in the design grid, so you only need to specify the sort order for the two fields.

   First, you need to specify an ascending sort order for the City field. Even though the records are already sorted by the values in this field, you need to modify the query so that this sort order, and the sort order you will specify for the VisitDate field, are part of the query's design. Any time the query is run, the records will be sorted according to these specifications.

2. Click the right side of the **City Sort** box to display the arrow and the sort options, and then click **Ascending**. You've selected an ascending sort order for the City field, which will be the primary sort field. The City field is a Short Text field, and an ascending sort order will display the field values in alphabetical order.

3. Click the right side of the **VisitDate Sort** box, click **Descending**, and then click in one of the empty text boxes below the VisitDate field to deselect the setting. You've selected a descending sort order for the VisitDate field, which will be the secondary sort field because it appears to the right of the primary sort field (City) in the design grid. The VisitDate field is a Date/Time field, and a descending sort order will display the field values with the most recent dates first. See Figure 3-12.

> **TIP**
> In Design view, the sort fields do not have to be adjacent, and fields that are not sorted can appear between the sort fields.

Figure 3-12   Selecting two sort fields in Design view

Tutorial 3 Maintaining and Querying a Database | Access   AC 135

You have finished your query changes, so now you can run the query and then save the modified query with the same name.

4. In the Results group on the DESIGN tab, click the **Run** button. Access runs the query and displays the query datasheet. The records appear in ascending order based on the values in the City field. Within groups of records with the same City field value, the records appear in descending order by the values of the VisitDate field. See Figure 3-13.

Figure 3-13   Datasheet sorted on two fields

primary sort field   *secondary sort field*

City	First Name	Last Name	Date of Visit	Reason/Diagnosis
Bloomfield	Cathy	Engber	4/13/2016	Varicella
Bloomfield	Isobel	Kirk	4/8/2016	Hypertension monitoring
Bloomfield	Drea	Gorski	4/8/2016	Fifth Disease follow-up
Bloomfield	Pam	Fielder	4/6/2016	Pertussis
Bloomfield	Drea	Gorski	4/1/2016	Fifth Disease
Bloomfield	Isobel	Kirk	3/9/2016	Hypertension monitoring
Bloomfield	Siyang	Li	3/3/2016	Allergies - environmental follow-up
Bloomfield	Isobel	Kirk	2/25/2016	Hypertension monitoring
Bloomfield	Troy	Smith	2/24/2016	Follow-up - cast removal
Bloomfield	Isobel	Kirk	2/11/2016	Hypertension
Bloomfield	Troy	Smith	1/13/2016	Broken leg
Bloomfield	Pam	Fielder	12/1/2015	Influenza
Bloomfield	Edward	Darcy	11/30/2015	Influenza
Bloomfield	Siyang	Li	11/9/2015	Allergies - environmental
Hartford	Steve	Kervin	4/18/2016	Tinea pedis follow-up
Hartford	Michael	Caputo	4/15/2016	Removal of sutures from left eyelid
Hartford	Jane	Ropiak	4/14/2016	COPD management visit
Hartford	Susan	Hawes	4/12/2016	Joint pain/arthritis
Hartford	Michael	Caputo	4/8/2016	Laceration of left eyelid -sutured
Hartford	Sera	Torres	4/8/2016	Conjunctivitis follow-up
Hartford	Matthew	Weiss	4/7/2016	Diabetes mellitus Type 2 - serum glucose check
Hartford	Steve	Kervin	4/4/2016	Tinea pedis
Hartford	Sera	Torres	4/1/2016	Conjunctivitis
Hartford	Jessica	Wallner	3/28/2016	UTI follow-up
Hartford	Jerome	Taylor	3/23/2016	Onychocryptosis follow-up

records grouped by City are shown in descending order by VisitDate

When you save the query, all of your design changes—including the selection of the sort fields—are saved with the query. The next time Kelly runs the query, the records will appear sorted by the primary and secondary sort fields.

5. On the Quick Access Toolbar, click the **Save** button to save the revised PatientVisits query.

Kelly knows that Chatham Community Health Services has seen an increase in the number of patients from Windsor. She would like to focus briefly on the information for patients in that city only. Also, she is interested in knowing how many patients from Windsor have had annual wellness exams. She is concerned that, although more patients are coming to the clinic from this city, not enough of them are scheduling wellness visits. Selecting only the records with a City field value of "Windsor" and a Reason field value beginning with "Annual" is a temporary change that Kelly wants in the datasheet, so you do not need to switch to Design view and change the query. Instead, you can apply a filter.

Filtering Data

A **filter** is a set of restrictions you place on the records in an open datasheet or form to *temporarily* isolate a subset of the records. A filter lets you view different subsets of displayed records so that you can focus on only the data you need. Unless you save a query or form with a filter applied, an applied filter is not available the next time you run the query or open the form.

The simplest technique for filtering records is Filter By Selection. **Filter By Selection** lets you select all or part of a field value in a datasheet or form, and then display only those records that contain the selected value in the field. You can also use the AutoFilter feature to filter records. When you click the arrow on a column heading, the menu that opens provides options for filtering the datasheet based on a field value or the selected part of a field value. Another technique for filtering records is to use **Filter By Form**, which changes your datasheet to display blank fields. Then you can select a value using the arrow that appears when you click any blank field to apply a filter that selects only those records containing that value.

REFERENCE

Using Filter By Selection

- In the datasheet or form, select the part of the field value that will be the basis for the filter; or, if the filter will be based on the entire field value, click anywhere within the field value.
- Make sure the HOME tab is displayed.
- In the Sort & Filter group, click the Selection button.
- Click the type of filter you want to apply.

For Kelly's request, you need to select a City field value of Windsor, and then use Filter By Selection to display only those records with this value. Then you will filter the records further by selecting only those records with a Reason value that begins with "Annual" (for Annual wellness visit).

To display the records using Filter By Selection:

1. In the query datasheet, locate the first occurrence of a City field containing the value **Windsor**, and then click anywhere within that field value.

2. In the Sort & Filter group on the HOME tab, click the **Selection** button. A menu opens with options for the type of filter to apply. See Figure 3-14.

Tutorial 3 Maintaining and Querying a Database | Access   AC 137

Figure 3-14 Using Filter By Selection

options for the type of filter to apply →

Selection menu options:
- Equals "Windsor"
- Does Not Equal "Windsor"
- Contains "Windsor"
- Does Not Contain "Windsor"

current field is the basis for the filter →

PatientVisits

City	First Name	Last Name	Date of Visit	Reason/Diagnosis
Hartford	Julia	Ingram	11/12/2015	Transverse fracture of left ulna
Hartford	Thomas	Booker	11/10/2015	Seborrheic dermatitis
Hartford	Matthew	Weiss	11/9/2015	Diabetes mellitus Type 2 - initial diagnosis
West Hartford	Henry	O'Brien	4/11/2016	Idiopathic abdominal pain
West Hartford	Magdalena	Cruz	3/18/2016	Migrane headache follow-up
West Hartford	Magdalena	Cruz	2/18/2016	Migrane headache
West Hartford	Anna	Diaz	2/2/2016	Brachial neuritis
West Hartford	Henry	O'Brien	2/1/2016	Annual wellness visit
West Hartford	Daniel	Castro	1/13/2016	Cardiac monitoring
West Hartford	Daniel	Shaw	1/11/2016	Nasopharyngitis
West Hartford	Malcolm	Belanger	1/8/2016	Hypertension monitoring
West Hartford	Daniel	Castro	12/3/2015	Annual wellness visit
West Hartford	Malcolm	Belanger	11/30/2015	Hypertension
Windsor	Chaney	Franklin	4/15/2016	Elevated blood lipids-monitoring meds
Windsor	Maria	Rodriguez	4/6/2016	Wound care for patellar abrasion
Windsor	Maria	Rodriguez	4/1/2016	Severe abrasion of left patella

The menu provides options for displaying only those records with a City field value that equals the selected value (in this case, Windsor); does not equal the value; contains the value somewhere within the field; or does not contain the value somewhere within the field. You want to display all the records whose City field value equals Windsor.

3. In the Selection menu, click **Equals "Windsor"**. Access displays the filtered results. Only the 24 records that have a City field value of Windsor appear in the datasheet. See Figure 3-15.

Figure 3-15 Datasheet after applying the filter

PatientVisits

City	First Name	Last Name	Date of Visit	Reason/Diagnosis
Windsor	Chaney	Franklin	4/15/2016	Elevated blood lipids-monitoring meds
Windsor	Maria	Rodriguez	4/6/2016	Wound care for patellar abrasion
Windsor	Maria	Rodriguez	4/1/2016	Severe abrasion of left patella
Windsor	Andreas	Mendez	3/30/2016	Annual wellness visit
Windsor	Chaney	Franklin	3/23/2016	Elevated blood lipids-monitoring meds
Windsor	Patrice	Lewis	3/21/2016	Eczema erythematosum follow-up
Windsor	Alex	Delgado	3/18/2016	Hypertension monitoring
Windsor	Christina	Rowe	3/11/2016	Annual wellness visit
Windsor	Patrice	Lewis	3/7/2016	Eczema erythematosum
Windsor	Chaney	Franklin	2/24/2016	Elevated blood lipids-monitoring meds
Windsor	Davis	Hallick	2/22/2016	Follow-up - gastric reflux
Windsor	Robert	Goldberg	2/9/2016	Sinusitis
Windsor	Davis	Hallick	2/8/2016	Gastric reflux
Windsor	Alex	Delgado	2/8/2016	Hypertension monitoring
Windsor	Christina	Rowe	1/28/2016	Nasopharyngitis
Windsor	Max	Sutherland	1/26/2016	Acute viral rhinopharyngitis
Windsor	Nancy	Bennett	1/25/2016	Nasopharyngitis
Windsor	Alex	Delgado	1/25/2016	Hypertension
Windsor	Patrice	Lewis	1/22/2016	Acute sinusitis follow-up
Windsor	Ashley	Garrett	1/15/2016	Annual wellness visit
Windsor	Patrice	Lewis	1/13/2016	Acute sinusitis
Windsor	Davis	Hallick	12/7/2015	Annual wellness visit
Windsor	Patrice	Lewis	11/25/2015	Influenza
Windsor	Amrita	Mehta	11/24/2015	Influenza

click to display more options for filtering the field

indicate that a filter has been applied to the datasheet

datasheet displays only records with a City value of Windsor

The button labeled "Filtered" to the right of the navigation buttons and the notation "FILTERED" on the status bar both indicate that a filter has been applied to the datasheet. Also, notice that the Toggle Filter button in the Sort & Filter group on the HOME tab is active; you can click this button or the Filtered button next to the navigation buttons to toggle between the filtered and unfiltered displays of the query datasheet. The City column heading also has a filter icon on it; you can click this icon to display additional options for filtering the field.

Next, Kelly wants to view only those records with a Reason field value beginning with the word "Annual" so she can view the records for annual wellness visits. You need to apply an additional filter to the datasheet.

4. In any Reason field value beginning with the word "Annual," select only the word **Annual**.

5. In the Sort & Filter group, click the **Selection** button. The same four filter types are available for this selection as when you filtered the City field.

6. On the Selection menu, click **Begins With "Annual"**. The second filter is applied to the query datasheet, which now shows only the four records for customers located in Windsor who have had annual wellness visits at the clinic.

Now you can redisplay all the query records by clicking the Toggle Filter button, which you use to switch between the filtered and unfiltered displays.

7. In the Sort & Filter group, click the **Toggle Filter** button. Access removes the filter and redisplays all 85 records in the query datasheet.

8. Close the PatientVisits query. Access asks if you want to save your changes to the design of the query—in this case, the filtered display, which is still available through the Toggle Filter button. Kelly does not want the query saved with the filter because she doesn't need to view the filtered information on a regular basis.

9. Click the **No** button to close the query without saving the changes.

10. If you are not continuing to Session 3.2, click the **FILE** tab, and then click **Close** in the navigation bar to close the Chatham database.

> **TIP**
> The ScreenTip for this button is Remove Filter.

Session 3.1 Quick Check

REVIEW

1. In Datasheet view, what is the difference between navigation mode and editing mode?
2. What command can you use in Datasheet view to remove the display of one or more fields from the datasheet?
3. What is a select query?
4. Describe the field list and the design grid in the Query window in Design view.
5. How are a table datasheet and a query datasheet similar? How are they different?
6. For a Date/Time field, how do the records appear when sorted in ascending order?
7. When you define multiple sort fields in Design view, describe how the sort fields must be positioned in the design grid.
8. A(n) _____ is a set of restrictions you place on the records in an open datasheet or form to isolate a subset of records temporarily.

Session 3.2 Visual Overview:

When creating queries in Design view, you can enter criteria so that Access will display only selected records in the query results.

Field:	PatientID	LastName	FirstName	BirthDate	City
Table:	Patient	Patient	Patient	Patient	Patient
Sort:					
Show:	✓	✓	✓	✓	✓
Criteria:					"Bloomfield"
or:					

To define a condition for a field, you place the condition in the field's Criteria box in the design grid.

To tell Access which records you want to select, you must specify a condition as part of the query. A **condition** is a criterion, or rule, that determines which records are selected.

Field:	InvoiceNum	InvoiceDate	InvoiceAmt	
Table:	Billing	Billing	Billing	
Sort:				
Show:	✓	✓	✓	☐
Criteria:			>250	
or:				

A condition usually consists of an operator, often a comparison operator, and a value. A **comparison operator** asks Access to compare the value in a field to the condition value and to select all the records for which the condition is true.

Field:	VisitID	PatientID	VisitDate	Reason
Table:	Visit	Visit	Visit	Visit
Sort:				
Show:	✓	✓	✓	✓
Criteria:			Between #12/1/2015# And #12/31/2015#	
or:				

Most comparison operators (such as Between...And...) ask Access to select records that match a range of values for the condition—in this case, all records with dates that fall within the range shown.

Selection Criteria in Queries

The results of a query containing selection criteria include only the records that meet the specified criteria.

BloomfieldPatients

Patient ID	Last Name	First Name	Date of Birth	City
22501	Darcy	Edward	7/15/1986	Bloomfield
22506	Gorski	Drea	2/19/2005	Bloomfield
22513	Smith	Troy	1/31/1956	Bloomfield
22521	Engber	Cathy	4/7/2006	Bloomfield
22522	Li	Siyang	7/25/1986	Bloomfield
22549	Fielder	Pam	12/6/1978	Bloomfield
22557	Kirk	Isobel	11/18/1965	Bloomfield

The results of this query show only patients from Bloomfield because the condition "Bloomfield" in the City field's Criteria box specifies that Access should select records only with City field values of Bloomfield. This type of condition is called an *exact match* because the value in the specified field must match the condition exactly in order for the record to be included in the query results.

LargeInvoiceAmts

Invoice Num	Invoice Date	Invoice Amt
35815	11/16/2015	$300.00
35900	01/20/2016	$300.00
36002	03/15/2016	$450.00
36074	04/12/2016	$450.00
		$0.00

The results of this query show only those invoices with amounts greater than $250 because the condition >250, which uses the greater than comparison operator, specifies that Access should select records only with InvoiceAmt field values over $250.

DecemberVisits

Visit ID	Patient ID	Date of Visit	Reason/Diagnosis
1550	22549	12/1/2015	Influenza
1552	22511	12/3/2015	Annual wellness visit
1555	22520	12/7/2015	Annual wellness visit
1557	22526	12/10/2015	Annual wellness visit
1560	22514	12/15/2015	Influenza
1562	22516	12/22/2015	COPD management visit

The results of this query show only those patient visits that took place in December 2015 because the condition in the VisitDate's Criteria box specifies that Access should select records only with a visit date between 12/1/2015 and 12/31/2015.

Defining Record Selection Criteria for Queries

Cindi wants to display patient and visit information for all patients who live in Bloomfield. She is considering having the clinic hold a health fair in Bloomfield, with a special emphasis on hypertension, so she is interested in knowing more about the patients from this city. For this request, you could create a query to select the correct fields and all records in the Patient and Visit tables, select a City field value of Bloomfield in the query datasheet, and then click the Selection button and choose the appropriate filter option to display the information for only those patients in Bloomfield. However, a faster way of displaying the data Cindi needs is to create a query that displays the selected fields and only those records in the Patient and Visit tables that satisfy a condition.

Just as you can display selected fields from a database in a query datasheet, you can display selected records. To tell Access which records you want to select, you must specify a condition as part of the query, as illustrated in the Session 3.2 Visual Overview. A condition usually includes one of the comparison operators shown in Figure 3-16.

Figure 3-16   **Access comparison operators**

Operator	Meaning	Example
=	equal to (optional; default operator)	="Hall"
<>	not equal to	<>"Hall"
<	less than	<#1/1/99#
<=	less than or equal to	<=100
>	greater than	>"C400"
>=	greater than or equal to	>=18.75
Between … And …	between two values (inclusive)	Between 50 And 325
In ()	in a list of values	In ("Hall", "Seeger")
Like	matches a pattern that includes wildcards	Like "706*"

© 2014 Cengage Learning

Specifying an Exact Match

For Cindi's request, you need to create a query that will display only those records in the Patient table with the value Bloomfield in the City field. This type of condition is an exact match because the value in the specified field must match the condition exactly in order for the record to be included in the query results. You'll create the query in Design view.

To create the query in Design view:

1. If you took a break after the previous session, make sure that the Chatham database is open and the Navigation Pane is closed.
2. On the ribbon, click the **CREATE** tab.
3. In the Queries group, click the **Query Design** button. The Show Table dialog box opens. You need to add the Patient and Visit tables to the Query window.
4. Click **Patient** in the Tables list, click the **Add** button, click **Visit**, click the **Add** button, and then click the **Close** button.

Tutorial 3 Maintaining and Querying a Database | Access AC 143

5. Use the ↕ pointer to resize both field lists so that all the fields are displayed and the vertical scroll bars disappear.

6. Add the following fields from the Patient table to the design grid in the order shown: **LastName**, **FirstName**, **Phone**, **Address**, **City**, and **Email**.

   Cindi also wants information from the Visit table included in the query results.

7. Add the following fields from the Visit table to the design grid in the order shown: **VisitID**, **VisitDate**, and **Reason**. See Figure 3-17.

Figure 3-17   Design grid after adding fields from both tables

Field:	LastName	FirstName	Phone	Address	City	Email	VisitID	VisitDate	Reason
Table:	Patient	Patient	Patient	Patient	Patient	Patient	Visit	Visit	Visit
Sort:									
Show:	✓	✓	✓	✓	✓	✓	✓	✓	✓
Criteria:									
or:									

enter condition here

The field lists for the Patient and Visit tables appear in the top portion of the window, and the join line indicating a one-to-many relationship connects the two tables. The fields you selected appear in the design grid.

To display the information Cindi wants, you need to enter the condition for the City field in its Criteria box (see Figure 3-17). Cindi wants to display only those records with a City field value of Bloomfield.

To enter the exact match condition, and then save and run the query:

1. Click the **City Criteria** box, type **Bloomfield**, and then press the **Enter** key. The condition changes to "Bloomfield".

   Access automatically enclosed the condition you typed in quotation marks. You must enclose text values in quotation marks when using them as selection criteria. If you omit the quotation marks, however, Access will include them automatically in most cases. Some words—including "in" and "select"—are special keywords in Access that are reserved for functions and commands. If you want to enter one of these keywords as the condition, you must type the quotation marks around the text or Access will display an error message and will not allow the condition to be entered.

2. On the Quick Access Toolbar, click the **Save** button 💾 to open the Save As dialog box.

3. In the Query Name box, type **BloomfieldPatients** and then press the **Enter** key. Access saves the query with the specified name and displays the name on the object tab.

4. In the Results group on the DESIGN tab, click the **Run** button. Access runs the query and displays the selected field values for only those records with a City field value of Bloomfield. A total of 14 records is selected and displayed in the datasheet. See Figure 3-18.

Figure 3-18 Datasheet displaying selected fields and records

(Datasheet screenshot showing BloomfieldPatients query results with columns: Last Name, First Name, Phone, Address, City, Email, Visit ID, Date of Visit, Reason/Diagnosis. 14 records are selected; only records with a City field value of Bloomfield are selected.)

Cindi realizes that it's not necessary to include the City field values in the query results. The name of the query, BloomfieldPatients, indicates that the query design includes all patients who live in Bloomfield, so the City field values are unnecessary and repetitive. Also, she decides that she would prefer the query datasheet to show the fields from the Visit table first, followed by the Patient table fields. You need to modify the query to produce the results Cindi wants.

Modifying a Query

After you create a query and view the results, you might need to make changes to the query if the results are not what you expected or require. First, Cindi asks you to modify the BloomfieldPatients query so that it does not display the City field values in the query results.

To remove the display of the City field values:

1. In the Views group on the HOME tab, click the **View** button. The BloomfieldPatients query opens in Design view.

   You need to keep the City field as part of the query design because it contains the defined condition for the query. You only need to remove the display of the field's values from the query results.

2. Click the **City Show** check box to remove the checkmark. The query will still find only those records with the value Bloomfield in the City field, but the query results will not display these field values.

Next, you need to change the order of the fields in the query so that the visit information is listed first.

To move the Visit table fields to precede the Patient table fields:

1. Position the pointer on the VisitID field selector until the pointer changes to a ⬇ shape, and then click to select the field. See Figure 3-19.

Figure 3-19   Selected VisitID field

Show check box is cleared

VisitID field selector

entire column is selected

2. Position the pointer on the VisitID field selector, and then click and hold down the mouse button; notice that the pointer changes to ▹ and a black vertical line appears to the left of the selected field. This line represents the selected field when you drag the mouse to move it.

3. Drag to the left until the vertical line representing the selected field is positioned to the left of the LastName field. See Figure 3-20.

Figure 3-20   Dragging the field in the design grid

line representing selected field

drag pointer to here

selected field being moved

TIP
Instead of moving a field by dragging, you can also delete the field and then add it back to the design grid in the location you want.

4. Release the mouse button. The VisitID field moves to the left of the LastName field.

   You can also select and move multiple fields at once. You need to select and move the VisitDate and Reason fields so that they follow the VisitID field in the query design. To select multiple fields, you click and drag the mouse over the field selectors for the fields you want.

5. Click and hold the pointer ⬇ on the VisitDate field selector, drag the pointer to the right to select the Reason field, and then release the mouse button. Both fields are now selected. See Figure 3-21.

Figure 3-21   **Multiple fields selected to be moved**

Field:	VisitID	LastName	FirstName	Phone	Address	City	Email	VisitDate	Reason		
Table:	Visit	Patient	Patient	Patient	Patient	Patient	Patient	Visit	Visit		
Sort:											
Show:	☑	☑	☑	☑	☑	☐	☑	☑	☑	☐	☐
Criteria:						"Bloomfield"					
or:											

6. Position the pointer anywhere near the top of the two selected fields, and then click and drag to the left until the vertical line representing the selected fields is positioned to the left of the LastName field.

7. Release the mouse button. The three fields from the Visit table are now the first three fields in the query design.

   You have finished making the modifications to the query Cindi requested, so you can now run the query.

8. In the Results group on the DESIGN tab, click the **Run** button. Access displays the results of the modified query. See Figure 3-22.

Figure 3-22   **Results of the modified query**

Visit ID	Date of Visit	Reason/Diagnosis	Last Name	First Name	Phone	Address	Email
1549	11/30/2015	Influenza	Darcy	Edward	860-305-3985	723 Oxford Ave	edarcy@example.org
1667	4/1/2016	Fifth Disease	Gorski	Drea	860-305-8394	83 Everett Ln	
1683	4/8/2016	Fifth Disease follow-up	Gorski	Drea	860-305-8394	83 Everett Ln	
1575	1/13/2016	Broken leg	Smith	Troy	860-305-0384	16 Ravine Rd	t_smith@example.edu
1626	2/24/2016	Follow-up - cast removal	Smith	Troy	860-305-0384	16 Ravine Rd	t_smith@example.edu
1690	4/13/2016	Varicella	Engber	Cathy	860-305-3048	58 Deering Pl	
1527	11/9/2015	Allergies - environmental	Li	Siyang	860-305-6548	225 Krauss Rd	li.siyang@example.org
1634	3/3/2016	Allergies - environmental follow-up	Li	Siyang	860-305-6548	225 Krauss Rd	li.siyang@example.org
1550	12/1/2015	Influenza	Fielder	Pam	860-305-2689	39 Unger Ave	pfielder@example.org
1673	4/6/2016	Pertussis	Fielder	Pam	860-305-2689	39 Unger Ave	pfielder@example.org
1613	2/11/2016	Hypertension	Kirk	Isobel	860-305-7384	48 Grafton St	
1628	2/25/2016	Hypertension monitoring	Kirk	Isobel	860-305-7384	48 Grafton St	
1640	3/9/2016	Hypertension monitoring	Kirk	Isobel	860-305-7384	48 Grafton St	
1679	4/8/2016	Hypertension monitoring	Kirk	Isobel	860-305-7384	48 Grafton St	

fields from the Visit table are now listed first in the query datasheet

City field values are no longer displayed

Note that the City field values are no longer displayed in the query results.

9. Save and close the BloomfieldPatients query.

After viewing the query results, Cindi decides that she would like to see the same fields, but only for those records with a VisitDate field value before 1/1/2016. She is interested to know which patients of Chatham Community Health Services in all cities have not been to the clinic recently, so that her staff can follow up with these patients by sending them reminder notes or emails. To create the query that will produce the results Cindi wants, you need to use a comparison operator to match a range of values—in this case, any VisitDate value less than 1/1/2016.

Tutorial 3 Maintaining and Querying a Database | Access   AC 147

Using a Comparison Operator to Match a Range of Values

After you create and save a query, you can double-click the query name in the Navigation Pane to run the query again. You can then click the View button to change its design. You can also use an existing query as the basis for creating another query. Because the design of the query you need to create next is similar to the BloomfieldPatients query, you will copy, paste, and rename this query to create the new query. Using this approach keeps the BloomfieldPatients query intact.

To create the new query by copying the BloomfieldPatients query:

1. Open the Navigation Pane. Note that the BloomfieldPatients query is listed in the Queries section.

   You need to use the shortcut menu to copy the BloomfieldPatients query and paste it in the Navigation Pane; then you'll give the copied query a different name.

2. In the Queries section of the Navigation Pane, right-click **BloomfieldPatients** to select it and display the shortcut menu.

3. Click **Copy** on the shortcut menu.

4. Right-click the empty area near the bottom of the Navigation Pane, and then click **Paste** on the shortcut menu. The Paste As dialog box opens with the text "Copy Of BloomfieldPatients" in the Query Name box. Because Cindi wants the new query to show data for patients who have not visited the clinic recently, you'll name the new query "EarlierVisits."

5. In the Query Name box, type **EarlierVisits** and then press the **Enter** key. The new query appears in the Queries section of the Navigation Pane.

6. Double-click the **EarlierVisits** query to open, or run, the query. The design of this query is currently the same as the original BloomfieldPatients query.

7. Close the Navigation Pane.

Next, you need to open the query in Design view and modify its design to produce the results Cindi wants—to display only those records with VisitDate field values that are earlier than, or less than, 1/1/2016.

To modify the design of the new query:

1. In the Views group on the HOME tab, click the **View** button to display the query in Design view.

2. Click the **VisitDate Criteria** box, type **<1/1/2016** and then press the **Tab** key. See Figure 3-23.

Figure 3-23   Criteria entered for the VisitDate field

Field:	VisitID	VisitDate	Reason	LastName	FirstName	Phone	Address	Email	City
Table:	Visit	Visit	Visit	Patient	Patient	Patient	Patient	Patient	Patient
Sort:									
Show:	✓	✓	✓	✓	✓	✓	✓	✓	☐
Criteria:		<#1/1/2016#							"Bloomfield"
or:									

new condition entered

original condition needs to be deleted

Note that Access automatically encloses the date criteria with number signs. The condition specifies that a record will be selected only if its VisitDate field value is less than (earlier than) 1/1/2016. Before you run the query, you need to delete the condition for the City field. Recall that the City field is part of the query, but its values are not displayed in the query results. When you modified the query to remove the City field values from the query results, Access moved the field to the end of the design grid. You need to delete the City field's condition, specify that the City field values should be included in the query results, and then move the field back to its original position following the Address field.

3. Press the **Tab** key six times until the condition for the City field is highlighted, and then press the **Delete** key. The condition for the City field is removed.

4. Click the **Show** check box for the City field to insert a checkmark so that the field values will be displayed in the query results.

5. Use the pointer to select the City field, drag the selected field to the left of the Email field, and then click in an empty box to deselect the City field. See Figure 3-24.

Figure 3-24 Design grid after moving the City field

6. In the Results group on the DESIGN tab, click the **Run** button. Access runs the query and displays the selected fields for only those records with a VisitDate field value less than 1/1/2016. The query displays a total of 18 records. See Figure 3-25.

Tutorial 3 Maintaining and Querying a Database | Access   AC 149

Figure 3-25   Running the modified query

Visit ID	Date of Visit	Reason/Diagnosis	Last Name	First Name	Phone	Address	City	Email
1527	11/9/2015	Allergies - environmental	Li	Siyang	860-305-6548	225 Krauss Rd	Bloomfield	li.siyang@example.org
1528	11/9/2015	Diabetes mellitus Type 2 - initial diagnosis	Weiss	Matthew	860-426-7492	38 German St	Hartford	matt.weiss@example.org
1530	11/10/2015	Seborrheic dermatitis	Booker	Thomas	860-661-2539	59 Nicola Ave	Hartford	
1535	11/12/2015	Transverse fracture of left ulna	Ingram	Julia	860-661-4937	834 Kiefer Rd	Hartford	
1536	11/17/2015	Gastroenteritis	Swenson	Lucia	860-226-0293	83 Osage Ave	Hartford	
1538	11/17/2015	Migraine	Student Last	Student First	860-538-2822	501 Perkins Dr	Hartford	student1@example.edu
1539	11/18/2015	Annual wellness visit	Aguilar	Lilian	860-374-5724	329 Fairchild Ave	Hartford	laguilar@example.com
1541	11/24/2015	Gastroenteritis - follow up	Swenson	Lucia	860-226-0293	83 Osage Ave	Hartford	
1542	11/24/2015	Influenza	Mehta	Amrita	860-552-0375	28 Aiken Ave	Windsor	a.mehta@example.com
1544	11/25/2015	Influenza	Lewis	Patrice	860-552-5830	83 Highland St	Windsor	plewis5@example.org
1548	11/30/2015	Hypertension	Belanger	Malcolm	860-637-3927	723 Nicola Ave	West Hartford	
1549	11/30/2015	Influenza	Darcy	Edward	860-305-3985	723 Oxford Ave	Bloomfield	edarcy@example.org
1550	12/1/2015	Influenza	Fielder	Pam	860-305-2689	39 Unger Ave	Bloomfield	pfielder@example.org
1552	12/3/2015	Annual wellness visit	Castro	Daniel	860-637-0430	61 Osmond Way	West Hartford	d_castro@example.com
1555	12/7/2015	Annual wellness visit	Hallick	Davis	860-552-4495	84 Churchill Pl	Windsor	dhallick@example.com
1557	12/10/2015	Annual wellness visit	Swenson	Lucia	860-226-0293	83 Osage Ave	Hartford	
1560	12/15/2015	Influenza	Parker	Ian	860-938-1873	12 Adelbert St	Hartford	ian_parker@example.org
1562	12/22/2015	COPD management visit	King	Susan	860-661-9347	48 Fenton St	Hartford	susan.king@example.edu

only records with a VisitDate field value less than 1/1/2016 are selected

18 records are selected

7. Save and close the EarlierVisits query.

Cindi continues to analyze patient visits to Chatham Community Health Services. She is especially concerned about being proactive and reaching out to older patients well in advance of flu season. With this in mind, she would like to see a list of all patients who are age 60 or older and who have visited the clinic suffering from influenza. She wants to track these patients in particular so that her staff can contact them early for flu shots. To produce this list, you need to create a query containing two conditions—one for the patient's date of birth and another for the reason/diagnosis for each patient visit.

Defining Multiple Selection Criteria for Queries

Multiple conditions require you to use **logical operators** to combine two or more conditions. When you want a record selected only if two or more conditions are met, you need to use the **And logical operator**. In this case, Cindi wants to see only those records with a BirthDate field value less than or equal to 12/31/1956 *and* a Reason field value of "Influenza." If you place conditions in separate fields in the *same* Criteria row of the design grid, all conditions in that row must be met in order for a record to be included in the query results. However, if you place conditions in *different* Criteria rows, a record will be selected if at least one of the conditions is met. If none of the conditions are met, Access does not select the record. When you place conditions in different Criteria rows, you are using the **Or logical operator**. Figure 3-26 illustrates the difference between the And and Or logical operators.

Figure 3-26   Logical operators And and Or for multiple selection criteria

design grid using the And logical operator

Criteria: condition   condition

or:

conditions are placed in the same row

Are both conditions satisfied? — YES → select record — NO → do not select record

design grid using the Or logical operator

Criteria: condition

or: condition

conditions are placed in different rows

Are one or more conditions satisfied? — YES → select record — NO → do not select record

© 2014 Cengage Learning

The And Logical Operator

To create the query for Cindi, you need to use the And logical operator to show only the records for patients who were born on or before 12/31/1956 *and* who have visited the clinic because of influenza. You'll create a new query based on both the Patient and Visit tables to produce the necessary results. In the query design, both conditions you specify will appear in the same Criteria row; therefore, the query will select records only if both conditions are met.

To create a new query using the And logical operator:

1. On the ribbon, click the **CREATE** tab.
2. In the Queries group, click the **Query Design** button.
3. Add the **Patient** and **Visit** tables to the Query window, and then close the Show Table dialog box. Resize both field lists to display all the field names.
4. Add the following fields from the Patient field list to the design grid in the order shown: **FirstName**, **LastName**, **BirthDate**, **Phone**, and **City**.
5. Add the **VisitDate** and **Reason** fields from the Visit table to the design grid.

   Now you need to enter the two conditions for the query.

6. Click the **BirthDate Criteria** box, and then type **<=12/31/1956**.
7. Press the **Tab** key four times to move to the **Reason Criteria** box, type **Influenza**, and then press the **Tab** key. See Figure 3-27.

Tutorial 3 Maintaining and Querying a Database | Access AC 151

Figure 3-27 — Query to find older patients who have had influenza

And logical operator with conditions entered in the same row

The design grid shows fields: FirstName (Patient), LastName (Patient), BirthDate (Patient) with Criteria `<=#12/31/1956#`, Phone (Patient), City (Patient), VisitDate (Visit), Reason (Visit) with Criteria `"Influenza"`. All Show boxes are checked.

8. Run the query. Access displays only those records that meet both conditions: a BirthDate field value less than or equal to 12/31/1956 *and* a Reason field value of Influenza. Two records are selected for two different patients. See Figure 3-28.

Figure 3-28 — Results of query using the And logical operator

First Name	Last Name	Date of Birth	Phone	City	Date of Visit	Reason/Diagnosis
Ian	Parker	6/3/1953	860-938-1873	Hartford	12/15/2015	Influenza
Jane	Ropiak	2/7/1950	860-938-7830	Hartford	3/3/2016	Influenza

9. On the Quick Access Toolbar, click the **Save** button, and then save the query as **OlderAndFluPatients**.

10. Close the query.

Cindi meets with staff member Ethan to discuss the issue of influenza and keeping patients informed about receiving flu shots at the clinic. After viewing the results of the OlderAndFluPatients query, Ethan suggests that the clinic should reach out to all elderly patients regarding flu shots, because this segment of the population is particularly susceptible to the flu. In addition, he thinks they should contact any patient who has visited the clinic suffering from influenza to keep these patients informed about flu shots well in advance of flu season. To help with their planning, Cindi and Ethan have asked you to produce a list of all patients who were born on or before 12/31/1956 or who visited the clinic because of influenza. To create this query, you need to use the Or logical operator.

The Or Logical Operator

To create the query that Cindi and Ethan requested, your query must select a record when either one of two conditions is satisfied or when both conditions are satisfied. That is, a record is selected if the BirthDate field value is less than or equal to 12/31/1956 *or* if the Reason field value is Influenza *or* if both conditions are met. You will enter the condition for the BirthDate field in the Criteria row and the condition for the Reason field in the "or" criteria row, thereby using the Or logical operator.

AC 152 Access | Tutorial 3 Maintaining and Querying a Database

To display the information Cindi and Ethan want to view, you'll create a new query based on the existing OlderAndFluPatients query, since it already contains the necessary fields. Then you'll specify the conditions using the Or logical operator.

To create a new query using the Or logical operator:

1. Open the Navigation Pane. You'll use the shortcut menu to copy and paste the OlderAndFluPatients query to create the new query.

2. In the Queries section of the Navigation Pane, right-click **OlderAndFluPatients** to select it and display the shortcut menu.

3. Click **Copy** on the shortcut menu.

4. Right-click the empty area near the bottom of the Navigation Pane, and then click **Paste** on the shortcut menu. The Paste As dialog box opens with the text "Copy Of OlderAndFluPatients" in the Query Name box. Because Cindi wants the new query to show data for all older patients or patients who have visited the clinic due to influenza, you'll name the new query "OlderOrFluPatients."

5. In the Query Name box, type **OlderOrFluPatients** and then press the **Enter** key. The new query appears in the Queries section of the Navigation Pane.

6. In the Navigation Pane, right-click the **OlderOrFluPatients** query to select it and display the shortcut menu, and then click **Design View** on the shortcut menu to open the query in Design view.

7. Close the Navigation Pane.

   The query already contains all the fields Cindi and Ethan want to view, as well as the first condition—a BirthDate field value less than or equal to 12/31/1956. Because you want records selected if either the condition for the BirthDate field or the condition for the Reason field is satisfied, you must delete the existing condition for the Reason field in the Criteria row and then enter this same condition in the "or" row of the design grid for the Reason field.

8. In the design grid, click at the end of the **Reason Criteria** box and then press the **Backspace** key until the condition "Influenza" is deleted.

9. Press the ↓ key to move to the "or" row for the Reason field, type **Influenza**, and then press the **Tab** key. See Figure 3-29.

Figure 3-29 Query window with the Or logical operator

Or logical operator with conditions entered in different rows

Cindi wants the list displayed in descending order by BirthDate to better analyze the data.

▶ **10.** Click the right side of the **BirthDate Sort** box, and then click **Descending**.

▶ **11.** Run the query. Access displays only those records that meet either condition: a BirthDate field value less than or equal to 12/31/1956 *or* a Reason field value of Influenza. Access also selects records that meet both conditions. The query displays a total of 38 records. The records in the query datasheet appear in descending order based on the values in the BirthDate field. See Figure 3-30.

Figure 3-30   Results of query using the Or logical operator

datasheet selector

First Name	Last Name	Date of Birth	Phone	City	Date of Visit	Reason/Diagnosis
Patrice	Lewis	7/15/1991	860-552-5830	Windsor	11/25/2015	Influenza
Amrita	Mehta	6/3/1989	860-552-0375	Windsor	11/24/2015	Influenza
Edward	Darcy	7/15/1986	860-305-3985	Bloomfield	11/30/2015	Influenza
Pam	Fielder	12/6/1978	860-305-2689	Bloomfield	12/1/2015	Influenza
Lisa	Chang	10/5/1955	860-226-6034	Hartford	1/5/2016	Annual wellness visit
Caroline	Greene	6/12/1954	860-938-8295	Hartford	3/1/2016	Annual wellness visit
Chaney	Franklin	1/18/1954	860-552-2409	Windsor	4/15/2016	Elevated blood lipids-monitoring meds
Chaney	Franklin	1/18/1954	860-552-2409	Windsor	3/23/2016	Elevated blood lipids-monitoring meds
Chaney	Franklin	1/18/1954	860-552-2409	Windsor	2/24/2016	Elevated blood lipids-monitoring meds
Ian	Parker	6/3/1953	860-938-1873	Hartford	1/14/2016	Hypertension monitoring
Ian	Parker	6/3/1953	860-938-1873	Hartford	12/15/2015	Influenza
Malcolm	Belanger	10/17/1950	860-637-3927	West Hartford	11/30/2015	Hypertension
Malcolm	Belanger	10/17/1950	860-637-3927	West Hartford	1/8/2016	Hypertension monitoring
Jane	Ropiak	2/7/1950	860-938-7830	Hartford	1/11/2016	COPD management visit
Jane	Ropiak	2/7/1950	860-938-7830	Hartford	3/3/2016	Influenza
Jane	Ropiak	2/7/1950	860-938-7830	Hartford	4/14/2016	COPD management visit
Amber	Finnerty	5/7/1946	860-226-4930	Hartford	1/26/2016	Annual wellness visit
Susan	Hawes	6/22/1945	860-661-7193	Hartford	4/12/2016	Joint pain/arthritis
Davis	Hallick	3/26/1944	860-552-4495	Windsor	2/8/2016	Gastric reflux
Davis	Hallick	3/26/1944	860-552-4495	Windsor	12/7/2015	Annual wellness visit
Davis	Hallick	3/26/1944	860-552-4495	Windsor	2/22/2016	Follow-up - gastric reflux
Olivia	Brown	11/24/1943	860-938-7482	Hartford	2/16/2016	Plantar faciitis follow-up
Olivia	Brown	11/24/1943	860-938-7482	Hartford	2/1/2016	Plantar faciitis
Lucia	Swenson	5/1/1943	860-226-0293	Hartford	11/24/2015	Gastroenteritis - follow up
Lucia	Swenson	5/1/1943	860-226-0293	Hartford	11/17/2015	Gastroenteritis

Record: 1 of 38

records with a Reason field value of Influenza

records that meet both criteria

records with BirthDate field values less than or equal to 12/31/1956

38 records are selected

INSIGHT

Understanding the Results of Using And vs. Or

When you use the And logical operator to define multiple selection criteria in a query, you *narrow* the results produced by the query because a record must meet more than one condition to be included in the results. For example, the OlderAndFluPatients query you created resulted in only 2 records. When you use the Or logical operator, you *broaden* the results produced by the query because a record must meet only one of the conditions to be included in the results. For example, the OlderOrFluPatients query you created resulted in 38 records. This is an important distinction to keep in mind when you include multiple selection criteria in queries, so that the queries you create will produce the results you want.

Cindi would like to spend some time reviewing the results of the OlderOrFluPatients query. To make this task easier, she asks you to change how the datasheet is displayed.

Changing a Datasheet's Appearance

You can make many formatting changes to a datasheet to improve its appearance or readability. Many of these modifications are familiar types of changes you can also make in Word documents or Excel spreadsheets, such as modifying the font type, size, color, and the alignment of text. You can also apply different colors to the rows and columns in a datasheet to enhance its appearance.

Modifying the Font Size

Depending on the size of the monitor you are using or the screen resolution, you might need to increase or decrease the size of the font in a datasheet to view more or fewer columns of data. Cindi asks you to change the font size in the query datasheet from the default 11 points to 14 points so that she can read the text more easily.

To change the font size in the datasheet:

1. In the Text Formatting group on the HOME tab, click the **Font Size** arrow, and then click **14**. The font size for the entire datasheet increases to 14 points.

   Next, you need to resize the columns to their best fit, so that all field values are displayed. Instead of resizing each column individually, you'll use the datasheet selector to select all the columns and resize them at the same time.

2. Click the **datasheet selector**, which is the box to the left of the First Name column heading (see Figure 3-30). All the columns in the datasheet are highlighted, indicating they are selected.

3. Position the pointer ↔ on the vertical line on the right of any column in the datasheet, and then double-click the vertical line. All the columns visible on the screen are resized to their best fit. Scroll down and repeat the resizing, as necessary, to make sure that all field values are fully displayed.

   Trouble? If all the columns are not visible on your screen, you need to scroll the datasheet to the right to make sure all field values for all columns are fully displayed. If you need to resize any columns, click a field value first to deselect the columns before resizing an individual column.

4. Click any value in the First Name column to make it the current field and to deselect the columns in the datasheet.

Changing the Alternate Row Color in a Datasheet

TIP
When choosing a row color, be sure not to select a color that is too dark because it might obscure the data rather than enhance it.

Access uses themes to format the objects in a database. A **theme** is a predefined set of formats including colors, fonts, and other effects that enhance an object's appearance and usability. When you create a database, Access applies the Office theme to objects as you create them. By default, the Office theme formats every other row in a datasheet with a gray background color to distinguish one row from another, making it easier to view and read the contents of a datasheet. The gray alternate row color provides a subtle difference compared to the rows that have the default white color. You can change the alternate row color in a datasheet to something more noticeable using the Alternate Row Color button in the Text Formatting group on the HOME tab. Cindi suggests that you change the alternate row color in the datasheet to see the effect of using this feature.

Tutorial 3 Maintaining and Querying a Database | Access   AC 155

To change the alternate row color in the datasheet:

1. In the Text Formatting group on the HOME tab, click the **Alternate Row Color** button arrow to display the gallery of color choices. See Figure 3-31.

Figure 3-31   Gallery of color choices for alternate row color

modified Font Size setting
select this color
gallery with color choices (yours might differ)

TIP
The name of the color appears in a ScreenTip when you point to a color in the gallery.

The Theme Colors section provides colors from the default Office theme, so that your datasheet's color scheme matches the one in use for the database. The Standard Colors section provides many standard color choices. You might also see a Recent Colors section, with colors that you have recently used in a datasheet. At the bottom of the gallery, you could also choose the No Color option, which sets each row's background color to white; or the More Colors option, which creates a custom color. You'll use one of the theme colors.

2. In the Theme Colors section, click the color box for **Orange, Accent 2, Lighter 60%** (third row, sixth color box). The alternate row color is applied to the query datasheet. See Figure 3-32.

Figure 3-32   Datasheet formatted with alternate row color

orange color applied to every other row
first row is active, so it appears selected (highlighted in blue)

> Every other row in the datasheet uses the selected theme color. Cindi likes how the datasheet looks with this color scheme, so she asks you to save the query.
>
> **3.** Save and close the OlderOrFluPatients query. The query is saved with both the increased font size and the orange alternate row color.

Next, Cindi turns her attention to some financial aspects of operating the clinic. She wants to use the Chatham database to perform calculations. She is considering imposing a 2% late fee on unpaid invoices and wants to know exactly what the late fee charges would be, should she decide to institute such a policy in the future. To produce the information for Cindi, you need to create a calculated field.

Creating a Calculated Field

In addition to using queries to retrieve, sort, and filter data in a database, you can use a query to perform calculations. To perform a calculation, you define an **expression** containing a combination of database fields, constants, and operators. For numeric expressions, the data types of the database fields must be Number, Currency, or Date/Time; the constants are numbers such as .02 (for the 2% late fee); and the operators can be arithmetic operators (+ – * /) or other specialized operators. In complex expressions, you can enclose calculations in parentheses to indicate which one should be performed first; any calculation within parentheses is completed before calculations outside the parentheses. In expressions without parentheses, Access performs basic calculations using the following order of precedence: multiplication and division before addition and subtraction. When operators have equal precedence, Access calculates them in order from left to right.

To perform a calculation in a query, you add a calculated field to the query. A **calculated field** is a field that displays the results of an expression. A calculated field that you create with an expression appears in a query datasheet or in a form or report; however, it does not exist in a database. When you run a query that contains a calculated field, Access evaluates the expression defined by the calculated field and displays the resulting value in the query datasheet, form, or report.

To enter an expression for a calculated field, you can type it directly in a Field box in the design grid. Alternately, you can open the Zoom box or Expression Builder and use either one to enter the expression. The **Zoom box** is a dialog box that you can use to enter text, expressions, or other values. To use the Zoom box, however, you must know all the parts of the expression you want to create. **Expression Builder** is an Access tool that makes it easy for you to create an expression; it contains a box for entering the expression, an option for displaying and choosing common operators, and one or more lists of expression elements, such as table and field names. Unlike a Field box, which is too narrow to show an entire expression at one time, the Zoom box and Expression Builder are large enough to display longer expressions. In most cases, Expression Builder provides the easiest way to enter expressions because you don't have to know all the parts of the expression; you can choose the necessary elements from the Expression Builder dialog box, which also helps to prevent typing errors.

Tutorial 3 Maintaining and Querying a Database | Access   AC 157

> **REFERENCE**
>
> ### Using Expression Builder
>
> - Create and save the query in which you want to include a calculated field.
> - Open the query in Design view.
> - In the design grid, click the Field box in which you want to create an expression.
> - In the Query Setup group on the DESIGN tab, click the Builder button.
> - Use the expression elements and common operators to build the expression, or type the expression directly in the expression box.
> - Click the OK button.

To produce the information Cindi wants, you need to create a new query based on the Billing and Visit tables and, in the query, create a calculated field that will multiply each InvoiceAmt field value by .02 to calculate the proposed 2% late fee.

To create the new query and the calculated field:

1. On the ribbon, click the **CREATE** tab.

2. In the Queries group, click the **Query Design** button. The Show Table dialog box opens.

   Cindi wants to see data from both the Visit and Billing tables, so you need to add these two tables to the Query window.

3. Add the **Visit** and **Billing** tables to the Query window, and then close the Show Table dialog box. The field lists appear in the Query window, and the one-to-many relationship between the Visit (primary) and Billing (related) tables is displayed.

4. Resize the two field lists so that all field names are visible.

5. Add the following fields to the design grid in the order given: **VisitID**, **PatientID**, and **VisitDate** from the Visit table; and **InvoiceItem**, **InvoicePaid**, and **InvoiceAmt** from the Billing table.

   Cindi is interested in viewing data only for unpaid invoices because a late fee would apply only to them, so you need to enter the necessary condition for the InvoicePaid field. Recall that InvoicePaid is a Yes/No field. The condition you need to enter is the word "No" in the Criteria box for this field, so that Access will retrieve the records for unpaid invoices only.

6. In the **InvoicePaid Criteria** box, type **No**. As soon as you type the letter "N," a menu appears with options for entering various functions for the criteria. You don't need to enter a function, so you can close this menu.

7. Press the **Esc** key to close the menu.

   You must close the menu or you'll enter a function, which will cause an error.

8. Press the **Tab** key. The query name you'll use will indicate that the data is for unpaid invoices, so you don't need to include the InvoicePaid values in the query results.

9. Click the **InvoicePaid Show** check box to remove the checkmark.

10. Save the query with the name **UnpaidInvoiceLateFee**.

Now you can use Expression Builder to create the calculated field for the InvoiceAmt field.

To create the calculated field:

1. Click the blank Field box to the right of the InvoiceAmt field. This field will contain the expression.

2. In the Query Setup group on the DESIGN tab, click the **Builder** button. The Expression Builder dialog box opens.

   > **TIP**
   > You must first save and name a query in order for its fields to be listed in the Expression Categories section.

   The insertion point is positioned in the large box at the top of the dialog box, ready for you to enter the expression. The Expression Categories section of the dialog box lists the fields from the query so you can include them in the expression. The Expression Elements section contains options for including other elements in the expression, including functions, constants, and operators. If the expression you're entering is a simple one, you can type it in the box; if it's more complex, you can use the options in the Expression Elements section to help you build the expression.

   The expression for the calculated field will multiply the InvoiceAmt field values by the numeric constant .02 (which represents a 2% late fee).

3. In the Expression Categories section of the dialog box, double-click **InvoiceAmt**. The field name is added to the expression box, within brackets and with a space following it. In an expression, all field names must be enclosed in brackets.

   Next you need to enter the multiplication operator, which is the asterisk (*), followed by the constant.

4. Type * (an asterisk) and then type **.02**. You have finished entering the expression. See Figure 3-33.

Figure 3-33 — Completed expression for the calculated field

If you're not sure which operator to use, you can click Operators in the Expression Elements section to display a list of available operators in the center section of the dialog box.

5. Click the **OK** button. Access closes the Expression Builder dialog box and adds the expression to the design grid in the Field box for the calculated field.

   When you create a calculated field, Access uses the default column name "Expr1" for the field. You need to specify a more meaningful column name so it will appear in the query results. You'll enter the name "LateFee," which better describes the field's contents.

6. Click to the left of the text "Expr1:" at the beginning of the expression, and then press the **Delete** key five times to delete the text **Expr1**. *Do not delete the colon*; it is needed to separate the calculated field name from the expression.

7. Type **LateFee**. Next, you'll set this field's Caption property so that the field name will appear as "Late Fee" in the query datasheet.

8. In the Show/Hide group on the DESIGN tab, click the **Property Sheet** button. The Property Sheet for the current field, LateFee, opens on the right side of the window. See Figure 3-34.

Figure 3-34   **Property Sheet for the calculated field**

9. Click in the Caption box of the Property Sheet, type **Late Fee** and then close the Property Sheet.

10. Run the query. Access displays the query datasheet, which contains the specified fields and the calculated field with the caption "Late Fee." See Figure 3-35.

Figure 3-35 Datasheet displaying the calculated field

Visit ID	Patient ID	Date of Visit	Invoice Item	Invoice Amt	Late Fee
1535	22546	11/12/2015	Radiograph	$250.00	5
1538	22500	11/17/2015	Pharmacy	$125.00	2.5
1548	22519	11/30/2015	Office visit	$100.00	2
1550	22549	12/1/2015	Pharmacy	$85.00	1.7
1550	22549	12/1/2015	Radiograph	$250.00	5
1555	22520	12/7/2015	Office visit	$100.00	2
1555	22520	12/7/2015	Pharmacy	$72.00	1.44
1557	22526	12/10/2015	Phlebotomy	$45.00	0.9
1557	22526	12/10/2015	Lab work	$32.00	0.64
1562	22516	12/22/2015	Office visit	$100.00	2
1562	22516	12/22/2015	Respiratory therapy	$150.00	3
1563	22548	1/4/2016	Cast removal	$75.00	1.5
1570	22561	1/11/2016	Pharmacy	$85.00	1.7
1570	22561	1/11/2016	Phlebotomy	$45.00	0.9
1570	22561	1/11/2016	Pharmacy	$68.00	1.36
1570	22561	1/11/2016	Lab work	$125.00	2.5
1572	22560	1/13/2016	Office visit	$100.00	2
1575	22513	1/13/2016	Radiograph	$250.00	5
1575	22513	1/13/2016	Bone setting and cast	$300.00	6
1576	22514	1/14/2016	Office visit	$100.00	2
1580	22552	1/15/2016	Pharmacy	$68.00	1.36
1585	22555	1/25/2016	Office visit	$100.00	2
1585	22555	1/25/2016	Pharmacy	$85.00	1.7
1585	22555	1/25/2016	Lab work - culture	$125.00	2.5
1586	22523	1/25/2016	Office visit	$100.00	2

specified caption for the calculated field

calculated field values

Trouble? If a dialog box opens noting that the expression contains invalid syntax, you might not have included the required colon in the expression. Click the OK button to close the dialog box, resize the column in the design grid that contains the calculated field to its best fit, change your expression to LateFee: [InvoiceAmt]*0.02 and then repeat Step 10.

The LateFee field values are currently displayed without dollar signs and decimal places. Cindi wants these values to be displayed in the same format as the InvoiceAmt field values for consistency.

Formatting a Calculated Field

You can specify a particular format for a calculated field, just as you can for any field, by modifying its properties. Next, you'll change the format of the LateFee calculated field so that all values appear in the Currency format.

To format the calculated field:

1. Switch to Design view.

2. In the design grid, click in the **LateFee** calculated field to make it the current field, if necessary.

3. In the Show/Hide group on the DESIGN tab, click the **Property Sheet** button to open the Property Sheet for the calculated field.

    You need to change the Format property to Currency, which displays values with a dollar sign and two decimal places.

4. In the Property Sheet, click the right side of the **Format** box to display the list of formats, and then click **Currency**.

5. Close the Property Sheet for the calculated field, and then run the query. The amounts in the LateFee calculated field are now displayed with dollar signs and two decimal places.

Tutorial 3 Maintaining and Querying a Database | Access   AC 161

> **6.** Save and close the UnpaidInvoiceLateFee query.

PROSKILLS

Problem Solving: Creating a Calculated Field vs. Using the Calculated Field Data Type

You can also create a calculated field using the Calculated Field data type, which lets you store the result of an expression as a field in a table. However, database experts caution users against storing calculations in a table for several reasons. First, storing calculated data in a table consumes valuable space and increases the size of the database. The preferred approach is to use a calculated field in a query; with this approach, the result of the calculation is not stored in the database—it is produced only when you run the query—and it is always current. Second, the Calculated Field data type provides limited options for creating a calculation, whereas a calculated field in a query provides more functions and options for creating expressions. Third, including a field in a table using the Calculated Field data type limits your options if you need to upgrade the database at some point to a more robust DBMS, such as Oracle or SQL Server, that doesn't support this data type; you would need to redesign your database to eliminate this data type. Finally, most database experts agree that including a field in a table whose value is dependent on other fields in the table violates database design principles. To avoid such problems, it's best to create a query that includes a calculated field to perform the calculation you want, instead of creating a field in a table that uses the Calculated Field data type.

To better analyze costs at Chatham Community Health Services, Cindi wants to view more detailed information about patient invoices. Specifically, she would like to know the minimum, average, and maximum invoice amounts. She asks you to determine these statistics from data in the Billing table.

Using Aggregate Functions

You can calculate statistical information, such as totals and averages, on the records displayed in a table datasheet or selected by a query. To do this, you use the Access aggregate functions. **Aggregate functions** perform arithmetic operations on selected records in a database. Figure 3-36 lists the most frequently used aggregate functions.

Figure 3-36 Frequently used aggregate functions

Aggregate Function	Determines	Data Types Supported
Average	Average of the field values for the selected records	AutoNumber, Currency, Date/Time, Number
Count	Number of records selected	AutoNumber, Currency, Date/Time, Long Text, Number, OLE Object, Short Text, Yes/No
Maximum	Highest field value for the selected records	AutoNumber, Currency, Date/Time, Number, Short Text
Minimum	Lowest field value for the selected records	AutoNumber, Currency, Date/Time, Number, Short Text
Sum	Total of the field values for the selected records	AutoNumber, Currency, Date/Time, Number

© 2014 Cengage Learning

Working with Aggregate Functions Using the Total Row

If you want to quickly perform a calculation using an aggregate function in a table or query datasheet, you can use the Totals button in the Records group on the HOME tab. When you click this button, a row labeled "Total" appears at the bottom of the datasheet. You can then choose one of the aggregate functions for a field in the datasheet, and the results of the calculation will be displayed in the Total row for that field.

Cindi wants to know the total amount of all invoices for the clinic. You can quickly display this amount using the Sum function in the Total row in the Billing table datasheet.

To display the total amount of all invoices in the Billing table:

1. Open the Navigation Pane, open the **Billing** table in Datasheet view, and then close the Navigation Pane.
2. Make sure the HOME tab is displayed.
3. In the Records group, click the **Totals** button. Access adds a row with the label "Total" to the bottom of the datasheet.
4. Scroll to the bottom of the datasheet to view the last records in the datasheet and the Total row. You want to display the sum of all the values in the Invoice Amt column.
5. In the Total row, click the **Invoice Amt** column. An arrow appears on the left side of the field.
6. Click the **arrow** to display the menu of aggregate functions. The functions displayed depend on the data type of the current field; in this case, the menu provides functions for a Currency field. See Figure 3-37.

Figure 3-37   Using aggregate functions in the Total row

Tutorial 3 Maintaining and Querying a Database | Access   AC 163

> 7. Click **Sum** in the menu. Access adds all the values in the Invoice Amt column and displays the total $20,603.00 in the Total row for the column.
>
>   Cindi doesn't want to change the Billing table to always display this total. You can remove the Total row by clicking the Totals button again; this button works as a toggle to switch between the display of the Total row with the results of any calculations in the row, and the display of the datasheet without this row.
>
> 8. In the Records group, click the **Totals** button. Access removes the Total row from the datasheet.
>
> 9. Close the Billing table without saving the changes.

Cindi wants to know the minimum, average, and maximum invoice amounts for Chatham Community Health Services. To produce this information for Cindi, you need to use aggregate functions in a query.

Creating Queries with Aggregate Functions

Aggregate functions operate on the records that meet a query's selection criteria. You specify an aggregate function for a specific field, and the appropriate operation applies to that field's values for the selected records.

To display the minimum, average, and maximum of all the invoice amounts in the Billing table, you will use the Minimum, Average, and Maximum aggregate functions for the InvoiceAmt field.

> **To calculate the minimum of all invoice amounts:**
>
> 1. Create a new query in Design view, add the **Billing** table to the Query window, and then close the Show Table dialog box. Resize the Billing field list to display all fields.
>
>   To perform the three calculations on the InvoiceAmt field, you need to add the field to the design grid three times.
>
> 2. In the Billing field list, double-click **InvoiceAmt** three times to add three copies of the field to the design grid.
>
>   You need to select an aggregate function for each InvoiceAmt field. When you click the Totals button in the Show/Hide group on the DESIGN tab, a row labeled "Total" is added to the design grid. The Total row provides a list of the aggregate functions that you can select.
>
> 3. In the Show/Hide group on the DESIGN tab, click the **Totals** button. A new row labeled "Total" appears between the Table and Sort rows in the design grid. The default entry for each field in the Total row is the Group By operator, which you will learn about later in this tutorial. See Figure 3-38.

Figure 3-38   **Total row inserted in the design grid**

Total row

InvoiceAmt field included three times in the design grid

In the Total row, you specify the aggregate function you want to use for a field.

4. Click the right side of the first column's **Total** box, and then click **Min**. This field will calculate the minimum amount of all the InvoiceAmt field values.

   When you run the query, Access automatically will assign a datasheet column name of "MinOfInvoiceAmt" for this field. You can change the datasheet column name to a more descriptive or readable name by entering the name you want in the Field box. However, you must also keep the InvoiceAmt field name in the Field box because it identifies the field to use in the calculation. The Field box will contain the datasheet column name you specify followed by the field name (InvoiceAmt) with a colon separating the two names.

5. In the first column's Field box, click to the left of InvoiceAmt, and then type **MinimumInvoiceAmt:** (including the colon).

   Be sure to type the colon following the name or the query will not work correctly.

6. Using the ↔ pointer, double-click the column dividing line between the first two columns so that you can see the complete field name, MinimumInvoiceAmt:InvoiceAmt.

   Next, you need to set the Caption property for this field so that the field name appears with spaces between words in the query datatsheet.

7. In the Show/Hide group on the DESIGN tab, click the **Property Sheet** button to open the Property Sheet for the current field.

8. In the Caption box, type **Minimum Invoice Amt** and then close the Property Sheet.

You'll follow the same process to complete the query by calculating the average and maximum invoice amounts.

To calculate the average and maximum of all invoice amounts:

1. Click the right side of the second column's **Total** box, and then click **Avg**. This field will calculate the average of all the InvoiceAmt field values.

2. In the second column's Field box, click to the left of InvoiceAmt, and then type **AverageInvoiceAmt:**.

3. Resize the second column to fully display the field name, AverageInvoiceAmt:InvoiceAmt.

4. Open the Property Sheet for the current field, and then set its Caption property to **Average Invoice Amt**. Leave the Property Sheet open.

5. Click the right side of the third column's **Total** box, and then click **Max**. This field will calculate the maximum amount of all the InvoiceAmt field values.

6. In the third column's Field box, click to the left of InvoiceAmt, and then type **MaximumInvoiceAmt:**.

7. Resize the third column to fully display the field name, MaximumInvoiceAmt:InvoiceAmt.

8. In the Property Sheet for the current field, set the Caption property to **Maximum Invoice Amt** and then close the Property Sheet. See Figure 3-39.

Figure 3-39 — Query with aggregate functions entered

functions entered and columns resized

Field:	MinimumInvoiceAmt: InvoiceAmt	AverageInvoiceAmt: InvoiceAmt	MaximumInvoiceAmt: InvoiceAmt
Table:	Billing	Billing	Billing
Total:	Min	Avg	Max
Sort:			
Show:	✓	✓	✓
Criteria:			
or:			

Trouble? Carefully compare your field names to those shown in the figure to make sure they match exactly; otherwise the query will not work correctly.

9. Run the query. Access displays one record containing the three aggregate function results. The single row of summary statistics represents calculations based on all the records selected for the query—in this case, all 203 records in the Billing table.

10. Resize all columns to their best fit so that the column names are fully displayed, and then click the field value in the first column to deselect the value and view the results. See Figure 3-40.

Figure 3-40 — Result of the query using aggregate functions

Minimum Invoice Amt	Average Invoice Amt	Maximum Invoice Amt
$30.00	$101.49	$450.00

11. Save the query as **InvoiceAmtStatistics**.

Cindi would like to view the same invoice amount statistics (minimum, average, and maximum) as they relate to both scheduled appointments and walk-in visits to the clinic.

Using Record Group Calculations

In addition to calculating statistical information on all or selected records in selected tables, you can calculate statistics for groups of records. For example, you can determine the number of patients in each city or the average invoice amount by city.

To create a query for Cindi's latest request, you can modify the current query by adding the WalkIn field and assigning the Group By operator to it. The **Group By operator** divides the selected records into groups based on the values in the specified field. Those records with the same value for the field are grouped together, and the datasheet displays one record for each group. Aggregate functions, which appear in the other columns of the design grid, provide statistical information for each group.

You need to modify the current query to add the Group By operator to the WalkIn field from the Visit table. The Group By operator will display the statistical information grouped by the values of the WalkIn field for all the records in the query datasheet. To create the new query, you will save the InvoiceAmtStatistics query with a new name, keeping the original query intact, and then modify the new query.

To create a new query with the Group By operator:

1. Display the InvoiceAmtStatistics query in Design view. Because the query is open, you can use Backstage view to save it with a new name, keeping the original query intact.

2. Click the **FILE** tab to display Backstage view, and then click **Save As** in the navigation bar. The Save As screen opens.

3. In the File Types section on the left, click **Save Object As**. The right side of the screen changes to display options for saving the current database object as a new object.

4. Click the **Save As** button. The Save As dialog box opens, indicating that you are saving a copy of the InvoiceAmtStatistics query.

5. Type **InvoiceAmtStatisticsByWalkIn** to replace the highlighted name, and then press the **Enter** key. The new query is saved with the name you specified and displayed in Design view.

   You need to add the WalkIn field to the query. This field is in the Visit table. To include another table in an existing query, you open the Show Table dialog box.

6. In the Query Setup group on the DESIGN tab, click the **Show Table** button to open the Show Table dialog box.

7. Add the **Visit** table to the Query window, close the Show Table dialog box, and then resize the Visit field list.

8. Drag the **WalkIn** field from the Visit field list to the first column in the design grid. When you release the mouse button, the WalkIn field appears in the design grid's first column, and the existing fields shift to the right. Group By, the default option in the Total row, appears for the WalkIn field.

9. Run the query. Access displays 2 records—one for each WalkIn group, Yes and No. Each record contains the WalkIn field value for the group and the three aggregate function values. The summary statistics represent calculations based on the 203 records in the Billing table. See Figure 3-41.

> **TIP**
> You could also open the Navigation Pane and drag the Visit table from the pane to the Query window.

Figure 3-41 Aggregate functions grouped by WalkIn

record groups → (checkbox rows)
aggregate function results → (Minimum/Average/Maximum Invoice Amt columns)

Walk-in?	Minimum Invoice Amt	Average Invoice Amt	Maximum Invoice Amt
☑	$35.00	$115.78	$450.00
☐	$30.00	$88.16	$150.00

Cindi notes that the invoice amounts for walk-in visits are higher than those for scheduled appointments.

▶ 10. Save and close the query.

▶ 11. Open the Navigation Pane.

You have created and saved many queries in the Chatham database. The Navigation Pane provides options for opening and managing the queries you've created, as well as the other objects in the database, such as tables, forms, and reports.

Working with the Navigation Pane

As noted earlier, the Navigation Pane is the main area for working with the objects in a database. As you continue to create objects in your database, you might want to display and work with them in different ways. The Navigation Pane provides options for grouping database objects in various ways to suit your needs. For example, you might want to view only the queries created for a certain table or all the query objects in the database.

The Navigation Pane divides database objects into categories, and each category contains groups. The groups contain one or more objects. The default category is **Object Type**, which arranges objects by type—tables, queries, forms, and reports. The default group is **All Access Objects**, which displays all objects in the database. You can also choose to display only one type of object, such as tables.

The default group name, All Access Objects, appears at the top of the Navigation Pane. Currently, each object type—Tables, Queries, Forms, and Reports—is displayed as a heading, and the objects related to each type are listed below the heading. To group objects differently, you can select another category by using the Navigation Pane menu. You'll try this next.

> **TIP**
> You can hide the display of a group's objects by clicking the button to the right of the group name; click the button again to expand the group and display its objects.

To group objects differently in the Navigation Pane:

▶ 1. At the top of the Navigation Pane, click the **All Access Objects** button ⌄. A menu is displayed for choosing different categories and groups. See Figure 3-42.

Figure 3-42 | **Navigation Pane menu**

default category selected → Object Type (checked)

Menu contents:
- Navigate To Category
  - Custom
  - ✓ Object Type
  - Tables and Related Views
  - Created Date
  - Modified Date
- Filter By Group
  - Tables
  - Queries
  - Forms
  - Reports
  - ✓ All Access Objects

category options point to the Navigate To Category section.
group options point to the Filter By Group section.
default group selected → All Access Objects

PatientVisits

The top section of the menu provides the options for choosing a different category. The Object Type category has a checkmark next to it, signifying that it is the currently selected category. The lower section of the menu provides options for choosing a different group; these options might change depending on the selected category.

2. In the top section of the menu, click **Tables and Related Views**. The Navigation Pane is now grouped into categories of tables, and each table in the database—Visit, Billing, and Patient—is its own group. All database objects related to a table are listed below the table's name. See Figure 3-43.

Figure 3-43 Database objects grouped by table in the Navigation Pane

All Tables group selected

each table name appears as a heading

an object based on more than one table appears in the group of objects for each table

Some objects appear more than once. When an object is based on more than one table, that object appears in the group for each table. For example, the UnpaidInvoiceLateFee query is based on both the Visit and Billing tables, so it is listed in the group for both tables.

You can also choose to display the objects for only one table to better focus on that table.

3. At the top of the Navigation Pane, click the **All Tables** button to display the Navigation Pane menu, and then click **Patient**. The Navigation Pane now shows only the objects related to the Patient table—the table itself plus the six queries you created that include fields from the Patient table.

4. At the top of the Navigation Pane, click the **Patient** button, and then click **Object Type** to return to the default display of the Navigation Pane.

5. Compact and repair the Chatham database, and then close the database.

   Trouble? If a dialog box opens and warns that this action will cause Microsoft Access to empty the Clipboard, click the Yes button to continue.

The default All Access Objects category is a predefined category. You can also create custom categories to group objects in the way that best suits how you want to manage your database objects. As you continue to build a database and the list of objects grows, creating a custom category can help you to work more efficiently with the objects in the database.

The queries you've created and saved will help Cindi, Kelly, Ethan, and other staff members to monitor and analyze the business activity of Chatham Community Health Services and its patients. Now any staff member can run the queries at any time, modify them as needed, or use them as the basis for designing new queries to meet additional information requirements.

Session 3.2 Quick Check

1. A(n) _____ is a criterion, or rule, that determines which records are selected for a query datasheet.
2. In the design grid, where do you place the conditions for two different fields when you use the And logical operator, and where do you place them when you use the Or logical operator?
3. To perform a calculation in a query, you define a(n) _____ containing a combination of database fields, constants, and operators.
4. Which Access tool do you use to create an expression for a calculated field in a query?
5. What is an aggregate function?
6. The _____ operator divides selected records into groups based on the values in a field.
7. What is the default category for the display of objects in the Navigation Pane?

SAM Projects

Put your skills into practice with SAM Projects! SAM Projects for this tutorial can be found online. If you have a SAM account, go to www.cengage.com/sam2013 to download the most recent Project Instructions and Start Files.

Review Assignments

Data File needed for the Review Assignments: Vendor.accdb *(cont. from Tutorial 2)*

Cindi asks you to update some information in the Vendor database and also to retrieve specific information from the database. Complete the following:

1. Open the **Vendor** database you created and worked with in Tutorials 1 and 2, and then click the Enable Content button next to the security warning, if necessary.
2. Open the **Supplier** table in Datasheet view, and then change the following field values for the record with the Supplier ID GRE364: Address to **1550 W Main St**, Contact Phone to **401-625-2745**, Contact First Name to **Andrew**, and Contact Last Name to **Kline**. Close the table.
3. Create a query based on the Supplier table. Include the following fields in the query, in the order shown: Company, Category, ContactFirst, ContactLast, Phone, and InitialContact. Sort the query in ascending order based on the Category field values. Save the query as **ContactList**, and then run the query.
4. Use the ContactList query datasheet to update the Supplier table by changing the Phone field value for Aresco Surgical, Inc. to **203-335-0054**.
5. Change the size of the font in the ContactList query datasheet to 12 points. Resize columns, as necessary, so that all field values and column headings are visible.
6. Change the alternate row color in the ContactList query datasheet to the Theme Color named Green, Accent 6, Lighter 60%, and then save and close the query.
7. Create a query based on the Supplier and Product tables. Select the Company, Category, and State fields from the Supplier table, and the ProductName, Price, Units, and Weight fields from the Product table. Sort the query results in descending order based on price. Select only those records with a State field value of CT, but do not display the State field values in the query results. Save the query as **CTSuppliers**, run the query, and then close it.
8. Create a query that lists all products that cost more than $200 and are sterile. Display the following fields from the Product table in the query results: ProductID, ProductName, Price, Units, and TempControl. (*Hint:* The Sterile field is a Yes/No field that should not appear in the query results.) Save the query as **HighPriceAndSterile**, run the query, and then close it.
9. Create a query that lists information about suppliers who sell equipment or products that require temperature control. Include the Company, Category, ContactFirst, and ContactLast fields from the Supplier table; and the ProductName, Price, TempControl, and Sterile fields from the Product table. Save the query as **EquipmentOrTempControl**, run the query, and then close it.
10. Create a query that lists only those products that cost $1000 or more, along with a 5% discount amount based on the price of the product. Include the Company field from the Supplier table and the following fields from the Product table in the query: ProductID, ProductName, and Price. Save the query as **HighPriceWithDiscount**. Display the discount in a calculated field named **DiscountAmt** that determines a 5% discount based on the Price field values. Set the Caption property **Discount Amt** for the calculated field. Display the query results in descending order by Price. Save and run the query.

11. Modify the format of the DiscountAmt field in the HighPriceWithDiscount query so that it uses the Standard format and two decimal places. Run the query, resize all columns in the datasheet to their best fit, and then save and close the query.
12. Create a query that calculates the lowest, highest, and average prices for all products using the field names **LowestPrice**, **HighestPrice**, and **AveragePrice**, respectively. Set the Caption property for each field to include a space between the two words in the field name. Run the query, resize all columns in the datasheet to their best fit, save the query as **PriceStatistics**, and then close it.
13. In the Navigation Pane, copy the PriceStatistics query, and then rename the copied query as **PriceStatisticsBySupplier**.
14. Modify the PriceStatisticsBySupplier query so that the records are grouped by the Company field in the Supplier table. The Company field should appear first in the query datasheet. Save and run the query, and then close it.
15. Compact and repair the Vendor database, and then close it.

Case Problem 1

APPLY

Data File needed for this Case Problem: Gopher.accdb *(cont. from Tutorial 2)*

GoGopher! Amol Mehta needs to modify a few records in the Gopher database and analyze the data for members enrolled in his company's various plans. To help Amol, you'll update the Gopher database and create queries to answer his questions. Complete the following:

1. Open the **Gopher** database you created and worked with in Tutorials 1 and 2, and then click the Enable Content button next to the security warning, if necessary.
2. In the **Member** table, find the record for MemberID 1251, and then change the Street value to **75 Hemlock Ln** and the Phone to **303-553-1847**.
3. In the **Member** table, find the record for MemberID 1228, and then delete the record. Close the Member table.
4. Create a query that lists members who did not have to pay a fee when they joined. In the query results, display the FirstName, LastName, and DateJoined fields from the Member table, and the PlanCost field from the Plan table. Sort the records in descending order by the date joined. Select records only for members whose fees were waived. (*Hint:* The FeeWaived field is a Yes/No field that should not appear in the query results.) Save the query as **NoFees**, and then run the query.
5. Use the NoFees query datasheet to update the Member table by changing the Last Name value for Kara Murray to **Seaburg**.
6. Use the NoFees query datasheet to display the total Plan Cost for the selected members. Save and close the query.
7. Create a query that lists the MemberID, FirstName, LastName, DateJoined, PlanDescription, and PlanCost fields for members who joined GoGopher! between April 1, 2016 and April 30, 2016. Save the query as **AprilMembers**, run the query, and then close it.
8. Create a query that lists all members who live in Louisville and whose memberships expire on or after 1/1/2017. Display the following fields from the Member table in the query results: MemberID, FirstName, LastName, Phone, and Expiration. (*Hint:* The City field values should not appear in the query results.) Sort the query results in ascending order by last name. Save the query as **LouisvilleAndExpiration**, run the query, and then close it.
9. Copy and paste the LouisvilleAndExpiration query to create a new query named **LouisvilleOrExpiration**. Modify the new query so that it lists all members who live in Louisville or whose memberships expire on or after 1/1/2017. Display the City field values in the query results following the Phone field values, and sort the query results in ascending order by city (this should be the only sort in the query). Save and run the query.
10. Change the size of the font in the LouisvilleOrExpiration query datasheet to 14 points. Resize columns, as necessary, so that all field values and column headings are visible.

11. Change the alternate row color in the LouisvilleOrExpiration query datasheet to the Theme Color named Blue, Accent 1, Lighter 80%, and then save and close the query.
12. Create a query that calculates the lowest, highest, and average cost for all plans using the field names **LowestCost**, **HighestCost**, and **AverageCost**, respectively. Set the Caption property for each field to include a space between the two words in the field name. Run the query, resize all columns in the datasheet to their best fit, save the query as **CostStatistics**, and then close it.
13. Copy and paste the CostStatistics query to create a new query named **CostStatisticsByCity**.
14. Modify the CostStatisticsByCity query to display the same statistics grouped by City, with City appearing as the first field. (*Hint:* Add the Member table to the query.) Run the query, and then save and close it.
15. Compact and repair the Gopher database, and then close it.

Case Problem 2

Data File needed for this Case Problem: OBrien.accdb *(cont. from Tutorial 2)*

O'Brien Educational Services After reviewing the OBrien database, Karen O'Brien wants to modify some records and then view specific information about the students, tutors, and contracts for her educational services company. She asks you to update and query the OBrien database to perform these tasks. Complete the following:

1. Open the **OBrien** database you created and worked with in Tutorials 1 and 2, and then click the Enable Content button next to the security warning, if necessary.
2. In the **Tutor** table, change the following information for the record with TutorID 79-0678: Degree is **BA** and Hire Date is **9/15/2015**. Close the table.
3. In the **Student** table, find the record with the StudentID MCS8051, and then delete the related record in the subdatasheet for this student. Delete the record for StudentID MCS8051, and then close the Student table.
4. Create a query based on the Student table that includes the LastName, FirstName, and CellPhone fields, in that order. Save the query as **StudentCellList**, and then run the query.
5. In the results of the StudentCellList query, change the cell phone number for Haley Gosnold to **574-252-1973**. Close the query.
6. Create a query based on the Tutor and Contract tables. Display the LastName field from the Tutor table, and the StudentID, ContractDate, SessionType, Length, and Cost fields, in that order, from the Contract table. Sort first in ascending order by the tutor's last name, and then in ascending order by the StudentID. Save the query as **SessionsByTutor**, run the query, and the close it.
7. Copy and paste the SessionsByTutor query to create a new query named **GroupSessions**. Modify the new query so that it displays the same information for records with a Group session type only. Do not display the SessionType field values in the query results. Save and run the query, and then close it.
8. Create and save a query that produces the results shown in Figure 3-44. Close the query when you are finished.

Access | Tutorial 3 Maintaining and Querying a Database

Figure 3-44   SouthBendPrivate query results

- show only records for students from South Bend who are taking private sessions
- sort by Last Name
- format with a font size of 12 and the Gold, Accent 4, Lighter 60% alternate row Theme Color

SouthBendPrivate

Student ID	Last Name	First Name	Contract Date
MAH8053	Mahlau	Albert	7/16/2016
OAT8010	Oates	Kyle	1/26/2016
PAP8024	Pappas	Zach	7/10/2016
SPE8022	Spence	Ross	2/1/2016
TUR8005	Turner	Lynne	9/15/2016
VAR8027	Vargas	Vera	9/20/2016
VAR8027	Vargas	Vera	4/3/2016

9. Create and save a query that produces the results shown in Figure 3-45. Close the query when you are finished.

Figure 3-45   OscelaOrSemi query results

- show only records for students from Oscela or students taking semi-private sessions
- sort in descending order by Contract Date
- Total row shows the sum of the Cost values

OscelaOrSemi

Student ID	First Name	Last Name	Contract Date	Cost
DRO8048	Emma	Drouin	9/15/2016	$720
NAS8012	Andre	Nastasia	9/12/2016	$800
GUS8002	Michael	Gustafson	9/10/2016	$900
RIV8011	Marco	Rivera	8/10/2016	$1,080
DEN8042	David	DeNardo	8/1/2016	$800
CAR8059	Carol	Carlson	7/15/2016	$1,200
YEN8035	Lila	Yen	6/22/2016	$1,440
MAS8056	Kimberly	Mase	5/8/2016	$960
STI8038	Lily	Stiefel	3/15/2016	$720
BIE8000	Joshua	Biega	3/14/2016	$1,800
HIN8040	Erica	Hinkle	3/1/2016	$960
NAS8012	Andre	Nastasia	2/1/2016	$960
GUS8002	Michael	Gustafson	1/28/2016	$720
MUE8041	Bart	Mueller	1/15/2016	$1,440
YEN8035	Lila	Yen	1/7/2016	$1,280
HEC8018	Eric	Hecht	12/17/2015	$900
WOO8071	Jon	Woodburn	12/15/2015	$1,800
NUN8084	Rodrigo	Nunez	9/30/2015	$800
Total				$19,280

10. Create and save a query to display statistics for the Cost field, as shown in Figure 3-46. Close the query when you are finished.

Figure 3-46   CostStatistics query results

- set captions to include spaces between words
- format values as Standard with two decimal places

CostStatistics

Minimum Cost	Average Cost	Maximum Cost
720.00	1,086.67	1,920.00

11. Copy and paste the CostStatistics query to create a new query named **CostStatisticsByCity**.
12. Modify the CostStatisticsByCity query to display the same statistics grouped by City, with City appearing as the first field. (*Hint:* Add the Student table to the query.) Run the query, and then save and close it.
13. Compact and repair the OBrien database, and then close it.

Case Problem 3

Data File needed for this Case Problem: Shelter.accdb *(cont. from Tutorial 2)*

Rosemary Animal Shelter   Ryan Lang needs to modify some records in the Shelter database, and then he wants to find specific information about the animals, patrons, and donations for his not-for-profit agency. Ryan asks you to help him update the database and create queries to find the information he needs. Complete the following:

1. Open the **Shelter** database you created and worked with in Tutorials 1 and 2, and then click the Enable Content button next to the security warning, if necessary.
2. **Explore** In the **Patron** table, delete the record with PatronID 36064. (*Hint:* Delete the related record in the Donation subdatasheet first, which you need to display using the Insert Subdatasheet dialog box.) Close the Patron table without saving changes to the table layout.
3. Create a query based on the Animal table that includes the AnimalID, AnimalName, AnimalType, Gender, and ArrivalDate fields, in that order. Save the query as **AnimalsByType**, and then run it.
4. Modify the AnimalsByType query design so that it sorts records in ascending order first by AnimalType and then by Gender. Save and run the query.
5. In the AnimalsByType query datasheet, find the record for the animal with Animal ID D23, and then change the arrival date for this animal to **5/19/2016**. Close the query.
6. Create a query that displays the PatronID, FirstName, and LastName fields from the Patron table, and the Description and DonationValue fields from the Donation table for all donations over $150. Sort the query in ascending order by donation value. Save the query as **LargeDonations**, run the query, and then close it.
7. Copy and paste the LargeDonations query to create a new query named **LargeCashDonations**.
8. **Explore** Modify the LargeCashDonations query to display only those records with donations valuing more than $150 in cash. Do not include the Description field values in the query results. Use the query datasheet to calculate the average cash donation. Save and close the query.
9. Create a query that displays the PatronID, FirstName, and LastName fields from the Patron table, and the AnimalName, AnimalType, Age, Gender, and Adopted fields from the Animal table. Specify that the results show records for only those animals that have been adopted. Do not display the Adopted field values in the query results. Save the query as **CatAdoptions**, and then run the query.
10. Filter the results of the CatAdoptions query datasheet to display records for cats only.
11. **Explore** Format the datasheet of the CatAdoptions query so that it does not display gridlines, uses an alternate row Standard Color of Purple 2, and displays a font size of 12. (*Hint*: Use the Gridlines button in the Text Formatting group on the HOME tab to select the appropriate gridlines option.) Resize the columns to display the complete field names and values, if necessary. Save and close the query.

Explore 12. Create a query that displays the PatronID, FirstName, and LastName fields from the Patron table, and the Description, DonationDate, and DonationValue fields from the Donation table. Specify that the query include records for noncash donations only or for donations made in the month of June 2016. Sort the records first in ascending order by the patron's last name, and then in descending order by the donation value. Save the query as **NonCashOrJuneDonations**, run the query, and then close it.

13. Copy and paste the NonCashOrJuneDonations query to create a new query named **DonationsAfterStorageCharge**.

Explore 14. Modify the DonationsAfterStorageCharge query so that it displays records for noncash donations made on all dates. Create a calculated field named **NetDonation** that displays the results of subtracting $3.50 from the DonationValue field values to account for the cost of storing each noncash donated item. Set the Caption property **Net Donation** for the calculated field. Display the results in ascending order by donation value. Run the query, and then modify it to format both the DonationValue field and the calculated field as Currency with two decimal places. Run the query again and resize the columns in the datasheet to their best fit, as necessary. Save and close the query.

Explore 15. Create a query based on the **Donation** table that displays the sum, average, and count of the DonationValue field for all donations. Then complete the following:

   a. Specify field names of **TotalDonations**, **AverageDonation**, and **NumberofDonations**. Then specify captions to include spaces between words.
   b. Save the query as **DonationStatistics**, and then run it. Resize the query datasheet columns to their best fit.
   c. Modify the field properties so that the values in the Total Donations and Average Donation columns display two decimal places and the Standard format. Run the query again, and then save and close the query.
   d. Copy and paste the DonationStatistics query to create a new query named **DonationStatisticsByDescription**.
   e. Modify the DonationStatisticsByDescription query to display the sum, average, and count of the DonationValue field for all donations grouped by Description, with Description appearing as the first field. Sort the records in descending order by Total Donations. Save, run, and then close the query.

16. Compact and repair the Shelter database, and then close it.

Case Problem 4

TROUBLESHOOT

Data File needed for this Case Problem: Stanley.accdb *(cont. from Tutorial 2)* and Tour.accdb

Stanley EcoTours Janice and Bill Stanley need your help to maintain and analyze data about the clients, reservations, and tours for their ecotourism business. Additionally, you'll troubleshoot some problems in another database containing tour information. Complete the following:

1. Open the **Stanley** database you created and worked with in Tutorials 1 and 2, and then click the Enable Content button next to the security warning, if necessary.
2. In the **Guest** table, change the phone number for Paul Barry to **406-497-1068**, and then close the table.
3. Create a query based on the Tour table that includes the TourName, Location, Country, PricePerPerson, and TourType fields, in that order. Sort in ascending order based on the PricePerPerson field values. Save the query as **ToursByPrice**, and then run the query.
4. Use the ToursByPrice query datasheet to display the total Price Per Person for the tours. Save and close the query.

5. Create a query that displays the GuestLast, City, and State/Prov fields from the Guest table, and the ReservationID, StartDate, and People fields from the Reservation table. Save the query as **GuestTourDates**, and then run the query. Change the alternate row color in the query datasheet to the Theme Color Green, Accent 6, Lighter 40%. In Datasheet view, use an AutoFilter to sort the query results from oldest to newest Start Date. Save and close the query.

6. Create a query that displays the GuestFirst, GuestLast, City, ReservationID, TourID, and StartDate fields for all guests from Montana (MT). Do not include the State/Prov field in the query results. Sort the query in ascending order by the guest's last name. Save the query as **MontanaGuests** and then run it. Close the query.

7. Create a query that displays data from all three tables in the database, as follows: the GuestLast, City, State/Prov, and Country fields from the Guest table; the StartDate field from the Reservation table; and the TourName, Location, and TourType fields from the Tour table. Specify that the query select only those records for guests from Canada or guests who are taking Jeep tours. Sort the query in ascending order by Location. Save the query as **CanadaOrJeep**, and then run the query. Resize datasheet columns to their best fit, as necessary, and then save and close the query.

8. Copy and paste the CanadaOrJeep query to create a new query named **IdahoAndJuly**.

9. Modify the IdahoAndJuly query to select all guests from Idaho who are taking a tour starting sometime in the month of July 2016. Do not include the State/Prov field values or the Country field values in the query results. Run the query. Resize datasheet columns to their best fit, as necessary, and then save and close the query.

10. Create a query that displays the ReservationID, StartDate, and People fields from the Reservation table, and the TourName, Location, Country, PricePerPerson, and SingleSupplement fields from the Tour table for all reservations with a People field value of 1. Save the query as **SingleReservations**. Add a field to the query named **TotalCost** that displays the results of adding the SingleSupplement field values to the PricePerPerson field values. Set the Caption property **Total Cost** for the calculated field. Display the results in descending order by TotalCost. Do not include the People field values in the query results. Run the query. Modify the query by formatting the TotalCost field to show 0 decimal places. Run the query, resize datasheet columns to their best fit, as necessary, and then save and close the query.

11. Create a query based on the Tour table that determines the minimum, average, and maximum price per person for all tours. Then complete the following:
    a. Specify field names of **LowestPrice**, **AveragePrice**, and **HighestPrice**.
    b. Set the Caption property for each field to include a space between the two words in the field name.
    c. Save the query as **PriceStatistics**, and then run the query.
    d. In Design view, specify the Standard format and two decimal places for each column.
    e. Run the query, resize all the datasheet columns to their best fit, save your changes, and then close the query.
    f. Create a copy of the PriceStatistics query named **PriceStatisticsByTourType**.
    g. Modify the PriceStatisticsByTourType query to display the price statistics grouped by TourType, with TourType appearing as the first field. Save your changes and then run and close the query.

12. Compact and repair the Stanley database, and then close it.

Troubleshoot 13. Open the **Tour** database located in the Access1 ▶ Case4 folder provided with your Data Files, and then click the Enable Content button next to the security warning, if necessary. Run the BookingByDateAndState query in the Tour database. The query is not producing the desired results. Fix the query so that the data from the Booking table is listed first, the data is sorted only by StartDate in ascending order, and the results do not display country values. Save and close the corrected query.

Troubleshoot 14. Run the WYGuestsFewerPeople query, which displays no records in the results. This query is supposed to show data for guests from Wyoming with fewer than four people in their booking. Find and correct the error in the query design, run the query, and then close it.

Troubleshoot 15. Run the CanadaOrSeptStart query. This query should display the records for all guests who are from Canada or whose booking start date is on or after 9/1/2016. Find and correct the errors in the query design, run the query, and then close it. Compact and repair the Tour database, and then close it.

TUTORIAL 5

Creating Advanced Queries and Enhancing Table Design

Making the Clinic Database Easier to Use

OBJECTIVES

Session 5.1
- Review object naming standards
- Use the Like, In, Not, and & operators in queries
- Filter data using an AutoFilter
- Use the IIf function to assign a conditional value to a calculated field in a query
- Create a parameter query

Session 5.2
- Use query wizards to create a crosstab query, a find duplicates query, and a find unmatched query
- Create a top values query

Session 5.3
- Modify table designs using lookup fields, input masks, and data validation rules
- Identify object dependencies
- Review a Long Text field's properties
- Designate a trusted folder

Case | Chatham Community Health Services

Chatham Community Health Services is a nonprofit health clinic located in Hartford, Connecticut. It provides a range of medical services to patients of all ages. The clinic specializes in the areas of pulmonology, cardiac care, and chronic disease management. Cindi Rodriguez, the office manager for Chatham Community Health Services, oversees a small staff and is responsible for maintaining the medical records of the clinic's patients.

Cindi and her staff rely on Microsoft Access 2013 to manage electronic medical records for patient information, billing, inventory control, purchasing, and accounts payable. The Chatham staff developed the Clinic database, which contains tables, queries, forms, and reports that Cindi and other staff members use to track patient, visit, and billing information.

Cindi is interested in taking better advantage of the power of Access to make the database easier to use and to create more sophisticated queries. For example, Cindi wants to obtain lists of patients in certain cities. She also needs a summarized list of invoice amounts by city. In this tutorial, you'll modify and customize the Clinic database to satisfy these and other requirements.

STARTING DATA FILES

Access2 → Tutorial
Clinic.accdb

Review
Supplier.accdb

Case1
Task.accdb

Case2
Tutoring.accdb

Case3
Rosemary.accdb

Case4
Ecotour.accdb

AC 234 Access | Tutorial 5 Creating Advanced Queries and Enhancing Table Design

Session 5.1 Visual Overview:

A Select query selects the records in the fields that satisfy the criteria.

The tbl prefix tag identifies a table object.

The qry prefix tag identifies a query object.

The frm prefix tag identifies a form object.

The rpt prefix tag identifies a report object.

A calculated field contains an expression that calculates the values of the data in the field.

The design grid contains the fields and criteria that will be used in the query.

Tutorial 5 Creating Advanced Queries and Enhancing Table Design | Access   AC 235

Calculated Field

The name of the new calculated field is placed to the left of the expression, separated with a colon.

The **IIf function** tests a condition and returns one of two values. The function returns the first value if the condition is true, and the second value if the condition is false.

The Expression Builder can be used to create an expression for a calculated field.

Expression Builder

Enter an Expression to define the calculated query field:
(Examples of expressions include [field1] + [field2] and [field1] < 5)

Patient: IIf(IsNull([Parent]),[LastName] & ", " & [FirstName],[Parent] & " (Parent)")

OK
Cancel
Help
<< Less

The falsepart of this IIf function will concatenate the data in the Parent field to the string "(Parent)".

Expression Elements
- qryPatientsByName
- Functions
- Clinic.accdb
- Constants
- Operators
- Common Expressions

Expression Categories
- <Parameters>
- Patient
- PatientID
- LastName
- FirstName
- Parent
- BirthDate
- Phone
- Address
- City
- State
- Zip
- EmailAddress

Expression Values

The truepart of this IIf function will concatenate the data in the LastName field to a string with a comma and space. It will then concatenate the result to the data in the FirstName field.

The **IsNull function** will return a value of true if the field is empty and will return a value of false if the field is not empty.

Reviewing the Clinic Database

TIP
Read the Microsoft Access Naming Conventions section in the appendix titled "Relational Databases and Database Design" for more information about naming conventions.

Cindi and her staff had no previous database experience when they created the Clinic database; they simply used the wizards and other easy-to-use Access tools. As business continued to grow at Chatham Community Health Services, Cindi realized she needed a database expert to further enhance the Clinic database. She hired Raj Gupta, who has a business information systems degree and nine years of experience developing database systems. Raj spent a few days reviewing the Clinic database, making sure the database adhered to simple naming standards for the objects and field names to make his future work easier.

Before implementing the enhancements for Cindi, you'll review the naming conventions for the object names in the Clinic database.

To review the object naming conventions in the Clinic database:

1. Make sure you have the Access starting Data Files on your computer.

   Trouble? If you don't have the Access Data Files, you need to get them before you can proceed. Your instructor will either give you the Data Files or ask you to obtain them from a specified location (such as a network drive). If you have any questions about the Data Files, see your instructor or technical support person for assistance.

2. Start Access, and then open the **Clinic** database from the Access2 ▸ Tutorial folder where your starting Data Files are stored.

   Trouble? If a security warning is displayed below the ribbon, click the Enable Content button next to the warning text to dismiss it. The security warning may appear because there is active content (a query) in the file and it may not be in a trusted folder.

As shown in Visual Overview 5.1, the Navigation Pane displays the objects grouped by object type. Each object name has a prefix tag—a tbl prefix tag for tables, a qry prefix tag for queries, a frm prefix tag for forms, and a rpt prefix tag for reports. All three characters in each prefix tag are lower case. The word immediately after the three-character prefix begins with an upper case letter. Using object prefix tags, you can readily identify the object type, even when the objects have the same base name—for instance, tblPatient, frmPatient, and rptCustomersAndBilling. In addition, object names have no spaces, because other database management systems, such as SQL Server and Oracle, do not permit spaces in object and field names. It is important to adhere to industry standard naming conventions, both to make it easier to convert your database to another DBMS in the future, if necessary, and to develop personal habits that enable you to work seamlessly with other major DBMSs. If Chatham Community Health Services needs to upscale to one of these other systems in the future, using standard naming conventions means that Raj will have to do less work to make the transition.

PROSKILLS

Teamwork: Following Naming Conventions

Most Access databases have hundreds of fields, objects, and controls. You'll find it easier to identify the type and purpose of these database items when you use a naming convention or standard. Most companies adopt a standard naming convention, such as the one used for the Clinic database, so that multiple people can develop a database, troubleshoot database problems, and enhance and improve existing databases. When working on a database, a team's tasks are difficult, if not impossible, to perform if a standard naming convention isn't used. In addition, most databases and database samples on Web sites and in training books use standard naming conventions that are similar to the ones used for the Clinic database. By following the standard naming convention established by your company or organization, you'll help to ensure smooth collaboration among all team members.

Now you'll create the queries that Cindi needs.

Using a Pattern Match in a Query

You are already familiar with queries that use an exact match or a range of values (for example, queries that use the > or < comparison operators) to select records. Access provides many other operators for creating select queries. These operators let you build more complicated queries that are difficult or impossible to create with exact-match or range-of-values selection criteria.

Cindi created a list of questions she wants to answer using the Clinic database:

- Which patients have the 860 area code?
- What is the patient information for patients located in Bloomfield, Windsor, or Meriden?
- What is the patient information for all patients except those located in Bloomfield, Windsor, or Meriden?
- What is the patient and visit information for patients in Hartford or West Hartford who have invoice amounts for less than $100 or who visited during the winter?
- What are the first and last names of Chatham Community Health Services' patients, or the parent name if it is listed? Children should not be contacted directly.
- What is the patient information for patients in a particular city? This query needs to be flexible to allow the user to specify the city.

Next, you will create the queries necessary to answer these questions. Cindi wants to view the records for all patients located in the 860 area code. These patients are located nearby and Cindi would like to start planning to arrange transportation for any of these patients who have difficulty travelling to the clinic. To answer Cindi's question, you can create a query that uses a pattern match. A **pattern match** selects records with a value for the designated field that matches the pattern of a simple condition value—in this case, patients with the 860 area code. You do this using the Like comparison operator.

The **Like comparison operator** selects records by matching field values to a specific pattern that includes one or more of these wildcard characters: asterisk (*), question mark (?), and number symbol (#). The asterisk represents any string of characters, the question mark represents any single character, and the number symbol represents any single digit. Using a pattern match is similar to using an exact match, except that a pattern match includes wildcard characters.

To create the new query, you must first place the tblPatient table field list in the Query window in Design view.

Access | Tutorial 5 Creating Advanced Queries and Enhancing Table Design

To create the new query in Design view:

1. If necessary, click the **Shutter Bar Open/Close Button** « at the top of the Navigation Pane to close it.
2. On the ribbon, click the **CREATE** tab.
3. In the Queries group, click the **Query Design** button. Access opens the Show Table dialog box in front of the Query window in Design view.
4. Click **tblPatient** in the Tables box, click the **Add** button, and then click the **Close** button. Access places the tblPatient table field list in the Query window and closes the Show Table dialog box.
5. Drag the bottom border of the tblPatient window down until you can see the full list of fields.
6. Double-click the **title bar** of the tblPatient field list to highlight all the fields, and then drag the highlighted fields to the first column's Field box in the design grid. Access places each field in a separate column in the design grid, in the same order that the fields appear in the table. See Figure 5-1.

> **TIP**
> You can also double-click a table name to add the table's field list to the Query window.

Figure 5-1 Adding the fields for the pattern match query

[Screenshot of Query1 Design view showing tblPatient field list with PatientID, LastName, FirstName, Parent, BirthDate, Phone, Address, City, State, Zip, EmailAddress. Callouts: "all tblPatient table fields in the design grid" and "Phone Criteria box"]

Trouble? If tblPatient.* appears in the first column's Field box, you dragged the * from the field list instead of the highlighted fields. Press the Delete key, and then repeat Step 6.

Now you will enter the pattern match condition Like "860*" for the Phone field. Access will select records with a Phone field value of 860 in positions one through three. The asterisk wildcard character specifies that any characters can appear in the remaining positions of the field value.

Tutorial 5 Creating Advanced Queries and Enhancing Table Design | Access   AC 239

TIP

If you omit the Like operator, Access automatically adds it when you run the query.

To specify records that match the indicated pattern:

1. Click the **Phone Criteria** box, and then type **L**. The Formula AutoComplete menu displays a list of functions beginning with the letter L, but the Like operator is not one of the choices in the list. You'll finish typing the condition.

2. Type **ike "860*"**. See Figure 5-2.

Figure 5-2   Record selection based on matching a specific pattern

pattern match selection criterion → Like "860*"

3. Click the **Save** button on the Quick Access Toolbar to open the Save As dialog box.

4. Type **qry860AreaCode** in the Query Name box, and then press the **Enter** key. Access saves the query and displays the name on the object tab.

5. On the DESIGN tab, in the Results group, click the **Run** button. The query results are displayed in the query window. Access finds 46 records with the area code 860 in the Phone field. Not all records fit in the window, and you can scroll down to see more records. See Figure 5-3.

Figure 5-3   tblPatient table records for area code 860

46 records total

scroll down to see more records that match the criteria

Note that Raj removed the hyphens from the Phone field values; for example, 8609382822 in the first record used to be 860-938-2822. You'll modify the Phone field later in this tutorial to format its values with hyphens.

> **6.** Change the first record in the table, with Patient ID 22500, so the Last Name and First Name columns contain your last and first names, respectively.
>
> **7.** Close the qry860AreaCode query.

Next, Cindi asks you to create a query that displays information about patients who live in Bloomfield, Windsor, or Meriden. She wants a printout of the patient data for her administrative assistant, who will contact these patients. To produce the results Cindi wants, you'll create a query using a list-of-values match.

Using a List-of-Values Match in a Query

A **list-of-values match** selects records whose value for the designated field matches one of two or more simple condition values. You could accomplish this by including several Or conditions in the design grid, but the In comparison operator provides an easier and clearer way to do this. The **In comparison operator** lets you define a condition with a list of two or more values for a field. If a record's field value matches one value from the list of defined values, then Access selects and includes that record in the query results.

To display the information Cindi requested, you want to select records if their City field value equals Bloomfield, Windsor, or Meriden. These are the values you will use with the In comparison operator. Cindi wants the query to contain the same fields as the qry860AreaCode query, so you'll make a copy of that query and modify it.

> **To create the query using a list-of-values match:**
>
> **1.** Open the Navigation Pane.
>
> **2.** In the Queries group on the Navigation Pane, right-click **qry860AreaCode** and then click **Copy** on the shortcut menu.
>
> **Trouble?** If you don't see the qry860AreaCode query in the Queries group, press the F5 function key to refresh the object listings in the Navigation pane.
>
> **3.** Right-click in the empty area in the Navigation Pane below the report and click **Paste**.
>
> **4.** In the Query Name box, type **qryBloomfieldWindsorMeridenPatients** and then press the **Enter** key.
>
> To modify the copied query, you need to open it in Design view.
>
> **5.** In the Queries group on the Navigation Pane, right-click **qryBloomfield WindsorMeridenPatients** to select it and display the shortcut menu.
>
> **6.** Click **Design View** on the shortcut menu to open the query in Design view, and then close the Navigation Pane.
>
> You need to delete the existing condition from the Phone field.
>
> **7.** Click the **Phone Criteria** box, press the **F2** key to highlight the entire condition, and then press the **Delete** key to remove the condition.
>
> Now you can enter the criterion for the new query using the In comparison operator. When you use this operator, you must enclose the list of values you want to match within parentheses and separate the values with commas. In addition, for fields defined using the Text data type, you enclose each value in quotation marks, although Access adds the quotation marks if you omit them. For fields defined using the Number or Currency data type, you don't enclose the values in quotation marks.

8. Right-click the **City Criteria** box to open the shortcut menu, click **Zoom** to open the Zoom dialog box, and then type **In ("Bloomfield","Windsor","Meriden")**, as shown in Figure 5-4.

| Figure 5-4 | Record selection based on matching field values to a list of values |

list-of-values selection criteria → In ("Bloomfield","Windsor","Meriden")

TIP
After clicking in a box, you can also open its Zoom dialog box by holding down the Shift key and pressing the F2 key.

9. Click the **OK** button to close the Zoom dialog box, and then save and run the query. Access displays the recordset, which shows the 20 records with Bloomfield, Windsor, or Meriden in the City field.

10. Close the query.

Cindi also asks her assistant to contact Chatham Community Health Services patients who don't live in Bloomfield, Windsor, or Meriden. You can provide Cindi with this information by creating a query with the Not logical operator.

Using the Not Logical Operator in a Query

The **Not logical operator** negates a criterion or selects records for which the designated field does not match the criterion. For example, if you enter *Not "Windsor"* in the Criteria box for the City field, the query results show records that do not have the City field value Windsor—that is, records of all patients not located in Windsor.

To create Cindi's query, you will combine the Not logical operator with the In comparison operator to select patients whose City field value is not in the list *("Bloomfield", "Windsor","Meriden")*. The qryBloomfieldWindsorMeridenPatients query has the fields that Cindi needs to see in the query results. Cindi doesn't need to keep the qryBloomfieldWindsorMeridenPatients query, so you'll rename and then modify the query.

TIP
You can rename any type of object, including a table, in the Navigation Pane using the Rename command on the shortcut menu.

To create the query using the Not logical operator:

1. Open the Navigation Pane.

2. In the Queries group, right-click **qryBloomfieldWindsorMeridenPatients**, and then on the shortcut menu click **Rename**.

3. Position the insertion point after "qry," type **Non**, and then press the **Enter** key. The query name is now qryNonBloomfieldWindsorMeridenPatients.

4. Open the **qryNonBloomfieldWindsorMeridenPatients** query in Design view, and then close the Navigation Pane.

You need to change the existing condition in the City field to add the Not logical operator.

5. Click the **City Criteria** box, open the Zoom dialog box, click at the beginning of the expression, type **Not**, and then press the **spacebar**. See Figure 5-5.

Figure 5-5 Record selection based on not matching a list of values

Zoom dialog box showing: Not In ("Bloomfield","Windsor","Meriden")

Callout: Not logical operator with list-of-values selection criteria

6. Click the **OK** button, and then save and run the query. The recordset displays only those records with a City field value that is not Bloomfield, Windsor, or Meriden. The recordset includes a total of 31 patient records.

7. Scroll down the datasheet to make sure that no Bloomfield or Windsor or Meriden patients appear in your results.

Now you can close and delete the query, because Cindi does not need to run this query again.

8. Close the query, and then open the Navigation Pane.

9. Right-click **qryNonBloomfieldWindsorMeridenPatients**, click **Delete** on the shortcut menu, and then click **Yes** in the dialog box warning that deleting this object will remove it from all groups.

TIP
You can delete any type of object, including a table, in the Navigation Pane using the Delete command on the shortcut menu.

You now are ready to answer Cindi's question about patients in Hartford or West Hartford that have invoice amounts for less than $100 or that visited during the winter.

Using an AutoFilter to Filter Data

Cindi wants to view the patient last and first names, cities, visit dates, walk-in statuses, and visit reasons for patients in Hartford or West Hartford who either walked in without an appointment or visited during the first week in January. The qryJanuaryOrWalkin query contains the same fields Cindi wants to view. This query also uses the Or logical operator to select records if the Walkin field has a value of true or if the VisitDate field value is between 1/1/2016 and 1/7/2016. These are two of the conditions needed to answer Cindi's question. You could modify the qryJanuaryOrWalkin query in Design view to further restrict the records selected to patients located only in Hartford or West Hartford. However, you can use the AutoFilter feature to choose the city restrictions faster and with more flexibility. You previously used the AutoFilter feature to sort records, and you previously used Filter By Selection to filter records. Now you'll use the AutoFilter feature to filter records.

To filter the records using an AutoFilter:

1. Open the **qryJanuaryOrWalkin** query in Design view, and then close the Navigation Pane.

Tutorial 5 Creating Advanced Queries and Enhancing Table Design | Access   AC 243

The true condition for the Walkin field selects records for patients who walked in without an appointment, and the Between #1/1/2016# And #1/7/2016# condition for the VisitDate field selects records for patients whose visit date was in the first week of January 2016. Although the Walkin field is a yes/no field, these values are represented by true (yes) and false (no). Because the conditions are in two different rows, the query uses the Or logical operator. If you wanted to answer Cindi's question in Design view, you would add a condition for the City field, using either the Or logical operator—"Hartford" Or "West Hartford"—or the In comparison operator—In ("Hartford","West Hartford"). If you were to use Like *Hartford instead of the In function, the asterisk wildcard (*) would include East Hartford as well as Hartford and West Hartford. You'd place the condition for the City field in both the Criteria row and in the Or row. The query recordset would include a record only if both conditions in either row are satisfied. Instead of changing the conditions in Design view, though, you'll choose the information Cindi wants using an AutoFilter.

2. Run the query, and then click the **arrow** on the City column heading to display the AutoFilter menu. See Figure 5-6.

Figure 5-6   **Using an AutoFilter to filter records in the query recordset**

The AutoFilter menu lists all City field values that appear in the recordset. A check mark next to an entry indicates that records with that City field value appear in the recordset. To filter for selected City field values, you uncheck the cities you don't want selected and leave checked the cities you do want selected. You can click the "(Select All)" check box to select or deselect all field values. The "(Blanks)" option includes null values when checked and excludes null values when unchecked. (Recall that a null field value is the absence of a value for the field.)

3. Click the **(Select All)** check box to deselect all check boxes, click the **Hartford** check box, and then click the **West Hartford** check box.

   The two check boxes indicate that the AutoFilter will include only Hartford and West Hartford City field values.

4. Click the **OK** button. Access displays the 18 records for patients in Hartford and West Hartford who walked in without an appointment, or who had a visit in the first week in January. See Figure 5-7.

Figure 5-7   **Using an AutoFilter to filter records in the query recordset**

You click the Toggle Filter button in the Sort & Filter group on the HOME tab to remove the current filter and display all records in the query. If you click the Toggle Filter button a second time, you reapply the filter.

5. On the HOME tab, in the Sort & Filter group, click the **Toggle Filter** button. Access removes the filter, and all 37 records appear in the recordset.

6. Click the **Toggle Filter** button. Access applies the City filter, displaying the 18 records for patients in Hartford and West Hartford.

7. Save the query and close it.

Next, Cindi wants to view all fields from the tblPatient table, along with the patient name or the parent name if the patient is a child.

Assigning a Conditional Value to a Calculated Field

If a field in a record does not contain any information at all, it has a null value. Such a field is also referred to as a null field. A field in a record that contains any data at all—even a single space—is nonnull. Records for patients who are adults have nonnull FirstName and LastName field values and null Parent field values in the tblPatient table, while records for children have nonnull values for all three fields. Cindi wants to view records from the tblPatient table in order by the Parent value, if it's nonnull, and at the same time in order by the LastName and then FirstName field values, if the Parent field value is null. To produce this information for Cindi, you need to create a query that includes all fields from the tblPatient table and then add a calculated field that will display the patient name—either the Parent field value, which is input using the form LastName, FirstName, or the LastName and FirstName field values, separated by a comma and a space.

To combine the LastName and FirstName fields, you'll use the expression *LastName & ", " & FirstName*. The **& (ampersand) operator** is a concatenation operator that joins text expressions. **Concatenation** refers to joining two or more text fields or characters encapsulated in quotes. When you join the LastName field value to the string that contains the comma and space, you are concatenating these two strings. If the LastName field value is Fernandez and the FirstName field value is Sabrina, for example, the result of the expression *LastName & ", " & FirstName* is *Fernandez & ", " & Sabrina* which results in *Fernandez, Sabrina*.

> **INSIGHT**
>
> ### Using Concatenation
>
> IT professionals generally refer to a piece of text data as a string. Most programming languages include the ability to join two or more strings using concatenation.
>
> Imagine you're working with a database table that contains Title, FirstName, and LastName values for people who have made donations, and you've been asked to add their names to a report. You could add each individual field separately, but the data would look awkward, with each field in a separate column. Alternatively, you could create a calculated field with an expression that combines the fields with spaces into a more readable format, such as "Mr. Jim Sullivan". To do this, you would concatenate the fields with a space separator. The expression to perform this task might look like *=Title & " " & FirstName & " " & LastName*.

To display the correct patient value, you'll use the IIf function. The IIf (Immediate If) function assigns one value to a calculated field or control if a condition is true, and a second value if the condition is false. The IIf function has three parts: a condition that is true or false, the result when the condition is true, and the result when the condition is false. Each part of the IIf function is separated by a comma. The condition you'll use is *IsNull(Parent)*. The IsNull function tests a field value or an expression for a null value; if the field value or expression is null, the result is true; otherwise, the result is false. The expression *IsNull(Parent)* is true when the Parent field value is null, and is false when the Parent field value is not null.

For the calculated field, you'll enter *IIf(IsNull(Parent),LastName & ", " & FirstName, Parent & " (Parent)")*. You interpret this expression as follows: If the Parent field value is null, then set the calculated field value to the concatenation of the LastName field value and the text string ", " and the FirstName field value. If the Parent field value is not null, then set the calculated field value to the Parent field value and the text string "(Parent)" to indicate the patient name is the parent of a child patient.

Now you're ready to create Cindi's query to display the patient name.

AC 246 Access | Tutorial 5 Creating Advanced Queries and Enhancing Table Design

To create the query to display the patient name:

1. Click the **CREATE** tab, and then in the Queries group, click the **Query Design** button. The Show Table dialog box opens on top of the Query window in Design View.

2. Click **tblPatient** in the Tables box, click the **Add** button, and then click the **Close** button. The tblPatient table field list is placed in the Query window and the Show Table dialog box closes.

   Cindi wants all fields from the tblPatient table to appear in the query recordset, with the new calculated field in the first column.

3. Drag the bottom border of the tblPatient field list down until all fields are visible, double-click the **title bar** of the tblPatient field list to highlight all the fields, and then drag the highlighted fields to the second column's Field box in the design grid. Access places each field in a separate column in the design grid starting with the second column, in the same order that the fields appear in the table.

   Trouble? If you accidentally drag the highlighted fields to the first column in the design grid, click the PatientID Field box, and then in the Query Setup group, click the Insert Columns button. Continue with Step 4.

4. Right-click the blank Field box to the left of the PatientID field, and then click **Build** on the shortcut menu. The Expression Builder dialog box opens.

   Cindi wants to use "Patient" as the name of the calculated field, so you'll type that name, followed by a colon, and then you'll choose the IIf function.

5. Type **Patient:** and then press the **spacebar**.

6. Double-click **Functions** in the Expression Elements (left) column, and then click **Built-In Functions**.

7. Scroll down the Expression Categories (middle) column, click **Program Flow**, and then in the Expression Values (right) column, double-click **IIf**. Access adds the IIf function with four placeholders to the right of the calculated field name in the expression box. See Figure 5-8.

TIP

After clicking in a box, you can also open its Expression Builder dialog box by holding down the Ctrl key and pressing the F2 key.

Make sure you double-click instead of single-click the IIf function.

Figure 5-8 | **IIf function inserted for the calculated field**

Tutorial 5 Creating Advanced Queries and Enhancing Table Design | Access

The expression you will create does not need the leftmost placeholder (<<Expr>>), so you'll delete it. You'll replace the second placeholder (<<expression>>) with the condition using the IsNull function, the third placeholder (<<truepart>>) with the expression using the & operator, and the fourth placeholder (<<falsepart>>) with the Parent field name and expression to include the " (Parent)" text.

▸ 8. Click **<<Expr>>** in the expression box, and then press the **Delete** key. The first placeholder is deleted.

▸ 9. Click **<<expression>>** in the expression box, and then click **Inspection** in the Expression Categories (middle) column.

▸ 10. Double-click **IsNull** in the Expression Values (right) column, click **<<expression>>** in the expression box, and then type **Parent**. You've completed the entry of the condition in the IIf function. See Figure 5-9.

Figure 5-9 After entering the condition for the calculated field's IIf function

After you typed the first letter of "Parent," the Formula AutoComplete box displayed a list of functions beginning with the letter P, and a ScreenTip for the IsNull function was displayed above the box. The box closed after you typed the third letter, but the ScreenTip remains on the screen.

Instead of typing the field name of Parent in the previous step, you could have double-clicked Clinic.accdb in the Expression Elements column, double-clicked Tables in the Expression Elements column, clicked tblPatient in the Expression Elements column, and then double-clicked Parent in the Expression Categories column.

Now you'll replace the third placeholder and then the fourth placeholder.

TIP
The expression "[tblPatient]![Parent]", meaning the Parent field in the tblPatient table, is the same as "Parent".

▸ 11. Click **<<truepart>>**, and then type **LastName & ", " & FirstName** to finish creating the calculated field. Be sure you type a space after the comma within the quotation marks.

▸ 12. Click **<<falsepart>>**, and then type **Parent & " (Parent)"**. Be sure you type a space after the first quotation mark. See Figure 5-10.

AC 248 Access | Tutorial 5 Creating Advanced Queries and Enhancing Table Design

Figure 5-10   Completed calculated field

truepart expression → Patient: IIf(IsNull(Parent) , LastName & ", " & FirstName, Parent & " (Parent)") ← *falsepart expression*

Cindi wants the query to sort records in ascending order by the Patient calculated field.

To sort, save, and run the query:

1. Click the **OK** button in the Expression Builder dialog box to close it.

2. Click the right side of the **Patient Sort** box to display the sort order options, and then click **Ascending**. The query will display the records in alphabetical order based on the Patient field values.

   The calculated field name of Patient consists of a single word, so you do not need to set the Caption property for it. However, you'll review the properties for the calculated field by opening its property sheet.

3. On the DESIGN tab, in the Show/Hide group, click the **Property Sheet** button. The property sheet opens and displays the properties for the Patient calculated field. See Figure 5-11.

Figure 5-11   Property sheet for the Patient calculated field

Tutorial 5 Creating Advanced Queries and Enhancing Table Design | Access   AC 249

Among the properties for the calculated field, which is the current field, is the Caption property. Leaving the Caption property set to null means that the column name for the calculated field in the query recordset will be Patient, which is the calculated field name. The Property Sheet button is a toggle, so you'll click it again to close the property sheet.

4. Click the **Property Sheet** button again to close the property sheet.

5. Save the query as **qryPatientsByName**, run the query, and then resize the Patient column to its best fit. Access displays all records from the tblPatient table in alphabetical order by the Patient field. See Figure 5-12.

Figure 5-12   Completed query displaying the Patient calculated field

Patient	Patient ID	Last Name	First Name	Parent	Date of Birth
Aguilar, Lilian	22504	Aguilar	Lilian		8/16/1938
Belanger, Malcolm	22519	Belanger	Malcolm		10/17/1950
Billings, Claire	22541	Billings	Claire		11/16/1990
Booker, Thomas	22510	Booker	Thomas		8/25/1966
Boucher, Sam	22543	Boucher	Sam		3/11/1975
Brown, Olivia	22530	Brown	Olivia		11/24/1943
Caputo, Michael	22536	Caputo	Michael		10/19/1998
Castro, Daniel	22511	Castro	Daniel		9/23/1933
Chang, Lisa	22512	Chang	Lisa		10/5/1955
Cruz, Magdalena	22550	Cruz	Magdalena		7/24/1984
Darcy, Edward	22501	Darcy	Edward		7/15/1986
Delgado, Alex	22535	Delgado	Alex		7/16/1960
Diaz, Anna	22542	Diaz	Anna		9/25/1987
Engber, Jim (Parent)	22521	Engber	Cathy	Engber, Jim	4/7/2006
Fielder, Pam	22549	Fielder	Pam		12/6/1978
Finnerty, Amber	22505	Finnerty	Amber		5/7/1946
Franklin, Chaney	22551	Franklin	Chaney		1/18/1954
Fraser, Nancy	22523	Fraser	Nancy		11/8/1977
Garrett, Ashley	22552	Garrett	Ashley		3/24/1989

patient names are the concatenation of LastName, FirstName for null Parent values

patient names are the same as nonnull Parent values with the additional "(Parent)" text

6. Save and close the query.

You're now ready to create the query to satisfy Cindi's request for information about patients in a particular city.

Creating a Parameter Query

Cindi's next request is for records in the qryPatientsByName query for patients in a particular city. For this query, she wants to specify a city, such as Windsor or Hartford, each time she runs the query.

To create this query, you will copy, rename, and modify the qryPatientsByName query. You could create a simple condition using an exact match for the City field, but you would need to change it in Design view every time you run the query. Alternatively, Cindi or a member of her staff could filter the qryPatientsByName query for the city records they want to view. Instead, you will create a parameter query. A **parameter query** displays a dialog box that prompts the user to enter one or more criteria values when the query is run. In this case, you want to create a query that prompts for the city and selects only those patient records with that City field value from the table. You will enter the prompt in the Criteria box for the City field. When Access runs the query, it will open a dialog box and prompt you to enter the city. Access will then create the query results, just as if you had changed the criteria in Design view.

> **REFERENCE**
>
> **Creating a Parameter Query**
> - Create a select query that includes all fields to appear in the query results.
> - Choose the sort fields and set the criteria that do not change when you run the query.
> - Decide which fields to use as prompts when the query runs. In the Criteria box for each of these fields, type the prompt you want to appear in a dialog box when you run the query, and enclose the prompt in brackets.

You'll copy and rename the qryPatientsByName query now, and then you'll change its design to create the parameter query.

To create the parameter query based on an existing query:

1. Open the Navigation Pane, copy and paste the qryPatientsByName query, and then name the new copy **qryPatientsByCityParameter**.

2. Open the **qryPatientsByCityParameter** query in Design view, and then close the Navigation Pane.

   Next, you must enter the criterion for the parameter query. In this case, Cindi wants the query to prompt users to enter the city for the patient records they want to view. You need to enter the prompt in the Criteria box for the City field. Brackets must enclose the text of the prompt.

3. Click the **City Criteria** box, type **[Type the city:]**, and then press the **Enter** key. See Figure 5-13.

Figure 5-13 Specifying the prompt for the parameter query

prompt text enclosed in brackets

4. Save and run the query. Access displays a dialog box prompting you for the name of the city. See Figure 5-14

Tutorial 5 Creating Advanced Queries and Enhancing Table Design | Access   AC 251

Figure 5-14   **Enter Parameter Value dialog box**

prompt — Type the city:
type value here —

TIP

You must enter a value that matches the spelling of a City field value, but you can use either lowercase or uppercase letters.

The bracketed text you specified in the Criteria box of the City field appears above a box, in which you must type a City field value. Cindi wants to see all patients in Waterbury.

5. Type **Waterbury**, press the **Enter** key, and then scroll the datasheet to the right, if necessary, to display the City field values. The recordset displays the data for the two patients in Waterbury. See Figure 5-15.

Figure 5-15   **Results of the parameter query**

Waterbury patients selected

Patient	Patient ID	Last Name	First Name	Parent	Date of Birth	Phone	Address	City	State	Zip	Email Address
Garrett, Ashley	22552	Garrett	Ashley		3/24/1989	475-552-8429	372 Higbee Ct	Waterbury	CT	06704	agarrett@example.org
Rodriguez, Maria	22525	Rodriguez	Maria		2/11/1936	475-552-9023	624 Noyes St	Waterbury	CT	06704	marodrig13@example.net

Cindi asks what happens if she doesn't enter a value in the dialog box when she runs the qryPatientsByCityParameter query. You can run the query again to show Cindi the answer to her question.

6. Switch to Design view, and then run the query. The Enter Parameter Value dialog box opens.

If you click the OK button or press the Enter key, you'll run the parameter query without entering a value for the City field criterion.

7. Click the **OK** button. Access displays no records in the query results.

When you run the parameter query and enter "Waterbury" in the dialog box, Access runs the query just as if you had entered "Waterbury" in the City Criteria box in the design grid, and displays all Waterbury patient records. When you do not enter a value in the dialog box, Access runs the query as if you had entered "null" in the City Criteria box. Because none of the records has a null City field value, Access displays no records. Cindi asks if there's a way to display records for a selected City field value when she enters its value in the dialog box and to display all records when she doesn't enter a value.

Creating a More Flexible Parameter Query

Most users want a parameter query to display the records that match the parameter value the user enters or to display all records when the user doesn't enter a parameter value. To provide this functionality, you can change the value in the Criteria box in the design grid for the specified column. For example, you could change an entry for a City field from *[Type the city:]* to *Like [Type the city:] & "*"*. That is, you can prefix the Like operator to the original criterion and concatenate the criterion to a wildcard character. When you run the parameter query with this new entry, Access will display one of the following recordsets:

- If you enter a specific City field value in the dialog box, such as *Windsor*, the entry is the same as *Like "Windsor" & "*"*, which becomes *Like "Windsor*"* after the concatenation operation. That is, Access selects all records whose City field values have Windsor in the first nine positions and any characters in the remaining positions. If the table on which the query is based contains records with City field values of Windsor, Access displays only those records. However, if the table on which the query is based also contains records with City field values of Windsor City, then Access would display both the Windsor and the Windsor City records.
- If you enter a letter in the dialog box, such as *W*, the entry is the same as *Like "W*"*, and the recordset displays all records with City field values that begin with the letter W, which would include Waterbury, West Hartford, Windsor, and Windsor City.
- If you enter no value in the dialog box, the entry is the same as *Like Null & "*"*, which becomes *Like "*"* after the concatenation operation, and the recordset displays all records.

Now you'll modify the parameter query to satisfy Cindi's request and you'll test the new version of the query.

To modify and test the parameter query:

1. Switch to Design view.

2. Click the **City Criteria** box, and then open the Zoom dialog box.

    You'll use the Zoom dialog box to modify the value in the City Criteria box.

3. Click to the left of the expression in the Zoom dialog box, type **Like**, press the **spacebar**, and then press the **End** key.

4. Press the **spacebar**, type **&**, press the **spacebar**, and then type "*" as shown in Figure 5-16.

> Be sure you type "*" at the end of the expression.

Figure 5-16 | **Modified City Criteria value in the Zoom dialog box**

Zoom dialog box showing: Like [Type the city:] & ""*

Now you can test the modified parameter query.

5. Click the **OK** button to close the Zoom dialog box, save your query design changes, and then run the query.

    First, you'll test the query to display patients in Windsor.

6. Type **Windsor**, and then press the **Enter** key. The recordset displays the data for the 10 patients in Windsor.

    Now you'll test the query without entering a value when prompted.

7. Switch to Design view, run the query, and then click the **OK** button. The recordset displays all 51 original records from the tblPatient table.

   Finally, you'll test how the query performs when you enter W in the dialog box.

8. On the HOME tab, in the Records group, click the **Refresh All** button to open the Enter Parameter Value dialog box.

9. Type **W**, press the **Enter** key, and then scroll to the right, if necessary, to display the City field values. The recordset displays the 19 records for patients in Windsor, West Hartford, and Waterbury.

10. Close the query.

11. If you are not continuing on to the next session, close the Clinic database and click the **Yes** button if necessary to empty the Clipboard.

The queries you created will make the Clinic database easier to use. In the next session, you'll create a top values query and use query wizards to create three additional queries.

Session 5.1 Quick Check

1. According to the naming conventions used in this session, you use the _____ prefix tag to identify queries.
2. Which comparison operator selects records based on a specific pattern?
3. What is the purpose of the asterisk (*) in a pattern match query?
4. When do you use the In comparison operator?
5. How do you negate a selection criterion?
6. The _____ function returns one of two values based on whether the condition being tested is true or false.
7. When do you use a parameter query?

Session 5.2 Visual Overview:

A **crosstab query** uses aggregate functions such as Sum and Count to perform arithmetic operations on selected records.

A simple query selects records from one of more tables that satisfy criteria.

A **find duplicates query** is a select query that finds duplicate records in a table or query.

A **find unmatched query** is a select query that finds all records in a table or query that have no related records in a second table or query.

New Query

- Simple Query Wizard
- Crosstab Query Wizard
- Find Duplicates Query Wizard
- Find Unmatched Query Wizard

This wizard creates a select query from the fields you pick.

OK   Cancel

Each column and row intersection will display the sum of the InvoiceAmt values.

The selected field (InvoiceAmt) is used in the calculations for each column and row intersection.

This option determines whether to display an overall totals column in the crosstab query.

The crosstab query will display one column for the paid invoices and a second column for the unpaid invoices.

The crosstab query will display one row for each unique City field value.

Crosstab Query Wizard

What number do you want calculated for each column and row intersection?

Fields:
- LastName
- FirstName
- **InvoiceAmt**

Functions:
- Avg
- Count
- First
- Last
- Max
- Min
- StDev
- **Sum**
- Var

For example, you could calculate the sum of the field Order Amount for each employee (column) by country and region (row).

Do you want to summarize each row?

☑ Yes, include row sums.

Sample:

City	InvoicePaid1	InvoicePaid2	InvoicePaid3
City1	Sum(InvoiceAmt)		
City2			
City3			
City4			

Cancel   < Back   Next >   Finish

Advanced Query Wizards

Find Unmatched Query Wizard

What piece of information is in both tables?

For example, a Customers and an Orders table may both have a CustomerID field. Matching fields may have different names.

Select the matching field in each table and then click the <=> button.

Fields in 'tblVisit':
- VisitID
- PatientID
- VisitDate
- Reason
- WalkIn

Fields in 'tblBilling':
- InvoiceNum
- VisitID
- InvoiceDate
- InvoiceAmt
- InvoiceItemID
- InvoicePaid
- Insurance

Matching fields: VisitID <=> VisitID

[Cancel] [< Back] [Next >] [Finish]

This find unmatched query will find all records that do not have matching records in both the tblVisit and tblBilling tables.

The tblVisit and tblBilling tables are joined on the VisitID field.

This list contains the remaining fields in the tblVisit table that will not be considered for duplicate values.

Find Duplicates Query Wizard

Which fields might contain duplicate information?

For example, if you are looking for cities with more than one customer, you would choose City and Region fields here.

Available fields:
- VisitID
- PatientID
- Reason
- WalkIn

Duplicate-value fields:
- VisitDate

[Cancel] [< Back] [Next >] [Finish]

This find duplicates query will find records that have the same VisitDate field value.

Creating a Crosstab Query

Cindi wants to analyze the Chatham Community Health Services invoices by city, so she can view the paid and unpaid invoice amounts for all patients located in each city. Crosstab queries use the aggregate functions shown in Figure 5-17 to perform arithmetic operations on selected records. A crosstab query can also display one additional aggregate function value that summarizes the set of values in each row. The crosstab query uses one or more fields for the row headings on the left and one field for the column headings at the top.

Figure 5-17 Aggregate functions used in crosstab queries

Aggregate Function	Definition
Avg	Average of the field values
Count	Number of the nonnull field values
First	First field value
Last	Last field value
Max	Highest field value
Min	Lowest field value
StDev	Standard deviation of the field values
Sum	Total of the field values
Var	Variance of the field values

© 2014 Cengage Learning

Figure 5-18 shows two query recordsets—the first recordset (qryPatientsAndInvoices) is from a select query and the second recordset (qryPatientsAndInvoicesCrosstab) is from a crosstab query based on the select query.

Tutorial 5 Creating Advanced Queries and Enhancing Table Design | Access   AC 257

| Figure 5-18 | Comparing a select query to a crosstab query |

results of a select query — qryPatientsAndInvoices

Last Name	First Name	City	Invoice Amt	Invoice Paid
Lewis	Patrice	Windsor	$85.00	✓
Lewis	Patrice	Windsor	$48.00	✓
Belanger	Malcolm	West Hartford	$100.00	☐
Darcy	Edward	Bloomfield	$100.00	✓
Darcy	Edward	Bloomfield	$85.00	✓
Fielder	Pam	Bloomfield	$100.00	✓
Fielder	Pam	Bloomfield	$85.00	☐
Fielder	Pam	Bloomfield	$250.00	☐
Castro	Daniel	West Hartford	$100.00	✓
Hallick	Davis	Windsor	$100.00	☐
Hallick	Davis	Windsor	$72.00	☐
Swenson	Lucia	Hartford	$100.00	✓
Swenson	Lucia	Hartford	$85.00	✓
Swenson	Lucia	Hartford	$45.00	☐
Swenson	Lucia	Hartford	$32.00	☐
Parker	Ian	Hartford	$100.00	✓
Parker	Ian	Hartford	$85.00	✓
King	Susan	Meriden	$100.00	☐
King	Susan	Meriden	$150.00	☐
Ingram	Julia	Hartford	$100.00	✓
Ingram	Julia	Hartford	$75.00	☐
Chang	Lisa	Hartford	$100.00	✓
Chang	Lisa	Hartford	$85.00	✓
Belanger	Malcolm	West Hartford	$100.00	✓
Ropiak	Jane	Hartford	$100.00	✓
Ropiak	Jane	Hartford	$150.00	✓
Shaw	Daniel	West Hartford	$100.00	✓

Record: 1 of 204

- West Hartford record with unpaid invoice
- individual West Hartford records
- West Hartford records with paid invoices

results of a crosstab query — qryPatientsAndInvoicesCrosstab

paid invoices | unpaid invoices

City	Total Of InvoiceAmt	Paid	Unpaid
Bloomfield	$2,953.00	$1,273.00	$1,680.00
Hartford	$9,040.00	$4,681.00	$4,359.00
Meriden	$1,336.00	$748.00	$588.00
Waterbury	$528.00	$460.00	$68.00
West Hartford	$2,153.00	$1,395.00	$758.00
Windsor	$4,693.00	$3,591.00	$1,102.00

one row for West Hartford invoice amounts

The qryPatientsAndInvoices query, a select query, joins the tblPatient, tblVisit, and tblBilling tables to display selected data from those tables for all invoices. The qryPatientsAndInvoicesCrosstab query, a crosstab query, uses the qryPatientsAndInvoices query as its source query and displays one row for each unique City field value. The City column in the crosstab query identifies each row. The crosstab query uses the Sum aggregate function on the InvoiceAmt field to produce the displayed values in the Paid and Unpaid columns for each City row. An entry in the Total Of InvoiceAmt column represents the sum of the Paid and Unpaid values for the City field value in that row.

PROSKILLS

Decision Making: Using Both Select Queries and Crosstab Queries

Companies use both select queries and crosstab queries in their decision making. A select query displays several records—one for each row selected by the select query—while a crosstab query displays only one summarized record for each unique field value. When managers want to analyze data at a high level to see the big picture, they might start with a crosstab query, identify which field values to analyze further, and then look in detail at specific field values using select queries. Both select and crosstab queries serve as valuable tools in tracking and analyzing a company's business, and companies use both types of queries in the appropriate situations. By understanding how managers and other employees use the information in a database to make decisions, you can create the correct type of query to provide the information they need.

> **TIP**
> Microsoft Access Help provides more information on creating a crosstab query without using a wizard.

The quickest way to create a crosstab query is to use the **Crosstab Query Wizard**, which guides you through the steps for creating one. You could also change a select query to a crosstab query in Design view using the Crosstab button in the Query Type group on the DESIGN tab.

REFERENCE

Using the Crosstab Query Wizard

- In the Queries group on the CREATE tab, click the Query Wizard button.
- In the New Query dialog box, click Crosstab Query Wizard, and then click the OK button.
- Complete the Wizard dialog boxes to select the table or query on which to base the crosstab query, select the row heading field (or fields), select the column heading field, select the calculation field and its aggregate function, and enter a name for the crosstab query.

The crosstab query you will create, which is similar to the one shown in Figure 5-18, has the following characteristics:

- The qryPatientsAndInvoices query in the Clinic database is the basis for the new crosstab query. The base query includes the LastName, FirstName, City, InvoiceAmt, and InvoicePaid fields.
- The City field is the leftmost column in the crosstab query and identifies each crosstab query row.
- The values from the InvoicePaid field, which is a Yes/No field, identify the rightmost columns of the crosstab query.
- The crosstab query applies the Sum aggregate function to the InvoiceAmt field values and displays the resulting total values in the Paid and Unpaid columns of the query results.
- The grand total of the InvoiceAmt field values appears for each row in a column with the heading Total Of InvoiceAmt.

Next you will create the crosstab query based on the qryPatientsAndInvoices query.

To start the Crosstab Query Wizard:

1. If you took a break after the previous session, make sure that the Clinic database is open and the Navigation Pane is closed.

   Trouble? If the security warning is displayed below the ribbon, click the Enable Content button next to the security warning.

Tutorial 5 Creating Advanced Queries and Enhancing Table Design | Access   AC 259

> 2. Click the **CREATE** tab on the ribbon.
> 3. In the Queries group, click the **Query Wizard** button. The New Query dialog box opens.
> 4. Click **Crosstab Query Wizard**, and then click the **OK** button. The first Crosstab Query Wizard dialog box opens.

You'll now use the Crosstab Query Wizard to create the crosstab query for Cindi.

To finish the Crosstab Query Wizard:

> 1. Click the **Queries** option button in the View section to display the list of queries in the Clinic database, and then click **Query: qryPatientsAndInvoices**. See Figure 5-19.

Figure 5-19   Choosing the query for the crosstab query

[Screenshot of Crosstab Query Wizard dialog box with qryPatientsAndInvoices query selected and Queries option button selected]

> 2. Click the **Next** button to open the next Crosstab Query Wizard dialog box. This is the dialog box where you choose the field (or fields) for the *row* headings. Because Cindi wants the crosstab query to display one row for each unique City field value, you will select that field for the row headings.
> 3. In the Available Fields box, click **City**, and then click the **>** button to move the City field to the Selected Fields box.

TIP
When you select a field, Access changes the sample crosstab query in the dialog box to illustrate your choice.

> 4. Click the **Next** button to open the next Crosstab Query Wizard dialog box, in which you select the field values that will serve as *column* headings. Cindi wants to see the paid and unpaid total invoice amounts, so you need to select the InvoicePaid field for the column headings.
> 5. Click **InvoicePaid** in the box, and then click the **Next** button.
>
> In the next Crosstab Query Wizard dialog box, you choose the field that will be calculated for each row and column intersection and the function to use for the calculation. The results of the calculation will appear in the row and column intersections in the query results. Cindi needs to calculate the sum of the InvoiceAmt field value for each row and column intersection.

6. Click **InvoiceAmt** in the Fields box, click **Sum** in the Functions box, and then make sure that the "Yes, include row sums" check box is checked. The "Yes, include row sums" option creates a column showing the overall totals for the values in each row of the query recordset. See Figure 5-20.

Figure 5-20 — Completed crosstab query design

- selected field for crosstab calculation
- Sum aggregate function selected
- InvoicePaid field values in columns
- option to display an overall totals column in the crosstab query
- City field values in rows

7. Click the **Next** button to open the final Crosstab Query Wizard dialog box, in which you choose the query name.

8. Click in the box, delete the underscore character so that the query name is qryPatientsAndInvoicesCrosstab, be sure the option button for viewing the query is selected, and then click the **Finish** button. Access saves the crosstab query, and then displays the query recordset.

9. Resize all the columns in the query recordset to their best fit, and then click the City field value in the first row (**Bloomfield**). See Figure 5-21.

Figure 5-21 — Crosstab query recordset

- unpaid invoices by city
- paid invoices by city

City	Total Of InvoiceAmt	-1	0
Bloomfield	$2,953.00	$1,273.00	$1,680.00
Hartford	$9,040.00	$4,681.00	$4,359.00
Meriden	$1,336.00	$748.00	$588.00
Waterbury	$528.00	$460.00	$68.00
West Hartford	$2,153.00	$1,395.00	$758.00
Windsor	$4,693.00	$3,591.00	$1,102.00

Tutorial 5 Creating Advanced Queries and Enhancing Table Design | Access   AC 261

The query recordset contains only one row for each City field value. The Total Of InvoiceAmt column shows the total invoice amount for the patients in each city. The columns labeled -1 and 0 show the sum total paid (-1 column) and sum total unpaid (0 column) invoice amounts for patients in each city. Because the InvoicePaid field is a Yes/No field, by default, Access displays field values in datasheets, forms, and reports in a check box (either checked or unchecked), but stores a checked value in the database as a -1 and an unchecked value as a 0. Instead of displaying check boxes, the crosstab query displays the stored values as column headings.

Cindi wants you to change the column headings of -1 to Paid and 0 to Unpaid. You'll use the IIf function to change the column headings, using the expression *IIf (InvoicePaid,"Paid","Unpaid")*—if the InvoicePaid field value is true (because it's a Yes/No field or a True/False field), or is checked, use "Paid" as the column heading; otherwise, use "Unpaid" as the column heading. Because the InvoicePaid field is a Yes/No field, the condition *InvoicePaid* is the same as the condition *InvoicePaid = -1*, which uses a comparison operator and a value. For all data types except Yes/No fields, you must use a comparison operator in a condition.

To change the crosstab query column headings:

1. Click the **HOME** tab on the ribbon, and then switch to Design view. The design grid has four entries. See Figure 5-22.

Figure 5-22   **Crosstab query in the design grid**

Field:	[City]	[InvoicePaid]	[InvoiceAmt]	Total Of InvoiceAmt: [InvoiceAmt]
Table:	qryPatientsAndInvoices	qryPatientsAndInvoices	qryPatientsAndInvoices	qryPatientsAndInvoices
Total:	Group By	Group By	Sum	Sum
Crosstab:	Row Heading	Column Heading	Value	Row Heading
Sort:				
Criteria:				
or:				

- produces row headings
- produces column headings
- produces total values
- produces grand total column heading and values

From left to right, the [City] entry produces the row headings, the [InvoicePaid] entry produces the column headings, the [InvoiceAmt] entry produces the totals in each row/column intersection, and the Total Of InvoiceAmt entry produces the row total column heading and total values. The field names are enclosed in brackets; the Total Of InvoiceAmt entry is the name of this calculated field, which displays the sum of the InvoiceAmt field values for each row.

You need to replace the Field box value in the second column with the IIf function expression to change the -1 and zero column headings to Paid and Unpaid. You can type the expression in the box, use Expression Builder to create the expression, or type the expression in the Zoom dialog box. You'll use the last method.

2. Right-click the **InvoicePaid Field** box, and then open the Zoom dialog box.

3. Delete the InvoicePaid expression, and then type **IIf (InvoicePaid,"Paid", "Unpaid")** in the Zoom dialog box. See Figure 5-23.

Figure 5-23 | IIf function for the crosstab query column headings

[Zoom dialog box showing: IIf (InvoicePaid,"Paid","Unpaid")]

4. Click the **OK** button, and then save and run the query. Access displays the completed crosstab query with Paid and Unpaid as the last two column headings, in alphabetical order, as shown in Figure 5-18.

5. Close the query, and then open the Navigation Pane.

TIP
Point to an object in the Navigation Pane to display the full object name in a ScreenTip.

In the Navigation Pane, Access uses unique icons to represent different types of queries. The crosstab query icon appears in the Queries list to the left of the qryPatientsAndInvoicesCrosstab query. This icon looks different from the icon that appears to the left of the other queries, which are all select queries.

INSIGHT

Using Special Database Features Cautiously

When you create a query in Design view or with a wizard, Access automatically constructs an equivalent SQL statement and saves only the SQL statement version of the query. **SQL (Structured Query Language)** is a standard language used in querying, updating, and managing relational databases. If you learn SQL for one relational DBMS, it's a relatively easy task to begin using SQL for other relational DBMSs. However, differences exist between DBMSs in their versions of SQL—somewhat like having different dialects in English—and in what additions they make to SQL. The SQL-equivalent statement that Access creates for a crosstab query is one such SQL-language addition. If you need to convert an Access database to SQL Server, Oracle, or another DBMS, crosstab queries created in Access will not work in these other DBMSs. You'd have to construct a set of SQL statements in the other DBMS to replace the SQL statement automatically created by Access. Constructing this replacement set of statements is a highly technical process that only an experienced programmer can complete, so you should use special features of a DBMS judiciously.

Next, Cindi wants to identify any visit dates that have the same visit dates as other patients because these are the ones that might have potential scheduling difficulties. To find the information Cindi needs, you'll create a find duplicates query.

Creating a Find Duplicates Query

A find duplicates query is a select query that finds duplicate records in a table or query. You can create this type of query using the **Find Duplicates Query Wizard**. A find duplicates query searches for duplicate values based on the fields you select

Tutorial 5 Creating Advanced Queries and Enhancing Table Design | Access   AC 263

when answering the Wizard's questions. For example, you might want to display all employers that have the same name, all students who have the same phone number, or all products that have the same description. Using this type of query, you can locate duplicates to avert potential problems (for example, you might have inadvertently assigned two different numbers to the same product), or you can eliminate duplicates that cost money (for example, you could send just one advertising brochure to all patients having the same address).

REFERENCE

Using the Find Duplicates Query Wizard

- In the Queries group on the CREATE tab, click the Query Wizard button.
- In the New Query dialog box, click Find Duplicates Query Wizard, and then click the OK button.
- Complete the Wizard dialog boxes to select the table or query on which to base the query, select the field (or fields) to check for duplicate values, select the additional fields to include in the query results, enter a name for the query, and then click the Finish button.

You'll use the Find Duplicates Query Wizard to create and run a new query to display duplicate visit dates in the tblVisit table.

To create the query using the Find Duplicates Query Wizard:

1. Close the Navigation Pane, click the **CREATE** tab on the ribbon, and then, in the Queries group, click the **Query Wizard** button to open the New Query dialog box.

2. Click **Find Duplicates Query Wizard**, and then click the **OK** button. The first Find Duplicates Query Wizard dialog box opens. In this dialog box, you select the table or query on which to base the new query. You'll use the tblVisit table.

3. Click **Table: tblVisit** (if necessary), and then click the **Next** button. Access opens the next Find Duplicates Query Wizard dialog box, in which you choose the fields you want to check for duplicate values.

4. In the Available fields box, click **VisitDate**, click the > button to select the VisitDate field as the field to check for duplicate values, and then click the **Next** button. In the next Find Duplicates Query Wizard dialog box, you select the additional fields you want displayed in the query results.

   Cindi wants all remaining fields to be included in the query results.

5. Click the >> button to move all fields from the Available fields box to the Additional query fields box, and then click the **Next** button. Access opens the final Find Duplicates Query Wizard dialog box, in which you enter a name for the query. You'll use qryDuplicateVisitDates as the query name.

6. Type **qryDuplicateVisitDates** in the box, be sure the option button for viewing the results is selected, and then click the **Finish** button. Access saves the query, and then displays the 50 records for visits with duplicate visit dates. See Figure 5-24.

Figure 5-24   **Query recordset for duplicate visit dates**

Date of Visit	Visit ID	Patient ID	Reason/Diagnosis	Walk-in?
11/9/2015	1528	22507	Diabetes mellitus Type 2 - initial diagnosis	☑
11/9/2015	1527	22522	Allergies - environmental	☑
11/17/2015	1536	22526	Gastroenteritis	☐
11/17/2015	1538	22500	Migraine	☑
11/24/2015	1541	22526	Gastroenteritis - follow up	☐
11/24/2015	1542	22537	Influenza	☑
11/30/2015	1548	22519	Hypertension	☐
11/30/2015	1549	22501	Influenza	☑
1/11/2016	1569	22558	COPD management visit	☐
1/11/2016	1570	22561	Nasopharyngitis	☑
1/13/2016	1573	22511	Cardiac monitoring	☐
1/13/2016	1575	22513	Broken leg	☑
1/13/2016	1572	22560	Acute sinusitis	☑
1/25/2016	1586	22523	Nasopharyngitis	☑
1/25/2016	1588	22535	Hypertension	☐
1/25/2016	1585	22555	Acute viral rhinopharyngitis	☑
1/26/2016	1590	22505	Annual wellness visit	☐
1/26/2016	1591	22544	Acute viral rhinopharyngitis	☑
2/1/2016	1597	22517	Annual wellness visit	☐
2/1/2016	1598	22530	Plantar faciitis	☑
2/8/2016	1605	22535	Hypertension monitoring	☐
2/8/2016	1606	22520	Gastric reflux	☑
2/9/2016	1610	22529	Sinusitis	☑
2/9/2016	1608	22527	UTI	☑
2/9/2016	1607	22507	Diabetes mellitus Type 2 - serum glucose che	☐
2/24/2016	1626	22513	Follow-up - cast removal	☐
2/24/2016	1625	22551	Elevated blood lipids-monitoring meds	☐

▶ **7.** Close the query.

Cindi now asks you to find the records for patients with no visits. These are patients who have been referred to Chatham Community Health Services but have not had a first visit. Cindi wants to contact these patients to see if they would like to book initial appointments. To provide Cindi with this information, you need to create a find unmatched query.

Creating a Find Unmatched Query

A find unmatched query is a select query that finds all records in a table or query that have no related records in a second table or query. For example, you could display all patients who have had an appointment but have never been invoiced, or all students who are not currently enrolled in classes. Such a query provides information for a medical office to ensure all patients who have received services have also been billed for those services, and for a school administrator to contact the students to find out their future educational plans. You can use the **Find Unmatched Query Wizard** to create this type of query.

> **REFERENCE**
>
> *Using the Find Unmatched Query Wizard*
>
> - In the Queries group on the CREATE tab, click the Query Wizard button.
> - In the New Query dialog box, click Find Unmatched Query Wizard, and then click the OK button.
> - Complete the Wizard dialog boxes to select the table or query on which to base the new query, select the table or query that contains the related records, specify the common field in each table or query, select the additional fields to include in the query results, enter a name for the query, and then click the Finish button.

Cindi wants to know which patients have no visits. She will contact these patients to determine if they will be visiting Chatham Community Health Services Clinic or whether they are receiving their medical services elsewhere. To create a list of patients who have not had a visit to the clinic, you'll use the Find Unmatched Query Wizard to display only those records from the tblPatient table with no matching PatientID field value in the related tblVisit table.

To create the query using the Find Unmatched Query Wizard:

1. On the CREATE tab, in the Queries group, click the **Query Wizard** button to open the New Query dialog box.

2. Click **Find Unmatched Query Wizard**, and then click the **OK** button. The first Find Unmatched Query Wizard dialog box opens. In this dialog box, you select the table or query on which to base the new query. You'll use the qryPatientsByName query.

3. In the View section, click the **Queries** option button to display the list of queries, click **Query: qryPatientsByName** in the box to select this query, and then click the **Next** button. The next Find Unmatched Query Wizard dialog box opens, in which you choose the table that contains the related records. You'll select the tblVisit table.

4. Click **Table: tblVisit** in the box (if necessary), and then click the **Next** button. The next dialog box opens, in which you choose the common field for both tables. See Figure 5-25.

Access | Tutorial 5 Creating Advanced Queries and Enhancing Table Design

Figure 5-25 Selecting the common field

- matching field in the tblVisit table
- matching field in the qryPatientsByName query
- click to confirm after selecting matching fields
- matching fields will appear here

The common field between the query and the table is the PatientID field. You need to click the common field in each box, and then click the <=> button between the two boxes to join the two objects. The Matching fields box then will display PatientID <=> PatientID to indicate the joining of the two matching fields. If the two selected objects already have a one-to-many relationship defined in the Relationships window, the Matching fields box will join the correct fields automatically.

> Be sure you click the Patient ID field in both boxes.

5. In the Fields in 'qryPatientsByName' box click **PatientID**, in the Fields in 'tblVisit' box click **PatientID**, click the <=> button to connect the two selected fields, and then click the **Next** button. The next Find Unmatched Query Wizard dialog box opens, in which you choose the fields you want to see in the query recordset. Cindi wants the query recordset to display all available fields.

6. Click the >> button to move all fields from the Available fields box to the Selected fields box, and then click the **Next** button. The final dialog box opens, in which you enter the query name.

7. Type **qryInactivePatients**, be sure the option button for viewing the results is selected, and then click the **Finish** button. Access saves the query and then displays four records in the query recordset. See Figure 5-26.

Figure 5-26 Query recordset displaying four patients without visits

Patient	Patient ID	Last Name	First Name	Parent	Date of Birth	Phone	Address	City	State	Zip	Email Address
Billings, Claire	22541	Billings	Claire		11/16/1990	860-661-2053	786 Kidder Rd	Hartford	CT	06105	
Boucher, Sam	22543	Boucher	Sam		3/11/1975	860-226-5920	92 Bunnell Pl	Hartford	CT	06112	sambchr2@cengage.com
Grus, Mateo	22556	Grus	Mateo		3/11/1959	860-226-8472	18 Norman Rd	Hartford	CT	06112	matgrus5@example.com
Morales, Jose	22559	Morales	Jose		12/25/1965	860-637-2015	251 Lilac St	West Hartford	CT	06117	

8. Close the query.

Next, Cindi wants to contact those patients who have the highest invoice amounts to make sure that Chatham Community Health Services is providing satisfactory service. To display the information Cindi needs, you will create a top values query.

Creating a Top Values Query

Whenever a query displays a large group of records, you might want to limit the number to a more manageable size by displaying, for example, just the first 10 records. The **Top Values property** for a query lets you limit the number of records in the query results. To find a limited number of records using the Top Values property, you can click one of the preset values from a list, or enter either an integer (such as 15, to display the first 15 records) or a percentage (such as 20%, to display the first fifth of the records).

For instance, suppose you have a select query that displays 45 records. If you want the query recordset to show only the first five records, you can change the query by entering a Top Values property value of either 5 or 10%. If the query contains a sort and the last record that Access can display is one of two or more records with the same value for the primary sort field, Access displays all records with that matching key value.

Cindi wants to view the same data that appears in the qryLargeInvoiceAmounts query for patients with the highest 25 percent contract amounts. Based on the number or percentage you enter, a top values query selects that number or percentage of records starting from the top of the recordset. Thus, you usually include a sort in a top values query to display the records with the highest or lowest values for the sorted field. You will modify the query and then use the Top Values property to produce this information for Cindi.

To set the Top Values property for the query:

1. Open the Navigation Pane, open the **qryLargeInvoiceAmounts** query in Datasheet view, and then close the Navigation Pane. Access displays 14 records, all with InvoiceAmt field values greater than $200, in descending order by InvoiceAmt.

2. Switch to Design view.

3. In the Query Setup group on the DESIGN tab, click the **Return** arrow (with the ScreenTip "Top Values"), and then click **25%**. See Figure 5-27.

Access | Tutorial 5 Creating Advanced Queries and Enhancing Table Design

Figure 5-27 Creating the top values query

[Screenshot of Access query design view showing the qryLargeInvoiceAmounts query with the Return arrow dropdown showing values 5, 25, 100, 5%, 25%, All with "25% selected" callout. The design grid shows fields InvoiceAmt (tblBilling), LastName, FirstName, Parent, Phone, Address, City, State, Zip (tblPatient). InvoiceAmt has Descending sort order and criteria >=200, with a "Descending sort order" callout.]

If the number or percentage of records you want to select, such as 15 or 20%, doesn't appear in the Top Values list, you can type the number or percentage in the Return box.

4. Run the query. Access displays four records in the query recordset; these records represent the patients with the highest 25 percent of the invoice amounts (25 percent of the original 14 records). See Figure 5-28.

Figure 5-28 — Top values query recordset

Invoice Amt	Last Name	First Name	Parent	Phone	Address	City	State	Zip
$450.00	Caputo	Michael		8603749347	96 Vega Dr	Hartford	CT	06114
$450.00	Taylor	Jerome		8602262037	598 Belleflower Ave	Hartford	CT	06112
$300.00	Smith	Troy		8603050384	16 Ravine Rd	Bloomfield	CT	06002
$300.00	Ingram	Julia		8606614937	834 Kiefer Rd	Hartford	CT	06105

5. Save and close the query.

6. If you are not continuing on to the next session, close the Clinic database.

Cindi will use the information provided by the queries you created to analyze the Chatham Community Health Services business and to contact patients. In the next session, you will enhance the tblPatient and tblVisit tables.

Session 5.2 Quick Check

1. What is the purpose of a crosstab query?
2. What are the four query wizards you can use to create a new query?
3. What is a find duplicates query?
4. What does a find unmatched query do?
5. What happens when you set a query's Top Values property?
6. What happens if you set a query's Top Values property to 2 and the first five records have the same value for the primary sort field?

Session 5.3 Visual Overview:

The tblInvoiceItem query supplies the field values for the lookup field in the tblBilling table. A **lookup field** lets the user select a value from a list of possible values to enter data into the field.

tblInvoiceItem

Invoice Item ID	Invoice Item
DG111	Lab work
DG115	Lab work - culture
DG118	Lab work - glycated hemoglobin (A1C)
DG119	Lab work - urine glucose
DG225	Lab - culture
DG287	Lab - serum glucose
DG424	EKG with interpretation
DG532	Radiograph
OST145	Bone setting and cast
OST150	Cast of fracture

The tblBilling table contains the lookup field.

The InvoiceItemID and InvoiceItem fields from the tblInvoiceItem table are used to look up InvoiceItemID values in the tblBilling table.

tblBilling

Invoice Num	Visit ID	Invoice Date	Invoice Amt	Invoice Item	Invoice Paid	Insurance
35801	1527	11/10/2015	$100.00	Office visit	✓	$50.00
35802	1528	11/10/2015	$100.00	Lab - culture	DG225	$0.00
35803	1528	11/10/2015	$45.00	Lab - serum glucose	DG287	$0.00
35804	1528	11/13/2015	$238.00	EKG with interpretation	DG424	$0.00
35805	1528	11/13/2015	$48.00	Radiograph	DG532	$0.00
35808	1530	11/12/2015	$100.00	Bone setting and cast	OST145	$0.00
35809	1530	11/12/2015	$85.00	Cast of fracture	OST150	$0.00
35810	1530	11/12/2015	$65.00	Cast removal	OST158	$0.00
35811	1530	11/13/2015	$48.00	Pharmacy	PRM712	$0.00
35813	1535	11/13/2015	$100.00	Office visit	REP001	$0.00
35814	1535	11/13/2015	$45.00	IM injection	REP139	$0.00
35815	1535	11/16/2015	$300.00	Physical therapy	REP187	$0.00
35816	1535	11/16/2015	$250.00	Phlebotomy	REP298	$0.00
35818	1536	11/18/2015	$100.00	Influenza vaccine	REP725	$100.00
35819	1536	11/18/2015	$65.00	Respiratory therapy	REP752	$0.00
35821	1538	11/18/2015	$100.00	Surgery	SUR001	$0.00
35822	1538	11/18/2015	$125.00	Suture removal	SUR145	$0.00
35825	1539	11/19/2015	$100.00	Office visit	✓	$0.00

Values in the lookup field appear in alphabetical order, sorted by Invoice Item.

Only the InvoiceItemID values are stored in the InvoiceItemID field in the tblBilling table even though the user also sees the InvoiceItem values in the datasheet.

Tutorial 5 Creating Advanced Queries and Enhancing Table Design | Access AC 271

Lookup Fields and Input Masks

The tblPatient table contains the field that displays values with an input mask. An **input mask** is a predefined format that is used to enter and display data in a field.

tblPatient

Field Name	Data Type	
PatientID	Short Text	Primary key
LastName	Short Text	
FirstName	Short Text	
Parent	Short Text	Parent or Guardian
BirthDate	Date/Time	
Phone	Short Text	
Address	Short Text	
City	Short Text	
State	Short Text	
Zip	Short Text	
EmailAddress	Short Text	

The Phone field uses an input mask to format displayed field values.

You can create an input mask for any field with the Short Text or Number data type.

The 9 character in an input mask indicates a digit or space in the field value whose entry is optional.

Field Properties

General Lookup

Field Size	14
Format	
Input Mask	999\-000\-0000;; _
Caption	
Default Value	
Validation Rule	
Validation Text	
Required	No
Allow Zero Length	Yes
Indexed	No
Unicode Compression	No
IME Mode	No Control
IME Sentence Mode	None
Text Align	General

The \ indicates that the character that follows is a literal display character.

The character after the ;; indicates what character to display as the user is entering data. In this case the _ will be displayed.

The 0 character in an input mask indicates that only a digit can be entered and the entry is mandatory.

Creating a Lookup Field

The tblBilling table in the Clinic database contains information about patient invoices. Cindi wants to make entering data in the table easier for her staff. In particular, data entry is easier if they do not need to remember the correct InvoiceItemID field value for each treatment. Because the tblInvoiceItem and tblBIlling tables have a one-to-many relationship, Cindi asks you to change the tblBilling table's InvoiceItemID field, which is a foreign key to the tblInvoiceItem table, to a lookup field. A lookup field lets the user select a value from a list of possible values. For the InvoiceItemID field, a user will be able to select an invoice item's ID number from the list of invoice item names in the tblBilling table rather than having to remember the correct InvoiceItemID field value. Access will store the InvoiceItemID field value in the tblBilling table, but both the invoice item and the InvoiceItemID field value will appear in Datasheet view when entering or changing an InvoiceItemID field value. This arrangement makes entering and changing InvoiceItemID field values easier for users and guarantees that the InvoiceItemID field value is valid. You use a **Lookup Wizard field** in Access to create a lookup field in a table.

Cindi asks you to change the InvoiceItemID field in the tblBilling table to a lookup field. You'll begin by opening the tblBilling table in Design view.

To change the InvoiceItemID field to a lookup field:

1. If you took a break after the previous session, make sure that the Clinic database is open.

   Trouble? If the security warning is displayed below the ribbon, click the Enable Content button next to the warning.

2. If necessary, open the Navigation Pane, open the **tblBilling** table in Design view, and then close the Navigation Pane.

TIP
You can display the arrow and the menu simultaneously if you click the box near its right side.

3. Click the **Data Type** box for the InvoiceItemID field, click the drop-down arrow to display the list of data types, and then click **Lookup Wizard**. A message box appears, instructing you to delete the relationship between the tblBilling and tblInvoiceItem tables if you want to make the InvoiceItemID field a lookup field. See Figure 5-29.

Figure 5-29 | **Warning message for an existing table relationship**

Lookup Wizard
You can't change the data type or field size of this field; it is part of one or more relationships. If you want to change the data type of this field, first delete its relationships in the Relationships window.
OK

Access will use the lookup field to form the one-to-many relationship between the tblBilling and tblInvoiceItem tables, so you don't need the relationship that previously existed between the two tables.

4. Click the **OK** button and then close the tblBilling table, clicking the **No** button when asked if you want to save the table design changes.

5. Click the **DATABASE TOOLS** tab on the ribbon, and then in the Relationships group, click the **Relationships** button to open the Relationships window.

6. Right-click the join line between the tblBilling and tblInvoiceItem tables, click **Delete**, and then click the **Yes** button to confirm the deletion.

Tutorial 5 Creating Advanced Queries and Enhancing Table Design | Access   AC 273

Trouble? If the Delete command does not appear on the shortcut menu, click a blank area in the Relationships window to close the shortcut menu, and then repeat Step 6, ensuring you right-click on the relationship line.

7. Close the Relationships window.

Now you can resume changing the InvoiceItemID field to a lookup field.

To finish changing the InvoiceItemID field to a lookup field:

1. Open the **tblBilling** table in Design view, and then close the Navigation Pane.

2. Click the right side of the **Data Type** box for the InvoiceItemID field, if necessary click the drop-down arrow, and then click **Lookup Wizard**. The first Lookup Wizard dialog box opens.

   This dialog box lets you specify a list of allowed values for the InvoiceItemID field in a record in the tblBilling table. You can specify a table or query from which users select the value, or you can enter a new list of values. You want the InvoiceItemID values to come from the tblInvoiceItem table.

3. Make sure the option for "I want the lookup field to get the values from another table or query" is selected, and then click the **Next** button to display the next Lookup Wizard dialog box.

4. Click the **Tables** option button in the View section to display the list of tables, if it is not already displayed, click **Table: tblInvoiceItem**, and then click the **Next** button to display the next Lookup Wizard dialog box. See Figure 5-30.

Figure 5-30   Selecting the lookup fields

select these two fields

click to select all fields

This dialog box lets you select the lookup fields from the tblInvoiceItem table. You need to select the InvoiceItemID field because it's the common field that links the tblInvoiceItem table and the tblBilling table. You also must select the InvoiceItem field because Cindi wants the user to be able to select from a list of invoice item names when entering a new contract record or changing an existing InvoiceItemID field value.

5. Click the >> button to move the InvoiceItemID and InvoiceItem fields to the Selected Fields box, and then click the **Next** button to display the next Lookup Wizard dialog box. This dialog box lets you choose a sort order for the box entries. Cindi wants the entries to appear in ascending Invoice Item order. Note that ascending is the default sort order.

6. Click the **arrow** for the first box, click **InvoiceItem**, and then click the **Next** button to open the next dialog box.

   In this dialog box, you can adjust the widths of the lookup columns. Note that when you resize a column to its best fit, Access resizes the column so that the widest column heading and the visible field values fit the column width. However, some field values that aren't visible in this dialog box might be wider than the column width, so you must scroll down the column to make sure you don't have to repeat the column resizing.

7. Click the Hide key column check box to remove the checkmark and display the InvoiceItemID field.

8. Click the InvoiceItemID column heading to select it. With the mouse pointer on the InvoiceItemID heading, drag it to the right of the InvoiceItem field to move the InvoiceItemID field to the right.

9. Place the pointer on the right edge of the InvoiceItem field column heading, and then when the pointer changes to ↔, double-click to resize the column to its best fit.

10. Scroll down the columns and repeat Step 9 as necessary until the InvoiceItem column accommodates all contents, and then press **Ctrl + Home** to scroll back to the top of the InvoiceItem column. See Figure 5-31.

Figure 5-31 Adjusting the width of the lookup column

11. Click the **Next** button.

    In the next dialog box, you select the field you want to store in the table. You'll store the InvoiceItemID field in the tblBilling table because it's the foreign key to the tblInvoiceItem table.

12. Click **InvoiceItemID** in the Available Fields box if it's not already selected, and then click the **Next** button.

Tutorial 5 Creating Advanced Queries and Enhancing Table Design | Access   AC 275

In the next dialog box, you specify the field name for the lookup field. Because you'll be storing the InvoiceItemID field in the table, you'll accept the default field name, InvoiceItemID.

▶ 13. Click the **Finish** button, and then click Yes to save the table.

The Data Type value for the InvoiceItemID field is still Short Text because this field contains text data. However, when you update the field, Access uses the InvoiceItemID field value to look up and display in the tblBilling table datasheet both the InvoiceItem and InvoiceItemID field values from the tblInvoiceItem table.

In reviewing patient visits recently, Cindi noticed that the InvoiceItemID field value stored in the tblBilling table for visit number 1552 is incorrect. She asks you to test the new lookup field to select the correct field value. To do so, you need to switch to Datasheet view.

To change the InvoiceItemID field value:

▶ 1. Switch to Datasheet view, and then resize the **Invoice Item** column to its best fit.

Notice that the Invoice Item column displays InvoiceItem field values, even though the InvoiceItemID field values are stored in the table.

▶ 2. For Visit Num 1552, click **Office visit** in the Invoice Item column, and then click the **arrow** to display the list of InvoiceItem and InvoiceItemID field values from the tblInvoiceItems table. See Figure 5-32.

Figure 5-32   List of InvoiceItem and InvoiceItemID field values

scrollable list of values for the lookup field

The invoice item for visit 1552 is Pharmacy, so you need to select this entry in the list to change the InvoiceItemID field value.

> 3. Scroll through the list if necessary, and then click **Pharmacy** to select that value to display in the datasheet and to store the InvoiceItemID field value of PRM712 in the table. The list closes and "Pharmacy" appears in the InvoiceItemID column.
>
> 4. Save and close the tblBilling table.

Next, Cindi asks you to change the appearance of the Phone field in the tblPatient table to a standard telephone number format.

Using the Input Mask Wizard

The Phone field in the tblPatient table is a 10-digit number that's difficult to read because it appears with none of the special formatting characters usually associated with a telephone number. For example, the Phone field value for Darcy Edward, which appears as 8603053985, would be more readable in any of the following formats: 860-305-3985, 860.305.3985, 860/305-3985, or (860) 305-3985. Cindi asks you to use the (860) 305-3985 style for the Phone field.

Cindi wants the parentheses and hyphens to appear as literal display characters whenever users enter Phone field values. A literal display character is a special character that automatically appears in specific positions of a field value; users don't need to type literal display characters. To include these characters, you need to create an input mask, which is a predefined format used to enter and display data in a field. An easy way to create an input mask is to use the **Input Mask Wizard**, an Access tool that guides you in creating a predefined format for a field. You must be in Design view to use the Input Mask Wizard.

> **To use the Input Mask Wizard for the Phone field:**
>
> 1. Open the **tblPatient** table, close the Navigation Pane, and then, if necessary, switch to Design view.
>
> 2. Click the **Phone Field Name** box to make that row the current row and to display its Field Properties options.
>
> 3. Click the **Input Mask** box in the Field Properties pane. The Build button [...] appears at the right edge of the Input Mask box.
>
> 4. Click the **Build** button [...] in the Input Mask box. The first Input Mask Wizard dialog box opens. See Figure 5-33.

Figure 5-33 | **Input Mask Wizard dialog box**

- scrollable list of predefined input masks
- sample values for the corresponding input masks
- practice area

You can scroll the Input Mask box, select the input mask you want, and then enter representative values to practice using the input mask.

5. If necessary, click **Phone Number** in the Input Mask box to select it.

6. Click the far left side of the **Try It** box. (___) ___-____ appears in the Try It box. As you type a phone number, Access replaces the underscores, which are placeholder characters.

   Trouble? If your insertion point is not immediately to the right of the left parenthesis, press the ← key until it is.

7. Type **8603053985** to practice entering a sample phone number. The input mask formats the typed value as (860) 305-3985.

8. Click the **Next** button. The next Input Mask Wizard dialog box opens. In it, you can change the input mask and the placeholder character. Because you can change an input mask easily after the Input Mask Wizard finishes, you'll accept all wizard defaults.

9. Click the **Finish** button, and then click to the right of the value in the Input Mask box to deselect the characters. The Input Mask Wizard creates the phone number input mask, placing it in the Input Mask box for the Phone field. See Figure 5-34.

Figure 5-34   **Phone number input mask created by the Input Mask Wizard**

The characters used in a field's input mask restrict the data you can enter in the field, as shown in Figure 5-35. Other characters that appear in an input mask, such as the left and right parentheses in the phone number input mask, are literal display characters.

Figure 5-35 Input mask characters

Input Mask Character	Description
0	Digit only must be entered. Entry is required.
9	Digit or space can be entered. Entry is optional.
#	Digit, space, or a plus or minus sign can be entered. Entry is optional.
L	Letter only must be entered. Entry is required.
?	Letter only can be entered. Entry is optional.
A	Letter or digit must be entered. Entry is required.
a	Letter or digit can be entered. Entry is optional.
&	Any character or a space must be entered. Entry is required.
C	Any character or a space can be entered. Entry is optional.
>	All characters that follow are displayed in uppercase.
<	All characters that follow are displayed in lowercase.
"	Enclosed characters treated as literal display characters.
\	Following character treated as a literal display character. This is the same as enclosing a single character in quotation marks.
!	Input mask is displayed from right to left, rather than the default of left to right. Characters typed into the mask always fill in from left to right.
;;	The character between the first and second semicolons determines whether to store the literal display characters in the database. If the value is 1 or if no value is provided, the literal display characters are not stored. If the value is 0, the literal display characters are stored. The character following the second semicolon is the placeholder character that appears in the displayed input mask.

© 2014 Cengage Learning

Cindi wants to view the Phone field with the default input mask.

To view and change the input mask for the Phone field:

1. Save the table, and then switch to Datasheet view. The Phone field values now have the format specified by the input mask.

   Cindi decides that she would prefer to omit the parentheses around the area codes and use only hyphens as separators in the displayed Phone field values, so you'll change the input mask in Design view.

2. Switch to Design view.

   The input mask is set to !\(999") "000\-0000;;_. The backslash character (\) causes the character that follows it to appear as a literal display character. Characters enclosed in quotation marks also appear as literal display characters. (See Figure 5-35.) The exclamation mark (!) forces the existing data to fill the input mask from right to left instead of left to right. This does not affect new data. This only applies to the situation when data already exists in the table and a new input mask is applied. For instance, if the existing data is 5551234 and the input mask fills from left to right, the data with the input mask would look like: (555) 123-4. If the input mask fills from right to left, the data with the input mask applied would look like: () 555-1234.

   If you omit the backslashes preceding the hyphens, Access will automatically insert them when you press the Tab key. However, Access doesn't add backslashes automatically for other literal display characters, such as periods and slashes, so it's best to always type the backslashes. Since all of the existing data includes the area code, it will not make a difference whether the input mask applied to the data fills the data from left to right or from right to left, so you'll omit the ! symbol.

3. In the Input Mask box for the Phone field, change the input mask to **999\-000\-0000;;_** and then press the **Tab** key.

   Because you've modified a field property, the Property Update Options button appears to the left of the Input Mask property.

4. Click the **Property Update Options** button. A menu opens below the button, as shown in Figure 5-36.

Figure 5-36   Property Update Options button menu

5. Click **Update Input Mask everywhere Phone is used**. The Update Properties dialog box opens. See Figure 5-37.

Figure 5-37   Update Properties dialog box

Because the frmPatient form displays the Phone field values from the tblPatient table, Access will automatically change the Phone field's Input Mask property in this object to your new input mask. If other form objects

Tutorial 5 Creating Advanced Queries and Enhancing Table Design | Access   AC 281

included the Phone field from the tblPatient table, they would be included in this dialog box as well. This capability to update field properties in objects automatically when you modify a table field property is called **property propagation**. Although the Update Properties dialog box displays no queries, property propagation also does occur with queries automatically. Property propagation is limited to field properties such as the Decimal Places, Description, Format, and Input Mask properties.

▶ **6.** Click the **Yes** button, save the table, switch to Datasheet view, and then resize the Phone column to its best fit. The Phone field values now have the format Cindi requested. See Figure 5-38.

Figure 5-38   After changing the Phone field input mask

Patient ID	Last Name	First Name	Parent	Date of Birth	Phone	Address	City	State	Zip	Email Address	Click to Add
22506	Student Last	Student First		2/28/1994	860-938-2822	501 Perkins Dr	Hartford	CT	06120	student2@example.com	
22501	Darcy	Edward		7/15/1986	860-305-3985	723 Oxford Ave	Bloomfield	CT	06002	edarcy@cengage.com	
22502	Mendez	Andreas		3/1/1934	860-552-6893	57 Wallace Rd	Windsor	CT	06095	amendios@example.com	
22504	Aguilar	Lilian		8/16/1938	860-374-5724	329 Fairchild Ave	Hartford	CT	06114	laguilar@cengage.com	
22505	Finnerty	Amber		5/7/1946	860-226-4930	37 Noyes Ct	Hartford	CT	06112	amberglo@example.com	
22506	Gorski	Drea	Samson, Mary	2/19/2005	860-305-8394	83 Everett Ln	Bloomfield	CT	06002		
22507	Weiss	Matthew	Weiss, Jordan	6/7/1997	860-426-7492	38 German St	Hartford	CT	06106	matt.weiss@cengage.com	
22509	Kervin	Steve		4/6/1993	860-938-0025	49 Davenport St	Hartford	CT	06120	skervin@example.com	

Phone field with input mask

Because Cindi wants her staff to store only standard 10-digit U.S. phone numbers for patients, the input mask you've created will enforce the standard entry and display format that Cindi desires.

INSIGHT

Understanding When to Use Input Masks

An input mask is appropriate for a field only if all field values have a consistent format. For example, you can use an input mask with hyphens as literal display characters to store U.S. phone numbers in a consistent format of 987-654-3210. However, a multinational company would not be able to use an input mask to store phone numbers from all countries because international phone numbers do not have a consistent format. In the same way, U.S. zip codes have a consistent format, and you could use an input mask of 00000#9999 to enter and display U.S. zip codes such as 98765 and 98765-4321, but you could not use an input mask if you need to store and display foreign postal codes in the same field. If you need to store and display phone numbers, zip/postal codes, and other fields in a variety of formats, it's best to define them as Short Text fields without an input mask so users can enter the correct literal display characters.

After the change to the Phone field's input mask, Access gave you the option to update, selectively and automatically, the Phone field's Input Mask property in other objects in the database. Cindi is thinking about making significant changes to the way data is stored in the tblPatient table, and wants to understand which other elements those changes might impact. To determine the dependencies among objects in an Access database, you'll open the Object Dependencies pane.

Identifying Object Dependencies

An **object dependency** exists between two objects when a change to the properties of data in one object affects the properties of data in the other object. Dependencies between Access objects, such as tables, queries, and forms, can occur in various ways. For example, the tblVisit and tblBilling tables are dependent on each other because they have a one-to-many relationship. In the same way, the tblVisit table uses the qryPatientsByName query to obtain the Patient field to display along with the PatientID field, and this creates a dependency between these two objects. Any query, form, or other object that uses fields from a given table is dependent on that table. Any form or report that uses fields from a query is directly dependent on the query and is indirectly dependent on the tables that provide the data to the query. Large databases contain hundreds of objects, so it is useful to have a way to easily view the dependencies among objects before you attempt to delete or modify an object. The **Object Dependencies pane** displays a collapsible list of the dependencies among the objects in an Access database; you click the list's expand indicators to show or hide different levels of dependencies. Next, you'll open the Object Dependencies pane to show Cindi the object dependencies in the Clinic database.

To open and use the Object Dependencies pane:

1. Click the **DATABASE TOOLS** tab on the ribbon.
2. In the Relationships group, click the **Object Dependencies** button to open the Object Dependencies pane, and then drag the left edge of the pane to the left until the horizontal scroll bar at the bottom of the pane disappears. See Figure 5-39.

Figure 5-39   After opening the Object Dependencies pane

Trouble? If the "Objects that depend on me" option button is not selected, click the option button to select it.

The Object Dependencies pane displays the objects that depend on the tblPatient table, the object name that appears at the top of the pane. If you change the design of the tblPatient table, the change might affect objects in the pane. Changing a property for a field in the tblPatient table that's also used by a listed object affects that listed object. If a listed object does not use the field you are changing, that listed object is not affected.

Objects listed in the Ignored Objects section of the box might have an object dependency with the tblPatient table, and you'd have to review them individually to determine if a dependency exists. The Help section at the bottom of the pane displays links for further information about object dependencies.

3. Click the **frmPatient** link in the Object Dependencies pane. The frmPatient form opens in Design view. All the fields in the form are fields from the tblPatient table, which is why the form has an object dependency with the table.

4. Switch to Form view for the frmPatient form. Note that the Phone field value is displayed using the input mask you applied to the field in the tblPatient table. Access propagated this change from the table to the form.

5. Close the frmPatient form, open the Navigation Pane, open the **tblVisit** table in Datasheet view, and then click the **Refresh** link near the top of the Object Dependencies pane. The Object Dependencies box now displays the objects that depend on the tblVisit table.

6. Click the **Objects that I depend on** option button near the top of the pane to view the objects that affect the tblVisit table.

7. Click the **Objects that depend on me** option button and then click the **expand indicator** ▷ for the qryPatientsByName query in the Object Dependencies pane. The list expands to display the tblPatient table, which is another table that the query depends upon.

8. Close the tblVisit table, close the Object Dependencies pane, and then save and close the tblPatient table.

Cindi now better understands object dependencies and how to identify them by using the Object Dependencies pane. She's decided to leave the tblPatient table the way it is for the moment to avoid making changes to forms and/or queries.

Defining Data Validation Rules

Cindi wants to minimize the amount of incorrect data in the database caused by typing errors. To do so, she wants to limit the entry of InvoiceAmt field values in the tblBilling table to values greater than $10 because Chatham Community Health Services does not invoice patients for balances of $10 or less. In addition, she wants to make sure that the Insurance field value entered in each tblBilling table record is either the same or less than the InvoiceAmt field value. The InvoiceAmt value represents the total price for the visit or procedure, and the Insurance value is the amount covered by the patient's insurance. The Insurance value may be equal to or less than the InvoiceAmt value, but it will never be more, so comparing these numbers is an additional test to ensure the data entered in a record makes sense. To provide these checks on entered data, you'll set field validation properties for the InvoiceAmt field in the tblBilling table and set table validation properties in the tblBilling table.

Defining Field Validation Rules

To prevent a user from entering an unacceptable value in the InvoiceAmt field, you can create a **field validation rule** that verifies a field value by comparing it to a constant or to a set of constants. You create a field validation rule by setting the Validation Rule and the Validation Text field properties. The **Validation Rule property** value specifies the valid values that users can enter in a field. The **Validation Text property** value will be displayed in a dialog box if a user enters an invalid value (in this case, an InvoiceAmt field value of $10 or less). After you set these two InvoiceAmt field properties in the tblBilling table, Access will prevent users from entering an invalid InvoiceAmt field value in the tblBilling table and in all current and future queries and future forms that include the InvoiceAmt field.

You'll now set the Validation Rule and Validation Text properties for the InvoiceAmt field in the tblBilling table.

To create and test a field validation rule for the InvoiceAmt field:

1. Open the **tblBilling** table in Design view, close the Navigation Pane, and then click the **InvoiceAmt Field Name** box to make that row the current row.

   To make sure that all values entered in the InvoiceAmt field are greater than 10, you'll use the > comparison operator in the Validation Rule box.

2. In the Field Properties pane, click the **Validation Rule** box, type **>10**, and then press the **Tab** key.

   You can set the Validation Text property to a value that appears in a dialog box that opens if a user enters a value not listed in the Validation Rule box.

3. In the Validation Text box, type **Invoice amounts must be greater than 10**. See Figure 5-40.

Figure 5-40 | Validation properties for the InvoiceAmt field

tblBilling

Field Name	Data Type	
InvoiceNum	Short Text	Primary key
VisitID	Short Text	Foreign key
InvoiceDate	Date/Time	
InvoiceAmt	Currency	← current field
InvoiceItemID	Short Text	
InvoicePaid	Yes/No	
Insurance	Currency	

Field Properties

General / Lookup

Format	Currency
Decimal Places	2
Input Mask	
Caption	Invoice Amt
Default Value	
Validation Rule	>10
Validation Text	Invoice amounts must be greater than 10
Required	No
Indexed	No
Text Align	General

(validation properties ↑)

Design view. F6 = Switch panes. F1 = Help.

You can now save the table design changes and then test the validation properties.

4. Save the table, and then click the **Yes** button when asked if you want to test the existing InvoiceAmt field values in the tblBilling table against the new validation rule.

   Access tests the existing records in the tblBilling table against the validation rule. If any existing record violated the rule, you would be prompted to continue testing or to revert to the previous Validation Rule property setting. Next, you'll test the validation rule.

5. Switch to Datasheet view, select **$100.00** in the first row's InvoiceAmt field box, type **5**, and then press the **Tab** key. A dialog box opens containing the message "Invoice amounts must be greater than 10," which is the Validation Text property setting you created in Step 3.

6. Click the **OK** button, and then press the **Esc** key. The first row's InvoiceAmt field reverts to its original value, $100.00.

7. Close the tblBilling table.

Now that you've finished entering the field validation rule for the InvoiceAmt field in the tblBilling table, you'll enter the table validation rule for the date fields in the tblVisit table.

Defining Table Validation Rules

To make sure that the Insurance field value that a user enters in the tblBilling table is not larger than the InvoiceAmt field value, you can create a **table validation rule**. Once again, you'll use the Validation Rule and Validation Text properties, but this time you'll set these properties for the table instead of for an individual field. You'll use a table validation rule because this validation involves multiple fields. A field validation rule is used when the validation involves a restriction for only the selected field, and does not depend on other fields.

To create and test a table validation rule in the tblBilling table:

1. Open the tblBilling table in Design view and then on the DESIGN tab, in the Show/Hide group, click the **Property Sheet** button to open the property sheet for the table.

   > Be sure "Table Properties" is listed as the selection type in the property sheet.

   To make sure that each Insurance field value is less than or equal to the InvoiceAmt field value, you use the Validation Rule box for the table.

2. In the property sheet, click the **Validation Rule** box.

3. Type **Insur**, press the **Tab** key to select Insurance in the AutoComplete box, type **<= InvoiceAm**, and then press the **Tab** key.

4. In the Validation Text box, type **Insurance coverage cannot be larger than the invoice amount**, and then if necessary widen the Property Sheet so the Validation Rule text is visible. See Figure 5-41.

Figure 5-41   Setting table validation properties

You can now test the validation properties.

5. Close the property sheet, save the table, and then click the **Yes** button when asked if you want to test the existing dates in the tblBilling table against the new validation rule.

6. Close the Navigation Pane, switch to Datasheet view, and then click the Insurance column value in the first record. Edit the Insurance value to change it to $150.00, and then press the **Tab** key to complete your changes to the record. A dialog box opens containing the message "**Insurance coverage cannot be larger than the invoice amount**," which is the Validation Text property setting you entered in Step 4.

Tutorial 5 Creating Advanced Queries and Enhancing Table Design | Access   AC 287

Unlike field validation rule violations, which Access detects immediately after you finish a field entry and advance to another field, Access detects table validation rule violations only when you finish all changes to the current record and advance to another record.

7. Click the **OK** button, and then press the **Esc** key to undo your change to the Insurance column value.

8. Close the tblBilling table.

PROSKILLS

Problem Solving: Perfecting Data Quality

It's important that you design useful queries, forms, and reports and that you test them thoroughly. But the key to any database is the accuracy of the data stored in its tables. It's critical that the data be as error-free as possible. Most companies employ people who spend many hours tracking down and correcting errors and discrepancies in their data, and you can greatly assist and minimize their problem solving by using as many database features as possible to ensure the data is correct from the start. Among these features for fields are selecting the proper data type, setting default values whenever possible, restricting the permitted values by using field and table validation rules, enforcing referential integrity, and forcing users to select values from lists instead of typing the values. Likewise, having an arsenal of queries—such as find duplicates and top values queries—available to users will expedite the work they do to find and correct data errors.

Based on a request from Cindi, Raj added a Long Text field to the tblVisit table, and now you'll review Raj's work.

Working with Long Text Fields

You use a Long Text field to store long comments and explanations. Short Text fields are limited to 255 characters, but Long Text fields can hold up to 65,535 characters. In addition, Short Text fields limit you to plain text with no special formatting, but you can define Long Text fields to store plain text similar to Short Text fields or to store rich text, which you can selectively format with options such as bold, italic, and different fonts and colors.

You'll review the Long Text field, named Comments, that Raj added to the tblVisit table.

To review the Long Text field in the tblVisit table:

1. Open the Navigation Pane, open the **tblVisit** table in Datasheet view, and then close the Navigation Pane.

2. Increase the width of the **Comments** field so most of the comments fit in the column.

   Although everything fits on the screen size and resolution shown in the figure, on some computer systems freezing panes is necessary to be able to view everything at once. On a smaller screen, if you scroll to the right to view the Comments field, you'll no longer be able to identify which patient applies to a row because the Patient ID column will be hidden. You'll also see this effect if you shrink the size of the Access window. You'll freeze the Visit ID, Patient ID, and Date of Visit columns so they remain visible in the datasheet as you scroll to the right.

3. Click the **Visit ID** column selector, press and hold down the **Shift** key, click the **Date of Visit** column selector, and then release the **Shift** key. The Visit ID, Patient ID, and Date of Visit columns should be selected.

4. On the HOME tab, in the Records group, click the **More** button, and then click **Freeze Fields**.

5. Scroll to the right until you see the Comments column. If all columns fit in the Access window, size the Access window smaller until the horizontal scroll bar is visible and not all columns are visible. Notice that the Visit ID, Patient ID, and Date of Visit columns, the three leftmost columns, remain visible. See Figure 5-42.

Figure 5-42   **Freezing three datasheet columns**

The Comments column is a Long Text field that Chatham Community Health Services clinicians use to store observations and other commentary about each patient. Note that the Comment for Visit ID 1548 displays rich text using a bold and blue font. Comments field values are partially hidden because the datasheet column is not wide enough. You'll view a record's Comments field value in the Zoom dialog box.

6. Click the **Comments** box for the record for Visit ID 1548, hold down the **Shift** key, press the **F2** key, and then release the **Shift** key. The Zoom dialog box displays the entire Comments field value.

7. Click the **OK** button to close the Zoom dialog box.

INSIGHT

Viewing Long Text Fields with Large Contents in Datasheet View

For a Long Text field that contains many characters, you can widen the field's column to view more of its contents by dragging the right edge of the field's column selector to the right or by using the Field Width command when you click the More button in the Records group on the HOME tab. However, increasing the column width reduces the number of other columns you can view at the same time. Further, for Long Text fields containing thousands of characters, you can't widen the column enough to be able to view the entire contents of the field at one time across the width of the screen. Therefore, increasing the column width of a Long Text field isn't necessarily the best strategy for viewing table contents.

Alternatively, you can increase the row height of a datasheet by dragging the bottom edge of a row selector down or by using the Row Height command when you click the More button in the Records group on the HOME tab. Increasing the row height causes the text in a Long Text field to wrap to the next line, so that you can view multiple lines at one time. Once again, however, for a Long Text field containing thousands of characters, you can't increase the row height enough to ensure that you can view the entire contents of the field at one time on screen. Additionally, you'd view fewer records at one time, and the row height setting for a table propagates to all queries that have an object dependency with the table. Thus, you generally shouldn't increase the row height of a table datasheet to accommodate a Long Text field.

What is the best way to view the contents of a Long Text field that contains a large number of characters? It is best to use the Zoom dialog box in a datasheet, or to use a large scrollable box on a form. It's really a matter of your own preference.

Now you'll review the property settings for the Comments field Raj added to the tblPatient table.

To review the property settings of the Long Text field:

1. Save the table, switch to Design view, click the **Comments Field Name** box to make that row the current row, and then, if necessary, scroll to the bottom of the list of properties in the Field Properties pane.

2. Click the **Text Format** box in the Field Properties pane, and then click its **arrow**. The list of available text formats appears in the box. See Figure 5-43.

Figure 5-43 Viewing the properties for a Long Text field

(Screenshot of tblVisit table in Design view showing fields VisitID, PatientID, VisitDate, Reason, Walkin, Comments. The Comments field is highlighted as "current field, a Long Text field" and the Text Format property is set to "Rich Text".)

Raj set the **Text Format property** for the Comments field to Rich Text, which lets you format the field contents using the options in the Font group on the HOME tab. The default Text Format property setting for a Long Text field is Plain Text, which doesn't allow text formatting.

3. Click the **arrow** on the Text Format box to close the list, and then click the **Append Only** box.

   The **Append Only property,** which appears at the bottom of the list of properties, enables you to track the changes that you make to a Long Text field. Setting this property to Yes causes Access to keep a historical record of all versions of the Long Text field value. You can view each version of the field value, along with a date and time stamp of when each version change occurred.

   You've finished your review of the Long Text field, so you can close the table.

4. Close the tblVisit table.

When employees at Chatham Community Health Services open the Clinic database, a security warning might appear below the ribbon, and they must enable the content of the database before beginning their work. Cindi asks if you can eliminate this extra step when employees open the database.

Designating a Trusted Folder

A database is a file, and files can contain malicious instructions that can damage other files on your computer or files on other computers on your network. Unless you take special steps, Access treats every database as a potential threat to your computer. One special step that you can take is to designate a folder as a trusted folder. A **trusted folder** is a folder on a drive or network that you designate as trusted and where you place databases you know are safe. When you open a database located in a trusted folder, Access treats it as a safe file and no longer displays a security warning. You can also place files used with other Microsoft Office programs, such as Word documents and Excel workbooks, in a trusted folder to eliminate warnings when you open them.

Tutorial 5 Creating Advanced Queries and Enhancing Table Design | Access **AC 291**

Because the Clinic database is from a trusted source, you'll specify its location as a trusted folder to eliminate the security warning when a user opens the database.

To designate a trusted folder:

1. Click the **FILE** tab, and then click **Options** in the navigation bar. The Access Options dialog box opens.
2. In the left section of the dialog box, click **Trust Center**. The Trust Center options are displayed in the dialog box.
3. In the right section of the dialog box, click the **Trust Center Settings** button to open the Trust Center dialog box.
4. In the left section of the Trust Center dialog box, click **Trusted Locations**. The trusted locations for your installation of Access and other trust options are displayed on the right. See Figure 5-44.

Figure 5-44 Designating a trusted folder

Existing trusted locations appear in the list at the top, and options to add, remove, and modify trusted locations appear at the bottom.

Trouble? Check with your instructor before adding a new trusted location. If your instructor tells you not to create a new trusted location, skip to Step 8.

5. Click the **Add new location** button to open the Microsoft Office Trusted Location dialog box.
6. In the Microsoft Office Trusted Location dialog box, click the **Browse** button, navigate to the Access2 ▶ Tutorial folder where your Data Files are stored, and then click the **OK** button.

You can also choose to designate subfolders of the selected location as trusted locations, but you won't select this option. By default, files in subfolders are not trusted.

▸ 7. Click the **OK** button. Access adds the Access2 ▸ Tutorial folder to the list of trusted locations.

▸ 8. Click the **OK** button to close the Trust Center dialog box, and then click the **OK** button to close the Access Options dialog box.

You've created several queries and completed several table design changes, so you should compact and repair the Clinic database. Raj doesn't use the Compact on Close option with the Clinic database because it's possible to lose the database if there's a computer malfunction when the Compact on Close operation runs. As a precaution, you'll make a backup copy of the database before you compact and repair it. Making frequent backup copies of your critical files safeguards your data from hardware and software malfunctions, which can occur at any time.

To backup, compact, and repair the Clinic database:

First, you'll make a backup of the Clinic database.

▸ 1. Click the **FILE** tab on the ribbon, and then click the **Save As** menu item.

▸ 2. Click the **Back Up Database** option, and then click the **Save As** button. The Save As dialog box opens with a suggested filename of Clinic_date in the File name box, where date is the current date in the format year-month-day. For instance, if you made a backup on February 15, 2016, the suggested filename would be Clinic_2016-02-15.

▸ 3. Navigate to the location of a USB drive or other external medium, if available, and then click the **Save** button to save the backup file.

Next, you'll verify that the trusted location is working.

▸ 4. Click the **FILE** tab on the ribbon, and then click the **Close** command to close the Clinic database.

▸ 5. Click the **FILE** tab on the ribbon, click **Open** on the navigation bar, and then click **Clinic.accdb** in the Recent list. The database opens, and no security warning appears below the ribbon because the database is located in the trusted location you designated.

Next, you'll compact and repair the database.

▸ 6. Click the **FILE** tab on the ribbon, and then click the **Compact & Repair Database** button.

▸ 7. Close the Clinic database.

You've completed the table design changes to the Clinic database, which will make working with it easier and more accurate.

Session 5.3 Quick Check

1. What is a lookup field?
2. A(n) _____ is a predefined format you use to enter and display data in a field.
3. What is property propagation?
4. Define the Validation Rule property, and give an example of when you would use it.
5. Define the Validation Text property, and give an example of when you would use it.
6. Setting a Long Text field's Text Format property to _____ lets you format its contents.
7. A(n) _____ folder is a location where you can place databases that you know are safe.

SAM Projects

Put your skills into practice with SAM Projects! SAM Projects for this tutorial can be found online. If you have a SAM account, go to www.cengage.com/sam2013 to download the most recent Project Instructions and Start Files.

Review Assignments

Data File needed for the Review Assignments: Supplier.accdb

Cindi asks you to create several new queries and enhance the table design for the Supplier database. This database contains information about the vendors that Chatham Community Health Services works with to obtain medical supplies and equipment for the clinic, as well as the vendors who service and maintain the equipment. Complete the following steps:

1. Open the **Supplier** database located in the Access2 ▸ Review folder provided with your Data Files.
2. Modify the first record in the **tblSupplier** table datasheet by changing the Contact First Name and Contact Last Name field values to your first and last names. Close the table.
3. Create a query to find all records in the tblSupplier table in which the City field value starts with the letter T. Display all fields in the query recordset, and sort in ascending order by CompanyName. Save the query as **qryTSelectedCities**, run the query, and then close it.
4. Make a copy of the qryTSelectedCities query using the new name **qryOtherSelectedCities**. Modify the new query to find all records in the tblSupplier table in which the City field values are not Dayton, Madison, or Edison. Save and run the query, and then close it.
5. Create a query to find all records from the tblSupplier table in which the State value is CT, NJ, or NY. Use a list-of-values match for the selection criteria. Display all fields in the query recordset, and sort in descending order by CompanyName. Save the query as **qrySelectedStates**, run the query, and then close it.
6. Create a query to display all records from the tblSupplier table, selecting the CompanyName, City, and ContactPhone fields, and sorting in ascending order by CompanyName. Add a calculated field named **ContactName** as the first column that concatenates the ContactFirstName, a space, and the ContactLastName. Set the Caption property for the ContactName field to **Contact Name**. Save the query as **qryCompanyContacts**, run the query, resize the Contact Name column to its best fit, and then save and close the query.
7. Create a parameter query to select the tblSupplier table records for a State field value that the user specifies. If the user doesn't enter a State field value, select all records from the table. Display the CompanyName, Category, City, State, ContactFirstName, ContactLastName, and ContactPhone fields in the query recordset, sorting in ascending order by City. Save the query as **qryStateParameter**. Run the query and enter no value as the State field value, and then run the query again and enter **CT** as the State field value. Close the query.
8. Create a find duplicates query based on the tblProduct table. Select ProductName as the field that might contain duplicates, and select the ProductID, SupplierID, Price, and Units fields as additional fields in the query recordset. Save the query as **qryDuplicateProductTypes**, run the query, and then close it. Because the tblProduct table does not have any duplicate ProductName values, running this query should show that no duplicate records are found.
9. Create a find unmatched query that finds all records in the tblSupplier table for which there is no matching record in the tblProduct table. Display the SupplierID, CompanyName, City, State, ContactPhone, ContactFirstName, and ContactLastName fields from the tblSupplier table in the query recordset. Save the query as **qrySuppliersWithoutMatchingProducts**, run the query, and then close it. Because the tblSupplier and tblProduct tables do not have unmatched records, running this query should show that no unmatched records are found.

10. Create a query to display all records from the tblProduct table, selecting the ProductID, SupplierID, ProductName, and Price fields, and sorting in descending order by Price. Use the Top Values property to select the top 25 percent of records. Save the query as **qryTop25Price** run the query, and then close it.

11. In the **tblProduct** table, change the SupplierID field to a lookup field. Select the CompanyName field and then the SupplierID field from the tblSupplier table. Sort in ascending order by the CompanyName field, do not hide the key column, make sure the Company Name column is the leftmost column, resize the lookup columns to their best fit, select SupplierID as the field to store in the table, and accept the default label for the lookup column. View the tblProduct table datasheet, resize the Supplier ID column to its best fit, test the lookup field without changing a value permanently, and then save and close the table.

12. Use the Input Mask Wizard to add an input mask to the ContactPhone field in the **tblSupplier** table. The ending input mask should use periods as separators, as in 987.654.3210 with only the last seven digits required; do not store the literal display characters, if you are asked to do so. Update the Input Mask property everywhere the ContactPhone field is used. Resize all columns in the datasheet to their best fit, and then test the input mask by typing over an existing Phone field value, being sure not to change the value by pressing the Esc key after you type the last digit in the Phone field.

13. Designate the Access2 ▸ Review folder as a trusted folder. (*Note:* Check with your instructor before adding a new trusted location.)

14. Make a backup copy of the database, compact and repair the database, and then close it.

Case Problem 1

Data File needed for this Case Problem: Task.accdb

GoGopher! Amol Mehta, a recent college graduate living in Boulder, Colorado, spent months earning money by running errands and completing basic chores for family members and acquaintances, while looking for full-time employment. As his list of customers needing such services continued to grow, Amol decided to start his own business called GoGopher! The business, which Amol operates completely online from his home, offers customers a variety of services—from grocery shopping and household chores to yard work and pet care—on a subscription basis. Clients become members of GoGopher! by choosing the plan that best suits their needs. Each plan provides a certain number of tasks per month to members for a specified period of time. Amol created an Access database named Task to store data about members, plans, and contracts. He wants to create several new queries and make design changes to the tables. Complete the following steps:

1. Open the **Task** database located in the Access2 ▸ Case1 folder provided with your Data Files.

2. Modify the first record in the **tblMember** table datasheet by changing the First Name and Last Name column values to your first and last names. Close the table.

3. Create a query to find all records in the tblPlan table in which the PlanCost field is 600, 900, or 1500. Use a list-of-values match for the selection criterion, and include all fields from the table in the query recordset. Sort the query in descending order by the PlanID field. Save the query as **qryLowVolumePlans**, run the query, and then close it.

4. Make a copy of the qryLowVolumePlans query using the new name **qryHighVolumePlans**. Modify the new query to find all records in the tblPlan table in which the PlanCost field is not 600, 900, or 1500. Save and run the query, and then close it.

5. Create a query to display all records from the tblMember table, selecting the LastName, FirstName, Street, and Phone fields, and sorting in ascending order by LastName and then in ascending order by FirstName. Add a calculated field named **MemberName** as the first column that concatenates FirstName, a space, and LastName. Set the Caption property for the MemberName field to **Member Name**. Do not display the LastName and FirstName fields in the query recordset. Create a second calculated field named **CityLine**, inserting it between the

Street and Phone fields. The CityLine field concatenates City, a space, State, two spaces, and Zip. Set the Caption property for the CityLine field to **City Line**. Save the query as **qryMemberNames**, run the query, resize all columns to their best fit, and then save and close the query.

6. Create a query to display all matching records from the tblPlan and tblMember tables, selecting the LastName and FirstName fields from the tblMember table and the PlanDescription and PlanCost fields from the tblPlan table. Add a calculated field named **FeeStatus** as the last column that equals *Fee Waived* if the FeeWaived field is equal *to yes*, and that equals *Fee Not Waived* otherwise. Set the Caption property for the calculated field to **Fee Status**. Sort the list in ascending order on the LastName field. Save the query as **qryFeeStatus**, run the query, resize all columns to their best fit, and then save and close the query.

7. Create a query based on the tblPlan and tblMember tables, selecting the LastName, FirstName, and City fields from the tblMember table and the FeeWaived, PlanDescription, and PlanCost fields from the tblPlan table. The query should find the records in which the City field value is Boulder or Erie and the FeeWaived field value is *Yes*. Save the query as **qryBoulderAndErieFeeWaived**. Save and run the query, and then close the query.

8. Create a parameter query to select the tblMember table records for a City field value that the user specifies. If the user doesn't enter a City field value, select all records from the table. Display all fields from the tblMember table in the query recordset. Save the query as **qryMemberCityParameter**. Run the query and enter no value as the City field value, and then run the query again and enter **Boulder** as the City field value. Close the query.

9. Create a find duplicates query based on the tblMember table. Select Expiration as the field that might contain duplicates, and select all other fields in the table as additional fields in the query recordset. Save the query as **qryDuplicateMemberExpirationDates**, run the query, and then close it.

10. Create a find unmatched query that finds all records in the tblMember table for which there is no matching record in the tblPlan table. Select FirstName, LastName, and Phone fields from the tblMembers table. Save the query as **qryMembersWithoutPlans**, run the query, and then close it.

11. Create a new query based on the tblMember table. Display the FirstName, LastName, Phone, Expiration, and PlanID fields, in this order, in the query recordset. Sort in ascending order by the Expiration field, and then use the Top Values property to select the top 25 percent of records. Save the query as **qryUpcomingExpirations**, run the query, and then close it.

12. Use the Input Mask Wizard to add an input mask to the Phone field in the **tblMember** table. Create the input mask such that the phone number is displayed with a dot separating each part of the phone number. For instance, if the phone number is (303) 123-4567 it should be displayed as 303.123.4567 for new entries. Test the input mask by typing over an existing Phone column value, being certain not to change the value by pressing the Esc key after you type the last digit in the Phone column, and then save and close the table.

13. Define a field validation rule for the PlanCost field in the **tblPlan** table. Acceptable field values for the PlanCost field are values greater than 500. Enter the message **Value must be greater than 500** so it appears if a user enters an invalid PlanCost field value. Save your table changes, and then test the field validation rule for the PlanCost field; be certain the field values are the same as they were before your testing, and then close the table.

14. Define a table validation rule for the **tblMember** table to verify that DateJoined field values precede Expiration field values in time. Use an appropriate validation message. Save your table changes, and then test the table validation rule, making sure any tested field values are the same as they were before your testing.

15. Add a Long Text field named **MemberComments** as the last field in the tblMember table. Set the Caption property to **Member Comments** and the Text Format property to Rich Text. In the table datasheet, resize the new column to its best fit, and then add a comment in the Member Comments column in the first record about a job you would do for someone else, formatting the text with blue, italic font. Save your table changes, and then close the table.

16. Designate the Access2 ▸ Case1 folder as a trusted folder. (*Note:* Check with your instructor before adding a new trusted location.)

17. Make a backup copy of the database, compact and repair the database, and then close it.

Case Problem 2

Data File needed for this Case Problem: Tutoring.accdb

O'Brien Educational Services After teaching English in a public high school for 15 years, Karen O'Brien decided to channel her experience in education in a new direction and founded O'Brien Educational Services, a small educational consulting company located in South Bend, Indiana. The company offers tutoring services to high school students to help prepare them for standardized tests, such as the SAT and the ACT. The company provides group, private, and semiprivate tutoring sessions to best meet the needs of its students. To make the database easier to use, Karen wants you to create several queries and modify its table design. Complete the following steps:

1. Open the **Tutoring** database located in the Access2 ▶ Case2 folder provided with your Data Files.
2. Change the record in the **tblTutor** table datasheet that contains Student First and Student Last so the First Name and Last Name field values contain your first and last names. Close the table.
3. Create a query to find all records in the tblStudent table in which the LastName field value begins with M. Display the FirstName, LastName, City, and HomePhone fields in the query recordset, and sort in ascending order by LastName. Save the query as **qryLastNameM**, run the query, and then close it.
4. Create a query that finds all records in the tblTutor table in which the Degree field value is either BA or MA. Use a list-of-values criterion and include the fields First Name, Last Name, and Degree in the recordset, sorted in ascending order on the LastName field. Save the query using the name **qrySelectedDegrees**. Run the query, and then close it.
5. Create a query to find all records in the tblStudent table in which the City field value is not equal to South Bend. Display the FirstName, LastName, City, and HomePhone fields in the query recordset, and sort in ascending order by City. Save the query as **qryNonSouthBend**, run the query, and then close it.
6. Create a query to display all records from the tblTutor table, selecting all fields, and sorting in ascending order by LastName and then in ascending order by FirstName. Add a calculated field named **TutorName** as the second column that concatenates FirstName, a space, and LastName for each teacher. Set the Caption property for the TutorName field to **Tutor Name**. Do not display the FirstName and LastName fields in the query recordset. Save the query as **qryTutorNames**, run the query, resize the Tutor Name column to its best fit, and then save and close the query.
7. Create a parameter query to select the tblContract table records for a SessionType field value that the user specifies. If the user doesn't enter a SessionType field value, select all records from the table. Include all fields from the tblContract table in the query recordset. Save the query as **qrySessionTypeParameter**. Run the query and enter no value as the SessionType field value, and then run the query again and enter **Private** as the SessionType field value. Close the query.
8. Create a crosstab query based on the tblContract table. Use the SessionType field values for the row headings, the Length field values for the column headings, and the count of the ContractID field values as the summarized value, and include row sums. Save the query as **qrySessionTypeCrosstab**. Change the column heading for the row sum column to **Total Number of Sessions.** Resize the columns in the query recordset to their best fit, and then save and close the query.
9. Create a find duplicates query based on the tblContract table. Select StudentID and SessionType as the fields that might contain duplicates, and select all other fields in the table as additional fields in the query recordset. Save the query as **qryMultipleSessionsForStudents**, run the query, and then close it.
10. Create a find unmatched query that finds all records in the tblStudent table for which there is no matching record in the tblContract table. Display all fields from the tblStudent table in the query recordset. Save the query as **qryStudentsWithoutContracts**, run the query, and then close it.

11. In the **tblContract** table, change the TutorID field data type to Lookup Wizard. Select the FirstName, LastName, and TutorID fields from the tblTutor table, sort in ascending order by LastName, resize the lookup columns to their best fit, select TutorID as the field to store in the table, and accept the default label for the lookup column. View the tblContract table datasheet, resize the Tutor ID column to its best fit, and then save and close the table.

12. Use the Input Mask Wizard to add an input mask to the HomePhone field in the **tblStudent** table. The ending input mask should use periods as separators, as in 987.654.3210, with only the last seven digits required; do not store the literal display characters, if you are asked to do so. Resize the Home Phone column to its best fit, and then test the input mask by typing over an existing Phone field value, being sure not to change the value permanently by pressing the Esc key after you type the last digit in the Phone field.

13. Define a field validation rule for the Gender field in the tblStudent table. Acceptable field values for the Gender field are F or M. Use the message "Gender value must be F or M" to notify a user who enters an invalid Gender field value. Save your table changes, test the field validation rule for the Gender field, making sure any tested field values are the same as they were before your testing, and then close the table.

14. Designate the Access2 ▸ Case2 folder as a trusted folder. (*Note:* Check with your instructor before adding a new trusted location.)

15. Make a backup copy of the database, compact and repair the database, and then close it.

Case Problem 3

Data File needed for this Case Problem: Rosemary.accdb

Rosemary Animal Shelter Ryan Lang is the director of the Rosemary Animal Shelter in Cobb County, Georgia. The main goals of the shelter, which has several locations in the county, are to rescue dogs and cats and to find people who will adopt them. The shelter was established by Rosemary Hanson, who dedicated her life to rescuing pets and finding good homes for them. Residents of Cobb County generously donate money, food, and equipment in support of the shelter. Some of these patrons also adopt animals from the shelter. Ryan has created an Access database to manage information about the animals, patrons, and donations. Ryan now wants to create several queries and to make changes to the table design of the database. You'll help Ryan by completing the following steps:

1. Open the **Rosemary** database located in the Access2 ▸ Case3 folder provided with your Data Files.

2. Modify the first record in the **tblPatron** table datasheet by changing the Title, FirstName, and LastName column values to your title and name. Close the table.

3. Create a query to find all records in the tblAnimal table for dogs that have been adopted. Display the AnimalName, AnimalGender, AnimalType, AdoptionDate, and Adopted fields in the query recordset. Sort by ascending order by AnimalName. Save the query as **qryDogsAdopted**, run the query, and then close it.

4. Create a query to find all records in the tblDonation table in which the DonationDesc field value is not equal to Cash Donation. Display the Title, FirstName, and LastName, from the tblPatron table, and DonationDesc from the tblDonation table. Sort in ascending order by LastName. Save the query as **qryNonCashDonations**, run the query, and then close it.

5. Create a query called **qryNetDonationsAprilOrLater** that will contain all fields from the tblDonation and tblPatron tables except for PatronID and DonationID, for all donations that are on or after April 1, 2016. Sort this query by DonationValue in descending order. Save and run the query, and then close it.

6. Create a query to display all records from the tblPatron table, selecting the Title and Phone fields. Add a calculated field named **PatronName** that concatenates FirstName, a space, and LastName. Position this column as the second column, and sort the recordset in ascending order by LastName. Set the Caption property for the PatronName field to **Patron Name**. Save the query as **qryPatronNames**, run the query, resize the new column to its best fit, and then save and close the query.

7. Create a parameter query to select the tblAnimal table records for an AnimalType field value that the user specifies. If the user doesn't enter an AnimalType field value, select all records from the table. Display all fields from the tblAnimal table in the query recordset, and sort in ascending order by AnimalName. Save the query as **qryAnimalTypeParameter**. Run the query and enter no value as the AnimalType field value, and then run the query again and enter **Cat** as the AnimalType field value. Close the query.

8. Create a crosstab query based on the qryNetDonationsAprilOrLater query. Use the DonationDate field values for the row headings, the DonationTypeID field values for the column headings, and the sum of the DonationValue field values as the summarized value, and include row sums. Save the query as **qryNetDonationsAprilOrLaterCrosstab**. Change the format of the displayed values (DonationValue and Total Of DonationValue columns in Design view) to Fixed. Resize the columns in the query recordset to their best fit, and then save and close the query.

9. Create a find duplicates query based on the qryNetDonationsAprilOrLater query. Select FirstName and LastName as the fields that might contain duplicates, and select the DonationTypeID and DonationValue fields in the query as additional fields in the query recordset. Save the query as **qryMultipleDonorDonations**, run the query, and then close it.

10. Create a find unmatched query that finds all records in the tblPatron table for which there is no matching record in the tblDonation table. Include all fields from the tblPatron table, except for PatronID, in the query recordset. Save the query as **qryPatronsWithoutDonations**, run the query, and then close it.

11. Make a copy of the qryNetDonationsAprilOrLater query using the new name **qryTopNetDonations**. Modify the new query by using the Top Values property to select the top 40 percent of the records. Save and run the query, and then close the query.

12. Use the Input Mask Wizard to add an input mask to the Phone field in the **tblPatron** table. The ending input mask should use hyphens as separators, as in 987-654-3210, with only the last seven digits required; do not store the literal display characters, if you are asked to do so. Update the Input Mask property everywhere the Phone field is used. Test the input mask by typing over an existing Phone field value, being sure not to change the value permanently by pressing the Esc key after you type the last digit in the Phone field. Close the table.

13. Designate the Access2 ▸ Case3 folder as a trusted folder. (*Note:* Check with your instructor before adding a new trusted location.)

14. Make a backup copy of the database, compact and repair the database, and then close it.

Case Problem 4

Data File needed for this Case Problem: Ecotour.accdb

Stanley EcoTours Janice and Bill Stanley live in Pocatello, Idaho, and are the proud owners and operators of Stanley EcoTours. Their passion is to encourage people to visit natural areas around the world in a responsible manner that does not harm the environment. Their advertising has drawn clients from Idaho, Wyoming, Montana, and Canada. As the interest in ecotourism grows, Janice and Bill's business is also expanding to include more tours in Africa and South America. Janice and Bill have created an Access database for their business and now want you to create several queries and modify the table design. To do so, you'll complete the following steps:

1. Open the **Ecotour** database located in the Access2 ▸ Case4 folder provided with your Data Files.
2. Modify the first record in the **tblGuest** table datasheet by changing the Guest First Name and Guest Last Name column values to your first and last names, and then close the table.
3. Create a query to find all records in the tblGuest table in which the GuestLast field value starts with the letter G, sorted in ascending order by GuestLast. Display all fields except the GuestID field in the query recordset. Save the query as **qryGuestLastNameG**, run the query, and then close it.
4. Create a query to find all records in the tblTour table where the country is not Brazil or Peru. Name this query **qryNonBrazilOrPeruTours**. Display all fields, sorting by Country and then by Location. Save and run the query, and then close it.

5. Create a query to find all records in the tblGuest table in which the StateProv field value is MT, WY, or ID and display all fields from the tblGuest table in the query recordset, sorted by GuestLast in ascending order. Save the query as **qrySelectedStates**, run the query, and then close it.
6. Create a query to select all records from the tblTour with tour rates of $5,000 or less, where the TourType is either Hiking or Jeep. Display all fields in the query recordset, sorted by Nights in descending order. Save the query as **qryHikingOrJeepSelectedTours**, run the query, and then close it.
7. Create a parameter query to select the tblTour table records for a Country field value that the user specifies. If the user doesn't enter a Country field value, select all records from the table. Display all fields from the tblTour table in the query recordset, and sort in ascending order by TourName. Save the query as **qryCountryParameter**. Run the query and enter no value as the Country field value, and then run the query again and enter **Peru** as the Country field value. Close the query.
8. Create a query that contains all records from the tblGuest table and all matching records from the tblReservation table. Display all fields from the tblGuest table and all fields except GuestID from the tblReservation table. Save the query as **qryGuestsAndReservations**, run the query, and then close it.
9. Create a crosstab query based on the qryGuestsAndReservations query. Use the TourID field values for the row headings, the Country field values for the column headings, and the sum of the People field as the summarized value, and include row sums. Save the query as **qryReservationsCrosstab**, resize the columns in the query recordset to their best fit, and then save and close the query.
10. Create a find duplicates query based on the **qryGuestsAndReservations** query. Select GuestID as the field that might contain duplicates, and select the fields GuestFirst, GuestLast, TourID, StartDate, and People in the table as additional fields in the query recordset. Save the query as **qryMultipleReservations**, run the query, and then close it.
11. Create a find unmatched query that finds all records in the tblGuest table for which there is no matching record in the tblReservation table. Display the GuestFirst, GuestLast, City, StateProv. and Phone fields from the tblGuest table in the query recordset. Save the query as **qryGuestsWithoutReservations**, run the query, and then close it.
12. Copy the **qryHikingOrJeepSelectedTours** and save it as **qryTopHikingOrJeepSelectedTours.** Use the Top Values property to select the top 30 percent of the records. Save and run the query, and then close it.
13. In the **tblReservation** table, change the TourID field data type to Lookup Wizard. Select the TourID, TourName, Location, and Country fields from the tblTour table, sort in ascending order by TourName, hide the key column, resize the lookup columns to their best fit, select TourID as the field to store in the table, and accept the default label for the look up column. View the tblReservation datasheet, resize the TourID column to its best fit, test the lookup field without changing a field value permanently, and then close the table.
14. Define a field validation rule for the People field in the **tblReservation** table. Acceptable field values for the People field are values less than or equal to 12. Display the message **Please book a custom tour for large groups.** when a user enters an invalid People field value. Save your table changes, and then test the field validation rule for the People field; be certain the field values are the same as they were before your testing.
15. Define a table validation rule for the **tblTour** table to verify that SingleSupplement field values are less than the PricePerPerson values. Use an appropriate validation message. Save your table changes, test the table validation rule, making sure any tested field values are the same as they were before your testing, and then close the table.
16. Designate the Access2 ▶ Case4 folder as a trusted folder. (*Note:* Check with your instructor before adding a new trusted location.)
17. Make a backup copy of the database, compact and repair the database, and then close it.

TUTORIAL 8

Sharing, Integrating, and Analyzing Data

Importing, Exporting, Linking, and Analyzing Data in the Clinic Database

OBJECTIVES

Session 8.1
- Export an Access query to an HTML document and view the document
- Import a CSV file as an Access table
- Use the Table Analyzer
- Import a table from another Access database
- Import and export XML files
- Save and run import and export specifications

Session 8.2
- Create a tabbed form using a tab control
- Understand the difference between importing, embedding, and linking external objects
- Embed a chart in a form
- Create and use an application part
- Export a PDF file
- Link data from an Excel workbook

Case | Chatham Community Health Services

Cindi Rodriguez, Kelly Schwarz, and Ethan Ward are pleased with the design and contents of the Clinic database. Cindi feels that other employees would benefit from gaining access to the Clinic database and from sharing data among the different programs employees use. Cindi and Kelly would also like to be able to analyze the data in the database.

In this tutorial, you will import, export, link, and embed data, and you will create application parts. You will also explore the charting features of Access.

STARTING DATA FILES

Access2 → Tutorial
Clinic.accdb (*cont.*)
NewPatientReferrals.accdb
peoplecalled.csv
Referral.xml
Volunteer.xlsx

Review
Ads.xlsx
Partners.accdb
Payables.csv
Payments.xml
Vendor.accdb (*cont.*)

Case1
CreditCard.xml
Schedule.xlsx
Task.accdb (*cont.*)

Case2
AddSubject.xml
NewStudentReferrals.accdb
Room.xlsx
Subject.csv
Tutoring.accdb (*cont.*)

Case3
Facility.csv
Rosemary.accdb (*cont.*)
Volunteer.accdb

Case4
Ecotour.accdb (*cont.*)
Personnel.xlsx
PotentialTours1.xml
PotentialTours2.xml

Session 8.1 Visual Overview:

Extensible Markup Language (XML) is a programming language that uses customizable tags to describe the data it contains and how that data should be structured.

Each piece of data is encapsulated in paired tags.

Access includes tools for exporting data on the EXTERNAL DATA tab.

The field names from the table are used as XML tags to identify data.

Each record begins with the tag `<tblReferral>` and ends with the tag `</tblReferral>`.

Access table exported as an XML file

```
<tblReferral>
<PatientID>36229</PatientID>
<FirstName>Larissa</FirstName>
<LastName>Waller</LastName>
<Phone>860-661-3098</Phone>
<Address>7297 Dolor St</Address>
<City>Hartford</City>
<State>CT</State>
<Zip>06105</Zip>
<Email>lwaller@example.com</Email>
</tblReferral>
<tblReferral>
<PatientID>36232</PatientID>
<FirstName>Maria</FirstName>
<LastName>Marquez</LastName>
<Phone>860-938-1123</Phone>
<Address>27 Frankfurt St</Address>
<City>Hartford</City>
<State>CT</State>
<Zip>06120</Zip>
<Email>mmarq@example.com</Email>
</tblReferral>
<tblReferral>
<PatientID>36239</PatientID>
<FirstName>Betty</FirstName>
<LastName>Gallagher</LastName>
<Phone>860-552-2987</Phone>
<Address>127 Rain Ct</Address>
<City>Windsor</City>
<State>CT</State>
<Zip>06095</Zip>
<Email>bettyg@example.com</Email>
</tblReferral>
<tblReferral>
<PatientID>36241</PatientID>
<FirstName>Jonathan</FirstName>
<LastName>Holloway</LastName>
<Phone>860-552-2341</Phone>
<Address>128 Charning Ave</Address>
```

PatientID	FirstName	LastName	Phone	Address	City	State
36229	Larissa	Waller	860-661-3098	7297 Dolor St	Hartford	CT
36232	Maria	Marquez	860-938-1123	27 Frankfurt St	Hartford	CT
36239	Betty	Gallagher	860-552-2987	127 Rain Ct	Windsor	CT
36241	Jonathan	Holloway	860-552-2341	128 Charning Ave	Windsor	CT
36247	Lapfong	Wong	860-374-2521	129 Devon Ave	Hartford	CT
36599	Randy	Hawes	860-661-7193	26 Edwin Ct	Hartford	CT
36602	Maria	Torres	860-938-2098	27 Reno Dr	Hartford	CT
36609	Chung	Ho	860-552-5846	127 Tracey Ct	Windsor	CT
36611	Victor	Park	860-552-0395	228 Aiken Ave	Windsor	CT
36617	Sam	Lew	860-374-9342	129 Fairchild Ave	Hartford	CT
36618	Mandy	Lin	860-637-5800	332 Agnes Ct	West Hartford	CT
36621	Arthur	Scott	860-228-4992	317 Noyes Ct	Hartford	CT

Exporting data to XML and HTML

The table field names are used as column headings in the table on the web page.

The Export to HTML tool generates an HTML document, embedding the Access content in the document. An HTML document contains tags and other instructions that a web browser processes and displays as a web page.

The name of the table is used as a heading on the web page.

The values are formatted using the formatting property for each field.

Access table exported as an HTML file

The Export to HTML tool creates a static web page, which reflects the state of the query at the time you created it. If the data in the query changed, you would need to export the query as an HTML document again.

Exporting an Access Query to an HTML Document

Cindi wants to display the summary data in the qryPatientsAndInvoicesCrosstab query on the company's intranet so that all employees working in the office are able to view it. To store the data on the company's intranet, you'll create a web page version of the qryPatientsAndInvoicesCrosstab query.

An HTML document contains tags and other instructions that a Web browser, such as Microsoft Internet Explorer, Apple Safari, or Google Chrome, processes and displays as a Web page. Creating the necessary HTML document to provide Cindi with the information she wants is not as difficult as it might appear at first. You can use Access to export the query and convert it to an HTML document automatically.

REFERENCE

Exporting an Access Object to an HTML Document

- In the Navigation Pane, right-click the object (table, query, form, or report) you want to export, point to Export on the shortcut menu, and then click HTML Document; or in the Navigation Pane, click the object (table, query, form, or report) you want to export, click the EXTERNAL DATA tab, in the Export group click the More button, and then click HTML Document.
- In the Export – HTML Document dialog box, click the Browse button, select the location where you want to save the file, enter the filename in the File name box, and then click the Save button.
- Click the Export data with formatting and layout check box to retain most formatting and layout information, and then click the OK button.
- In the HTML Output Options dialog box, if using a template click the Select a HTML Template check box, click the Browse button, select the location for the template, click the template filename, and then click the OK button.
- Click the OK button, and then click the Close button.

You'll export the qryPatientsAndInvoicesCrosstab query as an HTML document. The qryPatientsAndInvoicesCrosstab query is a select query that joins the tblPatient, tblVisit, and tblBilling tables to display selected data from those tables for all invoices. The query displays one row for each unique City field value.

To export the qryPatientsAndInvoicesCrosstab query as an HTML document:

1. Start Access, and then open the **Clinic** database you worked with in Tutorials 5–7.

2. Open the Navigation Pane (if necessary), right-click **qryPatientsAndInvoicesCrosstab** to display the shortcut menu, point to **Export**, and then click **HTML Document**. The Export - HTML Document dialog box opens.

3. Click the **Browse** button to open the File Save dialog box, navigate to the **Access2 ▸ Tutorial** folder in the location where your data files are stored, select the text in the File name box, type **Crosstab.html**, and then click the **Save** button. The File Save dialog box closes, and you return to the Export – HTML Document dialog box.

TIP

Always select the "Export data with formatting and layout" option, or the HTML document you create will be poorly formatted and difficult to read.

Figure 8-1 Export - HTML Document dialog box

destination file location and filename (your file location might be different) → File name: E:\Access2\Tutorial\Crosstab.html

click the Browse button to select the save location for the new HTML file → Browse...

export options for an HTML document:

- ☐ **Export data with formatting and layout.**
  Select this option to preserve most formatting and layout information when exporting a table, query, form, or report.
- ☐ **Open the destination file after the export operation is complete.**
  Select this option to view the results of the export operation. This option is available only when you export formatted data.
- ☐ **Export only the selected records.**
  Select this option to export only the selected records. This option is only available when you export formatted data and have records selected.

The dialog box provides options for exporting the data with formatting and layout, opening the exported file after the export operation is complete, and exporting selected records from the source object (available only when you select records in an object instead of selecting an object in the Navigation Pane). You need to select the option for exporting the data with formatting and layout.

▶ **4.** Click the **Export data with formatting and layout** check box to select it, and then click the **OK** button. The Export - HTML Document dialog box closes and the HTML Output Options dialog box opens. See Figure 8-2.

Figure 8-2 HTML Output Options dialog box

HTML Output Options

☐ Select a HTML Template:
Browse...

Choose the encoding to use for saving this file:
- ⦿ Default encoding ← *data encoding options*
- ○ Unicode
- ○ Unicode (UTF-8)

▶ **5.** Click the **OK** button. The HTML Output Options dialog box closes, the HTML document named Crosstab is saved in the Access2 ▶ Tutorial folder, and the Export - HTML Document dialog box is displayed with an option to save the export steps. You won't save these export steps.

▶ **6.** Click the **Close** button in the dialog box to close it without saving the steps and to close the Navigation Pane.

Now you can view the web page.

Viewing an HTML Document Using Internet Explorer

Cindi asks to see the web page you created. You can view the HTML document that you created using any web browser.

To view the Crosstab web page:

1. Open Windows File Explorer, and then navigate to and open the **Access2 ▸ Tutorial** folder, which is where you saved the exported HTML document.

2. Right-click **Crosstab** in the file list to open the shortcut menu, click **Open with**, click the name of your web browser, such as **Internet Explorer**, and then click the **OK** button (if necessary). Internet Explorer starts and opens the Crosstab web page. The Session 8.1 Visual Overview shows the web page in Internet Explorer.

   Trouble? You may see different column widths than the ones shown in the Session 8.1 Visual Overview, depending on the size of your web browser window. This difference is not an issue of concern.

Any subsequent changes that employees make to the Clinic database will not appear in the Crosstab web page that you created because it is a static web page—that is, it reflects the state of the qryPatientsAndInvoicesCrosstab query in the Clinic database at the time you created it. If data in the qryPatientsAndInvoicesCrosstab query changes, you will need to export the query as an HTML document again.

Because this static web page is not linked to the qryPatientsAndInvoicesCrosstab query on which it is based, you cannot use your browser to make changes to its data. Before closing the Crosstab web page, you'll verify this by trying to change one of its field values.

To attempt to change a field value in the web page:

1. Double-click **Hartford** in the City column for the second record, type **D**, and then notice that no change occurs. The value of Hartford remains highlighted and unchanged because the Crosstab web page is a static page.

2. Click the **Close** button ⊠ on the Internet Explorer window title bar to close it and to return to Windows File Explorer.

3. Click the **Close** button ⊠ on the Windows File Explorer window title bar to close it and to return to Access.

   Trouble? If the Access window is not active on your screen, click the Microsoft Access program button on the taskbar.

Now that you've completed your work creating the web page, Kelly has a file containing information for potential new patients that she needs to add to the Clinic database. Instead of typing the information into new records, she asks you to import the data into the Clinic database.

Importing a CSV File as an Access Table

Kelly has been maintaining an Excel workbook containing contact information for people who have called the Chatham Community Health Services clinic to inquire about the services, but have not yet booked appointments. She has exported the Excel data to a CSV file. A **CSV (comma-separated values) file** is a text file in which commas separate values, and each line is a record containing the same number of values in the same positions. This is a common format for representing data in a table and is used by spreadsheet applications such as Excel as well as database applications. Many people use Excel to manage a simple table, such as a table of contact information or product information. They may not want to provide the entire Excel file if it also contains formulas or other data that they do not want to distribute. Instead, they may choose to save one worksheet of the Excel workbook as a CSV file so you can import it into Access.

REFERENCE

Importing a CSV File as an Access Table

- On the EXTERNAL DATA tab, in the Import & Link group, click the Text File button to open the Get External Data - Text File dialog box.
- Click the Browse button in the dialog box, navigate to the location where the file to import is stored, click the filename, and then click the Open button.
- Click the "Import the source data into a new table in the current database" option button, and then click the OK button.
- In the Import Text Wizard dialog box, click the Delimited option button, and then click the Next button.
- Make sure the Comma option button is selected. If appropriate, click the First Row Contains Field Names check box to select it, and then click the Next button.
- For each field, if necessary, select the column, type its field name and select its data type, and then click the Next button.
- Choose the appropriate option button to let Access create a primary key, to choose your own primary key, or to avoid setting a primary key, click the Next button, type the table name in the Import to Table box, and then click the Finish button.

Access can import data from a CSV file directly into a database table. Kelly's CSV file is named peoplecalled.csv, and you'll import the data as a new table in the Clinic database.

To view and import the CSV file as an Access table:

1. Open Windows File Explorer, navigate to the **Access2 ▸ Tutorial** folder included with your Data Files, right-click **peoplecalled.csv** in the file list to open the shortcut menu, click **Open with**, and then click **Notepad**.

   Trouble? If Notepad isn't an option when you click Open with, click More options, and then click Notepad in the expanded list that is displayed.

2. Examine the contents of the peoplecalled.csv file. The file contains rows of data, with commas separating pieces of data.

3. Close the Notepad window.

   Trouble? If a dialog box appears prompting you to save the file, click **Don't Save**. You may have accidentally added or deleted a character, and you don't want to save this change to the file.

4. In Access, click the **EXTERNAL DATA** tab, and then in the Import & Link group, click the **Text File** button (with the ScreenTip "Import text file") to open the Get External Data - Text File dialog box.

   Trouble? If the Export - Text File dialog box opens, you clicked the Text File button in the Export group. Click the Cancel button and then repeat Step 4, being sure to select the Text File button from the Import & Link group.

5. Click the **Browse** button, navigate to the **Access2 ▸ Tutorial** folder, click **peoplecalled.csv**, click the **Open** button, and then click the **Import the source data into a new table in the current database** option button (if necessary). The selected path and filename appear in the File name box. See Figure 8-3.

Figure 8-3 — Get External Data - Text File dialog box

path and filename for selected CSV file (your path might be different)

import options for a CSV file

The dialog box provides options for importing the data into a new table in the database, appending a copy of the data to an existing table in the database, and linking to the source data. In the future, Kelly wants to maintain the potential new patient data in the Clinic database, instead of using her Excel workbook, so you'll import the data into a new table.

6. Click the **OK** button to open the first Import Text Wizard dialog box, in which you designate how to identify the separation between field values in each line in the source data. The choices are the use of commas, tabs, or another character to separate, or delimit, the values, or the use of fixed-width columns with spaces between each column. The wizard has correctly identified that values are delimited by commas.

7. Click the **Next** button to open the second Import Text Wizard dialog box, in which you verify the delimiter for values in each line. See Figure 8-4.

Figure 8-4 Verifying the delimiter for values in the CSV file

select this check box when the first row contains field (column) names

selected delimiter

ten fields in the source file

this file does not contain field names in the first row

The CSV source file contains eight records with ten fields in each record. A comma serves as the delimiter for values in each line, so the Comma option button is selected. The first row in the source file contains the first record, not field names, so the "First Row Contains Field Names" check box is not checked. If the source file used either single or double quotation marks to enclose values, you would click the Text Qualifier arrow to choose the appropriate option.

8. Click the **Next** button to open the third Import Text Wizard dialog box, in which you enter the field name and set other properties for the imported fields. You will import all fields from the source file and use the default data type and indexed settings for each field, except for the first field's data type.

9. Type **PatientID** in the Field Name box, click the **Data Type** arrow, click **Short Text** in the list, and then click **Field2** in the table list. The heading for the first column changes to PatientID (partially hidden) in the table list, and the second column is selected.

10. Repeat Step 9 for the remaining nine columns, making sure Short Text is the data type for all fields, except for DOB, which should be Date With Time, typing **LastName**, **FirstName**, **DOB**, **Phone**, **Address**, **City**, **State**, **Zip**, and **Email** in the Field Name box. See Figure 8-5.

Be sure the data type for DOB is Date With Time, and the data type for Phone and Zip is Short Text.

Figure 8-5 After setting field names for the ten fields in the source file

[Screenshot of Import Text Wizard dialog with callouts:]
- field name for selected column
- leave this option unchecked for all fields
- field names for the ten columns

Field Name: Email   Data Type: Short Text
Indexed: No   ☐ Do not import field (Skip)

PatientID	LastName	FirstName	DOB	Phone	Address	City	State	Zip	Email
36108	Ali	Jaspreet	2/12/1996	8609382834	505 Perkins Dr	Hartford	CT	06120	jasali
36112	Alvarez	Maria	7/10/1991	8603053985	735 Oxford Ave	Bloomfield	CT	06002	malvar
36117	Sweeney	Patrick	3/4/1932	8605526832	5 Wallace Rd	Windsor	CT	06095	psween
36119	Higgins	Jim	8/16/1942	8603745742	329 Fairchild Ave	Hartford	CT	06114	jhiggi
36120	Morales	Juan	5/8/1943	8602264954	33 Noyes Ct	Hartford	CT	06112	juanm@
36125	Go	Bae	2/21/2001	8603055494	183 Everett Ln	Bloomfield	CT	06002	chingo
36128	Ma	Dae	6/7/1999	8604267653	138 German St	Hartford	CT	06106	daema@
36129	Zhang	Guang	4/6/1943	8609380142	29 Davenport St	Hartford	CT	06120	zguang

▶ 11. Click the **Next** button to open the fourth Import Text Wizard dialog box, in which you select the primary key for the imported table. PatientID, the first column, will be the primary key. When you select this column as the table's primary key, Access will delete the ID column it created.

▶ 12. Click the **Choose my own primary key** option button, make sure **PatientID** appears in the box for the option, click the **Next** button, type **tblPeopleCalled** as the table name in the Import to Table box, click the **I would like a wizard to analyze my table after importing the data** check box to select it, and then click the **Finish** button. An Import Text Wizard dialog box opens asking if you want to analyze the table; you'll continue working with this dialog box in the next set of steps.

After importing data and creating a new table, you can use the Import Text Wizard to analyze the imported table. When you choose this option, you start the Table Analyzer.

Analyzing a Table with the Table Analyzer

TIP
Read the Normalization section in the appendix titled "Relational Databases and Database Design" for more information about normalization and third normal form.

The **Table Analyzer** analyzes a single table and, if necessary, splits it into two or more tables that are in third normal form. The Table Analyzer looks for redundant data in the table. When the Table Analyzer encounters redundant data, it removes redundant fields from the table and then places them in new tables. The analyzer results must always be reviewed carefully by the database designer to determine if the suggestions are appropriate.

Tutorial 8 Sharing, Integrating, and Analyzing Data | Access   AC 453

To use the Table Analyzer to analyze the imported table:

> **TIP**
> You can start the Table Analyzer directly by clicking the DATABASE TOOLS tab, and then in the Analyze group clicking the Analyze Table button.

1. Click the **Yes** button to close the dialog box and to open the first Table Analyzer Wizard dialog box. The wizard identifies duplicate data in your table and displays a diagram and explanation in the dialog box describing the potential problem.

2. Click the first **Show me an example** button [»], read the explanation, close the example box, click the second **Show me an example** button [»], read the explanation, close the example box, and then click the Next button to open the second Table Analyzer Wizard dialog box. The diagram and explanation in this dialog box describe how the Table Analyzer solves the duplicate data problem.

3. Again, click the first **Show me an example** button [»], read the explanation, close the example box, click the second **Show me an example** button [»], read the explanation, close the example box, and then click the **Next** button to open the third Table Analyzer Wizard dialog box. In this dialog box, you choose whether to let the wizard decide the appropriate table placement for the fields, if the table is not already normalized. Normalizing is the process of identifying and eliminating anomalies from a collection of tables. You'll let the wizard decide.

4. Make sure the **Yes, let the wizard decide** option button is selected, and then click the **Next** button. The wizard indicates that the City and State fields should be split into a separate table. Although this data is redundant, it is an industry practice to keep the city, state, and zip information with the address information in a table, so you'll cancel the wizard rather than split the table.

5. Click the **Cancel** button to close the message box and exit the wizard. Access returns you to the Get External Data - Text File dialog box, in which you are asked if you want to save the import steps. You don't need to save these steps because you're importing the data only this one time.

6. Click the **Close** button to close the dialog box.

The tblPeopleCalled table is now listed in the Tables section in the Navigation Pane. You'll open the table to verify the import results.

To open the imported tblPeopleCalled table:

1. Open the Navigation Pane and double-click **tblPeopleCalled** to open the table datasheet, resize all columns to their best fit, and then click **36108** in the first row in the PatientID column to deselect all values. Close the Navigation Pane. See Figure 8-6.

Figure 8-6   Imported tblPeopleCalled table datasheet

PatientID	LastName	FirstName	DOB	Phone	Address	City	State	Zip	Email
36108	Ali	Jaspreet	2/12/1996	8609382834	505 Perkins Dr	Hartford	CT	06120	jasali@example.com
36112	Alvarez	Maria	7/10/1991	8603053985	735 Oxford Ave	Bloomfield	CT	06002	malvarez@example.com
36117	Sweeney	Patrick	3/4/1932	8605526832	5 Wallace Rd	Windsor	CT	06095	psweeney@example.com
36119	Higgins	Jim	8/16/1942	8603745742	329 Fairchild Ave	Hartford	CT	06114	jhiggins@example.com
36120	Morales	Juan	5/8/1943	8602264954	33 Noyes Ct	Hartford	CT	06112	juanm@example.com
36125	Go	Bae	2/21/2001	8603055494	183 Everett Ln	Bloomfield	CT	06002	chingo@example.com
36128	Ma	Dae	6/7/1999	8604267653	138 German St	Hartford	CT	06106	daema@example.com
36129	Zhang	Guang	4/6/1943	8609380142	29 Davenport St	Hartford	CT	06120	zguang@example.com

▶ 2. Save and close the table.

Kelly has received a file from another clinic that contains a table of referral patients in an Access database. She'd like you to import this table into the Clinic database, creating a new table called tblReferral.

Importing a table from an Access Database

You can import tables, queries, reports, and other Access database objects. While you can import only a table's structure to create a blank new table, Kelly wants the data in the referral file imported into the Clinic database as well. You'll import the structure and data of the table into the Clinic database as a new table.

To import an Access table:

▶ 1. Click the **EXTERNAL DATA** tab (if necessary), and then in the Import & Link group, click the **Access** button. The Get External Data-Access Database dialog box opens.

Trouble? If the Export - Access File dialog box opens, you clicked the Access File button in the Export group. Click the Cancel button and then repeat Step 1, being sure to select the Access File button from the Import & Link group.

▶ 2. Click the **Browse** button. The File Open dialog box opens. The Access database file from which you need to import the table structure is named NewPatientReferrals and is located in the Access2 ▶ Tutorial folder provided with your Data Files.

▶ 3. Navigate to the **Access2 ▶ Tutorial** folder where your starting Data Files are stored, click the **NewPatientReferrals** database file to select it, and then click the **Open** button.

▶ 4. Make sure the **Import tables, queries, forms, reports, macros, and modules into the current database** option button is selected, and then click the **OK** button. The Import Objects dialog box opens.

▶ 5. Click the **Options** button in the dialog box to see all the options for importing tables.

Tutorial 8 Sharing, Integrating, and Analyzing Data | Access   AC 455

There is only one table in the NewPatientReferrals database. You'll import the tblReferral table and all of its data.

6. On the Tables tab, click **tblReferral** to select this table. See Figure 8-7.

Figure 8-7 Import Objects dialog box showing tblReferral

- select to import the table including all records
- imports only the structure of the table without the records

7. In the Import Tables section of the dialog box, click the **Definition and Data** option button if necessary, and then click the **OK** button. Access creates the tblReferral table in the Clinic database using the structure and contents of the tblReferral table in the NewPatientReferrals database, and opens a dialog box asking if you want to save the import steps.

8. Click the **Close** button to close the dialog box without saving the import steps.

9. Open the Navigation Pane (if necessary) and note that the tblReferral table is listed in the Tables section.

10. Double-click **tblReferral** to open the table. The tblReferral table opens in Datasheet view. See Figure 8-8.

Figure 8-8 Imported tblReferral table datasheet

- new table imported

11. Close the tblReferral table.

Next, Kelly would like you to import data from another file containing new patient referrals from another clinic. However, this data is not in an Access table; instead, it's stored in XML format.

Using XML

Chatham Community Health Services occasionally receives patient referrals from other clinics. Kelly was provided an XML document that contains patient contact information from another clinic, which she wants to add to the Clinic database. XML (Extensible Markup Language) is a programming language that is similar in format to HTML, but is more customizable and is suited to the exchange of data between different programs. Unlike HTML, which uses a fixed set of tags to describe the appearance of a web page, developers can customize XML to describe the data it contains and how that data should be structured.

PROSKILLS

Decision Making: Exchanging Data Between Programs

If all companies used Access, you could easily exchange data between any two databases. However, not all companies use Access. One universal and widely used method for transferring data between different database systems is to export data to XML files and import data from XML files. XML files are used to exchange data between companies, and they are also used to exchange data between programs within a company. For example, you can store data either in an Excel workbook or in an Access table or query, depending on which program is best suited to the personnel working with the data and the business requirements of the company. Because the XML file format is a common format for both Excel and Access—as well as many other programs—whenever the data is needed in another program, you can export the data from one program as an XML file and then import the file into the other program. You should consider the needs of the users and the characteristics of the programs they use when deciding the best means for exchanging data between programs.

Importing Data from an XML File

Access can import data from an XML file directly into a database table. Kelly's XML file is named Referral.xml, and you'll import it into the tblReferral table in the Clinic database, adding the XML records to the end of the table.

REFERENCE

Importing an XML File as an Access Table

- On the EXTERNAL DATA tab, in the Import & Link group, click the XML File button to open the Get External Data - XML File dialog box; or right-click the table name in the Navigation pane, click Import, and then click XML File.
- Click the Browse button, navigate to the location of the XML file, click the XML filename, and then click the Open button.
- Click the OK button in the Get External Data - XML File dialog box, click the table name in the Import XML dialog box, click the appropriate option button in the Import Options section, and then click the OK button.
- Click the Close button; or if you need to save the import steps, click the Save import steps check box, enter a name for the saved steps in the Save as box, and then click the Save Import button.

Tutorial 8 Sharing, Integrating, and Analyzing Data | Access   AC 457

Now you will import the Referral XML document as an Access database table.

To import the contents of the XML document:

1. In the Navigation Pane, right-click the **tblReferral** table name in the Tables objects listing, point to **Import**, then click **XML File**. The Get External Data - XML File dialog box opens.

2. Click the **Browse** button, navigate to the **Access2 ▸ Tutorial** folder, click **Referral**, and then click the **Open** button. The selected path and filename now appear in the File name box.

3. Click the **OK** button. The Import XML dialog box opens. See Figure 8-9.

Figure 8-9   Import XML dialog box

select to import the data into the table that was selected initially

From the XML file, you can import only the table structure to a new table, import the table structure and data to a new table, or append the data in the XML file to an existing table. You'll import the data to the tblReferral table, which you selected to begin this import process.

TIP
To add records from an XML file to an existing table, in the Import XML dialog box click the Append Data to Existing Table(s) option button.

4. Make sure the **Append Data to Existing Table(s)** option button is selected, click **tblReferral** in the box, and then click the **OK** button. The Import XML dialog box closes, and the last Get External Data - XML File dialog box is displayed. You'll continue to work with this dialog box in the next set of steps.

Saving and Running Import Specifications

If you need to repeat the same import procedure many times, you can save the steps for the procedure and expedite future imports by running the saved import steps without using a wizard. Because the other clinic will send Kelly additional lists of patient referrals in the future, you'll save the import steps for Kelly so she can reuse them whenever she receives a new list.

To save the XML file import steps:

1. In the Get External Data – XML File dialog box, click the **Save import steps** check box to select it. The dialog box displays additional options for the save operation. See Figure 8-10.

Figure 8-10 Saving the import steps

- path and filename of the imported file (your path might be different)
- click this check box to display additional options in the dialog box
- default name for the saved import steps
- option to create a reminder task in Outlook

Get External Data - XML File

Save Import Steps

Finished importing document 'E:\Access2\Tutorial\Referral.xml'.

Do you want to save these import steps? This will allow you to quickly repeat the operation without using the wizard.

☑ S_a_ve import steps

Save as: Import-Referral

Description:

Create an Outlook Task.

If you regularly repeat this saved operation, you can create an Outlook task that reminds you when it is time to repeat this operation. The Outlook task will include a Run Import button that runs the import operation in Access.

☐ Create O_u_tlook Task

Hint: To create a recurring task, open the task in Outlook and click the Recurrence button on the Task tab.

[Manage Data Tasks...]   [Save Import]   [Cancel]

You can accept the default name for the saved import steps or specify a different name, and you can enter an optional description. If the import will occur on a set schedule, you can also create a reminder task in Microsoft Outlook. You'll accept the default name for the saved steps, and you won't enter a description or schedule an Outlook task.

2. Click the **Save Import** button. The import steps are saved as Import-Referral, the Get External Data - XML File dialog box closes, and the tblReferral records from the Referral.xml file have been imported into the tblReferral table in the Clinic database. Before reviewing the imported table, you'll add a description to the saved import steps.

3. On the EXTERNAL DATA tab, in the Import & Link group, click the **Saved Imports** button. The Manage Data Tasks dialog box opens. See Figure 8-11.

Tutorial 8 Sharing, Integrating, and Analyzing Data | Access **AC 459**

Figure 8-11 **Manage Data Tasks dialog box**

- path and filename for the saved file (your path might be different)
- selected saved import
- click to add or modify a description for the saved import

[Manage Data Tasks dialog box showing Saved Imports tab with "Import-Referral" entry and path "file:///E:\Access2\Tutorial\Referral.xml" with "Click here to edit the description." Buttons: Run, Create Outlook Task..., Delete, Close]

In this dialog box, you can change the name of a saved import, add or change its description, create an Outlook task for it, run it, or delete it. You can also manage any saved export by clicking the Saved Exports tab. You'll add a description for the saved procedure.

4. Click the **Click here to edit the description** text to open a box that contains an insertion point, type **XML file containing patient referrals from other clinics**, click an unused portion of the highlighted selection band to close the box and accept the typed description, and then click the **Saved Exports** tab. You have not saved any export steps, so no saved exports are displayed.

5. Click the **Close** button to close the Manage Data Tasks dialog box.

6. Double-click the **tblReferral** table in the Navigation Pane to open the table datasheet, close the Navigation Pane, resize all columns to their best fit, and then click **36229** in the first row in the PatientID column to deselect all values. See Figure 8-12.

AC 460 Access | Tutorial 8 Sharing, Integrating, and Analyzing Data

Figure 8-12 Imported XML records added to the tblReferral table

records from both the imported table and the imported XML file

7. Save and close the table.

Next, Kelly asks you to export the tblBilling table as an XML file.

Exporting an Access Table as an XML File

Chatham Community Health Services uses an accounting package that accepts data in XML files. Kelly wants to test this capability by exporting the tblBilling table as an XML file and giving the XML file to the company's accounting manager for testing with the accounting package.

REFERENCE

Exporting an Access Object as an XML File

- Right-click the object (table, query, form, or report) in the Navigation Pane, point to Export, and then click XML File; or click the object (table, query, form, or report) in the Navigation Pane, and then on the EXTERNAL DATA tab, in the Export group, click XML File button.
- Click the Browse button in the Export - XML File dialog box, navigate to the location where you will save the XML file, and then click the Save button.
- Click the OK button in the dialog box, select the options in the Export XML dialog box or click the More Options button and select the options in the expanded Export XML dialog box, and then click the OK button.
- Click the Close button; or if you need to save the export steps, click the Save export steps check box, enter a name for the saved steps in the Save as box, and then click the Save Export button.

You'll export the tblBilling table as an XML file now.

To export the tblBilling table as an XML file:

1. Open the Navigation Pane (if necessary), right-click **tblBilling**, point to **Export** on the shortcut menu, and then click **XML File**. The Export - XML File dialog box opens.

Tutorial 8 Sharing, Integrating, and Analyzing Data | Access   AC 461

   2. Click the **Browse** button, navigate to the **Access2 ▶ Tutorial** folder included with your data files, change the name in the File name box to **Billing.xml**, and then click the **Save** button. The selected path and filename now appear in the File name box in the Export-XML File dialog box.

   3. Click the **OK** button. The Export XML dialog box opens.

   Clicking the More Options button in the Export XML dialog box expands the dialog box and lets you view and change detailed options for exporting a database object to an XML file.

   4. Click the **More Options** button to reveal detailed export options in the Export XML dialog box. See Figure 8-13.

Figure 8-13   **Data tab in the Export XML dialog box**

- click to display lookup tables for the tblBilling table
- click to display a list of files containing custom formats
- location in which to export the table (your path might be different)
- choices for which records to export
- default character encoding method

   The "Export Data" check box, the "Export Location" box, and the "Records To Export" option group display the selections you made in the previous steps. You're exporting all records from the tblBilling table, including the data in the records and the structure of the table, to the Billing.xml file in the Access2 ▶ Tutorial folder. The encoding option determines how characters will be represented in the exported XML file. The encoding choices are UTF-8, which uses 8 bits to represent each character, and UTF-16, which uses 16 bits to represent each character. You can also click the Transforms button if you have a special file that contains instructions for changing the exported data.

   The accounting package doesn't have a transform file and requires the default encoding, but Kelly wants to review the tables that contain lookup data.

   5. In the Data to Export box, click the plus box to the left of [Lookup Data], and then verify that the tblVisit check box is not checked. The tblVisit table contains lookup data because it's the primary table in the one-to-many relationship with the related tblBilling table. The accounting package requirements don't include any lookup data from the tblVisit table, so you don't want the tblVisit check box to be checked.

   The Data tab settings are correct, so next you'll verify the Schema tab settings.

   6. Click the **Schema** tab. See Figure 8-14.

Figure 8-14   Schema tab in the Export XML dialog box

option to export the table structure

option to include the table structure in the XML file

Along with the data from the tblBilling table, you'll be exporting its table structure, including information about the table's primary key, indexes, and table and field properties. An **XSD (XML Structure Definition) file** is a file that defines the structure of the XML file, much like the Design view of a table defines the fields and their data types. You can include this structure information in a separate XSD file or you can embed the information in the XML file. The accounting package expects a single XML file, so you'll embed the structure information in the XML file.

▶ 7. Click the **Embed schema in exported XML data document** option button. The "Create separate schema document" option button is now grayed out.

▶ 8. Click the **Presentation** tab. See Figure 8-15.

Figure 8-15   Presentation tab in the Export XML dialog box

option to export formatting instructions

The Presentation tab options let you export a separate **XSL (Extensible Stylesheet Language) file** containing the format specifications for the tblBilling table data. The accounting package contains its own formatting instructions for any imported data, so you will not export an XSL file.

9. Make sure that the **Export Presentation (HTML 4.0 Sample XSL)** check box is not checked, and then click the **OK** button. Access closes the Export XML dialog box, exports the data in the tblBilling table as an XML file to the Access2 ▸ Tutorial folder, and returns you to the final Export - XML File dialog box. You'll see the results of creating this file in the next set of steps.

Kelly plans to make further tests exporting the tblBilling table as an XML file, so you'll save the export steps.

INSIGHT

Importing and Exporting Data

Access supports importing data from common file formats such as an Excel workbook, a text file, and an XML file. Additional Access options include importing an object from another Access database, importing data from other databases (such as Microsoft SQL Server, mySQL, and others), and importing an HTML document, an Outlook folder, or a SharePoint list.

In addition to exporting an Access object as an XML file or an HTML document, Access includes options for exporting data to another Access database, other databases (Microsoft SQL Server, mySQL), an Excel workbook, a text file, a Word document, a SharePoint list, or a PDF or XPS file. You can also export table or query data directly to Word's mail merge feature, or export an object to an e-mail message.

The steps you follow for other import and export options work similarly to the import and export steps you've already used.

Saving and Running Export Specifications

Saving the steps to export the tblBilling table as an XML file will save time and eliminate errors when Kelly repeats the export procedure. You'll save the export steps and then run the saved steps.

To save and run the XML file export steps:

1. Click the **Save export steps** check box. The dialog box displays additional options for the save operation.

   The dialog box has the same options you saw earlier when you saved the XML import steps. You'll enter a description, and you won't create an Outlook task because Kelly will be running the saved export steps on an as-needed basis.

2. In the Description box, type **XML file accounting entries from the tblBilling table**. See Figure 8-16.

Figure 8-16 Saving the export steps

path and filename of the exported file (your path might be different) → Finished exporting 'tblBilling' to file 'E:\Access2\Tutorial\Billing.xml' successfully.

Export - XML File

Save Export Steps

Do you want to save these export steps? This will allow you to quickly repeat the operation without using the wizard.

click this check box to display additional options in the dialog box → ☑ Save export steps

Save as: Export-Billing

Description: XML file accounting entries from the tblBilling table ← *description you entered*

default name of the saved export steps

Create an Outlook Task.

If you regularly repeat this saved operation, you can create an Outlook task that reminds you when it is time to repeat this operation. The Outlook task will include a Run Export button that runs the export operation in Access.

☐ Create Outlook Task

Hint: To create a recurring task, open the task in Outlook and click the Recurrence button on the Task tab.

[Manage Data Tasks...]   [Save Export] [Cancel]

3. Click the **Save Export** button. The export steps are saved as Export-Billing and the Export - XML File dialog box closes.

    Now you'll run the saved steps.

4. Click the **EXTERNAL DATA** tab (if necessary), and then in the Export group, click the **Saved Exports** button. The Manage Data Tasks dialog box opens with the Saved Exports tab selected. See Figure 8-17.

    Trouble? If the Saved Imports tab is visible, then you selected the Saved Imports button instead of the Saved Exports button. Click the Close button and repeat Step 4.

Figure 8-17 Manage Data Tasks dialog box

- Saved Exports tab selected
- selected saved export
- path and filename for the saved file (your path might be different)

5. Verify that the Export-Billing procedure you created in Step 3 is selected, and then click the **Run** button. The saved procedure runs and a message box opens, asking if you want to replace the existing XML file you created earlier.

6. Click the **Yes** button to replace the existing XML file. A message box informs you that the export was completed successfully.

7. Click the **OK** button to close the message box, and then click the **Close** button to close the Manage Data Tasks dialog box.

8. Open Windows File Explorer, navigate to the **Access2 ▸ Tutorial** folder, right-click **Billing.xml** in the file list to open the shortcut menu, click **Open with**, and then click **Notepad**.

   The Billing.xml file contains the data itself, along with code that describes the data, as shown in Visual Overview 8.1.

9. Close the Notepad window.

10. If you are not continuing on to the next session, close the Clinic database.

You've imported and exported data, analyzed a table's design, and saved and run import and export specifications. In the next session, you will analyze data by working with a chart, create and use an application part, link external data, and add a tab control to a form.

Session 8.1 Quick Check

REVIEW

1. What is HTML?
2. What is an HTML template?
3. What is a static web page?
4. What is a CSV file?
5. What is the Table Analyzer?
6. _____ is a programming language that describes data and its structure.

Session 8.2 Visual Overview:

Tabbed Control with a Chart

This chart has one data series with 4 data items.

The Chart Title appears at the top of the chart.

This chart is embedded as an object on the second page of the tab control.

Data markers represent the data value of each data item.

The name of each data item is listed under the data marker in a column chart.

The y-axis is the vertical axis containing numbers that represent a range of data values in the data series.

The x-axis is the horizontal axis containing labels that describe each of the data items.

frmVisitsAndInvoices

Visits and Invoices

Select Visit: 1535

- Patient ID: Ingram, Julia
- Visit ID: 1535
- Date of Visit: 11/12/2015
- Reason/Diagnosis: Transverse fracture of left ulna
- Comments:
- Walk-in? ☑

Invoice Data | Invoice Chart

Invoices for this Visit

- DG532
- OST150
- PRM712
- REP001

(y-axis: 0, 100, 200, 300, 400)

- Number of Invoices: 4
- Invoice Amount Total: $695.00

Visit: 4 of 86 — No Filter — Search

Form View

Creating a Tabbed Form Using a Tab Control

Kelly wants you to enhance the frmVisitsAndInvoices form to enable users to switch between different content. Specifically, she wants users to be able to choose between viewing the frmBillingSubform subform or viewing a chart showing the invoices associated with the displayed visit.

You can use the **Tab Control tool** to insert a tab control, which is a control that appears with tabs at the top, with one tab for each form. Users can switch between forms by clicking the tabs. You'll use a tab control to implement Kelly's requested enhancements. The first tab will contain the frmBillingSubform subform that is currently positioned at the bottom of the frmVisitsAndInvoices form. The second tab will contain a chart showing the invoice amounts for the invoices associated with the displayed visit.

> ### INSIGHT
> ### Working with Large Forms
>
> When you want to work with a form that is too large to display in the Access window, one way to help you navigate the form is to manually add page breaks, where it makes sense to do so. You can use the **Page Break tool** to insert a page break control in the form, which lets users move between the form pages by pressing the Page Up and Page Down keys.

To expedite placing the subform in the tab control, you'll first cut the subform from the form, placing it on the Clipboard. You'll then add the tab control, and finally you'll paste the subform into the left tab on the tab control. You need to perform these steps in Design view.

To add the tab control to the form:

1. If you took a break after the previous session, make sure that the Clinic database is open with the Navigation Pane displayed.

2. Open the **frmVisitsAndInvoices** form in Form view to review the form, switch to Design view, and then close the Navigation Pane.

3. Scroll down to the subform (if necessary), right-click the top edge of the subform control to open the shortcut menu, and then click **Cut** to delete the subform control and place it on the Clipboard.

   Trouble? If you do not see Subform in New Window as one of the options on the shortcut menu, you did not click the top edge of the subform control correctly. Right-click the top edge of the subform control until you see this option on the shortcut menu, and then click Cut.

4. Increase the length of the Detail section to 6.5 inches.

5. Select the Number of Invoices label and control, the Invoice Amount Total label and control, and the rectangle shape surrounding them, and then move them below the 6-inch horizontal line in the grid.

6. On the DESIGN tab, in the Controls group, click the **Tab Control** tool.

7. Position the + portion of the pointer in the Detail section at the 2.75-inch mark on the vertical ruler and three grid dots from the left edge of the grid, and then click the mouse button. Access places a tab control with two pages in the form.

8. Right-click in the middle of the tab control, and then when an orange outline appears inside the tab control, click **Paste** on the shortcut menu. The subform is pasted in the tab control. See Figure 8-18.

Figure 8-18 | Subform on the tab control in the Detail section

- tab for second page of tab control (your page number might be different)
- tab for first page of tab control (your page number might be different)
- Tab Control tool
- tab control in form
- pasted subform with the tab control

9. Switch to Form view, and then click **1527** in the VisitID text box to deselect all controls. The left tab, which represents the first page in the tab control, is the active tab. See Figure 8-19.

Figure 8-19 Subform on the tab control in Form view

Annotations on figure:
- tab for first page of tab control is active
- subform on the first tab of tab control
- controls moved down

The subform is now displayed on the first page of the tab control, and the form displays the same content as it did before you inserted the tab control.

10. Click the **right tab** of the tab control to display the second page. The page is empty because you haven't added any controls to it yet.

After viewing the form in Form view, Kelly's staff finds the two sets of navigation buttons confusing—they waste time determining which set of navigation buttons applies to the subform and which to the main form. To clarify this, you'll set the Navigation Caption property for the main form and the subform. The **Navigation Caption property** lets you change the navigation label from the word "Record" to another value. Because the main form displays data about visits and the subform displays data about invoices, you'll change the Navigation Caption property for the main form to "Visit" and for the subform to "Invoice."

You'll also edit the labels for the tabs in the tab control, so they indicate the contents of each page.

To change the captions for the navigation buttons and the tabs:

1. Switch to Design view.

2. Click the **form selector** for the main form to select the form control in the main form, open the property sheet to display the properties for the selected form control, click the **All** tab (if necessary), click the **Navigation Caption** box, and then type **Visit**. See Figure 8-20.

Tutorial 8 Sharing, Integrating, and Analyzing Data | Access   AC 471

Figure 8-20   Setting the Navigation Caption property for the main form

3. Click the **form selector** for the subform to select the subform, click the **form selector** for the subform again to select the form control in the subform and to display the properties for the selected form control, on the Property Sheet click the **Navigation Caption** box, and then type **Invoice**. Navigation buttons don't appear in Design view, so you won't see the effects of the Navigation Caption property settings until you switch to Form view.

4. Click the **left tab** in the subform, click the **left tab** in the subform again to select it, on the Property Sheet in the Caption box type **Invoice Data**, and then press the **Tab** key. The Caption property value now appears in the left tab. See Figure 8-21.

Figure 8-21   Setting the Caption property for the left tab

5. Click the **right tab** in the subform to select it, on the Property Sheet in the Caption box, type **Invoice Chart**, and then close the property sheet.

6. If necessary, adjust the alignment of the form controls so the form has a balanced look. You may need to adjust the vertical spacing between the form controls so the controls are evenly spaced, and adjust the placement of the heading controls so they align with the left and right margins. Decrease the vertical spacing between form controls to fit the form on the screen as much as possible.

7. Save your form design changes, switch to Form view, select VisitID 1527 in the combo box, click **1527** in the VisitID text box to deselect all controls, and then scroll to the bottom of the form. The tabs and the navigation buttons now display the new caption values. See Figure 8-22.

Figure 8-22   Caption properties and aligned form controls

Next, Kelly wants you to add a simple chart to the second page of the tab control. This chart will be created by another program that's part of Microsoft Office, called Microsoft Graph. Before creating and adding the chart, it's important to understand the different ways of integrating external data with Access.

Integrating Access with Other Programs

When you create a form or report in Access, you include more than just the data from the record source table or query. You've added controls such as lines, rectangles, tab controls, and graphics in your forms and reports to improve their appearance and usability. You can also add charts, drawings, and other objects to your forms and reports, but Access doesn't have the capability to create them. Instead, you create these objects using other programs and then place them in a form or report using the appropriate integration method.

When you integrate information between programs, the program containing the original information, or object, is called the **source program**, and the program in which you place the information created by the source program is called the **destination program**. Access offers three ways for you to integrate objects created by other programs.

- **Importing**. When you import an object, you include the contents of a file in a new table or append it to an existing table, or you include the contents of the file in a form, report, or field. For example, when you add a picture to a form, you import it into the form; likewise, in this tutorial you imported CSV and XML files as new tables in the Clinic database. An imported picture is a file with a .bmp extension that was created by a graphics program, and the CSV and XML files you imported were also created by other programs. After importing an object, it no longer has a connection to the program that created it. Any subsequent changes you make to the object using the source program are not reflected in the imported object.
- **Embedding**. When you embed an object in a form, report, or field, you preserve its connection to the source program, which enables you to edit the object, if necessary, using the features of the source program. However, any changes you make to the object are reflected only in the form, report, or field in which it is embedded; the changes do not affect the original object in the file from which it was embedded. Likewise, if you start the source program outside Access and make any changes to the original object, these changes are not reflected in the embedded object. The features of the source program determine which features are available for the embedded object.
- **Linking**. When you link an object to a form, report, or field, you include a connection in the destination program to the original file maintained by the source program; you do not store data from the file in the destination program. Any changes you make to the original file using the source program are reflected in the linked file version in the destination program.

PROSKILLS

Decision Making: Importing, Embedding, and Linking Data

How do you decide which method to use when you need to include in an Access database data that is stored in another file or format? When you intend to use Access to maintain the data and no longer need an updated version of the data in the source program, you can import a file as a new table or append the records in the file to an existing table. You link to the data when the source program will continue to maintain the data in the file, and you need to use an updated version of the file at all times in the destination program. When linking to the data, you can also maintain the data using the destination program, and the source program will always use the updated version of the file.

- For objects in forms or reports, you import an object (such as a picture) when you want a copy of the object in your form or report and you don't intend to make any changes to the object. You embed or link an object when you want a copy of the object in your form or report and you intend to edit the object using the source program in the future. You embed the object when you do not want your edits to the object in the destination program to affect any other copies of the object used by other programs. You link the object when you want your edits to the object in the destination program to affect the object used by other programs.
- The decision to import, embed, or link to data depends on how you will use the data in your database, and what connection is required to the original data. You should carefully consider the effect of changes to the original data and to the copied data before choosing which method to use.

To add the chart that Kelly wants on the second page of the tab control, you'll embed data from another program.

Embedding a Chart in a Form

The Chart Wizard in Access helps you to embed a chart in a form or report. The chart is actually created by another program, Microsoft Graph, but the Chart Wizard does the work of embedding the chart. After embedding the chart in a form or report, you can edit it using the Microsoft Graph program.

> **REFERENCE**
>
> ### Embedding a Chart in a Form or Report
> - In Design view, on the DESIGN tab, in the Controls group, click the More button, and then click the Chart tool.
> - Position the + portion of the pointer where you want to position the upper-left corner of the chart, and then click the mouse button to start the Chart Wizard.
> - Select the record source, fields, and chart type.
> - Edit the chart contents, and select the fields that link the object and chart, if necessary.
> - Enter a chart title, select whether to include a legend, and then click the Finish button.

The tblBilling table contains the information needed for the chart Kelly wants you to include in the form's right tab in the tab control.

To add a chart in the tab control and start the Chart Wizard:

1. Switch to Design view, then on the Invoice Chart tab on the tab control click the **subform**, and then click the **subform** again to ensure the tab content is selected.

2. On the DESIGN tab, in the Controls group, click the **Chart** tool, and then move the pointer to the tab control. When the pointer is inside the tab control, the rectangular portion of the tab control you can use to place controls is filled in black.

3. Position the + portion of the pointer in the upper-left corner of the black portion of the tab control, and then click the mouse button. Access places a chart control in the form and opens the first Chart Wizard dialog box, in which you select the source record for the chart.

Kelly wants the chart to provide her staff with a simple visual display of the relative proportions of the invoice amounts for the invoice items for the currently displayed patient visit. You'll use the tblBilling table as the record source for the chart and select the InvoiceAmt and InvoiceItem fields as the fields to use in the chart.

The order of the items is important. Be sure to add InvoiceItemID first, then InvoiceAmt. If you make a mistake, move both back to the Available Fields and start again.

To create the chart with the Chart Wizard:

1. Click **Table: tblBilling** in the box, and then click the **Next** button to display the second Chart Wizard dialog box.

2. Add the InvoiceItemID and InvoiceAmt fields to the Fields for Chart box, in that order, and then click the **Next** button to display the third Chart Wizard dialog box, in which you choose the chart type.

Tutorial 8 Sharing, Integrating, and Analyzing Data | Access   AC 475

3. Click the **Pie Chart** button (row 4, column 1) to select the pie chart as the chart type to use for Kelly's chart. The box on the right displays a brief description of the selected chart type. See Figure 8-23.

| Figure 8-23 | Selecting the chart type |

description of the selected chart type

click to select the Pie Chart chart type

4. Click the **Next** button to display the next Chart Wizard dialog box, which displays a preview of the chart and options to modify the data and its placement in the chart. You'll use the default layout based on the two selected fields. You can easily modify the chart after you create it.

5. Click the **Next** button to display the next Chart Wizard dialog box, which lets you choose the fields that link records in the main form (which uses the tblVisit table as its record source) to records in the chart (which uses the tblBilling table as its record source). You don't need to make any changes in this dialog box, as the wizard has already identified VisitID as the common field linking these two tables. You can use the VisitID field as the linking field even though you didn't select it as a field for the chart.

6. Click the **Next** button to display the final dialog box, which allows you to enter the title that will appear at the top of the chart and choose whether to include a legend in the chart.

7. Type **Invoices for this Visit**, make sure the **Yes, display a legend** option button is selected, and then click the **Finish** button. The completed chart appears in the tab control.

You'll view the form in Form view, where it's easier to assess the chart's appearance.

8. Save your form design changes, switch to Form view, in the combo box select Visit ID **1535**, click the **Invoice Chart** tab to display the chart, and then scroll down to the bottom of the form (if necessary). See Figure 8-24.

Figure 8-24   Embedded chart in Form view

[Screenshot of frmVisitsAndInvoices form showing Visits and Invoices with Patient ID: Ingram, Julia; Visit ID: 1535; Date of Visit: 11/12/2015; Reason/Diagnosis: Transverse fracture of left ulna; Walk-in checked. Invoice Chart tab displays a pie chart labeled "Invoices for this Visit" with legend entries DG532, OST150, PRM712, REP001. Number of Invoices: 4; Invoice Amount Total: $695.00. Callouts point to "chart title," "pie chart," and "legend."]

Linking Record Sources

INSIGHT

The record source for a primary main form must have a one-to-many relationship to the record source for a related subform or chart. The subform or chart object has its Link Master Fields property set to the primary key in the record source for the main form and its Link Child Fields property set to the foreign key in the record source for the subform or chart.

After viewing the chart, Kelly decides it needs some modifications. She wants you to change the chart type from a pie chart to a bar chart, remove the legend, and modify the chart's background color. To make these changes, you'll switch to Design view and then you'll start Microsoft Graph.

To edit the chart using Microsoft Graph:

1. Switch to Design view, right-click an edge of the chart object to open the shortcut menu, point to **Chart Object**, and then click **Open**. Microsoft Graph starts and displays the chart. See Figure 8-25.

    Trouble? If Chart Object doesn't appear on the shortcut menu, right-click the edge until it does.

Tutorial 8 Sharing, Integrating, and Analyzing Data | Access   AC 477

Figure 8-25   Editing the chart with Microsoft Graph

Microsoft Graph is the source program that the Chart Wizard used to create the chart. Because the chart was embedded in the form, editing the chart object starts Graph and allows you to edit the chart using the Graph menu bar and toolbar. In addition to displaying the selected chart, the Graph window displays a datasheet containing the data on which the chart is based. You'll now make Kelly's chart changes using Graph.

2. On the Graph menu bar, click **Chart**, click **Chart Type** to open the Chart Type dialog box, and then click **Column** in the Chart type box to display the types of column charts. See Figure 8-26.

Figure 8-26   Chart Type dialog box

- click to create a custom chart type
- selected chart type
- subtypes of the selected chart type
- description of selected chart subtype
- click and hold to view sample of selected chart subtype

The column chart is the selected chart type, and the clustered column chart is the default chart subtype (row 1, column 1). A description of the selected chart subtype appears below the chart subtypes. You can create a custom chart by clicking the Custom Types tab. If you click and hold on the Press and Hold to View Sample button, you'll see a sample of the selected subtype.

3. Click the **Press and Hold to View Sample** button to view a sample of the chart, release the mouse button, and then click the **OK** button to close the dialog box and change the chart to a column chart in the Graph window and in the form.

4. On the Graph menu bar, click **Chart**, click **Chart Options** to open the Chart Options dialog box, click the **Legend** tab to display the chart's legend options, click the **Show legend** check box to clear it, and then click the **OK** button. The legend is removed from the chart object in the Graph window and in the form.

To change the color or other properties of a chart control—the chart background (or chart area), axes, labels to the left of the y-axis, labels below the x-axis, or data markers (columnar bars for a column chart)—you need to double-click the control.

TIP

A data marker is a bar, dot, segment, or other symbol that represents a single data value.

5. In the Chart window, double-click one of the blue data markers inside the chart to open the Format Data Series dialog box, and then in the Area section, in the color palette, click the orange box (row 2, column 2). The sample color in the dialog box changes to orange to match the selected color in the color palette. See Figure 8-27.

Trouble? If you click off the chart in MS Graph, and the chart disappears, just click View on the menu bar, and then click Datasheet to bring the chart back.

Figure 8-27 Format Data Series dialog box

- selected color
- color palette
- sample of selected color

6. Click the **OK** button to close the dialog box. The color of the data markers in the chart in the Graph window and in the form changes to orange.

   Trouble? If only one of the bars changed color, you selected one bar instead of the entire series. Click Edit, click Undo, and then repeat Steps 5 and 6.

7. In the Chart window, double-click the white chart background to the left of the title to open the Format Chart Area dialog box, in the Area section in the color palette click the light orange box (row 5, column 2), and then click the **OK** button. The chart's background color changes from white to light orange in the chart in the Graph window and in the form.

8. Click **File** on the Graph menu bar, and then click **Exit & Return to frmVisitsAndInvoices** to exit Graph and return to the form.

9. Save your form design changes, switch to Form view, in the combo box select Visit ID **1535** and then click the **Invoice Chart** tab to display the chart. See Figure 8-28.

Figure 8-28   **Completed chart in Form view**

> **10.** Close the form.

Kelly has found the tblReferral table so useful that she'd like to be able to use the same table structure in other databases. One option would be to import the table structure from the NewPatientReferrals.accdb database file into each database. Another option is to create an application part from the NewPatientReferrals database, which could then easily be included in any Access database file on Kelly's computer.

Using Templates and Application Parts

A template is a predefined database that can include tables, relationships, queries, forms, reports, and other database objects. When you create a new database using Backstage view, Access displays a list of predefined templates. You can also create your own template from an existing database file. In addition to creating a standard template, you can also create an **application part**, which is a specialized template that can be imported into an existing database. A standard template would be used to create a new database file. An application part is used when you already have a database file that you're working with, and would like to include the content from an application part in your existing database. Like a template, an application part can contain tables, relationships, queries, forms, reports, and other database objects.

Tutorial 8 Sharing, Integrating, and Analyzing Data | Access   AC 481

Kelly would like to reuse the tblReferral table structure to store a table of referrals from local pharmacists. You'll use the NewPatientReferrals.accdb database file to create an Application Part for the tblReferral table structure, then you'll import the new application part into the Clinic database to use for referrals from local pharmacists.

To create an application part from a database file:

1. Click the **CREATE tab**, and then in the Templates group, click the **Application Parts** button to open the gallery of predefined application parts. See Figure 8-29.

Figure 8-29 **Predefined Application Parts**

templates that create forms

templates that create multiple database objects including tables, forms, and queries

Note that there are Blank Forms and Quick Start Application Parts, but there are no user-defined application parts.

Trouble? If you see user-application parts listed in the Application Parts gallery it could be that these application parts were created by other users. Access will store Application Parts created from any Access database file and they will be available in all Access database files on the computer. You can disregard any user-defined application parts that you may see on your local computer.

2. Close the Clinic database file.

3. Open the NewPatientReferrals database file from the Access2 ▶ Tutorial folder included with your Data Files.

   When you save this file as a template, all database objects that are in the file will be included in the template file. This file contains only the tblReferral table.

4. Click the **FILE** tab to display Backstage view, and then click **Save As**.

5. Click **Save Database As** (if necessary) and then in the Save Database As box in the Database File Types list click **Template**. See Figure 8-30.

Figure 8-30   Saving a database as a template

(Screenshot of the Save As screen in Access backstage view, showing File Types with "Save Database As" selected, and Save Database As options including Access Database (.accdb), Access 2002-2003 Database (*.mdb), Access 2000 Database (*.mdb), Template (*.accdt), Package and Sign, Back Up Database, Make ACCDE, and SharePoint. A callout points to "database file type options".)*

> **6.** Click the **Save As** button. Access displays the **Create New Template from This Database** dialog box.
>
> **7.** In the Name text box, type **Referral**. In the Description text box, type **New patient referral**, and then click the Application Part check box to select it. See Figure 8-31.

Figure 8-31   Create New Template from This Database dialog box

(Screenshot of the Create New Template from This Database dialog box with Name: Referral; Description: New patient referral; Category: User Templates; Icon, Preview, Primary Table, and Instantiation Form fields; Application Part check box selected; Include Data in Template check box unselected. Callouts: "this text will appear as a ScreenTip for this application part" points to the Description field; "check to save this template as an application part" points to the Application Part check box.)

AC 482   Access | Tutorial 8 Sharing, Integrating, and Analyzing Data

Tutorial 8 Sharing, Integrating, and Analyzing Data | Access AC 483

> 8. Click the **OK** button to close the dialog box. An alert box opens indicating that the template has been saved.
>
> 9. Click the **OK** button to close the message box, and then close the NewPatientReferrals database.

Now that you've created the application part, you'll use it in the Clinic database to create the referral table for patients who have been referred to the clinic by a pharmacist.

To use the application part to create the referral table:

> 1. Open the **Clinic** database, click the **CREATE** tab, and then click the **Application Parts** button. The Referral template is displayed in the User Templates section in the Application Parts list. See Figure 8-32.

Figure 8-32   **Application Parts showing Referral template**

user-defined template added as an Application Part

> 2. Click **Referral**. The Create Relationship dialog box opens because the application part includes a table.
>
> 3. Click the **There is no relationship** option button. This indicates that the new table is not related to other tables in the current database. See figure 8-33.

Figure 8-33   **Create Relationship dialog box**

use these options to create a relationship between the table in the application part and a table in the current database

4. Click the **Create** button to insert the Referral database object into the current database, and then open the Navigation Pane.

   Only the tblReferral table will be inserted into the current database since the Referral template contains only one database object, which is the tblReferral table. Because the Clinic database already contains a table called tblReferral, the newly inserted table is named tblReferral1, to avoid overwriting the table that already exists. The newly inserted tblReferral1 will be used to store the patient information for patients referred by pharmacists. You'll rename this table as tblReferralPharm.

5. In the Navigation Pane, right-click the **tblReferral1** table, click **Rename**, change the name to **tblReferralPharm**, and then press **Enter**.

6. In the Navigation Pane, double-click **tblReferralPharm** to open it in Datasheet view.

   Note that the tblReferralPharm table contains the same fields as the tblReferral table but does not contain any records.

7. Close the tblReferralPharm table.

Kelly would like to be able to send an electronic copy of the rptVisitDetails report that other people can read on their computers, rather than distributing printed reports. You can export tables, queries, reports, and other database objects as files that can be opened in other programs such as Excel and PDF readers. Kelly would like to distribute rptVisitDetails as a PDF and asks you to export the report in this format.

Tutorial 8 Sharing, Integrating, and Analyzing Data | Access **AC 485**

Exporting a Report to a PDF File

PDF (portable document format) is a file format that preserves the original formatting and pagination of its contents no matter where it's viewed. Current versions of all major operating systems for desktop computers and handheld devices include software that opens PDF files. Most web browsers allow you to view PDF files as well. You'll create a PDF document from the rptVisitDetails report so Kelly can send this report to colleagues.

To export the rptVisitDetails report to a PDF file:

▸ **1.** In the Navigation Pane, right-click **rptVisitDetails**, point to **Export** on the shortcut menu, and then click **PDF or XPS**. The Publish as PDF or XPS dialog box opens.

▸ **2.** Navigate to the **Access2 ▸ Tutorial** folder included with your Data Files, and then change the name in the File name box to **Visit Details Report.pdf**. See Figure 8-34.

Figure 8-34 Publish as PDF or XPS file dialog box

file size is reduced to minimize downloading time

Kelly would like people who are visually impaired to be able to use the PDF document with their screen readers. When a PDF file is saved using the minimum size option, there is no additional functionality for screen readers. You can include document structure tags that allow people using screen readers to navigate the document easily. Screen reader software voices the structure tags, such as a tag that provides a description of an image. Structure tags also reflow text so that screen readers understand the flow of information and can read it in a logical order. For instance, a page with a sidebar shouldn't be read as two columns; the main column needs to be read as a continuation of the previous page.

In order to add this functionality, you'll specify that document structure tags should be included.

3. Click the **Options** button. The Options dialog box opens.

4. Click the **Document structure tags for accessibility** check box to select it. See Figure 8-35.

Figure 8-35   Options dialog box for PDF file export

this option allows you to select individual pages from a multi-page report

this option includes the document structure tags

5. Click the **OK** button to close the Options dialog box, and then click the **Publish** button to close the Publish as PDF or XPS dialog box and to create the PDF file. The Export – PDF dialog box opens.

   Trouble? Depending on the operating system you're using, the PDF file may open. If it does, close the PDF file and return to Access.

6. In the Export – PDF dialog box, click the **Close** button to close the dialog box without saving the export steps.

7. Open Windows File Explorer, navigate to the **Access2 ▸ Tutorial** folder, double-click the **Visit Details Report.pdf** to open the PDF file, examine the results, and then close the PDF file.

Kelly is pleased to know that she can export database objects as PDF files. Now she would like your help with one additional external data issue. Her staff maintains an Excel workbook that contains contact information for people who volunteer at Chatham Community Health Services. Kelly wants to be able to use this data in the Clinic database.

Linking Data from an Excel Worksheet

Kelly's staff has extensive experience working with Excel, and one of her staff members prefers to maintain the data for people who volunteer in the Volunteer workbook using Excel. However, Kelly needs to reference the volunteer data in the Clinic database on occasion, and the data she's referencing must always be the current version of the worksheet data. Importing the Excel workbook data as an Access table would provide Kelly with data that's quickly out of date unless she repeats the import steps each time the data in the Excel workbook changes. Because Kelly doesn't personally need to update the volunteer data in the Clinic database, you'll link to the workbook from the database. When the staff changes the Volunteer workbook, the changes will be reflected automatically in the linked version of the database table. At the same time, Kelly won't be able to update the volunteer data from the Clinic database, which ensures that only the staff members responsible for maintaining the volunteer workbook can update the data.

To link to the data in the Excel workbook:

1. Click the **EXTERNAL DATA** tab, and then in the Import & Link group, click the **Excel** button (with the ScreenTip "Import Excel spreadsheet"). The Get External Data - Excel Spreadsheet dialog box opens.

   Trouble? If the Export - Excel File dialog box opens, you clicked the Excel File button in the Export group. Click the Cancel button and then repeat Step 1, being sure to select the Excel File button from the Import & Link group.

2. Click the **Browse** button, navigate to the **Access2 ▸ Tutorial** folder included with your Data Files, click **Volunteer**, click the **Open** button, and then click the **Link to the data source by creating a linked table** option button. This option links to the data instead of importing or appending it. The selected path and filename are displayed in the File name box. See Figure 8-36.

Figure 8-36 Linking to data in an Excel workbook

path and filename of the linked file (your path might be different)

option to link to the file

3. Click the **OK** button. The first Link Spreadsheet Wizard dialog box opens.

   The first row in the worksheet contains column heading names, and each row in the worksheet represents the data about a single product.

4. Click the **First Row Contains Column Headings** check box to select it. See Figure 8-37.

AC 488 Access | Tutorial 8 Sharing, Integrating, and Analyzing Data

Figure 8-37   Link Spreadsheet Wizard dialog box

- option to use the first row in the worksheet as column heading names
- data in the worksheet to be linked

5. Click the **Next** button to open the final Link Spreadsheet Wizard dialog box, in which you choose a name for the linked table.

6. Change the default table name to **tblVolunteer** and then click the **Finish** button. A message box informs you that you've created a table that's linked to the workbook.

7. Click the **OK** button to close the message box. The tblVolunteer table is displayed in the Navigation Pane. The icon to the left of the table name identifies the table as a linked table.

You can open and view the tblVolunteer table and use fields from the linked table in queries, forms, and reports, but you can't update the products data using the Clinic database. You can update the products data only from the Excel workbook.

Next, you'll make a change to data in the workbook and see the update in the linked table. Kelly tells you that the volunteer Crawford had not been able to volunteer for a while, so her Active status was **no**. She's now able to volunteer, and Kelly would like to change her Active status to **yes**.

To update the Excel workbook and view the data in the linked table:

1. Open Windows File Explorer, navigate to the **Access2 ▸ Tutorial** folder, right-click **Volunteer.xlsx**, and then open the file using **Microsoft Excel**. The Volunteer workbook opens and displays the Volunteer worksheet.

   Trouble? If you attempt to open the table in Access before you open the workbook in Excel, you'll get an error message and won't be able to open the workbook. Make sure you always open the workbook or other source file before you open a linked table.

Tutorial 8 Sharing, Integrating, and Analyzing Data | Access   AC 489

▶ 2. Switch to the Clinic database, and then open the **tblVolunteer** datasheet. The fields and records in the tblVolunteer table display the same data as the Volunteer worksheet.

▶ 3. Switch to the Volunteer workbook, select the value **no** in the Active column for Maria Crawford (row 7), type **yes** to replace the value, and then press the **Enter** key.

▶ 4. Switch to the Clinic database. Maria Crawford's Active status is now **yes**.

You've completed your work for Kelly and her staff.

▶ 5. Close the tblVolunteer table in Access.

▶ 6. Switch to the Volunteer workbook, save your worksheet change, and then exit Excel.

▶ 7. Make a backup copy of the database, compact and repair the database, and then close it.

Knowing how to create tabbed form controls and Application Parts, export data to PDF documents, and link to data maintained by other programs will make it easier for Kelly and her staff to work efficiently and manage their data.

Session 8.2 Quick Check

REVIEW

1. The _____ property lets you change the default navigation label from the word "Record" to another value.
2. What is the Microsoft Graph program?
3. What is a PDF file?
4. What is an application part?
5. What is the difference between an application part and a template?
6. How can you edit data in a table that has been linked to an Excel file?

SAM Projects

Put your skills into practice with SAM Projects! SAM Projects for this tutorial can be found online. If you have a SAM account, go to www.cengage.com/sam2013 to download the most recent Project Instructions and Start Files.

Review Assignments

Data Files needed for the Review Assignments: Ads.xlsx, Partners.accdb, Payables.csv, Payments.xml, and Supplier.accdb *(cont. from Tutorial 7)*

Kelly wants you to integrate the data in the Supplier database with other programs, and she wants to be able to analyze the data in the database. Complete the following steps:

1. Open the **Supplier** database you worked with in Tutorials 5–7.
2. Export the qrySupplierProducts query as an HTML document to the Access2 ▶ Review folder provided with your Data Files, saving the file as **qrySupplierProducts.html**. Do not save the export steps.
3. Import the CSV file named Payables, which is located in the Access2 ▶ Review folder, as a new table in the database. Use the names in the first row as field names, use Currency as the data type for the numeric fields, choose your own primary key, name the table **tblPayable**, run the Table Analyzer, record the Table Analyzer's recommendation, and then cancel out of the Table Analyzer Wizard without making the recommended changes. Do not save the import steps.
4. Import the data and structure from the XML file named Payments, which is located in the Access2 ▶ Review folder, as a new table named **tblPayments** in the database. Save the import steps, and then rename the table **tblPayment**.
5. Export the tblSupplier table as an XML file named **Supplier.xml** to the Access2 ▶ Review folder; do not create a separate XSD file. Save the export steps.
6. The Chatham Community Health Services clinic also pays for advertisements. Link to the Ads.xlsx workbook, which is located in the Access2 ▶ Review folder, using **tblAd** as the table name. Change the cost of the flyer for Ad Num 5 to $300 and save the workbook.
7. Modify the **frmSuppliersWithProducts** form in the following ways:
   a. Size the text box controls for SupplierID, Company Name, Category, City, State, and Zip so that they are all the same width as the Address text box.
   b. Size the text box controls for ContactPhone, ContactFirstName, and ContactLastName so that they are all the same width as the InitialContact text box.
   c. Move the Number of Products label, text box, and rectangle so the right edge of the rectangle is aligned with the right edge of the InitialContact text box.
   d. Add a tab control to the bottom of the Detail section, so the left edge is aligned with the left edge of the Company Comments label, and then place the existing subform on the first page of the tab control.
   e. Change the caption for the left tab to **Product Data** and for the right tab to **Product Chart**.
   f. Change the caption for the main form's navigation buttons to **Supplier**.
   g. Add a chart to the second page of the tab control. Use the tblProduct table as the record source, select the ProductName and Price, use the 3-D Column Chart type (row 1, column 2), do not include a legend, and use **Products Offered** as the chart title.
   h. Change the chart to a 3-D Bar chart, and change the blue colored data markers to pink.
8. Export the **tblPayment** table as a PDF file called Payments.pdf, using document structure tags for accessibility. Do not save the export steps.

9. Open the **Partners** database from the Access2 ▸ Review folder, and then create and implement an application part as follows:
   a. Create an application part called **vendor** with the description **New vendor**, and do not include the data.
   b. Close the **Partners** database.
   c. Open the **Supplier** database and import the **vendor** application part, which has no relationship to any of the other tables. Open the tblNewVendor table to verify the data has been imported.
10. Make a backup copy of the database, compact and repair the database, and then close it.

Case Problem 1

Data Files needed for this Case Problem: CreditCard.xml, Task.accdb (*cont. from Tutorial 7*), **and Schedule.xlsx.**

GoGopher! Amol Mehta wants you to integrate the data in the Task database with other programs, and he wants to be able to analyze the data in the database. Complete the following steps:

1. Open the **Task** database you worked with in Tutorials 5–7.
2. Export the qryMemberNames query as an HTML document to the Access2 ▸ Case1 folder using a filename of **MemberNames.html**. Save the export steps.
3. Export the rptPlanMembership report as a PDF document with a filename of **Plan.pdf** to the Access2 ▸ Case1 folder. Include the document structure tags for accessibility, and do not save the export steps.
4. Import the data and structure from the XML file named CreditCard, which is located in the Access2 ▸ Case1 folder, as a new table. Save the import steps. Rename the table as **tblCreditCard**.
5. Export the tblPlan table as an XML file named **Plan** to the Access2 ▸ Case1 folder; do not create a separate XSD file. Save the export steps.
6. Link to the Schedule workbook, which is located in the Access2 ▸ Case1 folder, using **tblSchedule** as the table name. For TaskID 301, change the Day value to **F**.
7. Modify the **frmPlansWithMembers** form in the following ways:
   a. Add a tab control to the bottom of the Detail section, and place the existing subform on the first page of the tab control.
   b. Change the caption for the left tab to **Member Data** and for the right tab to **Member Chart**.
   c. Change the caption for the main form's navigation buttons to **Plan** and for the subform's navigation buttons to **Member**.
   d. Add a chart to the second page of the tab control. Use the tblPlan table as the record source, select the PlanID and PlanCost fields, use the Column Chart chart type, do not include a legend, and use **Plan Cost** as the chart title.
   e. Change the color of the data marker to red (row 3, column 1).
8. Make a backup copy of the database, compact and repair the database, and then close it.

Case Problem 2

Data Files needed for this Case Problem: AddSubject.xml, NewStudentReferrals.accdb, Tutoring.accdb (*cont. from Tutorial 7*), **Room.xlsx and Subject.csv.**

O'Brien Educational Services Karen O'Brien wants you to integrate the data in the Tutoring database with other programs, and she wants to be able to analyze the data in the database. Complete the following steps:

1. Open the **Tutoring** database you worked with in Tutorials 5–7.
2. Export the rptTutorSessions report as a PDF document with a filename of **TutorSessions.pdf** to the Access2 ▸ Case2 folder. Include the document structure tags for accessibility, and do not save the export steps.
3. Import the CSV file named Subject.csv, which is located in the Access2 ▸ Case2 folder, as a new table in the database. Use the names in the first row as field names, set the third column's data type to Currency and the other fields' data types to Short Text, choose your own primary key, name the table **tblSubject**, run the Table Analyzer, and record the Table Analyzer's recommendation, but do not accept the recommendation. Do not save the import steps.
4. Export the tblTutor table as an XML file named **Tutor** to the Access2 ▸ Case2 folder; do not create a separate XSD file. Save the export steps.
5. Link to the Room workbook, which is located in the Access2 ▸ Case2 folder, using **tblRoom** as the table name. Add the following new record to the Room workbook: Room Num 5, Rental Cost **$25**, and Type **Private**.
6. **Explore** Import the **AddSubject.xml** file, which is located in the Access2 ▸ Case2 folder, appending the records to the tblSubject table. Do not save the import steps. Open the tblSubject table in Datasheet view and then verify that the record with SubjectID 50 and Subject Math4 has been appended, along with other records. Close the tblSubject table and then close the Tutoring database.
7. **Explore** Open the **NewStudentReferrals** database from the Access2 ▸ Case2 folder, and then create and work with an application part as follows:
   a. Create an application part called **NewStudentContact** with the description **New student referrals** and include the data.
   b. Close the **NewStudentReferrals** database.
   c. Open the **Tutoring** database and import the **NewStudentContact** Application Part, which has no relationship to any of the other tables. Open the tblContact table to verify the data has been imported.
   d. Karen would like to import an empty tblContact table in the future. Delete the **NewStudentContact** Application Part by clicking on the Application Parts button, right-clicking on the **NewStudentContact** template, selecting **Delete Template Part from Gallery**, and then clicking **Yes** in the dialog box that opens.
   e. Save and close the Tutoring database.
   f. Open the **NewStudentReferrals** database, then create an Application Part called **Contact** with the description **Contact** information and do not include the data.
   g. Close the NewStudentReferrals database.
   h. Open the Tutoring database and then add the Contact Application Part. Open the tblContact1 table to verify that it does not contain records.
8. Make a backup copy of the database, compact and repair the database, and then close it.

Case Problem 3

Data Files needed for this Case Problem: Facility.csv, Rosemary.accdb (*cont. from Tutorial 7*), **and Volunteer.accdb.**

Rosemary Animal Shelter Ryan Lang wants you to integrate the data in the Rosemary database with other programs, and he wants to be able to analyze the data in the database. Complete the following steps:

1. Open the **Rosemary** database you worked with in Tutorials 5–7.
2. Export the qryNetDonationsAprilOrLaterCrosstab query as an HTML document named **Crosstab** to the Access2 ▸ Case3 folder. Save the export steps.

3. Export the rptPatronDonations report as a PDF document with a filename of **PatronDonations.pdf** to the Access2 ▶ Case3 folder. Include the document structure tags for accessibility, and do not save the export steps.

Explore 4. Import the CSV file named Facility, which is located in the Access2 ▶ Case3 folder, as a new table in the database. Use the Short Text data type for all fields, choose your own primary key, name the table **tblTemporary**, and run the Table Analyzer. Accept the Table Analyzer's recommendations, which will be to create two tables. Rename the tables as **tblStorage** and **tblFacility**. (*Hint*: Use the Rename Table button to the right of "What name do you want for each table?") Make sure each table has the correct primary key. (*Hint*: Use the Set Unique Identifier button to set a primary key if necessary.) Let the Table Analzyer create a query. Do not save the import steps. Review the tblTemporary query, review the tblTemporary table (it might be named tblTemporary_OLD), and then review the tblStorage and tblFacility tables. Close all tables.

5. Export the tblDonation table as an XML file named **Donation.xml** to the Access2 ▶ Case3 folder; do not create a separate XSD file. Save the export steps.

6. Modify the **frmPatronDonations** form in the following ways:
   a. Add a tab control to the bottom of the Detail section, and place the existing subform on the first page of the tab control.
   b. Change the caption for the left tab to **Donation Data** and for the right tab to **Donation Chart**.
   c. Change the caption for the main form's navigation buttons to **Donor** and for the subform's navigation buttons to **Donation**.
   d. Add a chart to the second page of the tab control. Use the tblDonation table as the record source, select the PatronID, DonationValue, and DonationDate fields, use the 3-D Column Chart type, include a legend, and use **Donations by Patron** as the chart title.
   e. Change the chart to a Clustered Bar chart.

7. Close the Rosemary database.

8. Open the **Volunteer** database, which is located in the Access2 ▶ Case3 folder. Create an application part called **Volunteer** with the description **Volunteer information**, and do not include the data. Close the Volunteer database.

9. Open the **Rosemary** database. Create a table called **tblPotentialVolunteer** from the Volunteer application part.

10. Make a backup copy of the database, compact and repair the database, and then close it.

Case Problem 4

CHALLENGE

Data Files needed for this Case Problem: Personnel.xlsx, PotentialTours1.xml, PotentialTours2.xml, and Ecotour.accdb (*cont. from Tutorial 7*)

Stanley EcoTours Janice and Bill Stanley want you to integrate the data in the Stanley database with other programs, and they want to be able to analyze the data in the database. Complete the following steps:

1. Open the **Ecotour** database you worked with in Tutorials 5–7.
2. Export the qryGuestsWithoutReservations query as an HTML document named **GuestsWithoutReservations.html** to the Access2 ▶ Case4 folder. Do not save the export steps.
3. Import the data and structure from the XML file named **PotentialTours1.xml**, which is located in the Access2 ▶ Case4 folder, as a new table in the database. Do not save the import steps. Open the PotentialTours table to verify the records were imported. Close the PotentialTours table.

Explore 4. Import the data from the XML file named **PotentialTours2.xml**, which is located in the Access2 ▶ Case4 folder, appending the data to the **PotentialTours** table. Rename the table as **tblPotentialTours**. Open the tblPotentialTours table to verify the records were appended. Close the tblPotentialTours table.

5. Export the qryTourReservations query as an XML file named **TourReservations** to the Access2 ▸ Case4 folder; do not create a separate XSD file. Do not save the export steps.
6. Link to the Personnel Excel workbook, which is located in the Access2 ▸ Case4 folder, using **tblPersonnel** as the table name. Change the Job Title in the last record from Staff Manager to **HR Staff Manager**.
7. Modify the **frmGuestsWithReservations** form in the following ways:
   a. Add a tab control to the bottom of the Detail section, and place the existing subform on the first page of the tab control.
   b. Change the caption for the left tab to **Reservation Data** and for the right tab to **Reservation Chart**.
   c. Change the caption for the main form's navigation buttons to **Guest** and for the subform's navigation buttons to **Reservation**.
   d. Add a chart to the second page of the tab control. Use the tblReservation table as the record source, select the StartDate, TourID, and People fields, use the Column Chart chart type, do not include a legend, and use **Reservations** as the chart title.
8. Export the rptTourReservations report as a PDF document with a filename of **TourReservations.pdf** to the Access2 ▸ Case4 folder. Include the document structure tags for accessibility, and do not save the export steps.
9. Make a backup copy of the database, compact and repair the database, and then close it.

Decision Making

Deciding When to Create a Personal Database

Decision making is a process of choosing between alternative courses of action. When you make decisions, you normally follow these steps:

1. Gather information relevant to the decision
2. Consider viable alternatives
3. Select the best alternative
4. Prepare an implementation action plan
5. Take action and monitor results
6. Verify the accuracy of the decision

For some decisions, you might combine some steps, and you might even skip steps for the simplest decisions.

Gathering Information, Considering Alternatives, and Selecting the Best Alternative

Suppose you were charged with tracking volunteers and their jobs for a service organization or other entity that requires coordination of a large group of people. The first step in decision making—gathering relevant information—starts with the choice of how to organize the people and their jobs. For example, if your information shows that each person completes only one job, few people are involved in the process, and volunteers all report to the same coordinator, then you could use a Word document or an Excel workbook to manage the volunteers and their jobs.

However, what if your information shows a very large number of volunteers, and many volunteers work in multiple jobs and report to more than one coordinator? When the relevant information changes so that one volunteer is no longer completing only one job and no longer reporting to a single coordinator, managing the data in a Word document or Excel workbook becomes problematic.

When making the decision to use a database to manage your data, at first you might find that some data exists in another format, such as in an Excel workbook. After considering the data that you have already collected (such as in a workbook) or data that you will collect in the future, consider the types of decisions you need to make. These decisions might include determining whether a database will effectively and efficiently manage your data, deciding which DBMS you will use, and evaluating the ability of users to manage and use the database to get the information they need.

Preparing an Implementation Action Plan

Once you have made the choice to use a DBMS, determine the steps needed to design and create the database. The first step is to analyze the data you have collected or will collect and start compiling it into tables. Then, you can begin identifying the primary and foreign keys in the tables to create the relationships between those tables. Finally, you can determine the field properties in anticipation of making data entry easier and reducing the likelihood of errors. For example, you might use the Default Value property to enter a city or state field value if all of your volunteers reside in the same area.

Taking Action and Monitoring Results

The next step in decision making involves implementation, which includes creating the database, defining the tables, and entering the data. After designing and installing the database, you need to make decisions about the types of queries, forms, and reports to create to produce the data in the format that users need. After implementation, you should make decisions about how the database will be updated so it remains current and ready for any future decisions you need to make.

Verifying the Accuracy of the Decision

At the end of your decision-making process, review your steps and evaluate how well they worked. Did you discover data you wish you had originally collected and stored in the database, but didn't have available? How did that limitation affect your ability to make a good decision? What changes do you need to make to your database so that it will provide better information for future decisions?

PROSKILLS

Create a Personal Database

Most businesses use databases for decision making, and you can also use databases to track data in your personal life. Examples of personal database use include tracking personal collections, such as music or books; hobby data, such as crafts or antiques; or items related to sports teams, theater clubs, or other organizations to which you might belong. In this exercise, you'll use Access to create a database that will contain information of your choice, using the Access skills and features you've learned in these tutorials.

Note: Please be sure *not* to include any personal information of a sensitive nature in the database you create to be submitted to your instructor for this exercise. Later on, you can update the data in your database with such information for your own personal use.

1. Consider your personal interests and activities, school-related functions, and work-related duties, and select from them one set of requirements that includes data that is best tracked using a DBMS. (If you completed Tutorials 1–4 of this book and the ProSkills Exercise at the end of Tutorial 4, you can use and enhance the database you've already created, and you can skip this step and the next step.) Make sure the data is sufficiently complex that a Word document or Excel workbook would not be viable alternatives to store and manage the data.
2. Create a new Access database to contain the data you want to track. The database must include two or more tables that you can join through one-to-many relationships. Define the properties for each field in each table. Make sure you include a mix of data types for the fields (for example, do not include only Text fields in each table). Specify a primary key for each table, define the table relationships with referential integrity enforced, and enter records in each table.
3. Create queries that include at least one of each of the following: pattern query match, list-of-values match, parameter, crosstab, find duplicates, find unmatched, and the use of a conditional value in a calculated field.
4. For one or more fields, apply an input mask and specify field validation rules.
5. Create a split form and modify the form.
6. Create a custom form that uses at least one of each of the following: combo box for a lookup, combo box to find records, subform, lines and rectangles, and tab control. Add one or more calculated controls to the main form based on the subform's calculated control(s), and add a chart, if appropriate. Check the main form's tab order, and improve the form's appearance.
7. Create a custom report that uses at least one of each of the following: grouping field, sort field(s), lines, and rectangles. Hide duplicates, and add the date, page numbers, and a report title.
8. Export two or more objects in different formats, and save the step specifications.
9. Designate a trusted folder, make a backup copy of the database, and compact and repair it.
10. Submit your completed database to your instructor as requested. Include printouts of any database objects, if required. Also, prepare a document that addresses the specific data you selected to store and track and why a DBMS was the best choice.

GLOSSARY/INDEX

Microsoft Access 2013, Comprehensive — REF 1

SPECIAL CHARACTERS

\ (backslash), AC 279, FM 11
< (left angle bracket), AC 142, AC 279
> (right angle bracket), AC 142, AC 279
! (exclamation point), AC 195, AC 279
" (double quotation mark), AC 279
(number symbol), AC 195, AC 237, AC 279
& (ampersand), AC 245, AC 279
* (asterisk), AC 195, AC 196, AC 237
+ (plus sign), AC 123–124
- (minus sign), AC 123, AC 195
= (equal sign), AC 142
? (question mark), AC 195, AC 237, AC 279
[] (square brackets), AC 195
. (dot), FM 16
; (semicolon), AC 279

A

.accdb file extension, AC 9

ACCDE file A special version of an Access database that runs as a normal database, but in which the VBA code can't be viewed or edited. In addition, users can't view, modify, or create forms, reports, or modules in Design view, and can't import or export forms, reports, or modules. The ACCDE file has an .accde extension instead of the usual .accdb extension. AC 697

Access. *See* Microsoft Access 2013

access
    to database objects, restricting, AC 574
    exclusive, to a database, AC 691

Access Help Information on Access commands and features as well as instructions for using them. AC 25, AC 40–41

Access Options dialog box, AC 693–694

Access window The program window that appears when you start the Access program to create a new database or open an existing database. AC 3

accuracy, data, AC 287

action An instruction to Access to perform an operation. AC 548
    adding to macros, AC 553–557

Action Catalog button A toggle to open and close the Action Catalog pane, which lists all actions by category and all macros in a database. AC 548

action query A query that adds, changes, or deletes multiple table records at a time. AC 498–515
    append, AC 498, AC 506–508
    delete, AC 499, AC 509–512
    deleting, AC 515
    make-table, AC 498, AC 501–505
    update, AC 499, AC 512–515

Add & Delete group A group on the FIELDS tab in Table Datasheet view that contains options for adding different types of fields to a table. AC 2

Address Quick Start selection The Quick Start Selection that adds a collection of fields related to an address to the table at one time. AC 86

Advanced Filter/Sort A form and datasheet tool that lets you specify multiple selection criteria and specify a sort order for selected records in the Filter window, in the same way you specify record selection criteria and sort orders for a query in Design view. AC 650

AfterUpdate event An event that occurs after changed data in a control or a record is updated. AC 607, AC 616, AC 625

aggregate function A function that performs an arithmetic operation on selected records in a database. AC 161–167
    creating queries using, AC 163–166
    record group calculations, AC 166–167
    Total row, AC 162–163
    used in crosstab queries, AC 256

alignment
    aligning controls, AC 332–333
    field values, changing, AC 213–214

All Access Objects The default category in the Navigation Pane; it lists all the objects in the database grouped by type (tables, queries, forms, reports, and so on). AC 40, AC 167–170

Allow Full Menus property A database property that specifies whether all options are available on the Ribbon. AC 671

Allow Multiple Values property The property that controls whether a field can store more than one value. AC 648

Allow Zero Length property A property that controls whether a field can store a zero length string value in a field. AC 676–677
    setting to No, AC 677

alternate key A candidate key that was not chosen to be the primary key. AC A3

ampersand (&), input mask character, AC 279

ampersand (&) operator A concatenation operator that joins text expressions. AC 245

Anchor property A form and report property that resizes a control and places it in the chosen position on a form. AC 303

Anchoring gallery, AC 319–320

And logical operator The logical operator you use in a query when you want a record selected only if two or more conditions are met. AC 149, AC 150–151
    Or logical operator vs. AC 153

anomaly Undesirable irregularity of a table caused by data redundancy and by partial and transitive dependencies. Anomalies are of three types: insertion, deletion, and update. AC A14–A15

Append Only property A field property for a Long Text field that lets you edit the field value and, when set to Yes, causes Access to keep a historical record of all versions of the field value. You can view each version of the field value, along with a date and time stamp of when each version change occurred. AC 290

append query An action query that adds records from existing tables or queries to the end of another table. AC 498, AC 506–508

application part A specialized template that can be imported into an existing database. You use an application part when you already have a database file that you're working with, and would like to include the content from an application part in your existing database. AC 480–484

Application Title property A database property that specifies the name for a database that appears in the Access window title bar. AC 670

ApplyFilter action, AC 550

archive A special type of folder containing compressed files. FM 26

argument A piece of data that is required by an action. AC 553

argument (for VBA) A value passed to a VBA function and used in place of a parameter when the function is executed. AC 617
    naming, AC 617

arrow button, FM 2, FM 3, FM 11

artificial key A field that you add to a table to serve solely as the primary key and that is visible to users. AC A21–A23

assignment statement A VBA statement that assigns the value of an expression to a field, control, or property. AC 604

asterisk (*), wildcard character, AC 195, AC 196, AC 237

Attachment data type A data type used to attach one or more files to a table record. AC 672–674

Attachments dialog box, AC 673–674

attribute The formal term for a column in a relation (table). AC A2

AutoFilter An Access feature, available by clicking the arrow to the right of a field name in Datasheet view for a table or query, that enables you to quickly sort and display the field's values in various ways. AC 132, AC 242–244

AutoNumber An Access data type that automatically assigns a unique number to a record. AC 13, AC 57
    sorting results, AC 131
    using AutoNumber fields, AC 674–676
Average function, AC 161, AC 164–165
Avg function, AC 256

B

back-end database A database that contains the tables that are needed for an application. AC 687

Background Color button A button in the Font group on the FORMAT tab that you use to change the background color of an object (form or report) or of a specific section or control in the object. AC 371

backing up Making a copy of a database file to protect your database against loss or damage. AC 43

backslash (\)
    file path, FM 11
    input mask character, AC 279

Backstage view The FILE tab of the ribbon, which provides access to file-level options and program settings. AC 8

backup A duplicate copy of a file. FM 25

BCNF. *See* Boyce-Codd normal form

Beep action, AC 550

BeforeUpdate event, AC 607

Between...And... operator, AC 142

Boolean data type, AC 633

border, removing from report in Design view, AC 415–416

bound control A control that is connected, or bound, to a field in the database based on the record source, or the underlying table or query, and that is used to display and maintain a table field value. AC 322

bound form A form that has a table or query as its record source and is used for maintaining and displaying table data. AC 325

Boyce-Codd normal form (BCNF) A second normal form table is in Boyce-Codd normal form if every determinant is a candidate key. BCNF is also called third normal form in this book, although BCNF is an improvement over the original version of third normal form. AC A19

bubble diagram A diagram that graphically shows a table's functional dependencies and determinants. Also known as a data model diagram or a functional dependency diagram. AC A12–A13

button
    command. *See* command button
    ribbon, AC 13

Byte The Field Size property that stores whole numbers from 0 to 255 in one byte. AC 58
Byte data type, AC 633

C

calculated control A control that displays a value that is the result of an expression. The expression usually contains one or more fields, and the calculated control is recalculated each time any value in the expression changes. AC 326, AC 356–364
    adding to main form, AC 358–360
    adding to subform's form footer section, AC 356–358
    enhancing information, AC 367
    formatting, AC 360–364
    moving, AC 361–364
    resizing, AC 361–364

calculated field A field that you create with an expression that displays the results of the expression in a datasheet, form, or report, but does not exist as a field in the database. AC 156–161
    Calculated Field data type vs. AC 161
    conditional values, AC 245–249
    formatting, AC 160–161

Calculated Field data type, calculated fields vs. AC 161

Can Grow property A property that controls the appearance of a control or section in a form or report when viewed, printed, or previewed. When you set the property to Yes, the control or section expands vertically to print or preview all the data within the control or section. When you set the property to No, the data that doesn't fit within the fixed size of the control or section isn't visible, printed, or previewed. AC 414, AC 415

candidate key A column, or a collection of columns, whose values are non-changing and whose values uniquely and minimally identify each row of a table, but that has not necessarily been chosen as the primary key. AC A3

caption, labels, changing, AC 338–340

Caption property A field property that specifies how the field name is displayed in database objects, including table and query datasheets, forms, and reports. AC 58, AC 576

Cascade Delete Related Records option An option you can set to enforce the referential integrity rule that permits a record in the primary table to be deleted and also deletes all records in related tables that have matching foreign key values. AC 99

Cascade Update Related Fields option An option you can set to enforce the referential integrity rule that permits a change in value to the primary key and changes the appropriate foreign key values in related tables. AC 99

cascades A referential integrity option in which the DBMS, when you change a primary key value, automatically changes the matching foreign key values to the new primary key value, and when you delete a record, automatically deletes the matching foreign key rows. AC A11

case
    field values, changing, AC 637–638
    VBA code, AC 619

Case control structure A conditional control structure that evaluates an expression, and then performs one of several alternative actions based on the resulting value of the evaluated expression. AC 605, AC 634

Case statement A VBA statement that designates the start of an alternative set of actions for the Case control structure. AC 604

Change your view button, FM 2

Charms bar, FM 4

chart
    embedding in forms, AC 474–480
    selecting type, AC 474–475

Chart Type dialog box, AC 477–478

Choose Builder dialog box, AC 589

class module A VBA module that is usually associated with a particular form or report. AC 609
    adding procedures, AC 631–637

clear filter button A button used to clear the search box and display all actions and objects in the Action Catalog pane. AC 549

Click event, AC 607

Click to Add column In Datasheet view for a table, the datasheet column you can use to create a new field in the table. AC 2

Clipboard A temporary storage area for files and information that you have copied or moved from one place and plan to use somewhere else. FM 21
    moving files, FM 22–23

Close Button property, AC 576

CloseWindow action, AC 550

closing tables, AC 22–23

code from other sources, reusing, AC 640

Code window The window in which you create, modify, and display VBA procedures. AC 605

coding The process of writing instructions in a programming language such as VBA. AC 606

color
    alternate rows in datasheets, changing, AC 154–156
    controls, changing, AC 639–643
    form title, AC 191–192

report rows, AC 415–416
text on reports, AC 216
color value, assigning to control property, AC 614
column
    newspaper-style (snaking), AC 433
    reports, resizing and renaming in layout view, AC 406–407

column selector In a datasheet, the column heading (also called the field selector) that you click to select the entire column. AC 16

combo box A control that provides the features of a text box and a list box; you can choose a value from the list or type an entry. AC 304
    adding to forms, AC 336–342
    to find records, AC 348–355
    modifying in Design and Layout views, AC 340–342
    using for foreign keys, AC 336

Combo Box tool A tool you use in Design view to add a combo box to a form. AC 336

command button A button that performs an action when a user clicks it. AC 551
    adding to forms, AC 567–568, AC 584–588
    with attached macro, AC 559–562
    attaching submacros, AC 568–571

comma-separated values. *See* CSV

comment A text description in a macro that has no effect on the macro. AC 548, AC 549

comment (VBA), AC 619

common field A field that appears in more than one table, allowing you to connect the records in the separate tables. AC 4, AC 55

compacting A process that rearranges the data and objects in a database to decrease its file size, thereby making more space available and enhancing the performance of the database. AC 42–43

comparison operator In a query, an operator that asks Access to compare the value in a database field to the condition value and to select all the records for which the relationship is true. AC 140, AC 142, AC 147–149

compilation The process of translating modules from VBA to a translated form that a computer processor can understand. AC 629–630

compile To translate a module from VBA to a translated form that a computer processor can understand. AC 629–630

composite key A primary key that consists of two or more fields. AC A4, AC 55

composite primary key A multiple-column primary key. AC A4, AC A5

compressed file, FM 26–28
    compressing files and folders, FM 26, FM 27
    extracting, FM 26, FM 27–28

compressed folder A folder that stores files in a format that requires less disk space. FM 2

Computer icon, FM 3

concatenated key A multiple-column key. Also known as a composite key. AC A4, AC A5

concatenation The process of joining two or more text fields or characters encapsulated in quotes. AC 245

condition A criterion, or rule, that determines which records are selected in a query. AC 140

conditional control structure A VBA control structure that evaluates an expression and then performs one of several alternative actions based on the resulting value of the evaluated expression. AC 613

conditional formatting Special formatting applied to field values that meet specified conditions. AC 217
    reports, AC 217–221

conditional value, calculated fields, AC 245–249

contextual tab A tab that appears and provides options for working with a specific object that is selected. AC 13

control An item on a form, report, or other database object that you can manipulate to modify the object's appearance. AC 189
    aligning, AC 332–333
    allowing users to make selections, AC 594
    anchoring in forms, AC 319–321
    assigning color values, AC 614
    calculated. *See* calculated control
    changing color, AC 639–643
    deleting, AC 333–335
    Design view, AC 412–417
    hiding, AC 639–643
    moving, AC 329–330, AC 331–332
    positioning in forms and reports, AC 587
    resizing, AC 333–335
    selecting, AC 329–330
    unbound, AC 326

control layout A set of controls grouped together in a form or report so that you can manipulate the set as a single control. AC 190, AC 316–317

Control Margins property A form and report property that controls the spacing around the text inside a control. AC 303

Control Padding property A form and report property that controls the spacing around the outside of a control. AC 303

Control Source property A property that you use to specify the source of the data that appears in a control. You can set this property to a field name or an expression. AC 357

control structure A set of VBA statements that work together as a unit. AC 613

Control Wizard A wizard that asks a series of questions and then uses your answers to create a control in a form or report. AC 336

Controls gallery, AC 337

ControlTip Text property A property that you use to specify the text that appears in a ScreenTip when users hold the mouse pointer over a control in a form. AC 360

Copy command, FM 21

Copy to button, FM 21

copying (file) To place a file in a new location that you specify without removing it from its current location. FM 20
    files and folders in File Explorer, FM 20–21, FM 24–25

copying records from another Access database, AC 26–29

Count function A function that determines the number of occurrences of an expression. AC 161, AC 256, AC 346

Create New Template from This Database dialog box, AC 482–483

Create Relationship dialog box, AC 483–484

CREATE tab A tab on the ribbon that provides options for creating various database objects, including tables, forms, and reports. AC 24

crosstab query A query that uses aggregate functions to perform arithmetic operations on the values of one database field and displays the results in a spreadsheet format. AC 254, AC 256–262
    changing query column headings, AC 260–261
    starting, AC 258–259

Crosstab Query Wizard A wizard that guides you through the steps for creating a crosstab query. AC 258–261

CSV (comma-separated values) file A text file in which commas separate values, and each line is a record containing the same number of values in the same positions. AC 449–454

Ctrl + ' A keyboard shortcut that lets you insert in the current field the value from the same field in the previous record. AC 79

Currency data type, AC 57, AC 633
    sorting results, AC 131

Current event The event that occurs when the focus shifts to the next record loaded in a form, making it the current record. AC 607, AC 610

Current Record box The box that appears at the bottom of a datasheet or form and that indicates the current record and total number of records displayed. AC 22

custom form An existing form that you modify or a new form that you create from scratch in Layout View or in Design view. AC 304, AC 346–372

adding lines, AC 367–368
adding rectangles, AC 369–370
combo boxes for finding records, AC 348–355
creating in Design view, AC 324–329
designing, AC 324
displaying subform calculated controls in main form, AC 356–364
modifying visual effects of controls, AC 370–372
planning, AC 324

custom report An existing report that you modify, or a new report that you create from scratch in Layout view or in Design view. AC 381–434
creating, AC 405–412
creating queries for, AC 403–404
customizing existing reports. *See* customizing existing reports
design modifications, AC 405
Design view. *See* Design view (forms)
designing, AC 402–403
hiding duplicate values, AC 418–419
sorting and grouping data, AC 407–412

Cut command, FM 21

D

data accuracy, AC 287

Data Mode argument An action argument that specifies a table's data-entry options. Allowable settings for this argument are Add (users can add new records but can't change or delete existing records), Edit (users can change and delete existing records and can add new records), and Read Only (users can only view records). Edit is the default setting. AC 563

data model diagram. *See* bubble diagram

data redundancy A condition that occurs when you store the same data in more than one place; it wastes space and can cause inconsistencies. AC A14, AC 55

data type The field property that determines what field values you can enter for the field and what other properties the field will have. AC 13–14
assigning, AC 56–57
changing in Design view, AC 90–93
sorting results, AC 131

Data Type gallery An Access tool that allows you to add a group of related fields to a table at the same time, rather than adding each field individually. AC 86–87

data validation rule, AC 283–287
defining, AC 286–287
field validation rule, AC 284–285

database A collection of related tables stored in the same file. AC 4, AC 26
back-end, AC 687
backing up and restoring, AC 43
compacting and repairing, AC 42–43
creating, AC 4, AC 8–10

deleting dab objects, AC 505
designing, guidelines, AC 54–56
exchanging data between programs, AC 456
front-end, AC 687
importing tables from, AC 454–455
large, creating, AC 104
opening, AC 26
performance analysis, AC 678–681
prohibiting design changes, AC 574
relational. *See* relational database
relationships, AC 4–6
restricting access, AC 574
saving. *See* saving a database
securing, AC 690–692
setting properties, AC 692–697
splitting, AC 687–690
themes, AC 154, AC 425
updating (maintaining), AC 118–124

database design The process of determining the content and structure of data in a database in order to support some activity on behalf of a user or group of users. AC A15

database management system (DBMS) A software program that lets you create databases and then manipulate data in them. AC 6–7
naming conventions, AC A25–A27

Database Splitter An Access tool that splits an Access database into two files: one file contains the tables, and the other file contains the queries, forms, reports, and other database objects. AC 687–690

datasheet The display of a table's contents in rows and columns, similar to a table or spreadsheet; each row is a separate record in the table, and each column contains the field values for one field in the table. AC 3
changing alternate row color, AC 154–156
finding data, AC 194
modifying font size, AC 154
navigating, AC 29–30
query datasheet vs. table datasheet, AC 129

datasheet selector A box in the upper-left corner of a datasheet that lets you select the entire datasheet. AC 27

Datasheet tool A form tool that creates a form in a datasheet format that contains all the fields in the source table or query. AC 311–313

Datasheet view (for a table) The Access view that shows a table's contents as a datasheet in rows and columns. AC 2
changing Format property, AC 71–73
creating tables, AC 11–23
viewing long text fields with large contents, AC 289

Datasheet View button, AC 117

date, adding to reports in Design view, AC 422–428

Date data type, AC 633

Date function A function that returns the current date. AC 420, AC 422, AC 423, AC 424

Date/Time data type, AC 57
sorting results, AC 131

DB2 naming conventions, AC A27

DblClick event, AC 607

DBMS. *See* database management system

debugging Testing the VBA code you create. AC 622

Decimal The Field Size property that stores positive and negative numbers to precisely 28 decimal places in 12 bytes. AC 58

Decimal data type, AC 633

Decimal Places property The property that specifies the number of decimal places that are displayed to the right of the decimal point. AC 62

Declarations section The VBA statements at the beginning of a module that apply to all procedures in the module. AC 608

decrypting The translation by Access of encrypted data in a database into a normal form that users can understand. AC 690

Default Value property The property that specifies what value will appear, by default, for a field in each new record you add to a table. AC 93–95

Delete button, AC 122

Delete event, AC 607

delete query An action query that deletes a group of records matching the criteria you specify from one or more tables. AC 499, AC 509–512

deleting
action queries, AC 515
controls, AC 333–335
dab objects, AC 505
fields from table structure, AC 87–89
files and folders, FM 25
records, AC 122–124

deletion anomaly Deleting data from a table and unintentionally losing other critical data. AC A15

delimited text file A type of text file in which fields of data are separated by a character such as a comma or tab. AC 96

dependency, AC A12–A14

Description property The optional property you can use to enter a description for a field to explain its purpose or usage. AC 52

design grid The portion of the Query window in Design view in which you specify the fields and record selection criteria for the query you are creating. AC 116
adding fields, AC 126–127, AC 128

DESIGN tab, Query Type group, AC 117

Design view (for a form)
adding fields to forms, AC 327–328
creating custom forms, AC 324–329

Form window, AC 325–327
    modifying combo boxes, AC 340–342
Design view (for a report), AC 420–434
    adding dates to reports, AC 422–428
    adding titles to reports, AC 428–430
    controls, AC 412–417
    creating mailing labels, AC 430–434
    modifying reports, AC 395–398
Design view (for a table) The Access view you use to define or modify a table structure or the properties of the fields in a table. AC 52
    adding fields, AC 69–71
    changing data type for fields, AC 90–93
    changing field properties, AC 73–75
    creating queries, AC 238
    creating tables, AC 59–68
    deleting fields, AC 88–89
    moving fields, AC 68
    renaming fields, AC 89–90
    specifying primary key, AC 67
desktop, Windows 8 and Windows 7 compared, FM 4
destination program The program in which you place the information, or object, that's created by another program when you integrate information between programs. AC 473
detail record In a report based on two tables, the set of field values displayed for each field in the related table. AC 206
detail report A report that displays fields in the Detail section for every record from the record source. AC 402
Detail section The main body of a form or report in which you place bound controls and calculated controls. AC 323
Detail section bar The bar at the top of the Detail section in Design view that you use to select the entire Detail section. AC 322
Details pane The pane in Windows Explorer that displays the characteristics of the folder or selected object. FM 2
determinant A field, or a collection of fields, whose values determine the values of another field. AC A12
Dim statement A VBA statement used to declare variables and their associated data types in a procedure. AC 633
disk A computer device for storing data. FM 5
Display Control property A property that specifies the default control used to display a field. AC 305
Display Form property A database property that specifies the form that opens automatically when you open a database. AC 670
Display Navigation Pane property A database property that controls whether the Navigation Pane is available in the Access window. AC 671

Documenter An Access tool you use to create detailed documentation of all, or selected, objects in a database. AC 307–310
domain The set of values that are permitted for a field. AC A11
domain integrity constraint A rule you specify for a field. AC A11
dot (.), filenames, FM 16
Double The Field Size property that stores positive and negative numbers to precisely 15 decimal places in eight bytes. AC 58
Double data type, AC 633
double quotation mark ("), input mask character, AC 279
dragging moving files, FM 21–22
drive A computer device that can retrieve and sometimes record data on a disk. FM 6

E

Edit Relationships dialog box, AC 101, AC 681
editing mode The mode in which you can insert or delete characters in a field value based on the location of the insertion point. AC 118
editor. See Visual Basic Editor
embedding Creating or copying an object in a form, report, or field and preserving the object's connection to the source program, which enables you to edit the object, if necessary, using the features of the source program. AC 473
    charts in forms, AC 474–480
Enable design changes for tables in Datasheet view property A database property that allows you to change a table's design in Datasheet view. AC 670
Enable error checking property A database property that checks for design errors in forms and reports and alerts you to errors by displaying the Error Checking Options button. AC 692
Enable Layout View property A database property that shows or hides the Layout View button on the Access status bar and on shortcut menus. AC 670
encryption The translation of the data in a database to a scrambled format that's indecipherable to a word processor or other program. AC 690–692
End Function statement The last statement in a VBA function. AC 617
End Select statement A VBA statement that designates the end of a Case control structure. AC 604
End Sub statement A VBA statement that designates the end of a VBA Sub procedure. AC 604
Enter parameter Value dialog box, AC 251

entity A person, place, object, event, or idea for which you want to store and process data. AC A2
entity integrity The condition that exists when a primary key has been specified for a table, whereby Access forces you to enter a value for the primary key field in every record in the table. AC 68
entity integrity constraint The rule that none of the individual fields comprising the primary key can contain nulls. AC A11
entity subtype A table whose primary key is a foreign key to a second table and whose fields are additional fields for the second table. AC A8–A9, AC 520–521
entity-relationship diagram (ERD) A symbolic, visual way to show a database's entities and the relationships among the entities. AC A9–A11
equal sign (=), comparison operators, AC 142
equal to operator (=), AC 142
ERD. See entity-relationship diagram
event A state, condition, or occurrence detectable by Access. AC 560–562, AC 606–607
event procedure A procedure that Access executes when an event occurs. AC 561, AC 624–643
    adding, AC 628–629, AC 634–637
    compiling modules, AC 629–630
    creating, AC 626–631
    designing, AC 627–628
    displaying, AC 610–614
    modifying, AC 614–615
    testing, AC 630–631
event property The property that specifies how an object responds when an event occurs. AC 561
event-driven language A programming language that executes a set of instructions when a specific event occurs. AC 606
exact match A type of query in which the value in the specified field must match the condition exactly in order for the record to be included in the query results. AC 141
    specifying, AC 142–144
Excel. See Microsoft Excel 2013
exclamation point (!)
    input mask character, AC 279
    wildcard character, AC 195
exclusive access Opening a database in a way that prevents other users from opening and using the database at the same time. AC 691
exiting Access, AC 22–23
expand indicator In a datasheet, the plus sign that lets you display the related records in the subdatasheet. AC 123, AC 359
Export - HTML Document dialog box, AC 447
Export XML dialog box, AC 461–463

exporting, AC 473
file formats, AC 463
queries to HTML documents, AC 446–448
reports to PDF files, AC 485–486
saving and running export specifications, AC 463–465

expression A statement containing a combination of database fields, constants, and operators that you define in a query to perform a calculation. AC 154

Expression Builder An Access tool that makes it easy to create an expression by providing boxes for entering the expression, options for displaying and selecting common operators, and one or more lists of expression elements, such as table and field names. AC 156–157, AC 158–160

Expression Builder dialog box, AC 359

Extensible Markup Language (XML) A programming language that uses customizable tags to describe the data it contains and how that data should be structured. AC 444, AC 456–465
exporting Access tables as, AC 460–463
importing data from XML files, AC 456–457
saving and running export specifications, AC 463–465
saving and running import specifications, AC 457–460

Extensible Stylesheet Language. *See* XSL

extension The three or four characters that follow the dot in a filename and identify the file's type. FM 16

extract To create an uncompressed copy of a compressed file in a folder you specify. FM 26, FM 27–28

F

F1 key The function key you press to display Help information, such as for the current property in Table Design view. AC 53

F2 key The function key you press to switch between navigation mode and editing mode in a datasheet. AC 118

F6 key The function key you press to move from the Table Design grid to the Field Properties pane of the Table window in Design view. AC 52

false-statement group The group of VBA statements executed when an If statement condition is false. AC 627

field A single characteristic or attribute of a person, place, object, event, or idea. AC 2
adding in Design view, AC 69–71
adding to forms, AC 327–328
adding using Data Type gallery, AC 86–87
calculated. *See* calculated field
changing alignment of values, AC 213–214
changing data type in Design view, AC 90–93
common, AC 4, AC 55

data types, AC 56–57
defining, AC 59–66
deleting from table structure, AC 87–89
grouping, AC 389
indexes. *See* index
modifying properties, AC 71–75
moving in Design view, AC 69
moving on reports, AC 214–215
multivalued, AC 648, AC 661–668
naming, AC 12–13, AC 56, AC 58
new, adding, AC 14–16
nonkey, AC A5
properties, AC 56–58
renaming in Design view, AC 89–90
resizing on reports, AC 214–215
selecting for queries, AC 126–127
setting Default Value property, AC 93–95
sort, AC 133
sorting on multiple fields in Design view, AC 133–135

field list A list containing the fields for a table, with the table name at the top and the fields listed in the order in which they appear in the table. AC 77, AC 116

field name The unique name for a column in a table. The table name allows you to access a specific column without needing to know its position within the table. AC A2

Field Properties pane The part of the Table window in Design view that contains the properties for the selected field. AC 53

Field Size property The property that defines a field's maximum storage size for Short Text, Number, and AutoNumber fields. AC 57–58

field validation procedure, designing, AC 632–634

field validation rule Setting A rule to prevent a user from entering an unacceptable value in a field by comparing user input to a constant or to a set of constants. AC 284–285

field value The specific value, or content, of a field in a record. AC 4
changing case, AC 637–638

FIELDS tab A tab on the Ribbon that provides options for adding, removing, and formatting the fields in a table. AC 2
Formatting group, AC 13

file A collection of data that has a name and is stored on a computer. FM 5
backup copy, FM 25
compressed, FM 2, FM 26–28
copying, FM 20–21, FM 24–25
deleting, FM 25
determining where to store, FM 8
moving, FM 20–24
multiple, selecting, FM 24
opening, FM 15–16
organizing files, FM 6–8
saving, FM 16–18
text. *See* text file

File Explorer A Windows 8 tool that displays the contents of your computer and uses icons to represent drives, folders, and files. FM 3, FM 8–14
changing views, FM 12–13
compressed files, FM 26–28
copying files and folders, FM 20–21, FM 24–25
creating folders, FM 19–20
deleting files and folders, FM 25
expanding ribbon, FM 13–14
moving files and folders, FM 20–24
navigating to data files, FM 10–12
opening, FM 10
opening files, FM 15–16
panes, FM 8
renaming files, FM 26
saving files, FM 16–18

file format, importing and exporting data, AC 463

file icon An icon that indicates a file's type. FM 3

file path A notation that indicates a file's location. FM 2, FM 3, FM 10–12

file system An operating system's hierarchy of folders and files, which ensures system stability and enables Windows to find files quickly. FM 6, FM 7

FILE tab, Print button, AC 39

file type, databases, AC 9

filename The name of a file; provides important information about the file, including its contents and purpose. FM 3, FM 16–17

filter A set of restrictions you place on the records in an open datasheet or form to temporarily isolate a subset of the records. AC 136
AutoFilter, AC 132, AC 242–244
filtering data, AC 136–138, AC 650–657
saved as queries, applying, AC 656–657
saving as queries, AC 654–656

Filter By Form A filtering technique that changes a datasheet or form to display blank fields, allowing you to select a value from a list in any blank field to apply a filter that selects only those records containing that value. AC 136, AC 651–654

Filter By Selection A filtering technique that lets you select all or part of a field value in a datasheet or form, and then display only those records that contain the selected value in the field. AC 136–138

filtered record, creating Word documents containing, AC 387

Find and Replace dialog box, AC 121–122, AC 181, AC 195

Find button, AC 181

Find command A command you use to search for data in a form or a table or query datasheet so that you can locate a specific field value or part of a field value. AC 121–122

find duplicates query A select query that finds duplicate records in a table or query. You specify the fields in the query or table you want to compare and, if two or more records have the same values for those fields, those records appear in the query recordset. AC 254, AC 255, AC 262–264

Find Duplicates Query Wizard A wizard that guides you through the steps for creating a find duplicates query. AC 262–264

find unmatched query A select query that finds all records in a table or query that have no related records in a second table or query. AC 254, AC 255, AC 264–266

Find Unmatched Query Wizard A wizard that guides you through the steps for creating a find unmatched query. AC 264–266

finding data
    combo boxes to find records, AC 348–355
    datasheets, AC 194
    forms, AC 194–196
    tables, AC 121–122

FindRecord action An action that finds the first record, or the next record if the action is used again, that meets the specified criteria. AC 550, AC 553–557

First function, AC 256

first normal form (1NF) A table is in first normal form if it does not contain repeating groups. AC A15–A17

focus When an object, record(s), or control(s) in a form are currently selected and thus active and awaiting user interaction, they are said to have focus. AC 364

folder A container for files and subfolders. FM 5
    backup copy, FM 25
    copying, FM 20–21, FM 24–25
    creating, FM 19–20
    deleting, FM 25
    moving, FM 20–24
    multiple, selecting, FM 24
    organizing folders, FM 6–8
    trusted, AC 290–292

font, report titles, changing color, AC 216

Font group, AC 191

ForeColor property A property that determines a control's foreground, or font, color. AC 605

foreign key A primary key field from one table that you include as a field in a second table to form a relationship between the two tables. AC A4–A5, AC 5

form A database object you can create and customize to maintain, view, and print records in a database in different and useful ways. AC 24, AC 180–205

    adding event procedures, AC 628–629
    adding fields, AC 327–328
    adding lines, AC 367–368
    adding pictures, AC 189–191

    adding rectangles, AC 369–370
    adding subforms, AC 352–355
    anchoring controls, AC 319–321
    applying themes, AC 185–189
    bound, AC 325
    building, suggestions, AC 329
    changing from title color, AC 191–192
    combo boxes, AC 336–342
    command buttons, AC 567–568, AC 584–588
    creating using Datasheet tool, AC 311–313
    creating using Form Wizard, AC 82–84
    creating using Multiple Items tool, AC 313–314
    creating using Split Form tool, AC 314–315
    creating with main form and subform, AC 200–205
    custom. *See* custom form
    design, AC 193
    design modifications, AC 336
    designing, AC 304–306
    embedding charts, AC 474–480
    finding data, AC 194–196
    formatting controls, AC 568
    formatting print layout, AC 598
    list boxes, AC 577–579
    macros, AC 588–592
    main. *See* main form
    maintaining table data, AC 196–198
    modifying design in Layout view, AC 185–193
    modifying visual effects of controls, AC 370–372
    multiple, creating, AC 311
    navigating, AC 193–194
    positioning controls, AC 587
    previewing, AC 199
    printing, AC 199–200
    saving, AC 35
    simple, creating, AC 33–35
    split. *See* split form
    tab order, AC 364–367
    tabbed, creating using Tab Control tool, AC 468–472
    testing, AC 592–593
    titles, AC 343–345
    unbound, AC 325

Form Footer section The section that appears at the bottom of a form in Form view and used to is display titles, instructions, command buttons, and other controls. AC 342–343
    subforms, adding calculated controls, AC 356–358

Form Header section The section that appears at the top of a form in Form view and is used to display titles, a logo, the date and time, instructions, command buttons, and other controls. AC 342–343

form selector The square selector at the intersection of the horizontal and vertical rulers in Design view that you click to select and set properties for the entire form. AC 344

Form tool An Access tool that creates a form containing all the fields in the table or query on which the form is based. AC 24, AC 33–35

Form view The Access view you use to view, enter, and maintain data in the table on which a form is based. AC 181

Form window, Design view, AC 325–327

Form Wizard An Access tool that asks you a series of questions, and then creates a form based on your answers. AC 24, AC 181
    creating forms, AC 182–184

Format property, modifying in Datasheet view, AC 71–73

Format Series dialog box, AC 478–479

FORMAT tab, AC 212, AC 568
    Font group, AC 191

formatting
    calculated controls, AC 360–364
    calculated fields, AC 160–161
    conditional, reports, AC 217–221
    controls in forms and reports, AC 568
    print layout for forms, AC 598

Formatting group, AC 13

front-end database A database that contains the user interface and other objects, but not the tables that are needed for an application. AC 687

function A procedure that performs operations, returns a value, accepts input values, and can be used in expressions. Also known as a user-defined function or a Function procedure. AC 607
    aggregate. *See* aggregate function
    creating, AC 617–620
    naming, AC 617
    saving, AC 620–621
    starting, AC 617–618

function call A statement that contains the name of a function plus any parameters required by the function. AC 626

Function statement The first statement in a VBA function. AC 617

functional dependency diagram. *See* bubble diagram

functionally related Two fields are functionally related if a value for a particular field gives you a single value for another field. AC A12

G

GB. *See* gigabyte

gesture, FM 4–5

Get External Data - Excel Spreadsheet dialog box, AC 81

Get External Data - Text File dialog box, AC 450

gigabyte (GB) 1 billion bytes of data. FM 6

GotFocus event, AC 607
GoToControl action, AC 550
grand total, reports, AC 393–395
greater than operator (>), AC 142
greater than or equal to operator (>=), AC 142
grid The area in Design view with dotted and solid lines that helps you position controls precisely in a form. AC 322
Group, Sort, and Total pane A pane in Layout and Design views for a report in which you can modify the report's grouping fields and sort fields, and the report calculations for the groups. AC 389, AC 407, AC 408, AC 409
group band field A report field that is used to group detail items. AC 401
Group By operator In a query, an operator that divides the selected records into groups based on the values in the specified field. AC 166–167
Group Footer section A report section that appears after each group of records that share the same sort field value, and that usually displays subtotals or counts for the records in that group. AC 389, AC 396
Group Header section A report section that appears before each group of records that share the same sort field value, and that usually displays the group name and the sort field value for the group. AC 389, AC 396
grouped report A report in which the data from a record in the primary table appears as a group, followed on subsequent lines of the report by the joined records from the related table. AC 206
grouping data in reports, AC 407–412
grouping field A report sort field that includes a Group Header section before a group of records that has the same sort field value and that includes a Group Footer section after the group of records. AC 389, AC 407–410

H

hard disk A storage device permanently housed inside the computer case. FM 6
Hide Duplicates property A property you use to hide a control in a report when the control's value is the same as that of the preceding record in the group. AC 418–419
Hide Fields In Datasheet view, the command that allows you to remove the display of one or more fields. AC 119
hiding
  controls, AC 639–643
  fields, AC 119–120
history table A table that contains data that is no longer needed for current processing but that you might need to reference in the future. AC 500

HOME tab
  Delete button, AC 122
  Totals button, AC 163
HTML document A text document that contains tags and other instructions that a web browser, such as Microsoft Internet Explorer or Mozilla Firefox, processes and displays as a web page. You usually save an HTML document with the .htm or .html file extension. AC 445
  exporting Access queries to, AC 446–448
  viewing using Internet Explorer, AC 448
HTML Output Options dialog box, AC 447
Hyperlink data type, AC 57

I

icon, Windows 8 and Windows 7 compared, FM 4
ID field The default field Access creates to serve as the primary key field for all new tables. AC2, AC 11, AC 12–13
If statement A VBA statement that executes one of two groups of statements based on a condition. If the condition is true, the true-statement group executes. If the condition is false, the false-statement group executes. AC 627
IIf (Immediate If) function A function that test a condition and returns one of two values based on whether the condition being tested is true or false. AC 235, AC 245–248
Immediate window A Visual Basic Editor window that lets you enter different values to test the procedures you create without changing any data in the database. AC 604
  testing procedures, AC 621–623
Import Objects dialog box, AC 84–85, AC 455
Import Spreadsheet Wizard dialog box, AC 82
importing A process that allows you to copy the data from a source, without having to open the source file, and to add the imported data in an Access table, form, report, for field. AC 80, AC 473
  adding data to tables by importing text files, AC 95–97
  data from Excel worksheet to tables, AC 80–83
  existing table structure, AC 83–85
  file formats, AC 463
  saving and running import specifications, AC 457–460
  tables from Access databases, AC 454–455
  XML files as Access tables, AC 456
In comparison operator A comparison operator that defines a condition with a list of two or more values for a field. If a record's field value matches one value from the list of defined values, then Access selects and includes that record in the query results. AC 240
In () operator, AC 142
indenting VBA code, AC 619

index A list that relates field values to the records that contain those values. AC 534–535
  existing, viewing, AC 536–540
  tradeoffs of using, AC 535
inner join A join between two tables in which the DBMS selects records from the tables only when the records have the same value in the common field that links the tables. AC 525–526
inner query. See subquery
input mask A field property used to define a predefined format to enter and display data in a field. AC 269
  when to use, AC 281
Input Mask Wizard An Access tool that guides you in creating a predefined format for a field. AC 276–281
insertion anomaly The inability to add a record to a table because you do not know the entire primary key value. AC A14
insertion point A flashing cursor that shows where text you type will be inserted. AC 13
Integer The Field Size property that stores whole numbers from -32,768 to 32,767 in two bytes. AC 58
Integer data type, AC 633
integrating Access with other programs, AC 472–474. See also embedding; exporting; importing; linking
integrity A database has integrity if its data follows certain rules, known as integrity constraints. AC A11
integrity constraint A rule that must be followed by data in a database. AC A11
intelligent key. See natural key
Internet Explorer, viewing HTML documents, AC 448
intersection table A table that connects two other tables having a many-to-many relationship; its primary key is a composite key, consisting of the primary keys of the other two tables. AC A6
IsNull function A function that tests a field value or an expression for a null value; if the field value or expression is null, the result is true; otherwise, the result is false. AC 235, AC 628

J

join line In the Relationships window, the line that connects the common field that joins two tables. AC 77
Join Properties dialog box, AC 529, AC 532
joining To relate tables using a common field. AC 98, AC 525–534
  inner and outer joins, AC 525–529
  self-joins, AC 529–534
junction table. See intersection table

K

Keep Together property A property for a group in a report to keep parts of the group together on the same page. Settings for the property are "do not keep together on one page" (default), "keep whole group together on one page" (prints the group header, detail, and group footers on the same page), and "keep header and first record together on one page" (prints the group header on a page only if it can also print the first detail record). For a section, this property specifies whether the section starts printing on a new page if the entire section doesn't fit entirely on the current page. AC 409–410

key
    artificial, AC A21–A23
    foreign, AC A4–A5, AC 5
    natural (logical, intelligent), AC A21
    primary. *See* primary key
    surrogate (synthetic), AC A23–A25

key (function). *See* F1 key; F2 key; F6 key

keyboard, Windows 8 and Windows 7 compared, FM 4

keyboard shortcut A key or combination of keys you press to complete an action more efficiently. AC 79

L

label An unbound control that displays text. AC 326
    changing caption, AC 338–340

label (mailing), AC 430–434

label (ribbon), AC 13

Label Wizard An Access tool that asks you a series of questions, and then creates a mailing label report based on your answers. AC 430–434

landscape orientation The orientation where the page is wider than it is tall. AC 206

Large icons view button, FM 3

Last function, AC 256

layout
    stacked, AC 302
    tabular, AC 302

Layout view The Access view in which you can make design changes to a form or report while it is displaying data so that you can immediately *see* the effects of changing the design. AC 34, AC 181
    modifying combo boxes, AC 340–342
    modifying form design, AC 185–193
    modifying report design, AC 212–216
    modifying reports, AC 388–395
    modifying split forms, AC 315–319
    resizing and renaming columns, AC 406–407

LCase function A built-in Access function that accepts a single string argument as input, converts the value of the argument to lowercase letters, and then returns the converted value. AC 618

left angle bracket (<)
    comparison operators, AC 142
    input mask character, AC 279

Left function A function that provides the first character(s) in a text string. The format of the Left function is Left (text string, number of characters). AC 582

less than operator (<), AC 142

less than or equal to operator (<=), AC 142

library In File Explorer, a container for folders and files that organize files by category-documents, music, pictures, and videos, no matter where these files are stored, such as your hard disk, removable drives, and network. FM 2, FM 3

Like comparison operator A comparison operator that selects records by matching field values to a specific pattern that includes one or more wildcard characters. AC 237

Like operator, AC 142

line
    adding to forms, AC 367–368
    adding to reports, AC 416–417

Line tool A tool in Design view that you use to add a line to a form or report. AC 346

Link Spreadsheet dialog box, AC 488

link table. *See* intersection table

Link Tables dialog box, AC 683

linked table A table that is stored in a file outside the open database and that can be updated from the open database. You can retrieve and update (add, change, and delete) records in a linked table, but you can't change its structure. AC 682–687

Linked Table Manager An Access tool you use to change the filename or disk location for linked tables in an Access database. AC 683–687

linking Creating a connection in a destination program to an original file maintained by a source program. Linked data is not stored in the destination program, and any changes you make to the original file using the source program are reflected in the linked version in the destination program. AC 473
    data from Excel worksheets, AC 486–489
    record source, AC 476

list box A control that displays a scrollable list of values. AC 572
    adding to forms, AC 577–579
    SQL statements, AC 582–584

list-of-values match A selection of records whose value for the designated field matches one of two or more simple condition values. AC 240–241

Load event An event that occurs when Access opens a form or report. AC 588, AC 607

local procedure. *See* private procedure

locking Denying access by other users to data while Access processes one user's updates to the database. AC 691–692

logic error A coding error that occurs when a VBA procedure produces incorrect results. AC 621

logical key. *See* natural key

logical operator In a query, an operator that allows you to combine two or more conditions. AC 149–153

Long data type, AC 633

Long Integer The Field Size property that stores whole numbers from -2,147,483,648 to 2,147,483,647 in four bytes. AC 58

Long Text data type, AC 57

long text field, AC 287–290

lookup field A field that lets the user select a value from a list of possible values to enter data into the field. AC 272–276
    changing to short text field, AC 304–306

Lookup Wizard field A field that uses the Lookup Wizard data type, which lets you create a lookup field in a table. AC 272–276

M

1:M relationship. *See* one-to-many relationship

macro A recorded action, or a set of actions, that Access can perform automatically for you. AC 547–598
    adding actions, AC 553–557
    with associated command buttons, AC 559–562
    converting to Visual Basic, AC 623
    creating, AC 588–592
    deciding when to use, AC 550
    forms, AC 588–592
    running, AC 550–553
    single stepping, AC 548, AC 557–559
    submacros. *See* submacro

Macro Builder The name of the Build button when you use it to work with macros. AC 562

Macro Designer A development environment built into Access that allows you create and modify macros. AC 551–553

mailing label, AC 430–434

main form In a form based on two related tables, the form that contains data from the primary table. AC 100–205
    adding calculated controls, AC 358–360

maintaining (a database) To add, change, and delete records in database tables to keep them current and accurate. AC 118–128

Make Table dialog box, AC 504

make-table query An action query that creates a new table by copying selected fields in records from one or more existing tables. AC 498, AC 501–505

Manage Data Tasks dialog box, AC 458–459, AC 464–465

many-to-many relationship (M:N) A relationship between two tables in which each record in the first table matches many records in the second table, and each record in the second table matches many records in the first table. For many-to-many relationships, you create a third table and form one-to-many relationships between the two original primary tables and the new related table. AC A6–A7, AC 516, AC 519–520
    defining, AC 522–524

margins, reports, AC 212

Max function, AC 256

Maximum function, AC 161, AC 165

message box A special dialog box that contains a message and a command button, but no options. A message box remains on the screen until the user clicks the OK button. AC 551

MessageBox action, AC 550

method An action that operates on specific objects or controls. AC 634

Microsoft Access 2013 A database program you use to enter, organize, display, and retrieve related information. AC 1, AC 7
    .accdb file extension, AC 9
    Excel vs. AC 44
    exiting, AC 22–23
    naming conventions, AC A25–A27
    starting, AC 7

Microsoft Access Help button, AC 24

Microsoft Excel 2013
    Access vs. AC 44
    importing data to tables from, AC 80–83
    linking data from, AC 486–489

Min function, AC 256

Minimum function, AC 161, AC 163–164

minus sign (-)
    in datasheet, AC 123
    wildcard character, AC 195

M:N relationship. *See* many-to-many relationship

module A group of related procedures that are stored together in a single object. AC 608–609
    class, AC 609
    compiling, AC 629–630
    standard. *See* standard module

mouse interaction, FM 4–5

MouseDown event, AC 607

move handle The large square handle in a selected control's upper-left corner that you use to move the control. AC 322

Move to button, FM 21, FM 23–24

moving
    calculated controls, AC 360–364
    controls, AC 329–330, AC 331–332

fields in Design view, AC 68
fields on reports, AC 214–215
report controls in Design view, AC 413–415

moving (file) To remove a file from its current location and place it in a new location. FM 20
    in File Explorer, FM 20–24

MSysObjects table A system table that keeps track of the names, types, and other characteristics of every object in an Access database. AC 582

Multiple Items tool A form tool that creates a customizable form that displays multiple records from a source table or query in a datasheet format. AC 313–314

multiple-column report A report that prints the same collection of field values in two or more sets across the page. AC 384

multivalued field A lookup field that allows you to store more than one value in a field in a record. AC 649, AC 661–668

N

1:N relationship. *See* one-to-many relationship

Name property A property that specifies the name of a control, section, or object in a form or report. AC 340

naming
    fields, AC 56, AC 58
    objects, AC 56

naming conventions, AC 237

naming rule, VBA, AC 617

natural key A primary key the consists of a field, or a collection of fields, that is an inherent characteristic of the entity described by the table and that is visible to users. Also known as a logical key or an intelligent key. AC A21

navigating
    to data files in File Explorer, FM 10–12
    datasheets, AC 29–30
    forms, AC 193–194

navigation button A button found at the bottom of a table datasheet or form that you use to move through the records in the table. AC 29
    changing captions, AC 470–472

Navigation Buttons property, AC 576

Navigation Caption property A form property that you can set to change the label for the navigation buttons from the word "Record" to another value. AC 470–472

navigation form A form with tabs that allows you to display database objects in an organized way to users. AC 572, AC 593–598

navigation mode The mode in which Access selects an entire field value, and your typed entry replaces the highlighted field value. AC 118

Navigation Pane (Access) The area on the left of the Access program window that lists all the objects in the database and is the main control center for opening and working with database objects. AC 2, AC 167–170
    viewing objects, AC 40

navigation pane (Windows) The left pane of the File Explorer window that provides access to resources and locations on your computer. FM 2, FM 3, FM 9

newspaper-style column A multiple-column report that prints with the "down, then across" layout, with the first label printed in the upper-left corner on the first page, the second label printed to its right, the third label printed below the first label, and so on. Also called snaking column. AC 433

NoData event, AC 607

nonkey field A field that is not part of the primary key. AC A5

nonunique (sort field) A sort field for which more than one record can have the same value. AC 133

normal form The sets of rules applied to a collection of tables during normalization to eliminate anomalies and to produce a new collection of problem-free tables. AC A15–A21
    1NF, AC A15–A17
    2NF, AC A17–A19
    3NF, AC A19–A21

normalization The process of identifying and eliminating anomalies in a collection of tables. AC A15

not equal to operator (<>), AC 142

Not logical operator A logical operator that negates a criterion or selects records for which the designated field does not match the criterion. AC 241–244

null The absence of a value in a particular table entry. AC A4

null value The value that results from not entering a value for a field; a null value is not permitted for a primary key. AC 68

nullifies A referential integrity option in which the DBMS, when you change or delete a primary key value, automatically sets all matching foreign key values to null. AC A11

Number data type, AC 57
    Field Size property, AC 58
    sorting results, AC 131

number symbol (#)
    input mask character, AC 279
    wildcard character, AC 195, AC 237

O

Object data type, AC 633

Object Dependencies pane A task pane that displays a collapsible list of the dependencies among the objects in an Access database; you click the list's expand indicators to show or hide different levels of dependencies. AC 282–283

object dependency A relationship that exists between two objects when a change to the properties of data in one object affects the properties of data in the other object. AC 282–283

Object Type The default category in the Navigation Pane; it arranges objects by type (tables, queries, forms, reports, and so on). AC 167

object-oriented language A programming language that operates on objects. AC 606

OnCurrent property The property that specifies how a control or object responds when the Current event occurs. AC 610–612

1NF. *See* first normal form

one-to-many relationship The type of database relationship that exists between two tables when one record in the first table matches zero, one, or many records in the second table, and when one record in the second table matches at most one record in the first table. AC A5–A6, AC 76, AC 98–99, AC 100–104, AC 518–519, AC 520–522
    defining, AC 524–525

1:1 relationship. *See* one-to-one relationship

one-to-one relationship (1:1) A relationship between two tables in which each record in the first table matches at most one record in the second table, and each record in the second table matches at most one record in the first table. AC A7–A8, AC 520–522

Open command, FM 15

Open event, AC 607

OpenForm action A macro action that opens a specified form in a specified view. AC 548, AC 550

opening
    File Explorer, FM 10
    files, FM 15–16
    tables, AC 22

Or logical operator The logical operator you use in a query when you want a record selected if at least one of the specified conditions is met. AC 149, AC 151–153
    And logical operator vs. AC 153

Oracle naming conventions, AC A27

orphaned footer section A report footer section that appears by itself at the top of a page; the detail lines for the section appear on the previous page. AC 411

orphaned header section A report header section that appears by itself at the bottom of a page. The first detail record that follows the orphaned header section appears at the top of the next page. AC 412

orphaned record A record whose matching record in either the primary or related table has been deleted. AC 99

outer join A join between two tables in which the DBMS selects all records from one table and only those records from the second table that have matching common field values. AC 526–529

outer query. *See* parent query

P

Page Break tool An Access tool that you use to place a page break in a form so that users can move between the form pages by pressing the Page Up and Page Down keys. AC 468

Page Footer section A section that appears at the bottom of each page of a report and is used for page numbers, brief explanations of symbols or abbreviations, or other information such as a company name. AC 343, AC 396

Page Header section A section that appears at the top of each page of a report and is used for page numbers, column headings, report titles, and report dates. AC 396
    adding title, AC 428–430
    placing title, date, and page number in, AC 422

page number, reports, AC 426–428

Page Numbers dialog box, AC 427

page orientation, reports, AC 206, AC 212

Page Setup dialog box, AC 434

pane, Windows Explorer, FM 8

parameter A placeholder used in a VBA procedure that is assigned an argument value when the procedure is executed. AC 617

parameter query A query that displays a dialog box that prompts the user to enter one or more criteria values when the query is run. AC 249–253

parent query A query that contains a subquery. AC 657

partial dependency A functional dependency on part of the primary key, instead of the entire primary key. AC A13

password A string of characters assigned to a database that users must enter before they can open the database. AC 690–691
    setting and unsetting, AC 692

Paste Table As dialog box, AC 662

pattern match A selection of records with a value for the designated field that matches the pattern of a simple condition value. AC 237–240

PDF (portable document format) A file format that preserves the original formatting and pagination no matter where it's viewed. AC 485
    exporting reports to, AC 485–486

pencil symbol The symbol that appears in a row selector to indicate that the record is being edited. AC17, AC 197

Performance Analyzer An Access tool that you can use to optimize the performance of an Access database. AC 678–681

picture
    forms, AC 189–191
    reports, AC 216

Picture Builder dialog box, AC 569

Picture Caption Arrangement property A property for a command button that specifies how a command button's Caption property value is arranged in relation to the picture placed on the command button. The choices are No Picture Caption, General, Top, Bottom, Left, and Right. AC 569

plus sign (+) In a datasheet, a symbol indicating that a record has related records in another table. AC 123–124

Popular searches section, Access Help, AC 24

portable document format. *See* PDF

portrait orientation The orientation where the page is taller than it is wide. AC 206

previewing
    reports, AC 219
    selected form records, AC 199

primary key A field, or a collection of fields, whose values uniquely identify each record in a database table. AC A3–A4, AC A5, AC 5
    alternate, AC A3
    candidate, AC A3
    composite (concatenated), AC A4, AC A5
    default, renaming, AC 12–13
    determining, AC 55
    importance, AC 68
    specifying, AC 67

primary sort field The first sort field specified that determines the order of records in an object. AC 133

primary table The "one" table in a one-to-many relationship. AC A5, AC 77

Print button, AC 39

Print Preview The view of a report, form, or datasheet that shows you what the object will look like when printed. AC 38–39

PRINT PREVIEW tab, AC 212

Print Table Definition dialog box, AC 309

printing
    database relationships, AC 307–310
    reports, AC 39–40
    selected form records, AC 199–200

PrintSelection argument An action argument that prints the selected form record. AC 564

private procedure A procedure in a VBA class module for a form or report that is used only by that form or report. Also known as a local procedure. AC 609

procedure A group of statements using VBA code. AC 561, AC 607–608
    adding to class modules
    compiling, AC 630–637
    event. *See* event procedure
    existing, using, AC 609–615
    local (private), AC 609
    public, AC 608
    testing in Immediate window, AC 621–623

Procedure box A box in the VBA Code window that displays the event name for the current event procedure. AC 605

programming language
    event-driven, AC 606
    object-oriented, AC 606
    statements, AC 606
    VBA. *See* Visual Basic for Applications
    writing instructions, AC 606
    XML. *See* Extensible Markup Language

propagating Updating field property changes made in Table Design view to the corresponding property on forms and reports that include the modified field. AC 91

property Characteristic of each field in a table. AC 56
    changing in Design view, AC 73–75
    modifying in Datasheet view, AC 71–73
    setting, guidelines, AC 56
    setting in Property Sheet, AC 361

property propagation An Access feature that updates control properties in objects when you modify a table field property. AC 281

Property Sheet, setting properties, AC 361

public procedure A procedure in a VBA standard module that more than one object can use. AC 608

Q

QBE. *See* query by example

query A question you ask about the data stored in a database. In response, Access displays the specific records and fields that answer your question. AC 24
    action. *See* action query
    append, AC 498, AC 506–508
    applying filters saved as, AC 656–657
    calculated field, AC 245–249
    creating reports based on, AC 208
    creating using aggregate functions, AC 163–166
    crosstab. *See* crosstab query
    for custom reports, AC 403–404
    designing, Query Wizard vs. AC 124
    find duplicates. *See* find duplicates query
    find unmatched. *See* find unmatched query
    joins. *See* joining tables
    list-of-values matches, AC 240–241
    matching a range of values, AC 147–149
    modifying, AC 144–146
    multitable, AC 129–131
    Not logical operator, AC 241–244
    parameter, AC 249–253
    pattern matches, AC 237–240
    saving, AC 35
    saving filters as, AC 654–656
    select, AC 116, AC 258
    simple, creating, AC 30–33
    SQL statements, viewing, AC 580–582
    top values, AC 267–269
    updating data using, AC 128–129

query by example (QBE) A method of constructing a query by giving Access an example of the information you are requesting. AC 117

query datasheet, table datasheet vs. AC 129

QUERY TOOLS DESIGN tab, AC 117

Query Type group, AC 116, AC 117

Query Wizard An Access tool that prompts you for information by asking a series of questions and then creates the appropriate query based on your answers. AC 124

Query Wizard button The button on the CREATE tab that opens a dialog box with different types of wizards that guide you through the steps to create a query. AC 24

question mark (?)
    input mask character, AC 279
    wildcard character, AC 195, AC 237

Quick Access Toolbar A row of buttons on a program's title bar that provides one-click access to commonly used commands, such as Save. AC 2, FM 3

Quick Start selection The name given to the group of fields you add to a table at the same time using the Data Type gallery. AC 86

QuitAccess action, AC 550

quotation mark ("), input mask character, AC 279

R

reading Any database action that does not involve updating a database, such as running queries (but not action queries) and viewing table records. AC 691

record A complete set of field values for a specific person, place, object, event, or idea. AC A2, AC 4
    adding, AC 16–19
    adding to new table, AC 78–80
    combo boxes to find, AC 348–355
    copying from another Access database, AC 26–29
    deleting, AC 122–123
    modifying, AC 118–119
    selected, previewing, AC 199
    selected, printing, AC 199–200
    selection criteria. *See* selection criteria

record selector In a datasheet, the small square at the beginning of a row (also called the row selector) that you click to select the entire row. AC 16

Record Selectors property, AC 576

record source, linking, AC 476

Record Source property A property that specifies the table or query that provides the fields for a form or report. AC 304

recordset The set of records that results from running a query. AC 124

rectangle, adding to forms and reports, AC 369–370

Rectangle tool A tool in Design view that you use to add a rectangle to a form or report. AC 346, AC 369–370

Recycle Bin, FM 25

referential integrity A set of rules that Access enforces to maintain consistency between related tables when you update data in a database. AC A11, AC 99

refresh the link To change the stored file location (drive, folder, and filename) for a linked table in an Access database. AC 683

related table The "many" table in a one-to-many relationship. AC A5, AC 77

relation The formal term for a table in a relational database. AC A2

relational database A collection of related tables stored in the same file. AC A2, AC 4
    DBMSs, AC 6–7

relational database management system A software program in which data is organized as a collection of tables, and relationships between tables are formed through a common field. AC 6–7

relationship, database, AC A5–A9
    many-to-many, AC A6–A7
    one-to-many, AC A5–A6, AC 76, AC 98–99, AC 100–104
    one-to-one, AC A7–A8
    printing, AC 307–310

relationship table A table created for the sole purpose of specifying a many-to-many relationship between two other tables. For many-to-many relationships, you form one-to-many relationships between the two original primary tables and the relationship table. AC 517

Relationships window The Access window in which you define and view the relationships among a database's tables. AC 76

Rename command, FM 26

renaming
    columns in reports, AC 406–407
    default primary key field, AC 12–13
    fields in Design view, AC 89–90

repairing a database, AC 42–43

repeating group A field, or a collection of fields, that can have multiple values at a single location in a table. AC A15–A16

Replication ID The Field Size property that establishes a unique identifier for replication of tables, records, and other objects in databases created using Access 2003 and earlier versions in 16 bytes. AC 58

report A formatted printout (or screen display) of the contents of one or more tables or queries in a database. AC 25, AC 206–221
    adding event procedures, AC 628
    adding lines, AC 367–368
    adding rectangles, AC 369–370
    applying themes, AC 212–213
    changing field value alignment, AC 213–214
    changing title font color, AC 216
    conditional formatting, AC 217–221
    creating using Report Wizard, AC 208–212
    custom. *See* custom report; Design view (reports)
    detail, AC 402
    exporting to PDF files, AC 485–486
    formatting controls, AC 568
    inserting pictures, AC 216
    margins, AC 212
    modifying design in Layout view, AC 212–216
    moving and resizing fields, AC 214–215
    multiple-column, AC 384
    page orientation, AC 206, AC 212
    positioning controls, AC 587
    previewing, AC 219
    printing, AC 39–40
    saving, AC 35
    simple, creating, AC 35–40
    summary, AC 402

Report Footer section A section that appears once at the end of a report and is used for report totals and other summary information. AC 396

Report Header section A report section that appears once at the beginning of a report and is used for report titles, company logos, report introductions, dates, visual elements such as lines, and cover pages. AC 396

Report tool An Access tool that places all the fields from a table or query on a report. AC 25, AC 35–38
    enhancing reports created by, AC 388

Report view The Access view that provides an interactive view of a report. You can use Report view to view the contents of a report and to apply a filter to the data in a report. You can also copy selected portions of the report to the Clipboard and use the selected data in another program. AC 384–388

Report Wizard An Access tool that asks you a series of questions, and then creates a report based on your answers. AC 25, AC 206, AC 208–212
    enhancing reports created by, AC 388
resizing
    calculated controls, AC 360–364
    columns in reports, AC 406–407
    controls, AC 333–335

    fields on reports, AC 214–215
    report controls in Design view, AC 413–415
restoring a database, AC 43

restricted A referential integrity option in which the DBMS changes or deletes a primary key value only if there are no matching foreign key values. AC A11

RGB function A built-in function that returns an RGB (red, green, blue) color value, indicating the relative intensity of red (first value), green (second value), and blue (third value) in color of a property for a control. AC 605

ribbon (Access) The main set of commands, located at the top of the Access window, organized into tabs and groups that you click to execute tasks. AC 3
    buttons and labels, AC 13
ribbon (Windows), FM 3
    expanding, FM 13–14
right angle bracket (>)
    comparison operators, AC 142
    input mask character, AC 279

root directory The location at the top of the file system hierarchy where Windows stores folders and important files that it needs when you turn on the computer. FM 6, FM 7

row selector In a datasheet, the small square at the beginning of a row (also called the record selector) that you click to select the entire row. AC 16

Row Source property A property that specifies the data source, such as a table, a query, or an SQL statement, for a control in a form or report, for a field in a table or query, or for a list box or other controls. AC 305, AC 583

row-level locking Denying access by other users to the table rows one user is in the process of updating; other users can update the database simultaneously as long as the rows they need to update are not being updated, and therefore not being locked, by other users at the same time. AC 691–692

RunMacro action, AC 550

RunMenuCommand action An action that selects and runs a command on the ribbon. AC 564
running (a macro), AC 550–553

running (a query) Answering a query and displaying the results. AC 116, AC 127

S

Save As dialog box, FM 17, FM 18
saving
    database objects, AC 35
    databases. *See* saving a database
    export specifications, AC 463–465
    files, FM 16–18
    filters as queries, AC 654–656

    functions, AC 620–621
    import specifications, AC 457–460
    table structure, AC 68
    tables, AC 19–21
saving a database, AC 23
    as ACCDE file, AC 697
    as previous version, AC 23, AC 677–678
    as template, AC 481–482

scope The specification of a VBA procedure as either a public procedure or a private procedure. AC 612
scrolling, Windows 8 and Windows 7 compared, FM 4
Search box, AC 180, FM 2

search box A box in the Action Catalog pane that allows you to enter a filter term to limit the actions and objects displayed. AC 549

second normal form (2NF) A first normal form table is in second normal form if it does not contain any partial dependencies. First normal form tables with a single-field primary key are automatically in second normal form. AC A17–A19

secondary sort field A second field that determines the order of records in an object that are already sorted by the primary sort field. AC 133

section selector The square to the left of a section bar in Design view for forms and reports that you click to select and set properties for the entire section. AC 344

security The protection of a database against unauthorized access, either intentional or accidental. AC 690–692

select query A query in which you specify the fields and records you want Access to select, and the results are returned in the form of a datasheet. AC 116, AC 258

SELECT statement A SQL statement used to define what data is retrieved from a database and how that data is presented. AC 580–584
selecting
    controls, AC 329–330
    fields for queries, AC 126–127
    multiple files or folders, FM 24
selection criteria, AC 142–153
    comparison operators, AC 142, AC 147–149
    exact matches, AC 142–144
    modifying queries, AC 144–146
    multiple, AC 149–153

SelectObject action An action that selects a specified object so that you can run an action that applies to the object. AC 550, AC 564

self-join An inner or outer join between a table and itself. AC 529–534

semantic object modeling The study within the database field of the meanings and relationships of data. AC A14 semicolon (;), input mask character, AC 279

SendKeys action, AC 550

setting (a property) To select or enter a value for a property of a field. AC 56

shared access Opening a database in a way that allows other users to open and use the same database at the same time. AC 691

Short Text An Access data type that allows field values containing letters, digits, and other characters. AC 14, AC 57
    sorting results, AC 131

shortcut menu A menu that opens when you right-click an object and provides options for working with that object. AC 12

Shortcut Menu property, AC 576

Show Table button A button on the RELATIONSHIP TOOLS DESIGN tab that you click to open the Show Table dialog box, where you can add tables to the Relationships window. AC 76

Show Table dialog box, AC 125

Shutter Bar Open/Close Button The button on the Navigation Pane that you click to open and close the pane. AC 2

Sign in link The link below the window buttons that lets you sign into your Office account. AC 3

Simple Query Wizard An Access wizard that lets you quickly select the records and fields to display in a query datasheet. AC 24, AC 31–33

Single The Field Size property that stores positive and negative numbers to precisely seven decimal places in four bytes. AC 58

Single data type, AC 633

single step To use single step mode to execute a macro one action at a time. AC 548, AC 557–559

single step mode The Access mode in which a macro is executed one action at a time, pausing between actions, to test the accuracy of the macro. AC 557

sizing handle One of the squares that appears on three of the four corners (all corners except the upper-left corner) and at the midpoints of the four edges of a control when you select it and that you use to resize the control. AC 323

SkyDrive A Microsoft service that provides online storage space for your files. FM 17

snaking column. See newspaper-style column

sort To list files and folders in a particular order, such as alphabetically by name or type or chronologically by their modification date. FM 14

sort field The field used to determine the order of records in a datasheet. AC 131

sorting To rearrange records in a specified order or sequence. AC 131–135
    AutoFilter, AC 132
    data in reports, AC 407–412
    sorting on multiple fields in Design view, AC 133–135

source program The program that contains the original information, or object, when you integrate information between programs. AC 473

Special Effect property A property that you use to specify the type of special effect applied to a control in a form or report. Choices for this property are Flat, Raised, Sunken, Etched, Shadowed, and Chiseled. AC 370

split form
    creating with Split Form tool, AC 314–315
    modifying in Layout view, AC 315–319

Split Form tool A form tool that creates a customizable form that simultaneously displays the data from in both Form view and Datasheet view. The two views are synchronized with each other at all times. AC 302, AC 314–315

SQL. See Structured Query Language

SQL Server, naming conventions, AC A27

square brackets ([]), wildcard character, AC 195

stacked layout A control layout in which text box controls are arranged vertically with a label to the left of each text box control. AC 302

standard module A VBA module that is a database object stored in memory with other database objects when you open a database and that is listed in the Navigation Pane. AC 608
    creating, AC 616–617
    creating functions, AC 617–621

star symbol The symbol that appears in a row selector to indicate that the row is the next one available for a new record. AC 17

Start menu, Windows 8 and Windows 7 compared, FM 4

startup options The set of actions that take place when a database opens. AC 692
    setting, AC 692–697

statement An individual instruction in a programming language such as VBA. AC 606

static web page A web page that reflects the state of a database object at the time the page was created. Any subsequent changes made to the database object, such as updates to field values in records, are not reflected in a static web page. AC 445

status bar An area at the top of the Access window that provides information about the program, open file, or current task or selection; it also contains buttons and other controls for working with the file and its content. AC 3

StDev function, AC 256

storage
    files, determining location, FM 8
    Windows 8 and Windows 7 compared, FM 4

StrConv function A function that converts the letters in a string to a form indicated in the second argument in the function. AC 625, AC 637

string A VBA value made up of one or more characters that could include alphabetic characters, numbers, spaces, and punctuation. AC 616

String data type, AC 633

Structured Query Language (SQL) A standard language used in querying, updating, and managing relational databases. AC 262, AC 579–584
    using SQL statements for list boxes, AC 582–584
    viewing SQL statements for queries, AC 580–582

Sub procedure A procedure that executes instructions and accepts input values, but does not return a value and cannot be used in expressions. AC 604, AC 608–609
    naming, AC 617

Sub statement The first statement in a VBA Sub procedure, which specifies the scope and name of the procedure. AC 604

subdatasheet A datasheet that displays the records related to the current record. AC 123

subfolder A folder contained within another folder. FM 6, FM 7
    viewing in File Explorer, FM 9

subform In a form based on two related tables, the form that contains data from the related table. AC 200–205, AC 566
    adding to forms, AC 352–355
    calculated controls. See calculated control

Subform/Subreport tool A tool in Design view that you use to add a subform to a form or a subreport to a report. AC 347

submacro A complete macro with a Submacro header within a macro. Using submacros allows you to consolidate related macros and to manage large numbers of macros. AC 562–566
    adding, AC 563–566
    attaching to command buttons, AC 568–571

subquery A SQL SELECT statement placed inside another SELECT statement. AC 566, AC 657–661

subreport, AC 566

Sum function A function that calculates the total of an expression. AC 161, AC 163, AC 256, AC 346

summary report A report that displays no detailed information; only grand totals and possibly subtotals are displayed based on calculations using fields from the record source. AC 403

surrogate key A system-generated primary key that is hidden from users. Also known as a synthetic key. AC A23–A25

synthetic key. See surrogate key

system table Special table maintained by Access that stores information about the characteristics of a database and about the structure of the objects in a database. AC 582

T

Tab Control tool An Access tool that you use to place a tab control in a form so that users can move between the form pages by clicking the tabs. AC 468–472

tab order The order in which you move from control to control, or change the focus, in a form when you press the Tab key. AC 364–367
    changing in forms, AC 364–367

Tab Stop property A property that you use to specify whether users can use the Tab key to move to a control on a form. AC 360

tabbed form, creating using Tab Control tool, AC 468–472

table A collection of fields that describes a person, place, object, event, or idea. AC A2, AC 4
    adding data by importing text files, AC 95–97
    analyzing with Table Analyzer, AC 452–454
    anomalies, AC A14–A15
    closing, AC 22–23
    creating in Datasheet view, AC 11–23
    creating in Design view, AC 59–68
    defining relationships, AC 98–104
    dependencies, AC A12–A14
    determinants, AC A12
    finding data, AC 121–122
    grouping data into, AC 54
    history, AC 500
    imported, modifying, AC 87–93
    importing data from Excel worksheets, AC 80–83
    importing from Access databases, AC 454–455
    importing XML files as, AC 456
    intersection (junction, link), AC A6
    joining. *See* joining tables
    linked, AC 682–687
    maintaining data using a form, AC 4, AC 196–198
    modifying structure, AC 68–71
    naming fields, AC 12–13
    new, adding records, AC 78–80
    opening, AC 22
    primary, AC A5, AC 77
    related, AC A5, AC 77
    relationships, AC 4–6
    saving, AC 19–21
    structure. *See* table structure
    temporary, AC 501
    viewing CSV files as, AC 4

Table Analyzer An Access tool that analyzes a single table, looks for redundant data in the table, and (if necessary) splits it into two or more tables that are in third normal form. AC 452–454

table datasheet, query datasheet vs. AC 129

Table Design grid The part of the Table window in Design view that contains the values for the Field Name, Data Type, and Description field properties. AC 52

Table Name argument An action argument that specifies the name of a table that will be opened when the macro is run. AC 563

table structure
    deleting fields, AC 87–89
    importing existing table structure, AC 83–85
    saving, AC 68

TABLE TOOLS tab, AC 13

table validation rule A rule that compares one field value in a table record to another field value in the same record to verify their relative accuracy. AC 286–287

tabular layout A control layout in which text box controls are arranged in a datasheet format with labels above each column. AC 302

template A predefined database that includes professionally designed tables, forms, reports, and other objects. AC 8, AC 480–484

text, long text field, AC 287–290

text box A control that lets users type an entry. AC 304

Text Box tool A Design view tool that you use to add a text box and associated label to a form or report. AC 357

text file
    adding data to tables by importing, AC 95–97
    delimited, AC 96

Text Format property A field property for a Long Text field that determines whether you can format the field contents (Rich Text setting) or cannot format the field contents (Plain Text setting). AC 290

theme A predefined set of formats including colors, fonts, and other effects that enhance a database object's appearance and usability. AC 154
    databases, AC 154, AC 425
    forms, AC 185
    reports, AC 212–213

third normal form (3NF) A second normal form table is in third normal form if every determinant is a candidate key. This definition for third normal form is referred to as Boyce-Codd normal form (BCNF) and is an improvement over the original version of 3NF. AC A19–A21

3NF. *See* third normal form

thumbnail image, FM 2, FM 3

tile, FM 4

time, adding to report in Design view, AC 422

title
    adding to reports in Design view, AC 428–430
    changing font color in reports, AC 216
    forms, AC 343–345

title bar The area at the top of the Access window that displays the name of the open file and identifies the program. AC 3

toolbar A set of buttons for completing current tasks. FM 2

Top Values property A query property that lets you limit the number of records in the query results to a specific number or percentage. AC 267–269

Totals button, AC 163

touch interaction, FM 4–5

Touch Mode, AC 9–10

Track name AutoCorrect info property A database property that stores information about changes to the names of fields, controls, and objects. AC 671

transitive dependency A functional dependency between two nonkey fields, which are both dependent on a third field. AC A14

true-statement group The group of VBA statements executed when an If statement condition is true. AC 627

trusted folder A folder on a drive or network that you designate as trusted and where you place databases you know are safe. When you open a database located in a trusted folder, Access no longer displays a security warning. AC 290–292

tuple The formal term for a row in a relation (table). AC A2

2NF. *See* second normal form

U

unbound control A control that is not connected to a field in the database and that is used to display a form title, instructions, lines, rectangles, or graphics. AC 325, AC 326

unbound form A form that does not have a record source, which is usually a form that helps users navigate among the objects in a database. AC 325

Unhide Columns dialog box, AC 120

Unhide Fields In Datasheet view, the command that allows you to redisplay any hidden fields. AC 119

unhiding fields, AC 120

unique (sort field) A sort field whose value is different for each record. AC 133

unnormalized relation A table that contains repeating groups. AC A15

update anomaly Inconsistent data as a result of changing one field value that forces the DBMS to make more than one change to the database, and a failure by the database to make all the changes. AC A15

Update Properties dialog box, AC 280

update query An action query that changes selected field values from selected records in one or more tables based on the criteria you specify. AC 499, AC 512–514

updating (a database) To add, change, and delete records in database tables to keep them current and accurate. AC 118–124
  updating data using queries, AC 128–129

USB drive A removable disk you can plug into your computer and use to store files. FM 6

Use Access Special Keys property A database property that enables or disables the F11 key (show/hide the Navigation Pane), the Ctrl+G key combination (show/hide the Immediate window in the Visual Basic Editor), and the Alt+F1 key combination (start VB Editor). AC 670

user interface What you see and use when you communicate with a computer program. AC 574

user-defined function. *See* function

V

Validation Rule property A field property value that specifies the valid values that users can enter in a field. AC 284

Validation Text property A field property value that will be displayed in a dialog box if a user enters an invalid value for the field. AC 284

Value property A property that displays a multivalued field in a query in expanded form so that each value is displayed in a separate row. AC 667

Var function, AC 256

variable A named location in computer memory that can contain a value and that is declared in the Declarations section or in the procedure where the variable is used. AC 633

Variant data type, AC 633

VBA constant A predefined memory location that is initialized to a value that doesn't change. AC 613

VBE. *See* Visual Basic Editor

vbLowerCase constant A VBA constant that specifies the conversion of a string to all lowercase letters. AC 637

vbProperCase constant A VBA constant that specifies the conversion of the first letter in every word in a string to uppercase letters and the conversion of all other letters to lowercase letters. AC 625, AC 637

vbUpperCase constant A VBA constant that specifies the conversion of a string to all uppercase letters. AC 637

view
  changing in File Explorer, FM 12–13
  choosing, to use for a report, AC 384

View argument An action argument that specifies the view in which an object opens. AC 563

View tab A tab on the File Explorer window's ribbon that contains options for specifying the view of the window. FM 3

viewing
  CSV files as Access tables, AC 449–452
  files in File Explorer, FM 9
  HTML documents using Internet Explorer, AC 448
  objects in Navigation Pane, AC 40

Visible property A property that determines when Access displays a control or section in a form or report. You set the Visible property to Yes to display the item, and set the Visible property to No to hide it. AC 342

Visual Basic Editor (VBE, editor) The program you use to create and modify VBA code. AC 612

Visual Basic for Applications (VBA) The programming language for Microsoft Office programs. AC 604–643
  case for code, AC 619
  changing case of field values, AC 637–638
  commenting, AC 619
  controls, AC 639–643
  converting macros to, AC 623
  data types, AC 632–633
  deciding when to use, AC 550
  events. *See* event
  indenting code, AC 619
  modules. *See* module; standard module
  procedures. *See* event procedure; procedure

Visual Basic window The program window that opens when you use the Visual Basic Editor. AC 612

W

wildcard character A placeholder you use when you know only part of a search value or when you want the search value to start or end with a specific character or match a certain pattern. AC 195–196, AC 237

Windows 8, Windows 7 compared, FM 4–5

Windows Explorer A Windows 7 tool that displays the contents of your computer and uses icons to represent drives, folders, and files. FM 2

Word document, containing filtered records, creating, AC 387

worksheet, linking data from, AC 486–489

X

XML. *See* Extensible Markup Language

XSD (XML Structure Definition) file A file that contains the data structure information (field definitions, primary key identification, indexes, and so on) for an XML document. AC 462

XSL (Extensible Stylesheet Language) file A file that contains format specifications for an XML document so that a browser or another program can display the data in an XML file in a readable way. AC 462–463

Y

Yes/No data type, AC 57
  sorting results, AC 131

Z

Zoom box A dialog box you can use to enter text, expressions, or other values. AC 154